INTERNATIONAL PRIVATE LAW IN SCOTLAND

D1332711

AUSTRALIA
Law Book Co.
Sydney

CANADA and USA
Carswell
Toronto

HONG KONG
Sweet & Maxwell Asia

NEW ZEALAND
Brookers
Wellington

SINGAPORE and MALAYSIA
Sweet & Maxwell Asia
Singapore and Kuala Lumpur

INTERNATIONAL PRIVATE LAW IN SCOTLAND

Elizabeth B. Crawford, LL.B. (Hons), Ph.D.,
Solicitor
Professor of International Private Law,
University of Glasgow

and

Janeen M. Carruthers, LL.B. (Hons), Dip.L.P.,
Ph.D., Solicitor
Reader in Conflict of Laws,
University of Glasgow

THOMSON
TM
W. GREEN

Published in 2006
by W. Green & Son Ltd
21 Alva Street Edinburgh EH2 4PS

www.wgreen.thomson.com

Typeset by LBJ Typesetting Ltd,
Kingsclere
Printed and bound in Great Britain by MPG Books, Bodmin,
Cornwall

No natural forests were destroyed to make this product;
only farmed timber was used and replanted

A CIP catalogue record for this book is available from
the British Library.

ISBN-10 0414 01608 4
ISBN-13 9780 414 01608 8

TO

DAVID M. WALKER
CBE, QC, LLD, FBA, FRSE

Regius Professor Emeritus of Law
in the University of Glasgow

PREFACE TO THE SECOND EDITION

Many changes have occurred in Scots conflict rules since publication of the first edition of this book at the end of 1998.

In the first place, the development by the European Union of an "area of freedom, security and justice" has justified and necessitated, *inter alia*, the assimilation of the conflict rules of Member States across an increasing number of areas of private law. The European programme affects all aspects of the conflict of laws, viz. jurisdiction, choice of law, and recognition and enforcement of judgments, as well as procedural matters.

A programme of work was set for the period 1999 to 2004 at an Extraordinary European Council Meeting at Tampere, Finland. Important legislative reform under the Tampere agenda includes the conversion of the 1968 Brussels Convention on jurisdiction and the enforcement of judgments in civil and commercial matters into Council Regulation (EC) No 44/2001; Council Regulation (EC) No. 1346/2000 on Insolvency Proceedings; and, significantly, moving into Family Law, Council Regulation (EC) No 2201/2003 ("Brussels II Bis") concerning jurisdiction and the recognition and enforcement of judgments in matrimonial matters and matters of parental responsibility. These are weighty changes concerning substantive conflict rules. There have been also a number of changes to procedural conflict rules, including those relating to service of documents, and taking of evidence abroad.

This programme is to be pursued without pause under the Hague Programme, adopted by the European Council in 2004, for the period 2005–2009. Negotiations continue on the conversion into a Regulation of the 1980 Rome Convention on the Law Applicable to Contractual Obligations; and upon a Proposal for a Regulation on the Law Applicable to Non-Contractual Obligations ("Rome II"). Green Papers recently have been presented by the European Commission on applicable law and jurisdiction in divorce matters; on succession and wills; and on maintenance.

Secondly, a number of important changes have been made to Scottish and English domestic law, requiring concomitant conflict rules. Where such rules are lacking, expert commentary must be provided. The prime examples in this category arise in Family Law, in particular with regard to the creation of the new status of civil partner under the Civil Partnership Act 2004; and the statutory regulation in Scots law of certain aspects of *de facto* cohabitation.

Thirdly, the Family Law (Scotland) Act 2006 has placed on a statutory basis for the first time a number of Scots conflict rules in Family Law, such as those relating to validity of marriage, and matrimonial property, thereby crystallising them, and in so doing changing conflict rules by seemingly foreclosing the operation of certain options which existed at common law. The Act has added rules on a number of particular points of conflict significance, including a new provision concerning void marriages, and a different rule for ascribing the domicile of persons under 16. It is fortunate that the publication schedule of this book has permitted us to take full account of this major new Act.

The material has been re-ordered, and the book is presented now in two parts. Part A deals with matters such as methodology; connecting factors; and the pre-eminent subject of civil and commercial jurisdiction, including full analysis of UK and ECJ case law such as *Gasser v Misat, Turner v Grovit and Owusu*. The subjects of evidence and procedure and foreign decree enforcement, included in Part A, reflect the importance of these rules, and their inter-relationship with jurisdictional rules. Part B gives a full account of the conflict rules of Scots law in all major areas of private law. Substantial re-writing has occurred, particularly in the chapters on marriage and other adult relationships; consistorial causes; property and financial consequences of adult relationships; children; contractual obligations; non-contractual obligations; and insolvency.

It has been our aim to provide a comprehensive account of Scots conflict rules in all major areas of private law. This must be done within reasonable compass, and the decision was made to excise chapters on company law and criminal law to compensate for the increase in text which the changes outlined above demand.

We wish to record our thanks to our research assistant, Michael Thomson, who ably assisted us during the summer of 2005.

As is obvious, this book is now a co-authored composition. EBC expresses her gratitude to JMC for joining her in this venture. Our friends will know that differences of opinion between us are seldom found (the most profound being Burns's/Burns' poems; by great forbearance EBC has allowed the case of *Dinwoodie's Executrix v Carruthers' Executor* to pass unchanged, in deference to Dr Carruthers's opinion). There has been no division of labour or writing tasks; the work is entirely jointly authored.

At the University of Glasgow in recent years the authors have greatly expanded the conflict of laws teaching provision. We are privileged to teach in an area which is that of our prime research interest; teaching and writing are best when they are interlinked. The authors acknowledge the benefit which accrues to them through teaching, and trust that the mutual advantage is apparent also from the student perspective.

This book is dedicated to David M. Walker, *Regius Professor Emeritus of Law in the University of Glasgow*, whose contribution to legal scholarship in Scots law and legal education is immense. For EBC, Professor Walker was an inspirational teacher; for JMC, of the next generation, a mentor in her early research; to both of us, a friend whose kind interest and encouragement we appreciate. We are honoured that Professor Walker has accepted this dedication. We have endeavoured to state the law as at 8 June 2006, although it has been possible to take account of some later developments.

EBC
JMC
University of Glasgow

June 2006

PREFACE TO THE FIRST EDITION

This book is the product of the Printed Notes provided annually for the class of International Private Law at Glasgow University. Originally, and for many years, they were the work of Alex Donaldson, my predecessor as lecturer in that class. Thereafter they were updated and enlarged by me until there came a time at which it seemed appropriate to develop them further into book form. The text is intended principally for students, but I hope that it may be of wider use and interest. I have sought to state the law as at the date of this Preface.

The account presented is of Scottish conflict rules. A Scots forum is assumed, and accordingly the substantive domestic legal background as well as the system of conflict rules is that of Scottish private law. Nevertheless, since in my view much in the conflict of laws is held in common with England, many English conflict cases are cited, for interest and by way of illustration. They may be persuasive. Differences between Scots conflict rules and English conflict rules, in common law or statute, in substance or procedure, in emphasis or in nuance, I have tried to identify at appropriate points in the text.

I am grateful to my colleagues in the Stair building for their advice and expertise in many areas of law; to my researchers—successively, Paul Sheehan, Susan Mitchell, Shaheed Fatima and Jacqueline Donald—for their help; and to the editorial team at W. Green for bringing the book to publication.

Above all, I thanks Moira Smith, who has converted many versions of this text into its final form, and without whose great skill and patience the book would not have been completed.

Finally I record my gratitude to all the students over the years to whom I have had the pleasure and the privilege of speaking on the subject of International Private Law. The classes have been a joy to me, as I know they were to Alex Donaldson. Mr Donaldson's death occurred in April 1998, after the completion of the text but before production of the book. International Private Law in Scotland is dedicated to him, by a pupil to a teacher.

Elizabeth B. Crawford
University of Glasgow

30 September 1998

CONTENTS

	Page
Preface to 2nd edition	vii
Preface to 1st edition	xi
Table of Cases	xv
Table of Statutes	lxxxi
Table of Statutory Instruments	xciii
Table of International Conventions	xcvii
Table of EU Instruments	ciii
Select Bibliography	cxi

PART A—GENERAL TOPICS

1. Nature of the Subject	1
2. History	13
3. Operation of Foreign Law: Theories of Inclusion and Rules of Exclusion	23
4. Method	45
5. *Renvoi*	63
6. Domicile and Residence	79
7. Jurisdiction in Civil and Commercial Matters	119
8. Evidence and Procedure	181
9. Enforcement of Foreign Decrees	205

PART B—PARTICULAR TOPICS

10. Status and Capacity	259
11. The Law of Marriage and Other Adult Relationships	267
12. Consistorial Causes	301
13. Proprietary and Financial Consequences of Marriage and Other Adult Relationships	347
14. Conflict Rules Affecting Children	373
15. The Law of Contractual Obligations	419
16. The Law of Non-contractual Obligations	471
17. The Law of Property	505
18. The Law of Succession	543
Index	579

TABLE OF CASES

A (A Child) (Temporary Removal from Jurisdiction), Re; sub nom. W v A
  [2004] EWCA Civ 1587; [2005] 1 F.L.R. 639; [2005] Fam. Law 215,
  CA (Civ Div) 14–46
A (A Minor) (Abduction: Non-Convention Country), Re. *See* JA (A
  Minor) (Child Abduction: Non—Convention Country), Re.
A (Infants), Re [1970] Ch. 665; [1970] 3 W.L.R. 142; [1970] 3 All E.R. 184,
  CA (Civ Div) 14–25
A (Minors) (Abduction: Custody Rights), Re [1992] Fam. 106; [1992] 2
  W.L.R. 536; [1992] 1 All E.R. 929, CA (Civ Div) 14–31
A (Minors) (Abduction: Habitual Residence), Re; sub nom. A (Abduction:
  Habitual Residence), Re [1996] 1 W.L.R. 25; [1996] 1 All E.R. 24,
  Fam Div 14–48
A v S (Financial Relief after Overseas US Divorce) [2002] EWHC 1157;
  [2003] 1 F.L.R. 431; [2003] Fam. Law 155, Fam Div 13–24
ACE Insurance SA—NV (formerly Cigna Insurance Co of Europe SA
  NV) v Zurich Insurance Co [2001] EWCA Civ 173; [2001] 1 All
  E.R. (Comm) 802, CA (Civ Div) 7–46
A De Bloos SPRL v Bouyer SA (C14/76) [1976] E.C.R. 1497; [1977] 1
  C.M.L.R. 60, ECJ 7–13
AIG Europe (UK) Ltd v Ethniki; sub nom. AIG Europe (UK) Ltd v
  Anonymous Greek Co of General Insurances; Anonymous Greek
  Co of General Insurances v AIG Europe (UK) Ltd [2000] 2 All
  E.R. 566; [2000] 1 All E.R. (Comm) 65, CA (Civ Div) 7–13, 7–29
AJ v FJ, unreported, April 29, 2005, 2nd Div 14–29
AM Luther Co v James Sagor and Co; sub nom. Aksionairnoye
  Obschestvo AM Luther Co v James Sagor and Co [1921] 3 K.B.
  532; (1921) 7 Ll. L. Rep. 218, CA 3–04
A/S D/S Svenborg v Wansa [1997] 1 C.L. 122 7–58
A Frenchman against an Englishman (1550) Mor. 7323 2–03
Abate v Abate (otherwise Cauvin) [1961] P. 29; [1961] 2 W.L.R. 221;
  [1961] 1 All E.R. 569; 105 S.J. 210, PDAD 14–61
Abbasi v Abbasi [2006] All E.R.(D.) 92, CA 12–17
Aberdeen Artic Co v Sutter 1862) 4 Macq. 355; (1862) 24 D (H.L.)4 16–14
Abidin Daver, The. See Owners of the Las Mercedes v Owners of the
  Abidin Daver.
Abkco Music and Records Inc v Jodorowski; sub nom. Abkco Music and
  Records Inc v Jodorowsky [2003] E.C.D.R. 3; [2003] C.L.Y.B. 598,
  Ch D 7–39
Abnett v British Airways Plc; Joined Cases Sidhu v British Airways Plc
  [1997] A.C. 430; [1997] 2 W.L.R. 26; 1997 S.L.T. 492, HL 1–06
Abodi Mendi, The [1939] P. 178; (1939) 63 Ll. L. Rep. 100, CA 3–05
Abouloff v Oppenheimer and Co (1882–83) L.R. 10 Q.B.D. 295, CA 9–12
Abusaif v Abusaif, 1984 S.L.T. 90, IH (1 Div) 14–46
Achillopoulos, Re; Joined Cases Johnson v Mavromichall [1928] Ch. 433,
  Ch D 5–01, 5–06, 18–01, 18–03
Ackerman v Blackburn (No.1); sub nom. Ackerman v Logan's Executors
  (No.1), 2002 S.L.T. 37; 2001 Fam. L.R. 90, IH (Ex Div) 11–24
Ackerman v Logan's Executors (No.1). *See* Ackerman v Blackburn (No.1).
Acrux, The (No.3); sub nom. Casa Nazionale Della Previndenza Marinara v
  The Proceeds of the Sale of the Italian Steamship Acrux [1965] P.
  391; [1965] 3 W.L.R. 80, PDAD 8–22
Acutt v Acutt, 1935 S.C. 525; 1935 S.L.T. 347, IH (1 Div) 12–04

Adams v Cape Industries Plc [1990] Ch. 433; [1990] 2 W.L.R. 657; [1991] 1
    All E.R. 929, CA (Civ Div) 9–09, 9–12
Adams v Clutterbuck (1882–83) L.R. 10 Q.B.D. 403, QBD 17–07
Adams v National Bank of Greece and Athens SA; sub nom. Prudential
    Assurance Co Ltd v National Bank of Greece and Athens SA;
    Joined Cases Darling v National Bank of Greece SA [1961] A.C.
    255; [1960] 3 W.L.R. 8, HL 3–01, 4–05, 15–23, 15–25
Addison v Brown [1954] 1 W.L.R. 779; [1954] 2 All E.R. 213; 98 S.J. 338,
    QBD 3–06, 15–26
Adelaide Electric Supply Co Ltd v Prudential Assurance Co Ltd [1934]
    A.C. 122, HL 15–07, 15–50
Administrator of Austrian Property v Von Lorang. *See* Salvesen (otherwise
    Van Lorang) v Administrator of Austrian Property; Administrator
    of Austrian Property v Von Lorang.
Adriatic, The [1931] P. 241, PDAD 15–32
Aeolian Shipping SA (*The Aeolian*) [2001] EWCA Civ 1162; [2001] 2 Ll
    Rep. 641, CA (Civ Div) 15–13
Aeolian Shipping SA v ISS Machinery Services Ltd (*The Aeolian*); sub
    nom. ISS Machinery Services Ltd v Aggeliki Charis Compania
    Maritima SA v Pagnan SpA (The Angelic Grace) [1995] 1 Ll Rep.
    87, CA (Civ Div); affirming [1994] 1 Ll Rep. 168, QBD (Comm) 7–47,
    9–76
Agnew v Lansforsakringsbolagens AB [2001] 1 A.C. 223; [2000] 2 W.L.R.
    497, HL; affirming [1997] 4 All E.R. 937; [1997] L.R.L.R. 671, CA
    (Civ Div); affirming [1996] 4 All E.R. 978; [1996] L.R.L.R. 392,
    QBD (Comm) 7–13
Agnew v Norwest Construction Co Ltd, 1935 S.C. 771; 1935 S.L.T. 517, IH
    (2 Div) 7–04
Agrafax Public Relations Ltd v United Scottish Society Inc [1995] C.L.C.
    862; [1995] I.L.Pr. 753; [1995] C.L.Y.B. 703, CA (Civ Div) 7–29
Agulian v Cyganik. *See* Cyganik v Agulian.
Ahmed v Ahmed; sub nom. Syed v Ahmed, 2006 S.C. 165; 2006 S.L.T. 135,
    IH (Ex Div) 12–23, 12–27, 12–28
Aiglon Ltd v Gau Shan Co Ltd; Joined Cases L'Aiglon SA v Gau Shan Co
    Ltd [1993] 1 Ll Rep. 164; [1993] B.C.L.C. 321, QBD (Comm) 7–46
Aikman v Aikman (1859) 21 D. 757; affirmed (1861) 23 D.(H.L.)3 14–04
Airbus Industrie GIE v Patel [1997] I.L.Pr. 191 7–47
Aitchison v Dixon (1870) L.R. 10 Eq. 589, Ct of Chancery 6–14
Akram v Akram, 1979 S.L.T. (Notes) 87, OH 11–01, 12–38
Al Wahab, The. See Amin Rasheed Shipping Corp v Kuwait Insurance Co.
Al-Bassam v Al-Bassam [2004] EWCA Civ 857; [2004] W.T.L.R. 757;
    (2004) 148 S.J.L.B. 826; *The Times*, July 22, 2004, CA (Civ Div) 18–12
Albeko Schuhmaschinen AG v Kamborian Shoe Machine Co (1961) 111
    L.J. 519 15–19
Alberti, In the Estate of [1955] 1 W.L.R. 1240; [1955] 3 All E.R. 730
    (Note), PDAD 18–22, 18–29
Albion Insurance v Covills (1828) 3 W. & S. 218 15–40
Alcock v Smith [1892] 1 Ch. 238, CA 5–07, 17–10, 17–29
Alcom v Columbia [1984] A.C. 580; [1984] 2 W.L.R. 750; [1984] 2 All E.R.
    6, HL 7–03, 3–05
Aldridge v Aldridge, 1954 S.C. 58; 1954 S.L.T. 84, OH 12–33
Alexander v Badenoch (1843) 6 D. 322 8–08
Alexander v Bennet's Trs (1829) 7 S. 817 18–34
Alexandria, The [1972] 1 Ll Rep. 399 15–24
Al-Fayed v Al-Tajir [1988] Q.B. 712; [1987] 3 W.L.R. 102; [1987] 2 All
    E.R. 396, CA (Civ Div) 7–03, 16–10

Alfonso-Brown v Milwood [2006] EWHC 642; [2006] All E.R. (D.) 420,
Fam Div 11–16, 11–31, 12–38
Alfred C Toepfer International GmbH v Société Cargill France; sub nom.
Toepfer International GmbH v Société Cargill France [1998] 1 Ll
Rep. 379; [1998] C.L.C. 198, CA (Civ Div) 9–76
Alfred Dunhill Ltd v Diffusion Internationale de Maroquinerie de Prestige
SARL [2002] 1 All E.R. (Comm) 950; [2001] C.L.C. 949; [2001]
C.L.Y.B. 812, QBD (Comm) 7–14
Al-Habtoor (Rashid) v Fotheringham [2001] EWCA Civ 186; [2001] 1
F.L.R. 951; [2001] 1 F.C.R. 385, CA (Civ Div) 14–27
Alhaji Mohamed v Knott; sub nom. M v Knott; Mohamed v Knott [1969] 1
Q.B. 1; [1968] 2 W.L.R. 1446; [1968] 2 All E.R. 563, DC 11–05
Ali v Ali [1968] P. 564; [1966] 2 W.L.R. 620; [1966] 1 All E.R. 664, PDAD .. 4–05,
11–10, 11–23
Alison's Trusts, Re (1874) 31 L.T. 638 11–25
Allan's Trs (1896) 24 R. 238; (1896) 24 R. 718 18–52
Allen's Estate; Joined Cases Prescott v Allen and Beaumont [1945] 2 All
E.R. 264, Ch D 13–02, 18–26, 18–34
Almeda, Re (1902) 18 T.L.R. 414 6–09
Al-Najjar, Petr, 1993 G.W.D. 27–1661 14–44
Aluminium Industrie Vaassen BV v Romalpa Aluminium 30196 [1976] 1
W.L.R. 676; [1976] 2 All E.R. 552, CA (Civ Div) 8–03, 17–16
Amalia, The (1863) 1 Moore P.C. (N.S.) 471 16–14
American Motorists Insurance Co (AMICO) v Cellstar Corp [2003]
EWCA Civ 206; [2003] 2 C.L.C. 599; [2003] I.L.Pr. 22, CA (Civ Div) .. 7–51
Amin Rasheed Shipping Corp v Kuwait Insurance Co (The Al Wahab)
[1984] A.C. 50; [1983] 3 W.L.R. 241; [1983] 2 All E.R. 884, HL 5–07,
15–11, 15–12, 15–22
Anchor Line (Henderson Bros) Ltd, Re; sub nom. Companies Act 1929,
Re [1937] Ch. 483; [1937] 2 All E.R. 823, Ch D 17–08, 17–53, 17–58
Anderson (A Bankrupt), Re [1911] 1 K.B. 896, KBD 17–56
Anderson v Equitable Life Ass Co (1926) 41 T.L.R. 123 15–53
Anderson v Eric Anderson Radio and TV Pty Ltd (1965) 114 C.L.R. 20 ... 16–13
Andrew Weir Shipping Ltd v Wartsila UK Ltd [2004] EWHC 1284; [2004]
2 Ll Rep. 377, QBD (Comm) 7–17
Anglo Iranian Oil Co Ltd v Jaffrate (The Rose Mary) [1953] 1 W.L.R. 246;
97 S.J. 81, Sup Ct (Aden) 3–04
Anglo-Austrian Bank (Vogel's Application), Re; Joined Cases Dresdner
Bank (Ellert's Application), Re; Direction Der Disconto
Gesellschaft (Gutschow's Application), Re [1920] 1 Ch. 69, Ch D .. 15–25,
15–37
Anglo-Dutch Petroleum International Inc v Ramco Energy Plc 2006 S.L.T.
334; 2006 G.W.D. 5–90, OH 7–58
Annesley, Re; sub nom. Davidson v Annesley [1926] Ch. 692, Ch D .. 4–02, 4–03,
5–01, 5–04, 5–06, 5–07, 5–09, 5–10, 6–04, 12–20
Anselme Dewavrin Fils et Cie v Wilsons and North Eastern Railway
Shipping Co Ltd (1931) 39 Ll. L. Rep. 289, KBD 15–11
Anton Durbeck GmbH v Den Norske Bank ASA, unreported, June 13,
2002, QBD (Comm) 16–20
Anton Durbeck GmbH v Den Norske Bank ASA [2005] EWHC 2497;
[2006] 1 Ll Rep. 93; [2005] 2 C.L.C. 783, QBD (Comm) 16–18, 16–20
Anton Durbeck GmbH v Den Norske Bank ASA; sub nom. Durbeck
GmbH v Den Norske Bank ASA [2003] EWCA Civ 147; [2003]
Q.B. 1160; [2003] 2 W.L.R. 1296, CA (Civ Div); reversing [2002]
EWHC 1173, QBD (Comm) 7–15, 16–18
Anton Piller KG v Manufacturing Processes Ltd [1976] Ch. 55; [1976] 2
W.L.R. 162, CA (Civ Div) 7–58

Anton v Bartolo (1891) Clunet 1171 4–03
Antony Gibbs and Sons v Société Industrielle et Commerciale des Métaux
    (1890) L.R. 25 Q.B.D. 399, CA 4–05, 15–25, 17–53, 17–59
Anziani, Re; sub nom. Herbert v Christopherson [1930] 1 Ch. 407, Ch D .. 17–10,
    17–26
Apple Corps Ltd v Apple Computer Inc [2004] EWHC 768; [2004] 2
    C.L.C. 720; [2004] I.L.Pr. 34, Ch D 7–55, 15–16
Apt (otherwise Magnus) v Apt [1948] P. 83; [1974] 2 All E.R. 677, CA 4–04,
    11–14, 11–24
Arab Bank Ltd v Barclays Bank (Dominion, Colonial and Overseas) [1954]
    A.C. 495; [1954] 2 W.L.R. 1022; [1954] 2 All E.R. 226, HL .. 15–23, 15–26,
    17–17
Arab Monetary Fund v Hashim (No.3) [1991] 2 A.C. 114; [1991] 2 W.L.R.
    729; [1991] 1 All E.R. 871, HL 7–03, 10–03, 10–04
Arab Monetary Fund v Hashim (No.9) [1996] 1 Ll Rep. 589, CA (Civ Div);
    affirming in part [1993] 1 Ll Rep. 543, QBD (Comm) 16–30
Arantzazu Mendi, The. See Spain v Owners of the Arantzazu Mendi.
Araya v Coghill, 1921 S.C. 462; 1921 1 S.L.T. 321, IH (1 Div) 17–57, 17–58
Arbitration between the Owners of the Steamship Catalina and the
    Owners of the Motor Vessel Norma, Re (1938) 61 Ll. L. Rep. 360,
    KBD 9–12
Arcado SPRL v Haviland SA (9/87) [1988] E.C.R. 1539; [1989] E.C.C. 1,
    ECJ (6th Chamber) 7–13
Argyllshire Weavers Ltd v A Macaulay (Tweeds) Ltd (No.1) 1962 S.C. 388;
    1962 S.L.T. 310, IH (1 Div) 7–45
Ark Therapeutics Plc v True North Capital Ltd [2005] EWHC 1585; [2006]
    1 All E.R. (Comm) 138, QBD (Comm) ... 7–44, 7–45, 7–55, 15–15, 16–18,
    16–20
Arkwright Mutual Insurance Co v Bryanston Insurance Co Ltd [1990] 2
    Q.B. 649; [1990] 3 W.L.R. 705; [1990] 2 All E.R. 335, QBD 7–46
Armagas Ltd v Mundogas SA (*The Ocean Frost*) [1986] A.C. 717; [1986] 2
    W.L.R. 1063; [1986] 2 All E.R. 385; [1986] 2 Ll Rep. 109; (1986) 83
    L.S.G. 2002; (1986) 130 S.J. 430, HL 16–21
Armar Shipping Co v Caisse Algerienne d'Assurance et de Reassurance
    (*The Armar*) [1981] 1 W.L.R. 207; [1981] 1 All E.R. 498, CA (Civ
    Div) 15–06
Armitage v Armitage (1866) L.R. 3 Eq. 343 11–02
Armitage v Attorney General; sub nom. Gillig v Gillig [1906] P. 135,
    PDAD 5–01, 5–02, 5–06, 12–18, 14–61
Armour v Thyssen Edelstahlwerke AG [1991] 2 A.C. 339; [1990] 3 W.L.R.
    810; 1990 S.L.T. 891, HL; reversing 1989 S.L.T. 182, IH (2 Div);
    affirming 1986 S.L.T. 452, OH 4–01, 15–22, 17–16
Armour v Thyssen Edelstahlwerke AG (Preliminary Procedure), 1986
    S.L.T. 94, OH 15–22
Armstrong v Armstrong [1892] P. 98, PDAD 7–47
Arnott v Lord Advocate, 1932 S.L.T. 46, OH 12–17
Arnott v Groom (1846) 9 D. 142 6–04
Arnott v Redfern (1825) 2 Car. & P. 88 15–37
Artic Fish Sales Co Ltd v Adam (No.2), 1996 S.L.T. 970; 1995 G.W.D.
    25–1351, OH 9–40
Ascot Commodities NV v Northern Pacific Shipping (*The Irini A*) (No.2)
    [1999] 1 Ll Rep. 189, QBD (Comm) 9–08
Ashbury v Ellis [1893] A.C. 339, PC (NZ) 9–10
Ashurst v Pollard; sub nom. Pollard v Ashurst [2001] Ch. 595; [2001] 2
    W.L.R. 722, CA (Civ Div) 7–27
Askew, Re; sub nom. Majoribanks v Askew [1930] 2 Ch. 259, Ch D .. 5–04, 5–06,
    5–11, 14–04

Askin v Absa Bank Ltd [1999] I.L.Pr. 471; (1999) 96(13) L.S.G. 32, CA
(Civ Div) 7–45
Assitalia SpA v Frahuil SA (C265/02). *See* Frahuil SA v Assitalia SpA
(C265/02).
Assunzione, The [1954] P. 150; [1954] 2 W.L.R. 234; [1954] 1 All E.R. 278,
CA 15–12, 15–24, 15–32
Astilleros Zamakona SA v MacKinnons, 2002 S.L.T. 1206; 2002 S.C.L.R.
1018, OH 7–31
Astro Exito Navegacion SA v WT Hsu (*The Messiniaki Tolmi*) [1984] 1 Ll
Rep. 266; (1984) 128 S.J. 265, CA (Civ Div); reversing [1983] 1 Ll
Rep. 666, QBD (Comm) 7–45
Astro Vencedor v Babanaft. *See* Astro Vencedor Compania Naviera SA of
Panama v Mabanaft GmbH (*The Damianos*).
Astro Vencedor Compania Naviera SA of Panama v Mabanaft GmbH
(*The Damianos*) [1971] 2 Q.B. 588; [1971] 3 W.L.R. 24; [1971] 2 All
E.R. 1301, CA (Civ Div) 15–21
Astro Venturoso Compania Naviera v Hellenic Shipyards SA (*The Marian-
nina*) [1983] 1 Ll Rep. 12, CA (Civ Div) 15–12, 15–22
Atherstane's Trs (1896) 24 R. 39 18–10
Atlantic Song, The [1983] 2 Ll Rep. 394, QBD (Admlty) 7–45
Atlantic Telecom GmbH, Noter, 2004 S.L.T. 1031; 2004 G.W.D. 30–623,
OH 4–02
Atlas Shipping Agency (UK) Ltd v Suisse Atlantique Société d'Armement
Maritime SA (*The Gulf Grain* and *The El Amaan*) [1995] 2 Ll Rep.
188; [1995] C.L.C. 633, QBD (Comm) 15–02
Attorney General for Canada v William Schulze and Co (1901) 9 S.L.T. 4,
OH 3–02, 3–06
Attorney General of Alberta v Cook [1926] A.C. 444, PC (Can) 6–25
Attorney General of Alberta v Huggard Assets Ltd [1953] A.C. 420; [1953]
2 W.L.R. 768, PC (Can) 1–02
Attorney General of Ceylon v Reid [1965] A.C. 720; [1965] 2 W.L.R. 671;
[1965] 1 All E.R. 812, PC (Cey) 11–10
Attorney General of New Zealand v Ortiz [1984] A.C. 1; [1983] 2 W.L.R.
809; [1983] 2 All E.R. 93, HL; affirming [1982] 3 W.L.R. 570; [1982]
3 All E.R. 432, CA (Civ Div) 3–03, 3–04, 3–05
Attorney General v Dunn (1840) 6 M. & W. 511 6–17
Attorney General v Heniemann Publishers Australia PTY Ltd [1988]
C.L.Y. 1982 3–03
Attorney General v HRH Prince Ernest Augustus of Hanover; sub nom.
Prince Ernest of Hanover v Attorney General [1957] A.C. 436;
[1957] 2 W.L.R. 1, HL; affirming [1956] Ch. 188; [1955] 3 W.L.R.
868, CA; reversing [1955] Ch. 440; [1955] 2 W.L.R. 613, Ch D 6–38
Attorney General v Kent (1862) 1 H. & C. 12 6–31
Attorney General v Nissan; sub nom. Nissan v Attorney General [1970]
A.C. 179; [1969] 2 W.L.R. 926, HL; affirming [1968] 1 Q.B. 286;
[1967] 3 W.L.R. 1044, CA (Civ Div); reversing in part [1967] 3
W.L.R. 109; [1967] 2 All E.R. 200, QBD 3–06
Attorney General v Pottinger (1861) 6 H. & N. 733 6–31
Attorney General v Rowe (1862) 1 H. & C. 31 6–31
Attorney General v Yule and Mercantile Bank of India (1931) 145 L.T. 9 .. 6–14
Auckland Corp v Alliance Assurance Co Ltd . *See* Mayor of Auckland v
Alliance Assurance Co Ltd.
August, The [1891] P. 328, PDAD 15–32
Australian Commercial Research and Development Ltd v ANZ
McCaughan Merchant Bank Ltd [1989] 3 All E.R. 65, Ch D 7–47
Austrian Lloyd Steamship Co v Gresham Life Assurance Society Ltd
[1903] 1 K.B. 249, CA 15–12

B (A Minor) (Adoption Order: Nationality), Re [1999] 2 A.C. 136; [1999]
   2 W.L.R. 714; [1999] 2 All E.R. 576; [1999] 1 F.L.R. 907, HL 14–52
B (Abduction) (Article 13 Defence), Re; sub nom. B (Article 13 Defence),
   Re [1997] 2 F.L.R. 573; [1997] Fam. Law 780, Fam Div 14–31
B (Minors) (Residence Order), Re; sub nom. B (A Minor) (Residence
   Order: Ex parte), Re [1992] Fam. 162; [1992] 3 W.L.R. 113; [1992]
   3 All E.R. 867, CA (Civ Div) 14–45
B's Settlement, Re; sub nom. B v B [1940] Ch. 54, Ch D 14–25
B v B (Injunction: Restraint on Leaving Jurisdiction); sub nom. B v B
   (Passport Surrender: Jurisdiction) [1998] 1 W.L.R. 329; [1997] 3 All
   E.R. 258, Fam Div 7–58
B v B (Sist), 1998 S.L.T. 1245; 1998 G.W.D. 15–740, OH 14–44
B v France (A/232–C) [1992] 2 F.L.R. 249; (1993) 16 E.H.R.R. 1, ECHR .. 11–01
B v T (No.1) 2002 C.L.Y.B. 637 9–21
BJ Mann (Advertising) Ltd v Ace Welding and Fabrications Ltd, 1994
   S.C.L.R. 763, Sh Pr 7–20
BP International Ltd v Energy Infrastructure Group Ltd [2003] EWHC
   2924; [2004] 1 C.L.C. 539, QBD (Comm) 7–46
BRAC Rent—A—Car International Inc, Re; sub nom. BRAC
   Rent—A—Car Ltd, Re [2003] EWHC 128; [2003] 1 W.L.R. 1421;
   [2003] 2 All E.R. 201, Ch D (Companies Ct) 17–40
BSA Co v De Beers. *See* De Beers Consolidated Mines Ltd v British South
   Africa Co.
Babanaft International Co SA v Bassatne [1990] Ch. 13; [1989] 2 W.L.R.
   232; [1989] 1 All E.R. 433, CA (Civ Div) 7–58
Babcock v Jackson, 12 N.Y. 2d 473; 191 N.E. 2d 279 (1963) 16–08
Babington v Babington; sub nom. Babington, Petr, 1955 S.C. 115; 1955
   S.L.T. 170, IH (1 Div) 14–25
Baccus Srl v Servicio Nacional del Trigo [1957] 1 Q.B. 438; [1956] 3
   W.L.R. 948100 S.J. 872, CA 7–03
Baelz v Public Tr. [1926] Ch. 863, Ch 17–31
Baily v Baily (1884) 13 Q.B.D.855 9–12
Bain v Bain, 1971 S.C. 146; 1971 S.L.T. 141, OH 12–18
Bain v Whitehaven and Furness Junction Ry Co (1850) 3 H.L. 1 8–12
Baindail v Baindail [1946] P. 122, CA 11–03, 11–07
Balkanbank v Taher (No.2) [1995] 1 W.L.R. 1056; [1995] 2 All E.R. 904,
   CA (Civ Div) 7–58
Ballachulish Slate Quarries Co Ltd v Bruce (1908) 16 S.L.T. 48, IH
   (1 Div) 17–08
Ballantyne v MacKinnon [1896] 2 Q.B. 455, CA 9–04
Balshaw v Kelly; sub nom. Balshaw v Balshaw, 1967 S.C. 63; 1967 S.L.T.
   54, IH (1 Div) 12–33
Bamberski v Krombach (C7/98); sub nom. Krombach v Bamberski (C7/98)
   [2001] Q.B. 709; [2001] 3 W.L.R. 488; [2001] All E.R. (EC) 584;
   [2000] E.C.R. I—1935;, ECJ 7–02, 9–81, 9–90
Bambino Holdings Ltd v Speed Investments Ltd. *See* Speed Investments
   Ltd v Formula One Holdings Ltd (No.2).
Bamgbose v Daniel [1955] A.C. 107; [1954] 3 W.L.R. 561; [1954] 3 All E.R.
   263, PC (West Africa) 11–04, 11–06, 14–02
Banco Atlantico SA v British Bank of the Middle East [1990] 2 Ll Rep.
   504; Financial Times, June 5, 1990, CA (Civ Div) 7–45
Banco De Vizcaya v Don Alfonso De Borbon y Austria [1935] 1 K.B. 140,
   KBD 3–03
Bangoura v Washington Post, 2005 (25) T.L.W.D. 2522–006 [2005] O.J.
   No. 5428, CA Ont 7–15, 16–18
Bank of Africa Ltd v Cohen [1909] 2 Ch. 129, CA 10–07, 17–05

Bank of Baroda v Vysya Bank Ltd [1994] 2 Ll Rep. 87; [1994] 3 Bank. L.R.
216, QBD (Comm) 15–15, 15–16, 17–29
Bank of British West Africa Ltd, Petrs, 1931 S.L.T. 83, OH 9–20
Bank of China v NBM LLC [2001] EWCA Civ 1933; [2002] 1 W.L.R. 844;
[2002] 1 All E.R. 717, CA (Civ Div) 7–58
Bank of Credit and Commerce International (Overseas) Ltd (In Liquida-
tion) v Price Waterhouse (No.1) [1997] 4 All E.R. 108, Ch D 1–01,
3–05, 7–03
Bank of Credit and Commerce International SA (In Liquidation) (No.11),
Re [1997] Ch. 213; [1997] 2 W.L.R. 172; [1996] 4 All E.R. 796, Ch
D 17–53
Bank of East Asia Ltd v Scottish Enterprise 1997 S.L.T. 1213; [1996] 5
Bank. L.R. 93, HL 8–17, 15–22
Bank of Montreal v Exhibit and Trading Co (1906) 22 T.L.R. 722 17–29
Bank of Scotland v Investment Management Regulatory Organisation Ltd,
1989 S.C. 107; 1989 S.L.T. 432, IH (Ex Div) 7–13
Bank of Scotland v SA Banque Nationale de Paris, 1996 S.L.T. 103; [1996]
I.L.Pr. 668, OH 7–29, 7–38, 7–39
Bank of Scotland v Seitz, 1990 S.L.T. 584; 1990 S.C.L.R. 418, IH 7–13
Bank of Scotland v Youde (1908) 15 S.L.T. 847, Bill Chamber (SC) 17–35
Bank of Tokyo-Mitsubishi Ltd v Baskan Gida Sanayi Ve Pazarlama AS
[2004] EWHC 945; [2004] 2 Ll Rep. 395; [2004] I.L.Pr. 26, Ch D ... 7–38,
7–44
Bank Polski v KJ Mulder and Co [1942] 1 K.B. 497, CA; affirming [1941] 2
K.B. 266, KBD 17–29
Bank voor Handel en Scheepvaart NV v Slatford (No.2); sub nom. Bank
voor Handel en Scheepvaart NV v Administrator of Hungarian
Property [1954] A.C. 584; [1954] 2 W.L.R. 867; [1954] 1 All E.R.
969, HL; reversing [1953] 1 Q.B. 248; [1952] 2 All E.R. 956, CA 3–04,
3–07, 17–10
Bankers Trust International v Todd Shipyards Corp (*The Halcyon Isle*)
[1981] A.C. 221; [1980] 3 W.L.R. 400, PC (Sing) 8–23, 8–24
Bankes, Re; sub nom. Reynolds v Ellis [1902] 2 Ch. 333, Ch D 13–04, 13–06,
13–07
Bankhaus H Aufhauser v Scotboard Ltd 1973 S.L.T. (Notes) 87, OH 17–25,
17–27
Bannerton Holdings Pty Ltd v Sydbank Soenderjylland A/S (Australia)
(1997) 5 C.L. 102 7–47
Banque Cantonale Vaudoise v Waterlily Maritime Inc [1997] 2 Ll Rep.
347; [1997] 5 C.L. 103, QBD (Comm) 7–47
Banque des Marchands de Moscou (Koupetschesky) (No.3), Re [1954] 1
W.L.R. 1108; [1954] 2 All E.R. 746, Ch D 17–03, 17–17
Barclay v Sweeney [1999] I.L.Pr. 288, C d'A (Paris) 7–15
Barclays Bank International Ltd v Levin Bros (Bradford) Ltd [1977] Q.B.
270; [1976] 3 W.L.R. 852, QBD (Comm) 8–21
Baring Bros and Co Ltd v Cunninghame DC, 1996 G.W.D. 25–1405 16–30
Barker, Re [1995] 2 V.R. 439 18–30
Barnett, Re [1902] 1 Ch. 867 18–14
Baron Emanuel de Almeda, Re (1902) 18 T.L.R. 414 6–21
Baroness Lloyd, Petrs 1963 S.C. 37; 1963 S.L.T. 231, IH (1 Div) 18–51
Barratt International Resorts Ltd v Martin, 1994 S.L.T. 434, OH 7–27, 7–29,
9–03
Barretto v Young [1900] 2 Ch. 339, Ch D 18–40
Barros Mattos Junior v MacDaniels Ltd; sub nom. Mattos Junior v
MacDaniels Ltd; Joined Cases Barros Mattos Junior v General
Securities and Finance Co Ltd [2004] EWHC 1188; [2005] 1 W.L.R.
247; [2004] 2 Ll Rep. 475, Ch D 5–07, 16–30, 16–31

Barry v Bradshaw [2000] C.L.C. 455; [2000] I.L.Pr. 706, CA (Civ Div) 7–13
Bartlett v Bartlett [1925] A.C. 377, PC (Egy) 5–01, 5–06
Bartley v Hodges (1861) 1 B. & S. 375 17–59
Base Metal Trading Ltd v Shamurin [2004] EWCA Civ 1316; [2005] 1
    W.L.R. 1157; [2005] 1 All E.R. (Comm) 17, CA (Civ Div); affirming
    [2003] EWHC 2419; [2004] 1 All E.R. (Comm) 159; [2004] I.L.Pr. 5,
    QBD (Comm) 16–15
Basinski v Basinski, 1993 G.W.D. 8–533 14–47
Bata v Bata [1948] W.N. 366; 92 S.J. 574, CA 16–18
Battaglia v Battaglia (Jurisdiction: Custody of children), 1967 S.L.T. 49;
    1966 S.L.T. (Notes) 85, OH 14–25
Batthyany v Walford (1887) L.R. 36 Ch. D. 269, CA 16–30
Battye's Tr. v Battye's Administrator; sub nom. Battye's Tr. v Battye, 1917
    S.C. 385; 1917 1 S.L.T. 189, IH (1 Div) 13–07
Beach Petroleum NL v Johnson [1996] C.L.Y. 1104 9–17
Beamish v Beamish (1861) 9 H.L. Cas. 274 11–28
Beattie v Beattie (1866) 5 M. 181 11–21
Beatty v Beatty [1924] 1 K.B. 807, CA 9–12
Beazley v Horizon Offshore Contractors Inc [2004] EWHC 2555; [2005]
    I.L.Pr. 11; [2005] Ll Rep. I.R. 231, QBD (Comm) 7–30
Beckford v Wade (1805) 17 Ves. Un. 87 17–07
Belgian International Insurance Group SA v McNicoll, 1999 G.W.D.
    22–1065, IH (2 Div) 7–13, 7–31
Bell Electric Ltd v Aweco Appliance Systems GmbH and Co KG (Appli-
    cation to Stay Appeal) [2002] EWCA Civ 1501; [2003] 1 All E.R.
    344; [2003] C.P. Rep. 18, CA (Civ Div) 7–03
Bell v Bell [1992] 2 I.R. 152 6–13
Bell v Kennedy (1868) 6 M. (H.L.) 69 .. 2–04, 4–05, 6–01, 6–04, 6–06, 6–07, 6–12,
                                        6–30, 6–40, 13–02, 18–06
Bellinger v Bellinger [2003] UKHL 21; [2003] 2 A.C. 467; [2003] 2 W.L.R.
    1174, HL; affirming [2001] EWCA Civ 1140; [2002] Fam. 150;
    [2002] 2 W.L.R. 411, CA (Civ Div) 11–01
Benaim and Co v Debono [1924] A.C. 514, PC (M) 15–12, 15–22
Benarty (No.1), The. See RA Lister and Co Ltd v EG Thomson (Shipping)
    Ltd and PT Djkarta Lloyd (The Benarty) (No.1).
Benincasa v Dentalkit Srl (C269/95) [1998] All E.R. (EC) 135; [1997]
    E.C.R. I—3767, ECJ (6th Chamber) 7–13, 7–20, 7–44
Bennett v Inveresk Paper Co (1891) 18 R.975 15–40
Berchtold, Re; Joined Cases Berchtold v Capron [1923] 1 Ch. 192, Ch D .. 17–02
Berezovsky v Forbes Inc (No.1); sub nom. Berezovsky v Michaels;
    Glouchkov v Michaels; Joined Cases Glouchkov v Forbes Inc [2000]
    1 W.L.R. 1004; [2000] 2 All E.R. 986, HL 7–15
Berezovsky v Forbes Inc [1999] C.L.Y.B. 717 7–45
Bergerem v Marsh (1921) L.T. 630 17–56
Berkovits v Grinberg [1995] Fam. 142; [1995] 2 W.L.R. 553; [1995] 2 All
    E.R. 681, Fam Div 12–29, 12–30
Berliner Industriebank AG v Jost [1971] 2 Q.B. 463; [1971] 3 W.L.R. 61,
    CA (Civ Div) 9–12
Bernaben and Co v Hutchison (1902) 18 Sh.Ct.Rep. 72 .... 8–05, 8–07
Bernhard v Harrah's Club, 128 Cal. Rptr. 215; 546 P. 2d 709 (1976) 16–08
Berthiaume v Dame Dastous [1930] A.C. 79, PC (Can) 11–24
Besix SA v Wasserreinigungsbau Alfred Kretzschmar GmbH and Co KG
    (WABAG) (C256/00) [2003] 1 W.L.R. 1113; [2004] All E.R. (EC)
    229, ECJ 7–13
Bethell, Re; sub nom. Bethell v Hildyard (1888) L.R. 38 Ch. D 220, Ch D .. 11–02
Bettinson's Question, Re; sub nom. Bettinson v Bettinson [1956] Ch. 67;
    [1955] 3 W.L.R. 510, Ch D 3–01, 13–10

Bibi v Chief Adjudication Officer [1998] 1 F.L.R. 375; [1998] 1 F.C.R. 301;
     The Times, July 10, 1997, CA (Civ Div)   11–08
Birkdale SS Co Ltd v Compania Naviera Vascongada (1923–24) 17 Ll. L.
     Rep. 41; 1923 S.L.T. 719, OH   16–14
Birtwhistle v Vardill (1840) 7 Cl. & F. 895   14–02
Bischoffsheim, Re; sub nom. Cassel v Grant [1948] Ch. 79; [1947] 2 All
     E.R. 830, Ch D 4–06, 14–02
Biskra, The [1983] 2 Ll Rep. 59, QBD (Admlty)   7–45
Bitwise Ltd v CPS Broadcast Products BV, 2003 S.L.T. 455; 2002 G.W.D.
     34–1155, OH   7–13
Black v Black's Trs, 1950 S.L.T. (Notes) 32, OH 10–07, 13–05, 13–07, 17–05,
                                                                                          18–48
Black v Yates [1992] Q.B. 526; [1991] 3 W.L.R. 90; [1991] 4 All E.R. 722,
     QBD   16–12
Black Clawson International Ltd v Papierwerke Waldhof-Aschaffenburg AG
     [1975] A.C. 591; [1975] 2 W.L.R. 513; [1975] 1 All E.R. 810, HL   9–12,
                                                                                          9–32
Blair v Kay's Trs, 1940 S.L.T. 464, OH   14–04
Bliersbach v McEwen; sub nom. Bliersbach v MacEwen 1959 S.C. 43; 1959
     S.L.T. 81, IH (1 Div) 4–02, 11–14, 11–17, 11–24, 11–34
Bloch v Bloch [2003] 1 F.L.R. 1   12–11
Blohn v Desser [1962] 2 Q.B. 116; [1961] 3 W.L.R. 719, QBD 9–10, 9–12
Blue Nile Shipping Co Ltd v Iguana Shipping and Finance Inc (*The Happy
     Fellow*) [1998] 1 Ll Rep. 13; [1997] C.L.C. 1391, CA (Civ Div)   7–39
Bodley Head Ltd v Alec Flegon (t/a Flegon Press) [1972] 1 W.L.R. 680;
     [1972] F.S.R. 21, Ch D   15–20
Boe v Anderson (1857) 20 D. 11   9–13
Boe v Anderson (1862) 24 D. 732   18–25
Boeing Co v PPG Industries [1988] 3 All E.R. 839; (1988) 138 N.L.J. Rep.
     259, CA (Civ Div)   8–16
Boettcher v Carron C (1861) 23 D. 322   16–14
Boissevain v Weil [1950] A.C. 327; [1950] 1 All E.R. 728, HL; affirming
     [1949] 1 K.B. 482; [1949] 1 All E.R. 146, CA 3–07, 15–12, 15–53
Boldrini v Boldrini [1932] P. 9, CA 6–09, 6–30
Bonacina, Re; sub nom. Le Brasseur v Bonacina [1912] 2 Ch. 394, CA   4–02,
                                                                                     15–01, 15–22, 16–16
Bondholders Securities Corp v Manville (1933) 4 D.L.R. 699 . . . . .   15–20, 16–05
Bonnier Media Ltd v Smith; sub nom. Bonnier Media Ltd v Kestrel
     Trading Corp, 2003 S.C. 36; 2002 S.C.L.R. 977, OH 7–14, 7–15
Bonnor v Balfour Kilpatrick Ltd 1974 S.C. 223; 1975 S.L.T. (Notes) 3, IH
     (1 Div); affirming 1974 S.L.T. 187, OH 1–01, 4–01, 8–17
Bonython v Commonwealth of Australia [1951] A.C. 201; 66 T.L.R. (Pt. 2)
     969; [1948] 2 D.L.R. 672; 94 S.J. 821, PC (Aus) 15–24, 15–50
Bordera v Bordera, 1995 S.L.T. 1176, OH   14–29
Boss Group Ltd v Boss France SA [1997] 1 W.L.R. 351; [1996] 4 All E.R.
     970, CA (Civ Div) 7–13, 7–44
Bouygues Offshore SA v Caspian Shipping Co (No.2) [1997] I.L.Pr. 472,
     CA (Civ Div) [1997] 2 Ll Rep. 485, QBD (Admlty)   7–30
Bowler v John Mowlem and Co Ltd [1954] 1 W.L.R. 1445; [1954] 3 All
     E.R. 556, CA   18–01
Boys v Chaplin; sub nom. Chaplin v Boys [1971] A.C. 356; [1969] 3 W.L.R.
     322; [1969] 2 All E.R. 1085, HL; affirming [1968] 2 Q.B. 1; [1968] 2
     W.L.R. 328; [1968] 1 All E.R. 283, CA (Civ Div) 8–20, 16–05, 16–12,
                                                                                          16–28
Bozzelli's Settlement, Re; sub nom. Husey—Hunt v Bozzelli [1902] 1 Ch.
     751, Ch D 4–05, 11–16
Bradfield v Swanton [1931] I.R. 446 . . . .   6–13, 6–21

Bradford v Young (1884) 11 R. 1135 18–17
Bradford v Young (1885) L.R. 29 Ch. D. 617, CA 18–26
Brady v Murray, 1933 S.L.T. 534, OH 12–38
Brassard v Smith; sub nom. Levesque v Smith [1925] A.C. 371, PC (Can) ... 17–03,
                                                                       17–31
Breadalbane's Trs, Marquess of (1843) 15 S.L. 389 17–02
Breavington v Godleman (1988) 880 A.L.R. 362 16–11
Breen (otherwise Smith) v Breen [1964] P. 144; [1961] 3 W.L.R. 900,
    PDAD 3–06, 11–18
Bremer v Freeman (1857) 10 Moo. P.C. 306 .... 5–02, 18–17, 18–18
Breuning v Breuning [2002] EWHC 236; [2002] 1 F.L.R. 888; [2002] Fam.
    Law 519, Fam Div 6–25, 6–39, 12–11, 12–13
Brianchon v Occidental Petroleum (Caledonia) Ltd, 1990 S.L.T. 322; 1989
    S.C.L.R. 760, OH 8–05
Briesemann, In the Goods of [1894] P. 260, PDAD 18–01
Brinkibon v Stahag Stahl und Stahlwarenhandels GmbH; sub nom.
    Brinkibon Ltd v Stahag Stahl und Stahlwarenhandelsgesellschaft
    mbH [1983] 2 A.C. 34; [1982] 2 W.L.R. 264; [1982] 1 All E.R. 293,
    HL 15–12, 15–43
Brinkley v Attorney General (1890) L.R. 15 P.D. 76, PDAD 11–02
Bristow v Sequeville (1850) 5 Ex. 275 8–12
Bristow Helicopters Ltd v Sikorsky Aircraft Corp [2004] EWHC 401; [2004]
    2 Ll Rep. 150; [2005] 2 C.L.C. 856, QBD (Comm) 7–44, 7–46
British Airways Board v Laker Airways Ltd; sub nom. Laker Airways Ltd v
    Secretary of State for Trade and Industry; Joined Cases British
    Caledonian Airways Ltd v Laker Airways Ltd [1985] A.C. 58; [1984]
    3 W.L.R. 413; [1984] 3 All E.R. 39, HL 7–47, 9–34
British Controlled Oilfields v Stagg [1921] W.N. 319 15–11
British Linen Co v Drummond (1830) 10 B.C. 903 8–09
British Nylon Spinners v ICI [1953] Ch. 19; [1952] 2 All E.R. 780, CA 9–03
British Phonographic Industry Ltd v Cohen 1983 S.L.T. 137; [1984] E.C.C.
    279; [1984] F.S.R. 159, IH (1 Div) 7–55
British South Africa Co v Companhia de Moçambique; sub nom. Com-
    panhia de Moçambique v British South Africa Co; Joined Cases De
    Sousa v British South Africa Co [1893] A.C. 602; [1891–94] All E.R.
    Rep. 640, HL 7–04
British South Africa Co v De Beers Consolidated Mines Ltd. *See* De Beers
    Consolidated Mines Ltd v British South Africa Co.
British Steel Corp v Allivane International Ltd, 1989 S.L.T. (Sh. Ct.) 57;
    1988 S.C.L.R. 562, Sh Ct (South Strathclyde) 7–30
British Sugar Plc v Fratelli Babbini di Lionello Babbini and Co SAS; sub
    nom. Fratelli Babbini di Lionello Babbini and Co SAS v BF
    Engineering SpA [2004] EWHC 2560; [2005] 1 All E.R. (Comm)
    55; [2005] 1 Ll Rep. 332, QBD (TCC) 7–29
Brodie v Barry (1813) 3 Ves. B. 127 18–08
Brodin v A/R Seljan, 1973 S.C. 213; 1973 S.L.T. 198, OH 16–24
Brokaw v Seatrain UK Ltd; sub nom. United States v Brokaw [1971] 2
    Q.B. 476; [1971] 2 W.L.R. 791; [1971] 2 All E.R. 98, CA (Civ Div) .. 3–02
Brook v Brook (1861) 9 H.L. Cas. 193 .... 4–05, 11–14, 11–16, 11–17, 11–37
Brooks v Brooks Trs. *See* Marchioness of Huntly v Gaskell.
Brown (1744) Mor 4604 18–12
Brown (Samuel Marshall) v Brown (Emily McGregor), 1928 S.C. 542; 1928
    S.L.T. 339, IH (1 Div) 6–04
Brown v Brown, 1913 2 S.L.T. 314, OH 13–04, 13–07
Brown v Brown (Husband and wife: Jurisdiction), 1967 S.L.T. (Notes) 44,
    OH 6–10

Brown v Brown (Parent and child: Custody); sub nom. Brown v Brown
 (Child: Custody), 1948 S.C. 5; 1948 S.L.T. 129, IH (2 Div) 14–25
Brown v Gregson; sub nom. Brown's Trs v Gregson [1920] A.C. 860; 1920
 S.C. (H.L.) 87; 1920 1 S.L.T. 311, HL 18–08, 18–34
Brown v Smith (1852) 15 Beav. 444 6–31
Brown's Trs (1890) 17 R. 1174 13–07
Bruce v Bruce (1790) 3 Pat. 163 18–12
Brunel v Brunel (1871) L.R. 12 Eq. 298, Ct of Chancery 6–13, 6–21
Buchanan v Rucker (1808) 9 East. 192 9–10
Buckland v Buckland (otherwise Camilleri) [1968] P. 296; [1967] 2 W.L.R.
 1506; [1967] 2 All E.R. 300, PDAD 11–31, 12–36
Buckle v Buckle (otherwise Williams) [1956] P. 181; [1955] 3 W.L.R. 898;
 [1955] 3 All E.R. 641; 99 S.J. 913, PDAD 10–06, 11–21
Bullock v Caird (1874–75) L.R. 10 Q.B. 276, QBD 8–05
Bumper Development Corp v Commissioner of Police of the Metropolis
 [1991] 1 W.L.R. 1362; [1991] 4 All E.R. 638, CA (Civ Div) . . . 3–01, 7–03,
 8–05, 8–17,
Burke v Burke, 1983 S.L.T. 331, OH 11–24
Burke v Uvex Sports GmbH [2005] I.L.Pr. 26, HC (Irl) 7–14
Burns v Campbell [1952] 1 K.B. 15; [1951] 2 All E.R. 965; [1951] 2 T.L.R.
 1007; 95 S.J. 743, CA 18–01
Buron v Denman (1848) 2 Ex. 167 3–06
Burton v Fisher (1828) Milward's Rep. 183 6–29
Bus Berzelius Umwelt Service AG v Chemconserve BV Reakt Ltd
 (C99/245 HR) [2004] I.L.Pr. 9, HR (NL) 7–14
Bushby v Munday (1821) 5 Madd. 297 7–47
Butler v Butler (No.2) [1998] 1 W.L.R. 1208; [1997] 2 All E.R. 822, CA
 (Civ Div) 12–11

C (A Child), Re [2006] EWHC 1229, Fam Div 14–30, 14–31
C (An Infant), Re [1959] Ch. 363; [1958] 3 W.L.R. 309, Ch D 7–03
C (Minors) (Abduction: Consent), Re [1996] 1 F.L.R. 414; [1996] 3 F.C.R.
 222; [1996] Fam. Law 266, Fam Div 14–31
C, Petr, 1997 G.W.D. 23–1132, OH 14–21
C v C (Divorce: Jurisdiction); sub nom. C v C (Brussels II: French
 Conciliation and Divorce Proceedings) [2005] EWCA Civ 68; [2005]
 1 W.L.R. 469; [2005] 2 F.L.R. 38, CA (Civ Div) 12–12
C v C (Divorce: Stay of English Proceedings) [2001] 1 F.L.R. 624; [2001]
 Fam. Law 181, Fam Div 13–09
C v C, 2003 S.L.T. 793; 2003 G.W.D. 16–497, OH 14–31
C v FC (Brussels II: Freestanding Application for Parental Responsibility)
 [2004] 1 F.L.R. 317; [2004] Fam. Law 101, Fam Div 14–14
C v FC (Children Proceedings: Costs) [2004] 1 F.L.R. 362; [2004] Fam.
 Law 104, Fam Div 6–39
CEB Draper and Son Ltd v Edward Turner and Son Ltd [1965] 1 Q.B. 424;
 [1964] 3 W.L.R. 783; [1964] 3 All E.R. 148, CA 1–02
Cabel v Cabel (Divorce: Jurisdiction), 1974 S.L.T. 295, OH 6–39
Cable (Lord) (Deceased) Will Trusts, Re (No.1); sub nom. Garratt v
 Waters; Cable (Lord) (Deceased), Re [1977] 1 W.L.R. 7; [1976] 3
 All E.R. 417, Ch D 3–02
Caithness, Re (1890) 7 T.L.R. 354 18–33
Caldwell v Van Vlissengen (1851) 9 Hare 415 3–01
Caledonia Subsea Ltd v Micoperi Srl; sub nom. Caledonia Subsea Ltd v
 Micoperi Srl, 2003 S.C. 70; 2002 S.L.T. 1022, IH (1 Div) 15–16
Calleja v Calleja, 1996 S.C. 479; 1997 S.L.T. 579, IH (1 Div) 14–48
Callwood v Callwood [1960] A.C. 659; [1960] 2 W.L.R. 705; [1960] 2 All
 E.R. 1, PC (WI) 13–02

Caltex Singapore Pte Ltd v BP Shipping Ltd [1996] 1 Ll Rep. 286, QBD
 (Admlty) 8–12
Calvin's Case (1608 7 Co. Rep.1; 2 St. Tr. 559 2–02
Cambridge Bionutritional Ltd v VDC Plc, 2000 G.W.D. 6–230, Sh Ct 7–27
Camdex International Ltd v Bank of Zambia [1997] 1 C.L. 123 8–23
Camdex International Ltd v Bank of Zambia (No.2) [1997] 1 W.L.R. 632;
 [1997] 1 All E.R. 728, CA (Civ Div) 7–58
Cameron v Cameron (No.1), 1996 S.C. 17; 1996 S.L.T. 306, IH (2 Div) ... 14–27,
 14–29
Cameron v Cameron (No.2), 1997 S.L.T. 206; 1996 S.C.L.R. 552, OH 14–27,
 14–31
Cameron v Mackie (1833) 7 W. & S. 16 18–29
Cammell v Sewell (1858) 3 Hurl. & N. 617 9–04
Cammell v Sewell (1860) 5 H. & M. 728 .... 3–04, 17–12
Campbell v Campbell (1861) 23 D. 256 6–31
Campbell v Campbell (1866) L.R. 1 Eq. 383 18–27
Campbell v Campbell, 1977 S.C. 103; 1977 S.L.T. 125, OH 14–25, 14–47
Campbell v Mirror Group Newspapers Ltd (Costs); sub nom. Campbell v
 MGN Ltd (Costs); Campbell v MGN Ltd (No.2) [2005] UKHL 61;
 [2005] 1 W.L.R. 3394; [2005] 4 All E.R. 793, HL 16–21
Campbell v Mirror Group Newspapers Ltd; sub nom. Campbell v MGN
 Ltd [2004] UKHL 22; [2004] 2 A.C. 457; [2004] 2 W.L.R. 1232;
 [2004] 2 All E.R. 995, HL 16–21
Campbell Connelly and Co v Noble [1963] 1 W.L.R. 252; [1963] 1 All E.R.
 237; 107 S.J. 135, Ch D 17–22, 17–32
Campbell-Wyndham-Long's Trs, Petrs 1951 S.C. 685; 1952 S.L.T. 43, IH (1
 Div) 18–52
Campins-Coll, Petr, 1988 S.C. 305; 1989 S.L.T. 33, OH 14–33
Canada Trust Co v Stolzenberg (No.2) [2002] 1 A.C. 1; [2000] 3 W.L.R.
 1376; [2000] 4 All E.R. 481, HL 7–10, 7–17, 7–41
Canadian Pacific Railway Co v Parent [1917] A.C. 195, PC (Can) 16–12
Cannon v Cannon; sub nom. C (Abduction: Settlement) (No.1), Re [2004]
 EWCA Civ 1330; [2005] 1 W.L.R. 32; [2005] 1 F.L.R. 169, CA (Civ
 Div) 14–30
Cantiere San Rocco SA (Shipbuilding Co) v Clyde Shipbuilding and
 Engineering Co Ltd; sub nom. Cantiere San Rocco SA (Shipbuild-
 ing Co) v Clyde Shipbuilding and Engineering Co Ltd [1924] A.C.
 226; (1923) 16 Ll. L. Rep. 327; 1923 S.C. (H.L.) 105, HL 16–30
Capdevielle, Re (1864) 2 H. & C. 985 .... 6–10, 6–14
Carl Zeiss Stiftung v Rayner and Keeler Ltd; Joined Cases Rayner and
 Keeler Ltd v Courts and Co [1967] 1 A.C. 853; [1966] 3 W.L.R. 125,
 HL 9–07, 9–13
Carlson v Rio Tinto Plc [1999] C.L.C. 551; [1999] C.L.Y.B. 718, QBD 7–45
Carnegie v Giessen [2005] EWCA Civ 191; [2005] 1 W.L.R. 2510; [2005]
 C.P. Rep. 24, CA (Civ Div) 8–21
Carnoustie Universal SA v International Transport Workers Federation;
 Joined Cases Craddock Continental Ltd v Finnish Seamen's Union
 [2002] EWHC 1624; [2002] 2 All E.R. (Comm) 657; [2003] I.L.Pr. 7,
 QBD (Comm) 7–38
Carr v Fracis Times and Co [1902] A.C. 176, HL 3–06, 16–12, 16–13
Carron Iron Co v McLaren (1855) 5 H.L. Cxas 416 7–47
Carse (Liquidator) v Coppen, 1951 S.C. 233; 1951 S.L.T. 145, IH (1 Div) ... 17–08,
 17–17
Carswell v Carswell (1881) 8 R. 901 .... 4–05, 6–10
Casey v Casey, 1968 S.L.T. 56; 1967 S.L.T. (Notes) 106, OH 6–04, 6–13
Casio Computer Co Ltd v Sayo (No.3) [2001] EWCA Civ 661; [2001]
 I.L.Pr. 43, CA (Civ Div) 7–14

Castaneda v Clydebank Engineering and Shipbuilding Co Ltd; sub nom.
   Clydebank Engineering Co v Don Jose Yzquierdo Y Castanada
   [1902] A.C. 524; (1902) 4 F.(H.L.) 31; (1902) 10 S.L.T. 237, HL 8–05
Castanho v Brown and Root (UK) Ltd [1981] A.C. 557; [1980] 3 W.L.R.
   991, HL 7–45
Castree v ER Squibb and Sons Ltd [1980] 1 W.L.R. 1248; [1980] 2 All E.R.
   589; 124 S.J. 743, CA (Civ Div) 16–18
Castrique v Imrie (1869-70) L.R. 4 H.L. 414, HL . . . 9–04, 9–11, 9–13, 17–10, 17–12
Catalina (Owners) v MV Norma (Owners). *See* Re Arbitration between
   the Owners of the Steamship Catalina and the Owners of the Motor
   Vessel Norma, Re.
Caterpillar Financial Services Corp v SNC Passion [2004] EWHC 569;
   [2004] 2 Ll Rep. 99, QBD (Comm) 15–17, 15–57
Cathcart v Cathcart (1904) 12 S.L.T. 12 7–04
Catterall v Sweetman (1845) 1 Rob. Ecc. 304 11–28
Century Credit Corp v Richard (1962) 24 D.L.R. (2d) 291 17–13
Ceskoslovenska Obchodni Banka AS v Nomura International Plc [2002]
   I.L.Pr. 321 7–45
Chamberlain v Napier (1880) L.R. 15 Ch. D. 614, Ch D 13–04, 13–07
Chamberlain's Settlement, Re; sub nom. Chamberlain v Chamberlain
   [1921] 2 Ch. 533, Ch D 6–37
Channel Tunnel Group Ltd v Balfour Beatty Construction Ltd; Joined
   Cases France Manche SA v Balfour Beatty Construction Ltd [1993]
   A.C. 334; [1993] 2 W.L.R. 262, HL 7–47, 7–48
Chaparral, The. See Zapata Offshore Co v Bremen.
Chappelle v Chappelle [1950] P. 134; [1950] 1 All E.R. 236, Assizes
   (Liverpool) 12–23, 12–36
Charman v Charman [2005] EWCA Civ 1606; [2006] 1 W.L.R. 1053; [2006]
   W.T.L.R. 1, CA (Civ Div) 8–16
Charron v Montreal Trust (1985) 15 D.L.R. (2d.) 240 . . . . 15–20, 17–05
Chartered Mercantile Bank of India, London and China v Netherlands
   India Steam Navigation Co Ltd (1882–83) L.R. 10 Q.B.D. 521,
   CA 15–32, 16–14
Chatenay v Brazilian Submarine Telegraph Co Ltd [1891] 1 Q.B. 79, CA . . 15–12,
   15–40
Chaudhary v Chaudhary [1985] Fam. 19; [1985] 2 W.L.R. 350; [1984] 3 All
   E.R. 1017, CA (Civ Div) 12–27
Chaudhry v Chaudhry [1976] 1 W.L.R. 221; [1976] 1 All E.R. 805, CA (Civ
   Div); affirming [1976] Fam. 148; [1975] 3 W.L.R. 559; [1975] 3 All
   E.R. 687, Fam Div 11–05, 11–08
Chebaro v Chebaro [1987] Fam. 127; [1987] 2 W.L.R. 1090; [1987] 1 All
   E.R. 999, CA (Civ Div) 13–24
Cheni (otherwise Rodriguez) v Cheni [1965] P. 85; [1963] 2 W.L.R. 17,
   PDAD 4–05, 11–11, 11–17
Chesterman's Trusts, Re; Joined Cases Mott v Browning [1923] 2 Ch. 466,
   CA 15–09
Chetti v Chetti [1909] P. 67, PDAD 3–06, 10–07, 11–21
China National Star Petroleum Co v Tor Drilling (UK) Ltd 2002 S.L.T.
   1339; 2002 G.W.D. 12–348, OH 7–58
Chisholm v Chisholm, 1949 S.C. 434; 1949 S.L.T. 394, OH 18–17
Chiwell v Carlyon (1897) 14 S.C. (S.A.) 61 . . . . 13–02, 13–10
Chorley v Chorley. *See* C v C (Divorce: Jurisdiction).
Chris Hart (Business Sales) Ltd v Niven, 1992 S.L.T. (Sh. Ct.) 53; 1992
   S.C.L.R. 534, Sh Pr 7–20
Chung Chi Cheung v R.[1929] A.C. 16 16–14
Church of Scientology of California v Commissioner of Police of the
   Metropolis (No.1) (1976) 120 S.J. 690, CA (Civ Div) 16–12

Ci4Net.com.Inc, Re; Joined Cases DBP Holdings, Re [2004] EWHC 1941;
    [2005] B.C.C. 277, Ch D (Companies Ct) 17–40
Cie europeenne des petroles SA v Sensor Nederlands BV Hague, 1982
    (1983) 23 Int. Legal Mat. 66 15–26
City Bank v Barrow (1879–80) L.R. 5 App. Cas. 664, HL 17–15
Claim by a German Lottery Company, Re (6 U 135/03) [2005] I.L.Pr. 35,
    OLG (Koln) 7–38
Claim by Helbert Wagg and Co Ltd, Re; sub nom. Prudential Assurance
    Co Ltd, Re [1956] Ch. 323; [1956] 2 W.L.R. 183, Ch D . . 3–02, 3–04, 3–07,
                                15–22, 15–24, 15–53, 17–17
Clare and Co v Dresdner Bank [1915] 2 K.B. 576, KBD 17–17
Clark v Bowring and Co. *See* Clark v Hine.
Clark v Hine; sub nom. Clark v Bowring and Co, 1908 S.C. 1168; (1908) 16
    S.L.T. 326, IH (1 Div) 8–22
Clarke v Clarke, 1993 G.W.D. 16–1030 14–21
Clarke v Fennoscandia Ltd (No.1), 1998 S.C. 464; 1998 S.L.T. 1014, IH (2
    Div) 9–08
Clarke v Fennoscandia Ltd (No.2), 2001 S.L.T. 1311; 2000 G.W.D. 11–377,
    OH 9–12
Clarke v Fennoscandia Ltd (No.3), 2005 S.L.T. 511; 2005 S.C.L.R. 322, IH
    (2 Div) 9–12
Clarke v Newmarsh (1836) 14 S. 488 .... 6–31, 13–10
Clarke's Trs, Petrs 1966 S.L.T. 249, IH (1 Div) 18–47
Cleveland Museum of Art v Capricorn Art International SA [1990] 2 Ll
    Rep. 166; (1989) 5 B.C.C. 860, QBD (Comm) 7–45
Cloncurry's (Lord) Case (1811) 6 St. Tr. (N.S.) 87 11–28
Cloncurry's (Lord) Estate, Re [1932] I.R. 687 13–07
Clore (Deceased) (No.2), Re; sub nom. Official Solicitor v Clore [1984]
    S.T.C. 609, Ch D 6–04, 6–10
Clydesdale Bank v Anderson (1890) 27 S.L.R. 493 17–53
Clydesdale Bank Ltd v Schroder and Co [1913] 2 K.B. 1, KBD 9–11
Coast Lines v Hudig and Veder Chartering NV [1972] 2 Q.B. 34; [1972] 2
    W.L.R. 280; [1972] 1 All E.R. 451, CA (Civ Div) 15–12, 15–32
Cochrane v Moore (1890) L.R. 25 Q.B.D. 57, CA 17–07
Cohen v Rothfield [1919] 1 K.B. 410, CA 7–47
Cohn, Re [1945] Ch. 5, Ch D 4–04, 8–01, 8–18, 18–25
Coin Controls Ltd v Suzo International (UK) Ltd [1999] Ch. 33; [1998] 3
    W.L.R. 420; [1997] 3 All E.R. 45, Ch D 17–32
Coleman v Shang, alias Quartey [1961] A.C. 481; [1961] 2 W.L.R. 562, PC
    (Gha) 11–04
Collens (Deceased), Re; sub nom. Royal Bank of Canada (London) Ltd v
    Krogh [1986] Ch. 505; [1986] 2 W.L.R. 919; [1986] 1 All E.R. 611,
    Ch D 18–04, 18–06
Collier v Rivaz, (1841) 2 Curt. 855 5–02
Collins Trs v Collins; sub nom. Anderson (Collins Trs) v Collins (1913) 1
    S.L.T. 219, OH 18–37, 18–40
Colonial Bank v Cady; sub nom. Williams v Colonial Bank; Williams v
    London Chartered Bank of Australia; Joined Cases London Char-
    tered Bank of Australia v Cady (1890) L.R. 15 App. Cas. 267, HL;
    affirming (1888) L.R. 38 Ch. D. 388, CA 17–31
Colorado, The [1923] P. 102, CA 8–22
Colt Industries Inc v Sarlie (No.2) [1966] 1 W.L.R. 1287; [1966] 3 All E.R.
    85, CA 9–12
Comber v Maclean (1881) 9 R. 215 9–13
Comex Houlder Diving v Colne Fishing Co, 1987 S.C. (H.L.) 85; 1987
    S.L.T. 443, HL 16–24
Commercial Bank of South Australia, Re (1887) L.R. 36 Ch. D. 522, Ch D   17–29

Commerzbank AG v Large, 1977 S.C. 375; 1977 S.L.T. 219, IH (1 Div) 8–21, 15–54

Compagnie Commerciale Andre SA v Artibell Shipping Co Ltd (No.1) 1999 S.L.T. 1051; 1999 S.C.L.R. 349, OH 7–45, 7–54

Compagnie Tunisienne de Navigation SA v Compagnie d'Armement Maritime SA; sub nom. Compagnie d'Armement Maritime SA v Compagnie Tunisienne de Navigation SA [1971] A.C. 572; [1970] 3 W.L.R. 389; [1970] 3 All E.R. 71, HL 15–06, 15–12, 15–32

Compania Colombiana de Seguros v Pacific Steam Navigation Co (*The Colombiana*); Joined Cases Empressa de Telefona de Bogota v Pacific Steam Navigation Co (The Colombiana) [1965] 1 Q.B. 101; [1964] 2 W.L.R. 484; [1964] 1 All E.R. 216, QBD (Comm) 17–17

Compania Naviera Micro SA v Shipley International Inc (*The Parouth*) [1982] 2 Ll Rep. 351, CA (Civ Div) 15–19

Compania Naviera Vascongada v Cristina, The [1938] A.C. 485; [1938] 1 All E.R. 719, HL 3–05, 7–03

Comsite Projects Ltd v Andritz AG [2003] EWHC 958; (2004) 20 Const. L.J. 24, QBD (TCC) 7–29

Connal and Co v Loder (1868) 6 M. 1095 17–15

Connel's Trs v Connel (1872) 10 M. 627 18–17

Connelly v RTZ Corp Plc (No.2) [1998] A.C. 854; [1997] 3 W.L.R. 373; [1997] 4 All E.R. 335, HL 7–45

Continental Bank NA v Aeakos Compania Naviera SA [1994] 1 W.L.R. 588; [1994] 2 All E.R. 540, CA (Civ Div) 7–29, 7–30

Continuity Promotions Ltd v O'Conner's Nenagh Shopping Centre Ltd [2006] All E.R.(D.) 39 .... 7–13, 9–41

Convery v Lanarkshire Tramways Co (1905) 8 F. 117; (1905) 13 S.L.T. 512, IH (1 Div) 16–10

Cood (1863) 33 Beav. 314 .... 15–12, 17–06

Coode, In the Goods of (1865–69) L.R. 1 P. & D. 449, Ct of Probate 18–01

Cooke's Trs, Re (1887) 56 L.T. 737 6–25

Cooke's Trusts, Re (1887) 3 T.L.R. 558 13–05

Cooney v Cooney, 1950 S.L.T. (Notes) 1, IH (2 Div) 6–31

Cooney v Dunne, 1925 S.L.T. 22, OH 9–12

Cooper v Baillie (1878) 5 R.564 17–49

Cooper v Cooper (1888) L.R. 13 App. Cas. 88; (1888) 15 R. (H.L.) 21, HL 13–05

Coote v Jecks (1871–72) L.R. 13 Eq. 597, Ct of Chancery 17–08

Copin v Adamson; Joined Cases Copin v Strachan (1875–76) L.R. 1 Ex. D. 17, CA; affirming (1873–74) L.R. 9 Ex. 345, Ex Ct 9–10

Corbet v Waddell (1879) 7 R. 200 13–07

Corbett v Corbett [1957] 1 W.L.R. 486; [1957] 1 All E.R. 621, PDAD 3–06, 10–05

Corbett v Corbett (otherwise Ashley) (No.1) [1971] P. 83; [1970] 2 W.L.R. 1306; [1970] 2 All E.R. 33, PDAD 11–01

Cordova Land Co Ltd v Victor Bros Inc; Joined Cases Cordova Land Co v Black Diamond Steamship Corp [1966] 1 W.L.R. 793; 110 S.J. 290, QBD 16–18

Coreck Maritime GmbH v Handelsveem BV (C387/98); sub nom. Handelsveem BV v Coreck Maritime GmbH (C387/98) [2000] E.C.R. I—9337; [2001] C.L.C. 550; [2001] C.L.Y.B.795, ECJ (5th Chamber) .. 7–29

Cornelius v Banque Franco—Serbe [1942] 1 K.B. 29; [1941] 2 All E.R. 728,
  KBD 17–29
Corocraft Ltd v Pan American Airways Inc; sub nom. Corocraft v Pan
  American World Airways Inc; Corocraft and Vendome Jewels v Pan
  American Airways Inc [1969] 1 Q.B. 616; [1968] 3 W.L.R. 1273;
  [1969] 1 All E.R. 82, CA (Civ Div) 15–24
Cottington's Case (1678) 2 Swans. 326 2–02
Cottrell v Cottrell (1872) L.R. 2 P. & D. 397 18–29
Countess of Findlater and Seafield v Seafield Grant, February 8, 1814, FC ... 13–07
Coupland v Arabian Gulf Oil Co [1983] 1 W.L.R. 1136; [1983] 3 All E.R.
  226, CA (Civ Div) 16–24
Courtney Ex p. Pollard, Re (1840) Mont. & Ch. 239 .... 17–08, 17–53, 17–58
Cox v Army Council; sub nom. R. v Cox [1963] A.C. 48; [1962] 2 W.L.R.
  950, HL 3–07
Cox v Owners of the Esso Malaysia (*The Esso Malaysia*) [1975] Q.B. 198;
  [1974] 3 W.L.R. 341; [1974] 2 All E.R. 705, QBD (Admlty) ... 3–07, 16–14
Craig, Re, 86 L.J. Ch. 62 17–56
Craignish, Re; sub nom. Craignish v Hewitt [1892] 3 Ch. 180, CA 6–06
Craven's Estate (No.1), Re; sub nom. Lloyds Bank Ltd v Cockburn (No.1)
  [1937] Ch. 423; [1937] 3 All E.R. 33, Ch D 17–12
Credit Chimique v James Scott Engineering Group Ltd 1979 S.C. 406;
  1982 S.L.T. 131, OH 7–45
Credit Lyonnais v New Hampshire Insurance Co Ltd [1997] 2 Ll Rep. 1;
  [1997] 2 C.M.L.R. 610, CA (Civ Div) 15–16
Credit Suisse Fides Trust SA v Cuoghi [1998] Q.B. 818; [1998] 1 W.L.R.
  474; [1997] 3 W.L.R. 871; [1997] 3 All E.R. 724, CA (Civ Div) 7–58
Cripps's Trs v Cripps, 1926 S.C. 188; 1926 S.L.T. 188, IH (2 Div) 18–26
Cristina, The. See Compania Naviera Vascongada v Cristina, The.
Croft v Royal Mail Group Plc (formerly Consignia Plc) [2003] EWCA Civ
  1045; [2003] I.C.R. 1425; [2003] I.R.L.R. 592, CA (Civ Div) 11–01
Cronos Containers NV v Palatin; Joined Cases Cronos Equipment (Ber-
  muda) Ltd v Palatin [2002] EWHC 2819; [2003] 2 Ll Rep. 489,
  QBD (Comm) 7–14
Crookenden v Fuller (1859) 1 Sw. & Tr. 441 6–16
Cross Construction Sussex Ltd v Tseliki [2006] EWHC 1056; [2006] All
  E.R. (D.) 334, Ch D 17–40
Crowe v Crowe [1937] 2 All E.R. 723 3–06
Cruh v Cruh [1945] 2 All E.R. 545, PDAD 6–09, 6–30
Cruickshanks v Cruickshanks [1957] 1 W.L.R. 564; [1957] 1 All E.R. 889,
  PDAD 6–31
Crumpton's Judicial Factor v Finch-Noyes, 1918 S.C. 378; 1918 1 S.L.T.
  254, IH (1 Div) 6–24
Cruse v Chittum (formerly Cruse) [1974] 2 All E.R. 940; (1974) 4 Fam.
  Law 152, Fam Div 6–40
Cullen v Gossagge (1850) 12 D. 633 11–24
Cumming v Scottish Daily Record and Sunday Mail Ltd [1995] E.M.L.R.
  538; *The Times*, June 8, 1995, QBD 7–46
Cunningham, Ex p.; sub nom. Mitchell Ex p. Cunningham, Re (1883–84)
  L.R. 13 Q.B.D. 418, CA 6–31
Cunnington, Re; sub nom. Healing v Webb [1924] 1 Ch. 68, Ch D 18–26
Curling v Thorton (1823) 2 Add. 6 6–17
Currie v McKnight (1897) 24 R. (H.L.) 1 16–14
Custom Made Commercial Ltd v Stawa Metallbau Gmbh [1993] I.L.Pr.
  490, BGH (Ger) 7–13
Customs and Excise Commissioners v Barclays Bank Plc [2004] EWCA Civ
  1555; [2005] 1 W.L.R. 2082; [2005] 3 All E.R. 852, CA (Civ Div) 7–58

Cutcliffe's Will Trusts, Re; Joined Cases Brewer v Cutcliffe [1940] Ch. 565,
Ch D 17–02
Cutcliffe, Re [1940] Ch.565 17–02
Cyganik v Agulian; sub nom. Agulian v Cyganik [2006] EWCA Civ 129;
[2006] 1 F.C.R. 406; [2006] W.T.L.R. 565, CA (Civ Div) 6–04, 6–06,
6–11, 6–15, 6–16, 6–22, 6–34, 18–09

D (a child)(abduction: Custody rights) [2006] All E.R. (D.) 355 14–29
D v D (Child Abduction: Non Convention Country) [1994] 1 F.L.R. 137;
[1994] 1 F.C.R. 654; [1994] Fam. Law 126, CA (Civ Div) 14–48
D v D (Parent and Child: Residence), 2002 S.C. 33; 2001 S.L.T. 1104, IH
(1 Div) 14–27
DSM Anti-Infectives BV v SmithKline Beecham Plc; Joined Cases DSM
Anti-Infectives Sweden AB v SmithKline Beecham Corp [2004]
EWCA Civ 1199; [2004] 2 C.L.C. 900; (2004) 27(10) I.P.D. 27080,
CA (Civ Div); affirming [2004] EWHC 1309, Ch D 7–51
DWS (Deceased), Re; sub nom. S (Deceased), Re; S (A Child) v G; Joined
Cases EHS (Deceased), Re; TWGS (A Child) v JMG [2001] Ch.
568; [2000] 3 W.L.R. 1910; [2001] 1 All E.R. 97, CA (Civ Div) 18–25
Dadourian Group International Inc v Simms [2006] EWCA Civ 399; [2006]
1 All E.R. (Comm) 709; *The Times*, May 23, 2006, CA (Civ Div) 7–58
Dailey Petroleum Services Corp v Pioneer Oil Tools Ltd 1994 S.L.T. 757,
OH 7–55
Daisytek-ISA Ltd, Re [2003] B.C.C. 562; [2004] B.P.I.R. 30, Ch D 17–40
Dallal v Bank Mellat [1986] Q.B. 441; [1986] 2 W.L.R. 745; [1986] 1 All
E.R. 239, QBD (Comm) 9–11
Dallas and Co (Transport) Ltd v McArdle, 1949 S.C. 481; 1949 S.L.T. 375,
IH (1 Div) 7–03
D'Almeida Araujo LDA v Sir Frederick Becker and Co Ltd. *See* J
D'Almeida Araujo LDA v Sir Frederick Becker and Co Ltd.
Dalrymple v Dalrymple (1811) 2 Hag. Con.54 3–01
Daly v Irish Group Travel Ltd (t/a Crystal Holidays) [2003] I.L.Pr. 38, HC
(Irl) 7–17
Daniel v Foster, 1989 S.L.T. (Sh. Ct.) 90; 1989 S.C.L.R. 378, Sh Ct (North
Strathclyde) 7–10, 7–53
Danmarks Rederiforening v LO Landsorganisationen i Sverige (C18/02);
sub nom. DFDS Torline A/S v SEKO Sjofolk Facket for Service och
Kommunikation [2004] All E.R. (EC) 845; [2004] 2 Ll Rep. 162,
ECJ (6th Chamber) 7–14
Dansommer A/S v Gotz (C8/98) [2001] 1 W.L.R. 1069; [2000] E.C.R.
I—393, ECJ (6th Chamber) 7–27
Davidson v Davidson, 1997 G.W.D. 2–39, OH 14–25
Davidson, Re (1873) L.R. 15 Eq. 383 17–56
Davidsson v Hill [1901] 2 K.B. 606; [1900-1903] All E.R. 997, KBD .. 3–07, 16–14
Davies v Rayner. *See* Rayner v Davies.
Dawodu v Danmole [1962] 1 W.L.R. 1053; 106 S.J. 628, PC (Nig) 11–04
Dawson, Re; Joined Cases Pattisson v Bathurst [1915] 1 Ch. 626, CA 18–25
Dawson's Trs v Macleans (1860) 22 D. 685, IH (1 Div) 7–47
De Beeche v South American Stores (Gath and Chaves) Ltd; Joined Cases
De Beeche v Chilian Stores (Gath and Chaves) Ltd [1935] A.C. 148,
HL 15–26
De Beer v Kanaar and Co (No.1) [2001] EWCA Civ 1318; [2003] 1 W.L.R.
38; [2002] 3 All E.R. 1020, CA (Civ Div) 7–03
De Beers Consolidated Mines Ltd v British South Africa Co; sub nom.
British South Africa Co v De Beers Consolidated Mines Ltd [1912]
A.C. 52, HL; reversing [1910] 2 Ch. 502, CA 15–12, 17–06

De Bloos SPRL v Bouyer SA. *See*A De Bloos SPRL v Bouyer SA (C14/76).

De Bonneval (1838) 1 Curt. 856 . . . . 6–16, 6–30

De Cavel v De Cavel (143/78) [1979] E.C.R. 1055; [1979] 2 C.M.L.R. 547, ECJ 13–18

De Cavel v De Cavel (120/79) [1980] E.C.R. 731; [1980] 3 C.M.L.R. 1, ECJ (3rd Chamber) 7–09, 13–08

De Cosse Brissac v Rathbone (1861) 6 H. & N. 301 9–11

De Dampierre v De Dampierre [1988] A.C. 92; [1987] 2 W.L.R. 1006; [1987] 2 All E.R. 1, HL 11–23, 12–11

De Fogassieras v Duport (1881) 11 L.R. Ir. 123 . . . . 17–02, 18–17

De Hosson, Re [1937] I.R. 467 6–10

De la Vega v Vianna (1830) 1 B. & Ad. 284 . . . . 7–03, 8–01

De Mulder v Jadranska Linijska (Jadrolinija) 1989 S.L.T. 269, OH 7–45

De Nicols v Curlier (No.1); sub nom. De Nicols, Re [1900] A.C. 21, HL . . . 4–03, 13–02, 15–01

De Nicols v Curlier (No.2); sub nom. De Nicols, Re [1900] 2 Ch. 410, Ch D 13–02

De Noailles, Re (1916) 114 L.T. 1089 18–25

De Reneville (otherwise Sheridan) v De Reneville [1948] P. 100; [1948] 1 All E.R. 56, CA 1–01, 4–01, 6–25, 11–09, 11–17, 12–36

De Wilton, Re; sub nom. De Wilton v Montefiore [1900] 2 Ch. 481, Ch D . . . 4–05, 11–16

De Wolf v Harry Cox BV (C42/76) [1976] E.C.R. 1759; [1977] 2 C.M.L.R. 43, ECJ 9–37, 9–59

Deans (Joseph) v Deans (Morag), 1988 S.C.L.R. 192, Sh Pr 14–49

Debaecker v Bouwman (49/84) [1985] E.C.R. 1779; [1986] 2 C.M.L.R. 400, ECJ (4th Chamber) 9–40

Deep Vein Thrombosis and Air Travel Group Litigation, Re [2005] UKHL 72; [2006] 1 A.C. 495; [2005] 3 W.L.R. 1320; [2006] 1 All E.R. 786, HL 1–06

Def Lepp Music v Stuart—Brown [1986] R.P.C. 273, Ch D 16–12

Definitely Maybe (Touring) Ltd v Marek Lieberberg Konzertagentur GmbH (No.2); sub nom. Definitely Maybe (Touring) Ltd v Marek Lieberberg Konzertagentur GmbH (No.2) [2001] 1 W.L.R. 1745; [2001] 4 All E.R. 283, QBD (Comm) 15–16

Dehn v Dehn, 1998 G.W.D. 2–59; 1998 G.W.D. 35–705, OH 14–33

Delaurier v Wyllie (1889) 17 R. 167 15–40

Dent v Smith (1868–69) L.R. 4 Q.B. 414, QB 9–11

Derby and Co Ltd v Weldon (No.1) [1990] Ch. 48; [1989] 2 W.L.R. 276; [1989] 1 All E.R. 469, CA (Civ Div) 7–58

Derby and Co Ltd v Weldon (Nos.3 and No.4) [1990] Ch. 65; [1989] 2 W.L.R. 412, CA (Civ Div) 7–58

Desert Sun Loan Corp v Hill [1996] 2 All E.R. 847; [1996] 5 Bank. L.R. 98, CA (Civ Div) 9–12

Despatie v Tremblay [1921] 1 A.C. 702, PC (Can) 11–16

Despina, R, The. See Services Europe Atlantique Sud (SEAS) v Stockholms Rederi AB Svea: *Despina, R, The: Folias, The.*

Det Norske v McLaren (1885) 22 S.L.R. 861 9–12

Deutz Engines v Terex (1984) 1984 S.L.T. 273, OH 17–16

Dewar v Dewar, 1995 S.L.T. 467, OH 11–24

Dexter Ltd (In Administrative Receivership) v Harley [2001] C.L.Y.B. 810; *The Times*, April 2, 2001, Ch D 7–14

Di Rollo v Di Rollo, 1959 S.C. 75; 1959 S.L.T. 278, OH 11–31, 12–38, 12–39

Diamond v Bank of London and Montreal [1979] Q.B. 333; [1979] 2 W.L.R. 228; [1979] 1 All E.R. 561; [1979] 1 Ll Rep. 335, CA (Civ Div) 16–18, 16–21

Dickson v Dickson (Parent and child: Evidence), 1990 S.C.L.R. 692, IH
(Ex Div) 6–40, 14–27
Dinwoodie's Exr v Carruthers' Exr (1895) 23 R. 234 17–28
Disley v Levine (t/a Airtrak Levine Paragliding) [2001] EWCA Civ 1087;
[2002] 1 W.L.R. 785; [2001] C.L.C. 1694, CA (Civ Div) 1–06
Distillers Co (Biochemicals) Ltd v Thompson (Laura Anne); sub nom.
Distillers Co (Bio—chemicals) Ltd v Thompson (by her next friend
Arthur Leslie Thompson) [1971] A.C. 458; [1971] 2 W.L.R. 441;
[1971] 1 All E.R. 694, PC (Aus) 16–18
Dobree v Napier (1836) 2 Bing. N.C. 781 .... 3–06, 16–12
Doglioni v Crispin; sub nom. Crispin v Doglioni (1866) L.R. 1 H.L. 301,
HL 9–04, 10–07, 18–03, 18–10
Dollfus Mieg et Compagnie SA v Bank of England (No.1); sub nom.
United States v Dollfus Mieg et Cie SA [1952] A.C. 582; [1952] 1
All E.R. 572, HL 7–03
Domicrest Ltd v Swiss Bank Corp [1999] Q.B. 548; [1999] 2 W.L.R. 364;
[1998] 3 All E.R. 577, QBD 7–15
Dominion Bridge Co v British American Nickel Co Ltd (1925) 2 D.L.R.
138 17–04
Don v Lippmann (1837) 5 Cl. & F. (HL) 13; (1837) 2 Sh. & Macl. 682 8–02,
8–09
Don's Estate, Re (1857) 4 Drewry 194 14–02
Donaldson v McClure (1857) 20 D. 207 6–04
Donaldson v Ord (1855) 17 D. 1053 17–28
Donaldson (otherwise Nichols) v Donaldson [1949] P. 363; 65 T.L.R. 233,
PDAD 6–31
Donofrio v Burrell, 2000 S.L.T. 1051; 2000 S.C.L.R. 465, IH (Ex Div) 14–21
Donohue v Armco Inc [2001] UKHL 64; [2002] 1 All E.R. 749; [2002] 1
All E.R. (Comm) 97, HL 7–30, 7–47
Dornoch Ltd v Mauritius Union Assurance Co Ltd [2006] EWCA Civ 389,
CA (Civ Div) 7–45, 16–20
Dorward v Dorward, 1994 S.C.C.R. 928, Sh Pr 14–44
Doucet v Geoghegan (1878) L.R. 9 Ch. D. 441, CA 6–13, 6–15
Douglas v Douglas; Joined Cases Douglas v Webster (1871) L.R. 12 Eq.
617, CA in Chancery 6–21
Douglas v Hello! Ltd (No.6); sub nom. Douglas v Hello! Ltd (Trial Action:
Breach of Confidence) (No.3) [2005] EWCA Civ 595; [2006] Q.B.
125; [2005] 3 W.L.R. 881; [2005] 4 All E.R. 128, CA (Civ Div) 16–16,
16–20, 16–29, 16–31, 16–33
Douglas-Menzies v Umphelby [1908] A.C. 224, PC (Aus) 18–34
Dowds, In the Estate of Arthur [1948] P. 256; 64 T.L.R. 244, PDAD 8–12
Downie v Downie's Trs (1866) 4 M. 1067 17–02
Dow's Trs, Petrs 1947 S.C. 524; 1947 S.L.T. 293, IH (1 Div) 18–52
Dramgate Ltd v Tyne Dock Engineering Ltd 2000 S.C. 43; 1999 S.L.T.
1392; 1999 G.W.D. 31–1452, IH (Ex Div) 7–58
Drammeh v Drammeh (1970) 78 Cey. L.W. 55 11–10
Dresser UK Ltd v Falcongate Freight Management Ltd (The Duke of
Yare) [1992] Q.B. 502; [1992] 2 W.L.R. 319; [1992] 2 All E.R. 450,
CA (Civ Div) 7–29, 7–41
Drevon v Drevon (1834) 34 L.J. Ch. 129 .... 6–04, 6–13, 6–15m 6–21
Drouot Assurances SA v Consolidated Metallurgical Industries (CMI
Industrial Sites) (C351/96) [1999] Q.B. 497; [1999] 2 W.L.R. 163;
[1998] All E.R. (EC) 483, ECJ (5th Chamber) 7–38
Drummond v Bell-Irving; sub nom. Drummond v Peel's Trs, 1929 S.C. 484;
1929 S.L.T. 450; 1930 S.C. 704; 1930 S.L.T. 466, IH (2 Div) ... 13–07, 13–09
Dublin Finance Corp v Rowe [1943] N.I. 1 3–07
Duc de Frias v Pichon (1886) 13 Journal du Droit International 593 17–04

Duchess of Buckingham v Winterbottom (1851) 13 D. 1129 13–10
Dulaney v Merry and Son [1901] 1 Q.B. 536, QBD 3–07
Dulles Settlement, Re (No.2); sub nom. Dulles (An Infant) v Vidler;
    Dulles Settlement Trusts, Re (No.2) [1951] Ch. 842; [1951] 2 All
    E.R. 69, CA 9–10
Dumez France SA v Hessische Landesbank (220/88) [1990] E.C.R. I—49;
    [1990] I.L.Pr. 299, ECJ (6th Chamber) 7–14
Dunbee Ltd v Gilman and Co (Australia) Pty Ltd [1968] 2 Ll Rep. 394; 118
    N.L.J. 1126, Sup Ct (NSW) 15–12
Duncan v Lawson (1889) L.R. 41 Ch. D. 394, Ch D 17–02
Duncan v Motherwell Bridge and Engineering Co Ltd, 1952 S.C. 131; 1952
    S.L.T. 433, IH (2 Div) 3–07
Dundas v Dundas (1830) 3 Dow. & B. 349. HL 18–08, 18–34
Dungannon v Hackett (1702) 1 Eq. Cas.Abrs. 289 2–02
Dunne v Saban [1955] P. 178; [1954] 3 W.L.R. 980; [1954] 3 All E.R. 586;
    98 S.J. 888, PDAD 6–25
Dunstan v Dunstan (1858) 28 L.J.C.P. 97 6–29
Durie's Trs v Osborne, 1960 S.C. 444; 1961 S.L.T. 53, IH (2 Div) .. 18–33, 18–37,
    18–40, 18–43
Duyrewaardt v Barber (1992) 43 R.F.L. (3d.) 139, BC CA 13–08
Dyas, Re [1937] I.R. 479 18–01
Dynamit AG (Vormals Alfred Nobel Co) v Rio Tinto Co Ltd; Vereingte
    Koenigs v Rio Tinto Co Ltd. *See* Ertel Bieber and Co v Rio Tinto
    Co Ltd.

E (D) (An Infant), Re; sub nom. E (An Infant), Re [1967] Ch. 761; [1967]
    2 W.L.R. 1370; [1967] 2 All E.R. 881, CA (Civ Div); affirming
    [1967] Ch. 287; [1967] 2 W.L.R. 445; [1967] 1 All E.R. 329, Ch D .. 14–25
E Pfeiffer Weinkellerei-Weineinkauf GmbH and Co v Arbuthnot Factors
    Ltd [1988] 1 W.L.R. 150; (1987) 3 B.C.C. 608, QBD 17–16
Eadie's Trs v Henderson, 1919 1 S.L.T. 253, OH 13–04, 13–07
Earl, Re (1867) L.R. 1 P. & D. 450 18–01
Earl Iveagh v Inland Revenue Commissioners; sub nom. Iveagh Trusts, Re
    [1954] Ch. 364; [1954] 2 W.L.R. 494; [1954] 1 All E.R. 609, Ch D .. 13–04
Earl Middleton v Baron Cottesloe; sub nom. Cottesloe (Lord) v Attorney
    General; Middleton's Settlement, Re [1949] A.C. 418; [1949] 1 All
    E.R. 841, HL; affirming [1947] Ch. 583; [1947] 2 All E.R. 134, CA ... 17–02,
    17–31
Earl of Stair v Head (1844) 6 D. 904 .... 13–07, 15–01, 15–11
East India Trading Co Inc v Carmel Exporters and Importers Ltd [1952] 2
    Q.B. 439; [1952] 1 All E.R. 1053, QBD 9–07
Eddie v Alpa Srl, 2000 S.L.T. 1062; 2000 G.W.D. 11–397, OH 7–13
Edgar v Fisher's Trs (1893) 21 R.59 14–46
Edmunds v Simmonds [2001] 1 W.L.R. 1003; [2001] R.T.R. 24, QBD 16–20
Egan, Re (1918) L.J. 633 18–25
Egerton's Will Trusts, Re; sub nom. Lloyds Bank v Egerton [1956] Ch. 593;
    [1956] 3 W.L.R. 453;, Ch D 4–05, 11–17, 13–10
Egon Oldendorff v Libera Corp (No.2) [1996] 1 Ll Rep. 380; [1996] C.L.C.
    482, QBD (Comm) 9–76
EI Du Pont de Nemours and Co v Agnew (No.1) [1987] 2 Ll Rep. 585;
    [1987] F.L.R. 376, CA (Civ Div) 15–06
EI Du Pont de Nemours and Co v Agnew (No.2) [1988] 2 Ll Rep. 240;
    [1990] E.C.C. 9; [1988] 2 F.T.L.R. 39, CA (Civ Div) 7–47
El Ajou v Dollar Land Holdings Plc (No.1) [1994] 2 All E.R. 685; [1994]
    B.C.C. 143, CA (Civ Div); reversing [1993] 3 All E.R. 717; [1993]
    B.C.C. 698, Ch D 7–58, 16–30
Electronic Arts CV v CTO SpA [2003] EWHC 1020, QBD (Comm) 7–09

Elefanten Schuh GmbH v Jacqmain (150/80) [1981] E.C.R. 1671; [1982] 3
 C.M.L.R. 1, ECJ 7–49
Elf Caledonia Ltd v London Bridge Engineering Ltd, 1997 G.W.D.
 33–1686 9–08
Eliades v Lewis (No.9) [2005] EWHC 2966, QBD 7–58
Ellerman Lines Ltd v Read [1928] 2 K.B. 144; 64 A.L.R. 1128, CA 9–04
Elliot, Re (1891) 39 W.R. 297 18–25
Ellis v McHenry (1870-71) L.R. 6 C.P. 228, CCP 9–11, 15-25, 17–59
Elmquist v Elmquist, 1961 S.L.T. (Notes) 71, OH 6–10
Emanuel v Symon [1908] 1 K.B. 302, CA 7–04, 9–10
Embiricos v Anglo Austrian Bank; sub nom. Embiricos v Anglo Austrian
 Bank [1905] 1 K.B. 677, CA; affirming [1904] 2 K.B. 870, KBD
 (Comm Ct) 5–07, 17–29
Emerald Stainless Steel Ltd v South Side Distribution Ltd 1982 S.C. 61;
 1983 S.L.T. 162, OH 17–16
Emery's Investment Trusts, Re; sub nom. Emery v Emery [1959] Ch. 410;
 [1959] 2 W.L.R. 461, Ch D 3–02, 3–06
Emin v Yeldag [2002] 1 F.L.R. 956; [2002] Fam. Law 419, Fam Div 12–20,
 13–24
Emperor Napoleon Bonaparte, Re the late (1853) 2 Rob. Ecc. 606 6–29
Employers Liability Assurance Corp Ltd v Sedgwick Collins and Co Ltd;
 sub nom. Sedgwick Collins and Co Ltd v Rossia Insurance Co of
 Petrograd (Employers Liability Assurance Corp Ltd) [1927] A.C.
 95; (1926) 25 Ll. L. Rep. 453, HL 15–25
Engdiv Ltd v G Percy Trentham Ltd, 1990 S.C. 53; 1990 S.L.T. 617, OH ... 7–13
Engler v Janus Versand GmbH (C27/02) [2005] E.C.R. I—481; [2005]
 C.E.C. 187; [2005] 7 C.L. 76, ECJ (2nd Chamber) 7–13, 7–20
English v Donnelly, 1958 S.C. 494; 1959 S.L.T. 2, IH (1 Div) 15–11, 15–23,
 15–33
English Scottish and Australian Bank Ltd v Inland Revenue Commis-
 sioners [1932] A.C. 238, HL 17–03
Ennstone Building Products Ltd v Stanger Ltd; sub nom. Ennstone
 Building Products Ltd (formerly Natural Stone Products Ltd) v
 Stanger Ltd (formerly TBV Stanger Ltd) (No.2) [2002] EWCA Civ
 916; [2002] 1 W.L.R. 3059; [2002] 2 All E.R. (Comm) 479, CA (Civ
 Div) 7–13, 15–14, 15–16, 16–15, 16–18
Ennstone Building Products Ltd v Stanger (No.1) [2002] C.L.Y.B. 624 7–14,
 7–46
Enochin v Wylie (1862) 10 H.L. Cas. 1 .... 9–04, 18–03
Entores Ltd v Miles Far East Corp; sub nom. Newcomb v De Roos [1955]
 2 Q.B. 327; [1955] 3 W.L.R. 48; [1955] 2 All E.R. 493, CA .. 15–12, 15–43
Equitable Trust Co of New York v Henderson (1930) 47 T.L.R. 90; (1930)
 38 Ll. L. Rep. 187, KBD 15–22
Equitas Ltd v Wave City Shipping Co Ltd [2005] EWHC 923; [2005] 2 All
 E.R. (Comm) 301, QBD (Comm) 7–14, 7–44, 16–17
Erich Gasser GmbH v MISAT Srl (C116/02) [2005] Q.B. 1; [2004] 3
 W.L.R. 1070, ECJ 7–29, 7–30, 7–31, 7–42, 7–43, 7–44, 7–49
Erie Beach Co Ltd v Attorney General of Ontario [1930] A.C. 161, PC
 (Can) 17–31
Ertel Bieber and Co v Rio Tinto Co Ltd; Joined Cases Dynamit AG
 (Vormals Alfred Nobel Co) v Rio Tinto Co Ltd; Vereingte Koenigs
 v Rio Tinto Co Ltd [1918] A.C. 260, HL 8–17
Esso Malaysia, The. See Cox v Owners of the Esso Malaysia (*The Esso
 Malaysia*).
Et Plus SA v Welter [2005] EWHC 2115; [2006] 1 Ll Rep. 251; [2006]
 I.L.Pr. 18, QBD (Comm) 7–17

Etablissement Baudelot v RS Graham and Co [1953] 2 Q.B. 271; [1953] 2
     W.L.R. 180, CA 8–05
Euro-Diam Ltd v Bathurst [1990] 1 Q.B. 1; [1988] 2 W.L.R. 517; [1988] 2
     All E.R. 23, CA (Civ Div); affirming [1987] 2 W.L.R. 1368; [1987] 2
     All E.R. 113, QBD (Comm) 15–19
Eurofood IFSC Ltd, unreported, May 2, 2006, ECJ 17–40, 17–47
Europs Ltd v Sunshine Lifestyle Products Ltd [1998] C.L.Y.B. 750 7–45
Eva, The; sub nom. Eva, The (Question of Priorities) [1921] P. 454; (1921)
     8 Ll. L. Rep. 315, PDAD 3–02
Evans and Sons v John G Stein and Co (1904) 7 F. 65; (1904) 12 S.L.T.
     462, IH (1 Div) 16–11, 16–21
Evans (Deceased), Re; sub nom. National Provincial Bank v Evans [1947]
     Ch. 695; [1948] L.J.R. 498; 177 L.T. 585, Ch D 6–04, 6–17, 6–22, 6–29,
                                                                          6–30
Evialis SA v SIAT [2003] EWHC 863; [2003] 2 Ll Rep. 377; [2003] 2
     C.L.C. 802, QBD (Comm) 7–39
Ewin, Re (1830) 1 Cr. & J. 151 17–10
Ewing v Orr Ewing (No.1) (1883–84) L.R. 9 App. Cas. 34, HL 18–01, 18–03
Ewing's Trs v Ewing; sub nom. Ewing v Orr Ewing (No.2) (1884–85) L.R.
     10 App. Cas. 453; (1885) 13 R. (H.L.) 1, HL 9–04, 18–03

F (A Minor) (Abduction: Custody Rights), Re; sub nom. F (A Minor)
     (Abduction: Jurisdiction), Re [1991] Fam. 25; [1990] 3 W.L.R. 1272;
     [1990] 3 All E.R. 97, CA (Civ Div) 14–48
F (A Minor) (Child Abduction: Rights of Custody Abroad), Re; sub nom.
     F (A Minor) (Child Abduction: Risk if Returned), Re [1995] Fam.
     224; [1995] 3 W.L.R. 339; [1995] 3 All E.R. 641, CA (Civ Div) 14–31
F v F (Ancillary Relief: Substantial Assets) [1995] 2 F.L.R. 45; [1996] 2
     F.C.R. 397, Fam Div 13–09
F v F (Minors) (Custody: Foreign Order: Enforcement) [1989] Fam. 1;
     [1988] 3 W.L.R. 959; [1989] 1 F.L.R. 335; [1989] F.C.R. 232; (1989)
     153 J.P.N. 307; (1988) 132 S.J. 1323, Fam Div 14–33
F and K Jabbour v Custodian of Israeli Absentee Property [1954] 1 W.L.R.
     139; [1954] 1 All E.R. 145, QBD 3–07, 17–08, 17–10, 17–18, 17–28
F Koechlin et Cie v Kestenbaum Bros; sub nom. Koechlin et Cie v
     Kestenbaum Bros [1927] 1 K.B. 889, CA 5–07, 17–29
Fab Tek Engineering Ltd v Carillion Construction Ltd 2002 S.L.T. (Sh Ct)
     113; 2002 G.W.D. 13–390, Sh Ct (Tayside) 7–58
Fabbri v Fabbri (No.1) [1962] 1 W.L.R. 13; [1962] 1 All E.R. 35, PDAD .. 14–25
Fairbairn v Neville (1897) 25 R. 192; (1897) 5 S.L.T. 224, IH (1 Div) 6–31
Farrell v Long (C295/95) [1997] Q.B. 842; [1997] 3 W.L.R. 613; [1997] All
     E.R. (E.C.) 449, ECJ (6th Chamber) 7–09, 9–38, 13–18
Faulkner (Michael Stanislaus) v Hill, 1942 J.C. 20; 1942 S.L.T. 159, HCJ
     Appeal 8–17
Faye v IR (1961) 40 T.C. 103 6–25
Feist v Société Intercommunale Belge d'Electricité; sub nom. Société
     Intercommunale Belge d'Electricité, Re [1934] A.C. 161; 88 A.L.R.
     1524, HL 15–11
Felixstowe Dock and Railway Co v United States Lines Inc; Joined Cases
     Freightliners v United States Lines Inc; Europe Container Ter-
     minus BV v United States Lines Inc [1989] Q.B. 360; [1989] 2
     W.L.R. 109; [1988] 2 All E.R. 77, QBD (Comm) 17–36
Fennoscandia Ltd v Clarke, 1995 G.W.D. 39–3032 9–08
Fenston's Settlement, Re; sub nom. Max Muller v Simonsen [1971] 1
     W.L.R. 1640; [1971] 3 All E.R. 1092; 115 S.J. 741, Ch D 18–43
Fenton v Livingstone (1859) 3 Macq. 497 18–11

Ferdinand Wagner v Laubscher Bros and Co; sub nom. Wagner v
    Laubschner Bros and Co; Wagner (Ferdinand) (A Firm) v
    Laubscher Bros and Co (A Firm) [1970] 2 Q.B. 313; [1970] 2
    W.L.R. 1019, CA (Civ Div) 9–25
Ferguson v Littlewoods Pools Ltd, 1997 S.L.T. 309, OH 3–06
Ferguson v Marjoribanks (1853) 15 D. 637 18–25
Ferguson Shipbuilders Ltd v Voith Hydro GmbH and Co KG, 2000 S.L.T.
    229; 1999 G.W.D. 31–1500, OH 7–13, 15–16
Fergusson's Will, Re [1902] 1 Ch. 483, Ch D 5–02, 18–27
Fibrosa Spolka Akcyjna v Fairbairn Lawson Combe Barbour Ltd; sub nom.
    Fibrosa Société Anonyme v Fairbairn Lawson Combe Barbour Ltd
    [1943] A.C. 32; [1942] 2 All E.R. 122; (1942) 73 Ll. L. Rep. 45; 144
    A.L.R. 1298, HL 16–30
Finance One Public Co. Ltd v Lehman Bros Special Financing Inc., 414 F.
    3d 325 (2nd Cir. 2005) .... 8–24, 15–13.
Findlay (Margaret) v Findlay (John) (No.1), 1994 S.L.T. 709; 1994
    S.C.L.R. 523, IH (2 Div) 14–29, 14–30
Findlay (Margaret) v Findlay (John) (No.2), 1995 S.L.T. 492, OH .. 14–29, 14–30
Finnegan v Cementation Co Ltd [1953] 1 Q.B. 688; [1953] 2 W.L.R. 1015;
    [1953] 1 All E.R. 1130, CA 18–01
First American Corp v Al—Nahyau (1998) 6 C.L. Week, issue 54.
    September 25, 1998 8–16
First Fidelity Bank NA v Hudson, 1995 G.W.D. 28–1499 9–08
Fisher v Unione Italiana de Riassicurazione SPA [1998] C.L.C. 682; [1988]
    C.L. 71, QBD 7–13
Fitzgerald, Re; sub nom. Surman v Fitzgerald [1904] 1 Ch. 573, CA 13–04,
                                                                        13–07
Fleming v Horniman (1928) 44 T.L.R. 315 6–19
Flynn (No.1), Re; sub nom. Flynn v Flynn (No.1) [1968] 1 W.L.R. 103;
    [1968] 1 All E.R. 49, Ch D 6–06, 6–22, 6–30
FMC Corp v Russell 1999 S.L.T. 99; 1998 G.W.D. 11–521, OH 7–45, 7–47,
                                                                8–05, 16–25
Folliot v Ogden (1789) 1 Ll.Bl. 123 3–03
Forbes v Official Receiver in Bankruptcy 1924 S.L.T. 522, OH 17–28
Fordyce v Bridges (1848) 2 Ph. 497 18–25
Forrest v Forrest (1910) 54 S.J. 737 18–52
Forsikringsaktieselskapet Vesta v Butcher [1989] A.C. 852; [1989] 2
    W.L.R. 290; [1989] 1 All E.R. 402, HL; affirming [1988] 3 W.L.R.
    565; [1988] 2 All E.R. 43; [1988] 1 Ll Rep. 19, CA (Civ Div);
    affirming [1986] 2 All E.R. 488; [1986] 2 Ll Rep. 179, QBD
    (Comm) 15–07, 15–11
Foster v Driscoll; Joined Cases Lindsay v Attfield; Lindsay v Driscoll
    [1929] 1 K.B. 470, CA 3–06.15–26
Fourman v Fourman, 1998 G.W.D. 32–1638, Sh Ct 14–29
Fowler v Fowler (No.2), 1981 S.L.T. (Notes) 78, OH 14–46
Foxen v Scotsman Publications Ltd [1995] E.M.L.R. 145; The Times,
    February 17, 1994, QBD 7–46
Frahuil SA v Assitalia SpA (C265/02); sub nom. Assitalia SpA v Frahuil
    SA (C265/02) [2004] All E.R. (EC) 373; [2004] C.E.C. 222; [2004]
    I.L.Pr. 11, ECJ (5th Chamber) 7–13
Francke and Rasch, Re [1918] 1 Ch. 470, Ch D 17–29
Frankel v CIR (1950) 1 S.A.L.R. 220 11–17
Frankel v The Master (1950) 1 S.A.L.R. 220 13–10
Frankfurther v WL Exner Ltd [1947] Ch. 629; [1948] L.J.R. 553; 177 L.T.
    257; 91 S.J. 532, Ch D 3–04
Fratelli Babbini di Lionello Babbini and Co SAS v BF Engineering SpA.
    See British Sugar Plc v Fratelli Babbini di Lionello Babbini and Co.

Freeman v The East India Co (1822) 5 B. & Ald. 617 17–13
Freke v Carbery (1873) L.R. 16 Eq. 461 17–02
Frere v Frere (1847) 5 Notes of Cases 593 5–02
Fried Krupp AG, Re [1917] 2 Ch. 188, Ch D 3–03
Front Comor, The. See West Tankers Inc v RAS Riunione Adriatica di
 Sicurta SpA.
Fry (Deceased), Re; Joined Cases Chase National Executors and Trs Corp
 v Fry [1946] Ch. 312, Ch D 17–31
Fuld (Deceased) (No.3), In the Estate of; sub nom. Hartley v Fuld
 (Conflict of Laws) [1968] P. 675; [1966] 2 W.L.R. 717, PDAD 4–04,
                      4–05, 5–01, 5–06, 6–10, 6–13, 8–01, 8–12, 8–18, 18–16
Fullemann v McInnes's Executors, 1993 S.L.T. 259, OH 8–21
Furness Withy (Australia) Ltd v Metal Distributors (UK) Ltd (*The
 Amazonia*) [1990] 1 Ll Rep. 236; *Independent*, December 4, 1989
 (C.S.), CA (Civ Div) 15–12
Furse (Deceased), Re; sub nom. Furse v Inland Revenue Commissioners
 [1980] 3 All E.R. 838; [1980] S.T.C. 596, Ch D 6–19
Fyffe v Ferguson (1841) 2 Rob. 267 8–20

G (Abduction: Rights of Custody), Re [2002] 2 F.L.R. 703; [2002] Fam.
 Law 732, Fam Div 14–29
G v Caledonian Newspapers Ltd 1995 S.L.T. 559, OH 7–57
G v Caledonian Newspapers Ltd, 1995 S.L.T. 559, OH 9–03
GIE Groupe Concorde v Master of the Vessel Suhadiwarno Panjan
 (C440/97); sub nom. GIE Group Concorde v Master of the Vessel
 Suhadiwarno Panjan (C440/97) [2000] All E.R. (EC) 865; [1999] 2
 All E.R. (Comm) 700, ECJ 7–13
GKN Westland Helicopters Ltd v Korean Air Lines Co Ltd; Joined Cases
 Press Tech Controls Ltd v Korean Air Lines Co Ltd [2003] EWHC
 1120; [2003] 2 All E.R. (Comm) 578; [2003] 2 Ll Rep. 629, QBD
 (Comm) 1–06
Gadd v Gadd [1984] 1 W.L.R. 1435; [1985] 1 All E.R. 58, CA (Civ Div) ... 12–11
Gaetano and Maria, The (1882) L.R. 7 P.D. 137, CA 8–12, 15–32
Gaillard v Chekili (C518/99) [2001] E.C.R. I—2771; [2001] I.L.Pr. 33, ECJ
 (6th Chamber) 7–27
Galbraith v Galbraith (Divorce), 1971 S.C. 65; 1971 S.L.T. 139, OH 12–18
Galbraith v Grimshaw [1910] A.C. 508, HL 17–49, 17–55
Gantner Electronic GmbH v Basch Exploitatie Maatschappij BV
 (C111/01) [2003] E.C.R. I—4207; [2003] I.L.Pr. 37, ECJ (5th
 Chamber) 7–38
Garcia v Garcia [1992] Fam. 83; [1992] 2 W.L.R. 347; [1991] 3 All E.R.
 451, CA (Civ Div) 13–24
Garden decd, Re (1895) 11 T.L.R. 167 .... 6–14, 6–21, 6–32
Gardiner v Houghton (1862) 2 B. & S. 743 17–59
Gascoine v Pyrah [1994] I.L.Pr. 82, CA (Civ Div) 7–15
Geiger v D and J Macdonald Ltd 1932 S.L.T. 70, OH 9–09
General Star International Indemnity Ltd v Stirling Cooke Brown Rein-
 surance Brokers Ltd [2003] EWHC 3; [2003] I.L.Pr. 19; [2003] Ll
 Rep. I.R. 719, QBD (Comm) 7–47
General Steam Navigation Co v Guillou (1843) 11 M. & W. 877 8–05
Gentili, Re (1875) I.R. 9 Eq. 541 .... 17–02, 18–11
George Monro Ltd v American Cyanamid and Chemical Corp [1944] K.B.
 432, CA 16–18
Georges v Georges (1921) 65 S.J. 311 18–52
Ghosh v D'Rozario [1963] 1 Q.B. 106; [1962] 3 W.L.R. 405, CA 7–03

Gibbs and Sons v Société Industrielle et Commerciale des Métaux. *See* Antony Gibbs and Sons v Société Industrielle et Commerciale des Métaux.

Gibson v Munro (1894) 21 R. 840 17–56

Gill and Duffus Landauer Ltd v London Export Corp [1982] 2 Ll Rep. 627, QBD (Comm) 15–22

Gill v Culter (1895) 23 R. 371 7–47

Gingi v Secretary of State for Work and Pensions [2001] EWCA Civ 1685; [2002] 1 C.M.L.R. 20; [2002] Eu. L.R. 37, CA (Civ Div) 6–39, 6–40

Girvin Roper and Co v Monteith (1895) 23 R. 129; (1895) 3 S.L.T. 148, IH (1 Div) 15–12, 15–40

Glencore International AG v Metro Trading International Inc (No.1); Joined Cases Metro Trading International Inc v Itochu Petroleum Co (S) PTE Ltd (No.1) [1999] 2 All E.R. (Comm) 899; [1999] 2 Ll Rep. 632, QBD (Comm) 7–38

Glencore International AG v Metro Trading International Inc (No.2); sub nom. Glencore International AG v Metro Trading International Inc (formerly Metro Bunkering and Trading Co) (No.2) [2001] 1 All E.R. (Comm) 103; [2001] 1 Ll Rep. 284, QBD (Comm) 16–20, 17–09, 17–10, 17–14

Glencore International AG v Shell International Trading and Shipping Co Ltd [1999] 2 All E.R. (Comm) 922; [1999] 2 Ll Rep. 692, QBD (Comm) 7–38

Godard v Gray (1870–71) L.R. 6 Q.B. 139, QB 9–11, 9–13

Godfrey v Demon Internet Ltd (Application to Strike Out) [2001] Q.B. 201; [2000] 3 W.L.R. 1020, QBD 7–15

Goenaga, Re [1949] P. 367; 93 S.J. 28, PDAD 4–01, 18–03

Goetschuis v Brightman, 245 N.Y. 186, 156 N.E. 660 (1927) 3–07, 17–13

Goetze, Re; sub nom. National Provincial Bank v Mond [1953] Ch. 96; [1953] 2 W.L.R. 26; [1953] 1 All E.R. 76, CA 18–03, 18–26

Goetze v Aders and Co (1874) 2 R.100 .... 17–35, 17–55, 17–58

Golden Acres v Queensland Estates (1969) St. R. Qd. 738 15–11

Goodman v LNWR (1877) 15 S.L.R. 449 .... 8–09, 16–11, 16–13

Goodman's Trusts, Re (1881) L.R. 17 Ch. D. 266, CA 4–05, 14–04, 18–10

Goodwin v Robarts (1875–76) L.R. 1 App. Cas. 476, HL 17–30

Goodwin v United Kingdom (28957/95) [2002] I.R.L.R. 664; [2002] 2 F.L.R. 487; (2002) 35 E.H.R.R. 18, ECHR 11–01

Goold Stuart's Trs v McPhail, 1947 S.L.T. 221, OH .. 13–04, 13–07, 18–14, 18–27

Gould v Gould (No.2), 1968 S.L.T. 98, OH 6–10

Gould v Lewal. *See* Lewal's Settlement Trusts, Re.

Gourdain (Liquidator) v Nadler (C133/78) [1979] E.C.R. 733; [1979] 3 C.M.L.R. 180, ECJ 17–38

Gow v Caledonian Scrap Company (1893) 7 Sh. Ct. Rep. 65 15–22

Gowans (Mitchell's Tr.) v Rule, (1908) 16 S.L.T. 189, OH 5–02, 18–27

Grant v Easton (1883–84) L.R. 13 Q.B.D. 302, CA 9–07

Grant v Gordon Falconer and Fairweather, 1932 48 Sh.Ct.Rep. 155 18–03

Grant v Grant (Divorce: Domicile), 1931 S.C. 238; 1931 S.L.T. 180, IH (1 Div) 6–06, 6–09

Grant's Trs v Ritchie's Exr (1886) 13 R. 646 17–22

Grassi, Re; sub nom. Stubberfield v Grassi [1905] 1 Ch. 584, Ch D 18–17

Gray (otherwise Formosa) v Formosa; sub nom. Formosa v Formosa [1963] P. 259; [1962] 3 W.L.R. 1246, CA 3–01, 11–25, 12–23, 12–24, 12–36, 12–39

Green, Re; Noyes v. Pitkin (1909) 25 T.L.R. 222 11–24

Greer v Poole (1879–80) L.R. 5 Q.B.D. 272, QBD 15–07

Grell v Levy (1864) 16 C.,B. (N.S.) 73 .... 3–06, 10—5

Grey's Trusts, Re; sub nom. Grey v Stamford [1892] 3 Ch. 88, Ch D 14–02

Griffiths v United Airlines Inc., 203 A. 2d 796 (1964) 16–08
Griffiths JF v Griffiths Exrs (1905) 7 F. 470 18–26
Groos, In the Estate of [1904] P. 269, PDAD 18–16, 18–17
Groos, Re; sub nom. Groos v Groos [1915] 1 Ch. 572, Ch D 4–05, 11–24,
                                     18–06, 18–16, 18–25, 18–32, 18–33
Grovit v De Nederlandsche Bank; Joined Cases Thorncroft v De
     Nederlandsche Bank [2005] EWHC 2944; [2006] 1 All E.R.
     (Comm) 397, QBD 7–03
Gruppo Torras SA v Sheik Fahad Mohammed Al—Sabah [1995] 1 Ll Rep.
     374 7–10
Guaranty Trust Co of New York v Hannay and Co [1918] 2 K.B. 623, CA;
     affirming [1918] 1 K.B. 43, KBD 17–29
Gubisch Maschinenfabrik KG v Palumbo (C144/86) [1987] E.C.R. 4861;
     [1989] E.C.C. 420, ECJ (6th Chamber) 7–38
Guepratte v Young (1851) 4 De G. & Sm. 217 .... 13–06, 15–21
Guiard v De Clermont and Donner [1914] 3 K.B. 145, KBD 9–10, 17–53
Gulbenkian v Gulbenkian [1937] 4 All E.R. 618 6–10
Gully v Dix; sub nom. Dix (Deceased), Re [2004] EWCA Civ 139; [2004] 1
     W.L.R. 1399; [2004] 1 F.L.R. 918, CA (Civ Div) 18–09
Gunn and Co v Couper (1871) 10 M. 116 7–03
Guthrie (Ann) v Guthrie (William), 1954 S.L.T. (Sh. Ct.) 58; (1954) 70 Sh.
     Ct. Rep. 173, Sh Ct (Tayside) 14–46
Gutnick v Dow Jones [2002] HCA 56, HC (Aus) 7–15, 16–18

H, Re [2005] All E.R. (D.) 17 14–31
H (A Minor) (Abduction: Rights of Custody), Re; sub nom. H (A Child)
     (Removal from Jurisdiction), Re [2000] 2 A.C. 291; [2000] 2 W.L.R.
     337; [2000] 2 All E.R. 1, HL 14–29
H (A Minor) (Adoption: Non-Patrial), Re (1983) 4 F.L.R. 85; (1982) 12
     Fam. Law 218, CA (Civ Div) 14–52
H (A Minor) (Foreign Custody Order: Enforcement), Re [1994] Fam. 105;
     [1994] 2 W.L.R. 269; [1994] 1 All E.R. 812, CA (Civ Div) 14–21
H (Infants) (No.1), Re [1966] 1 W.L.R. 381; [1966] 1 All E.R. 886, CA ... 14–25
H (Minors) (Abduction: Custody Rights), Re; Joined Cases S (Minors)
     (Abduction: Custody Rights), Re [1991] 2 A.C. 476; [1991] 3
     W.L.R. 68; [1991] 3 All E.R. 230, HL 14–29, 14–47
H v H [1928] P. 206, PDAD 12–03
H v H [1954] P. 258; [1953] 3 W.L.R. 849, PDAD 11–31, 12–36
H v H, 2006 G.W.D.18– 14–31
H v H (Child Abduction: Acquiescence); sub nom. H (Minors) (Abduc-
     tion: Acquiescence), Re [1998] A.C. 72; [1997] 2 W.L.R. 563; [1997]
     2 All E.R. 225, HL 14–31
Hack v Hack (1976) 6 Fam. Law 177 .... 12–23, 12–27
Hacker v Euro-Relais GmbH (C280/90) [1992] E.C.R. I—1111; [1992]
     I.L.Pr. 515, ECJ 7–27
Hagerbaum, Re [1933] I.R. 198 18–10
Haiti v Duvalier (Mareva Injunction) (No.2) [1990] 1 Q.B. 202; [1989] 2
     W.L.R. 261; [1989] 1 All E.R. 456, CA (Civ Div) 7–58
Haji-Ioannou v Frangos [1999] 2 All E.R. (Comm) 865; [1999] 2 Ll Rep.
     337; [1999] C.L.C. 1075, CA (Civ Div) 7–10, 7–38, 7–39, 7–52
Hakeem v Hussain. *See* SH v KH.
Halcyon Isle, The. See Bankers Trust International v Todd Shipyards Corp.
Halcyon the Great, The (No.1) [1975] 1 W.L.R. 515; [1975] 1 All E.R. 882,
     QBD (Admlty) 8–21
Haldane v Eckford (No.2) (1869) L.R. 8 Eq. 631, Ct of Chancery 6–08, 6–13,
                                      6–14, 6–15, 6–16, 6–21

Halki Shipping Corp v Sopex Oils Ltd (*The Halki*) [1998] 1 W.L.R. 726;
    [1998] 2 All E.R. 23, CA (Civ Div); affirming [1997] 1 W.L.R. 1268;
    [1997] 3 All E.R. 833, QBD (Admlty) 7–13
Hall (Deceased), Re; sub nom. Hall v Knight; Hall, In the Estate of [1914]
    P. 1, CA 18–10
Hall's Trs v Hall (1854) 16 D. 1057 .... 17–02, 18–33
Halley, The (1868) L.R. 2 P.C. 193 .... 16–12, 16–13, 16–17
Halpern v Halpern [2006] All E.R. (D.) 389 .... 15–13, 18–12
Hamed el Chiaty and Co (t/a Travco Nile Cruise Lines) v Thomas Cook
    Group Ltd (The Nile Rhapsody) [1994] 1 Ll Rep. 382; [1994] I.L.Pr.
    367, CA (Civ Div) 7–46
Hamill v Hamill, unreported, July 24, 2000 16–20
Hamilton v Dallas (1875) 1 Ch.D. 257 6–13
Hamilton v Wakefield, 1993 S.L.T. (Sh Ct) 30, Sh Ct (Grampian) .. 15–12, 15–31,
                                                                    17–06
Hamlyn and Co v Talisker Distillery; sub nom. Talisker Distillery v Hamlyn
    and Co [1894] A.C. 202; (1894) 21 R. (H.L.) 21, HL ... 8–01, 8–02, 15–12,
                                                                    15–22
Hammer and Sohne v HWT Realisations Ltd, 1985 S.L.T. (Sh. Ct.) 21, Sh
    Ct (Glasgow) 15–55, 17–16
Handelswekerij GJ Bier BV v Mines de Potasse d'Alsace SA (21/76) [1978]
    Q.B. 708; [1977] 3 W.L.R. 479; [1976] E.C.R. 1735, ECJ 7–14
Hansen v Dixon (1906) 96 L.T. 32; (1906) 23 T.L.R. 56 ..... 8–04, 11–17, 15–12,
                                                                    15–22
Happy Fellow, The. See Blue Nile Shipping Co Ltd v Iguana Shipping and
    Finance Inc.
Harding v Wealands [2004] EWCA Civ 1735; [2005] 1 W.L.R. 1539; [2005]
    1 All E.R. 415, CA (Civ Div); [2006] UKHL 32 .. 8–20, 8–21, 16–20, 16–28
    Hari Bhum, (No.1), The. *See* Through Transport Mutual Insurance
        Association (Eurasia) Ltd v New India Assurance Co Ltd (*The Hari
        Bhum*) (No.1)
    Hari Bhum, (No.2), The. *See* Through Transport Mutual Insurance
        Association (Eurasia) Ltd v New India Assurance Co Ltd (*The Hari
        Bhum*) (No.2).
Harris v Harris [1949] 2 All E.R. 318; 65 T.L.R. 519, DC 13–21
Harris v Quine (1869) L.R. 4 Q.B. 653 .... 8–09, 9–12
Harris v Taylor [1915] 2 K.B. 580, CA 9–10
Harris Trs, Petrs (Trust: International law); sub nom. Harris Trs, 1919 S.C.
    432; (1919) 1 S.L.T.220, IH (2 Div) 18–52
Harrison v Harrison [1953] 1 W.L.R. 865; 97 S.J. 456, PDAD .. 6–05, 6–11, 6–26,
                                                                    6–27
Harrods (Buenos Aires) Ltd (No.2), Re [1992] Ch. 72; [1991] 3 W.L.R.
    397, CA (Civ Div) 7–30, 7–46, 7–51, 12–13
Harrop (John) v Harrop (Mabel) [1920] 3 K.B. 386, KBD 9–12
Har-Shefi (otherwise Cohen Lask) v Har-Shefi (No.2) [1953] P. 220; [1953]
    3 W.L.R. 200; [1953] 2 All E.R. 373, PDAD 12–27
Harvey (otherwise Farnie) v Farnie (1882–83) L.R. 8 App. Cas. 43, HL ... 11–09
Hashmi v Hashmi [1972] Fam. 36; [1971] 3 W.L.R. 918; [1971] 3 All E.R.
    1253, Assizes (Leeds) 14–02
Hay v Hay (1861) 23 D. 1291 14–51
Hay-Balfour v Scotts (1793) 3 Pat. 300 18–08
Hayward (Deceased), Re [1997] Ch. 45; [1996] 3 W.L.R. 674; [1997] 1 All
    E.R. 32, Ch D 7–27
Heidberg (No.2), The. *See* Partenreederei M/S Heidberg v Grosvenor Grain
    and Feed Co Ltd (*The Heidberg*) (No.2).
Helbert Wagg and Co Ltd, Re. *See* Helbert Wagg and Co Ltd, Re.

Hellman's Will, Re (1866) L.R. 2 Eq. 363 18–10
Hemain v Hemain [1988] 2 F.L.R. 388; [1988] Fam. Law 432, CA (Civ Div) .. 7–47,
    12–11
Henaff v Henaff [1966] 1 W.L.R. 598; 110 S.J. 269, PDAD 8–12
Henderson v Henderson (1843) 3 Hare. 100 9–11
Henderson v Henderson [1967] P. 77; [1965] 2 W.L.R. 218, PDAD ... 6–05, 6–27
Henderson v Jaouen [2002] EWCA Civ 75; [2002] 1 W.L.R. 2971; [2002] 2
    All E.R. 705, CA (Civ Div) 4–05, 7–14, 16–18
Henderson v Merrett Syndicates Ltd (No.1); sub nom. McLarnon Deeney
    v Gooda Walker Ltd; Gooda Walker Ltd v Deeny; Joined Cases
    Hallam—Eames v Merrett Syndicates Ltd; Hughes v Merrett Syndi-
    cates Ltd; Feltrim Underwriting Agencies Ltd v Arbuthnott; Deeny
    v Gooda Walker Ltd (Duty of Care) [1995] 2 A.C. 145; [1994] 3
    W.L.R. 761; [1994] 3 All E.R. 506, HL 16–24
Henry v Geoprosco International Ltd; sub nom. Henry v Geoprosco
    International Ltd [1976] Q.B. 726; [1975] 3 W.L.R. 620, CA (Civ
    Div) 9–10
Herd v HM Advocate, 1993 G.W.D. 24–1504 3–03
Herd v Herd [1936] P. 205, PDAD 12–03
Heriz v Riera (1840) 11 Sum. 318 15–26
Hermanos, Artola, Ex p. Chale, Re (1890) L.R. 24 Q.B.D. 640, CA 17–36
Hernando, Re; sub nom. Hernando v Sawtell (1884) L.R. 27 Ch. D. 284,
    Ch D 13–07
Hesperides Hotels v Muftizade; sub nom. Hesperides Hotels v Aegean
    Turkish Holidays [1979] A.C. 508; [1978] 3 W.L.R. 378, HL 7–04
Hewit's Trs v Lawson (1891) 18 R. 793 .... 7–04, 18–08, 18–25, 18–34
Hewitson v Hewitson [1995] Fam. 100; [1995] 2 W.L.R. 287; [1995] 1 All
    E.R. 472, CA (Civ Div) 13–24
Hewitson v Hewitson [1999] 2 F.L.R. 74; [1999] Fam. Law 450, QBD 13–24
Hewitt's Settlement, Re; sub nom. Hewitt v Hewitt [1915] 1 Ch. 228,
    Ch D 13–04, 13–07
Higgins v Ewing's Trs; sub nom. Higgins v Bruce, 1925 S.C. 440; 1925
    S.L.T. 329, IH (2 Div) 8–08
Hill, Re (1870) L.R. 2 P. & D. 89 18–01
Hill v Hill [1959] 1 W.L.R. 127; [1959] 1 All E.R. 281, PC (Bar) 11–30
Hill v Hill, 1991 S.L.T. 189; 1990 S.C.L.R. 238, OH 14–44
Hodgson v De Beauchesne (1858) 12 Moore P.C. 285 6–21
Hoffmann v Krieg (145/86) [1988] E.C.R. 645; [1990] I.L.Pr. 4, ECJ 9–40
Hogg Insurance Brokers Ltd v Guardian Insurance Co Inc [1997] 1 Ll Rep.
    412, QBD (Comm) 15–16
Holman v Johnson Holman v Johnson (1775) 1 Cowp. 341; (1775–1802)
    E.R. 98 3–02
Holmes v Bank of Scotland; sub nom. Davidson v Bank of Scotland, 2002
    S.L.T. 544; 2002 S.C.L.R. 481, OH 18–24
Holmes v Holmes [1989] Fam. 47; [1989] 3 W.L.R. 302; [1989] 3 All E.R.
    786, CA (Civ Div) 13–24
Home's Tr. v Home's Trs, 1926 S.L.T. 214, OH 17–58
Hooper v Gumm; Joined Cases McLellan v Gumm (1866–67) L.R. 2 Ch.
    App. 282, CA in Chancery 3–01, 17–10
Hooper (otherwise Harrison) v Hooper [1959] 1 W.L.R. 1021; [1959] 2 All
    E.R. 575, PDAD 5–07, 11–25
Hope, Re (1857) 8 De G.M. & G. 731 3–06
Hope v Hope (1857) 8 De G.M. & G. 731 15–26
Hope Todd and Kirk v Bruce (1899) 6 S.L.T. 310, OH 6–14
Hope Vere v Hope Vere (1907) 15 S.L.T. 361, HL; affirming (1907) 14
    S.L.T. 772, IH (2 Div); reversing (1906) 13 S.L.T. 774, OH 13–07

Hopkins v Hopkins (Divorce: Domicile) [1951] P. 116; [1950] 2 All E.R.
1035, PDAD 6–39
Horn Linie GmbH and Co v Panamericana Formas e Impresos SA [2006]
EWHC 373, QBD (Comm) 7–45, 7–47, 15–13
Hornett v Hornett [1971] P. 255; [1971] 2 W.L.R. 181, PDAD 9–12
Hoskins v Matthews (1855) 25 L.T. (O.S.) 78 6–32
Hough v P and O Containers Ltd [1999] Q.B. 834; [1998] 3 W.L.R. 851;
[1998] 2 All E.R. 978, QBD (Admlty) 7–29
House of Spring Gardens Ltd v Waite (No.2) [1991] 1 Q.B. 241; [1990] 3
W.L.R. 347, CA (Civ Div) 9–12
Hoy v Hoy (Interim interdict: Discretion of Lord Ordinary), 1968 S.C. 179;
1968 S.L.T. 413; 1968 S.L.T. (Notes) 36, IH (1 Div) 11–32
Hoyles (No.1), Re; sub nom. Row v Jagg (No.1); Hoyles, Re [1911] 1 Ch.
179, CA 17–02
Huber v Steiner (1835) 2 Bing N.C. 202 .... 8–05, 8–09
Hulse v Chambers [2001] 1 W.L.R. 2386; [2002] 1 All E.R. (Comm) 812,
QBD 16–17, 16–20
Hume's Trs v Hume Trs, 1926 S.L.T. 214 17–35
Humphries, In the Estate of [1934] P. 78, PDAD 18–01
Hunter v Murrow; sub nom. H v M (Abduction: Rights of Custody) [2005]
EWCA Civ 976; [2005] 2 F.L.R. 1119; [2005] 3 F.C.R. 1, CA (Civ
Div) 14–29
Huntington v Attrill; sub nom. Huntingdon v Attrill [1893] A.C. 150, PC
(Can) 3–03
Hussain (Aliya) v Hussain (Shahid) [1983] Fam. 26; [1982] 3 W.L.R. 679;
[1982] 3 All E.R. 369, CA (Civ Div) 11–09, 11–11
Hutchison v Aberdeen Bank (1837) 15 S. 1100 18–01
Hyde v Hyde; sub nom. Hyde v Hyde and Woodmansee (1865–69) L.R. 1
P. & D. 130; [1861–73] All E.R. Rep. 175, Divorce Ct 11–01, 11–02
Hydraload Research and Developments Ltd v Bone Connell and Baxters
Ltd 1996 S.L.T. 219, OH 7–58
Hyslops v Gordon (1824) 2 Sh. App. 451, HL 8–21, 15–54

I, Petr, 2004 S.L.T. 972; 2004 G.W.D. 7–129, OH 14–31
I, Petr, 1999 G.W.D.21–272 14–31
Igra v Igra [1951] P. 404; [1951] 2 T.L.R. 670; 95 S.J. 563, PDAD ... 9–12, 10–05
Iman Din v National Assistance Board [1967] 2 Q.B. 213; [1967] 2 W.L.R.
257; [1967] 1 All E.R. 750; 110 S.J. 906; *The Times*, November 22,
1966, QBD 11–05
Immanuel v Denholm and Co (1887) 15 R. 152 8–12
Import Export Metro Ltd v Compania Sud Americana de Vapores SA
[2003] EWHC 11; [2003] 1 All E.R. (Comm) 703; [2003] 1 Ll Rep.
405, QBD (Comm) 7–30
India v Taylor; sub nom. Delhi Electric Supply and Traction Co Ltd, Re
[1955] A.C. 491; [1955] 2 W.L.R. 303, HL 3–02
Indian and General Investment Trust Ltd v Borax Consolidated Ltd [1920]
1 K.B. 539, KBD 3–02
Industrie Tessili Italiana Como v Dunlop AG (12/76); sub nom. Firma
Industrie Tessili Italiana Como v Firma Dunlop AG (12/76) [1976]
E.C.R. 1473; [1977] 1 C.M.L.R. 26; *The Times*, October 11, 1976,
ECJ 7–13
Industrie, The [1894] P. 58, CA 15–12, 15–32
Indyka v Indyka [1969] 1 A.C. 33; [1967] 3 W.L.R. 510; [1967] 2 All E.R.
689; 111 S.J. 456, HL 9–09, 12–18, 12–39
Inglis v Robertson; sub nom. Irvine v Inglis; Irvine and Robertson v Baxter
and Inglis [1898] A.C. 616; (1898) 25 R. (H.L.) 70; (1898) 6 S.L.T.
130, HL 17–15

Inglis v Usherwood (1801) 1 East 515 17–12
Ingmar GB Ltd v Eaton Leonard Technologies Inc [2001] All E.R. (D.)
    448
Inland Revenue Commissioners v Bullock [1976] 1 W.L.R. 1178; [1976] 3
    All E.R. 353, CA (Civ Div) 6–10, 6–12
Inland Revenue Commissioners v Duchess of Portland [1982] Ch. 314;
    [1982] 2 W.L.R. 367; [1982] 1 All E.R. 784, Ch D 4–05, 6–09, 6–10,
                                                       6–12, 6–25
Inland Revenue Commissioners v Gordon's Exs (1850) 12 D. 657 6–31
Inland Revenue Commissioners v Muller and Co's Margarine Ltd; sub
    nom. Muller and Co's Margarine Ltd v Inland Revenue Commis-
    sioners [1901] A.C. 217, HL 17–32
Inland Revenue Commissioners v Stype Investments (Jersey) Ltd; Joined
    Cases Clore (Deceased) (No.1), Re [1982] Ch. 456; [1982] 3 W.L.R.
    228; [1982] 3 All E.R. 419, CA (Civ Div) 18–01
Interdesco SA v Nullifire Ltd [1992] 1 Ll Rep. 180; [1992] I.L.Pr. 97, QBD
    (Comm) 9–12, 9–36, 9–40
International Credit and Investment Co (Overseas) Ltd v Adham (Jurisdic-
    tion) [1994] 1 B.C.L.C. 66; *The Times*, March 26, 1993, Ch D 17–31
International Credit and Investment Co (Overseas) Ltd v Adham (Share
    Ownership) [1999] I.L.Pr. 302, CA (Civ Div) 7–45
Iomega Corp v Myrica (UK) Ltd (No.2); sub nom. Iomega Corp, Petrs
    1998 S.C. 636; 1999 S.L.T. 796, IH (1 Div) 7–55, 7–57
Iran Continental Shelf Oil Co v IRI International Corp [2002] EWCA Civ
    1024; [2004] 2 C.L.C. 696, CA (Civ Div) 15–16
Irini A (No.2), The. *See* Ascot Commodities NV v Northern Pacific
    Shipping (*The Irini A*) (No.2).
Irving v Snow, 1956 S.C. 257; 1956 S.L.T. 328, IH (1 Div) 18–17, 18–25
Irwin v Caruth [1916] P. 23, PDAD 18–01
Israel Discount Bank of New York v Hadjipateras [1984] 1 W.L.R. 137;
    [1983] 3 All E.R. 129, CA (Civ Div) 9–12
Italian Leather SpA v Weco Polstermobel GmbH and Co (C80/00) [2002]
    E.C.R. I—4995; [2003] E.T.M.R. 10; [2003] C.L.Y.B. 620, ECJ (5th
    Chamber) 9–40
Ivan Zagubanski, The. *See* Navigation Maritime Bulgare v Rustal Trading
    Ltd.
Ivenel v Schwab (133/81) [1982] E.C.R. 1891; [1983] 1 C.M.L.R. 538, ECJ.. 7–13

J (A Child) (Custody Rights: Jurisdiction), Re; sub nom. Jomah v Attar; J
    (Child Returned Abroad: Human Rights), Re; J (A Child) (Return
    to Foreign Jurisdiction: Convention Rights), Re; J (A Child) (Child
    Returned Abroad: Convention Rights) [2005] UKHL 40; [2006] 1
    A.C. 80; [2005] 3 W.L.R. 14; [2005] 3 All E.R. 291, HL 14–48
J (A Minor) (Abduction: Custody Rights), Re; sub nom. C v S (Minors)
    (Abduction: Illegitimate Child) [1990] 2 A.C. 562; [1990] 3 W.L.R.
    492; [1990] 2 All E.R. 961, HL 6–39, 6–40
J (A Minor) (Abduction: Ward of Court), Re; sub nom. J (A Minor)
    (Abduction), Re [1989] Fam. 85; [1989] 3 W.L.R. 825; [1989] 3 All
    E.R. 590, Fam Div 14–21
J (Children) (Abduction: Child's Objections to Return), Re; sub nom. J
    (Children) (Child Abduction: Child Appellant), Re [2004] EWCA
    Civ 428; [2004] 2 F.L.R. 64; [2004] 1 F.C.R. 737, CA (Civ Div) 14–31
J v C; sub nom. C (An Infant), Re [1970] A.C. 668; [1969] 2 W.L.R. 540;
    [1969] 1 All E.R. 788; 113 S.J. 164, HL 14–25
J v K (Child Abduction: Acquiescence); sub nom. J, Petr, 2002 S.C. 450;
    2002 G.W.D. 18–583, OH 14–31, 14–35

JA (A Minor) (Child Abduction: Non-Convention Country), Re; sub nom.
A (A Minor) (Abduction: Non-Convention Country), Re [1998] 1
F.L.R. 231; [1998] 2 F.C.R. 159; *The Times*, July 3, 1997, CA (Civ
Div) 14–48
JB (Child Abduction: Rights of Custody: Spain), Re [2003] EWHC 2130;
[2004] 1 F.L.R. 796; [2004] Fam. Law 241, Fam Div 5–07
J D'Almeida Araujo LDA v Sir Frederick Becker and Co Ltd; sub nom. J
D'Almaido Aruajo LDA v Sir Frederick Becker and Co Ltd [1953]
2 Q.B. 329; [1953] 3 W.L.R. 57, QBD 8–20, 15–22, 16–28
JH Rayner (Mincing Lane) Ltd v Department of Trade and Industry;
Joined Cases Maclaine Watson and Co Ltd v Department of Trade
and Industry; Maclaine Watson and Co Ltd v International Tin
Council; TSB England and Wales v Department of Trade and
Industry; Amalgamated Metal Trading Ltd v International Tin
Council [1990] 2 A.C. 418; [1989] 3 W.L.R. 969; [1989] 3 All E.R.
523 [1989] Ch. 72; [1988] 3 W.L.R. 1033; [1988] 3 All E.R. 257, CA
(Civ Div) 15–40
JP Morgan Europe Ltd v Primacom AG [2005] EWHC 508; [2005] 2 All
E.R. (Comm) 764; [2005] 2 Ll Rep. 665, QBD (Comm) 7–38, 7–43
Jabbour v Custodian of Israeli Absentee Property. *See* F and K Jabbour v
Custodian of Israeli Absentee Property.
Jaber Elias Kotia v Katr Bint Jiryes Nahas [1941] A.C. 403, PC (Pal) 5–06
Jack v Jack (1862) 24 D, 467 12–02
Jacobs Marcus and Co v Credit Lyonnais (1884) 12 Q.B.D. 589 .... 15–22, 15–25
Jacobson v Frachon (1924) 44 T.L.R.103 .... 9–12, 9–13
Jakob Handte and Co GmbH v Traitements Mecano—Chimiques des
Surfaces SA (TMCS) (C26/91) [1992] E.C.R. I—3967; [1993] I.L.Pr.
5, ECJ 7–13, 15–02
Jameel v Dow Jones and Co Inc; sub nom. Dow Jones and Co Inc v Jameel
[2005] EWCA Civ 75; [2005] Q.B. 946; [2005] 2 W.L.R. 1614, CA
(Civ Div) 16–18
James, Re (1908) 98 L.T. 438 6–32
James Burrough Distillers Plc v Speymalt Whisky Distributors Ltd, 1989
S.L.T. 561; 1989 S.C.L.R. 255, OH 16–05, 16–11
James Miller and Partners Ltd v Whitworth Street Estates (Manchester)
Ltd. *See* Whitworth Street Estates (Manchester) Ltd v James Miller
and Partners Ltd.
Jarrett v Barclays Bank Plc; Joined Cases Jones v First National Bank Plc;
First National Bank Plc v Peacock [1999] Q.B. 1; [1997] 3 W.L.R.
654; [1997] 2 All E.R. 484, CA (Civ Div) 7–27
Jean Kraut AG v Albany Fabrics Ltd; sub nom. Kraut v Albany Fabrics
[1977] Q.B. 182; [1976] 3 W.L.R. 872, QBD 8–21
Jeannot v Fuerst (1909) 25 T.L.R. 424 9–12
Jenic Properties Ltd v Andy Thornton Architectural Antiques, 1992 S.L.T.
(Sh. Ct.) 5; 1992 S.C.L.R. 16, Sh Pr 7–30
Jenner v Sun Oil Co (1952) 2 D.L.R. 526 16–18
Jet Holdings Inc v Patel [1990] 1 Q.B. 335; [1988] 3 W.L.R. 295, CA (Civ
Div) 9–12
Joachimson (A Firm) v Swiss Bank Corp (Costs) [1921] 3 K.B. 110; (1921)
6 Ll. L. Rep. 435, CA 17–17
Joffre, 1992 G.W.D. 27–1522 14–21
Jogia (A Bankrupt), Re; sub nom. Tr. in Bankruptcy v D Pennellier and
Co [1988] 1 W.L.R. 484; [1988] 2 All E.R. 328, Ch D 16–30
Johannesburg v Stewart and Co (1902) Ltd, 1909 S.C. (H.L.) 53; 1909 2
S.L.T. 313, HL 15–12

Johannesburg Municipal Council v D Stewart and Co (1902) Ltd; sub nom.
    Municipal Council of John Walker and Sons Ltd v Henry Ost and
    Co Ltd [1970] 1 W.L.R. 917; [1970] 2 All E.R. 106, Ch D 16–12
Johnson v Coventry Churchill International Ltd [1992] 3 All E.R. 14,
    QBD 16–05, 16–12
Johnson (Mary Elizabeth), Re; sub nom. Roberts v Attorney General
    [1903] 1 Ch. 821, Ch D 4–06, 5–05
Johnstone v Beattie (1843) 10 Cl. & F. 42 . . . . 6–32, 10–04
Jones v Oceanic Steam Navigation Co Ltd [1924] 2 K.B. 730; (1924) 19 Ll.
    L. Rep. 348, KBD 15–11
Jones v Saudi Arabia; sub nom. Jones v Minister of the Interior
    Al—Mamlaka Al—Arabiya AS Saudiya; Joined Cases Mitchell v
    Al—Dali [2006] UKHL 26; *The Times*, June 15, 2006, HL; reversing
    in part [2004] EWCA Civ 1394; [2005] Q.B. 699; [2005] 2 W.L.R.
    808, CA (Civ Div) 3–05, 7–03
Jones v Somervell's Tr.; sub nom. Jones v Tait, 1907 S.C. 545; (1907) 14
    S.L.T. 759, IH (2 Div) 8–05
Jones' Estate, Re (1921) 182 N.W. 227 (Iowa SC) 6–07, 6–22
Jopp v Wood (1865) 34 L.J. Ch. 212 6–09
Jordan v Jordan [2000] 1 W.L.R. 210; [1999] 2 F.L.R. 1069; *The Times*, July
    29, 1999, CA (Civ Div) 13–24
Joyce v DPP [1946] A.C. 347, HL 6–38
Joyce v Joyce and O'Hare [1979] Fam. 93; [1979] 2 W.L.R. 770; [1979] 2
    All E.R. 156, Fam Div 12–23, 12–27
Juan Ysmael and Co Inc v Indonesia [1955] A.C. 72; [1954] 3 W.L.R. 531,
    PC (HK) 7–03
Judgment Debtor A, Re [1939] 1 All E.R. 1 9–25
Jugoslavenska Oceanska Plovidba v Castle Investment Co Inc (*The Kozara*)
    [1974] Q.B. 292; [1973] 3 W.L.R. 847, CA (Civ Div) 8–21
Jupiter, The (No.3) [1927] P. 250; (1927) 28 Ll. L. Rep. 233, CA; affirming
    [1927] P. 122; (1927) 27 Ll. L. Rep. 75, PDAD 3–04

KR (A Child) (Abduction: Forcible Removal by Parents), Re; sub nom.
    KR (A Minor) (Abduction: Forcible Removal), Re [1999] 4 All
    E.R. 954; [1999] 2 F.L.R. 542, Fam Div 12–38, 14–47, 14–48
K v K [1986] 2 F.L.R. 411; [1986] Fam. Law 329; *The Times*, April 24,
    1986, QBD 12–11
Kadel Chajkin and Ce De Ltd v Mitchell Cotts and Co (Middle East) Ltd
    (*The Stensby*) [1947] 2 All E.R. 786; (1947–48) 81 Ll. L. Rep. 124,
    KBD 15–32
Kahan v Pakistan Federation [1951] 2 K.B. 1003; [1951] 2 T.L.R. 697, CA . . 7–03
Kahler v Midland Bank Ltd [1950] A.C. 24; [1949] 2 All E.R. 621, HL 3–02,
                                                                    15–23, 15–26, 15–09
Kaiser Bautechnik GmbH v GA Group Ltd, 1993 S.L.T. 826, OH 7–03
Kalfelis v Bankhaus Schroder Munchmeyer Hengst and Co (t/a HEMA
    Beteiligungsgesellschaft GmbH) (189/87) [1988] E.C.R. 5565; [1989]
    E.C.C. 407, ECJ (5th Chamber) 7–14
Kamouh v Associated Electrical Industries International [1980] Q.B. 199;
    [1979] 2 W.L.R. 795, QBD 8–05, 8–12
Kamperman v MacIver, 1994 S.C. 230; 1994 S.L.T. 763, IH (2 Div) 11–24
Kanani (Deceased), Re; sub nom. Engledow v Davidson, 122 S.J. 611 18–20
Karnak, The (1869) L.R. 2 P.C. 505 15–32
Karoulias S.A. v The Drambuie Liqeuer Co. Ltd [2005] CSOH 112 16–35
Kassim (otherwise Widmann) v Kassim (otherwise Hassim) [1962] P. 224;
    [1962] 3 W.L.R. 865; [1962] 3 All E.R. 426, PDAD 11–31, 12–36
Kaufman v Gerson [1904] 1 K.B. 591, CA 3–06, 15–26

Kaufman (Gustav) (Deceased), Re [1952] P. 325; [1952] 2 All E.R. 261,
    PDAD 18–01
Kaye (Peter) v HM Advocate, 1957 J.C. 55; 1957 S.L.T. 357, HCJ 10–07
Keiner v Keiner [1952] 1 All E.R. 643; 45 R. & I.T. 174, QBD 15–22
Kell v Henderson, 26 A.D. 2d 595; 270 N.Y.S. 2d 552 (1966) 16–08
Kelly v Marks, 1974 S.L.T. 118, OH 14–05, 14–25
Kelly v Selwyn [1905] 2 Ch. 117, Ch D 17–28
Kelly Banks v CGU Insurance plc, unreported, November 5, 2004 ... 7–45, 7–46,
    16–32
Kenburn Waste Management Ltd v Bergmann [2002] EWCA Civ 98;
    [2002] C.L.C. 644; [2002] I.L.Pr. 33, CA (Civ Div); affirming [2002]
    F.S.R. 44; *The Times*, July 9, 2001, Ch D 15–16
Kendall v Kendall [1977] Fam. 208; [1977] 3 W.L.R. 251, Fam Div ... 12–23, 12–27
Kendrick v Burnett (Owners of the SS Marsden) (1987) 25 R. 82; (1897) 5
    S.L.T. 199, IH (1 Div) 8–20, 16–14
Kennedy v Bell (1864) 2 M. 587 13–10
Kennedy v London Express [1931] I.R. 532 15–12
Kennion v Buchan's Trs (1880) 7 R. 570; (1880) 17 S.L.R. 380, IH (2
    Div) 18–35, 18–40
Kenny v Ireland ROC Ltd [2005] 1 E.H.C. 241 15–42
Kenward v Kenward; Joined Cases Way v Way; Rowley v Rowley;
    Whitehead v Whitehead [1951] P. 124; [1950] 2 All E.R. 297, CA .. 11–09,
    11–17, 11–23, 11–24
Kernot (An Infant), Re; sub nom. Kernot v Kernot [1965] Ch. 217; [1964]
    3 W.L.R. 1210; [1964] 3 All E.R. 339, Ch D 14–25
Kerr v Coulthart (Richardson's Trs) (1898) 6 S.L.T. 245, OH 6–21
Keys v Keys [1919] 2 I.R. 160 9–12
Khan's Settlement, Re; sub nom. Coutts and Co v Bhopal [1966] Ch. 567;
    [1965] 3 W.L.R. 1291; [1966] 1 All E.R. 160, Ch D 18–41, 18–43
Khoo Hooi Leong v Khoo Chong Yeok [1930] A.C. 346, PC (Shanghai) ... 11–04
Khoo Hooi Leong v Khoo Hean Kwee [1926] A.C. 529, PC (Shanghai) ... 11–04,
    14–02
Kilgour v Kilgour, 1987 S.C. 55; 1987 S.L.T. 568, OH 14–25, 14–47
Killen v Killen, 1981 S.L.T. (Sh. Ct.) 77, Sh Ct (Glasgow) 13–21
King v Bristow Helicopters Ltd; sub nom. Hammond v Bristow Helicopters
    Ltd; Joined Cases Morris v KLM Royal Dutch Airlines [2002]
    UKHL 7; [2002] 2 A.C. 628; [2002] 2 W.L.R. 578; 2002 S.L.T. 378,
    HL 1–06
King v Crown Energy Trading AG [2003] EWHC 163; [2003] 2 C.L.C. 540;
    [2003] I.L.Pr. 28, QBD (Comm) 7–10
King v Foxwell (1876) L.R. 3 Ch. D. 518, Ch D 6–07
King Alfred, The [1914] P. 84, PDAD 16–14
Kinnear v Falconfilms NV [1996] 1 W.L.R. 920; [1994] 3 All E.R. 42, QBD .. 7–17
Kirchner and Co v Gruban [1909] 1 Ch. 413, Ch D 15–12
Kitechnology BV v Unicor GmbH Plastmaschinen [1994] I.L.Pr. 568;
    [1995] F.S.R. 765, CA (Civ Div) 7–14, 16–16
Kitson (Victor) v Kitson (Marjorie), 1945 S.C. 434; 1945 S.N. 59; 1946
    S.L.T. 109, IH (2 Div) 14–25
Klein v Rhodos Management Ltd (C73/04) [2005] E.C.R. I—8667; [2006]
    I.L.Pr. 2, ECJ (1st Chamber) 7–27
Klein v Rhodos Management Ltd [2005] I.L.Pr. 17, OLG (Hamm) 7–27
Kleinwort Benson Ltd v Glasgow City Council (C346/93); sub nom.
    Kleinwort Benson Ltd v Glasgow DC (City of) (C346/93) [1996]
    Q.B. 57; [1995] 3 W.L.R. 866; [1995] All E.R. (E.C.) 514, ECJ 16–30

Kleinwort Benson Ltd v Glasgow City Council (No.1); sub nom. Kleinwort
    Benson Ltd v Glasgow DC (City of); Barclays Bank Plc v Glasgow
    DC (City of); Joined Cases Barclays Bank Plc v Glasgow City
    Council [1994] Q.B. 404; [1994] 2 W.L.R. 466, CA (Civ Div) 7–13
Kleinwort Benson Ltd v Glasgow City Council (No.2) [1999] 1 A.C. 153;
    [1997] 3 W.L.R. 923; [1997] 4 All E.R. 641, HL . . 7–10, 7–13, 7–53, 16–30
Kleinwort Sons and Co v Ungarische Baumwolle Industrie AG; sub nom.
    Kleinwort Sons and Co v Hungarian General Creditbank [1939] 2
    K.B. 678, CA 15–23, 15–26
Kloebe, Re; sub nom. Kannreuther v Geiselbrecht (1885) L.R. 28 Ch. D.
    175, Ch D 8–22, 17–53, 18–03
Knight v Wedderburn (1778) Mor. 14545 .... 3–06, 10–05
Koch v Dicks [1933] 1 K.B. 307, CA 17–29
Kochanski v Kochanska [1958] P. 147; [1957] 3 W.L.R. 619; [1957] 3 All
    E.R. 142; 101 S.J. 763, PDAD 11–27
Kohnke v Karger [1951] 2 K.B. 670; [1951] 2 All E.R. 179, KBD 9–13, 16–28
Konamaneni v Rolls Royce Industrial Power (India) Ltd [2002] 1 W.L.R.
    1269; [2002] 1 All E.R. 979, Ch D 7–55
Koninklijke Zwavelzuurfabrieken V/H Ketjen NV v DA and DD Psy-
    choyos, Piraeus (*The Metamorphosis*); sub nom. Metamorfosis, The
    [1953] 1 W.L.R. 543; [1953] 1 All E.R. 723, PDAD 15–32
Konkola Copper Mines Plc v Coromin Ltd [2006] EWCA Civ 5; [2006] 1
    All E.R. (Comm) 437; [2006] 1 Ll Rep. 410, CA (Civ Div) 7–51
Kooperman, Re [1928] W.N. 101 .... 17–49, 17–57
Kornatzki v Oppenheimer [1937] 4 All E.R. 133 15–53
Korvine's Trust, Re; Joined Cases Levashoff v Block [1921] 1 Ch. 343, Ch
    D 4–04, 17–07, 17–12
Kozikowska v Kozikowski (No.1), 1996 S.L.T. 386, OH 4–03
Krajina v Tass Agency [1949] 2 All E.R. 274; [1949] W.N. 309; 93 S.J. 539,
    CA 7–03, 10–03
Kramer v Attorney General [1923] A.C. 528, HL 6–37
Kraus's Administrators v Sullivan, 1998 S.L.T. 963; 1997 G.W.D. 20–931,
    OH 4–01
Kremezi v Ridgway [1949] 1 All E.R. 662; 93 S.J. 287, KBD ... 11–17, 15–12, 15–22
Krombach v Bamberski (C7/98). *See* Bamberski v Krombach (C7/98).
Kronhofer v Maier (C168/02) [2004] All E.R. (EC) 939; [2004] 2 All E.R.
    (Comm) 759, ECJ (2nd Chamber) 7–14
Krupp Uhde GmbH v Weir Westgarth Ltd, 2002 G.W.D. 19–620, OH 15–01,
    15–16
Krzus v Crows Nest Pass Coal Co Ltd [1912] A.C. 590, PC (Can).... 1–02, 3–07
Kuwait Airways Corp v Iraqi Airways Co (No.1) [1995] 1 W.L.R. 1147;
    [1995] 3 All E.R. 694, HL 7–03
Kuwait Airways Corp v Iraqi Airways Co (No.6); sub nom. Kuwait Airways
    Corp v Iraq Airways Co (No.6); Joined Cases Kuwait Airways Corp
    v Iraqi Airways Co (No.5) [2002] UKHL 19; [2002] 2 A.C. 883;
    [2002] 2 W.L.R. 1353; [2002] 3 All E.R. 209, HL . . 1–01, 3–04, 3–06, 4–05,
    16–15
Kwok Chi Leung Karl v Commissioner of Estate Duty [1988] 1 W.L.R.
    1035; [1988] S.T.C. 728; (1988) 85(33) L.S.G. 44; (1988) 132 S.J.
    1118; *The Times*, July 16, 1988, PC (HK) 17–18

L/F Foroya Fiskasola v Charles Mauritzen Ltd, 1978 S.L.T. (Sh. Ct.) 27, Sh
    Pr; affirming 1977 S.L.T. (Sh. Ct.) 76, Sh Ct (Lothian) 8–21
LTU v Eurocontrol (C29/76). *See* Lufttransportunternehmen GmbH and
    Co KG v Organisation Européenne pour la Securité de la Naviga-
    tion Aérienne (Eurocontrol) (C29/76).
L'Affaire Forgo (1833) 10 Clun et 64 5–05

Labacianskas v Labacianskas 1949 S.C. 280; 1949 S.L.T. 199, IH (1 Div) . . . 6–22,
      6–29
Lacroix, In the Goods of (1876–77) L.R. 2 P.D. 94, PDAD 5–02
Lally v Comex (Diving) Ltd, unreported, May 5, 1976, OH 16–14
Lamb v Heath (1624) Mor. 4812 2–03
Land (Vivian) v Land (Geert), 1962 S.L.T. 316, OH 6–39
Laneuville v Anderson (1860) 2 Sw. & Tr. 24 5–02
Lang v Lang, 1921 S.C. 44; 1920 2 S.L.T. 353, IH (Ct of 7 judges) 11–32
Langley's Settlement Trusts, Re; sub nom. Lloyds Bank Ltd v Langley
    [1962] Ch. 541; [1961] 3 W.L.R. 1169, CA; affirming [1961] 1
    W.L.R. 41; [1961] 1 All E.R. 78, Ch D 10–05, 18–39
Larkins v National Union of Mineworkers [1985] I.R. 671 3–03
Las Mercedes v Abidin Daver. *See* Owners of the Las Mercedes v Owners
    of the Abidin Daver.
Lashley v Hog (1804) 4 Pat. 581 . . . . 13–02, 13–07, 13–10, 18–06, 18–12
Latchin (t/a Dinkha Latchin Associates) v General Mediterranean Hold-
    ings SA [2002] C.L.C. 330; [2003] C.L.Y.B. 601 7–16
Latta, Petr, 1954 S.L.T. (Notes) 74, IH (2 Div) 6–16, 6–21
Lauderdale Peerage Case (1884–85) L.R. 10 App. Cas. 692, HL 6–32
Laurie's Trs, Petrs 1946 S.L.T. (Notes) 31, IH (2 Div) 18–52
Law v Gustin [1976] Fam. 155; [1975] 3 W.L.R. 843; [1976] 1 All E.R. 113,
    Fam Div 12–38
Lawrence v Lawrence [1985] Fam. 106; [1985] 3 W.L.R. 125; [1985] 2 All
    E.R. 733, CA (Civ Div) 4–06, 10–06, 11–17, 12–26
Lawson, Re [1896] 1 Ch. 175 17–56
Lawson v Fox; sub nom. Fox v Lawson [1974] A.C. 803; [1974] 2 W.L.R.
    247, HL 3–07
Lazarewicz (otherwise Fadanelli) v Lazarewicz [1962] P. 171; [1962] 2
    W.L.R. 933, PDAD 11–27
Le Feuvre v Sullivan (1855) 10 Moo.P.C. 389 17–28
Le Mesurier v Le Mesurier [1895] A.C. 517, PC (Cey) 6–25, 11–23, 12–02,
    12–03, 12–18
Lecouturier v Rey; sub nom. Rey v Lecouturier [1910] A.C. 262, HL 3–04
Lee v Abdy (1886) L.R. 17 Q.B.D. 309, QBD 17–19, 17–23
Lee v Lau [1967] P. 14; [1964] 3 W.L.R. 750; [1964] 2 All E.R. 248,
    PDAD 11–01, 11–09, 12–27
Leguia Ex p. Ashworth, In the Estate of; Joined Cases Leguia Ex p.
    Meinertzhagen, In the Estate of [1934] P. 80, PDAD 18–01
Lemenda Trading Co Ltd v African Middle East Petroleum Co Ltd [1988]
    Q.B. 448; [1988] 2 W.L.R. 735; [1988] 1 All E.R. 513; [1988] 1 Ll Rep.
    361; [1988] 1 F.T.L.R. 123; (1988) 132 S.J. 538, QBD (Comm) 15–26
Lendrum v Chakravarti, 1929 S.L.T. 96, OH 11–01, 11–09, 11–11, 12–33
Leon, The (1881) L.R. 6 P.D. 148, PDAD 16–14
Leon XIII, The (1883) L.R. 8 P.D. 121, CA 15–22
Lepre v Lepre [1965] P. 52; [1963] 2 W.L.R. 735, PDAD 12–23, 12–36, 12–39
Leroux v Brown (1852) 12 C.B. 801 8–12
Levick's Will Trusts, Re; sub nom. Ffennell v Inland Revenue Commis-
    sioners; Levick, Re [1963] 1 W.L.R. 311; [1963] 1 All E.R. 95,
    Ch D 18–25, 18–26
Lewal's Settlement Trusts, Re; sub nom. Gould v Lewal [1918] 2 Ch. 391,
    Ch D 18–39, 18–43
Lewis v Eliades (No.2); sub nom. Eliades v Lewis [2003] EWCA Civ 1758;
    [2004] 1 W.L.R. 692; [2004] 1 All E.R. 1196 [2003] EWHC 368;
    [2003] 1 All E.R. (Comm) 850, QBD 9–34
Libertas-Kommerz GmbH v Johnson 1977 S.C. 191; 1978 S.L.T. 222,
    OH 17–22, 17–26

Libyan Arab Foreign Bank v Bankers Trust Co [1989] Q.B. 728; [1989] 3
    W.L.R. 314; [1989] 3 All E.R. 252, QBD (Comm) 15–06, 15–07
Liddell-Crainger's Will Trusts, Re [1936] 3 All E.R. 173 6–16
Lieber v Gobel (C292/93) [1994] E.C.R. I—2535; [1994] I.L.Pr. 590; *The
    Times,* July 9, 1994, ECJ (5th Chamber) 7–27
Lightbody v West (1903) 19 T.L.R. 319 11–28
Lindsay v Paterson (1840) 2 D. 1373 .... 17–47, 17–49
Liquidator of Salt Mines Syndicate Ltd. *See* Tait (Liquidator of Salt Mines
    Syndicate Ltd), Noter.
Liquidators of California Redwood Co Ltd v Walker (1886) 13 R. 810 7–47
Liquidators of Pacific Coast Mining Co Ltd v Walker (1886) 13 R. 816 7–47
Lister's Judicial Factor v Syme; sub nom. Lister's Judicial Factor v Burn,
    1914 S.C. 204; 1914 1 S.L.T. 12, IH (1 Div) 13–07
Little Olympian Each Ways Ltd (No.2), Re [1995] 1 W.L.R. 560; [1994] 4
    All E.R. 561, Ch D 7–03
Liverpool Marine Credit Co v Hunter (1867) L.R. 4 Eq. 62 17–10
Liverpool Royal Infirmary v Ramsay, *See* Ramsay v Liverpool Royal
    Infirmary.
Lloyd v Guibert (1865–66) L.R. 1 Q.B. 115, Ex Chamber 8–17, 15–32
Lloyd Evans, Re. *See* Evans (Deceased), Re.
Lolley's Case (1812) Russ. & Ry. 237 12–02
London and South American Investment Trust Ltd v British Tobacco Co
    (Australia) Ltd [1927] 1 Ch. 107, Ch D 17–31
London Joint Stock Bank v Simmons; sub nom. Simmons v London Joint
    Stock Bank; Joined Cases Little v London Joint Stock Bank [1892]
    A.C. 201, HL 17–30
Longworth v Hope (1865) 3 M. 1049, IH (1 Div) 7–45, 16–21
Lord v Colvin (1859) 4 Drew 366 6–10
Lord Advocate v Brown's Trs, 1907 S.C. 333; (1907) 14 S.L.T. 636, IH (1
    Div) 6–04, 6–12, 6–15
Lord Advocate, Petr. *See* Lord Advocate v Murdoch.
Lord Advocate, Petr (Evidence: Foreign Proceedings), 1998 S.C. 87; 1998
    S.L.T. 835, IH (Ex Div) 8–16
Lord Advocate v Jaffrey; sub nom. Mackinnon's Trs v Lord Advocate;
    Mackinnon's Trs v Inland Revenue Commissioners [1921] 1 A.C.
    146; 1920 S.C. (H.L.) 171, HL 6–25
Lord Advocate v Murdoch,; sub nom. Lord Advocate, Petr 1993 S.C. 638;
    1994 S.L.T. 852, IH (2 Div) 8–16
Lord Advocate v Tursi, 1998 S.L.T. 1035; 1997 S.C.L.R. 264; 1997 G.W.D.
    6–254, OH 3–02
Lorentzen v Lydden and Co Ltd [1942] 2 K.B. 202, KBD 3–04, 3–07
Lorrillard, Re; sub nom. Lorillard, Re; Joined Cases Griffiths v Catforth
    [1922] 2 Ch. 638, CA 8–22, 17–53, 18–03
Low, Re; sub nom. Bland v Low [1894] 1 Ch. 147, CA 8–08
Low v Low (1891) 19 R. 115 6–25
Low v Low (1893) 1 S.L.T. 43, OH 8–08
Lowenthal v Attorney General [1948] 1 All E.R. 295; 64 T.L.R. 145; (1948)
    65 R.P.C. 126; [1948] W.N. 66; 92 S.J. 141, Ch D 6–38
Lubbe v Cape Plc (No.2); Joined Cases Afrika v Cape Plc (Stay of
    Proceedings) [2000] 1 W.L.R. 1545; [2000] 4 All E.R. 268, HL   7–45, 7–51
Luck's Settlement Trusts, Re; sub nom. Luck's Will Trusts, Re; Walker v
    Luck [1940] Ch. 864; [1940] 3 All E.R. 307, CA 10–04, 14–05
Lufttransportunternehmen GmbH and Co KG v Organisation Européenne
    pour la Securité de la Navigation Aérienne (Eurocontrol) (C29/76);
    sub nom. LTU v Eurocontrol (C29/76) [1976] E.C.R. 1541; [1977] 1
    C.M.L.R. 88, ECJ 7–09, 8–16
Luigi Bianchi (In the Goods of) (1862) 3 Sw. & Tr. 16 6–22

Lushington v Sewell (1827) 1 Sim. 435 17–04
Lusk v Elder (1843) 5 D. 1279 8–22
Lynch v Provisional Government of Paraguay (1869–72) L.R. 2 P. & D.
 268, Ct of Probate 4–05, 6–04, 18–12
Lyndon v Lyndon, 1978 S.L.T. (Notes) 7, OH 14–25, 14–47
Lyne's Settlement Trusts, Re; sub nom. Gibbs, Re; Lyne v Gibbs [1919] 1
 Ch. 80, CA 17–02

M, Petr, 2005 S.L.T. 2; 2005 S.C.L.R. 396, OH 14–27
M, Petitition, 2000 G.W.D. 32–1242 14–29
M, Re [1937] N.I. 151 6–16
M (Abduction: Acquiescence), Re; sub nom. M (A Minor) (Abduction),
 Re [1996] 1 F.L.R. 315; [1995] 3 F.C.R. 99, Fam Div 14–31
M (A Child), Re; sub nom. Vigreux v Michel [2006] EWCA Civ 630;
 (2006) 103(22) L.S.G. 26; (2006) 150 S.J.L.B. 666, CA (Civ Div) 14–34
M (Minors) (Abduction: Psychological Harm), Re [1997] 2 F.L.R. 690;
 [1998] 2 F.C.R. 488, CA (Civ Div) 14–31
M (Minors)(Residence Order: Jurisdiction)[1995] 1 F.L.R. 495, CA 14–29
M v B [2005] EWHC 1681; [2006] 1 F.L.R. 117; [2005] Fam. Law 860, Fam
 Div 10–05, 11–16, 12–38
M v M [1995] 7 C.L. 64 13–24
M v M (Children: International Abduction); sub nom. MM v AMR
 (otherwise M), 2003 S.C. 252; 2003 S.L.T. 330, IH (2 Div) 14–31
M Isaacs and Sons Ltd v Cook [1925] 2 K.B. 391, KBD 16–12, 16–13
MBM Fabri—Clad Ltd v Eisen und Huttenwerke Thale AG [2000] C.L.C.
 373; [2000] I.L.Pr. 505; [2000] C.L.Y.B. 739, CA (Civ Div) 7–13
MT Group v James Howden and Co Ltd (Jurisdiction), 1993 S.L.T. 409,
 OH 7–29
McAdam v Boxpak Ltd, 2006 S.L.T. 217 15–42
McAllister v General Medical Council [1993] A.C. 388; [1993] 2 W.L.R.
 308; [1993] 1 All E.R. 982; 1993 S.C. 388; [1993] 4 Med. L.R. 29;
 (1993) 137 S.J.L.B. 12, PC (UK) 8–12
Macalpine v Macalpine [1958] P. 35; [1957] 3 W.L.R. 698, PDAD 9–12
Macartney, Re; sub nom. MacFarlane v Macartney (No.2) [1921] 1 Ch.
 522, Ch D 9–12
Macaulay v Macaulay [1991] 1 W.L.R. 179; [1991] 1 All E.R. 865, Fam Div 13–24
McBride's Trs, Special Case (International law: Succession), 1952 S.L.T.
 (Notes) 59, IH (1 Div) 18–26
McCabe v McCabe [1994] 1 F.L.R. 410; [1994] 1 F.C.R. 257; *Independent*,
 September 3, 1993, CA (Civ Div) 4–04, 11–14, 11–24
McCarron (George Wallace) v HM Advocate, 2001 J.C. 199; 2001 S.L.T.
 866, HCJ Appeal 3–03
McCarthy v Abowall (Trading) Ltd, 1992 S.L.T. (Sh. Ct.) 65; 1992 S.C.L.R.
 264, Sh Ct (Lothian) 7–30
McCarthy v McCarthy, 1995 S.L.T. 1176 14–29
McCarthy (Daniel) v McCarthy (Parent and Child : Custody), 1994 S.L.T.
 743, OH 14–29
McCormick v Rittmeyer (1869 7 M. 854 15–22
Macdonald v Cuthbertson (1890) 18 R. 101 18–17
Macdonald v Macdonald's Executrix; sub nom. Macdonald v Macdonald
 1932 S.C. (H.L.) 79; 1932 S.L.T. 381, HL 4–01, 17–02, 18–06
McDonnell v McDonnell [1912] 2 I.R. 148 9–12
McDouall v Adair (1852) 14 D. 525 14–04
MacDougall v Chitnavis, 1937 S.C. 390; 1937 S.L.T. 421, IH (1 Div) 3–06,
 10–05, 10–07, 11–09, 11–11, 11–21, 11–22, 12–33
McElroy v McAllister, 1949 S.C. 110; 1949 S.L.T. 139, IH (Ct of 7 judges .. 5–07,
 8–09, 16–06, 16–11, 16–12, 16–13, 16–26, 16–27

McEwan (George) v McEwan (Frances), 1969 S.L.T. 342, OH 6–10
McFarlane v McFarlane [2006] UKHL 26 13–09
Macfarlane v Norris (1862) 2 B.J. 783 8–24
McFeetridge v Stewarts and Lloyds Ltd, 1913 S.C. 773; 1913 1 S.L.T. 325,
    IH (2 Div) 15–20
McGowan v Summit at Lloyds, 2002 S.C. 638; 2002 S.L.T. 1258; *The Times*,
    July 15, 2002, IH (Ex Div) 7–29
Machado v Fontes [1897] 2 Q.B. 231, CA 16–12, 16–13
McHenry v Lewis (1883) L.R. 22 Ch. D. 397, CA 7–47
McKay v Walls, 1951 S.L.T. (Notes) 6, OH 5–02, 12–17
McKee (Mark) v McKee (Evelyn) [1951] A.C. 352; [1951] 1 All E.R. 942,
    Sup Ct (Can) 14–25, 14–47
Mackender v Feldia AG[1967] 2 Q.B. 590; [1967] 2 W.L.R. 119, CA   7–31, 15–19
Mackenzie, Re; sub nom. Mackenzie v Edwards Moss [1911] 1 Ch. 578, Ch
    D 6–25, 13–04, 13–07
Mackenzie v Hall (1854) 17 D. 164 8–18
Mackie v Darling (1871) L.R. 12 Eq. 319, Ct of Chancery 10–04
McKie v McKie [1933] I.R. 464 .... 9–04, 13–13
Mackinnon v Iberia Shipping Co [1954] 2 Ll Rep. 372; 1955 S.C. 20; 1955
    S.L.T. 49, IH (1 Div) 16–11, 16–13, 16–14
Mackinnon's Trs v Lord Advocate. *See* Lord Advocate v Jaffrey.
Mackintosh v May (1895) 22 R. 345; (1895) 2 S.L.T. 471, IH (2 Div) 15–12,
                                                                        17–06
McKiver (Children: Abduction) v McKiver (Fiona), 1995 S.L.T. 790, OH .. 14–29
Maclaine Watson and Co Ltd v International Tin Council (No.1) [1989]
    Ch. 253; [1988] 3 W.L.R. 1169; [1988] 3 All E.R. 257, CA (Civ Div);
    affirming [1988] Ch. 1; [1987] 3 W.L.R. 508; [1987] 3 All E.R. 787,
    Ch D 15–40
Maclarty v Steele (1881) 8 R. 435, IH (2 Div) 16–12, 16–21
McLean v McLean, 1947 S.C. 79; 1947 S.L.T. 36, IH (2 Div) 14–25
Maclean's Trs v McNair, 1969 S.C. 65; 1969 S.L.T. 146, IH (1 Div) 18–03
McLelland v McLelland, 1942 S.C. 502; 1943 S.L.T. 66, IH (1 Div) 6–10
Mcmillan v Canadian Northern Railway Co [1923] A.C. 120, PC (Can) ... 16–12,
                                                                        16–13
MacMillan v MacMillan, 1989 S.C. 53; 1989 S.L.T. 350, IH (Ex Div) 14–31,
                                                                        14–39
Macmillan Inc v Bishopsgate Investment Trust Plc (No.3) [1996] 1 W.L.R.
    387; [1996] 1 All E.R. 585, CA (Civ Div) 4–02, 5–07, 16–30, 17–02,
                                            17–03, 17–17, 17–19, 17–31
McMorran, Re; sub nom. Mercantile Bank of India v Perkins [1958] Ch.
    624; [1958] 2 W.L.R. 327; [1958] 1 All E.R. 186, Ch D 18–26, 18–43
McNeill v McNeill; sub nom. M'Neill v M'Neill 1919 2 S.L.T. 127, OH 6–10
Macreight, Re; sub nom. Paxton v Macreight (1885) L.R. 30 Ch. D. 165,
    Ch D 6–31
McShane v McShane, 1962 S.L.T. 221, OH 14–25
MacShannon v Rockware Glass Ltd; Joined Cases Fyfe v Redpath Dorman
    Long Ltd; Jardine v British Steel Corp; Paterson v Stone Man-
    ganese Marine Ltd [1978] A.C. 795; [1978] 2 W.L.R. 362; [1978] 1
    All E.R. 625, HL 7–45, 16–11
Mahadervan v Mahadervan; sub nom. Mahadevan v Mahadevan [1964] P.
    233; [1963] 2 W.L.R. 271, PDAD 8–12, 11–30
Maharanee Seethadevi Gaekwar of Baroda v Wildenstein [1972] 2 Q.B.
    283; [1972] 2 W.L.R. 1077, CA (Civ Div) 7–02, 7–04
Maher v Maher [1951] P. 342; [1951] 2 All E.R. 37, PDAD 12–27
Mahme Trust Reg v Lloyds TSB Bank Plc [2004] EWHC 1931; [2004] 2 Ll
    Rep. 637; [2004] I.L.Pr. 43, Ch D 7–51

Mahmood v Mahmood, 1993 S.L.T. 589; 1993 S.C.L.R. 64, OH 11–01, 11–31, 12–38

Mahmud v Mahmud, 1977 S.L.T. (Notes) 17, OH 11–01, 11–31

Mahmud v Mahmud, 1994 S.L.T. 599; 1993 S.C.L.R. 688, OH 11–01, 11–31, 12–38

Maimann v Maimann (Application for Freezing Order) [2001] I.L.Pr. 27, QBD 7–58

Mainschiffahrts Genossenschaft eG (MSG) v Les Gravières Rhenanes Srl (C106/95) [1997] Q.B. 731; [1997] 3 W.L.R. 179; [1997] All E.R. (EC) 385, ECJ (6th Chamber) 7–29, 7–43

Makouipour v Makouipour, 1967 S.C. 116; 1967 S.L.T. 101, OH 4–06, 12–27

Maldonado, In the Estate of; sub nom. Spain v Treasury Solicitor [1954] P. 223; [1954] 2 W.L.R. 64; [1953] 2 All E.R. 1579, CA 4–02, 4–04, 18–14

Male v Roberts (1800) 3 Esp. 163 15–20

Maltese Marriage Case. *See* Anton v Bartolo.

Maltman v Tarmac Civil Engineering Ltd, 1967 S.C. 177; 1967 S.L.T. 141, IH (1 Div) 9–12

Manifold, Re; sub nom. Slater v Chryssaffinis [1962] Ch. 1; [1961] 2 W.L.R. 456; [1961] 1 All E.R. 710, Ch D 18–03, 18–29

Manners, Re; sub nom. Manners v Manners [1923] 1 Ch. 220, Ch D 18–26

Manning v Manning [1958] P. 112; [1958] 2 W.L.R. 318, PDAD 12–27

Maples (formerly Melamud) v Maples; sub nom. Maples v Melamud [1988] Fam. 14; [1987] 3 W.L.R. 487; [1987] 3 All E.R. 188, Fam Div 9–21, 12–30

Marc Rich and Co AG v Impianti. *See* Marc Rich and Co AG v Societa Italiana Impianti SpA (*The Atlantic Emperor*) (No.2).

Marc Rich and Co AG v Societa Italiana Impianti SpA (The Atlantic Emperor) (No.2) [1992] 1 Ll Rep. 624; [1992] I.L.Pr. 544, CA (Civ Div) 9–76

Marc Rich and Co AG v Societa Italiana Impianti SpA (C190/89) [1992] 1 Ll Rep. 342; [1991] E.C.R. I—3855, ECJ 7–09, 9–76

Macey v Rozbicki, 18 N.T. 2d 289; 221 N.E. 2d 380 (1966) 16–08

Marchant v Marchant (Divorce: Jurisdiction), 1948 S.L.T. 143; 1948 S.L.T. (Notes) 1, OH 6–10

Marchioness of Hastings v Executors of Marquess of Hastings (1852) 15 D. 489 18–01

Marchioness of Huntly v Gaskell; sub nom. Marchioness of Huntly v Brooks Trs; Huntly (Lady) v Cunliffe Brooks Trs; Cunliffe Brooks v Gaskell (Cunliffe Brooks Tr.); Brooks v Brooks Trs; Joined Cases Cunliffe (Lady) Brooks v Cunliffe Brooks Trs; Marchioness of Huntly v Gaskell (Cunliffe Brooks Trs.) [1906] A.C. 56; (1905) 8 F. (H.L.) 4; (1905) 13 S.L.T. 600, HL; affirming (1902) 4 F. 1014; (1902) 10 S.L.T. 217, IH (1 Div) 6–04, 6–08, 6–09

Marconi Communications International Ltd v PT Pan Indonesia Bank TBK; sub nom. Marconi Communications International Ltd v PT Pan Indonesian Bank Ltd [2005] EWCA Civ 422; [2005] 2 All E.R. (Comm) 325, CA (Civ Div) 15–16, 17–29, 17–55

Mareva Compania Naviera SA v International Bulk Carriers SA (*The Mareva*) [1980] 1 All E.R. 213; [1975] 2 Ll Rep. 509, CA (Civ Div) . . 7–58

Marie Brizard et Roger International SA v William Grant and Sons (International) Ltd (Case C–126/96), unreported 9–50

Marie Brizzard et Roger International SA v William Grant and Sons Ltd (No.2); sub nom. Marie Brizard et Roger International SA v William Grant and Sons Ltd (No.2); Marie Brizzard et Roger International SA, Petr (No.2), 2002 S.L.T. 1365; 2002 S.C.L.R. 619, OH 9–40

Marinari v Lloyds Bank Plc (C364/93) [1996] Q.B. 217; [1996] 2 W.L.R.
   159; [1996] All E.R. (E.C.) 84, ECJ   7–14
Mark v Mark [2005] UKHL 42; [2006] 1 A.C. 98; [2005] 3 W.L.R. 111;
   [2005] 3 All E.R. 912, HL 6–09, 6–30, 6–39, 12–04, 12–27
Marlborough (Duke of)v Attorney General [1945] Ch. 78, CA 13–04, 13–07,
                                                                       18–51
Marodi Service de D Mialich v Mikkal Myklebusthaug Rederi A/S, 2002
   S.L.T. 1013; 2002 G.W.D. 13–398, OH   7–45
Maronier v Larmer [2002] EWCA Civ 774; [2003] Q.B. 620; [2002] 3
   W.L.R. 1060, CA (Civ Div)   9–90
Marrett, Re; sub nom. Chalmers v Wingfield (1887) L.R. 36 Ch. D. 400,
   CA   6–22
Marseilles Extension Railway and Land Co, Re; sub nom. Smallpage's
   Case; Brandon's Case (1885) L.R. 30 Ch. D. 598, Ch D   17–29
Marsh v Marsh, 2002 S.L.T. (Sh Ct) 87; 2002 S.C.L.R. 84, Sh Pr   6–10
Marshall, Re; sub nom. Barclays Bank Ltd v Marshall [1957] Ch. 507;
   [1957] 3 W.L.R. 538; [1957] 3 All E.R. 172, CA   14–61
Marshall v Marshall, 1996 S.L.T. 429, IH (2 Div)   14–31
Martin, Re; sub nom. Loustalan v Loustalan [1900] P. 211, CA 4–04, 6–30,
                                                                       18–33
Martin v Buret, 1938 S.L.T. 479, OH 10–06, 11–21
Martin-Dye v Martin-Dye [2006] EWCA Civ 681; [2006] All E.R.(D.) 369;
   (2006) 156 N.L.J. 917, CA (Civ Div)   13–09
Martin Peters Bauunternehmung GmbH v Zuid Nederlandse Aannemers
   Vereniging (C34/82) [1983] E.C.R. 987; [1984] 2 C.M.L.R. 605, ECJ . .   7–13
Mary Moxham, The (1876) 1 P.D. 107 . . . .   16–12, 16–13
Masinimport v Scottish Mechanical Light Industries Ltd, 1972 S.L.T.
   (Notes) 76, OH   7–03
Maspons y Hermano v Mildred Goyeneche and Co. *See* Mildred v
   Maspons.
Masri v Consolidated Contractors International (UK) Ltd; sub nom. Masri
   v Consolidated Contractors Group SAL [2005] EWCA Civ 1436;
   [2006] 1 W.L.R. 830; [2006] 1 All E.R. (Comm) 465, CA (Civ Div) . .   7–17
Matthews v Kuwait Bechtel Corp [1959] 2 Q.B. 57; [1959] 2 W.L.R. 702;
   [1959] 2 All E.R. 345, CA   16–24
Matznick v Matznick, 1998 S.L.T. 636; 1997 G.W.D. 27–1345, OH . .   14–31, 14–32
Maudslay Sons and Field, Re; sub nom. Maudslay v Maudslay Sons and
   Field [1900] 1 Ch. 602, Ch D   17–28
Maugham, Re (1885) 2 T.L.R. 115   15–12
Mauroux v Soc Com Abel Pereira Da Fonseca Srl [1972] 1 W.L.R. 962;
   [1972] 2 All E.R. 1085, Ch D 15–12, 15–40
Mawji v Queen, The; Joined Cases Mawji (Laila Jhina) v Queen, The
   [1957] A.C. 126; [1957] 2 W.L.R. 277, PC (EA)   11–05
Maxwell v McClure (1857) 20 D. 307; affirmed 3 Macq. 852   18–12
Maxwell Communications Corp (No.2), Re [1992] B.C.C. 757   7–47
May, Re [1943] 2 All E.R. 146 . . . .   6–29, 6–30
Mayo-Perrott v Mayo-Perrott [1958] I.R. 336   3–06
Mayor of Auckland v Alliance Assurance Co Ltd [1937] A.C. 587, PC (NZ) . . .   15–50
Mecklermedia Corp v DC Congress GmbH [1998] Ch. 40; [1997] 3 W.L.R.
   479; [1998] 1 All E.R. 148, Ch D 7–14, 7–38, 7–39
Medicopharma (UK) BV v Cairns, 1993 S.L.T. 386, OH   7–03
Medway Packaging Ltd v Meurer Maschinen GmbH and Co KG [1990] 2
   Ll Rep. 112; *The Times*, May 7, 1990, CA (Civ Div)   7–13
Mehta v Sutton (1913) 108 L.T. 514   17–13
Mehta (otherwise Kohn) v Mehta [1945] 2 All E.R. 690; 174 L.T. 63,
   PDAD 11–01, 11–03
Melbourne, Ex p. (1870) L.R. 6 Ch.App. 64   17–53

Mengel's Will Trusts, Re; sub nom. Westminster Bank Ltd v Mengel
    [1962] Ch. 791; [1962] 3 W.L.R. 311; [1962] 2 All E.R. 490, Ch D .. 13–02,
        18–34
Mercantile Mutual v Neilson [2004] WASCA 60 5–06
Mercedes—Benz AG v Leiduck [1996] A.C. 284; [1995] 3 W.L.R. 718;
    [1995] 3 All E.R. 929, PC (HK) 7–58
Merker v Merker [1963] P. 283; [1962] 3 W.L.R. 1389, PDAD 9–11, 11–27,
        12–32, 12–39
Merrick Homes Ltd v Duff (No.1), 1996 S.L.T. 932; 1995 S.C.L.R. 959;
    [1995] B.C.C. 954, IH (2 Div) 7–03
Messenger v Messenger, 1992 S.L.T. (Sh. Ct.) 29, Sh Pr 14–44, 14–45
Messier Dowty Ltd v Sabena SA [2000] 1 W.L.R. 2040; [2001] 1 All E.R.
    275, CA (Civ Div) 7–30, 7–44
Metal Industries (Salvage) Ltd v ST Harle (Owners), 1962 S.L.T. 114, OH .. 3–02
Metcalfe's Trusts, In the Matter of (1864) De G.J. and S. 122 10–05
Metliss v National Bank of Greece and Athens SA. *See* National Bank of
    Greece and Athens SA v Metliss.
Mette v Mette (1859) 1 Sw. & Tr. 416 .... 4–05, 11–14, 11–16
Meyer, Re; sub nom. Meyer v Meyer [1971] P. 298; [1971] 2 W.L.R. 401,
    PDAD 9–12, 10–05, 12–23
Meyer v Dresser (1864) 16 C.B. (N.S.) 646 8–24
Middleburg v Executors of Smith (1626) Mor. 12420 2–03
Middleton v Middleton [1967] P. 62; [1966] 2 W.L.R. 512; [1966] 1 All
    E.R. 168; 110 S.J. 170, PDAD 9–12
Midland Bank Plc v Laker Airways Ltd; sub nom. Midland Bank Plc and
    Clydesdale Bank Plc v Laker Airways Ltd, Morris and Laker
    Airways (International) Ltd [1986] Q.B. 689; [1986] 2 W.L.R. 707;
    [1986] 1 All E.R. 526, CA (Civ Div) 7–47
Mildred v Maspons; sub nom. Maspons y Hermano v Mildred Goyeneche
    and Co (1882–83) L.R. 8 App. Cas. 874, HL; affirming (1881–82)
    L.R. 9 Q.B.D. 530, CA 15–40
Miles Platts Ltd v Townroe Ltd; sub nom. Miles Platt Ltd v Townroe Ltd
    [2003] EWCA Civ 145; [2003] 1 All E.R. (Comm) 561; [2003] 2
    C.L.C. 589, CA (Civ Div) 7–39
Miliangos v George Frank (Textiles) Ltd (No.1) [1976] A.C. 443; [1975] 3
    W.L.R. 758, HL; affirming [1975] Q.B. 487; [1975] 2 W.L.R. 555,
    CA (Civ Div) 8–21
Millar v Mitchell Caddell and Co (1860) 22 D. 833 15–40
Miller v Deakin, 1912 1 S.L.T. 253, OH 11–14, 12–33
Miller (William), Re; sub nom. Bailie v Miller; Sir William Miller, Re;
    Miller (James), Re; Sir James Miller, Re [1914] 1 Ch. 511, Ch D .. 18–25,
        18–26
Minna Craig Steamship Co v Chartered Mercantile Bank of India London
    and China [1897] 1 Q.B. 460, CA; affirming [1897] 1 Q.B. 55, QBD .. 9–04
Minnesota v Philip Morris Inc (1997) 11 C.L. 100 8–16
Minster Investments Ltd v Hyundai Precision and Industry Co Ltd [1988] 2
    Ll Rep. 621; *The Times*, January 26, 1988, QBD (Comm) 7–14
Missouri Steamship Co, Re (1889) L.R. 42 Ch. D. 321, CA 15–12, 15–26
Mitchell v Burnett and Mowat (1746) Mor. 4468 8–24
Mitchell v McCulloch, 1976 S.C. 1; 1976 S.L.T. 2, OH 16–11, 16–13, 16–28
Mitchell v Mitchell (Divorce: Jurisdiction), 1992 S.C. 372; 1993 S.L.T. 123,
    IH (Ex Div) 12–11
Mitchell and Baxter v Davies (1875) 3 R. 208 18–26
Mitchell's Tr. v Rule. *See* Gowans (Mitchell's Tr.) v Rule.
Mohamed v Alaga and Co; sub nom. Mohammed v Alaga and Co [2000] 1
    W.L.R. 1815; [1999] 3 All E.R. 699, CA (Civ Div); reversing in part
    [1998] 2 All E.R. 720; (1998) 95(17) L.S.G. 29, Ch D 3–06

Mohammed v Bank of Kuwait and the Middle East KSC [1996] 1 W.L.R.
    1483; [1996] C.L.C. 1835, CA (Civ Div) 7–45
Montagu Evans (A Firm) v Young, 2000 S.L.T. 1083; 2000 G.W.D. 24–912,
    OH 7–13
Monteith v Monteith's Trs (1882) 9 R. 982 17–02
Monterosso Shipping Co v International Transport Workers' Federation
    (The Rosso) [1982] 3 All E.R. 841; [1982] 2 Ll Rep. 120, CA (Civ
    Div) 15–12, 15–22
Montgomery v Zarifi, 1918 S.C. (H.L.) 128; 1918 2 S.L.T. 110, HL   13–07, 13–09
Moorhouse v Lord (1863) 10 H.L. Cas. 272 6–32
Mora Shipping Inc v Axa Corporate Solutions Assurance SA [2005]
    EWCA Civ 1069; [2005] 2 Ll Rep. 769; [2005] 2 C.L.C. 349, CA
    (Civ Div) 7–13
Moran v Moran, 1997 S.L.T. 541, OH 14–29
Morgan v Cilento; sub nom. Morgan (Attorney of Shaffer) v Cilento [2004]
    EWHC 188; [2004] W.T.L.R. 457, Ch D 6–04, 6–22, 6–34, 18–09
Morin v Bonhams and Brooks Ltd [2003] EWCA Civ 1802; [2004] 1 All
    E.R. (Comm) 880; [2004] 1 Ll Rep. 702 [2003] EWHC 467; [2003] 2
    All E.R. (Comm) 36; [2003] I.L.Pr. 25, QBD (Comm) 7–55, 15–13,
                                                 16–01, 16–17, 16–18, 16–20
Morley's Tr. v Aitken, 1982 S.C. 73; 1983 S.L.T. 78, OH 17–52, 17–55, 17–57
Morris v KLM Royal Dutch Airlines; sub nom. KLM Royal Dutch Airlines
    v Morris [2001] EWCA Civ 790; [2002] Q.B. 100; [2001] 3 W.L.R.
    351, CA (Civ Div) 1–06
Morris v Murjani [1996] 1 W.L.R. 848; [1996] 2 All E.R. 384, CA (Civ Div) .. 7–58
Morrison v Panic Link Ltd, 1993 S.C. 631; 1994 S.L.T. 232, IH (Ex Div) ... 7–29,
                                                                       7–30
Morton v Morton (Divorce: Domicile) (1897) 5 S.L.T. 222, OH 4–05, 6–10
Moses, Re; sub nom. Moses v Valentine [1908] 2 Ch. 235, Ch D 18–17
Moss' Trs v Moss, 1916 2 S.L.T. 31, OH 17–02
Mostyn v Fabrigas (1774) 1 Coup. 161; 1 S.L.C. 615 2–02
Motala v Attorney General; Joined Cases Attorney General v Safiya and
    Faruce Motala [1992] 1 A.C. 281; [1991] 3 W.L.R. 903; [1991] 4 All
    E.R. 682, HL; reversing [1991] 2 All E.R. 312; [1991] Fam. Law 425,
    CA (Civ Div); affirming [1990] 2 F.L.R. 261, Fam Div 14–02
Moulis v Owen [1907] 1 K.B. 746, CA 17–29
Mount Albert BC v Australasian Temperance and General Mutual Life
    Assurance Society Ltd [1938] A.C. 224, PC (NZ) 15–07, 15–12, 15–25,
                                                                     15–50
Mountbatten v Mountbatten (No.1); sub nom. Marquess of Milford Haven
    v Marchioness of Milford Haven [1959] P. 43; [1959] 2 W.L.R. 128;
    [1959] 1 All E.R. 99, PDAD 5–02, 12–18
Muhammed v Suna, 1956 S.C. 366; 1956 S.L.T. 175, OH 11–02, 11–03
Muir v Collett (1862) 24 D. 1119 8–05
Muir v Matassa 1935 S.L.T. (Sh. Ct.) 55, Sh Ct 7–04
Muirhead and Turnbull v Dickson (1905) 7 F. 686; (1905) 13 S.L.T. 151,
    IH (1 Div) 12–38
Munro v Munro (1837) 16 S. 18; affirmed (1840) 1 Rob. 492, HL 14–04
Munster and Leinster Bank Ltd v O'Connor [1937] L.R. 462 6–21
Murphy v Murphy, 1994 G.W.D. 32–1893 14–31
Murphy's Tr., Petr, 1933 S.L.T. 632, OH 17–53
Murphy's Trs v Aitken. *See* Morley's Tr. v Aitken.
Murray v Champernowne [1901] 2 I.R. 232 .... 17–02, 18–17
Murray v Smith (1838) 6 S. 690 18–34
Musurus, In the Estate of [1936] 2 All E.R. 1666, PDAD 18–14

N v N (Jurisdiction: Pre Nuptial Agreement); sub nom. N v N (Divorce: Judaism); N v N (Divorce: Antenuptial Agreement) [1999] 2 F.L.R. 745; [1999] 2 F.C.R. 583, Fam Div 13–09

NV Daarnhouwer and Co, Handelmaatschappij v Boulos [1968] 2 Ll Rep. 259; (1968) 118 N.L.J. 1030, QBD 9–10

NV Kwik Hoo Tong Handel Maatschappij v James Finlay and Co Ltd [1927] A.C. 604, HL 15–12

NV Ondix International v Landay Ltd, 1963 S.C. 270; 1963 S.L.T. (Notes) 68, OH 7–03

Nabi v Heaton (Inspector of Taxes) [1983] 1 W.L.R. 626; [1983] S.T.C. 344, CA (Civ Div) 11–05

Nachimson v Nachimson [1930] P. 217; 74 A.L.R. 1517, CA 11–01

Naftalin v London Midland and Scottish Railway Co, 1933 S.C. 259; 1933 S.L.T. 193, IH (2 Div) 8–02, 16–11, 16–13

Narden Services Ltd v Inverness Retail and Business Park Ltd 2006 S.L.T. 338; 2005 S.C.L.R. 704; 2005 G.W.D. 33–620, OH 7–56

National Bank of Australia Ltd v Scottish Union and National Insurance Co Ltd [1952] A.C. 493; [1952] 2 T.L.R. 254; 96 S.J. 529; (1951) 24 A.L.J. 533, HC (Aus) 15–24

National Bank of Greece and Athens SA v Metliss [1958] A.C. 509; [1957] 3 W.L.R. 1056, HL 3–01, 4–05, 10–04, 15–12, 15–23

National Bank of Greece SA v Westminster Bank Executor and Tr. Co (Channel Islands); sub nom. Westminster Bank Executor and Tr. Co (Channel Islands) v National Bank of Greece SA [1971] A.C. 945; [1971] 2 W.L.R. 105; [1971] 1 All E.R. 233, HL 17–17

National Mutual Life Association of Australasia v Attorney General of New Zealand [1956] A.C. 369; [1956] 2 W.L.R. 532; [1956] 1 All E.R. 721, PC (NZ) 15–50

Navigation Maritime Bulgare v Rustal Trading Ltd (*The Ivan Zagubanski*) [2002] 1 Ll Rep. 106, QBD (Comm) 7–09

Navigators Insurance Co v Atlantic Methanol Production Co LLC [2003] EWHC 1706; [2004] Ll Rep. I.R. 418, QBD (Comm) 7–46

Nelson v Bridport (1846) 8 Beav. 547 .... 4–05, 18–25

Nesbitt, Re; sub nom. Dr Barnardo's Homes National Inc Association v Board of Governors of the United Newcastle-upon-Tyne Hospitals; Nesbitt's Will Trust, Re [1953] 1 W.L.R. 595; [1953] 1 All E.R. 936, Ch D 18–03.18–26

Nessa v Chief Adjudication Officer [1999] 1 W.L.R. 1937; [1999] 4 All E.R. 677, HL 6–39

Neste Chemicals SA v DK Line SA (*The Sargasso*) [1994] 3 All E.R. 180; [1994] 2 Ll Rep. 6, CA (Civ Div) 7–41

Netz v Ede [1946] Ch. 224, Ch D 7–03

New York Breweries Co Ltd v Attorney General; sub nom. Attorney General v New York Breweries Co Ltd [1899] A.C. 62, HL 18–01

New York Life Insurance Co v Public Tr. [1924] 2 Ch. 101, CA 17–17

Newlands v Chalmers' Trs (1832) 11 S. 65 18–12

Newmarch v Newmarch [1978] Fam. 79; [1977] 3 W.L.R. 832; [1978] 1 All E.R. 1, Fam Div 12–23, 12–27

Nguyen v Searchnet Associates Ltd, 2000 S.L.T. (Sh Ct) 83; 1999 S.C.L.R. 1075; [1999] 3 C.M.L.R. 413; 1999 G.W.D. 23–1106, Sh Pr 7–03

Niboyet v Niboyet (1878–79) L.R. 4 P.D. 1, CA 6–31, 10–01

Nielson v Overseas Projects Corporation of Victoria Ltd [2005] HCA 54 ... 5–06, 5–07

Nile Rhapsody, The. See Hamed el Chiaty and Co (t/a Travco Nile Cruise Lines) v Thomas Cook Group Ltd (The Nile Rhapsody).

Nina, The (1867) L.R. 2 P.C. 38 15–11

Nisbett v Nisbett's Trs (1835) 13 S. 517 18–11

Nissan v Attorney General. *See* Attorney General v Nissan.
Njegos, The [1936] P. 90; (1935) 53 Ll. L. Rep. 286, PDAD 15–32
Noble v Noble, 1947 S.L.T. (Notes) 62, OH 11–01
Nordglimt, The [1988] Q.B. 183; [1988] 2 W.L.R. 338; [1988] 2 All E.R. 531,
    QBD (Admlty) 7–45
Norske Atlas Insurance Co Ltd v London General Insurance Co Ltd
    (1972) 43 T.L.R. 541 15–12
North Scottish Helicopters Ltd v United Technologies Corp Inc (No.2)
    (Pleadings and Decree for Payment) 1988 S.L.T. 778, OH 8–21, 15–54
North Western Bank Ltd v John Poynter Son and MacDonalds [1895] A.C.
    56; (1894) 22 R. (H.L.) 1; (1894) 2 S.L.T. 311, HL ... 13–14, 17–15, 17–28
Northern Electricity Supply Corp (Private) Ltd v Jamieson, 1971 S.L.T. 22,
    IH (1 Div) 9–26
Norton v Florence Land and Public Works Co (1877–78) L.R. 7 Ch. D.
    332, Ch D 17–07
Norway's Application (Nos.1 and 2), Re. *See* State of Norway's Appli-
    cation. [
Nouvion v Freeman; sub nom. Henderson's Estate, Re; Henderson, Re
    (1890) L.R. 15 App. Cas. 1, HL 9–12
Novello and Co Ltd v Hinrichsen Edition Ltd [1951] Ch. 1026; [1951] 2 All
    E.R. 457, CA 3–04

O (A Minor), Re [1996[6 C.L. 73 14–31
O (A Minor) (Child Abduction: Custody Rights), Re [1997] 2 F.L.R. 702;
    [1997] 2 F.C.R. 465; *The Times*, June 24, 1997, Fam Div 14–29
O (Child Abduction: Re—Abduction), Re; sub nom. O (Minors) (Abduc-
    tion), Re; O (Child Abduction: Competing Orders), Re [1997] 2
    F.L.R. 712; [1998] 1 F.C.R. 107, Fam Div 14–27, 14–33
O v O (Appeal against Stay: Divorce Petition) [2002] EWCA Civ 949;
    [2003] 1 F.L.R. 192; [2002] 3 F.C.R. 123, CA (Civ Div) 12–11
OT Africa Line Ltd v Hijazy (The Kribi) (No.1) [2001] 1 Ll Rep. 76; [2001]
    C.L.C. 148, QBD (Comm) 7–29, 7–30
OT Africa Line Ltd v Magic Sportswear Corp [2005] EWCA Civ 710;
    [2006] 1 All E.R. (Comm) 32, CA (Civ Div) 7–46
O'Callaghan v Thomond (1810) 3 Taunt. 82 8–05
O'Connor v O'Connor, 1995 G.W.D. 3–113 .... 14–30, 14–31
O'Grady, Re (1941) 75 I.L.T.R. 119 18–01
Obers (Paton's Trs) v Paton's Trs (No.3) (1897) 24 R.719; (1897) 4 S.L.T.
    350, IH (1 Div) 17–49, 17–56m 17–58
Ocean Steamship Co v Queensland State Wheat Board [1941] 1 K.B. 402;
    (1940) 68 Ll. L. Rep. 136, CA 15–11
Ochsenbein v Papelier (1872–73) L.R. 8 Ch. App. 695, CA in Chancery 9–12
O'Connor v Erskine (1905) 13 S.L.T. 530; (1906) 22 Sh. Ct. Rep. 58, Sh Ct
    (Tayside) 9–09
Offshore International SA v Banco Central SA; sub nom. Offshore
    International SA v Banco Central SA and Hijos de J Barreras SA
    [1977] 1 W.L.R. 399; [1976] 3 All E.R. 749, QBD (Comm) 17–29
Ogden v Ogden; sub nom. Ogden v Ogden (otherwise Philip) [1908] P. 46;
    [1904–07] All E.R. Rep. 86, CA 11–14, 11–33
Ogilvie, Re; sub nom. Ogilvie v Ogilvie [1918] 1 Ch. 492, Ch D 18–06,18–25,
    18–34
Ogilvy v Ogilvy's Trs, 1927 S.L.T. 83, OH 10–07, 17–05, 18–10
Ohochuku v Ohochuku [1960] 1 W.L.R. 183; [1960] 1 All E.R. 253, PDAD .. 11–03
O'Keefe (Deceased), Re; Joined Cases Poingdestre v Sherman [1940] Ch.
    124, Ch D 5–06, 5–12
Oludimu v Oludimu, 1967 S.L.T. 105, OH 14–15, 14–25
Ommanney v Bingham (1836) 3 Pat. 448 18–25

Onobrauche v Onobrauche (1978) 8 Fam. Law 107; 122 S.J. 210 11–10
Opening of Insolvency Proceedings, Re (IX ZB 418/02) [2005] I.L.Pr. 4,
　　BGH (Ger) 17–40
Ophthalmic Innovations International (UK) Ltd v Ophthalmic Innovations
　　International Inc [2004] EWHC 2948; [2005] I.L.Pr. 10, Ch D 7–55,
　　　　　　　　　　　　　　　　　　　　　　　　　　　　　 15–15
Oppenheimer v Cattermole (Inspector of Taxes); sub nom. Nothman v
　　Cooper [1976] A.C. 249; [1975] 2 W.L.R. 347; [1975] 1 All E.R. 538,
　　HL; affirming [1973] Ch. 264; [1972] 3 W.L.R. 815, CA (Civ Div) ... 3–04,
　　　　　　　　　　　　　　　　　　　　　　4–01, 6–02, 6–37, 6–38
Oriental Island SS Co, Re (1874) L.R. 9 Ch. App. 557 17–53
Orlando v Castelli, 1961 S.L.T. 119 12–33
Orlando v Earl of Fingall [1940] I.R. 281 10–07
Orleans, Duchess of, Re (1859) 1 Sw. & Tr. 253 18–01
Orr Lewis v Orr Lewis [1949] P. 347; [1949] 1 All E.R. 504, PDAD 7–47
Orrell v Orrell (1871) 6 Ch. App. 302 18–08
Osborne v Matthan (No.3), 1998 S.C. 682; 1998 S.L.T. 1264, IH (1 Div) ... 14–48
Otobo v Otobo. *See* O v O (Appeal against Stay: Divorce Petition).
O'Toole v Whiterock Quarry Co Ltd, 1937 S.L.T. 521, OH 15–26
Overseas Union Insurance Ltd v New Hampshire Insurance Co (C351/89)
　　[1992] Q.B. 434; [1992] 2 W.L.R. 586; [1992] 2 All E.R. 138, ECJ
　　(6th Chamber) 7–38
Owens Bank Ltd v Bracco [1992] 2 A.C. 443; [1992] 2 W.L.R. 621; [1992] 2
　　All E.R. 193, HL 9–12
Owens Bank Ltd v Bracco (C129/92) [1994] Q.B. 509; [1994] 2 W.L.R. 759;
　　[1994] 1 All E.R. 336, ECJ (6th Chamber) 9–12, 9–37
Owens Bank Ltd v Etoile Commerciale SA [1995] 1 W.L.R. 44, PC (StV) .. 9–12
Owners of Cargo Lately Laden on Board the Playa Larga v Owners of the I
　　Congreso del Partido; sub nom. Owners of Cargo Lately Laden on
　　Board The Marble Islands v Owners of The I Congreso del Partido
　　[1983] 1 A.C. 244; [1981] 3 W.L.R. 328; [1981] 2 All E.R. 1064, HL .. 7–03
Owners of Cargo Lately Laden on Board the Siskina v Distos Compania
　　Naviera SA; Joined Cases Ibrahim Shanker Co v Distos Compania
　　Naviera SA [1979] A.C. 210; [1977] 3 W.L.R. 818, HL 7–58
Owners of Cargo Lately Laden on Board the Tatry v Owners of the Maciej
　　Rataj (C406/92) [1999] Q.B. 515; [1999] 2 W.L.R. 181, ECJ 7–38
Owners of the Atlantic Star v Owners of the Bona Spes (*The Atlantic Star*
　　and *The Bona Spes*) [1974] A.C. 436; [1973] 2 W.L.R. 795; [1973] 2
　　All E.R. 175, HL 7–45
Owners of the Bowditch v Owners of the Po (*The Po*) [1991] 2 Ll Rep. 206;
　　[1995] I.L.Pr. 52, CA (Civ Div) 7–46
Owners of the Cressington Court v Owners of the Marinero (*The
　　Marinero*) [1955] P. 68; [1955] 2 W.L.R. 607, PDAD 7–45, 7–47
Owners of the Las Mercedes v Owners of the Abidin Daver [1984] A.C.
　　398; [1984] 2 W.L.R. 196, HL 7–45
Owners of the Philippine Admiral v Wallem Shipping (Hong Kong) Ltd
　　(*The Philippine Admiral*); Joined Cases Telfair Shipping Corp v
　　Owners of the Ship Philippine Admiral [1977] A.C. 373; [1976] 2
　　W.L.R. 214, PC (HK) 7–03
Owners of the Seirstad v Hindustan Shipping Co Ltd (*The Waziristan* and
　　The Seristad) [1953] 1 W.L.R. 1446; [1953] 2 All E.R. 1213,
　　PDAD 16–12, 16–13
Owusu v Jackson (t/a Villa Holidays Bal Inn Villas) (C281/02) [2005] Q.B.
　　801; [2005] 2 W.L.R. 942; [2005] 1 Ll Rep. 452, ECJ 7–45, 7–46, 7–48,
　　　　　　　　　　　　　　　　　　　　　7–49, 7–51, 7–52, 12–13

P (A Child) (Abduction: Custody Rights), Re; sub nom. P (A Child)
(Abduction: Consent), Re; P (A Child) (Abduction: Acquiescence),
Re [2004] EWCA Civ 971; [2005] Fam. 293; [2005] 2 W.L.R. 201;
[2004] 2 F.L.R. 1057, CA (Civ Div) 14–29, 14–31
P (A Minor) (Child Abduction: Non—Convention Country), Re [1997]
Fam. 45; [1997] 2 W.L.R. 223; *The Times*, July 19, 1996, CA (Civ
Div) 14–48
P (GE) (An Infant), Re; sub nom. P (An Infant), Re [1965] Ch. 568; [1965]
2 W.L.R. 1; [1964] 3 All E.R. 977, CA 14–25
P and O v Shand (1865) 3 Moore P.C. (N.S.) 272 15–12
PT Pan Indonesian Bank Ltd v Marconi Communications International
Ltd. *See* Marconi Communications International Ltd v PT Pan
Indonesian Bank Ltd,
Padolecchia v Padolecchia [1968] P. 314; [1968] 2 W.L.R. 173, PDAD 12–26,
12–33
Paine, Re; Joined Cases Griffith v Waterhouse; Williams, Re [1940] Ch.
46, Ch D 4–05, 11–16
Pan American World Airways Inc v Andrews, 1992 S.L.T. 268; 1992
S.C.L.R. 257, OH 7–47
Panayiotou v Sony Music Entertainment (UK) Ltd [1994] Ch. 142; [1994] 2
W.L.R. 241; [1994] 1 All E.R. 755, Ch D 8–16
Papadopoulos v Papadopoulos [1930] P. 55, PDAD 11–25
Paramount Airways Ltd (No.2), Re; sub nom. Powdrill v Hambros Bank
(Jersey) Ltd [1993] Ch. 223; [1992] 3 W.L.R. 690; [1992] 3 All E.R.
1, CA (Civ Div) 3–07
Parkasho v Singh [1968] P. 233; [1967] 2 W.L.R. 946, DC 11–10
Parken v Royal Exchange Assurance Co (1846) 8 D. 365 15–22
Parkes v Lintec International Ltd [2006] CSIH 30, Ex Div 7–53
Parks v Esso Petroleum Co Ltd; sub nom. Parkes v Esso Petroleum Co Ltd
[2000] E.C.C. 45; [2000] Eu. L.R. 25; (1999) 18 Tr. L.R. 232, CA
(Civ Div) 15–42
Parlement Belge, The (1879–80) L.R. 5 P.D. 197; [1874–80] All E.R. Rep.
104, CA 7–03
Parnell v Walter (1889) 16 R. 917 16–21
Parojcic (otherwise Ivetic) v Parojcic [1958] 1 W.L.R. 1280; [1959] 1 All
E.R. 1; 102 S.J. 938, PDAD 11–31
Parouth, The. See Compania Naviera Micro SA v Shipley International Inc
(*The Parouth*).
Partenreederei M/S Heidberg v Grosvenor Grain and Feed Co Ltd (*The
Heidberg*) (No.2) [1994] 2 Ll Rep. 287, QBD (Comm) 9–12, 9–76
Patience, Re; sub nom. Patience v Main (1885) L.R. 29 Ch. D. 976, Ch D .. 6–31
Pattison v Mills (1828) 1 Dow & Cl. 342 15–40
Paul v Roy (1852) 15 Beav. 433 9–12
Payne v Payne, 2001 C.L.Y. 596 14–46
Payne v Payne [2005] Fam. Law 781 14–46
Peagram v Peagram [1926] 2 K.B. 165, KBD 13–21
Pearce v Ove Arup Partnership Ltd (Jurisdiction) [2000] Ch. 403; [2000] 3
W.L.R. 332; [1999] 1 All E.R. 769, CA (Civ Div); reversing in part
[1997] Ch. 293; [1997] 2 W.L.R. 779; [1997] 3 All E.R. 31, Ch D ... 17–32
Pease v Pease, 1967 S.C. 112, IH (1 Div) 11–32
Peat, Re (1869) L.R. 7 Eq. 302 17–07
Peer International Corp v Termidor Music Publishers Ltd (No.1); sub
nom. Peer International Corp v Termidor Music Publishers Co Inc
[2003] EWCA Civ 1156; [2004] Ch. 212; [2004] 2 W.L.R. 849, CA
(Civ Div) 3–04
Peer International Corp v Termidor Music Publishers Ltd (No.3) [2005]
EWHC 1048; [2006] C.P. Rep. 2; (2005) 28(7) I.P.D. 28050, Ch D ... 8–16

Pemberton v Hughes [1899] 1 Ch. 781, CA 9–11, 9–12, 12–23
Pena Copper Mines v Rio Tinto Co (1911) 103 L.T. 846 15–12
Pender v Commercial Bank of Scotland Ltd 1940 S.L.T. 306, OH 17–22
Pender's Trs, Petrs (1903) 5 F. 504; 1907 S.C. 207; (1906) 14 S.L.T. 555, IH
   (1 Div) 18–52
Pendy Plastic Products BV v Pluspunkt Handelsgesellschaft mbH
   (C228/81) [1982] E.C.R. 2723; [1983] 1 C.M.L.R. 665, ECJ (2nd
   Chamber) 9–40
Penhas (Isaac) v Tan Soo Eng [1953] A.C. 304; [1953] 2 W.L.R. 459, PC
   (Sing) 11–28
Pepin v Bruyere [1902] 1 Ch. 24, CA 17–02
Pepper v Pepper (1921) L.J. 413 11–24
Perendes v Sim, 1998 S.L.T. 1382; 1998 G.W.D. 15–735, OH 14–48
Perin v Perin 1950 S.L.T. 51, OH 12–23
Perrin v Perrin (Parent and Child : Custody), 1994 S.C. 45; 1995 S.L.T. 81;
   1993 S.C.L.R. 949, IH (Ex Div) 14–29, 14–30
Perrini v Perrini [1979] Fam. 84; [1979] 2 W.L.R. 472; [1979] 2 All E.R.
   323, Fam Div 4–06, 12–26, 12–39
Perry v Equitable Life Assurance Society (1929) 45 T.L.R. 468 ..... 15–12, 15–25
Peter Buchanan Ltd v McVey [1955] A.C. 516 (Note); [1954] I.R. 89, Sup
   Ct (Irl) 3–02
Petereit v Babcock International Holdings Ltd [1990] 1 W.L.R. 350; [1990]
   2 All E.R. 135, QBD 9–50
Petrotrade Inc v Smith (Jurisdiction); sub nom. Petrograde Inc v Smith
   [1999] 1 W.L.R. 457; [1998] 2 All E.R. 346, QBD (Comm) 7–10
Pharaon v Bank of Credit and Commerce International SA (In Liquida-
   tion); Joined Cases Price Waterhouse v Bank of Credit and
   Commerce International SA (In Liquidation) [1998] 4 All E.R. 455;
   (1998) 142 S.J.L.B. 251, Ch D 8–16
Philips v Eyre (1870) L.R. 6 Q.B. 1 .... 3–06, 16–12, 16–13
Philipson—Stow v Inland Revenue Commissioners [1961] A.C. 727; [1960]
   3 W.L.R. 1008; [1960] 3 All E.R. 814, HL 18–25, 18–26
Phillips v Air New Zealand Ltd [2002] EWHC 800; [2002] 1 All E.R.
   (Comm) 801; [2002] 2 Ll Rep. 403, QBD (Comm) 1–06
Phillips v Phillips (1921) 38 T.L.R. 150 11–28
Phillips v Symes (A Bankrupt); sub nom. Nussberger v Phillips [2006]
   EWCA Civ 654; (2006) 103(23) L.S.G. 28, CA (Civ Div); reversing
   [2005] EWHC 1880; [2006] I.L.Pr. 9, Ch D 7–41
Phipps v Phipps' Tr. 1914 1 S.L.T. 239, OH 18–52
Phosphate Sewage Co v Molleson (1876) 3 R. (H.L.) 77; 5 R. 1125; 6 R.
   (HL) 113 .... 9–12, 17–58
Phrantzes v Argenti [1960] 2 Q.B. 19; [1960] 2 W.L.R. 521; [1960] 1 All
   E.R. 778, QBD 3–01, 8–04
Picker v London and County Banking Co Ltd (1887) L.R. 18 Q.B.D. 515,
   CA 17–30
Pilinski v Pilinska [1955] 1 W.L.R. 329; [1955] 1 All E.R. 631; 99 S.J. 222,
   PDAD 11–24
Pilkington's Will Trusts, Re; sub nom. Pilkington v Harrison [1937] Ch.
   574; [1937] 3 All E.R. 213, Ch D 15–12, 18–49
Pirrie v Sawacki, 1997 S.L.T. 1160; 1997 S.C.L.R. 59, OH 14–29
Pitt v Acre (Lord) (1876) 3 Ch. D. 295 17–07
Pitt v Pitt (1864) 2 M. (H.L.) 28 12–02
Platt v Attorney General of NSW [1873] 3 A.C. 336 6–14
Platt v Platt, 1958 S.C. 95; 1958 S.L.T. 94, IH (1 Div) 9–13
Plumex v Young Sports NV (C473/04) [2006] I.L.Pr. 13; *The Times*,
   February 22, 2006, ECJ (3rd Chamber) 8–10

Plummer v Inland Revenue Commissioners [1988] 1 W.L.R. 292; [1988] 1 All
    E.R. 97; [1987] S.T.C. 698; 60 T.C. 452; (1988) 132 S.J. 54, Ch D 6–04,
                                    6–07, 6–26
Poll v Lord Advocate (1899) 1 F. 823 3–06
Ponder v Ponder, 1932 S.C. 233; 1932 S.L.T. 187, IH (2 Div) 14–25
Ponticelli v Ponticelli (otherwise Giglio) (by her Guardian) [1958] P. 204;
    [1958] 2 W.L.R. 439, PDAD 4–04, 11–14, 11–24, 12–36
Pordea v Times Newspapers Ltd [2001] C.L.Y.B. 818 ....
Pouey v Hordern [1900] 1 Ch. 492, Ch D 18–41
Powell Duffryn Plc v Petereit (C214/89) [1992] E.C.R. I—1745; [1992]
    I.L.Pr. 300, ECJ 7–13
Power Curber International Ltd v National Bank of Kuwait SAK [1981] 1
    W.L.R. 1233; [1981] 3 All E.R. 607, CA (Civ Div) 17–18, 17–29
Poyser v Minors (1880–81) L.R. 7 Q.B.D. 329, CA 8–02
Prawdziclazarska v Prawdziclazarski, 1954 S.C. 98; 1954 S.L.T. 41, OH 12–33,
                                        12–44
Prazie v Prazie [2006] All E.R. (D.) 246 7–27
Prescription Pricing Authority v Ferguson, 2005 1 S.C. 171; 2005 S.L.T. 63,
    IH (1 Div) 8–12
Presentaciones Musicales SA v Secunda [1994] Ch. 271; [1994] 2 W.L.R.
    660; [1994] 2 All E.R. 737, CA (Civ Div) 15–40
Preston (otherwise Putynski) v Preston (otherwise Putynska) (otherwise
    Basinska) [1963] P. 411; [1963] 2 W.L.R. 1435, CA; affirming [1963]
    P. 141; [1962] 3 W.L.R. 1401, PDAD 11–27
Price, Re; sub nom. Tomlin v Latter [1900] 1 Ch. 442, Ch D 18–26, 18–40,
                                        18–43
Price v Dewhurst (1837) Sim. 279 9–12
Priest (Deceased), Re; Joined Cases Belfield v Duncan [1944] Ch. 58, Ch
    D 18–25
Prifti v Musini Sociedad Anonima de Seguros y Reaseguros [2003] EWHC
    2796; [2004] 1 C.L.C. 517; [2004] Ll Rep. I.R. 528, QBD (Admin) ... 7–13
Princess Paley Olga v Weisz [1929] 1 K.B. 718, CA 3–04, 3–05, 17–12
Pringle's Trs v Pringle1913 S.C. 172; 1912 2 S.L.T. 367, IH (1 Div) 5–02
Print Concept GmbH v GEW (EC) Ltd [2001] EWCA Civ 352; [2002]
    C.L.C. 352, CA (Civ Div) 15–16
Prodexport State Co for Foreign Trade v ED and F Man Ltd [1973] Q.B.
    389; [1972] 3 W.L.R. 845; [1972] 1 All E.R. 355; [1972] 2 Ll Rep.
    375; 116 S.J. 663, QBD (Comm) 15–26
Prostar Management Ltd v Twaddle, 2003 S.L.T. (Sh Ct) 11; 2002 G.W.D.
    28–983, Sh Pr 7–20
Protea Leasing Ltd v Royal Air Cambodge Co Ltd; sub nom. Protea
    Leasing Ltd v Royal Air Cambode Co Ltd [2002] EWHC 2731; *The*
    Times, January 13, 2003, QBD (Comm) 16–17, 16–18
Provincial Treasurer of Alberta v Kerr [1933] A.C. 710, PC (Can) 17–10
Prudential Assurance Co Ltd, Petrs; sub nom. Horne's Trs, Petrs 1952 S.C.
    70; 1952 S.L.T. 121, IH (1 Div) 18–52
Pryce, Re; sub nom. Lawford v Pryce [1911] 2 Ch. 286, CA 18–41
Pryde v Proctor and Gamble Ltd 1971 S.L.T. (Notes) 18, OH ... 1–01, 4–01, 8–17
Pugh v Pugh (1951) ICLQ 478 .... 3–07, 11–16, 11–17
Purvis's Trs v Purvis's Executors (1861) 23 D. 812 .... 15–21, 18–17
Puttick v Attorney General [1980] Fam. 1; [1979] 3 W.L.R. 542; [1979] 3
    All E.R. 463, Fam Div 6–09, 6–30

Q, Petr, 2001 S.L.T. 243; 2000 G.W.D. 15–570, OH 14–31, 14–39
QRS 1 ApS v Frandsen [1999] 1 W.L.R. 2169; [1999] 3 All E.R. 289, CA
    (Civ Div) 3–02

Quantum Corp Inc v Plane Trucking Ltd; sub nom. Quantum Corp Ltd v
　　Plane Trucking Ltd [2002] EWCA Civ 350; [2002] 1 W.L.R. 2678;
　　[2003] 1 All E.R. 873; [2002] 2 Ll Rep. 25, CA (Civ Div) 1–06
Quazi v Quazi [1980] A.C. 744; [1979] 3 W.L.R. 833; [1979] 3 All E.R. 897,
　　HL 12–11, 12–27
Queensland Estates v Collas [1971] St. R. Qd. 75 15–11
Queensland Mercantile and Agency Co Ex p. Australian Investment Co,
　　Re; Joined Cases Queensland Mercantile and Agency Co Ex p.
　　Union Bank of Australia, Re [1892] 1 Ch. 219, CA 17–28
Quoraishi v Quoraishi [1985] Fam. Law 308, CA (Civ Div); affirming
　　(1983) 13 Fam. Law 86 11–10
Qureshi v Qureshi [1972] Fam. 173; [1971] 2 W.L.R. 518; [1971] 1 All E.R.
　　325; (1970) 114 S.J. 908, PDAD 11–09, 12–27

R, Re [1990] 1 F.L.R. 387 14–33
R, Re: *See* R (Abduction: Hague and European Conventions), Re.
R (Abduction: Hague and European Conventions), Re ; sub nom. AR (A
　　Minor) (Abduction), Re [1997] 1 F.L.R. 673, CA (Civ Div);
　　affirming [1997] 1 F.L.R. 663; [1997] 3 F.C.R. 29, Fam Div 14–27
R (Abduction: Immigration Concerns), Re [2004] EWHC 2042; [2005] 1
　　F.L.R. 33; [2004] Fam. Law 862, Fam Div 14–31
R v R (Divorce: Hemain Injunction) [2003] EWHC 2113; [2005] 1 F.L.R.
　　386, Fam Div 7–47
R v R (Divorce: Stay of Proceedings) [1994] 2 F.L.R. 1036; [1995] 1 F.C.R.
　　745, Fam Div 13–04, 13–09
R. v Atakpu (Austin); Joined Cases R. v Abrahams (Alister Victor) [1994]
　　Q.B. 69; [1993] 3 W.L.R. 812; [1993] 4 All E.R. 215, CA (Crim
　　Div) 3–03, 3–07
R. v Barnet LBC Ex p. Shah (Nilish); Joined Cases Akbarali v Brent LBC;
　　Abdullah v Shropshire CC; Shabpar v Barnet LBC; Shah (Jitendra)
　　v Barnet LBC; Ablack v Inner London Education Authority; R. v
　　Shropshire CC Ex p. Abdullah [1983] 2 A.C. 309; [1983] 2 W.L.R.
　　16, HL 6–40
R. v Bottrill Ex p. Kuechenmeister [1947] K.B. 41; [1946] 2 All E.R. 434,
　　CA 7–03
R. v Brentwood Superintendent Registrar of Marriages Ex p. Arias [1968]
　　2 Q.B. 956; [1968] 3 W.L.R. 531; [1968] 3 All E.R. 279, DC ... 4–06, 5–01,
　　　　　　　　　　　　　　　　　　　　　　　　　　　　　　　12–26
R. v Commanding Officer of the 30th Battalion Middlesex Regiment Ex p.
　　Freyberger [1917] 2 K.B. 129, CA 6–38
R. v Doutre (1883–84) L.R. 9 App. Cas. 745, PC (Can) 15–12
R. v Forsyth (Elizabeth) [1997] 2 Cr. App. R. 299; [1997] Crim. L.R. 581;
　　The Times, April 8, 1997, CA (Crim Div) 8–16
R. v Governor of Pentonville Prison Ex p. Teja [1971] 2 Q.B. 274; [1971] 2
　　W.L.R. 816S.J. 305, QBD 7–03
R. v Hammersmith Superintendent Registrar of Marriages Ex p.
　　Mir—Anwaruddin [1917] 1 K.B. 634, CA 11–09, 12–27
R. v Harrow Crown Court Ex p. UNIC Centre Sarl; sub nom. UNIC
　　Centre Sarl v Harrow Crown Court; UNIC Centre Sarl v Brent and
　　Harrow LBC Trading Standards Service [2000] 1 W.L.R. 2112;
　　[2000] 2 All E.R. 449, QBD 7–09
R. v Horseferry Road Mags' Court Ex p. Bennet (No.3), *The Times*,
　　January 14, 1994 8–16
R. v International Tr. for the Protection of Bondholders AG; sub nom.
　　International Tr. for the Protection of Bondholders AG v King, The
　　[1937] A.C. 500; (1937) 57 Ll. L. Rep. 145, HL 15–07, 15–12, 15–26
R. v Lynch [1903] 1 K.B. 444, KBD 6–38

R. v Martin (Alan) [1998] A.C. 917; [1998] 2 W.L.R. 1; [1998] 1 All E.R.
  193, HL 8–12
R. v Naguib [1917] 1 K.B. 359, CCA 11–09
R. v Peters (1886) 16 Q.B.D. 636 16–18
R. v Robert Millar (Contractors) Ltd; Joined Cases R. v Millar (Robert)
  [1970] 2 Q.B. 54; [1970] 2 W.L.R. 541; [1970] 1 All E.R. 577, CA
  (Crim Div); affirming [1969] 3 All E.R. 247; 133 J.P. 554, Crown Ct .. 16–18
R. v Sagoo (Mohinder Singh) [1975] Q.B. 885; [1975] 3 W.L.R. 267; [1975]
  2 All E.R. 926, CA (Crim Div) 11–07
R. v Sarwan Singh [1962] 3 All E.R. 612, Quarter Sessions 11–07
R. v Secretary of State for the Home Department Ex p. Bagga [1991] 1
  Q.B. 485; [1990] 3 W.L.R. 1013, CA (Civ Div) 7–03
R. v Secretary of State for the Home Department Ex p. Fatima (Ghulam);
  sub nom. R. v Immigration Appeal Tribunal Ex p. Secretary of State
  for the Home Department; Joined Cases R. v Secretary of State for
  the Home Department Ex p. Bi (Shafeena) [1986] A.C. 527; [1986] 2
  W.L.R. 693; [1986] 2 All E.R. 32, HL; affirming [1985] Q.B. 190;
  [1984] 3 W.L.R. 659; [1984] 2 All E.R. 458, CA (Civ Div) 12–29
R. v Secretary of State for the Home Department Ex p. L [1945] K.B. 7,
  KBD 6–38
R. v Williams [1942] A.C. 541, PC (Can) 17–03, 17–31
R. (on the application of Al-Skeini v Secretary of State for Defence [2005]
  All E.R. (D.) 337 3–07
R. (on the application of Baiai) v Secretary of State for the Home
  Department; Joined Cases R. (on the application of Bigoku) v
  Secretary of State for the Home Department; R. (on the application
  of Tilki) v Secretary of State for the Home Department; R. (on the
  application of Trzcinska) v Secretary of State for the Home Depart-
  ment [2006] EWHC 823; [2006] 2 F.C.R. 131, QBD (Admin) 12–38
R. (on the application of Thomson) v Minister of State for Children; sub
  nom. R. (on the application of Charlton Thomson) v Secretary of
  State for Education and Skills [2005] EWHC 1378; [2006] 1 F.L.R.
  175; [2005] 2 F.C.R. 603, QBD (Admin) 14–59
RA Lister and Co Ltd v EG Thomson (Shipping) Ltd and PT Djkarta
  Lloyd (*The Benarty*) (No.1) [1983] 1 Ll Rep. 361, CA (Civ Div) 7–45
RPS Prodotti Siderurgici Srl v Owners of the Sea Maas (*The Sea Maas*)
  [2000] 1 All E.R. 536; [1999] 1 All E.R. (Comm) 945, QBD
  (Admlty) 7–13
RTZ v Westinghouse Electric Corp. See Westinghouse Electric Corp
  Uranium Contract Litigation MDL Docket 235 (No.2).
Radhakrishna Hospitality Service Private Ltd v EIH Ltd; Joined Cases
  Eurest SA v EIH Ltd [1999] 2 Ll Rep. 249, QBD 7–45
Radoyevitch v Radoyevitch, 1930 S.C. 619; 1930 S.L.T. 404, IH (1 Div) 14–25
Radwan v Radwan (No.2) [1973] Fam. 35; [1972] 3 W.L.R. 939; [1972] 3
  All E.R. 1026, Fam Div 11–09, 11–11, 11–17
Raffenel, Re (1863) 3 Sw. & Tr. 49 .... 6–04, 6–07, 6–19, 6–22, 6–25
Rahimtoola v Nizam of Hyderabad; sub nom. Nizam of Hyderabad v Jung
  [1958] A.C. 379; [1957] 3 W.L.R. 884, HL 7–03
Raiffeisen Zentral Bank Osterreich AG v Tranos [2001] I.L.Pr. 9, QBD
  (Comm) 7–14
Raiffeisen Zentralbank Osterreich AG v Five Star General Trading LLC
  (*The Mount I*); sub nom. Raiffeisen Zentral Bank Osterreich AG v
  An Feng Steel Co Ltd; Raffeisen Zentralbank Osterreich AG v Five
  Star General Trading LLC (The Mount I) [2001] EWCA Civ 68;
  [2001] Q.B. 825; [2001] 1 Ll Rep. 597, CA (Civ Div); reversing in
  part [2000] 1 All E.R. (Comm) 897; [2000] 2 Ll Rep. 684, QBD
  (Comm) 4–02, 17–17, 17–19

Raiffeisen Zentralbank Osterreich AG v National Bank of Greece SA
    [1999] 1 Ll Rep. 408; *The Times*, September 25, 1998, QBD
    (Comm) 7–13
Rainford v Newell Roberts [1962] I.R. 95 9–10
Ralli Bros v Compania Naviera Sota y Aznar; sub nom. Compania Naviera
    Sota Y Aznar v Ralli Bros [1920] 2 K.B. 287; (1920) 2 Ll. L. Rep.
    550, CA 4–05, 15–26, 15–53
Ralston, Re [1906] V.L.R. 689 18–04
Ramsay v Liverpool Royal Infirmary; sub nom. Liverpool Royal Infirmary
    v Ramsay [1930] A.C. 588; 1930 S.C. (H.L.) 83, HL 6–09, 6–10, 6–18,
                                                        6–19, 6–20, 6–21
Rankin v Rankin, 1960 S.L.T. 308, OH 6–10
Rankine (Deceased), Re [1918] P. 134, CA 18–01
Raresby v SS Cobetas. *See* Birkdale SS Co Ltd v Compania Naviera
    Vascongada.
Rattray v White (1842) 4 D. 88– 17–57
Raulin v Fischer [1911] 2 K.B. 93, KBD 3–03
Rayner v Davies; sub nom. Davies v Rayner [2002] EWCA Civ 1880;
    [2003] 1 All E.R. (Comm) 394; [2003] 1 C.L.C. 169, CA (Civ Div);
    affirming [2002] 1 All E.R. (Comm) 620; [2002] C.L.C. 952, QBD ... 7–20
Rea, Re [1902] I.R. 451 .... 18–01, 18–04, 18–12
Red Sea Insurance Co Ltd v Bouygues SA [1995] 1 A.C. 190; [1994] 3
    W.L.R. 926; [1994] 3 All E.R. 749, PC (HK) 16–05, 16–12
Reddington v Riach's Executor, 2002 S.L.T. 537; 2002 G.W.D. 7–214,
    OH 6–04, 6–10, 6–16, 6–21
Reed v Reed (1969) 6 D.L.R. (3d.) 617 .... 4–01, 11–18
Refrew and Brown v Glasgow Mags (1861) 23 D. 1003 7–03
Regazzoni v KC Sethia (1944) Ltd; sub nom. Regazzoni v Sethia (KC)
    (1944) [1958] A.C. 301; [1957] 3 W.L.R. 752, HL 3–06, 3–26
Regie Nationale des Usines Renault SA v Maxicar SpA (C38/98) [2000]
    E.C.R. I—2973; [2000] E.C.D.R. 415; [2000] C.L.Y. 782, ECJ (5th
    Chamber) 9–40
Reich v Purcell 67 Cal. 2d 551; 423 P. 2d 727 (1967) 16–08
Reichert v Dresdner Bank (C115/88) [1990] E.C.R. I—27; [1990] I.L.Pr.
    105, ECJ (5th Chamber) 7–27
Reichhold Norway ASA v Goldman Sachs International [2000] 1 W.L.R.
    173; [2000] 2 All E.R. 679, CA (Civ Div) 7–30
Reid, Re (1866) L.R. 1 P. & D. 74 18–33
Reid v Reid (1887 24 S.L.R. 281 14–51
Reid v Ski Independence 1999 S.L.T. (Sh Ct) 62; 1998 G.W.D. 31–1576, Sh
    Ct (Lothian) 1–06
Reilly, Re [1942] I.R. 416 17–53
Rellis v Hart, 1993 S.L.T. 738, OH 14–45
Republica de Guatemala v Nunez [1927] 1 K.B. 669, CA ... 17–11, 17–19, 17–23,
                                                        17–24, 17–28
Réunion Européenne SA v Spliethoff's Bevrachtingskantoor BV (C51/97)
    [2000] Q.B. 690; [2000] 3 W.L.R. 1213[1998] C.L.Y.B. 769, ECJ
    (3rd Chamber) 7–14
Reuter v Mulhens (No.2) [1954] Ch. 50; [1953] 3 W.L.R. 789; [1953] 2 All
    E.R. 1160, CA 17–17, 17–32
Rev. Comms. v Matthews (1958) 92 I.T.L.R. 44 .... 6–16, 6–17, 6–22, 6–29, 6–30
Ricardo v Garcias (1845) 12 Cl. & F. 368; 65 R.R. 585 9–13
Richardson v Richardson; Joined Cases National Bank of India Ltd, Re
    [1927] P. 228, PDAD 17–17
Richmond's Trs v Winton (1864) 3 M. 95 18–29
Risk v Risk [1951] P. 50; [1950] 2 All E.R. 973, PDAD 11–03
Roberton v Roberton, 1998 S.L.T.408 14–31

Robertson, Ex p.; sub nom. Morton, Re (1875) L.R. 20 Eq. 733, Ct of
Chancery 17–53
Robertson, Petr, 1911 S.C. 1319; 1911 2 S.L.T. 201, IH (1 Div) 14–47
Robertson v Brandes Schonwald and Co (1906) 8 F. 815; (1906) 14 S.L.T.
90, IH (1 Div) 15–12
Robertson v McVean, February 18, 1817, FC 18–08
Robertson v Robertson, February 16, 1816, FC 18–08
Robertson v Robertson, 1988 S.L.T. 468 14–29
Robertson's Trs v Bairds (1852) 14 D.1010 8–24
Robins v Robins [1907] 2 K.B. 13, KBD 9–12
Robinson v Bird; sub nom. Robinson v Fernsby; Scott—Kilvert's Estate,
Re [2003] EWCA Civ 1820; [2004] W.T.L.R. 257, CA (Civ Div);
affirming [2003] EWHC 30; [2003] W.T.L.R. 529, Ch D 18–09
Robinson v Bland (1760) 2 Burr. 1077 2–02
Robinson v Fenner [1913] 3 K.B. 835, KBD 9–12
Robinson-Scott v Robinson-Scott [1958] P. 71; [1957] 3 W.L.R. 842; [1957]
3 All E.R. 473; 101 S.J. 887, PDAD 12–18
Rodden v Whatlings Ltd, 1961 S.C. 132; 1960 S.L.T. (Notes) 96,
OH 1–01, 4–01, 8–17, 16–11
Rodger v Adam's Trs (1885) 1 Sh. Ct. Rep. 202 18–01
Rodriguez v Parker [1967] 1 Q.B. 116; [1966] 3 W.L.R. 546, QBD 8–06
Roe v Roe, 1916 32 Sh. Ct. Rep. 30 13–10
Roerig v Valiant Trawlers Ltd [2002] EWCA Civ 21; [2002] 1 W.L.R. 2304;
[2002] 1 All E.R. 961; [2002] 1 Ll Rep. 681, CA (Civ Div) . . . 8–21, 16–20,
16–28
Rojas, Petr (Marriage: Legal impediment), 1967 S.L.T. (Sh. Ct.) 24, Sh Ct
(Lothian) 11–16
Roneleigh v MII Exports [1989] 1 W.L.R. 619; (1989) 86(14) L.S.G. 40,
CA (Civ Div) 7–45
Rooker v Rooker (1863) 3 Sw. & Tr. 526 11–24
Rose Mary, The. See Anglo Iranian Oil Co Ltd v Jaffrate.
Rosler v Rottwinkel (241/83) [1986] Q.B. 33; [1985] 3 W.L.R. 898, ECJ
(4th Chamber) 7–27
Ross, Re; sub nom. Ross v Waterfield [1930] 1 Ch. 377, Ch D . . 5–06, 5–07, 5–10,
5–12
Ross v Ross [1930] A.C. 1; 1930 S.C. (H.L.) 1; 1929 S.L.T. 560, HL . . 6–09, 6–13,
6–16
Ross v Ross's Trs, July 4, 1809, FC 17–02
Ross Smith v Ross Smith [1963] A.C. 280; [1962] 2 W.L.R. 388; [1962] 1
All E.R. 344, HL 12–33, 12–37
Rossano v Manufacturers Life Insurance Co [1963] 2 Q.B. 352; [1962] 3
W.L.R. 157, QBD (Comm) 3–02, 15–14, 15–23
Rosseel NV v Oriental Commercial and Shipping Co (UK) Ltd [1990] 1
W.L.R. 1387; [1990] 3 All E.R. 545, CA (Civ Div) 7–58
Rosses v Bhagvat Sinhjee (1891) 19 R. 31 . . . . 16–11, 16–13
Rossmeier v Mounthooly Transport, 2000 S.L.T. 208; [2000] I.L.Pr. 697, IH
(1 Div) 7–03
Rousillon v Rousillon (1880) L.R. 14 Ch. D. 351, Ch D 3–06, 15–26
Rousou's Tr. v Rousou [1955] 1 W.L.R. 545; [1955] 2 All E.R. 169, Ch D   17–53
Royal and Sun Alliance Insurance Plc v MK Digital FZE (Cyprus) Ltd
[2006] EWCA Civ 629, CA (Civ Div); reversing [2005] EWHC 1408;
[2005] 2 Ll Rep. 679; [2005] 2 C.L.C. 146, QBD (Comm) 7–38
Royal and Sun Alliance Insurance Plc v Retail Brand Alliance Inc [2004]
EWHC 2139; [2005] Ll Rep. I.R. 110, QBD (Comm) 7–46
Royal Bank of Canada v Cooperatieve Centrale
Raiffeisen—Boerenleenbank BA [2004] EWCA Civ 7; [2004] 2 All
E.R. (Comm) 847; [2004] 1 Ll Rep. 471, CA (Civ Div) 7–47

Royal Bank of Scotland v Assignees of Scott Stein and Co, Janury 20, 1813, FC 17–49
Russ v Russ; sub nom. Geffers v de Waele (Intervening) [1964] P. 315; [1962] 3 W.L.R. 930; [1962] 3 All E.R. 193, CA; affirming [1963] P. 87; [1962] 2 W.L.R. 708; [1962] 1 All E.R. 649, PDAD 12–27
Russell v FW Woolworth and Co Ltd, 1982 S.C. 20; 1982 S.L.T. 428, OH . . . 7–04
Rutherford v Miln and Co; sub nom. Rutherford and Son v Miln and Co, 1941 S.C. 125; 1941 S.L.T. 105, IH (2 Div) 15–12

S (A Child) (Abduction: Custody Rights), Re; sub nom. S (A Child) (Abduction: Grave Risk of Harm), Re; S (A Child) (Return to Jurisdiction: Israel), Re [2002] EWCA Civ 908; [2002] 1 W.L.R. 3355; [2002] 2 F.L.R. 815, CA (Civ Div) 14–31
S (A Minor) (Abduction: European Convention), Re; sub nom. S (A Minor) (Abduction: European and Hague Conventions), Re; S (A Minor) (Custody: Habitual Residence), Re [1998] A.C. 750; [1997] 3 W.L.R. 597; [1997] 4 All E.R. 251, HL; affirming [1997] 1 F.L.R. 958; [1997] 1 F.C.R. 588, CA (Civ Div); reversing [1996] 1 F.L.R. 660; [1996] 3 F.C.R. 115, Fam Div 14–33, 14–35
S (A Minor) (Child Abduction: Delay), Re [1998] 1 F.L.R. 651; [1998] 1 F.C.R. 17, Fam Div 14–31
S (A Minor) (Custody: Habitual Residence), Re. *See* S (A Minor) (Abduction: European Convention).
S (Hospital Patient: Court's Jurisdiction) (No.2), Re; sub nom. S (Hospital Patient: Foreign Curator), Re [1996] Fam. 23; [1995] 3 W.L.R. 596; [1995] 4 All E.R. 30, Fam Div 10–02, 10–05, 10–07
S (Hospital Patient: Foreign Curator), Re. *See* S (Hospital Patient: Court's Jurisdiction) (No.2), Re.
S (Minors) (Abduction), Re [1994] 1 F.L.R. 297; [1993] 2 F.C.R. 499; [1994] Fam. Law 245, CA (Civ Div) 14–48
S (Minors) (Convention on Civil Aspects of International Child Abduction: Wrongful Retention), Re; sub nom. S (Minors) (Child Abduction: Wrongful Retention), Re [1994] Fam. 70; [1994] 2 W.L.R. 228; [1994] 1 All E.R. 237, Fam Div 14–30
S v B [2005] All E.RD.(D.) 37 14–31
S v S (Matrimonial Proceedings: Appropriate Forum); sub nom. S v S (Divorce: Staying Proceedings) [1997] 1 W.L.R. 1200; [1997] 2 F.L.R. 100, Fam Div 13–09
S v S, unreported, March 31, 2006, OH 11–24
SA Consortium General Textiles v Sun and Sand Agencies [1978] Q.B. 279; [1978] 2 W.L.R. 1; [1978] 2 All E.R. 339, CA (Civ Div) . . . 3–02, 9–26
S and T Bautrading v Nordling [1997] 3 All E.R. 718; [1998] I.L.Pr. 151, CA (Civ Div) 7–58
S and W Berisford Plc v New Hampshire Insurance Co Ltd; sub nom. NGI International Precious Metals v New Hampshire Insurance Co [1990] 2 Q.B. 631; [1990] 3 W.L.R. 688; [1990] 2 All E.R. 321, QBD (Comm) 7–46
SH v KH (Hakeem v Hussain), 2006 S.C. 129; 2005 S.L.T. 1025, IH (Ex Div); reversing 2003 S.L.T. 515; 2003 G.W.D. 11–314, OH . . . 11–01, 12–38
SNI Aérospatiale (SNIA) v Lee Kui Jak. *See* Société Nationale Industrielle Aérospatiale (SNIA) v Lee Kui Jak.
Sabah Shipyard (Pakistan) Ltd v Pakistan [2002] EWCA Civ 1643; [2003] 2 Ll Rep. 571; [2004] 1 C.L.C. 149, CA (Civ Div) 7–30
Sadler v Robins (1808) 1 Camp.253 9–12
Salaman v Tod. *See* Tod's Tr. v Tod.
Salim Nasrallah Khoury (Syndic in Bankruptcy) v Khayat [1943] A.C. 507, PC (Pal) 17–29

Salvage Association, Re [2003] EWHC 1028; [2004] 1 W.L.R. 174; [2003] 3
All E.R. 246, Ch D 17–40
Salvesen or Van Lorang) v Administrator of Austrian Property. *See*Von
Lorang v Administrator of Austrian Property.
Salvesen's Trs, Petrs, 1993 S.C. 14; 1993 S.L.T. 1327, IH (1 Div) 18–27
Samcrete Egypt Engineers and Contractors SAE v Land Rover Exports
Ltd [2001] EWCA Civ 2019; [2002] C.L.C. 533, CA (Civ Div) 15–16
San Roman, The (1872) L.R. 3 A. & E. 583 15–32
Sanders v Van der Putte (C73/77) [1977] E.C.R. 2383; [1978] 1 C.M.L.R.
331, ECJ 7–27
Santos v Illidge (1860) 8 C.B. (N.S.) 861 .... 3–06, 10–05
Sargeant v Sargeant (Parent and child: Custody), 1973 S.L.T. (Notes) 27,
IH (1 Div) 14–25
Sarrio SA v Kuwait Investment Authority [1999] 1 A.C. 32; [1997] 3
W.L.R. 1143, HL 7–39, 7–52
Sasson v Sasson [1924] A.C. 1007, PC (Egy) 5–01, 12–27
Sawrey-Cookson v Sawrey-Cookson's Trs (1905) 8 F. 157; (1905) 13 S.L.T.
605, IH (1 Div) 10–07, 13–05
Sayce v Ameer Ruler Sadig Mohammed Abbasi Bahawalpur State [1952] 2
Q.B. 390; [1952] 2 All E.R. 64, CA 7–03
Sayers v International Drilling Co NV [1971] 1 W.L.R. 1176; [1971] 3 All
E.R. 163, CA (Civ Div) 15–37, 16–24
Scania Finance France SA v Rockinger Spezialfabrik fur Anhangerkup-
plungen GmbH and Co (C522/03) [2005] E.C.R. I—8639; [2006]
I.L.Pr. 1, ECJ (1st Chamber) 8–10
Scappaticci v Att-Gen [1955] P. 47; [1955] 2 W.L.R. 409, PDAD 6–16
Scarpetta v Lowenfeldt (1911) 27 T.L.R. 509 9–12
Scheibler Ex p. Holthausen, Re (1873–74) L.R. 9 Ch. App. 722, CA in
Chancery 17–08
Scherrens v Maenhout (158/87) [1988] E.C.R. 3791; *The Times*, September
5, 1988, ECJ 7–27
Schibsby v Westenholz (1870–71) L.R. 6 Q.B. 155, QB 9–07, 9–10
Schnapper, Re [1928] Ch. 420, Ch D 18–10
Schnapper [1936] 1 All E.R. 322 15–53
Schorsch Meier GmbH v Hennin [1975] Q.B. 416; [1974] 3 W.L.R. 823,
CA (Civ Div) 8–21
Schroeder [1949] I.R. 89 18–17
Schulhof, Re; Joined Cases Wolf, Re [1948] P. 66; [1947] 2 All E.R. 841,
PDAD 8–12, 18–01
Schultz v Robinson and Niven (1861) 24 D. 120 17–10
Schulze Gow and Co v Bank of Scotland, 1916 2 S.L.T. 207, IH (2 Div)
1914 2 S.L.T. 455, OH 7–03
Schwebel v Ungar (Or Schwebel) (1964) 48 D.L.R. (2d) 644, Sup Ct (Can);
affirming (1963) 42 D.L.R. (2d) 622 .... 4–06, 12–26
Scotmotors (Plant Hire) Ltd v Dundee Petrosea Ltd (Construction of
contractual condition), 1980 S.C. 351; 1982 S.L.T. 181, IH (2 Div) ... 7–30
Scott v Attorney General (1886) L.R. 11 P.D. 128, PDAD 10–06, 11–21
Scott v Pilkington (1862) 2 B. & S. 11 .... 9–11, 9–12
Scott v Seymour (1862) L.J. 61 16–13
Scott v Sinclair (1865) 3 M. 918 13–07
Scott, Re; sub nom. Scott v Scott; Scott, Re [1915] 1 Ch. 592,
CA 18–03, 18–26
Scottish National Orchestra Society Ltd v Thomson's Executor, 1969 S.L.T.
325, OH 3–02, 4–01, 18–03
Scottish Provident Institution v Cohen (1888) 16 R. 112 ..... 17–24, 17–26, 17–28
Scottish Provident Institution v Robinson (1892) 29 S.L.R. 733 ..... 13–14, 17–28
Scottish Union and National Insurance Co v James (1886) 13 R. 928 17–58

Scullard, Re; sub nom. Smith v Brock [1957] Ch. 107; [1956] 3 W.L.R.
1060; [1956] 3 All E.R. 898; 100 S.J. 928, Ch D 6–25, 11–24
Sea Maas, The. See RPS Prodotti Siderurgici Srl v Owners of the Sea Maas.
Seaconsar (Far East) Ltd v Bank Markazi Jomhouri Islami Iran (Service
Outside Jurisdiction) [1994] 1 A.C. 438; [1993] 3 W.L.R. 756, HL;
reversing [1993] 1 Ll Rep. 236; *The Times*, November 25, 1992, CA
(Civ Div) 7–55, 9–10
Seagull Manufacturing Co Ltd (In Liquidation) (No.1), Re [1993] Ch. 345;
[1993] 2 W.L.R. 872; [1993] 2 All E.R. 980, CA (Civ Div) 3–07
Seale's Marriage Settlement, Re [1961] Ch. 574; [1961] 3 W.L.R. 262;
[1961] 3 All E.R. 136, Ch D 18–51
Sealey (otherwise Callan) v Callan [1953] P. 135; [1953] 2 W.L.R. 910,
PDAD 7–47, 12–09
Secretary of State for Foreign Affairs v Charlesworth Pilling and Co [1901]
A.C. 373, PC (Zanzibar) 5–01
Seddon v Seddon (1891) 20 R. 675 18–10
Sehota (Deceased), Re; sub nom. Kaur v Kaur [1978] 1 W.L.R. 1506;
[1978] 3 All E.R. 385, Ch D 11–08
Selco Ltd v Mercier, 1996 S.L.T. 1247, OH 9–40
Sellar and Sons v Gladstone and Co (1868) 5 S.L.R. 417 15–22
Sellars v Sellars, 1942 S.C. 206; 1942 S.L.T. 171, IH (1 Div) 6–10, 6–15, 6–31
Selot's Trust, Re [1902] 1 Ch. 488, Ch D 10–05
Semple Fraser WS v Quayle, 2002 S.L.T. (Sh Ct) 33; 2001 G.W.D. 16–653,
Sh Ct (Glasgow) 7–20
Seroka v Bellah, 1995 S.L.T. 204, OH 14–29
Serra v Famous Lasky Film Service [1922] W.N. 44 15–37
Services Europe Atlantique Sud (SEAS) v Stockholms Rederi AB Svea:
Despina, R, The: Folias, The [1979] 1 All E.R. 421; [1979] A.C. 685 . . 8–21
Sethi v Sethi (Divorce: Maintenance), 1995 S.L.T. 104; 1993 S.C.L.R. 788,
OH 13–21
Settebello Ltd v Banco Totta and Acores [1985] 1 W.L.R. 1050; [1985] 2
All E.R. 1025, CA (Civ Div) 3–04
Settlement Corp v Hochschild (No.1) [1966] Ch. 10; [1965] 3 W.L.R. 1150;
[1965] 3 All E.R. 486; 109 S.J. 920, Ch D 7–47
Sfeir and Co v National Insurance Co of New Zealand Ltd; Joined Cases
Aschkar and Co v National Insurance Co of New Zealand; Aschkar
Bros v National Insurance Co of New Zealand [1964] 1 Ll Rep. 330,
QBD 9–17
Shafi v Shafi, unreported, August 18, 1977, Glasgow Sh Ct 11–07
Shahnaz v Rizwan [1965] 1 Q.B. 390; [1964] 3 W.L.R. 759; [1964] 2 All
E.R. 993, QBD 3–01, 11–05
Shamil Bank of Bahrain EC v Beximco Pharmaceuticals Ltd (No.1); sub
nom. Beximco Pharmaceuticals Ltd v Shamil Bank of Bahrain EC
[2004] EWCA Civ 19; [2004] 1 W.L.R. 1784; [2004] 4 All E.R. 1072,
CA (Civ Div) 15–13
Shand-Harvey v Bennet Clark, 1910 1 S.L.T. 133, Sh Ct 13–02, 13–08
Sharpe v Crispin (1865–69) L.R. 1 P. & D. 611, Ct of Probate 6–24, 6–31
Shaw v Gould; sub nom. Wilson's Trusts, Re (1868) L.R. 3 H.L. 55, HL . . . 4–06,
12–02, 12–18, 12–19
Shaw v Shaw [1979] Fam. 62; [1979] 3 W.L.R. 24; [1979] 3 All E.R. 1, Fam
Div 7–03
Sheaf Steamship Co Ltd v Compania Trasmediterranea (1930) 36 Ll. L.
Rep. 197; 1930 S.C. 660, IH (2 Div) 16–14
Shedden v Patrick (1854) 1 Macq. 535 . . . . 9–12, 14–02
Sheey v Professional Life Assurance Co (1857) 2 C.B. (N.S.) 211 9–12
Sheikh v Sheikh 2005 Fam. L.R. 7; 2005 G.W.D. 11–183, OH 11–24

Shekar v Satyam Computer Services Ltd [2005] I.C.R. 737, EAT 7–45, 15–38,
    15–49
Shell (UK) Exploration and Production v Innes 1995 S.L.T. 807, OH ... 7–45, 7–47
Shemshadfard v Shemshadfard [1981] 1 All E.R. 726; (1980) 10 Fam. Law
    189, Fam Div 12–11
Shenavai v Kreischer (266/85) [1987] E.C.R. 239; [1987] 3 C.M.L.R. 782,
    ECJ 7–13
Shetland Times Ltd v Wills 1997 S.C. 316; 1997 S.L.T. 669, OH 1–02, 15–43
Shevill v Presse Alliance SA [1996] A.C. 959; [1996] 3 W.L.R. 420; [1996] 3
    All E.R. 929, HL 7–14
Shields v Shields (1852) 15 D. 142 12–02
Shierson v Vlieland—Boddy [2005] EWCA Civ 974; [2005] 1 W.L.R. 3966,
    CA (Civ Div); reversing [2004] EWHC 2752; [2005] B.C.C. 416, Ch
    D 17–40
Showlag v Mansour [1995] 1 A.C. 431; [1994] 2 W.L.R. 615; [1994] 2 All
    E.R. 129, PC (Jer) 9–12
Siboti K/S v BP France SA [2003] EWHC 1278; [2003] 2 Ll Rep. 364;
    [2004] 1 C.L.C. 1, QBD (Comm) 7–29
Sierra Leone Telecommunications Co Ltd v Barclays Bank Plc; sub nom.
    Sierratel v Barclays Bank Plc [1998] 2 All E.R. 820; [1998] C.L.C.
    501, QBD (Comm) 1–01, 15–14
Sill v Worswick (1791) 1 H.B. 1 665 17–10
Sillar, Re; sub nom. Hurley v Wimbush [1956] I.R. 344 .... 6–10, 6–16, 6–20
Sim v Robinow (1892) 19 R. 665, IH (1 Div) 7–45
Sim v Sim (Process: Form of decree), 1968 S.L.T. (Notes) 15, OH 12–17
Simonin v Mallac (1860) 2 Sw. & Tr. 67 .... 11–14, 11–24, 11–33
Simpson v Fogo (1863) 1 H. & M. 195 17–10
Simpson's Trs v Fox, 1951 S.L.T. 412, OH 8–12, 9–02, 18–02
Sinclair v Sinclair, 1988 S.C. 19; 1988 S.L.T. 87, OH 14–47
Sinfra Ltd, Re [1939] 2 All E.R. 675 15–40
Singh v Singh, 1998 S.C. 68; 1998 S.L.T. 1084, IH (Ex Div) 14–31
Singh v Singh; sub nom. Kaur v Singh, 2005 S.L.T. 749; 2005 S.C.L.R.
    1000, OH 12–35, 12–38
Sinha Peerage Claim, Re [1946] 1 All E.R. 348 (Note), HL 11–02, 11–04
Sirdur Gurdyal Singh v Rajah of Faridkote [1894] A.C. 670, PC (Ind) 9–10
Sisro v Ampersand Software BV [1995] 10 C.L. 97 9–40
Skjevesland v Geveran Trading Co Ltd (No.4) [2002] EWHC 2898; [2003]
    B.C.C. 391; [2003] B.P.I.R. 924, Ch D 17–39
Slamen v Slamen, 1991 G.W.D. 34–2041 14–31
Slater v Mexican National Railroad Co, 194 U.S. 120 (1904) 3–01, 16–07
Smart v Registrar General; sub nom. Smart, Petr, 1954 S.C. 81; 1954 S.L.T.
    213, IH (2 Div) 12–17
Smelting Co of Australia Ltd v Inland Revenue Commissioners [1897] 1
    Q.B. 175, CA 17–03
Smijth v Smijth, 1918 1 S.L.T. 156, OH 7–06, 14–02
Smith, Re; sub nom. Lawrence v Kitson [1916] 2 Ch. 206, Ch D 17–06
Smith v Owners of the SS Zigurds [1934] A.C. 209; (1933) 47 Ll. L. Rep.
    267, HL; affirming [1933] P. 87; (1933) 45 Ll. L. Rep. 1, CA;
    reversing [1932] P. 113; (1932) 43 Ll. L. Rep. 387, PDAD 8–22
Smith v Smith (1891) 18 R. 1036 18–26
Smith Kline and French Laboratories Ltd v Bloch (Interlocutory Injunction)
    [1983] 1 W.L.R. 730; [1983] 2 All E.R. 72, CA (Civ Div) 7–45, 7–47
Smith's Trs v Macpherson's Trs, 1926 S.C. 983; 1926 S.L.T. 669, IH (1 Div) .. 5–02,
    18–27
Société Commerciale de Réassurance v Eras International Ltd (No.2); sub
    nom. Eras EIL Actions (No.2), Re [1995] 2 All E.R. 278; [1995] 1
    Ll Rep. 64, QBD (Comm) 7–47

Société Cooperative Sidmetal v Titan International [1966] 1 Q.B. 828;
  [1965] 3 W.L.R. 847; [1965] 3 All E.R. 494, QBD 9–26
Société des Hotels Réunis v Hawker (1913) 29 T.L.R. 578 . . . . 15–22, 15–26
Société du Gaz de Paris v Société Anonyme de Navigation "Les
  Armateurs Français" Paris; sub nom. Société du Gaz de Paris v SA
  de Navigation les Armateurs Français; Société du Gaz de Paris v
  Armateurs Français (1925) 23 Ll. L. Rep. 209; 1926 S.C. (H.L.) 13,
  HL 7–45
Société Financière et Industrielle du Peloux v Axa Belgium (C112/03)
  [2006] Q.B. 251; [2006] 2 W.L.R. 228, ECJ 7–19
Société Nationale Industrielle Aérospatiale (SNIA) v Lee Kui Jak [1987]
  A.C. 871; [1987] 3 W.L.R. 59; [1987] 3 All E.R. 510, PC (Bru) 7–47
Société Nouvelle des Papeteries de l'Aa SA v BV Machinenfabriek BOA,
  unreported, September 25, 1992 15–16
Sohio Supply Co v Gatoil (USA) Inc [1989] 1 Ll Rep. 588, CA (Civ Div) . . . 7–47
Sohrab v Khan, 2002 S.C. 382; 2002 S.L.T. 1255, OH 11–01, 12–38
Soleimany v Soleimany [1999] Q.B. 785; [1998] 3 W.L.R. 811; [1999] 3 All
  E.R. 847; [1998] C.L.C. 779; *The Times*, March 4, 1998, CA (Civ
  Div) 9–77, 15–26
Somerset v Stewart (1772) 20 St. Tr. 1 . . . . 3–06, 10–05
Sottomayor (otherwise De Barros) v De Barros (No.2) (1879–80) L.R. 5
  P.D. 94; [1874–80] All E.R. Rep. 97, PDAD 11–22
Soucie v Soucie, 1995 S.C. 134; 1995 S.L.T. 414, IH (Ex Div) 14–30, 14–31
Source Ltd v TUV Rheinland Holding AG [1998] Q.B. 54; [1997] 3 W.L.R.
  365; *The Times*, March 28, 1997, CA (Civ Div) 7–13
Soutar v Peters, 1912 1 S.L.T. 111, OH 4–05, 16–11, 16–18
South African Breweries Ltd v King [1900] 1 Ch. 273, CA; affirming [1899]
  2 Ch. 173, Ch D 15–37
South Carolina Insurance Co v Assurantie Maatshappij De Zeven Provin-
  cien NV; Joined Cases South Carolina Insurance Co v Al Ahlia
  Insurance Co; South Carolina Insurance Co v Arabian Seas Insur-
  ance Co; South Carolina Insurance Co v Cambridge Reinsurance
  Co Ltd [1987] A.C. 24; [1986] 3 W.L.R. 398; [1986] 3 All E.R. 487,
  HL 7–47
Sovfracht (V/O) v Van Udens Scheepvaart en Agentuur Maatschappij (NV
  Gebr); sub nom. NV Gerb Van Udens Scheepvaart en Agentuur
  Maatschappij v V/O Sovfracht [1943] A.C. 203; (1942) 74 Ll. L.
  Rep. 59, HL 7–03
Sowa v Sowa [1961] P. 70; [1961] 2 W.L.R. 313, CA 11–03
Soya Margareta, The; sub nom. Owners of Cargo on Board the Soya
  Lovisa v Owners of the Soya Margareta [1961] 1 W.L.R. 709; [1960]
  2 All E.R. 756, PDAD 7–45, 7–47
Spain v Christie Manson and Woods Ltd [1986] 1 W.L.R. 1120; [1986] 3
  All E.R. 28, Ch D 3–03
Spain v National Bank of Scotland (1939) 63 Ll. L. Rep. 330; 1939 S.C.
  413; 1939 S.L.T. 317, IH (2 Div) 3–04, 7–03
Spain v Owners of the Arantzazu Mendi [1939] A.C. 256; (1939) 63 Ll. L.
  Rep. 89; [1939] W.N. 69; 108 L.J. P. 55; 160 L.T. 513; 55 L.T.R. 454,
  HL 3–05
Speed Investments Ltd v Formula One Holdings Ltd (No.2); sub nom.
  Bambino Holdings Ltd v Speed Investments Ltd [2004] EWCA Civ
  1512; [2005] 1 W.L.R. 1936; [2005] 1 B.C.L.C. 455, CA (Civ Div) 7–27
Spence (Claudia) v Spence (Husband and Wife : Domicile), 1995 S.L.T.
  335, OH 6–04, 6–10, 6–15, 6–21
Spenceley, In the Goods of [1892] P. 255, PDAD 8–12
Spencer's Trs v Ruggles, 1981 S.C. 289; 1982 S.L.T. 165, IH (1 Div) 18–27
Sperling v Sperling, 1975 (2) S.A. 707 13–10

Spiliada Maritime Corp v Cansulex Ltd (The Spiliada) [1987] A.C. 460;
    [1986] 3 W.L.R. 972; [1986] 3 All E.R. 843, HL 7–45
Spurrier v La Cloche [1902] A.C. 446, PC (Jer) 15–12
Srini Vasan (otherwise Clayton) v Srini Vasan [1946] P. 67, PDAD 11–03
St Joseph, The [1933] P. 119; (1933) 45 Ll. L. Rep. 180, PDAD 15–32
St Pierre v South American Stores (Garth and Chaves) Ltd [1936] 1 K.B.
    382; [1937] 3 All E.R. 349, CA 7–45, 7–47, 15–22
Standard Bank London Ltd v Apostolakis (No.1) [2002] C.L.C. 933; [2000]
    I.L.Pr. 766, QBD (Comm) 7–20
Standard Bank London Ltd v Apostolakis (No.2) [2001] Ll Rep. Bank. 240;
    [2002] C.L.C. 939, QBD (Comm) 7–30
Standard Chartered Bank Ltd v Inland Revenue Commissioners [1978] 1
    W.L.R. 1160; [1978] 3 All E.R. 644; [1978] S.T.C. 272; [1978] T.R.
    45; 122 S.J. 698, Ch D 17–03
Standard Steamship Owners Protection and Indemnity Association (Ber-
    muda) Ltd v GIE Vision Bail [2004] EWHC 2919; [2005] 1 All E.R.
    (Comm) 618; [2005] 2 C.L.C. 1135, QBD (Comm) 7–29
Starkowski (otherwise Urbanski) v Attorney General; sub nom. Starkowski
    (otherwise Juszczkiewicz) [1954] A.C. 155; [1953] 3 W.L.R. 942,
    HL 3–07, 4–05, 11–24
Starr v Starr; sub nom. Starr, Petr, 1999 S.L.T. 335; 1998 S.C.L.R. 775, OH .. 14–31
State of Norway's Application [1990] 1 A.C. 723; [1989] 2 W.L.R. 458;
    [1989] 1 All E.R. 745, HL 3–02, 8–16
Staubitz-Schreiber, Re (C1/04) [2006] B.P.I.R. 510, ECJ 17–40
Stavert v Stavert (1882) 9 R. 519 .... 4–05, 6–10
Steer, Re (1858) 2 H. & N. 594 6–16
Stettin, Ethe (1889) 14 P.D. 142 15–32
Stevenson v Currie (Stevenson's Trs) (1905) 13 S.L.T. 457, OH 13–07
Stevenson v Stevenson's Trs. *See* Stevenson v Currie (Stevenson's Trs).
Stewart v Auld (1851) 13 D. 1337 17–53
Stewart v Callaghan, 1996 S.L.T. (Sh Ct) 12, Sh Pr 8–16
Stewart v Garnett (1830) 3 Sim. 398 17–04
Stewart v Royal Bank of Scotland Plc, 1992 G.W.D. 31–1799 8–23
Stirling, Re; sub nom. Stirling v Stirling [1908] 2 Ch. 344, Ch D 4–05
Stirling's Trs v Legal and General Assurance Society Ltd, 1957 S.L.T. 73,
    OH 8–08, 15–11, 15–33, 17–24
Stoeck v Public Tr. [1921] 2 Ch. 67, Ch D 6–37
Stone v Stone [1958] 1 W.L.R. 1287; [1959] 1 All E.R. 194, PDAD 6–31
Stoughton, Re [1941] I.R. 166 17–02
Strachan v McDougle (1835) 13 S. 954 17–28
Stransky v Stransky [1954] P. 428; [1954] 3 W.L.R. 123, PDAD 6–39
Strathaird Farms Ltd v GA Chattaway and Co, 1993 S.L.T. (Sh Ct) 36, Sh
    Pr 7–13, 16–30
Studd v Cook (1883) 10 R. (H.L.) 53 18–26
Submarine Telegraph Co v Dickson (1864) 15 C.B. (N.S.) 759 16–14
Sulaiman v Juffali [2002] 1 F.L.R. 479; [2002] 2 F.C.R. 427, Fam Div 12–29,
    12–30
Sussex Peerage Case (1844) 11 Cl. & F. 85 .... 3–07, 11–20, 11–37
Sutherland v Administrator of German Property (1934) 50 T.L.R. 107 17–17
Swaddling v Adjudication Officer (C90/97) [1999] All E.R. (EC) 217;
    [1999] E.C.R. I—1075, ECJ (5th Chamber) 6–39, 6–40
Swan's Will, Re (1871) 2 V.L.R. (I.E.&M.) 47 .... 4–03, 11–17
Swiss Bank Corp v Boehmische Industrial Bank [1923] 1 K.B. 673, CA ... 15–25,
    17–17
Swiss Reinsurance Co Ltd v United India Insurance Co (Jurisdiction)
    [2003] EWHC 741; [2004] I.L.Pr. 4, QBD (Comm) 7–44

Swithenbank Foods Ltd v Bowers [2002] EWHC 2257; [2002] 2 All E.R.
(Comm) 974, QBD (Merc) 7–14
Syal v Heyward [1948] 2 K.B. 443; [1948] 2 All E.R. 576, CA 9–12
Sydney Municipal Council v Bull [1909] 1 K.B. 7, KBD 3–02
Syndic in Bankruptcy of Khoury v Khayat. *See* Salim Nasrallah Khoury
(Syndic in Bankruptcy) v Khayat.
Szalatnay—Stacho v Fink [1947] K.B. 1; [1946] 2 All E.R. 231, CA 16–10
Szechter v Szechter [1971] P. 286; [1971] 2 W.L.R. 170, PDAD 4–05, 11–01,
11–31, 12–36

T (Infants), Re [1968] Ch. 704; [1968] 3 W.L.R. 430; [1968] 3 All E.R. 411,
CA (Civ Div) 14–25
T v T; sub nom. KT v JT, 2004 S.C. 323; 2003 S.L.T. 1316, IH (1 Div) 14–31
T and N Ltd (Jurisdiction), Re [2005] EWHC 2990, Ch D (Companies
Ct) 8–21, 16–15, 16–28
TSN Kunststoffrecycling GmbH v Jurgens; sub nom. Jurgens v TSN
Kunststoffrecycling GmbH [2002] EWCA Civ 11; [2002] 1 W.L.R.
2459; [2002] 1 All E.R. (Comm) 282, CA (Civ Div) 9–40
Taczanowska (otherwise Roth) v Taczanowski; sub nom. Holdowanski v
Holdowanska (otherwise Bialoszewska) and Price [1957] P. 301;
[1957] 3 W.L.R. 141; [1957] 2 All E.R. 563; 101 S.J. 534, CA ... 5–07, 11–27
Tagus, The [1903] P. 44, PDAD 8–22
Tahir v Tahir (Husband and wife: Divorce), 1993 S.L.T. 194; 1992 S.C.L.R.
746, OH 12–28, 13–24
Tahir v Tahir (No.2), 1995 S.L.T. 451, OH 12–11, 13–24
Tait (Liquidator of Salt Mines Syndicate Ltd), Noter (1895) 2 S.L.T. 489,
OH 15–12
Tatnall v Hankey, 2 Moo. P.C. 342 18–35
Tatry, The. See Owners of Cargo Lately Laden on Board the Tatry v
Owners of the Maciej Rataj
Tavoulareas v Alexander G Tsavliris and Sons Maritime Co (No.2) [2005]
EWHC 2643; [2006] 1 All E.R. (Comm) 130; [2005] 2 C.L.C. 848,
QBD (Comm) 7–38
Tayler v Scott (1847) 9 D. 1504 8–05
Taylor v Ford, 1993 S.L.T. 654, OH 14–29
Taylor v Hollard [1902] 1 K.B. 676, KBD 9–13
Tee v Tee [1974] 1 W.L.R. 213; [1973] 3 All E.R. 1105, CA (Civ Div) 6–22,
6–30
Tennekoon, Commissioner for Registration of Indian and Pakistani Res-
idents v Duraisamy [1958] A.C. 354; [1958] 2 All E.R. 479, PC (Cey) .. 6–16
Tezcan v Tezcan (1992) 87 D.L.R. 503, BC CA 13–07
Thai-Europe Tapioca Service Ltd v Pakistan Directorate of Agricultural
Supplies (*The Harmattan*); sub nom. Thai-Europe Tapioca Service
Ltd v Pakistan, Ministry of Food and Agriculture (The Harmattan)
[1975] 1 W.L.R. 1485; [1975] 3 All E.R. 961, CA (Civ Div) 7–03
Thoars Judicial Factor v Ramlort Ltd; sub nom. Reid v Ramlort Ltd 1998
S.C. 887; 1999 S.L.T. 1153, IH (Ex Div); reversing 1998 G.W.D.
20–1040, OH 17–38
Thomson (1917) 33 Sh. Ct. Rep. 84 .... 8–12, 18–49
Thomson, Petr, 1980 S.L.T. (Notes) 29, OH 14–25, 14–47
Thomson v Kindell, 1910 2 S.L.T. 442, OH 16–11, 16–21
Thornton v Thornton 106560 (1886) L.R. 11 P.D. 176, CA 7–47
Through Transport Mutual Insurance Association (Eurasia) Ltd v New
India Assurance Co Ltd (*The Hari Bhum*) (No.1) [2004] EWCA Civ
1598; [2005] 1 All E.R. (Comm) 715; [2005] 1 Ll Rep. 67, CA (Civ
Div); reversing in part [2003] EWHC 3158; [2004] 1 Ll Rep. 206,
QBD (Comm) 7–09, 7–30, 7–47

Through Transport Mutual Insurance Association (Eurasia) Ltd v New
    India Assurance Co Ltd (*The Hari Bhum*) (No.2) [2005] EWHC
    455; [2005] 2 Ll Rep. 378; [2005] 1 C.L.C. 376, QBD (Comm) 9–76
Thulin, Re [1995] 1 W.L.R. 165; (1995) 92(2) L.S.G. 35, Ch D 17–36
Thurburn v Steward (1869–71) L.R. 3 P.C. 478, PC (Cape) 17–53
Thyssen-Bornemisza v Thyssen-Bornemisza [1995] 1 All E.R. 58 12–11
Todd v Armour (1882) 9 R. 901 17–12
Tod's Tr. v Tod; sub nom. Salaman v Tod, 1911 S.C. 1214; 1911 2 S.L.T.
    172, IH (1 Div) 17–58
Tolofson v Jensen (1994) 120 D.L.R. (4th) 289 16–11
Tomalin v S Pearson and Son Ltd [1909] 2 K.B. 61, CA 3–07
Tooker v Lopez, 12 N.Y. 2d 569; 249 N.E. 2d 394 (1969) 16–08
Toprak Enerji Sanayi AS v Sale Tilney Technology Plc [1994] 1 W.L.R.
    840; [1994] 3 All E.R. 483; [1994] 1 Ll Rep. 303, QBD (Comm) 8–05
Torni, The [1932] P. 78; (1932) 43 Ll. L. Rep. 78; 48 T.L.R. 471; 101 L.J. P.
    44; 147 L.T. 208, CA 15–32
Torok v Torok [1973] 1 W.L.R. 1066; [1973] 3 All E.R. 101, Fam Div 13–24
Tracomin SA v Sudan Oil Seeds (No.1) [1983] 1 W.L.R. 1026; [1983] 3 All
    E.R. 137, CA (Civ Div); affirming [1983] 1 All E.R. 404; [1983] 1 Ll
    Rep. 560, QBD (Comm) 9–10, 9–12, 9–76
Tracomin SA v Sudan Oil Seeds Co Ltd (No.2) [1983] 3 All E.R. 140;
    [1983] 2 Ll Rep. 624, CA (Civ Div); reversing [1983] 1 W.L.R. 662;
    [1983] 2 All E.R. 129, QBD (Comm) 15–12
Train v Train's Exr (1899) 2 F. 146 .... 17–02, 18–04, 18–06, 18–11
Trasporti Castelletti Spedizioni Internazionali SpA v Hugo Trumpy SpA
    (C159/97) [1999] E.C.R. I—1597; [1999] I.L.Pr. 492, ECJ 7–44
Travelers Casualty and Surety Co of Europe Ltd v Sun Life Assurance Co
    of Canada (UK) Ltd [2004] EWHC 1704; [2004] I.L.Pr. 50; [2004]
    Ll Rep. I.R. 846, QBD (Comm) 7–51
Travers v Holley (otherwise Travers) [1953] P. 246; [1953] 3 W.L.R. 507;
    [1953] 2 All E.R. 794, CA 6–39, 9–10, 12–18
Trendtex Trading Corp v Central Bank of Nigeria [1977] Q.B. 529; [1977]
    2 W.L.R. 356, CA (Civ Div) 7–03
Trendtex Trading Corp v Crédit Suisse [1982] A.C. 679; [1981] 3 W.L.R.
    766; [1981] 3 All E.R. 520, HL 7–45, 17–17, 17–19, 17–20
Trepca Mines Ltd, Re [1960] 1 W.L.R. 1273; [1960] 3 All E.R. 304 (Note);
    104 S.J. 979, CA 9–04, 9–10
Trevelyan v Trevelyan (1873) 11 M. 516 18–06
Trinidad Shipping and Trading Co Ltd v GR Alston and Co [1920] A.C.
    888; (1920) 3 Ll. L. Rep. 210; [1920] 3 W.W.R. 221, PC (Trin) 15–26
Trotter v Trotter (1829) 3 Wils. & Sh. 407 18–34
Trufort, Re; sub nom. Trafford v Blanc (1887) L.R. 36 Ch. D. 600, Ch D .. 5–01,
                                                                    18–03
Tubantia, The (No.2) (1924) 18 Ll. L. Rep. 256, CA; affirming [1924] P. 78;
    (1924) 18 Ll. L. Rep. 158, PDAD 16–14
Tucker, Re (1864) 3 Sw. & Tr. 585 18–01
Turner v Grovit (C159/02); sub nom. Turner, Re (C159/02) [2005] 1 A.C.
    101; [2004] 3 W.L.R. 1193, ECJ 7–30, 7–31, 7–47, 7–48, 9–76
Tyburn Productions Ltd v Conan Doyle [1991] Ch. 75; [1990] 3 W.L.R.
    167; [1990] 1 All E.R. 909, Ch D 16–12, 17–32
Tzortzis v Monark Line A/B [1968] 1 W.L.R. 406; [1968] 1 All E.R. 949,
    CA (Civ Div) 15–12

Udny v Udny (1869) 7 M. (H.L.) 89 ... 2–04, 6–01, 6–06, 6–08, 6–29, 6–31, 14–04
Union Carbide Corp v BP Chemicals Ltd, 1995 S.C. 398; 1995 S.L.T. 972,
    IH (1 Div) 7–56, 8–16, 8–23

Union Transport v Continental Lines SA; sub nom. Cross AM Lines [1992]
    1 W.L.R. 15; [1992] 1 All E.R. 161, HL 7–13
United City Merchants (Investments) Ltd v Royal Bank of Canada (*The
    American Accord*) [1983] 1 A.C. 168; [1982] 2 W.L.R. 1039; [1982] 2
    All E.R. 720, HL 17–29
United Railways of Havana and Regla Warehouses Ltd, Re [1961] A.C.
    1007; [1960] 2 W.L.R. 969; [1960] 2 All E.R. 332, HL; reversing in
    part [1960] Ch. 52; [1959] 2 W.L.R. 251; [1959] 1 All E.R. 214, CA;
    affirming [1958] Ch. 724; [1958] 2 W.L.R. 229; [1957] 3 All E.R.
    641, Ch D 5–07, 8–21, 15–12, 15–25, 15–54
United States v A Ltd [2003] C.L.Y.B. 621 3–03
United States v Inkley [1989] Q.B. 255; [1988] 3 W.L.R. 304; [1988] 3 All
    E.R. 144; [1988] 2 F.T.L.R. 86; (1988) 132 S.J. 995, CA (Civ Div) ... 3–03
Universal Credit Co v Marks (1932) 163 A. 810 17–13
Universal General Insurance Co (UGIC) v Group Josi Reinsurance Co SA
    (C412/98); sub nom. Group Josi Reinsurance Co SA v Compagnie
    d'Assurances Universal General Insurance Co (UGIC) (C412/98)
    [2001] Q.B. 68; [2000] 3 W.L.R. 1625, ECJ (6th Chamber) 7–51
Urness v Minto (International Child Abduction), 1994 S.C. 249; 1994
    S.L.T. 988, IH (2 Div) 14–29, 14–31
Usher v Usher [1912] 2 I.R. 445 11–25

Vadala v Lawes (1890) L.R. 25 Q.B.D. 310, CA 9–12
Valentine's Settlement, Re; sub nom. Valentine v Valentine [1965] Ch.
    831; [1965] 2 W.L.R. 1015; [1965] 2 All E.R. 226, CA 14–61
Valery v Scott (1876) 3 R. 965 15–21
Van den Boogaard v Laumen (C220/95) [1997] Q.B. 759; [1997] All E.R.
    (E.C.) 517; [1997] E.C.R. I—1147, ECJ (5th Chamber) .. 7–09, 9–38, 13–18
Van Grutten v Digby (1862) 31 Beav. 561 .... 13–06, 13–07, 15–21
Van Uden Maritime BV (t/a Van Uden Africa Line) v Komman-
    ditgesellschaft in Firma Deco—Line (C391/95) [1999] Q.B. 1225;
    [1999] 2 W.L.R. 1181; [1998] E.C.R. I—7091, ECJ 7–57
Vanquelin v Bouard (1863) 15 C.B. (N.S.) 341 9–13
Vardopulo (1909) 25 T.L.R. 518 7–47
Varr v Smith (1879) 7 R. 247 17–53
Velasco v Coney [1934] P. 143, PDAD 18–31, 18–45
Verein fur Konsumenteninformation v Henkel (C167/00) [2003] All E.R.
    (EC) 311; [2003] 1 All E.R. (Comm) 606, ECJ (6th Chamber) .. 7–14, 7–20
Vervaeke v Smith [1983] 1 A.C. 145; [1982] 2 W.L.R. 855, HL 12–25, 12–38
Viditz v O'Hagan [1900] 2 Ch. 87, CA 13–05
Vigreux v Michel, *See* M (A Child), Re
Viking Line Abp v International Transport Workers Federation; sub nom.
    International Transport Workers Federation v Viking Line Abp
    [2005] EWCA Civ 1299; [2006] 1 Ll Rep. 303; [2005] 2 C.L.C. 720,
    CA (Civ Div); reversing [2005] EWHC 1222; [2005] 1 C.L.C. 951;
    [2005] 3 C.M.L.R. 29 [2006] I.L.Pr. 4, QBD (Comm) 7–51, 9–40
Vincent v Earl of Buchan (1889) 16 R. 637 6–04
Viola v Viola (Parent and child: International child abduction), 1988 S.L.T.
    7; 1987 S.C.L.R. 529, OH 14–31
Viskase Ltd v Paul Kiefel GmbH; sub nom. Viskase Ltd v Paul Kiefel
    GmbH [1999] 1 W.L.R. 1305; [1999] 3 All E.R. 362, CA (Civ Div) ... 7–13
Visser, Re; sub nom. Holland v Drukker [1928] Ch. 877, Ch D 3–02
Viswalingham v Viswalingham (1980) 1 E.L.R. 15, CA 12–23
Vita Food Products Inc v Unus Shipping Co Ltd (In Liquidation) [1939]
    A.C. 277; (1939) 63 Ll. L. Rep. 21, PC (Can) 5–07, 15–11, 15–23
Vogel v R and A Kohnstamm Ltd [1973] Q.B. 133; [1971] 3 W.L.R. 537,
    QBD 9–10

Von Hellfeld v Rechnitzer [1914] 1 Ch. 748, CA 8–05
Von Linden, In the Goods of [1896] P. 148, PDAD 18–01
Von Lorang v Administrator of Austrian Property; sub nom. Salvesen
    (otherwise Van Lorang) v Administrator of Austrian Property;
    Administrator of Austrian Property v Von Lorang [1927] A.C. 641;
    1927 S.C. (H.L.) 80; 1927 S.L.T. 438, HL 9–05, 11–18, 11–24, 12–16

W Petr, 2003 G.W.D. 28–772 14–27
W (A Child) (Abduction: Conditions for Return), Re; sub nom. W
    (Abduction: Domestic Violence), Re [2004] EWCA Civ 1366;
    [2005] 1 F.L.R. 727; [2004] 3 F.C.R. 559, CA (Civ Div); affirming
    [2004] EWHC 1247; [2004] 2 F.L.R. 499; [2004] Fam. Law 785, Fam
    Div 14–31
W v H (Child Abduction: Surrogacy) (No.1) [2002] 1 F.L.R. 1008; [2002]
    Fam. Law 345, Fam Div 10–04, 10–27
W v W; sub nom. PW v AL (or W), 2004 S.C. 63; 2003 S.L.T. 1253, IH (1
    Div) 14–31
WJ Alan and Co Ltd v El Nasr Export and Import Co [1972] 2 Q.B. 189;
    [1972] 2 W.L.R. 800; [1972] 2 All E.R. 127, CA (Civ Div) 15–24
Wahl v Attorney General (1932) 147 L.T. 382 .... 6–13, 6–14
Waite's Settlement Trusts, Re; sub nom. Westminster Bank Ltd v Brouard
    [1958] Ch. 100; [1957] 2 W.L.R. 1024; [1957] 1 All E.R. 629,
    Ch D 18–41, 18–43
Waldwiese Shiftung v Lewis [2004] EWHC 2589 17–20
Walford v Batthyany. *See* Batthyany v Walford.
Walker v Roberts, 1998 S.L.T. 1133; 1998 G.W.D. 14–721, OH 11–24, 13–13
Wall v De Thoren (1874) 1 R. 1036 11–21
Wallach (Deceased), Re; sub nom. Weinschenk v Treasury Solicitor [1950]
    1 All E.R. 199; 66 T.L.R. (Pt. 1) 132, PDAD 6–25
Walpole v Canadian Northern Railway Co [1923] A.C. 113, PC (Can) 16–12,
                                                                      16–13
Warrender v Warrender (1835) 2 Cl. & F. 488 .... 11–09, 12–15
Warter v Warter (1890) L.R. 15 P.D. 152, PDAD 10–06, 11–21
Waste Systems International Inc v Eurocare Environmental Services Ltd,
    1999 S.L.T. 198; 1998 G.W.D. 6–260, OH 9–03
Watson v First Choice Holidays and Flights Ltd; Joined Cases Aparta
    Hotels Caledonia SA v Watson [2001] EWCA Civ 972; [2001] 2 Ll
    Rep. 339, CA (Civ Div) 7–17
Watson v Jamieson, 1998 S.L.T. 180; 1997 G.W.D. 4–131, OH 14–27, 14–29
Watson v Renton (1792) M. 4582 15–25
Waygood and Co v Bennie (1885) 12 R. 615 .... 7–04, 9–03
Wayland (Deceased), Re [1951] 2 All E.R. 1041; [1951] W.N. 604,
    PDAD 18–01, 18–39
Webb v Clelland's Trs (1904) 41 S.L.R. 229 18–10
Webb (George Lawrence) v Webb (Lawrence Desmond) (C294/92) [1994]
    Q.B. 696; [1994] 3 W.L.R. 801, ECJ 7–27, 15–12
Weber v Universal Ogden Services Ltd (C37/00) [2002] Q.B. 1189; [2002] 3
    W.L.R. 931, ECJ (6th Chamber) 7–23
Weber's Trs v Riemer, 1947 S.L.T. 295; 1947 S.L.T. (Notes) 30, OH 7–03
Webster v Webster's Tr. (1886) 14 R. 90 11–16
Weinstock v Sarnat (2005–06) 8 I.T.E.L.R. 141; [2006] 3 C.L. 79, Sup Ct
    (NSW) 7–47, 18–03
Weiss, In the Estate of [1962] P. 136; [1962] 2 W.L.R. 353; [1962] 1 All
    E.R. 308, PDAD 17–03
Weiss v Weiss, 1940 S.L.T. 447, OH 7–03
Welch v Tennent [1891] A.C. 639; (1891 18 R. (H.L.) 72, HL 13–10

Wellington (Duke of), Re; sub nom. Glentanar v Wellington [1948] Ch.
    118; 64 T.L.R. 54; 92 S.J. 11, CA; affirming [1947] Ch. 506; [1947] 2
    All E.R. 854, Ch D 5–06, 5–10, 5–13, 17–03
Welsh, Re [1931] I.R. 161 18–01
Wendel v Moran, 1993 S.L.T. 44; 1992 S.C.L.R. 636, OH 7–04, 9–08, 9–10
West Tankers Inc v RAS Riunione Adriatica di Sicurta SpA (*The Front
    Comor*) [2005] EWHC 454; [2005] 2 All E.R. (Comm) 240; [2005] 2
    Ll Rep. 257, QBD (Comm) 7–30, 7–47, 16–17
Westergaard v Westergaard, 1914 S.C. 977; 1914 2 S.L.T. 167, IH (2 Div) ... 14–25
Westerman v Schwab (1905) 8 F. 132; (1905) 13 S.L.T. 594, IH (1 Div) 18–33
Western Digital Corp v British Airways Plc [1999] 2 All E.R. (Comm) 270;
    [1999] 2 Ll Rep. 380, QBD (Comm) 1–06
Western Provident v Norwich Union [1997] New L.J. Digest 1277 15–43
Westinghouse Electric Corp Uranium Contract Litigation MDL Docket
    235 (No.2); sub nom. Rio Tinto Zinc Corp v Westinghouse Electric
    Corp (Nos.1 and 2); Joined Cases RTZ Services Ltd v Westing-
    house Electric Corp [1978] A.C. 547; [1978] 2 W.L.R. 81; [1978] 1
    All E.R. 434, HL 8–16
Westland Helicopters Ltd v Arab Organisation for Industrialisation [1995]
    Q.B. 282; [1995] 2 W.L.R. 126; [1995] 2 All E.R. 387, QBD
    (Comm) 7–03, 10–04
Westminster Bank v McDonald, 1955 S.L.T. (Notes) 73, OH 8–06
Weston's Settlements, Re; sub nom. Weston v Weston [1969] 1 Ch. 223;
    [1968] 3 W.L.R. 786; [1968] 3 All E.R. 338, CA (Civ Div) 18–51
Whicker v Hume (1858) H.L. Cas. 124 .... 6–10, 6–16
Whiffin v Lees (1872) 10 N. 797 18–01
White v Jones [1995] 2 A.C. 207; [1995] 2 W.L.R. 187; [1995] 1 All E.R.
    691, HL; affirming [1993] 3 W.L.R. 730; [1993] 3 All E.R. 481, CA
    (Civ Div) 18–24
White v Tennant, 31 W.Va.790, 8 S.E. 596 (1888) 6–07
Whitley v Whitley, 1992 G.W.D. 15–843; 1992 G.W.D. 22–1248 14–31
Whitworth Street Estates (Manchester) Ltd v James Miller and Partners
    Ltd; sub nom. James Miller and Partners Ltd v Whitworth Street
    Estates (Manchester) Ltd [1970] A.C. 583; [1970] 2 W.L.R. 728;
    [1970] 1 All E.R. 796, HL 8–02, 9–76, 15–06, 15–12
Whyte v Whyte [2005] EWCA Civ 858; [2006] 1 F.L.R. 400; [2005] 3
    F.C.R. 21, CA (Civ Div) 14–46
Wiers Case (1607) 1 Rolle, Abridgmt. 530, 12 2–02
Wilby, Re; sub nom. In the Estate of Wilby [1956] P. 174; [1956] 2 W.L.R.
    262; [1956] 1 All E.R. 27; 100 S.J. 75, PDAD 14–61
Wilkie v Cathcart (1870) 9 M. 168 17–56
Wilkinson v Kitzinger [2006] EWHC 835; (2006) 103(19) L.S.G. 26, Fam
    Div 11–12
Wilkinson's Settlement, Re; sub nom. Butler v Wilkinson [1917] 1 Ch. 620,
    Ch D 18–40
Wilks, Re; sub nom. Keefer v Wilks [1935] Ch. 645, Ch D 4–01. 18–03
Willar v Willar 1954 S.C. 144; 1954 S.L.T. 267, IH (2 Div) 6–07, 6–09, 6–14,
                                                                6–17, 6–31
William Grant and Sons International Ltd v Marie Brizard Espana SA,
    1998 S.C. 536, OH 7–13, 15–16
William Grant and Sons Ltd v Glen Catrine Bonded Warehouse Ltd 1995
    S.L.T. 936, OH 1–01, 16–11
Williams, Petr (Parent and child: Custody) 1977 S.L.T. (Notes) 2, OH 6–06,
                                                                6–26
Williams v Jones (1845) 13 M. & W. 633 9–07

Williams and Humbert Ltd v W and H Trade Marks (Jersey) Ltd; Joined
Cases Rumasa SA v Multinvest (UK) [1986] A.C. 368; [1986] 2
W.L.R. 24, HL; affirming [1985] 3 W.L.R. 501; [1985] 2 All E.R.
619, CA (Civ Div); affirming [1985] 2 All E.R. 208; (1985) 129 S.J.
573, Ch D 3–04
Williamson v Taylor (1845) 8 D. 156 13–07
Wilson (Deceased), Re; sub nom. Grace v Lucas [1954] Ch. 733; [1954] 2
W.L.R. 1097; [1954] 1 All E.R. 997; 98 S.J. 372, Ch D 14–61
Wilson v Robertson (1884) 11 R. 893 9–12
Wilsons (Glasgow and Trinidad) Ltd v Dresdner Bank, 1913 2 S.L.T. 437,
OH 17–53
Winans v Attorney General (No.1) [1904] A.C. 287, HL .. 6–02, 6–09, 6–10, 6–14,
6–19, 6–20, 6–32
Windeatt's Will Trusts, Re; sub nom. Webster v Webster [1969] 1 W.L.R.
692; [1969] 2 All E.R. 324, Ch D 18–51
Winkworth v Christie Manson & Woods Ltd [1980] Ch. 496; [1980] 2
W.L.R. 937, Ch D 4–05, 5–07, 17–03, 17–10, 17–12, 17–13, 17–14
Winter Maritime Ltd v North End Oil Ltd (The Winter); Joined Cases
Winter Maritime Ltd v Maritime Oil Trading Ltd [2000] 2 Ll Rep.
298, QBD (Comm) 7–38
Wolfenden v Wolfenden [1946] P. 61, PDAD 11–28
Wolff v Oxholm (1817) 6 M. & S. 92 3–03
Wood v Wood (Foreign Divorce: Maintenance Order) [1957] P. 254;
[1957] 2 W.L.R. 826, CA 10–06
Woodbury v Sutherland's Trs, 1939 S.L.T. 93, OH 6–06, 6–16
Woodcock v Woodcock, 1990 S.C. 267; 1990 S.L.T. 848, IH (1 Div) 14–45
Woodhouse AC Israel Cocoa SA v Nigerian Produce Marketing Co Ltd;
sub nom. Woodhouse v Nigerian Produce Marketing Co Ltd [1972]
A.C. 741; [1972] 2 W.L.R. 1090; [1972] 2 All E.R. 271, HL;
affirming [1971] 2 Q.B. 23; [1971] 2 W.L.R. 272; [1971] 1 All E.R.
665, CA (Civ Div) 15–24, 15–51
Woodward v Woodward (Husband and wife: Jurisdiction), 1957 S.C. 415;
1958 S.L.T. 213, OH 12–33
Worms v De Valdor (1880) 49 L.J. Ch. 261 10–05
Wright's Trs v Callender, 1993 S.C. (H.L.) 13; 1993 S.L.T. 556, HL;
reversing 1992 S.C. 48; 1992 S.L.T. 498, IH (Ex Div) 5–02, 18–27
Wynn (Deceased), Re [1984] 1 W.L.R. 237; [1983] 3 All E.R. 310, Ch D .. 18–20

X v Fortis Bank (Nederland) NV [2004] I.L.Pr. 37, HR (NL) 17–40
X's Settlement, Re [1945] Ch. 44, Ch D 14–25
XN Corp Ltd v Point of Sale Ltd [2001] I.L.Pr. 35, Ch D 7–45

Yachya v Levi [2002] C.L.Y.B. 640, Royal Ct of Jersey 7–47
Yahoo! v Ligue Contra le racisme et l'Antisimitisme, 433 F. 3d; 2006 U.S.
App. Lexis 668 3–03
Yahuda, In the Estate of [1956] P. 388; [1956] 3 W.L.R. 20; [1956] 2 All
E.R. 262; 100 S.J. 382, PDAD 18–01
Yelverton v Yelverton (1859) 1 Sw. & Tr. 574 6–31
Yorke v British & Continental Steamship Co Ltd (1945) 78 Ll. L. Rep.
181, CA 1–02, 3–07
Young v Barclay (1846) 8 D. 774, IH (1 Div) 7–47
Yzquierdo v Clydebank Engineering Co. *See* Castanada Castanada v
Clydebank Engineering and Shipbuilding Co Ltd.

Z (Abduction: Non-Convention Country), Re [1999] 1 F.L.R. 1270; [1999]
1 F.C.R. 251, Fam Div 14–48

Z Ltd v A-Z and AA-LL; sub nom. Mareva Injunction, Re [1982] Q.B.
558; [1982] 2 W.L.R. 288; [1982] 1 All E.R. 556, CA (Civ Div) 7–58
Zahnrad Fabrik Passau GmbH v Terex Ltd, 1985 S.C. 364; 1986 S.L.T. 84,
OH 15–22, 17–16
Zanelli v Zanelli, 64 T.L.R. 556; [1948] W.N. 381, CA 4–05, 6–30, 12–15
Zapata Offshore Co v Bremen, The (*The Chaparral*) [1972] 2 Ll Rep. 315;
[1971] 2 Ll Rep. 348, US Ct 7–31
Zarine v Ramava [1942] I.R. 148 3–05
Zebrarise Ltd v De Nieffe [2004] EWHC 1842; [2005] 2 All E.R. (Comm)
816; [2005] 1 Ll Rep. 154, QBD (Comm) 15–02, 15–12
Zelger v Salinitri (129/83) [1984] E.C.R. 2397; [1985] 3 C.M.L.R. 366, ECJ
(4th Chamber) 7–41
Zenel v Haddow, 1993 S.C. 612; 1993 S.L.T. 975, IH (Ex Div) 14–29, 14–31
Zivnostenska Banka National Corp v Frankman; sub nom. Frankman v
Prague Credit Bank [1950] A.C. 57; [1949] 2 All E.R. 671, HL 3–02

TABLE OF STATUTES

1431 (C.128) 2–02
1436 (C.145) 2–02
1587 (c.105) 2–02
1753 Clandestine Marriages
     Act (c.37) 11–14
1772 Royal Marriages Act (12
     Geo.3 c.11) 11–20
1824 Slave Trade Act (5 Geo.4
     c.113)
     s.2 10–05
1855 Intestate Moveable Suc-
     cession (Scotland)
     Act (18 & 19 Vict.
     c.23)
     s.6 13–02
1856 Marriage (Scotland) Act
     (19 & 20 Vict.
     c.96) 11–14
1861 Offences against the Per-
     son Act (24 & 25
     Vict. c.100)
     s.57 11–07
     Wills Act (24 & 25 Vict.
     c.114) 18–17, 18–18,
              18–19, 18–26, 18–29
1868 Judgments Extension Act
     (31 & 32 Vict.
     c.54) 9–14, 9–61
     Titles to Land Consolida-
     tion (Scotland) Act
     (31 & 32 Vict. c.101)
     s.117 17–02
1882 Inferior Courts Judg-
     ments Extension Act
     (45 & 46 Vict.
     c.31) 9–14, 9–61
     Bills of Exchange Act (45
     & 46 Vict c.61) 17–29
     s.3 17–29
     s.4 17–29
     s.21 17–29
     s.72 17–29
     s.72(2) 17–29
     s.72(3) 17–29
     s.72(5) 17–29
     Married Women's Prop-
     erty Act (45 & 46
     Vict. c.75) 17–22
     s.17 11–08
1892 Colonial Probates Act (55
     & 56 Vict. c.6) 18–01,
                          18–02
     s.22 18–02

1892 Foreign Marriage Act (55
     & 56 Vict. c.23) 11–27
1907 Sheriff Courts (Scotland)
     Act (7 Edw.7 c.51)
     s.6(f) 7–04
1913 Bankruptcy (Scotland)
     Act (3 & 4 Geo.5
     c.20) 10–07, 17–50
1920 Maintenance Orders
     (Facilities for Enfor-
     cement) Act (10 &
     11 Geo.5 c.33) 13–21
     Administration of Justice
     Act (10 & 11 Geo.5
     c.81) 3–01, 9–06, 9–07,
               9–08, 9–09, 9–12,
               9–14, 9–15, 9–21,
               9–34, 9–61, 9–77,
                             9–94
     Pt II 9–15
     s.9(1) 9–16
     s.9(2) 9–17
     s.9(2)(d) 9–12
     s.9(2)(e) 9–12
     s.9(3) 9–18
     s.9(4) 9–19
     s.9(5) 9–09
     s.10 9–20
     s.14 9–14
1926 Indian and Colonial
     Divorce Jurisdiction
     Act (16 & 17 Geo.5
     c.40) 12–03, 12–18
     Legitimacy Act (16 & 17
     Geo.5 c.60) ... 4–05, 14–04
     s.1 14–04
     s.8 14–04
1927 Colonial Probate (Pro-
     tected States and
     Mandated Territo-
     ries) Act (17 & 18
     Geo.5 c.43) 18–01
1933 Foreign Judgments
     (Reciprocal Enforce-
     ment) Act (23 & 24
     Geo.5 c.13) ... 3–01, 9–06,
               9–07, 9–08, 9–14,
               9–21, 9–34, 9–61,
               9–77, 9–94, 12–30
     Pt I 9–32
     s.1(1) 9–22
     s.1(2) 9–23
     s.1(2)(a) 9–12

1933 Foreign Judgments
 (Reciprocal Enforce-
 ment) Act—*cont.*
  s.1(2A) 9–21, 9–37
  s.1(3) 9–17, 9–24
  s.2(a) 9–28
  s.2(b) 9–28
  s.2(c) 9–28
  s.2(1) 9–21, 9–25
  s.2(2) 9–25
  s.2(4) 9–21
  s.4(1)(a) 9–26
  s.4(1)(b) 9–27
  s.4(2) 9–28
  s.4(2)(a)(i)—(v) 9–17
  s.4(3) 9–28
  s.5(1) 9–29
  s.5(2) 9–30
  s.6 .... 9–09, 9–31
  s.8(1) 9–32
  s.9 .... 9–07, 9–33
1937 Matrimonial Causes Act
 (1 Edw.8 & 1 Geo.6
 c.57) 12–03
  s.13 6–30
1939 Marriage (Scotland) Act
 (2 & 3 Geo.6 c.34) 11–14
1940 Indian and Colonial
 Divorce Jurisdiction
 Act (3 & 4 Geo.6
 c.35) 12–03, 12–18
 Law Reform (Mis-
 cellaneous Pro-
 visions) (Scotland)
 Act (3 & 4 Geo.6
 c.42)
  s.3(2) 16–24
1944 Matrimonial Causes (War
 Marriages) Act (7 &
 8 Geo.6 c.43)
  s.1 12–03
  s.2 12–03
1947 Foreign Marriage Act (10
 & 11 Geo.6 c.33) ... 11–27
1948 British Nationality Act
 (11 & 12 Geo.6
 c.56) 6–38
1949 Law Reform (Mis-
 cellaneous Pro-
 visions) Act (12, 13
 & 14 Geo.6 c.100)
  s.1 .... 6–39, 12–03
  s.2 .... 6–39, 12–03
  s.4 14–01
1950 Arbitration Act (14 Geo.6
 c.27)
  Pt III 9–77
  s.26 9–77

1950 Colonial and Other Territories (Divorce)
 Jurisdiction Act (14
 Geo.6 c.20) 12–03
 Maintenance Orders Act
 (14 Geo.6 c.37) 13–20,
                      13–28
1952 Visiting Forces Act (15 &
 16 Geo.6 & 1 Eliz.2
 c.67) 7–03
1955 Army Act (3 & 4 Eliz.2
 c.18) 8–12
1961 Carriage by Air Act (9 &
 10 Eliz.2 c.27) 1–06
 Trusts (Scotland) Act (9
 & 10 Eliz.2 c.57) ... 18–47
1962 Law Reform (Husband
 and Wife) Act (10 &
 11 Eliz.2 c.48) 8–03
  s.2(1) 4–03
  s.2(2) 4–03
1963 Wills Act (c.44) .. 18–05, 18–19,
                  18–40, 18–56
  s.1 .... 4–05, 5–07
  s.1(1) 18–20
  s.2 18–21
  s.2(1)(a) 18–21
  s.2(1)(b) 18–21
  s.2(1)(c) 18–22, 18–29
  s.2(1)(d) 18–22
  s.2(2) 18–22, 18–40
  ss.2–6 18–22
  s.3 18–22
  s.4 ..... 18–22, 18–26, 18–32
  s.6 18–22
  s.6(1) 18–20
  s.6(2) 18–22
1964 Succession (Scotland) Act
 (c.41) 1–02, 11–12,
       13–16, 18–04, 18–11,
                       18–13
  s.8 .... 18–11, 18–13
  s.8(2) 18–13
  s.8(4) 18–13
1965 Carriage of Goods by
 Road Act (c.37) 1–06
1967 Uniform Laws on International Sales Act
 (c.45) 1–10, 15–39
 Sch.1, art.1 ..... 1–10, 15–39
1968 Consular Relations Act
 (c.18) 7–03
 Legitimation (Scotland)
 Act (c.22)
  s.1 14–04
  s.4 14–04
  s.5(2) 14–04
  s.5(3) 14–04

1968	Legitimation (Scotland) Act—*cont.*	
	s.8(4)	14–02
	1968 60. Theft Act (c.60)	3–03
1970	Law Reform (Miscellaneous Provisions) Act (c.33)	14–01
	s.1	4–03
	Conveyancing and Feudal Reform (Scotland) Act (c.35)	17–02
1971	Carriage of Goods by Sea Act (c.19)	15–33
	Administration of Estates Act (c.25)	18–02
	s.3(1)	18–01
	National Insurance Act (c.50)	
	s.12	11–05
	Recognition of Divorces and Legal Separations Act 1971 (c.53)	1–02, 12–18, 12–19, 12–27
	s.2–6	12–27
	s.7	4–06, 11–17, 12–26
	s.8	12–23
	Law Reform (Jurisdiction in Delict) Act (c.55)	2–02, 7–04
	Diplomatic and other Privileges Act (c.64)	7–03
	Immigration Act (c.77)	12–04
1972	Maintenance Orders (Reciprocal Enforcement) Act (c.18)	13–21, 13–28
	Pt I	13–21, 13–28
	Pt II	9–08, 13–21, 13–28
	Pt III	13–21, 13–23, 13–28
	s.6	13–21
	ss.6–11	13–21
	s.8	13–21
	Matrimonial Proceedings (Polygamous Marriages) Act (c.38)	11–10, 11–42
	s.2	11–03, 11–09
	Administration of Justice (Scotland) Act (c.59)	
	s.1	7–56
	Companies (Floating Charges and Receivers) (Scotland) Act (c.67)	17–08
1972	European Communities Act (c.68)	
	s.2(2)	2–04
1973	Matrimonial Causes Act (c.18)	12–28
	s.11(c)	11–12
	s.16	14–01
	s.47	11–03
	Domicile and Matrimonial Proceedings Act (c.45)	1–02, 6–09, 6–25, 12–04, 12–05, 12–06, 12–09, 12–13, 12–32, 12–35, 14–16
	s.1	6–04, 6–25, 11–10
	s.1(1)	4–05, 6–40
	s.1(2)	4–05, 6–25, 6–40
	s.3	6–07, 6–40
	s.3(a)	6–04
	s.4	6–04, 6–06, 6–26, 6–27
	s.5	6–39, 12–04, 12–09, 12–13, 12–34
	s.5(2)	6–09, 12–04
	s.7	6–39, 9–05, 12–04, 12–34, 12–50
	s.7(2A)	12–06
	s.7(3)	12–06, 12–35
	s.7(3A)	12–06, 12–35
	s.7(3A)(a)	12–35
	s.7(3A)(b)	12–35
	s.7(3B)	12–35
	s.8	12–50
	s.8(1)	12–04
	s.8(2)	12–04
	s.9	6–39
	s.11	12–09
	s.11(2)	12–11
	s.12(5)(b)	12–05
	s.12(5)(d)	12–08
	s.13	12–04, 12–34
	s.14	6–40
	s.16	12–20
	Sch.1	12–09
	Sch.3	12–09, 12–11, 12–45, 12–50
	Sch.3, para.3	12–10
	Sch.3, para.7	12–11
	Sch.3, para.8	12–10, 12–14
	Sch.3, para.9	12–11
	Prescription and Limitation (Scotland) Act (c.52)	4–02, 8–06, 8–08
	s.23A	8–06
1975	Arbitration Act (c.3)	9–77, 9–94
	s.1(1)	9–76
	s.1(4)	9–76
	ss.2–6	9–77

1975 Finance Act (c.7)
s.45 6–03
Social Security Act (c.14)
s.25 11–08
s.162(b) 11–08
Evidence (Proceedings in
Other Jurisdictions)
Act (c.34) 3–02, 8–16,
8–25
s.1 3–02
Child Benefit Act (c.61)
s.9(2)(a) 11–08
Inheritance (Provision for
Family and Depen-
dants) Act (c.63) 6–34,
11–08, 18–09
1976 Damages (Scotland) Act
(c.13) 11–38, 16–26
s.2 16–26
s.2(2) 16–26
s.2(3) 16–26
s.2(4) 16–26
s.2A 16–26
s.3 16–26
Legitimacy Act (c.31)
s.2 14–04
s.3 14–04
Divorce (Scotland) Act
(c.39) 12–41
s.3 12–28
1977 Marriage (Scotland) Act
(c.15) 11–16, 11–22,
11–24, 11–37
s.2(1) 11–18
s.2(3)(b) 11–11
s.3(5) 5–02
s.5(4)(b) 11–11
s.5(4)(e) 11–12
s.20 11–31
s.23A 11–30
Presumption of Death
(Scotland) Act (c.27)
s.1(3) 12–35
s.1(4) 12–35
s.10 . . . . 8–12, 9–02
Unfair Contract Terms
Act (c.50) 3–07, 15–34
s.27 15–13
s.27(1) 15–34
s.27(2) 15–34
1978 Adoption (Scotland) Act
(c.28) 14–52, 14–60,
14–61, 14–62
Pt IV 14–52
s.14(2) 14–52
s.38(1)(c) 14–53
s.47 14–52

1978 Adoption (Scotland)
Act—*cont.*
s.47(2)(a) 14–60
s.49 14–52
s.56(3) 14–52
s.65 14–60
State Immunity Act (c.33) . . . .
3–05, 7–03, 9–39
ss.1–2 3–05
s.2 3–05
s.3 3–05
s.3(3) 7–03
s.4 3–05
s.5 3–05
s.6 3–05
s.7 3–05
s.8 3–05
s.9 3–05
s.10 3–05
s.11 3–05
s.14(2) 10–03
Employment Protection
(Consolidation) Act
(c.44) 15–34
1979 Merchant Shipping Act
(c.39) 1–06
1980 Protection of Trading
Interests Act (c.11) . . 9–34,
9–94
s.5 . . . . 9–34, 9–35
s.5(2) 9–35
s.5(3) 9–35
s.5(4) 9–35
s.6 9–35
s.6(2) 9–35
s.6(5) 9–35
s.6(6) 9–35
Law Reform (Mis-
cellaneous Pro-
visions) (Scotland)
Act (c.55)
s.20 12–04
1981 British Nationality Act
(c.61) 6–38
1982–1991 Civil Jurisdiction
and Judgments Act . . 7–53,
7–54, 9–36
1982 Civil Jurisdiction and
Judgments Act
(c.27) . . . 1–02, 1–08, 3–01,
6–03, 6–40, 7–04,
7–54, 9–06, 9–07,
9–14, 9–59, 17–38
s.2(2) 9–62
s.3B(1) 9–60
s.18 . . 9–14, 9–61, 9–75, 9–77,
9–94

1982 Civil Jurisdiction and Judgments Act—*cont.*
s.18(2)(a) 9–61
s.18(2)(e) 9–61, 9–77
s.18(3) 9–61
s.18(5) 9–61
s.18(6) 9–61
s.18(7) 9–61
s.18(8) 9–75
s.19 9–75
s.20 9–76
s.25 7–57
s.25(1) 7–58
s.30 7–04
s.31 7–04
s.32 .... 9–12, 9–76
s.32(2) 9–12
s.32(4) 9–12
s.33 9–10
s.34 9–07
s.41 .... 7–10, 7–59
ss.41–46 .... 6–03, 7–06
s.43 17–38
s.49 7–46
Sch.1 ..... 7–04, 7–53, 7–54,
7–59, 9–94
Sch.1, art.2 7–53
Sch.1, art.5.3 7–53
Sch.4 ..... 7–04, 7–06, 7–10,
7–13, 7–14, 7–30, 7–46,
7–53, 7–54, 7–59, 17–38,
17–41
Sch.4, r.3(h) 7–53, 7–54
Sch.4, rr.3–10 7–53
Sch.4, r.10 7–53
Sch.4, r.11 7–53
Sch.4, r.12 .... 7–29, 7–53
Sch.6 ..... 9–14, 9–61, 9–75,
9–77, 9–94
Sch.6, para.2(1) 9–62
Sch.6, para.3 9–63
Sch.6, para.4 9–64
Sch.6, para.5 9–65
Sch.6, para.6(1) 9–66
Sch.6, para.9 9–67
Sch.6, para.10 9–68
Sch.7 ..... 9–14, 9–61, 9–69,
9–75, 9–77, 9–94
Sch.7, para.2(1) 9–69
Sch.7, para.5(1) 9–70
Sch.7, para.5(5) 9–71
Sch.7, para.6(1) 9–72
Sch.7, para.8 9–73
Sch.7, para.9 9–74
Sch.8 ..... 7–04, 7–06, 7–52,
7–53, 7–54, 7–59, 13–28

1982 Civil Jurisdiction and Judgments Act—*cont.*
Sch.8, Pt 1 7–06
Sch.8, Pt 2 7–06
Sch.8, r.2(b) 7–54
Sch.8, r.2(e) 7–54, 13–18
Sch.8, r.2(o) 7–54
Sch.8, r.2(l) 7–04
Sch.8, r.2(m) 9–75
Sch.8, r.2(8)(b) 9–10
Sch.8, r.5 7–54
Sch.8, r.6 7–54
Sch.8, r.6(2) 9–10
Sch.10 .... 9–21, 9–37
Administration of Justice Act (c.53) 18–47
s.14(4) 11–38
ss.23–25 18–23
s.27 18–23
s.28 18–23
Sch.2 18–23
Sch.2, art.1 18–23
Sch.2, arts 2–5 18–23
1983 Divorce Jurisdiction, Court Fees and Legal Aid (Scotland) Act (c.12) 12–04
s.6(2) 11–03
International Transport Conventions Act (c.14) 1–06
1984 Law Reform (Husband and Wife) (Scotland) Act (c.15)
s.1 4–03
s.9(1) 11–03
Foreign Limitation Periods Act (c.16) 4–02, 8–06, 8–09
s.3 9–32
Child Abduction Act (c.37) 14–49
Pt I 14–49
Pt 2 14–49
s.6 .... 14–47, 14–49
s.8 14–49
Matrimonial and Family Proceedings Act (c.42) .. 1–02, 3–07, 12–11, 12–28, 13–24, 13–28
Pt 3 .... 2–04, 13–24
Pt 4 .... 2–04, 13–24
s.13 13–24
s.28 .... 13–24, 13–25
s.29 .... 13–24, 13–25
s.29A 13–24
s.30 13–24

1984	Prescription and Limitation (Scotland) Act (c.45)	8–09
	s.4	8–06, 8–09
	Inheritance Tax Act (c.51)	
	s.18(1)	18–25
	s.267	6–03.18–25
1985	Companies Act (c.6)	17–48
	Family Law (Scotland) Act (c.37)	13–16, 13–24, 13–25
	ss.1–7	13–19
	s.9	13–09
	s.14(2)(h)	13–09, 13–14
	s.16	13–09, 13–14
	s.17	13–09, 13–14
	s.24	13–01
	s.25	13–01
	Child Abduction and Custody Act (c.60)	1–02, 6–02, 14–23, 14–62
	Pt 1	14–27
	Pt 2	14–27
	s.4	14–28
	s.16(4)(c)	14–27
	Sch.1	14–27
	Sch.2	14–27
	Bankruptcy (Scotland) Act (c.66)	17–48, 17–50, 17–60
	s.2(2)(a)	17–51
	s.2(2)(b)	17–51
	s.3(b)	17–51
	s.9	17–50
	s.10	17–50
	s.16	17–50
	s.17	17–50
	s.24(d)	17–51
	s.29(6)	17–51
	s.29(9)(a)	17–51
	s.31	17–52
	s.31(8)	17–52
	ss.34–37	17–58
	s.36	17–53
	s.48	17–53
	s.49	17–53
	s.54	15–25
	s.55(1)	15–25
	Law Reform (Miscellaneous Provisions) (Scotland) Act (c.73)	
	s.19	7–56
1986	Law Reform (Parent and Child) (Scotland) Act (c.9)	6–04, 6–06, 14–01, 14–02
1986	Law Reform (Parent and Child) (Scotland) Act—*cont.*	
	s.1	14–01
	s.9(1)(a)	6–04, 6–06
	s.21	6–04
	s.22	6–04
	Sch.2	14–02
	Insolvency Act (c.45)	17–38, 17–48, 17–50, 17–60
	Pt 4	17–50
	s.72	17–49
	s.281(1)	15–25
	s.426	17–49
	s.426(1)	17–49
	s.426(2)	17–49
	s.426(3)	17–49
	s.426(4)	17–49
	s.426(5)	17–49
	Wages Act (c.48)	15–34
	Family Law Act (c.55)	1–02, 3–07, 10–04, 10–08, 12–16, 12–18, 12–20, 12–27, 12–30, 12–32, 14–23, 14–43, 14–44
	Pt I	14–25, 14–43
	Pt II	9–05, 9–94, 12–32, 12–39, 14–46
	Chap.III	14–43, 14–44
	Chap.V	14–45
	Chap.VI	14–46
	s.7	14–02
	ss.8–18	14–62
	s.9	14–44
	ss.9–12	14–50
	ss.9–14	14–43
	ss.9–18	14–16
	s.10	14–14, 14–44
	s.11	14–44
	s.12	14–14, 14–44
	s.13	14–44
	s.14	14–44
	s.15(2)	14–44
	s.16	14–51
	s.16(3)	14–51
	s.17	14–44, 14–47
	s.18(1)	14–44
	s.25(1)	14–45
	s.26	6–02, 14–45, 14–47
	s.27	14–44
	s.27(1)	14–45
	s.27(2)	14–45
	ss.27–29	14–43, 14–62
	s.28(1)	11–03
	s.29	14–45
	s.29(1)	14–45
	s.32	14–45

1986 Family Law Act—*cont.*
s.33 14–46
ss.33–37 14–47
s.34 14–46
s.35 14–46
s.37 14–46
s.41 14–46
s.41(1) 14–46
s.41(2) 14–46
s.41(2)(a) 14–46
s.44(1) 12–19, 12–29,
            12–30, 12–47
s.44(2) . . 12–16, 12–19, 12–47
ss.44–51 . . . . 12–18, 12–50
ss.44–54 12–39
s.45 12–23
s.45(2) 12–19, 12–39
s.46 . . . . . 6–03, 12–20, 12–21,
       12–22, 12–25, 12–29,
                 12–48
s.46(1)   12–20, 12–21, 12–27,
            12–39, 14–61
s.46(2)   12–20, 12–27, 12–28,
                 12–39
s.46(2)(b) 6–39
s.46(2)(b)(ii) 5–02
s.46(3)(b) 12–20
s.46(5) 4–02, 4–03, 6–04,
       12–20, 12–26, 12–48
s.47 . . . . 12–21, 12–22
s.47(2) 12–21, 12–31
s.48 9–02
s.50 . . . . . 4–06, 10–06, 11–17,
       11–18, 12–26, 12–48
s.51 . . . . 12–19, 12–23, 12–28,
                 12–48
s.51(1) 12–19
s.51(2) 12–19
s.51(3)(a) 12–28
s.51(3)(b) 12–28
s.51(3)(b)(ii) 5–02
s.51(3)(c) 12–25, 12–28
s.52 12–23
s.55 . . . . . 9–05, 11–12, 12–17
1987 Recognition of Trusts Act
(c.14) . . 1–02, 5–07, 13–04,
       15–04, 18–46, 18–47,
       18–52, 18–53, 18–56
s.1(1) 18–53
s.1(2) 18–53
Sch. 18–53
Sch, art.2 . . . . . . 18–47, 18–53
Sch, art.3 18–53
Sch, art.4 18–53
Sch, art.5 18–53
Sch, art.6 . . . . . . 18–52, 18–53
Sch, art.7 . . . . . . 18–52, 18–53

1987 Recognition of Trusts
Act—*cont.*
Sch, art.8 18–53
Sch, art.8(a)—(j) 18–53
Sch, art.8(d) 18–52
Sch, art.11 18–53
Sch, art.11(d) 18–53
Sch, art.14 18–52
Sch, art.15 18–52
Sch, art.15(d) 18–53
1988 Housing (Scotland) Act
(c.43)
s.31(4) 11–38
Foreign   Marriage
(Amendment)   Act
(c.44) 11–27
1989 Children Act (c.41) 11–32,
                 14–25
1990 Contracts   (Applicable
Law) Act (c.36) 1–02,
       3–07, 5–07, 15–02,
       15–03, 15–05, 15–18,
       15–34, 15–58, 17–06,
       17–20, 17–24, 17–60
s.2 1–10
s.2(3) 15–02
s.3(1) 15–03
s.3(2) 15–03
s.3(3)(a) 15–03
s.5 15–34
s.12 17–20
Sch.1 13–04
Sch.4, para.4 15–34
Law   Reform   (Mis-
cellaneous   Pro-
visions)   (Scotland)
Act (c.40)
s.66 9–77
Sch.7 9–77
1991 Civil   Jurisdiction   and
Judgments Act
(c.12) . . . 1–02, 1–08, 3–01,
       6–03, 6–40, 7–07,
                 17–38
s.20(5) 7–54, 9–06, 9–14
Foreign Corporations Act
(c.44) 1–01
Age of Legal Capacity
(Scotland) Act
(c.50) 3–07, 10–07,
            14–50, 15–20
s.1(3)(f) 14–50
s.2(2) 10–07, 18–16
s.7 6–04
Sch.2, para.46 14–51

1992 Social Security Contribu-
      tions and Benefits
      Act (c.4)
      s.37 11–08
      Timeshare Act (c.35) 3–07,
                                    15–13
      Maintenance   Orders
      (Reciprocal Enforce-
      ment) Act (c.56) . . . 13–21
1993 Damages (Scotland) Act
      (c.5) 16–26
      Criminal   Justice   Act
      (c.36)
      s.71 3–02
1994 Sale and Supply of Goods
      Act (c.35)
      Sch.2, para.3 15–39
1995 Merchant Shipping Act
      (c.21) 16–14
      Children (Scotland) Act
      (c.36) 14–23, 14–25.14–50,
                                    14–51
      Pt 3 14–52
      s.2(3) 14–46
      s.7 14–50
      s.8 14–50
      s.9 14–51
      s.10 14–51
      s.11 . . . . 14–29, 14–51
      s.11(2)(h) 14–50
      s.11(3)(a)(i) 14–50
      s.13 14–51
      s.14 . . . . . 6–02, 14–51, 14–62
      s.14(4) 14–51
      Law Reform (Succession)
      Act (c.41) 18–25
      s.1(2) 18–08
      s.(3) 18–09
      Private International Law
      (Miscellaneous Pro-
      visions) Act 1995
      (c.42) . . . 1–02, 2–02, 3–07,
              4–05, 16–12, 16–14,
              16–15, 16–16, 16–17,
              16–18, 16–19, 16–20,
              16–21, 16–24, 16–27,
                                    16–30
      Pt I 8–21, 15–54, 16–05
      Pt III 8–03, 16–36
      ss.5–7 . . . . 11–09, 11–11
      s.7 . . . . 11–11, 11–42
      s.9 . . . . 16–16, 16–19
      s.9(1) 16–16
      s.9(2) 15–01, 16–16
      s.9(4) 16–16
      s.9(5) 5–07, 16–27
      s.9(6) 16–23

1995 Private International Law
      (Miscellaneous Pro-
      visions)   Act
      1995—*cont.*
      s.10 . . . . 16–15, 16–22, 16–23,
                                    16–36
      s.11 . . . . 16–14, 16–15, 16–17,
              16–19, 16–20, 16–36,
                                    18–24
      s.11(1) 16–17
      s.11(2) 16–18
      s.11(2)(c) 16–18, 16–20
      s.12 . . . . . 4–03, 16–14, 16–15,
              16–19, 16–20, 16–23,
                                16–36, 18–24
      s.12(2) 16–19
      s.13 . . . . 16–15, 16–21, 16–29,
                                    16–36
      s.14 . . . . . . 4–03, 8–20, 16–15,
                            16–19, 16–22
      s.14(2) . . 16–14, 16–23, 16–28
      s.14(3)(b) 8–12, 16–28
      s.14(4) 16–14
      s.92 4–02
1996 Arbitration Act (c.23) . . . 9–77,
                                    9–94
      Pt I 9–77
      Pt II 9–77
      s.2 7–58
      s.85 9–76
      ss.99–104 9–77
      Sch.4 9–77
      Sexual Offences (Conspir-
      acy and Incitement)
      Act (c.29) 1–02
1997 British Nationality (Hong
      Kong) Act (c.20) 6–38
      Contract (Scotland) Act
      (c.34) 8–12
      Sex Offenders Act (c.51) . . 1–02
1998 Scotland Act (c.46) 2–04
      Pt IV (ss.73–79) 3–02
      s.29 2–04
      s.29(2)(b) 2–04
      s.29(3) 2–04
      s.29(4)(b) 2–04
      s.30 2–04
      s.57 2–04
      s.73 3–02
      s.73(1)(b) 3–02
      s.75 3–02
      s.126(4)(a) 2–04
      Sch.5 2–04
      Sch.5, Pt 1, para.7 2–04
      Human Rights Act (c.42)
      s.4 11–12

1999 Adoption (Intercountry
        Aspects) Act (c.18) .. 6–02,
            14–52, 14–54, 14–61,
                        14–62
    s.14 14–55
    Contracts (Rights of
        Third Parties) Act
        (c.31)
2000 Electronic Communica-
        tions Act (c.7) 15–44,
                15–45, 15–58
    Pt I 15–44
    Pt II 15–44
    Pt III 15–44
    s.7 15–44
    Adults with Incapacity
        (Scotland) Act (asp
        4) 6–24, 10–05
    s.80 6–24
    Sch.3, para.3 10–05
    Sch.4, para.1 6–24
2001 Mortgage Rights
        (Scotland) Act (asp
        11) 11–38
2002 British Overseas Territo-
        ries Act (c.8) 6–38
    Divorce (Religious Mar-
        riages) Act (c.27)
    s.1 12–28
    Adoption and Children
        Act (c.38) 14–62
    s.41 15–52
    s.48 14–52
    s.83(7) 14–52
    s.87 14–60
    s.105–14 53
    Enterprise Act (c.40) ... 17–48,
                        17–60
    Nationality, Immigration
        and Asylum Act
        (c.41) 6–38
    Marriage (Scotland) Act
        (asp 8) 11–09, 11–24
    Debt Arrangement and
        Attachment
        (Scotland) Act (asp
        17) 8–23
    App.2 7–58
2003 Electronic Communica-
        tions Act (c.7) 15–44
2004 Gender Recognition Act
        (c.7) 11–01
    Asylum and Immigration
        (Treatment of Claim-
        ants, etc.) Act (c.19)
    ss.19–25 12–38
    s.21 12–38
    s.22 12–38

2004 Civil Partnership Act
        (c.33) .. 1–02, 2–04, 11–01,
            11–12, 11–35, 11–37,
            11–38, 11–46, 12–48,
                        13–25
    Pt 1 11–36
    Pt 2 11–36
    Pt 2, Chap.3 13–16
    Pt 3 ... 11–36, 11–37, 12–40,
                        12–41
    Pt 3, Chap.3 13–16
    Pt 4 11–36
    Pt 5 ... 11–36, 11–42, 12–25,
            12–40, 12–41, 12–42,
                        12–48
    Chap.2 .... 12–43, 12–46
    Chap.3 12–44
    s.50 12–46
    ss.50–51 12–46
    s.71 18–09
    s.86 .... 11–37, 12–43, 12–46
    s.86(1) 11–37
    s.117 .... 12–41, 12–50
    ss.117–122 12–40
    s.121 12–46
    s.123 ... 11–37, 12–40, 12–46
    s.124 ... 12–40, 12–46, 12–50
    s.124(7) 12–46
    s.124(8) 12–46
    s.124(10) 5–07, 12–46, 12–48
    s.125 .... 13–25, 13–28
    s.128 11–17
    s.131 11–12
    s.174 12–46
    s.210 11–27
    s.211 11–27
    s.212 12–43
    s.212(2) 12–42
    s.213 12–42
    s.214 12–42
    s.215 .... 11–12, 12–43
    s.216(1) 11–37, 12–43
    s.217 12–43
    s.217(2) 12–43
    s.217(5) 12–43
    s.218 12–43
    s.219 ... 12–44, 12–45, 12–48,
                        12–50
    s.225 12–44
    s.225(1)(c) 12–41
    s.225(3) 12–44
    ss.225–227 .... 12–41, 12–46,
                        12–50
    s.226 .... 12–45, 12–50
    s.233 .... 12–47, 12–50
    s.234 12–48
    s.234(1) 12–50

2004 Civil   Partnership
        Act—*cont.*
      s.234(2) 12–48, 12–50
      s.235 12–48
      s.236 12–48
      s.236(3)(c) 12–48
      s.237 12–48
      s.237(2) 12–48
      s.237(2)(b)(i) 12–48
      s.238 12–48
      s.161 13–25
      s.261(2) 13–16
      Sch.4 18–09
      Sch.10 11–37
      Sch.11 13–25
      Sch.11, Pt 3 13–25
      Sch.20 11–12
      Sch.28 13–16
      Sch.28, Pt 2 13–25
2005 International   Organisa-
        tions Act (c.20) 7–03
2006 Family Law (Scotland)
        Act 2006 (asp 2) 1–02,
                3–07, 5–07, 6–03,
                6–04, 6–05, 6–06,
                6–07, 6–22, 6–26,
                6–27, 6–34, 6–40,
             11–21, 11–38, 11–40,
             11–42, 12–17, 12–38,
             13–10, 13–13, 13–14,
             13–16, 13–19, 13–27,
                              14–01
      s.2 ..... 11–18, 11–31, 11–42,
                       12–38, 12–50
      s.3 11–24
      s.3(2) 11–24
      s.3(3) 11–24
      s.3(4) 11–24
      s.4 12–32
      s.15 12–28
      s.21 14–01
      s.21(2)(a) 14–01

2006 Family Law (Scotland)
        Act 2006—*cont.*
      s.22 .. 6–03, 6–04, 6–05, 6–06,
             6–07, 6–27, 6–36, 6–40m
                              14–01
      s.22(1) 6–06, 6–27
      s.22(3) 6–04, 6–27
      s.22(4) 6–04, 6–07, 6–40
      s.25 .... 11–38, 13–13, 13–14
      s.25(1) .. 11–39, 11–40, 13–13
      s.25(2) 11–40, 13–13
      ss.25–30 ...... 11–38, 11–41,
                   12–49, 13–12, 13–13
      s.26 .... 11–38, 13–13
      ss.26–30 11–40
      s.27 .... 11–38, 13–13
      s.28 .... 11–38, 11–41, 12–49,
                              13–13
      s.29 .... 11–38, 11–41, 13–13
      s.29(1)(b)(i) 13–13
      s.33 11–37
      s.37 .... 9–05, 12–17
      s.37(3) 9–05
      s.38 ...... 2–04, 5–07, 11–17,
                              11–18
      s.38(1) .. 11–24, 11–29, 11–42
      s.38(2) 11–16, 11–42
      s.38(2)(a) 11–16, 11–31
      s.38(3) 11–16, 11–18
      s.38(4) .. 11–16, 11–21, 11–42
      s.38(5) 11–34, 11–42
      s.39 .... 13–01, 13–11, 13–26
      s.39(1) 13–11
      s.39(2) 13–11
      s.39(3) 13–11
      s.39(4) 13–11
      s.39(5) 13–11
      s.39(6)(b) 13–01, 13–14
      s.40 13–19
      s.41 .... 14–01, 18–27
      Sch.3 6–04

BILLS

2005 Children and Adoption
      Bill 2005
      cll.9–12   14–59
2006 Adoption and Children
      (Scotland) Bill   14–52
      Chap.6   14–52
      cl.73   14–60

TABLE OF STATUTORY INSTRUMENTS

1946 Bretton Woods Agree-
ments Order in
Council (SR & O
1946/36) 15–26
1975 Social Security and Family Allowances
(Polygamous Mar-
riage) Regulations
(SI 1975/561) 11–08
1985 Carriage of Goods by Sea
(Parties to Conven-
tion) Order (SI
1985/443) 15–33
1986 Co—operation of Insolvency Courts (Desig-
nation of Relevant
Countries and Ter-
ritories) Order (SI
1986/2123) 17–49
1987 Reciprocal Enforcement
of Foreign Judg-
ments (Canada)
Order
(SI 1987/468) 7–05
1988 Small Claims (Scotland)
Order 1988 (SI
1988/1999) 9–87
1993 Reciprocal Enforcement
of Maintenance
Orders (Hague Con-
vention Countries)
Order
(SI 1993/593) 13–21
Civil Jurisdiction and
Judgments (Authen-
tic Instruments and
Court Settlements)
Order
(SI 1993/604) 13–22
Adoption (Designation of
Overseas Adoptions)
(Variation) Order
1993
(SI 1993/690) 14–60
Act of Sederunt (Sheriff
Court Ordinary
Cause Rules) (SI
1993/1956)
r.5.5 8–11
Commercial Agents
(Council Directive)
Regulations (SI
1993/3053) 15–42
reg.2 15–42

1993 Commercial Agents
(Council Directive)
Regulations—cont.
reg.2(1) 15–42
Commercial Agents
(Council Directive)
(Amendment) Regu-
lations (SI
1993/3173) 15–42
1994 EC Commercial Agents
Regulations (SI
1994/33) 15–42
Act of Sederunt (Rules of
the Court of Session)
(SI 1994/1443) .. 9–77, 9–84
r.16.2 8–11
r.62.37 6–62
r.62. 38–9–69
r.62.41 9–62
r.62.42 9–69
r.62.82 9–84
r.62.83 9–84
r.62.84 9–84
r.62.88 9–84
Reciprocal Enforcement
of Foreign Judg-
ments (Australia)
Order 1994 (SI
1994/1901) 7–05
1995 Reciprocal Enforcement
of Foreign Judg-
ments (Canada)
(Amendment) Order
1995
(SI 1995/2708) 7–05
Act of Sederunt
(Reciprocal Enforce-
ment of Maintenance
Orders) (United
States of America)
(SI 1995/3345) 13–21
1997 Civil Jurisdiction and
Judgments Act 1982
(Gibraltar) Order (SI
1997/2602) 9–16
Civil Jurisdiction and
Judgments Act 1982
(Provisional and Pro-
tective Measures)
(Scotland) Order (SI
1997/2780) 7–56, 7.57
1998 Civil Procedure Rules (SI
1998/3132) 7–55
r.6.20 .... 7–55, 9–10

2000 Consumer Protection (Distance Selling) Regulations (SI 2000/2334) .. 15–46, 15–47, 15–58

    reg.3(1) 15–47

    reg.12(2) 15–47

    reg.25(1) 15–47

    reg.25(5) 15–47

    Civil Jurisdiction and Judgments (Authentic Instruments and Court Settlements) Order

    (SI 2001/3928) 13–22

    Civil Jurisdiction and Judgments Order (SI 2001/3929) 1–08, 7–08, 7–54, 9–06, 9–14, 9–94, 13–18, 17–38

    art.7 9–76

    art.9 .... 6–03, 7–53

    Sch.1, para.9 7–10

    Sch.1, para.10 .... 7–10, 7–27

    Sch.1, r.4 9–59

    Sch.2 7–53

    Sch.2, para.1(c) 9–60

    European Communities (Matrimonial Jurisdiction and Judgments) (Scotland) Regulations (SSI 2001/36) 12–05, 12–06, 12–08

    reg.2(5)(d) 12–08

    Act of Sederunt (Ordinary Cause Rules) Amendment (European Matrimonial and Parental Responsibility Jurisdiction and Judgments) (SSI 2001/144) 12–05

    Adoption of Children from Overseas (Scotland) Regulations (SSI 2001/236) 14–52

2002 Electronic Commerce (EC Directive) Regulations (SI 2002/2013) .. 15–46, 15–58

    reg.4 15–46

2003 British Nationality (British Overseas Territories)(Amendment) Regulations (SI 2003/539) 6–38

2003 British Nationality (General) Regulations (SI 2003/548) 6–38

    Insolvency (Scotland) Regulations (SI 2003/2109) 17–48

    Insolvency (Scotland) Amendment Rules (SI 2003/2111) 17–48

    Intercountry Adoption (Hague Convention) (Scotland) Regulations (SSI 2003/19) 14–52

    Foreign Adoptions (Scotland) Regulations (SSI 2003/67) 14–52

2004 Contracts (Applicable Law) Act 1990 (Commencement No.2) Order (SI 2004/3448) ... 1–10, 15–02, 15–03

    Act of Sederunt (Ordinary Cause, Summary Application, Summary Cause, and Small Claim Rules) Amendment (Miscellaneous) (SSI 2004/197)

    r.2(4) 8–11

2005 Prior Rights of Surviving Spouse (Scotland) Order (SI 2005/252) 18–13

    European Communities (Jurisdiction and Judgments in Matrimonial and Parental Responsibility Matters) Regulations (SI 2005/265) 2–04

    Civil Partnership Act 2004 (Consequential Amendments) (Scotland) Order (SI 2005/623) 11–36

    Civil Partnership Act 2004 (Overseas Relationships) Order (SI 2005/3135) .. 11–12, 12–42

2005   Civil Partnership (Jurisdiction and Recognition of Judgments) Regulations (SI 2005/3334) .. 12–44, 12–48
        European Communities (Matrimonial and Parental Responsibility Jurisdiction and Judgments) (Scotland) Regulations (SSI 2005/42) .. 2–04, 2–05, 12–06, 14–23, 14–43
        reg.4 14–44
        reg.5 14–51
        Act of Sederunt (Ordinary Cause Rules) Amendment (European Matrimonial and Parental Responsibility Jurisdiction and Judgments) (SSI 2005/135) 12–05

2005   Act of Sederunt (Sheriff Court European Enforcement) Order Rules (SSI 2005/523)
        Act of Sederunt (Rules of the Court of Session Amendment No.8) (Miscellaneous) (SSI 2005/521) 9–84
2006   Family Law (Scotland) Act 2006 (Commencement, Transitional Provisions and Savings) Order (SI 2006/212) 6–06, 13–13
        art.4 6–06
        Divorce (Religious Bodies)(Scotland) Regulations (SI 2006/253) 12–28
        Cross—Border Insolvency Regulations (SI 2006/1030) 17–54
        reg.7 17–49

TABLE OF INTERNATIONAL CONVENTIONS

1886	Berne Convention for the Protection of Literary and Artistic Work	1–02
1923	Geneva Protocol	9–77
1924	Hague—Visby Rules on Carriage of Goods by Sea	1–06
1927	Geneva Convention	9–77
1929	Warsaw Convention for the Unification of Certain Rules relating to International Carriage by Air (as amended at The Hague, 1955)	1–06
1950	European Convention on Human Rights	
	Art.8	11–01
	Art.12	11–01, 12–38
	Art.14	12–38
	Art.24	14–08
1955	Hague Convention on the Law Applicable to International Sales of Goods	15–39
1956	Geneva Convention on the Contract for the International Carriage of Goods by Road	1–06
1956	New York (UN) Convention on the Recovery Abroad of Maintenance	13–21, 13–22, 13–23, 13–28
1957	Treaty of Rome	8–21
	Title IIIa	1–07, 12–05
	Art.12	7–03
	Art.65	13–23
	Art.67.2	13–23
	Art.67.5	13–23
	Art.251	13–23
1958	Hague Convention on the Jurisdiction of Selected Forum in the case of International Sales of Goods	15–39
	Hague Convention on the Law governing Transfer of Title in International Sales of Goods	15–39
1958	New York Convention on the Recognition and Enforcement of Foreign Arbitral Awards	9–77, 9–94
1961	Guadalajara Convention	1–06
	Hague Convention concerning the Powers of Authorities and the Law Applicable in respect of the Protection of Minors	14–06
	Hague Convention on the Conflict of Laws relating to the Form of Testamentary Disposition	1–09, 18–05, 18–19
1964	Hague Uniform Law on the Formation of Contracts for the International Sale of Goods	15–39
	Hague Uniform Law on the International Sale of Goods	15–39
1965	Hague Convention on Jurisdiction, Applicable Law and Recognition of Decrees relating to Adoptions	14–52
	Hague Convention on the Service Abroad of Judicial and Extrajudicial Documents in Civil and Commercial Matters	8–10, 8–11
	Art.15	7–37, 9–49
1968	Brussels Convention on Jurisdiction and the Enforcement of Judgments in Civil and Commercial Matters	1–08, 3–02, 7–02, 7–04, 7–05, 7–06, 7–07, 7–10, 7–11, 7–18, 7–23, 7–45, 7–46, 7–48, 7–51, 7–53, 9–06, 9–36, 9–37, 9–60, 9–77, 9–83, 10–02, 12–05, 17–32, 17–38, 18–47

1968 Brussels Convention on
Jurisdiction and the
Enforcement of
Judgments in Civil
and Commercial
Matters—*cont.*
Title 1 10–02
Art.1 ..... 3–02, 7–51, 10–02
Art.1.1 13–18
Art.2 ...... 7–43, 7–48, 7–51
Art.3 .... 7–02, 7–05
Art.5.1 .... 7–43, 7–48, 7–51,
15–01, 15–02, 15–16
Art.5.5 7–48
Art.17 7–43
Art.21 .... 7–38, 7–43
Art.24 7–57
Art.25 9–37
Art.26 9–38
Art.27 .... 9–40, 9–49
Art.27.1 9–76
Art.27.2 8–10
Art.27.4 9–40
Art.28 .... 9–41, 9–49
Art.29 9–42
Art.30 .... 9–43, 9–51
Art.31 9–44
Art.32 9–45
Art.33 9–46
Art.34 .... 9–47, 9–49
Art.35 9–48
Art.36 9–48
Art.37 .... 9–48, 9–50
Art.37(1) 9–49
Art.38 .... 9–51, 9–52
Art.39 9–53
Art.40 9–48
Art.42 9–54
Art.43 9–55
Art.44 9–56
Art.45 .... 7–03, 9–57
Art.46–49 9–46
Art.50 9–37
Art.51 9–37
Art.52(2) 6–03
Art.54 7–06
Art.59 ..... 7–05, 7–52, 9–37
1970 Hague Convention on the
Recognition of
Divorces and Legal
Separations 1–09
Hague Convention on the
Taking of Evidence
Abroad in Civil or
Commercial
Matters .. 1–09, 8–15, 8–16

1971 Hague Convention on the
Law Applicable to
Traffic
Accidents 16–15
Protocol on Interpreta-
tion of the Brussels
Convention ... 7–06, 15–02
1972 UNIDROIT Convention
on the Establishment
of a Scheme of
Registration of
Wills 18–23
European Convention on
State Immunity 3–05
1973 Hague Convention con-
cerning the Inter-
national
Administration of
the Estates of
Deceased Persons .. 18–02
Hague Convention on the
Law Applicable to
Products Liability ... 16–15
Hague Convention on the
Recognition and
Enforcement of
Decisions relating to
Maintenance
Obligations 13–21,
13–22, 13–23
Washington Convention
on International
Wills
Annex 18–23
1974 Athens Convention relat-
ing to the Carriage of
Passengers and their
Luggage by
Sea 1–06
1976 Hague Marriage Conven-
tion 11–01
1978 Hague Convention on the
Law Applicable to
Matrimonial Prop-
erty Regimes 13–01
UK Danish and Irish
Accession Conven-
tion [1978] O.J.
L304/1 .... 1–08, 7–06
UN Convention on the
Carriage of Goods by
Sea (Hamburg
Rules) 1–06
1980 Berne Convention con-
cerning International
Carriage by Rail 1–06

1980 Council of Europe Convention on the Recognition and Enforcement of Decisions concerning Custody of Children 14–06, 14–27, 14–33, 14–34, 14–62
Art.10(c) 14–33
Art.11 14–21
Hague Convention on the Civil Aspects of International Child Abduction ... 1–09, 1–10, 2–04, 3–01, 5–07, 6–39, 14–06, 14–21, 14–23, 14–24, 14–27, 14–28, 14–33, 14–34, 14–35, 14–36, 14–46, 14–48, 14–55, 14–62
Art.3 ... 14–27, 14–29, 14–30
Art.7 14–32
Art.9 14–27
Art.12 .. 14–30, 14–34, 14–37
Art.13 .. 14–31, 14–34, 14–35, 14–37, 14–41, 14–48
Art.13.b 14–39
Art.19 14–27
Art.21 14–21
Art.26 14–32
Art.60 14–27
Rome Convention on the Law Applicable to Contractual Obligations 1–08, 1–10, 7–13, 7–20, 13–04, 13–26, 15–02, 15–03, 15–13, 15–15, 15–17, 15–21, 15–42, 15–48, 15–49, 15–58, 16–24, 16–29, 16–30, 16–31, 16–33, 17–16, 17–29, 17–30, 17–46
Art.1 .... 1–10, 15–02, 15–04
Art.1.2 15–04
Art.1.2.b 13–04
Art.1.2.c 17–29
Art.1.2.f 15–41
Art.1.2.h 8–18, 15–27
Art.1.3 15–04
Art.1.4 15–04
Art.2 15–02
Art.3 ... 15–13, 15–14, 15–36, 15–38, 15–41, 15–42, 15–49, 16–29, 17–25, 17–26
Art.3.1 .... 15–07, 15–48

1980 Rome Convention on the Law Applicable to Contractual Obligations—*cont.*
Art.3.2 .... 6–39, 15–08
Art.3.3 15–13, 15–17, 15–26, 15–42, 15–48, 15–49, 16–29
Arts 3–6 15–22
Art.4 ... 15–14, 15–36, 15–38, 15–41, 15–48, 15–49, 17–25, 17–26
Art.4.2 .... 15–15, 15–16, 15–31, 15–33, 15–49, 16–20, 17–29
Art.4.3 15–16, 15–31, 17–06, 17–60
Art.4.4 .... 15–16, 15–33
Art.4.5 .... 15–14, 15–16, 15–31, 15–33, 15–48, 15–49, 16–20
Art.5 ... 15–21, 15–35, 15–36, 15–48
Art.5.2 .. 6–39, 15–21, 15–35, 15–48
Art.5.3 15–48
Art.5.4.a 15–33
Art.5.5 15–33
Art.6 15–38
Art.7 .... 15–17, 15–36
Art.7.1 .... 15–02, 15–13, 15–17, 15–26, 15–42, 15–49
Art.7.2 .... 15–13, 15–17, 15–23, 15–26, 15–42, 15–49, 15–53, 15–58
Art.8 ... 15–13, 15–18, 15–19, 15–26, 15–48, 15–58
Art.8.1 15–19
Art.8.2 .... 6–39, 15–19
Art.8.21 15–58
Art.9 ..... 4–05, 8–12, 15–13, 15–18, 15–21, 15–26, 15–58, 17–24
Art.9.1 .... 2–03, 15–48
Art.9.2 15–48
Art.9.6 .. 17–06, 17–07, 17–60
Art.10 .. 15–02.15–22, 15–23, 15–58
Art.10.1.a 15–24, 15–58
Art.10.1.c 8–20, 8–24, 15–58
Art.10.1d 8–06, 8–24, 15–25, 15–58
Art.10.1.e 15–02, 15–22
Art.11 .. 10–07, 15–02, 15–04, 15–13, 15–18, 15–20. 15–58, 17–05, 17–23

1980 Rome Convention on the
        Law Applicable to
        Contractual
        Obligations—*cont.*
        Art.12 .. 15–22, 15–49, 17–21,
                                    17–60
        Art.12.1 .... 17–25, 17–26
        Art.12.2 ...... 15–49, 17–22,
                            17–25, 17–27
        Art.14 .... 15–04, 15–27
        Art.14.1 .... 8–18, 8–19
        Art.14.2 8–12
        Art.15 ... 5–07, 15–28, 15–49
        Art.15.1 15–49
        Art.16 .. 15–13, 15–19, 15–23,
                    15–26, 15–29, 15–58
        Art.17 15–02
        Art.18 15–02
        Art.19.2 15–02
        Art.21 .... 15–33, 15–39
      UN Convention on Con-
        tracts for the Inter-
        national   Sale   of
        Goods (Vienna Con-
        vention) 15–39, 15–49
1982 Greek Accession Conven-
        tion   [1982]   O.J.
        L388/1 .... 1–08, 7–06
1985 UNCITRAL Model Law
        on   International
        Commercial Arbitra-
        tion 9–77
1986 Hague Convention on the
        Law Applicable to
        Trusts and on their
        Recognition ... 1–09, 5–07,
                    13–04, 18–53
        Art.2 18–53
        Art.3 18–53
        Art.17 5–07
1988 Lugano Convention on
        Jurisdiction and the
        Enforcement   of
        Judgments in Civil
        and   Commercial
        Matters 1–08, 7–07,
                    7–08, 7–17, 7–41,
                    7–46, 7–54, 9–06,
                    9–21, 9–76, 9–77,
                                    9–94
        Art.1.4 9–76
        Art.3.2 9–60
        Art.4 9–76
        Art.5.1 15–02
        Art.16.1.b 7–27

1988 Lugano Convention on
        Jurisdiction and the
        Enforcement   of
        Judgments in Civil
        and   Commercial
        Matters—*cont.*
        Art.25 9–37
        Art.26 9–39
        Art.27 9–40
        Art.27.4 9–40
        Art.28 9–41
        Art.29 9–42
        Art.30 .... 9–43, 9–51
        Art.31 9–44
        Art.32 9–60
        Art.33 9–46
        Art.34 9–47
        Art.35 9–48
        Art.36 9–48
        Art.37 ..... 9–48, 9–50, 9–60
        Art.38 9–52
        Art.39 9–53
        Art.40 .... 9–48, 9–60
        Art.42 9–54
        Art.43 9–55
        Art.44 9–56
        Art.45 9–57
        Arts 46–49 9–46
        Art.50 9–37
        Art.51 9–37
        Art.54B 9–60
        Art.54B.2(c) 9–60
        Art.54B.3 9–60
        Art.57(4) 9–60
        Art.59 9–60
        Protocol, para.1(1)(b) .. 9–60
        Luxembourg Protocol .. 9–60
1989 Hague Convention on the
        Law Applicable to
        the   Estates   of
        Deceased Persons .. 18–04,
                        18–05, 18–56
      Spanish and Portuguese
        Accession   Conven-
        tion (San Sebastian
        Convention)[1989]
        O.J. L285/1 ... 1–08, 7–06,
                                    7–54
1990 Istanbul Convention of
        Certain International
        Aspects of Bank-
        ruptcy 17–39
1992 Maastricht Treaty 7–08
        Title IV 7–08

1993 Hague Convention on Protection of Children and Co—operation in Respect of Intercountry Adoption .. 14–52, 14–54, 14–55, 14–56, 14–59, 14–60, 14–61, 14–62

1993 Hague Convention on Protection of Children and Co—operation in Respect of Intercountry Adoption—*cont.*
Chap.VI 14–59
Art.2(1) 14–56
Art.2(2) 14–56
Art.3 14–56
Art.4 . . . . 14–57, 14–58
Art.5 . . . . 14–57, 14–58
Arts 6–13 14–55
Art.14 14–58
Art.17 14–58
Art.21 14–58
Art.23 14–58
Art.24 14–58
Art.26(1) 14–58
Art.26(2) 14–58
Art.26(3) 14–58
Art.27(1) 14–58
Art.28 14–59
Art.32 14–59

1996 Austrian, Finnish and Swedish Accession Convention [1997] O.J. C15/1 7–06
Geneva Copyright Treaty 1–02
Hague Convention on Jurisdiction, Applicable Law, Recognition, Enforcement and Cooperation in respect of Parental Responsibility Measures for the Protection of Children 1–09, 3–01, 6–02, 14–06, 14–09, 14–24
Art.5 14–24
Arts 5–14 14–62
Arts 7–14 14–24
Arts 15–22 . . . . 14–24, 14–62
Arts 23–28 14–62

1997 Treaty of Amsterdam . . 12–15
Arts 61–67 1–07
Art.65 1–07

1999 Montreal Convention for the Unification of Certain Rules relating to International Carriage by Air 1–06

2000 Hague Convention on International Protection of Adults 2–04

2001 UNIDROIT Convention on International Interests in Mobile Equipment and Aircraft Equipment Protocol 17–10

2002 Hague Convention on the Law Applicable to Certain Rights in Respect of Securities Held with an Intermediary 1–09, 17–31
Art.4 17–31
Art.5 17–31
Art.6 17–31

2004 [Draft] Treaty establishing a Constitution for Europe 1–07
Art.III—269 1–07

2005 Hague Convention on Choice of Court Agreements . . . 1–09, 7–31, 7–33, 7–34, 7–59, 9–76
Art.1 9–88
Art.1.2.d 9–76
Art.2 7–31
Art.3 7–31
Art.3.d 7–31
Art.3.1 9–76
Art.4.5 9–76
Art.5 . . . . 7–31, 7–32
Art.5.1 7–34
Art.5.3 7–32
Art.6 . . . . 7–31, 7–33
Art.6(a) 7–34
Art.6(b) 7–34
Art.7 7–33
Art.8 7–34
Art.9(a) 7–34
Art.9(b) 7–33, 7–34
Art.19 7–34
Art.20 7–34
Art.26 7–34
Art.26.1 7–34
Art.26.2 7–34
Art.26.3 7–34
Art.29 7–34
Art.31 7–31

TABLE OF EU INSTRUMENTS

REGULATIONS

1346/2000 Regulation on Insolvency Proceedings 15–25,
    17–39, 17–42, 17–48,
    17–55, 17–60
    Recital 13 ..... 15–25, 17–40
    Recital 14 ..... 15–25, 17–40
    Recital 15 17–51
    Recital 19 17–42
    Recital 23 ..... 15–25, 17–45
    Recital 25 ... —15–26, 17–46
    Recital 28 17–46
    Art.1 17–39
    Art.2(h) 17–42
    Art.3 ... 15–25, 17–40, 17–47
    Art.3.1 .... 17–40, 17–43
    Art.4 17–45
    Art.4.2 .... 15–25, 17–45
    Arts 5–15 17–46
    Art.7 17–46
    Art.8 .... 15–25, 17–46
    Art.10 17–46
    Arts 16–26 17–47
    Art.25 17–47
    Art.26 17–47
    Art.28 17–45
    Art.31 17–44
    Art.32 17–44
    Art.33 17–44
    Art.35 17–44
    Art.39 .... 3–02, 17–47
    Art.40 17–47
    Annex A 17–39
1347/2000 Regulation on Jurisdiction and the Recognition and Enforcement of Judgments in Matrimonial Matters and in Matters of Parental Responsibility for Children of Both Spouses [2000] O.J. L160/9 (Brussels II) 1–08, 10–02,
    12–05, 12–06, 12–13, 12–14,
    12–30, 12–39, 14–06, 14–07,
    14–08, 14–23, 14–33
    Art.1.2 12–30
    Art.2 .... 12–13, 12–30
    Art.2.1.a 12–35
    Art.11 12–12
    Art.37 1–10

1348/2000 Regulation on the Service in the Member States of Judicial and Extrajudicial Documents in Civil or Commercial Matters [2000] O.J. L160/37 ..... 1–08, 7–37, 8–10,
    8–25, 9–49, 9–84, 9–86, 9–86
    Art.19 9–49
44/2001 Regulation on Jurisdiction and the Recognition and Enforcement of Judgments in Civil and Commercial Matters (Brussels I) [2001] O.J. L12/1 .. 1–08, 1–10, 3–02, 4–01,
    7–02, 7–03, 7–04, 7–08, 7–13,
    7–18, 7–34, 7–35, 7–42, 7–44,
    7–48, 7–49, 7–51, 7–52, 7–53,
    7–54, 7–59, 8–10, 9–06, 9–08,
    9–14, 9–37, 9–38, 9–39, 9–49,
    9–59, 9–76, 9–77, 9–79, 9–83,
    9–86, 9–91, 9–94, 12–05,
    13–18, 13–22, 13–23, 13–28,
    14–08, 14–51, 15–02, 15–46,
    15–48, 17–38
    Chap.II, Sect.3 .. 7–02, 7–18,
    7–19, 9–02, 9–41, 9–82,
    9–90
    Chap.II, Sect.4 .. 7–02, 7–18,
    9–02, 9–41, 9–82
    Chap.II, Sect.5 .. 7–02, 7–23,
    9–82
    Chap.II, Sect.6 .. 7–18, 9–02,
    9–41, 9–82, 9–90
    Chap.III (Arts 32–56) .. 9–37
    Chap.IV (Arts 57, 58) .. 9–37
    Rectial 11 7–10
    Art.1 3–02, 7–09, 7–52, 9–37
    Art.1.1 9–38
    Art.1.2 .... 8–10, 9–38
    Art.1.2.a 13–18
    Art.1.2.b 17–38
    Art.1.2.d 9–76
    Art.2 ...... 7–10, 7–15, 7–59,
    13–18, 13–28
    Art.3 7–11
    Art.4 ...... 7–11, 7–20, 7–52,
    15–48
    Art.4.2 8–10
    Art.4.3 8–10

44/2001 Regulation on Juris-
diction and the Recogni-
tion and Enforcement of
Judgments in Civil and
Commercial
Matters—*cont.*
　Arts 4–11 . . . .　8–10
　Art.5　7–02, 7–12, 7–49, 7–59
　Art.5.1 . . . .　7–13, 7–53, 8–10,
　　　　　　　　　　　　15–49
　Art.5.1.a . . . .　7–13
　Art.5.1.b . . . .　7–08, 7–13
　Art.5.1.c . . . .　7–13
　Art.5.2 . . .　7–09, 9–38, 13–18,
　　　　　　13–23, 13–28, 15–04
　Art.5.3 . . . .　7–13, 7–14, 16–18
　Art.5.5 . . . .　7–20, 15–48
　Art.6 . . . .　7–17
　Art.6.1 . . . .　8–10
　Art.7.1 . . . .　8–10
　Art.8 . . . .　8–10
　Arts 8–14 . . . .　7–19
　Art.9 . . . .　7–19
　Art.9.1 . . . .　8–10
　Art.9.2 . . . .　8–10
　Arts 9–21 . . . .　7–59
　Art.10 . . . .　7–19
　Art.11 . . . .　7–19
　Art.12 . . . . .　7–08, 7–19, 8–10
　Art.12.1 . . . .　7–19
　Art.12.2 . . . .　7–19
　Art.13 . . . . .　7–19, 7–19, 7–29,
　　　　　　　　　　　7–49, 8–10
　Art.14 . . . .　7–19, 8–10
　Art.15 . . . .　7–20, 8–10, 15–48,
　　　　　　　　　　　　15–49
　Arts 15–17 . . . .　7–20
　Art.16 . . . .　7–21, 8–10
　Art.17 . . . . .　7–22, 7–29, 7–30,
　　　　　　　　　　　　　7–49
　Art.18.2 . . . .　7–23
　Arts 18–21 . . . .　7–23
　Art.19 . . . .　7–24
　Art.19.1 . . . .　8–10
　Art.19.2 . . . .　8–10
　Art.19.4 . . . .　8–10
　Art.20 . . . .　7–25
　Art.21 . . . . .　7–26, 7–29, 7–49
　Art.21(2) . . . .　9–85
　Art.22 . . . . .　7–02, 7–11, 7–27,
　　　　　　7–29, 7–30, 7–35, 7–36,
　　　　　　　7–49, 7–52, 7–59
　Art.22.1 . . . .　7–27
　Art.22.2 . . . .　7–10, 17–38
　Art.23 . . . . .　7–02, 7–11, 7–28,
　　　　　　7–30, 7–43, 7–49, 7–53,
　　　　　　　　　　　　　7–59

44/2001 Regulation on Juris-
diction and the Recogni-
tion and Enforcement of
Judgments in Civil and
Commercial
Matters—*cont.*
　Art.23.3 . . . .　7–28, 7–29
　Arts 23–27 . . . . . .　7–49, 7–59
　Art.24 . . . . .　7–02, 7–18, 7–30,
　　　　　　7–35, 7–49, 7–59, 9–10
　Art.25 . . . . .　7–36, 7–38, 9–37
　Arts 25–30 . . . .　7–59
　Art.26 . . . .　7–37
　Art.26(2)—(4) . . . .　9–49
　Art.26.3 . . . .　7–37
　Art.26.4 . . . .　7–37
　Art.27 . . . . .　7–28, 7–38, 7–43
　Arts 27–30 . . . .　7–46
　Art.28 . . . .　7–39, 9–76
　Art.29 . . . .　7–27, 7–40
　Art.30 . . . .　7–38, 7–41
　Art.31 . . . .　7–57
　Arts 32–56 . . . .　9–37
　Art.33 . . . .　9–39
　Art.33.1 . . . .　9–49
　Art.33.3 . . . .　9–38
　Art.34 . . . . .　9–40, 9–47, 9–49,
　　　　　　　　　　　9–51, 9–59
　Art.34.1 . . . .　9–41
　Art.34.2 . . . .　8–10
　Art.35 . . . . .　9–41, 9–47, 9–49,
　　　　　　　　　　　9–51, 9–59
　Art.35.1 . . .　7–17, 7–18, 9–07,
　　　　　　　9–41, 9–82, 12–24
　Art.35.2 . . . .　9–02
　Art.35.3 . . . .　7–02, 7–18
　Art.36 . . . .　9–05, 9–42, 13–22
　Art.37 . . . .　9–43
　Art.38 . . . .　9–44
　Art.38(1) . . . .　9–50
　Art.38.2 . . . .　9–47, 9–50
　Art.39 . . . .　9–45
　Art.40 . . . .　9–46
　Art.41 . . . .　9–44, 9–47, 9–53
　Art.42 . . . .　9–48
　Art.43 . . . . .　9–49, 9–51, 9–52
　Art.43(5) . . . .　9–53
　Art.44 . . . . .　9–50, 9–51, 9–52
　Art.45 . . . .　9–51
　Art.46 . . . .　9–52
　Art.47 . . . .　9–53
　Art.48 . . . .　9–54
　Art.49 . . . .　9–55
　Art.50 . . . .　9–56
　Art.51 . . . .　7–03, 9–57
　Art.52 . . . .　9–58

44/2001 Regulation on Jurisdiction and the Recognition and Enforcement of Judgments in Civil and Commercial Matters—*cont.*

Art.53 ..... 9–44, 9–46, 9–47, 9–49
Art.54 9–46
Art.55 9–46
Art.56 9–44
Art.57 9–37
Art.58 9–37
Art.59 9–82
Art.59(2) 3–03
Art.60 ..... 7–08, 7–10, 7–27, 17–38
Art.62.37 9–62
Art.62.41 9–62
Art.67 13–22
Art.72 ..... 7–05, 7–52, 9–37, 9–41
Annex I 7–11
Annex II 9–45
Annex III 9–49
Annex IV 9–50
Annex V 9–46

1206/2001 Regulation on Cooperation between the Courts of the Member States in the Taking of Evidence in Civil or Commercial Matters [2001] O.J. L174/1 .. 1–08, 8–13, 8–16, 8–25
Art.1.2 8–13
Art.3 8–15
Art.4 .... 8–14, 8–15
Art.4.2 8–14
Art.5 8–14
Art.6 8–14
Art.7.1 8–14
Art.7.2 8–14
Art.8 8–14
Art.8.1 8–14
Art.9 8–14
Art.10 8–14
Art.10.2 8–14
Art.10.3 8–14
Art.10.4 8–14
Art.11 8–14
Art.12.4 8–14
Art.13 8–14
Art.14 8–14
Art.14.2 8–14
Art.14.3 8–14
Art.15 8–14

1206/2001 Regulation on Cooperation between the Courts of the Member States in the Taking of Evidence in Civil or Commercial Matters—*cont.*
Art.16 8–14
Art.17 8–15
Art.17.2 8–15
Art.17.5 8–15
Art.18 8–14
Art.18.3 8–14
Art.21 8–15

2201/2003 Regulation concerning Jurisdiction and the Recognition and Enforcement of Judgments in Matrimonial Matters and in Matters of Parental Responsibility [2003] O.J. L338/1(Brussels II *Bis*) ... 1–08, 6–02, 9–05, 9–94, 10–02, 10–04, 10–08, 11–12, 12–05, 12–06, 12–11, 12–14, 12–15, 12–16, 12–21, 12–24, 12–25, 12–26, 12–30, 12–32, 12–35, 12–39, 12–44, 12–48, 12–50, 13–23, 14–06, 14–07, 14–08, 14–09, 14–11, 14–19, 14–22, 14–23, 14–24, 14–27, 14–33, 14–34, 14–43, 14–50, 14–51, 14–62
Chap.II 14–08, 14–10
Chap.II, Sect.2   14–10, 14–43
Chap.II, Sect.3 14–43
Chap.III 14–08, 14–43
Chap.IV 14–08, 14–22
Recital 8 13–18
Recital 9 14–51
Recital 10 14–08
Recital 11 14–08
Recital 12 14–10
Recital 17 14–34
Recital 19 14–37
Art.1.1 12–30
Art.1.1.b 14–08
Art.1.2 .... 14–08, 14–09
Art.1.2.b 14–50
Art.1.2.e 14–50, 14–51
Art.1.3.e 13–18, 14–08
Art.2.11 14–34
Art.2.7 .... 14–08, 14–09
Art.2.9 14–09
Art.2.10 14–09
Art.3 .... 6–39, 12–07, 12–13, 12–24, 12–25, 12–30, 12–44, 14–16

2201/2003 Regulation concerning Jurisdiction and the Recognition and Enforcement of Judgments in Matrimonial Matters and in Matters of Parental Responsibility—*cont.*

Art.3.2 12–07
Art.5 12–31
Art.7 ... 12–08, 12–15, 12–44
Art.8 .... 14–11, 14–12
Arts 8–13 14–16
Arts 8–15 ..... 14–10, 14–43, 14–51, 14–62
Art.9 14–12
Arts 9 *et seq* 14–11
Art.10 .... 6–39, 6–40, 14–12, 14–13, 14–35
Art.10.a 14–35
Art.10.b 14–35
Art.10 14–62
Art.11 .. 14–13, 14–34, 14–36, 14–42, 14–62
Art.11.2 14–37
Art.11.2–11.8 14–36
Art.11.3 14–38
Art.11.4 .... 14–31, 14–39
Art.11.5 14–40
Art.11.6 14–41
Art.11.7 .... 14–35, 14–41
Art.11.8 14–42
Art.12 .... 14–14m 14–15
Art.12(1) 14–14
Art.12(1)(b) 14–14
Art.12(2) 14–14
Art.12(3) 14–14
Art.12(3)(b) 14–14
Art.13 14–15
Art.14 .. 14–16, 14–43, 14–50
Art.15 .. 12–12, 12–15, 14–17, 14–23, 14–44
Art.15(2)(6) 14–17
Art.16 12–12
Art.19 .. 12–12, 12–13, 12–14, 12–50, 13–09, 14–18
Art.21 ... 9–05, 12–17, 14–62
Art.21.4 12–17
Arts 21–27 .... 12–50, 14–45
Art.22 .... 12–24, 12–25
Art.22(d) 12–26
Arts 22–24 14–20
Art.23 .... 14–19, 14–62
Art.24 .. 12–24, 12–25, 14–19
Art.25 .... 2–06, 13–23
Art.26 12–24
Art.28 .... 9–05, 14–20
Art.31 14–20

2201/2003 Regulation concerning Jurisdiction and the Recognition and Enforcement of Judgments in Matrimonial Matters and in Matters of Parental Responsibility—*cont.*

Art.33 14–20
Art.40 14–42
Art.41.1 14–45
Art.42 .... 14–41, 14–42
Art.42.1 14–45
Art.48 14–21
Art.56 14–19
Arts 59–63 14–23
Art.60 .... 1–10, 2–04, 14–23, 14–33, 14–35
Art.61 14–24
Art.66 12–16

805/2004 Regulation creating a European Enforcement Order for Uncontested Claims [2004] O.J. L143/15 ..... 9–78, 9–79, 9–80, 9–84, 9–86, 9–87, 9–90m 9–91, 9–93, 9–94, 13–22, 13–23
Chap.III 9–82, 9–84
Recital 5 9–81
Recital 6 9–81
Recital 7 9–80
Recital 8 9–85
Recital 9 9–86
Recital 12 9–84
Recital 13 9–84
Recital 14 9–84
Recital 17 9–84
Recital 19 9–84
Recital 20 9–86
Recital 21 9–86
Recital 24 9–78
Recital 25 9–78
Art.1 9–78
Art.2 9–80
Art.3 9–80
Art.4(4) 9–82
Art.4(5) 9–83
Art.5 9–83
Art.6 9–82
Art.6(1) 9–84
Art.8 .... 9–82, 9–84
Art.9 9–82
Art.12 9–84
Art.13 9–84
Art.14 9–84
Art.20 9–85
Art.21 8–85
Art.21(2) 9–86

805/2004 Regulation creating a European Enforcement Order for Uncontested Claims—*cont.*

Art.23 9–86
Art.24 9–84
Art.25(1) 9–84
Art.26 9–78
Art.27 9–86
Art.28 9–86
Art.33 9–78
Annex I 9–82

2116/2004 Regulation concerning Jurisdiction and the Recognition and Enforcement of Judgments in Matrimonial Matters and the Matters of Parental Responsibility [2004] O.J. L367/1 .... 12–05, 12–39

PROPOSED EU REGULATIONS

2003 Proposal for a Regulation on the Law Applicable to Non—contractual Obligations (Rome II) COM (2003) 427 final .. 15–49, 16–10, 16–16, 16–23, 16–29, 16–31, 16–32, 16–36
Chap.III 16–35, 16–36
Chap.IV 16–29
Recital 7 16–29
Recital 9 16–29
Recital 16 16–29
Art.A.3 16–32
Art.1.2 16–30
Art.2 16–29
Art.3 .... 6–39, 16–29
Art.3.1 16–29
Art.3.2 16–29
Art.3.3 .... 7–34, 16–29
Art.3A.1 16–29
Art.3A.3 16–29
Arts 4–8a 16–29
Art.9 16–32
Art.9.1 16–32
Art.9.2 16–32
Art.9.3 16–32
Art.9.4 16–32
Art.9.5 16–32
Art.9.6 16–32
Art.9A 16–32, 16–35
Art.9A.1 16–35
Art.9B 16–32, 16–36

2003 Proposal for a Regulation on the Law Applicable to Non—contractual Obligations—*cont.*
Art.9C 15–48
Art.10 16–01
Art.11 16–29
Art.12 16–29
Art.12(e) 8–20
Art.19.1 8–18
Art.20 16–29
Art.22 16–29
Art.23 16–29
ex Art.24 3–06
Art.21 5–07
Art.23 8–20
Art.26B 16–29
Art.27 16–30

2004 Proposed Regulation creating a European Order for Payment Procedure COM (2004) 173 final/3 (Brussels, May 25, 2004) 9–93
Recital 5 9–93
Proposed Regulation on Jurisdiction, Applicable Law, Recognition and Enforcement of Decisions and Co—operation in Matters relating to Maintenance Obligations COM (2004) 254 final ... 13–23
Chap.III 13–23
Recital 13 13–23
Art.3 13–23
Arts 3–5 13–23
Art.4 13–23
Art.5 13–23
Art.6 13–23
Arts 7–9 13–23
Art.12 13–23
Art.13 13–23
Art.13.1 13–23
Art.13.2 13–23
Art.13.3 13–23
Art.14 13–23
Art.18 13–23
Art.19 13–23
Art.20 13–23
Art.25 13–23
Art.33 13–23
Art.34 13–23
Arts 40–47 13–23
Art.49 13–23

2005 Proposed Regulation
establishing a European
Small Claims Procedure
COM (2005) 87 final
(Brussels, March 15,
2005) ... 9–87, 9–88, 9–89, 9–91
 Recital 4 9–87
 Recital 6 9–92
 Recital 7 9–92
 Recital 13 9–90
 Recital 15 9–90
 Recital 19 9–88
 Recital 20 9–88
 Art.1 9–88
 Art.3.1 9–89
 Art.3.3 9–89
 Art.3.4 9–89
 Art.4 9–89
 Art.4.1 9–89
 Art.5 .... 9–89, 9–92
 Art.6 9–89
 Art.7 9–89
 Art.10 9–89
 Art.12 9–89
 Art.13 9–90
 Art.18 9–90
 Art.18.1–18.4 9–90
Proposal for a Regulation
on the Law Applicable to
Contractual Obligations
(Rome I Regulation)
COM (2005) 650 final .. 15–49,
      15–58, 16–16
 Art.1 15–49
 Art.1.2(i) 15–48, 15–49
 Art.3 15–49
 Art.3.1 15–49
 Art.3.2 15–49
 Art.3.4 .... 15–49, 16–29
 Art.3.5 15–49
 Art.4 15–49
 Art.4.1 15–49
 Art.4.1.a 15–49
 Art.4.2 15–49
 Art.5 15–49
 Art.5.2 15–49
 Art.5.3 15–49
 Art.7 15–49
 Art.7.1 15–49
 Art.7.2 15–49
 Art.7.3 15–49
 Art.7.4 15–49
 Art.8 15–49
 Art.8.2 15–49
 Art.8.3 15–49
 Art.10 15–49
 Art.11 15–49

2005 Proposal for a Regulation
on the Law Applicable to
Contractual
Obligations—*cont.*
 Art.13 15–49
 Art.13.2 15–49
 Art.13.3 15–49
2006 Proposal for a Regulation
on applicable law and
jurisdiction in divorce
matters (Rome III) 12–15,
      12–25, 12–50

DIRECTIVES

73/239 Directive Relating to
the Taking-up and Pursuit
of the Business of Direct
Insurance other than Life
Insurance [1973] O.J.
L228/3 7–19
76/308 Directive on Mutual
Assistance on Recovery
of Claims [1976] O.J.
L73/18 3–02
86/653 Directive on the
Co—ordination of the
Laws of the Member
States relating to
Self—employed Commer-
cial Agents (Commercial
Agents Directive) [1986]
O.J. L382/17 15–42
97/7 Directive on the Protec-
tion of Consumers in
Relation to Distance
Contracts [1997] O.J.
L144/19 15–47
99/93 Electronic Signatures
Directive [2000] O.J.
L13/12 15–44
2000/31 Directive on Certain
Legal Aspects of Informa-
tion Society Services in
particular Electronic
Commerce in the Internal
Market [2000] O.J.
L178/1 .... 15–45, 15–46, 15–58
 Recital 18 15–46
 Recital 23 15–45
 Recital 55 .... 15–45, 15–46,
      15–48
 Recital 58 15–45
 Art.1.4 15–45
 Art.9 15–45
 Art.9.2 15–45

DECISIONS

2003 Decision by EU Council authorising Member States to sign 1996 Hague Convention in the interests of the Community [2003] O.J. L48/1 1–10

2006 Decision 6922/06 noting Agreement Concerning the Extension to Denmark of Regulation 44/2001 7–08

SELECT BIBLIOGRAPHY

GENERAL

AE Anton, *Private International Law (A treatise from the standpoint of Scots law* (1st ed., 1967)

AE Anton with PR Beaumont, *Private International Law* (2nd ed., 1990)

AE Anton ad PR Beaumont, *Civil Jurisdiction in Scotland* (2nd ed., 1995)

W Binchy, *Irish Conflict of Laws* (2nd ed., forthcoming 2006)

A Briggs, *The Conflict of Laws* (2002)

A Briggs and P Rees, *Civil Jurisdiction and Judgments* (4th ed., 2005)

CMV Clarkson and J Hill, *Jaffey on the Conflict of Laws* (2nd ed., 2002)

J Collier, *Conflict of Laws* (3rd ed., 2001)

L Collins and others, *Dicey & Morris, The Conflict of Laws* (13th ed., 2000) ("Dicey & Morris")

C Forsyth, *Private International Law* (4th ed., 2003)

RH Graveson, *Private International Law* (7th ed., 1974)

J Hill, *International Commercial Disputes in English Courts* (3rd ed., 2005)

RD Leslie, *Stair Memorial Encyclopaedia of the Law of Scotland*, Vol. 17, *Private International Law* (1989)

G McBain (ed.), *Butterworths International Litigation Handbook* (1999)

D McClean and K Beevers, *Morris, The Conflict of Laws* (6th ed., 2005)

North and Fawcett, *Cheshire and North's Private International Law* (13th ed., 1999) ("Cheshire and North")

FC von Savigny, *A Treatise on the Conflict of Laws* (WM Guthrie, transl., 2nd ed., 1880)

L Van Bar, *The Theory and Practice of Private International Law* (GR Gillespie, transl., 2nd ed., 1892)

J Westlake, *A Treatise on Private International Law* (7th ed., 1925)

M Wolff, *Private International Law* (2nd ed., 1950)

REFLECTIVE/ SPECIFIC

R Aird and JNStC Jameson, *The Scots Dimension to Cross-Border Litigation* (1996)

PR Beaumont and P McEleavy, *The Hague Convention on International Child Abduction* (1999)

A Bell, *Forum Shopping and Venue in Transnational Litigation* (2003)

JM Carruthers, *The Transfer of Property in the Conflict of Laws* (2005)

L Collins, *Essays in International Litigation and the Conflict of Laws* (1994)

DF Cavers, *The Choice of Law Process* (1966)

B Currie, *Selected Essays on the Conflict of Laws* (1963)

T Einhorn and K Siehr (eds), *Intercontinental Cooperation through Private International Law: Essays in Memory of Peter E Nygh* (2004)

J Falconbridge, *Essays on the Conflict of Laws* (Toronto, 1954)

JJ Fawcett (ed.), *Declining Jurisdiction in Private International Law* (1995)

JJ Fawcett, *Reform and Development of Private International Law: Essays in Honour of Sir Peter North* (2002)

JJ Fawcett, JM Harris, and M Bridge, *International Sale of Goods in the Conflict of Laws* (2005)

JJ Fawcett and P Torremans, *Intellectual Property and Private International Law* (1998)

R Fentiman, *Foreign Law in English Courts* (1998)

IF Fletcher, *Insolvency in Private International Law: National and International Approaches* (2005)

S Geeroms, *Foreign Law in Civil Litigation* (2004)

JM Harris, *The Hague Trusts Convention: The Private International Law of Trusts* (2002)

O Kahn-Freund, *General Problems of Private International Law* (1980)

W Kennett, *The Enforcement of Judgments in Europe* (2000)

P Lalive, *The Transfer of Chattels in the Conflict of Laws* (1955)

F Mann, *Foreign Affairs in English Courts* (1986)

M Meston, *The Succession (Scotland) Act* 1964 (4th ed., 1993)

CGJ Morse, *Torts in Private International Law* (1978)

PM North, *Essays in Private International Law* (1993)

PM North, *Private International Law Problems in Common Law Jurisdictions* (1993)

P Nygh, *Autonomy in International Contracts* (1998)

M Ooi, *Shares and other Securities in the Conflict of Laws* (2003)

G Panagopoulos, *Restitution in Private International Law* (2000)

R Plender and M Wilderspin, *The European Contracts Convention* (2nd ed., 2001)

AH Robertson, *Characterization in the Conflict of Laws* (1940)

F Rose, *Restitution and the Conflict of Laws* (1995)

E Scobbie, *Currie on Confirmation of Executors* (8th ed., 1995)

GA Zaphiriou, *The Transfer of Chattels in Private International Law: A Comparative Study* (1956)

CHAPTER 1

NATURE OF THE SUBJECT

NATURE

International private law is also known as conflict of laws and its **1–01**
rules are known as conflict rules. Each legal system has its own
conflict rules, which exist to regulate the treatment of conflict cases
arising for decision in the courts of that legal system. Conflict cases
are those which contain a foreign element, but not all cases
containing a foreign element are conflict cases: they may reveal
themselves on the facts to be domestic,[1] or they may be treated as
domestic cases if no offer,[2] or no timeous offer,[3] is made to prove
foreign law. In such an event, the court may proceed on the basis
that the content of the foreign law is the same as its own.[4]
Generally, therefore, international private law is that branch of the
law of any system which is applied to determine questions which
involve foreign elements. More particularly, it is the branch of the
private law of any country which consists of the rules which enable
its courts to determine the following matters:

(a) the rules of jurisdiction to be followed by its courts;
(b) the system of law which is to be applied to determine the
    rights of the parties in cases involving foreign elements
    ("choice of law"); and
(c) the extent to which recognition is to be given to decrees of
    foreign courts, and the manner of enforcement of such
    recognised decrees if enforcement be necessary.

In other words, in cases involving relevant foreign elements, a legal
system's conflict rules determine which court has jurisdiction,
which law is applicable and whether the decree of a foreign court
should be recognised. A key element in the last of these topics is

---

[1] *William Grant & Sons Ltd v Glen Catrine Bonded Warehouse Ltd*, 1995 S.L.T. 936.
[2] *Pryde v Proctor and Gamble Ltd*, 1971 S.L.T. (Notes) 18.
[3] *Bonnor v Balfour Kilpatrick Ltd*, 1974 S.L.T. 187 and 1975 S.L.T. (Notes) 3.
[4] *De Reneville v De Reneville* [1948] P. 100; see also *Rodden v Whatlings Ltd*, 1960
S.L.T. (Notes) 96. See Ch.8.

the consideration of whether the foreign court had jurisdiction, in the view of the forum's conflict rules: clearly, the foreign court itself thought it had jurisdiction.

The subject, therefore, is concerned with the relationship among different systems of private law, rather than with the relationship among sovereign states as political units. Only occasionally will the subjects of public international law (which in its nature is international, and not peculiar to each legal system) and international private law meet[5]; they will not usually conflict with each other, though it may be found that their approaches to a problem common to both may differ.[6]

Even if viewed originally as akin to public international law, international private law is truly a branch of the private law of a legal system. This means that they are likely to differ from one another, unless and until the harmonisation process supervenes, in any given area and to a full or limited extent. It means also that there is no affront to the sovereignty of the forum in entertaining the notion of upholding foreign acquired rights because the matter is regulated by a branch of the forum's own law.

1–02   As the twentieth century progressed, legislation in the United Kingdom showed an increasing awareness of conflict issues and of the matter of territorial application. Since 1970, the subject of Scots and English international private law has been transformed from one largely regulated by common law to one largely regulated by statute. There has been much legislation specifically concerned with international private law subjects in all areas, personal[7] and commercial.[8]

---

[5] *e.g.* sovereign immunity; international personality; jurisdiction (not, perhaps, as that word is understood in a domestic or conflict of laws sense, but used to express *locus standi*, the legality of expression of interest by a state in an incident which takes place within its own borders, or to one of its nationals outside its own borders or otherwise outside its borders). Sometimes, the two branches are involved jointly in a question: an example is the extent to which English and Scots law should recognise private law "events", such as the celebration or termination of a marriage, the conclusion of a contract, and rights which would normally flow therefrom, if the event has taken place within a state the government of which is not formally recognised by the UK ("the problem of unrecognised governments"). See Leslie, "The Existence of Governments and the Conflict of Laws: The Republic of Somalia Case", 1997 J.R. 110. See *Sierra Leone Telecommunications Co. Ltd v Barclays Bank Plc* [1998] 2 All E.R. 820; see also (incidentally) *BCCI (Overseas) Ltd v Price Waterhouse* [1997] 4 All E.R. 108. *Cf.* Foreign Corporations Act 1991.

[6] *e.g. Kuwait Airways Corporation v Iraqi Airways Company (No.6)* [2002] 3 All E.R. 209, discussed in J.M. Carruthers and E.B. Crawford, 2003 (52) I.C.L.Q. 761.

[7] *e.g.* Recognition of Divorces and Legal Separations Act 1971, superseded by Family Law Act 1986; Domicile and Matrimonial Proceedings Act 1973; Matrimonial and Family Proceedings Act 1984; Child Abduction and Custody Act 1985 Civil Partnership Act 2004; and Family Law (Scotland) Act 2006.

[8] *e.g.* Contracts (Applicable Law) Act 1990; Private International Law (Mis-

Traditionally, UK statutes do not have extra-territorial operation unless this is express or a necessary implication,[9] and this is especially strongly held in certain branches such as criminal law,[10] but in recent years there have been more examples of extra-territoriality, especially in criminal law.[11] It must always be remembered that British statutes have a silent or implicit extraterritorial dimension by virtue of our conflict choice of law rules, as later explained. If Scots or English law be the law governing the substance of the question (the *lex causae*), the relevant Scots or English or U.K. statute will apply, *e.g.* if the deceased died domiciled in Scotland, the distribution, testate or intestate, of his moveable estate, *wherever situated*, will be subject to the provisions of the Succession (Scotland) Act 1964.

Technological and electronic advances pose immense difficulties of jurisdiction and choice of law, particularly in matters of intellectual property, and copyright,[12] and with regard to the dissemination of defamatory[13] or pornographic or otherwise offensive material. In 1996, negotiations took place in Geneva under the auspices of the World Intellectual Property Organisation, with the aim of reaching agreement to extend the copyright protection of the Berne Convention 1886 for the Protection of Literary and Artistic Work, to material transmitted over the Internet, which resulted in the 1996 Geneva Copyright Treaty. However, technology is well in advance

---

cellaneous Provisions) Act 1995; Civil Jurisdiction and Judgments Act 1982–1991; and Recognition of Trusts Act 1987.

[9] Crabbe, *Understanding Statutes* (1994), pp.176–177; Bell and Eagle, *Cross on Statutory Interpretation* (3rd ed., 1995), pp.5–6; Bennion, *Statutory Interpretation* (1984), pp.453 *et seq.* (and 2nd ed., 1992). The position seems to be that UK statutes apply geographically intra-territorially and bind British subjects and aliens within the Realm—but whether an Act binds British subjects in their activities abroad depends upon the intention of the legislature, there being no presumption either way except that criminal statutes in the main are local. See, *e.g. Att.-Gen. for Alberta v Huggard Assets Ltd* [1953] A.C. 420, *per* Lord Asquith of Bishopstone at 441; *C.E.B. Draper & Son Ltd v Edward Turner & Son Ltd* [1964] 3 All E.R. 148, *per* Lord Denning at 150; *Yorke v British and Continental Steamship Co.* (1945) 78 Ll.L.Rep. 181. The terms of a statute may have the effect that a foreigner is entitled to take advantage of UK legislation even if not subject to it: *Krzus v Crow's Nest Pass Coal Co. Ltd* [1912] A.C. 590.

[10] Most conflict of laws textbooks are chary of including within their treatment the subject of criminal law. An exception is the first edition of this work: *International Private Law in Scotland* (W.Green, 1998), Ch.20.

[11] *e.g.* Sex Offenders Act 1997 and Sexual Offences (Conspiracy and Incitement) Act 1996. See *IPL in Scotland* (1st ed.), above, para.20.06.

[12] cf. *Shetland Times Ltd v Wills*, 1997 S.L.T. 669.

[13] See C. Waelde and L. Edwards, "Defamation and the Internet: A Case Study of Anomalies and Difficulties in the Information Age" (1996) 10 International Review of Law, Computers and Technology 263. In the matter of offensive material, the principles of protection of innocence and the provision of freedom of speech are at war. See Edwards and Waelde, *Law and the Internet: Regulating Cyberspace* (2nd ed., 2000).

of legal thinking on the subject. The same may be said of (electronic) commerce (*i.e.* contractual matters) and of related property problems, *e.g.* the transfer of securities held with an intermediary, where modern holding practice typically is "dematerialised" and "immobilised".[14]

Therefore, the subject of conflict of laws, which hitherto has been characterised by respect for territorial boundaries, must continue to respond to the challenge of finding appropriate solutions to the growing number of legal problems, of jurisdiction and choice of law, prompted by rapidly increasing technological and electronic advances.

THE NAME

1–03 The names "international private law", "private international law" and "conflict of laws" are each suitable descriptions of this branch of law, but conflict lawyers, being particularly fond of disputation, like to disagree first on the name of their subject of study.[15] It has been said of the subject that "dispute starts from the title page". In this treatment of the subject, we shall use the term international private law, as it is believed to be the name traditionally used in Scotland, and it brings to mind more quickly the nature of the subject.

TERMINOLOGY

1–04 Traditionally, treatments of international private law are characterised by the use of Latin terminology, though it can be observed that it is less frequently employed in modern instruments. The following is a list of expressions frequently used:

Lex fori	The *internal* (or local or domestic) law of the country in which an action is raised.
Lex causae	The legal system which governs the subject matter of an action or the rights of parties, that is, the law in accordance with which the substance of a legal question is to be determined.
Lex domicilii	The law of a person's domicile.

---

[14] J. Benjamin, *Interests in Securities* (2000); J.M. Carruthers, *The Transfer of Property in the Conflict of Laws* (2005), Ch.7.

[15] Wolff, *Private International Law* (2nd ed., 1950), p.10 rightly predicted that the German suggestion of "demarcation law" was unlikely to become popular. He notes that Baty considered the term "polarized law".

Lex patriae	The law of a person's nationality.
Lex loci celebrationis	The law of the country where a marriage is celebrated.
Lex situs and lex loci rei sitae	The law of the country in which immoveable property or moveable assets are situated: the latter term used to be considered the correct one with regard to moveables, but nowadays *lex situs* is used in all property cases.
Lex loci actus	The law of the country where a legal act or transaction takes place.
Lex actus	The law with which a legal act or transaction has the most real connection. This may or may not be also the *lex loci actus*: in many cases the two coincide.
Lex loci contractus	The law of the country in which a contract technically is said to have been made.
Lex loci solutionis	The law of the country in which performance of a contract is to take place.
Lex loci delicti	The law of the country where a delict or tort has allegedly been committed.
Lex successionis	The law in accordance with which rights of succession to an estate are to be determined.

THE LAW OF A COUNTRY

The expression "the law of a country" is ambiguous because its **1–05** meaning may be either of the following:

(a) *Narrow sense*: in this sense it means the internal, or domestic, law of a country, excluding all conflict rules providing for the recognition of foreign elements and rights under foreign laws.

(b) *Wide sense*: in this sense it means the internal law as above, as well as the conflict rules of the country in question.

The term "country" should be taken to mean law unit, or legal system, having an independent body of law.[16] The expression "law

---

[16] Hence in the UK there are the three separate law units of England and Wales, Scotland and Northern Ireland; and in the "British Islands" there are in addition Jersey, Guernsey, Alderney and Sark (the latter often subsumed under Guernsey), and the Isle of Man. Dicey and Morris, *The Conflict of Laws* (13th ed., 2000), pp.28–29. Similarly, there are Canadian and South African provinces and Australian States. For some purposes, e.g. consistorial causes or company law, the law may be the same for all the component parts and so the meaning of "country" in that context is the composite unit. The situation in the USA is doubly complex, since there may be State/Federal and US/international conflicts.

of a country" will always be used in this work in its narrow sense, except in the context of discussion of the methodological problems of *renvoi* and the incidental question.[17]

Scottish international private law, therefore, is that body of Scots private law rules in use to decide questions which raise foreign issues, of jurisdiction, choice of law, or recognition of foreign judgments. It is still true to say that each body of conflict rules is peculiar to its own legal system, but each is affected now more than ever before by international legal, commercial and political developments, and by technological advances.

HARMONISATION

1–06 The subject is undergoing fundamental change. The nature of Scots and English conflict rules until as late as the end of the twentieth century, paradoxically, were national in nature, despite their international purpose and despite the provision in the twentieth century of certain examples of international co-operation in the treatment of private law problems which cross the boundaries of legal systems, *e.g.* commercial codes on carriage or insurance, such as the conventions on the carriage of goods by sea,[18] by air,[19] by rail,[20] or by road.[21] Henceforward we witness the creation and development of a supranational body of conflict rules, as evidenced by international co-operation in the harmonisation of conflict rules, which is the outstanding feature of the modern age.

---

[17] See Chaps 4 and 5, below.

[18] Athens Convention relating to the Carriage of Passengers and their Luggage by Sea 1974 (Merchant Shipping Act 1979); Hague-Visby Rules on Carriage of Goods by Sea (Carriage of Goods by Sea Act 1971); UN Convention on the Carriage of Goods by Sea (1978) (the "Hamburg Rules"); and UN Draft Instrument on the Carriage of Goods [Wholly or Partly] [By Sea] (multimodal carriage of goods).

[19] Warsaw Convention for the Unification of Certain Rules relating to International Carriage by Air 1929, as amended at The Hague, 1955, supplemented by the Guadalajara Convention 1961 (Carriage by Air Act 1961), and modernised by the Montreal Convention for the Unification of Certain Rules relating to International Carriage by Air 1999. *Sidhu v British Airways plc*; *Abnett v British Airways plc* 1997 S.L.T. 492 (HL: no remedy available except under convention). See also *Reid v Ski Independence* 1998 S.L.T. (Sh.Ct.) 62; *Western Digital Corp. v British Airways plc* [1999] 2 Ll Rep. 380; *Phillips v Air New Zealand Ltd* [2002] 2 Ll Rep. 403; *Quantum Corp Inc v Plane Trucking Ltd* [2002] 2 Ll Rep. 25; *King v Bristow Helicopters Ltd*, 2002 S.L.T. 278; *Disley v Levine T/A Airtrack Levine Paragliding* [2002] 1 W.L.R. 785; *Morris v KLM Royal Dutch Airlines* [2002] Q.B. 100; *GKN Westland Helicopters Ltd v Korean Airlines Co Ltd* [2003] 2 Ll Rep. 629; *Re Deep Vein Thrombosis and Air Travel Group Litigation* [2006] 1 All E.R. 786.

[20] Berne Convention concerning International Carriage by Rail 1980 (International Transport Conventions Act 1983), revised 1999.

[21] Geneva Convention on the Contract for the International Carriage of Goods by Road 1956 (Carriage of Goods by Road Act 1965).

The impetus comes principally from the European Union and the Hague Conference on Private International Law.

EUROPEAN HARMONISATION

The most striking change in the content of the conflict rules of **1–07** Scotland and England has been occasioned by the ambitious and wide-ranging programme of harmonisation of law undertaken by the EU in its Justice and Home Affairs portfolio, with the aim of creating an "Area of Freedom, Security and Justice". The central policy is the removal of barriers to the free movement of persons, goods, services and capital. The legal basis for the development of this area is founded upon the Treaty of Amsterdam, Articles 61 to 67. Measures in the field of judicial co-operation in civil matters having cross-border implications are authorised by Article 65 "insofar as necessary for the proper functioning of the internal market".[22] The Treaty establishing a Constitution for Europe, signed on October 29, 2004, further entrenches the establishment of the European common judicial area, confirming the purpose and accelerating the pace of achieving it. In terms of Article III-269 of the Constitutional Treaty, judicial co-operation in civil matters shall be developed, including "the adoption of measures for the approximation of the laws and regulations of the Member States", "*particularly* when necessary for the proper functioning of the internal market" (emphasis added). The future of the Constitutional Treaty is unclear.

In detail, the aims in the period 1999 to 2004 were pursued under the heading of the "Tampere Agenda". 2005 marked the beginning of a follow-up, "second generation" agenda, the "Hague Programme".[23] Priorities for the period 2005 to 2009 have been agreed, and will be adverted to throughout the text. The attainment of the aims is to be monitored on a "scoreboard".[24]

---

[22] See Protocol No 4 on the position of the UK and Ireland (OJ 1997 C340/99), in terms of which the default position for the UK and Ireland is one of opt-out, but within three months of presentation of a proposal under Title IIIa of the Treaty establishing the European Community, either jurisdiction may intimate the wish to opt in. Contrast Protocol No 5 on the position of Denmark (OJ 1997 C340/101), in terms of which Denmark shall not take part in the adoption of proposed measures pursuant to Title IIIa of the Treaty establishing the European Community.

[23] Draft Multiannual Programme (Brussels, October 27, 2004) (JAI 408 13993/04– LIMITE). See E.B. Crawford and J.M. Carruthers, "Conflict of Loyalties in the Conflict of Laws: the Cause, the Means and the Cost of Harmonisation", 2005 J.R. 251.

[24] *http://europa.eu.int/comm/justice_home/doc_centre/scoreboard_en.htm*.

Instruments (actual and proposed) to achieve the European agenda

1–08   The European Regulation is the legislative tool of choice in order to achieve the harmonisation of European conflict laws, in view of the desired speed of change and the benefits which the Regulation extends, namely, uniform date of entry into force, uniform application, and automatic right of appeal to the European Court of Justice on points of interpretation. Although the basis of EU actings in the area of harmonisation of law is regional, many instruments adopt a principle of universality, meaning that in the forum of an EU Member State the harmonised rules must apply, no matter that the law identified as applicable under the EU instrument in question is that of a third country.

The instruments which are concerned with the allocation of jurisdiction and the enforcement of judgments fall under the "Brussels" family name, since in philosophy and detail they stem from the 1968 Brussels Convention on Jurisdiction and the Enforcement of Judgments in Civil and Commercial Matters[25] (henceforth "Brussels I").[26] In 2001, certain amendments were made to the text of Brussels I upon its conversion into a Regulation, termed Council Regulation (EC) No 44/2001 (December 22, 2000) on Jurisdiction and the Recognition and Enforcement of Judgments in Civil and Commercial Matters (henceforth Council Regulation 44/2001). [27]

Corresponding measures have been introduced in family law, governing jurisdiction and the recognition of judgments emanating from Member States: Council Regulation (EC) No 2201/2003 (November 27, 2003) concerning Jurisdiction and the Recognition and Enforcement of Judgments in Matrimonial Matters and in Matters of Parental Responsibility ("Brussels II *Bis*").[28]

---

[25] Entry into force in 1973 among the original six (Belgium, France, Germany, Italy, Luxembourg and the Netherlands). See also Accession Convention 1978, signed by the UK, Denmark and Ireland (into effect for the UK by Civil Jurisdiction and Judgments Act 1982 ("CJJA 1982")); Greek Accession Convention 1982; Spanish and Portuguese Accession Convention 1989 (the San Sebastian Convention, bringing certain substantive changes). Then the Lugano Convention 1988 makes parallel provision for the EFTA bloc (then Austria, Finland, Iceland, Norway, Sweden and Switzerland). Lugano was implemented for the UK by Civil Jurisdiction and Judgments Act 1991 ("CJJA 1991"). Austria, Finland and Sweden have now become members of the EU.

[26] Implemented in the UK by means of the Civil Jurisdiction and Judgments Act 1982. See Ch.7.

[27] OJ 2001 L12/1. See also the Civil Jurisdiction and Judgments Order 2001 (SI 2001/3929).

[28] Repealing Council Regulation (EC) No 1347/2000 (May 29, 2000) on Jurisdiction and the Recognition and Enforcement of Judgments in Matrimonial Matters and in Matters of Parental Responsibility for Children of Both Spouses, known as "Brussels II" OJ 2000 L160/19.

Proposed to be treated similarly are the subjects of: matrimonial property ("Brussels III"[29]); succession ("Brussels IV"[30]) and maintenance obligations ("Brussels V"[31]).

The most significant instrument in choice of law is the 1980 Rome Convention on the Law Applicable to Contractual Obligations ("Rome I"). Proposed measures in choice of law, their names deriving from Rome I, comprise the following proposals: choice of law concerning non-contractual obligations ("Rome II"[32]), choice of law in divorce ("Rome III"[33]), choice of law concerning matrimonial property ("Rome IV"[34]) and choice of law in succession ("Rome V"[35]).

Additionally, the EU has enacted a number of important procedural law instruments, such as Regulations on the Taking of Evidence Abroad,[36] and the Service of Documents.[37]

The details of these instruments, actual and proposed, will be discussed at appropriate points in the text.

Global harmonisation

The EU operates on a regional level, but the Hague Conference **1–09** on Private International Law operates at a global level, among its Member States. The Hague Conference is an inter-governmental body, founded in 1893, dedicated to the harmonisation of the conflict rules of different legal systems, and the development and service of multilateral legal instruments. In 1955 the Conference was put on a statutory footing, and now has more than sixty

---

[29] Hague Programme, para.3.4.2.

[30] Hague Programme, para.3.4.2. See now EU Green Paper on Succession and Wills COM (2005) 65 final.

[31] Green Paper issued April 15, 2004: COM (2004) 254/final. See now Proposal for Council Regulation on jurisdiction, applicable law, recognition and enforcement of decisions, and co-operation in matters relating to maintenance obligations COM (2005) 649 final.

[32] COM (2003) 427 final (2003/0168 [COD]). See also the European Parliament's Committee on Legal Affairs and the Internal Market Draft Report (Revised Version) on the Commission Proposal, COM (2003) 427–1.C5-0338/2003-2003/0168 (COD), April 5, 2004. The latest version is the Amended Proposal of February 21, 2006 (COM (2006) 83 final).

[33] EU Green Paper on Applicable Law and Jurisdiction in Divorce Matters issued March 14, 2005: COM (2005) 82 final.

[34] Hague Programme, para.3.4.2.

[35] *ibid.*, para.3.4.2.

[36] Council Regulation (EC) No. 1206/2001 (May 18, 2001) on Cooperation between the Courts of the Member States in the Taking of Evidence in Civil or Commercial Matters OJ 2001 L174/1.

[37] Council Regulation (EC) No. 1348/2000 (May 29, 2000) on the Service in the Member States of Judicial and Extrajudicial Documents in Civil or Commercial Matters OJ 2000 L160/37.

Member States from all continents. The main participation by the United Kingdom has been in the period after 1951.[38]

The Conference's chosen mode of proceeding is by multilateral treaty or convention, to which Member States may accede, occasionally under reservation as to particular provisions. Conventions may be simple, double, sometimes triple or even quadruple: see the cumbrously named 1996 Convention, below.

Since 1955 36 conventions have been finalised, notable examples of which are: 1961 Convention on the Conflict of Laws relating to the Form of Testamentary Dispositions; 1970 Convention on the Recognition of Divorces and Legal Separations; 1970 Convention on the Taking of Evidence Abroad in Civil or Commercial Matters; 1980 Convention on the Civil Aspects of International Child Abduction; 1985 Convention on the Law Applicable to Trusts and on their Recognition; 1996 Convention on Jurisdiction, Applicable Law, Recognition, Enforcement and Cooperation in respect of Parental Responsibility Measures for the Protection of Children; 2002 Convention on the Law Applicable to Certain Rights in Respect of Securities Held with an Intermediary; and 2005 Convention on Choice of Court Agreements. A true measure of the success of a Convention is the extent to which it is acceptable internationally, as expressed in the number of states acceding to the instrument, an excellent example being the 1980 Convention, above.

Engines for law reform—potential for duplication and rivalry

1–10   Clearly there is potential for over-regulation and duplication where different law reform agencies operate in the same subject area. A complicating feature of modern conflict of laws is the "layering phenomenon", which is seen most plainly where international instruments overlap, in terms of substance and geography, giving rise to the need to rank potentially applicable sets of rules.[39] The phenomenon also is seen in demarcation questions which necessitate a decision as to whether the factual matrix of the instance is to be governed by one or other potentially applicable body of rules, each of which is concerned with the same general subject matter.[40] Thirdly, a problem may arise in the EU context

---

[38] See Lipstein, "One Hundred Years of Hague Conferences on Private International Law" (1993) 42 I.C.L.Q. 553. For background information, and operation detail, see *www.hcch.net*.

[39] While ranking of provisions may give rise to problems of hierarchy within instruments, the ranking of different instruments *inter se* in the same subject area normally is set out in a disconnection clause within the latest instrument, *e.g.* Brussels II, Art.37; and Brussels II *Bis*, Art.60.

[40] *e.g.* in the matter of choice of law in contract, whether the case falls to be regulated by Rome 1, or by residual national law rules, as being excluded by reason of its nature from the scope of the convention (Art.1).

concerning the application in the United Kingdom (or in any other multi-legal system Member State) of a particular set of harmonised conflict rules, *i.e.* in intra-UK cases, should the harmonised "regional" rules apply?

The relationship between the Hague Conference, on the one hand, and the EU Council and Commission and EU Member States, on the other, is of moment. Each EU Member State, as a result of opting in to the European harmonisation scheme, has lost its capacity to act independently in any matter concerning judicial co-operation in civil law which falls within EU competence. For example, the entry by the EU into family law regulation has removed from EU Member States their autonomy in the signature and ratification of Hague instruments concerning family law.[41] Moreover, the Community, having at present only observer status, now seeks full membership of the Hague Conference.[42]

Insofar as efforts by the EU Council and Commission and the Hague Conference have as their goal the harmonisation of *choice of law* (conflict) rules, they aim to produce the result that the courts of all contracting states will agree as to which law shall apply in any given situation. The purpose of harmonisation of the *substantive* rules of legal systems would have the result that the issue of choice of law would matter less, because the substantive content of each law which potentially could be chosen would be the same.[43] The latter purpose would seem to be a longer-term and more ambitious one, but it is clear that both harmonisation aims can be viewed as facilitating large-scale legal, political and eco-

---

[41] See decision by EU Council authorising Member States to sign 1996 Hague Convention in the interests of the Community: OJ 2003 L48/1 (February 21, 2003).

[42] See Hague Conference Prel. Doc. No. 20 (February 2005), Note on the Admission of the European Community to the Hague Conference on Private International Law, and Prel. Doc. No 21B (February 2005), Draft Recommendation to the Twentieth Session of the Hague Conference on Private International Law on the Admission of the European Community to the Hague Conference on Private International Law. Further, Council of the European Union Press Release 8402/06. But see also developing use in international instruments of the "Regional Economic Integration Organisation" clause, in terms of which such a body, constituted by sovereign states and with competence over certain matters within the scope of a particular Convention, is able to sign, accept, approve or accede to the Convention. The European Community qualifies as a Regional Economic Integration Organisation.

[43] We are beginning to see signs of substantive harmonisation. A Commission on European Contract Law has been engaged for many years in the task of drafting principles of European contract law. There are earlier examples, e.g. agreement on a uniform law on the international sale of goods available for selection by parties (under the Uniform Laws on International Sales Act 1967: international sale is defined in Sch. 1, Art. 1). For a consideration of the problems arising from the interaction of the two types of harmonisation: see S. Knöfel, "EC Legislation on Conflict of Laws: Interactions and Incompatibilities between Conflict Rules" (1998) 47 I.C.L.Q. 439.

nomic objectives. But even if harmonisation of conflict of laws is "achieved" in major areas of private law, the interpretation of harmonisation instruments will vary from contracting state to contracting state. The degree of interpretative guidance differs from instrument to instrument, depending upon the availability and status of accompanying expert reports,[44] and upon the rules concerning appeal to international court.[45] Even if harmonisation of conflict rules across all major areas and within a particular political grouping such as the EU were achieved, conflict problems of a different (interpretative) type would arise.

---

[44] As regards interpretation of Rome I, the Giuliano & Lagarde Report may be relied upon by the courts (M. Giuliano and P. Lagarde, "Report on the Convention on the Law Applicable to Contractual Obligations" OJ C282 23 (1980)), and authoritative interpretative rulings may be handed down by the European Court of Justice (Contracts (Applicable Law) Act 1990, s.3; and The Contracts (Applicable Law) Act 1990 (Commencement No. 2) Order 2004, bringing into force in the United Kingdom on March 1, 2005 the 1988 Brussels Protocol, which will enable appellate courts to refer cases to the European Court of Justice for interpretative rulings on the Rome Convention). Contrast the position concerning, *e.g.* 1980 Hague Convention on the Civil Aspects of International Child Abduction, for which there is no central court of over-arching authority. The national courts may derive assistance from the Perez-Vera Report (*Actes et Documents*, Fourteenth Session of the Hague Conference) and the INCADAT database of decisions maintained by the Hague Conference on Private International Law.

[45] The question in each case is by which national court(s) reference may be made. In the interpretation of Council Regulation (EC) No. 44/2001 (December 22, 2000) on Jurisdiction and the Recognition and Enforcement of Judgments in Civil and Commercial Matters, reference may be made only by a national court "against whose decisions there is no judicial remedy under national law" (*i.e.* in the UK, only the House of Lords). See generally *New Rules on Civil Jurisdiction*, 2002 S.L.T. (News) 39.

CHAPTER 2

HISTORY

One of the earliest examples of a system of conflict rules is to be **2–01** found, preserved in the Louvre Museum, carved on a black pillar: it is the Code of Hammurabi, King of Babylon. He became king in 2400 B.C. The Code includes rules of international private law in the areas of property law, family law and the law of contract. Hammurabi distinguished between persons and things, and applied different choice of law rules to each; thus Hammurabi law governed all contracts made in Babylon regardless of the personal law of the parties whereas capacity to marry was governed by the law of the religion provided that the religion was that of the God of the sun or the God of justice. Where the religion was neither, Hammurabi law applied: in the earliest days, as now, the forum preferred to keep overall control. Whatever religion, the form of marriage, if celebrated in Babylon, was governed by the *lex loci celebrationis* (a normal rule down the years). The distinction between that which pertains to persons ("permanent") and that which pertains to things ("transient") is a most useful starting point in any consideration of choice of law and forms the basis of the distinction drawn in the early Middle Ages by the Post-Glossator, Bartolus, who distinguished between Statutes Personal and Statutes Real. By the sixth century Hammurabi's Kingdom drew a different distinction—that between Islam and infidel. The personal law of the Muslim was to be the law of Islam, no matter where he or she might be domiciled.

Roman law is not a fertile source of conflict rules or thinking. Martin Wolff[1] notes that the *Corpus Juris Civilis*, that repository of answers to "practically every conceivable legal question", says little on the subject of the application of foreign laws. Rome's promising circumstances, of legal ability and extensive empire, produced little, as Graveson points out,[2] largely because Roman law was so dominant that if one party to a dispute was a Roman citizen, the application of no other system would be considered. Roman citizens alone had the privilege of being governed by the *jus civile* of Rome: provincials were subject to their own provincial laws.

---

[1] Wolff (2nd ed.), p.19.
[2] Graveson, p.30.

Hence, the *jus civile* governed the rights *inter se* (and against the world) of Roman citizens; where the dispute was between provincials from different provinces the *jus gentium*, the law of nations, "which bore little relation to the provincial laws of either party",[3] would regulate the outcome.

In A.D. 212, by the Edict of Caracalla, which increased greatly the number of persons entitled to the status of Roman citizen and liable to pay citizens' taxes, the ambit of the civil law of Rome was extended to include all people living within the Roman Empire. Hence, that system of private law became territorial—that is to say, it was the same for all people, of whatever race, living within the rule of Rome.

Next came the Barbarian Invasion, which overthrew the Roman Empire, and settled different tribes in territories previously Roman: law became personal, and those few who travelled took their personal laws with them like a cloak. This era of personal law, existing from about the sixth to tenth centuries, was succeeded by a period (eleventh to twelfth centuries) when territorial laws prevailed. The meaningful development was the emergence of the powerful Italian city states in the thirteenth century. As these cities (of Bologna, Florence, Genoa, Padua, Milan, Modena, Venice and others) developed, they began to pass their own statutes or legal codes which applied over and above the common law. Problems arose in conflicts between the statutes of different cities or between statutes and the common law and the true origin of conflict of laws is to be found in such problems, and in the necessity to identify the applicable law.

Even before this, it is thought that the presence of a number of races in Italy had resulted in the practice of expressing a choice of law in contract. Trade has always fostered the development of conflict rules. So too has scholarship.[4] In the thirteenth century, the subject was exciting interest among scholars. Of the Glossators, and post-Glossators[5] the greatest contribution to the development of thinking in the conflict of laws was made by Bartolus of Saxoferrato (1314–1357). He made the distinction, in his "Statute Theory", between *statutes personal* (affecting a person in his personal and domestic life wherever he might go), and *statutes real* (concerning *things*: such laws applied only within the territory of the enacting state, and would affect also all persons transacting

---

[3] *ibid.*, p.30.

[4] Wolff, "Private International Law was a product of the Italian Universities of the thirteenth century" (2nd ed.), p.21.

[5] Or better, Kunkel, "Commentators" in *Roman Legal and Constitutional History* (Clarendon Press, 1966), pp.171–172. Kunkel argues that the work of putting a gloss on the Roman texts was creative work and a significant contribution, not merely "laborious erudition".

with things within that state, but might extend also to moveable property outside the jurisdiction but belonging to subjects of that state). However difficult it may be in a particular case to make this classification, the distinction which Bartolus drew is essential to an understanding of the nature and content of orthodox conflict rules. It is essential to grasp that the law which we may expect to have applied to our situation in the fundamental things of life is not necessarily the appropriate law to govern that which is commercial and/or relatively transient.

The statute theory was applied by the French jurists of the **2–02** sixteenth century, with varying approaches. D'Argentré, of the Breton (territorial) background, favoured the extension of the scope of the statute real, and the ascription of doubtful cases to that category, while Dumoulin (Molinaeus) advocated what we should now call "party autonomy" (a permissive attitude towards choice of law by parties).

The developments in France were followed by a corresponding development in the Netherlands, by jurists of the Dutch School, such as Burgundus (d. 1649), Paul Voet (d. 1677), John Voet, his son (1647–1714), and Huber (1636–94). The last mentioned was a professor and judge from Friesland, whose treatise on the subject, entitled *De Conflictu Legum* (1689) was only five quarto pages in length but immensely influential. By Huber's time, political considerations and notions of sovereignty had begun to impinge. Why should a sovereign admit the application within his kingdom of the laws of another sovereign? Huber provided the following guide and explanation in his maxims:

(1) The laws of each state have force within the limits of that government, and bind all subject to it, but not beyond.
(2) All persons within the limits of a government, whether they live there permanently or temporarily, are deemed to be subjects thereof.
(3) Sovereigns will so act by way of comity that rights acquired within the limits of a government retain their force everywhere so far as they do not cause prejudice to the power or rights of such government or of its subjects.

It should be noted that in his third maxim, Huber made two suggestions to explain the extra-territorial application of law. The first is comity which may be translated as international goodwill into which is mixed a measure of reciprocal advantage, and the second is the use of the phrase *"rights acquired"*. The second concept later gave support to that theory (called the "vested rights theory") which is based upon the proposition that it is not foreign law *per se*, but a right acquired under a foreign legal system, which is enforced *extra territorium*.

In England, there is little trace of any attempt to apply conflict rules and principles before 1603. There could be little private law conflict between England and Scotland because the gates were closed. The Scots Act of 1431 c. 128 made it treason to live in England without permission of the King of Scotland, that of 1436 c. 145 forbade Scots from buying English goods "under pain of escheat"; that of 1587 c.105 prohibited a Scot from marrying an Englishwoman. (When the gates were opened, the differences in the domestic laws of persons of the neighbouring countries made the conflict cases particularly interesting.[6]) In addition, England had not the beneficial exposure to the influence of the continental jurists. The English practice was to apply English law to all disputes coming before English courts, whether or not the case contained a foreign element.

When the Crowns were unified in 1603, a problem was posed for Huber's sovereignty theory in that the king was sovereign of two legal systems. Previously, the English courts had applied English law to all disputes whether or not foreign elements were involved: surely some validity now must be accorded in England to the king's law in/of Scotland? In *Calvin's Case*,[7] it was held by the Exchequer Chamber in England that Scots born after the accession of James to the throne of England did not have the status of aliens in England. Many would consider this a constitutional, or international, law case rather than a conflict case. The first true conflict case may be that of *Dungannon*[8] upon the question of which law should govern the rate of interest under an Irish bond. It indicates the beginning of a readiness to accept that perhaps the *lex loci actus* ("the law of the paper transfer") or the *lex situs* might apply, in preference to the English law of the forum.

In the 1760s, the great Anglo-Scottish lawyer, Lord Mansfield, made valuable contributions to early conflict of laws thinking, for example in the identification of the law which should govern substantive questions pertaining to a contract, where no choice of law has been made (*Robinson v Bland*[9]). In these early days—for despite Hammurabi's black pillar, the subject is not old[10]—English courts were troubled by the taking of jurisdiction in a case of alleged civil wrongdoing where the actings complained of had been committed abroad. They devised, therefore, the fiction of "local

---

[6] Gibb, *Law from Over The Border* (W. Green, 1950), p.89.

[7] (1608) 7 Co. Rep. 1; 2 St. Tr. 559.

[8] *Dungannon v Hackett* (1702) 1 Eq. Cas.Abr. 289. See also *Cottington's Case* [1678] 2 Swans. 326, and (1607) *Wiers Case* 1 Rolle, Abridgmt. 530, 12, admitting the obligation in principle to recognise and give effect to foreign judgments: Wolff (2nd ed.), p.30.

[9] (1760) 2 Burr 1077.

[10] Still something of a teenager: Morse, "Retention of Title in English Private International Law" [1992] J.B.L. 168. One might comment in 2006 that the conflict rules of Scotland and England have been required to grow up, and adapt, fast since 1992.

venue", and would accept the plea that the event had taken place "in the Parish of St Mary le Bow" (laying the venue) (*Mostyn v Fabrigas*[11]). This fiction also tended to lead the English courts to the view that the *lex fori* was the natural law to apply. The consequences of this were far reaching both for England and Scotland, and even after the revision of our conflict rules in tort/ delict by the Private International Law (Miscellaneous Provisions) Act 1995, the influence of the *lex fori* is not extinguished.[12] The fiction of "local venue" was abandoned in English law and was never present in Scots law which found no difficulty with the assumption of jurisdiction in a case relating to a foreign delict so long as a personal link would justify it.[13]

After 1707 the two systems have grown together in all areas, including international private law, and in truth, are closer in their conflict rules than in many other areas. The English rules in this area were slower to emerge, and developed later in a typically pragmatic and remedy-based manner (although Morris[14] was of the view that the attention paid in the decision of cases to the writings of jurists was unusual in English law). Of the Anglo-American school the greatest debt is owed to the jurist Joseph Story (1779– 1845)[15] who drew the strands together. He was followed by Dicey and Westlake, a long line of learned English writers[16] and a wealth of nineteenth and twentieth-century case law.

DEVELOPMENT OF CONFLICT RULES IN SCOTLAND

In consequence of the close ties between Scotland and France **2–03** before the Reformation and between Scotland and the Netherlands after the Reformation, the Scots courts had to deal with conflict

---

[11] (1774) 1 Coup. 161: 1 S.L.C. 615, in which Lord Mansfield again brought the law forward by taking the view that a justification by the *lex loci delicti* could be pleaded as a defence to an action in England. But see Graveson, p.135, on the matter of taking jurisdiction where the conduct complained of related to immovable property in Nova Scotia (a "local" (land) action as opposed to a "transitory" (with the potential to arise anywhere) action, in English parlance). Morse, *Torts in Private International Law* (1978), p.9.

[12] Because the common law "Double Rule" is retained by s.13 in relation to actions pertaining to defamation, and in other less obvious ways. See Ch.16.

[13] And until 1971 (when this requirement was removed by the Law Reform (Jurisdiction in Delict) Act 1971) so long as the defender was served within the jurisdiction.

[14] Morris, *The Conflict of Laws* (4th ed., McClean, 1993), p.6. Dicey's *Conflict of Laws* (1896) is regarded as the first systematic English treatment.

[15] *Commentaries on the Conflict of Laws* (1834).

[16] Through Cheshire, Graveson and Morris, the distinguished list continues up to the expertise of the present day. The subject becomes larger and the experts specialists within it.

problems at an earlier date than the English courts.[17] The diction-aries of Morison, Kilkerran and others contain reports of Scots conflict cases[18] a century ahead of English cases.

Knowledge of conflict thinking grew through scholarship[19] and through trade, the latter perhaps even more valuable in the view of Gibb.[20] It is gratifyingly evident in the early case of *Stranger from Middleburg v Executors of Smith*,[21] a case concerning a bond which the deceased Smith, a Scot, had made in Flanders, but had failed to honour, and from whose estate in Scotland the Flemish creditor had been obliged to seek satisfaction. The Scots court upheld the bond as valid, though it lacked witnesses, "because the pursuer offered to prove that it was the custom of the country that such bonds, albeit wanting witnesses, yet were effectual against the subscribers thereof", a matter to be proved, not by declarations of witnesses, but by a testimonial by the judges of the country.[22] In *A Frenchman against an Englishman*[23] it was held that the Scottish Lords of Council were competent judges between stranger and stranger, in all civil actions, "even concerning transactions outside the realm", and should decide according to "the common law, and not after the municipal law of this realme": the choice of law therefore was not to be Scots law despite the fact that Scotland was the forum. Possibly what was intended was the application of the "Law of Nations"; that is, principles of right reason generally accepted internationally.

The links achieved as a result of trade demonstrated at an early date the problems which systems of international private law exist to try to solve. It was the practice in Scotland to confer upon one town in the Low Countries a monopoly of trade: this was the "Scottish Staple", established at various times at Middleburg, Campvere, Antwerp, Bruges, and at Vere, from 1541, with two breaks, until the practice died out. All Scots merchants had to use the favoured town, and in return it would keep the channel safe, and provide warehouse accommodation and wharfage.[24] Hence,

---

[17] Gibb, "International Private Law in Scotland in the 16th and 17th Centuries" (1927) 39 J.R. 369; A. Donaldson, "Some Conflict Rules of Scots Law" in "Problems of Public and Private International Law" (1953) 39, *The Grotius Society*, 145 at 145–148.

[18] See Anton with Beaumont, pp.9–13. But also in the later Victorian years, Scotland produced significant and helpful cases: see MacKinnon, *Leading Cases in the International Private Law of Scotland* (W. Green, 1934); and see Gibb, *op. cit.*, pp.89–91.

[19] It is well established that many Scottish students resorted to European univer-sities in the Low Countries such as Franeker and Leyden: Walker, *The Scottish Legal System* (8th ed., revised 2001), p.163.

[20] Gibb, p.373.

[21] (1626) Mor. 12420.

[22] This accords with the modern practice: Rome Convention, Art. 9(1). See Ch.13.

[23] (1550) Mor. 7323.

[24] Gibb, p.375, who comments that English merchants were never other than private adventurers.

there grew up a little Scottish colony which had a Governor, the Lord Conservator of the Scottish privileges, with jurisdiction to hear disputes between Scots litigants and to apply Scots law. Gibb notes how remarkable it is to find a judge exercising exclusive jurisdiction and using his own law in a foreign country.[25] The Scots community *lege Scotica viverunt*. There was appeal to the Scots courts. Where the parties were Scots and Dutch, a mixed court of local magistrates and arbiters appointed by the Conservator would decide, but it is uncertain according to which law. We know that when a Scotsman married a Dutchwoman, she came under the jurisdiction of the Conservator and became subject to Scots law. It has been pointed out,[26] however, that there was a loophole (closed in 1696) which gave advantages for the potentially insolvent Scots merchant: if he became bankrupt, his property would escape safe to his wife.

When a community is transferred out of its usual abode, it is compelled to consider the conflict of laws. Conversely, when the gates are closed between neighbours, conditions do not encourage development of conflict thinking.

Donaldson[27] concluded that, although Scotland by the end of the seventeenth century could not be said to be furnished with a complete set of conflict rules, certain principles were clearly established, namely, the pre-eminence of the *lex situs* in property matters,[28] and of the *lex fori* in procedure, and the universality of bankruptcy.

HOW SCOTTISH ARE OUR CONFLICT RULES?

In contrast with the early days, for many years there has been a **2–04** spirit of co-operation and sympathy between English and Scots law and between their law reform agencies in the matters of the aims and content of their conflict rules. Not only can there be identified swathes of conflict rules which long have been similar in content and mutually supportive,[29] there is now also, in an increasing

---

[25] Indeed it is hard to think of a parallel, though the Court of Session in the person of Lord Milligan transported itself in 1992, with the co-operation of the Lithuanian Supreme Court, to Vilnius, in Latvia, to hear a case concerning alleged war crimes. This was done in view of the age and infirmity of the witnesses (although the original pursuer, alleged to be a war criminal, participated in the proceedings by satellite telephone link from Edinburgh, in view of *his* age and infirmity).

[26] Gibb, p.377.

[27] Donaldson, p.147.

[28] *Lamb v Heath* (1624) Mor. 4812.

[29] *e.g.* in family law, obligations, property and succession (while there remain many differences between the domestic laws of Scotland and England in these areas).

number of areas, uniformity attributable to the europeanisation of the subject.[30] Further, there is within the UK mutual recognition of consistorial decrees,[31] of parental responsibility orders and adoption orders,[32] and of confirmation and probate/letters of administration.[33] Strictly speaking, conflict decisions of one legal system of the UK are merely persuasive in the other, but the conflict decisions of the one jurisdiction are likely to be followed in the other if on a point common to both sets of conflict rules. If the decision be of the House of Lords on a matter of general principle, Professor Anton[34] notes that for all practical purposes the decisions will be of equal authority in both countries: in this way there have become "naturalised" in England, Scottish House of Lords cases and *vice versa*. The twin Victorian domicile pillars of *Udny v Udny*[35] and *Bell v Kennedy*[36] (both Scottish House of Lords cases) represent a very British view of domicile. A caveat perhaps should be inserted: where a substantial body of interpretative case law has been developed in Scotland in a particular subject matter (*e.g.* concerning the 1980 Hague Convention on the Civil Aspects of International Child Abduction), there is less need and less inclination to refer to English authority. The approach taken in this book is that the conflict rules of Scots and English law in many areas have more to unite them than to divide them: where there are differences, or have been differences, these will be mentioned in the text. This is not intended to detract in any way from the status of the body of Scots conflict rules as a complete and independent system, capable of providing an answer to any conflict problem.

Account must be taken of the fundamental constitutional change effected by the Scotland Act 1998, as a result of which matters of Scottish civil law fall within the legislative competence of the Scottish Parliament.[37] Section 126(4)(a) interprets the civil law of Scotland as a reference to the general principles of private law, including private international law.[38] An Act of the Scottish Parliament is not law insofar as any provision thereof is outside the legislative competence of the Parliament; reserved matters are expressly excluded from the legislative competence of the Scottish

---

[30] See Ch.1.

[31] See Ch.12.

[32] See Ch.14.

[33] See Ch.18.

[34] Anton with Beaumont, p.9.

[35] (1869) 7 M. (H.L.) 89.

[36] (1868) 6 M. (H.L.) 69.

[37] s.29 (legislative competence) establishes what the Scottish Parliament may not do rather than what it may do. Section 29(2)(b) provides that reserved matters (s.30 and Sch.5) are outside Scottish Parliamentary competence.

[38] Family Law (Scotland) Act 2006, s.38 serves as an example of Holyrood utilisation of this competence.

Parliament. The question whether a provision relates to a reserved matter is to be determined by reference to the purpose of the provision.[39] Although international private law generally is a devolved matter falling within the legislative competence of the Scottish Parliament, the private international law aspects of reserved matters also are reserved (section 29(4)(b); *e.g.* the international private law rules concerning intellectual property).

In terms of section 57 ("Community law and Convention rights"), despite the transfer to the Scottish Ministers of functions in relation to implementing obligations under Community law, any function of a Minister of the Crown in relation to any matter shall be continued to be exercisable by him as regards Scotland for the purposes of section 2(2) of the European Communities Act 1972. In this context, therefore, there is "shared power" between Scottish and UK Ministers. Furthermore, Schedule 5, Part 1, paragraph 7 "reserves" foreign affairs, including relations with the EU, but excepting implementation of obligations under Community law.[40] Moreover, it is intended[41] that the Scottish Executive will be involved closely in policy formation and negotiation of EU legislation.

With regard to participation in and ratification of initiatives of the Hague Conference on Private International Law, it remains the case that the United Kingdom is the Hague Conference Contracting State. Nevertheless, on occasion, as a result of differences in the content of certain areas of domestic law of Scotland and England, it may happen that the United Kingdom will sign a Hague Convention on behalf of one constituent legal system only.[42]

By constitutional convention,[43] it is possible for the UK Parliament, with consent of the Scottish Parliament, to legislate for

---

[39] s.29(3).

[40] Secondary legislation may be required separately in Scotland and in England, *e.g.* pertaining to Council Regulation (EC) No 2201/2003 concerning Jurisdiction and the Recognition and Enforcement of Judgments in Matrimonial Matters and in Matters of Parental Responsibility for Children of Both Spouses, repealing Regulation (EC) No 1347/2000 (27 November 2003) (OJ 2003 L338/1): The European Communities (Jurisdiction and Judgments in Matrimonial and Parental Responsibility Matters) Regulations 2005 (SI 2005 No 265) (England and Wales); and The European Communities (Matrimonial and Parental Responsibility Jurisdiction and Judgments) (Scotland) Regulations 2005 (SI 2005 No 42).

[41] *Scotland's Parliament* CM. 3658 (1997) (White Paper), Ch.8.

[42] *e.g.* 2000 Hague Convention on International Protection of Adults, signed by the UK separately for Scotland and for England, and now ratified by Scotland only.

[43] The "Sewel Convention". See generally N. Burrows, "This is Scotland's Parliament: Let Scotland's Parliament Legislate", 2002 J.R. 213. In October 2005, the Scottish Parliament's Procedures Committee proposed that existing procedures "should be replaced with a framework of new rules to improve transparency and to enhance the opportunity for parliamentary security". Under the proposal, "Sewel motions" in future would be known as "Legislative Consent Motions" (Procedure Committee, 7th Report, 2005 (session 2) SP Paper 428).

Scotland in devolved matters. In the context of the conflict of laws, particularly in family law, there may be perceivable benefits from having the UK Parliament legislate for the entire UK, thus lessening the likelihood of intra-UK conflict problems. The resultant UK legislation may contain separate provision for each legal system within the UK, but even if that is the case, it is hoped that the legislation will demonstrate internal UK coherence.[44]

Even in the post-devolution era, therefore, the relationship between Scots and English conflict of laws and their continuing development (independently, intra-UK and vis-à-vis third states) still is characterised by a subtle interaction and inter-dependence.

---

[44] The Civil Partnership Act 2004, which affects reserved matters as well as devolved matters, was referred to Westminster by means of a Sewel motion. The Act, however, makes bespoke provision for the different legal systems within the UK. See Ch.9. *cf* Matrimonial and Family Proceedings Act 1984, Pt 3 (England) and Pt 4 (Scotland).

CHAPTER 3

OPERATION OF FOREIGN LAW: THEORIES OF INCLUSION AND RULES OF EXCLUSION

Why should the domestic law of one legal system be recognised **3–01** and given effect to in another? It is surely a sufficient reply that there is in each developed legal system a system of rules, known as its international private law, or conflict of laws, rules, which regulates these matters: the operation of the rules of one legal system within the bounds of another stems from the law of the latter. There is therefore no affront to sovereignty.

However, over the course of the relatively young life of the subject, various theories have been advanced to explain the extra-territorial effect of a rule:

(1) The International Theory (comity) finds the nature of the subject in the notion of international goodwill or reciprocity, a "do as you would be done by" spirit of international co-operation,[1] which indeed is present in many modern international legislative exercises,[2] as well as in longer-established bodies of rules based on mutual assistance,[3] the more so if the legal systems involved are each members of a supranational body.[4]

(2) The Statutory or Neo-Statutory Theory is derived from the distinction made by Bartolus[5] between Statutes Real (affecting only property situated within the enacting State) and Statutes Personal (affecting the individual in his personal life wherever he or she might go). The distinction remains illuminating.

---

[1] See L. Collins, "Comity in Modern Private International Law" in J. Fawcett, ed., *Reform and Development in Private International Law. Essays in Honour of Sir Peter North* (2002), Ch.4.

[2] *e.g.* 1980 Hague Convention on the Civil Aspects of International Child Abduction and 1996 Hague Convention on Jurisdiction, Applicable Law, Recognition, Enforcement and Cooperation in respect of Parental Responsibility Measures for the Protection of Children.

[3] *e.g.* in foreign judgment enforcement: Administration of Justice Act 1920 and Foreign Judgments (Reciprocal Enforcement) Act 1933; and Civil Jurisdictions and Judgments Acts 1982 and 1991.

[4] See Ch.1 above.

[5] See para. 2–01 above.

(3) Savigny's Theory of the Natural Seat of an Obligation[6] holds that every relationship is by its nature connected more strongly with one legal system than with any other. That legal system, therefore, being the source of rights and obligations, should determine the outcome wherever it is litigated.

Savigny's view was "universalist" and supranational, seeking uniformity in the treatment of conflict cases. Savigny's work (adapted[7]) had a Scottish follower in James Lorimer (1818–90), writer on international law (favouring the law of nature).[8]

(4) Mancini's Theory of Nationality. The movements for political unification of Italy and Germany in the latter part of the nineteenth century brought with them a natural enthusiasm for nationality as the most suitable choice of personal law. Mancini argued that nationality was the basis of international law (propounding this at a famous lecture at the University of Turin in 1851) and that a person should be entitled, under limited exceptions, to be governed by the law of his nationality even when abroad.

(5) The Territorial Theory originated in the writings of the Dutch jurists and in particular those of Huber.[9] This theory, which reflects the concerns of the time at which Huber was writing (1689), and which is founded upon the dignity of sovereigns, and their power and authority within their own realms, continues to influence many areas of the subject, *e.g.* property matters. In effect the theory means that a state has complete power over all persons and property within its territory, that within its territory only its own law applies, and that it has no power over persons and property outside its own territory: "The Laws of a foreign State have no coercive force *extra territorium*."[10] It follows from this that, if foreign rights are to be recognised in Scotland, they must be regarded as being part of Scots law and/or as acquiring recognition under Scots conflict rules.

(6) The Local Law Theory, which arose from the observations and writings of the American jurist Cook, suggests that the forum, when asked to lend its aid to enforce a foreign right

---

[6] Von Savigny, *System of Modern Roman Law* (1849), Vol. 8, translated by Sheriff Wm Guthrie, *A Treatise on the Conflict of Laws* (1869). cf. in similar vein, American view expressed by Holmes and Cardozo JJ. that foreign law constitutes an *obligatio* which "follows the person and may be enforced wherever the person may be found": *Slater v Mexican National Railway* (1904) 194 U.S. 120 at 126.

[7] Walker, *The Scottish Jurists*, p.369.

[8] Walker, *op. cit.*, p.370.

[9] See above at para. 2–02.

[10] *Morison's Dictionary*, 4453.

which has originated in a foreign system, does not apply foreign law, but uses an analogous right of its own domestic law to achieve the same end.[11]

(7) The Theory of Justice. It may be that the true basis of the subject is simply the desire and necessity to ensure that the ends of justice are served and in particular that justice is done to the individual whose personal or business life has led him or her to experience the conflict of laws. "Conflicts justice" would seem to include considerations such as meeting party expectations, and achieving certainty, predictability and uniformity of result. Graveson writes that this is the major basis of the subject.[12] It is doubtful whether the grand aim of uniformity of result regardless of forum is ever capable of being accomplished—and indeed whether that is, or should be, the grandest aim of the subject.

(8) American policy evaluation theories, discussed and debated in the USA since the 1930s (termed "The American Revolution"[13]), and which constitute a fundamental change in thinking (both as to theory and as to method).

There are many approaches, and there has been much writing.[14] Essentially the policy evaluation thinking seeks to depart from the traditional jurisdiction-selecting[15] approach of "blind" or "blinkered" selection of the law to be applied

---

[11] Cases may be found in which the theory seems to be borne out by the circumstances and outcome, *e.g. Re Bettinson* [1956] Ch. 67.

[12] Graveson, p.7. He cites at p.9 the "Greek Bank Case" of *National Bank of Greece and Athens v Metliss* [1958] A.C. 509, *per* Viscount Simonds at 525. This case, together with *Adams v National Bank of Greece and Athens* [1961] A.C. 255, narrates a lengthy story, at the end of which English creditors under an English bond made with Greek debtors were held by the House of Lords to be entitled to enforce their debt in England against the debtor's successors, Greek moratoriums notwithstanding: cf. *Gray v Formosa* [1963] P.259 (status: see Ch.10).

[13] See Morris, 6th ed. (2005), Ch.21; and PM North, "Family Law and the American Revolution" in *Essays in Private International Law* (1993), Ch.6.

[14] Though the writing may be said to be concerned particularly with inter-state conflicts. The federal structure, wherever found (but especially in the USA) is likely to produce conflict disputes. The American Law Institute brought together, in a Restatement, the most important principles. The Restatement is persuasive, not binding on states, but has been influential for good. The first Restatement (1934, with Reporter Beale) was certain in tone and favoured the Vested Rights approach; the second Restatement (1971, with Reporter Reese) is more open to the new theories and methods.

[15] This is a term used to describe the orthodox choice of law process which seeks to apply the law indicated as applicable, category by category, according to the forum's choice of law rules. This method is not intended to take account of the outcome in the instant case. The term is confusing because "jurisdiction" in this context must be interpreted, unusually, as a reference to the rules of a particular legal system and does not pertain to the allocation or exercise of jurisdiction by a particular forum.

which is appropriate in the abstract (in the view of the
forum) to adjudicate upon the type of problem in question,
and instead to have regard to the nature and desirability (in
view of the forum, presumably) of the particular outcome,
i.e. to consider the effect in the concrete case of the
application of such law.

Every forum has to struggle against the view, conscious
or subconscious, that its own law is best. Commentators,
and courts themselves, must be alert to incidents of a
"homeward trend" on the part of the forum, that is to say,
a tendency of the forum to favour its own law and/or its
"own" litigant. It has been suggested that often the effect
of the policy evaluation theories—or, properly, methods—
is that the forum wends its way home, albeit by a circuitous
route.

Examples of the policy evaluation methods include the
theories of "Government Interest Analysis" (can the policies of the competing laws be ascertained? How reasonable is it for each respective state to assert an interest in
the application of its law?), "Comparative Impairment" (if
policies conflict, there should be applied the law of the
state whose interest would be more/most gravely impaired
if not applied), "Principles of Preference"[16] and "Choice
Influencing Factors", which proceed on the basis that
agreement on certain general aims, for example protection
of justified expectations, or uniformity of result, should aid
choice of law.

All such policy evaluation methods involve "rule-
selection", that is, "looking up to see the finishing tape",
which is at odds with the orthodox or classical "jurisdiction-
selection" method traditionally held to provide the benefits
of neutrality and distance. Quite apart from the question of
acceptability in principle of such a rule-selection approach,
it is thought unsuitable in an international, as opposed to
an inter-state, context.[17]

(9) The Theory of the Vested or Acquired Right, based on the
Territorial Theory, was advocated by Dicey. The effect of
the theory is that, if a question should arise in Scotland as
to the enforcement of a "foreign right", in solving the

---

[16] Cavers's suggestions are concerned principally with the law of obligations,
offering guidance to the forum on grounds of general policy (the higher standard
of conduct being usually, but not always, preferred) in choosing between or
among the rules of interested states.

[17] Morris, p.533 (re principles of preference) "[H]ow could a judge express a
preference for the rules adopted by one country or another when those countries
are not component parts of a federal system but are linked only by diplomatic
relations or (perhaps) by a common cultural heritage?"

problem the Scots court must determine the origin of the foreign right and ascertain whether it is a right which has been validly acquired under its own law. If that is so, the right will be enforceable in Scotland provided that its enforcement does not fall within any of the exceptions, discussed in paragraph 3–02 below. Whatever the merits and standing of the theory (or of any theory of extra-territorial validity and enforceability of rights), at least the exceptions or limitations are well known, well understood, and well vouched:[18] no Scots or English court will recognise or give effect to a foreign right if this would involve:

(a) the enforcement of foreign revenue laws;
(b) the enforcement of foreign penal laws;
(c) the enforcement extra-territorially of foreign confisca-tory laws; or
(d) making a decision inconsistent with the public policy or morality of this country, or detrimental to its political and judicial institutions.

The procedure available by Scots law must be appropriate for the enforcement of the right, and a foreign right, which is otherwise valid, will not be enforced if its enforcement would involve any question of discretion or some other element which would be exercised more appropriately by a foreign court.[19]

The theory has been the subject of trenchant criticism.[20] The germ of the vested rights theory (as well as of the comity theory) can be found in Huber's third maxim (paragraph 2–02, above). The premise is that it is not the foreign law *per se* which is being enforced *extra-territorium*, but rights acquired under the foreign law; but it is difficult to see how the rights conferred by a legal system can be dissociated from the law which created them. Moreover, if the forum is to set itself to implement foreign acquired rights, so far as its own public policy and procedure allow, it must ascertain the law by which the right is to be tested to determine whether it has vested or has been acquired. The theory contains no choice of law rules. The forum cannot start from the right and work backwards, assuming/supposing that the right should be enforced, because the law whence the right has sprung may not be (in the view of the forum) the correct choice of law to

---

[18] Though nowadays, while the core of the exceptions (a)—(c) holds firm, the edges, as a result of harmonisation and globalisation, are not so well defined.

[19] *Phrantzes v Argenti* [1960] 1 Q.B. 19; contrast *Shahnaz v Rizwan* [1965] 1 Q.B. 390.

[20] Supporters are Schmitthof, pp.32 and 35 *et seq.*, and Beale, *Treatise on the Conflict of Laws* (1935); the theory has been criticised by Cheshire, various editions, and see 13th ed., pp.20–22, Wolff, p.2, moderately by Graveson, p.38 and others.

apply.[21] Therefore, if the acquired rights theory is to be used at all, it seems suitable only for simpler cases where all seemingly relevant factors (apart from the identity of the forum) pertain to one legal system, and the remedy available in the legal system of origin is sought elsewhere: there are a number of cases in the conflict of laws catalogue which satisfy this test,[22] but a much greater number which do not. However, there is no doubt that the vested rights theory, as encapsulated in a form of words as a guide, instils the correct attitude of international co-operation and open-mindedness.[23] Novelty in itself should be no bar to the enforcement of a foreign acquired right,[24] nor to the recognition of a foreign status unknown but unexceptionable.[25]

THE EXCEPTIONS TO THE ENFORCEMENT OF FOREIGN RIGHTS
(THE EXCLUSION OF FOREIGN LAW)

REVENUE LAWS

3–02 As a general rule, the revenue laws of a foreign country are not enforceable in the United Kingdom because such laws are regarded as being essentially local in their application and not appropriate for enforcement in any other country.[26] The rule applies as regards the revenue laws of all other countries whatsoever whether foreign countries or countries of the British Commonwealth.[27] As a result of the overarching jurisdiction of the

---

[21] cf. Guthrie's translation of Savigny: Anton with Beaumont, p.28.

[22] *e.g. Dalrymple v Dalrymple* (1811) 2 Hag. Con. 54 at 58; *Caldwell v Van Vlissengen* (1851) 9 Hare 415 at 425; *Hooper v Gumm* (1867) I.R. 2 Ch. 282, *per* Turner, L.J. at 289–290; *Slater v Mexican National Railroad Co.* (1904) 194 U.S. 120 at 125; *Re Bettinson* [1956] Ch. 67; *Phrantzes v Argenti* [1960] 1 Q.B. 19; *Shahnaz v Rizwan* [1965] 1 Q.B. 390.

[23] See Cheshire & North, p.22.

[24] *Shahnaz v Rizwan*, above: contrast *Phrantzes v Argenti*, above.

[25] *Bumper Development Corporation v Commissioner of Police of the Metropolis* [1991] 1 W.L.R. 1362.

[26] See *Holman v Johnson* [1775–1802] All E.R. Rep. 98, *per* Lord Mansfield CJ at 99: "no country ever takes note of the revenue laws of another"; *The Eva* [1921] P. 454; *Re Visser* [1928] Ch. 877; *Rossano v Manufacturers' Life Ins. Co.* [1963] 1 Q.B. 352; and *Lord Advocate v Tursi*, 1998 S.L.T. 1035. The principal authority is *Government of India v Taylor* [1955] A.C. 491.

[27] *Attorney-General for Canada v Schulze*, 1901 9 S.L.T. 4, *per* Lord Stormonth-Darling at 5: "It is no doubt rather anomalous that the King, through his Courts in Scotland, should refuse to recognise a debt due to himself in Canada, merely because it arises out of the execution of a Revenue Statute. But it was not maintained, and I think is not maintainable, that in the sense of international law, the mother country and her self-governing colonies stand in different relationship from that which exists between two foreign states. If that relationship is ever to be modified it must be done by reciprocal legislation." See also *Government of India v Taylor*, above.

Westminster Parliament and the common exchequer, revenue laws are enforceable throughout the UK. However, in view of section 73 of the Scotland Act 1998, which confers upon the Scottish Parliament tax-varying power,[28] the Scottish Parliament has power to vary, "for Scottish taxpayers",[29] the basic rate of income tax by up to 3 per cent.[30] The question which in time may require to be answered is whether the Inland Revenue in Scotland may pursue a claim against a Scottish taxpayer, later resident in England, for any unpaid tax due by him/her, arising under a provision made by the Scottish Parliament. While it may be anomalous that it should not be able to do so, by reason of the "revenue law exception", this may indeed be the case since a distinction can still be drawn between tax legislation passed on a UK basis by the Westminster Parliament under its superior authority, and that passed by the Scottish Parliament under its tax-varying powers.

The revenue law exception applies only to the *collection of money*, with the result that foreign revenue laws may be recognised and receive effect indirectly. Foreign revenue laws therefore have received effect as regards currency laws,[31] sufficiency of stamp duty, or forgery of coins or banknotes. Double taxation treaties exist with the aim of ensuring that the income of corporate bodies or individuals is subjected to taxation only by one of the signatory states: they provide the detailed regulation required to assess the income according to its source. When considering the claim the forum will categorise its nature as "revenue", or not. It does not matter in what light the claim is viewed in its legal system of "origin". Lord Cameron stated in *Metal Industries (Salvage) Ltd v Owners of the S.T. Harle*[32]: "It is a general rule of law that no state will act as a tax gatherer for another or permit its courts to be used for that purpose, and it is a corollary of that rule that what is a revenue or fiscal claim is to be determined by the Courts of the country where the claim is sought to be enforced and in accordance with the *lex fori*."

The forum will not knowingly be deluded by the manner in which the claim comes to court, or by its form, but rather will seek

---

[28] Pt IV, ss.73–79.
[29] s.75 defines "Scottish taxpayer" essentially on the basis of the proportion of days during which a person has resided in Scotland in the tax year in question.
[30] s.73(1)(b).
[31] *Re Helbert Wagg* [1956] Ch. 323; *Kahler v Midland Bank* [1950] A.C. 24; *Zivnostenka Banka v Frankman* [1950] A.C. 57; contrast *Indian and General Inv. Trust Co. v Borax Consolidated Ltd* [1920] 1 K.B. 539 and *Rossano v Manufacturers Life Ins. Co.* [1963] 1 Q.B. 352.
[32] 1962 S.L.T. 114, 116.

to ascertain its true nature.[33] A claim for local rates has been classified as "revenue"[34]; so too has been a claim in a Scottish multiplepoinding for employers' contributions, unpaid, to a French government Benefit Scheme for seamen.[35] However, where the *lex causae* has the effect of permitting its exchange control laws to discharge a contractual obligation, the contract will be discharged according to Scots and English conflict rules,[36] nor will our courts connive at an attempt to deprive a foreign government of its revenue.[37] A most instructive example is provided by the case of *Re State of Norway's Application*,[38] a tax investigation into the affairs of the late AJ, a Norwegian. With the agreement of the late AJ's family, the Norwegian tax authorities sought to have evidence taken in England from two merchant bankers for use in a tax litigation in Norway. This was done by means of "letters of request" under the Evidence (Proceedings in Other Jurisdictions) Act 1975.[39] The House of Lords permitted the application on the view that this was not an attempt to collect foreign revenue but rather a request for assistance in a tax investigation. As to the warring principles of banker/client confidentiality on the one hand, and the demands of international comity on the other, the court favoured the latter, while protecting the former by a careful monitoring of the terms of the questions to be asked. Moreover, trustees or executors who decide to pay foreign inheritance tax may be exonerated (though the foreign government could not stand in our courts to claim the sum), if by their action they have taken the only means of giving effect to the wishes of the testator or testatrix.[40]

---

[33] *Peter Buchanan Ltd v McVey* [1954] I.R. 89, [1955] A.C. 516; cf. *QRS 1 Aps v Frandsen* [1999] 3 All E.R. 289. See also *Brokaw v Seatrain UK Ltd* [1971] 2 All E.R. 98, *per* Lord Denning at 100: "It is well established in English law that our courts will not give their aid to enforce, directly or indirectly, the revenue law of another country. That was decided in the times of Lord Mansfield C.J.": *Holman v Johnson* [1775–1802] All E.R. Rep. 98 at 99. "Classification" or "characterisation" of an issue is discussed below at Ch.4.

[34] *Municipal Council of Sydney v Bull* [1909] 1 K.B. 7.

[35] *Metal Industries (Salvage) Ltd v Harle*, 1962 S.L.T. 114.

[36] See *Re Helbert Wagg* and *Kahler* above.

[37] e.g. by affording a party who had divested himself in America of shares in favour of his wife the opportunity to attempt to prove the true position by trying to rebut the presumption of gift: *Re Emery* [1959] Ch. 410.

[38] [1989] 1 All E.R. 745.

[39] With regard to the classification of a fiscal case as being of a "civil or commercial" nature, in order to satisfy the 1975 Act, s.1, the House of Lords held that classification of the proceedings was to be referred to the laws of both states (the requesting state and the state addressed), since there was no internationally acceptable classification. Lord Goff, giving the leading speech, concluded that the 1975 Act would apply only if both states agreed that the proceedings were to be categorised as civil. A dual approach to classification is unusual.

[40] *Scottish National Orchestra Society Ltd v Thomson's Executor*, 1969 S.L.T. 325; *Re Lord Cable deceased* [1977] 3 All E.R. 417.

Therefore, there are many exceptions to the revenue law exception, or limitations on it. Some of these result from the EU harmonisation programme.[41]

PENAL LAWS

Penal laws are regarded also as being strictly local and therefore **3–03** they are not enforceable in another state.[42] In the sense of this rule, a penal law is a measure directed by a state against a particular individual or group of individuals. Hence it does not include a penalty in a private contract,[43] nor on the other hand does it include a general enactment confiscating all property, such an enactment falling under the heading of "confiscatory laws" below.

The classic definition was given by the Privy Council in *Huntington v Attrill*[44]: the "penal law exception" refers to "a penalty imposed by the State for some criminal violation of its rules". The (excluded) proceeding "must be in the nature of a suit in favour of the State whose law has been infringed, and the penalties must be recoverable at the instance of the State, or a State official, or a

---

[41] *e.g.* in terms of Council Regulation (EC) No 1346/2000 on Insolvency Proceedings, Art. 39, any creditor who has his habitual residence, domicile or registered office in a Member State, other than the State of the opening of insolvency proceedings, including the tax authorities and social security authorities of Member States, shall have the right to lodge claims in the insolvency proceedings in writing. There is also the concept of the "Community duty or tax", enforceable across boundaries of Member States (EC Directive 76/308: Mutual Assistance on Recovery of Claims). In terms of Criminal Justice Act 1993, s.71, a person who in the UK assists in, or induces, any conduct outside the UK which contravenes *inter alia* the determination, discharge or enforcement of any liability for any of the following Community duties or taxes commits an offence (that is to say, any Community customs duty, agricultural levy, value added tax under the law of any Member State, excise duty in another Member State or any duty or tax which is imposed by or in pursuance of any Community instrument or the movement of goods into or out of any Member State). In *QRS 1 Aps v Frandsen* [1999] 3 All E.R. 289, the Court of Appeal ruled that the principle of "the revenue law exception" as a fundamental of English law, could be objectively justified and therefore that it was not incompatible with European Community law. Neither the 1968 Brussels Convention nor Council Regulation 44/2001 extends to revenue, customs or administrative matters (Art.1). It was made clear in *QRS 1 Aps v Frandsen*, above, that the exception encompasses attempted indirect enforcement of revenue claims.

[42] "The courts of no country execute the penal laws of another"—*The Antelope, per* Marshall C.J. quoted in *Huntington v Attrill* [1893] A.C. 150. *Ogden v Folliot* (1790) 3 Term Rep. 726; affirming *sub nom. Folliot v Ogden* (1789) 1 H B1 123. For the problems which may arise in modern electronic conditions, see *Yahoo! Inc. v La Ligue Contra Le racisme et L'Autismitisme* 433 F 3d.; 2006 U.S. App. Lexis 668.

[43] *S.A. Consortium General Textiles v Sun and Sand Agencies Ltd* [1978] Q.B. 279, *per* Lord Denning at 299–300.

[44] [1893] A.C. 150.

member of the public acting in the public interest". This means that criminal law is intra-territorial. A person should face trial (if necessary following extradition) in the legal system where he allegedly committed the offence. There can be no conviction in Scotland on the ground of breach of a foreign criminal law, nor enforcement of a judgment given in foreign criminal proceedings.[45]

Sometimes the question of *where* an offence has taken place becomes of essential importance for the purpose of the meaning and operation of a statute. With regard to British statutes, there is a strong presumption against extra-territorial effect in the case of criminal statutes. Thus, on interpretation of the (English) Theft Act 1968, in circumstances where a criminal plan had been devised to bring stolen cars into Britain from Germany, it has been held that since the statutory crime of theft was a "once and for all" and not a "continuing" act, there could be no conviction in England, the criminal activity having been completed abroad.[46] It may be possible to sever the civil from the criminal aspect of a foreign award granted in a legal system which has a unified procedure, and there is no objection to enforcing the award of civil damages.[47]

To classify the nature of the foreign law is the function of the forum.[48] In *Huntington v Attrill*, the question was whether the New York-imposed liability on promoters for making misrepresentations in company reports was penal (criminal) in nature, or remedial (protective of private interests). The Privy Council, exercising the power of classification on appeal from the Court of Ontario, found it was not penal within the relevant conflict rule (or exception).

In this connection, therefore, "penal" should be understood as meaning "criminal" rather than in its other possible meaning of unfair or discriminatory.[49] A case may arise in which a foreign law can be regarded as "penal" in both senses, as illustrated by *Banco de Vizcaya v Don Alfonso*.[50] The Spanish Republican Government purported to confiscate the property in England of the former King Alfonso, founding on a Spanish decree declaring the King guilty of high treason and an outlaw. The English forum refused to enter-

---

[45] Though an instance of account being taken in Scotland, for the purpose of sentencing, of an individual's criminal history in England is to be found in the case of *Herd v H.M. Advocate*, 1993 G.W.D. 24–1504. cf. shrieval jurisdiction in relation to a statutory offence allegedly committed abroad: *McCarron v H.M. Advocate*, 2001 S.L.T. 866.

[46] *R v Atakpu* [1993] 4 All E.R. 215. See para.3–07, below.

[47] *Raulin v Fischer* [1911] 2 K.B. 93.

[48] See, *e.g.*, exercise of this function by the Irish court in *Larkins v National Union of Mineworkers* [1985] I.R. 671.

[49] Though early cases used it in this way: *Wolff v Oxholm* (1817) 6 M. & S. 92; see also *Re Fried Krupp Aktien-Gesellschaft* [1917] 2 Ch. 188.

[50] [1935] 1 K.B. 140.

tain the Spanish claim (which came to court in the form of a claim by a bank). In whatever form it appeared, it was an attempt to have enforced extra-territorially a foreign "penal" (and confiscatory) law. Again, in *USA v Inkley*,[51] the attempt by the U.S. Government to recover an "appearance bond" (security for appearance in forthcoming American criminal proceedings), granted by Inkley when in America, was irrecoverable from him when resident in England, because in the view of the English court the bond was inextricably linked with American public, criminal procedure.

Certain foreign statutory provisions, such as prohibitions on export without licence of historic artefacts, may be difficult to classify. In the leading case of *Attorney-General of New Zealand v Ortiz*,[52] Maori carvings, having been removed from New Zealand without the requisite certificate under the (New Zealand) Historic Articles Act 1962, the plaintiff sought to restrain the sale of these articles in London. Two principal questions arose: (1) the nature of the New Zealand statutory provision; and (2) interpretation of the wording of the provision, and in particular of the word "forfeit". In the Court of Appeal[53] the majority view was that the provision was "penal" (criminal), although Lord Denning placed it in a broad grouping which he termed "other public law" (and hence concurred with his brother judges in finding it not enforceable *extra-territorium*).[54] The speeches in the House of Lords were concerned only with interpretation of the word "forfeit", and the view taken of the meaning was that the carvings fell into the ownership of the Crown in right of New Zealand only if seized within the territorial bounds of New Zealand; on interpretation, there could be no notional forfeiture upon export from New Zealand without a licence.[55] Hence, to have conceded the Attorney-General's argument would have amounted to giving effect extra-territorially to a foreign law.

CONFISCATORY LAWS

There are three manifestations of confiscatory law: **3–04**

    (a) *expropriation or confiscation*: the taking by a state of property belonging to a private individual or body for public purposes without adequate compensation;

---

[51] [1989] Q.B. 255. See also *United States v A. Ltd* [2003] C.L.Y.B. 621.
[52] [1983] 2 All E.R. 93.
[53] [1982] 3 All E.R. 432.
[54] *Att.-Gen. v Heniemann Publishers Australia PTY Ltd* [1988] C.L.Y. 1982; and *United States v A. Ltd*, above.
[55] cf. and contrast *Kingdom of Spain v Christie, Manson & Woods Ltd* [1986] 1 W.L.R. 1120.

(b) *nationalisation*: the taking of private property for public purposes in the same circumstances upon payment of compensation;

(c) *requisitioning*: the taking of private property for public purposes with compensation for a limited period such as the duration of a war.[56]

Modern instances tend to concern the first of these.

The general principle is that the act of any recognised government[57] is accepted as being effective as regards all property situated within its territory, but as having no effect on property situated outside such territory. Hence, a confiscatory act directed against an individual or a class of individuals will be deemed to be completely effective as regards property belonging to such persons within the territory of the "confiscating" state,[58] but will not receive any effect in the view of Scots law as regards assets situated outside that territory.[59] The question, therefore, may simply be one as to the location of property, the territorial limits of the state which has purported to confiscate,[60] or as to the effective completion of the purported confiscation within those limits.[61] The suggestion made in *Anglo-Iranian Oil Co. v Jaffrate; The Rose Mary*,[62] that another requirement of an effective confiscation was that the persons divested of their property must be nationals of the confiscating state, was shortlived, and was disapproved in *Re Helbert Wagg*.[63] Intra-territorial compulsory acquisitions by recognised governments therefore are recognised.

Should a state purport to confiscate property beyond its territorial bounds, there will be a question of interpretation as to the intended extent of the confiscatory order; but even if extra-territorial ambit is intended, it is unlikely to receive effect. In *Lecouturier v Rey*[64] a French confiscation was interpreted by the

---

[56] As to which see anomalous wartime case of *Lorentzen v Lydden & Co. Ltd* [1942] 2 K.B. 202.

[57] See R. Leslie, "The Existence of Governments and the Conflict of Laws: the *Republic of Somalia* Case", 1997 J.R. 110.

[58] *Luther v Sagor* [1921] 3 K.B. 532; *Princess Paley Olga v Weisz* [1929] 1 K.B. 718; *Frankfurther v Exner* [1947] Ch. 629; *Novello v Hinrichsen* [1951] Ch. 1026.

[59] *Bank voor Handel v Slatford* [1953] 1 Q.B. 248.

[60] *The Jupiter* [1927] P. 122 and 250.

[61] *Williams & Humbert Ltd v W. & H. Trade Marks (Jersey) Ltd; Rumasa v Multinvest* [1986] A.C. 368: in complex circumstances, it was held by the House of Lords that a Spanish compulsory acquisition had in fact been completed within the territorial boundaries of Spain. But see F. Mann, "The Effect in England of the Compulsory Acquisition by a Foreign State of the Shares in a Foreign Company", 1987 L.Q.R. 191.

[62] [1953] 1 W.L.R. 246.

[63] [1956] Ch. 323.

[64] [1910] A.C. 262, at 265.

House of Lords as having been intended to be only of intra-territorial effect. However, in the words of Lord Macnaghten: "[t]o me it seems perfectly plain that it must be beyond the power of any foreign Court or any foreign legislature to prevent the monks from availing themselves in England of the benefit of the reputation which the liqueurs of their manufacture have acquired here".

It may be asked whether any inquiry can be made by the forum of the "immoral" quality of intra-territorial confiscation,[65] so as to provide justification for the forum in refusing recognition; or, in the obverse situation, whether a "benevolent" quality of an extra-territorial confiscation should permit recognition thereof.[66] It is thought that each submission is only superficially attractive and on reflection erroneous. There is found in *Oppenheimer v Cattermole*[67] condemnation of Nazi removal of Jewish German Citizenship.[68] Morris[69] raises the possibility that if a confiscation be regarded as discriminatory and unfair, there might be some means of circumventing the established conflict rule as to title to property if the confiscated property should find its way to Britain. However, on the whole it has to be concluded that there seems to be little support in case authority for this suggestion.[70] The House of Lords in *Williams & Humbert* took the view that expropriation is a common occurrence and that the forum should be concerned only with the territoriality principle.[71] The position is regulated in the general case by the principle of territoriality, and the resultant

---

[65] Consider the attempt made by Nourse J. in *Williams & Humbert Ltd*, above, at first instance to categorise governmental decrees according to degrees of unacceptability on moral grounds: [1985] 2 All E.R. 208 at 213–215; and see *per* Sir John Donaldson M.R. in *Settebello Ltd v Banco Totta & Acores* [1985] 1 W.L.R. 1050 at 1056–1057.

[66] See *Peer International Corp. v Termidor Music Publishers Ltd* [2004] Ch. 212: Morris, p.425. Contrast the clear decision against extra-territorial effect of a New Zealand statute of essentially benevolent intent in *Attorney General for New Zealand v Ortiz* [1983] 2 All E.R. 93.

[67] [1975] 1 All E.R. 538 (H.L.).

[68] The majority of their Lordships were in agreement with Wolff (2nd ed.), p.129: *e.g. per* Lord Hodson, at 557, "The courts of this country are not in my opinion obliged to shut their eyes to the shocking nature of such legislation as the 1941 decree if and when it falls for consideration." Yet in the circumstances the removal of citizenship was held to be effective; in consequence, in this tax case, the taxpayer was not entitled to tax relief under the relevant double taxation agreement.

[69] Morris, pp.425–426. But see *Frankfurther v Exner* [1947] Ch. 629, *per* Romer J. at 644 (strict territorial approach): it is in the nature of confiscations to be unfair.

[70] Morris, p.414. However, in the case of Nazi confiscations, the pressure of international opinion and the efforts of investigators seem likely to result in compensation, disbursement and/or restoration of property.

[71] *Williams & Humbert Ltd*, above, *per* Lord Templeman at 427, 428 and 431. As to human rights infringement and condemnation by opinion of international community, see *Kuwait Airways Corporation v Iraqi Airways Company* [2002] 3 All E.R. 209.

principle found in moveable property that he who takes a good title by the *lex situs* obtains a good title against the world.[72]

It has been established above that extra-territorial purported confiscations will not be viewed by courts in the UK as effective[73]; and it has been suggested that intra-territorial governmental confiscations will be regarded by courts in the UK as valid. An important difficulty arises in some cases where it is not clear whether the purported confiscation took place extra-territorially or intra-territorially, the most notable example being *Kuwait Airways Corporation v Iraqi Airways Company*,[74] which featured human rights argumentation, and concerted and expressed opprobrium by the international community.

Kuwait Airways Corporation v Iraqi Airways Company illustrates various points: the meaning of intra-territoriality; the application of the rule of intra-territoriality; the appropriate use of public policy to recognise or not intra-territorial confiscations; the appropriate use of public policy to exclude the application of an otherwise applicable foreign law in terms of the choice of law rule in tort; application of the common law choice of law rule of double actionability in tort; application of the choice of law rule in property; and interaction of international private law and public international law. The student of the rules of jurisdiction might also note the general lack of connection between the forum and the circumstances of the alleged tort. The first three of these issues shall be discussed in this chapter, and the remaining issues at relevant points throughout the text.

3–05　　The case arose out of the circumstances of the 1990 Gulf War. After lengthy litigation, including a trial of jurisdictional issues, it came before the House of Lords in the form of an action laid in the English tort of conversion (wrongful interference with the property of another). Iraqi military forces having occupied Kuwait, the Iraqi authorities passed resolutions proclaiming Iraqi sovereignty over Kuwait, and seized from Kuwait airport and removed to Iraq, a number of commercial aircraft belonging to Kuwait Airways Corporation ("KAC"). One month later, the Revolutionary Command Council of Iraq passed Resolution 369 dissolving KAC, and purporting to transfer all of its property, wherever situated, to the Iraqi Airways Company ("IAC"). Early in 1991, KAC began litigation against IAC and the Republic of Iraq, seeking return of the aircraft, or payment of the value, and damages.

---

[72] *Cammell v Sewell* (1860) 5 H. & N. 728 (Exchequer Chamber); *Princess Paley Olga v Weisz* [1929] 1 K.B. 718. See Ch.17.

[73] *Spain v National Bank of Scotland*, 1939 S.C. 413.

[74] [2002] 3 All E.R. 209. See E.B. Crawford and J.M. Carruthers, "*Kuwait Airways Corporation v Iraqi Airways Company*" 2003 (52) I.C.L.Q. 761.

The question of fundamental importance at the outset was whether the seizure of the aircraft was to be regarded as *intra-territorium* Iraq, in light of Iraq's purported annexation of Kuwait. The purported annexation was universally condemned, and United Nations Security Council resolutions called on member states to give no recognition, directly or indirectly, to the annexation.

Many conflict confiscation cases arose from turbulent events of the twentieth century, such as the Russian Revolution, the Spanish Civil War, and seizure of property by the Nazi regime. An important strand in the conflict reasoning of any Scots or English forum called upon to adjudicate upon such cases was whether the UK recognised the authority of the government which performed the confiscation in question, or which subsequently ratified the confiscatory actings, as *de jure* or *de facto*[75] in control of the territory in question.[76] A summary of twentieth century cases must conclude that the courts in Scotland and England recognised the actings of a governing body subsequently recognised (politically) by the UK Government, and all the private law consequences which flowed from such initial confiscation, without commenting upon the "morality" of the confiscatory event.

On this reasoning, had Kuwait been recognised, sooner or later, as Iraqi territory, then precedent suggests that a Scottish or English court would have recognised the confiscation and its private law consequences.[77] Conversely, the annexation of Kuwait not having been accorded recognition, had the litigation presented as a confiscation one, precedent would have required that the confiscation be refused recognition as an extra-territorial purported seizure. But the litigation presented in tort, and there was little discussion of these important anterior points.

A final point which may be relevant in this area of law is the position with regard to taking suit against a foreign government.[78] Historically, a Scots or English court could not proceed with an action against a foreign government in cases such as these if the foreign government had been recognised (politically) by the UK government as the *de jure* or *de facto* government, and was in peaceful possession of the property in question.[79] The subject of

---

[75] As a result of a parliamentary announcement in 1980 the British Government stated that it would no longer give formal recognition to new governments, although it would continue formally to recognise new states where appropriate. Henceforward, the status of a new regime must be inferred from the manner of the British Government's dealings with it, as to which the Foreign and Commonwealth Office will provide information. See Leslie, *op.cit.*, at 112.

[76] *Princess Paley Olga v Weisz* [1929] 1 K.B. 718.

[77] Subject to a scintilla of doubt about the proper reaction to "immoral"/evil conduct.

[78] See Cheshire & North, pp.388 *et seq.*

[79] *The Cristina* [1938] A.C. 485; *The Arantzazu Mendi* [1939] A.C. 256; *The Abodi Mendi* [1939] P. 178; *Zarine v Ramava* [1942] I.R. 148. See Leslie, *op.cit.*, 110.

sovereign immunity has been placed on a statutory basis following the European Convention on State Immunity (1972), which resulted in the passing of the State Immunity Act 1978. "The basic principle of the 1978 Act is that a foreign state is immune from the jurisdiction of the English courts and effect is to be given to that immunity whether or not the State appears in the proceedings."[80] Hence, a state is immune from the jurisdiction of the UK courts, unless it submits to the jurisdiction thereof,[81] but there are certain important exceptions from immunity.[82]

Where the foreign government is the pursuer, no question of immunity from suit arose at common law, or arises under statute.[83] However, in terms of substance, a foreign state or its official representative will not be able to secure from a Scottish or English court an order which gives effect extra-territorially to a foreign government act.[84]

Public Policy

3–06   It is a well-settled principle that the courts of this country will not apply a foreign rule if its terms, or the result which follows from the application thereof, would be contrary to the British conceptions of public policy, notwithstanding that the right which is sought to be enforced may have been validly acquired under the law of the country in which it had its origin.[85] This bar to the enforcement of a foreign right may derive from statute or public policy at common law:

---

[80] Cheshire and North, p.390. As to Sovereigns and heads of state, in public and private capacities, see *Bank of Credit and Commerce International (Overseas) Ltd (in liquidation) v Price Waterhouse* [1997] 4 All E.R. 108.

[81] ss.1–2.

[82] s.3–commercial transactions and contracts to be performed in the UK (see *Alcom Ltd v Republic of Columbia* [1984] 2 All E.R. 6); s.4–contracts of employment between the state and an individual; s.5–proceedings in respect of personal injury, death or damage to property; s.6–proceedings relating to property in the UK; s.7–proceedings relating to patents and trade marks; s.8–proceedings relating to a state's membership of a body corporate incorporated under the law of the UK; s.9–proceedings relating to agreement to submit to arbitration; s.10–admiralty proceedings; and s.11–state liability for value added tax, customs duty or excise duty. The subject of the extent of immunity where not expressly excluded arose in *Jones v Saudi Arabia* [2004] EWCA Civ 1394, with regard to the question whether an implied exception to immunity exists in the case of alleged torture.

[83] State Immunity Act 1978, s.2.

[84] See *Att.-Gen. of New Zealand v Ortiz* [1983] 2 All E.R. 93.

[85] Morris, p.41.

(a) Statute

A British Act of Parliament directly or indirectly may render a foreign right void as regards its enforcement in this country[86]; so too may a British act of indemnity or government declaration. [87]

(b) Public policy at common law

Public policy in this sense means British conceptions of morality and justice. In practice, the courts have applied this restraint in the following circumstances[88]:

(1) where the fundamental conceptions of British justice have been disregarded[89];

(2) where British conceptions of morality have been infringed;

(3) where the enforcement of a transaction would prejudice the interests of the United Kingdom or its good relations with foreign powers[90];

(4) where the recognition of a penal[91] condition of status or its incidents would offend British conceptions of human liberty and freedom of action.

It is accepted that the use of public policy in the conflict of laws should be more restricted than in domestic law, its scope narrower. The conflict of laws is not about conflict, but about the resolution of disputes in as fair-minded and non-partisan a manner as can be achieved by any given forum. This (even) more restrictive attitude

---

[86] *Philips v Eyre* (1870) L.R. 6 Q.B. 1; *Poll v Lord Advocate* (1899) 1 F. 823; *Foster v Driscoll* [1929] 1 K.B. 470.

[87] *Dobree v Napier* (1836) 2 Bing. N.Cas. 781; *Buran v Denman* (1848) 2 Ex. 167; *Carr v Fracis Times & Co.* [1902] A.C. 176; *Nissan v Att.-Gen.* [1963] 3 W.L.R. 1044.

[88] See P.B. Carter, "The Role of Public Policy in English Private International Law" 1993 (42) I.C.L.Q. 1; and R. Leslie, "The Relevance of Public Policy in Legal Issues Involving Other Countries and Their Laws", 1995 J.R. 477.

[89] *Re Hope* (1857) 8 De G.M. & G. 731 (collusive divorce); contrast *Crowe v Crowe* [1937] 2 All E.R. 723; *Grell v Levy* (1864) 16 C.B. (N.S.) 73 (*pactum de quota litis*); *Kaufman v Gerson* [1904] 1 K.B. 591 (*pactum illicitum*, unenforceable in England, even if acceptable by its French proper law); *Roussillon v Roussillon* (1880) 14 Ch.D. 51. Contrast *Addison v Brown* [1954] 1 W.L.R. 779. See more recently *Mohamed v Alaga & Co.* [1998] 2 All E.R. 720 (domestic case with foreign aspects).

[90] *Regazzione v Sethia* [1958] A.C. 301 (refusal of English court to allow the normal contractual remedies where the terms of the contract, to the knowledge of both parties, contravened Indian legislation prohibiting export of jute to South Africa); *Re Emery's Investment Trust* [1959] Ch. 410.

[91] In this sense, "penal" should be taken to mean (excessively) punitive, unfair or discriminatory. Examples arise in relation to prohibitions on marriage out of religion or out of caste: *Chetti v Chetti* [1909] P. 67; *MacDougall v Chitnavis*, 1937 S.C. 390. See Ch.11.

towards public policy in the international private law context is termed external public policy. There is a particular danger of public policy making mischief and running counter to the aims of the subject. Nevertheless, public policy must exist as a tool or a mechanism, available for use in any subject area of the conflict of laws, in order that the forum may avoid a result which, though identified as the "correct" result by its appropriate conflict rule, is fundamentally unacceptable to it. One question which arose from the case of *Kuwait Airways Corporation v Iraqi Airways Company* [92] was whether, and why, excision of part of the *lex loci delicti* was thought to be justified. The dissenting speech of Lord Scott preferred to proceed on the basis that the forum must accept and apply the whole content of the *lex loci delicti* as it stood in the eyes of Iraqi law. The majority view held that Resolution 369[93] constituted a fundamental breach of international law, this view strengthened by background circumstances of public international law as expressed in condemnatory UN Security Council resolutions.

In this matter of policy objection, we should remember that the domestic policy of the forum upon a certain matter may change from time to time (*e.g.* in relation to contingent fees, perhaps, or (not), to gaming contracts,[94] or recognition of same-sex relationships), and further that the forum must strive so far as possible to be consistent.[95] Moreover, in conflict cases, the ranking of policies may vary according to context and period of history.[96] Nevertheless, the right of any forum to act in the light of its own conscience is an essential part of its conflict rules, and the availability of exercise of such discretion by the forum serves to secure participation by contracting states in international co-operative projects since the international instruments to date invariably contain a public policy discretion. Normally this discretion may be used only where the rule in question is "manifestly contrary to public policy"; while this phrase has become formulaic, it is undeniable that it contains a

---

[92] [2002] 3 All E.R. 209.

[93] See para.3–05, above.

[94] *Ferguson v Littlewoods Pools Ltd*, 1997 S.L.T. 309.

[95] It can be shown that we are not always consistent: one hundred years after refusing to recognise the status of slave (*Sommerset v Stewart* (1772) 20 St. Tr. 1, *Knight v Wedderburn* (1778) Mor. 14545), the English courts enforced a contract for the sale of slaves, because the contract was valid by its Brazilian proper law (*Santos v Illidge* (1860) 8 C.B. (N.S.) 861). Again, we appear to have recognised, in *Corbett v Corbett* [1957] 1 All E.R. 621, a foreign prohibition of marriage between Jew and Gentile, imposed by the law of the then Palestine, while generally not approving such restrictions, though strictly the court was more concerned with being satisfied that the district court in Jerusalem had jurisdiction than with the ground of annulment. See generally Ch.10 below.

[96] See J.M. Carruthers and E.B. Crawford, "*Kuwait Airways Corporation v Iraqi Airways Company*", 2003 (52) I.C.L.Q. 761 at 768, n.57.

warning against over-use. Since its exercise is a manifestation of individual state discretion, attempts to formulate a fixed, pre-determined, regionally-harmonised view on a matter *sub nom.* public policy are inappropriate and paradoxical.[97]

It is possible to employ flexibility. The court in Scotland might accept a foreign status without being obliged to accept all its incidents, or to recognise a foreign divorce without accepting all the terms imposed by the foreign court. [98]

The effect of a successful plea to public policy in any given forum is normally negative, that is to say, it operates to exclude application of the rule of the otherwise applicable *lex causae*, and thereby to revert to the default position of applying the *lex fori*. But a positive use also can be envisaged, that is, where the public policy of the forum insists upon application of the domestic *lex fori*, overriding the otherwise applicable foreign law in order to supply a remedy or fill a gap. The presence and use of public policy will be discussed in context throughout this work.

THE OPERATION OF STATUTE LAW AND THE CONFLICT OF LAWS:
AMBIT OF STATUTES

Both British[99] and foreign statutes are presumed to have a strictly **3–07** limited territorial effect so that in general they apply respectively only to persons and property in British or foreign territory.[1] In many conflict cases it will be found that the answer to a problem depends upon the scope of a statute[2] and that the real question is

---

[97] "Community public policy", Rome II, Art.22, ex-Art.24. However, in the Amended Proposal of February 21, 2006 (COM (2006) 83 final), express reference to Community public policy has been deleted. See Ch.16, and E.B. Crawford and J.M. Carruthers, "Reflections on Rome II", Pt I, 2005 (9) Edin. L.R. 65. The harmonisation exercise of the European regime may require the suppression of the normally available freedom to refuse to recognise a judgment on the ground of differing substantive law (Brussels II *Bis*, Art.25) and therefore represents a further incursion into independent judgment.

[98] cf. *Att.-Gen. for Canada v Schulze*, above, where the expenses of a foreign revenue action could not be recovered in Scotland, as they were tainted by the excluded nature of the principal action. See also *Mayo-Perrott v Mayo-Perrott* [1958] I.R. 336, and contrast *Breen* [1964] P. 144.

[99] *Tomalin v Pearson* [1909] 2 K.B. 61; *Yorke v British and Continental Steamship Co. Ltd* (1945) 78 Ll. L. Rep. 181 (Digest 144). It may happen, however, that foreigners may be entitled to benefits under British statutory provisions— *Davidsson v Hill* [1901] 2 K.B. 606; *Krzus v Crow's Nest Pass Coal Co.* [1912] A.C. 590; *The Esso Malaysia* [1974] 3 W.L.R. 341.

[1] Contrast the situation in which British forces occupy foreign territory in order to maintain security: *R. (on the application of Al-Skeini and Ors v Secretary of State for Defence* [2005] All E.R. (D.) 337.

[2] Statutes imposing licensing requirements are particularly likely to be intra-territorial. *Dublin Finance Corp. v Rowe* [1943] N.I. 1; *Goetschuis v Brightman*, 245 N.Y. 186, 156 N.E. 660 (1927). And see *Dulaney v Merry* [1901] 1 Q.B. 536.

one of interpretation as to whether or not a particular statute is intended to apply, *e.g.* only to persons domiciled or resident in a particular country, or to contracts made or to be performed in, or to actings which took place in, some particular country.[3] In order to resolve a cross-border instance, a question of statutory interpretation may arise of a statute which Parliament did not consciously enact as a conflict of laws provision;[4] the problem is one of extent of operation. Traditionally, the British Parliament passed Acts with intended extra-territorial operation only in relation to nationality, status and capacity, [5] and exchange control,[6] but it is notable that many incursions have been made into the principle of intra-territoriality of Scottish or English statutes pertaining to criminal law.[7] British courts apply equivalent principles to the operation of foreign statutes[8]: it is probable that a foreign statute dealing with a matter of nationality, status and capacity, or exchange control would receive extra-territorial effect in Scotland,[9] subject to the forum's public policy.

It is important to appreciate that the corpus of Scots and English conflict rules, specifically so designated, now is largely statutory. These statutes may be entirely "conflict" law,[10] or may be general statutes, containing particular provisions of conflict of laws implication, which consciously[11] (or possibly inadvertently[12]) adhere to or cut across pre-existing conflict rules or reasoning.

The final point to make at this juncture is that as a matter of technical or orthodox conflict reasoning in a Scots or English forum, any rule, common law or statutory, of the applicable law (*lex causae*) *must* apply, if it is substantive in nature and in its terms

---

[3] Consider, *e.g.*, the scope of the Age of Legal Capacity (Scotland) Act 1991; see Nichols, "Can They or Can't They? Children and the Age of Legal Capacity (Scotland) Act 1991", 1991 S.L.T. 395.

[4] *Fox v Lawson* [1974] A.C. 803; *Cox v Army Council* [1963] A.C. 48; and *Duncan v Motherwell Bridge Engineering Co.*, 1952 S.L.T. 433. See also *R. v Atakpu* [1993] 4 All E.R. 215; consider also *Re Seagull Manufacturing Co. Ltd (in liquidation)* [1993] 2 All E.R. 980. And see *In re Paramount Airways Ltd (In Administration) (No.2)* [1992] 3 All E.R. 1.

[5] *e.g. Sussex Peerage Case* (1884) 11 Cl. & Fin. 85; and *Pugh v Pugh* [1951] P. 482.

[6] *Boissevain v Weil* [1950] A.C. 327.

[7] In respect of which see *International Private Law* (1st ed.), Ch.20.

[8] *Bank voor Handel v Slatford (No.2)* [1953] 1 Q.B. 248; *Jabbour v Custodian of Israeli Property* [1954] 1 W.L.R. 139. A decree of the Dutch government in wartime exile in England was not capable, in the view of the English court of the *lex fori* and *lex situs*, of affecting gold physically in England. Contrast *Lorentzen v Lydden & Co. Ltd* [1942] 2 K.B. 202, now discredited.

[9] See *Starkowski v Att.-Gen.* [1954] A.C. 155; and *Re Helbert Wagg* [1956] Ch. 323.

[10] *e.g.* Matrimonial and Family Proceedings Act 1984; Family Law Act 1986; Contracts (Applicable Law) Act 1990; Private International Law (Miscellaneous Provisions) Act 1995.

[11] Unfair Contract Terms Act 1977. Family Law (Scotland) Act 2006.

[12] Timeshare Act 1992.

not offensive to the policy of the forum. A more complex point is that modern conflict of laws instruments employ as a drafting device the concept of "mandatory rules".[13] Since the forum must give effect to these mandatory provisions of its own law or of a third law,[14] the result is that rules, usually statutory, of legal systems over and above the *lex causae*, sometimes must be applied. Hence, by reason of conflict of laws methodology, a Scots or English forum in a suitable case, potentially in any branch of law, may be required to give effect to a foreign statutory provision.

SUMMARY 3

A foreign right validly acquired under its proper/applicable law **3–08** (that is, by the law which in the view of a Scottish forum is the *lex causae*) will be enforceable in Scotland provided that the form of procedure available under Scots law is not inappropriate to the enforcement of the right and that the right does not fall within any of the areas where the operation of foreign law is excluded.

---

[13] These are specific rules, as opposed to general policy attitudes, the application of which the parties may not by their own agreement avoid. See further Ch.15.
[14] See Ch.15.

CHAPTER 4

METHOD

THE STAGES IN A CONFLICT CASE

(1) *Jurisdiction* over both the subject matter and the defender **4–01**
is always determined by the *lex fori*, in accordance with the
rules applicable in any given situation (in many cases as
directed by Council Regulation (EC) No 44/2001).[1]
(2) *Form of action* is decided by the *lex fori*.
(3) *Classification* of the issue is also decided by the *lex fori*.[2]
(4) *Choice of law rule* is indicated by the *lex fori* after classification of the nature of the point at issue has been determined
as in (3) above. It may be that the question has several
"strands", each of which may properly be referred by the
forum, in the exercise of its conflict rules, to a different law.
This is termed *dépeçage* or, by the Americans, "picking and
choosing"—an "issue by issue", segregated approach. [3]
(5) *Connecting factor* or point of contact is indicated by the
choice of law rule. The connecting factor is a legal concept
or localising agent, such as domicile, *locus celebrationis*,
habitual residence of the child, or applicable law (of a
contract), upon which a choice of law rule is based. It is the
link between an event or transaction or person, on the one
hand, and a legal system, on the other. The connecting
factor and all legal concepts or elements are determined by
the *lex fori* with two exceptions:

(a) the nature of property as moveable or immoveable is
always decided by the *lex situs*[4];

---

[1] See Ch.7, below.
[2] At least in practice. For doubts and theories, see below.
[3] See the Canadian case of *Reed v Reed* (1969) 6 D.L.R. (3d.) 617 in which legal
capacity to marry (consanguinity) was referred to the British Columbian ante-
nuptial domiciles alone, and the requirement of parental consent to the Washington State *lex loci celebrationis* alone, thereby producing the positive result of a
valid marriage. *Dépecage* is seen most clearly in the context of choice of law rules
concerning the law of obligations, and its application will be discussed in Chs 15
and 16.
[4] *Macdonald v Macdonald*, 1932 S.C. (H.L.) 79.

(b) nationality (except in time of war) is always decided by the law of the country the nationality of which is in question.[5]

(6) *Procedure*. Foreign rules of a purely procedural nature must be excluded. The possibly applicable rules therefore are classified as pertaining to procedure or substance: foreign rules of procedure are ignored and domestic rules applied.[6]

(7) *Substance*. The existence and extent of the rights of the parties are determined in accordance with the *lex causae*, by applying the substantive law indicated by the conflict rule. Strictly the function of the conflict lawyer is complete when he or she has answered the question of which law applies. If the *lex causae* happens to be the law of the forum, the matter will be determined by the domestic law on the point; if the *lex causae* is a foreign law, the onus lies upon the interested party to aver and prove foreign law to the satisfaction of the court. If no evidence is led of foreign law, the court is entitled to proceed on the basis that it is the same as its own law.[7]

(8) *Proof of foreign law*.[8] Foreign law is a question of fact in a British court and therefore it must be proved.[9] There is a presumption[10] that the law of a foreign country is the same as the *lex fori* and the onus is on a person who maintains otherwise to aver the foreign law and to prove it.[11] This rule of Scots and English law has fundamental implications for the conduct of litigation, and arguably stunts the development of UK conflict rules, for it means that a case will proceed as a domestic case if neither side offers to plead and prove foreign law. By inadvertence, negligence or complicity between the adversaries, the conflict dimension

---

[5] *Oppenheimer v Cattermole* [1973] Ch. 264, rev'd [1975] 2 W.L.R. 347; [1975] 1 All E.R. 538 (H.L.).

[6] *Re Wilks* [1935] 1 Ch. 645; and *In the Estate of Goenaga* [1949] P. 367.

[7] See Ch.8, below.

[8] See, for detail, Ch.8, below.

[9] See R. Fentiman, *Foreign Law in English Courts*, Oxford Monographs in Private International Law (1997), beginning "How foreign law is pleaded and proved is the crux of the conflict of laws".

[10] A. Briggs, *The Conflict of Laws* (2002), p.6, robustly declares that the better view is that the domestic law is the default position, *faute de mieux*. See T.C. Hartley, "Pleading and Proof of Foreign Law: the Major European Systems Compared", 1996 (45) I.C.L.Q. 271.

[11] *De Reneville v De Reneville* [1948] P. 100. See also *Pryde v Proctor and Gamble Ltd*, 1971 S.L.T. (Notes) 18; *Bonnor v Balfour Kilpatrick Ltd*, 1975 S.L.T. (Notes) 3; *Faulkner v Hill*, 1942 J.C. 20; *Scottish National Orchestra Soc. Ltd v Thomson's Executor*, 1969 S.L.T. 325; *Armour v Thyssen Edelstahlwerke AG*, 1986 S.L.T. 182 and in HL, 1990 S.L.T. 891; *Rodden v Whatlings Ltd*, 1960 S.L.T. (Notes) 96; and *Kraus's Administrators v Sullivan*, 1998 S.L.T. 963.

of a case may be lost. While Scots judges have judicial knowledge of Scots law, including its conflict rules, a court cannot of its own initiative order a proof of the content of foreign law. Hence although the court will apply the appropriate conflict rule (even if the parties fail to plead it), in the absence of proof of foreign law, operation of the conflict rule effectively will be frustrated. However, where the foreign law is "proved", it should not be supposed that a forum proceeds always on an accurate understanding of its content.[12]

CLASSIFICATION OR CHARACTERISATION

The problem, or method (or method, with problems) of classifica- **4–02** tion is as old as law itself. It is the natural inclination of the lawyer to categorise a legal problem. In domestic law, the matter must be placed under a particular *nomen juris*, or more than one. Of course, the issue may cross boundaries, and the problem as a whole will be likely to do so. For example, in domestic law a grievance may find its legal basis in contract or delict or both (travel accident), or in contract and property (loss of or mistaken re-sale of property entrusted for repair), or matrimonial law and succession (testamentary provisions rendered inoperative through occurrence of subsequent marriage by testator).[13] In domestic cases, advice will be offered to the potential litigant whether to sue, for example, in contract or delict (assuming both bases of action are available) based upon perceived financial or tactical advantage, *e.g.* a head of damage (such as *pretium affectionis*) may be available in delict but not in contract.

The classification exercise in the conflict of laws has a much deeper significance than in domestic law. In the first place, the rules of jurisdiction of the proposed forum must be satisfied, and these will vary in content according to the nature of the action, as personal or commercial, and within the many subdivisions of the latter, as, for example, pertaining to contract, delict or property.

When the forum is seised of jurisdiction, it must decide upon its classification of the problem, for that classification will determine the choice of law rule to be applied, upon which, in turn, will depend availability (in principle) of remedy, and all further substantive matters concerning constitution of the claim, defences and heads of damage.

---

[12] Briggs, *op. cit.*, p.6.
[13] By English domestic law, though not by Scots domestic law, later marriage revokes earlier will unless the will was made in contemplation of the later marriage. See Ch.18.

The choice of law rule is likely to differ from forum to forum, a fact which brings to its proper prominence the importance of the identity of the forum. Moreover, even if the conflict rule of different legal systems should appear to be the same, the classifications adopted by the different courts in the operation of the rule may differ. There may be wide agreement that in respect of marriage, matters of formal validity should be referred to the *lex loci celebrationis*, and that matters of capacity, essentials, or substance, are governed by the personal law—but is there any reason to suppose that these courts will assign a particular problem, such as lack of parental consent, to the same category?[14] How many courts would characterise the matter as relating to form, and how many as relating to essence? It might be argued that the only view which matters is that of the legal system in which the case is litigated, given that decree enforcement internationally is now well regulated, but in the law of persons, there are further aspects to be considered: not only nowadays is more than one court likely to be competent (leading to conflicts as to jurisdiction), but the outcome, if competent courts should disagree on the choice of law rule to be applied and/or upon classification of issues within that choice, is likely to be limping status.

If competent courts should agree that a matter will be governed by an individual's personal law, will they agree upon the identity of that law? Nationality, domicile, and habitual residence may each be contenders. If courts should agree upon domicile, will their rules for determining domicile, and application thereof, be identical? Where the connecting factor is the same, *ex facie* differences in interpretation thereof may give rise to what are known as "latent conflicts".[15] If, on the other hand, the choice of law rules, or the connecting factors *ex facie* be different, the conflict is more clearly seen and therefore is said to be "patent".

It becomes apparent that the hopes of success of each party will vary according to forum, and that in a conflict case the problem of classification is more acute, and the importance and complexity of the task is much greater, than in a domestic case. The importance of the classification exercise in traditional conflict methodology cannot be over-stated.

In Scots and English courts, the characterisation exercise is performed, in practice, by the forum in accordance with its own law, but taking an "international" or "enlightened" view.[16] Very

---

[14] *Bliersbach v McEwen*, 1959 S.L.T. 81: after careful consideration, a Dutch rule requiring parental consent to marriage was categorised as a (mere) prohibitive rather than an irritant impediment (in the canon law terminology).

[15] *Re Annesley* [1926] Ch. 692.

[16] *Re Bonacina* [1912] 2 Ch. 394; Private International Law (Miscellaneous Provisions) Act 1995, s.9(2).

few inroads upon this practice have been made,[17] but in terms of theory, there are other views on the proper solution of the characterisation problem.[18] The literature on the subject is immense.[19]

Additionally, one must ask what it is that the forum must characterise: facts, issues, and/or rules of law? Generally, one might say that it is the facts which lead the court to the categorisation of the issue. Although, in complex cases,[20] judges may disagree about the issue(s) presented, and may look behind the form in which the case is pleaded. In the initial question of jurisdiction, the putative forum may be required to make a provisional characterisation.[21] Possibly the most helpful explanation is that there are different stages in the choice of law process, and it seems that what the forum must characterise varies according to the stage it has reached. Initially, the forum must allocate the question raised by the factual situation to its correct legal category,[22] but later in the process, one might say that the subject of a conflict rule is a legal question arising from a factual situation and that the focus of characterisation is a legal matter, being the determination of the question to which the rule of law relates. The relationship of fact and law in this exercise is inter-dependent.

Wolff has noted that "each general conception has a firm and stable nucleus but an indistinct periphery, and it would be prac-

---

[17] *e.g.* Family Law Act 1986, s.46(5). See also Prescription and Limitation (Scotland) Act 1973, as amended, and Foreign Limitation Periods Act 1984, enjoining a Scots or English court, subject to public policy, to apply the limitation period prescribed by the *lex causae*, without reference to the characterisation of the foreign rule as substantive or procedural, whether in its own view or in that of the forum. See also, exceptionally, characterisation by the *lex situs* of the nature of property, and by the putative *lex patriae* the meaning of nationality.

[18] Most prominently the *lex causae* theory, as upheld by Wolff, at pp.154–6, that characterisation be performed according to the applicable law, though this has an obvious difficulty of circularity of reasoning. For an example of classification by the *lex causae*, see *Re Maldonado* [1954] P. 223. A refinement on the forum-centred approach was urged by Robertson, to the effect that the court must initially characterise according to its own law (primary characterisation), but having been led by its own choice of law rule to the foreign law which it considers relevant, it must thereafter adopt the classification of the foreign law (secondary characterisation) (Robertson, *Characterization in the Conflict of Laws* (1940)).

[19] Robertson, above; Falconbridge's *"via media"*: the forum in characterising must take into account the part which a foreign rule of law plays in its own system, *Selected Essays on the Conflict of Laws* (2nd ed., 1954), Chaps 3–5; Lederman, "Classification in Private International Law", 29 Can. Bar Rev. 3, comprise a distinguished sample.

[20] *e.g. Macmillan Inc v Bishopsgate Investment Trust plc (No. 3)* [1996] 1 All E.R. 585, *per* Staughton L.J. at 589, endorsed by Mance L.J. in *Raiffeisen Zentralbank Osterreich A.G. v Five Star General Trading LLC* [2001] I Ll. Rep. 597; *Atlantic Telecom GmbH, Noter*, 2004 S.L.T. 1031, *per* Lord Brodie at 1041.

[21] See Crawford, "The Uses of Putativity and Negativity in the Conflict of Laws", 2005 (54) I.C.L.Q. 829. Also *Burke v Uvex Sports GmbH* [2005] I.L.Pr. 26.

[22] Cheshire and North term this "classification of the cause of action" (p.36).

tically impossible for any legislator or court to establish a rigid and precise delimitation."[23] In more recent years, Mance L.J. has called for a "more nuanced analysis": "the overall aim is to identify the most appropriate law to govern a particular issue. The classes or categories of issue which the law recognises . . . are man-made, not natural. They have no inherent value, beyond their purpose in assisting to select the most appropriate law."[24] The characterisation task must be undertaken with perceptiveness and a sensitivity to the goal of the choice of law process, which is to identify and apply to the problem the appropriate law in the view of the forum.

4–03   The conflict lawyer should be alert to the presence of "false conflicts" that is, to note that there is only a conflict problem if there is a conflict, and that there is no conflict problem if there is a coincidence of outcome. Three examples can be provided. First, there is a false conflict if the result of application of different connecting factors (*e.g.* domicile and habitual residence) by different legal systems would be to apply the same law. This is the opposite of the latent conflict outlined above; it is rather latent harmony. Secondly, there is a false conflict where, of two contending legal systems, only one has an "interest" in the application of its own law in the particular case. If the outcome was that neither law was applied, both would be frustrated, for the two laws have a common interest that one of the laws be applied. An example of the second type of false conflict is as follows: if, by the law of country A, the loan of a car were to impose on the owner liability for negligent driving by the borrower, but only if the negligent driving occurred within country A, and if the borrower drove the car negligently in country B, which imposed the same liability but only if the contract of loan had been made in country B.[25] A third example of false conflict results from the interaction of certain sets of rules, choice of law and/or domestic: *e.g.*, where, by the Arcadian *locus delicti* there is inter-spousal immunity in tort, but by the Utopian *lex fori* there is a policy objection to such immunity, and where by Utopian law parties involved in a road accident in Utopia are husband and wife, but by Arcadian law are not married, there is no reason by either law why the woman, injured through the negligent driving of the man, should not sue him for damages in Utopia or in Arcadia. A similar situation arises where the principal point at issue is whether a will has been revoked by a subsequent marriage[26]: if by the *lex causae/lex successionis* (being the law which contains the revocation rule) the marriage is invalid, but by the *lex fori* (which has no such revocation rule) the marriage is valid, the

---

[23] Wolff, p.150.
[24] *Raiffeisen*, above, paras 27–28.
[25] This example is taken from Morris (4th ed.), p.422.
[26] cf. *Re Swan's Will* (1871) 2 V.L.R. (I.E.&M.) 47.

same concatenation of circumstances is present. The forum should note the coincidence of outcome regardless of the path of reasoning, and heed should be paid to what lies in common rather than to what divides.

Where a conflict rule is inflexible (by pointing to a "hard" single-contact connecting factor, such as nationality) and thereby unsatisfactory, the forum may chafe under its restrictions and may be tempted to reclassify the problem, by taking it out of its natural category and placing it in another category, thereby delivering a different and more acceptable result. This is termed "manipulative classification". It may be argued, for example, that a rule presented as delictual in its legal system of origin, which prohibits suits between spouses, is overlaid with a family law purpose; and further, that it might be reasonable that it was not intended to apply to a married couple passing through the enacting legal system, who are strangers to that legal system.[27] If a wife should choose to sue her husband for damages arising out of his culpable lack of care, in a forum which has a choice of law rule in delict of strict application of the *lex loci delicti*, reclassification by the forum of the interspousal immunity rule of the *locus delicti* as one of family law and not delictual, may permit circumvention by the claimant of the prohibition.

To summarise:

(a) Different laws may classify the same set of facts in different ways, *e.g.* breach of promise of marriage.[28]

---

[27] This is the type of factual scenario against which American conflict theorists tested their policy evaluation theories. A traditional solution in such a case may arise not through identification of a false conflict but in a threshold "disapplication" of the *lex loci delicti* as applicable law in tort (*cf.* Private International Law (Miscellaneous Provisions) Act 1995, s.12), or through exclusion of the foreign rule through operation of the forum's public policy (s.14). See Ch.16. In Scots domestic law, the prohibition upon spouse suing spouse in delict was removed by the Law Reform (Husband and Wife) Act 1962, s.2(1), except where, in the view of the court, it appears that no substantial benefit would accrue to either party from the continuation of the action (s.2(2)). See *Kozikowska v Kozikowski (No.1)*, 1996 S.L.T. 386.

[28] Though breach of promise of marriage might be regarded in France as civil wrongdoing, if sued upon in Scotland or England, the case would have proceeded as an action founded in breach of contract, no matter that the pursuer might be "French". However, all such suits in British forums now are barred, by overriding legislation of Scotland (Law Reform (Husband and Wife) (Scotland) Act 1984, s.1) and England (Law Reform (Miscellaneous Provisions) Act 1970, s.1) which provides that no action will lie, whatever be the law governing the agreement to marry.

    (b) Different legal systems may attach different meanings to the same legal terms, *e.g.* domicile.[29]

    (c) Some legal systems contain legal rights or remedies which are unknown to others.

    (d) The conflict rules of two legal systems may be the same and yet the two laws may classify the same legal issue in different ways so as to produce entirely different results, *e.g.* whether the requirement of parental consent to marriage is one of essential or formal validity; or whether a wife's rights in property upon her husband's death should be categorised as rights of succession or rights arising out of the matrimonial relationship.[30]

APPLICATIONS OF CLASSIFICATION

4–04 This central matter of classification is most easily understood through examples.

From the law of marriage, the cases of *Apt v Apt*[31] and *Ponticelli v Ponticelli*[32] demonstrate the orthodox, jurisdiction selection approach to solving a conflict problem. If an English domiciliary be party (the absent party) to a proxy marriage celebrated abroad, and the question of validity of the marriage comes before an English court, the English forum must categorise the problem (*marriage—formal validity*). Once the problem has been accommodated within a legal category, the relevant choice of law rule is applied. The connecting factor to govern form of marriage indicated by the choice of law rule under English and Scots conflict rules is the *lex loci celebrationis*. If by the foreign *lex loci celebrationis*, a proxy marriage is acceptable, the marriage will be regarded as valid in England, subject to public policy, even though by domestic English

---

[29] It is not to be thought that one meaning is correct and another wrong; rather the forum must ascertain which definition ought to apply in a given case. This is the problem of "latent conflict" (*cf.* Kahn Freund's "hidden homonym"). The English or Scots forum will insist upon deciding, according to its own rules, what is the domicile of an individual: *Re Annesley* [1926] Ch. 692: though see Family Law Act 1986, s.46(5).

[30] As in the notable case of *Anton v Bartolo* (the Maltese Marriage Case) (1891) Clunet 1171. A question famously arose in this area in the House of Lords: *De Nicols v Curlier (No.1)* [1900] A.C. 21. Clear evidence was led of French law that the community established by the code transcended any change of domicile during the marriage. The court abided by the French rule that community rights were not disturbed by change of domicile but there seems no evidence of a dispute between French law and the English law of the forum on the issue of classification. Indeed in many such cases, as in *De Nicols*, the word classification may not be mentioned, the rôle of the forum hardly or not expressly noticed.

[31] [1948] P. 83.

[32] [1958] P. 204.

law marriages may not be validly celebrated by proxy. An English court has held that the foreign *lex loci celebrationis* governs validity of marriage where neither party was present, though this may be doubted, because though a celebration took place abroad, the better view would seem to be that the true place of celebration of marriage (constituted by the exchange of consent) was the English *lex loci contractus*.[33]

From the law of property, where a man of Russian domicile, a patient in a London hospital, transferred, in contemplation of death, money and jewellery to his mistress and one month later died, the grievances of his widow and sons, brought to an English court, depended on whether the court viewed the matter as one of succession, to be referred to the Russian last domicile of the deceased as the appropriate connecting factor, or as one of transfer of moveable property, in which case the connecting factor would be the English *lex situs* of the property at the time. The court classified the point as one of property and applied English domestic law by which the gift was valid.[34]

From the law of succession, *Re Martin*[35] concerned the classification of the English domestic rule that marriage revokes a will, unless the will is made in express contemplation of a particular marriage which does take place. Does this rule belong to the rules of marriage or to the rules of succession? The testatrix, of French domicile, made a will in England in English form. Later she married a professor of French origin, a fugitive from French justice. When the French criminal prescriptive period expired, he returned to France without her. They were not divorced, and since unity of domicile between spouses then prevailed, she, predeceasing him, died possessed of the French domicile of her husband. Had her will been revoked by her marriage? The English court held that the matter was one of marriage law, to be referred to the connecting factor of her domicile immediately after marriage (surprisingly, held to be English) and not to her French domicile at death (being the applicable law in succession).

In *Re Cohn*,[36] Uthwatt J. held that a rule governing sequence of death in a common calamity was a matter of the substantive succession law of the German *lex causae/lex successionis*. Its classification as substantive under English succession law did not matter. Since the parties died domiciled in Germany, the rule of the German *lex causae* must prevail. Similarly in *Re Fuld, dec'd (No. 3)*,[37] the effect of "undue influence" (however termed) upon a

---

[33] *McCabe v McCabe* [1994] 1 F.C.R. 257, CA; *The Independent*, September 3, 1993. R Leslie, "Foreign Consensual Marriages", 1994 S.L.T. (News) 87.
[34] *Re Korvine's Trusts* [1921] 1 Ch. 343.
[35] [1900] P. 211.
[36] [1945] Ch. 5.
[37] [1968] P. 675.

testator was a matter of substantive succession law to be governed by Peter Fuld's last (German) domicile. Scarman J. assigned rules of burden of proof, in this instance at least, to the category of procedure.[38]

Re Maldonado[39] is unusual in that the Court of Appeal accepted the Spanish classification of the nature of the Spanish government's claim to ownerless property. Spanish law was the lex causae/lex successionis: "it has been found (and the Crown has accepted the finding) that the State of Spain is, in the eye of Spanish law, the true heir"[40]; (as opposed to the fiscal recipient of ownerless property).

These examples serve to give an indication of the traditional conflict of laws method of working. It can be seen that the connecting factor is a buffer between forum and outcome. The forum draws back from choosing directly the "best" or "better" rule from home and foreign contenders.

TIME

4–05 Time may be a relevant factor in the forum's resolution of a conflict problem.[41] The temporal dimension may be important as a result of one of a number of eventualities:

(a) The *content of the forum's choice of law rule may change* (*le conflit transitoire*), *e.g.* the choice of law rule applicable in a Scots court in a matter of delict will vary according to the date of the act or omission giving rise to the claim. If this occurred prior to May 1, 1996, the rule of double actionability requirement must operate; conversely,[42] if after that date, the case will be governed by the Private International Law (Miscellaneous Provisions) Act 1995.[43]

(b) The *connecting factor may require to be defined by time.* [44] Connecting factors may be fixed, constant or static, on the

---

[38] *ibid., per* Scarman J. at 696–697. However, the categorisation of burden of proof generally is not uncontroversial. See Ch.8.

[39] [1954] P. 223.

[40] *ibid., per* Jenkins L.J. at 250.

[41] For a clear exposition of this topic generally, see F. Mann, "The Time Element in the Conflict of Laws" (1954) 31 B.Y.B.I.L. 217.

[42] *Kuwait Airways Corporation v Iraqi Airways Co. (No.6)* [2002] 3 All E.R. 209.

[43] Where change in the choice of law rule of the forum is effected by legislative means, transitional provisions normally will be found, but these too may give rise to interpretative difficulty, *e.g.* unity of domicile between husband and wife was thought to have been removed by the Domicile and Matrimonial Proceedings Act 1973, s.1(1) and (2), but the case of *IRC v Duchess of Portland* [1982] Ch. 314 reveals an imperfection in the drafting of the rule governing the domicile after January 1, 1974, of women married before January 1, 1974.

[44] For the purposes of jurisdiction and/or choice of law and/or recognition of decrees.

one hand, or variable/dynamic on the other. Examples of the former are the *lex situs* of immoveable property,[45] *lex loci contractus*,[46] *lex loci actus*,[47] and *lex loci celebrationis*.[48] Examples of the latter are the *lex situs* of moveables, and domicile/habitual residence/nationality of persons. *Locus delicti* (place of occurrence of harm) may be a fixed connecting factor depending on the circumstances (e.g. a road accident), but in more complex cases of multi-locational harm the case is more likely to be regarded properly as "spread over" space rather than time. Admittedly, delicts having a continuing quality, on the facts or in their constituent elements, may display both spatial and temporal elements.[49]

Within the category of variable/dynamic factors, a distinction perhaps can be drawn between a connecting factor such as the *situs* of moveable property, which, by nature, may change from time to time, but in respect of the identification of which at any one time, only that time is relevant[50]; and a connecting factor such as domicile which also by nature may change from time to time, but in respect of the identification of which at any one time, review will have to be made of earlier events. The domicile or habitual residence of the *propositus* is a "variable" as opposed to "static" connecting factor, and is useless as a guide unless the rule specifies the date at which domicile or habitual residence is to be determined. Thus, legal capacity to marry is referred to the law of the domicile immediately before marriage,[51] legal testamentary capacity (age, sanity) to the law of the domicile at testing,[52] and proprietary testamentary capacity (freedom to disinherit one's family) to the law

---

[45] The *situs* of land obviously can never change, unless politically, by means of territorial re-alignment, a rare occurrence.

[46] Rome 1, Art.9: see Ch.15.

[47] See *e.g.* Wills Act 1963, s.1, which, however, also exemplifies the use, alternatively, of the variable connecting factors of domicile or habitual residence or nationality, each qualified in terms of time. See Ch.18.

[48] Except perhaps in relation to marriage by cohabitation with habit and repute: see Ch.11.

[49] *Soutar v Peters*, 1912 1 S.L.T. 111; *Henderson v Jaouen* [2002] 2 All E.R. 705.

[50] See *Winkworth v Christie, Manson & Woods Ltd* [1980] 1 Ch. 496: Ch.17.

[51] *Brook v Brook* (1861) 9 H.L.C. 193; *Mette v Mette* (1859) 1 Sw. & Tr. 416; *Re Paine* [1940] Ch. 46; *Re Bozzelli* [1902] 1 Ch. 751; *Re De Wilton* [1900] 2 Ch. 481. See Ch.11.

[52] This point is not completely vouched but see *Re Fuld (No.3)* [1968] P. 675; Scot. Law Com. Memo. No. 71 (1986), para. 6.14 and Scot. Law Com. No. 124 (1990) (heritage and moveables).

of the deceased's domicile at death.[53] It is necessary therefore to determine the domicile or habitual residence of the *propositus* at a particular point of time[54] for the purpose of resolving the particular conflict problem before the court; there is a *tempus inspiciendum*, and for this reason the forum may not have regard to events which post-date that time.

The necessity to identify a variable connecting factor at a particular time does not impinge upon the choice between *leges situs* which a conflict rule on occasion may require to make.[55]

(c) *The substantive content of the lex causae may change*, in such a way as to have significance for the case (*le conflit mobile*

---

[53] *Re Groos* [1915] 1 Ch. 572. The very idea of an instrument being "inchoate" is interesting. A will is inchoate: one cannot say that it is the last will of the testator until his death occurs (assuming lucidity to the end): similarly, one cannot say whether its provisions are essentially valid until that date, because its essential validity will be judged by the law of his last domicile, which can only be ascertained with certainty at the date of death.

[54] *cf. Bell v Kennedy* (1868) 6 M. (H.L.) 69. The crucial year being 1838 for the establishment of Bell's domicile, the House of Lords could not look forward to view Bell's life thereafter, which clearly showed adoption of Scots domicile. On the other hand, investigation had to be made of Bell's life up to 1838 and of his father's life in order to reach a conclusion as to his domicile at the relevant date.

[55] *e.g.* Security rights over moveables are governed by the *lex situs*: should the governing law be the situation of the moveables when the terms of the contract and relevant security are concluded (perhaps Germany), or the *situs* (perhaps Scotland) of the moveables when an issue of bankruptcy arises and the validity of rights in security become commercially and practically important? See Stewart, "Romalpa Clauses", 1985 S.L.T. (News) 149. Then again, with regard to choice of law in annulment of marriage, the court if it chooses to apply the law of the domicile (a variable connecting factor) of either or both parties, should make explicit whether it seeks to apply the domicile at the date of the purported marriage or at the date of litigation. Principle suggests that the former is the correct approach, but in jurisdictional terms, it has happened that the parties have benefited from the acquisition of domicile in the legal system of the forum by the date of litigation. *Cf. Szechter v Szechter* [1971] P. 286 and see a polygamy case such as *Cheni v Cheni* [1965] P. 85. Thus, the *tempus inspiciendum* in a litigation of this type will vary according to whether the purpose is one of choice of law or jurisdiction. In matrimonial property questions, an argument exists between those legal systems which adhere to the immutability approach (which is that parties' rights in moveable property are fixed, being regulated by whatever touchstone is preferred, as to which time again may be relevant: see *Re Egerton's Trusts* [1956] Ch. 593), and those (principally in the USA) which consider that rights in moveables may change with changes in the domicile of the spouses during the marriage. Sometimes a choice of law rule contains within it a reference to more than one *tempus, e.g.* the English choice of law rule concerning legitimation by subsequent marriage, which prevailed before the Legitimacy Act 1926, and which required legal capacity in the father to legitimate by this manner by his personal law both at the date of the birth of the child, and at the date of the marriage: see *Re Goodman's Trusts* (1881) 17 Ch.D. 266. These examples are concerned with the articulation of the temporal requirements of a conflict rule where that temporal element is of significance.

dans le temps). Parties' choice of applicable law to govern their contract is a choice of that body of law as it may prevail from time to time. It follows from this that the passage of time may bring the occurrence of supervening illegality of contractual terms.[56] In other cases the choice falls upon the domestic content at a defined date (*e.g.* in distribution of an estate in accordance with the domiciliary law at death).[57] A consequence of change of content of the applicable law may be positive, in that defects in formalities of marriage may be removed by subsequent retrospective legislation or government decree, recognised by our conflict rules.[58]

(d) *Innominate cases.* Divorce yields interesting examples of the significance of time. If the forum has jurisdiction, according to current law it will apply its own law to the grounds on which divorce may be obtained.[59] Consequently, it does not matter whether the acts complained of were of legal significance as grounds of marriage dissolution when and/or where committed.[60] It does not matter that they took place before a change of domicile, the divorce court having taken jurisdiction on the basis of a new domicile.[61]

---

[56] *cf. Ralli Bros v Compania Naviera Sota y Aznar* [1920] 2 K.B. 287: another example from contract is that moratoria on debtor's payments, or defences such as supervening bankrupt status are heeded by the Scots or English forum only if these decrees or effects flow from the proper law of the obligation: *Adams v National Bank of Greece and Athens* [1961] A.C. 255; *National Bank of Greece and Athens v Metliss* [1958] A.C. 509; *Gibbs & Sons v La Société Industrielle et Commercialle des Metaux* (1890) 25 Q.B.D. 399.

[57] *Lynch v Provisional Government of Paraguay* [1871] L.R. 2 P. & D. 268 in which the English court, concerned with the property in England of Lopez who died domiciled in Paraguay, did not give effect to Paraguayan legislation which confiscated all his property after his death. It is fair to say, however, that this case equally could be explained as a refusal to give extra-territorial effect to foreign expropriatory legislation, or on policy grounds, or as a simple affirmation of our choice of ultimate domicile as *lex successionis*. But see *Nelson v Bridport* (1846) 8 Beav. 547, where the necessity to defer at all times to the *lex situs* is affirmed. Practicalities on which the theory of the supremacy of the *lex situs* is based require recognition even of post-death changes.

[58] *Starkowski v Att.-Gen.* [1954] A.C. 155. See Ch.11.

[59] *Zanelli v Zanelli* [1948] W.N. 381. See choice of law in divorce and nullity contrasted, Ch.12.

[60] Though see in specialised circumstances *Ali v Ali* [1968] P. 564 where the English court was unwilling to take into consideration any alleged matrimonial offences pre-dating the conversion by Ali of the nature of "his" marriage to monogamous.

[61] *Carswell v Carswell* (1881) 8 R. 901 (alleged desertion took place in Canada: divorce forum in Scotland); *Morton v Morton* (1897) 5 S.L.T. 222 (divorce forum in Scotland: place of alleged adultery probably Ireland but report does not specify). But equally (*Stavert v Stavert* (1882) 9 R. 519) commission of the offence within the forum is not enough! Jurisdiction cannot be founded in such cases *ratione delicti*.

Grounds of annulment are quite a different matter as they are inextricably linked to earlier matters relating to the essential or formal constitution of marriage, as to each of which the forum will have a conflict rule.

The significance of time is easy to see when the matter is pointed out. However, though all the points made above may be valid considerations, the "primary dimension" (Graveson) of conflict problems is space.

THE INCIDENTAL QUESTION

4–06 An incidental or preliminary question may arise in a conflict problem if the choice of law rule of the forum relating to a matter refers to a foreign law, but, before the main question can be answered, it is necessary to obtain an answer to another question also containing foreign elements. The problem which arises is whether this incidental or preliminary question is to be solved by application of the same foreign law (*i.e.* by use of the *lex causae*'s conflict rules) as is applied by the forum to the main question, or by application of the conflict rules of the *lex fori* upon the incidental question. Should the forum permit its chosen law to regulate not only the main, but also the preliminary question?

This problem arises only[62] if the following conditions are present:

(a) the main question must be referred to a foreign law under the conflict rule of the *lex fori*;

(b) the main question cannot be answered until an incidental question has been answered;

(c) choice of law rules of *lex causae* (main question) and *lex fori* lead to different results as to the answer to the incidental question.

It may be that the problem is present in a case, but this is not noted by the court.[63] The problem seems to be an unavoidable one in certain sets of circumstances.[64]

---

[62] The problem does not arise frequently, or at least is not discussed often: *Shaw v Gould* (1868) L.R. 3 H.L. 55; *Re Johnson* [1903] 1 Ch. 821; *Re Stirling* [1908] 2 Ch. 344; *Re Bischoffscheim* [1948] Ch. 79; *Schwebel v Ungar* (1963) 42 D.L.R. (20) 622 (Ont.C.A.) aff'd. (1964) 48 D.L.R. (20) 644 (Sup. Ct. Can.); *R. v Brentwood Registrar* [1968] 2 Q.B. 956 (note—although *Brentwood Registrar* illustrates the problem it was superseded by Recognition of Divorces and Legal Separations Act 1971, s.7, itself superseded by Family Law Act 1986, s.50).

[63] Consider, *e.g. Shaw v Gould*, above; *Perrini v Perrini* [1979] 2 All E.R. 323; *Lawrence v Lawrence* [1985] 2 All E.R. 733.

[64] Morris, p.499.

This deeper mystery of the conflict of laws is most readily understood if set in narrative form. The classic exposition concerns the distribution by a Scots court (*qua* forum) of that part of the intestate moveable estate situated in Scotland, of the deceased X, who died domiciled in Attica. Since by Scots choice of law rules the distribution of moveable estate is governed by the law of the deceased's last domicile, the *lex causae* in this example is the law of Attica. Attican law has conflict rules of its own, likely to differ in many areas from those of the Scots *lex fori*.

What if by Attican law a portion of moveables falls to the widow of the deceased; but we discover in *fact* that X had a complex matrimonial history, that she who on first sight appears to be X's widow, is X's second (or third or subsequent) "wife", and that the marriage(s) to the earlier wife (or wives) has/have been terminated by divorce(s) or annulment(s), upon the validity of some or all of which the conflict laws of Scotland and of Attica do not agree? Should the Scottish forum permit the law of Attica to regulate not only the rules of intestate moveable succession with regard to its domiciliary,[65] but also to answer the incidental or preliminary question of "who *is* X's widow?" If prepared to cede to Attican law the decision upon both questions, the Scots court would follow the *lex causae* theory; if preferring to apply its own conflict rule on validity of/recognition of consistorial decrees, it would use the *lex fori* theory. If the divorce between X and his first wife had been obtained from a Scots court, a later Scots court is likely to find it difficult in effect to deny its own decree.[66]

There is no definitive answer. There is general agreement upon the pursuit of the aims of justice and expediency, but which manner of proceeding best serves the case/produces a positive outcome (and for whom?) is a matter of conjecture.

Parliament, in removing one related problem,[67] has left unanswered the question of what is to happen when the Scots court hears a case where a party has legal capacity to marry in the view of his domiciliary law, but has been divorced by a decree not worthy of recognition by Scots law. No such case appears yet to have presented itself to a Scots forum, but is exactly the situation in the classic incidental question found in the case of *Schwebel v Ungar*.[68] A husband and wife, both Jews domiciled in Hungary, decided to emigrate to Israel. *En route*, in Italy, they were divorced

---

[65] Who the law of Attica may not consider to be its domiciliary, and in any case the law of Attica may consider the law of the last nationality to be the appropriate *lex successionis*—but that is another story, told in Ch.5.

[66] But see *R v Brentwood Superintendent Registrar of Marriages, ex p. Arias* [1968] 2 Q.B. 956.

[67] See Family Law Act 1986, s.50. Ch.12, below.

[68] (1963) 42 D.L.R. (20) (Ont. C.A.) aff'd (1964) 48 D.L.R. (20) 644 (Sup. Ct Can.).

by *ghet* (Jewish religious divorce).[69] Such a divorce was worthy of recognition by the law of Israel, but not by the law of Hungary, the personal law of the parties at the time. Each party later acquired domicile of choice in Israel. Later still, the woman removed to Canada where she purported to re-marry in Toronto, she being still of Israeli domicile.

The law of Ontario referred capacity to marry to the Israeli law of the ante-nuptial domicile, but, in the matter of the incidental or preliminary question—of the validity of the antecedent divorce which was capable of having its own conflict rule—the Ontarian court was not willing by its own conflict rules on the particular issue of religious divorces to recognise as valid the *ghet* (since it was not valid by the Hungarian law of the husband's domicile at the time: this would have been the Scottish view also at that date).[70]

The dilemma is clear to see. The decision by the Supreme Court of Canada, affirming the Ontario Court of Appeal, was to have the Israeli law, governing the main question of capacity to marry, regulate also the incidental question of validity of antecedent divorce. The case therefore provides an example of the *lex causae* approach. But one might say that overall control was still with the forum, which chose to take that path, the conflict rules of Ontario containing the possibility, on occasion, at their own option, to defer to the conflict rules of the foreign system which they had them-selves selected to answer the main question.

Writers are divided in approach. The *lex causae* approach, as well as being internationally minded, has an attraction. It concedes that a foreign law has a conflict of laws dimension (and that that dimension is equipped with detailed conflict rules), and is willing to remit all aspects of the problem to the entirety of that foreign law, which the forum has itself selected in the first place: perhaps that is what "application" of the *lex causae* entails.[71] But conversely, one notes that there are two or more identifiable conflict problems in this example, each with its own *lex causae*, and that the (secondary) *lex causae* preferred by the forum has a claim to be applied.

It has been said that the natural approach of the Scots lawyer is to refer the entire matter to the *lex causae*.[72] It may be that such an approach is preferable, in the interests of international harmony and universality of status, unless the price in terms of internal

---

[69] As to Scots and English conflict rules on recognition of religious (extra-judicial) divorces, see Ch.12.

[70] See *Makouipour*, 1967 S.L.T. 101 (form of divorce valid by Iranian law of the husband).

[71] See Ch.5.

[72] Anton with Beaumont, p.86–but subject, in the end, to justice and convenience, pp.88–89.

dissonance is too high,[73] but few would advise a rigid, predetermined attitude in this area where instances in any event are rare. *Potior et utilior*, we might say, had we not let go of the Latin.

THE END OF THE BEGINNING

The aim of each system of conflict rules is to identify the **4-07** appropriate law to govern a question which has arisen for decision in the court of that system, and which contains foreign elements. The content of the conflict rules of systems of law will vary from system to system, though as the years go on, the "harmonisation" impetus will bring about a measure of agreement (*ex facie* if not necessarily in interpretation) among consenting states in an increasing number of areas of choice of law.

That which remains to be considered is the meaning of the word "law", as used in the expression "choice of law". For, if every developed legal system has both domestic law, and conflict law, its law "flat", and its law "in the round"—then, for example, when the Scots forum chooses "French" law to govern an issue, is it within the Scots court's contemplation that French *conflict* law should be proved and followed? This is the celebrated problem of *renvoi*, the pleasures of which will now be tasted.

SUMMARY 4

1. The forum having accepted jurisdiction, the *lex fori* governs:

    (a) form of action;
    (b) classification of point at issue;
    (c) selection of choice of law rule, including identification and ascertainment of connecting factor;
    (d) application of choice of law rule; and
    (e) matters of procedure (whereas the *lex causae* governs matters of substance).

2. Foreign law must be averred and proved.

3. The element of time may be relevant.

4. The circumstances may present an incidental question.

---

[73] Wolff, p.209.

CHAPTER 5

RENVOI

NATURE OF THE SUBJECT

Renvoi means a dismissal, a sending away, or sending back. The **5–01** word denotes a mystery which lies at the heart of the conflict of laws. The problem springs from the dual meaning of the expression *the law of a country*. This term may be used in a narrow sense or in a wide sense. It may mean the law of country X in its narrow domestic sense or the law of country X "in the round", including its conflict rules. Hence, in suggesting a choice of the law of country X as the applicable law in a given problem, we can be criticised for lack of specification.

The natural home of *renvoi* is the law of succession.[1] A classic example of the *renvoi* problem concerns the question of the succession to the moveable estate in Scotland of a British subject who dies domiciled in a foreign country, by the law of which succession to moveables is governed by the law of the nationality instead of by the law of the domicile. If, according to the Scots choice of law rule governing succession to moveable property, the estate of the deceased will be distributed according to the French law of his domicile, ought we to include within our understanding of "the law of the domicile", the French conflict rule concerning succession to moveable estate, so as to secure the outcome that the distribution of the moveables in Scotland shall be effected according to the law of the nationality?[2]

The *renvoi* problem in general may be said to arise whenever, within the permitted scope of operation of *renvoi* as noted below, a question of law is referred notionally by one law to another law and that other law either refers it back to the original law (*renvoi*

---

[1] The *renvoi* process was used without success in *In the Estate of Fuld, dec'd (No. 3)* [1968] P. 675 to attempt to save two (of the four) codicils from a finding of formal invalidity.

[2] It seems, however, that we are never prepared fully to put ourselves into the position of the foreign law: there is always a holding-back in that the deceased's domicile is identified according to the rules of the *lex fori*. *Re Annesley* [1926] Ch. 692.

remission) or refers it to still another law (*renvoi* transmission).[3] The narrow range of potentially usable connecting factors in any given problem lying within the permitted range of operation of the *renvoi* doctrine probably accounts for the small number of instances of *renvoi* transmission.

HISTORY OF THE PROBLEM

5–02 The problem of *renvoi* entered the consciousness of the English judiciary as a means of circumventing the rigid rule then operative concerning formal validity of wills, which required that in order to be valid as to form, a will had to satisfy the formal validity rules of the legal system of the last domicile of the testator.[4] The courts were reluctant to strike down a will on a matter of form if, by reference to the "total" law of a country in which the deceased died domiciled, a positive outcome might be obtained by permitting onward reference to another law, thereby enlarging the number of potentially applicable laws governing formal validity. "The fountain-head of authority is *Collier v Rivaz*"[5]: "the court sitting here . . . must consider itself sitting in Belgium."[6] The English court, by so doing, rendered itself able to come to the view that codicils formally invalid by the Belgian law of the domicile but valid under English law, could be admitted to probate in England, for Belgian law "in the round" would have referred the matter to the (English) law of the nationality.

A grand Scottish *renvoi* case is there none,[7] though there is evidence that the Scots courts would accept transmission, that is to say, that they would be prepared to apply the law of a third country

---

[3] *Re Trufort* (1887) 36 Ch.D. 600; *Sec. of State for Foreign Affairs v Charlesworth Pilling & Co.* [1901] A.C. 377; *Armitage v Att.-Gen.* [1906] P. 135; *Sasson v Sasson* [1924] A.C. 1007; *Bartlett v Bartlett* [1925] A.C. 377; and *Re Achillopoulos* [1928] 1 Ch. 433. These are cases decided in the era in which the English courts adopted the single *renvoi* theory (see below). A more modern example is *R. v Brentwood Superintendent Registrar of Marriages, ex p. Arias* [1968] 3 All E.R. 279.

[4] See, for example, early cases such as: *Collier v Rivaz* (1841) 2 Curt. 855; *Laneuville v Anderson* (1860) 2 Sw. & Tr. 24; *Bremer v Freeman* (1857) 10 Moore P.C. 306; *Frere v Frere* (1847) 5 Notes of Cases 593; *In the Goods of Lacroix* (1877) 2 P.D. 94. *Collier* was disapproved firmly but on no easily decipherable grounds in *Bremer*.

[5] Dicey and Morris, pp.67 and 68.

[6] *per* Sir Herbert Jenner at 859.

[7] Though Anton with Beaumont, p.75 notes that the requisite elements were present in *Pringle's Trs v Pringle*, 1913 S.C. 172.

if referred thereto by the foreign law identified by the Scottish choice of law rule.[8]

If there is value in the *renvoi* exercise, there is no reason in principle for its exclusion from other areas, although there may be persuasive reasons of time, expense, complexity and uncertainty; and incontrovertible reasons of prohibition contained in statute, convention or regulation.

THE THEORIES

There are many variations and there is much writing on this **5-03** acclaimed subject.[9] The following is an outline of three basic approaches.

(1) INTERNAL LAW THEORY

The question should be solved by the simple application of the **5-04** forum-identified *lex causae*, in its narrow domestic sense. This is not so much a theory of *renvoi* as a refusal to entertain it. This approach is supported by *obiter dicta* in *Re Askew* [10] and in *Re Annesley*,[11] in which it was commended as avoiding the "endless oscillation"[12] which other theories entail.

(2) PARTIAL *RENVOI*, *RENVOI* OR SINGLE *RENVOI* THEORY

The starting point is the *lex fori* in its wide sense from which the **5-05** question is referred (*envoi*) to another law (usually the law of the domicile) which in turn may refer it back (*renvoi*) to the *lex fori*

---

[8] See *e.g.*, *McKay v Walls* 1951 S.L.T. (Notes) 6; *Armitage v A.G.* [1906] P. 135; *Mountbatten v Mountbatten* [1959] 1 All E.R. 99. Reference to the personal law of the institute on a question of status, as opposed to the law of the testator, shows the same "open" attitude: *Mitchell's Tr. v Rule* (1908) 16 S.L.T. 189; *Smith's Trs v Macpherson*, 1926 S.C. 983; *cf. Wright's Trs v Callander*, 1992 S.L.T. 498 (Ex. Div.); 1993 S.L.T. 556, HL. Contrast *Re Fergusson's Will* [1902] 1 Ch. 483. See generally the "recognition by" mode of reasoning used to extend the range of courts considered by our common law rules competent to grant divorce: Family Law Act 1986, ss.46(2)(b)(ii) and 51(3)(b)(ii). See also Marriage (Scotland) Act 1977, s.3(5): certificate of legal capacity required for a foreign domiciliary intending to marry in Scotland will be acceptable if issued by a competent authority in a state other than the domicile if by the law of the latter the law of that other state is the personal law.

[9] *e.g.* Bate, *Note on the Doctrine of Renvoi* (1904); Griswold, "*Renvoi* Revisited" 51 Harv. L.R. 1165; Falconbridge, *Conflict of Laws* (2nd ed., 1954), Chaps 6–10; Munro, "The Magic Roundabout of the Conflict of Laws" 1978 J.R. 65; and Sauveplanne "International Encyclopaedia of Comparative Law" Volume III, Ch.6 (1990).

[10] [1930] 2 Ch. 259.

[11] [1926] 1 Ch. 692.

[12] *ibid., per* Russell J. at 708–709. However, this preference for the simple approach was *obiter*, for *Annesley* marks the beginning of the favour shown by English law to the double *renvoi* theory, *qv*. But the *effect* of applying the internal law theory and the double *renvoi* theory may often be the same.

(usually *qua lex patriae*). If the *lex fori* accepts the *renvoi* or reference back, at that stage the court applies (its own) *lex fori* in its narrow sense. The essentials of this theory are that:

(a) the starting point for the forum is the *lex fori*;
(b) proof is required of the choice of law rules of the foreign law; and
(c) at the third stage the reference/application is always to/of a law in its narrow sense.

The effect of applying this theory is that one legal system *defers* to another legal system's conflict rules.[13] At one time this theory was approved in England,[14] but it is not now applied by the English courts. There seems no particular logic in stopping the game at this point, but once having started down the road of *renvoi* reasoning, it would be hard to say when it is logical to stop.[15]

L'Affaire Forgo[16] provides an example of the French attitude to the problem. Forgo was a national of Bavaria who had lived in France since the age of five and who had a *de facto* domicile there. He was illegitimate. He died intestate. Under the Code Napoleon his whole estate fell to the French government because of his illegitimate status, but under the law of Bavaria it passed to his collaterals. The French *lex fori*, holding that the question was referred by French conflict rules to the Bavarian law of the nationality, found that that law referred the question back to French law, as the law of the domicile or habitual residence: at that point France accepted the *renvoi* or reference back and applied its own domestic law.

(3) FOREIGN COURT THEORY OR TOTAL *RENVOI* OR DOUBLE *RENVOI* THEORY

5–06 The forum endeavours to place itself at the outset in the position of the foreign court and to decide the question as that court would decide it.[17] In succession cases, according to the Scottish choice of

---

[13] But it depends what one means by the forum's choice of "law"; it might reasonably mean a choice of the foreign law in its entirety. On a simple view, however, the "British" preference for domicile to govern matters of status and succession represents a conscious policy decision. See Ch.6.

[14] *Re Johnson* [1903] 1 Ch. 821.

[15] Collier, p.24. Anton with Beaumont, p.79 recommends that it be terminated at the point indicated by convenience.

[16] (1833) 10 Clunet 64.

[17] *Armitage v A.G.* [1906] P. 135; *Bartlett* [1925] A.C. 377; *Re Achillopoulos* [1928] 1 Ch. 433; *Re Annesley* [1926] 1 Ch. 692; *Re Ross* [1930] 1 Ch. 377; *Re Askew* [1930] 2 Ch. 259; *Re O'Keefe* [1940] Ch. 124; *Re Duke of Wellington, dec'd* [1947] Ch. 506, *affd* [1948] Ch. 118; *Jaber Elias Kotia v Katr Bint Jiryes Nahas* [1941] A.C. 403; *In the Estate of Fuld, dec'd (No. 3)* [1968] P. 675.

law rule, the relevant foreign court will be the court of the domicile of the deceased as regards moveables and the court of the *lex situs* as regards immoveables. The first reference is therefore from that foreign law in its wide sense to the law indicated by its conflict rule and, if the latter would refer the matter back to the law of that foreign court, the question is whether the foreign court will accept the *renvoi*. The essentials of this theory are that:

(a) the starting point is (notionally) the foreign court;
(b) it is necessary to know not only the choice of law rule of the foreign law, but also whether or not the foreign law accepts *renvoi*; and
(c) at the third stage the reference/application is always to/of a law in its narrow sense.

If the foreign court accepts the principle of *renvoi*, it will accept (notionally) the reference back and the forum will consider itself entitled to apply that (foreign) law in its narrow sense[18]; but, if it will not accept a *renvoi*,[19] there can be no reference back. In such a case, an English court applies, in its narrow sense, the law indicated by the foreign conflict rule which is usually the law of the nationality. Where the country of nationality includes units with different laws, the English courts have applied the law of the territorial unit thereof in which the deceased had his domicile of origin. It has often been remarked that a *renvoi* remission may cause difficulty because there is no "British" law, nor "English" nationality.[20] *Re O'Keefe*[21] provides an example of difficulties which may be encountered, if the link with the *lex patriae* is tenuous and there has been a change of political status in the domicile of origin. However, the problem of ascribing the law of the nationality where the state is not unitary, and the problems of proof of foreign law, are secondary problems: one must first decide whether one is going to have any truck with this dimension.

A major stumbling block with regard to this theory is that it "works" only if the foreign court is not applying the same theory. If it should do so, the forum should have to seek to impersonate a foreign court which is seeking to impersonate the forum: this is a problem too far even for the enthusiasts to solve. But this theoretical objection to the theory remains theoretical; there are few *renvoi* cases, and none it seems in which the English court has found the foreign court to be playing the same double *renvoi* game. The foreign court has been found to be playing single *renvoi*

---

[18] *Re Annesley* [1926] 1 Ch. 692 (France).
[19] *Re Ross* [1930] 1 Ch. 337 (Italy).
[20] Chuah and Kaczarowska, *Conflict of Laws* (Cavendish, 1996), p.6.
[21] [1940] Ch. 124.

(France, Germany), or not to be playing at all (Italy), or not to know whether it is playing or not (Spain). Hence, the "mirror effect", or the "after you, Claud; no, after you, Montmorency" scenario, or *circulus inextricabilis* has not arisen.[22] The Scots attitude to *renvoi*, in principle and in practice, is unknown.[23]

THE SCOPE OF *RENVOI*

5–07 The doctrine of *renvoi* in English conflict of laws jurisprudence has been applied to questions involving intestacy, legal rights, formal validity of wills (and of marriage), essential validity of wills, succession to immoveables, and status (in particular legitimation cases). Even in this area, however, archetypically appropriate for the operation of *renvoi*, the trend, later emerging, has been expressly to exclude it. [24] The Wills Act 1963, section 1, provides that a will shall be treated as properly executed if its execution conformed to the internal law of the various possible laws regulating execution. The effect of this is to eliminate *renvoi* in questions relating to formal validity. As to matters of essential validity of wills, the effect of harmonisation of choice of law rules at a European level, "will obviate the need for *renvoi* where all the connecting factors are situated in a Member State."[25] In cases where the (harmonised) choice of law rule designates the law of a third country, it is not yet clear whether *renvoi* will be admitted. The Hague Trusts Convention (given effect in Scots and English law by the Recognition of Trusts Act 1987) by Article 17 excludes *renvoi*.

There have been suggestions from time to time that *renvoi* might also be applied in other branches of law—as for example in *Vita Food Products Inc. v Unus Shipping Co.*[26] (contract), and *Alcock,*

---

[22] Forsyth, *Private International Law* (4th ed., 2003), p.89 notes that if there is no proof of foreign law, it must be presumed to be the same as the law of the forum!

[23] Binchy, *Irish Conflict of Laws* (1988), p.38, speculates that the dearth of Irish *renvoi* cases may be due to the trend for Irish emigration to take place to countries such as Canada, USA, Australia, New Zealand, South Africa and Argentina, which belong to the family of "domicile" countries. He suggests that there may be cases in the future as a result of greater interaction between Continental Europe and Ireland. Note also *Neilson v Overseas Projects Corporation of Victoria Ltd* [2005] HCA 54 (and earlier *Mercantile Mutual v Neilson* [2004] WASCA 60) for an up-to-date consideration of Australia's position on *renvoi*.

[24] The query then arises whether the express exclusion in any instrument of *renvoi* means that incidental questions presenting within the ambit of such an instrument must be determined by the forum adopting a *lex fori* approach (see Ch.4, above): Anton with Beaumont, p.77.

[25] Green Paper, *Succession and Wills* (COM (2005) 65 final), para.2.7.

[26] [1939] A.C. 277. *cf. Amin Rasheed Shipping Corp. v Kuwait Insurance Co*; *The Al Wahab* [1983] 2 All E.R. 884, *per* Lord Diplock, p.888.

Embiricos and *Koechlin* (bills of exchange).[27] However, in *Re United Railways of Havana and Regla Warehouses Ltd*,[28] the Court of Appeal made it clear that "the principle of *renvoi* finds no place in the field of contract",[29] and the matter has been put beyond doubt by the Contracts (Applicable Law) Act 1990, bringing into United Kingdom law the Rome Convention on the law applicable to contractual obligations, Article 15 of which excludes the application of *renvoi*.

Similarly, in delict, *renvoi* was not thought to be applicable.[30] The point is now regulated for Scots and English conflict law by statute, the operation of *renvoi* being excluded by section 9(5) of the Private International Law (Miscellaneous Provisions) Act 1995.[31]

With regard to property problems, Dicey and Morris[32] considers that *renvoi* should be available in cases involving title to land abroad, because if there is one certainty in the conflict of laws, it is that, in matters pertaining to land, effectiveness of the conflict rule requires that the *lex situs* be entirely satisfied. Hence, choice of the *lex situs* may in the end mean choice of the entirety of that law.[33] As regards moveable property, it can be noted that in *Winkworth v Christie Manson & Woods Ltd*,[34] counsel argued strongly for a departure from the *lex situs* rule in problems of ownership of moveable property; the judge of first instance, though unconvinced, expressly made it clear that, at the trial, use might be made of *renvoi* reasoning to suggest that the Italian *lex situs* itself might not consider that it applied. However, such a hint of openness to the *renvoi* argument should be contrasted with the more recent dictum of Staughton L.J. in *Macmillan Inc. v Bishopsgate Investment Trust plc (No 3)*.[35] In relation to unjust enrichment, an argument (held to be premature) was made in *Barros Mattos Junior v MacDaniels Ltd*[36] that the applicable law should be understood as meaning the applicable law in its totality.

In Family Law, the Law Commissions commented[37] that *renvoi* reasoning may be useful when referring to the *lex loci celebrationis*

---

[27] *Alcock v Smith* [1892] 1 Ch. 238; *Embiricos v Anglo-Austrian Bank* [1905] 1 K.B. 677; *Koechlin et Cie v Kestenbaum Bros* [1927] 1 K.B. 889.

[28] [1960] Ch. 52; [1961] A.C. 1007 (House of Lords).

[29] [1960] Ch. 52, *per* Jenkins L.J. at 96–97; Willmer L.J. *diss.* at 115.

[30] *McElroy v McAllister*, 1949 S.C. 110, *per* Lord Russell at 126.

[31] See also Rome II, Art.21. But see *Neilson v Overseas Projects Corp. of Victoria Ltd* [2005] HCA 54.

[32] Dicey and Morris, pp.79–80.

[33] Though see *In re Ross* [1931] Ch 377: the effect of application of the Italian *lex situs* "in the round" led to the application, by the English forum, of the English law of succession.

[34] [1980] 1 Ch. 496

[35] [1996] 1 W.L.R. 387, at 405.

[36] [2005] I.L.Pr. 45, *per* Collins J. at para. 121.

[37] Law Com., Working Paper No. 89 and Scot. Law. Com. Memo., No. 64, *Private International Law Choice of Law Rules in Marriage*, paras 2.12–13 and 2.39–2.42.

(formal validity of marriage[38]), with the aim of promoting greater uniformity of status (to avoid "limping marriages") and of allowing a greater number of marriages to be upheld. "On the whole, we think that these arguments should prevail [against those of inconvenience, delay and cost in litigation, and theoretical problems]. Our provisional recommendation is that the reference made by our choice of law rules to the law of the country of celebration should in the case of marriages celebrated abroad be construed as a reference to the whole law of that country (including its choice of law rules) and not merely to its domestic rules."[39] Similarly,[40] in the matter of capacity to marry, the Law Commissions were amenable to the *renvoi* argument.

Where *renvoi* is not expressly excluded, care must be taken to construct a reasoned view as to the possible application of *renvoi* in the given situation. It is a rule of Hague Convention drafting that the word "law" includes rules of private international law and that reference is to internal rules only if that is explicitly stated.[41] In other legislation, the reasonable conclusion is that, if not expressly excluded, *renvoi* is available by default. Thus, for example, in the Family Law (Scotland) Act 2006, which contains certain provisions of conflict of laws significance, there is contained in section 38 (validity of marriages) a rule concerning the treatment in a Scots court of a foreign rule requiring parental consent to marriage, *viz* "If the law of the place in which a person is domiciled requires a person under a certain age to obtain parental consent before entering into a marriage, that requirement shall not be taken to affect the capacity of a person to enter into a marriage in Scotland unless failure to obtain such consent would render invalid any marriage that the person purported to enter into in any form anywhere in the world." It would appear that the reference to the "law of the place in which such a person is domiciled" must therefore encompass the conflict rules of that legal system.[42]

The *renvoi* process may be seen as the antithesis of what business requires (which is certainty and speed). Therein lies the explanation for its exclusion generally from the commercial sphere,

---

[38] See *Taczanowska v Taczanowski* [1957] P. 301; and *Hooper v Hooper* [1959] 1 W.L.R. 1021.

[39] Para.2.39.

[40] Para.3.39.

[41] The Peréz-Vera Report on the 1980 Hague Abduction Convention emphasised that the applicable law includes rules of private international law so as to expand the potential reach of the Convention.

[42] The provenance of this provision is *Report on Family Law* Scot. Law Com. No 135 (1992) paras 14.8–14.10, recommendation 70(a). Notably the Civil Partnership Act 2004, s.124(10) provides that, in testing the validity of civil partnerships registered outside Scotland, where reference is made to the "relevant law", that means "the law of the country or territory where the overseas relationship was registered (including its rules of private international law)".

because if there is any validity in *renvoi* thinking, it should surely apply in principle across the whole range of private law subjects. Yet the effect of judicial openness to *renvoi* normally is positive.[43] It has been a notable claim by *renvoi* proponents that the operation of the doctrine is capable of producing uniformity of result regardless of forum (*i.e.* harmony of decision), but a brief analysis of an hypothetical problem of intestate moveable succession reveals that diversity of result often may emerge, depending upon the approach to *renvoi* taken in each of the "forums" where is situated moveable estate of the deceased requiring to be distributed. As Munro demonstrates,[44] where one forum (the situation of the bulk of the deceased's moveable estate) favours the internal law theory, and the other (which *qua situs* is required to distribute the remainder of the deceased's moveable estate) favours the partial *renvoi* theory, a uniform approach to the distribution of the whole estate appears likely to be the outcome. Where, however, both systems favour the partial *renvoi* approach, the result would be diversity. Where both systems prefer the double *renvoi* approach, there is an *impasse*. Moreover, results other than such as these may eventuate in a particular case, by reason of different approaches which legal systems may take to characterisation and interpretation, and which may act as obstacles to achieving, in practice, a uniform result. The simple point can be made that the legal systems involved may differ in their definition of their preferred connecting factor(s)[45]; and there is the more complex point that an incidental question may arise which affects the validity of the claim of an heir, especially *qua* widow.[46]

Yet, in any given case of this type the search for uniformity of **5–08** treatment by the interested forums is said to be worth attempting. However, in argumentative mode, one might ask whether uniformity of treatment of an estate is always absolutely desirable. If the deceased had significant legal links with two legal systems, one of which strongly endorses the principle of family protection, and the other the principle of freedom of testation, advocates of harmony of decision, by seeking to secure a uniform distribution, necessarily would exclude the policy of one of those laws. Moreover, it must be queried how often these transnational succession problems arise.

---

[43] Though it may be productive of mischief: see *Re JB (Child Abduction) (Rights of Custody: Spain)* [2004] 1 F.L.R. 796 (English forum permitted application of Spanish law "in the round", resulting in a remission to English law by which the unmarried, bereft father, had no parental rights such as to justify a petition for return of the child under the 1980 Hague Convention on the grounds of wrongful removal).

[44] See Munro, "The Magic Roundabout of the Conflict of Laws", 1978 J.R. 65 at 78–80.

[45] *Re Annesley* [1926] 1 Ch. 692 (France).

[46] See Ch.4.

The EU in its harmonisation programme proceeds on the basis that there is a need for harmonisation of approach within Member States to govern such trans-European cases, and proposes a system of harmonised choice of law rules in succession, asserting that if this were achieved, the need for *renvoi* in these cases at Community level will fall away.

While the status of *renvoi* as an intellectual plaything in the subject cannot be denied, its potential use as a tool, to positive effect (ie in providing a legitimate escape route to a more positive result), or as a corrective (*i.e.* to seek to neutralise the effects of forum-shopping[47]) should be recognised.

RENVOI CASES

5-09 The following is a summary of the English cases (in which the foreign court theory of *renvoi* has been applied).

Re Annesley [1926] 1 Ch. 692

Mrs Annesley, an Englishwoman, lived in France from 1866 until her death there in 1924. By the date of her death, she had not taken the steps prescribed by the French Civil Code to acquire French domicile; the requisite form, not completed, was found among her papers. She made a will in France in English form in which she declared that she intended to remain a British subject, and that she had not any intention of abandoning her English domicile. By the will she left the residue of her estate to one daughter absolutely, but she had another child who was excluded from the will. By English law she could dispose of all her estate as she wished, but by French law she could dispose by will of only one-third of her moveable estate, and the question at issue was whether her will had effectively conveyed the whole of the residue to that daughter.

The question giving rise to the *renvoi* issue was the devolution of her moveable property, and the essential validity of her testamentary provisions pertaining thereto, which, by the conflict rule of English law, is determined by the law of the domicile. Russell J. arrived at his decision that Mrs Annesley's freedom of testation was governed by French law, by the following reasoning:

(a) The connecting factor was domicile, which must be identified by the English law of the forum, no matter what any other law might provide as to domicile.

(b) By English law, Mrs Annesley died domiciled in France.

---

[47] See A. Briggs, "In Praise and Defence of *Renvoi*", 1998 I.C.L.Q. 877.

(c) Applying the law of France as the law of the domicile, the English court must endeavour to place itself in the same position as a French court and decide the matter as a French court would decide it. Starting then from French law as the law of the domicile in its wide sense, that law referred the matter (*i.e.* the essential validity of the will) to "British law" as the law of the nationality and the only meaning which could be given to "British law" in the circumstances was English law, which, in turn, would refer the matter back to the law of France. According to expert evidence preferred by Russell J., French law accepted a reference back and so the English court sitting, as it were, in the position of the French court accepted the *renvoi* and applied French law in its narrow sense, with the result that it was held that Mrs Annesley's will could dispose of only one-third of her estate.

(d) It would have been possible to have arrived at the same result by ignoring *renvoi* and simply applying French law directly in its narrow sense as the law of the domicile. Indeed Russell J. commended this route, although single-handedly, it seems, he introduced into English conflict rules by this decision the doctrine of double *renvoi*.

Re Ross [1930] 1 Ch. 377

Mrs Ross was a British subject who died domiciled in Italy **5–10** leaving English and Italian wills by which she bequeathed the residue of her (moveable) estate in England to a niece and her (moveable and immoveable) estate in Italy to a grand-nephew. By doing so she excluded her son and he raised this action in England for payment of his legal rights, available under Italian law. Luxmoore J. decided as follows:

(a) As regards moveables, the connecting factor was domicile and the case must be decided in the same way as an Italian court would decide it, because the deceased died domiciled in Italy.

(b) Starting with Italian law (in its wide sense), that law referred the question to "British law" as the law of the nationality which, as in *Annesley*, could mean only English law, because the testatrix had her domicile of origin in England and had no other connection with Britain. English law would refer the question back to the law of Italy. The expert evidence, however, showed that the law of Italy could not accept a *renvoi*, so the matter could not proceed beyond the reference from Italian law, as the starting point, to "British law". As the Italian court could not accept a *renvoi*, it would apply "British law", so the English court did the same thing and applied English law in its narrow or domestic sense. In effect, therefore, the English court perforce applied the law of the domicile of origin in preference to the law of the last domicile. Was this the result of excessive care and politeness, or did the English court thereby truly give effect to its conception of Italian law?

(c) As regards immoveable property in Italy, the same decision was arrived at by the same reasoning, the only difference being that the starting point again was the law of Italy, this time *qua lex situs*.[48]

NOTE that the essential difference between *Annesley* and *Ross* lies simply in the fact that French law accepted the doctrine of *renvoi* whereas Italian law did not do so.

Re Askew [1930] 2 Ch. 259

5–11   Under an English marriage contract the husband, who was domiciled in England, had a power of appointment of the trust fund among the children of the marriage and also children of any subsequent marriage. Later he went to Germany where he acquired a domicile and became the father of an illegitimate child. He divorced his wife and married the child's mother. This child was included in the exercise of the power and the question was whether it could succeed to a share of the estate; had it been legitimated by the marriage of its parents? It was held that the child could succeed by the following process of reasoning:

(a) The question at issue was one of status, and so the connecting factor was domicile and the father and the child were both domiciled in Germany.

(b) Starting with German law in its wide sense, that law referred the matter to the law of the nationality, "British law", which, once again, could mean only English law.

(c) English law referred the matter back to the law of Germany, which accepted *renvoi*, and so German law was applied in its narrow sense; as the child had been legitimated by that law, despite its adulterine status, it could succeed. This was a positive outcome obviously, but the more so because by English domestic law at the time the child, being an "adulterine bastard", could not be legitimated.

---

[48] This produced the extremely unusual result that rights of succession to land in Italy were governed by the law of England; *cf.* with regard to the devolution of immoveables in Spain, *In re Duke of Wellington* [1947] 1 Ch. 506, aff'd [1948] 1 Ch. 118.

Re O'Keefe [1940] Ch. 124

This case is often cited to demonstrate that the operation of *renvoi* **5–12** may have artificial results.

Miss O'Keefe died intestate in Italy in 1937. Her father was born in County Clare, Ireland, and he lived first in India for many years and then in other countries. Miss O'Keefe, born in Calcutta, lived in India, France, England, Spain, Tangier and the Channel Islands, but for the last 47 years of her life in Italy, where she had acquired a domicile. Her domicile of origin was in Ireland, in the part which became Eire, now the Republic of Ireland, but she had not been in Ireland since a holiday visit when she was 18 years of age. At the time of her death she was a British—not Irish—subject. This case concerned the intestate succession to her estate, in respect of which the law of Ireland was applied, by the same reasoning as in *Ross*, as follows:

(a) English law as the law of the forum (where the assets were situated) decided that domicile was the connecting factor and that Miss O'Keefe had died domiciled in Italy.

(b) Italian law in its wide sense referred the matter to "British law" as the law of the nationality. "British law" would refer the matter back to the law of Italy, but Italian law could not accept a *renvoi*, so the question had to be decided according to "British law", whatever that might mean.

(c) Following *Ross*, the judge held that the law of the domicile of origin, the law of Ireland, was the only law which could be applied (though it will be noted that Miss O'Keefe was not a citizen of Ireland). An alternative in such a case would have been to hold the deceased domiciled in that part of the British Commonwealth in which he or she last had a domicile before acquiring a foreign domicile. The case attracts comment because in lay terms the choice of Irish law had little connection with the facts of the deceased's life, and in technical terms the English court could hardly be said to be applying the law of her nationality as was the rule of Italian law. Nevertheless, the unusual outcome reflects the unusual personal and political circumstances of the case and it is submitted that the task of applying the law of the nationality in relation to a multi-legal system state will not normally be productive of such difficulty.

Re Duke of Wellington, dec'd. [1947] Ch. 506, aff'd [1948] Ch. 118

The sixth Duke of Wellington, domiciled in England, left assets in **5–13** England and Spain and made two wills dealing respectively with those assets. By the Spanish will he left his land in Spain to the person who was to succeed jointly to the English dukedom and the

Spanish dukedom. He died unmarried and it transpired, therefore, that while his uncle succeeded to the English title, it was his sister who succeeded to the Spanish title, with the result that the destination in the Spanish will failed because there was no one beneficiary to succeed to both titles. The question arose at first instance and on appeal in England as to the determination of the manner in which the Spanish estate, moveable and immoveable, should devolve. By Spanish law succession to moveables and immoveables was governed by the law of the nationality. Wynn-Parry J. held that in these circumstances (of application of English law), the Spanish property, moveable and immoveable, ineffectually disposed of by the Spanish will, must fall to be distributed in accordance with the English will, which the sixth Duke had made in order to dispose of the remainder of his property, specifically excepting the property (competently) disposed of under the Spanish will. The court at first instance dealt with the case of moveable property on the simple view that it would descend in accordance with the English law of the ultimate domicile of the deceased. Therefore, by inference, it can be deduced that the English court felt under no obligation to dwell upon the consequences of the Spanish preference for a unity of succession rule.

The significance of the case resides in the treatment of the succession to immoveables which provoked a notable *renvoi* discussion. In relation to immoveable property, Wynn-Parry J., starting with Spanish law as the *lex situs*, held that the law referred the matter to "British law" as the law of the nationality, which could mean only English law. English law would refer the matter back to the *lex situs*, but each side produced conflicting expert evidence as to whether or not Spanish law would accept a *renvoi*. One of the experts died before the hearing, but no objection was taken to his affidavit being read and relied on on behalf of the current Duke. The judge had to decide the point for himself and held, on balance, that Spanish law did not accept a *renvoi*, and so he applied English law. In the Court of Appeal the only matters raised pertain to the construction and effect of the two wills in English law; by application of English law the seventh Duke was entitled under the English will to the Spanish property, moveable and immoveable, comprised in, but ineffectually disposed of by, the Spanish will. English law regulated the devolution to Spanish immoveable property, and in the view of the English court, the Spanish courts would be bound to register the title of the seventh Duke as the absolute owner of the Spanish immoveable property.[49]

---

[49] See *per* Wynn-Parry J. [1947] 1 Ch. 506 at 524. Contrast the general authority of the *lex situs* in matters pertaining to immoveable property (as to which see Ch.17, below). Note, however, that certain incursions into this principle are identifiable, from which it can be seen that the *lex situs* sometimes is required to be compliant: see Carruthers, *The Transfer of Property in the Conflict of Laws*, paras 02.76 *et seq.*

The judgment of Wynn-Parry J. contains a very well-known conflict of laws lament:

> "[I]t would be difficult to imagine a harder task than that which faces me, namely, of expounding for the first time either in this country or in Spain the relevant law of Spain as it would be expounded by the Supreme Court of Spain, which up to the present time has made no pronouncement on the subject, and having to base that exposition on evidence which satisfies me that on this subject there exists a profound cleavage of legal opinion in Spain, and two conflicting decisions of courts of inferior jurisdiction".[50]

SUMMARY 5–*RENVOI*

Renvoi: remission and transmission

1. The classic example is a question of succession to moveable **5–14** estate in Scotland belonging to a British subject who has died intestate domiciled in a foreign country, the law of which refers questions of succession to the law of the nationality.

2. Theories:

    (a) internal law theory
    (b) partial *renvoi* theory
    (c) foreign court theory—which requires knowledge of

      (i) choice of law rule of foreign law; and
      (ii) whether or not it accepts *renvoi*.

3. English courts have applied the foreign court theory. The starting point is the foreign court: if foreign law accepts *renvoi*, that law in the narrow sense is applied by the English court; if not, in the reported cases the forum resorts to application of its own domestic law.

4. The Scottish view of *renvoi* is untested.

5. The doctrine has been applied in succession cases, and also to questions of status. Although it may confer certain benefits, it is unlikely to be permitted wider application. Its operation is excluded specifically from the Scots and English conflict rules of contract and delict.

---

[50] p.515.

CHAPTER 6

DOMICILE AND RESIDENCE

THE NATURE OF DOMICILE

Every person in the course of his life becomes concerned in **6-01** matters with legal implications, some of which are passing or temporary, and others intended to be of a more permanent nature. It is necessary to find a connecting factor of some permanence for the regulation of the latter. The country to which a person "belongs" suggests itself as suitable. In continental European countries such matters have tended, in the past at least, to be governed by the law of the nationality, but in the English speaking countries, which usually contain various states, provinces or units, each with its own law, there is no such thing as the law of nationality. As a result, the laws of English speaking countries generally, and some others (*e.g.* Scandinavia), provide that questions of status and personal law are, in general, to be governed by the law of a person's domicile,[1] which is the place where he has his permanent home, in the legal sense. It has been estimated that allegiance to the factors of nationality and domicile, respectively, is equally divided,[2] but it should be noted that all European states now must employ also the connecting factor of habitual residence, as a result of the high incidence of the use of this factor in modern EU harmonisation instruments.

In the case of *Udny v Udny*,[3] which, with *Bell v Kennedy*,[4] forms the twin-pillared arch on which the Scots and English rules of domicile are built, there is found the following explanation in the judgment of Lord Westbury at p.99:

"The law of England, and of almost all civilised countries, ascribes to each individual at his birth two distinct legal states or conditions; one by virtue of which he becomes the subject

---

[1] See, *e.g.* K. Norrie, "Personal Law: Concept and Development", 1983 S.L.T. (News) 53.
[2] *ibid.*, at p.54.
[3] (1869) 7 M. (H.L.) 89.
[4] (1868) 6 M. (H.L.) 69.

of some particular country, binding him by the tie of natural allegiance, which may be called his political status; another by virtue of which he has ascribed to him the character of a citizen of some particular country, and as such is possessed of certain municipal rights, and subject to certain obligations, which latter character is the civil status or condition of the individual, and may be quite different from his political status, for the political status may depend upon different laws in different countries, whereas the civil status is governed universally by one specific principle. Domicile or the place of settled residence of an individual is the criterion established by law for the purpose of determining the legal condition of the person, for it is on this basis that the personal rights of the parties—that is, the law which determines his majority or minority, marriage, succession, testacy or intestacy—must depend."

DOMICILE, NATIONALITY AND RESIDENCE

6–02 *Domicile* is the tie or connection between an individual and an area or a territorial society governed by a common body of law. It is a relationship between an individual and a system of law. Because domicile implies a connection between a person and a territory having a common body of law, it follows that there is no such thing as British, Canadian, Australian or American domicile. A person may only have a domicile in a territory subject to one system of law such as Scotland, England (and Wales), the Provinces of Quebec or Ontario, etc. in Canada, the States of New South Wales, Victoria, etc., in Australia, New York, Ohio, etc., in USA or one of the Channel Islands.[5]

Domicile is a personal matter and may be changed without state authorisation. Cases of doubt can be resolved only by adjudication of the court, for there is no paper "evidence" of a person's domicile.

It is notoriously difficult to define domicile. Broadly, in its classic (*i.e.* common law) sense, the domicile of any person is the legal system which is considered by law to be his "permanent" (*i.e.* established) home. It is, in general, the country which is in fact his home, but in some cases it is the country which, whether it is in fact his home or not, is determined to be such by a rule of law.

---

[5] As the rules stand at present, an emigrant from Scotland to USA cannot be said to have acquired a new domicile until he has settled in a particular State. The Law Commissions have proposed a change: Law Com. No. 168 and Scot. Law Com. Memo. No. 107 (1987) 7.8. For certain purposes, *e.g.* divorce, legislation within a non-unitary state may speak of, say, "Australian domicile", Cheshire and North, p.136.

The concept of domicile and its rules remain the same wherever they are encountered—marriage, succession, legitimacy or other area of personal law.[6]

Nationality is the tie of allegiance which binds an individual to a state and involves reciprocal duties of obedience and protection. State authorisation is required before nationality may be changed.[7]

Residence is a mere physical fact independent of will or intention, but it may involve legal consequences such as liability to pay income tax or becoming subject to the jurisdiction of a particular court.

Habitual Residence is a modern contender for the role of personal law.[8] It might be thought that the use of the adjective "habitual" denotes substantial factual connection, not only more than sojourn,[9] but also more than mere "residence" or "ordinary residence".

STATUTORY DEFINITION OF DOMICILE

"Domicile" may be given a special meaning, defined by statute for **6–03** a particular purpose. This is a modern occurrence. An artificial conception of domicile was introduced by the Finance Act 1975, section 45 (now repealed) for Inland Revenue purposes only. This is now contained in the Inheritance Tax Act 1984, section 267, which provides that a person who is not domiciled in the UK at any given time shall be treated for inheritance tax purposes as if he were domiciled in the UK (and not elsewhere) at the relevant time if either:

(a) he was domiciled in the United Kingdom within the three years immediately preceding the relevant time; or
(b) he was resident in the United Kingdom in not less than 17 of the 20 years of assessment ending with the year of assessment in which the relevant time falls.

---

[6] "The single conception theory": see Cheshire and North, pp.134–135.

[7] *i.e.* for a person desiring change of nationality, the outcome (acquisition of the new; continuance of the old?) will depend on the laws of the states involved, including their attitudes to dual nationality. Further, the decision on who is a national of a state is a matter for the law of the state the nationality of which is in question: *Oppenheimer v Cattermole* [1975] 1 All E.R. 538.

[8] See Child Abduction and Custody Act 1985; Family Law Act 1986, ss. 26 and 46; Children (Scotland) Act 1995, s.14; Brussels II *Bis*; 1996 Hague Convention; Adoption (Intercountry Aspects) Act 1999.

[9] Wolff (2nd ed.), p.110 defines residence as "habitual physical presence in a place . . . more than sojourn (physical presence) and less than domicile. It is a purely factual conception and requires no legal capacity". In *Winans v Att.-Gen.* [1904] A.C. 287, Lord Macnaghten at 298 described Winans as "a sojourner and stranger" when he came to England, and "a sojourner and a stranger in it" when he died.

In this connection, exceptionally, domicile is that of the "United Kingdom", or not.

A much more important example for our purposes is the use of "domicile" for the purpose of ascertaining jurisdiction in terms of the Civil Jurisdiction and Judgment Acts 1982 and 1991, and the Brussels I Regulation.[10] "Domicile" in this context bears no relation to domicile in its classic meaning.

The remainder of this chapter is concerned with domicile in the classic sense.[11]

Family Law (Scotland) Act 2006 ("the 2006 Act")

The development of the rules of domicile in Scots and English law has been characterised by steady common law progression, punctuated by legislative intervention on particular matters. It is important to note at this juncture that there is a provision (section 22) of the 2006 Act, which effects a change in the domicile rules of Scots law concerning the domicile of persons under 16 years of age. Potentially this provision may undermine long-established rules of domicile, and its influence will be further reaching, and its consequences more radical, than the name of the section (domicile of persons under 16) and its ostensible purpose suggests. The rules to be set out in this chapter therefore must be read against the potential for change which section 22 contains.

THE RULES OF DOMICILE—A PRÉCIS

6–04 Knowledge of the subject of domicile requires a grasp of its technical rules and familiarity with the case authorities in which the topic is rich. The rules of domicile are a construct of the common law. Statutory reform of the classic domicile rules, though significant in content, is late in date and specific in nature.

A summary of the rules is set out below.

(a) No person can be without a domicile, though they may lack a home and may have no knowledge of the concept of a

---

[10] Civil Jurisdiction and Judgments Act 1982, ss.41–46; and now Civil Jurisdiction and Judgments Order 2001 (SI 2001/3929), reg.9. See Ch.7 below. The definition or *indicia* of domicile in its classic sense, including capacity to acquire domicile, is the prerogative of the forum to decide. But a Member State forum's role with regard to the meaning of domicile within the Brussels regime is different. If the individual is not domiciled in the forum, Art.52(2) of the Brussels Convention requires the forum (if need be) to ascertain whether the individual is domiciled in another Contracting State by application of the rules of "domicile" of that other Contracting State. See now in relation to Council Regulation 44/2001, Art.59(2).

[11] See regarding its use in jurisdiction, Ch.7 below.

legal home.[12] Equally, where an individual has two or more homes, the fact that his chief and favourite residence is situated in country A may not dissuade the court from finding him to be domiciled, by application of the forum's rules, in country B.[13] No person can have more than one domicile (in the classic sense) at any one time.

(b) *Domicile of origin* is ascribed according to fixed rules. Prior to the coming into force of the 2006 Act, these rules rested on the distinction between legitimacy and illegitimacy. The Law Reform (Parent and Child) (Scotland) Act 1986, by section 9(1)(a),[14] retained the rule of law whereby a child born outside marriage took the domicile of his mother as a domicile of origin, affirming therefore the common law rule (applying still in England), that domicile of origin is ascribed according to status as legitimate or illegitimate, the former taking as his/her domicile of origin the domicile of his/her father at the date of the child's birth.

One of the aims of the 2006 Act was to complete the process of removal from the law of Scotland of the status of illegitimacy. Abolition of the status has been effected by section 21.[15] In consequence, a new rule for the ascription of domicile at birth has been provided by section 22. The implications of this section are considered fully below, but essentially the new general rule is that if a child's parents are domiciled in the same country as each other, and the child has a home with either/both parent(s), the child shall be domiciled in the same country as his/her parents.

(c) There is a presumption in favour of an existing domicile. The onus of proof of change lies therefore on the party arguing that change has taken place.[16]

(d) Every person *sui juris*[17] may acquire a *domicile of choice* by a combination of a change of residence to a different legal

---

[12] Thus, where the *propositus* was found to have led a nomadic existence, living in lodgings or with friends, she was held not to have lost her Scots domicile of origin: *Arnott v Groom* (1846) 9 D. 142.

[13] *Marchioness of Huntly v Gaskell* (1905) 8 F. (H.L.) 4 (affirming *sub nom. Brooks v Brooks's Trs* (1902) 4 F. 1014 in Court of Session); also *Donaldson v McClure* (1857) 20 D. 207. *Re Clore dec'd (No. 2)* [1984] S.T.C. 609. See also the special circumstances and dual residence decision in *Plummer v IRC* [1988] 1 All E.R. 97.

[14] Repealed by Family Law (Scotland) Act 2006, Sch.3.

[15] In cases where the person's status is governed by Scots law. See further Chs 14 and 18, below.

[16] *Bell v Kennedy*, above; *Vincent v Earl of Buchan* (1889) 16 R. 637; *Lord Advocate v Brown's Trs*, 1907 S.C. 333; *Casey v Casey*, 1968 S.L.T. 56; *Spence v Spence*, 1995 S.L.T. 335; and *Reddington v Riach's Executor*, 2002 S.L.T. 537.

[17] That is, of full legal capacity, unaffected by a legal disability caused, *e.g.* by non-age or insanity. In English law, a person becomes *sui juris* for the purposes of domicile, at the age of 16 (Domicile and Matrimonial Proceedings Act 1973,

system and the intention to reside in that system, for as long as can be seen ahead. Any circumstances, even the seemingly trivial,[18] which seem to bear upon residence and/ or intention may be considered by the court in assessing domicile, and it is the duty of counsel to bring all potentially relevant matters to the attention of the court.[19]

(e) Domicile of choice is lost by a combination of loss of residence in, and loss of intention for, a legal system. Retention of either[20] will result in retention of domicile of choice.

(f) In all types of case in which the connecting factor of domicile is used, there is a *tempus inspiciendum* according to the choice of law rule in question (*e.g.* capacity to marry; succession to moveables). In the ascertainment of intention, the court is precluded from taking into account factors pertaining to residence or deemed intention which post-date that time.[21]

(g) In Scots law prior to the 2006 Act, and in English law still, an individual's domicile, during nonage, would/will be dependent upon the domicile of his father or mother, depending on the child's status, and the applicability of Domicile and Matrimonial Proceedings Act 1973, section 4 (*qv*), his/her domicile changing if a change should occur in the domicile of the relevant parent.[22] By virtue of section 22 of the 2006 Act, an individual's domicile at any given point under the age of 16, will be determined by application of that section at the time in question. It is important to note that the 2006 Act, in Schedule 3, repeals (for Scotland only) section 4 of the DMPA 1973.

Prior to the 2006 Act, and still in English law, it was/is thought that the domicile of persons under the age of 16 both of whose parents are dead, probably cannot be changed. Though the 2006 Act is silent on the point, the situation would appear to fall within section 22(3), permitting the court to find the child domiciled in the country

---

s.3(a)). In Scots law, legal capacity arises at the age of 16, but authority for this rests now not on the Age of Legal Capacity (Scotland) Act 1991, s.7 (repealed by 2006 Act, Sch.3), but rather on the 2006 Act, s.22(4).

[18] *Drevon v Drevon* (1834) 34 L.J. Ch. 129, *per* Kindersley V.-C. at 133.

[19] *Brown v Brown*, 1928 S.L.T. 339, *per* Lord President Clyde at 341.

[20] *Re Raffenel* (1863) 3 Sw. & Tr. 49 (loss of intention, but no sufficient loss of residence); *Re Lloyd Evans* [1947] Ch. 695 (loss of residence, but continuing intention for Belgium); and *Morgan v Cilento*, 2004 EWHC 188.

[21] *Bell v Kennedy*, above; *Morgan v Cilento*, 2004 EWHC 188; and *Lynch v Provisional Government of Paraguay* (1871) L.R. 2 P.&D. 268 and *Agulian & Anr v Cyganik* [2006] EWCA Civ. 129, *per* Mummery L.J. at para.46.

[22] The rules of dependent domicile rested upon both common law and statute (Domicile and Matrimonial Proceedings Act 1973, s.4).

with which s/he has for the time being the closest connection.

(h) Legal capacity in Scots law to have an independent domicile depends upon having attained the age of 16 and upon being of sufficient mental capacity to form the requisite intention.[23]

(i) Until January 1, 1974 the domicile of married women was dependent upon the domicile of their husbands, but the Domicile and Matrimonial Proceedings Act 1973, section 1 abolished the "unity of domicile" rule in cases of those persons married after that date.[24]

(j) In questions which have arisen in the courts of Scotland and England, domicile is always ascertained in accordance with the rules thereon of *lex fori*.[25] This will include determination of legal capacity to acquire a new domicile, although there is a lack of authority, and in principle, it might have seemed preferable that an individual's capacity to acquire a new domicile should be determined by the law of his present domicile.[26] On the other hand, in domicile cases before a Scots or English forum, no question ever arises of the individual's legal capacity to change his domicile throughout his life being determined by the conflict rules of any system other than that of the forum. Such conjecture would add greatly to the cost and complexity of the case, and would increase uncertainty.

CLASSES OF DOMICILE

Traditional view

Every person *sui juris* (the *"propositus"*) has a domicile which may **6–05** be either a domicile of origin or a domicile of choice. A domicile of origin is ascribed by law to every person at birth and is involuntary. Even if it is superseded by the acquisition of a new domicile, the domicile of origin is never entirely extinguished and, if the new domicile subsequently is lost, the domicile of origin will revive. Domicile of choice is the domicile which a person *sui juris*

---

[23] 2006 Act, s.22(4) (Scots law); and Domicile and Matrimonial Proceedings Act 1973, s.3 (English law: age 16 or if married before that date—being necessarily therefore not of English domicile).

[24] The situation is considered more fully below at para.6–25.

[25] *Re Annesley* [1926] Ch. 692. See, however, Family Law Act 1986, s.46(5) which in the matter of recognition of a foreign court as competent to dissolve a marriage, in extending to the foreign court of the domicile that recognition, permits "domicile" to be understood in either the "home" or "foreign" meaning.

[26] See Graveson, p.193.

may acquire by a change of residence and intention. A person who is not *sui juris* may acquire a derivative or dependent domicile, according to rules outlined below governing the years of legal incapacity.

Impact of Family Law (Scotland) Act 2006

The 2006 Act makes no reference to the terms "domicile of origin" and "domicile of choice". The express extent of section 22 is to effect the ascription of domicile of persons under 16. By inference, therefore, the rules contained in section 22 cease to be applicable to a person once s/he attains the age of 16. In the absence of further statutory intervention, it is presumed that in any domicile litigation occurring in Scotland concerning the domicile of someone over the age of 16, the Scots court is entitled to hold that such a person has legal capacity to change his under-16 domicile to a different domicile (of choice), or any number of subsequent changes of domicile of choice. It is assumed that where the individual has made no such change after s/he has attained 16 years, s/he will be held to have retained his/her under-16 domicile.[27]

It is regrettable that full consideration has not, it seems, been given to the implications of this *ad hoc* incursion into the framework of the domicile rules. The silence about the name of the under-16 domicile, and its place in the general scheme, is damaging to the coherence of the domicile rules. As will be explained below, in Scots law prior to the 2006 Act, and still in English law, the domicile of origin so called acted/acts as an "anchor" domicile, providing certainty at times of uncertainty. It is an essential part of an evolved system of rules of personal law.

DOMICILE OF ORIGIN

Traditional rules of English Law, and of Scots law prior to the Family Law (Scotland) Act 2006

6–06   A domicile of origin is the domicile ascribed by law to every person at birth[28] in accordance with the following rules:

> (1) *Legitimate child*—The domicile is that of the father as at the date of the child's birth.[29] It is thought[30] that the

---

[27] *cf. Harrison* [1953] 1 W.L.R. 865; and *Henderson* [1967] P. 77.
[28] *Woodbury v Sutherland's Trs*, 1939 S.L.T. 93. *Re Craignish v Hewitt* [1892] 3 Ch. 180. The only example of the ascribing of domicile of origin at a date later than birth is that of adoption.
[29] *Udny v Udny* (1869) 7 M. (H.L.) 89.
[30] Cheshire and North, p.155; though see *contra* Dicey & Morris, pp.115–116.

legitimate child born after a divorce must take his father's domicile as a domicile of origin, but his mother's domicile (of dependency) assuming thereafter the child has his home with the mother.

(2) *Illegitimate or posthumous child*—The domicile is that of the mother as at the date of the child's birth.[31] Changes brought about in Scottish domestic rules concerning illegitimacy and legal equality of children by the Law Reform (Parent and Child) (Scotland) Act 1986 did not produce any alteration in the rules governing the ascribing of domicile of origin or dependence.[32]

(3) *Child legitimated per subsequens matrimonium*—The domicile of origin remains that of the mother as at the date of the child's birth, but the child takes the domicile of the father as from the date of the marriage as a derivative or dependent domicile.

(4) *Child of putative marriage*—The child of a putative marriage takes the domicile of the innocent party.[33]

(5) *Adopted child*—It is thought that an adopted child will acquire from the date of the adoption the domicile of the adopting father and that on his death the domicile of the child will follow that of the adopting father's widow provided that she was a party to the adoption order. Generally, since an adopted child is treated as the legitimate child of the adoptive parent(s), his domicile should be determined in accordance with the legitimate child rule.

It follows from all above, that *place* of birth has no necessary relevance. Indeed it may be found on occasion (though less commonly nowadays) that the court must trace a family history in order to provide a reasoned judgment as to the domicile of origin of the *propositus*.[34]

Family Law (Scotland) Act 2006

The aim was that there would "no longer be a link between a child's domicile and that of his parent's marital status in relation to both the domicile of origin and dependant [sic] domicile."[35]

In terms of section 22, the domicile of a person under 16 is ascribed according to the following rules:

A child shall be domiciled in the same country as his/her parents where:

---

[31] *Udny*, above.
[32] Law Reform (Parent and Child) (Scotland) Act 1986, s.9(1)(a); and Domicile and Matrimonial Proceedings Act 1973, s.4.
[33] *Smijth v Smijth*, 1918 1 S.L.T. 156. But see Anton, (1st ed.), pp.343–344.
[34] *Grant v Grant*, 1931 S.C. 238; *Re Flynn (No.1)* [1968] 1 W.L.R. 103.
[35] Explanatory Notes to Family Law (Scotland) Bill, para.30.

(a) his/her parents are domiciled in the same country as each other; and

(b) s/he has a home with a parent or a home (or homes) with both of them.

Where these conditions are not satisfied, the child shall be domiciled in the country with which s/he has for the time being the closest connection.

The following observations may be made:

(a) Section 22 is much terser than its antecedent (clause 16 of the Bill, which contained a number of rebuttable presumptions, and gave a misleading impression of comprehensive treatment). The use of presumptions has been abandoned.

(b) Reliance is placed on the test "having a home with", which suggests an emotional tie (wishes/intention), rather than a purely factual tie. One would assume that where a child is sent away from his parents' home to another country for education, or for reasons of safety, his "home" (notional) must yet be held to be with his parents. Speculation would suggest that, on the basis of section 22, such a child would be held to "have his home with" his parents, although he may not generally reside with them, and so his domicile will follow that of his parents, who may or may not be domiciled in the place to which they have been posted. This example underlines the importance of interpretation of the key test of "having a home with".[36]

(c) Thirdly, as has been seen above, domicile of origin has been in Scotland, and remains in England, the default position to which recourse is had in cases of doubt and uncertainty. Seeking to legislate under the heading of "domicile of persons under 16", without appreciating the repercussions thereof in relation to the ascertainment of domicile at subsequent points in the individual's life, is ill-advised. It must be remembered what purpose the rules of domicile serve. The difficulty of establishing, at the time of death of a nonagenarian, for the purpose of distribution of his estate, his domicile of origin according to these proposed rules, does not seem to have been appreciated;[37] identification of the childhood "home" of such a person in many cases may be impossible to prove.

The Law Commissions' 1987 proposals, whatever view one takes of their desirability, contained a suggested corpus

---

[36] *cf. Williams, Petr*, 1977 S.L.T. (Notes) 2.

[37] *Agulian & Anr v Cyganik* [2006] EWCA Civ. 129. To quote Mummery L.J., at para.46, in turn quoting Kierkegaard: "[l]ife must be lived forwards, but can only be understood backwards".

of rules on domicile, including the abolition of domicile of origin,[38] whereas that which is contained in the 2006 Act purports to be restricted to the alteration of the rules in a particular area. The problem is that domicile at the start of life is fundamental, and has pivotal importance throughout the legal life of the *propositus*.[39]

(d) In the terms in which section 22 has been drafted, the location of the child's home, for the purpose of the general rule, is not important; only if the general rule in section 22(1) is not satisfied, at which point the forum can exercise a discretion hitherto unknown in this area, may the location of the child's home be relevant.

(e) If the ascription of domicile of origin according to status as legitimate or illegitimate was deemed unacceptable, nevertheless, in substituting another criterion, certainty has been lost. A wiser approach in the view of the authors, and one capable of application to all children regardless of status, would have been to ascribe to a child as his domicile of origin, the domicile of his mother at the date of birth, capable of rebuttal only in exceptional cases.[40] Favouring the matrilineal line has an ancient pedigree. Alternatively, absent a common domicile of the parents at the date of birth, the child, in the general case, could have taken the domicile of the mother at the date of birth as his/her domicile of origin. In this way, a new rule could have been devised, which in its content did not discriminate between children according to the marital status of their parents, without damaging the existing structure of domicile rules.

(f) The tacit assumption is that the new rule will apply, not only for the purposes of ascription of domicile at birth, but at any time during the first 16 years of the *propositus*'s life, if an issue of domicile should arise. Express repeal of the statutory amendment to dependent domicile effected by Domicile and Matrimonial Proceedings Act 1973, section 4, means that section 22 governs situations governed previously in a Scots court thereby. This provides a shifting test according to changing factual circumstances. One must seek to identify however factual and legal scenarios in which the domicile of an under 16 might arise before assessing the extent of the detrimental effect of the new

---

[38] Para.4.24.
[39] See *Bell v Kennedy* (1868) 6 M. (H.L.) 69.
[40] *e.g.* cases of death of mother in childbirth, or adopted children, in respect of whom the current rule would still apply. The 2006 Act does not provide a special rule for adopted children; nor, in s.22, does the Act make it clear whether the word "parent" includes adoptive parent.

rule on the old (capacity of the "minor" to succeed to land or moveables; to make a will; to marry). These are temporal issues, of *tempus inspiciendum*; but a much larger issue of time is the absence of any transitional arrangements.

(g) The question as to the time at which the new rule is to take effect is one in respect of which the Act is silent. One would have hoped that it would take effect from its date of commencement forward,[41] to regulate the domiciles of those who, at the date of coming into force of the Act, are under 16 and those at that date not yet born. Litigation to determine the ultimate domicile of an octogenarian *propositus* who dies after commencement of the Act, by inference of The Family Law (Scotland) Act 2006 (Commencement, Transitional Provisions and Savings) Order 2006, may require to be carried out, regrettably, according to the new rules contained in the Act.

(h) It is a matter of regret that the rules of domicile, in Scots law on the one hand, and in the law of England and Wales, on the other, now diverge. As a matter of necessity, the preferred personal law connecting factor within UK law, has been domicile not nationality, and a common approach to the ascription of domicile surely is desirable.

DOMICILE OF CHOICE

6–07 Every person who is *sui juris*[42] may acquire a domicile of choice in any country (other than the country of his domicile of origin) which has a system or body of law of its own, by a combination of residence (*factum*) and intention (*animus*) to reside there for as long as can be seen ahead, but not otherwise.

Acquisition of a domicile of choice involves a *change* of *both* residence *and* intention.[43]

---

[41] Though this is by no means borne out by The Family Law (Scotland) Act 2006 (Commencement, Transitional Provisions and Savings) Order 2006 (SSI 2006/212), which in Art.4 enacts that the provisions of s.22, *inter alia*, shall not apply in relation to any proceedings which commenced before May 4, 2006.

[42] After the age of 16, in Scots law, by inference of the Family Law (Scotland) Act 2006, s.22(4); and expressly in English law, at the age of 16, *per* Domicile and Matrimonial Proceedings Act 1973, s.3.

[43] "[W]here intention is absolutely clear, a minimum of residence in the ordinary case at any rate is enough": *Willar v Willar*, 1954 S.C. 144, *per* L.J.-C. Thomson at 147; and *King v Foxwell* (1876) 3 Ch.D. 518. Consider the extreme circumstances of *White v Tennant*, 31 W.Va. 790, 8 S.E. 596 (1888) in which "residence" of a few hours' duration, as evidenced by deposit of belongings in the new house in the new State, was sufficient for the *propositus* to have acquired domicile in that State, although that night, having returned to the State of his previous residence to lodge with relatives, he died there. See also the special circumstances of *Plummer v IRC* [1988] 1 All E.R. 97 (*chief* residence was not moved to new country).

Retention of a domicile of choice involves *retention* of *either* residence *or* intention.

Loss of a domicile of choice involves a *change* of *both* residence *and* intention.

The acquisition of a domicile of choice merely supersedes the domicile of origin, but does not obliterate it because, if the former is lost, the latter will revive.[44] Hence, if in the view of the court, the *propositus* has established a domicile of choice *animo et facto* in legal system A, a change of heart or mind the next day will change nothing: the change must be acted upon sufficiently, that is, by departure in a final manner beyond the territorial limits of legal system A.[45]

It cannot be emphasised too strongly that, under current rules, departure in a final manner from the domicile of origin effects no change unless/until domicile of choice is established clearly elsewhere.[46] In this context only, there is a "continuance" rule (*i.e.* continuance of domicile of origin). In all other situations, where a domicile of choice is lost *animo et facto*, the domicile of origin revives to fill any gap. This is the rule of revival of domicile of origin, which has been favoured in the UK. It is *not* the case that one domicile of choice subsists until a new one is acquired.[47] Although the revival rule in recent years has been criticised, it still operates. After the 2006 Act, however, there will be difficulties for a Scottish court in ascertaining with certainty the "domicile of origin"[48] of the *propositus*.

PROOF OF ACQUISITION OF DOMICILE OF CHOICE

It is clear, therefore, that a person averring a change of domicile **6–08** either of himself or of a third party must show that there has been a change of both *residence* and *intention*. All relevant factors regarding these two matters must be considered.[49] Residence may

---

[44] The Family Law (Scotland) Act 2006 makes no overt change to this fundamental rule, but in future, when a Scots forum seeks to ascertain the domicile of origin of an individual whose domicile at the outset of life will have been affected by that Act, it will be required to apply s.22 to ascertain the first domicile of the *propositus* (*i.e.* at date of birth).

[45] *cf. Raffenel* (1863) 3 Sw. & Tr. 49.

[46] *Bell v Kennedy*, above.

[47] Contrast US rule *In Re Jones' Estate* (1921) 182 N.W. 227 (Supreme Court of Iowa); but see Law Commission proposals below at para.6.26. Law Com. No. 168 and Scot. Law Com. Memo. No. 107, para.5.25. The difference between the two systems, as Collier suggests at p.51, stems from the different attitudes of a country whose sons went out to travel the world and were expected to return, and those of an immigrant country from which people were not expected to depart.

[48] As noted above, not so termed in the 2006 Act, s.22.

[49] The case of *Brooks v Brooks's Trs* (1902) 4 F. 1014 is a useful example which has been set in poetic terms by W.M. Gloag, *Carmina Legis* (1920): "A domicile at birth we all acquire, True, we may change it if we so desire".

throw some light on intention and expressed intention may throw some light on residence; intention may grow as residence lengthens. The two factors are interconnected, but are considered separately.[50]

Residence

6–09   Actual physical residence of some kind is necessary, but residence by itself, no matter for how long, is ineffective without intention.[51] Graveson remarked[52] that the word does not command its Victorian meaning of 10–roomed villa. Nourse, J. in *IRC v Duchess of Portland*[53] said that "Residence in a country for the purposes of the law of domicile is physical presence in that country as an inhabitant of it."

A modern example is provided by a divorce jurisdiction case, *Mark v Mark*,[54] in which the parties were Nigerian. The wife issued a divorce petition in an English forum, relying for jurisdiction initially solely upon her habitual residence in England over the previous 12 months, but her petition was later amended so as to include the claim that she had acquired a domicile of choice in England. The husband admitted that the English court had jurisdiction, but later changed his mind on this point, and applied for a stay of the English proceedings, on the basis that he had commenced proceedings in Nigeria. The husband argued that the habitual residence of the wife in England for 12 months prior to the petition could not clothe the court with jurisdiction because the wife's presence in England was unlawful. The judge at first instance held that while the wife could not be regarded as habitually resident in England, by reason of the unlawfulness of her presence, she could rely upon presence in England as a basis for the acquisition of a domicile of choice. The Court of Appeal dismissed the husband's appeal on the ground that the wife had not only acquired an English domicile of choice by the time of litigation, but also had been habitually resident in England for the previous 12 months. In the House of Lords, on the residence point, Baroness Hale held that for the purpose of the 1973 Act, section 5(2) (but

---

[50] *Haldane v Eckford (No.2)* (1869) L.R. 8 Eq. 631, as expressed in the rubric derived from Lord Westbury's judgment in *Udny*: "Residence originally temporary, and intended for a limited period, may afterwards become general and unlimited, and in such a case, so soon as the change of purpose, or *animus manendi*, can be inferred, the fact of domicil is established."

[51] *Jopp v Wood* (1865) 34 L.J. Ch. 212; *Brooks v Brooks's Trs* (1902) 4 F. 1014; *Re Almeda*, (1902) 18 T.L.R. 414; *Winans v Att.-Gen. (No.1)* [1904] A.C. 287; *Ross*, 1930 S.C. (H.L.) 1; *Liverpool Royal Infirmary v Ramsay*, 1930 S.C. (H.L.) 83; *Grant v Grant*, 1931 S.C. 238; *Willar*, 1954 S.C. 144.

[52] Graveson, p.201.

[53] [1982] 1 Ch. 314 at 318–319.

[54] [2005] 3 All E.R. 912.

not necessarily for other statutory provisions), the residence of the petitioner need not be lawful residence. On the question of domicile, her Ladyship found that there was little English case authority until *Puttick*,[55] though she drew on authorities from other Commonwealth jurisdictions. Treating the matter, therefore, as one of principle, and having regard to the object of the rules of domicile (which is to discover the system of law with which the *propositus* is most closely connected); and further noting that the state (of the projected domicile) has no particular interest one way or another, her Ladyship concluded that there was no reason in principle why a person whose presence in England is unlawful cannot there acquire a domicile of choice. As a matter of fact, the wife's position was precarious, in the same way as was found in *Boldrini*[56] and *Cruh*.[57] In view of this decision, which was unanimous, previously held views based upon *Puttick*, and as expressed in Dicey & Morris,[58] must be regarded now with caution.

Intention

There must be an intention to settle in a new country having a **6–10** separate body of law of its own. Although a person must regard his new home as being in that country for the foreseeable future, such an intention need not be irrevocable or everlasting because an everlasting intention cannot reasonably be required of anybody. However, there will not be a change of domicile if the person always had at the back of his mind the intention to leave the country at some indefinite future date, for example on retiral, and to go back to his original country.[59] The decision in *Re Capdevielle*[60] in 1864 marked the change to a stricter test; from that date the Scots and English courts have required what may be termed "conscious adoption" of the new legal system as home, whereas before that date residence of indefinite duration would suffice. Hence, lingering doubts and wishes are important, and may preclude acquisition of a domicile of choice.[61] *Motive* is not a bar

---

[55] *Puttick v Att.-Gen.* [1979] 3 All E.R. 463.

[56] [1932] P. 9.

[57] [1945] 2 All E.R. 545.

[58] Para. 6–037, where the authors opine that the forum cannot permit a person to acquire a domicile in the forum by means which include defiance of the *lex fori*, distinguishing the case where the forum is adjudicating upon a question of domicile acquisition which involves illegal residence in that second or third country.

[59] *IRC v Bullock* [1976] 3 All E.R. 353; *cf. Re De Hosson* [1937] I.R. 467. Contrast the outcome in *IRC v Duchess of Portland* [1982] 1 Ch. 314.

[60] (1864) 2 H. & C. 985.

[61] *Winans v Att.-Gen.*, above; *Liverpool Royal Infirmary v Ramsay*, above; *Gulbenkian* [1937] 4 All E.R. 618; *Re Clore (dec'd) (No. 2)* [1984] S.T.C. 609 (English domicile (of origin) retained); *IRC v Bullock* [1976] 3 All E.R. 353; *Lord v Colvin* (1859) 4 Drew 366 at 376; *Whicker v Hume* (1858) 7 H.L.C. 124; *Sillar* [1956] I.R. 344.

to change of domicile so long as the *propositus*, for whatever reason, had the requisite intention to settle in the new country.[62] The individual must be capable mentally of forming that intention, though no specialised knowledge of the significance of forming such intention is necessary.

The court will not draw the inference of sufficient intention for acquisition of a domicile of choice if it appears that an individual lives "between" legal systems, and if "his complex hesitant mind" has not decided between them[63]: in that case, domicile of origin remains. It must not be thought that the test is impossibly high nor that it cannot be satisfied in a relatively short time.[64] In the Scots decision of *Spence v Spence*,[65] a nicely balanced case, the court took the view that a period of 10 years residence in Spain and connections through business and family (though without social connection) was not sufficient to justify a finding of acquisition of a Spanish domicile of choice. However, the more recent decision of *Reddington v Riach's Executor*[66] held that the domicile of the deceased (who died in Bournemouth, England, at the age of 95) was an English domicile of choice. His domicile of origin had been Scottish, but from 1976 he had been resident in Bournemouth, continuing to reside there after the death of his wife in 1987, visiting Scotland only once or twice since 1976 and never having expressed a desire to return. A distinguishing factor between *Spence* and *Reddington* is that the alleged change of domicile in *Reddington* was between legal systems of one territorial unit of the UK to another; it has been said that it is easier to establish a change from one law unit to another in the same political state than to a legal system in which one will be an alien. The similarity of circumstance and difference of outcome between the cases of *Liverpool Royal Infirmary v Ramsay*[67] and that of *Reddington* is striking, and may be explicable not only in terms of the differing attitude of mind of the *propositus* in each case, but also by reason of the elapse in time between the two decisions, perhaps exemplifying a softening in the attitude of the courts.

Standard of proof

6–11 The standard of proof is the normal civil standard of the balance of probabilities. Nevertheless, under the current rules, a variation in difficulty of proof can be seen. It is relatively easy for an individual

[62] Intention is not compromised by the reason for entertaining the intention; *Carswell* (1881) 8 R. 901; *Stavert* (1882) 9 R. 519; *Morton* (1897) 5 S.L.T. 222; *Sellars*, 1942 S.C. 206; *McLelland*, 1943 S.L.T. 66; *Marchant*, 1948 S.L.T. 143.
[63] *In the Estate of Fuld* [1968] P. 675, *per* Scarman J. at 689.
[64] *McNeill v McNeill*, 1919 2 S.L.T. 127; *Elmquist*, 1961 S.L.T. (Notes) 71; *Rankin*, 1960 S.L.T. 308; *Gould v Gould (No.2)*, 1968 S.L.T. 98; *McEwan v McEwan*, 1969 S.L.T. 342; contrast *Brown v Brown*, 1967 S.L.T. (Notes) 44.
[65] 1995 S.L.T. 335. Also *Marsh v Marsh*, 2002 S.L.T. (Sh.Ct.) 87.
[66] 2002 S.L.T. 537.
[67] [1930] A.C. 588.

to shed, after 16, the domicile of dependence (or "under-16" domicile) that he has acquired perforce through a change of domicile on the part of the person on whom his domicile was dependent.[68] At the other extreme, the most striking feature of the current rules is the "limpet-like quality" of the domicile of origin, and the difficulty of discharging the burden of showing that a domicile of choice has replaced it.[69]

Stronger evidence is required to establish a change from a domicile of origin to a domicile of choice than from one domicile of choice to a new domicile of choice.

FACTORS WHICH HAVE TO BE CONSIDERED IN DETERMINING CHANGE OF DOMICILE

Value of authorities

Domicile cases make a review of the life of an individual, **6–12** frequently at the end of that life, or sometimes at a particular point in the course of it.[70] Since all lives are unique, it is said that the *corpus* of domicile cases does not form a body of precedent in the normal way; each decision is a guide only.[71] Yet, common themes recur and similar mind-sets[72] are found, and a wide knowledge of domicile decisions is the foundation of a fine domicile opinion.

(1) Nationality

There is no necessary link between domicile and nationality.[73] **6–13** Peter Fuld died domiciled in Germany, a Canadian citizen.[74] William Swanton died domiciled in Ireland, a US citizen.[75] In

---

[68] *Harrison v Harrison* [1953] 1 W.L.R. 865.

[69] *Agulian & Anr v Cyganik* [2006] EWCA Civ. 129.

[70] See, *e.g. Bell v Kennedy* (1868) 6 M. (H.L.) 69.

[71] *per* Lord McLaren in *Lord Advocate v Brown's Trs*, 1907 S.C. 333 at 338: "In view of the weight which is so often attributed to authorities in such questions it may not be superfluous that I should begin by stating what is almost a truism, that every question of domicile is essentially a question of fact. Judicial expositions, I need hardly say, may be of great value as guides to the relative weights to be attributed to different elements of a life history in the question of domicile; but in the determination of the whole question of the domicile, each case, as I think, must be considered by itself and in the light of the facts proved."

[72] Compare the fervour for Canada of the *propositus* in each of *IRC v Duchess of Portland* [1982] 1 All E.R. 784 and *IRC v Bullock* [1976] 3 All E.R. 353, and contrast the decisions.

[73] *Hamilton v Dallas* (1875) 1 Ch.D. 257; *Doucet v Geoghegan* (1879) 9 Ch.D. 441; *Bell* [1992] 2 I.R. 152; *Ross*, 1930 S.C. (H.L.) 1; *Haldane v Eckford (No.2)* (1869) L.R. 8 Eq. 631; *Brunel* (1871) L.R. 12 Eq. 298; *Drevon* (1864) 34 L.J.Ch. 129; *Wahl v Att.-Gen.* (1932) 147 L.T. 382; *Casey*, 1968 S.L.T. 56.

[74] *In the Estate of Fuld* [1968] P. 675.

[75] *Bradfield v Swanton* [1931] I.R. 446.

Wahl,[76] the enthusiasm evident in the application by the *propositus* for British citizenship did not persuade the English forum that he was of English domicile. The proposed U.S. citizenship of the Chief of the Clan Ross[77] was a matter separate from his (Scottish) domicile, and was likely to have been desired tactically for tax reasons.

(2) Residence

6–14 Residence may be "colourless"; but perhaps more often the nature of the residence may throw light on the intention to settle "permanently" or otherwise.[78] Taking lodgings is less positive a step than renting, and renting less strong than purchase.[79]

(3) Exercise of political rights, entry into social life, religion, custom

6–15 Wholehearted entry into the political and social life of a new country is a significant factor in acquisition of domicile there.[80] One may contrast the adoption by a Frenchman of the customs of an English village, in the old case of *Drevon*, with Winans' enforced and aloof life in Brighton. The *propositus* in *Lord Advocate v Brown's Trs* was "at home" in the social life of Ceylon: *contra*, Lord Cullen noted in *Spence*[81] that the pursuer's uncontradicted evidence was that her husband's social circles in Spain were made up of British and (in particular, Scottish) people. Nevertheless, a person who has entered into the local community may remain, in law, a stranger in a strange land, and may not be held to be domiciled there.[82]

4. Declaration of intention

6–16 A declaration as to domicile or as to intention to settle in a particular country may be relevant, but too much reliance should not be placed on such a declaration without first considering any possible motive behind it. In many of the cases declarations have been disregarded. Moreover, it is not the prerogative of the

---

[76] *Wahl v Att.-Gen.* (1932) 147 L.T. 382.
[77] 1930 S.C. (H.L.) 1.
[78] *Aitchison v Dixon* (1870) L.R. 10 Eq. 589; *Haldane v Eckford* (1869) L.R. 8 Eq. 631; *Platt v Att.-Gen. of NSW* [1873] 3 A.C. 336; *Re Garden (dec'd)* (1895) 11 T.L.R. 167; *Hope, Todd & Kirk v Bruce* (1899) 6 S.L.T. 310; *Att.-Gen. v Yule & Mercantile Bank of India* (1931) 145 L.T. 9; *Wahl v Att. Gen.* (1932) 147 L.T. 382; *Willar*, 1954 S.C. 144.
[79] *Re Capdevielle* (1864) 2 H. & C. 985 (29 years lodging in Manchester); see also *Winans*.
[80] *Drevon*; compare generally *Doucet*, above.
[81] 1995 S.L.T. 335 at 338. See also *Agulian*, above.
[82] *Sellars*, 1942 S.C. 206; contrast *Haldane v Eckford*, above, where intention had grown.

individual, but rather the court, to pronounce conclusively upon domicile.[83] The statement of the rule is to be found in the speech of Lord Buckmaster in *Ross*, often quoted:

> "Declarations as to intention are rightly regarded in determining the question of a change of domicile, but they must be examined by considering the person to whom, the purposes for which, and the circumstances in which they are made, and they must further be fortified and carried into effect by conduct and action consistent with the declared intention."[84]

In many cases, declarations assert the acquisition of a new domicile, but in others,[85] declarations of retention of an old domicile were made—and disregarded. Declarations may be made *inter vivos*, or *mortis causa* as the last clause in a will,[86] but in no case can they be regarded as more than a dubious guide for the court. Declarations may be tactical, or tactful, to please the listener. They may be contradictory (to please different listeners), and the court may consider some to be convincing and others not. If made many years before, by a speaker now dead, there is the problem of incomplete recollection or bias in the listener.[87]

Their value as dispassionate assessments of domicile is diminished by perceived self-interest or ignorance of the law, the author or speaker using the term domicile where he may not be aware of the technical meaning thereof. Nevertheless, on occasion,[88] declarations may tip the balance.

---

[83] Though see *In Re M.* [1937] N.I. 151 where the highly unusual step in unusual circumstances was taken of permitting the petitioner to choose whether his domicile was that of the Irish Free State or of Northern Ireland. He chose the latter, thereby clothing the court with jurisdiction to hear his petition of divorce.

[84] 1930 S.C. (H.L.) 1 at 6; see also *De Bonneval* (1838) 1 Curt. 856; *Whicker v Hume* (1858) 7 H.L.C. 124; *Crookenden v Fuller* (1859) 1 Sw. & Tr. 441; *Woodbury v Sutherland's Trs*, 1939 S.L.T. 93; *Latta*, 1954 S.L.T. (News) 74–declarations in favour of Glasgow vague, those in favour of Manchester convincing; *Scappaticci v Att.-Gen.* [1955] P.47; *Re Sillar* [1956] I.R. 344; *Tennekoon v Duraisamy* [1958] A.C. 354; *Rev. Comms. v Matthews* (1958) 92 I.T.L.R. 44.

[85] *Re Steer* (1858) 3 H. & N. 594; *Re Liddell-Grainger's Will Trusts* [1936] 3 All E.R. 173; *Re Sillar* [1956] I.R. 344.

[86] In *Reddington v Riach's Executor*, the court accepted evidence that the deceased had made repeated remarks that his move to England was to be his last move, and noted the fact that the deceased directed in his will that his remains should be buried in Bournemouth. Lord Clarke took the view that a declaration in a will dated 1976 that the *propositus* was domiciled in Scotland "was a statement carried over from previous wills without, perhaps, any clear thought being given to its purpose and meaning", relying also on the fact that the circumstances did not pass the test set in *Ross*.

[87] *Agulian*, above. However, it is in the nature of domicile cases that persons are found who can report significant remarks, *e.g. Haldane v Eckford* above, where evidence was offered of what the *propositus* had said about whether the burial vault could accommodate *him* when the time came.

[88] *Woodbury v Sutherland's Trs*, above.

(5) Depositing of moveables

6–17   Depositing of moveables in a place or leaving them there in a time of emergency may indicate a mental attitude towards that place as home.[89]

In his flight from the Nazi invasion of the Channel Islands, Captain Clarke[90] left his home in Sark, furnished, and his proposed home in Guernsey not yet complete, and in the war years lived briefly in Devon and then in Mull before his death in Scotland; it was held that he died domiciled in Sark. Domicile cases form intersecting circles. Captain Clarke's case also illustrates the weight to be given to the legal significance of physical departure under duress.[91] It is likely that, at least until it is safe to return, the *propositus* remains domiciled in the legal system which he has been forced to leave.[92] Of course, in accordance with the best established rule of all, departure from the domicile of origin, whether under pressure or not, effects no change unless/until a new domicile is acquired.

In *Willar*[93] it was held significant in establishing a soldier's domicile that he kept his belongings and his dog in a house in Glasgow belonging to the mother of a friend.

(6) Newspapers

6–18   Attention was paid in *Liverpool Royal Infirmary v Ramsay*[94] to the fact that the *propositus*, George Bowie, a Glasgow-born long-time resident of Liverpool, had taken a Glasgow weekly newspaper; the order by an expatriate of a newspaper from "home" indicates at the least an emotional attachment to that community and a continuing interest in it.

(7) Old age

6–19   Care must be exercised in the consideration of this factor. An individual may be compelled to remain in a place as a result of old age or infirmity. If (1) the view be taken that the *propositus* lived (and died) in the legal system of his domicile of origin, wishful thinking for another country can avail nothing. If (2) being of Scots domicile of origin, the *propositus* lived abroad, death abroad will not alter his retention of his domicile of origin at death, whether or

---

[89] *Curling v Thornton* (1823) 2 Add. 6; *Att.-Gen. v Dunn* (1840) 6 M. & W. 511; *Willar*, 1954 S.C. 144; *Rev. Comms. v Matthews* (1958) 92 1 T.L.R. 44; and *Haldane v Eckford (No.2)* (1869) L.R. 8 Eq. 631.
[90] *Rev. Comms v Matthews* (1958) 92 1 T.L.R. 44.
[91] *cf.* "Special Cases" where free will may be absent: paras 6–30 *et seq.*
[92] *Re Lloyd Evans, dec'd*, above.
[93] 1954 S.C. 144.
[94] 1930 S.C. (H.L.) 83.

not he longed to see Scotland again. However if (3) being of, say, French domicile of choice, he wished fervently to return to Scotland and was unable physically to do so, his French domicile will remain at death.[95] If (4) he sets up conditions for his departure from the country which arguably is his domicile of choice, in order to return "home", and seems loath to see these fulfilled, not only may such a condition (ever less likely to be satisfied) not preclude a finding of domicile of choice in that system, but also such a finding, once made, will mean that the *propositus* would be required physically to leave the system of his adoption before domicile of origin could revive.[96]

Domicile of choice, loss of which is later rued, cannot be reinstated except on the usual rules.[97]

(8) Bequests from a particular source

If, in his will, the *propositus* has directed that a specific item **6–20** situated in a certain room in a particular house be the subject of a bequest to XY, then the view may be taken that the *propositus* did not contemplate removal from that house and, at least while the will remained unaltered, had "intention" for the legal system in which that house was situated.[98] But even in formalising such a commonplace thought, one can see its limitations. On a "proper" interpretation,[99] the domicile may in any event be elsewhere; further, a man may change his domicile intention without changing his will. This factor, therefore, like each of those on these pages, is only a factor, and one factor among many.

(9) Lairs and directions for burial or cremation

Such directions may be relevant in so far as they show that the **6–21** person contemplated death in a particular district, but the whole surrounding circumstances must be considered including the time interval between the direction and the date of death.[1]

---

[95] *Raffenel*, above. See, generally, *Ramsay* and *Winans* above. Contrast *Re Furse v IRC* [1980] 3 All E.R. 838 where Fox J. at 843 concluded that the deceased's intention to return to the US from Sussex only when he was physically unable to continue an active life on the farm. He intended to live out his days in England subject to a contingency so vaguely expressed that it could not limit his intention (p. 848).

[96] *Re Furse*, above.

[97] *Fleming v Horniman* (1928) 44 T.L.R. 315.

[98] *Re Sillar* [1956] I.R. 344.

[99] *cf., e.g. Winans* and *Ramsay* above.

[1] *Hodgson v De Beauchesne* (1858) 12 Moore. P.C. 285; *Drevon* (1864) 34 L.J.Ch. 129; *Haldane v Eckford* (1869) L.R. Eq. 631; *Brunel* (1871) L.R. 12 Eq. 298; *Douglas* (1871) L.R. 12 Eq. 617; *Kerr v Richardson's Trs*, 1898 6 S.L.T. 245; *Re Garden (dec'd)* (1895) 11 T.L.R. 167; *Re Baron Emanuel de Almeda* (1902) 18 T.L.R. 414; *Liverpool Royal Infirmary v Ramsay*, 1930 S.C. (H.L.) 83; *Bradfield v Swanton* [1931] I.R. 446; *Munster & Leinster Bank Ltd v O'Connor* [1937] L.R. 462; *Latta*, 1954 S.L.T. (Notes) 74; *Spence* 1995 S.L.T. 335; *Reddington v Riach's Executors*, 2002 S.L.T. 537.

LOSS OF DOMICILE OF CHOICE

6–22 A domicile of origin (and presumably, though not expressly stated in the 2006 Act, an "under-16" domicile) is retained until a domicile of choice has been acquired. A domicile of choice is retained unless/until it is abandoned by a change of both residence and intention whereupon either—

(1) a new domicile of choice is acquired; or
(2) the domicile of origin revives.[2]

A domicile of choice is lost by *leaving* a country *animo non revertendi*[3] (or possibly *sine animo revertendi*).[4] Both elements, mental and physical, are required.[5] It is not lost, at least at the outset, by departure from a country under duress.[6] There is likely to be at least a small gap until a new domicile is acquired: under current rules the domicile of origin "under-16" domicile revives to fill that gap. Death *in itinere* (having travelled outside the domicile of choice) may or may not result in a change of domicile: it will have this effect if a person leaves a domicile of choice *animo non revertendi*, and death occurs outside the territorial waters of the domicile of choice.[7]

It is important to note, therefore, that domicile of choice may be retained by the mental link alone, while resident elsewhere.[8] The

---

[2] *i.e.* in cases in future in Scotland, the "under-16" domicile revives (presumably the domicile ascribed at birth, and not any subsequent domicile acquired in terms of s.22 up to the age of 16). It must be emphasised that the 2006 Act makes no such express provision; in the absence of abolition by statute of the doctrine of revival, that doctrine must prevail.

[3] See *Labacianskas*, 1949 S.C. 280 in which the relevant date of domicile for the purpose of declarator of presumed death was the last date on which the husband was known to be alive. Since departure from Scotland merely to look for work was held not to be sufficient to establish an intention to abandon Scots domicile, the deceased was held to have retained at the relevant date his Scottish domicile of choice.

[4] *Tee* [1974] 1 W.L.R. 213; *Re Flynn (No.1)* [1968] 1 W.L.R. 103. How clear a negative is required? Megarry J. *obiter* in *Flynn* at 113 took the view that a "withering away" of intention would suffice, and this is supported by Dicey & Morris, Rule 13. Contrast Cheshire and North, p. 151, where it is said that irresolution effects nothing, and that therefore if there is any doubt about return, domicile of choice must remain. With respect, surely the latter approach must be correct, though perhaps the difficulty has been exaggerated. In many cases, the whole life will be laid before the court and intention will then be clear. Graveson, p. 207.

[5] *Raffenel*, above; *Re Marrett* (1887) 36 Ch. D. 400.

[6] *Re Lloyd Evans, dec'd* [1947] Ch. 695; *Rev. Comm. v Matthews*, above.

[7] *In the Goods of Luigi Bianchi* (1862) 3 Sw. & Tr. 16; contrast *Re Raffenel* (1863) 3 Sw. & Tr. 49 in which the *propositus* was compelled by ill health to disembark from a boat which was to carry her to England, and then died in France, domiciled there. The American rule is one of continuance in these cases: see *Re Jones' Estate* (1921) 182 N.W. 227 (Supreme Court of Iowa).

[8] *Re Lloyd Evans*, above.

domicile of choice, once established, will be retained also, it is submitted, notwithstanding an ambivalent attitude by the *propositus* towards that legal system. Hence, if a significant event such as death occurs, before the *animus* for the domicile of choice can be said to have disappeared, the domicile of choice will remain in place at the death. Thus in *Morgan v Cilento*,[9] where the deceased, of English domicile of origin, had acquired a domicile of choice in Queensland, Australia, but whose links with England persisted, was found by Lewison, J. to be domiciled at death in Queensland: "I must attempt to assess [the *propositus's*] state of mind up to the day he died. To use the language of Megarry J., it may be that his intention to return to Queensland was withering. But I do not consider that it died before Anthony did. I conclude that Anthony died domiciled in Queensland."[10]

PERSONS NOT *SUI JURIS*

A person who is not *sui juris* does not have the legal capacity to **6–23** acquire a new domicile, but his domicile may be changed through the actings of some relation. Because such a change in domicile results from the actings of another person and is involuntary, it is known as a derivative or dependent domicile. Such a domicile is acquired, therefore, quite independently of residence and intention of the *propositus*.

(1) Mental *incapaces*

There is little authority, but the rule appears to be that a mental **6–24** *incapax* retains the domicile which he had at the date when he became "insane". If it can be changed, it can be changed only through the actings of a parent or other natural guardian, not through the actings of a non-related guardian such as *curator bonis*,[11] and even then probably only if the *incapax* became "insane" before attaining majority. The cases are few,[12] and it is suggested that not only does the state of the law here seem to be unsatisfactory, impractical, and unsympathetic, but also speculative. Where the *propositus* has fluctuating periods of lucidity and incapacity, the problems increase. It seems likely that, in a modern case, the court would concern itself with ascertaining the degree of

---

[9] 2004 E.W.H.C. 188. *cf. Agulian*, above.

[10] Para. 76.

[11] The new term in Scots domestic law, by virtue of the Adults with Incapacity (Scotland) Act 2000, s.80, is "guardian', with powers as set out in that Act (Sch.4, para.1).

[12] *Sharpe v Crispin* (1869) 1 P. & D. 611; *Crumpton's J.F. v Finch-Noyes*, 1918 S.C. 378.

mental incapacity to find out if the *incapax* was capable of forming the requisite intention at the relevant time, and would seek to act in what it perceived to be the best interests of the *incapax*.

The Law Commissions suggested new rules in 1987,[13] to the effect that:

(a) A person who has reached the age of 16, but who lacks the mental capacity to acquire a domicile of choice should be domiciled in the country with which he is for the time being most closely connected.[14]

(b) An adult who lacked the capacity to acquire a domicile should, on restoration of that capacity, retain the domicile he had before his capacity was restored.[15]

(c) Whether a person has the mental capacity to acquire a domicile of choice should be a question of fact in each case.[16]

(d) No special protective provisions are required to qualify the recommendation that the domicile of a mentally incapable person should be in the country with which he has for the time being the closest connection.[17]

The Adults with Incapacity (Scotland) Act 2000 makes no provision with regard to the domicile of incapable persons, within the meaning of the Act.[18] The 2006 Act governs the domicile of all persons under 16, but makes no further or specific provision for the domicile of *incapaces* in their lives thereafter.

(2) Married women

6–25 The law was changed by the Domicile and Matrimonial Proceedings Act 1973. In order to appreciate the effect of the Act, it is helpful to state the law up to December 31, 1973 which still affects questions relating to the domicile of women married before January 1, 1974:

(a) If the marriage was valid, a wife's domicile followed that of her husband.[19] If the marriage was void, her domicile did

---

[13] The Law Commissions produced (September, 1987) recommendations contained in L.C. No. 168 and Scot. Law Com. (No. 107) Private International Law: The Law of Domicile.

[14] Para.6.6; r.4(1).

[15] Para.6.7; r.4(2).

[16] Para.6.9.

[17] Para.6.12.

[18] As to other matters, see Chap.10 (status and capacity).

[19] *Re Cooke's Trs* (1887) 56 L.T. 737; *Low* (1891) 19 R. 115; *Le Mesurier* [1895] A.C. 517; *Mackenzie* [1911] 1 Ch. 578; *Mackinnon's Trs v Lord Advocate*, 1920 S.C. (H.L.) 171; *Att.-Gen. for Alberta v Cook* [1926] A.C. 444; *Dunne v Saban* [1955] P. 178; *Re Scullard* [1957] Ch. 107; *Faye v I.R.* (1961) 40 T.C. 103.

not become that of her husband, but in that case she might acquire a new domicile of choice, in the same way as a single woman, in the legal system in which she was living with him. If the marriage was voidable, the wife's domicile changed with that of the husband, and she would retain that domicile even after pronouncement of a nullity decree, unless/until she changed it, *animo et facto*.[20]

(b) Widows and divorcées. In this case a woman, being *sui juris*, might acquire a new domicile, in the usual way, by a change of residence and intention, upon the termination of the marriage. However, there would be no change if she continued to live in "his" legal system.[21]

(c) Separation. The domicile of a wife changed with that of the husband after a separation whether the separation was voluntary or judicial.[22]

(d) As domicile is determined by the *lex fori*, it was irrelevant that a wife might have been able to acquire a domicile separate from her husband in the country where she resided.[23]

(e) Cases may yet arise in which it is necessary to apply the common rules in order to ascertain the domicile of a married woman for the purpose before the court.[24]

By section 1 of the 1973 Act the position now is as follows:

(a) Subject to (b) below, the domicile of a married woman at any time after the coming into force of this section shall, instead of being the same as her husband's by virtue only of marriage, be ascertained by reference to the same factors as in the case of any other individual capable of having an independent domicile.

(b) Where immediately before this section came into force a woman was married and then had her husband's domicile by dependence, she is to be treated as retaining that domicile (as a domicile of choice, if it is not also her

---

[20] *De Reneville* [1948] P. 100.

[21] *Raffenel*, above; *Re Wallach* [1950] 1 All E.R. 199. But see *Re Scullard* [1957] Ch. 107, in which the separated spouses had been living in different jurisdictions; upon the death of the husband, albeit unknown to the wife, she became *sui juris* and her newly validated intention when added to her residence in Guernsey created acquisition of Guernsey domicile of choice which she held at her death six weeks later. Until two weeks before her death she retained all her mental faculties. Sufficient mental capacity being present, her status as a widow rendered her intention effective.

[22] *Att.-Gen. for Alberta v Cook* [1926] A.C. 444; *Mackinnon's Trs v Lord Advocate*, 1920 S.C. (H.L.) 171.

[23] *Att.-Gen. for Alberta v Cook*, above.

[24] *e.g. Breuning v Breuning*, 2002 E.W.H.C. 236 (divorce).

domicile of origin) unless and until it is changed by acquisition or revival of another domicile, either on or after the coming into force of this section.

(c) This section extends to England and Wales, Scotland and Northern Ireland.

This change, expected to be the last word on the matter, has proved not to be so. Where a woman was married before January 1, 1974, her domicile would change, on interpretation of section 1(2), only in accordance with the usual rules for loss of domicile of choice. There is to be no more lenient rule: *IRC v Duchess of Portland*.[25] Hence, in the case of the Duchess, while it was always clear that her intention was to return ultimately to Canada, her practice of taking long holidays in Quebec did not mean, after January 1, 1974 upon a proper construction of the Act, that she had ceased to reside in England.

In any future alteration to the rules of domicile, a different approach should be taken in the drafting of the transitional provisions,[26] to the effect that changes in the rules of domicile should apply to determine the domicile of a person as at any time *after* the legislation comes into force; those rules should *also* apply to times *before* the legislation comes into force, but only for the purpose of determining where, at a time *after* the legislation comes into force, a person is domiciled.

---

[25] [1982] Ch. 314, *per* Nourse J. at 318: "I will now attempt some general observations on section 1(2) of the Act of 1973. First, it is a deeming provision. Secondly, that which is deemed in a case where the domicile of dependency is not the same as the domicile of origin is the retention of the domicile of dependency as a domicile of choice. I think that that must mean that the effect of the subsection is to reimpose the domicile of dependency as a domicile of choice. The concept of an imposed domicile of choice is not one which it is very easy to grasp, but the force of the subsection requires me to do the best I can. It requires me to treat the taxpayer as if she had acquired an English domicile of choice, even though the facts found by the commissioners tell me that that would have been an impossibility in the real world. In my judgment it necessarily follows that the question whether, after January 1, 1974, the taxpayer abandoned her deemed English domicile of choice must be determined by reference to the test appropriate to the abandonment of a domicile of choice and not by reference to the more lenient test appropriate to the abandonment of one of dependency." See Wade, "Domicile: A Re-examination of Certain Rules" 1983 (32) I.C.L.Q. 1. Presumably, though, the physical return to her domicile of origin with or without her husband must mean the resumption by a woman married before January 1, 1974 of her domicile of origin, unless the mental element does not support this (s. 1(2)).

[26] 1987 Law Commission Proposals, para.8.7 and cl.1(2) and 2(3).

(3) Under-age parties

Derivative or dependent domicile[27]

Domicile and Matrimonial Proceedings Act 1973, section 4

The Domicile and Matrimonial Proceedings Act 1973, section 4, **6–26** which until the coming into force of the 2006 Act on May 4, 2006 applied to Scotland, England and Northern Ireland, but now applies only to the latter two, provides as follows:

> (1) when his father and mother are alive, but living apart, a child's domicile shall be that of his mother if:
>
> > (a) he then has his home with her and has no home with his father,[28] or
> > (b) he has at any time had his mother's domicile under rule (a) above and has not since had a home with his father;
>
> (2) if a child's mother is dead, his domicile shall be the domicile which she had at her death, if he then had her domicile under rule (a) above and has not since had a home with his father.

This statutory change was limited to domicile of dependence and applied only to legitimate and adopted children.

Consequently, the common law rules governing the domicile of persons of nonage remained applicable to those children to whom section 4 did not apply, by reason of the chronology or status.

The 2006 Act repeals section 4, on the rationale that the **6–27** domicile rule for persons under 16 inserted by section 22 of that Act, shall cover all questions of domicile of such persons, without making the distinction between domicile of origin and domicile of dependence. For details of the rules now applicable, see paragraph 6–03 above.

---

[27] *Harrison* [1953] 1 W.L.R. 865 but see the case of *Plummer v IRC*, above, which considers the difficult subject of dual residence in this area and requires careful consideration.

[28] "Home"—see *Williams*, 1977 S.L.T. (Notes) 2. The word "home" is clearly central to this provision and was used by the Law Commissions in their 1987 proposals for change in the domicile rules affecting children. A curious result was produced in *Williams*: the child having been removed from his mother's care in England to the house of his father's aunt in Scotland, the Lord Ordinary at subsequent custody proceedings found him domiciled in Scotland. In interpreting s.4, he held the *tempus inspiciendum* to be the "present" time and not the date of separation: the latter was merely the requisite precondition for the coming into force of s.4. Thus the term child's "home" was satisfied by a possibly temporary home in which he had spent at the date of litigation only two months.

Prior to the 2006 Act, and still in English law, on attaining legal capacity a young person retained/s the domicile, of origin or dependence, which he had/s at that date until such time as he acquired/s a new domicile of choice. The domicile held by the young adult emerging into legal maturity hitherto has been the easiest domicile to lose.[29] Subsequent to the 2006 Act, it is thought that if the domicile of the person under 16 has been established by use of the fixed rule in section 22(1), there is no reason why the pre-existing approach should not continue. Equally, if the under-16 domicile has been established by means of section 22(3) (the flexible exception), the outcome will depend upon the strength of connection of the individual with a legal system at the *tempus inspiciendum*.

Particular Cases

6–28 Particular cases are governed by the same rules, but bearing in mind that the specialities of a situation are likely to have an effect upon the extent to which the *propositus* is able to form (or is prevented from forming) an intention to change his home.

(1) Prisoners[30]

(2) Debtors[31]

6–29 Flight from creditors may be a sufficient reason to doubt the free will of the *propositus*, yet in *Udny* which contains Lord Westbury's classic dictum,[32] it does not seem to have been suggested that

---

[29] If the *propositus's* dependent domicile has followed that of his parent to a foreign land, but he has not followed in person, his domicile of origin will easily be found to have revived, or he may take steps to acquire a domicile of choice. *Henderson* [1967] P. 77, though in the circumstances Sir Jocelyn Simon held that the *propositus* retained his English dependent domicile "of quasi-choice". However it was said at pp.82–83 that "[t]he abandonment of a domicile of choice acquired dependently in favour of a domicile of origin reacquired by personal volition must, in the nature of things, generally be of all changes of domicile, the one the least onerous of proof." See *Harrison*, below.

[30] *Burton v Fisher* (1828) Milward's Rep. 183; *Dunstan* (1858) 28 L.J.C.P. 97. The judgment in *Re the late Emperor Napoleon Bonaparte* (1853) 2 Rob. Ecc. 606, concerning the custody of Napoleon's will and codicils concluded, not surprisingly, that he formed no voluntary intention to settle in the British territory of St Helena, and that he died domiciled in France. Napoleon was born in Corsica; after his defeat at Leipzig, he abdicated and was given the right to rule Elba. Having escaped from Elba he advanced on Paris and ruled for the "100 days" ending at Waterloo. Then he was conveyed to St Helena as a prisoner of war and died there six years later, perhaps as a result of poison ("Scheele's Green", arsenic dye) leaking out of the wallpaper (or perhaps not).

[31] *Udny*, above.

[32] "There must be a residence freely chosen, and not prescribed or dictated by any external necessity, such as the duties of office, the demand of creditors, or the relief from illness", at p.99.

Colonel Udny retained his English domicile of choice (if indeed he had acquired such a domicile) because of the enforced nature of his departure from England.[33]

(3) Persons seeking asylum[34]

Where the *propositus* has fled his domicile of origin, it will survive **6–30** his departure, and will remain until clearly superseded, on the principle of *Bell*.[35] Where the *propositus* leaves his domicile of choice, the enforced nature of his leaving will mean that he retains that domicile by *animus* alone; political or other conditions in his domicile of choice may explain his disinclination to return.[36] Strictly, in all cases where lack of free will is a factor, there is no need to explain failure to return, the onus of proof lying on the party averring change. However, it may be necessary to try to refute the argument that the intention of the *propositus* for his domicile of choice has "withered away".[37] Continuing spiritual attachment to the domicile of choice may be easier to show, against a background of hostile political conditions or diminishing physical strength.

A refugee has had the option of remaining in difficult circumstances, or of flight; the state of mind of the *propositus* might be one of desire positively to adopt the legal system of refuge, or one simply of seeking refuge, careless of the legal system in which such refuge might be found. In the latter case, domicile of choice will not be acquired. In *Martin*[38] a French professor of French, a fugitive from French justice, married in England during the period of the French criminal prescription. Upon its expiry, he returned to France. In certain cases, of which this was one, the court must judge the state of intention at a particular point in time and is not permitted to reflect on the life as a whole. The Court of Appeal (Lindley M.R. dissenting) found him domiciled in England at the time of his marriage.

Liability to be deported does not preclude the acquisition of a new domicile,[39] nor even does the grant of a deportation order

---

[33] *cf. Re Lloyd Evans*, above; *Rev. Comms v Matthews*, above; (even) *Labacianskas*, 1949 S.C. 280.

[34] *De Bonneval* (1838) 1 Curt. 856; *Re Martin* [1900] P. 211; *Boldrini* [1932] P. 9; *May* [1943] 2 All E.R. 146; *Cruh* [1945] 2 All E.R. 545; *Zanelli* [1948] 64 T.L.R. 556; *Re Lloyd Evans* [1947] Ch. 695; *Rev. Comms v Matthews* (1958) 92 I.L.T.R. 44; *Puttick v Att.-Gen.* [1979] 3 All E.R. 463.

[35] (1868) 6 M. (H.L.) 69.

[36] *Re Lloyd Evans*, above: *propositus* did not return to his beloved Belgium during the war years, and died, domiciled of choice in Belgium, in 1944. See also *Rev. Comms v Matthews*, above: war precluded return to Sark. Deceased died in Scotland domiciled in Sark. See Binchy, *Irish Conflicts of Law* (1988), p. 76.

[37] *Flynn, Tee*, above.

[38] [1900] P. 211.

[39] *May* [1943] 2 All E.R. 146.

until it is carried out.[40] Such residence would be "precarious", and the *propositus* could entertain validly the intention of remaining so long as the authorities permit. It was held in *Putticle* that illegal residence based on illegal entry cannot found residencee—or intention—for the purpose of domicile acquisition.[41] This statement now is qualified by the unanimous decision of the House of Lords in *Mark v Mark*,[42] in which, in the case of a wife "overstayer" in England, the court held that unlawful presence in England was not a bar in the circumstances to acquisition of a domicile of choice in England.

(4) Ambassadors and consuls[43]

(5) Service personnel

6–31   A member of the armed forces may acquire a domicile in a country to which he has been posted if there is the necessary change of intention as well as residence[44]: "there may co-exist with a residence, which has begun and is continued under military orders, facts and circumstances which establish a residence voluntary in character and chosen by the soldier, although it is a residence in the place in which he is stationed by the order of his military superiors."[45] In principle, the same reasoning is applicable to posted workers.[46]

---

[40] *Cruh* [1945] 2 All E.R. 545, *per* Lord Denning at 546.
[41] *Puttick v Att.-Gen.* [1979] 3 All E.R. 463. Contrast *Boldrini* [1932] P. 9 (an Italian alien might acquire an English domicile of choice and further, had discharged the onus of proving he had done so).
[42] [2005] 3 All E.R. 912.
[43] *Heath v Samson* (1851) 14 Beav. 441; *Att.-Gen.v. Kent* (1862) 1 H. & C. 12; *Sharpe v Crispin* [1869] L.R. 1 P. & D. 611; *Niboyet* (1878) 4 P.D. 1; *Udny* (the father of Col. Udny was British Consul at Leghorn (Livorno) in Italy at the time of his son's birth, but Col. Udny had Scottish domicile of origin).
[44] *Yelverton* (1859) 1 Sw. & Tr. 574; *Campbell* (1861) 23 D. 256; *Brown v Smith* (1852) 15 Beav. 444; *Ex parte Cunningham, in re Mitchell* (1884) 13 Q.B.D. 418; *Re Patience* (1885) 29 Ch. D. 976; *Re Macreight* (1885) 30 Ch. D. 165; *Sellars*, 1942 S.C. 206; *Donaldson v Donaldson* [1949] P. 363 (acquisition by R.A.F. officer posted to Florida of domicile of choice there); *Willar*, 1954 S.C. 144; *Cruickshanks* [1957] 1 W.L.R. 564; *Stone* [1958] 1 W.L.R. 1287 (acquisition by American soldier, Ohio domiciled of origin, of English domicile of choice).
[45] *Sellars*, above, *per* Lord President Normand at 211.
[46] Old cases concerning servants and officials such as government officials include *Commissioners of Inland Revenue v Gordon's Exrs* (1850) 12 D. 657; *Att.-Gen. v Pottinger* (1861) 6 H. & N. 733; *Att.-Gen. v Rowe* (1862) 1 H. & C. 31; *Fairbairn v Neville* (1897) 25 R. 192; *Cooney*, 1950 S.L.T. (Notes) 1; *Clarke v Newmarsh* (1836) 14 S. 488 (in which an English officer, appointed lieutenant-governor of Fort Augustus in 1746 after the second Jacobite rebellion, remained there for 51 years until his death in 1797, married a Scots woman, cultivated a farm, and was held to have acquired a Scottish domicile of choice).

(6) Invalids—health residence

Each case must be considered on its own merits, but the test, in **6–32** the words of Turner, L.J. in *Hoskins v Matthews*,[47] is whether the person acted upon a necessity or merely exercised a preference. The intention to stay for an indefinite time in a beneficial climate may transmute into the *animus* requisite for a change of domicile and, if so, that change will occur when *animus manendi* is established.

(7) Old age and infirmity

This area is potentially difficult and requires care. Place of death **6–33** may be found to have a significance in domicile litigation which place of birth rarely has.

REFORM

The rules of domicile, often criticised, provide a delicate tool to aid **6–34** the securing of an appropriate result. In 1985, proposals were made to reform the rules of domicile.[48] After consultation, the Law Commissions produced (September, 1987) recommendations contained in Law Com. (No. 168) and Scot. Law Com. (No. 107) Private International Law: The Law of Domicile. The scope of that report was confined to the domicile of natural persons. The Commissions concluded that domicile should be retained as a connecting factor in the international private law of England and Wales, Scotland and Northern Ireland. However, they wished substantial changes to be made in the detail of the present law of domicile. These changes were not implemented.[49] As has been seen

---

[47] (1855) 25 L.T. (O.S.) 78: on the death of the *propositus* after 12 years' residence in Florence, a choice of residence beneficial but not essential, prompted by a spinal complaint, the English court found him domiciled at his death at the age of 60, in Tuscany. The *propositus* "was exercising a preference, and not acting upon a necessity". *Johnstone v Beattie* (1843) 10 Cl. & F. 42, at 139; *Moorhouse v Lord* (1863) 10 H.L.C. 272; *The Lauderdale Peerage* [1885] 10 A.C. 692 at 740; *Re Garden, dec'd* (1895) 11 T.L.R. 167; *Winans v Att.-Gen.* [1904] A.C. 287; *Re James* (1908) 98 L.T. 438.

[48] Law Com. (No.168) and Scot. Law Com. (No.107), 8.7.

[49] Law Com., Working Paper No. 88 and Scot. Law Com. Memo., No. 63. There had been earlier attempts to reform the rules. The report of the Wynn-Parry Committee (1954) (Cmd. 9068) recommended abolition of domicile of origin, a continuance rule, independent domicile for judicially separated wives, and the dependence of a child's domicile upon that of the party having custody. Domicile Bills were introduced in 1958 and 1959, but each was withdrawn. Further thoughts on domicile were contained in the Seventh Report of the Lord Chancellor's Private International Law Committee, 1963 (Cmnd. 1955), the chief proposal of which was a shift in the onus of proof: a person would be presumed to be domiciled in the place where he lived. The recommendation was not taken up. Fundamental reform of domicile law has revenue implications.

above, the domicile change effected in Scots law by the 2006 Act, prompted by the desire to treat all children equally, in domicile as in other matters, has weakened, by inadvertence or design, the previously strong structure of the domicile rules. This factor, combined with the expanding European conflict of laws family law programme, which favours the connecting factor of habitual residence (*qv*), suggests that the failure to adopt the Law Commissions' recommendations to "modernize" the rules of domicile is less significant than would have been thought, because the area in which domicile in its traditional sense is used as a connecting factor is being eroded.[50] But if that is the case, it is predicted that there will be found to be a concomitant need for the rules of acquisition and loss of habitual residence to be more firmly drawn.

DOMICILE AND NATIONALITY

6–35 Although in English-speaking countries the law of domicile applies generally in questions of personal law, nationality is a connecting factor under the conflict rules of many other countries. Originally, domicile was pre-eminent throughout, but nationality was substituted as the personal law in France by the Code Napoleon 1804, and this approach was adopted in Belgium and Luxembourg, with similar provisions following in Austria and Holland.

Dogmatism is out of place and different rules suit different systems. It is clear, though, that each factor has disadvantages:

DOMICILE

6–36

    (a) A person's domicile may be in a place which has little or no connection with his home in the colloquial sense.
    (b) It is difficult to supersede domicile of origin.
    (c) Revival of domicile of origin may produce anomalies.
    (d) Long residence in itself is of no avail (leading to unpredictability).
    (e) Intention is difficult to prove (leading to unpredictability).
    (f) Uncertainty until judicial decision. Judicial consideration will be sensitive and careful, but lengthy and expensive.
    (g) The effect of s.22 of the 2006 Act is de-stabilising.

---

[50] Though there is a seam of cases arising as a result of claims under the Inheritance (Provision for Family and Dependants) Act 1975, such claims being competent only where the deceased died domiciled in England and Wales. These cases afford the opportunity for the writing of fine domicile judgments: *Morgan v Cilento* [2004] EWHC 188; and *Agulian & Anr v Cyganik* [2006] EWCA Civ. 129.

NATIONALITY

(a) A person's nationality may have no connection with the **6–37** country where he lives.
(b) Dual nationality.
(c) Statelessness.[51]
(d) Nationality cannot be applied to questions of personal law in countries containing different units which each have different systems of law.

Each country has its own rules as to nationality and when any question arises as to whether a person is a subject of a particular state, the matter is determined by the law of that state and (unlike domicile) not by the law of the forum.[52] This is subject only to the exception that changes of nationality are not regarded as being effective during war,[53] although they become effective on the termination of war.

BRITISH NATIONALITY[54]

The rules regarding British Nationality were based on two **6–38** principles:

(a) birth within the territory of Great Britain; and
(b) descent.[55]

The modern period of the law on this subject might be said to begin with the British Nationality Act 1948 which introduced the status of citizen of the United Kingdom and Colonies. The position is governed now by the British Nationality Act 1981,[56] which abolished that citizenship and substituted three categories of citizenship, namely:

(a) British citizenship[57];

---

[51] *Kramer v Att.-Gen.* [1923] A.C. 528; *Re Chamberlain's Settlement* [1921] 2 Ch. 533.
[52] *Stoeck v Public Trustee* [1921] 2 Ch. 67.
[53] *Oppenheimer v Cattermole* [1975] 1 All E.R. 538.
[54] *R. v Lynch* [1903] 1 K.B. 444; *R. v Commanding Officer, 30th Battalion Middlesex Regiment, ex p. Freyberger* [1917] 2 K.B. 129; *Joyce v DPP* [1946] A.C. 347; *R. v Home Sec., Ex p. L.* [1945] K.B. 7; *Lowenthal v Att.-Gen.* [1948] 1 All E.R. 295; *Oppenheimer v Cattermole* [1975] 1 All E.R. 538.
[55] See *The Laws of Scotland Stair Memorial Encyclopaedia*, Vol.14, Nationality and Citizenship (T. Mullen).
[56] For a full review of authorities, see *Att.-Gen. v Prince Ernest Augustus of Hanover* [1957] A.C. 436 (affirming [1956] Ch. 188, reversing [1955] Ch. 440).
[57] Wade & Bradley, *Constitutional and Administrative Law* (11th ed., 1993), pp.432–433; the 1981 Act also provided for two residual categories of citizenship, *viz.*, British subjects under the Act, and British protected persons. See also Wade & Forsyth, *Administrative Law* (7th ed., 1994), p. 229.

(b) citizenship of British Dependent Territories;
(c) British Overseas citizenship.[58]

RESIDENCE

6–39 Residence occasionally has been found to be a useful connecting factor in legislation. From the mid-twentieth century onwards,[59] its importance has tended to assert itself in the area of consistorial jurisdiction, and consequently in the rules of recognition of foreign decrees, where the granting court had assumed jurisdiction on a corresponding basis.[60] In some instances Parliament has specified the length of time necessary to satisfy the residence rule in question[61]; in such cases the main problem likely to arise is the extent to which interruptions can be tolerated.[62] Such time specifications ensure the existence of what is thought to be a sufficient link between the petitioner and the court which he seeks to access, or the decree of which he wishes to have enforced.[63]

Increasingly in modern conflict rules, the connecting factor of habitual residence is employed, particularly in family law (custody and abduction; guardianship and protection of children; adoption; divorce and nullity jurisdiction and recognition). There cannot, however, yet be said to be agreement on its meaning.[64] There is now a wealth of academic discussion upon the meaning and nature of "habitual residence", debates upon whether its meaning differs

---

[58] See also now British Nationality (Hong Kong) Act 1997; British Overseas Territories Act 2002; British Nationality (British Overseas Territories) (Amendment) Regulations 2003; British Nationality (General) Regulations 2003; and Nationality, Immigration and Asylum Act 2002.

[59] *e.g.* Matrimonial Causes Act 1937, s.13; Law Reform (Miscellaneous Provisions) Act 1949, ss.1 and 2 (clothing the court in England or Scotland with jurisdiction to grant a consistorial decree to a wife whose foreign-domiciled husband had deserted her, on the ground of her ordinary residence in the jurisdiction for three years).Crawford, "A Day is Not Enough", 2000 J.R. 89 at pp.90 *et seq.*

[60] *Travers v Holley* [1953] P. 246.

[61] DMPA 1973, ss.5, 7 and 9.

[62] *Land v Land*, 1962 S.L.T. 316 (*cf. Hopkins v Hopkins* [1951] P. 116); contrast *Cabel v Cabel*, 1974 S.L.T. 295 (*cf. Stransky v Stransky*, 1954 P. 428).

[63] Family Law Act 1986, s.46(2)(b).

[64] See E.B. Crawford, "Habitual Residence of the Child as the Connecting Factor in Child Abduction Cases: A Consideration of Recent Cases", 1992 J.R. 177; E.B. Crawford "A Day is Not Enough: Further Views on the Meaning of Habitual Residence", 2000 J.R. 89; E.B. Crawford, "Case Analysis: *Ginghi v Secretary of State for Work and Pensions*" (2003) 10 Journal of Social Security 52; R. Leslie, "Recent Scottish Cases on Habitual Residence", 1996 S.L.T. (News) 145; E. Clive, "The Concept of Habitual Residence", 1997 J.R. 137, and "The New Hague Convention on Children", 1998 J.R. 169; and P. Rogerson, "Habitual Residence: The New Domicile?" (2000) 49 I.C.L.Q. 86.

from that of "residence" or "ordinary residence",[65] and upon its *indicia* generally in matters such as the necessity for "voluntariness" (at the outset? or throughout?); for "settled intention"; for "lawfulness" of residence[66]; the conditions required for its acquisition and loss; the hunt for guidelines as to how long it takes to qualify as habitual as opposed to ordinary residence; whether a person can be without an habitual residence, or whether s/he can have more than one habitual residence simultaneously.[67] In other words, it seems necessary to furnish this connecting factor with a number of fixed rules[68], of the type of which "domicile" has been possessed for more than a century; and this despite the fact it is the vaunted characteristic of habitual residence that it is a factual, common sense notion, readily understandable by the man in the street.

In addition to this it must be asked whether, unlike domicile, the meaning of habitual residence varies according to context[69]. One must assume that its meaning is likely to vary according to forum. It may be that the same forum is required to adopt a different interpretation of the term according to the context in which it arises.[70] Lastly, one must be aware of the preferred status of this factor in international instruments; it is a favourite of Convention and Regulation, and as a matter of deliberate intent has been left undefined in such instruments.

The impetus for the upsurge in the use of habitual residence as a connecting factor can be traced to the 1980 Hague Convention on the Civil Aspects of International Child Abduction, where the "habitual residence of the child" is the key factor, prompting in many forums the consideration of the characteristics of habitual

---

[65] It has been said that there is no evidence in the cases of duration longer than one year being rejected as insufficiently long to be habitual, and even that projected future residence might be relevant. See E. Clive, "The Concept of Habitual Residence", 1997 J.R. 137, and "The New Hague Convention on Children", 1998 J.R. 169; E.B. Crawford, "'Habitual Residence of the Child' as the Connecting Factor in Child Abduction Cases: A Consideration of Recent Cases", 1992 J.R. 177; R. Leslie, "Recent Scottish Cases on Habitual Residence", 1996 S.L.T. (News) 145; and Rogerson, *ibid.*, pp.96 *et seq.*

[66] There was a tendency to consider that lawfulness of presence was not a prerequisite of a finding of habitual residence. This has received support in the most recent House of Lords decision *Mark v Mark* [2005] 3 All E.R. 912 at least with regard to its meaning for the purposes of s.5 of the DMPA 1973. The view that domicile, on the other hand, could not be founded upon illegal residence, is now in doubt following the unanimous decision of their Lordships in *Mark*.

[67] *C. v F.C.* [2004] 1 F.L.R. 362.

[68] Crawford, "A Day is Not Enough", 2000 J.R. 89, at pp.94–95.

[69] E.B. Crawford, "Case Analysis: *Gingi v Secretary of State for Work and Pensions*" (2003) 10 Journal of Social Security Law 52.

[70] *Gingi* [2001] EWCA Civ. 1685. See *Nessa v Chief Adjudication Officer* [1999] 1 W.L.R. 1937 and contrast *Swaddling v Adjudication Officer*, Case C-90/97 [1999] ECR 1–1075.

residence, and in particular how it may be lost and may be gained. Since it is not usual for a child to be financially independent, his residence is almost always dependent (factually; and therefore legally?) upon the wishes and actings of the parent upon whom he is dependent. Where wrongful removal or retention[71] is said to have occurred, the question whether the removing parent may establish for the child an habitual residence in the "new" country is a crucial one.[72] Examples can be found of legislative provisions designed to secure (for a limited period, by means of a "deeming" provision[73]) for the court of the abandoned legal system, continuing jurisdiction to adjudicate upon the case. The existence of such legislative devices does not mean that the point is conceded that a change of habitual residence may be effected by wrongful actings.[74] Similarly, the rule that the court addressed must take account of the fact that the child may have "settled" in its new environment, and also of factors such as alleged acquiescence by the bereft parent, means that provisions of the 1980 Hague Convention may operate to produce a situation in which the elapse of time produces a new *status quo*, resulting effectively in a (potentially) unwelcome incursion into the principle that a child's habitual residence may not be affected by wrongful actings. These examples have been taken from the context of international child abduction, but they lead to a more general conclusion that it may plausibly be argued that a finding of habitual residence in any context ultimately depends upon the facts laid before the court. It would seem to be agreed that there will come a point in a life history at which it would be perverse to regard a person as habitually resident at any place other than that of his established presence, whatever view be taken of the need for free will at the outset (inception of residence). This would mean that habitual residence initially brought about by coercion of any kind must take longer to establish, but must be capable of being established.

Habitual residence is a relevant connecting factor in the context of jurisdiction and recognition of overseas consistorial decrees.[75] In relation to jurisdiction and recognition of decrees of divorce, legal separation and marriage annulment among EU Member States, almost total reliance has been placed upon the concept of habitual

---

[71] See Ch.14, below.

[72] E.B. Crawford, "'Habitual residence of the Child' as the Connecting Factor in Child Abduction cases: A Consideration of Recent Cases", 1992 J.R. 177.

[73] Either that the child will be deemed still to be habitually resident, or that the jurisdiction of the "former" habitual residence will be clothed with a continuing (but usually limited) jurisdiction to hear the substance of the case. See, *e.g.* Council Regulation (EC) 2201/2003, Art.10. See Ch.14, below.

[74] *In re J (A Minor) (Abduction)* [1990] 2 A.C. 562.

[75] Which may elicit discussion of the concept: *Breuning v Breuning*, 2002 E.W.H.C. 236 (Fam.). See Chap.12.

residence as a basis. For example,[76] in matrimonial matters it is enacted that jurisdiction shall lie with the court of the Member State in which, *inter alia*, there is joint spousal habitual residence, or recent habitual residence by both spouses with continuing residence by one spouse, or habitual residence of either. This founding rule of jurisdiction contains examples where, in particular situations, draftsmen have added a time requirement (*e.g.* where the applicant is habitually resident if he or she resided there for at least a year before the application was made[77]). Such provisions exemplify the use to which, in a modern context, the factor of habitual residence can be put, and its versatility. It is not the concept itself which varies as to meaning in a list such as this, but rather that the draftsmen, seeking justice in each situation, make different demands in different circumstances.

The factor has some application in the commercial sphere also. In contract, the principal presumption for establishing the applicable law in the absence of choice is the habitual residence of the party whose performance is characteristic of the contract.[78] The factor is a favoured criterion in contract on policy grounds, usually with protective purposes.[79] In the drafting of proposed harmonised choice of law rules concerning non-contractual obligations, one may note a trend towards use of "commonality" (*i.e.* the fact that claimant and defendant have a common habitual residence at the time of occurrence of damage) as a principal exception to application of the main rule proposed (*e.g.* place of occurrence of damage).[80]

THE RULES OF HABITUAL RESIDENCE—A PRÉCIS

Proper use of the connecting factor of habitual residence requires **6–40** an understanding of the degree to which opinion varies on this topic, and a familiarity with the contexts in which increasingly the concept is used. Though use of the concept normally is authorised by statute, convention or regulation, its meaning appears to vary according to context.[81] A summary of that which, with reasonable confidence, can be said to be agreed, is as follows:

---

[76] Council Regulation (EC) 2201/2003, Art.3. See Ch.12, below.

[77] Council Regulation (EC) 2201/2003, Art.3, indent 5.

[78] Rome I, Art.4.2. In this connection litigation has tended to concern identification of the performance which is characteristic of the contract, rather than of the habitual residence of the party effecting such performance. See Ch.15, below.

[79] See *e.g.* Art.5.2 concerning the protection of consumers by the law of his/her habitual residence; and Art.8.2. See Ch.15, below.

[80] See Rome II, Art.3. Ch.16, below.

[81] It is suggested that there is no unitary concept; contrast domicile. See Rogerson, *op. cit.*, p.87.

(a) The concept has been left to judicial interpretation, by domestic court, or ECJ, as appropriate in the individual case.[82] To date there has been a deliberate absence of definition of the term in the legislative instruments in which it is employed, allowing great scope for judicial freedom within the bounds of the rules of precedent.[83]

(b) British judges[84] on occasion have attempted to define the concept, *e.g.* "a regular physical presence which must endure for some time".[85] "In our opinion a habitual residence is one which is being enjoyed voluntarily for the time being and with the settled intention that it should continue for some time".[86] There is perhaps agreement that the words habitual residence should bear their ordinary and natural meaning; it is said that the term is not a term of art, but rather a matter of fact.[87] Unfortunately, it is usually necessary to require for the purpose in hand some characteristics of a term of art. British judges might concur with the opinion of Lord Brandon in *Re J. (A Minor) (Abduction)*[88]: "an appreciable period of time and a settled intention will be necessary to enable him to become [habitually resident]."

(c) Many might concur with Lord Brandon that a person may cease to be habitually resident in country A in a single day if there is settled intention not to return to A, but to take up long term residence in country B.[89]

(d) Many would agree that such a person, having left country A with the settled intention not to return, cannot become habitually resident in country B in a single day.[90] The

---

[82] As to the extent to which the domestic court is bound by the ECJ definition, see *Gingi*, above, and Crawford (2003), above.

[83] There may also be a conflict aspect to the rules of binding precedent, as evidenced in *Gingi*, above.

[84] Though a different interpretation was used by the ECJ in *Swaddling*.

[85] *Cruse v Chittum* [1974] 2 All E.R. 940

[86] Lord President Hope in *Dickson v Dickson*, 1990 S.C.L.R. 692 at 703, agreeing with Lord Scarman in *R v London Borough Council, ex p. Shah* [1983] 2 A.C. 309, at 342/343, that the concept is the same for all practical purposes as ordinary residence. Contrast Lane J. in *Cruse v Chittum*, above, who considered that habitual residence is something more than ordinary residence. This difference of opinion is symptomatic of the controversies which underlie this apparently simple phrase.

[87] Rogerson, *op. cit.*, p89.

[88] *Re J. (A Minor) (Abduction)* [1990] 2 A.C. 562 (in the House of Lords *sub nom. C v S.* [1990] 2 All E.R. 961 (HL).

[89] *C v S.* [1990] 2 All E.R. 961 (HL), *per* Lord Brandon.

[90] *ibid.*

favoured adjective to qualify "period of time" is "appreciable".[91]

(e) "Voluntariness" is a question of degree.[92] While free will may be necessary at the outset to establish residence, and while a complete lack of consent may be preclude "settled intention", it is certainly arguable that, over time, factual residence "overwhelms all other, subjective, arguments".[93]

(f) In the specialised context of rules pertaining to children, habitual residence of a child cannot (normally) be lost through unilateral wrongful actings (*e.g.* of a parent).[94]

(g) There is no rule of continuance of habitual residence.[95] The loss of an existing habitual residence may leave a vacuum. A person can be without an habitual residence. While acquisition of a new habitual residence in most cases will extinguish an earlier habitual residence, concurrent habitual residence seems possible.

(h) It is not conceded that in light of the above the advantages of the connecting factor of habitual residence are self-evident. Nevertheless, the incidence of its use is certain to increase.

Summary 6–Domicile

1. Domicile is a relationship between a person and a territory with a common body of law: every person must have a domicile, but cannot have more than one operative domicile for the same purpose at any one time. There are no formalities for acquisition of domicile.

2. Prior to the Family Law (Scotland) Act 2006, and still in England, a domicile of origin was acquired at birth from a person's father's domicile at that date if the child is legitimate. Otherwise, and if posthumous, it would have been acquired from his mother's domicile at that date. Domicile at birth is ascribed now in Scots law in accordance with section 22 of the 2006 Act.

3. Onus of proof of a change of domicile rests on the person averring a change.

---

[91] See Rogerson, *op. cit.*, pp.91–93. See also *per* Lord Donaldson in *C v S*. [1990] 2 All E.R. 961 (HL), in the Court of Appeal at 454, *sub nom. Re J. (A Minor) (Abduction)* [1990] 2 A.C. 562 at 571.

[92] See Rogerson, *op. cit.*, pp.94 *et seq.*

[93] Clive, 1997 J.R. 307, wherein it is stated that factual residence of longer than one year has never been found insufficient by the courts. See Rogerson, *op. cit.*, p.94.

[94] See Ch. 14, below relating to Council Regulation 2201/2003, Art.10.

[95] Contrast *Bell v Kennedy*, above.

4. Domicile of choice is acquired by a combination of residence and intention, and is lost by a change of the same two factors.

5. Particular cases are governed by the same rules.

6. Prior to the Family Law (Scotland) Act 2006, and still in England, a derivative or dependent domicile was acquired from the actings of another person and was independent of the *propositus'* intention. Domicile up to 16 years is ascribed now in Scots law in accordance with section 22 of the 2006 Act. In English law the matter is governed by a combination of DMPA 1973, section 14, and the common law.

7. An individual becomes *sui juris* with regard to domicile at the age of 16. Scots law by inference of section 22(4) of the 2006 Act; English law: DMPA 1973, section 3.

8. Married women became *sui juris* with regard to domicile with effect from January 1, 1974, within the terms of DMPA 1973, section 1(1) and (2).

9. Special meanings exist for domicile for the purposes of Inland Revenue law and the Civil Jurisdiction and Judgments Acts 1982–91 (jurisdiction in civil and commercial matters falling within the Brussels regime).

10. Reform of domicile rules has been effected piecemeal by legislation. Wholesale reform has not come about. Yet so widespread is the use to-day of the connecting factor of habitual residence in modern instruments that, though the classic rules of domicile may remain largely intact, the ambit of operation of domicile itself seems likely to be cut down.

CHAPTER 7

JURISDICTION IN CIVIL AND COMMERCIAL MATTERS

INTRODUCTION

This chapter deals with that area of the conflict of laws which is of **7–01** greatest moment to litigants and their advisers. The subject of conflict of laws is built upon the three pillars of jurisdiction, choice of law, and recognition of foreign decrees. Although all three areas may contribute to the securing of a remedy in a conflict dispute, attention nowadays is directed to securing the most advantageous forum, and enforcement of the remedy there granted.[1]

Rules of jurisdiction clothe the forum with its great powers to classify the nature of the problem, segregate the substantive from the procedural, provide pre-trial safeguards, and identify the applicable law, as well as with its most obvious power to provide or withhold a remedy.[2]

OUTLINE

Jurisdiction means the power of a court to hear an action and **7–02** make a decision. The entitlement is conferred by common law or statute of the legal system of which the putative forum forms part, augmented in the UK, by the rules of civil and commercial jurisdiction[3] contained in Council Regulation (EC) No 44/2001 on Jurisdiction and the Recognition and Enforcement of Judgments in Civil and Commercial Matters (henceforth "the Regulation"), which are operative where the defender is "domiciled" in an EU Member State, or regardless of the domicile of the defender, if the

---

[1] In respect of which, see Chap.9, below.
[2] Reference generally may be made to J. Hill, *International Commercial Disputes in English Courts* (3rd ed., 2005); A. Briggs and P. Rees, *Civil Jurisdiction and Judgments* (4th ed., 2005); A. Anton and P.R. Beaumont, *Civil Jurisdiction in Scotland* (2nd ed., 1995); and R.E. Aird and JNSC Jameson, *The Scots Dimension to Cross-Border Litigation* (1996).
[3] As to consistorial jurisdiction, see Chap.12, below.

court of a Member State has exclusive jurisdiction in terms of Article 22 of the Regulation, or special jurisdiction under Article 5 (by nature of the subject matter of the dispute), or by choice of the parties under Article 23 (or by submission under Article 24).

In a conflict of laws text, the subject of jurisdiction connotes the allocation of jurisdiction between courts, internationally, or between the constituent legal systems of a multi-legal system State, but such problems of ascertainment and allocation of jurisdiction arise also in domestic law (as, for example, in Scotland, geographically among sheriffdoms, or hierarchically, in civil and criminal matters, between the lower and higher courts).

In general terms, the grounds upon which British courts exercise jurisdiction depend on three basic principles:

(a) *actor sequitur forum rei*[4];
(b) *effectiveness* of any decree which may be pronounced; and/or
(c) *submission*, that is, whether the defender has agreed to submit to the jurisdiction.

Forum actoris rules of jurisdiction, based upon a personal link between the *pursuer* and the court, have no place in "national" Scots rules of jurisdiction.[5]

In general and in theory (and usually borne out in practice), there must be a connection between the defender or the subject matter of the dispute and the court before which it is heard. If the connection is fragile, a rule of jurisdiction based upon it may be regarded internationally as objectionable.[6] Nevertheless, it is not always necessary that the defender be resident in the jurisdiction in question for the case to proceed there, for there are certain rules, based on the subject matter of the litigation, which permit the identification of a different court(s) as (equally) suitable, a fact

---

[4] Literally, that the pursuer must have recourse to the court where the subject matter of the dispute is situated; and colloquially, that the pursuer must seek out the defender in the place of the latter's place of residence or business.

[5] *i.e.* those rules of jurisdiction in Scots law existing before, and continuing to co-exist with, the system of jurisdictional rules put in place by the 1968 Brussels Convention, *q.v.* That system contains examples of *forum actoris* rules where these are considered justified to protect disadvantaged parties (ss.3, 4 and 5), but in principle such rules are not permitted under the Brussels regime to operate against persons domiciled in an EU Contracting/Member State (Art.3), being classed as "exorbitant". Nevertheless, if used, the general prohibition of review of the jurisdiction of the court of origin (Reg.44/2001, Art.35.3) renders it impossible for a court in an EU Member State in which enforcement is sought, to refuse enforcement on that ground alone: see *Krombach v Bamberski* [2001] All E.R. (EC) 584.

[6] *cf.* temporary presence in England only long enough for the service of a writ: *Maharanee of Baroda v Wildenstein* [1972] 2 Q.B. 283.

which may afford the pursuer an alternative forum in which to sue.[7] Similarly, the "national" English rules of jurisdiction permit "service out of the jurisdiction" in non-Brussels cases, upon a defendant resident abroad, if the subject matter of the litigation and the facts of the case, in the discretion of the English court, warrant this.[8] This is an example of "long arm" jurisdiction.

Broadly, the subject of jurisdiction covers three aspects:

(a) jurisdiction over the *parties* to litigation and restrictions thereon;
(b) jurisdiction over the *subject matter* of litigation and restrictions thereon;
(c) power/duty to decline jurisdiction.

Restrictions on parties (to sue or be sued)

The following restrictions may apply: **7–03**

(a) Immunity from suit may be claimed by[9] foreign sovereigns, governments,[10] and government departments;[11] diplomatic agents and agents of foreign sovereigns.[12] Ambassadors, their agents, their household, and staff in course of duty, are immune so long as they act in their respective capa-

---

[7] *e.g.* the Brussels regime provides special or exclusive grounds of jurisdiction in addition to, although in derogation from, the principal ground of personal jurisdiction, namely that a defender domiciled in an EU Member State shall be sued in that State. See para.7–10, below.

[8] See para.7–55, below.

[9] Though it may be waived, expressly or impliedly: M.N. Shaw, *International Law* (4th ed., 1997), pp.516–517. Institution of proceedings by a State would be an implied waiver. Waiver of diplomatic immunity must be express (Shaw, p.536), and by the State, not the individual: *Fayed v Al-Tajir* [1987] 2 All E.R. 396.

[10] See *Parlement Belge* (1880) 5 P.D. 197; *The Cristina* [1938] A.C. 485; *Government of the Republic of Spain v National Bank of Scotland*, 1939 S.C. 413; *Kahan v Pakistan* [1951] 2 K.B. 1003; *USA v Dollfus Mieg* [1952] A.C. 582; *Sayce v Ameer Ruler etc.* [1952] 2 Q.B. 390; and *Rahimtoola v Nizam of Hyderabad* [1958] A.C. 379 (though, *per* Lord Denning in HL: "it is more in keeping with the dignity of a foreign sovereign to submit himself to the rule of law than to claim to be above it"). Contrast *Juan Ysmael & Co. v Government of Indonesia* [1955] A.C. 72; *Baccus v Servico National* [1957] 1 Q.B. 438; and *Thai Europe Tapioca Service Ltd v Government of Pakistan* [1975] 1 W.L.R. 1485. See also *Jones v Minister of the Interior Al Mamlaka Al Arabiya AS Saudiya* [2006] UKHL 26.

[11] *Krajina v Tass Agency (of Moscow)* [1949] 2 All E.R. 274; *Baccus v Servico National* [1957] 1 Q.B. 438. Contrast *The Philippine Admiral* [1977] A.C. 373; *Trendtex Trading Corporation v Central Bank of Nigeria* [1977] Q.B. 529; *I Congreso del Partido* [1981] 2 All E.R. 1064; and *Alcom Ltd v Republic of Colombia* [1984] 2 All E.R. 6.

[12] *Re C (an infant)* [1959] Ch. 363; and *Ghosh v D'Rozario* [1963] 1 Q.B. 106. Consuls and their staff have immunity from suit in respect of official (not private) acts by virtue of the Consular Relations Act 1968, as amended by Diplomatic and Other Privileges Act 1971.

cities.[13] Their functions having come to an end, privileges and immunities normally will cease when they leave the receiving country, or on expiry of a reasonable period in which to do so.[14]

The matter of state immunity is governed by the State Immunity Act 1978, which provides generally for state immunity from suit, with exceptions on certain grounds, *e.g.* in respect of "commercial transactions".[15] The crucial distinction latterly at common law had been between a State's actions in the exercise of its sovereign authority (*acta jure imperii*), and its actions in the course of its commercial activities (*acta jure gestionis*).[16] The 1978 Act takes the same approach, but the distinction is less clear-cut. Shaw concludes that "the enumeration of non-immunity situations is so long that the situation of a rapidly diminishing exception to jurisdiction should be appreciated."[17] It has been held in England that Council Regulation 44/2001 should be read as subject to the international law of state immunity, and therefore not as precluding reliance upon state immunity.[18]

(b) By virtue of the Visiting Forces Act 1952, visiting forces may not be tried in UK courts.

(c) Enemy aliens may not be pursuers in a Scots forum,[19] unless resident in Scotland,[20] but it is open to such persons to defend actions.

(d) A foreign pursuer may be called upon to "sist a mandatory" as security for expenses. The function of a mandatory, appointed by the foreign party on the instruction of the court, is to perform any order of the court made during the

---

[13] However, a foreign State's unilateral action in purporting to confer some similar status upon an individual did not bind the court in England to accept that such a person had diplomatic status and immunity from suit: *R. v Governor of Pentonville Prison, ex p. Teja* [1971] 2 Q.B. 274; and *R. v Secretary of State for Home Department, ex p. Bagga* [1991] 1 Q.B. 485.

[14] See *Shaw v Shaw* [1979] 3 All E.R. 1.

[15] Defined in State Immunity Act 1978, s.3(3).

[16] See *Alcom Ltd v Republic of Colombia* [1984] 2 All E.R. 6, *per* Lord Diplock at 8; and more recently *BCCI (Overseas) Ltd v Price Waterhouse* [1997] 4 All E.R. 108; and *Kuwait Airways Corp. v Iraqi Airways Co.* [1995] 1 W.L.R. 1145 HL, *per* Lord Goff at 1156.

[17] At p.522; also pp.506 *et seq.*

[18] *Grovit v De Nederlandsche Bank* [2006] 1 All E.R. (Comm) 397.

[19] *Weber's Trs v Riemer*, 1947 S.L.T. 295; *Netz v Ede* [1946] Ch. 224; and *R. v Bottrill* [1947] K.B. 41.

[20] *Schulze Gow & Co. v Bank of Scotland* (1914) 2 S.L.T. 455; and *Weiss*, 1940 S.L.T. 447. Status as enemy alien depends on voluntary residence in an enemy-controlled state: *Sovfracht (V/O) v Van Udens* [1943] A.C. 203.

litigation, and to be personally liable for the expenses of the action. The matter is within the discretion of the court; one relevant factor is "whether arrangements exist for the mutual enforcement of judgments in the country in which the party resides or not."[21]

Alternatively, provision of caution (security) may be ordered. A balance must be kept between taking reasonable precautions to ensure that any decree pronounced against a foreign party can be satisfied, on the one hand, and, on the other, imposing unreasonably onerous conditions not applicable to native litigants. While it is true that a party who chooses a British jurisdiction must take the procedural, conflict and substantive law as he finds it, it is axiomatic that he should not be subject to a disadvantage not imposed on a native litigant. Nor should he enjoy an advantage not available to a native litigant.[22] The imposition of a requirement to sist a mandatory arguably may be discriminatory, at least in an EU context, falling foul of the EC Treaty, Article 12, and unjustified in terms of the Brussels jurisdiction and judgments regime.[23] Security or caution is not appropriate in respect of enforcement proceedings under Regulation 44/2001.[24]

Outside the EU context, is it right for the forum to seek to predict the possible outcome of a case, the likelihood of failure by the foreign party, and the chance of his inability to pay the expenses? This dilemma was described by Lindsay J. in *Re Little Olympian Each Ways Ltd (No.2)*,[25] where an order was made for security for costs. Recent examples in Scotland suggest that where there is no reason to doubt the financial standing of the foreign parties, caution will *not* be required.[26]

These cases apart, the court in Scotland or England will not be restrictive in attitude, nor offended by novelty, but rather will seek

---

[21] Aird and Jameson, p.128. See *Renfrew and Brown v Magistrates of Glasgow* (1861) 23 D. 1003; *Gunn & Co. v Couper* (1871) 10 M. 116; *N.V. Ondix International v. James Lindsay Ltd*, 1963 S.L.T. (Notes) 68; *Masinimport v Scottish Medical Light Industries Ltd*, 1972 S.L.T. (Notes) 76; and *Rossmeier v Mounthooly Transport*, 2000 S.L.T. 208.

[22] *cf. De la Vega v. Vianna* (1830). As to the position of the native litigant see, *e.g. Merrick Homes Ltd v Duff (No.1)*, 1996 S.L.T. 932.

[23] See *Rossmeier v Mounthooly Transport*, 2000 S.L.T. 208; *Nguyen v Searchnet Associates Ltd*, 2000 S.L.T. (Sh Ct) 83; *De Beer v Kanaar & Co (No.1)* [2003] 1 W.L.R. 38; and *Bell Electric Ltd v Aweco Appliance Systems GmbH* [2003] 1 All E.R. 344.

[24] Art.51; *cf.* Brussels Convention, Art.45.

[25] [1994] 4 All E.R. 561 at 576.

[26] *Kaiser Bautechnik GmbH v GA Group Ltd*, 1993 S.L.T. 826; and *Medicopharma (UK) BV v Cairns*, 1993 S.L.T. 386.

to act in accordance with the principles of comity, so far as public policy permits.[27] With regard to the status of international organisations, and their capacity to sue, reference may be made to *Arab Monetary Fund v Hashim (No. 3)*,[28] and *Westland Helicopters Ltd v Arab Organisation for Industrialisation*,[29] and also to the International Organisations Act 2005.

SCOTS COMMON LAW RULES OF JURISDICTION

7–04 At common law, the grounds upon which the Scots courts assumed jurisdiction were, with only a few exceptions, grounds which generally were recognised in other countries. The likely result was that a Scots decree would be recognised and enforced in such other countries. The grounds were as follows:

(a) domicile of succession[30] (consistorial actions and actions involving status);

(b) domicile of citation (*i.e.* residence);

(c) in relation to itinerants, presence of defender in Scotland, if personally cited (this ground is not, however, universally recognised)[31];

(d) place of performance of contract[32] (*ratione contractus*)[33];

(e) place of occurrence of delict[34] (*ratione delicti*)[35];

---

[27] *e.g. Bumper Development Corp. Ltd v Commissioner of Police of the Metropolis* [1991] 4 All E.R. 638, where the Court of Appeal permitted a Hindu temple to sue in England to recover its property, the temple having legal personality under the law where it was situated. It was entitled to sue in the person of the officer properly appointed under its own law. The matter was described as being within the inherent jurisdiction of the court.

[28] [1991] 1 All E.R. 871 HL.

[29] [1995] 2 All E.R. 387.

[30] *i.e.* domicile in the classic sense. See Ch.6, above.

[31] See now Civil Jurisdiction and Judgments Act 1982–1991, Sch.8, r.2(1), para.7–54, below.

[32] *Dallas & Co. v McArdle*, 1949 S.L.T. 375, *per* LP Cooper at 378.

[33] Jurisdiction *ratione contractus* (regarded as meaning that the place of execution or place of performance of the contract was within the jurisdiction) was subject to the essential condition that there had to be personal service within Scotland or within the sheriffdom: Sheriff Courts (Scotland) Act 1907, s.6(f) (now repealed to the extent that it determines jurisdiction in respect of any matter to which Civil Jurisdiction and Judgments Act 1982, Sch.8 applies). See, generally, Duncan and Dykes, *Principles of Civil Jurisdiction* (1911); and Dobie, *Law and Practice of the Sheriff Courts in Scotland* (1986), pp.75–76.

[34] *Waygood & Co. v Bennie* (1885) 12 R. 615. In *Wendel v Moran*, 1993 S.L.T. 44, the Scots court, having referred to internationally recognised jurisdiction, was *not* willing to accept that the New York court of the *locus delicti* was competent on that ground alone, without the presence of the defender in that jurisdiction, or submission thereto by him.

[35] The need for personal citation was removed by the Law Reform (Jurisdiction in Delict) (Scotland) Act 1971; also *Russell v F.W. Woolworth & Co. Ltd*, 1982 S.L.T. 428.

(f) moveables situated in Scotland[36] (*ratione rei sitae*);

   At common law, the courts of the *situs* alone had jurisdiction in questions relating to immoveable property because they alone have power to grant effective decrees. In English law, the Civil Jurisdiction and Judgments Acts 1982—1991, section 30, abolished the rule in *British South Africa Co. v Companhia de Mocambique*[37] which had excluded (though there were always certain exceptions) the jurisdiction of the English court to entertain an action concerning damages for trespass to foreign land, though no question of title was involved. Under section 31, the court in England and Wales or Northern Ireland has jurisdiction to hear proceedings for trespass to immoveable property situated outside that part of the United Kingdom (and hence in another part of the United Kingdom as well as outside the United Kingdom[38]) unless the proceedings principally are concerned with title, or right to possession of the property.

(g) prorogation (party choice of forum)[39];

(h) reconvention[40];

(i) interdict to prevent the commission of a wrong in Scotland, on that ground alone, or of a wrong abroad, if possessed of jurisdiction over the defender on another ground[41]; and

(j) in relation to trusts, the place of the domicile of a trust.

The following grounds of jurisdiction did *not* receive international recognition:

(a) possession of heritage in Scotland in an action unrelated to the heritage[42];

(b) arrestment of moveable property of the defender in Scotland in order to found jurisdiction[43]; and

---

[36] *Muir v Matassa*, 1935 S.L.T. (Sh.Ct) 55.

[37] [1893] A.C. 602. Upheld by the House of Lords in *Hesperides Hotels Ltd v Muftizade* [1978] 3 W.L.R. 378. See, for Scotland, *Hewit's Trs v Lawson* (1891) 18 R. 793; and *Cathcart v Cathcart* (1904) 12 S.L.T. 12.

[38] A.E. Anton, *Civil Jurisdiction in Scotland* (1st ed.), para. 11.21, noting as a *caveat* that a plea of *forum non conveniens*, *qv*, might readily be upheld.

[39] *i.e.* agreement supplies a lack of jurisdiction over the person, not the type of action or subject-matter.

[40] Jurisdiction which a foreign litigant, by raising an action in Scotland, is held to call down upon himself, in order to permit the defender to raise a counter-action, if the latter is necessary to do justice between the parties.

[41] D.M. Walker, *Principles of Scottish Private Law* (4th ed), p. 157; and see Sch.8, r.2(10), and Anton with Beaumont, pp.197–198.

[42] *Baron Hume's Lectures*, Vol. V (Stair Society), p. 249. *Cf.* in English law *Emanuel v Symon* [1908] 1 K.B. 302.

[43] *Baron Hume's Lectures*, p.250. *Agnew v. Norwest Construction Co.*, 1935 S.C. 771.

(c) temporary presence of the defender within the jurisdiction.[44]

At the behest of the Maxwell Committee,[45] the "residual" rules[46] of jurisdiction now in use in Scotland are set out in Schedule 8 of the Civil Jurisdiction and Judgments Act 1982, as amended.[47] By reason of the 1968 Brussels Convention, and Regulation 44/2001, the ambit of operation of the "native" Scots rules is much attenuated.

LEGISLATIVE CHANGES TO RULES OF JURISDICTION

1968 Brussels Convention on jurisdiction and the enforcement of judgments in civil and commercial matters

7–05 The 1968 Convention was intended to regulate both the jurisdiction of courts of Contracting States, and the enforcement in one Contracting State of judgments given in another. It is known for this reason as a "double" Convention, the two sets of rules having an interdependent relationship.[48]

The committee of experts engaged in drafting the Convention identified certain grounds of jurisdiction used in Contracting States which were unlikely to meet international standards of acceptability. These "exorbitant" grounds (*e.g.* the nationality of the pursuer—a *forum actoris* rule; service during temporary presence of the defendant in the UK; presence within the UK of property belonging to the defendant in actions not concerning such property) may not be used against persons domiciled in a Contracting State[49]; a category which includes a defendant "domiciled" elsewhere in the UK, and a defender "domiciled" in Scotland. The Brussels Convention prescribed the *only* grounds of jurisdiction, as from time to time interpreted and amended, which could be used

---

[44] Not a feature of Scots common law jurisdictional rules (the jurisdiction over itinerants being different in purpose and nature), but found in English law: *Maharanee of Baroda v Wildenstein* [1972] 2 Q.B. 283.

[45] Report of the Scottish Committee on Jurisdiction and Enforcement (1980).

[46] *i.e.* subject to CJJA 1982, as amended, Schs 1 and 4.

[47] See para.7–54, below.

[48] See Jenard Report on the Convention on Jurisdiction and the Enforcement of Judgments in Civil and Commercial Matters (OJ C59 5.3.79). The enforcement provisions have proved less productive of litigation than have the jurisdiction provisions.

[49] 1968 Convention, Art.3.

against such persons. Other grounds, however, could be used against defenders *not* domiciled in a Contracting State.[50]

Civil Jurisdiction and Judgments Act 1982[51]

The 1982 Act gave the force of law within the UK to the 1968 **7–06** Brussels Convention. The scheme of the Act is:

Part 1: Implementation of the 1968 Convention (in terms of international allocation).

Part 2: Jurisdiction, and Recognition and Enforcement of Judgments, within the United Kingdom (ie subordinate to the 1968 Convention; Schedule 4 "Modified" Convention).

Part 3: Jurisdiction in Scotland (subordinate to Parts 1 and 2; Schedule 8).

The text of the Brussels Convention changed over the years as more countries acceded to the EU.[52] Thus, in any dispute thought to fall within the Brussels Convention, it is necessary to find the date of commencement of proceedings to ascertain which version of the Convention applies.[53] Furthermore, decisions of the ECJ have put an interpretative gloss and ruling on many significant phrases of the jurisdictional rules, of which account must be taken.[54]

Civil Jurisdiction and Judgments Act 1982, Schedule 4 (as amended)

See paragraph 7–53, below.

Civil Jurisdiction and Judgments Act 1982, Schedule 8 (as amended)

See paragraph 7–54, below.

---

[50] If a judgment emanates from a court in a Contracting State, the enforcement procedures of the Convention may be used against assets situated in a Contracting State belonging to someone who is not "domiciled" in a Contracting State. See criticism in Briggs and Rees, 7.04. Non-Contracting States, especially USA, expressed concern about this matter. For this reason, Art.59 exists to enable non-Contracting States to make bilateral arrangements with Contracting States to protect their nationals; relevant treaties have been concluded between the UK and Canada (SI 1987/468 and SI 1995/2708), and the UK and Australia (SI 1994/1901). Treaties made under Art.59 are honoured in Reg.44/2001, Art.72.

[51] Henceforth "CJJA 1982".

[52] UK, Danish & Irish Accession Convention 1978 (OJ 1978 L304/1; see Schlosser Report OJ C59 5.3.79); Greek Accession Convention 1982 (OJ 1982 L388/1); Spanish and Portuguese Accession Convention 1989 (OJ 1989 L285/1); and Austrian, Finnish & Swedish Accession Convention 1996 (OJ 1997 C15/1).

[53] Brussels Convention, Art.54.

[54] See 1971 Protocol on Interpretation of the Brussels Convention.

Lugano Convention

Civil Jurisdiction and Judgments Act 1991

7–07 A parallel scheme of rules of jurisdiction and judgment enforcement was brought into force for the European Free Trade Association (EFTA) area[55] by the 1988 Lugano ("Parallel") Convention on Jurisdiction and Enforcement of Judgments in Civil and Commercial Matters, which was extended to operate in the UK by means of the Civil Jurisdiction and Judgments Act 1991.

To a large extent, the Lugano Convention repeated the text of the 1968 Brussels Convention, but the provisions though similar are not identical: "treacherously different one from another".[56] Moreover, the Lugano Convention confers no jurisdiction upon the ECJ to interpret its provisions.

COUNCIL REGULATION 44/2001[57]

7–08 The completion and implementation of the 1968 Brussels Convention and subsequent Conventions was a signal achievement. Although certain of the rules of the Brussels Convention, particularly those concerning jurisdiction, generated much interpretative litigation (both domestically, within the UK and in other Contracting States, but also as a result of references to the ECJ for preliminary rulings), when the Convention was transformed, with effect from March 1, 2002, into a Council Regulation, there was no fundamental change in its structure or provisions, but rather a process of refinement in light of experience.

EU rules of jurisdiction and judgment enforcement now are contained primarily in Regulation 44/2001, the preamble to which states that in order to attain the objective of free movement of judgments in civil and commercial matters, it is necessary and appropriate that the rules be governed by a Community instrument which is binding and directly applicable in Member States.

It was a feature of the 1968 Convention that certain key terms were allotted a "Community" or autonomous definition for use in all Contracting States. Definition and interpretation of certain other provisions were left to the discretion of individual States, in accordance with their own conflict rules. As might be expected, the

---

[55] Now comprising, for the purposes of Lugano, Iceland, Norway and Switzerland. The principality of Liechtenstein, an EFTA Contracting State, did not satisfy the Lugano Convention.

[56] A Briggs, *The Conflict of Laws*, p.53, commenting upon the fragmentation of jurisdictional schemes.

[57] On Jurisdiction and the Recognition and Enforcement of Judgments in Civil and Commercial Matters (henceforth "the Regulation").

incidence of ascription of Community meanings to particular terms has increased in the Regulation.[58]

Civil Jurisdiction and Judgments Order 2001[59]

Necessary changes to the CJJA 1982—1991, pursuant to Regulation 44/2001, were implemented in the UK by means of the Civil Jurisdiction and Judgments Order 2001.[60]

Denmark

Denmark did not participate in the adoption of Regulation 44/2001,[61] and therefore is not bound by it. Thus, the allocation of jurisdiction and enforcement of judgments vis-à-vis Denmark has continued to be governed by the 1968 Convention. However, in terms of an agreement between the European Community and Denmark on Jurisdiction and the Recognition and Enforcement of Judgments in Civil and Commercial Matters,[62] the provisions of Regulation 44/2001, with certain amendments of a fairly minor nature, will apply between the EC and Denmark.[63] Accordingly, application of the 1968 Convention now is almost spent, and the system put in place by Regulation 44/2001 soon will apply among *all* EU Member States.[64]

Proposed changes to the Lugano Convention

Textual revision work, in parallel with that undertaken in relation to the 1968 Brussels Convention, has been ongoing. Conclusion of a new Lugano Convention has been held by the full court of the ECJ (at the request of the Council of the EU) to fall entirely within the sphere of exclusive competence of the European Community,[65] and not within any shared competence.

Henceforth in this chapter all references, unless otherwise stated, are to Regulation 44/2001.

---

[58] *e.g.* Arts 5.1.b and 60.

[59] SI 2001/3929.

[60] Henceforth "CJJO 2001".

[61] Danish citizens having rejected the Maastricht Treaty in 1992, Denmark does not participate in the adoption of measures under Title IV of the Treaty establishing the European Community, though in a number of areas co-operation has been established; and see also n.62 below.

[62] OJ 2005 L299/62 (November 16, 2005). See further Council of the European Union Press Release 8402/06 (re. Luxembourg meeting, April 2006), noting agreement concerning the extension to Denmark of Reg.44/2001 (Council Decision 6922/06).

[63] For date of entry into force, see Art.12.

[64] Taking the form of a Regulation, the instrument applies to new Member States automatically upon admission as such.

[65] Opinion of the Court (Full Court), February 7, 2006 (Competence of the Community to conclude the new Lugano Convention on Jurisdiction and the Recognition and Enforcement of Judgments in Civil and Commercial Matters).

COUNCIL REGULATION 44/2001—SELECTED PROVISIONS

Scope

Article 1

7–09 The Regulation applies in civil and commercial matters, whatever the nature of the court or tribunal. It shall not extend, in particular, to revenue, customs or administrative matters.
Specifically excluded from its scope are:

(a) the status or legal capacity of natural persons, rights in property arising out of a matrimonial relationship,[66] wills and succession;
(b) bankruptcy, proceedings related to the winding up of insolvent companies or other legal persons, judicial arrangements, compositions and analogous proceedings;
(c) social security;
(d) arbitration.[67]

An important term at the outset is "civil and commercial matters". One aid to interpreting this phrase is the negative one of specific exclusions from the scope of the Regulation, of revenue, customs or administrative matters. Apart from such expressly excluded cases, ECJ concern has been to distinguish, and exclude, public law from private law cases, and to ensure that this is done according to a distinction made by the Community, rather than by individual legal systems. The test is "functional", rather than "institutional",[68] and classification of potentially "public law" cases depends upon whether a public authority is acting in exercise of its public law powers. Reference should be made to *Lufttransportunternehmen GmbH & Co. KG v Organisation Européenne pour la Securité de la Navigation Aérienne (Euro-Control)*.[69]

---

[66] Note particular problem with regard to the categorisation of maintenance. The special treatment accorded to it by Art.5.2 of the Regulation suggests that it is intended to be included in the instrument's scope as a civil and commercial matter only peripherally connected with status: *De Cavel v De Cavel* [1980] E.C.R. 731; *Van den Boogard v Laumen* Case C220/95 [1997] E.C.R. 1–1147; and *Farrell v Long* [1997] All E.R. (E.C.) 449.

[67] See *Marc Rich & Co AG v Societe Italiana Impianti SpA* Case C190-89 [1992] 1 Ll's Rep 342; *Navigation Maritime Bulgare v Rustal Trading Ltd (The Ivan Zagubanski)* [2002] 1 Ll's Rep 106; *Electronic Arts CB v CTO SpA* [2003] EWHC 1020; and *Through Transport Mutual Insurance Association (Eurasia) Ltd v New India Assurance Co Ltd (The Hari Bhum)* [2004] 1 Ll's Rep 206, and (No 2), [2005] 1 Ll's Rep 67.

[68] J. Hill, *International Commercial Disputes in English Courts* (3rd ed., 2005), p.337.

[69] C29-76 [1976] ECR 1541. Distinguished in *R v Harrow Crown Court, ex p. Unic Centre Sarl* [2000] 1 W.L.R. 2112.

General rule

Article 2

    (1) Subject to this Regulation, persons domiciled[70] in a Mem- **7–10**
ber State shall, whatever their nationality, be sued in the
courts of that Member State.

    (2) Persons who are not nationals of the Member State in
which they are domiciled shall be governed by the rules of
jurisdiction applicable to nationals of that State.[71]

Article 2 is the pre-eminent jurisdictional provision, to which all
others are derogations. Moreover, should other optional grounds
of jurisdiction fail for any reason, Article 2 remains.[72]

Recital 11 of the preamble to the Regulation states that rules of
jurisdiction in the Regulation should be highly predictable. Jurisdiction must always be available on this ground of defendant's
domicile, except in a few well-defined situations (*qv*), where the
subject matter of the dispute, or the exercise of party autonomy,
warrants a different linking factor.

The 1968 Brussels Convention left the definition of the
"domicile" of natural persons to the discretion of individual States.
For the UK, the definition of domicile of individuals now is to be
found in CJJO 2001, Schedule 1, paragraph 9.[73]

The definition of the "domicile" of juristic persons has received
a community definition, found in Article 60 of the Regulation.[74]

Significance of defendant's domicile

Article 3

    (1) Persons domiciled in a Member State may be sued in the **7–11**
courts of another Member State only by virtue of the rules
set out in sections 2 to 7 of this chapter.

    (2) In particular the rules of national jurisdiction set out in
Annex I shall not be applicable as against them.

Annex I of the Regulation details the exorbitant "national"
grounds of jurisdiction of Member States. Unacceptable grounds in

---

[70] See *Daniel v Foster*, 1989 S.L.T. 90 (Sch.4 case); *Gruppo Torras SA v Sheik Fahad Mohammed Al-Sabah* [1995] 1 Ll's Rep 374 at 444–446; *Haji-Ioannou v Frangos* [1999] 2 All E.R. (Comm) 865; *Petrotrade Inc. v Smith* [1999] 1 W.L.R. 457; and *Canada Trust v Stolzenberg* (No 2) [2000] 4 All E.R. 481.

[71] See Jenard Report, p.19.

[72] *Kleinwort Benson Ltd v City of Glasgow D.C. (No.2)* [1997] 4 All E.R. 641.

[73] Amending CJJA 1982, s.41. See Ch.6, above.

[74] *King v Crown Energy Trading AG* [2003] EWHC 163. See also CJJO 2001, Sch.1, para.10 (seat of company or other legal person or association for purposes of Art.22.2).

the UK are as follows: rules which enable jurisdiction to be founded on.

(a) the document instituting the proceedings having been served on the defendant during his temporary presence in the UK; or
(b) the presence within the UK of property belonging to the defendant; or
(c) the seizure by the plaintiff of property situated in the UK.

Article 4

(1) If the defendant is not domiciled in a Member State, the jurisdiction of the courts of each Member State shall, subject to Articles 22 and 23, be determined by the law of that Member State.
(2) As against such a defendant, any person domiciled in a Member State may, whatever his nationality, avail himself in that State of the rules of jurisdiction there in force, and in particular those specified in Annex I[75] in the same way as nationals of that State.

Special jurisdictions

Article 5

7–12 The Regulation permits a claimant to pursue his claim in a forum other than that of the defendant's domicile, in certain specified circumstances, according to the nature of the litigation. The most important special jurisdictions concern those for contract and delict, respectively.

Article 5.1—matters relating to a contract

7–13 An optional, "special" jurisdiction under the 1968 Brussels Convention is found in Article 5.1, concerning disputes relating to a contract. According to that provision, "a person domiciled in a Contracting State may, in another Contracting State be sued: 1. in matters relating to a contract, in the courts for the place of performance of the obligation in question". The meaning of these words generated much litigation, since each forum putatively seised was directed to use its own conflict rules to interpret the phrase

---

[75] *i.e.* the exorbitant jurisdictions.

"place of performance".[76] In contrast, the neighbouring phrases, "matters relating to a contract"[77] and "obligation in question"[78] received "Community" definitions. This necessitated the putative forum adopting a two-step method of reasoning: (i) the applicable law of the contract was ascertained by means of application of the 1980 Rome Convention; (ii) the law thereby identified was used to identify the place of performance. If the place of performance was the legal system of the forum, the forum concluded that it had jurisdiction in terms of Article 5.1.[79]

The special jurisdiction in contract appears in Regulation 44/2001, where, however, a Community meaning has been ascribed to the phrase "place of performance", to remove complexities which arose under the Convention version of the text. There is a large bank of cases interpretative of Article 5.1, but pre-Regulation authorities must be viewed in light of subsequent changes. Thus, in terms of the Regulation:

---

[76] *e.g. Industrie Tessili v Dunlop* (12/76) [1976] E.C.R. 1473; *Ivenel v Schwab* (133/81) [1982] E.C.R. 1891; *Shenavai v Kreischer* (266/85) [1987] E.C.R. 239; *Bank of Scotland v IMRO Ltd*, 1989 S.L.T. 432; *Custom Made Commercial Ltd v Stawa Metallbau GmbH* [1994] I.L.P. Pr. 516; *Fisher v Unione Italiana de Riassicurazione Spa* [1998] 8 C.L. 71 (denial of obligation to perform); *Viskase Ltd v Paul Kiefel* [1999] 3 All E.R. 362; *MBM Fabri-clad Ltd v Eisen und Huttenwerke Thale AG* [2000] CLYB 739; *Barry v Bradshaw* [2000] I.L.Pr. 706; *GIE Groupe Concorde v Master of the Vessel Suhadiwarno Panjan* Case C 440/97 [2000] All ER (EC) 865; *Montagu Evans v Young*, 2000 S.L.T. 1083; *Ennstone Building Products Ltd v Stanger (No.1)* [2002] C.L.Y.B. 624; *Besix SA v Wasserreinigungsbau Alfred Kretzschmar GmbH & Co* C256/00 [2003] 1 W.L.R. 1113 (ECJ); *Prifti v Musini* [2003] EWHC 2796; *Engler v Janus Versand GmbH* Case 27/02 [2005] 7 C.L. 76 (ECJ).

[77] *e.g. Peters v Zuid Nederlandse Aannemers Vereniging* [1983] E.C.R.987; *Arcado v Haviland* (9/87) [1988] E.C.R. 1539; *Engdiv Ltd v G. Percy Trentham Ltd*, 1990 S.L.T. 617; *Powell Duffryn v Petereit* [1992] 1 E.C.R. 1745; *Jakob Handte & Co GmbH v TMCS* [1992] E.C.R. 1–3967; *Boss Group Ltd v Boss France SA* [1996] 4 All E.R. 970; *cf. Halki Shipping Corp v. Sopex Oils Ltd* (arbitration) [1997] 3 All E.R. 833; *Source v TUV Rhineland Holding, The Times*, March 28, 1997 (CA); *Belgian International Insurance Group SA v McNicoll*, 1999 G.W.D. 22–1065; *Eddie v Alpa Srl*, 2000 S.L.T. 1062; and *Assitalia SpA v Frahuil SA* Case 265/02 [2004] All E.R. (E.C.) 373 (ECJ) (ostensible authority to enter into contract).

[78] *e.g. De Bloos v Bouyer* (14/76) [1976] E.C.R. 1497; *Medway Packaging Ltd v Meurer Maschinen GmbH & Co. KG* [1990] 2 Ll's Rep. 112; *Union Transport Group plc v Continental Lines SA* [1992] 1 All E.R. 161 (where there are several obligations, the "obligation in question" is the principal one); *Agnew & Others v Lansförsäkringbølagens AB* [1996] 4 All E.R. 978 (no express distinction between obligations arising during negotiation of a contract, and those arising under or after the contract); *AIG Group (UK) Ltd v The Ethniki* [2000] 2 All E.R. 566; *Raiffeisen Zentralbank Osterreich AG v National Bank of Greece SA* [1999] 1 Ll's Rep 408; and *RPS Prodotti Sidrurgici Srl v Owners of the Seamaas (The Sea Maas)* [2000] 1 All E.R. 536; and *Bitwise Ltd v CPS Broadcast Products BV*, 2003 S.L.T. 455.

[79] See *William Grant & Sons Ltd v Marie-Brizard & Roger International SA*, 1998 S.C. 536; and *Ferguson Shipbuilders Ltd v Voith Hydro*, 2000 S.L.T. 229. Currently in Sch.4 (the Modified Convention), the original Brussels Convention wording of Art.5.1 remains.

A person domiciled in a Member State may, in another Member State, be sued:

(1) (a) in matters relating to a contract, in the courts for the place of performance of the obligation in question[80];

(b) for the purpose of this provision, and unless otherwise agreed, the place of performance of the obligation in question shall be:

- in the case of the sale of goods, the place in a Member State where, under the contract, the goods were delivered or should have been delivered,
- in the case of the provision of services, the place in a Member State where, under the contract, the services were provided or should have been provided,

(c) if subparagraph (b) does not apply then subparagraph (a) applies.

The re-casting of Article 5.1 and insertion of a Community definition of "place of performance" constitutes an improvement. However, if the case does not fall within Article 5.1.b, Article 5.1.c directs that 5.1.a applies, which means that the default position and reasoning remains the same as the original Brussels Convention approach. One cautionary comment[81] is that while, under earlier authority,[82] the place of performance of a debtor's obligation to pay was held to be the creditor's place of business (clothing his home court with jurisdiction if an unpaid British seller should pursue a claim for payment against a foreign purchaser), under the Regulation, it is more likely that the forum will be that of the place of delivery of the goods, which usually will be the legal system of the purchaser.[83]

Regarding interpretation of the phrase "matters relating to a contract", it should be noted that the disputed existence of a contract is a "matter relating to a contract" so long as the claimant can satisfy the court that there is a "good arguable case" that a matter relating to a contract is in issue between the parties. Similarly, repudiation of a contract is a "matter relating to a contract".[84] This has an obvious implication in a *lis pendens* system (*qv*), which tolerates the use of negative actings to initiate litigation

---

[80] *Mora Shipping Inc. of Monrovia v Axa Corporate Solicitors Assurance SA* [2005] EWCA Civ. 1069.

[81] D. McClean and K. Beevers, *Morris, The Conflict of Laws* (6th ed.), para.4-026.

[82] *Bank of Scotland v Seitz*, 1990 S.L.T. 584.

[83] cf. *Continuity Promotions Ltd v O'Conner's Nenagh Shopping Centre Ltd* [2006] All E.R. (D) 39.

[84] *Boss Group Ltd v Boss France SA* [1996] 4 All E.R. 970.

in an available jurisdiction of choice, even of a party who wishes to deny the existence of a contract. This has important tactical implications.[85]

Doubt arose in England on the question whether a restitution claim for money paid under error was a matter relating to a contract,[86] but the point appears to have been laid to rest by the House of Lords in *Kleinwort Benson Ltd*,[87] to the effect that such a claim to qualify under Article 5.1 must be based upon a particular contractual obligation, and therefore a claim for restitution based simply on unjust enrichment did not qualify. Nor, *per* Lord Goff, could such a claim fall under Article 5.3 (*qv*), since, in general, unjust enrichment does not presuppose a harmful event or a threatened wrong. Ante-dating this decision is a shrieval decision, *Strathaird Farms v G.A. Chattaway Co.*,[88] that a claim under the *condictio indebiti* does not qualify as a "matter relating to a contract". Perhaps surprisingly, no bespoke special jurisdiction in unjust enrichment cases was created in the revised rules of special jurisdiction contained in the Regulation.

Where the parties to a contract have agreed to refer disputes arising therefrom, or in connection therewith, to arbitration, any subsequent claim made by one of the parties in relation to the contract, which the other does not admit, is a relevant dispute which the claimant is both entitled and bound to refer to arbitration. The belief or contention by the claimant that the defendant has no arguable defence does not take the matter out of the category of "dispute between the parties".[89]

Article 5.3—matters relating to tort, delict or quasi-delict

A person domiciled in a Member State may, in another Member State, be sued: **7–14**

---

[85] See para.7–44, below.

[86] *e.g. Kleinwort Benson Ltd v City of Glasgow D.C. (No.2)* [1997] 4 All E.R. 641. The question whether restitution was to be regarded as falling under quasi-delict was referred by the Court of Appeal to the ECJ in *Barclays Bank plc v Glasgow C.C. (No.1)* [1994] 2 W.L.R. 466, but the ECJ held that it had no jurisdiction to give a ruling on the interpretation of the "Modified Convention" (Sch.4): [1995] All E.R. (E.C.) 514.

[87] [1997] 4 All E.R. 641.

[88] 1993 S.L.T. (Sh.Ct) 36. Note fine distinction made by Sheriff Principal Ireland between matters "related" and "relating" to a contract.

[89] *Boss Group Ltd v Boss France SA* [1996] 4 All E.R. 970; *Halki Shipping Corp. v Sopex Oils Ltd* [1997] 3 All E.R. 833; and *Benincasa v Dentalkit Srl* (Case C-269/95) [1998] All E.R. (E.C.) 135.

(3) in matters relating to tort, delict or quasi-delict,[90] in the courts for the place where the harmful event occurred or may occur[91];

Interpretative difficulties have arisen in jurisdiction (and in choice of law[92]) in identifying the *locus* of double or multi-locality delicts, *i.e.* where elements of the delict occur in different legal systems; most commonly where the place of acting differs from the place of effect, but also where an act or omission giving rise to injury in one jurisdiction, is followed in another by deterioration.[93] The point was famously discussed in *Bier BV v Mines de Potasse d'Alsace SA*[94] (in circumstances where the pollution of the Rhine in France harmed the plants of a market gardener in Holland),[95] to the effect that Article 5.3 confers jurisdiction on the courts both for the place of acting, and the place where the effect(s) is/are felt, affording an option (within an option) to the aggrieved party.

Whether an event is harmful is to be decided by the domestic law of the legal system chosen to govern the issue by the conflict rules of the court seised.[96] So long as some primary harm occurs within the jurisdiction, that will suffice,[97] though consequential, tangential or secondary economic loss suffered in a Member State will not be enough to confer Article 5.3 jurisdiction upon it.[98]

---

[90] Tort etc has an independent Community meaning: *Kalfelis v Bankhaus, Schroder, Munchmeyer Hengst & Co* [1988] ECR 5565; and *Burke v Uvex Sports GmbH* [2005] I.L.Pr. 26. See also *Swithenbank Food Ltd v Bowers* [2002] 2 All E.R. (Comm) 974; *Verein für Konsumenteninformation v Henkel* Case C 167-1000 [2003] All E.R. (EC) 311 (ECJ); and *Danmarks Rederiforening v Landsorganisationen I Sverige* Case C18-02 [2004] All E.R. (E.C.) 845 (ECJ).

[91] *cf.* under Sch.4, *Bonnier Media Ltd v Kestral Trading Corp.*, 2002 S.C.L.R. 977.

[92] See Ch.16, below.

[93] *e.g. Henderson v Jaouen* [2002] 2 All E.R. 705.

[94] [1976] E.C.R. 1735

[95] See also *Mecklermedia Corp. v D.C. Congress GmbH* [1998] 1 All E.R. 148; *Reunion Europeene SA v Spliethoffs Bevrachtingskantoor BV* Case C-51/97 [1998] CLYB 769; *Raiffeisen Zentral Bank Osterreich AG v Tranos* [2001] I.L.Pr. 9; *Casio Computer Co v Sayo (No 3)* [2001] I.L.Pr. 43; *Dexter Ltd (in administrative receivership) v Harley* [2001] CLYB 810; *Alfred Dunhill Ltd v Diffusion Internationale di Maroquinerie de Prestige Sarl* [2001] CLYB 812; *Ennstone Building Products Ltd v Stanger (No 1)* [2002] C.L.Y.B. 624; *Cronos Containers MV v Palatin* [2003] 2 Ll's Rep 489; *Bus Berzelius Umwelt Service AG v Chemconserve BV Reakt Ltd* C99/245 HR (Hoge Raad) [2004] I.L.Pr. 9; and *Kronhofer v Maier* C168/02 [2004] All E.R. (E.C.) 939. These authorities are in line with interpretation of the jurisdiction rule which has emerged in respect of the delict of defamation (*qv*).

[96] *Kitechnology BV v Unicor GmbH Plastmaschininen* [1994] I.L.Pr. 568; and *Dumez France and Tracoba v Hessische Landesbank* Case C220/88 [1990] E.C.R. 49. See R.D. Leslie, "Jurisdiction in Tort or Delict", 1997 S.L.T. 133.

[97] *Minster Investments Ltd v Hyundai Precision and Industry Co. Ltd* [1988] 2 Ll's Rep. 621 and *Equitas Ltd v Wave City Shipping Co. Ltd* [2005] All E.R. (Comm.) 301.

[98] *Marinari v Lloyd's Bank plc* [1996] All E.R. (E.C.) 84.

Defamation claims

Shevill v Presse Alliance[99] is authority for the proposition that a **7-15** claimant may sue, under Article 2, a publisher for defamation in the publisher's place of business for *all* damage wherever alleged to have been suffered. Alternatively, the defendant may be sued in the jurisdiction where any (even small) circulation of the allegedly defamatory matter occurred, but *only* to the extent of the damage allegedly suffered by the claimant in that jurisdiction. This "separate" or "pluralist" approach, rather than "global" or "universal" approach, has been favoured also in non-EU cases.[1]

Other special jurisdictions

A person domiciled in a Member State may, in another Member **7-16** State, be sued:

> (2) [in matters relating to maintenance[2]]
>
> (4) as regards a civil claim for damages for restitution which is based on an act giving rise to criminal proceedings, in the courts seised of those proceedings, to the extent that that court has jurisdiction under its own law to entertain civil proceedings;
>
> (5) as regards a dispute arising out of the operations of a branch, agency or other establishment, in the courts for the place in which the branch, or agency or other establishment is situated. . .[3]

Related actions

Article 6

A person domiciled in a Member State may also be sued: **7-17**

> (1) where he is one of a number of defendants, in the courts for the place where any one of them is domiciled, provided the claims are so closely connected that it is expedient to

---

[99] [1996] 3 All E.R. 929.

[1] *cf. Barclay v Sweeney* [1999] I.L.Pr.288 (Court of Appeal, Paris); and *Berezovsky v Michaels (No.1)* [2000] 1 W.L.R. 1004. Contrast *Domicrest Ltd v Swiss Bank Corp.* [1998] 3 All E.R. 577. See, for England and Wales, Law Commission Scoping Study No. 2, "Defamation and the Internet: A Preliminary Investigation" (December 2002). Also *Godfrey v Demon Internet Ltd* [2001] Q.B. 201; *Bonnier Media v Smith*, 2003 S.C.36; and *King v Lewis* [2004] I.L.Pr.31. As to the position in Australia, see *Gutnick v Dow Jones* [2002] HCA 56; and in Canada, *Bangoura v Washington Post* 2005 (25) T.L.W.D. 2522-006 (CA (Ont) [2005] O.J. No.5428).

[2] See Ch.13, below.

[3] *cf. Latchin (T/A Dinkha Latchin Associates) v General Mediterranean Holdings SA* [2003] C.L.Y.B. 601; and *Durbeck v Den Norske Bank ASA* [2003] Q.B. 1160.

hear and determine them together to avoid the risk of irreconcilable judgments resulting from separate proceedings[4];

(2) as a third party in an action on a warranty or guarantee or in any other third party proceedings, in the court seised of the original proceedings, unless these were instituted solely with the object of removing him from the jurisdiction of the court which would be competent in his case[5];

(3) on a counter-claim arising from the same contract or facts on which the original claim was based, in the court in which the original claim is pending;

(4) in matters relating to a contract, if the action may be combined with an action against the same defendant in matters relating to rights *in rem* in immovable property, in the court of the Member State in which the property is situated.

Disadvantaged parties

7–18 A feature of the Regulation is the inclusion of rules providing grounds of jurisdiction protective of potentially disadvantaged parties. While the 1968 Convention afforded special protection to consumers and to insured parties, and the Lugano Convention contained a provision favouring employees, the Regulation has gathered these provisions together, creating a protective framework for insured parties (including, under the Regulation, the beneficiaries under insurance policies, if different from the policyholder), consumers, and employees, respectively. These sets of rules share common characteristics, for example in restrictions on parties' ability to contract out of them to their detriment; and in the principle that the "weak" may be sued only in his/her domicile, whereas s/he may sue the "strong" party in his/her own domicile, as an alternative to suing in the State where the "strong" defendant is domiciled.

A significant protection afforded to "weak" parties is contained in Chapter 3 (recognition and enforcement), Article 35.1, to the effect that a judgment shall not be recognised if the jurisdictional provisions contained in Sections 3 (insured parties), 4 (consumers) or 6 (exclusive jurisdictions) (*qv*) have not been met. One rationale of the Brussels regime is that at the enforcement stage the

---

[4] *Gascoine v Pyrah* [1994] I.L.Pr. 82; *Canada Trust v Stolzenberg (No 2)* [2000] 4 All E.R. 481; *Watson v First Choice Holidays & Flights Ltd* [2001] 2 Ll's Rep 339; *Daly v Irish Group Travel Ltd (T/A Crystal Holidays)* [2003] I.L.Pr. 38; *Andrew Weir Shipping Ltd v Wartsila UK Ltd* [2004] 2 Ll's Rep. 337; *Et plus SA v Welter* [2005] EWHC 2115 and *Masri v Consolidated Contractors International (UK) Ltd* [2006] 1 W.L.R. 830.
[5] See, *e.g. Kinnear v Falconfilms MV* [1994] 3 All E.R. 42.

jurisdiction of the court of the Member State of origin may not be reviewed,[6] and to this principle the "weaker parties" protections are the only exceptions. The omission of employees (Section 5) from this privileged list in Article 35.1 is thought to be inadvertent, not intentional.

Disadvantaged parties are not protected from the effect of Article 24 (*qv*), which is to confer entitlement to hear the action upon a court of a Member State to which a party has submitted (other than merely to contest the jurisdiction thereof).[7]

Articles 8—14 (jurisdiction in matters relating to insurance)

Article 9

    (1) An insurer domiciled in a Member State may be sued: (a) **7–19** in the courts of the Member State where he is domiciled, or (b) in another Member State, in the case of actions brought by the policyholder, the insured or a beneficiary, in the courts for the place where the plaintiff is domiciled, (c) if he is a co-insurer, in the courts of a Member State in which proceedings are brought against the leading insurer.

    (2) An insurer who is not domiciled in a Member State, but has a branch, agency or other establishment in one of the Member States shall, in disputes arising out of the operations of the branch, agency or establishment, be deemed to be domiciled in that Member State.

Article 10 lays down special provisions in respect of liability insurance,[8] and insurance of immoveable property.

Article 12 completes, with Article 13, the protective structure which the Regulation provides for insurance cases. In terms of Article 12.1, an insurer may bring proceedings only in the courts of the Member State in which the defendant is domiciled, irrespective of whether he is the policyholder, the insured or a beneficiary. Article 12.2 states that the provisions of Section 3 shall not affect the right to bring a counter-claim in the court in which, in accordance with the Section, the original claim is pending.

There follow in Article 13 rules concerning the extent to which the "beneficiaries" of the provisions of Section 3 may depart from them,[9] namely, only by an agreement which:

---

[6] Art.35.3. For it is understood that the grounds of jurisdiction are intrinsically acceptable, and that each Member State will apply them competently and in good faith. This is the paradigm example of the mutual trust and confidence said to imbue the Brussels system.

[7] J. Hill, *International Commercial Disputes in English Courts*, paras 5.2.1, and 5.8.24.

[8] In respect of which, see also Art.11.

[9] *Societé Financière et Industriclle du Peloux v Axa Belgium* [2006] 2 Q.B. 251 (ECJ).

(1) is entered into after the dispute has arisen; or

(2) allows the policyholder, the insured or a beneficiary to bring proceedings in courts other than those indicated in this Section; or

(3) is concluded between a policyholder and an insurer, both of whom are at the time of conclusion of the contract domiciled or habitually resident in the same Member State, and . . . has the effect of conferring jurisdiction on the courts of that State even if the harmful event were to occur abroad, provided that such an agreement is not contrary to the law of that State; or

(4) is concluded with a policyholder who is not domiciled in a Member State, except in so far as the insurance is compulsory or relates to immoveable property in a Member State; or

(5) relates to a contract of insurance in so far as it covers one or more of the risks set out in Article 14.

Article 14 excludes certain categories of risk, such as loss to seagoing ships, and "large" risks,[10] because certain specific risks are governed by sector-specific instruments, and it was accepted that the London insurance market should not suffer.

Articles 15—17 (jurisdiction over consumer contracts)

Article 15

7–20   (1) In matters relating to a contract concluded by a person, the consumer,[11] for a purpose which can be regarded as being outside his trade or profession, jurisdiction shall be determined by this Section, without prejudice to Article 4 and point 5 of Article 5 if:

(a) it is a contract for the sale of goods on instalment credit terms; or

(b) it is a contract for a loan repayable by instalments, or for any other form of credit, made to finance the sale of goods; or

---

[10] As defined in Council Directive 73/239/EEC, as amended (and as may be amended).

[11] See *Benincasa v Dentalkit Srl* Case C-269/95 [1998] All E.R. (E.C.) 135, and *Engler v Janus Versand GmbH* Case 27/02 [2005] 7 C.L. 76 (ECJ). Contrast *Chris Hart (Business Sales) Ltd v Niven* 1992 S.L.T. (Sh. Ct) 53; *B.J. Mann (Advertising) Ltd v Ace Welding & Fabrications Ltd*, 1994 S.C.LR. 763; *Standard Bank London Ltd v Apostolakis (No 1)* [2000] I.L.Pr. 766; *Davies v Rayner* [2002] 1 All E.R. (Comm) 620; *Semple Fraser v Quayle*, 2002 S.L.T. (Sh. Ct) 33; *Prostar Management Ltd v Twaddle*, 2003 S.L.T. (Sh. Ct) 11; and *Verein für Konsumenteninformation v Henkel* Case C 167-1000 [2003] All E.R. (EC) 311 (ECJ).

(c) in all other cases the contract has been concluded with a person who pursues commercial or professional activities in the Member State of the consumer's domicile or, by any means, directs such activities to that Member State or to several States including that Member State and the contract falls within the scope of such activities.

(2) Where a consumer enters into a contract with a party who is not domiciled in the Member State but has a branch, agency or other establishment in one of the Member States, that party shall, in disputes arising out of the operations of the branch, agency or establishment, be deemed to be domiciled in that State.

(3) This section shall not apply to a contract of transport other than a contract which, for an inclusive price, provides for a combination of travel and accommodation.

Article 16

(1) A consumer may bring proceedings against the other party **7–21** to a contract either in the courts of the Member State in which that party is domiciled or in the courts for the place where the consumer is domiciled.

(2) Proceedings may be brought against a consumer by the other party to the contract only in the courts of the Member State in which the consumer is domiciled.

(3) This Article shall not affect the right to bring a counter-claim in the court in which, in accordance with this Section the original claim is pending.

Article 17

The provisions of this Section may be departed from only by an **7–22** agreement:

(1) which is entered into after the dispute has arisen; or

(2) which allows the consumer to bring proceedings in courts other than those indicated in this Section; or

(3) which is entered into by the consumer and the other party to the contract, both of whom are at the time of conclusion of the contract domiciled or habitually resident in the same Member State, and which confers jurisdiction on the courts of that Member State, provided that such an agreement is not contrary to the law of that Member State.

Articles 18–21 (jurisdiction over individual contracts of employment[12])

7–23 Section 5 governs individual contracts of employment, including the situation (Article 18.2) where an employee enters into an individual contract of employment with an employer who is not domiciled in a Member State, but has a branch, agency or other establishment in one of the Member States. In such cases, the employer shall be deemed, in disputes arising out of the operations of the branch, agency, or establishment, to be domiciled in that Member State. Thus:

Article 19

7–24 An employer domiciled in a Member State may be sued:

(1) in the courts of the Member State where he is domiciled; or

(2) in another Member State:

(a) in the courts for the place where the employee habitually carries out his work or in the courts for the place where he last did so; or

(b) if the employee does not or did not habitually carry out his work in any one country, in the courts for the place where the business which engaged the employee is or was situated.

Article 20

7–25 (1) An employer may bring proceedings only in the courts of the Member State in which the employee is domiciled.

(2) The provisions of this Section shall not affect the right to bring a counter-claim in the court in which, in accordance with this Section, the original claim is pending.

Article 21

7–26 The provisions of this Section may be departed from only by an agreement on jurisdiction:

(1) which is entered into after the dispute has arisen; or

(2) which allows the employee to bring proceedings in courts other than those indicated in this section.

Exclusive jurisdiction

Article 22

7–27 The following courts shall have exclusive jurisdiction, regardless of domicile:

---

[12] *cf.* under 1968 Convention, *Weber v Universal Ogden Services Ltd* Case C 37-00 [2002] Q.B. 1189 (ECJ).

(1) In proceedings which have as their object rights *in rem*[13] in immoveable property,[14] or tenancies[15] of immoveable property, the courts of the Member State in which the property is situated.[16]

However, in proceedings which have as their object tenancies of immovable property concluded for temporary private use for a maximum period of six consecutive months, the courts of the Member State in which the defendant is domiciled shall also have jurisdiction, provided that the tenant is a natural person and that the landlord and the tenant are domiciled in the same Member State.[17]

(2) In proceedings which have as their object the validity of the constitution, the nullity or the dissolution of companies or other legal persons or associations of natural or legal persons, or of the validity of the decisions of their organs, the courts of the Member State in which the company, legal person or association has its seat. In order to determine that seat, the court shall apply its rules of private international law.[18]

(3) In proceedings which have as their object the validity of entries in public registers, the courts of the Member State in which the register is kept.

(4) In proceedings concerned with the registration or validity of patents, trade marks, designs, or other similar rights required to be deposited or registered, the courts of the Member State in which the deposit or registration has been applied for, has taken place or is under the terms of a community instrument or an international convention deemed to have taken place.

Without prejudice to the jurisdiction of the European Patent Office . . . ;

---

[13] See, *e.g. Barratt International Resorts Ltd v Martin*, 1994 S.L.T. 434; *Webb v Webb* [1994] Q.B. 696; *Lieber v Gobel* Case C292/93 [1994] I.L. Pr. 590; *Re Hayward (dec'd)* [1997] 1 All E.R. 32; *Cambridge Bionutritional v VDC plc*, 2000 G.W.D. 6–230; *Gaillard v Chekili* Case C-518/99 [2001] I.L.Pr 33 (ECJ); *Dansommer A/S v Gotz* Case C-8/98 [2001] I W.L.R. 1069 (ECJ); and *Ashurst v Pollard* [2001] 2 W.L.R. 722; and *Prazie v Prazie* [2006] All E.R.(D) 246.

[14] *e.g. Reichert v Dresdner Bank* Case C115/88 [1990] E.C.R. 1–27; *Webb v Webb* [1994] Q.B. 696; and *Barratt International Resorts Ltd v Martin*, 1994 S.L.T. 434.

[15] *Sanders v van der Putte* (Case 73/77) [1977] E.C.R. 2383; and *Klein v Rhodos Management* [2005] I.L.Pr.17 and [2006] I.L.Pr.2.

[16] See *Rosler v Rottwinkel* [1986] Q.B. 33; *Scherrens v Maenhout* Case 158/87 [1988] ECR 3791; *Hacker Euro Relais GmbH* [1992] ECR 1-1111; and *Jarrett v Barclays Bank plc* [1997] 2 All E.R. 484.

[17] Under Art.16.1.b of the Lugano Convention the concluding proviso is different, namely: that neither party is domiciled in the Contracting State in which the property is situated.

[18] For this purpose, the seat is to be determined by the national conflict rules. For the UK, see CJJO 2001, Sch.1, para.10, and *cf*. Art.60 of the Regulation. See *Bambino Holdings Ltd v Speed Investments Ltd* [2004] EWCA Civ. 1512.

(5) in proceedings concerned with the enforcement of judgments, the courts of the Member State in which the judgment has been or is to be enforced.

It can be seen from the current (and earlier) versions of the short-term tenancy provision contained in Article 22.1 that liberties have been taken with use of the word "exclusive". It is clear on the face of the provision that "exclusive" in this context does not mean "unique".[19]

CHOICE OF COURT CLAUSES

7-28 If parties, one or more of whom is domiciled in a Member State, have agreed that the court of a Member State is to have jurisdiction in any dispute arising between them, it is provided by Article 23 of the Regulation that such jurisdiction shall be exclusive unless the parties have agreed otherwise. The Article provides certain requirements, set out below, as to form, which must be complied with before the agreement will qualify as a valid prorogation.

Article 23.3 deals with the situation where such an agreement is concluded by parties, *none* of whom is domiciled in a Member State.

There are certain permutations as to choice of court clauses which Article 23 does not address, and to which thought must be given.[20]

Prorogation of jurisdiction

Article 23[21]

7-29 (1) If the parties, one or more of whom is domiciled in a Member State, have agreed[22] that a court or the courts of a Member State are to have jurisdiction to settle any disputes

---

[19] This is the explanation for Art.29 (*lis pendens*), which allocates jurisdiction among courts with exclusive jurisdiction on a priority in date basis.

[20] As to relationship between Arts 23 and 27, see paras 7–42 and 7–49, below.

[21] *Siboti K/S v BP France SA* [2003] 2 Ll's Rep 364; contrast *OT Africa Line Ltd v Hijazy ("The Kribi") (No. 1)* [2001] 1 Ll's Rep 76; *Comsite Projects Ltd v Andritz AG* [2003] EWHC 958; and *Standard Steamship Owners Protection & Indemnity Association (Bermuda) Ltd v GIA Vision Bail* [2005] 1 All E.R. (Comm) 618.

[22] Where there was/is no presumption of exclusivity, a number of authorities demonstrate the drafting difficulty of securing that end: *Dresser UK Ltd v Falcongate Freight Ltd* [1992] 2 All E.R. 450; *M.T. Group v James Howden & Co. Ltd,* 1993 S.L.T. 409; *Barratt International Resorts Ltd v Martin*, 1994 S.L.T. 434; *Morrison v Panic Link Ltd*, 1994 S.L.T. 232; *Continental Bank NA v Aeakos Cia Naviera SA* [1994] 2 All E.R. 540; *Agrafax Public Relations v United Scottish Society* [1995] C.L.Y.B. 703; *Bank of Scotland v SA Banque Nationale de Paris*, 1996 S.L.T. 103; *MSG v Les Gravières Rhenanes SARL* Case C-106/95 [1997] All E.R. (E.C.) 385; *Hough v P & O Containers Ltd* [1998] 2 All E.R. 978; *AIG Group (UK) Ltd v The Ethniki* [2000] 2 All E.R. 566. *McGowan v Summit at Lloyds*, 2002 S.L.T. 1258; and *Fratelli Babbini Di Lionello Babbini & Co SAS v BF Engineering Spa* [2005] 1 All E.R. (Comm) 55.

which have arisen or which may arise in connection with a particular legal relationship, that court or those courts shall have jurisdiction. Such jurisdiction shall be exclusive unless the parties have agreed otherwise. Such an agreement conferring jurisdiction shall be either:

(a) in writing or evidenced in writing; or
(b) in a form which accords with practices which the parties have established between themselves; or
(c) in international trade or commerce, in a form which accords with a usage of which the parties are or ought to have been aware and which in such trade or commerce is widely known to, and regularly observed by, parties to contracts of the type involved in the particular trade or commerce concerned.[23]

(2) Any communication by electronic means which provides a durable record of the agreement shall be equivalent to "writing".

(3) Where such an agreement is concluded by parties, none of whom is domiciled in a Member State, the courts of other Member States shall have no jurisdiction over their disputes unless the court or courts chosen have declined jurisdiction.

(4) The court or courts of a Member State on which a trust instrument has conferred jurisdiction shall have exclusive jurisdiction in any proceedings brought against a settlor, trustee or beneficiary, if relations between these persons or their rights or obligations under the trust are involved.

(5) Agreements or provisions of a trust instrument conferring jurisdiction shall have no legal force if they are contrary to Articles 13, 17 or 21, or if the courts whose jurisdiction they purport to exclude have exclusive jurisdiction by virtue of Article 22.

Exclusivity of choice

One distinction between the prorogation rules contained in the **7–30** Regulation and those in Schedule 4 (the Modified Convention, *qv*[24]) is that in the former, Article 23 provides a rebuttable presumption of exclusivity of jurisdiction. While this is advant-

---

[23] *cf. Coreck Maritime GmbH v Handelsveen BV* Case C-387/98 [2001] CLYB 795; and *Erich Gasser Gmbh v Misat Srl* [2005] Q.B. 1.
[24] Sch.4 (r.12; ex-Art.17) choice of court clause cases include: *Scotmotors (Plant Hire) Ltd v Dundee Petrosea Ltd*, 1982 S.L.T. 181; *BSC v Allivane International Ltd*, 1989 S.L.T. (Sh. Ct) 57; *Jenic Properties v Andy Thornton Architectural Antiques*, 1992 S.L.T. (Sh.Ct) 5; and *McCarthy v Abowall (Trading) Ltd*, 1992 S.L.T. (Sh.Ct) 65

ageous both in terms of certainty and clarity, in that it should operate to exclude doubt[25] as to whether parties intended their chosen court to be *additional* to those generally available, or (as is now the case) in *substitution* therefor, the limits of the advantage which it confers should be appreciated. That is to say:

The promise of exclusivity must bow before the provisions of Articles 22 and 24; and the extent to which disadvantaged parties may depart by agreement from what is provided for their benefit in the Regulation is circumscribed.[26] Moreover, as will be seen, the strength of the *lis pendens* system, as interpreted by the ECJ, is such that a choice of court clause cannot prevail against a different court which has been seised first by either party, unless the court first seised decides (by reason of the jurisdiction clause, or otherwise) that it does not have jurisdiction. Nowhere in Article 23, or elsewhere in the Regulation,[27] is it provided that, as a matter of principle, in the face of proof of the existence of a choice of court clause in favour of a different court, the court first seised need defer to that earlier "chosen". There are opportunities for argument in the court first seised that a particular prorogation clause is not formally valid, or is inapplicable in the circumstances, but, these questions aside, one must balance the much-vaunted principle of mutual trust and confidence, with the absence of a civilian tradition, or indication in the Regulation, such as to encourage the court first seised to defer to a Member State court having an allegedly stronger claim to hear the case. Nevertheless, following the principle of mutual trust and confidence, it is assumed that the courts of each Member State are equally competent to judge on jurisdiction, and that the court first seised, if persuaded that a valid and applicable exclusive choice of court clause exists, will defer thereto. The length of time spent pondering jurisdiction will not affect the rightness and acceptability of the principle of priority of process: the "Italian torpedo".[28] If the alternative court (that court selected by the parties in a choice of court agreement) is that of a non-Member State, a species of the *Harrods*-type problem is produced.[29]

---

[25] *cf. Morrison v Panic Link Ltd*, 1994 S.L.T. 232.

[26] See further para.7–18, above.

[27] *Erich Gasser Gmbh v Misat Srl* [2005] Q.B. 1. See para.7–43, below.

[28] Hartley, "The European Union and the Systematic Dismantling of the Common Law of Conflict of Laws" (2005) 54 I.C.L.Q. 813, at p.815. *Cf. Gasser v Misat*, above, para.24.

[29] *Re Harrods (Buenos Aires) Ltd (No.2)* [1992] Ch. 72. See J. Hill, *International Commercial Disputes in English Courts*, paras 9.5.13 *et seq*.

Prorogation clauses are found also outside the Brussels regime.[30] These will usually,[31] but not always,[32] be enforced. Under the Brussels regime, in light of *Turner v Grovit*,[33] the use by an English or Scottish forum of an anti-suit injunction to seek to prevent a party from reneging on an agreement by suing in a different jurisdiction, in defiance of the prorogation clause, now has been confirmed as inappropriate. However anti-suit injunctions remain competent where they are issued to enforce arbitration clauses inside[34] or outside the EU.

2005 Hague Convention on choice of court agreements[35]

This Convention represents that which could be salvaged of 7–31 international cooperation and agreement generated in advance of the collapse of negotiations instigated by the Hague Conference on Private International Law to achieve a "worldwide" convention on jurisdiction and the enforcement of judgments. It was admitted in 2003 that this ambitious project should be set aside. Thereafter the more restricted aim was to build upon a basis of what could be agreed at the broadest level of generality. What has emerged is a Convention the provisions of which seek to ensure the effectiveness of exclusive choice of court agreements between parties to commercial transactions, and which govern the recognition and enforcement thereof.

The rationale of these Hague rules is in striking contrast to the position which lately has emerged as confirmation of the nature of

---

[30] As to privity of agreement (*i.e.* who is entitled to enforce the agreement?), see *Bouygues Offshore SA v Caspian Shipping Co (No.2)* [1997] 2 Ll's Rep 485.

[31] *Continental Bank NA v Aeakos Cia Naviera SA* [1994] 2 All E.R. 540; *Reichhold Norway ASA v Goldman Sachs International* [2000] 1 W.L.R. 173; *Messier Dowty Ltd v Sabena SA* [2000] 1 W.L.R. 2040; *OT Africa Line Ltd v Hijazy ("The Kribi") (No.1)* [2001] 1 Ll's Rep 76; *Import Export Metro Ltd v Compania Sud Americana de Vapores SA* [2003] 1 All E.R. (Comm) 703; *Sabah Shipyard (Pakistan) Ltd v Pakistan* [2003] 2 Ll's Rep 571; and *Beazley v Horizon Offshore Contractors Inc.* [2005] I.L.Pr. 11.

[32] *Standard Bank London Ltd v Apostolakis (No.2)* [2001] Ll's Rep (Bank.) 240; and *Donohue v Armco Inc* [2002]1 All E.R. 749.

[33] [2005] 1 A.C. 101.

[34] *Through Transport Mutual Insurance Association (Eurasia) Ltd v New India Assurance Co Ltd (The Hari Bhum)* [2004] 1 Ll's Rep 206; and (No.2), [2005] 1 Ll's Rep 67. This was endorsed strongly in *West Tankers Inc v RAS Riunione Adriatica Di Securta SpA ("The Front Comar")* [2005] 2 Ll's Rep 257: "The fact that a foreign court would treat an anti suit injunction order as an impermissible exercise of jurisdiction by the English courts, was, as a matter of English conflict rules, not in itself any reason to withhold such an order to procure compliance with an agreement to arbitrate."

[35] Presently there are no Contracting States to this Convention. The Convention shall enter into force on the first day of the month following the expiration of three months after the deposit of the second instrument of ratification, acceptance, approval or accession (Art.31).

the system operating under the Brussels regime, as expressed in the judgments of the ECJ in *Gasser v Misat*[36] and *Turner v Grovit*.[37] As will be seen, under these decisions, the initiative lies with the court first seised to adjudge its own jurisdiction, both generally and in light of argument that the parties had made an exclusive choice of court in favour of another jurisdiction.

By contrast, the Hague Convention, after setting out[38] a lengthy list of excluded matters to which its provisions shall not apply, defines[39] "exclusive choice of court agreement" (with a presumption of exclusivity) and provides, usefully, that an exclusive choice of court agreement that forms part of a contract shall be treated as an agreement independent of the other terms of the contract.[40] The validity of the choice of court agreement cannot be contested solely on the ground that the "principal" contract is not valid.[41]

The essential differences introduced by this Convention are that it places the court selected by the parties in a position of authority, even though that authority sometimes is shared with the court first seised, though not "chosen". These important provisions are contained in Articles 5 and 6.

Article 5 (Jurisdiction of the chosen court)

7-32

(1) The court or courts of a Contracting State designated in an exclusive choice of court agreement shall have jurisdiction to decide a dispute to which the agreement applies, unless the agreement is null and void under the law of that State.[42]

(2) A court that has jurisdiction under paragraph 1 shall not decline to exercise jurisdiction on the ground that the dispute should be decided in a court of another State.

These provisions therefore set down the power and the duty[43] of the court selected.

---

[36] *Erich Gasser Gmbh v Misat Srl* [2005] Q.B. 1.

[37] [2005] 1 A.C. 101. See para.7–48, below.

[38] Art.2.

[39] Art.3.

[40] *cf.* doubts which arise in this area: *Mackender v Feldia* [1967] 2 Q.B. 590; *Zapata Off-Shore Company v The Bremen and Unterweser Reederei Gmbh, The Chaparral* [1972] 2 Ll's Rep 315 (US Sup. Ct); *Belgian International Insurance Group SA v McNicoll*, 1999 G.W.D. 22–1065; and *Astilleros v Zamakona SA v MacKinnons*, 2002 S.L.T. 1206. See E.B. Crawford, "The Uses of Putativity and Negativity in the Conflict of Laws" (2005) 54 I.C.L.Q. 829.

[41] Art.3.d.

[42] In terms of Art.5.3 this rule shall not affect rules of the court selected on jurisdiction related to subject matter or value of claim; nor on the internal allocation of jurisdiction among the courts of a Contracting State. "However, where the chosen court has discretion as to whether to transfer a case, due consideration shall be given to the choice of the parties" (Art.5.3).

[43] See Hill, *op.cit.*, para.9.3.2, and Cheshire and North, p.350.

Article 6 (Obligations of a court not chosen)

A court in a Contracting State other than that of the chosen court **7–33** shall suspend or dismiss proceedings to which an exclusive choice of court agreement applies unless:

   (a) the agreement is null and void under the law of the State of the chosen court;

   (b) a party lacked the capacity to conclude the agreement under the law of the State of the court seised[44];

   (c) giving effect to the agreement would lead to a manifest injustice[45] or would be manifestly contrary to the public policy of the State of the court seised[46];

   (d) for exceptional reasons beyond the control of the parties, the agreement cannot reasonably be performed; or

   (e) the chosen court has decided not to hear the case.

The 2005 Convention does not deal with interim measures of protection.[47]

Recognition and enforcement under the 2005 Convention

With regard to recognition and enforcement of judgments, Article **7–34** 8 of the Convention provides that a judgment given by a court of a Contracting State designated in an exclusive choice of court agreement shall be recognised in other Contracting States, and may be refused effect only on the grounds specified in the Convention. In general, there shall be no review of the merits of the judgment, except insofar as necessary for the application of the provisions of the Convention. The court addressed shall be bound by the findings of fact on which the court of origin based its jurisdiction, unless that judgment was given by default. A number of the grounds of refusal of recognition rest upon natural justice, but the relationship of power between the chosen court and the court seised, as expressed in Articles 6(a) and (b) and 9(a) and (b), repays study.[48]

---

[44] Note that the question of capacity (mental and legal, presumably) is to be governed by the law of the court seised. Contrast, at the stage of recognition, the rule under Art.9(b) that one reason for the requested State's refusal to recognise or enforce a resulting judgment is that a party lacked capacity to conclude the choice of court agreement under the law of the requested State.

[45] By which law? Does the clause to be found at the end of proviso (c) qualify the earlier part?

[46] Note the power which the public policy discretion gives to the court seised.

[47] Art.7.

[48] *i.e.* validity of agreement is determined by the law of the chosen court, at the stages both of jurisdiction allocation and judgment recognition; but the question of capacity is referred, at the stage of jurisdiction allocation, to the law of the court seised, and at the stage of judgment recognition, to the law of the court requested.

Articles 19 and 20 lay open the possibility of State reservations, to the effect (Article 20) that the courts of a State may refuse to recognise or enforce a judgment given by a court in another Contracting State if the parties were resident in the requested State, and the relationship of the parties and all other elements relevant to the dispute, other than the location of the chosen court, were connected only with the requested State.[49] More remarkable is Article 19, which permits a State to declare that its courts may refuse to determine disputes to which an exclusive choice of court agreement applies if, except for the location of the chosen court, there is no connection between that State and the parties or the dispute. If a State were to enter such a reservation, it would effectively be adding a mandatory rule of its own to the principal jurisdiction provision contained in Article 5.1.

Finally, at this early stage of assessing the strength of the Convention, Article 26 (relationship with other international instruments) should be considered. This "disconnection clause", which is lengthy, and opaque, begins, aspirationally, and in very general terms, by stating in Article 26.1 that the Convention shall be interpreted so far as possible to be compatible with other treaties in force for Contracting States, whether concluded before or after this Convention. Thereafter, Article 26.2 provides that the Convention shall not affect the application by a Contracting State of a treaty, whether concluded before or after the Convention, in cases where none of the parties is resident in a Contracting State that is not a party to the treaty.[50]

The EC having expressed a wish to become a Member of the Hague Conference on Private International Law, and the Conference having stated that it is desirable that the 1955 Statute of the Conference be amended, so as to make membership of the Conference possible for the EC (as well as for any other Regional Economic Integration Organisation) ("REIO"), the Conference, at its twentieth session, adopted certain amendments to its founding statute. It may be expected, therefore, that the EC will make use of Article 29 of the 2005 Convention, permitting signature and ratification by REIOs.[51]

---

[49] This is an interesting insight into the anticipated objection by some States to parties' unfettered choice of court. It militates against forum shopping, and in spirit has something in common with the anti-avoidance provision in Rome I, Art.3.3, which inhibits complete freedom of choice of law in contract.

[50] *e.g.* application of Regulation 44/2001will not be affected where all parties to the litigation are residents of EU Member States. The tenor of Art.26.3 tends to reinforce the inference that Reg.44 would prevail. If, however, only one party is an EU resident, and the other is a non-EU resident, Art.26 suggests that the 2005 Convention will apply. But would not this fall foul of *Owusu*-type reasoning?

[51] See Council of the European Union Press Release (Justice and Home Affairs), April, 2006: 84 02/06 (Presse 106).

SUBMISSION TO THE JURISDICTION

Regulation 44/2001 honours the well-established principle of **7–35** founding jurisdiction upon the basis of submission.

Article 24

Apart from jurisdiction derived from other provisions of this Regulation, a court of a Member State before which a defendant enters an appearance shall have jurisdiction. This rule shall not apply where appearance was entered solely to contest the jurisdiction, or where another court has exclusive jurisdiction by virtue of Article 22.

CONFLICTING JURISDICTIONS AND APPROPRIATE FORUM

Conflicts of jurisdiction under Regulation 44/2001

Lis pendens

Article 25

Where a court of a Member State is seised of a claim which is **7–36** principally concerned with a matter over which the courts of another Member State have exclusive jurisdiction by virtue of Article 22, it shall declare of its own motion that it has no jurisdiction.

Article 26

(1) Where a defendant domiciled in one Member State is sued **7–37** in a court of another Member State and does not enter an appearance, the court shall declare of its own motion that it has no jurisdiction unless its jurisdiction is derived from the provisions of this Regulation.

(2) The court shall stay the proceedings so long as it is not shown that the defendant has been able to receive the document instituting the proceedings or an equivalent document in sufficient time to enable him to arrange for his defence, or that all necessary steps have been taken to this end.[52]

---

[52] Art.26.3 and 4 pertain to Council Regulation (EC) No 1348/2000 on the Service in Member States of Judicial and Extrajudicial Documents in Civil or Commercial Matters; where that Regulation does not apply, Art.15 of the 1965 Hague Convention on the Service Abroad of Judicial and Extrajudicial Documents shall apply, if the document instituting the proceedings had to be transmitted pursuant to that Convention.

Article 27[53]

7–38   (1) Where proceedings involving the same cause of action[54] and between the same parties[55] are brought in the courts of different Member States,[56] any court other than the court first seised[57] shall of its own motion stay its proceedings until such time as the jurisdiction of the court first seised is established.[58]

(2) Where the jurisdiction of the court first seised is established, any court other than the court first seised shall decline jurisdiction in favour of that court.

---

[53] See *Owners of Cargo lately laden on board the Tatry v Owners of the Maciej Rataj* [1999] Q.B. 515; *Winter Maritime Ltd v North End Oil Ltd ("The Winter")* [2000] 2 Ll's Rep 298; *J.P. Morgan Europe Ltd v Primacom AG* [2005] 2 All E.R. (Comm.) 764; *Tavoulareas v Tsavliris & Sons Maritime Co.* [2005] EWHC 2643 (Comm); and *Re Claim by a German Lottery Company* [2005] I.L.Pr. 35.

[54] *e.g. Gubisch Maschinenfabrik v Giulio Palumbo* [1987] E.C.R. 4861 (in which the ECJ held that an action for the rescission or discharge of a contract involved the same cause of action as an action to enforce the same contract); *Bank of Scotland v SA Banque Nationale de Paris*, 1996 S.L.T. 103; *Mecklermedia Corp. v D C Congress GmbH* [1998] 1 All E.R. 148; *The Maciej Rataj*, above; *Haji-Ioannou v Frangos* [1999] 2 All E.R. (Comm) 865; *Carnoustie Universal SA v International Transport Workers Federation* [2002] 2 All E.R. (Comm) 657 (Lugano); *Gantner Electronic GmbH v Basch Exploitatie Maatschappij BV* Case 111/01 [2003] I.L.Pr. 37 (ECJ); *Bank of Tokyo-Mitsubishi Ltd v Baskan* [2004] 2 Ll's Rep 395; and *Royal & Sun Alliance Insurance plc v MK Digital FZE (Cyprus) Ltd* [2005] EWHC 1408.

[55] *e.g. Drouot Assurances SA v. Consolidated Metallurgical Industries (CMI Industrial Sites)* [1998] All E.R. (E.C.) 483 (There may be such a degree of identity between the interests of insurer and insured that they must be considered to be the same party for the purposes of Art.21, Brussels Convention). Contrast *Mecklermedia Corp. v D.C. Congress GmbH* [1998] 1 All E.R. 148; *Glencore International AG v Metro Trading Inc (No.1)* [1999] 2 All E.R. (Comm) 899; *Glencore International AG v Shell International Trading and Shipping Co Ltd* [1999] 2 All E.R. (Comm) 922; and *Owners of Cargo lately laden on board the Tatry v Owners of the Maciej Rataj* [1999] Q.B. 515.

[56] The question is whether the courts in the different Member States have jurisdiction, not whether either or both party(ies) is/are domiciled in a Member State: *Overseas Union Insurance Ltd v New Hampshire Ins. Co.* [1992] 2 All E.R. 138.

[57] As to which, see Art.30. See operation of *lis pendens* system *per* Court of Appeal in *(1) Royal Sun Alliance Insurance plc (2) Exel Logistique SA v MK Digital FZE (Cypus) Ltd & Ors* [2006] EWCA Civ. 629.

[58] Generally therefore the only judge of the jurisdiction of the court first seised is that court itself (and see Art.25, above). However, the ECJ decision in *Overseas Union Insurance Ltd v New Hampshire Ins. Co.* [1992] 2 All E.R. 138, to the effect that the rule that one Member State may not examine the jurisdiction of the court of another Member State which has been first seised, nevertheless held that this was without prejudice to the case where the court second seised has exclusive jurisdiction.

Article 28

(1) Where related[59] actions are pending in the courts of **7–39** different Member States, any court other than the court first seised may stay its proceedings.

(2) Where these actions are pending at first instance, any court other than the court first seised may also, on the application of one of the parties, decline jurisdiction if the court first seised has jurisdiction over the actions in question and its law permits the consolidation thereof.

(3) For the purposes of this Article, actions are deemed to be related where they are so closely connected that it is expedient to hear and determine them together to avoid the risk of irreconcilable judgments resulting from separate proceedings.

Article 29

Where actions come within the exclusive jurisdiction of several **7–40** courts,[60] any court other than the court first seised shall decline jurisdiction in favour of that court.

Article 30

For the purposes of this Section, a court shall be deemed to be **7–41** seised:

(1) at the time when the document instituting the proceedings or an equivalent document is lodged with the court, provided that the plaintiff has not subsequently failed to take the steps he was required to take to have service effected on the defendant; or

(2) if the document has to be served before being lodged with the court, at the time when it was received by the authority responsible for service, provided that the plaintiff has not subsequently failed to take the steps he was required to take to have the document lodged with the court.

This provision is a new, autonomous ("Community") definition of the date at which a court shall be deemed to be seised. It is

---

[59] *Sarrio SA v. Kuwait Investment Authority* [1999] 1 A.C. 32; *Haji-Ioannou v Frangos* [1999] 2 All E.R. (Comm) 865; *Bank of Scotland v. SA Banque Nationale de Paris*, 1996 S.L.T. 103; *Mecklermedia Corp. v D.C. Congress GmbH* [1998] 1 All E.R. 148; *Blue Nile Shipping Co Ltd v Iguana Shipping & Finance Inc. (The Happy Fellow)* [1998] 1 Ll's Rep. 13; *Abkco Music & Records Inc. v Jodorowsky* [2003] C.L.Y.B. 598; *Evialis SA v Siat* [2003] 2 Ll's Rep 377; and *Miles Platt Ltd v Townroe Ltd* [2003] 1 All E.R. (Comm) 561.

[60] See para.7–27, above.

essential in a priority of process system that there be clarity on this matter.[61] The rule is bifurcated to reflect two differing modes of practice among Member States.

Interpretation

7–42 A number of interpretative questions reasonably may still arise about the meaning of terms of the Regulation, and/or the ranking of its provisions *inter se*. Upon reference to the ECJ (which under the Regulation is the prerogative, in the UK, of the House of Lords), the court is required to provide interpretative rulings.[62] But the ECJ will respond solely to the issues in question and the questions asked. At this stage of development of a relatively new jurisdictional regime, it is often the case that an ECJ judgment may leave open to speculation related areas of doubt not presenting in the immediate case.

Erich Gasser GmbH v Misat Srl[63]

7–43 The parties in this case, Misat, an Italian company, based in Rome, and Gasser, an Austrian company, had done business together for a number of years in the matter of the supply by Gasser, and purchase by Misat, of children's clothing. In April 2000, Misat brought proceedings against Gasser in a court in Rome (arguing apparently that, in the circumstances, its jurisdiction was available under Article 2 of the 1968 Brussels Convention), seeking, essentially, 'negative declarations' to the effect that the contract between the parties had terminated by operation of law, or as a result of disagreement between the two companies; further, to find that Misat had not failed to perform the contract; and seeking also an order for damages plus expenses against Gasser in relation to its failure to fulfil its obligations of good faith.

In December 2000, Gasser brought an action against Misat in the Regional Court in Austria for payment of outstanding invoices, asserting that the jurisdiction of the Austrian court was established, not only on the basis of 1968 Brussels Convention, Article 5.1, but also on the basis that the parties had agreed a choice of court for Austria, as evidenced by a prorogation clause appearing on the back of all invoices sent by Gasser to Misat without any objection

---

[61] Identification of the point at which the court is seised having proved contentious under the 1968 Brussels Convention: *Neste Chemicals SA v DK Line (The Sargasso)* [1994] 3 All E.R. 180; *Dresser UK Ltd v Falcongate Freight Management Ltd* [1992] 1 Q.B. 502, overtaken by *Canada Trust v Stolzenberg (No.2)* [2000] 4 All E.R. 481; and *Zelger v Salinitri* [1984] ECR 2397. As to the Lugano Convention, see *Phillips v Symes (A Bankrupt)* [2006] I.L.Pr.9.

[62] *Gasser*, para.23.

[63] [2005] Q.B. 1; See application of *Gasser* in *J P Morgan Europe Ltd v Primacom AG* [2005] 2 All E.R. (Comm.) 764.

having been raised in that matter by Misat.[64] Misat denied this, contending that there had been no choice of court agreement, and further, that the litigation in Italy, being earlier in time, must take precedence.

The Austrian court decided of its own motion to stay its proceedings until the jurisdiction of the Italian court had been established. The Austrian court's view was that it had jurisdiction under Article 5.1 as the court for the place of performance of the contract, but it did not rule upon the question whether there had been an agreement to confer jurisdiction on the Austrian court. On appeal against that decision by *Gasser*, the Overlandsgericht Innsbruck referred these questions of interpretation to the ECJ for a preliminary ruling. In essence, this was a request for a ranking of Article 17 of the Brussels Convention (prorogation of jurisdiction)[65] and Article 21 (court first seised).[66]

It was decided that a national court could refer to the ECJ a request for interpretation even where the basis, factual and legal, for the reference relied upon submissions the merits of which had not yet been examined, ie in this case, that the choice of court clause printed on the back of the invoices, neither acknowledged nor denied by Misat, was sufficient to satisfy Article 17 as a choice which was in accordance with the parties' practice and trade usage prevailing between Austria and Italy.[67]

But more importantly, the decision of the ECJ is that the system set in place by the *lis pendens* rule is pre-eminent. Therefore, where a court had been first seised, any court second seised, even one the jurisdiction of which the parties had prorogued in terms of Article 17, must stay its proceedings until the court first seised has ruled upon its own jurisdiction. If the court first seised decides that it has jurisdiction, the court second seised must decline jurisdiction in favour of that court. This is the case even where the proceedings before the court first seised are protracted.

The initiative taken by Misat took the form of actings of a negative nature. A system of priority of process lends itself to such behaviour.[68]

This most significant decision has provoked comment in the UK.[69]

---

[64] *cf. MSG v Les Gravières Rhenanes SARL* (Case C-106/95) [1997] All E.R. (E.C.) 385.

[65] *cf.* Reg.44/2001, Art.23.

[66] *cf.* Reg.44/2001, Art.27.

[67] See *Gasser*, para.42. Also E.B. Crawford, "The Uses of Putativity and Negativity in the Conflict of Laws" (2005) 54 ICLQ 829.

[68] See A.S. Bell, *Forum Shopping and Venue in Transnational Litigation* (2003), Ch.4 (Reverse Forum Shopping).

[69] *e.g.* T.C. Hartley, "The European Union and the Systematic Dismantling of the Common Law of Conflict of Laws" (2005) 54 ICLQ 813.

Negative declarations

7–44 The *lis pendens* system places in an advantageous position a party
who is able to initiate the process in a forum of his choice, so far as
the facts and the law admit choice. It is necessary to assess the
extent to which it is reasonable for a litigant to seize the initiative
by seising a forum in which to seek a declaration of a negative
nature (*e.g.*, that he has *not* breached the contract: a declaration of
non-liability).

Initiation of litigation by means of negative proceedings was a
feature of *Gasser v Misat*.[70] The ECJ accepted[71] that the cause of
action later brought before the Austrian court involved the same
cause of action as the action brought previously in Rome, although
the latter was for a negative declaration.

The device seems to be indulged, or tolerated, so long as, in the
view of the instant forum, there has not been a gross abuse of
process. But what *is* an abuse of process?[72] The English courts in
their operation of the English residual rules (*q.v.*),[73] are not
inexperienced in dealing with this matter. Increasingly, while
advocating caution, the effect of recent pronouncements has been
to suggest that negative actings in litigation should not necessarily
be viewed negatively. Sometimes justice requires acceptance of the
seeking of a negative declaration in order to avoid further, perhaps
indefinite, delay.[74] It is difficult to avoid the conclusion that the
matter must be treated on a case-by-case basis. It was noted *per*
Morison J. in *Bristow Helicopters Ltd v Sikorsky Aircraft Corp.*[75] that
whether such a claim is proper or not proper is not to be
determined by the form of the claim, but by its substance. Where
the "defendant" (*i.e.* the "natural" claimant) had been "temporis-
ing", the seeking of such a negative declaration was appropriate.

Such toleration within the Brussels regime has been confirmed
by a decision of Collins J., in *The Bank of Tokyo-Mitsubishi Ltd v*

---

[70] One which attracted comment from Advocate General Léger: paras 68 and 69.
The ECJ in its judgment (para.53; also at 68) declined to engage with the
problem.

[71] Para.46. Hartley, above, explains that the ruling effectively condones the use of
delaying tactics by means of seeking a negative declaration in a legal system
which is available under Reg.44/2001 and which is known to be slow: *Transporti
Castellatti v Hugo Trumpy* Case C-159/97 [1999] ECR I-1597.

[72] *Messier Dowty Ltd v Sabena SA* [2000] 1 W.L.R. 2040.

[73] For use of the device is not limited to the Brussels scheme: see *Bristow
Helicopters Ltd v Sikorsky Aircraft Corp* [2004] 2 Ll's Rep 150; *Swiss Reinsurance
Co. Ltd v United India Insurance Co. (Jurisdiction)* [2004] I.L.Pr. 4; and *Ark
Therapeutics Plc v True North Capital Ltd* [2006] 1 All E.R. (Comm.) 1381.

[74] *Swiss Reinsurance Co. Ltd v United India Insurance Co. (Jurisdiction)* [2004]
I.L.Pr. 4.

[75] [2004] 2 Ll's Rep 150.

Baskan Gida Sanayi Ve Pazarlama.[76] Indeed the judge stated that "Pre-emptive proceedings for a negative declaration in a preferred jurisdiction are entirely legitimate."[77] Hence the paradoxical situation has resulted that, even within EU, forum shopping by the use of actions for negative declarations has been encouraged[78]; forum shopping is not eradicated by the use of a *lis pendens* system.

Conflicts of jurisdiction outside the Brussels regime

The plea of forum non conveniens

Much has been written on the subject of *forum non conveniens*.[79]   **7–45** Choice of forum is a fiercely fought issue because the same forum is unlikely to be in the best interests of all the parties. The starting point for Scots conflict law is taken to be the famous dictum by Lord Kinnear in *Sim v Robinow*,[80] where his Lordship said: "the plea can never be sustained unless the Court is satisfied that there is some other tribunal, having competent jurisdiction, in which the case may be tried more suitably for the interests of all the parties and for the ends of justice." This form of words was quoted with approval by Lord Goff in *Spiliada Maritime Corporation v Consulex*,[81] which decision of the House of Lords represents the acceptance by English law that its position in this area is indis-

---

[76] [2004] 2 Ll's Rep 395. Also *Boss Group Ltd v Boss France SA* [1996] 4 All E.R. 970; *Benincasa v Dentalkit Srl* Case C-269/95 [1998] All E.R. (E.C.) 135; and *Equitas Limited v Wave City Shipping Co. Ltd* [2005] 2 All E.R. (Comm.) 301.

[77] Para.114; see also 244.

[78] Para.198.

[79] See *Declining Jurisdiction in Private International Law* (JJ Fawcett ed., 1995); R Schuz (1986) 34 ICLQ 374; Verheul, "The *Forum (Non) Conveniens* in English and Dutch law and Under Some International Conventions" (1986) 35 ICLQ 413; Prince, "Bhopal, Bogainville and OK Tedi: Why Australia's *forum non conveniens* Approach is Better" (1998) 47 ICLQ 573.

[80] (1892) 19 R. 665, 668. Later notable Scottish cases are *Longworth v Hope* (1865) 3 M. 1049 (where the Bench noted the infelicity of the formerly used term *forum non competens*; still, *conveniens* should not be translated as convenient, but rather as appropriate, fit for, or suitable); *Société du Gaz de Paris v Armateurs Francais*, 1926 S.C. (H.L.) 13; *Argyllshire Weavers v Macaulay (No.1)*, 1962 S.C. 388; *Crédit Chemique v James Scott Engineering Group*, 1979 S.C. 406; *De Mulder v Jadranska Linijska (Jadrolinija)*, 1989 S.L.T. 269; *Shell (UK) Exploration and Production Ltd v Innes*, 1995 S.L.T. 807; *FMC Corporation v Russell*, 1999 S.L.T. 99; *Compagnie Commerciale Andre SA v Artibell Shipping Co Ltd (No.1)*, 1999 S.L.T. 1051; and *Kelly Banks v CGU Insurance plc*, unreported, November 5, 2000.

[81] [1986] 3 All E.R. 843, 853.

tinguishable from the Scots plea.[82] Useful consideration of the subject in Scotland is found in *De Mulder v Jadranska Linijska (Jadrolinija)*,[83] where the considerations appeared to be straightforward, for example convenience of witnesses, and language difficulties.

The onus of proof is shared in the following manner: the case having been properly laid in Scotland, the onus is on the defender[84] making the plea to show that there is a competent and more appropriate forum elsewhere. If this be established to the satisfaction of the original forum, in terms of expense and convenience of witnesses etc,[85] the onus shifts to the pursuer to show "objectively by cogent evidence"[86] that to require him to litigate abroad would remove from him a personal or juridical advantage of such importance that it would cause injustice to deprive him of it[87]: "a general principle may be derived, which is that, if a clearly more appropriate forum overseas has been identified, generally speaking the plaintiff will have to take that forum as he finds it, even if it is

---

[82] The trend of English judicial thinking can be traced from the strict (or avid) *St Pierre v S. American Stores (Gath and Chaves) Ltd* [1936] 1 K.B. 382; through *The Marinero* [1955] P. 68; *The Soya Margareta* [1961] 1 W.L.R. 709; *The Atlantic Star* [1973] 2 All E.R. 175; *MacShannon v Rockware Glass* [1978] A.C. 795 (the "natural forum"); *Castanho v Brown and Root (UK) Ltd* [1981] A.C. 557; *Trendtex Trading Corp. v Credit Suisse* [1982] A.C. 679; *Smith Kline & French Laboratories v Bloch* [1983] 2 All E.R. 72; *Astro Exito Navegacion SA v WT HSU: The Messiniaki Tolmi* [1983] 1 Ll's Rep. 666; *The Biskra* [1983] 2 Ll's Rep. 59; *The Benarty (No.1)* [1983] 1 Ll's Rep. 361; *The Atlantic Song* [1983] 2 Ll's Rep. 394; *Las Mercedes v Abidin Daver* [1984] 2 W.L.R. 196, HL; to *Spiliada Maritime Corporation v Consulex*, above. Post-*Spiliada* cases include: *The Nordglimt* [1988] 2 All E.R. 531; *Roneleigh Ltd v Mill Exports Inc.* [1989] 1 W.L.R. 619; *Cleveland Museum of Art v Capricorn Art International SA* [1990] 2 Ll's Rep. 166; *Banco Atlantico SA v The British Bank of the Middle East* [1990] 2 Ll's Rep. 504; *Connelly v RTZ Corp. plc (No.2)* [1998] A.C. 854, HL; *Europs Ltd v Sunshine Lifestyle Products Ltd* [1998] CLYB 750; *Carlson v Rio Tinto plc* [1999] CLYB 718; *Berezovsky v Forbes* [1999] CLYB 717; *Radhakrishna Hospitality Service Private Ltd v EIH Ltd* [1999] 2 Ll's Rep 249; *Askin v Absa Bank Ltd* [1999] I.L.Pr. 471; *International Credit & Investment Co (Overseas) Ltd v Adham (Share Ownership)* [1999] I.L.Pr. 302; *Lubbe v Cape plc (No 2)* [2000] 1 W.L.R. 1545; *XN Corp Ltd v Point of Sale Ltd* [2001] I.L.Pr 35; *Ceskoslovenska Obchodni Banka AS v Nomura International plc* [2002] I.L.Pr. 321; *Owusu v Jackson t/a Villa Holidays Bal-Inn Villas* [2005] 2 Q.B. 801; *Shekar v Satyam Computer Services Ltd* [2005] I.C.R. 737; *Dornoch Ltd v Mauritius Union Assurance Company Ltd* [2006] EWCA Civ. 389; and *Ark Therapeutics Plc v True North Capital Ltd* [2006] 1 All E.R. (Comm.) 138.

[83] 1989 S.L.T. 269.

[84] A pursuer having selected a forum will not normally be permitted, upon a change of mind, to plead *forum non conveniens* with a view to having his chosen Scots court defer to another court: *Marodi v Mikkal*, 2002 G.W.D. 13–398.

[85] If this is not established (see *e.g. Kelly Banks v CGU Insurance plc*, unreported, 5 November 2004), the case will not be sisted.

[86] *De Mulder v Jadranska Linijska (Jadrolinija)*, 1989 S.L.T. 269, *per* Lord Kincraig at 274.

[87] The principles which govern the identification of the appropriate forum in non-Brussels consistorial cases are similar: see Ch.12, below.

in certain respects less advantageous to him than the English forum".[88]

Level of damages, nature of the system of discovery, and content of the rules of evidence will not normally be relevant factors. In contrast, expiry of a limitation period in the alternative forum is an ambivalent factor, the weight attributed to which depends on circumstances, especially the court's assessment of the conduct of the party potentially disadvantaged by it, for example degree of culpability or motive in failing to act expeditiously.[89] The court may take into account the amount of legal and technical work done in one jurisdiction, or in one jurisdiction in relation to a similar case (the "Cambridgeshire factor").[90] The existence of a jurisdiction clause in favour of the forum will render it unlikely that the forum would accede to a plea of *forum non conveniens*.[91]

"Only if the plaintiff can establish that substantial justice cannot be done in the appropriate forum will the court refuse to grant a stay."[92] Availability in England of legal aid, or the benefit of a conditional fee agreement (*i.e.* availability of financial assistance absolutely necessary, and absolutely lacking in Namibia in *Connelly v RTZ Corp. plc (No.2)*) was held, in two House of Lords cases, to be good reason not to defer to the jurisdiction of the objectively natural forum.[93]

Hence, assessment of what constitutes personal or juridical advantage is the crucial and most difficult issue,[94] but there arises also the question *when* particular factors ought to be considered—at the first, or second, stage of the plea.[95] It is thought that at the

---

[88] *Connelly*, above *per* L. Goff at 872.
[89] *Spiliada* at 860. In *Kelly Banks v CGU Insurance plc*, above, Lady Smith declined to accede to the plea of *forum non conveniens* in respect of the English court, taking the view that the connections with England were no stronger than with Scotland. However, had the first stage plea been accomplished successfully for the defender, her Ladyship then would have had to consider whether the interests of justice required that the plea be not sustained, given that the pursuer was time-barred in England. The onus would have been on the pursuer to show this, and the hint was given that the onus in the circumstances might not have been discharged.
[90] At the time of the *Spiliada* decision, litigation was ongoing in England concerning a similar action for damage to a cargo of sulphur, involving the same defendant shippers, but a different ship, "The Cambridgeshire". Hence, this factor has become known as the "Cambridgeshire factor".
[91] *Horn and Linie GmbH & Co. Ltd v Panamericana Formas E Impresos SA, Ace Seguros SA* [2006] EWHC 373 (Comm).
[92] *Connelly*, above, *per* L. Goff at 853.
[93] *Lubbe v Cape plc (No.2)* [2000] 1 W.L.R 1545; and *Connelly v RTZ Corp. plc (No.2)* [1997] 4 All E.R. 335 (Lord Hoffman diss.).
[94] *Per* Lord Goff in his classic judgment in *Spiliada*, and in *Connelly v RTZ Corp.*, above at 345.
[95] See L. Merrett, "Uncertainties in the First Limb of the *Spiliada* Test" (2005) 54 ICLQ 211.

first stage availability of alternative forum means availability *in principle*; at the second stage, it will be open to the claimant to seek to establish that, *in reality*, the alternative forum is not open to him, by reason for example of: time bar; absence of public funding; or that for political or other reasons the claimant will not be afforded a fair hearing, or any hearing at all, in the alternative forum.[96]

The court may grant or refuse the sist; and if the former, it may dismiss the Scottish proceedings.

When may the plea be used?

7–46 Section 49 of CJJA 1982-1991, enacts that "[n]othing in this Act shall prevent any court in the United Kingdom from staying, sisting, striking out or dismissing any proceedings before it, on the ground of *forum non conveniens* or otherwise, where to do so is not inconsistent with the 1968 Convention, or as the case may be, the Lugano Convention."

Generally, a stay *will* be inconsistent with the Brussels/Lugano regime, but the question which has arisen in England is whether the plea can be used in an English/Scottish (CJJA 1982, Schedule 4) context. There are two conflicting decisions (of the same judge) on the question, the later decision favouring the continuing competence of the plea within the UK being preferred by commentators,[97] and having suffered no contradiction in the intervening years. Lady Smith gave no indication that the plea would not be competent within the UK, in her judgment in *Kelly Banks v CGU Insurance plc*.[98]

Subject to the UK situation of use of the plea among the legal systems of a Contracting/Member State, it can be said, therefore, that the plea of *forum non conveniens* is not available within the Brussels/Lugano regime.[99] But a doubt which had arisen[1] about

---

[96] *Askin v Absa Bank Ltd* [1999] I.L.Pr. 471; and *Mohammed v Bank of Kuwait and the Middle East* [1996] 1 W.L.R. 1483.

[97] *Foxen v Scotsman Publications, The Times*, February 17, 1994 and *Cumming v Scottish Daily Record, The Times*, June 8, 1995, both *per* Drake J., the latter in favour of the use of the plea as not inconsistent with CJJA 1982, s.49 (supported in Clarkson and Hill, *Jaffey on the Conflict of Laws*, p.132). See Collins and Davenport, "*Forum Conveniens* within the United Kingdom" (1994) 110 L.Q.R. 325.

[98] Unreported, November 5, 2004. See also *Ennstone Building Products Ltd v Stanger (No.1)* [2002] C.L.Y.B. 624.

[99] Reg.44/2001, Arts 27–30; *Arkwright Mutual Ins. Co. v Bryanston Ins. Co.* [1990] 2 All E.R. 335; *S and W Berisford v New Hampshire Ins. Co.* [1990] 2 All E.R. 321; and *Aiglon Ltd v Gau Shan Co. Ltd* [1993] 1 Ll's Rep 164.

[1] *Re Harrods (Buenos Aires) Ltd (No.2)* [1992] Ch. 72 (in which appeal to the ECJ was abandoned). The decision was followed in *The Po* [1991] 2 Ll's Rep. 206 (where the HL referred the question to the ECJ, but again the case was settled) and *The Nile Rhapsody* [1994] 1 Ll's Rep 382. See also *Ace Insurance SA-NV v Zurich Insurance Co.* [2001] 1 All E.R. (Comm) 802.

availability of the *forum non conveniens* discretion where it is attempted to use the plea in the court of a Member State, and the alternative forum is in a non-EU/EFTA state,[2] has been resolved by the ECJ (in the negative) in *Owusu v Jackson t/a Villa Holidays Bal Inn Villas* (*qv*),[3] which, in turn, is of assistance in understanding the reach of the Brussels regime.

Restraint of foreign proceedings (anti-suit injunction)

By way of contrast with *forum non conveniens*, the plea for restraint **7–47** of foreign proceedings relates to the common law power of a Scots[4] or English court to prevent a person who is subject to its jurisdiction from raising, or proceeding with, an action in a foreign court between the same parties and relating to the same subject matter as that before the Scots court. Although the Scots/English courts have no power to restrain a foreign *court* from proceeding to hear any action, they have power to restrain a *person* subject to their jurisdiction from proceeding with an action in a foreign court. This power will be exercised only if the foreign proceedings are considered to be vexatious and oppressive.[5]

If an order is granted restraining foreign proceedings, the foreign court, nevertheless, may still hear the action (for it is part of its sovereignty so to do), but if the party against whom the order of restraint is granted proceeds with the action abroad, s/he will be acting in contempt of the British court and will receive no assistance in attempting to enforce the resultant decree. The remedy has come to be known as an anti-suit injunction.

Generally, the court will not exercise this power if to do so would deprive a party of an advantage in the foreign court which the Scots forum considers legitimate. There is greater likelihood of the power being exercised in a case in which the pursuer in

---

[2] *BP International Ltd v Energy Infrastructure Group Ltd* [2003] EWHC 2924; *Navigators Insurance Co v Atlantic Methanol Production Co. LLC* [2004] Ll's Rep I.R. 418; *Bristow Helicopters Ltd v Sikorsky Aircraft Corp.* [2004] 2 Ll's Rep 150; *Royal & Sun Alliance Insurance plc v Retail Brand Alliance Inc* [2005] Ll's Rep I.R. 110; and *OT Africa Line Ltd v Magic Sportswear Corp.* [2005] EWCA Civ. 710.

[3] [2005] 2 Q.B. 801. Decided under the 1968 Brussels Convention, even though a 2005 decision. See para.7–51, below.

[4] *Young v Barclay* (1846) 8 D. 774; *Dawson's Trs v Macleans* (1860) 22 D. 685; *Pan American World Airways v Andrews*, 1992 S.L.T. 268, *per* Lord Kirkwood at 271; *Shell UK Exploration & Production Ltd v Innes*, 1995 S.L.T. 807; and *FMC Corp. v Russell*, 1999 S.L.T. 99. See Brown, "Interdict Proceedings in Scotland to Prevent or Restrain Court Actions in the United States", 1995 S.L.T. (News) 253 (quoting Lord Denning in *Smith Kline and French Laboratories Ltd v Bloch* [1983] 2 All E.R. 72, 74: "As a moth is drawn to the light, so is a litigant drawn to the United States").

[5] *Cohen v Rothfield* [1919] 1 K.B. 410.

Scotland is also the pursuer abroad.[6] Further, if no choice of forum is open to the claimant in that in only one (foreign) court is a remedy available, the claimant remaining also amenable to the home court, the English court has shown that it will hesitate before making an order to restrain the party: it would have to be shown that the defendant's being sued in the foreign forum would infringe a legal or equitable right of the defendant not to be sued.[7]

The reported cases fall into three classes:

(a) bankruptcy[8];
(b) consistorial actions[9]; and
(c) miscellaneous commercial.[10]

The modern interest arises principally in commercial matters.[11] In

---

[6] *Australian Commercial Research and Development Ltd v. ANZ McCaughan Merchant Bank Ltd* [1989] 3 All E.R. 65. In *Cohen v Rothfield* [1919] 1 K.B. 410 (where the test vexatious *or* oppressive is used) Scrutton L.J. at 414 said: "It is not *prima facie* vexatious for the same plaintiff to commence two actions relating to the same subject-matter, one in England and one abroad. The applicant must prove a substantial case of vexation resulting from the identity of proceedings, remedies, and benefits, or from the existence of some motive other than a *bona fide* desire to determine disputes."

[7] *British Airways Board v Laker Airways Ltd* [1984] 3 All E.R. 39; *Midland Bank plc v Laker Airways* [1986] 1 All E.R. 527; *South Carolina Ins. Co. v Assurantie Maatschappij "de Zeven Provincien" NV* [1986] 3 All E.R. 487; *SNI Aerospatiale v Lee Kui Jak* [1987] 3 All E.R. 510; *Channel Tunnel Group Ltd v Balfour Beatty Construction Ltd* [1993] A.C. 334; *Donohue v Armco Inc.* [2002] 1 All E.R. 749; *Yachya v Levi* (Royal Court of Jersey) [2002] C.L.Y.B. 640; and *Royal Bank of Canada v Cooperatieve Centrale Raiffeisen- Boerenleen Bank BA* [2004] 1 Ll's Rep 471.

[8] *e.g. Lindsay v Paterson* (1840) 2 D. 1373.

[9] *Thornton* (1886) 11 P.D. 176; *Armstrong* [1892] P. 98; *Vardopulo* (1909) 25 T.L.R. 518; *Orr-Lewis* [1949] P. 347; *Sealey v Callan* [1953] P. 135. *Cf.* the cognate subject of mandatory and discretionary sists, Ch.12, below, and Hemain injunctions in England: *Hemain v Hemain* [1988] 2 F.L.R. 388, and *R v R* [2005] 1 F.L.R. 386. See also, in the context of administration of a deceased person's estate, *Weinstock v Sarnat* (NSW) 2006 3 C.L. 79.

[10] *Bushby v Munday* (1821) 5 Madd. 297; *Carron Iron Co. v McLaren* (1855) 5 H.L.C. 416; *Dawson's Trs v MacLean* (1860) 22 D. 685; *McHenry v Lewis* (1883) 22 Ch. D. 397; *Liquidators of California Redwood Co. Ltd v Walker* (1886) 13 R. 810; *Liquidators of Pacific Coast Mining Co. Ltd v Walker* (1886) 13 R. 816; *Gill v Culter* (1895) 23 R. 371; *Cohen v Rothfield* [1919] 1 K.B. 410; *The Marinero* [1955] P. 68; *The Soya Margareta* [1961] 1 W.L.R. 709; *Settlement Corp. v Hochschild (No.1)* [1966] Ch. 10; and *Smith Kline & French Laboratories v Bloch* [1983] 2 All E.R. 72.

[11] *SNI Aerospatiale v Lee Kui Jak* [1987] 3 All E.R. 510; *El Du Pont de Nemours & Co. v Agnew CA* [1988] 2 Ll's Rep 240; *Sohio Supply Co. v Gatoil (U.S.A.) Inc.* [1989] 1 Ll's Rep. 588; *Re Maxwell Communications Corp. (No.2)* [1992] B.C.C. 757; *Société Commerciale de Reassurance v Eras International Ltd (No.2)* [1995] 2 All E.R. 278; *Airbus Industrie v Patel* [1997] I.L.Pr. 191; *Bannerton Holdings Pty Ltd v Sydbank Soenderjylland A/S (Australia)* (1997) 5 C.L. 102; *Banque*

SNI Aerospatiale v Lee Kui Jak,[12] on appeal from Brunei, the Privy Council ordered a party to desist from her suit in Texas because Brunei was the natural forum and the defendants would be unfairly disadvantaged if prevented from presenting their defence in Brunei. The leading opinion was given by Lord Goff who said that the principles governing an order by the English court to restrain foreign proceedings were not the same as those which govern the decision whether or not to accede to a plea under *forum non conveniens*. The restraint will be ordered only if the parallel double procedure is regarded as vexatious and oppressive, a test which has been abandoned by English law, both in substance and in its verbal formulation, as the plea of *forum non conveniens* has been received and developed.[13]

In *The Angelic Grace*,[14] the Court of Appeal held that there was no difference in principle between restraining a party from commencing/continuing foreign proceedings in breach of an exclusive jurisdiction clause and doing likewise in respect of foreign proceedings raised in contravention of an arbitration clause: the restraint should be effected as promptly as possible and without diffidence.

The unfolding of events has revealed that while there may be no difference in principle between these two instances, within a Brussels context, only restraints in relation to foreign arbitration proceedings remain available to a Scots or English court.[15]

It is clear from *Turner v Grovit*[16] that the use by one EU forum of an anti-suit injunction to seek to restrain a party from litigating in the court of another Member State is not acceptable.

Turner v Grovit

Turner, an English solicitor, was an employee of Harada Ltd, a **7–48** company incorporated in Ireland and having its place of central management in England, and under the control of a group of companies of which Grovit was the director. The companies carried on the business of operating *bureaux de changes* in Spain.

Cantonale Vaudoise v Waterlily Maritime Inc. [1997] 5 C.L. 103; *General Star International Indemnity Ltd v Stirling Cooke Brown Reinsurance Brokers* Ltd [2003] I.L.Pr. 19; *West Tankers Inc v RAS Riunione Adriatica Di Sicurta SpA ("The Front Comor")* [2005] 2 Ll's Rep 257; and *Horn and Linie GmbH & Co. Ltd v Panamericana Formas E Impresos SA, Ace Seguros SA* [2006] EWHC 373 (Comm).

[12] [1987] 3 All E.R. 510.
[13] *St Pierre v South American Stores (Gath and Chaves) Ltd* [1936] 1 K.B. 382.
[14] [1994] 1 Ll's Rep 168.
[15] *Through Transport Mutual Insurance Association (Eurasia) Ltd v New India Assurance Co. Ltd (The Hari Bhum)* [2004] 1 Ll's Rep 206, and (No.2), [2005] 1 Ll's Rep 67.
[16] [2005] 1 A.C. 101.

In 1997, Turner was sent to work in Madrid at the office of Changepoint SA, a Spanish company in the same group of companies as Harada. Turner remained employed by Harada Ltd, though Changepoint paid Harada for his services. Shortly after commencing work in Madrid, Turner resigned because his work involved his colluding in illegal conduct (tax fraud). Having returned to England, Turner brought constructive unfair dismissal proceedings against Harada Ltd before an English employment tribunal (which considered that it had jurisdiction under Articles 2, 5.1 and 5.5 of the 1968 Brussels Convention). In response, Grovit (in the name of Changepoint) sued Turner in Spain for damages for "unjustified departure" and for professional misconduct, claiming substantial damages. On the basis that the litigation brought in Spain was vexatious and oppressive, the Court of Appeal, at the request of Turner, granted an anti-suit injunction against Grovit. Grovit appealed to the House of Lords, which, in turn, referred the matter to the ECJ for a preliminary ruling on the following question: "[i]s it inconsistent with the Convention on Jurisdiction and the Enforcement of Judgments in Civil and Commercial Matters signed at Brussels on 27 September 1968 (subsequently acceded to by the United Kingdom) to grant restraining orders against defendants who are threatening to commence or continue legal proceedings in another Convention country when those defendants are acting in bad faith with the intent and purpose of frustrating or obstructing proceedings properly before the English courts?"

The decision of the ECJ was that a prohibition issued by one Member State court upon the commencement or continuation of legal proceedings in another is tantamount to interference with the jurisdiction of the foreign court and, with regard to the 1968 Brussels Convention, incompatible with the principle of mutual trust between legal systems of Contracting States, and the general prohibition of review of the jurisdiction of the court of one Contracting State by the court of another.

Therefore the Brussels Convention, and by implication, the Regulation, precludes the grant by a court in a Contracting/ Member State of an injunction prohibiting a party to proceedings pending before it, from commencing or continuing proceedings before a court of another Contracting/Member State,[17] even where that party is acting in bad faith.

---

[17] Presumably, the grant of anti-suit injunctions by Scots or English courts remains competent in respect of proceedings in a non Contracting/Member State; though after *Owusu v Jackson (t/a Villa Holidays Bal Inn Villas)* [2005] 2 Q.B. 801 no British lawyer can state with confidence the extent of the EU's reach (see para.7–50, below).

This decision, like *Gasser*, has provoked comment and criticism in the UK,[18] although its content was not unexpected. The two decisions are consistent *inter se*, and coherent, but concerns may be expressed about the human rights and natural justice consequences of the unrelenting rigidity of the ECJ's approach.

RANKING OF THE JURISDICTIONAL RULES IN REGULATION 44/2001

A subject of great importance is the ranking or hierarchy of the **7–49** provisions of Regulation 44/2001 *inter se*, and also of ranking in a wider sense, *i.e.* delineation of the ambit of the Brussels regime, as now enshrined in the Regulation, in relation to other systems of jurisdiction.

Within Regulation 44, Article 23 (prorogation of jurisdiction) yields to Article 24 (submission to the jurisdiction), on the rationale that submission by a party, other than merely to contest the jurisdiction, amounts to acquiescence in the jurisdiction of that court, being a manifestation of "submission", which is a recognised principle of jurisdiction. When submission post-dates the making of a choice of court agreement, the appearance in a different court by both parties, or by one party at the behest of the other, is taken to constitute later agreement (the latest indication) of a party's intentions as to choice of court, superseding earlier (even written) agreement.[19]

Moreover, agreements made under Article 23 have no legal force if they are contrary to the protective rules enshrined in Articles 13 (insured persons), 17 (consumers) and 21 (employees); and such agreements cannot override the jurisdiction conferred exclusively on certain courts by Article 22.

The effect of the ECJ decision in *Gasser* is to subordinate Article 23 to Article 27. The ECJ held that the pre-eminent position of the court first seised shall *not* be dislodged by a choice of court agreement between the parties which selects a different court (unless and until the court first seised should decide that it has no jurisdiction). The principle of mutual trust and confidence demands that trust be reposed in the court of the Member State first seised to adjudicate upon its jurisdiction, competently and in good faith, and to defer to the court exclusively chosen, if persuaded that the prorogation clause is valid and applicable. This trust is likely to be tested by the lack of any requirement that the court first seised should arrive at its decision with reasonable speed.[20]

---

[18] *e.g.* T.C. Hartley, "The European Union and the Systematic Dismantling of the Common Law of Conflict of Laws" (2005) 54 ICLQ 813.

[19] *Elefanten Schuh GmbH v Jacqmain* Case 150/80 [1981] ECR 1671.

[20] See para.7–44, above.

Even though the growing jurisprudence of the ECJ continues to enlarge our understanding of the Brussels system and its reach, there still exist, however, situations which can be envisaged as realistic possibilities in respect of which the outcome is in doubt. For example, where parties, one or more of whom is domiciled in a Member State, have agreed that the court of a non-Member State is to have jurisdiction in any dispute arising between them, and one party reneges and has resort to an EU Member State court on a ground such as Article 5, Article 23 is silent on this scenario, but that which is produced surely is an *Owusu* situation, leading to preference being shown to the court first seised? Similarly, if parties, one or more of whom is domiciled in a Member State, have agreed that the courts of, say, Spain, are to have jurisdiction in any dispute arising between them, and one party reneges, having resort to a non-EU court on a ground available in the circumstances, the Regulation makes no provision. One could expect that the Spanish proceedings would continue, possibly concurrently with the non-EU proceedings, leading potentially to irreconcilable judgments. Whilst the Regulation system of *lis pendens* is geared to avoiding irreconcilable judgments within the European legal space, it cannot operate so as to avoid such irreconcilability as between a court in Europe, and a non-EU court. The Brussels rules may impinge on litigation outside Europe (*e.g.* so as to preclude it), but there is a limit to EU control. Concurrent litigation between the same parties, about the same matter, conducted in an EU State and a non-EU State, are likely to run in parallel, without touching, except perhaps if it should come to a question of enforcement of the resultant decree within an EU State, at which point Article 34.4 might be relevant.

Presumably a situation of choice by parties (EU or non-EU), of the court of one non-EU State, where one party reneges in favour of the court of another non-EU State, is beyond European control, and a court to which the dishonouring party is subject may be petitioned for an anti-suit injunction or similar remedy, if such remedy is at that court's disposal.

In any event, the manner of development of ECJ interpretative authority will have an influence on the popularity of the choice of London under exclusive choice of court clauses.[21] This is what is meant by the hidden reach of the Brussels rules.

---

[21] *e.g.* Hartley, above, at 823: "In view of these cases businessmen may no longer want to choose the courts of England as the forum for litigation under international contracts. The European court has succeeded in making them unattractive. New York might now appear a better alternative, since it is outside the reach of the ECJ."

DELINEATION OF THE EUROPEAN LEGAL SPACE

An equally difficult subject, and one which is engaging the atten- **7–50** tion of courts and writers, is the delineation of the area of operation, respectively, of the Brussels regime, and of the system established by pre-existing, national rules of jurisdiction. For example, when assessing the respective merits and demerits of the opposing systems of rules for dealing with cases of conflicting jurisdiction (*lis pendens* and *forum non conveniens*), a crucial debate concerns the delimitation of the area of operation of each system: where does one system end and the other begin?

Owusu v Jackson (t/a Villa Holidays Bal Inn Villas)[22]

The claimant, a "UK domiciliary", who rented from the first **7–51** defendant, also domiciled in "the UK", a holiday villa in Jamaica with access to a private beach, suffered severe injuries following a diving accident. Mr Owusu walked into the sea and, diving under the water when it was at waist level, struck his head against a submerged sandbank, sustaining grave injuries rendering him tetraplegic. A similar accident, with the same outcome, allegedly occurred two years earlier to another English holidaymaker.

In 2000, Mr Owusu brought an action in England against Mr Jackson, the owner of the holiday villa, in contract; and against several Jamaican companies, including the owner and licensed users of the beach, in tort. The ground of argument in contract was that there was an implied term that the beach would be reasonably safe, or free from hidden dangers; and in tort, that it was the duty of the owner/occupier of the beach to warn swimmers of the unseen hazard constituted by the submerged sandbank.

Proceedings were commenced in Sheffield District Registry of the High Court, served on Jackson in the UK, and leave granted to serve the proceedings out of the jurisdiction on the other defendants in Jamaica. In response, a number of the six defendants, including Jackson, applied to the English court for a declaration that it should not exercise its jurisdiction in relation to them, on the argument that the case had closer links with Jamaica, and that Jamaica constituted a competent forum in which the case might be tried more suitably for the interests of all the parties and the ends of justice.[23]

The judge at first instance held that he had no power to stay proceedings, and that the application to a dispute of the jurisdictional rules in the 1968 Brussels Convention depended, in

---

[22] [2005] 2 Q.B. 801. See also *DSM Anti-Infectives BV v SmithKlein Beecham plc* [2004] EWHC 1309.
[23] Para.15.

principle, on whether the defendant had its seat or was domiciled
in a Contracting State, and that the Convention applied to a
dispute between a defendant domiciled in a Contracting State and
a claimant domiciled in a non-Contracting State.[24]

Is it competent for an English/Scots court to accede to the plea
of *forum non conveniens* in these circumstances?[25] How "European" must a case be before the plea is incompetent? It is assumed
that in an entirely European case[26] (which, however, does not, it
seems, include an intra-UK case) the plea is certainly
inappropriate.

As noted above, the matter had been in doubt in the UK since
the case of *Re Harrods Buenos Aires Ltd*.[27] The judge at first
instance, having no power to refer the question to the ECJ, ruled
that it was not open to him to stay the action because Jackson was
domiciled in a Contracting State. Similarly, he held that he could
not stay the action in relation to the other defendants, notwithstanding the fact that they were Jamaican domiciled, because of the
risk of conflicting decisions in related actions. On that basis of
reasoning, he held (using non-Brussels terminology) that a court in
the UK was a more appropriate forum than one in Jamaica.

Jackson and the other defendants appealed to the Court of
Appeal, which stayed its proceedings in order to refer the following
question to the ECJ for a preliminary ruling[28]: "(1) Is it inconsistent with the Brussels Convention, where a claimant contends
that jurisdiction is founded on article 2, for a court of a contracting
state to exercise a discretionary power, available under its national
law, to decline to hear proceedings brought against a person
domiciled in that state in favour of the courts of a non-contracting
state, (a) if the jurisdiction of no other contracting state under the
1968 Convention is in issue, (b) if the proceedings have no
connecting factors to any other contracting state? (2) If the answer
to question 1(a) or (b) is yes, is it inconsistent in all circumstances
or only in some and if so which?"

In relation to the first question, the ECJ held that on the
interpretation and applicability of Article 2, nothing in the wording

[24] Para.16.
[25] *cf. Lubbe v Cape plc* [2000] 1 W.L.R. 1545, *per* Lord Bingham at 1563.
[26] Which, for present purposes, could be taken to be one where each available
contending court is a court in an EU Member State.
[27] [1992] Ch. 72. *Cf. American Motorists Insurance Co (AMICO) v Cellstar Corp*
[2003] 1 I.L.Pr. 22; *Travelers Casualty & Surety Co of Europe Ltd v Sun Life
Assurance Co of Canada (UK) Ltd* [2004] I.L.Pr. 50. The ECJ position as
expressed in *Owusu* was foreshadowed in relation to the Lugano Convention in
Mahme Trust Reg v Lloyds TSB Bank plc [2004] 2 Ll's Rep 637.
[28] This being competent in relation to the Brussels Convention; questions of
interpretation with regard to Reg.44 may be requested only by the House of
Lords.

of Article 2 suggested that application of the general rule of jurisdiction there laid down on the basis of the defendant's domicile in a Contracting State is subject to the condition that there should be a legal relationship involving only the courts of Contracting States. Article 2 is mandatory in nature (meaning that the English court cannot stay its proceedings against a defendant domiciled there when it takes the view that another forum in a non-Member State is more appropriate[29]), and there can be no derogation from the principle it lays down, except in the cases expressly provided for by the Convention. No exception on the basis of *forum non conveniens* was provided by the authors of the Convention. Respect for the principle of legal certainty would not be fully guaranteed if the court having jurisdiction under the Convention were allowed to apply the *forum non conveniens* doctrine. Application of the doctrine would undermine predictability, and affect the uniform application of the rules within the Community since the doctrine of *forum non conveniens* is recognized only in a limited number of Member States. The ECJ held that to permit any incursion of judicial discretion into the system would undermine the legal protection of persons established in the Community (although it is notable that the UK-domiciled defendant wished to have the case proceed in Jamaica in this instance).

In summary, it was held in *Owusu* that the Brussels Convention (and henceforth, by inference, the Regulation) precludes a court of a Contracting State from declining the jurisdiction conferred on it by Article 2, on the ground that the court of a non-Contracting/ Member State would be a more appropriate forum for the trial of the action, even if the jurisdiction of no other Contracting/Member State is in issue, or the proceedings have no connecting factors to any other Contracting/Member State.

This decision resolves, in a negative way, points of dubiety. Strictly the decision is concerned with the ambit of authority of Article 2, the key provision of *in personam* jurisdiction under Brussels. But to suggest faintly[30] that the plea might still be utilised in a future case in which jurisdiction has been founded on a special jurisdiction such as Article 5.1, seems to invite disappointment.[31]

---

[29] Para.20.

[30] But less faintly when there is evidence of an exclusive jurisdiction clause: *Konkola Copper Mines plc v Coromin* [2006] EWCA Civ. 5, *per* Rix, L.J. at para.71. See also *Viking Line ABP v The Internaitonal Transport Worker Fedration* [2006] I.L.Pr. 4.

[31] This case and these matters are treated by J. Harris, "Stays of Proceedings and the Brussels Convention" (2005) 54 ICLQ 933.

Owusu raises complex questions about the applicability of the Brussels regime given different permutations of circumstance and identity of parties.[32]

At a simple level, if the claimant sues a defendant on the basis of Article 2, it is his legitimate expectation that all the rules and principles of the Brussels regime should apply. However, to ascribe to the defendant a similar expectation seems at times inappropriate and disingenuous. There are many reasons, some of them to do with factual evidence, why *Owusu* arguably would have been more appropriately dealt with in Jamaica. On the other hand, for a claimant so grievously injured, speed of resolution of the dispute in some reasonably appropriate court is most desirable. However, as has been seen, the speed of the Brussels system can be subverted.

The key

7–52   The key to understanding the extent of the Brussels regime may be that of appreciating the special status of persons domiciled in Member States. It is axiomatic within the regime that such persons, in their litigations, as claimants or defendants, are bound by and have the benefit of Regulation 44.

In the face of desire on the part of the defendant to transfer the case to a non-EU forum, the ECJ in *Owusu*, as part of its insistence upon maintaining the coherence of the Brussels system, relied upon principles such as legal certainty, predictability, and the legal protection of persons established in the Community: "a defendant, who is generally better placed to conduct his defence before the courts of his domicile, would not be able, in circumstances such as those of the main proceedings, reasonably to foresee before which other court he may be sued."[33]

An EU domiciliary, however, may utilise "non-Brussels" grounds of jurisdiction against a non-EU domiciliary (or in a non-qualifying EU case, *per* Article 1 of the Regulation) and in such instances, would operate outside the Brussels regime, though he may enforce any resulting judgment in any EU Member State in which the defendant has assets, using the Brussels enforcement scheme (subject to bilateral international arrangements made under Article 59/72 of the Brussels Convention/Regulation). However, *Owusu* reveals that even a defendant domiciled in a non-EU Member State may require to submit to the Brussels rules even though, as in *Owusu*, he would prefer not to do so.

As against non-EU domiciliaries (or in cases against EU domiciliaries which fall outside the subject-matter scope of

---

[32] It was held by the ECJ in *Universal General Insurance Co v Group Josi Reinsurance Co SA* Case C-412/98 [2001] Q.B. 68, that the 1968 Convention applied even where the claimant was domiciled in a non-Contracting State, so long as the defendant was domiciled within a Contracting State.

[33] Case C-281/02, para.42.

Brussels, *per* Article 1), national rules (*i.e.* for Scotland, CJJA 1982, Schedule 8), including the plea of *forum non conveniens* can be used,[34] with the result that in *that* situation, a court in the UK might find itself deferring *sub nom forum non conveniens*, to a court in another EU Member State.[35]

In addition to the determining factor of domicile of the defendant is the indefeasible claim to jurisdiction put forward in Article 22, namely that based upon irrefutable territorial connection, regardless of domicile, *i.e.* in geographical terms land situated within the territorial bounds of the EU.

The UK, being an EU Member State but having, in conflict of laws terms at least, a generally Anglo-American legal background and preference for the use of judicial discretion in this and many other matters, and being a favoured place of resort for commercial litigation, inevitably will find itself a "Janus".[36]

CIVIL JURISDICTION AND JUDGMENTS ACT 1982

SCHEDULE 4[37]

There are three regimes regulating the rules in use in Scotland **7–53** concerning civil and commercial jurisdiction, namely:

(a) Regulation 44/2001 *per* Civil Jurisdiction and Judgments Act 1982, Schedule 1 (noting the special position of Denmark[38]);

(b) CJJA 1982, Schedule 4: the Modified Convention, allocating jurisdiction within the UK; and

(c) CJJA 1982, Schedule 8, being the residual, "national", Scottish rules.

Schedule 4 applies when the nature of the proceedings comes within the scope of the Brussels regime, *and* the defendant is "domiciled" in the "UK", *or* where special jurisdiction can be established (under rules 3 to 10), *or* the proceedings come under the exclusive jurisdiction rules contained in rule 11 *or* jurisdiction is prorogued under rule 12.

---

[34] Art.4.

[35] *Sarrio SA v Kuwait Investment Authority* [1999] 1 A.C. 32; and *Haji-Iannou v Frangos* [1999] 2 Ll's Rep 337. See *Morris on the Conflict of Laws* (6th ed.), pp.126–127.

[36] *i.e.* the vigilant gatekeeper, looking in two directions.

[37] As amended by Civil Jurisdiction and Judgments Order 2001 (SI 2001/3929), Sch.2.

[38] Though see Agreement between the European Community and Denmark on Jurisdiction and the Recognition and Enforcement of Judgments in Civil and Commercial Matters (OJ 2005 L299/62, November 16, 2005).

Schedule 4 has two main functions: first, where under Schedule 1 jurisdiction is allotted to the "UK" generally, but not to a particular territorial unit thereof,[39] Schedule 4 supplies the lack. Secondly, it is utilised in cases which arise within the UK, but are related to more than one territorial unit within the UK.

The provisions of Schedule 4 follow those of Schedule 1, and in rationale and detail are frequently the same, or similar. Amendment of Schedule 4 was effected by the CJJO 2001, so as to mirror, so far as appropriate,[40] the changes made to the jurisdiction provisions of Regulation 44/2001. In one instance (special jurisdiction in delict), the re-cast rule in Schedule 1, Article 5.3, extending jurisdiction in the case of anticipated wrongs provides for Schedule 1 cases what, from the outset, was the rule in Schedule 4.

However, there are certain differences between the detail of Schedule 1 and Schedule 4, for example the Community definition of "place of performance" (of a contract) provided in Article 5.1 of the Regulation was not extended, in the meantime, by the CJJO 2001 to Schedule 4.[41] Similarly, the presumption of exclusivity of choice of court clauses, inserted into the prorogation provision of the Regulation (Article 23), is not found in the equivalent prorogation provision of Schedule 4.

Certain "national" rules of jurisdiction of Member States were proscribed by the 1968 Brussels Convention, and now by the Regulation, and may not be used against persons domiciled in a Member State, or in a territorial unit within a Member State. This means that a Scots rule such as arrestment to found jurisdiction can be utilised only if the property sought to be arrested is situated in Scotland, and the owner/defender is not domiciled in Scotland, England, or in any other Member State. There remains, however, one ground of jurisdiction which does not feature in Schedule 1, but yet is not a proscribed ground, and therefore deserves mention as an example of a distinction in the rules between Schedules 1 and 4, namely, the special jurisdiction conferred on the parts of the UK *qua lex situs*, where the proceedings concern a debt secured on immoveable property, or which are brought to assert, declare, or determine proprietary or possessory rights, or rights of security, in

---

[39] *e.g.* for the provision of jurisdiction on the basis of the defendant's domicile under Sch.1, Art.2, the international allocation of jurisdiction *per* Sch.1 is satisfied by a finding that the defendant is domiciled in the UK. Thereafter, identification of the domicile of the defendant as, *e.g.* between Scotland, and England and Wales, is determined by Sch.4: *Daniel v Foster*, 1989 S.C.L.R. 378. *Parkes v Lintec International Ltd* [2006] CSIH 30 (Extra Division).

[40] *e.g.* consumer protection rules. *Cf.* the introduction by Reg.44/2001 of rules to protect employees, which is carried through by CJJO 2001 into Sch.4, r.10. On the other hand, protective rules for insured parties and beneficiaries, equivalent to those found in Sch.1 are *not* present in Sch.4.

[41] See "New Rules on Civil Jurisdiction", 2002 S.L.T. (News) 39 at 41.

or over movable property, or to obtain authority to dispose of movable property.[42]

Recourse cannot be had to the ECJ for interpretation of the provisions of Schedule 4.[43]

CIVIL JURISDICTION AND JUDGMENTS ACT 1982

SCHEDULE 8

Schedule 8 (the "residual" Scottish rules) takes effect, subject to **7–54** Regulation 44/2001, the Lugano and San Sebastian etc. Conventions (allocating jurisdiction among EU/EFTA Member States), and to Schedule 4 (the "Modified Convention", allocating jurisdiction within the UK).

The introduction of a set of rules for Scotland was recommended by the Maxwell Committee,[44] which recommended that the grounds of jurisdiction in use in Scotland be rationalised and set out in a single code.[45] The scheme of jurisdiction for Scotland introduced by the CJJA 1982, as now amended, by CJJO 2001[46] supersedes all existing rules of jurisdiction in matters covered by the Act, subject to retention of the *nobile officium* of the Court of Session. Although Schedule 8 contains the "Scottish rules", the key to operation of these rules is not the Scottish location of the putative litigation, but rather the personal/legal characteristic of the defender, or the subject matter of the litigation. The provisions of Schedule 8 are termed "rules", not "Articles".

Schedule 8 contains the native or idiosyncratic rules of Scots law which are capable of being utilised against persons not domiciled in an EU or EFTA Member State. A defence which can be offered for retention of these native grounds is that their effect may be mitigated by the plea of *forum non conveniens*, where it remains available and competent. There is another, unexceptional ground available at Scots common law (in cases concerning moveable property, jurisdiction being based on the situation thereof[47]), which may be used not only against persons domiciled in a non-Member State, but also against persons domiciled in any part of the UK.

---

[42] Sch.4, r.3(h).

[43] European Convention, Art.234. Also *Kleinwort Benson Ltd v City of Glasgow D.C.* [1997] 4 All E.R. 641.

[44] Report of the Scottish Committee on Jurisdiction and Enforcement (1980) ("Maxwell Report").

[45] Maxwell Report, paras 2.16 (h), 2.23–2.24.

[46] SI 2001/3929.

[47] As to jurisdiction in proprietary and possessory actions relating to moveables, based on presence of the moveable within the jurisdiction, see Anton and Beaumont, paras 10.41–10.42, pointing out that this may be used against a UK domiciliary. *Cf.* corresponding provision in Sch.4, r.3(h).

Some rules in Schedule 8 are identical to their counterpart in Schedule 1 (the Regulation)[48]; some rules in Schedule 8 remain in the original Brussels Convention form, unamended to reflect the modifications effected internationally by the Regulation[49]; and some rules in Schedule 8 are similar to those in Schedule 1, but not identical.[50]

Where the rules in Schedule 8 are derived from provisions contained in the Regulation, the Scottish courts must have regard to relevant principles and decisions handed down by the ECJ, and to the expert reports (Jenard and Schlosser etc).[51]

It is particularly important to be clear upon which ground of jurisdiction a Scots (or English) court has taken jurisdiction, given the growing jurisprudence derived from the ECJ, to the effect that if jurisdiction is laid on a Brussels ground, no other system (for example the discretionary plea of *forum non conveniens*) may be adopted by the court in its decision whether to take the case. In cases said to be founded on a Brussels ground, the *lis pendens* system and none other must obtain.[52]

English law—Civil Procedure Rules[53]

7-55 Unlike the Scottish "residual" rules, the English "residual" rules are not contained in a Schedule to the Civil Jurisdiction and Judgments Act 1982. Rather, the pre-existing rules remain operative where the Brussels regime does not apply. In such cases, jurisdiction is assumed on a wide and liberal basis, namely presence of the defendant within the jurisdiction; submission of the defendant to the jurisdiction of the court; and "service out" of the English jurisdiction in cases in which the Civil Procedure Rules permit such service at the discretion of the court.[54]

---

[48] *e.g.* Sch.8, r.2(c) (special jurisdiction in matters relating to a delict) and r.2(o) (multiple defenders), as to which see *Compagnie Commerciale Andre SA v Artibell Shipping Co. Ltd*, 1999 S.L.T. 1051.

[49] *e.g.* Sch.8, r.2(b) (special jurisdiction in matters relating to a contract).

[50] *e.g.* Sch.8, r.5 (exclusive jurisdiction). Notably, Sch.8, r.6 (prorogation) does not include a presumption of exclusivity.

[51] CJJA 1982 and 1991, s.20(5).

[52] See para.7-50, above.

[53] See J. Hill, *International Commercial Disputes in English Courts*, Ch.7.

[54] CPR 6.20; as to the exercise of the discretion, a guide was provided by Lord Goff in *Seaconsar v Bank Markazi* [1993] I Ll's Rep 236. See also *Konamaneni v Rolls Royce Industrial Power (India) Ltd* [2002] 1 W.L.R. 1269; *Morin v Bonhams and Brooks Ltd* [2003] 2 All E.R. (Comm) 36; *Apple Corps. Ltd v Apple Computer Inc.* [2004] EWHC 768; *Ophthalmic Innovations International Ltd v Ophthalmic Innovations International Inc* [2005] I.L.Pr. 10; *PT Pan-Indonesia Bank TBK v Marconi Communications International Ltd* [2005] 2 All E.R. (Comm.) 325; and *Ark Therapeutics Plc v True North Capital Ltd* [2006] 1 All E.R. (Comm.) 138.

PRE-TRIAL MEASURES AND PREVENTIVE MEASURES AND SAFEGUARDS[55]

The reason for the existence of such rules and remedies in any **7–56** legal system is, *first*, to obtain and preserve evidence for the litigation and, *secondly*, to preserve the defender's assets for satisfaction of the claim and expenses.

Preservation of evidence

Evidence may be obtained under authority of a commission and diligence authorised by the Scots court at common law. Further, the Administration of Justice (Scotland) Act 1972, section 1,[56] permits the Scots court in its discretion to order commission and diligence[57] for the inspection, photographing, etc. and custody of documents or other property, including land, which appear to the court to be property in respect of which a question may arise in civil proceedings (*i.e.* the process of "recovery" in Scots law, or "discovery" in English law).

The First Division in *Iomega Corp. v Myrica (UK) Ltd (No.2)*,[58] overruling *Dailey Petroleum Services Corp. v Pioneer Oil Tools Ltd*,[59] permitted material so recovered to be used in foreign proceedings.[60] While the party recovering evidence was impliedly restricted in his use of the evidence to the proceedings in respect of which it had been recovered, the court had power to permit such evidence to be used in other proceedings in Scotland or elsewhere, provided it was satisfied that such use was in the interests of justice.[61]

By section 19 of the Law Reform (Miscellaneous Provisions) (Scotland) Act 1985, the court is empowered to order a party to disclose such information as s/he possesses as to the identity of possible witnesses or defenders.

Preservation of assets

By virtue of Article 24 of the 1968 Brussels Convention,[62] and **7–57** Article 31 of Regulation 44/2001, application may be made to the court in Scotland for such provisional, including protective, mea-

---

[55] Aird and Jameson, Ch.18; G. Maher, "Provisional and Protective Measures in Respect of Foreign Proceedings", 1998 S.L.T. (News) 225.

[56] See, in cases of urgency, s.1(3), the "dawn raid": *British Phonographic Industry Ltd v Cohen*, 1983 S.L.T. 137 (application for such remedy granted *ex parte* where there is danger that the possessor is likely to remove or destroy the property).

[57] See *Union Carbide Corporation v BP Chemicals Ltd*, 1995 S.L.T. 972. See Aird and Jameson, paras 14.06 *et seq*, and 18.59. As to human rights challenge, see *Narden Services Ltd v Inverness Retail and Business Park Ltd*, 2006 S.L.T. 338.

[58] 1999 S.L.T 796.

[59] 1994 S.L.T. 757.

[60] See now extension of powers of Court of Session by CJJA 1982 (Provisional and Protective Measures) (Scotland) Order 1997 (SI 1997/2780).

[61] *per* L.P. Rodger at 804, admitting the lack of precedent.

[62] See CJJA 1982, s.25.

sures as may be available under the law of that State, even if the court of another Member State has jurisdiction as to the substance of the matter under the Regulation.[63] Hence, not only does the Brussels system provide an effective procedure for enforcing judgments, it provides also a system of safeguarding the claimant's interests before and during litigation or arbitration.[64]

In accordance with the decision of the ECJ in *Van Uden Maritime BV v Firma Deco-Line*,[65] authorisation of provisional measures under Article 31 of the Regulation must be founded upon a real connection between the subject matter of the measures sought and the territorial jurisdiction of the requested forum.

Scots and English remedies

7–58 Scots law offers the remedy of arrestment. By arrestment, a litigant may restrain the payment to his opponent of money or property, in the hands of a third party, due to him.[66] Except in the case of ships, arrestment does not operate directly on the assets of the opponent. Arrestment of the defender's property in the hands of a third party, to await the outcome of litigation, is a provisional security measure, frequently manifested in the attaching of a credit balance held by the defender at a bank, to the amount sought in the decree. There is a triangular relationship among arrester, arrestee and debtor. The arrestee (*e.g.* bank) must not permit operation on the account by the defender, and will be liable to the arrester should this occur.[67] While the debtor at the outset may be unaware that the creditor intends to effect, or has effected, arrestment on the dependence,[68] it is open to the debtor to apply to the court for recall of the arrestment on the ground that it is nimious and oppressive.[69]

---

[63] *G v Caledonian Newspapers Ltd*, 1995 S.L.T. 559 (even though the Scots court was being asked to make an order where there would have been no ground of action in Scots law, it might lend its aid to grant an order similar to the English one so long as there was a *prima facie* case in the originating jurisdiction). See *Iomega Corp. v Myrica (No.2)*, 1999 S.L.T. 796. And see CJJA 1982 (Provisional and Protective Measures) (Scotland) Order 1997 (SI 1997/2780).

[64] See *Van Uden Maritime BV v Firma Deco-Line* Case C-391/95 [1998] ECR 1-7091.

[65] See concerns expressed by Clarkson & Hill, *Jaffey on the Conflict of Laws*, at p.143, and P. Rogerson, *All ER Annual Review 2004* at p.97.

[66] *e.g. Hydraload Research and Developments Ltd v Bone Connell & Baxters Ltd*, 1996 S.L.T. 219; *Dramgate Ltd v Tyne Dock Engineering Ltd*, 1999 S.L.T. 1392; and *China National Star Petroleum Co. v Tor Drilling (UK) Co.*, 2002 S.L.T. 1339. Cf. English garnishee order, and contrast English (Mareva) "freezing injunction".

[67] *cf.* duty of care owed by a bank in terms of an English freezing order: *Customs & Excise Commissioners v Barclays Bank* [2004] EWCA Civ. 1555.

[68] A court order granting (until a final court decision) a temporary security over goods, or funds, *e.g.* in a bank account, held on behalf of the defender by a third party (Debt Arrangement and Attachment (Scotland) Act 2002, Appendix 2).

[69] *Fab-Tek Engineering Ltd v Carillion Construction Ltd*, 2002 S.L.T. (Sh. Ct) 113.

Arrestment on the dependence depends upon litigation having commenced. *Dramgate Ltd v Tyne Dock Engineering Ltd*[70] demonstrates that, in a conflict of laws situation, the provisional safeguard of arrestment on the dependence cannot be sought or granted unless and until the jurisdiction of the Scots court over the defender is properly founded. [71]

Other remedies in Scots law are inhibition (which prevents a defender from disposing of, or burdening, his heritable property to the prejudice of the inhibitor), and interdict (interim or permanent) granted, like the English injunction, against "reasonable apprehension of wrong".[72]

English remedies, available from the High Court and above, of freezing orders (formerly "Mareva injunctions")[73] and search warrants (formerly "Anton Piller orders"[74]), exist respectively to prevent dissipation or removal of a defendant's assets, or to permit inspection of premises to discover documents relevant to the forthcoming litigation.

The "worldwide Mareva" until recently meant an injunction preventing the defendant from disposing of his assets *wherever situated*, granted in the discretion of the English forum in a case where, in its view, the remedy was merited, and where the principal litigation was to take place in England or, if the litigation were to take place abroad, the case was justiciable in England.[75] The English court now has power to make such order in support of foreign arbitral[76] or judicial[77] proceedings, even though the issue is

---

[70] 1999 S.L.T. 1392.

[71] In *Dramgate* a warrant for arrestment on the dependence could not be effective unless there had first been a warrant for arrestment to found jurisdiction. Hence provisional measures while available, in principle, in a jurisdiction, cannot be utilised unless and until jurisdiction over the defender of the granting court has been established. The safeguard sought was premature and contained an inherent vice. Absence of malice made no difference. All formalities must be strictly complied with in matters of diligence: *Anglo-Dutch Petroleum International Inc. v Ramco Energy Plc*, 2006 S.L.T. 334.

[72] Aird and Jameson, paras 18.02, and 18.45.

[73] *Mareva Compania Naviera SA v International Bulk Carriers SA* [1975] 2 Ll's Rep 509. Also *Z Ltd v A–Z* [1982] 1 All E.R. 556; *Babanaft International Co SA v Bassatne* [1989] 2 W.L.R. 232; *Rosseel NV v Oriental Commercial Shipping (UK) Ltd* [1990] 1 W.L.R. 1387; *S & T Bau Trading v Nordling* [1997] 3 All E.R. 718; *Maimann v Maimann* [2001] I.L.Pr 27; and *Bank of China v NBM LLC* [2002] 1 All E.R. 717.

[74] *Anton Piller K.G. v Manufacturing Processes Ltd* [1976] Ch. 55; *Republic of Haiti v Duvalier* [1989] 1 All E.R. 456; *Derby & Co. Ltd v Weldon (No.1)* [1989] 1 All E.R. 469; and *Balkanbank v Taher (No.2)* [1995] 2 All E.R. 904. This is a burgeoning area of development in English commercial and conflict rules. See e.g. *Camdex International Ltd v Bank of Zambia (No.2)* [1997] 1 All E.R. 728; and *A/S D/S Svenborg v Wansa etc.* [1997] 1 C.L. 122.

[75] Clarkson & Hill, pp.141–143.

[76] Arbitration Act 1996, s.2.

[77] CJJA 1982, s.25(1).

not justiciable in England.[78] The English court may grant an injunction restraining a party from leaving the country pending proceedings.[79]

Lord Donaldson in *Derby & Co. Ltd v Weldon (Nos 3 & 4)*[80] said "[w]e live in a time of rapidly growing commercial and financial sophistication and it behoves the courts to adapt their practices to meet the current wiles of those defendants who are prepared to devote as much energy to making themselves immune to the courts' orders as to resisting the making of such orders on the merits of their case."

Summary 7—Jurisdiction

1. Allocation of jurisdiction

7–59 There are three regimes regulating the rules in use in Scotland concerning civil and commercial jurisdiction, namely:

(a) Regulation 44/2001, *per* Civil Jurisdiction and Judgments Act 1982, Schedule 1 (noting the special position of Denmark[81]) (effecting international allocation);

(b) CJJA 1982, Schedule 4: the Modified Convention (allocating jurisdiction within the UK); and

(c) CJJA 1982, Schedule 8 (the residual, "national", Scottish rules, available only where the defender cannot be sued under (a) or (b) above).

2. Allocation of international jurisdiction among EU Member States is governed by Council Regulation 44/2001:

(a) The main ground of jurisdiction is "domicile" of the defendant (Article 2), which for this purpose, for the UK, is

---

[78] *Credit Suisse Fides Trust SA v Cuoghi* [1997] 3 All E.R. 724 (departing from the decision in *The Siskina* [1979] 2 A.C. 210 which had been followed in *Mercedes Benz AG v Leiduck* [1995] 3 All E.R. 929. See in development of the topic, *Channel Tunnel Group Ltd v Balfour Beatty Construction Ltd* [1993] A.C. 334). Consider *Republic of Haiti v Duvalier* [1989] 1 All E.R. 456. The effect of *Van Uden* may be to inhibit an English forum's use of this injunction in Brussels cases: see Clarkson & Hill, p.143. See also *Dadourian Group International Inc. v Simms* [2006] EWCA Civ. 399.

[79] *Morris v Murjani* [1996] 2 All E.R. 384; and *B v B* [1997] 3 All E.R. 258 (consistorial).

[80] [1989] 2 W.L.R. 412 at 420. Also *El Ajou v Dollar Land Holdings (No.1)* [1994] 2 All E.R. 685; and *Eliades v Lewis (No. 1)* [2005] EWHC 2966.

[81] Though see Agreement between the European Community and Denmark on Jurisdiction and the Recognition and Enforcement of Judgments in Civil and Commercial Matters (OJ 2005 L299/62, November 16, 2005).

defined in CJJO 2001, Schedule 1, paragraph 9 (amending CJJA 1982, section 41).

(b) There are alternative "special" grounds of jurisdiction, for example in matters relating to contract and delict (Article 5).

(c) There are protective jurisdictional rules for disadvantaged parties (Articles 9 to 21).

(d) Article 22 contains rules conferring exclusive jurisdiction on a court of a Member State in specified cases, for example proceedings which have as their object rights *in rem* in immoveable property.

(e) Article 23 permits prorogation of jurisdiction by parties.

(f) Article 24 endows with jurisdiction the court of a Member State to which a party has entered appearance, provided appearance was not solely for the purpose of contesting the jurisdiction.

(g) The *lis pendens* system of priority of process (Articles 25—30) regulates problems of conflicting jurisdiction.

(h) The hierarchy of provisions is as follows: Article 22 takes precedence over Articles 23 and 24. Article 24 takes precedence over Article 23. Articles 9—21 take precedence over Article 23, but are subordinate to Article 24. The effect of the ECJ decision in *Grasser* is to subordinate Article 23 to Article 27. In terms of personal jurisdiction, Article 2 is the pre-eminent ground to which all others are derogations.

(i) Cases handed down by the ECJ in 2004/05 have the effect of strictly guarding the Brussels system, with the aim of avoiding irreconcilable judgments within the EU legal area.

3. The Hague Conference in 2005 concluded the Convention on Choice of Court Agreements.

4. Resolution of conflicts of jurisdiction occurring "outside the Brussels regime" are treated by Scots and English courts as a matter arising within judicial discretion, expressed in the acceding to, or refusing of, a plea by the defender of *forum non conveniens*.

5. "Outside the Brussels regime", the Scots/English courts have power to order a party who is subject to Scots/English jurisdiction to desist from commencing or continuing proceedings abroad. This power is expressed by means of grant of an anti-suit injunction.

6. Scots and English law provide (different) mechanisms to safeguard the defender's assets pending litigation, and for preserving evidence.

CHAPTER 8

EVIDENCE AND PROCEDURE

INTRODUCTION

There is a basic and crucial distinction between *substance or right* **8–01** on the one hand and *procedure or remedy* on the other.

Substance or right is governed by the *lex causae*, the law which governs the right, such as the applicable law of contract or delict, the *lex successionis*, etc. For example, in the case of *Re Cohn*,[1] though both the German and the English rules of succession in the case of *commorientes* (deaths in a common calamity) were held to be substantive, the English court, applying the English conflict rule, deferred to the German rule of the *lex causae*. In the case of *Re Fuld*[2] any requirement that a testator have "a free view" and that he be not unduly influenced as to the terms of his will, was regarded as a substantive rule, and therefore the German rule of the domicile (probably at testing rather than at death, though this cannot be affirmed beyond doubt, because Fuld was held to be domiciled at all material times in Germany) was applied. Scarman J. assigned burden of proof in this instance to the category of procedure—the English Probate Court "must in all matters of burden of proof follow scrupulously its own *lex fori*"[3]—though this is not a categorisation about which all the authorities agree.

Procedure or remedy is governed by the *lex fori*. Foreign rules of procedure are ignored by a Scots forum. The reason for this rule was explained in *De La Vega v Vianna*[4] by Lord Tenterden, who said that if a person comes to raise an action in England he must take the (procedural) law as he finds it; he cannot enjoy an advantage over a native-born or resident litigant, nor should he be deprived of advantages normally available.

Further, it is feared that if a Scots or English forum should attempt to apply foreign procedural law, it may tear it out of context, misunderstand and misapply it. It would not be suitable to

---

[1] [1945] Ch. 5.
[2] [1968] P. 675.
[3] *ibid.* at 697.
[4] (1830) 1 B. & Ad. 284.

have litigations proceeding in Scotland according to a variety of legal systems' rules of evidence and procedure. Moreover, how "foreign" would a case have to be before application of foreign procedure seemed fair?

Hence, although a party sometimes may be able to choose the forum to his perceived best advantage, s/he is not entitled to choose the procedure which that forum uses to resolve the dispute.[5]

There is a danger that a forum may be too quick to categorise a foreign rule as procedural. This is a means of justifying disapplication of a rule of the *lex causae*. Professor Anton[6] has said that justice in conflict cases occasionally may be rough, but that the worst cases may be eliminated by a careful delimitation of what is procedural. The wording of a foreign rule may be deceptive, and the forum must look to the true nature of the rule.

Sometimes Parliament has intervened, as for example in the case of foreign limitation of actions rules, where the English and Scottish courts are directed to apply the prescription/limitation rule of the *lex causae* without attempting to classify its nature either by Scots law or by the foreign law.[7]

MEANING OF "PROCEDURE"

8–02 There are few definitions of procedure. One which may serve is *per* Lush L.J. in *Poyser v Minors*,[8] which is as follows: "'[p]ractice' . . . like 'procedure' . . . denotes the mode of proceeding by which a legal right is enforced, as distinguished from the law which gives or defines the right."[9] Lord Murray in *Naftalin v LMS Railway*[10] described procedure thus: "[n]o doubt procedure is a term of somewhat indefinite connotation but in his [Dicey's] opinion the true view is that any rule of law which affects, not the enforcement of a right, but the nature of the right itself, does not come under the head of procedure; or, in other words, is not governed by the *lex fori*."

Writers are sceptical of the possibility of making a definitive categorisation between matters of substance and matters of procedure.[11] The term "procedure" is used in a wide sense to cover

---

[5] Even though he/they may try to do so: *Hamlyn & Co. v Talisker Distillery* (1894) 21 R. (H.L.) 21, *per* Lord Herschell L.C. at 24.

[6] Anton with Beaumont, p.743.

[7] See para, 8–06, below (relating to 1984 Acts).

[8] (1881) 7 Q.B.D. 329 at 333.

[9] Another explanation can be found *per* Lord Brougham in *Don v Lippmann* (1837) 5 Cl. & F. (HL) at 13–14.

[10] 1933 S.L.T. 193 at 200.

[11] See W.W. Cook, "Substance and Procedure in the Conflict of Laws" (1932–1933) 42 Yale L.J. 333; and J.M. Carruthers, "Substance and Procedure in the Conflict of Laws: A Continuing Debate in relation to Damages", 2004 (53) ICLQ 691, at 694.

forms of action and remedies, including the laws of evidence, and diligence[12]; of this one can be confident. However, subjects such as actionability, and title to sue have a hybrid quality, and with regard to other topics, for example onus of proof and presumptions, opinions vary as to the proper categorisation.

MISCELLANEOUS MATTERS PERTAINING TO LITIGATION

ACTIONABILITY

The question whether an action may be raised at all is determined **8–03** by the *lex fori*. This can be seen, for example, from the Scottish and English prohibition upon suits for damages for breach of promise of marriage, no matter the identity and content of the law governing the promise.

However, so to confine the meaning of actionability is to emphasise the preliminary, procedural side of an issue which soon becomes substantive. Thus, a rule providing for inter-spousal immunity from suit, if part of the "applicable law" of delict, as determined in accordance with the Private International Law (Miscellaneous Provisions) Act 1995, Part III will preclude an action in delict in Scotland, unless re-characterised as, for example, a matter of family law, or judged contrary to public policy.[13] Similarly, where the Scots applicable law of contract confers a *jus quaesitum tertio*, the party so entitled by the *lex causae* may enforce his right against a contracting party in England (or elsewhere), whether or not he would be so entitled under the domestic law of England,[14] so long as the defendant was subject to the jurisdiction of the courts of England, and assuming that the foreign *lex fori* classifies the point as one of substance in contract, that its public policy is not outraged and that no other conflict rule of its own intervenes.[15]

Actionability in the broader sense of whether a cause of action arises (as determined by the *lex causae* identified by the *lex fori*)

---

[12] Including appeals (R.D. Leslie, *Stair Memorial Encyclopaedia*, p.359, arguing by analogy from *Whitworth Street Estates (Manchester) Ltd v James Miller & Partners Ltd* [1970] A.C. 583, where the point at issue was whether the award in an arbitration was subject to appeal to the courts, a matter classified as being part of the "curial law of the arbitration", *i.e.* of its procedure: *cf. Hamlyn v Talisker Distillery* (1894) 21 R. (H.L.) 21).

[13] Such an immunity was removed from Scots domestic law by the Law Reform (Husband and Wife) Act 1962. The effect in policy terms of the removal from the law of the forum of an equivalent rule to that of the *lex causae* which is under consideration is hard to predict.

[14] As to which, see now Contract (Rights of Third Parties) Act 1999.

[15] As, for example, where its own conflict rules of contract and property might collide in a *Romalpa* question. See para.17–16, below.

between claimant and defender is a substantive matter for decision by the *lex causae* as identified by and proved to the forum.

FORM OF ACTION

8–04 This is purely a matter of procedure to be decided by the *lex fori*.[16]

TITLE TO SUE/PARTIES

8–05 Title to sue and liability to be sued each contain elements both of the substantive and the procedural; the law governing the right which indicates the party who has the right or title to sue and the party who should be called as defender.[17] It is necessary, of course, to comply with the procedural requirements of the *lex fori*. For reasons of the (procedural) law of the forum, certain bodies or persons may be immune from suit, or prohibited from suing.[18]

The forum's requirements on occasion may reflect anxieties about the difficulties likely to be encountered in the place of enforcement. Thus in *Brianchon v Occidental Petroleum (Caledonia) Ltd*,[19] it was thought prudent for the Court of Session to appoint a curator *ad litem* to represent the children of a victim of the Piper Alpha disaster in litigation in Scotland where the principal litigant was their mother, in order that no question of conflict of interest should be raised later in the American courts. On the other hand, restrictions imposed by the *foreign* law upon a party's capacity to sue may be disregarded in Scotland as being local (of application only in the foreign jurisdiction), or penal.[20]

Unusual situations may arise, as for example, in *Toprak Enerji Sanayi AS v Sale Tilney Technology plc*,[21] in which the plaintiff foreign company ceased to exist during the course of the proceedings. In *Bumper Development Corporation v Commissioner of Police of the Metropolis*,[22] the Court of Appeal recognised, in accordance with the principle of comity of nations, the title to sue of an Hindu temple which had legal personality under its *lex situs* (its proper officer being responsible in the English process for security for costs). Novelty was no objection since the matter remained within the discretion and power of the forum.

---

[16] *Hansen v Dixon* (1906) 23 T.L.R. 56; *Phrantzes v Argenti* [1960] 2 Q.B. 19.
[17] *cf. FMC Corporation v Russell*, 1999 S.L.T. 99. See E.B. Crawford, "The Adjective and the Noun: Title and Right to Sue in International Private Law" 2000 J.R. 347.
[18] See Ch.7, above.
[19] 1990 S.L.T. 322.
[20] *Bernaben & Co. v Hutchison* (1902) 18 Sh.Ct. Rep. 72.
[21] [1994] 3 All E.R. 483. See also *Kamouh v AEI International Ltd* [1980] 1 Q.B. 199.
[22] [1991] 4 All E.R. 638.

The following cases may require special consideration: assignees,[23] foreign tutrix or "next friend",[24] ministerial representatives of foreign sovereign,[25] partnerships and companies.[26]

Prescription

From a conflict standpoint, the important distinction is between **8–06** those rules concerning the effect of lapse of time which extinguish the right (rules of prescription), and those which merely bar the remedy (rules of limitation).[27]

An early example in this area is *Huber v Steiner*[28] in which the English court interpreted the rule of the French *Code de Commerce* (that actions on promissory notes "prescribe themselves" after five years, reckoning from the day of protest if there had been no judgment or acknowledgment of the debt in that period), as no more than a limitation of the remedy and not an extinction of the contract, and therefore concluded that the enforceability of the French contract (in England) was governed by the limitation rule of the *lex fori*.[29]

In Scots domestic law, the rules on prescription were rationalised by the Prescription and Limitation (Scotland) Act 1973, as amended by the Prescription and Limitation (Scotland) Act 1984, section 4.[30] The choice of law rule contained now in section 23A requires the Scottish forum to apply, subject to public policy, any relevant rules upon extinction of obligations of the *lex causae*, in preference to domestic rules.[31]

---

[23] *Tayler v Scott* (1847) 9 D. 1504; *O'Callaghan v Thomond* (1810) 3 Taunt. 82.

[24] *Jones v Somervell's Trs*, 1907 S.C. 545.

[25] *Yzquierdo v Clydebank Engineering & Shipbuilding Co. Ltd* (1902) 4 F. (H.L.) 31.

[26] *Muir v Collett* (1862) 24 D. 1119; *Von Hellfeld v Rechnitzer* [1914] 1 Ch. 748; *Establissement Baudelot v Graham & Co. Ltd* [1953] 2 Q.B. 271; *Bullock v Caird* [1875] Q.B. 276; and *General Steam Navigation Co. v Guillou* (1843) 11 M. & W. 877.

[27] *The Westminster Bank Ltd v McDonald*, 1955 S.L.T. (Notes) 73, *per* Lord Hill Watson at 73: "[i]n considering whether a foreign law of a prescriptive nature is to be applied to a contract, a distinction must be drawn between a provision of that law which extinguishes a right and a provision which merely limits the time within which the right may be enforced"; *Rodriguez v Parker* [1967] 1 Q.B. 116.

[28] (1835) 2 Bing. N.C. 202–Tindal CJ; also [1835–42] All E.R.159.

[29] Contrast, therefore, the modern position under Foreign Limitation Periods Act 1984 and Prescription and Limitation (Scotland) Act 1973, as amended; consider also to the same effect Rome I, Art.10(1)(d).

[30] Inserting into the 1973 Act, s.23A.

[31] It should be noted that the Scottish statutory provision, unlike the English one, is limited to "obligations" and does not include "property rights"; see J.M. Carruthers, *The Transfer of Property in the Conflict of Laws* (2005), para.8.55. Also D.M. Walker, *The Law of Prescription and Limitation of Actions in Scotland* (1984).

Looking then at the matter from a Scottish perspective, the following would appear to be the position with regard to Scots domestic law.

Positive prescription

8–07   This involves acquisition of title to, or interest in, property (usually land) and is a matter of substance governed by the *lex situs*.[32]

Negative prescription[33]

8–08   The long negative prescription extinguishes an obligation. Hence, it is a matter of substance and is governed by the proper law of the right.

The 1973 Act has replaced a variety of earlier short prescriptions with two extinctive prescriptions, to which later were added two more. All of these, being, it is submitted, substantive in nature, will apply where the *lex causae* is Scots.

Limitation

8–09   At common law, the nature of the limitation had to be ascertained by the forum by referring to the (foreign) statute or rule in question to find out whether it affected the substance (and therefore the existence of the right) no matter where a party might seek to vindicate it, or whether it was merely a rule of procedure, effective only within the territory covered by the statute in question.[34] However, as noted above, since the coming into effect of the Prescription and Limitation (Scotland) Act 1984, the matter has been governed by statute,[35] and thereby assigned to the category of the substantive (insofar at least as concerns obligations).

The Legal Affairs Committee of the European Parliament, having noted "clear and significant divergence in respect of limita-

---

[32] See J.M. Carruthers, *The Transfer of Property in the Conflict of Laws* (2005), paras 8.52–8.66.

[33] *Alexander v Badenoch* (1843) 6 D. 322; *Low* (1893) 1 S.L.T. 43; [1894] 1 Ch. 147; *Higgins v Ewing's Trs*, 1925 S.C. 440; and *Stirling's Trs v Legal & General Assurance Society*, 1957 S.L.T. 73.

[34] *Huber v Steiner* (1835) 2 Bing. N.C. 202; *British Linen Co. v Drummond* (1830) 10 B.C. 903; *Don v Lippmann* (1837) 2 Sh. and Macl. 682; *Harris v.Quine* (1869) L.R. 4 Q.B. 653; *Goodman v LNWR* (1877) 15 S.L.R. 449; *McElroy v McAllister*, 1949 S.C. 110.

[35] Foreign Limitation Periods Act 1984 (England); Prescription and Limitation (Scotland) Act 1984, s.4 (Scotland). Both rules are subject to the public policy of the forum. The Legal Affairs Committee of the European Parliament in 2006 called upon the European Commission to recommend that in regard to personal injury and fatal accident claims in cross-border litigation, there should be a general limitation period throughout Europe of four years, under certain exceptions.

tion periods among Member States (*e.g.* as to commencement and running of period, interruption and suspension), has requested[36] the Commission to submit a legislative proposal on limitation in respect of personal injury and fatal accident claims in cross-border litigation. The Report is likely to be adopted in Plenary Session in autumn, 2006, whereupon the Commission will decide whether, and how, to take matters forward.

CITATION AND SERVICE OF WRITS

Service of documents within the EU

Service of documents within the EU[37] now is governed by **8–10** Council Regulation (EC) No. 1348/2000 on the Service in the Member States of Jud8icial and Extrajudicial Documents in Civil or Commercial Matters.[38] This instrument, the aim of which is to improve efficiency and speed in the transmission of such documents,[39] in order to aid the proper functioning of the internal market, entered into force on May 31, 2001, and takes precedence over the 1965 Hague Convention on the Service Abroad of Judicial and Extra-Judicial Documents in Civil and Commercial Matters (to which the UK is a party).[40]

In terms of the Regulation, transmission of documents is effected directly between "local bodies" (termed the transmitting and receiving agencies), rather than through the medium of "central bodies", as provided in the 1965 Convention. While in Scotland the central body is the Justice Department of the Scottish Executive, the transmitting agencies (*i.e.* local bodies) are the messengers-at-arms and accredited solicitors.

The document to be transmitted must have appended to it a form completed in the language of the Member State addressed, or in another language indicated by that Member State to be acceptable.[41] The use of all appropriate means of transmission are permitted,[42] provided that the content of the document received is

---

[36] See Report PE 367, 972v03–00.

[37] Excepting Denmark at the outset, but see now Council of the European Union Press Release 8402/06, noting decision approving agreement to extend to Denmark the provisions of Reg. 1348/2000 (Council Decision 6924/06).

[38] See generally *http://europa.eu.int/comm/justice—home/fsj/civil/documents*.

[39] The Regulation shall not apply where the address of the person to be served with the document is not known (Art.1.2).

[40] In respect of which, see Anton with Beaumont, pp.756–758. As to interrelationship of Art.27.2 of the 1968 Brussels Convention and the 1965 Hague Convention, see *Scania Finance France SA v Rockinger Specialfabrik GmbH*, ECJ 13 October 2005.

[41] Art.4.3.

[42] Art.4.2.

true and faithful to that of the document forwarded, and that all information in it is legible. The receiving agency (which must send a receipt within seven days to the transmitting agency[43]) will serve, or have served, the document in accordance with the law of the Member State addressed, or by a particular form requested by the transmitting agency, unless such a method is incompatible with the law of that Member State.[44] The receiving agency must inform the addressee that s/he may refuse to accept the document if it is in a language other than the official language of the Member State addressed, or a language of the transmitting state which the addressee understands.[45] When service has been effected, a certificate of completion will be sent to the transmitting agency. If it does not prove possible to effect service within one month of receipt, the receiving agency shall inform the transmitting agency by means of a standard form certificate.[46]

The date of service shall be the date on which it is served in accordance with the law of the Member State addressed.[47] However, where a document must be served within a particular period in the context of proceedings to be brought or pending in the Member State of origin, the date to be taken into account with respect to the applicant shall be that fixed by the law of that Member State.[48]

Other means of service remain competent: by consular or diplomatic channels,[49] post,[50] or direct service through the judicial officers, officials or other competent persons of the Member State addressed.[51]

Where a writ of summons has been transmitted under the provisions of the Regulation, and the defendant has not appeared, judgment shall not be given until it is established that the document was served by a method prescribed by the internal law of the Member State addressed for the service of documents in domestic actions upon persons within its territory; or the document was actually delivered to the defendant, or to his residence, by another method provided for by the Regulation; and that in either case, service or delivery was effected in sufficient time to enable

---

[43] Art.6.1.
[44] Art.7.1.
[45] Art.5.1; see also Art.8.
[46] Art.7.1.
[47] Art.9.1.
[48] Art.9.2.
[49] Arts 12 and 13.
[50] Art.14. The Regulation does not establish any hierarchy between the method of transmission and service under Arts 4 to 11 and that in Art.14. It is therefore possible to serve a judicial document by one or other or both of those methods: *Plumex v Young Sports NV* Case C473/04 [2006] (ECJ).
[51] Art.15.

the defendant to defend.[52] However, each Member State shall be free to make it known to the Commission that the judge, notwithstanding Article 19.1, may give judgment, even if no certificate of service or delivery has been received, if three conditions have been fulfilled, namely: (a) the document was transmitted by one of the methods provided for in the Regulation; (b) a period of not less than six months, considered adequate by the judge in the particular case, has elapsed since the date of the transmission; and (c) no certificate of any kind has been received, even though every reasonable effort has been made to obtain it through the competent authorities of the Member State addressed.[53]

Extrajudicial documents may be transmitted for service in another Member State in accordance with the Regulation.[54]

The operation of Regulation 1348/2000 is under review, but a report adopted by the EU Commission in 2004 concluded that its effect had been generally to expedite the transmission and service of documents.

Service of documents outside the EU

As regards service of documents in non-EU states, citation **8–11** "furth of Scotland" is governed by the Rules of Court,[55] assuming that the method of service does not contravene the local law or contradict the 1965 Hague Convention, where applicable.

EVIDENCE

All questions as to the requirements, extent and sufficiency of **8–12** evidence are determined by the *lex fori* alone, irrespective of the governing law of the matter. There is, however, an elaboration, namely, the particular rule in relation to contract contained in Rome I, Article 14(2).[56]

---

[52] Art.19.1.

[53] Art.19.2. See also Art.19.4 concerning expiry of time for appeal after non-appearance by the defendant. Consider also the inevitable inter-relationship between the detail of this Regulation, and Council Regulation 44/2001, Art.34.2 (defence to enforcement on grounds of natural justice).

[54] Art.16.

[55] See Act of Sederunt (Rules of the Court of Session 1994) 1994 (SI 1994/1443), r.16.2 (service furth of UK). For rules concerning service, intimation and diligence generally, see 1994 Rules, Ch.16. For Sheriff Court actions, see Act of Sederunt (Sheriff Court Ordinary Cause Rules) 1993 (SI 1993/1956), r.5.5 (service on persons furth of Scotland), as amended by Act of Sederunt (Ordinary Cause, Summary Application, Summary Cause, and Small Claim Rules) Amendment (Miscellaneous) 2004 (SSI 2004/197), r.2(4). See in detail Layton & Mercer, *European Civil Practice* (2004), Ch.4.

[56] "A contract or an act intended to have legal effect may be proved by any mode of proof recognised by the law of the forum or by any of the laws referred to in Article 9 under which that contract or act is formally valid, provided that such mode of proof can be administered by the forum" (Art.14(2)). Contrast traditional approach taken in Private International Law (Miscellaneous Provisions) Act 1995, s.14(3)(b).

The province of the governing law extends to all matters which involve substance rather than procedure. A distinction must be drawn between "the facts to be proved" (determined by the *lex causae*) and "the proof of the facts" (governed by the *lex fori*).[57]

The "whole point" of an evidential rule was said in *Re Fuld*[58] to be one "concerned with the approach required of the court to the evidence submitted for its consideration".

In *Immanuel v Denholm & Co.*[59] the question for the Scots court was whether the information contained in a bill of lading pertaining to a contract with a Danish proper law was conclusive on this matter, a point on which the *lex causae* and the *lex fori* differed. Since that point was classified by the forum as one of evidence, the Scots rule prevailed. There are many other cases which illustrate the rule.[60]

The following are particular aspects of the rule, the question in each case being whether the point truly involves substance or procedure[61]:

   (a) the *lex fori* determines whether or not a document is admissible in evidence, irrespective of whether or not it may be so under the proper law or any other law[62];

   (b) the *lex fori* determines whether extrinsic evidence will be allowed with a view to varying the terms of a contract, irrespective of the governing law, but its admissibility *to interpret* the terms of a contract is determined by the proper/applicable law of the contract[63];

   (c) at common law, proof of a death abroad was a matter of fact to be decided by the *lex fori*,[64] but in terms of the Presumption of Death (Scotland) Act 1977, section 10, where a foreign judgment of declaration of presumption of death emanates from a court in a foreign country in which

---

[57] *The Gaetano & Maria* (1882) 7 P.D. 137: "[n]ow the manner of proving the facts is matter of evidence, and, to my mind, is matter of procedure, but the facts to be proved are not matters of procedure; they are the matters with which the procedure has to deal", *per* Brett L.J. at 144.

[58] [1968] P. 675, *per* Scarman J. at 697.

[59] (1887) 15 R. 152.

[60] *Leroux v Brown* (1852) C.B. 801; *Bain v Whitehaven & Furness Junction Ry Co.* (1850) 3 H.L. 1; *Bristow v Sequeville* (1850) 5 Ex. 275; *Mahadervan* [1964] P. 233; *Fuld No. 3* [1968] P. 675; and *Caltex Singapore Pte Ltd v B.P. Shipping Ltd* [1996] 1 Ll's Rep. 286.

[61] *cf. Mahadervan*, above.

[62] *cf. Henaff v Henaff* [1966] 1 W.L.R. 598.

[63] *cf.* generally *Thomson* (1917) 33 Sh.Ct Rep. 84. See now for Scots domestic law, Contract (Scotland) Act 1997.

[64] *Simpson's Trs v Fox*, 1951 S.L.T. 412. See also *Spenceley* [1892] P.255; *Schulhof* [1948] P. 66; *Dowds* [1948] P. 256; and *Kamouh v AEI International Ltd* [1980] 1 Q.B. 199.

the person was domiciled or habitually resident on the date when he was last known to be alive, this raises a (rebuttable) presumption of death.

Professional conduct investigation/disciplinary procedure in respect of the medical profession has been held by the Privy Council[65] to be governed by English law (even though in the case in question the disciplinary committee sat in Glasgow), with the aim of having a single set of rules of evidence no matter where the committee might sit.[66] Similarly, British Army discipline by court-martial, wherever held, is governed by specialised UK rules.[67]

TAKING OF EVIDENCE ABROAD[68]

Taking of evidence within the EU

In this area too there is European legislation, in the form of **8–13** Council Regulation (EC) No 1206/2001 on Cooperation between the Courts of the Member States in the Taking of Evidence in Civil or Commercial Matters.[69] Regulation 1206/2001 entered into force on July 1, 2001, and thereby created a new system for the rapid transmission and execution of requests for the taking of evidence between Member State courts[70] and laying down precise criteria as to the form and content of the request. The Regulation applies in civil and commercial cases where a court of a Member State requests the competent court of another Member State to obtain evidence. A list of such courts competent for the purpose must be drawn up by each Member State. A request shall not be made to obtain evidence which is not intended for use in judicial proceedings, commenced or contemplated.[71] It is possible also for the requesting court to take evidence *directly* in another Member State.

As an aid to the working of the new scheme, Member States shall designate a "central body".

Evidence by request

Where evidence is to be taken by request, the request must be **8–14** made using a specific form[72] and must contain certain specific details such as details of the parties, and the nature of the case.

---

[65] *McAllister v The General Medical Council* [1993] 2 W.L.R. 388, PC; see Shiels, "*McAllister v The General Medical Council,* English Law in Scotland", 1993 S.L.T. (News) 102.

[66] *cf. Prescription Pricing Authority v Ferguson,* 2005 S.L.T. 63, concerning the jurisdiction of an industrial tribunal.

[67] Army Act 1955: see *R v Martin* [1998] 1 All E.R. 193.

[68] See, both as to EU Regulation and otherwise (from an English perspective) Layton & Mercer, *European Civil Practice,* Ch.7.

[69] See *http://europa.eu.int/comm/justice—home/fsj/civil/evidence—civil.*

[70] Except Denmark.

[71] Art.1.2.

[72] Art.4.

The request and all documents accompanying it shall be exempted from authentication or any equivalent formality.[73] The request must be presented in one of the official languages of the Member State requested, or in another language indicated by that State to be acceptable.[74] It is an aim of the new legislation that the taking of evidence should be done without delay. If it is not possible for the request to be executed by the requested court within ninety days of receipt of the request, the requested court should inform the requesting court, stating reasons. Representatives of the requesting court and of the parties may be physically present at the taking of evidence, but if this is not possible, technology, in particular video conferencing, may be used to permit their participation.

Communications pursuant to the Regulation shall be transmitted by the swiftest possible means, and may be carried out by any appropriate means provided that the document received accurately reflects the content of the document forwarded, and that all information in it is legible.[75]

Within seven days of receipt of the request, the requested competent court shall send by means of a particular form, an acknowledgement of receipt to the requesting court.[76] Where the request does not fall within the jurisdiction of the court to which it was transmitted, the latter shall forward the request to the competent court of its Member State, and shall inform the requesting court.[77] If the request cannot be executed because it does not contain all information required by Article 4, the requested court shall inform the requesting court thereof without delay, and at the latest within thirty days of receipt, using a particular form, and shall request it to send the missing information.[78] Similarly, if a request cannot be executed because a deposit or advance is necessary, the requested court shall inform the requesting court without delay, and at the latest within 30 days of receipt, using a particular form and informing the requesting court how the deposit or advance should be made.[79] With regard to the time limit (of execution of the request without delay and at the latest within 90 days of receipt) contained in Article 10, such time limit shall begin to run when the requested court receives the request duly completed.[80] The requested court shall execute the request in accordance with the law of its Member State, although if the requesting court calls for execution in accordance with a special procedure

---

[73] Art.4.2.
[74] Art.5.
[75] Art.6.
[76] Art.7.1.
[77] Art.7.2.
[78] Art.8.1.
[79] Art.18.
[80] Art.9.

provided for by the law of its Member State, the requested court shall comply unless this procedure is incompatible with its law, or would raise major practical difficulties.[81]

The requesting court may ask the requested court to use communications technology at the taking of evidence, in particular by using video conferencing and tele-conferencing.[82]

If, by the law of the requesting court, the parties and their representatives have the right to be present at the taking of evidence this shall be facilitated by the requested court.[83] If it is compatible with the law of the requesting court, representatives of the requesting court (including judicial personnel or experts), have the right to be present at the taking of evidence. If participation of such representatives is requested by the requesting court, the conditions under which such participation may take place shall be determined by the requested court.[84] Where necessary in executing a request, the requested court shall apply the appropriate coercive measures to the extent provided for by its law.[85]

With regard to refusal to give evidence, the Regulation provides in Article 14 that the request for the hearing of a person shall not be executed where s/he claims the right to refuse to give evidence, or to be prohibited from giving evidence, under the law of the requested court, or under the law of the requesting court (subject to confirmation by the requesting court).

The execution of a request may be refused only in exceptional circumstances, namely[86]:

(a) the request does not fall within the scope of the Regulation; or
(b) under the law of the requested court the execution of the request does not fall within the function of the judiciary; or
(c) the requesting court does not comply within thirty days with the request by the requested court to complete the request pursuant to Article 8; or
(d) a deposit or advance asked for in accordance with Article 18.3 has not been made within 60 days.[87]

---

[81] Art.10.2 and 10.3.
[82] Art.10.4
[83] Art.11.
[84] Art.12.4.
[85] Art.13.
[86] Art.14.2.
[87] Art.18 concerns costs: the execution of the request shall not give rise to a claim for any reimbursement of taxes or costs. However, the requested court may require that the requesting court ensure the reimbursement without delay of experts' and interpreters' fees, and costs associated with special procedures used, including use of communications technology. Where expert opinion is required,

Importantly, Article 14.3 provides that execution may not be refused by the requested court solely on the ground that under the law of its Member State a court of that State has exclusive jurisdiction over the subject matter of the action, or that the law of that Member State would not admit the right of action on it.[88] If execution of the request is refused on any of the grounds in Article 14.2, the requested court shall notify the requesting court thereof within 60 days of receipt.[89]

In terms of Article 16, the requested court shall send without delay to the requesting court the documents establishing the execution of the request, and where appropriate return documents received.

Direct taking of evidence

8–15 Where a court requests to take evidence *directly* in another Member State, it shall submit a request to the central body, or competent authority.[90] Direct taking of evidence may take place only if it can be performed on a voluntary basis without the need for coercive measures, and the requesting court shall inform participating persons that their performance shall take place on a voluntary basis.[91]

The taking of such evidence shall be performed by a member of the judicial personnel, or designated expert, in accordance with the law of the requesting court. The central body of the requested Member State shall advise within 30 days of receipt if the request is accepted, and, if necessary, under what conditions the performance is to be carried out. In particular, the central body may assign a court of its Member State to take part to ensure the proper application of this provision, and compliance with conditions.[92]

The central body may refuse direct taking of evidence only if[93]:

(a) the request does not fall within the scope of the Regulation; or

(b) the request does not contain all the necessary information pursuant to Article 4; or

(c) the direct taking of evidence requested is contrary to fundamental principles of law in its Member State.

---

the requested court may, before executing the request, ask the requesting court for an adequate deposit or advance towards costs. But in other cases, a deposit or advance shall not be a condition for the execution of a request. (However, a deposit or advance shall be made by the parties if that is a provision of the law of the requesting court.)

[88] Note the subservient position of the requested court in this regard.
[89] Art.15.
[90] Art.3.
[91] Art.17.2.
[92] Art.17.
[93] Art.17.5.

Without prejudice to the conditions mentioned above, the requesting court shall execute the request in accordance with the law of its Member State.

In terms of Article 21, this Regulation shall prevail over bilateral or multilateral agreements, and in particular, over the 1970 Hague Convention on the Taking of Evidence Abroad in Civil or Commercial Matters (to which the UK is a party), in relations between the Member States party thereto.

The operation of the Regulation is to be kept under review by the Commission.

Taking of evidence outside the EU

As regards taking of evidence from non-EU states, evidence in **8–16** the form of testimony, or documents[94] or both[95] may be obtained under the authority of, and by complying with the provisions in, the Evidence (Proceedings in Other Jurisdictions) Act 1975, implementing in the UK the 1970 Hague Convention on the Taking of Evidence Abroad in Civil or Commercial Matters. The practical problem is the degree of specification rightly required, but possibly lacking.[96]

The Court of Session, under the 1975 Act, may order (at the instance of a foreign court or tribunal by what is commonly known as a "letter of request"[97]) witnesses in Scotland to give evidence to be remitted abroad to aid foreign litigation.[98] The Extra Division has refused to accede to four letters of request from a Texas court, on the ground that the material sought related to pre-trial discov-

---

[94] *Stewart v Callaghan*, 1996 S.L.T. (Sh.Ct) 12; *Panayiotou v Sony Music Entertainment (UK) Ltd* [1994] 1 All E.R. 755.

[95] *RTZ v Westinghouse* [1978] 1 All E.R. 434; *Boeing Co. v PPG Industries Inc.* [1988] 3 All E.R. 839; and *Charman v Charman* [2005] EWCA Civ. 1606.

[96] Aird and Jameson, paras 18.62–18.68, concluding that there may be a difference between English and Scots rules here. See *Union Carbide Corp. v B.P. Chemicals Ltd*, 1995 S.L.T. 972.

[97] The leading case is *Re State of Norway's Application* [1989] 1 All E.R. 745, in which, *inter alia*, the House of Lords held that for the process to be initiated under the 1975 Act, the proceedings for which evidence was sought to be gathered must be regarded as concerning a "civil or commercial matter" in the view of both the requesting and the requested court, since there was no internationally acceptable classification. Contrast *LTU v Eurocontrol* [1976] E.C.R. 1541, at 1552, to the effect that for the purposes of interpretation of the Brussels Convention, and in particular the phrase "civil and commercial matters", reference must not be made to the law of one of the States concerned, but first, to the objectives and scheme of the Convention, and secondly, to the general principles which stem from the corpus of the national legal systems. See also *Pharaon v BCCI SA (in liquidation)* [1998] 4 All E.R. 455 as regards limits of disclosure.

[98] *Lord Advocate, Petr*, 1994 S.L.T. 852 but see *Lord Advocate, Petr*, 1998 S.L.T. 835; *Minnesota v Philip Morris Inc.* (1997) 11 C.L. 100 (request refused because terms of letter of request from Minnesota District Court too wide-ranging).

ery which might lead to a line of inquiry ultimately resulting in deposition testimony and did not relate directly to evidence for use at a trial.[99]

Outside the scope of the EU Regulation, there is also a precedent for use of video conferencing[1] and the sitting of a Scots court abroad. The former is an acknowledgment of the benefit in a suitable case of advances in technology. The latter is an exceptional event.[2]

PROOF OF FOREIGN LAW[3]

8–17 As noted above,[4] foreign law is a matter of fact, to be proved in Scots courts, the burden of proof lying on the party who wishes to rely on it. If there is failure to prove the foreign law, the forum will assume that the content of the foreign law is the same as its own.[5] It has been said that this state of law, which is found also in England, represents a presumption that the foreign law content is the same as that of the forum. There is a tendency now towards impatience with this manner of explanation: "[i]t is high time that such nonsense was eliminated from the discourse of the law. . . In default of proof . . . an English judge still has to adjudicate; and his

---

[99] *Lord Advocate, Petr*, 1998, above. Contrast *Lord Advocate, Petr*, 1994, above. And see in England, refusal to accede to letter of request from US District Court of Columbia, on the ground that the width of the questions made the letters oppressive. A balance had to be struck between international co-operation and oppression of witnesses: *First American Corp. v Al-Nahyau* [1998] 6 *C.L. Week*, issue 54, September 25, 1998.

[1] As to which in English law, see *R. v Horseferry Road Magistrates' Court, ex p. Bennet (No. 3)*, *The Times*, January 14, 1994; *R v Forsyth*, *The Times*, April 8, 1997, CA (evidence from abroad through television link).

[2] *e.g.* in 1992, when the Court of Session, in recognition of the age and frailty of witnesses, removed to Vilnius, Lithuania in order to hear a trial of alleged war crimes. More recently the Scots High Court removed to Camp Zeist in the Netherlands for the purposes of the Lockerbie trial, the territory being deemed part of Scotland for the purposes of the trial. Cf. *Peer International Corp. v Termidor Music Publishers Ltd (No. 3)* [2005] EWHC 1048.

[3] See generally, R. Fentiman, *Foreign Law in English Courts* (OUP); S. Geeroms, *Foreign Law in Civil Litigation* (OUP); Layton & Mercer, *European Civil Practice*, Ch.8; J. Hill, *International Commercial Disputes in English Courts* (2005), Ch.18; T.C. Hartley, "Pleading and Proof of Foreign Law: The Major European Systems Compared" (1996) 45 ICLQ 271; and Rodger and van Doorn, "Proof of Foreign Law: The Impact of the London Convention" (1997) 46 ICLQ 151.

[4] See also para.4–01.

[5] *Faulkner v Hill*, 1942 J.C. 20; *Rodden v Whatlings Ltd*, 1960 S.L.T. (Notes) 96; *Pryde v Proctor & Gamble Ltd*, 1971 S.L.T. (Notes) 18; *Bonnor v Balfour Kilpatrick Ltd*, 1975 S.L.T. (Notes) 3; *Lloyd v Guibert* (1865) L.R. 1 Q.B. 115; *Dynamit AG v Rio Tinto Co. Ltd* [1918] A.C. 260. See also, *e.g. Bumper Development Corp. Ltd v Commissioner of Police of the Metropolis* [1991] 4 All E.R. 638, *per* Purchas L.J. at 643–646.

default position is that he will apply English law, *faute de mieux*."[6] Moreover, it is recognised that this specialty of Scots and English pleading may operate as a tool in the conflict of laws, being consciously or unconsciously utilised as such, so as to enable an indirect choice to be made by the parties (or one of them), that the applicable law shall be that of the forum. [7]

The House of Lords, whatever its composition in a particular case, has knowledge of each of the laws of the constituent jurisdictions of the UK[8] (and must develop them[9]), with the result that that which was a matter of fact in the court(s) below may be a matter of law above.

ONUS OF PROOF

There is doubt whether this matter truly pertains to substance or **8–18** procedure.

Writers in their earlier editions[10] favoured classification as substantive, but latterly views are equivocal.[11] Again Rome I provides a particularity in that, while matters of evidence and procedure are excluded generally from its scope (Article 1(2)(h)), this is without prejudice to Article 14(1) which states that "[t]he law governing the contract under this Convention applies to the extent that it contains, in the law of contract, rules which raise presumptions of law or determine the burden of proof" (*i.e.* such rules are treated as substantive in this context).[12]

---

[6] A. Briggs, *The Conflict of Laws*, p.6.

[7] The UK approach has attracted criticism, and there have been calls for an international instrument to harmonise the treatment by courts of matters of foreign law.

[8] *Elliot v Joicey*, 1935 S.C. (H.L.) 57, see *per* Lord MacMillan at 68.

[9] *Bank of East Asia Ltd v Scottish Enterprise*, 1997 S.L.T. 1213.

[10] Cheshire and North (8th ed.), p.699 and (9th ed.), p.693. The 10th ed., at p707, does not express a firm view, nor does the latest edition at p.78. The case of *Cohn* [1945] Ch. 5 supports the view that it is substantive, but contrast Graveson, p.602 who, together with the cases of *Fuld (No. 3)* [1968] P. 675 and *Mackenzie v Hall* (1854) 17 D. 164, prefers to assign the topic to procedure. Wolff,pp.234–235 contributes the thought that the domain of substantive law covers all those rules on the burden of proof which are closely connected with the existence or non-existence of substantive rights. Hence, if it affects the whole nature of the distinction between the attributes of possession and of ownership (so that, if the burden of proof were to be removed, one of the main characteristics which the (continental) law attributes to possession would disappear), the classification of the rule in that case should be substantive.

[11] *e.g.* Anton with Beaumont, pp.746–747. Dicey & Morris, in a brief treatment at paras 7-026/027, conclude that there is "much to be said for treating questions relating to the burden of proof as substantive".

[12] *cf.* Amended Proposal of 21 February 2006 (COM (2006) 83 final) ("Rome II"), Art.19.1.

PRESUMPTIONS

8–19 Graveson[13] regarded all presumptions of law and fact as being procedural, governed by the *lex fori*, but, as has been seen above, this position has been overtaken, at least in relation to the particular (contractual) matter with which it deals, by Article 14(1) of Rome I. It is thought that irrebuttable presumptions contained within the *lex causae* are matters of substance. As regards rebuttable presumptions it is suggested, that they should also receive effect as matters involving substance unless they are clearly (foreign) rules of procedure.

DAMAGES

8–20 There are two elements in the assessment of damages, namely:

(a) liability,[14] which is a matter of substance, to be determined by the *lex causae*; and

(b) quantification of damages, which is a matter of procedure, to be determined by the *lex fori*.

The question whether a claim for a particular head of damages is competent is governed, therefore, by the *lex causae* (in contract, delict, or restitution, etc.). The monetary calculation of damages is a matter purely for the *lex fori*.[15]

This statement of the traditional conflict rule is subject to the specialty introduced by Rome I in respect of contracts within its scope, namely: "[w]ithin the limits of the powers conferred upon the court by its procedural law, the law applicable to the contract also governs the consequences of total or partial failure to perform these obligations, including the assessment of damages insofar as this is governed by rules of law" (Article 10(1)(c)).[16] Moreover, a

---

[13] p.602.

[14] *D'Almeida Araujo Lda v Becker & Co. Ltd* [1953] 2 Q.B. 329.

[15] *Fyffe v Ferguson* (1841) 2 Rob. 267; *Kendrick v Burnett* (1897) 25 R. 82; *pace Boys v Chaplin* [1971] A.C. 356, the *ratio* of which is, notoriously, a matter of individual opinion.

[16] According to Giuliano and Lagarde, p.33, the phrase of significance is "by rules of law": questions of fact in assessment of damages will always be for the forum, but international conventions or the terms of the contract itself may have provided "rules" for application in the instant matter, and these would be substantive. *Cf.* Amended Proposal of February 21, 2006 (COM (2006) 83 final) ("Rome II"), Art.12(e), which refers the "assessment of the damage in so far as prescribed by law" to the law applicable to the non-contractual obligation". However, as currently drafted Rome II adds to Art.23 (public policy of the forum) the provision that the application under Rome II of a law that would have the effect of awarding excessive, non-compensatory damages may be considered incompatible with the public policy of the forum.

change in approach to the treatment of damages in tort and delict is evident from the reasoning of the Court of Appeal,[17] particularly *per* Arden L.J., in *Harding v Wealands*[18]: the assessment of damages in delict, for the purposes of section 14 of the Private International Law (Miscellaneous Provisions) Act 1995, ought to be viewed, it seems, as a matter principally for the *lex causae*, and only exceptionally for the *lex fori*.[19]

CURRENCY IN WHICH JUDGMENT IS TO BE GIVEN

Money of account (which measures the substance of an obligation) **8–21** is a substantive matter governed by the *lex causae*, but *money of payment* (in which the debt is discharged) is procedural. For centuries it had been assumed without argument in Scotland[20] and England[21] that a British court could grant a decree for payment of money only as a sum of money expressed in sterling. In 1974,[22] however, the Court of Appeal decided unanimously that within the "Common Market" a judgment might be given in the foreign currency (being the currency of the governing law of the contract in question), and that to do otherwise would be contrary to the spirit and intent of the Treaty of Rome. Lord Denning also thought that there was no reason why a court should not now grant such a judgment in the currency of the governing law, whether or not the parties were from countries within the "Common Market".

This initiative was followed in many later cases, with refinements and advances, first and notably in *Miliangos v George Frank (Textiles) Ltd (No.1)*.[23] Later the same year, in *The Halcyon the Great (No.1)*,[24] the court ordered that a ship be sold and the proceeds paid in dollars into the English court.

In Scotland, these issues arose at the same point in the 1970s, first in *L/F Foroya Fiskasola v Charles Mauritzen Ltd*[25] (which was something of a false alarm as the case was felt not to fall squarely within *Miliangos*, a House of Lords decision arguably on a matter

---

[17] *cf. Roerig v Valiant Trawlers Ltd* [2002] 1 Ll's Rep. 681.
[18] [2005] All E.R. 415.
[19] See J.M. Carruthers, "Substance and Procedure in the Conflict of Laws: A Continuing Debate in relation to Damages" 2004 (53) ICLQ 691, at 694; and "Damages in the Conflict of Laws: The Substance and Procedure Spectrum: *Harding v Wealands*" (2005) J.Pr.I.L. 1. *Harding v Wealands*: however, Court of Appeal decision reversed on appeal ([2006] UKHL 32). See also *Re T and N Ltd* [2005] EWHC 2990 (Ch).
[20] *Hyslops v Gordon* (1824) 2 Sh. App. 451.
[21] *Re United Railways of Havana and Regla Warehouses* [1961] A.C. 1007.
[22] *Schorsch Meier GmbH v Hennin* [1974] 3 W.L.R. 823; [1975] Q.B. 416.
[23] [1975] Q.B. 487.
[24] [1975] 1 W.L.R. 515.
[25] 1977 S.L.T. (Sh.Ct) 76; 1978 S.L.T. (Sh.Ct) 27.

common to Scots and English law and therefore binding on the Scots court). However, soon thereafter in *Commerzbank Aktiengesellschaft v Large*[26] the point was clearly made that there was no reason why a foreign creditor suing for an undisputed money debt in the country of his debtor's residence should be disadvantaged by fluctuations in currency. He should be entitled to have his decree expressed in the currency of the debt. If conversion be necessary, it should take place at the latest date practicable, which would be the date of extracting the decree.[27]

There has been a "moving staircase" of judicial development, and in recognition of this the Law Commission concluded that it was inappropriate to propose substantial legislation, though minor amendments might be made.[28]

This, therefore, is one of the few areas of modern "British" conflict rules in which the legislature has refrained from itself effecting change where change was deemed necessary. There are many decisions,[29] and writing on the subject, especially at the time of principal change, is extensive.[30] One of the most useful guides is the conjoined contract/tort House of Lords decision, *The Despina R/The Folias*,[31] which held in tort (the tort aspect having been reserved by the House of Lords in *Miliangos*) that the plaintiff should have his judgment in the currency which best expressed his loss; and in contract, that the fact that payments under a contract were in a particular currency did not necessarily mean that damages for breach needed to be awarded in that same currency.

A significant Scottish decision is *Fullemann v McInnes's Executor*,[32] which concerned an award of damages to a Swiss pursuer injured in a road accident in Scotland as a result of the admitted

---

[26] 1977 S.L.T. 219.

[27] See *Carnegie v Giessen* [2005] 1 W.L.R. 2510, in which the Court of Appeal stated that conversion should be made as close as practicable to the date of payment, "having regard to realities of enforcement procedures".

[28] *Private International Law, Foreign Money Liabilities*, Law Com. No. 124 (1983). The question of interest on foreign currency judgment debts and arbitral awards was identified as an area where procedural change was needed: see now, for England and Wales only, Private International Law (Miscellaneous Provisions) Act 1995, Pt I.

[29] *Jugoslavenska Oceanska Plovidba v Castle Investments* [1974] Q.B. 292 (arbitration); *Barclays Bank International Ltd v Levin Bros. (Bradford) Ltd* [1977] Q.B. 270; *Jean Kraut AG v Albany Fabrics Ltd* [1977] Q.B. 182.

[30] White, "Judgments in Foreign Currency and the E.E.C. Treaty" (1976) J.B.L. 7; Marshall, "Judgments and Awards in Foreign Currency: Working out the *Miliangos* Rule" (1977) J.B.L. 225; Libling, "Questions and Answers (?): *Miliangos v Frank (Textiles) Ltd*" (1977) 93 L.Q.R. 212; Marshall, "Decrees in Foreign Currency. Following Craig—or Miliangos?", 1978 S.L.T. (News) 77; Forte, "Questions of General Jurisprudence: A Case in Point" (1977) 22 J.L.S. 377; Cusine, "Fair Exchange" (Court Report) (1977) 22 J.L.S. 397.

[31] [1978] 2 All E.R. 764; [1979] Q.B. 491.

[32] 1993 S.L.T. 259.

fault of the other driver. The pursuer suffered physical and patrimonial loss. Solatium was valued at £42,500 but the award for patrimonial loss was expressed in Swiss francs, or the sterling equivalent at the date of payment or of extracting decree, whichever was the earlier.[33]

PRIORITIES OF CREDITORS

In the distribution of assets under the supervision of the court, **8–22** priorities are decided by the *lex fori*.[34] In particular:

(a) as regards unsecured claims, the *lex fori* alone applies;
(b) as regards secured claims, the nature of each security is determined by its own applicable law and it is then translated into its nearest equivalent according to the *lex fori*, by which questions of priority are then decided.

Nevertheless, there is room for a little unease here. If all claims arise under the same law, perhaps the forum should defer to that law.[35]

DILIGENCE

This is governed entirely by the law of the place where a decree is **8–23** to be enforced.[36]

---

[33] *per* Lord Cullen at 267, contrasting *North Scottish Helicopters Ltd v United Technologies Corp. Inc. (No. 2)*, 1988 S.L.T. 778. With reference to arguments for the defender that it was illogical for the pursuer to accept decree in sterling for solatium but to seek decree in Swiss francs for the patrimonial loss, Lord Cullen at 268 said: "[t]here is no doubt in the present case that the patrimonial loss which was and will continue to be suffered by the pursuer is one suffered in Swiss currency." (The pursuer had had to sell his business which otherwise he might have expanded.) See Blaikie, "Personal Injuries Claims: Damages in Foreign Currency", 1993 S.L.T. (News) 184.

[34] *Lusk v Elder* (1843) 5 D. 1279 (forum governs ranking in bankruptcy); *Clark v Bowring & Co.*, 1908 S.C. 1168; *The Tagus* [1903] P. 44 (such questions are of remedy, for the *lex fori*); *The Colorado* [1923] P. 102; *The Zigurds* [1932] P. 113; *The Acrux* [1965] P.391; *Re Lorillard* [1922] 2 Ch. 638; *Re Kloebe* (1884) 28 Ch.D. 175.

[35] R.D. Leslie, *Stair Memorial Encyclopaedia*, p.359, citing Dicey & Morris (11th ed., 1987), pp.185–186; *cf.* doubts about the decision in *Re Lorillard* above. But see also *Re Kloebe*, above (ranking of creditors upon the estate of deceased was a matter of administration for the *lex fori*). *Cf.* Ch.17, below (relating to competing claimants).

[36] See *Stewart v The Royal Bank of Scotland plc*, 1992 G.W.D. 31–1799. Also *Union Carbide Corp. v BP Chemicals Ltd*, 1995 S.L.T. 972; *Camdex International Ltd v Bank of Zambia Ltd* [1997] 1 C.L. 123; and *Bankers Trust International v Todd Shipyards Corp (The Halcyon Isle)* [1981] A.C. 221 (Privy Council). See recently in Scots for domestic law Debt Arrangement and Attachment (Scotland) Act 2002.

SET-OFF/COMPROMISE

8–24   Early authorities tended to place this subject under the heading of procedure or remedy, governed by the *lex fori*.[37] However, instinct would suggest that an argument can be made for treating the topic as pertaining to substance, whether it be the applicable law in contract,[38] property or restitution.[39] Further, following the substantive, line, it is clear that rights in this area may be seen often to arise out of principles of property, or the fact of possession, for example lien.[40] It could be that the earlier decisions and later thoughts might meet on the rationalisation that an unpaid party's right to retain custody of an object of property pending payment for work done or a debt due, falls within the category of remedy or procedure, and frequently will be governed by the *lex fori qua lex situs*. Similarly, the right of a party to set off what he owes against what he is owed (as for example arising out of several contracts forming a course of dealing between two parties), arguably should be governed by the common applicable law, if there is one; and if there is not, it might be that the remedies available to the parties should be determined by the *lex fori qua situs* of the debt.[41]

Possibly any confusion which has arisen under this heading stems from the variety of circumstances which can be subsumed under it. Some of these issues are plainly procedural, for example, whether a counterclaim may be brought by the defender in an action against the pursuer without raising separate proceedings; and whether and under what circumstances an action may be settled by compromise.

Summary 8—Evidence and Procedure

8–25   1. Substance is governed by the *lex causae*; procedure by the *lex fori*. Classification between the two is for the forum in each instance, but certain matters are clearly procedural:

---

[37] *Mitchell v Burnett and Mowat* (1746) Mor. 4468; *Robertson's Trs v Bairds* (1852) 14 D. 1010; *Macfarlane v Norris* (1862) 2 B.J. 783; and *Meyer v Dresser* (1864) 16 C.B. (N.S.) 646. See also Anton with Beaumont, pp.748–749.

[38] At least if the circumstances involve only two parties in a matter which could be said to arise out of a contract or putative contract between them. *Finance One Public Co. Ltd v Lehman Bros Special Financing Inc.*, 414 F. 3d 325 (2nd Civ. 2005).

[39] *cf.* Rome I, Art.10(1)(c) and (d).

[40] See minority judgment of Lords Scarman and Salmon, in *Bankers Trust International v Todd Shipyards Corp. (The Halycon Isle)* [1981] A.C. 221 (Privy Council).

[41] These suggested solutions beg several questions, chief among them being "which debt?" (if the debts had different governing laws) and "which forum?" In practice, however, the forum probably would be that of the domicile (i.e. residence) of the debtor first sued.

form of action and of process, evidence, diligence. There is a certain doubt about the classification of other issues, such as onus of proof. Some matters (for example damages) are hybrid in nature.

2. Foreign prescriptive or limitation periods: the forum must defer to the rules of the *lex causae*, at least in matters relating to obligations.

3. The content of foreign law, if relied upon and not admitted, must be proved. In the absence of proof, it is presumed to be the same as the *lex fori*.

4. Service of judicial and extrajudicial documents within the EU now is governed by Council Regulation 1348/2000. Service furth of Scotland outside the EU is governed by Rules of Court of the Court of Session/Sheriff Court.

5. Among EU Member States evidence from another Member State may be obtained under authority of Council Regulation 1206/2001. Evidence from non-EU Member States, or to be remitted abroad, may be obtained provided by the "letter of request" procedure laid down by the Evidence (Proceedings in Other Jurisdictions) Act 1975.

6. Decrees expressed in foreign currency may be awarded by a Scots or English court.

CHAPTER 9

ENFORCEMENT OF FOREIGN DECREES

I. INTRODUCTION

The procedure for enforcement of judgments depends upon the **9–01** identity of the territory whence the judgment originated. However, the fact must also be noted, at the outset of consideration of this subject, that there are different types of judicial decrees, with different consequences for enforcement. Decrees *in rem* stand unaided *contra mundum*. Decrees *in personam* require further court procedure or registration in the state where the decree is to be enforced, if they are to take effect outside the jurisdiction which granted them. Not all judicial decrees are suitable for, or require, enforcement *extra territorium*.[1] Moreover, sometimes reliance is placed on a foreign judgment in a negative way, as a defence to an action in Scotland or England, under the heading of *res judicata*.

CLASSES OF DECREE

Decrees may be divided into the following classes:

(a) Declarators of fact

The courts in Scotland or England are not bound by findings of **9–02** fact in a foreign decree, and in any event a decree so limited will not as a rule create rights for a particular individual. Hence, a foreign declarator which merely purports to establish a fact is not necessarily conclusive, but may be accepted in non-contentious matters.[2]

---

[1] Morris, para.7-001: "[a] court must recognise every foreign judgment which it enforces, but it need not enforce every foreign judgment which it recognises. Some foreign judgments do not lend themselves to enforcement, but only to recognition."

[2] *Simpson's Trs v Fox*, 1951 S.L.T. 412 (death abroad; see now, in relation to proof of death abroad, Presumption of Death (Scotland) Act 1977, s.10: foreign declaration of presumption of death, from court of the domicile of the presumed deceased, or his habitual residence, on the date when he was last known to be alive, raises in Scotland a rebuttable presumption of death).

With regard to the jurisdictional competence of EU courts in civil and commercial matters, Council Regulation (EC) No 44/2001, Article 35.2 states that the court in which recognition/ enforcement is sought, in its examination of the grounds of jurisdiction utilised in a litigation falling under sections 3, 4 or 6 of Chapter II of the Regulation shall be bound by the findings of fact on which the court of a Member State of origin based its jurisdiction.[3]

(b) Interdicts

9–03   A decree of this class is generally enforceable only within the territorial limits of the court which granted it,[4] at least at common law, and generally in cases falling outside the ambit of the Brussels/ Lugano regime.[5] However, under that regime, orders for specific implement and interdict, as well as those which are purely money judgments, have the advantage of the enforcement scheme provided thereby among Contracting States.[6]

(c) Judgments *in rem*

9–04   Decrees of this class establish rights in property against the world at large, not simply between the two parties to a dispute.

The test of validity of such a decree turns upon the strength of the claim to jurisdiction of the foreign court, and this in turn depends upon the presence of the *res* within the jurisdiction,[7] with the result that if the *res* was within the jurisdiction at the time of pronouncement of the judgment, it is thought that the only ground upon which the judgment may be challenged is that of fraud.[8] It follows that the title of a third party who has acquired the *res* in compliance with that *lex situs* cannot be challenged.[9]

(d) Judgments affecting status

9–05   Judgments of this class although treated separately (*i.e.* possessing special statutory rules in conflict of laws, contained in the Family Law Act 1986, Part II (non-EU decrees) and Council

---

[3] *cf.* in consistorial causes Family Law Act 1986, s.48.

[4] *Waygood & Co. v Bennie* (1885) 12 R. 651; *British Nylon Spinners v ICI* [1953] Ch. 19. See generally *Waste Systems International Inc v Eurocare Environmental Services Ltd*, 1998 G.W.D. 6–260.

[5] See Ch.7, above .

[6] *Barratt International Resorts v Martin*, 1994 S.L.T. 434, *per* Lord Sutherland at 437: "[a]n interdict [granted in Scotland] therefore can be rendered effective even though the events being interdicted may occur in Spain." Also *G v Caledonian Newspapers Ltd*, 1995 S.L.T. 559 (intra-UK enforcement).

[7] Contrast the situation in *McKie v McKie* [1933] I.R. 464.

[8] *Ellerman Lines Ltd v Read* [1928] 2 K.B. 144.

[9] *Cammell v Sewell* (1858) 3 Hurl. & N. 617; *Castrique v Imrie* (1870) L.R. 4 H.L. 414; *Ballantyne v Mackinnon* [1896] 2 Q.B. 455; *Minna Craig S.S. Co. v Chartered Mercantile Bank of India* [1897] 1 Q.B. 55; *Re Trepca Mines Ltd* [1960] 1 W.L.R. 1273; *Enochin v Wyllie* (1882) 10 H.L.C. 1; *Orr-Ewing's Trs v Orr-Ewing* (1885) 13 R. (H.L.) 1; and *Doglioni v Crispin* (1866) L.R. 1 H.L. 301.

Regulation 2201/2003 (EU decrees)) are regarded as being equivalent in many respects to decrees *in rem* in that they establish rights which should be recognised internationally without the aid or intervention of a foreign court, and have standing in unrelated litigation. The case of *Administrator of Austrian Property v Von Lorang*[10] is particularly instructive as it demonstrates that a recognised foreign annulment may have a direct effect upon a property dispute taking place by way of multiplepoinding in Edinburgh. Viscount Dunedin in that case said "[a] metaphysical idea, which is what the status of marriage is, is not strictly a *res*, but, to borrow a phrase, it savours of a *res*, and has all along been treated as such."[11]

If there is doubt as to the validity in Scotland of a foreign, non-EU consistorial judgment, a party may seek declarator of status from the Court of Session.[12] In general, however, it follows from the decision in *Von Lorang*, above, that no such procedure should be necessary.[13]

In relation to EU judgments, in terms of Article 21 of Regulation 2201/2003, a judgment given in a Member State shall be recognised in the other Member States without any special procedure being required. Under the head of enforceable judgments, Article 28 of Regulation 2201/2003, provides that a judgment on the exercise of parental responsibility given in a Member State and enforceable there shall be enforceable in another Member State when, on the application of any interested party, it has been declared enforceable there.[14] Hence, a "declaration of enforceability" is required in such parental responsibility judgments; but the Regulation makes no mention of the use of such declarations in relation to any other type of judgment covered by the Regulation.

---

[10] 1927 S.C. (H.L.) 80.

[11] At 92.

[12] In English law a declarator may be sought in terms of the Family Law Act 1986, s.55.

[13] See, however, the Family Law (Scotland) Act 2006, s.37 of which contains amendments to the Domicile and Matrimonial Proceedings At 1973, s.7 (jurisdiction of Court of Session in certain consistorial causes) to the effect of providing jurisdiction in actions for declarator of recognition of a "relevant foreign decree" (meaning a decree of divorce, nullity or separation granted by a non-EU state). Shrieval jurisdiction to grant such declarator also is provided by s.37(3).

[14] *i.e.* a form of *exequatur* (registration) procedure. However special provision is made for the UK to the effect that such a judgment shall be enforced in England and Wales, in Scotland or in Northern Ireland only when, on the application of any interested party, it has been registered for enforcement in that part of the UK. The term "*exequatur*", in certain EU Member States encompassed a discretionary power in the state requested to subject the judgment to scrutiny on substance (Anton & Beaumont, *Civil Jurisdiction in Scotland*, paras 1.12–1.15). But this is no longer so: when enforcement is sought, there can be no review of the merits in terms of Council Regulation 44/2001, Art.36. The EU Commission wishes the registration process itself to be excluded in simpler cases (see below, para.9–78 *et seq*).

(e) Judgments *in personam*

9–06   Judgments of this class, such as claims for debts or for damages for breach of contract, establish personal rights between the litigants: a foreign decree *in personam*, if not complied with by the defender, may be enforced in Scotland only by invoking the assistance of the courts.

In Scotland, such a decree may be enforced in one of the following ways:

(1) by action for decree conform;
(2) by judgment registration (extension) under the Administration of Justice Act 1920 or the Foreign Judgments (Reciprocal Enforcement) Act 1933;
(3) by use of the system of judgment enforcement provided by Council Regulation 44/2001 (and, where appropriate, the Brussels/Lugano, etc. Conventions, *per* the Civil Jurisdiction and Judgments Acts 1982 and 1991[15]). There are significant differences between the rules of the European system and the rules which apply at common law and under the 1920 and 1933 Acts. This system now governs also the enforcement of English and Northern Ireland judgments in Scotland and *vice versa*; or
(4) European Enforcement Order for Uncontested Claims Procedure (or, it soon may be expected, the European Small Claims Procedure).

II. LEGAL BASIS OF ENFORCEMENT

9–07   The original basis of enforcement of any foreign decree in Scotland was simply comity (with reciprocity), but it is now generally accepted that comity alone is inadequate as a reason or basis for enforcement (though reciprocity remains relevant).[16] Later arose the doctrine that a foreign judgment imposed an *obligation*[17] enforceable in another jurisdiction, the burden lying on the defender to show why it should not be enforced.

Until recently in English conflict of laws, as contrasted with its domestic law, a foreign decree was not regarded as consuming the

---

[15] And Civil Jurisdiction and Judgments Order 2001 (SI 2001/3929). As to Brussels Convention and Denmark, see Ch.7. The Lugano Convention operates among EFTA countries.

[16] The statutory structure of foreign judgment recognition and enforcement inter-country (in terms of 1920 and 1933 Acts; and also under the Civil Jurisdiction and Judgments Act 1982) rests on reciprocity. See, *e.g.* Foreign Judgments (Reciprocal Enforcement) Act 1933, s.9.

[17] *Schibsby v Westenholz* (1870) L.R. 6 Q.B. 155.

cause of action. Hence, a claimant holding a foreign decree which he wished to enforce in England might sue either upon the decree itself, or ignore the decree and sue on the cause of action (the best course being to sue on both grounds as alternatives).[18] However, this *non-merger* rule was abolished by the Civil Jurisdiction and Judgments Acts 1982 and 1991, section 34.[19] The section does not apply to Scotland, possibly because it was not required, since the rule which it effected was already the rule in Scotland.[20]

Essentially, an unimpeachable foreign judgment creates rights and imposes obligations which should be enforceable across frontiers,[21] especially where a net of reciprocity has been woven, as by the 1920 and 1933 Acts and by the Brussels regime. The aim and rationale within the EU is the free movement of judgments, thereby facilitating the operation of the internal market.

Various principles of natural justice operate in the subject of judgment enforcement. For example, there should be finality in judgments so that a man be not required to "hawk his defence round Europe" (reputedly *per* Lord Braxfield). It follows from this that the "enforcing" court will not act as a further court of appeal from the foreign court. As a general rule, under any of the systems of judgment enforcement, review of substance will not be undertaken, nor will allegations of error on the part of the foreign court be investigated. The one important exception to this general rule against the re-opening of proceedings is in relation to alleged fraud (the opportunity to re-open on this ground being significantly more restricted under the Brussels regime). Review of jurisdictional competence is permitted under the common law rules and older statutory schemes, but under the Brussels regime only to a very limited extent:[22] *there* absence of a right to query the jurisdiction of the court of origin is a *leitmotif.*

---

[18] See *East India Trading Co. v Carmel Exporters & Importers* [1952] 2 Q.B. 439; and *Carl Zeiss Stiftung v Rayner & Keeler* [1967] A.C. 853.

[19] s.34: "[n]o proceedings may be brought by a person in England and Wales, or Northern Ireland on a cause of action in respect of which a judgment has been given in his favour in proceedings between the same parties, or their privies, in a court in another part of the United Kingdom or in a court of an overseas country, unless that judgment is not enforceable or entitled to recognition in England and Wales, or, as the case may be, in Northern Ireland."

[20] See Anton with Beaumont, pp.237–238. And *cf.* Maxwell Report (1980), para.6.186. Moreover, under the Brussels enforcement scheme, a party must sue on the judgment and not on the cause of action.

[21] *Williams v Jones* (1845) 13 M. & W. 633; *Schibsby v Westenholz* (1870) L.R. 6 Q.B. 155; *Grant v Easton* (1883) 13 Q.B.D. 302.

[22] Namely, to ensure that the rules with regard to disadvantaged parties and exclusive jurisdiction have been complied with: Council Regulation 44/2001, Art.35.1.

A. ENFORCEMENT OF JUDGMENTS AT COMMON LAW

9–08 The subject of judgment enforcement will be treated in the manner of the general to the particular, *i.e.* the common law first will be considered, and the differences between the common law and statutory systems thereby will be sought to be identified.

Enforcement via the common law route is required when a judgment emanates from a foreign country which is not bound by the Brussels/Lugano regime, nor linked by reciprocal arrangements with the UK in terms of the Administration of Justice Act 1920 or the Foreign Judgments (Reciprocal Enforcement) Act 1933.[23] Generally speaking, common law enforcement is required in respect of judgments from the USA,[24] Africa (except for Commonwealth countries), the Middle East and the Far East (including now Hong Kong[25]). Enlargement of the membership of the EU means that the enforcement of judgments emanating from the courts of new Member States proceed under the system contained in Council Regulation 44/2001.

The conditions set out below must be complied with in order that a foreign decree *in personam* may be enforceable in Scotland under the common law procedure:

(a) the decree must have been granted in a judicial process[26];

---

[23] Relevant countries in respect of each Act are listed at paras 9–15 and 9–21, below.

[24] Many such actions relate to attempted enforcement of USA awards, since at present there is no reciprocal arrangement of judgment extension between the UK and the USA (except in relation to reciprocal enforcement of maintenance awards under Maintenance Orders (Reciprocal Enforcement) Act 1972, Pt II). See, *e.g. First Fidelity Bank NA v Hudson*, 1995 G.W.D. 28–1499; *Wendel v Moran*, 1993 S.L.T. 44; *Fennoscandia Ltd v Clarke*, 1995 G.W.D. 39–3032; *Clarke v Fennoscandia Ltd (No.1)*, 1998 S.C. 464. Also *Elf Caledonia Ltd v London Bridge Engineering Ltd*, 1997 G.W.D. 33–1686.

[25] [1997] 12 C.L. 90.

[26] *Where* in the judicial process? It is not clear whether the judgment must emanate from a "superior" court. By inference of case law (on the question of the meaning of "final" decree: see below, para.9–12, it is clear that it is no bar to enforcement of a judgment that appeal from that judgment is competent in the legal system of the court of origin. This surely must mean that a decree from a medium ranking foreign court has sufficient status to be enforced in Scotland. It is arguable that, to found enforcement proceedings in Scotland/England, the decree must be "incapable of revision by the Court which pronounced it": *The Irini A (No. 2)* [1999] 1 Ll's Rep 189 (issue estoppel). See also Clarkson & Hill, p.165. Taking a purposive approach, it seems unlikely that objection would be raised to the status of the court of origin in its own hierarchy so long as the judgment in question meets the common law requirements as to the "finality" of the judgment. In a practical sense, decisions of the lower courts are more likely to be appealed domestically before being sought to be enforced abroad.

(b) the foreign court of origin must have had jurisdiction in the international sense[27];

(c) the decree must be final and *res judicata*;

(d) the decree must be for payment of a definite sum of money (a foreign decree for an indefinite sum or a decree *ad factum praestandum* is not enforceable at common law in Scotland);

(e) the subject-matter of the decree must not fall within any of the areas which form exclusions or exceptions to the extra-territorial effect of foreign law (revenue or penal laws etc[28]).

Action for decree conform

At common law, a foreign decree is enforced in Scotland by raising an action for *decree conform* to the decree of the foreign court. Certified translation of the foreign decree may be required. Decree conform may be granted only against a person who was party to the foreign proceedings.[29] Such an action may be raised only in the Court of Session because it is regarded as falling under the *nobile officium*.[30] **9–09**

If decree conform is sought in circumstances where judgment extension under the 1920 Act is available, expenses will not be awarded.[31] Under the Foreign Judgments (Reciprocal Enforcement) Act 1933, section 6, it is incompetent to proceed at common law if registration *per* the Act is possible.

Grounds of challenge to actions for decree conform

(a) No jurisdiction

This will always be the first challenge to be considered. **9–10**

In considering the sufficiency of the ground of jurisdiction assumed by a foreign court, there would be no point in referring only to the law of the foreign court because clearly that court regarded itself as having had jurisdiction; nor would there be any point in considering only the grounds assumed by the court where the decree is sought to be enforced because that would restrict

---

[27] See *Wendel v Moran*, 1993 S.L.T. 44, in which Lord Cullen refused to recognise as internationally jurisdictionally competent the New York court on the sole basis of the occurrence there of the delict, without presence of defender or express or implied submission by him; and noting that Brussels principles have no application in a common law case.

[28] Ch.3, above.

[29] Anton with Beaumont, p.238.

[30] *O'Connor v Erskine* (1905) 13 S.L.T. 530; *Geiger v D & J Macdonald Ltd*, 1932 S.L.T. 70.

[31] Administration of Justice Act 1920, s.9(5).

enforceability to cases where the two laws coincided. In practice, the courts of the enforcing country test the ground of jurisdiction in the foreign court according to whether or not it complies with a broad international standard of justice. By this standard certain grounds (domicile, residence,[32] presence,[33] prorogation or submission,[34] reconvention, place of performance of contract or occurrence of delict) generally are recognised,[35] whereas others (nationality,[36] arrestment to found jurisdiction, ownership of heritage in an action not relating to the heritage[37]) are not recognised.[38]

In the context of recognition of foreign divorces, Lord Pearce in *Indyka v Indyka*[39] said that insofar as a court limited its rules of recognition more strictly than it did its rules of taking jurisdiction, it was adding to the sum of limping marriages.[40] In commercial matters too, it may be reasonable to ask whether a legal system's own rules of exercising jurisdiction are consonant with the rules which it applies to assess the jurisdictional competence of another system's courts.[41]

---

[32] *Schibsby v Westenholz* [1870] L.R. 6 Q.B. 155. As to difficulties in the case of federal states, see Clarkson & Hill, pp.161–163.

[33] *Adams v Cape Industries plc* [1991] 1 All E.R. 929. See also in that case consideration of the application of the principle to corporations; see Clarkson & Hill, p.159.

[34] *cf. Copin v Adamson* (1874) L.R. 9 Ex. 345; *Blohn v Desser* [1962] Q.B. 116; contrast *Emanuel v Symon* [1908] 1 K.B. 302 and *Vogel v RA Kohnstamm* [1973] 1 Q.B. 133. See now for England Civil Jurisdiction and Judgments Act 1982, s.33.

[35] Though see *Wendel v Moran*, 1993 S.L.T. 44, above.

[36] *Rainford v Newell Roberts* [1962] I.R. 95; *Sirdar Gurdyal Singh v Rajah of Faridkote* [1894] A.C. 670; though see *Ashbury v Ellis* [1893] A.C. 339.

[37] Heritable or real property; possession of such property in Scotland is a general ground of jurisdiction in the Court of Session (Civil Jurisdiction & Judgments Act 1982, Sch.8, r.2(8)(b)) which might therefore recognise foreign decrees based on such a ground of jurisdiction; but this ground is not recognised in England and many other countries, and the English courts will not enforce a foreign judgment where it was the ground of jurisdiction, except when the action related to the property.

[38] See in English law *Emanuel v Symon* [1908] 1 K.B. 302, *per* Buckley L.J. at 309; see also *Trepca Mines Ltd* [1960] 1 W.L.R. 1273 and *Buchanan v Rucker* (1808) 9 East. 192, where the court in England refused to enforce a judgment from Tobago in respect of which service had been effected on the defendant by "substituted service"; namely by nailing a copy of the writ to the courthouse door, effective under that law though the defendant had never been to Tobago.

[39] [1969] 1 A.C. 33 at 78.

[40] Prior to *Indyka* the reciprocity basis of recognition known as the *Travers v Holley* doctrine had been influential; see Ch.12, below.

[41] The "long-arm" English jurisdiction rules (see *Seaconsar Far East Ltd v Bank Markazi Jomhouri Islami Iran* [1994] 1 A.C. 438) contained in Civil Procedure Rules, para.6.20 (permitting the court in its discretion to grant leave to the plaintiff to effect service outside the jurisdiction if he can show a good arguable case on the merits and the case falls within one of the nineteen categories specified) may attract criticism in this regard.

The case of appearance under protest (to contest the jurisdiction of the putative forum) is one which requires special consideration.[42] A controversy arose in England[43] upon the question whether appearance simply to deny that the court had jurisdiction amounted to submission. The matter has been clarified by the Civil Jurisdiction and Judgments Acts 1982–1991, section 33 (which does not apply to Scotland), to the effect that a person shall not be regarded as having submitted to the jurisdiction of the court by reason only of the fact that he appeared (conditionally or otherwise) in the proceedings (a) to contest the jurisdiction of the court and/or (b) to ask the court to dismiss or stay the proceedings on the ground that the dispute in question should be submitted to arbitration or to the determination of the courts of another country, *or* to protect, or obtain the release of, property seized or threatened with seizure in the proceedings.[44]

(b) Other grounds of challenge

As a foreign decree which, on the face of it, complies with the **9–11** "international" standards of jurisdiction, is regarded as conferring rights on the holder thereof, those rights generally will be recognised in Scotland, unless the other party satisfies the court that it would not be proper for it to recognise them. A Scots or English court will not act as a further court of appeal in relation to a foreign decree.[45] The foreign court must be regarded as having been able to try the case and as having pronounced a valid judgment. The result is that, broadly speaking, the grounds upon which a foreign decree may be challenged are restricted to those cases in which the court should be deemed not to have had jurisdiction in the international sense, as explained, or where it would be contrary to public policy to recognise the decree. A foreign judgment will be subject to challenge in Scotland or England only on some ground which goes to the very root and

---

[42] Common law cases *before* Civil Jurisdiction and Judgments Act 1982, s.33, demonstrating the controversy: *Guiard v De Clermont* [1914] 3 K.B. 145; *Harris v Taylor* [1915] 2 K.B. 580; *Re Dulles Settlement (No.2)* [1951] Ch. 842; *Daarnhouwer & Co. NV v Boulos* [1968] 2 Ll Rep. 259; finally *Henry v Geoprosco International Ltd* [1976] Q.B. 726; *thereafter*, see *Tracomin v Sudan Oil Seeds Ltd (No. 1)* [1983] 3 All E.R. 137.

[43] This is an area where different degrees of disquiet or interest have been produced in England and Scotland, respectively. With regard to this question in Scotland there is no clear statutory direction (though see Sch.8, r.6(2)); see Anton and Beaumont, para.9.28 and cases there cited. It seems unlikely that any other approach in any context would be taken by a Scots court: Anton and Beaumont, para.10.80.

[44] See at common law *Guiard v De Clermont* [1914] 3 K.B. 145. *Cf.* Council Regulation 44/2001, Art.24.

[45] Contrast continental doctrine of the *exequatur*, which in some forms permitted review of the merits (*révision au fond*).

essence: "[i]f a judgment is pronounced by a foreign Court over persons within its jurisdiction and in a matter with which it is competent to deal, English courts never investigate the propriety of the proceedings of the foreign Court unless they offend against English views of substantial justice."[46]

Thus the following challenges to enforcement are *not* available.

(1) Defence omitted.[47] The defender must make available all his defences in the foreign court; [48] if he fails to do so he will not be allowed to plead them afterwards in the court where enforcement is requested. There is one important exception to this principle; namely, defences founded on fraud.[49]

(2) Error in fact by the foreign court.

(3) Error in law by the foreign court as to its own law.[50] Whether the error is as to the substantive law of the foreign court, or as to its rules of jurisdiction, it does not serve as a defence against enforcement unless the "judgment" is a nullity by its own law.[51]

(4) Error as to Scots or English law.[52]

(5) Defective procedure. It behoves the enforcing court to pay regard to the *de minimis* principle. Natural justice must be secured, but the question is always whether substantial justice has been done in the instant case.[53]

9–12 The following are the only available defences:

(1) No jurisdiction—as above.

(2) Judgment not final and conclusive.[54] Particular attention should be paid to the meaning at common law of this

---

[46] *Pemberton v Hughes* [1899] 1 Ch. 781, *per* Lindley M.R. at 790.

[47] *Ellis v McHenry* (1871) 6 C.P. 228; *cf. Henderson* (1843) 3 Hare 100.

[48] *Clydesdale Bank Ltd v Schroder* [1913] 2 K.B. 1, *per* Bray J. at 5: if the party "desires to prove that he is not liable to pay the money, he must defend the action which has been brought for the very purpose of deciding whether the money is payable or not. He cannot by paying under protest reserve his right to raise the question of his liability in some subsequent proceedings".

[49] See para.9–12, below.

[50] *Henderson* (1843) 3 Hare 100; *Scott v Pilkington* (1862) 2 B. & S. 11; *Dent v Smith* [1869] 4 Q.B. 414, *per* Cockburn C.J. at 446; *De Cosse Brissac v Rathbone* (1861) 6 H. & N. 301; *Merker v Merker* [1963] P. 283.

[51] Thereby meeting challenge of *"judgment no longer (or not) extant"*, para.9–12, below.

[52] *Castrique v Imrie* (1870) L.R. 4 H.L. 414; *Godard v Gray* [1870] 6 Q.B. 139; *cf. Dallal v Bank Mellat* [1986] 1 All E.R. 239 (arbitration).

[53] *Pemberton v Hughes* [1899] 1 Ch. 781, *e.g. per* Lindley MR at 789–791.

[54] *Nouvion v Freeman* (1889) 15 App. Cas. 1; *Sheey v Professional Life Assurance Co.* (1857) 2 C.B. (N.S.) 211; *Paul v Roy* (1852) 15 Beav 433; *Scott v Pilkington* (1862) 2 B. & S. 11; *Shedden v Patrick* (1854) 1 Macq. 535; *Blohn v Desser* [1962] 2 Q.B. 116; *Colt Industries v Sarlie (No.2)* [1966] 1 W.L.R. 1287; *Berliner Industriebank v Jost* [1971] 2 Q.B. 463; *Harris v Quine* (1869) L.R. 4 Q.B. 653; *Black-Clawson International Ltd v Papierwerke* [1975] A.C. 591.

challenge. A foreign judgment will not be enforced in Scotland or England if the merits have not been exhausted,[55] but the fact that the judgment is appealable,[56] or even that an appeal is pending, will not necessarily render it unenforceable in Scotland or England at common law. However, a Scots court would be likely to sist the action for decree conform if foreign appeal was imminent.[57]

Aliment decrees intrinsically, however, are regarded as subject to change at any time, and enforcement will be permitted only of past instalments which have fallen due.[58]

(3) Decree for an indefinite amount[59] or *ad factum praestandum*[60] or for enforcement of a foreign revenue or penal or other public law excluded by Scots conflict rules from extra-territorial operation.[61]

(4) Judgment no longer extant (*e.g.* time-barred in foreign system, or satisfied, or otherwise no longer enforceable).[62]

(5) Fraud: *fraus omnia corrumpit*. Fraud may relate to the substantive issue, or it may reside in the fraudulent quality of the behaviour of the parties (collateral fraud).[63] Within the latter, another distinction[64] may be made, namely that between *dolus praesens* (by fraudulent *use* of the judgment as, for example, by falsely promising not to enforce it) and *dolus praeteritus* (consisting, for example, in fraud in the *getting* of the judgment, as by bribing the judge or producing perjured evidence).[65]

The alleged presence of fraud (by the court; on the court; by one party against another[66]) may vitiate a judg-

---

[55] *Nouvion v Freeman* above, in which it was found that an attempt was being made to enforce a preliminary Spanish judgment in circumstances where the Spanish legal system provided for preliminary *and* plenary proceedings.

[56] *Colt Industries v Sarlie* [1966] 1 W.L.R. 1287.

[57] As to the statutory position with regard to this matter, see Administration of Justice Act 1920, s.9(2)(e), and the Foreign Judgment (Reciprocal Enforcement) Act 1933, s.1(2)(a).

[58] *Harrop* [1920] 3 K.B. 386; *Keys* [1919] 2 I.R. 160; *McDonnell* [1912] 2 I.R. 148 (Binchy, p.114); *Re Macartney* [1921] 1 Ch. 522; *Beatty v Beatty* [1924] 1 K.B. 807; *Baily* (1884) 13 Q.B.D. 855; *Robins* [1907] 2 K.B. 13. See Ch.13 for specialised rules concerning maintenance.

[59] *Sadler v Robins* (1808) 1 Camp. 253 (amount definite to the last farthing, but expenses not taxed).

[60] *Beatty* [1924] 1 K.B. 807.

[61] See para.3–02, above.

[62] Anton with Beaumont, p.233.

[63] See, *e.g. Ochsenbein v Papelier* (1873) 8 Ch. App. 695.

[64] Made in *Jacobson v Frachon* (1924) 44 T.L.R. 103: see Wolff, p.268.

[65] Wolff, p.268; *MacAlpine v MacAlpine* [1958] P. 35; *Middleton v Middleton* [1967] P.62; and more recently, *Clarke v Fennoscandia Ltd (No. 2)*, 2002 S.L.T. 1311, and *(No. 3)*, 2005 S.L.T. 511.

[66] *Wilson v Robertson* (1884) 11 R. 893; *Price v Dewhurst* (1837) Sim. 279; *Abouloff v Oppenheimer* (1882) 10 Q.B.D. 295; *Vadala v Lawes* [1890] 25 Q.B. 310.

ment. In domestic law, a judgment may be impugned only if new evidence suggestive of fraud has been discovered since the hearing. In the conflict of laws, at least in cases falling outside the Brussels/Lugano regime, there seems to be no such requirement. Indeed, a defence relating to fraud may have been kept back in the original (foreign) proceedings, to be used in the subsequent enforcement proceedings,[67] and may then be admitted to proof. The right, or duty, of the enforcing/requested court to consider and pronounce upon the effect of some allegedly fraudulent element, brought to the notice of, and perhaps dismissed by the court of origin, was upheld ringingly by the Court of Appeal in *Jet Holdings v Patel*,[68] itself approved by the House of Lords in *Owens Bank Ltd v Bracco*.[69] But the same latitude to the defendant in permitting him to raise a defence previously held back in the foreign proceedings was not evident where the not dissimilar issue of undue influence was alleged,[70] nor in the Brussels/Lugano context does the challenge under the head of *ordre public* allow such a wide challenge. In *Interdesco S.A. v Nullifire*[71] it was held to be incompetent for the enforcing court to investigate an issue of fraud which had been subject to the scrutiny of the original EU court.

Clearly, there are warring principles of roughly equal weight: the desirability of finality of judgments is set against the undesirability of permitting a party to profit from his/her own wrongdoing. A modern understanding of comity, together with a desire for consistency, internally and in our conflict rules, may lead us,[72] when a suitable opportunity (in the House of Lords) arises, to place greater faith in the decision of the foreign court in such a matter.[73]

---

[67] *Syal v Hayward* [1948] 2 K.B. 443.

[68] [1990] 1 Q.B. 335.

[69] [1992] 2 All E.R. 193 (HL) (enforcement sought by means of 1920 Act) and [1994] 1 All E.R. 336 (ECJ), though contrast *House of Spring Gardens Ltd v Waite (No 2)* [1991] 1 Q.B. 241 (*res judicata*/estoppel).

[70] *Israel Discount Bank v Hadjipateras* [1984] 1 W.L.R. 137. Speaking generally, undue influence would be subsumed under public policy.

[71] [1992] 1 Ll's Rep. 180. Phillips J. did not favour review of the conclusions of the foreign court in a Convention case (p.187).

[72] But see Briggs and Rees, paras 7.49 and 7.50. Scots law, both conflict and domestic, seems to be the same, since *Owens Bank Ltd* is a decision upon the construction of the 1920 Act, s.9(2)(d) (a provision common to Scotland and England), to the effect of upholding the availability of a conflict challenge on fraud stronger than the domestic challenge. Scots domestic law on the point (*res noviter veniens ad notitiam: Maltman v Tarmac Civil Engineering Ltd*, 1967 S.C. 177) appears to be the same as English law.

[73] And see *Owens Bank v Etoile Commerciale SA* [1995] 1 W.L.R. 44, PC, *e.g. per* Lord Templeman at 48–51.

(6) Decree contrary to natural justice[74] The Scottish and English courts have recognised that it is unreasonable to expect Scottish/English procedural rules[75] to be replicated abroad. Though breach of natural justice must always be one of the prime justifications for refusal to enforce a foreign decree, the requested forum must be satisfied, before refusing to enforce, that substantial justice was not done in the granting of the decree. A complaint that the defendant in the foreign court was not allowed to give evidence on his own behalf may be answered sufficiently by an explanation that *neither* party, in the circumstances, was entitled by the law of the forum to give evidence.[76] The ends of comity are not served if one legal system is too quick to criticise the standards of another.[77]

Procedural irregularities *may* result in unfairness. A proof was ordered in *Det Norske v McLaren*.[78] A Scots sea captain, whose ship had run on to the rocks off the coast of Norway, was pursued in Scotland by a Norwegian "salvor" for decree conform to a Norwegian award of salvage, or alternatively to have the case tried again in Scotland as a salvage action. The sea captain defended not only on the ground that the pursuer was not a "salvor",[79] but also because he alleged that all the proceedings took place in the Norwegian language and that he could not understand them (and further that he had not agreed to have the question of salvage settled by a Norwegian court: what *was* the bargain made upon the rock?). Notwithstanding his lack of understanding of the language of the court, he averred that the evidence led was inadequate and that the judgment was erroneous in fact and in law. Normally it is advisable to have only one excuse or defence for fear of contradicting oneself.[80]

---

[74] *Jeannot v Fuerst* (1909) 25 T.L.R. 424; *Robinson v Fenner* [1913] 3 K.B. 835; *Re Macartney* [1921] 1 Ch. 522; *MacAlpine* [1958] P. 35; *Pemberton v Hughes* [1899] 1 Ch. 781; *S.S. Catalina (Owners) v MV Norma (Owners)* (1938) 61 Ll's Rep. 360 (prejudice of arbitrator openly expressed).

[75] *e.g.* on matters such as days of notice: *Jeannot v Fuerst* (1909) 25 T.L.R. 424.

[76] *Scarpetta v Lowenfeldt* (1911) 27 T.L.R. 509.

[77] *Igra v Igra* [1951] P. 404 (admittedly an odd case in which to issue such a guide, the foreign decree in question being a Gestapo-instigated divorce, intrinsically unfair to the husband, but recognised in England, for he had been represented at the proceedings and had acted upon the decree).

[78] (1885) 22 S.L.R. 861.

[79] By which law? The claim for salvage had been authorised by a maritime court in Norway, presumably in accordance with Norwegian law as to substantive issues and amount.

[80] Remembering the unsuccessful claim of the house insured who, when challenged that he himself had set fire to his property when drunk, replied that he was entirely sober and that the bed had been on fire when he got into it.

If, in the foreign system, there is a ladder of appeal which was not used by the party then or later declaring himself aggrieved, that fact will tell against him.[81] On the other hand, force and fear imposed on a litigant to persuade him/her to seek the remedy[82] may result in non-enforcement.[83]

(7) Decree contrary to public policy. For examples of public policy objection, reference may be made to Chapter 3, above. At common law, there is always the possibility of a public policy challenge to meet any circumstances which arise.[84]

Frequently, public policy defences merge with those founded on fraud, or unfair treatment of a litigant as a result of foreign rules of procedure. It is very rare in commercial circumstances for a Scots or English court *qua* court addressed to refuse recognition on the ground of objection to some rule of substance on which the foreign decree is founded. However, an example of an objection to the substance of a foreign decree (in family law) can be found in the case of *Re Macartney*,[85] in which the English court refused to enforce a Maltese award of "perpetual" aliment for a posthumously born child, out of the estate of her putative father. Novelty alone would not have rendered it unenforceable on policy grounds, but it was viewed in England, at least at that time, as unfair as well as unprecedented. It has been questioned whether it is right for a British forum to direct its attention to the policy acceptability of the underlying ground of decree, rather than of the judgment.[86] However in a case such as *Macartney* the objectionable rule gives rise to an objectionable judgment;

---

[81] *Cooney v Dunne*, 1925 S.L.T. 22; and *Jacobson v Frachon* (1924) 44 T.L.R. 103. Moreover, the decision of the foreign court on a procedural matter may bar the raising of that issue in the enforcement proceedings: *Desert Sun Loan Corporation v Hill* [1996] 2 All E.R. 847 ("issue estoppel" might operate in an English court as a result of an interlocutory judgment of a foreign court).

[82] *Re Meyer* [1971] 2 W.L.R. 401; *Hornett* [1971] P. 255.

[83] Similarly, where a Texas court awarded a global sum of damages, to be divided among a number of plaintiffs at the discretion of the plaintiffs' lawyers, the Texan judge making no decision upon the defendants' liability to each plaintiff, this constituted one of the grounds upon which the Court of Appeal refused to enforce the judgment: *Adams v Cape Industries plc* [1991] 1 All E.R. 929.

[84] However, see Briggs & Rees, para.7.52, where it is pointed out that there is no public policy bar to recognition (as opposed to enforcement) of a foreign judgment merely by reason of its being given upon the basis of a foreign penal or revenue law.

[85] [1921] 1 Ch. 522.

[86] Rubino-Sammartano and Morse, *Public Policy in Transnational Relationships* (1996), p.165.

in contractual cases there may be more distance between the rule and the judgment. In any event, the public policy challenge to a commercial judgment is rarely found.

(8) Decree taken contrary to agreement. Under the Civil Jurisdiction and Judgments Act 1982, section 32, a judgment given by a court in an overseas country[87] shall not be recognised or enforced in the UK if the bringing of those proceedings was contrary to an agreement,[88] by which the dispute in question was to be settled otherwise than by proceedings in the courts of that country; and those proceedings were not brought in that court by or with the agreement of the party against whom the judgment was given; and that party did not counterclaim in the proceedings or otherwise submit to the jurisdiction of that court.[89]

Res judicata

A foreign decree may be founded upon as a *defence* to an action **9–13** in Scotland[90] and in such a case, if the decree was in favour of the defender in the Scottish action, a defence of *res judicata* may be based on it. If in such a case the pursuer maintains that the decree should not be recognised, it may still be scrutinised, but the grounds on which it may be challenged are fewer in number; for example, the pursuer in a foreign action who is suing again in Scotland can hardly plead that the court which he himself selected had no jurisdiction.

The case of *Showlag v Mansour*[91] is Privy Council authority for the view that, where there are two conflicting foreign judgments on the same matter, apparently of equal standing, the first in date should be preferred.

B. Direct Enforcement of Foreign Judgments

In terms of the Judgments Extension Act 1868, and the Inferior **9–14** Courts Judgments Extension Act 1882, a system was established of registration in Edinburgh in a Register of English and Irish

---

[87] *i.e.* outside UK (s.32(4)) but not a judgment falling within the Brussels regime: *The Heidberg* [1994] 2 Ll's Rep. 287.

[88] So long as the agreement was not illegal, void, unenforceable or incapable of being performed for reasons not attributable to the fault of the party bringing the proceedings in which the judgment was given (s.32(2)).

[89] See *Tracomin v Sudan Oil Seeds Ltd (No. 1)* [1983] 3 All E.R. 137 (the first case on s.32).

[90] Scottish Cases: *Boe v Anderson* (1857) 20 D. 11; *Phosphate Sewage Co. v Molleson* (1878) 5 R. 1125; *Comber v Maclean* (1881) 9 R. 215. English Cases: *Ricardo v Garcois* (1845) 12 Cl. & F. 368 (reported at 65 R.R. 585); *Vanquelin v Bouard* (1863) 15 C.B. (N.S.) 341; *Castrique v Imrie* (1870) L.R. 4 H.L. 414; *Godard v Gray* (1870) L.R. 6 Q.B. 139; *Taylor v Hollard* [1902] 1 K.B. 676; *Jacobson v Frachon* (1927) 44 T.L.R. 103; *Kohnke v Karger* [1951] 2 K.B. 670; *Carl Zeiss Stiftung v Keeler Ltd (No. 2)* [1967] 1 A.C. 853.

[91] [1994] 2 All E.R. 129, PC.

Decrees of the Supreme (and, by the 1882 Act, the inferior) Courts of England and Ireland. After registration these decrees were given the same effect as decrees of the Court of Session, and might be enforced in the same way.

Both Acts have been repealed by the Civil Jurisdiction and Judgments Act 1982. Reciprocal enforcement of judgments within the United Kingdom is governed now by the 1982 Act, section 18 and Schedules 6 and 7.[92] These provisions replace the 1868 and 1882 Acts.

Within the Brussels/Lugano ambit, the system of enforcement is that prescribed by the Civil Jurisdiction and Judgments Act 1982 and 1991, as amended by Regulation 44/2001 (and the Civil Jurisdiction and Judgments Order 2001).[93]

There remain applicable to judgments emanating from countries outside the geographical ambit[94] of Brussels/Lugano two Acts concerning the registration of foreign judgments. These are the Administration of Justice Act 1920 and the Foreign Judgments (Reciprocal Enforcement) Act 1933.[95] The 1933 Act is more detailed than the 1920 Act[96] and is much more important in terms of geographical spread. Both Acts depend on reciprocity. Applicability of their provisions depends on their extension by Order in Council in suitable cases[97] to the country whence the judgment came.

The Administration of Justice Act 1920

9–15   Part II provides for the enforcement of judgments of superior courts within Commonwealth countries,[98] by means of registration (which is a matter of *discretion* and not of right). The provisions

---

[92] As amended by Civil Jurisdiction and Judgments Order 2001 SI 2001/3929. See below, para.9–61.

[93] See para.9–36, below.

[94] Where a judgment from an EU Member State falls outside the scope of Council Regulation 44/2001, or the Brussels Convention, as appropriate, and likewise where a judgment from an EFTA country falls outside the scope of the Lugano Convention, the 1933 Act will continue to apply.

[95] See, in detail, Rules of Court of Session (as at July 2005), Ch.62: Recognition, Registration, and Enforcement of Foreign Judgments, etc.—Part II.

[96] The contrasting features of the Acts of 1920 and 1933 are set out in a Table (fig.20.1) in Aird and Jameson, para.20.24.

[97] *i.e.* that in such country satisfactory provision for enforcement of UK judgments has been made: Administration of Justice Act 1920, s.14. In relation to the 1933 Act, see *Cheshire and North*, pp.464–465.

[98] New Zealand, Falkland Islands, Jamaica, Trinidad, Ghana, Nigeria, Kenya, Tanzania, Uganda, Zimbabwe, Zambia, Malawi, Botswana, Sri Lanka, Malaysia, Singapore. No countries will be added to the list. Gibraltar is now governed by the Civil Jurisdiction and Judgments Act 1982 (CJJA 1982 (Gibraltar) Order 1997; SI 1997/2602). Enforcement of Hong Kong judgments, previously falling under the Administration of Justice Act 1920, now proceeds at common law.

undernoted (paraphrased and abbreviated) are those of principal importance.

Section 9(1). A judgment[99] of a superior court of the Dominions **9–16** may be enforced on application to the High Court in England or [Northern] Ireland or the Court of Session in Scotland at any time within 12 months after its date or within such longer period as the (enforcing) court may allow: on any such application the court may order the judgment to be registered and enforced in the UK if it thinks it just and convenient to do so.

Section 9(2). No judgment may be registered if: **9–17**

    (a) the original court acted without jurisdiction[1]; or

    (b) the defender, being neither a person carrying on business nor ordinarily resident in the jurisdiction of the court of origin, did not voluntarily appear or submit or agree to submit to the jurisdiction of that court[2]; or

    (c) the defender was not duly served with the process of the original court and did not appear, notwithstanding that he was ordinarily resident or was carrying on business within the jurisdiction of that court or agreed to submit to the jurisdiction of that court; or

    (d) the judgment was obtained by fraud; or

    (e) the defender satisfies the registering court either that an appeal is pending, or that he is entitled and intends to appeal against the judgment[3]; or

    (f) the judgment was in respect of a cause of action which for reasons of public policy or some other similar reason could not have been entertained by the registering court.

Section 9(3). When registered the decree shall have as from the **9–18** date of registration the same force and effect, and proceedings may be taken thereon, as if it had been a judgment originally obtained in the registering court.

Section 9(4). If an action for decree conform is raised on a decree **9–19** which could have been registered the pursuer shall not be entitled to expenses unless an application for registration was refused or the court orders otherwise.

Section 10. When a decree has been obtained in a superior court **9–20** in the UK and the judgment creditor wishes to secure the

---

[99] See *Platt*, 1958 S.L.T. 94.
[1] See the more detailed prescription of the 1933 Act: s.4(2)(a)(i)—(v).
[2] *Sfeir v National Insurance Co. of New Zealand Ltd* [1964] 1 Ll's Rep. 330; and *Beach Petroleum NL v Johnson* [1996] C.L.Y. 1104.
[3] Contrast common law position, and the rule under 1933 Act, s.1(3).

enforcement of the judgment in a part of the Dominions outside the UK to which the Act extends, the court shall issue to the judgment creditor a certificated copy of the decree to enable him to enforce it.[4]

The Foreign Judgments (Reciprocal Enforcement) Act 1933

9–21   The Act applies to certain non-Commonwealth countries as well as to Commonwealth countries,[5] the hope being that ultimately it would supersede the 1920 Act. The Australian states have transferred from the 1920 to the 1933 system. European countries, in respect of which enforcement of decrees originally was governed by the 1933 Act, transferred to the Brussels system upon becoming EU Member States.[6]

Moreover, the 1933 Act governs the enforcement in the United Kingdom of judgments under certain sector-specific Conventions to which the UK is party.[7] But it does not cover the enforcement of a judgment of a relevant foreign country if the latter was simply for the enforcement of a judgment given in a third country.[8]

The Act may not be used for the recognition or enforcement of a foreign decree which does not relate to a commercial matter.[9]

Unlike the 1920 Act, registration is a matter of *right* not discretion, subject only to the provisos (section 2(1)) that registration shall not take place if at the date of the application—(a) a judgment has been wholly satisfied[10]; or (b) it could not be enforced by execution in the country of the original court.

The provisions undernoted (paraphrased and abbreviated) are of principal importance.

9–22   **Section 1(1).** The Act applies to foreign countries which give reciprocal treatment with regard to decrees of UK courts: such countries are to be specified by Order in Council.

---

[4] *Bank of British West Africa*, 1931 S.L.T. 83.
[5] The list comprises Australia, Bangladesh, Canada (except Quebec), India, Isle of Man, Israel, Jersey, Guernsey, Pakistan, Surinam and Tonga. Norway was on the original list, but the Lugano Convention now applies to Norwegian judgments. See special circumstances of the Bahamas in *B v T (No. 1)* 2002 C.L.Y.B. 637.
[6] Austria, Belgium, France, Germany, Italy, Netherlands. However, where the matter falls outside the scope of the Brussels regime, the 1933 Act continues to apply.
[7] Aird and Jameson, para.20.23, *e.g.* conventions concerning carriage by rail, road, concerning oil pollution.
[8] 1933 Act, s.1(2A), added by Civil Jurisdiction and Judgments Act 1982, Sch.10, pertaining to judgments at one remove, *e.g.* judgments of the foreign court on appeal from a court which is not a recognised court, or a judgment regarded as a judgment of the foreign court but made in another country.
[9] *Maples* [1987] 3 All E.R. 188 (concerning a Jewish divorce).
[10] If, at the date of application for registration, the judgment has been partially satisfied, judgment shall be registered only in respect of the balance remaining payable at that date (s.2(4)).

Section 1(2). A judgment of a recognised court will be governed by 9–23 this Act if it satisfied the following conditions:

(a) it is either final and conclusive as between the judgment debtor and the judgment creditor, or requires the former to make an interim payment to the latter; and

(b) there is payable thereunder a sum of money, not being a sum payable in respect of taxes or other charges of a like nature, or in respect of a fine or other penalty; and

(c) it is given after the coming into force of the Order in Council which made that court a recognised court.

Section 1(3). A judgment shall be deemed to be final and conclu- 9–24 sive notwithstanding that an appeal may be pending against it, or that it may still be subject to appeal, in the courts of the country of the original court.

Section 2(1). Application for registration may be made by the 9–25 judgment creditor to the Court of Session or the High Court within six years of the date of the decree or last judgment in the appeal proceedings; upon registration the decree has the same force and effect as a decree of the courts of this country.[11]

Section 4(1)(a). If a decree has been registered under the Act, on 9–26 application by the defender the registration *shall* be set aside[12] by the registering court if it is satisfied that:

(i) the Act does not apply to the judgment in question, or the judgment was registered in contravention of the above provisions of the Act; or

(ii) the courts of the country of the original court had no jurisdiction in the circumstances of the case; or

(iii) the defender (even if duly served in accordance with the law of the country of the original court) did not receive notice of the proceedings in sufficient time to enable him to defend the proceedings, and did not appear; or

(iv) the judgment was obtained by fraud; or

(v) the enforcement of the judgment would be contrary to public policy in the country of the registering court[13]; or

---

[11] 1933 Act, s.2(2): *Re a Judgment Debtor* [1939] 1 All E.R. 1; *Ferdinand Wagner v Laubscher Bros* [1970] 2 Q.B. 313.

[12] *Société Co-operative Sidmetal v Titan International Ltd* [1965] 3 All E.R. 494; *Northern Electricity Supply Corp. (Private) Ltd v Jamieson*, 1971 S.L.T. 22 (expenses).

[13] *SA Consortium General Textiles v Sun and Sand Agencies Ltd* [1978] 2 All E.R. 339.

(vi) the rights under the judgment are not vested in the person by whom the application for registration was made.

9–27 Section 4(1)(b). The judgment *may* be set aside if the registering court is satisfied that the matter in dispute in the proceedings in the original court had previously to the date of the judgment in the original court been the subject of a final and conclusive judgment by another court having jurisdiction in the matter (*res judicata*).

9–28 Section 4(2). Recognised grounds of jurisdiction in the original court are in essence[14] *in personam*—submission by voluntary appearance by the judgment debtor; or the debtor's residence or place of business in that place. In the case of a judgment given in an action in which the subject matter was immoveable property, or in an action *in rem* of which the subject matter was moveable property, if the property in question was at the time of the proceedings in the original court situate in the country of that court. In all other cases, if the jurisdiction of the original court is recognised by the law of the registering court, the original court will be taken to have been competent to hear the case subject to the provision below.

Notwithstanding all the above, the court is deemed not to have had jurisdiction if the subject matter was immoveable property outside the country of the original court, or if the defender was immune under the rules of public international law from the jurisdiction of the original court and did not submit to that jurisdiction.[15]

If the judgment debtor was the plaintiff in or counterclaimed in the proceedings of the original court, the court of origin will be deemed to have had jurisdiction.

9–29 Section 5(1). On an application to set aside registration, if the applicant satisfies the registering court either that an appeal is pending, or that he is entitled and intends to appeal against the judgment, the court may set aside the registration or adjourn the application until after the expiration of such period as appears to the court to be reasonably sufficient to enable the applicant to take the necessary steps to have the appeal disposed of by the competent tribunal.

9–30 Section 5(2). Where the registration of a judgment has been set aside, for any of the above reasons, or solely for the reason that at the date of application for registration the judgment was not enforceable by execution in the country of the original court, the

---

[14] For detail see 1933 Act, s.2(a), (b) and (c).
[15] *ibid.*, s.4(3).

setting aside shall not prejudice a further application to register the judgment when the appeal has been disposed of or if and when the judgment becomes enforceable by execution in that country.

Section 6. Foreign decrees which can be registered under the Act **9–31** are not enforceable by other means (*i.e.* action for decree conform is incompetent).

Section 8(1). A judgment to which Part I applies or would have **9–32** applied if a sum of money had been payable thereunder, whether it can be registered or not, or whether, if it can be registered, it is registered or not, shall be recognised in any court in the UK as conclusive between the parties thereto in all proceedings founded on the same cause of action and may be relied on by way of defence or counterclaim.[16]

Section 9. Should it appear to the Crown that the treatment **9–33** afforded by relevant foreign countries to UK judgments is substantially less favourable than that accorded by UK courts to judgments of that country, then, subject to Order in Council to the contrary, no proceedings shall be entertained in any UK court for the recovery of any sum alleged to be payable under a judgment given in such country. (This lays open the importance of reciprocity in these statutory provisions.)

The Protection of Trading Interests Act 1980

It can be seen that, although the statutes provide a structure, **9–34** essentially the system of judgment enforcement resembles that of the common law; common law authorities on matters such as fraud, natural justice or public policy therefore may be useful. All systems so far considered envisage the enforcement in the UK of fixed money judgments from courts of a foreign legal system which has jurisdiction according to an international test; and the registration system caters for those countries which have entered into reciprocal arrangements with the UK.

The enforcement system described hereto, at common law and under the Acts of 1920 and 1933, is subject to the Protection of Trading Interests Act 1980, section 5, in terms whereof no

---

[16] This provision was used in *Black-Clawson International Ltd v Papierwerke AG* [1975] 1 All E.R. 810, to persuade the Court of Appeal that a German judgment on its own limitation period was conclusive and binding on the English court. However, the House of Lords held that the extent of conclusiveness of the German judgment was as to the effect of the limitation period in German law, and not upon the substance of the case; the English limitation period being longer, the English court was not barred from hearing the substance of the case. But see now for England Foreign Limitation Periods Act 1984, s.3.

judgment to which section 5 applies shall be registered under the Acts of 1920 or of 1933, nor shall common law enforcement proceedings be entertained by any UK court.[17] The judgments affected are:

9–35 **Section 5(2)** (paraphrased and abbreviated)

    (a) a judgment for multiple damages[18];

    (b) a judgment based on a provision or rule of law specified or described in an order under section 5(4)[19];

    (c) a judgment on a claim for contribution in respect of damages awarded by a judgment falling within (a) or (b) above.

Section 6 applies where such a judgment for multiple damages has been made against a UK citizen, or company incorporated in the UK or person carrying on business in the UK, and where such a defendant has paid (or has yielded through process of execution (section 6(6)) an amount on account of the damages; *in such circumstances, unless*[20] the party (the "qualifying defendant") was ordinarily resident in the overseas country at the time of the institution of the judgment proceedings, or is a body corporate with its principal business there, or carried on business in the overseas country and the judgment proceedings concerned activities exclusively carried on in that country, the qualifying defendant *shall be entitled to recover from the judgment creditor so much of the amount as exceeds the part attributable to compensation.*[21] Further, by section 6(5), a court in the UK may entertain proceedings on such a claim even though the person against whom the proceedings are brought is not within the jurisdiction of the court.

This legislation, unusual in nature, and unusually specific, is designed to protect British individuals and companies from American anti-trust legislation which makes possible an award of multiple damages for losses caused by anti-competitive actings.[22] Section

---

[17] See *British Airways Board v Laker Airways Ltd* [1985] A.C. 58. Contrast *Lewis v Eliades (No.2)* [2003] 1 All E.R. (Comm) 850.

[18] *i.e.* a judgment for an amount arrived at by doubling, trebling or otherwise multiplying a sum assessed as compensation for the loss or damage sustained by the person in whose favour the judgment is given (s.5(3)).

[19] *i.e.* a judgment appearing to the Secretary of State to be concerned with the prohibition or regulation of agreements, arrangements or practices designed to restrain, distort or restrict competition in the carrying on of business of any description or to be otherwise concerned with the promotion of such competition.

[20] Emphasis added.

[21] As defined: s.6(2) (emphasis added).

[22] For explanation of background and details, see Cheshire and North, pp.448–450.

5 (and consequently section 6) does not apply within the Brussels/ Lugano ambit, nor, generally, does it appear to strike at other foreign awards of exemplary damages which do not fall within the definition provided by section 5(3).[23]

JUDGMENTS RENDERED IN EU MEMBER STATES OR EFTA STATES[24]

Civil Jurisdiction and Judgments Acts 1982 and 1991

It falls now to consider the system of free flow of judgments put **9–36** in place by the Brussels Convention, as augmented and amended. Since that Convention was a double convention, concerned to reach agreement on jurisdiction and then to proceed to a relatively simple enforcement method, certain differences from the systems earlier described are apparent, one at the outset being the small scope for query as to the foreign court's jurisdiction. Further, the mechanism is not limited to the enforcement of money judgments, but may extend to decrees *ad factum praestandum*; it does not matter that the judgment is not final, nor is the level of the hierarchy whence the decree comes significant. Finally, such defences as are made must fall within those specifically rendered available by the Convention: the "catch-all" defence of *ordre public* does not catch so much as does the common law defence of public policy.[25]

Council Regulation (EC) No 44/2001 (and Brussels Convention)

Introduction and general principles

The Brussels Convention laid down its own procedure for **9–37** enforcement, a procedure which has been streamlined, but not in essentials changed by Council Regulation 44/2001.

---

[23] *SA Consortium General Textiles v Sun and Sand Agencies* [1978] 2 All E.R. 339.

[24] See W. Kennett, *The Enforcement of Judgments in Europe* (OUP) 2000; and S. Cromie, *International Commercial Litigation* (2nd ed., 1997), Ch.XI, and J. Hill, *International Commercial Disputes in English Courts* (3rd ed., 2005). Also K. Lipstein (ed.), *Harmonisation of Private International Law by the EEC* (1978), chapters entitled "Judgments Convention: Jurisdiction" (L. Collins) and "Judgments Convention: Recognition" (T. Hartley); Anton and Beaumont, Ch.8; L. Collins, *The Civil Jurisdiction and Judgments Act 1982*; and Briggs and Rees, *Civil Jurisdiction and Judgments* (2nd ed., 1997).

[25] *Interdesco SA v Nullifire Ltd* [1992] 1 Ll's Rep. 180.

The recognition rules of the Regulation apply only to judg-ments[26] from Community countries,[27] and only to such judgments as fall within the scope of the Regulation (that is, *judgments in civil and commercial matters*, not specifically excluded by Article 1).[28] The rules of recognition and enforcement vis-à-vis all Member States except Denmark are contained in Chapter III, Articles 32 to 56 of the Regulation.

The ambit of the Brussels Convention is restricted to Denmark; as regards enforcement of Danish judgments in the UK and *vice versa*, reference (currently) must be made to the Brussels Convention.[29]

The enforcement mechanism under both the Regulation and the Convention applies to all qualifying judgments, whether or not the defendant was "domiciled" in a Contracting State/ Denmark. This feature of the original Convention made it necessary to allow therein for the possibility of bilateral agreements between Con-tracting States and non-Contracting States whose nationals live in Contracting States, in order to ensure that in the former States the enforcement procedures might not be used against them.[30] Such bilateral agreements continue to be respected under the Regulation.[31]

Where the Regulation (or Convention, as appropriate) is oper-ative, no other (*e.g.* common law) procedure is competent;[32] the Brussels system is obligatory. The claimant must apply to a court in his own country for an enforcement order. If granted, notice is given to the defendant, who has a right to appeal on the grounds that the judgment is outside the scope of the Regulation, that it is not enforceable in the country which granted the judgment, or that it is not entitled to recognition under the Regulation. A judgment

---

[26] Art.32: the recognition and enforcement scheme applies to any judgment given by a court or tribunal of a Member State, whatever the judgment may be called, including a decree, order, decision or writ of execution, as well as the determina-tion of costs or expenses by an officer of the court. *Cf.* Brussels Convention, Art.25. The system, therefore, may be taken to extend to the enforcement of judgments of a court of a Member State no matter the position of that court in the Member State's hierarchy. For provisions in the Regulation concerning authentic instruments and court settlements, see Ch.IV (Arts 57 and 58) (*cf.* Brussels Convention, Arts 50 and 51; and Lugano Convention, Arts 50 and 51).

[27] There can be no "laundering" of non-EU judgments: *Owens Bank Ltd v Bracco (No. 2)* [1994] 1 All E.R. 336. The convention enforcement procedure does not apply to judgments from a court of a non-contracting state (*cf.* exclusion of laundering in 1933 Act, s.1(2A), added by Civil Jurisdiction and Judgments Act 1982, Sch.10). Nor does it apply to interim decisions on procedure, or court settlements (Clarkson & Hill, p.185; *cf.* Lugano Convention, Art.25).

[28] Art.25.

[29] See para.7–08, above.

[30] Brussels Convention, Art.59.

[31] Regulation 44/2001, Art.72.

[32] *De Wolf v Cox* [1976] E.C.R. 1759.

must be recognised before it can be enforced: "a judgment cannot be enforced unless it is first recognised; but it may be recognised without being enforced."[33] There are various challenges to recognition, as explained below.

Henceforth in this chapter, reference shall be to the terms of the Regulation, with equivalent provisions of the Brussels Convention footnoted.

Scope

The scope of the Regulation encompasses *civil and commercial* **9–38** *matters*. It shall not extend (in particular) to revenue, customs or administrative matters.[34] The Regulation shall not apply to the following categories of decree[35]:

(a) the status or legal capacity of natural persons, rights in property arising out of a matrimonial relationship,[36] wills and succession;

(b) bankruptcy, proceedings relating to the winding-up of insolvent companies or other legal persons, judicial arrangements, compositions and analogous proceedings;

(c) social security;

(d) and arbitration.[37]

If the outcome of proceedings in a Member State court depends upon the determination of an incidental question of recognition, that court shall have jurisdiction over that question.[38]

Recognition rules in Council Regulation 44/2001

Article 33[39]

A judgment given in a Member State shall be recognised in the **9–39** other Member States without any special procedure being required.[40]

---

[33] Hartley, *op.cit.*, p.105.

[34] Art.1.1.

[35] Art.1.2.

[36] But maintenance is included; and where a matter falls in the area of maintenance and matrimonial property, questions of classification arise, one such case being *Van Den Boogard v Laumen* (Case C-220/95), *The Times*, March 26, 1997 (relating to Art.5.2). See also *Farrell v Long* (Case C-295/95) [1997] All E.R. (E.C.) 449. See Ch.12 concerning consistorial causes, and Ch.13 regarding matrimonial property issues.

[37] What is to happen if a foreign court takes jurisdiction in a case where ordinarily it would have jurisdiction were it not for an arbitration clause, on the view that the arbitration is invalid or not incorporated in the agreement? See below, paras 9–76 *et seq.*

[38] Art.33.3.

[39] *cf.* Brussels Convention, Art.26; and Lugano Convention, Art.26.

[40] Where a judgment is given against a state by a court in another state, this, to be enforceable, must be in conformity with the State Immunity Act 1978.

Any interested party who raises the recognition of a judgment as the principal issue in a dispute may, in accordance with the procedures provided for in sections 2 and 3 of this Chapter, apply for a decision that the judgment be recognised.

If the outcome of proceedings in a court of a Member State depends on the determination of an incidental question of recognition that court shall have jurisdiction over the question.

Article 34[41]

9–40   A judgment shall not be recognised:

(1) if such recognition is manifestly[42] contrary to public policy in the Member State in which recognition is sought[43];

(2) where it was given in default of appearance, if the defendant was not served[44] with the document which instituted the proceedings or with an equivalent document in sufficient time and in such a way as to enable him to arrange for his defence, unless the defendant failed to commence proceedings to challenge the judgment when it was possible for him to do so;

(3) if it is irreconcilable with a judgment given in a dispute between the same parties in the Member State in which recognition is sought[45];

(4) if it is irreconcilable with an earlier judgment given in another Member State or in a third State involving the same cause of action and between the same parties, provided that the earlier judgment fulfils the conditions

---

[41] *cf.* Brussels Convention, Art.27.

[42] The word "manifestly" does not appear in Brussels Convention, Art.27, or in Lugano Convention, Art.27.

[43] *Viking Line ABP v The International Transport Workers' Federation* [2006] I.L.Pr. 4, paras 78-81. See under Brussels Convention *Sisro v Ampersand Software BV* [1995] 10 C.L. 97. Under this heading of public policy/*ordre public* will be subsumed allegations of fraud, but the challenge is a muted version of the strong challenge available at common law: *Interdesco SA v Nullifire Ltd* [1992] 1 Ll's Rep. 180. Also *Regie Nationale des Usines Renault SA v Maxicar Spa* [2000] C.L.Y. 782. As to human rights challenges, see *Krombach v Bamberski* [2000] ECR I-1935; *Pordea v Times Newspapers Ltd* [2001] CLYB 818; and *Marie Brizard ETA Roger International SA v William Grant & Sons Ltd (No. 2)*, 2002 S.L.T. 1365.

[44] *cf.* Brussels Convention, Art.27 reference to "duly served" (and Lugano Convention, Art.27). *Arctic Fish Sales Co Ltd v Adam (No. 2)*, 1995 G.W.D. 25–1351, and *Selco Ltd v Mercier*, 1996 S.L.T. 1247; and earlier from ECJ *Pendy Plastic Products BV v Pluspunkt* (Case 228/81) [1982] E.C.R. 2723, to the effect that "duly served" is to be tested against the law of the originating court, and "sufficient time" by the law of the enforcing system. *Debaecker v Bouwman* [1985] E.C.R. 1779, and *TSN Kunststoffrecycling GmbH v Jurgens* [2002] 1 W.L.R. 2459. See, however, further, Clarkson & Hill, p.192.

[45] *Hoffmann v Krieg* (Case 145/86) [1988] E.C.R. 645.

necessary for its recognition in the Member State addressed.[46]

Article 35[47]

(1) Moreover, a judgment shall not be recognised if it conflicts **9–41** with Sections 3, 4 or 6 of Chapter II,[48] or in a case provided for in Article 72.[49]

(2) In its examination of the grounds of jurisdiction referred to in the foregoing paragraph, the court or authority applied to shall be bound by the findings of fact on which the court of the Member State of origin based its jurisdiction.

(3) Subject to paragraph 1, the jurisdiction of the court of the Member State of origin may not be reviewed.[50] The test of public policy referred to in point 1 of Article 34 may not be applied to the rules relating to jurisdiction.

Article 36[51]

Under no circumstances may a foreign judgment be reviewed as **9–42** to its substance.

Article 37[52]

(1) A court of a Member State in which recognition is sought **9–43** of a judgment given in another Member State may stay the proceedings if an ordinary appeal against the judgment has been lodged.

---

[46] The Regulation does *not* provide for refusal of recognition in circumstances where the judgment of the State of origin concerns a preliminary question on, *e.g.* the status or legal capacity of natural persons, or other topics excluded from the scope of the instrument. Contrast Brussels Convention, Art.27.4, and Lugano Convention, Art.27.4. Kennett (writing in anticipation of Reg.44/2001) notes that, in view of the process of approximation of laws in family law, achieved and contemplated, the removal of Art.27.4 had been accepted (Kennett, *op.cit*, p.222). See *Italian Leather SpA v Weco Polstermobel GmbH & Co* [2003] CLYB 620.

[47] *cf.* Brussels Convention, Art.28.

[48] That is to say, jurisdiction in matters relating to insurance (3); jurisdiction over consumer contracts (4); and exclusive jurisdiction provisions (6). Inexplicably, the limitation on recognition contained in Art.35.1 does not extend to cases falling under S.5 (jurisdiction over individual contracts of employment). There appears to be no reason for this omission, and it is thought to have arisen from mere oversight, probably because employees were not a protected category under the Brussels Convention, nor under Lugano (*cf.* Lugano Convention, Art.28).

[49] Art.72 ensures that agreements made by Member States with third States to protect defendants domiciled or habitually resident in those third States shall not be affected by the Regulation. It does not appear, however, that such special arrangements may be made in future (*cf.* n.31, above).

[50] See *Continuity Promotions Ltd v O'Connor's Nenagh Shopping Centre Ltd* [2006] All E.R. (D) 39, in which the English court declined to set aside a default judgment which had been entered against an Irish defendant in England without jurisdiction in terms of Reg.44/2001.

[51] *cf.* Brussels Convention, Art.29, and Lugano Convention, Art.29.

[52] *cf.* Brussels Convention, Art.30, and Lugano Convention, Art.30.

    (2) A court of a Member State in which recognition is sought of a judgment given in Ireland or the United Kingdom may stay the proceedings if enforcement is suspended in the State of origin, by reason of an appeal.

Enforcement rules in Council Regulation 44/2001

Article 38[53]

9–44   (1) A judgment given in a Member State and enforceable in that State shall be enforced in another Member State when, on the application of any interested party, it has been declared enforceable there.[54]

    (2) However, in the UK, such a judgment shall be enforced in England and Wales, in Scotland, or in Northern Ireland when, on the application of any interested party, it has been registered for enforcement in that part of the UK.[55]

Article 39[56]

9–45   (1) The application shall be submitted to the court or competent authority indicated in the list in Annex II.[57]

    (2) The local jurisdiction shall be determined by reference to the place of domicile of the party against whom enforcement is sought or to the place of enforcement.

Article 40[58]

9–46   (1) The procedure for making the application shall be governed by the law of the Member State in which enforcement is sought.

---

[53] *cf.* Brussels Convention, Art.31, and Lugano Convention, Art.31.

[54] This is the *exequatur* procedure ("declaration of enforceability"). In terms of Art.53 a party seeking recognition or applying for a declaration of enforceability shall produce a copy of the judgment, which satisfies the conditions necessary to establish its authenticity; together with a certificate [see note 59 below]. No legalisation or other similar formality shall be required in respect of the copy judgment, certificate, or translation thereof, or in respect of a document appointing a representative *ad litem* (Art 56).

[55] For the UK, reference is to the process of registration rather than to the declaration of enforceability (*qv* Art.41): J Hill, *International Commercial Disputes in English Courts*, para 13.4.10; and Jenard-Moller Report [1990] OJ C189/79 (para 68). This difference is attributable to the lack of an *exequatur* procedure in the UK, but the difference is largely one of terminology.

[56] *cf.* Brussels Convention, Art.32.

[57] Within the United Kingdom, application shall be submitted to: (a) In England and Wales, to the High Court of Justice, or in the case of a maintenance judgment to the Magistrates' Court on transmission by the Secretary of State; (b) in Scotland, to the Court of Session, or in the case of a maintenance judgment to the Sheriff Court on transmission by the Secretary of State; and (c) in Northern Ireland to the High Court of Justice, or in the case of a maintenance judgment to the Magistrates' Court on transmission by the Secretary of State.

[58] *cf.* Brussels Convention, Art.33, and Lugano Convention, Art.33.

(2) The applicant must give an address for service of process within the area of jurisdiction of the court applied to. However, if the law of the Member State in which enforcement is sought does not provide for the furnishing of such an address, the applicant shall appoint a representative *ad litem*.

(3) The documents referred to in Article 53 shall be attached to the application.[59]

Article 41[60]

The judgement shall be declared enforceable immediately on completion of the formalities in Article 53 (*qv*) without any review under Articles 34 and 35. The party against whom enforcement is sought shall not at this stage of the proceedings be entitled to make any submissions on the application. **9–47**

Article 42[61]

(1) The decision on the application for a declaration of enforceability shall forthwith be brought to the notice of the applicant in accordance with the procedure laid down by the law of the Member State in which enforcement is sought. **9–48**

(2) The declaration of enforceability shall be served on the party against whom enforcement is sought, accompanied by the judgment, if not already served on that party.

Article 43[62]

(1) The decision on the application for a declaration of enforceability may be appealed against by either party.[63] **9–49**

---

[59] *i.e.* a copy of the judgment, which satisfies the conditions necessary to establish its authenticity. A party applying for a declaration of enforceability shall also produce (without prejudice to Art.55) the certificate referred to in Art.54: the court or competent authority of a Member State where a judgment was given shall issue, at the request of any interested party, a certificate using the standard form in Annex V to the Regulation. Art.55 provides that if such certificate is not produced, the court or competent authority (by inference, of the state addressed) may specify a time for its production, or accept an equivalent document, or if it considers that it has sufficient information before it, dispense with its production. If that latter court so requires, a certified translation of the document shall be produced. *Cf.* Brussels Convention, Arts 46–49, and Lugano Convention, Arts 46–49.

[60] Compare and contrast Brussels Convention, Art.34, and Lugano Convention, Art.34. Note also Art.38.2, in relation to the UK.

[61] *cf.* Brussels Convention, Art.35, and Lugano Convention, Art.35.

[62] *cf.* Brussels Convention, Arts 36, 37 and 40, and Lugano Convention, Arts 36, 37 and 40.

[63] Under Reg.44/2001, it must be concluded that there are very few grounds upon

(2) The appeal is to be lodged with the court indicated in the list in Annex III.[64]

(3) The appeal shall be dealt with in accordance with the rules governing procedure in contradictory matters.

(4) If the party against whom enforcement is sought fails to appear before the appellate court in proceedings concerning an appeal brought by the applicant, Article 26(2) to (4) shall apply[65] even where the party against whom enforcement is sought is not domiciled in any of the Member States.

(5) An appeal against the declaration of enforceability is to be lodged within one month of service thereof. If the party against whom enforcement is sought is domiciled in a Member State other than that in which the declaration of enforceability was given, the time for appealing shall be two months and shall run from the date of service, either on him in person or at his residence. No extension of time may be granted on account of distance.

---

which the applicant shall be refused this declaration of enforceability; presumably the only possible ground would be failure to comply with the formalities of Art.53. This must be contrasted with the situation which obtained under the Brussels Convention, in which (*per* Art.34) although the party against whom enforcement was sought was not entitled at that stage to make any submissions on the application, the application might be refused for one of the reasons specified in Arts 27 and 28 of the Convention (*i.e.* the substantive grounds of refusal of recognition—public policy, natural justice, failure to observe the jurisdictional rules with regard to disadvantaged parties etc). Under Reg.44/2001, however, the judgment shall be declared enforceable immediately on completion of the formalities, without any review under Arts 34 and 35 (the equivalent non-recognition grounds). Arts 34 and 35 can be invoked only after the declaration of enforceability. Thus, it would seem that recognition under Art.33.1 is provisional in nature.

[64] *cf.* Brussels Convention, Art.37(1). In the UK, as follows: (a) in England and Wales, with the High Court of Justice or (maintenance judgment) Magistrates' Court; (b) in Scotland, with the Court of Session, or (maintenance judgment) Sheriff Court; and (c) in Northern Ireland with the High Court of Justice, or (maintenance judgment) Magistrates' Court.

[65] *i.e.* rules concerning the case where a defendant domiciled in one Member State is sued in a court of another Member State and does not enter an appearance: the court shall declare of its own motion that it has no jurisdiction unless its jurisdiction is derived from the provisions of Regulation 44/2001. If so, the court shall stay its proceedings unless it is shown that the defendant has received sufficient intimation in sufficient time to enable him to arrange for his defence, or that all necessary steps have been taken to this end (subject to Council Regulation No. 1348/2000 (Service of Documents), Art.19, where applicable; where Reg.1348/2000 is not applicable, the 1965 Hague Convention, Art.15 shall apply).

Article 44[66]

The judgment given on the appeal may be contested only by the **9–50** appeal referred to in Annex IV.[67]

Article 45[68]

(1) The court with which an appeal is lodged under Article 43 **9–51** and Article 44 shall refuse or revoke a declaration of enforceability only on one of the grounds specified in Articles 34 and 35. It shall give its decision without delay.

(2) Under no circumstances may the foreign judgment be reviewed as to its substance.

Article 46[69]

(1) The court with which an appeal is lodged under Article 43 **9–52** or Article 44 may, on the application of the party against whom enforcement is sought, stay the proceedings if an ordinary appeal has been lodged against the judgment in the Member State of origin or if the time for such an appeal has not yet expired. In the latter case, the court may specify the time within which such an appeal is to be lodged.

(2) Where the judgment was given in Ireland or the UK, any form of appeal available in the Member State of origin shall be treated as an ordinary appeal for the purposes of paragraph 1.

(3) The court may also make enforcement conditional on the provision of such security as it shall determine.

Article 47[70]

(1) When a judgment must be recognised in accordance with **9–53** this Regulation, nothing shall prevent the applicant from availing himself of provisional, including protective, mea-

---

[66] *cf.* Brussels Convention, Art.37, and Lugano Convention, Art.37.

[67] The court with which the appeal under Art.44 is lodged may on the application of the appellant (see *Petereit v Babcock International Holdings Ltd* [1990] 1 W.L.R. 350), stay the proceedings if an ordinary appeal has been lodged against the judgment in the state of origin or if the time for such an appeal has not yet expired; in the latter case, the court may specify the time within which such an appeal is to be lodged. Where the judgment was given in Ireland or the United Kingdom, any form of appeal available in the state of origin shall be treated as an ordinary appeal for the purposes of the first paragraph. The court may also make endorsement conditional on the provision of such security as it shall determine. (Referral by Court of Session on Art.38(1) and (2)—*Marie Brizard et Roger International SA v William Grant & Sons (International) Ltd* (Case C–126/96)).

[68] *cf.* Brussels Convention, Art.38, and Lugano Convention, Art.30.

[69] *cf.* Brussels Convention, Art.38, and Lugano Convention, Art.38.

[70] *cf.* Brussels Convention, Art.39, and Lugano Convention, Art.39.

sures in accordance with the law of the Member State requested without a declaration of enforceability under Article 41 being required.

(2) The declaration of enforceability shall carry with it the power to proceed to any protective measures.

(3) During the time specified for an appeal pursuant to Article 43(5) against the declaration of enforceability and until such appeal has been determined, no measures of enforcement may be taken other than protective measures against the property of the party against whom enforcement is sought.

Article 48[71]

9–54   (1) Where a foreign judgment has been given in respect of several matters and the declaration of enforceability cannot be given for all of them, the court of competent authority shall give it for one or more of them.

(2) An applicant may request a declaration of enforceability limited to parts of a judgment.

Article 49[72]

9–55   A foreign judgement which orders a periodic payment by way of a penalty shall be enforceable in the Member State in which enforcement is sought only if the amount of the payment has been finally determined by the courts of the Member State of origin.

Article 50[73]

9–56   An applicant who, in the Member State of origin has benefited from complete or partial legal aid or exemption from costs or expenses, shall be entitled, in the procedure provided for in this Section, to benefit from the most favourable legal aid or the most extensive exemption from costs or expenses provided for by the law of the Member State addressed.

Article 51[74]

9–57   No security, bond or deposit, however described, shall be required of a party who in one Member State applies for enforcement of a judgment given in another Member State on the grounds that he is a foreign national or that he is not domiciled or resident in the State in which enforcement is sought.

---

[71] *cf.* Brussels Convention, Art.42, and Lugano Convention, Art.42.
[72] *cf.* Brussels Convention, Art.43, and Lugano Convention, Art.43.
[73] *cf.* Brussels Convention, Art.44, and Lugano Convention, Art.44.
[74] *cf.* Brussels Convention, Art.45, and Lugano Convention, Art.45.

Article 52

In proceedings for the issue of a declaration of enforceability no **9–58** charge, duty or fee calculated by reference to the value of the matter at issue may be levied in the Member State in which enforcement is sought.

Summary of enforcement procedure under Council Regulation 44/2001[75]

The following is an outline of the procedure to be followed by a **9–59** claimant seeking to enforce a Member State judgment in Scotland. The claimant must sue on the judgment, and not on the cause of action.[76]

(1) Application for declaration of enforceability (*i.e.* registration) is made *ex parte* to the Court of Session. The defender has no right to be heard, or even to be informed. The element of surprise is intended to lessen the possibility of removal by the defender of his property from the enforcing state.

(2) The declaration of enforceability shall be granted (*i.e.* registration shall be made) immediately on completion of due formalities (ie production of relevant documents), without any review at this stage of matters such as public policy, natural justice, and such challenges to jurisdiction as the Regulation permits. The defender at this stage shall not be entitled to make any submissions.

(3) A declaration of enforceability (*i.e.* registration) shall carry with it the power to proceed to any protective measures.

(4) The declaration of enforceability (*i.e.* registered order) shall be served on the defender.

(5) The decision to grant or withhold the declaration of enforceability (registration) may be appealed by either party to the Court of Session within a period of one month (or two months, if he is domiciled in another Member State).

(6) The judgment given on the appeal may be contested only by a single further appeal on a point of law to the Inner House of the Court of Session.[77]

(7) In the case of appeal at stages (4) or (5), the grounds of appeal are limited to those specified in Articles 34 and 35

---

[75] See, in detail, Rules of Court of Session (as at July 2005), Chapter 62—Recognition, Registration, and Enforcement of Foreign Judgments, etc.—Part V—Recognition and Enforcement under the Civil Jurisdiction and Judgments Act 1982, or under Council Regulation (EC) No.44/2001.

[76] *De Wolf v Henry Cox BV* [1976] E.C.R. 1759.

[77] Civil Jurisdiction & Judgments Order 2001 (SI 2001/3929), Sch.1, r.4.

(public policy, natural justice, jurisdiction (so far as permitted)), except that the proceedings may be stayed if an ordinary appeal has been lodged against the judgment in the Member State of origin or if the time for such an appeal has not yet expired.

Enforcement procedures under the Lugano Convention[78]

9–60   Article 54B (Lugano Convention) governs the relationship between the Lugano Convention and the Brussels (and other) Conventions. In terms of Article 54B.2(c), in matters of recognition and enforcement, Lugano shall apply where either the State of origin, or the State addressed is not an EU Member State, but is a Contracting State to Lugano.

Lugano and Brussels enforcement provisions are generally the same except that Article 54B.3[79] provides that recognition or enforcement may be refused under Lugano if the ground of jurisdiction on which the judgment has been based differs from those contained in the Lugano Convention, *and* recognition or enforcement is sought against a party who is domiciled in a Contracting State (to Lugano) which is not a member of the European Communities, unless the judgment may otherwise be recognised or enforced under any rule of law in the State addressed.[80]

In Article 32, the relevant courts of relevant countries in respect of enforcement of judgments ordering the payment of a sum of money, and on the other hand, judgments ordering the performance other than the payment of a sum of money, are specified. So too in Articles 37 and 40, the appropriate courts for application for appeal against the decision authorizing enforcement and for further appeal are listed.

Article 59 remains, permitting bilateral arrangements to be made between a Lugano Contracting State and a third State, whereby it is agreed not to recognise and enforce judgments given in other Contracting States against defendants domiciled or habitually resident in the third State, where the judgment in question could be founded only on a ground of jurisdiction specified in Article 3.2 (*i.e.* so-called exorbitant jurisdictions).[81]

---

[78] See Chap.7 above for scope and rules of jurisdiction.

[79] See Civil Jurisdiction and Judgments Order 2001 (SI 2001/3929), Sch.2, para.1(c).

[80] See also Art.57(4), and Protocol 1(1)(b).

[81] However, a Contracting State may not assume an obligation towards a third State not to recognise a judgment given in another Contracting State by a court basing its jurisdiction on the presence within that State of property belonging to the defendant or the seizure by the plaintiff of property situated there: (1) if the action is brought to assert or declare proprietary or possessory rights in that property, seeks to obtain authority to dispose of it, or arises from another issue relating to such property; or (2) if the property constitutes the security for a debt which is the subject-matter of the action.

In essence, therefore, the Lugano Convention is more or less equivalent to the Brussels Convention. Consequently, it has not benefited from such advantages of speed and certainty which have followed as a result of the transformation of the Brussels Convention into a Regulation. Furthermore, in the matter of appeal to the European Court of Justice on points of interpretation of the instrument, there is a difference. While the Luxembourg Protocol permits a reference to the ECJ on a matter of interpretation of the Brussels Convention by a court from which there is no further domestic appeal, there is no such provision in relation to Lugano. Courts in Lugano Contracting States will have the benefit of the Jenard-Möller Report and must "take account" of relevant decisions in other states which are parties to Lugano,[82] but interpretation of Lugano is not under central control.

Reciprocal Enforcement within the United Kingdom

The relevant provisions, contained in Civil Jurisdiction and Judgments Act 1982, section 18 and Schedules 6 and 7, replace those contained in the Judgments Extension Act 1868 and the Inferior Courts Judgments Extension Act 1882. They apply to money (Schedule 6) and non-money (Schedule 7) judgments, and include, therefore, orders of interdict and specific implement. Arbitration awards also are included.[83] **9–61**

"Judgment" is defined positively in section 18(2), beginning (section 18(2)(a)) "any judgment or order (by whatever name called) given or made by a court of law in the United Kingdom", with derogations therefrom in section 18(3), (5), (6) and (7), excluding judgments *inter alia* regarding insolvency, maintenance, status or capacity, management of affairs of *incapaces*, and foreign judgments which have achieved status as UK judgments by virtue of legislation under statute, for example 1920 or 1933 Acts.[84]

Schedule 6 (money provisions)[85] (abbreviated extracts)

Paragraph 2(1). Any interested party who wishes to secure the enforcement in another part of the United Kingdom of any money provisions contained in a judgment may apply for a certificate under this Schedule (in the manner prescribed by section 2(2)). **9–62**

---

[82] The Civil Jurisdiction and Judgments Act 1982, s.3B(1). The report which accompanies the Brussels Convention is the Jenard Report; on the Accession Convention, the Schlosser Report; on the Greek Accession Convention, the Evrigemis and Kerameus Report; and on the San Sebastian Convention, the Cruz, Real and Jenard Report. (See *Jurisdiction, Foreign Judgments and Awards Handbook* (Butterworths, 1994).)

[83] s.18(2)(e).

[84] See Aird and Jameson, para.20.05.

[85] See, in detail, Rules of Court of Session (as at July 2005), Chap.62—Recognition, Registration, and Enforcement of Foreign Judgments, etc—Part V—Recognition and Enforcement under the Civil Jurisdiction and Judgments Act 1982, or under

9–63 Paragraph 3. A certificate shall not be issued under this Schedule in respect of a judgment unless under the law of the part of the UK in which the judgment was given either the time for bringing an appeal against the judgment has expired, no such appeal having been brought within that time, or, such an appeal having been brought within that time, that appeal has been finally disposed of, and provided further, that the enforcement of the judgment is not for the time being stayed or suspended, and the time available for its enforcement has not expired.

9–64 Paragraph 4. The proper officer shall issue to the applicant a certificate . . . stating the sum payable and such other particulars as may be prescribed, and stating that the above conditions have been satisfied.

9–65 Paragraph 5. Where a certificate has been issued under this Schedule in any part of the UK, any interested party may, within six months from the date of its issue, apply in the prescribed manner to the proper officer of the superior court[86] in any other part of the UK (*i.e.* Court of Session or, in relation to England and Wales, or Northern Ireland, the High Court) for the certificate to be registered in that court.

9–66 Paragraph 6(1). A certificate registered under this Schedule shall, for the purposes of its enforcement, be of the same force and effect, the registering court shall have in respect of its enforcement the same powers, and proceedings for or with respect to its enforcement may be taken, as if the certificate has been a judgment originally given in the registering courts and had (where relevant) been entered.

9–67 Paragraph 9. Where a certificate in respect of a judgment has been registered under this Schedule, the registering court may, if it satisfied that any person against whom it is sought to enforce the certificate is entitled and intends to apply under the law of the part of the UK in which the judgment was given for any remedy which would result in the setting aside or quashing of the judgment, stay (or, in Scotland, sist) proceedings for the enforcement of the certificate, on such terms as it thinks fit, for such period as appears to the court to be reasonably sufficient to enable the application to be disposed of.

9–68 Paragraph 10. Where a certificate has been registered under this Schedule, the registering court—

Council Regulation (EC) No 44/2001—rr.62.37 and 62.41.
[86] Even if the court of origin of the judgment was an inferior court.

(a) shall set aside the registration if, on an application made by any interested party, it is satisfied that the registration was contrary to the provisions of this Schedule;

(b) may set aside the registration if, on an application so made, it is satisfied that the matter in dispute in the proceedings in which the judgment in question was given, had previously been the subject of a judgment by another court or tribunal having jurisdiction in the matter.

Schedule 7 (non-money provisions)[87] (abbreviated extracts)

Paragraph 2(1). Any interested party who wishes to secure the enforcement in another part of the UK of any non-money provisions contained in a judgment may apply for a certified copy of the judgment (to the proper officer of the original court, who shall issue the certified copy, subject, however, to the same provisos as set out above regarding appeals etc.). **9–69**

Paragraph 5(1). Where a certified copy of a judgment has been issued under this Schedule in any part of the UK, any interested party may apply in the prescribed manner to the superior court in any other part of the UK (*i.e.* Court of Session or, in relation to England and Wales, or Northern Ireland, the High Court) for the judgment to be registered in that court. **9–70**

Paragraph 5(5). A judgment shall not be registered under this Schedule by the superior court in any part of the UK if compliance with the non-money provisions contained in the judgment would involve a breach of the law of that part of the UK. **9–71**

Paragraph 6(1). The non-money provisions contained in a judgment registered under this Schedule shall, for the purposes of their enforcement, be of the same force and effect, the registering court shall have in relation to their enforcement the same powers, and proceedings for or with respect to their enforcement may be taken, as if the judgment containing them had been originally given in the registering court and had (where relevant) been entered. **9–72**

Paragraph 8. Where a certificate in respect of a judgment has been registered under this Schedule, the registering court may, if it is satisfied that any person against whom it is sought to enforce the certificate is entitled and intends to apply under the law of the part **9–73**

---

[87] See, in detail, Rules of Court of Session (as at July 2005), Chap.62—Recognition, Registration, and Enforcement of Foreign Judgments, etc—Part V—Recognition and Enforcement under the Civil Jurisdiction and Judgments Act 1982, or under Council Regulation (EC) No.44/2001—rr.62.38 and 62.42.

of the UK in which the judgment was given for any remedy which would result in the setting aside or quashing of the judgment, stay (or, in Scotland, sist) proceedings for the enforcement of the certificate, on such terms as it thinks fit, for such period as appears to the court to be reasonably sufficient to enable the application to be disposed of.

9–74 Paragraph 9. Where a certificate has been registered under this Schedule, the registering court—

    (a) shall set aside the registration if, on an application made by any interested party, it is satisfied that the registration was contrary to the provisions of this Schedule;

    (b) may set aside the registration if, on an application so made, it is satisfied that the matter in dispute in the proceedings in which the judgment in question was given, had previously been the subject of a judgment by another court or tribunal having jurisdiction in the matter.

Summary

9–75 Thus, judgments to which section 18 applies may not be enforced except by registration under Schedules 6 or 7.[88] Moreover, reasons for *refusal to register* are strictly limited under both Schedules. Judgments to which section 18 apply, in the matter of intra-UK *recognition* (only), are governed by CJJA 1982, section 19: subject to the definition of judgment, and exclusions thereto contained in section 18, recognition of judgments in another part of the UK shall not be refused solely on the ground that the court of origin was not a court of competent jurisdiction according to the rules of private international law in force in that other part of the UK.

ARBITRATION[89]

9–76 The conflict aspects of resolution of commercial disputes by arbitration is important, complex and many-faceted. The subject is of significance at various points in a conflict of laws discussion. As a result of the exclusion from the scope of the Rome Convention of "arbitration agreements and agreements on the choice of court",[90] the validity of an arbitration clause in a contract is determined by its own (common law) proper law, separate from the applicable law which governs the contract of which is forms a

---

[88] s.18(8).
[89] See F.P. Davidson, *Arbitration* (W.Green, 2000).
[90] Rome Convention, Art.1.2.d.

part. Nevertheless, the existence of an arbitration clause may be an indication of the applicable law under the Rome Convention, Article 3.1[91] or Article 4.5.[92]

In terms of the Civil Jurisdiction and Judgments Act 1982, section 20, Schedule 8, rule 2(m),[93] the Court of Session has jurisdiction in proceedings concerning an arbitration if it was conducted in Scotland, or if the arbitration procedure was governed by Scots law.[94]

One specialised conflict aspect of arbitration is the potential conflict of jurisdiction between the court and the arbitration tribunal.

Council Regulation 44/2001 excludes from its scope arbitration,[95] as does the Lugano Convention.[96] If, therefore, after the parties have proceeded to arbitration as agreed, an attempt is made to have the award enforced as a judgment under the Brussels regime, the attempt should fail.[97] However, if, in the face of an arbitration clause, a court in a contracting state gives a decision—perhaps on the basis that the clause is essentially invalid or not incorporated in the agreement, or if persuaded that the matter in dispute does not fall within the arbitration clause[98]—is this to be enforceable in accordance with the Brussels enforcement procedure and with its benefits? Perhaps the party against whom the judgment was made was so unwise as to submit to the jurisdiction, but even if so, and especially if not, what is the position? The matter is not clear[99]— and in these cases, circularity of argument can occur.[1]

---

[91] *Egon Oldendorff v Libera Corp.* [1996] 1 Ll's Rep. 380. Note, however, that the curial (or procedural) law of the arbitration and the applicable/proper law to be applied by the arbiter to the substance of the dispute may differ, as happened in *James Miller & Partners Ltd v Whitworth Street Estates (Manchester) Ltd* [1970] 1 All E.R. 796. In *Egon Oldendorff*, English law was identified as both the applicable law and curial law. The curial law will govern matters such as whether there can be an appeal to the court from the decision of the arbiter/arbitrator.

[92] Or perhaps the reverse, symbiotically, that the applicable law established in the absence of choice under Art.4 should be presumed to apply also to the arbitration. See note 10 below.

[93] Civil Jurisdiction and Judgments Order 2001 (SI 2001/3929), para.7.

[94] See Davidson, *Arbitration*, para.15.10.

[95] Art.1.2.d.

[96] Art.1.4.

[97] Briggs & Rees, 7.08.

[98] Contrast *The Angelic Grace* [1995] 1 Ll's Rep. 87.

[99] On the one side see *Marc Rich v Impianti* [1992] 1 Ll's Rep. 624 and *The Heidberg* [1994] 2 Ll's Rep. 287 (favouring the convention state court decision over arbitration clause); on the other *Marc Rich v Imipianti* at [1991] E.C.R. 1–3855 in ECJ and Briggs & Rees discussion at 7.08 which prefers the latter view, but suggests that even if it may come to be clear that such a judgment is to be regarded as a Brussels judgment *prima facie* enforceable, there might be a public policy objection under Art.27(1) to flouting a binding arbitration agreement. *Cf. Tracomin v Sudan Oil Seeds (No. 1)* [1983] 1 All E.R. 404; *The Angelic Grace* [1995] 1 Ll's Rep. 87; *Alfred C. Toepfer International GmbH v Société Cargill France* [1998] 1 Ll's Rep 379 (circularity). See Hill, *op.cit.*, paras 3.3.26 *et seq.*

[1] *Alfred C. Toepfer International GmbH v Société Cargill France* [1998] 1 Ll Rep. 379.

It is at least clear that one benefit from exclusion of arbitration from the Brussels regime is that it remains open to the courts of EU Member States to seek to enforce arbitration agreements by means of anti-suit injunctions,[2] a remedy which in view of *Turner v Grovit*,[3] has ceased to be a competent policing remedy to uphold choice of court agreements in circumstances where an EU court other than that chosen by the parties has been seised first by one of them.

Outwith the Brussels regime, a foreign judgment obtained in *breach* of an arbitration agreement is not enforceable in the UK.[4] Where the arbitration is not a "domestic arbitration agreement",[5] the Scottish court must sist its proceedings if such an arbitration agreement exists, unless it is satisfied that the arbitration agreement is void or inoperative.[6]

Enforcement of foreign arbitration awards

9–77   A foreign arbitration award may be enforced at common law, but a scheme for recognition and enforcement of arbitration awards is contained in the New York Convention on the Recognition and Enforcement of Foreign Arbitral Awards 1958, replacing the Geneva Protocol 1923 and Geneva Convention 1927, except in relation to awards issued in countries which are parties thereto and not party to the New York Convention (which cases remain

---

[2] *Through Transport Mutual Insurance Association (Eurasia) Ltd v New India Assurance Co. Ltd* [2005] 2 Ll's Rep. 378. Tactically, therefore, it may be better for reasons of certainty for parties to choose to resolve possible disputes by a previously agreed arbitration clause. Another advantage of exclusion from the Brussels regime is that the related actions rule contained in Art.28 clearly would not apply where the subject matter though related or identical is being addressed by different (judicial and arbitral, respectively) means. Hence, the English court is under no obligation to stay arbitration proceedings which have been brought in England later than foreign judicial proceedings upon the same matter. Therefore, arbitration clauses have a double tactical advantage in that it is competent for an English/Scottish court to seek to enforce them by anti-suit injunction; and whatever their date they are not affected by the Brussels *lis pendens* rule.

[3] [2005] 1 A.C. 101.

[4] Civil Jurisdiction and Judgments Act 1982, s.32. But note that this provision does not extend to authorise the non-recognition of a judgment which is required to be recognised in terms of the Brussels regime. See *Tracomin SA v Sudan Oil Seeds Co. (Nos 1 & 2)* [1983] 1 W.L.R. 1026.

[5] Defined by Arbitration Act 1996, s.85.

[6] Arbitration Act 1975, s.1(1). If any party to an arbitration agreement (which is not a domestic arbitration agreement: s.1(4)) commences legal proceedings in any court against any other party to the agreement, in respect of any matter agreed to be referred, any party to the proceedings may at any time after appearance and before delivering any pleadings or taking any other steps in the proceedings, apply to the court to stay the proceedings; and the court shall "stay", unless satisfied that the arbitration agreement is null and void, inoperative or incapable of being performed or that there is not in fact any dispute between the parties with regard to the matter agreed to be referred.

governed by the Arbitration Act 1950, Pt III). The New York Convention was brought into UK law by the Arbitration Act 1975.

The 1975 Act continues to apply to Scotland,[7] and the Law Reform (Miscellaneous Provisions) (Scotland) Act 1990, section 66, Schedule 7 has given effect in Scots law to the UNCITRAL Model Law on International Commercial Arbitration.[8] However, for England and Wales and Northern Ireland only, the 1975 Act has been repealed and largely re-enacted in the Arbitration Act 1996.[9] Part 1 of the 1996 Act applies when the "seat" of the arbitration is in England and Wales or Northern Ireland, with modifications in Part II relating to "domestic arbitration" (to which none of the parties is a national of, or habitually resident in, a state other than the UK or a body corporate incorporated in or having central control and management exercised in a state other than the UK and under which the seat of the arbitration (if designated or determined) is in the UK). Recognition and enforcement of foreign arbitration awards under the New York Convention is governed by the 1996 Act, sections 99 to 104.

Broadly speaking, defences under the Conventions include breach of natural justice/public policy, the arbitration process being *ultra vires* or its procedure defective, or the award being not binding.[10]

An arbitration award made in a country the judgments of which are enforceable under the Administration of Justice Act 1920 or the Foreign Judgments (Reciprocal Enforcement) Act 1933 is enforceable in Scotland in the same way as judicial decrees.

Anomalously,[11] within the UK, an arbitration award from one part is enforceable in another part in terms of the Civil Jurisdiction and Judgments Act 1982, section 18, Schedules 6 and 7,[12] or at common law.

---

[7] Relevant provisions, ss.2–6.

[8] See, in detail, Rules of Court of Session (as at July 2005), Chap.62—Recognition, Registration, and Enforcement of Foreign Judgments, etc.—Part IX—Recognition and Enforcement of Arbitral Awards under the Model Law on International Commercial Arbitration.

[9] See generally McClean & Beevers, *Morris, The Conflict of Laws* (6th ed.), paras 8.014–8.016.

[10] Smith, paras 3–105 *et seq.* A foreign arbitration award may be refused effect if it offends public policy, as where the arbitration agreement was valid but the contract to which it pertained was illegal by its governing law or the law of place of performance (*Soleimany v Soleimany* [1999] Q.B. 785, decided with reference to Arbitration Act 1950, s.26 (curiously, since that section was repealed by Sch.4 of the Arbitration Act 1996). *Cf.* n.92, above).

[11] Because arbitration is excluded from the scope of Council Regulation 44/2001, and the Brussels and Lugano Conventions.

[12] s.18(2)(e): "judgment" includes an arbitration award which has become enforceable in the part of the UK in which it was given in the same manner as a judgment given by a court of law in that part.

The circumstances may be such that the claimant has an option as to which method of enforcement to invoke.

EUROPEAN ENFORCEMENT ORDER FOR UNCONTESTED CLAIMS

9–78 Regulation (EC) No.805/2004 of the European Parliament and of the Council of April 21, 2004 creating a European Enforcement Order for Uncontested Claims[13] came into force on January 21, 2004, and applies generally from October 21, 2005.[14]

Its purpose is to ensure, by laying down minimum procedural standards, that judgments, court settlements and authentic instruments on uncontested claims, can circulate freely throughout the Member States of the EU, without the need for intermediate proceedings in the Member State of enforcement prior to recognition and enforcement.[15] The Regulation applies to all Member States, including the UK and Ireland,[16] but excluding, at present, Denmark.[17]

Background

9–79 Whilst Council Regulation (EC) No. 44/2001 represents notable progress in the development of procedures for the recognition and enforcement of judgments in civil and commercial matters, it leaves in place the requirement for *exequatur* (declaration of enforceability) procedure.[18]

The European Council at its Tampere meeting agreed that, to simplify and expedite procedures for the recognition and enforcement of judgments among Member States, there should be introduced a form of automatic recognition without any intermediate proceedings, or grounds for refusal of enforcement, for certain specific types of claim.[19] The abolition of *exequatur* for uncontested claims was identified as one of the Community's priorities.

The Regulation has two distinct components, first, the creation of the European Enforcement Order; and second, the laying down of minimum procedural standards.

---

[13] [2004] OJ L143 15.

[14] Art.33. Art.26 provides that the Regulation applies only to judgments given, settlements approved and documents formally drawn up or registered as authentic instruments after the entry into force of the Regulation.

[15] Art.1.

[16] Recital 24.

[17] Recital 25.

[18] "It does not remove all the obstacles to the unhindered movement of judgments within the EU and leaves intermediate measures that are still too restrictive." (Proposal for a Council Regulation creating a European Enforcement Order for Uncontested Claims, Explanatory Memorandum, p.2 (COM (2002) 159 final (April 18, 2002)), henceforth "Explanatory Memorandum").

[19] Explanatory Memorandum, p.2.

Scope of instrument

The Regulation applies to judgments, court settlements and **9–80** authentic instruments on uncontested claims,[20] in civil and commercial matters, whatever the nature of the court or tribunal. It does not extend, however, to revenue, customs or administrative matters or the liability of the State for acts and omissions in the exercise of State authority.[21]

Uncontested claims

An uncontested claim is one: **9–81**

    (a) to which the debtor has expressly agreed by admission or by means of a settlement which has been approved by a court or concluded before a court in the course of proceedings; or

    (b) to which the debtor has never objected, in compliance with the relevant procedural requirements under the law of the Member State of origin, in the course of the court proceedings; or

    (c) in which the debtor has not appeared or been represented at a court hearing regarding that claim after having initially objected to the claim in the course of the court proceedings, provided that such conduct amounts to a tacit admission of the claim or of the facts alleged by the creditor under the law of the Member State of origin; or

    (d) to which the debtor has expressly agreed in an authentic instrument.

The concept of "uncontested claims" is intended to cover "all situations in which a creditor, given the verified absence of any dispute by the debtor as to the nature or extent of a pecuniary claim,[22] has obtained either a court decision against that debtor or an enforceable document that requires the debtor's express consent, be it a court settlement or an authentic instrument."[23] In other words, a claim will be treated as uncontested if the debtor has failed to object to it in the course of court proceedings (*i.e.* if decree were passed in absence,[24] or by default), or if he has

---

[20] Recital 7; and Art.3.

[21] Art.2.

[22] Amplified in recital (6), to the effect that the absence of objections from the debtor may take the form of decree by default (default of appearance at a court hearing), or decree in absence (failure to comply with an invitation by the court to give written notice of an intention to defend the case).

[23] Recital 5.

[24] *i.e.* absent or without representation. Contrast *Krombach v Bamberski* [2000] ECR I-1935.

expressly agreed (in court proceedings, or by means of a settlement or in an authentic instrument), that the claim exists and is justified.

European Enforcement Order

9–82   Article 6 lays down the requirements for certification as a European Enforcement Order ("EEO"), by the Member State of origin,[25] of a judgment delivered in that State on an uncontested claim.[26] Such a judgment shall, upon application at any time to the court of origin, be certified as an EEO if:

(a) the judgment is enforceable in the Member State of origin; and

(b) the judgment does not conflict with the rules on jurisdiction as laid down in Sections 3 and 6 of Chapter II of Regulation 44/2001[27]; and

(c) the court proceedings in the Member State of origin meet the requirements of Chapter III of Regulation 805 (minimum standards for uncontested claims procedures); and

(d) if the claim relates to a consumer contract and the debtor is the consumer, the judgment was given in the Member State of the debtor's domicile within the meaning of Article 59 of Regulation 44.

By Article 9, the EEO shall be issued in the standard form provided in Annex I of Regulation 805, and in the language of the judgment.

Abolition of *exequatur*

9–83   By virtue of Article 5, a judgment which has been certified as an EEO in the Member State of origin shall be recognised and enforced in the other Member State (the Member State of enforcement[28]), without the need for a declaration of enforceability, and without any possibility of opposing its recognition.

Thus, it can be said that the certification of a judgment as an EEO "renders obsolete" the *exequatur* procedure which, under the Brussels Convention and Council Regulation 44/2001, is a precondition of enforcement of a judgment in another Member State.[29]

---

[25] Defined in Art.4(4): the Member State of origin is the Member State in which the judgment has been given, the court settlement has been approved or concluded or the authentic instrument has been drawn up or registered, and is to be certified as a European Enforcement Order.

[26] Art.8 provides that if only parts of the judgment meet the requirements laid down in Art.6, a partial EEO certificate shall be issued for those parts.

[27] Note absence of reference to S.4 (consumers); S.5 (employees) is omitted in the protective provisions contained in Reg.44/2001, Art.35.1

[28] Art.4(5).

[29] Explanatory Memorandum, p.6.

The EEO has been described as "a comprehensive and transparent certificate of the fulfilment of all the conditions for enforcement throughout the Community without intermediate measures."[30]

Satisfaction of minimum procedural standards

As a corollary to the abolition of *exequatur* for uncontested **9–84** claims, and to ensure that the debtor is duly informed about the court action against him,[31] the Regulation lays down, in Chapter III, minimum standards with regard to the service of documents, covering admissible methods of service, the time of service enabling the preparation of a defence and the proper information concerning the debtor.[32]

Article 12 states that a judgment on an uncontested claim can be certified as an EEO only if the court proceedings in the Member State of origin satisfied the procedural requirements set out in the Regulation. It is said that due to differences among the Member States regarding their rules of civil procedure, and especially those governing the service of documents,[33] it is necessary to lay down a specific and detailed definition of those minimum standards.[34] Accordingly, Articles 13 and 14 provide for methods of service which are characterised,[35] respectively, by full certainty,[36] or by a very high degree of likelihood that the document served reached its addressee.[37]

The courts competent for scrutinising full compliance with the minimum procedural standards should, if satisfied, issue a standardised EEO certificate that makes that scrutiny and its result transparent.[38] The point to note is that it is the court of the Member State of *origin*, rather than that of the Member State of enforcement which is responsible for scrutiny of the judgment, and for deciding whether the judgment satisfies the conditions precedent to its being certified as an EEO.[39]

---

[30] Explanatory Memorandum, p.4.

[31] Recital 12.

[32] "Only the compliance with these minimum standards justifies the abolition of a control of the observation of the rights of the defence in the Member State where the judgment is to be enforced." (Explanatory Memorandum, p.4.)

[33] Though see Reg.1348/2000 (Chap.8, above). And see para.9–86, below.

[34] Recital 13.

[35] Recital 14.

[36] Art.13: service with proof of receipt by the debtor.

[37] Art.14: service without proof of receipt by the debtor.

[38] Recital 17.

[39] Contrast the position under the *exequatur* procedure, where responsibility rests with the court of the Member State of *enforcement* to determine whether the conditions for a declaration of enforceability have been met. *Cf.* Explanatory Memorandum, p.6. This characteristic of the EEO procedure is worthy of comment in that it is novel for the court addressed in effect to lose its power of scrutiny, but such a loss is inherent in the purpose of the Regulation and the mode adopted to fulfil it.

Recital 19 states that the Regulation does not imply an obligation upon Member States to ensure that their national legislation meets the minimum procedural standards set out therein, but rather that it provides an incentive to that end by making available a more efficient and rapid enforceability of judgments in other Member States only if those minimum standards are met.[40]

For Scotland, relevant provision has been made via secondary legislation, namely, Act of Sederunt (Rules of the Court of Session Amendment No. 8) (Miscellaneous) 2005[41] (whereby rules consequential upon the introduction of Regulation 805/2004 create a procedure for certifying certain judgments as EEOs,[42] and for enforcing EEOs in Scotland[43]); and Act of Sederunt (Sheriff Court European Enforcement Order Rules) 2005[44] (pertaining to applications under the Regulation where the sheriff court is the court of origin and introducing rules of equivalent procedure for applications for EEO certificates for enforcement of judgments in other Member States).

Enforcement

9–85   A judgment that has been certified as an EEO by a court of the Member State of origin should be treated, for enforcement purposes, as if it had been delivered in the Member State in which enforcement is sought.[45] Arrangements for the enforcement of judgments should continue to be governed by national law. Hence, recital 8 specifically provides that, "[i]n the United Kingdom, for example, the registration of a certified foreign judgment will therefore follow the same rules as the registration of a judgment from another part of the UK".

In terms of Article 20, the creditor shall be required to provide the competent enforcement authorities of the Member State of enforcement with (a) a copy of the judgment; (b) a copy of the

---

[40] "It is up to the Member States to decide whether or not to adjust their national legislation to the minimum standards of Chapter III in order to ensure the eligibility of the largest possible number of decisions on uncontested claims for certification as a European Enforcement Order." (Explanatory Memorandum, p.4.)

[41] SSI 2005/521, amending Rules of the Court of Session 1994 (SI 1994/1443). (Entry into force on October 21, 2005.)

[42] Procedure for certification under Art.6(1) (judgment on uncontested claim) or Art.8 (partial EEO) of decree in absence or decree by default (r.62.82); and for certification under Art.24 of court settlement (r.62.83); and for certification under Art.25(1) of authentic instrument (r.62.84).

[43] Registration for enforcement of a judgment, court settlement or authentic instrument certified as an EEO (r.62.88).

[44] SSI 2005/523 (entry into force October 21, 2005).

[45] Recital 8.

EEO certificate; and (c) where necessary, a transcription of the EEO certificate.

The grounds for refusal of enforcement, *per* Article 21, are very restricted, being limited to the existence of irreconcilable judgments.[46] Enforcement shall, upon application by the debtor, be refused by the competent court in the Member State of enforcement if the judgment certified as an EEO is irreconcilable with an earlier judgment given in another (Member State or non-Member State) country, provided that (a) the earlier judgment involved the same cause of action and was between the same parties; and (b) the earlier judgment was given in the Member State of enforcement or is recognised in that state; and (c) the irreconcilability was not and could not have been raised as an objection in the court proceedings in the Member State of origin.

Under no circumstances may a judgment or its certification as an EEO be reviewed as to its substance in the Member State of enforcement.[47]

Relationship with other Community instruments (in particular Regulation 44/2001 and Regulation 1348/2000)

Regulation 805/2004 provides Member States and, in turn, **9–86** creditors, with an additional, optional, rather than compulsory, means of seeking recognition and enforcement of a judgment, court settlement or authentic instrument on an uncontested claim.[48] In suitable cases, creditors can choose whether to seek a declaration of enforceability under Regulation 44/2001, or to utilise the more expeditious procedure laid down in Regulation 805. In terms of recital (9), the latter procedure should offer significant advantages as compared with the *exequatur* procedure provided for in Regulation 44, in that there is no need for approval by the judicial authorities in a second Member State, with the expense and delay which that entails.

Similarly, in terms of Article 28, Regulation 805 shall not affect the application of Regulation 1348/2000 concerning service of documents.[49]

---

[46] Art.23 provides, in exceptional cases, for the stay of enforcement proceedings, or for the limitation thereof to protective measures.

[47] Art.21(2).

[48] Art.27; *cf.* recital 20.

[49] See Chap.8, above. Recital (21) provides that when a document has to be sent from one Member State to another for service there, Reg.805 should apply *together with* Reg.1348.

EUROPEAN SMALL CLAIMS PROCEDURE

There is currently an EU Commission Proposal for a Regulation of the European Parliament and of the Council establishing a European Small Claims Procedure.[50]

Objective

9–87   The objective of the proposed Regulation is to simplify and speed up litigation concerning small claims, by establishing a European Small Claims Procedure ("ESCP"), and to reduce the costs associated with pursuing such a claim.[51] The Regulation is also intended to eliminate, by means of the ESCP, the intermediate measures which currently are necessary[52] to enable recognition and enforcement in one Member State of judgments given in another Member State.

Scope

9–88   It is proposed that the Regulation should apply in civil and commercial matters, whatever the nature of the court or tribunal, where the total value of the claim, monetary or non-monetary (and excluding interest, expenses and outlays), does not exceed EUR 2000 at the time the procedure is commenced. This limit contrasts with the small claims limit under Scots law which, at the time of writing, is £750.[53] The Regulation would not apply, however, to revenue, customs or administrative matters, or to what may be termed "standard" excluded matters.[54]

---

[50] COM (2005) 87 final (Brussels, March 15, 2005). Work on this draft instrument is set to continue under the Operational Programme of the EU Council for 2006 (under the Austrian and Finnish Presidencies) (Ref 16065/05, December 22, 2005, p.44). See amendments proposed by European Parliament Committee on Legal Affairs JURI/6/27155. PR-PE 368.105v01–00 AM-PE 371.891v01–00. This proposal is supported by H.L. EU Committee (15.2.06 Press Release).

[51] Recital 4 narrates that the "costs, delay and vexation connected with litigation do not necessarily decrease proportionally with the amount of the claim. The obstacles to obtaining a fast and inexpensive judgment are intensified in cross-border cases. It is therefore necessary to create a European Small Claims Procedure. The objective of such a European procedure should be to facilitate access to justice by purveying a procedure of moderate duration at affordable costs."

[52] Except as otherwise provided for by Regulation (EC) No. 805/2004 of the European Parliament and of the Council of April 21, 2004 creating a European Enforcement Order for Uncontested Claims.

[53] Small Claims (Scotland) Order 1988 (SI 1988/1999). Contrast England and Wales where the upper limit for small claims is £5,000. It is debateable whether there should be different upper limits for different types of case (*e.g.* personal injury claims as opposed to claims for arrears of payment).

[54] Art 2.2. *Cf.* Rome Convention, Art.1.

As at present advised, Denmark will not participate in the adoption of any resultant Regulation.[55] The position of the UK and Ireland is not yet clear.[56]

Nature of the proposed ESCP

It is proposed that a claimant would commence the claim **9–89** procedure[57] by completing a claim form in the style provided in the Regulation, and by lodging it with relevant supporting documents at the competent (home) court or tribunal.[58] That court or tribunal would register the claim immediately upon receipt; the court would be deemed to be seized when the claim form is registered.[59]

It is proposed that the procedure be, in the main, a written procedure, unless, for some reason, an oral hearing is deemed to be necessary by the court or tribunal.[60] A relatively tight timescale is set out in Articles 4, 5 and 10, in accordance with which the claim must be served on the defendant, his response submitted, and judgment delivered by the court or tribunal.[61] Article 6 permits, if the parties should agree, the holding of a hearing through audio, video or e-mail conference.[62]

Enforceability of judgments

Article 13 provides that the judgment rendered shall be immedi- **9–90** ately enforceable, notwithstanding any possible appeal.[63] It is intended to abolish the need for a declaration of enforceability (*exequatur* procedure).[64] Moreover, there will be no possibility

---

[55] Recital 20.

[56] Recital 19.

[57] Whether it seems to be a purely domestic claim, or a cross-border one. See para.9–92, below.

[58] Art.3.1.

[59] Art.3.3 and 3.4.

[60] Art.4.1.

[61] In particular, Art.10 provides that the judgment shall be rendered within six months following the registration of the claim form. A degree of flexibility is proposed in Art.12, by which, in "exceptional circumstances", the court or tribunal may prolong the time limits otherwise laid down, if that is necessary in order to guarantee an effective defence of the parties.

[62] *cf.* Art.7 by which the court or tribunal may determine the means of proof (including taking evidence via telephone, written witness statements and audio/video/e-mail conference) and the extent to which evidence is taken, according to its discretion. It may be expected that this could give rise to certain practical problems.

[63] *cf.* recital 13. Art.18

[64] Art.18. *Cf.* recital 15. Art.18.1–18.4 does not apply to judgments on uncontested claims within the meaning of Regulation (EC) No. 805/2004 of the European Parliament and of the Council of April 21, 2004 creating a European Enforcement Order for Uncontested Claims.

whatsoever (even, it seems, on a public policy basis[65]) of opposing recognition of the judgment if it has been certified by the court or tribunal of the Member State of origin as complying with the rules of jurisdiction in Chapter II, Sections 3 and 6 of Council Regulation No. 44/2001.

Relationship with other Community instruments

9–91   The proposed Regulation shall not affect the application of Regulation (EC) No. 805/2004 (creating a European Enforcement Order for Uncontested Claims), or of Regulation (EC) No. 44/2001.[66]

Territorial scope

9–92   It is said, in recital 5, that "[t]he distortion of competition within the internal market due to the disequilibrium with regard to the functioning of the procedural means afforded to creditors in different Member States entails the need for Community legislation which guarantees a level playing field for creditors and debtors throughout the EU." Given this rationale, the Commission's position is that it would be inappropriate and counterproductive to restrict the scope of application of the ESCP to cross-border cases[67]: "the creation of two different regimes for internal cases and for cases with cross-border aspects should be avoided.[68] Such a duality of regimes would be inconsistent with the objective of a single and coherent area of justice for all."[69] It is not clear, however, how the proposed ESCP would operate alongside existing, national, small claims procedures in typical "domestic" cases. It may be that the Commission's aim is for the ESCP, eventually, to supplant residual national systems, under the guise of an "optional"[70] tool, which makes it "simpler to obtain the recognition

---

[65] *i.e.* a policy on public policy objection, attributable to the size of the claim. It is noteworthy that in recent years important public policy cases in the area of judgment enforcement have arisen: *Maronier v Larmer* [2003] Q.B. 620; and *Krombach v Bamberski* [2000] ECR I-1935.

[66] In terms of which the public policy challenge, *inter alia*, to recognition and enforcement would remain.

[67] COM (2005) 87 final (Brussels, March 15, 2005), Explanatory Memorandum, para.2.2.1. *Cf.* recital (6) which states that "[t]he ESCP should apply also to purely domestic cases in order to eliminate distortions of competition between economic operators in different Member States and to facilitate access to justice under equal conditions in all Member States."

[68] If that were not the case, there would be difficulties of definition: how exactly would a cross-border case be defined? There is potential for every judgment to assume a cross-border nature if it should need to be enforced in another Member State.

[69] COM (2005) 87 final (Brussels, March 15, 2005), Explanatory Memorandum, para.2.2.1.

[70] *i.e.* in addition to the possibilities existing under the laws of the Member States, which will remain unaffected (recital 7).

and enforcement of a judgment given in an ESCP in another Member State, including judgments which were initially of a purely domestic nature."[71]

EUROPEAN ORDER FOR PAYMENT PROCEDURE

It is said that the expeditious recovery of uncontested outstanding **9–93** debts is of paramount importance to economic operators within the EU and for the proper functioning of the internal market.[72] Accordingly, as part of the programme of proposed reform, the European Commission has issued a Proposal for a Regulation of the European Parliament and of the Council creating a European Order for Payment Procedure.[73] The relationship between this Proposal and Regulation 805/2004 is rather complex and more opaque than the Commission suggests in its explanation now set forth:

> "The Commission has decided to pursue both objectives—the mutual recognition of decisions on uncontested claims on the one hand and the creation of a specific procedure for the attainment of decisions on the other—in two different legislative instruments. This two-tiered strategy does not entail the risk of an overlap or of contradictions between both projects since they are clearly demarcated by their strict limitation to the stages before (creation of an order for payment procedure) and after (recognition and enforcement) the delivery of the enforceable decision, respectively. Quite on the contrary, this approach offers a number of significant advantages over a legislative initiative combining both aspects. For example, it allows a broader scope of application for the abolition of exequatur, extending it to all judgments handed down in the verifiable absence of any dispute over the nature and extent of a debt and not only to decisions delivered in one specific procedure."[74]

---

[71] *ibid.*

[72] Recital (5), and also Council of the European Union, Press Release 247 (12645/05) (Luxembourg, October 12, 2005). It is said that "it is increasingly not the exception but the rule that in the verifiable absence of any dispute the creditor has to turn to the judiciary to attain an enforceable title allowing him to collect a claim by means of forced execution that the debtor is simply unwilling or unable to honour." (COM (2004) 173 final/3 (Brussels, May 25, 2004), para.2.1.1).

[73] COM (2004) 173 final/3 (Brussels, May 25, 2004). Like the small claims proposal, work on this proposal is set to continue under the Operational Programme of the EU Council for 2006. See now Amended Proposal COM (2006) 57 final (Brussels, February 7, 2006).

[74] COM (2004) 173 final/3, Explanatory Memorandum, para.1.1.

SUMMARY 9—ENFORCEMENT OF FOREIGN DECREES

9–94

1. Decrees *in rem* establish rights in property against all comers and stand unaided on their own strength: challenge of a foreign decree *in rem* is limited to the challenges of "no jurisdiction in the foreign court" or fraud. Jurisdiction in any court is established by the presence of the *res* within the jurisdiction at the time of pronouncement of the decree.

2. Judgments affecting status are treated as equivalent to decrees *in rem* but recognition is governed by special statutory provision, namely, the Family Law Act 1986, Part II, and Council Regulation 2201/2003.

3. Decrees *in personam* establish personal rights. Foreign decrees of this type, if not complied with where pronounced, require the assistance of our courts in order to be enforced in Scotland (by granting of decree conform to the foreign decree or by process of registration as described below).

4. Action for decree conform is necessary if the judgment emanates from a state with which the UK has no reciprocal arrangement of judgment enforcement under the Administration of Justice Act 1920 or the Foreign Judgments (Reciprocal Enforcement) Act 1933, and is not an EU Member State or an EFTA State.

5. A number of defences may be raised to an action for decree conform, on jurisdictional or natural justice/public policy grounds.

6. "Direct" enforcement may be effected of Commonwealth (1920 Act) or other foreign (1933 Act) judgments, by means of registration ("judgment extension"). Under the Act of 1920, registration is a matter of discretion and will not be permitted if the defender can establish any one of a number of defences (of a jurisdictional or natural justice/ public policy nature). Registration under the Act of 1933 is of right, but the registration may be set aside later on application by the defender if any one of a number of challenges (of a jurisdictional or natural justice/public policy nature) can be made. Challenges at common law and under each of these statutes are similar to each other but care must be taken as there are differences in detail, for example, the effect of pending or possible appeal.

7. The Protection of Trading Interests Act 1980 constitutes a specialised *caveat* to the above.

8. Judgments rendered by the court of an EU Member State are enforced in another Member State in accordance (only) with the procedures laid down by Council Regulation 44/2001, and subject to the proviso that the matter falls within the scope of that instrument. Arbitration is excluded. Enforcement is not limited to money judgments, nor to judgments of superior courts. See the Civil Jurisdiction and Judgments Acts 1982–1991, Schedule 1 (and Civil Jurisdiction and Judgments Order 2001 (SI 2001/3929)).

9. There is a parallel regime, contained in the Lugano Convention, for enforcement of judgments rendered by the courts of an EFTA State.

10. Among EU Member States, Council Regulation 805/2004 has created a European Enforcement Order for Uncontested Claims, and supporting procedures, operative from October 2005.

11. Reciprocal enforcement of money and non-money judgments within the UK is governed by the Civil Jurisdiction and Judgments Act 1982, section 18 and Schedules 6 and 7 (and Civil Jurisdiction and Judgments Order 2001 (SI 2001/3929)).

12. Enforcement of arbitration awards is governed principally by the New York Convention on the Recognition and Enforcement of Foreign Arbitral Awards 1958. See for Scotland, the Arbitration Act 1975, and for England, the Arbitration Act 1996.

CHAPTER 10

STATUS AND CAPACITY

STATUS

At any particular time every person has at least one status in law. **10–01**
Status may be defined as a person's legal condition in society: "The
status of an individual, used as a legal term, means the legal
position of the individual in or with regard to the rest of a
community."[1] Status may result either from a natural condition
such as age or insanity, or from a legal condition such as marriage.
It is a condition which has attached to it the capacity of an
individual to acquire and exercise legal rights and to perform legal
acts and duties. It carries with it rights and duties, capacities and
incapacities, powers and disabilities. The effect of allocation, by
application of the forum's conflict rules, of an individual to a
particular status automatically results in the acquisition, according
to the relevant applicable law, of corresponding rights, powers,
duties, capacities and incapacities.

GENERAL POINTS AS TO STATUS

Natural persons

The general rule is that a person's status (except to some extent his **10–02**
matrimonial status, in respect of which see Chapter 11, below[2]) is
determined by his personal law, that is, in the view of Scots law, by
the law of his domicile. Traditionally the court of the domicile[3] has
been the appropriate court to determine the existence and effects
of any status,[4] or alteration therein, and has been unlikely to yield
to another court its pre-eminence in this area.

The scope of the 1968 Brussels Convention does *not* include the
status or legal capacity of natural persons.[5] When the Brussels

---

[1] *Niboyet v Niboyet* (1878) L.R. 4 P.D., *per* Brett, L.J. at 11.
[2] There are also specialties with regard to bankruptcy; see Ch.17, below.
[3] Hence the Court of Session has jurisdiction to entertain a petition to determine
status if the petitioner avers sufficient evidence of a Scots domicile. D.M. Walker,
Civil Remedies (1974), pp.119 *et seq.*
[4] *Re S (hospital patient: foreign curator)* [1995] 4 All E.R. 30.
[5] Title 1, Art.1.

Convention was concluded, the rules of the Member States on jurisdiction in matrimonial matters "were considered so disparate as to preclude their effective unification in the 1968 Convention without major change to its nature".[6] However, account must now be taken of encroachment by the factor of habitual residence as directed by modern EU legislation.[7] Since March 1, 2001, matrimonial status[8] has been regulated by Regulation 1347/2000, itself superseded by Regulation 2201/2003, with effect from March 1, 2005. In terms of these instruments, an EU forum is clothed with jurisdiction in matrimonial matters, and in matters of parental responsibility, principally upon the basis of habitual residence and only residually on the basis of nationality or domicile.[9]

Non-natural persons

10–03 The status of foreign government departments is determined by the courts of the United Kingdom in accordance with evidence given by a representative of the foreign country.[10] Where by comity the courts of the United Kingdom recognised as having legal personality an international organisation created by the law of a foreign state itself recognised by the Crown, it was held that the body was entitled to be regarded in the English court as a juridical person with capacity to sue.[11]

THE THEORY OF THE UNIVERSALITY OF STATUS

10–04 The ideal is that status should be universal so that a condition of status which Scots conflict rules regard as having been validly conferred in one country (particularly if it is the country of a

---

[6] House of Laws European Communities Committee—Fifth Report, 22 July 1997, Pt 1, 1.

[7] Reg.2201/2003. See Ch.12.

[8] Insofar as concerns the allocation of jurisdiction, and recognition of judgments, in cases concerning divorce, legal separation, and marriage annulment, but not concerning capacity to marry which remains governed by Scots conflict rules. See Ch.11, below.

[9] See in detail Ch.12, below.

[10] At common law, see *Krajina v Tass Agency* [1949] 2 All E.R. 274. See now State Immunity Act 1978, s.14(2). From 1980, it has ceased to be the practice of the British Government to accord recognition to governments, but rather now to decide whether to have "dealings" with a regime. (Carrington Statement, *Hansard*, H.L. Vol. 408, cols 1121–1122; and H.L. Vol. 409, cols 107–109.) The system of seeking a certificate from the Foreign and Commonwealth Office still applies with regard to the recognition or not of States. With regard to Governments, it seems that the FCO will continue to provide a certificate, if so requested, as to whether the U.K. has the requisite dealings with a particular government, and this will be accepted by the courts. See Harris, *Cases and Materials on International Law* (4th ed., 1991) p.143. Also generally FA Mann, *Foreign Affairs in English Courts* (1986). See also para.3–05, above.

[11] *Arab Monetary Fund v Hashim (No.3)* [1991] 1 All E.R. 871 (H.L.).

person's domicile) should be recognised in all other countries.[12] This theory or ideal is the basis of a legal theory known as the theory of the universality of status.[13] The theory is an excellent starting point[14]: modern times still produce cases of a bizarre nature[15] and cases of international complexity which cross the boundaries of other branches of legal knowledge[16] where recourse to first principles is the best help. However, Viscount Simonds in *National Bank of Greece and Athens v Metliss*[17] attributes recognition of a foreign status to comity rather than to the universal quality of the status. Further, the theory of universality of status is often not sufficiently strong, subtle or detailed to provide solutions to modern problems of family law. Rather, resort must be had to technical rules of jurisdiction and recognition enshrined in the Family Law Act 1986 and Regulation 2201/2003 ("Brussels II *Bis*"). Nevertheless, these technical rules are inspired by the theory of universality.

PUBLIC POLICY

Though status and its incidents normally are governed by the individual's personal law, recognition thereof is a matter ultimately for the policy of the forum. By way of exception to the principle of recognition, the forum may refuse to accept a particular status conferred by another law, or any of its incidents. The exceptions to recognition correspond to the exceptions described in Chapter 3, of which the broadest in scope is the public policy exception.[18] **10–05**

The following conditions of status, for example, are not recognised on the ground that they are penal (*i.e.* discriminatory) or contrary to UK public policy:

(1) slavery[19];
(2) civil death;
(3) monastic celibacy[20];

---

[12] *Mackie v Darling* (1871) L.R. 12 Eq. 319 (but see *Johnstone v Beattie* (1843) 10 Cl. & F. 42).

[13] *Re. Luck's Settlement Trusts* [1940] Ch. 864, *per* Scott L.J. at 885–919, especially 889–891.

[14] *cf.* comments with regard to the vested rights theory: Ch.3, para.3–01.

[15] *e.g. W & B v H (Surrogacy)* [2002] 1 F.L.R. 1008.

[16] *e.g. Arab Monetary Fund v Hashim (No.3)* [1991] 1 All E.R. 871 (H.L.); *Westland Helicopters Ltd v Arab Organisation for Industrialisation* [1995] 2 All E.R. 387.

[17] [1958] A.C. 509 at 525.

[18] See paras 3–06, *et seq.*

[19] *cf. Somerset v Stewart* (1772) 20 St. Tr. 1; *Knight v Wedderburn* (1778) Mor. 1454; *Santos v Illidge* (1860) 8 C.B. (N.S.) 861.

[20] *cf. In the Matter of Metcalfe's Trusts* (1864) 2 De G.J. & S. 122 (property and free will, no specific mention of celibacy).

(4) conviction for treason abroad;

(5) the prodigal status.[21]

These categories may seem archaic, but the conflict rules of status may require still to be consulted, one example being *Re S*[22] in the matter of a physical *incapax* whose domicile was Norway and whose current residence was England; and another being *M v B*,[23] concerning mental incapacity. This is an instructive modern case on a question still governed by common law. In *Re S*, it was considered that the presence of the *incapax* in the jurisdiction, whatever his nationality or domicile, clothed the court with jurisdiction[24]; further, even though an appointment of a guardian by the date of litigation had been made under the Norwegian personal law, the English court still had a discretion to act in the best interests of the *incapax*. However, comity suggested that the *incapax* should be returned to his country of nationality and probable domicile, the onus of proof lying on those who argued to the contrary. Surprisingly, no reference appears to have been made to the case of *Re Langley*[25] where, after some doubt, the English court concluded that the status of "incompetent" and its concomitant capacities and incapacities, conferred by the Californian court of the domicile upon a person mentally capable but physically incapable, did not offend the forum's public policy, but rather was to be recognised by the forum as being protective of the individual, and not punitive.

Sometimes British courts have been inconsistent in their views. A century after it had been agreed that the status of slavery could not be recognised in the UK, the English court in *Santos v Illidge*[26] enforced a contract for the sale of slaves, despite that general stance and despite the provision of the Slave Trade Act 1824, section 2 making it unlawful for "any person" to purchase, sell or contract for the purchase or sale of slaves (a provision in its nature of intra-territorial effect only), because the contract was governed by the law of Brazil, by which it was valid. Both then and now,[27] a

---

[21] *Worms v De Valdor* (1880) 49 LJ Ch. 261; *Re Selot's Trusts* [1902] 1 Ch. 488; *Re Langley's Settlement Trusts* [1962] 1 Ch. 541; *Re S (hospital patient: foreign curator)* [1995] 4 All E.R. 30.

[22] [1995] 4 All E.R. 30.

[23] [2005] EWHC 1681: refusal by Sumner J. (Family Division) to permit the parents of an adult woman with severe learning disability to remove her from the jurisdiction, because there was a real risk that despite the parents' declared intentions they would arrange for her a marriage when she was in Pakistan.

[24] *cf*. Adults with Incapacity (Scotland) Act 2000, in which the jurisdiction of the Scots court is based upon habitual residence of the *incapax* (Sch.3, para.3).

[25] [1961] 1 All E.R. 78.

[26] (1860) 8 C.B.(N.S.) 861; contrast *Somerset v Stewart* (1772) 20 St. Tr. 1; *Knight v Wedderburn* (1778) Mor. 1454.

[27] *Grell v Levy* (1864) 16 C.B. (N.S.) 73.

provision valid by the proper/applicable law, but offensive to the public policy of the forum may be refused enforcement.

Similarly, in family law, while prohibitions on marriage out of caste are rejected by Scots and English courts as imposing incapacities unacceptable on public policy grounds,[28] it is possible to cite a case of overseas nullity recognition[29] in which a ground of nullity used by the court in Jerusalem was that the Jewish faith of the woman precluded marriage with a Christian. On the other hand, Nazi divorces of Jew and Gentile, obtained by duress or coercion, were not recognised by British courts.[30]

One should be aware of the dangerous potential of the public policy discretion, and of the risk of inconsistency, but should not be unduly concerned,[31] for it is well recognised by the courts that even greater delicacy and scrupulousness must be exercised in relation to public policy in international private law issues.

STATUS AND ITS INCIDENTS

Status must be distinguished from its incidents, that is, from the **10–06** effects, powers or disabilities attaching to it or resulting from it. Although a condition of status may be recognised in general, consequences following from it may or may not be recognised in certain circumstances, with the result that a condition of status may be recognised for some purposes but not for others. The question is always whether it will be recognised for the purpose before the court. Thus, a divorce may be recognised as having terminated a marriage,[32] but nevertheless, certain consequences normally following from a valid foreign decree may not eventuate.[33] Further, a condition (attached to divorce) considered by the (recognising) forum to be penal, may be regarded as *pro non scripto*.[34]

---

[28] *McDougall v Chitnavis*, 1937 S.C. 390.

[29] *Corbett v Corbett* [1957] 1 W.L.R. 486.

[30] *Re Meyer* [1971] P. 298 (duress); but regard must be had to all the circumstances—*Igra v Igra* [1951] P. 404.

[31] N. Enonchong, "Public Policy in the Conflict of Laws: A Chinese Wall Around Little England?" [1996] 45 ICLQ 633; and R.D. Leslie, "The Relevance of Public Policy in Legal Issues Involving Other Countries And Their Laws", 1995 J.R. 477.

[32] Indeed that is generally recognised to be the principal purpose of divorce. Scots conflict rules assume that this is a defining feature of a divorce decree as opposed to an award of judicial separation. *Cf.* Family Law Act 1986, s.50, and *Lawrence v Lawrence* [1985] 2 All E.R. 733.

[33] *Wood v Wood* [1957] P. 254 (pre-existing English award of maintenance kept in being by English court after pronouncement of Nevada divorce recognised in England).

[34] *Warter* (1890) 15 P.D. 152; *Martin v Buret*, 1938 S.L.T. 479. But see *Buckle v Buckle* [1956] P. 181; *Scott v Att.-Gen.* (1886) 11 P.D. 128. Further as to remarriage after divorce, see Ch.12, below.

CAPACITY

10–07 Status is the basis of capacity or incapacity so that a person's capacity to have legal rights and to perform legal acts depends upon his status. Status is a legal condition while capacity is a power which results from status. Whereas capacity is a power, incapacity is a disability which also follows from a condition of status. Although one law determines any particular status, different laws may determine different questions of capacity within the same degree of status. Thus, although the law of first recourse in a matter of status is that of an individual's domicile, different laws may determine his capacity to marry, to enter into a contract and to purchase land; domicile is the default position.[35]

A person may stand in a number of legal conditions of status at one and the same time; thus he may be in nonage, married, and bankrupt. The question whether he is in nonage for the purposes, respectively, of marriage and bankruptcy may be decided by different laws. This is so, even though strictly speaking, it is meaningless to say that a status of nonage exists *except* in relation to particular capacities, with regard to each of which conflict rules will provide a governing factor. Thus in Scots conflict rules, the capacity of a young person to test with regard to moveables is governed by the law of his domicile at the time of testing,[36] whereas his capacity to test with regard to immoveables is referred to the *lex situs*.[37] Therefore conflict rules direct to different legal systems, by means of different connecting factors, the question of *capacity* in respect of each "transaction" as it may arise. Some rules are more complex and/or uncertain than others.[38]

As in the case of penal or discriminatory conditions of status, penal incapacities are not recognised.[39] An incapacity imposed by the personal law may be found to have created an incapacity of strictly limited territorial extent and may not affect that person when outside the jurisdiction of his personal law.[40] The broad rule,

---

[35] *Re S (hospital patient: foreign curator)* [1995] 4 All E.R. 30; and *Ogilvy v Ogilvy's Trs*, 1927 S.L.T. 83.

[36] See Ch.18, below. The domestic law of Scotland sets that age at 12 years: Age of Legal Capacity (Scotland) Act 1991, s.2(2).

[37] See *e.g. Black v Black's Trs*, 1950 S.L.T. (Notes) 32; *Bank of Africa Ltd v Cohen* [1909] 2 Ch. 129.

[38] *e.g.* to reach a view on a person's capacity to contract, reference might have to be made not only to the domestic rules of the Scots personal law (say), which confers capacity at 16 (Age of Legal Capacity (Scotland) Act 1991), but also to the additions made by Art.11 of the Rome Convention on an already uncertain Scots conflict contract rule. See Ch.15, below.

[39] *Chetti v Chetti* [1909] P. 67; *McDougall v Chitnavis*, 1937 S.C. 390.

[40] See *Bernaben v Hutchison* (1902) 18 Sh. Ct. Rep. 72 (an incapacity, imposed by reason of failure to pay local taxes and failure to register the firm by the law of

however, is that a person's capacity to perform acts and have legal rights, depends upon the law of his domicile in relation to personal matters and proprietary matters concerning moveable property,[41] while, in general, proprietary matters relating to immoveable property depend upon the *lex situs*.[42]

SUMMARY 10—STATUS AND CAPACITY

1. Status in general is determined by the law of the domicile. **10–08**

2. Matrimonial status is affected now by Regulation 2201/2003, with the result that the court of an individual's habitual residence may determine his status.

3. The question is whether a particular status should be recognised for the purpose before the court (rather than in general).

4. A condition of status conferred by the law of the domicile should be recognised everywhere. There are exceptions corresponding generally to those outlined in relation to enforcement of foreign rights; and specialties, *e.g.* contained in Family Law Act 1986 and Regulation 2201/2003.

5. Status must be distinguished from its incidents.

6. Capacity follows from status and, while capacity to do a particular act is determined by the law applicable to the particular transaction, as a general guide, capacity is governed by the law of the domicile or habitual residence as regards matters of personal law and as regards dealings with moveable property, and by the *lex situs* as regards immoveable property.

Spain, upon a Spanish firm to sue for debt, was held not to preclude suit by the firm in Scotland in respect of a debt contracted in Spain). Consider also in a general sense the case of *Kaye v H.M. Advocate*, 1957 J.C. 55 (incapacity upon bankrupt imposed in English bankruptcy proceedings to obtain more than £10 credit without disclosing his status on pain of criminal penalty did not extend to his activities in Scotland, with the result that he could not be relevantly indicted for contravention of the (then current) Bankruptcy (Scotland) Act 1913).

[41] *Doglioni v Crispin* [1866] L.R. 1 H.L.C. 301; *Orlando v Earl of Fingall* [1940] I.R. 281; *Sawrey-Cookson v Sawrey-Cookson's Trs* (1905) 8 F. 157; *Ogilvy v Ogilvy's Trs*, 1927 S.L.T. 83 (where an American minor was bequeathed a pecuniary legacy, a discharge proffered by his father as his guardian by the New York law of the domicile was acceptable in Scotland since the matter pertained to moveables).

[42] *Black v Black's Trs*, 1950 S.L.T. (Notes) 32; *Bank of Africa Ltd v Cohen* [1902] 2 Ch. 129; *Ogilvy v Ogilvy's Trs*, 1927 S.L.T. 83 (where an American minor was bequeathed a house in Kirriemuir, Angus, a conveyancing opinion had to be sought as to the proper method by Scots law of discharging the trustees).

7. Offence to the public policy of the forum justifies refusal of recognition of any status and/or capacity.

CHAPTER 11

THE LAW OF MARRIAGE AND OTHER ADULT RELATIONSHIPS

A. NATURE OF THE RELATIONSHIP

I. MARRIAGE

In order that a decision can be made upon the validity of a **11–01** marriage in the view of Scots conflict law, it is necessary first that the relationship presented amounts in its nature to the Scots conception of marriage. If that test is satisfied, the adequacy of the "marriage" in terms of its essential and formal validity must be examined.

> "I conceive that marriage, as understood in Christendom, may for this purpose be defined as the voluntary union for life of one man and one woman, to the exclusion of all others."[1]

It follows from this famous definition, widely accepted in the common law world, that the nature of the union must be such that it is recognised as conferring the status of married persons on one man and one woman[2] in a relationship intended to be

---

[1] *Hyde v Hyde & Woodmansee* [1866] L.R. 1 P. & D. 130, *per* Lord Penzance at 133.
[2] In the domestic law of England and Scotland it is an essential of marriage that the parties be of different sexes. The Scottish Law Commission has recommended that it continue to be a ground of nullity in Scots law that the parties are of the same sex (Scot. Law Com. Report No. 135 (1992) *Report on Family Law*, 8.5 and recommendation 45). From *Corbett v Corbett (No.1)* [1970] 2 All E.R. 33, courts in the UK applied solely a biological test to determine a person's sex. However in *Bellinger v Bellinger* [2002] Fam. Law 150 (*cf. Croft v Royal Mail Group plc (formerly Consignia plc)* [2003] I.C.R. 1425) the Court of Appeal, in the case of an individual whose gender had been reassigned by surgery, pondered what policy demanded in the current state of medical knowledge, and concluded that it was for Parliament to address whether recognition should be given to a change of gender from that which had been correctly assigned at birth. In the instant case, the Court could not recognise the purported marriage between a transsexual female and a man because as the law then stood the petitioner's status for the purposes of marriage was male. In *Goodwin v United Kingdom*

permanent.[3] As a result of the dual domicile theory[4] no Scottish or English domiciliary has capacity to enter into "same sex marriage",[5] no matter that the *lex loci celebrationis* or the personal law of the other party permits such a "marriage".[6] Except in the special case of polygamous marriages,[7] the relationship of married persons must be exclusive. The law will not recognise sub-normal marriages, that is unions under which the wife does not have the status of a wife though the issue of such a union may be recognised as legitimate.[8]

Marriage must be entered into voluntarily, "with an agreeing mind". Marriage induced by coercion,[9] or under error,[10] is void.[11]

(2002) 35 E.H.R.R. 18 (and *cf. B v France* (1993) 16 E.H.R.R. 1) the ECtHR found that in applying purely biological criteria, the UK had breached the Convention rights of transsexual persons under Arts 8 (right to respect for private life) and 12 (right to marry), directing that the UK Government had an obligation to rectify these breaches. Consequently, the Gender Recognition Act 2004 was brought into force, providing legal recognition of the acquired gender of transsexual people. See para.11–12 in respect of same sex marriage.

[3] Ease of dissolution does not invalidate original intention: *Nachimson v Nachimson* [1930] P.217.

[4] Explained below at para.11–16. Since the effect of the dual domicile theory is not alternative but cumulative, the stricter rule prevails.

[5] Though registered (same sex) civil partnerships are permitted by Scots and English law by virtue of the Civil Partnership Act from December 2005. See para.11–35, below.

[6] Whether same sex foreign "marriages" will be recognised by Scots courts as equivalent to heterosexual marriages is a matter of conjecture and for the policy of the forum as it may view the matter at any particular date. Consider K. Norrie, "Reproductive Technology, Transsexualism and Homosexuality: New Problems for International Private Law" (1994) 43 ICLQ 757; and "Would Scots Law Recognise a Dutch Same-Sex Marriage?", 2003 Edin. L.R. 147. The introduction into UK law of same sex civil partnerships makes a successful public policy challenge to recognition of foreign same sex "marriage" less likely.

[7] And even there, the forum must decide whether the situation presented amounts to polygamy or concubinage; the forum's view will prevail over that of the *lex loci celebrationis: Lee v Lau* [1967] P. 14.

[8] M. Wolff, *Private International Law* (1950), p.316. The "morganatic" marriage is a term and concept derived from German law in its early treatment of legal relationships, many of which required the parties to be of equal social standing.

[9] *Mahmud v Mahmud*, 1994 S.L.T. 559; *Mahmood v Mahmood*, 1993 S.L.T. 589 (both treated as domestic cases); *Szechter v Szechter* [1971] P. 286; *Mahmud v Mahmud*, 1977 S.L.T. (Notes) 17; *Akram v Akram*, 1979 S.L.T. (Notes) 87 (marriages of expediency: no true consent); *Sohrab v Kahn*, 2002 S.L.T. 1255; and *SH v KH (Hakeem v Hussain)*, 2003 S.L.T. 515, and on appeal, unreported, October 13, 2005.

[10] *Lendrum v Chakravarti*, 1929 S.L.T. 96; *Mehta v Mehta* [1945] 1 All E.R. 690; *Noble v Noble*, 1947 S.L.T. (Notes) 62 (error by male party domiciled at marriage in Scotland in the matter of pregnancy *per alium* of his bride). Lord Birnam's choice of law was the Scots *locus celebrationis*, which afforded no remedy; he preferred to leave out of account averments by the man of change of domicile to English law in the period before litigation.

[11] See more fully below at para.11–31, and again in "choice of law" in "nullity" at para.12–38, below.

Forced marriage, however, must be distinguished from arranged marriage.

One would think Lord Penzance's definition to be both classic and comprehensive. His Lordship cannot have thought it necessary to state that both parties should be alive at the date of marriage. But a marriage may be valid in French law though one of the parties is dead, if certain conditions are satisfied, and to safeguard the succession rights of children.[12] It is probable that such marriage, though novel in the view of Scots law, would not be so offensive to Scots public policy as to preclude recognition, provided that by the personal laws of both parties such marriages are competent.[13]

THE SPECIAL CASE OF POLYGAMOUS RELATIONSHIPS

Polygamous marriages now are recognised for practically all pur- **11–02** poses, but such recognition is of relatively recent origin.[14] The older view was that such "marriages" should not be recognised at all.[15] The foundation for this view is found in the judgment of Lord Penzance in *Hyde*. Courts and commentators placed emphasis upon the first excerpt from his judgment cited below, to the expense of the second:[16]

> "Now, it is obvious that the matrimonial law of this country is adapted to the Christian marriage, and it is wholly inapplicable to polygamy"; and "[t]his Court does not profess to decide upon the rights of succession or legitimacy which it might be proper to accord to the issue of the polygamous unions, nor upon the rights or obligations in relation to third persons which people living under the sanction of such unions may have created for themselves. All that is intended to be here decided is that as between each other they are not

---

[12] See French Civil Code, Art.171.

[13] The Hague Marriage Convention 1976 (not signed or ratified by the UK nor by many other countries) excludes from its scope posthumous marriage (and proxy marriage). See Clive, pp.111–112; and C.A. Dyer, "The Hague Convention on celebration and recognition of the validity of marriages in perspective", *Grensoverschrijdend Privaatrecht Opstellen aangeloden aan Mu Y van Rijn Van Alkeumde* (Kluwer).

[14] Much of what follows describes the development of this subject in the English conflict of laws, but there is no reason to suppose that our smaller jurisdiction was not in agreement, if less often required to comment. See denial of remedy: *Muhammed v Suna* 1956 S.C. 366. Clive, p. 111 notes the lack of development in Scots law, while recommending "the widest possible recognition" (which is the point to which English law has been moving).

[15] *Hyde v Hyde and Woodmansee* [1866] L.R. 1 P. & D. 130; *Armitage* (1866) L.R. 3 Eq. 343; *Re Bethell* (1888) 38 Ch.D. 220; *Brinkley v Att.-Gen* (1890) 15 P.D. 76.

[16] *Hyde v Hyde and Woodmansee* [1866] L.R. 1 P. & D. 130 at 135.

entitled to the remedies, the adjudication, or the relief of the matrimonial law of England."[17]

After 1945, it was realised that there was a growing case for the recognition, for some purposes, of polygamous marriages if valid by their own laws, and it began to be appreciated that the question was not whether such a marriage should be recognised in general or in the abstract, but whether it should be recognised *for the particular purpose before the court*; that is, that the problem concerned the incidents of the status, not the status itself. This change was seen first in *The Sinha Peerage Case*,[18] in which, in a peerage claim with no precedent, the son of a Hindu marriage was entitled to succeed to the title. The marriage at its inception was potentially polygamous, but was never actually polygamous and had changed its nature through a change of religious sect by the parties before the birth of the son and, obviously, therefore, before the litigation.[19] From that date, polygamous marriages began to be recognised gradually over an increasingly wide field. The cases fall into the following groups:

(a) Consistorial actions

11–03 The consistorial remedies provided by Scots and English law were regarded as being essentially adapted to the concept of monogamous marriage and accordingly were not initially available to parties to a polygamous marriage.[20] Nevertheless, such a marriage was regarded as conferring upon the parties thereto the status of married persons, to the effect that such persons, being married, could not enter into subsequent monogamous unions. Hence annulments were granted of purported monogamous unions entered into by persons who previously had entered into polygamous marriages.[21] To this extent, therefore, the polygamous marriage was recognised.

The position was altered materially by the Matrimonial Proceedings (Polygamous Marriages) Act 1972,[22] section 2 of which

---

[17] *ibid*. at 138.

[18] 1939, reported [1946] 1 All E.R. 348.

[19] Hence, mutability of nature of a marriage received recognition as a concept; and the importance of *tempus inspiciendum* is clearly seen. See para.11–10, below relating to mutability.

[20] *Mehta* [1945] 2 All E.R. 690 (court had jurisdiction to grant remedy, marriage being essentially monogamous); *Risk* [1951] P.50; *Sowa* [1961] P.70; *Ohochuku* [1960] 1 W.L.R. 183; *Muhammad v Suna*, 1956 S.C. 366; Webb, "Potentially Polygamous Marriages and Capacity to Marry"; Cohen, "A Note on Potentially Polygamous Marriages" [1963] 12 I.C.L.Q. 672 and 1407. See also A.E. Anton, "The 'Christian Marriage' Heresy", 1956 S.L.T. (News) 201.

[21] *Srini Vasan* [1946] P. 67; *Baindail* [1946] P. 122.

[22] As amended by Divorce Jurisdiction, Court Fees and Legal Aid (Scotland) Act 1983, s.6(2); Law Reform (Husband and Wife) Act 1984, s.9(1); Family Law (Scotland) Act 1985, s.28(1). The equivalent English provisions are contained now in the Matrimonial Causes Act 1973, s.47.

provides that the fact that a marriage was entered into under a law which permits polygamy shall not preclude a British court from entertaining proceedings for:

(a) divorce;
(b) nullity of marriage;
(c) dissolution of marriage on the ground of presumed death;
(d) judicial separation;
(e) separation and aliment, adherence and aliment or interim aliment;
(f) declarator of marriage (that a marriage is valid or invalid);
(g) any other action involving a decision on the validity of a marriage.

Section 2 also states that it shall apply whether or not either party has taken an additional spouse, but that provision may be made by rules of court for requiring notice of the proceedings to any such other spouse and conferring on such a person the right to be heard.

(b) Legitimacy and succession

The children of polygamous marriages are regarded as having the **11–04** status of legitimate persons for the purpose of status generally, and of succession in particular, if they have such a status by the law of their domicile (that is, in view of the circularity problem, by the law(s) of the domicile(s) of each parent).[23]

(c) General

Polygamous marriages now are recognised as creating the status of **11–05** marriage in a large number of different areas of law, from criminal law to taxation.[24]
  Specialties arise with regard to the following matters:

---

[23] *Khoo Hooi Leong* [1926] A.C. 529; [1930] A.C. 346; *The Sinha Peerage Case*, 1939, reported [1946] 1 All E.R. 348; *Bamgbose v Daniel* [1955] A.C. 107; *Coleman v Shang* [1961] A.C. 481; *Dawodu v Danmole* [1962] 1 W.L.R. 1053. See Ch.14, below. And see Ch.6, above, for current Scots rules of domicile.

[24] *Mawji v The Queen* [1957] A.C. 126; *Imam Din v National Assistance Board* [1967] 2 Q.B. 213; *Alhaji Mohamed v Knott* [1968] 2 All E.R. 563; [1969] 1 Q.B. 1; *Chaudhry* [1975] 3 All E.R. 687, aff'd; [1976] 1 All E.R. 805; *Shahnaz v Rizwan* [1964] 2 All E.R. 993; *Nabi v Heaton* [1983] 1 W.L.R. 626, CA (husband of two concurrent wives entitled to personal relief from income tax in respect of both of them). *Cf.* statutory recognition of polygamous marriages in such provisions as the National Insurance Act 1971, s.12. But see re modern Social Security provision, para.11–18.

Succession to titles of honour, or of an heir in intestacy to immoveables

11–06 In such cases it must be ascertained whether the law of the title, or the *lex situs*, requires the heir to be legitimate; if so, he must be legitimate in the view of that law. This does not necessarily preclude claims by children of a polygamous marriage.[25]

Bigamy

11–07 In Scots law, bigamy is a crime at common law, while in English law it is a statutory offence under the Offences Against the Person Act 1861, section 57. In both cases the crime or offence is committed if a person who already has the status of a "married person" purports to enter into a subsequent marriage. Under Scots law a charge of bigamy can be preferred only if the second "marriage" takes place in Scotland because the common law of Scotland cannot apply elsewhere, whereas in England the Act of 1861 has extra-territorial effect, so as to affect the actings of a British subject abroad, and a charge of bigamy may be preferred even if the second marriage takes place abroad.

In the case of a person who is already a party to a polygamous marriage, there is a question as to what is meant by a "married person" in this (criminal) context, that is whether a party to a polygamous marriage is to be regarded as "married" in this sense, so as to forbid (or not) a subsequent "marriage".[26] In English civil law, at a point in the development of the conflict rules at which recognition was not generally afforded to potentially or actually polygamous marriages, the existence of a prior marriage of such a type was recognised to the extent of barring the celebration of a valid marriage in England (necessarily monogamous in nature) by one of the parties. The first marriage would be recognised there-fore, as regards civil law, to the effect of making the second marriage void, but criminal charges for bigamy in respect of the second "marriage" did not follow. In *R. v Sagoo*,[27] overruling *R. v Sarwan Singh*,[28] it was held that the offence of bigamy had been committed when the first (potentially polygamous) marriage had become monogamous by statute or by change of domicile before the second marriage, but there has been no decision when the first marriage has remained potentially polygamous. These matters are

---

[25] *cf. Bamgbose v Daniel* [1955] A.C. 107.
[26] *cf. Baindail*, above (civil action).
[27] [1975] 2 All E.R. 926.
[28] [1962] 3 All E.R. 612.

subtle and confusing, and one must note the disinclination of the authorities to prosecute, and of the Law Commissions to discuss.[29]

Social Security

The rule in benefits regulations is often that[30] (potentially) polyg- **11–08** amous marriage will be treated as monogamous for every day that the marriage remains actually monogamous. However, the British fisc will not pay widows' benefit to two widows,[31] nor invalidity benefit to one wife of a marriage proved to the satisfaction of the Commissioners to be polygamous in nature.[32] It has been decided[33] that one wife of an actually polygamous marriage contracted in Bangladesh was not entitled to widowed mother's allowance under the Social Security Act 1975, section 25 (now Social Security Contributions and Benefits Act 1992, section 37); it would have been different if the marriage had been merely potentially polygamous.[34] Generally British courts will not recognise marriages actually polygamous in nature as marriages for the purpose of such benefits.[35]

The result is therefore that a polygamous marriage now will be recognised for practically all purposes.[36] Finally, however, attention must be paid in any conflict of laws treatment of polygamy to the inter-related matters of (a) characterisation; and (b) capacity.

---

[29] But see, for Scotland, R.D. Leslie, "Polygamous Marriages and Bigamy", 1972 JR. 113, and the unreported case of *Shafi* (Glasgow Sheriff Court, August 18, 1977). The position seems unsatisfactory, but cases are rare and there seems to be no inclination to act further in the matter or to clarify it: Law Com. No. 83 and Scot. Law Com. Report No. 56 (1982), 4.46.

[30] Child Benefit Act 1975, s.9(2)(a); Social Security Act 1975, s.162(b).

[31] Social Security Acts 1975 to 1990: Decision No. R(G) 1/93.

[32] Decision No. R(S) 2/92.

[33] *Bibi v Chief Adjudication Officer, The Times*, July 10, 1997, CA.

[34] Social Security and Family Allowances (Polygamous Marriage) Regulations 1975 (SI 1975/561).

[35] See generally Inland Revenue Decision Makers Guides: DMG 11105; CG 22072–Transfer of Assets between Husband and Wife: Polygamy (to the effect that transfers between a husband and any wife with whom he is living will be at no gain/no loss); DMG 41003–Polygamy; and CBTM 11020–General and supplementary provisions: Polygamous marriages.

[36] Consider post-1972 cases in England of *Chaudhry v Chaudhry* [1975] 3 All E.R. 687 (extending to the polygamously married the remedy in English law provided by Married Women's Property Act 1882, s.17); *Re Sehota* [1978] 3 All E.R. 385 (permitting to one of two widows of the same man to claim under the Inheritance (Provision for Family and Dependants) Act 1975 in the estate of their husband, domiciled at death in England, he having favoured the other wife in his will). Why then should not such a wife (wives), validly married to a man who died domiciled in Scotland, claim legal rights? *Cf.* R.D. Leslie, *Stair Memorial Encyclopaedia*, 216.

Characterisation of the nature of a marriage

Which law characterises?

11–09 According to the balance of authorities, the character of a union as monogamous or polygamous is determined initially by the *lex loci celebrationis*,[37] though later, for the purpose before the court, the decision upon classification is for the forum.[38] A marriage bears a mark but not an indelible mark.

Notwithstanding absence of case authority, the nature of a marriage celebrated in Scotland is monogamous despite scope for a wide variation in *locus* and form of ceremony,[39] and regardless of the personal law(s) of the parties.

Until the decision by the Court of Appeal in *Hussain*,[40] the assumption was made that the initial character of a marriage was determined by the *lex loci celebrationis* (though there was some support for the application of the matrimonial domicile).[41] It should be noted that in *Hussain* the marriage was categorised as monogamous because the capacity of each party at the marriage (English male domiciliary; Pakistani female domiciliary) precluded the possibility of any other type of marriage. In other words, the test of the nature of the marriage was capacity of parties, and capacity of parties did not extend in either case to empower the parties to enter into the proposed union.[42] However, this decision may be regarded as a creative judicial solution to a problem solved shortly thereafter by Parliament by means of sections 5 to 7 of the Private International Law (Miscellaneous Provisions) Act 1995.

Mutability: change of character of marriage

11–10 It has been suggested above that different views may be taken about the character of a marriage, and that the view of the forum in the instant case governs that matter for the purposes of that case. It is also true that the nature of any marriage may *change*, from actually or potentially polygamous to monogamous[43]; less

---

[37] *R. v Hammersmith Superintendent Registrar of Marriages, ex p. Mir-Anwaruddin* [1917] 1 K.B. 634; *R. v Naguib* [1917] 1 K.B. 359; *Lendrum v Chakravarti*, 1929 S.L.T. 96; *MacDougall v Chitnavis*, 1937 S.C. 390; *Qureshi v Qureshi* [1971] 1 All E.R. 325 (*obiter*). *Cf.* wording of Matrimonial Proceedings (Polygamous Marriages) Act 1972, s.2.

[38] *Lee v Lau* [1967] P. 14, *per* Cairns, J. at 20.

[39] Extended by Marriage (Scotland) Act 2002.

[40] [1982] 3 All E.R. 369.

[41] *Warrender v Warrender* (1835) 2 Cl. & F. 488, *per* Lord Brougham at 535; *Harvey v Farnie* [1882] 8, A.C. 43, *per* Lord Selborne; *De Reneville* [1948] P. 100, *per* Lord Greene M.R.; *Kenward* [1951] P. 124, *per* Denning LJ at 144 and 146. *Cf.* the legal capacity issue: *Radwan No.2* [1972] 3 All E.R. 1026.

[42] See now assistance provided by Private International (Miscellaneous Provisions) Act, 1995, ss.5–7.

[43] See, *e.g. Cheni* [1965] P. 85; *Parkasho v Singh* [1968] P. 233. *Quoraishi v Quoraishi* (1983) 13 Fam. Law 86.

commonly the other way.[44] Since 1972, the issue of a marriage's character is less important (except in the area of Social Security legislation).

The change in character may be as a result of a change in the parties' personal circumstances, religion, religious sect, or joint change of domicile,[45] or a change by statutory provision. Such a change will not affect the marriage's validity, though in the past it would affect jurisdiction, and, consequently, remedies. In *Drammeh*,[46] a Gambian case upheld by the Privy Council, it was decided that the change from monogamous to polygamous, effected unilaterally by the husband through reversion to his original domicile and religion, did not affect the monogamous nature of the *original wife's* marriage.

Date of Determination of Character of Marriage

It was held in *Cheni*[47] that, if a question arises as to the character of a marriage, it is determined at the date, and for the purpose, of the litigation: if the marriage was monogamous at that date, it was no objection for jurisdictional purposes that the marriage was potentially polygamous when it was entered into.

These matters, although of interest, are of less importance in view of the 1972 Act which removes the necessity for the marriage to come before the court in monogamous form.

Capacity to marry

The effect of section 7 of the Private International Law (Miscellaneous Provisions) Act 1995[48] is that a person of Scots domicile may enter into a *potentially* polygamous marriage, which marriage shall be treated as a monogamous marriage for every day that it remains so. This removes doubt about the validity of marriages entered into abroad by persons of British residence and uncertain domicile, where, by the *lex loci celebrationis* (*e.g.* Pakistan), the nature of all marriages at the point of celebration is potentially   **11–11**

---

[44] *Drammeh v Drammeh* (1970) 78 Cey. L.W. 55; *Att.-Gen. of Ceylon v Reid* [1965] A.C. 720; *cf.* Anton with Beaumont, p.450, *cf. Onobrauche v Onobranche* (1978) 8 Fam. Law 107.

[45] *Ali* [1968] P. 564 (unilateral change by husband, but a case of short-lived fame in view of the breaking of the unity of domicile rule between husband and wife with effect from January 1, 1974 by Domicile and Matrimonial Proceedings Act 1973, s.1).

[46] (1970) 78 Cey. L.W. 55.

[47] [1965] P. 85.

[48] As to England and Wales, see ss.5 and 6 (retrospective effect, subject to conditions therein contained).

polygamous (*i.e.* giving one spouse, normally the husband, the legal entitlement to take concurrently more than one wife).[49]

No Scottish or English domiciliary has legal capacity by his or her personal law to enter an *actually* polygamous marriage, in Scotland or abroad.[50] Hence, if the dual domicile theory is used, no such purported marriage by someone whose personal law is Scots can be regarded as valid by Scots law. Authority exists for applying the intended matrimonial home theory (*qv*),[51] but the decision is an isolated one, and is not highly regarded.

SAME SEX MARRIAGE

11–12 It is not the policy of the Scottish Executive to change the requirement of Scots domestic law that to create a valid marriage under Scots law the participating parties must be of opposite sex.[52] However, it seems inevitable that since the laws of certain EU Member States, and other states,[53] permit "same sex marriage", questions can be expected on a number of conflict of laws issues, eg the capacity of Scottish parties to enter such a marriage abroad, the laws to regulate formal and essential validity of such marriages, and the recognition of such marriages and any incidents thereof by Scots law. These problems are likely to be complicated further by the issue of recognition of the purported divorces of such purported marriages, especially within the framework of Regulation 2201/2003.[54] Discussion of these matters is speculative, given the

---

[49] Unlike the equivalent English provisions, the rule is not retrospective: see B.J. Rodger, *Annotations to Statute*. The precursor to this provision is the Law Commissions' joint report (August 1985) entitled "Private International Law— Polygamous Marriages: Report on Capacity to Contract a Polygamous Marriage and Related Issues", Law Com. No. 146, Scot. Law Com. No. 96. See also *Hussain* [1982] 3 All E.R. 369.

[50] Scots law: *McDougall v Chitnavis*, 1937 S.C. 390; Law Com. No. 146 and Scot. Law Com. No. 96, 4.2–4.9. Marriage (Scotland) Act 1977, s.2(3)(b) and s.5(4)(b). English law: see Matrimonial Causes Act 1973, s.11(d), and *Hussain v Hussain* [1982] 3 All E.R. 369, now subject to Private International Law (Miscellaneous Provisions) Act 1995, ss.5, 6 and 7.

[51] *Radwan (No.2)* [1972] 3 All E.R. 1026 in which a woman domiciled in England was found by an English court to have contracted a valid marriage to an Egyptian, which marriage for a short time was actually polygamous. The marriage took place in the Egyptian Consulate-General in Paris. The parties intended to live in Egypt after their marriage and fulfilled that intention for a number of years before returning to England. Contrast *Lendrum v Chakravarti*, 1929 S.L.T. 96, *per* Lord Mackay at 99.

[52] Marriage (Scotland) Act 1977, s.5(4)(e). Scottish Executive White Paper, *Parents and Children* (2001), para.6.4.2. See note 2 above, however, in relation to transsexual individuals.

[53] *e.g.* Belgium, the Netherlands, certain provinces of Canada and States of the USA. A list of legal systems in which at least a form of same sex partnership has been introduced is contained in Civil Partnership Act 2004, Sch.20.

[54] See further, para.12–25, below.

absence of case law, but principle would direct that in accordance with the dual domicile theory outlined below, any such "marriage", purported to be entered into anywhere in the world, where one at least of the parties is of Scots domicile, will not be regarded as valid in a Scots court (by reason of lack of legal capacity). Where, however, such "marriages" are valid by the *lex loci celebrationis*, and where by his personal law each contracting party has legal capacity to enter into such a union, recognition is likely to be afforded in Scotland to the status, or at least to certain of the incidents thereof. This speculative view is reinforced by the existence and terms of the Civil Partnership Act 2004, which introduces the option in English and Scots law of the formation of same sex civil partnership (on condition that the parties are eligible so to do).[55] Although the 2004 Act does not introduce into the domestic laws of the United Kingdom same sex marriage,[56] it is impossible to overlook the fact that the structure of rules and the provenance of many of the terms of the 2004 Act find their foundation in domestic and conflict statutes concerning marriage and divorce.

There are many difficulties *en route* to *recognition* of same sex marriage, before the matter of policy is addressed. The forum in which the issue of recognition is raised will choose, define and identify the applicable law to govern legal capacity to enter into such a marriage. The fact that, by the *locus celebrationis*, the individuals concerned possessed legal capacity so to marry is irrelevant, at least according to orthodox conflicts methodology.

Important matters of policy are present, and there may be difficulties of ranking of interests. For example, in a question of succession to land in Scotland belonging to an intestate, same sex "spouse" domiciled abroad (a party to a "marriage" recognised by Scots law), there may be a competition between the surviving same sex "spouse", and other relations of the deceased having a ranking in terms of the Succession (Scotland) Act 1964. The position would be more complicated if, by his date of death, the deceased "spouse" had resumed his Scottish domicile and died possessed of moveable property in Scotland requiring to be distributed. Prob-

---

[55] See further, para.11–37, below.

[56] In terms of s.215 of the Civil Partnership Act 2004, the effect of recognition in the UK of a specified overseas relationship (including "marriage" in Belgium, the Netherlands and, under SI 2005/3135, Canada) qualifying under Sch.20 will be to treat such a union as equivalent to a UK civil partnership. Litigation is ongoing in England *sub nom. Wilkinson v Kitzinger* [2006] EWHC 835 (Fam) seeking declaration pursuant to the Family Law Act 1986, s.55, that a same sex marriage celebrated in British Columbia, Canada is a valid *marriage* worthy of recognition in the UK; and a declaration of incompatability, under the Human Rights Act 1998, s.4, in relation to the Matrimonial Causes Act 1973, s.11(c), which specifies that a marriage shall be void on the ground that parties are not respectively male and female.

lems such as these have not been overlooked by the Civil Partnership Act 2004.[57]

It is often said, with regard to the recognition of same sex marriage, that there are parallels with the history of recognition in Scots conflict rules of polygamous marriages, and the incidents thereof. While the pattern of growing recognition may be repeated, it should be borne in mind that legal capacity to enter into polygamous marriages remains confined to those individuals whose personal law permits this.

II. COHABITATION AND CIVIL PARTNERSHIP

11–13 Account must be taken of the incidence now of cohabitation as an alternative, or precursor to marriage, and of the introduction into UK law of the new institution of civil partnership. While *ex hypothesi* these two domestic relationships do not meet the Scots conception of marriage, the new legislative provision, especially with regard to civil partnerships, is modelled upon existing legislative provision concerning marriage. Equally with marriage, these new forms of adult relationship may have conflict of laws implications. These matters are discussed below at Sections C and D, below.

B. MARRIAGE: THE DISTINCTION BETWEEN ESSENTIALS AND FORM

11–14 Until about 1860, marriage was regarded as a matter of contract, the rights of the contracting parties being governed by the law of the place where the contract was entered into, that is the *lex loci celebrationis*. The result of this was that the *lex loci celebrationis* was applied to determine all questions as to the validity of a marriage. As the rules developed, however, it was recognised that marriage involves more than contract insofar as it creates a new status, and that the law of the domicile has an interest in being applied. When, after 1860,[58] questions concerning the validity of a marriage arose, not involving form, UK courts began to distinguish between essentials and form, in order to avoid making decisions inconsistent

---

[57] *e.g.* s.131.
[58] *e.g. Brook v Brook* (1861) 9 H.L.C. 193; and *Mette v Mette* (1859) 1 Sw. & Tr. 416.

with the "Gretna Green cases".[59] In questions involving essentials (in this sense meaning legal capacity to marry), the courts applied the law of the domicile, while in questions involving form they continued to apply the *lex loci celebrationis*.

Although essentials and form are quite distinct in theory, in some cases it may be difficult in practice to distinguish them; examples are the need for parental consent,[60] and marriage by proxy. The classification of a particular matter or element as pertaining to essentials or form is determined by the *lex fori*. Marriage by proxy has been classified as a matter of form, with the result that such marriages have been accepted by an English forum if this form of marriage is permitted by the foreign *lex loci celebrationis*.[61] Where neither of the parties was present, but a family celebration took place in the parties' "country of origin" (Ghana), while the parties themselves remained in London, the Court of Appeal recognised the marriage as valid[62] (though it is hard to see how it can be said with confidence that the conflict rule requiring compliance in matters of form with the *lex loci celebrationis* has been adhered to when the identity of the *lex loci* is by no means clear).[63] The novel question is whether the place of celebration (for there was certainly a celebration) was properly regarded as the place of marriage celebration if both principals were absent. Where is the *locus celebrationis* in such a case?

---

[59] Marriages at Gretna became popular when Lord Hardwicke's Act 1753, which was not extended to Scotland, ended the legality of clandestine marriages (originally meaning secret marriages without solemnities, but later signifying irregular marriage of less than full formality but celebrated by a priest or minister, possibly out of doors: D.M. Walker, *Oxford Companion to Law* (1980)) and also marriages *per verba de praesenti*. Though Lord Mansfield objected, it became accepted in England that the Act of 1753 was of effect in England only. The Scottish rule permitting marriage at an early age without parental consent also was an attraction. Some restrictions arose as a result of the Marriage (Scotland) Act 1856 which required 21 days' residence in Scotland by at least one party: see *Miller v Deakin* (1912) 1 S.L.T. 253. The Marriage (Scotland) Act 1939 removed from Scots domestic law irregular forms of marriage except marriage by cohabitation with habit and repute. This and further information and discussion from Anton and Francescakis, "Modern Scots Runaway Marriages", 1958 JR. 253. See also Anton (1st ed.), pp.273–274.

[60] *Bliersbach v McEwen*, 1959 S.L.T. 81; see also and contrast the English cases of *Simonin v Mallac* (1860) 2 Sw. & Tr. 67 and *Ogden v Ogden* [1908] P.46. See also para.11–33, below.

[61] *Apt v Apt* [1948] P. 83; *Ponticelli v Ponticelli* [1958] P. 204.

[62] *McCabe, The Independent*, September 3, 1993; [1994] 1 F.C.R. 257, CA.

[63] See R.D. Leslie, "Foreign Consensual Marriages", 1994 S.L.T. (News) 87. Dr Leslie would prefer to say that the *lex loci celebrationis* in such a case is the place where there was interchange of consent.

ESSENTIAL VALIDITY

11–15 The term "essentials" covers matters such as whether the parties have legal capacity to marry, the incidents of marriage, and rights and duties during marriage.[64] The majority of "essential" problems concern capacity to marry. Since this is a matter which arises before the marriage when the parties are separate, the majority view is that it is appropriate for it to be governed by the personal law of each party, that is, by the laws of their separate domiciles which are thought to provide a personal safeguard, and to have an interest. Matters which arise after the marriage, when the parties are deemed to be one, are governed by the law of the matrimonial domicile, that is, the law of the place where the parties have their permanent home.

Capacity to marry

There are two views as to which law governs:

(a) Traditional view: dual domicile theory

11–16 By this theory, each party must have legal capacity (*e.g.* in matters of consanguinity, sanity and nonage)[65] to marry in general, and to marry the other party, in particular, according to the law of his/her domicile immediately before the marriage (the ante-nuptial domicile).[66] This is termed "distributive application" of the personal law. It has been said that "this theoretical construct tumbles over its own heels in hilarious circularity",[67] for the reality is the cumulative application of the parties' personal laws, and hence the stricter rule (if two rules are involved) will prevail. Taking the example of the proposed marriage of an uncle and his niece: what does it benefit the uncle if his law permits him to marry his niece, if her law does not reciprocate?

The common law view that the Scottish forum defers to the law(s) of the parties' domicile(s), subject to a public policy

---

[64] As to matrimonial property matters see Ch.13.
[65] *Mette* (1859) 1 Sw. & Tr. 416; *Brook* (1861) 9 H.L. Cas. 193; *Webster v Webster's Tr.* (1886) 14 R. 90; *Re De Wilton* [1900] 2 Ch. 481; *Re Bozzelli's Settlement* [1902] 1 Ch. 751; *Despatie v Tremblay* [1921] 1 A.C. 702; *Re Paine* [1940] Ch. 46; *Pugh* [1951] P. 482; *Rojas, Petr*, 1967 S.L.T. (Sh.Ct) 24. It is noted often that the contract of marriage is an easy one to understand, but there may be cases where an individual is not capable of understanding the nature of marriage or giving his/her consent to be married: *M v B* [2005] EWHC 1681; *Alfonso-Brown v Milwood* [2006] EWHC 642 (Fam).
[66] And perhaps also according to the *lex loci celebrationis*: see para.(c) below.
[67] C.A. Dyer, First Secretary of the Hague Conference on Private International Law, "The Hague Convention on celebration and recognition of the validity of marriages in perspective", *Grensoverschrijdend Privaatrecht*, p.102.

discretion, was given legislative approval in effect by the Marriage (Scotland) Act 1977,[68] and more recently, and expressly, by the Family Law (Scotland) Act 2006, s.38(2). Scots law now, in section 38(2)(a) (which is subject to a public policy exception in section 38(4), and a saving for Scots domestic law where Scotland is the *lex loci celebrationis*, in section 38(3)) is that the question whether a person who enters into a marriage had capacity to enter into it shall be determined by the law of the place where, immediately before the marriage, that person was domiciled.

This forecloses any possibility of seeking to persuade a Scots court to apply in *favorem matrimonii* the matrimonial domicile theory, outlined below.

(b) Matrimonial domicile theory

According to this view, attributed first to Cheshire,[69] the relevant **11–17** law is the law of the place where the parties intend to live their married life, that is, the law of the intended matrimonial domicile. The intended matrimonial domicile is presumed to be the husband's domicile, but that presumption may be rebutted if it can be inferred that the parties, at the point of marriage, intended to settle in a different country, and proved that they did so within a reasonable time.[70]

According to this theory all questions of essentials arising before and after the marriage ceremony are governed by the law of the intended/actual matrimonial domicile.[71] There can be little doubt that the law of the matrimonial domicile applies to all matters of essentials arising after the marriage, but there is controversy as to whether it applies to capacity. Authority in favour of the matrimonial theory is scarce[72] and criticism of it not hard to find.[73]

---

[68] See E.M. Clive, "The Marriage (Scotland) Act 1977 2. International Private Law", 1977 S.L.T. (News) 225.

[69] G.C. Cheshire, *Private International Law* (5th ed., 1957), pp.305–320.

[70] *ibid.*, p.307.

[71] Although it is likely also to be necessary to comply with the *lex loci celebrationis* as to essentials, and certainly as to form. See paras 11–18 and 11–24, below.

[72] *De Reneville* [1948] P. 100, *per* Greene M.R., esp. at 114; *Kenward* [1951] P. 124, *per* Denning L.J. at 144 and 146; *In the Will of Swan* (1871) 2 V.R. 47 (Victoria, Australia); *Radwan (No.2)* [1972] 3 All E.R. 1026 (polygamous marriage); *Bliersbach v McEwen*, 1959 S.C. 43, *per* Lord Sorn at 55; C. Schmitthoff, *The English Conflict of Laws* (3rd ed., 1954), pp.312–314 (supportive of Cheshire's theory).

[73] Graveson, pp.265–269; Wolff (2nd ed.), pp.335–356; Cheshire & North, pp.724 *et seq.* (current edition of Cheshire admits that the weight of authority supports the dual domicile theory, though a number of decisions are inconclusive in that the same decision would have been reached by the application of either theory); Anton with Beaumont, pp.428–431; Bresler, "Note on *Pugh v Pugh*" (1951) 4 ICLQ 478, who notes that the celebrated South African case in matrimonial

However, dicta to support Cheshire's view can be produced, and decisions can be cited in which it is difficult to say whether the choice of a law has been made *qua* matrimonial domicile or *qua* ante-nuptial domicile(s), because the two coincide. In *Brook*,[74] one of the early leading authorities cited in support of the dual domicile theory, Lord Campbell, to determine the validity of a purported marriage in Denmark between a man and his deceased wife's sister, at a time when such marriages were void by English law, applied the law of England *qua* ante-nuptial domicile of the parties but also as the law "in which the matrimonial residence is contemplated". *Radwan (No.2)*[75] supports Cheshire's theory, but comes from the specialty of polygamous marriage, and is not well regarded. In the era, now gone, of breach of promise of marriage actions, English courts referred the question of remedy to the law of the territory in which the intended marriage was going to be performed (*i.e.* where the parties intended to set up home).[76]

A study of the case of *Lawrence*,[77] especially in the first instance judgment of Anthony Lincoln J.,[78] reveals approval of the intended matrimonial home theory, or at least of a criterion of "real and substantial connection" and a *favor matrimonii* approach, to the extent of expression of the view that there is equal support for each theory, but it may be that the exigencies of the case, and the state of the conflict rule principally under consideration[79] in that case contributed to the stance taken.

The balance of authority favoured the traditional view. Leaving on one side, however, the question of authority, there is the problem, also seen in the context of commercial contractual capacity,[80] of seeming to permit parties to confer capacity on themselves by virtue merely of their own choice.[81] Further, there is the danger[82] of creating uncertainty: how soon after the ceremony

---

property of *Frankel v CIR* (1950) 1 S.A.L.R. 220 is firmly against the use of the intended matrimonial home theory at least in that connection. In that case, after learned debate of the civilian authorities, the South African forum applied as *lex causae* the German domicile of the husband at marriage although the parties were settled in Johannesburg, South Africa, within four months.

[74] (1861) 9 H.L.C. 193.

[75] [1972] 3 All E.R. 1026.

[76] *Hansen v Dixon* (1906) 23 T.L.R. 56; *Kremezi v Ridgway* [1949] 1 All E.R. 662. *Cf.* Civil Partnership Act 2004, s.128.

[77] [1985] 2 All E.R. 733. See *per* Sir David Cairns at 746.

[78] [1985] 1 All E.R. 506 at 510–512 (review of authorities).

[79] Recognition of Divorces and Legal Separations Act 1972, s.7, now repealed and replaced by Family Law Act 1986, s.50.

[80] G.C. Cheshire, "David Murray lecture on International Contracts", University of Glasgow, March 4, 1948, pp.45–46.

[81] Anton with Beaumont, p.429.

[82] See, similarly, in the matrimonial property context: *Re Egerton's Will Trusts* [1956] Ch. 593, para.13–10, below.

must matrimonial domicile be established, and what is the status of the parties if they should die *en route*?

While section 38 of the 2006 Act provides more clarity, it has excluded the possibility in Scotland of advancing an alternative argument on choice of law which, if of sufficient merit in the circumstances, might have enabled the court to give a positive result. As yet there is no equivalent statutory provision in England having the effect of excluding the operation of the matrimonial domicile theory, though it is noted that the Law Commissions reviewed[83] the matter in the 1980s, and concluded[84] that the dual domicile test is preferable to the intended matrimonial domicile test and should be adopted as the test for all issues of legal capacity.

It may be foreseen that use may be made in future (*e.g.* with regard to new forms of domestic relationship) of the connecting factor of habitual residence, with the attendant difficulties of definition which that concept carries, and the doubts which arise with regard to date of commencement.[85] Whichever connecting factor is used, the forum retains its discretion not to require capacity by (or not to give effect to) the provisions of that personal law, if offensive to conscience[86] or common sense.

(c) *Requirement of capacity by* lex loci celebrationis

Where a marriage takes place in Scotland, there must be capacity **11–18** to marry by Scots law, in addition to there being no impediment by the law(s) of the domicile.[87] Whether a Scots court reviewing the validity of a marriage celebrated abroad would require capacity by the foreign *lex loci* is a matter of conjecture. This question was considered by the Scottish Law Commission,[88] but the 2006 Act is

---

[83] Law Commission, Working Paper No. 89 and *Private International Law: Choice of Law Rules in Marriage*, Scottish Law Commission, Memorandum No. 64 (1984), 3.3 and 3.4.

[84] Law Commission No. 165, *Private International Law, Report on Choice of Law Rules in Marriage*, Scottish Law Commission, No. 105 (1987) Scot. Law Com. No. 64, 3.36.

[85] See paras 6–41 *et seq.*, above.

[86] Prohibitions on marriage are more likely to yield examples, *e.g.* enforced celibacy, or prohibitions on marriage out of caste, but there are rules of consanguinity which Scots law would not countenance. However, uncle-niece marriage, if acceptable to the personal law, has been recognised. See discussion in *Cheni v Cheni* [1965] P. 85, *per* Sir Jocelyn Simon P. at 99.

[87] Marriage (Scotland) Act 1977, s.2(1). This has been reinforced by Family Law (Scotland) Act 2006, s.38(3), and further s.2 regarding party consent, which traditionally is regarded as a matter of essential validity.

[88] Law Com. No. 165, Scot. Law Com. No. 105 (1987), 2.6. Also Scot. Law Com., Discussion Paper No. 85 (1990), 9.5–9.6, 9.21. Also *Report on Family Law*, Scot. Law Com. No. 135 (1992), 14.5, 14.6 and 14.22. Conclusion that capacity by *lex loci* should not be required unless it is also the *lex fori*. And see Clive, p.125.

silent on the matter. It is tempting to argue that the role of the *lex loci* should be confined to matters of form and ceremony, including the evidencing of consent, and registration of the event. In the view of the participants, the role of the *lex loci* merely may be to provide an exotic backdrop. To what extent does that branch of the travel industry which arranges "marriage holiday packages" concern itself with matters of capacity as well as with those of form? On the other hand, the *leges domicilii* and the *lex loci celebrationis*, albeit exotic, may coincide. The question is open.[89]

The Canadian forum, in the instructive case of *Reed v Reed*,[90] directed the issue of consanguinity to the domicile of British Columbia, and the issue of parental consent to the *lex loci* in the State of Washington. By this reasoning, the purported marriage of first cousins, the female party according to her personal law being under the age of marriage without parental consent, avoided all difficulties and was held to be valid in a nullity petition brought by the female party in the British Columbian court of their (common[91]) domicile.[92]

A problem occurs if a legal system is antagonistic to divorce (though few legal systems now do not contain the remedy of divorce). Objection may be raised to the celebration in that country of the re-marriage of a divorced person. However, if the antecedent divorce is worthy of recognition by that legal system in the round, the policy objections of the *lex loci* must yield to direction by its own conflict rules.[93] The different, but related, problem, of the validity of a purported re-marriage, in respect of which one or both of the parties, previously divorced from other persons by virtue of divorce(s) not recognised by their personal law(s), will be solved now in the UK by use of the Family Law Act 1986, section 50 (or where the problem is the opposite—non-recognition of divorce by the forum—as an incidental question at common law[94]).

---

[89] Moreover, there are always other ways of looking at a situation. Dr Dyer, n.67, above, explains the American preference for permitting the place of celebration to judge both form and substance as the natural preference of an immigrant society whose members were far from their original home and did not intend to go back there. "The idea of holding up a marriage while waiting for a certificate of marriageability to come by slow boat from Europe would hardly appeal to these frontier societies where family life was hard and sometimes was cut very short."

[90] [1969] 6 D.L.R. (3d.) 617.

[91] Presumably on the facts, whatever the validity of the marriage and independent of any unity of domicile rule: *cf. Administrator of Austrian Property v Von Lorang*, 1927 S.C. (HL) 80.

[92] The case illustrates the process of teasing out the issues from the skein of a legal problem and treating them in the conflict of laws to different choice of law rules: *dépeçage*.

[93] *Breen v Breen* [1964] P. 144. Irish domestic law now permits divorce.

[94] See para.4–06, above.

Exceptions to the rule concerning capacity to marry

A Scots or English forum requires exceptions to be made to the **11–19** operation of either capacity theory in the following cases:

Royal marriages

A marriage is invalid if either of the parties, being a descendant (as **11–20** defined) of George II, marries in contravention of the Royal Marriages Act 1772, which requires the consent of the sovereign to the marriage of such persons, no matter where the purported marriage may take place.[95]

Penal incapacity

A marriage celebrated in Scotland or England is not invalid on **11–21** account of any incapacity, which, although existing under the law of the domicile of either/ both party/ies, is penal in the sense of discriminatory. Penal incapacities include restrictions or inca-pacities attributable to colour or race, rules of caste, or religion,[96] religious rules of celibacy, or prohibitions on re-marriage. A restriction on the re-marriage of one party (usually the guilty party) at any time or within the lifetime of the other (usually the innocent party) will be regarded in Scots law as penal,[97] and therefore will not be recognised in Scotland; but a restriction upon each party's re-marriage within a certain time limit, or until certain formalities have been complied with, will be regarded as affecting the capacity of either party to remarry, and such a condition will be respected, being an integral part of the divorce proceedings (probably imposed for the avoidance of doubt about paternity) and not uneven in application or otherwise objectionable.[98]

From the coming into effect of the 2006 Act, the public policy exception in Scots law vests upon section 38(4) of that Act.

---

[95] *The Sussex Peerage Case* (1844) 11 Cl. & F. 85. But see Farran, "The Royal Marriages Act 1772" (1951) 14 M.L.R. 53, cited in Wilson, "Validation of Void Marriages in Scots Law" (1964) J.R. 199, who considered that the force of the Act is spent. The point is also made there that many such descendants are likely to be foreign domiciliaries, even allowing for the exception contained in s.1 of the "issue of princesses who have married, or may hereafter marry into foreign families". The application extra-territorially to an individual of a personal law which is not his own is something new. See more recently Pugh and Samuels, "The Royal Marriages Act 1772: Its Defects and the Case for Repeal" (1994) 15 Statute Law Review 46; Cretney, 'The Royal Marriages Act 1772: A Footnote' (1995) 16 Statute Law Review 195.

[96] *Chetti* [1909] P. 67; *MacDougall v Chitnavis*, 1937 S.C. 390. See Clive, p.126.

[97] *Beattie* (1866) 5 M. 181 (prohibition upon any subsequent marriage by adul-teress); *Scott v Att.-Gen.* (1886) 11 P.D. 128 (prohibition upon the re-marriage of the guilty party while the innocent party remained unmarried). There was a similar prohibition in Scotland until 1964: Clive, p.130.

[98] *Warter* (1890) 15 P.D. 152; *Martin v Buret*, 1938 S.L.T. 479; but see *Buckle* [1956] P. 181; and see *Wall v De Thoren* (1874) 1 R. 1036.

Unknown incapacity

11–22 In English law there is authority[99] to the effect that a marriage
celebrated in England, according to local form, between parties of
whom one has an English domicile and the other a foreign
domicile, is not invalid on account of an incapacity affecting the
foreign party under the law of his/her domicile, which does not
exist under English law. Probably this rule is not part of Scots law
on the subject,[1] and it is one which the Law Commissions would
like to see removed from English law.[2]

Other matters of essential validity

11–23 With the exception of *Kenward*,[3] all the cases cited above involve
questions of capacity to marry. As regards other essentials, particularly those involving matters arising during the marriage, only
one law can apply to determine the rights of married parties, and
that is the law of the place where the parties have their home in
the legal sense, *i.e.* the law of the matrimonial domicile. Matrimonial domicile used to be presumed to be the law of the
husband's domicile and now must be decided on the facts. In
Kenward,[4] the view was put forward by Denning L.J. (though this
was not the foundation of the decision[5]) that as the right to
matrimonial consortium is an essential condition of marriage as
understood by English law, in circumstances where the personal
law of the woman would not permit her to leave Russia to cohabit
as a married woman with her "husband" in England, the marriage
failed in its essentials.

As a matter of principle all questions which may arise as to the
rights and duties of the spouses while the married relationship
subsists are governed by the law of the matrimonial domicile at the

---

[99] *Sottomayor v De Barros (No.2)* (1879) 5 P.D. 94.
[1] Walton, *A Handbook of Husband and Wife According to the Law of Scotland* (3rd
ed., 1951), p.325; Anton with Beaumont, pp.431–432; Clive, p.130. *Private
International Law Choice of Law Rules in Marriage*, Law Com. and Scot. Law
Com., Working Paper No. 89 and No. 64, and Report on 3.13(a), and report on
Family Law (1992), 14.14. Dr Clive at p.130, noting the words of L.P. Normand in
MacDougall v Chitnavis, 1937 S.C. 390, concludes: "[t]here is, therefore, regrettably some ground for saying that this supposed exception has been recognised in
Scottish law, though it can hardly be regarded as firmly entrenched", and notes
that it could not be acted upon practically by a registrar within the provisions of
the Marriage (Scotland) Act 1977.
[2] Law Com., *op. cit.*, 3.48. It has not taken matters further.
[3] [1951] P. 124.
[4] *ibid.* at 144 and 146.
[5] Ultimately, the marriage was annulled on the ground of a defect in form.

time in question.[6] Such questions include selection of home and allocation of the costs of running it, duty to adhere and duty to aliment.[7] Questions of the extent of property rights in wealth inherited by one spouse during the marriage, or as to ownership of items acquired by the parties during the marriage are within the province of conflict rules of matrimonial property.[8] Grounds of divorce or separation (as opposed to grounds of annulment) are regarded as the province of the forum in which the action is brought.[9] Hence, with regard to matrimonial offences, if the marriage is to be ended by divorce or judicial separation, the only offences worth mentioning will be those of legal significance in the forum in which the remedy is sought.[10]

FORMAL VALIDITY

The rule is well settled that in order for a marriage to be valid as to **11–24** form there must be compliance with the requirements of the *lex loci celebrationis* in all matters of form.[11] Form includes not only length of residence (and how to count the days), notice and

---

[6] *cf.* meaning of this connecting factor as understood by Cheshire (n.69, above). Consider also the denial of this connecting factor for the purposes of jurisdiction (*Le Mesurier* [1895] A.C. 517). In the present context, it is probable that the expression would be interpreted as meaning the place of fixed matrimonial residence at the time in question. Such an interpretation would obviate difficulties in identifying the domicile of each party at that time, and in reconciling potentially conflicting laws.

[7] See further for detail, Ch.13. Similarly, occupancy rights in the matrimonial home fall within the interest of the *lex situs*.

[8] See Ch.13.

[9] See Ch.12.

[10] This will be true not only of behaviour which if proved entitles a party to a remedy, but also (*De Dampierre v De Dampierre* [1987] 2 All E.R. 1) in relation to the significance or not of behaviour as affecting financial provision. In *Ali v Ali* [1968] P. 564 the English court addressed itself only to those matrimonial offences alleged to have been committed after the marriage changed its nature to monogamous, thereby fitting itself for the jurisdiction of that court (at that date). But *Ali* is now a special and historical example.

[11] *Bliersbach v McEwan*, 1959 S.C. 43; *Simonin v Mallac* (1860) 2 Sw. & Tr. 67; *Administrator of Austrian Property v Von Lorang*, 1927 S.C. (HL) 80; *Berthiaume v Dastous* [1930] A.C. 79: "[i]f a marriage is good by the laws of the country where it is effected, it is good all the world over, no matter whether the proceeding or ceremony which constituted marriage according to the law of the place would or would not constitute marriage in the country of the domicil of one or other of the spouses", *per* Lord Dunedin at 83; *Pepper* (1921) L.J. 413; *Kenward* [1951] P. 124; *Pilinski v Pilinska* [1955] 1 W.L.R. 329; *Burke v Burke*, 1983 S.L.T. 331 (in which there was an adminicle of evidence of a marriage on the Island of St Christopher. It was not for the pursuer, who was seeking nullity, having "married" the defender in ignorance of his first marriage, to prove its validity. The maxim *omnia praesumuntur rite et solemniter acta esse* applied). Where Scotland is the *locus celebrationis*, see Marriage (Scotland) Acts 1977 and 2002.

ceremony, but also irregular forms of marriage, such as marriage by cohabitation with habit and repute,[12] and proxy marriage,[13] or even marriage lacking the presence of the principal parties.[14] The Family Law (Scotland) Act 2006, section 38(1) confirms that, subject to the Foreign Marriage Act 1892 (*qv* below), the question of formal validity of a marriage shall be determined by the law of the place where it was celebrated. There may be advantage in remembering that since the Act does not expressly exclude the operation of *renvoi*,[15] a Scots court might be persuaded to apply the *lex loci celebrationis* or the *leges domicilii* in their entirety, "in the round", *i.e.* including their choice of law rules.[16]

The case of *Starkowski v AG*[17] held that if the formal validity of a marriage is called in issue, this falls to be determined in accordance with the *lex loci celebrationis* at the date when it is called in issue, not at the date of the marriage ceremony. The reason for this is that, although as a general rule the validity of a marriage must be determined as at the date of the ceremony (at which the formalities either have been complied with or not), in exceptional circumstances its validity may be affected for the better by subsequent legislation of the *lex loci*. Yet *Starkowski*, though long established and of high authority, is regarded as a case tied very closely to its facts. In particular, in considering whether the *ratio* could be extended to broader issues of status, it will be noted from the speech of Lord Tucker[18] that, in treating the effect of foreign retrospective legislation, his Lordship was inclined to distinguish between laws directly affecting status and those which deal with form and have only indirect or consequential effect on status.[19] It is to be expected that any decision on the formal validity of a marriage will have repercussions for the status of all parties involved. For example, in *Starkowski* the decision as to the effect of

---

[12] The 2006 Act, s.3, has abolished this form of irregular marriage in Scots domestic law. Older conflict cases on this matter include *Cullen v Gossage* (1850) 12 D. 633; *Rooker* (1863) 3 Sw. & Tr. 526; *Re Green, Noyes v Pitkin* (1909) 25 T.L.R. 222. Modern instances include *Kamperman v MacIver*, 1994 S.L.T. 763; *Dewar v Dewar*, 1995 S.L.T. 467; *Walker v Roberts*, 1998 S.L.T. 1133; *Ackerman v Logan's Executor (No.1)*, 2002 S.L.T. 37; *Sheikh v Sheikh*, 2005 G.W.D. 11–183; and *S v S*, unreported (OH) March 31, 2006. The transitional provisions are contained in s.3(2) and (3), and attention should be paid to the protective provisions in s.3(4).

[13] *Apt* [1948] P. 83; *Ponticelli* [1958] P. 204.

[14] So as to furnish sufficient evidence of a marriage to permit dissolution thereof in an English court: *McCabe v McCabe* [1994] 1 FLR 410; *sed quaere* R.D. Leslie, "Foreign Consensual Marriages", 1994 S.L.T. (News) 87.

[15] See Ch.5 for default position.

[16] See para.5–07 (scope—a redoubt for *renvoi*); R.D. Leslie, *Stair Memorial Encyclopaedia* 221. And see *Hooper v Hooper* [1959] 2 All E.R. 575.

[17] [1954] A.C. 155. See also and contrast *Pilinski v Pilinska* [1955] 1 W.L.R. 329. See Clive, pp.134–135.

[18] At 173 and 176.

[19] At 173.

Austrian legislation with regard to form (permitting retrospective validation by registration of purely religious marriages which lacked the civil component necessary by the *lex loci* at the date of celebration) had an effect on status in England. Had there been a "second" marriage in England, ante-dating the rectification of the "first" marriage in Austria, and celebrated validly as to form and with no incapacity as to persons by their then domicile, it is hard to see how a British court could have denied the validity of that "second" marriage.[20] However, the *Starkowski* principle clearly is capable of beneficial effect. It is a different matter to suggest that the later removal by the law(s) of the domicile of incapacities existing by that/those laws at the date of "marriage" can be effected *ratione Starkowsi* (which would amount to the recognition of a subsequent direct effect on status). Any extension of the principle to include recognition by the forum addressed, of enlargement of capacity after the purported marriage by the *lex domicilii*, would appear unwarranted,[21] and productive of uncertainty.

Religious Ceremonies

The *lex loci celebrationis* must be complied with if it requires **11–25** observance of the rules of the parties' religious denomination(s), but not if it requires compliance with the rules of some other denomination. Generally compliance or non-compliance with the religious beliefs of the parties does not affect the validity of a marriage unless the *lex loci celebrationis* insists upon observance of such forms.[22]

---

[20] This question was left open in the speeches of Lords Morton of Henryton, Tucker and Cohen. The decision concerns a defect of form, and does not extend to a consideration of capacity.

[21] Except perhaps in the rare case of marriage by cohabitation with habit and repute, where it might be said that a new *terminus a quo* occurs when an incapacity on the part of one "spouse" is removed, as *e.g.* by the death of a prior spouse. In this unusual situation, capacity overtakes incapacity, sometimes even without the knowledge of the parties (*cf. In re Scullard* [1957] Ch. 107; and *In re Groos* [1915] 1 Ch. 572). *Contra*, if in a foreign *locus celebrationis* of an irregular marriage (place of cohabitation of apparent spouses), the law were to be changed so as to forbid this form of marriage, a Scots forum would have to apply the *lex loci celebrationis* as at the date of litigation, subject to a public policy discretion.

[22] *Re Alison's Trusts* (1874) 31 L.T. 638 (compliance with parties' own religious denomination required); *Usher* [1912] 2 I.R. 445 (marriage valid by Irish law though invalid in the view of the Roman Catholic Church); *Papadopoulos* [1930] P. 55; *Hooper* [1959] 1 W.L.R. 1021 (compliance with the requirements of parties' nationality was the rule of the *lex loci celebrationis*); *Gray v Formosa* [1963] P. 259; as to marriages at sea, see Cheshire & North, pp.585–586 which takes a slightly more generous view than do the Scottish writers, *e.g.* Anton with Beaumont, p.428; Clive, p.123.

Exceptions to the rule on formal validity

11–26 The rule is subject to exceptions. A marriage celebrated abroad which does not comply with the *lex loci celebrationis* as to form nevertheless is valid[23] in the following cases:

Foreign Marriage Acts

11–27 The Foreign Marriage Acts 1892 and 1947, as amended[24] provide that certain marriages (of service personnel and marriages at foreign embassies) will be valid if they comply with formalities laid down in these Acts. In such cases it does not matter that there is no compliance with the *lex loci celebrationis*.[25]

Common law exceptions

A body of authority consisting of English conflict law cases exists, under the headings "belligerent occupation" and "local form impossible", to the effect that a benevolent exception operated in qualifying cases for the purpose of upholding the formal validity of a marriage otherwise defective. The former is to the effect that a marriage celebrated in accordance with the "requirements of common law"[26] in a country under the occupation of military forces and where one of the parties is a member of these forces, is formally valid.[27] The benefit of the rule is not extended to those whose intention was to comply with the local law, but who failed to achieve this.[28]

---

[23] Certainly in England; with regard to the first two exceptions, the cases are English, and Clive, pp.124–125 expresses doubt about their application in Scotland. But see Anton with Beaumont, p.428.

[24] By the Foreign Marriage (Amendment) Act 1988.

[25] For equivalent provision for civil partnerships, see Civil Partnership Act 2004, ss.210 and 211. In respect of marriage at British consulates, the prescribed officer of HM Diplomatic Service need not permit registration if, in his opinion, the formation of such a civil partnership would be "inconsistent with international law or the comity of nations."

[26] The basic minimum, one presumes, is mutual voluntary exchange of consent, in the presence of at least one witness. However, *cf.* the Scots irregular form of marriage by declaration *de praesenti* (removed with effect from July 1, 1940), in respect of which no witness was required, nor proof of time nor place at which consent was given, provided that the court was satisfied that the parties' true intention was to be married to each other.

[27] *Taczanowska v Taczanowski* [1957] P. 301; *Kochanski v Kochanska* [1958] P. 147; *Merker v Merker* [1963] P. 283; *Preston v Preston* [1963] P. 141.

[28] *Lazarewicz v Lazarewicz* [1962] P. 171.

Secondly, a number of cases stand as authority, at least for English **11–28** law,[29] that a marriage celebrated as nearly as possible in accordance with the "requirements of common law" in a country in which the use of the local form is impossible or in which there is no such form, is formally valid.

The question arises now, in light of the express formulation **11–29** contained in the 2006 Act, section 38(1) (that formal validity of a marriage shall be determined by the law of the place where the marriage was celebrated), whether that provision affords any exception other than that specifically mentioned in the section.

Presumption *in favorem matrimonii*

There is a presumption in law that if a marriage has been **11–30** celebrated, registered and a formal certificate produced, it will be formally valid, and the onus of proving otherwise rests upon any person who so avers.[30]

CONSENT TO MARRIAGE

Parties to the marriage

While evidencing consent is a matter for regulation by the *lex loci,* **11–31** the nature and extent of free will necessary to create a valid marriage are matters of substance for decision by the parties' personal law(s).[31] This broad statement is considered further in

---

[29] *Lord Cloncurry's Case* (1811), cited in 6 St. Tr. (N.S.) 87 (evidence of exchange of consent by Protestants in Rome held sufficient since local law made no provision for Protestant marriage); *Catterall v Sweetman* (1845) 1 Rob. Ecc. 304; *Beamish* (1861) 9 H.L.C. 274, at 348, 352; *Lightbody v West* (1903) 19 T.L.R. 319; *Phillips v Phillips* (1921) 38 T.L.R. 150; *Wolfenden v Wolfenden* [1945] P. 61 ("a British Subject takes to a colony only so much of English law as is applicable to his situation"); *Penhas v Tan Soo Eng* [1953] A.C. 304 (in the absence of a form appropriate to both, the parties devised a composite ceremony which they used in Singapore: the English forum accepted that a valid marriage had resulted, monogamous in nature). It will be noted that all these cases are English. Clive, pp.124–125 doubts the existence or at least the need for such an exception in Scots law. Scot. Law Com. has sought views but has made no firm recommendation: Law Com. No. 165, Scot. Law Com. No. 105 (1987), 2.5, 2.13, 2.15. But perhaps if it is not part of Scots law, it ought to be, as a harmless rule of potential benefit in the unusual case: Dr Clive takes the opposite view, p.125. The Family Law (Scotland) Act 2006 does not cede any exception to the rule now contained in s.38(1).

[30] *Hill v Hill* [1959] 1 W.L.R. 127; *Mahadervan v Mahadervan* [1964] P 233. *Cf.* Marriage (Scotland) Act 1977, s.23A: *omnia praesumuntur rite et solemniter acta esse.* See also s.20.

[31] 2006 Act, s.38(2)(a). But see the overriding rule contained in s.2 of the 2006 Act, amending Marriage (Scotland) Act 1977, s.20 ("void marriages"), which applies where a marriage is solemnised in Scotland. See further Ch.12, below.

Chapter 12. Parties may enter a marriage in mental states varying from joyful acceptance to rueful resignation (whether under the influence of ideals of family obedience and family honour, or under duress). Scots domestic law, while requiring "a willing mind" and while considering that the nature of the agreement is simple and easy to understand,[32] will not generally be prepared to give effect to unilateral mental reservation by granting an annulment. There are many fine distinctions, which are multiplied when the case is a conflict one giving rise to a number of choice of law options within the power of the forum to select.[33] The reported cases display a variety of approaches, from application by the forum of its own law without argument,[34] through application of the *lex fori* after useful argument,[35] and application of the *lex fori* as interpreted in the light of a cultural background foreign to the *lex fori*,[36] to application by the forum of the law(s) of the parties' domicile(s).[37] Moreover, two parties are involved: should the forum take account of the laws of both, or only of the party allegedly withholding consent?[38]

Third parties (parents)

11–32 Cases in which the validity of a marriage is dependent upon the consent of a third party, and of a parent in particular, require special consideration, particularly in view of the prevalence in earlier days of "runaway marriages" in Scotland, where one party is domiciled outside Scotland.[39]

---

[32] *Lang v Lang*, 1921 S.C. 44.

[33] There is even the possibility of conflict among the laws of the forum (also *qua lex loci celebrationis*), the religious laws of the Roman Catholic Church, and the laws of the domicile: *Di Rollo*, 1959 S.C. 75.

[34] *Buckland v Buckland* [1968] P. 296; *Kassim v Kassim* [1962] P. 224; or, oddly, of its own law *qua lex loci celebrationis* (or *lex loci contractus*—Davies J.), *Parojcic v Parojcic* [1958] 1 W.L.R. 1280.

[35] *H v H* [1954] P. 258.

[36] *Mahmud v Mahmud*, 1994 S.L.T. 599; *Mahmood v Mahmood*, 1993 S.L.T. 589; and *cf. Alfonso-Brown v Milwood* [2006] All E.R. (D.) 420. See also *Mahmud v Mahmud*, 1977 S.L.T. (Notes) 17.

[37] *Szechter v Szechter* [1971] P. 286 (all parties of Polish domicile at date of marriage of expediency/mercy in Poland).

[38] See further Ch.12, below.

[39] Most such cases concern foreign parties seeking to marry in Scotland. However, a specialty, now of historic interest only, is the problem which could arise where the party's or parties' age(s) is/are between 16 and 18 years (the parties being of English and Scots domicile), in that a young person of Scots domicile may marry at the age of 16 without parental consent, whereas by English law parental (or judicial) consent is required (or, after the Children Act 1989, the consent of the person with whom the child is living under a residence order). While the rule requiring parental consent rarely may be invoked, there is a possibility of friction if the English court should make a young person a ward of court and thereby seek to restrict his capacity to marry. A Scottish forum, while being inclined to the

In some countries parental consent to marriage is required up to the age of 21, in others to 25. In some, absence of consent makes a marriage void wherever it is celebrated, whilst in others, it may make a marriage voidable within a certain period wherever it is celebrated. In some, it may be overcome by following certain procedure; in others, lack of consent may have different effects according to whether the individual is under or above 21. The problem is the extent to which such consents as may be required by the law of the domicile of one or both parties are to receive effect in a Scots *locus celebrationis*.

English Law

The parental consent required by French law in the circumstances **11–33** of *Simonin v Mallac*[40] was of quite a different nature from that required in *Ogden*,[41] but in both cases it was held that the requirement was to be regarded as a foreign rule affecting form, and as having no effect upon the celebration of a marriage in England. In effect, the English courts decided that, no matter what might be the domicile of the parties, whether or not parental consent is a necessary condition for the validity of a marriage celebrated in England was a matter to be classified by English law (the *lex fori*), as a matter of form, governed by the *lex loci celebrationis*.

Scots Law

Scots domestic law, following Canon law, recognises two kinds of **11–34** impediments to marriage:

(a) irritant impediment (*impedimentum dirimens*), which is so fundamental that it bars a marriage altogether and makes any union void (suggestive of substance, to be referred to the personal law); and

(b) prohibitive impediment (*impedimentum impeditivum*), which is not so fundamental, merely prohibiting marriage until the impediment is removed (arguably formal or procedural).

---

view that "the writ of the Chancery Court does not run in Scotland" (*Hoy v Hoy*, 1968 S.L.T. 413, *per* Lord Robertson at 415) nevertheless may agree that delaying the marriage may be unwise (*Pease v Pease*, 1967 S.C. 112). The matter is within the discretion of the Scots court *qua lex fori, lex domicilii* and *lex loci celebrationis*; the point has been considered (T.B. Smith, *A Short Commentary on the Law of Scotland*, pp.315–316; and "Runaway Marriages", 1958 J.R. 253) but no solution suggested. The point seems likely to be eclipsed by conflict problems arising out of modern living patterns such as cohabitation.

[40] (1861) 2 Sw. & Tr. 67 (the consent requirement being in the nature merely of a delay).

[41] [1908] P. 46.

In *Bliersbach v McEwan*[42] the consent of parents required by the Dutch Civil Code was regarded as falling under class (b),[43] with the result that the proposed marriage in Scotland of a Dutch couple without such consent might proceed. The opinions in the case suggest a potentially different result if the requirement of consent were to fall within class (a). The decision as far as it goes is to the same effect as the English cases.

The Scottish Law Commission recommended in 1992 that a foreign parental consent rule should be regarded as resulting in a legal incapacity if, but only if, it precluded marriage by the person affected, anywhere in the world.[44]

The rule that is now contained in the Family Law (Scotland) Act 2006, section 38(5) follows that which was recommended by the Scottish Law Commission. In future cases, therefore, characterisation of the nature of the foreign rule will not be necessary; it will rather be a matter of proof of content of that law, and its intended ambit.

C. CIVIL PARTNERSHIP

11–35 In recent years conflict lawyers in the UK have been aware of the existence in other countries of forms of registered legal relationship (usually homosexual) unknown in Scots and English domestic law, and have noted the need for rules governing questions of capacity, formal validity and recognition. With effect from December 2005 the laws of Scotland and England will provide for a new institution of civil partnership, by virtue of the Civil Partnership Act 2004, which contains not only domestic, but also conflict of laws rules.

A civil partnership is defined as a legal relationship between two people of the same sex which is formed when they register as civil partners of each other, all in accordance with the relevant provisions of the 2004 Act, and which ends only on death, dissolution or annulment.

CIVIL PARTNERSHIP ACT 2004

11–36 The Act is in 8 parts and has 30 schedules.[45] Part 1 establishes the requirements for the creation of a valid civil partnership (both formal and essential validity). Separate provision is laid down for

---

[42] 1959 S.L.T. 81.

[43] But see criticism by Clive, pp.113–114.

[44] For Scotland—*Report on Family Law*, Scot. Law Com. No. 135, (1992), 14.8–14.10. Recommendation 70(a).

[45] And is accompanied by relevant secondary legislation making necessary consequential changes to primary law, *e.g.* the Civil Partnership Act 2004 (Consequential Amendments) (Scotland) Order 2005 (SSI 2005/623).

the different jurisdictions of the UK: Part 2 (England and Wales), Part 3 (Scotland), and Part 4 (Northern Ireland).[46]

Within each Part are special rules concerning formation and eligibility, registration, occupancy rights and tenancies, dissolution and financial arrangements. Part 5, containing the conflict of laws provisions, is concerned with civil partnerships formed or dissolved abroad, and is of particular relevance here.

Legal capacity to enter into a civil partnership

The choice of law rule as to capacity to enter into a civil **11–37** partnership differs according to the place of registration (*"lex loci registrationis"* used here for short reference). There are three potential scenarios, viz:

(1) where it is sought to register a civil partnership *in*[47] any territorial unit of the UK (by parties domiciled in a UK jurisdiction, or otherwise);

(2) where parties, one or both of whom is domiciled in a UK jurisdiction, seek(s) to register a civil partnership abroad (and thereafter to have it recognised in Scotland);

(3) where parties, neither of whom is domiciled in a UK jurisdiction, having registered a civil partnership abroad, seek to have it recognised in Scotland.

While in scenarios (1) and (3) legal capacity is determined according to the *lex loci registrationis*, scenario (2) is subject to the connecting factor of domicile. Where a party is domiciled in a UK jurisdiction, the provisions have the effect of ensuring that his personal law applies extra-territorially, meaning that the requirements as to eligibility contained in the 2004 Act will follow him wherever he may purport to register his partnership. This means that a Scottish domiciliary cannot evade, for example, Scottish rules of consanguinity or nonage by going abroad to register the partnership; this safeguard has an ancient lineage.[48]

Part 3—Scotland

Eligibility—section 86[49]

Legal capacity to enter a civil partnership is placed under the heading of "eligibility". Two parties are not eligible to register in Scotland as civil partners of each other if under s.86(1):

---

[46] Is it to be understood that the *locus* of registration alone determines which Part of the Act shall apply?

[47] The significance of location of registration will become apparent.

[48] See Ch.2, *Statutes Personal* in the writings of Bartolus. Cf. *Sussex Peerage Case* (1844) 11 Cl. & Fin. 85; and *Brook v Brook* (1961) 9 H.L.C. 193.

[49] As amended by Family Law (Scotland) Act 2006, s.33.

    (a) they are not of the same sex;
    (b) they are related in a forbidden degree[50];
    (c) either has not attained the age of 16 years;
    (d) either is married or already in civil partnership; or
    (e) either is incapable of understanding the nature of civil partnership, or validly consenting to its formation.[51]

One looks in vain for the connecting factor by which to judge the presence of eligibility.[52] Section 86 sets down these requirements with the qualification that they apply to registrations "in Scotland", which tends to suggest that we have returned to the pre-1860 (marriage) situation of having the law of the place of registration determine both form and capacity.

D. *DE FACTO* COHABITATION

11–38 Until the 2006 Act, there was no single body of rules in Scots domestic law governing the definition, constitution, and proprietary and other consequences, of cohabitation, although particular claims by one partner of a cohabiting couple may be recognised on occasion.[53] Provision was haphazard. As has been explained, with effect from December 21, 2005 in Scotland and England, homosexual partners may choose to register their relationship as a civil partnership, in terms of the Civil Partnership Act 2004. The effect of registering will be that parties become subject to the rules newly provided for the institution of civil partnership; this is a *de iure* relationship having specified consequences, which in the particular case will trump application of rules, current and proposed, regulating *de facto* cohabiting relationships.[54]

    As regards "*de facto*" cohabitation, the Family Law (Scotland) Act 2006 introduces in sections 25 to 30 a set of rules which, after defining "cohabitant" (section 25) provides certain rights for such persons in household goods (section 26); in money and property (section 27); upon termination of the relationship otherwise than by death (section 28); and upon termination of the relationship upon death intestate of one cohabitant (section 29).

---

[50] The forbidden degrees are set out in s.86 and Sch.10 to the Act in a similar manner to that found in the Marriage (Scotland) Act 1977, as amended (*mutatis mutandis*).

[51] s.123 provides that absence of consent is a ground rendering the civil partnership void.

[52] Except as regards final determination of gender: see s.216(1).

[53] *e.g.* Mortgage Rights (Scotland) Act 2001; the claim of a partner under the Damages (Scotland) Act 1976, as amended by the Administration of Justice Act 1982, s.14(4); and the Housing (Scotland) Act 1988, s.31(4).

[54] As to conflict of laws application, see speculation below.

The meaning of "cohabitant" is contained in the 2006 Act, **11–39** section 25(1), as follows: either member of a couple consisting of (a) a man and a woman who are (or were) living together as if they were husband and wife; or (b) two persons of the same sex who are (or were) living together as if they were civil partners.[55]

A problem with regard to the definition of cohabitation generally **11–40** is surely that of identifying the date of commencement, and possibly the date of termination; whilst both, presumably, are questions of fact, the former one might think more difficult of proof.

The Act takes the approach of providing in section 25(1) an abstract definition of those who are eligible to be regarded as "cohabitant", and of providing in section 25(2) factors which may be taken as sufficient to establish cohabitation so as to "trigger" sections 26 to 30. Section 25(2) states that the court shall have regard to (a) the length of the period during which A and B have been living together (or lived together); (b) the nature of their relationship during that period; and (c) the nature and extent of any financial arrangements subsisting, or which subsisted, during that period. It is therefore not possible to advise with certainty as to whether the law would regard a particular couple as being cohabitants for the purposes of the Act. On the other hand, it may be difficult for a couple to evade the status of cohabitant under the 2006 Act, even if that should be their choice, an outcome which is an affront to party autonomy.

Conflict problems arising from the incidence of *de facto* cohabitation

These notable changes in domestic Family Law have the potential **11–41** to generate conflict of laws problems, but in general sections 25 to 30 are "conflict of laws blind", except that for application to be made under section 29 the deceased cohabitant must have been domiciled in Scotland at death. It is implicit that application may be made for the rights provided for in the Act whenever Scots law is the *lex causae*. However, since generally the Act contains no jurisdiction or choice of law rules with regard to de facto cohabitation, it remains uncertain, e.g. which law governs an individual's legal capacity to attain the status of cohabitant. The essential antecedent question, not addressed in the Act, is in what circumstances the Scottish courts have jurisdiction to rule on these matters in the first place.[56]

---

[55] The manner in which this provision has been drafted suggests that the relationship between husband and wife is that between persons of different sexes.

[56] See J.M. Carruthers, in "Perspectives for the Unification and Harmonisation of Family Law in Europe" (ed. K Boele-Woelki, 2003) at p.322.

Furthermore, as conflict rules now stand, what arguments might a party approaching the Scots court deploy to persuade the court that a law other than Scots law should apply? The law of the domicile during cohabitation suggests itself, both as to jurisdiction and choice of law.[57] There is a strong argument for application, by the court of the country in which the parties cohabit, of the law of that country, to the consequences of cessation of de facto cohabitation; presumably that law also would determine when, and in what circumstances, such cohabitation is deemed to have ceased.[58] The conflict dimension of cohabitants' rights is dealt with further at Chapter 13 below.

SUMMARY 11—THE LAW OF MARRIAGE AND OTHER ADULT RELATIONSHIPS

11–42 1. Nature of the relationship

This must be tested by the *indicia* of marriage according to the Scots court acting as an enlightened *lex fori*.

2. Polygamous Marriages

Polygamous marriages are now recognised for virtually all purposes. In particular, consistorial actions between the parties to such a marriage have been competent since the Matrimonial Proceedings (Polygamous Marriages) Act 1972. Although no Scottish or English domiciliary has legal capacity to enter into an actually polygamous marriage, Private International Law (Miscellaneous Provisions) Act 1995, section 7 provides that such a person has legal capacity to enter into a marriage which is potentially polygamous.

3. Essential validity of marriage

In terms of the Family Law (Scotland) Act 2006, section 38(2), each party must have capacity to marry by the law of his/her domicile immediately before the marriage (and by section 38(3), where the *locus celebrationis* is Scots, provided that the parties have capacity by Scots law also), and subject always to public policy (section 38(4)).

In terms also of the 2006 Act, the question whether a party has consented to enter into a marriage is to be determined by his/her

---

[57] The courts will not entertain argument about the application of foreign rules concerning cohabitation unless one party were to aver that such foreign law is relevant and were to offer to prove its content.

[58] 2006 Act, s.28 gives lengthy consideration to the types of order which may be made on cessation of cohabitation and the criteria for awarding them, but no guidance to ascertain that cessation has occurred.

ante-nuptial domicile (section 38(2)), subject however to the provisions on void marriages inserted by section 2 of that Act.

4. Formal validity of marriage

Matters of form are governed by the *lex loci celebrationis* in terms of section 38(1) and the Family Law (Scotland) Act 2006.

5. Parental consent to marriage

In terms of section 38(5) of the Family Law (Scotland) Act 2006, a requirement of the law of a party's domicile that parental consent must be obtained to his/her marriage if s/he is under a certain age shall not be taken to affect his/her capacity to enter into a marriage in Scotland unless failure to obtain such consent would render invalid any marriage that the person purported to enter into in any form anywhere in the world.

6. *De facto* cohabitation

The Family Law (Scotland) Act 2006 sets out new rules for Scots domestic law in respect of the rights and duties of cohabitants. No jurisdiction or choice of law rules are contained in the Act.

7. Civil Partnership Act 2004

Part 5 contains conflict of laws provision in respect of civil partnerships formed or dissolved abroad. Legal capacity to enter a civil partnership is determined by the *lex loci registrationis*, although a party domiciled in a UK jurisdiction must have capacity also according to his personal law.

CHAPTER 12

CONSISTORIAL CAUSES

I. DIVORCE

The following will be considered in turn: **12–01**

(1) Jurisdiction of domestic courts;
(2) Choice of law; and
(3) Recognition of foreign decrees.

A. THE JURISDICTION OF SCOTS COURTS

Common law

At one time the Scots courts assumed jurisdiction on a wide basis, **12–02**
including residence, but Scots decrees were not recognised in
England unless the husband was domiciled in Scotland at the date
of the action.[1]

The Scots courts did not adopt this strict view at that time.
Between 1852 and 1895,[2] they developed a doctrine of matrimonial
domicile; that is, that the parties should be regarded as being
domiciled in the country where they resided, for the purpose of
consistorial actions only, and that the courts of that country should
be regarded as having jurisdiction in such actions. In *Le Mesurier*[3]
the Privy Council, on an appeal from Ceylon, held that there was
no such thing for this purpose as matrimonial domicile and that
only the courts of the husband's domicile had jurisdiction in actions
of divorce. This decision was accepted as applying both to Scotland
and England and in Scotland the doctrine of matrimonial domicile
as a ground of jurisdiction was abandoned after *Le Mesurier*.[4]

---

[1] *Lolley's Case* (1812) Russ. & Ry. 237; and *Shaw v Gould* (1868) L.R. 3 (H.L.) 55.
[2] *Shields v Shields* (1852) 15 D. 142; *Jack v Jack* (1862) 24 D. 467; *Pitt v Pitt* (1864)
2 M. (H.L.) 28; *Dombrowitzki v Dombrowitzki* (1895) 22 R. 906.
[3] [1895] A.C. 517.
[4] See McLaren's *Court of Session Practice* (1916), pp.57–58.

Statutory extension of grounds of jurisdiction

12–03 The practical difficulties of having to go to the court of the domicile, the problem of the deserted wife in England,[5] and the occurrence of wartime marriages to "foreigners", combined to demonstrate the undue strictness of the rule in *Le Mesurier*. As a result, a number of statutory extensions were made to permit access by the wife to the Scots or English courts on the basis of her residence in the jurisdiction.[6]

Current grounds of jurisdiction

Rules of jurisdiction up to March 1, 2001

12–04 The earlier statutory provisions were replaced by the Domicile and Matrimonial Proceedings Act 1973 ("the 1973 Act"), as now amended in light of EU harmonisation measures.

The 1973 Act specified a ground of jurisdiction additional to that of domicile. Section 7 provided that the Court of Session should have jurisdiction in actions of divorce, separation and declarators of freedom and putting to silence if and only if:

(a) either party was domiciled in Scotland at the date when the action began; or
(b) either party was habitually resident in Scotland throughout the period of one year ending with the date when the action is begun.[7]

Divorce jurisdiction was extended to the sheriff court by the Divorce Jurisdiction, Court Fees and Legal Aid (Scotland) Act

---

[5] The English courts regarded the husband's domicile *at the date of the raising of the action* as being the deciding factor: *H v H* [1928] P. 206 and *Herd v Herd* [1936] P. 205. In such cases in Scotland, however, the courts assumed jurisdiction if the husband was domiciled in Scotland *at the date of desertion*.

[6] Indian and Colonial Divorce Jurisdiction Acts 1926 and 1940; and Colonial and Other Territories (Divorce Jurisdiction) Act 1950; Matrimonial Causes Act 1937 (AP Herbert's Act) (introducing residence as a ground in England for a deserted wife); and Matrimonial Causes (War Marriages) Act 1944, s.1 (England), s.2 (Scotland). The last and most useful was the Law Reform (Miscellaneous Provisions) Act 1949, s.1 (England), s.2 (Scotland).

[7] There are similar provisions in ss.5 and 13 as regards the courts of England and Northern Ireland respectively. As to jurisdiction in nullity see para.12–34, below. See an important recent HL judgment, *Mark v Mark* [2005] 3 All E.R. 912, on the question whether a person can be either habitually resident or domiciled in England and Wales if her presence in the UK is a criminal offence under the Immigration Act 1971. Held that illegal residence by the wife as an "over-stayer" did not preclude her acquisition of a domicile of choice in England, and that residence for the purpose of s.5(2) of the 1973 Act need not be lawful residence. See further discussion in Ch.6.

1983.[8] Jurisdiction to reduce a decree of divorce granted by a court in Scotland is conferred on the Court of Session whether or not at that later date the court has jurisdiction independently to pronounce on the parties' status.[9]

Council Regulation 1347/2001

From March 1, 2001, there was put in place a discrete system of **12–05** allocation of jurisdiction in matrimonial matters and consistorial decree recognition among the then Member States of the EU, in the form of Council Regulation (EC) No.1347/2000 on Jurisdiction and the Recognition and Enforcement of Judgments in Matrimonial Matters and in Matters of Parental Responsibility for Children of Both Spouses (hereinafter "Regulation 1347", colloquially known as "Brussels II").[10] This system depends (as do its commercial law precursors, the 1968 Brussels Convention ("Brussels I") and Regulation 44/2001 ("Brussels I Regulation"), which provide the structure for the family law instrument) upon Member States' agreeing a set of rules of jurisdiction; if the decree in question emanates from a court of competent jurisdiction in terms of the instrument, recognition thereof is almost certain to follow in the other Member States. Regulation 1347 does not contain rules of choice of law.

Regulation 1347 was succeeded rapidly by Council Regulation (EC) No.2201/2003 concerning Jurisdiction and the Recognition and Enforcement of Judgments in Matrimonial Matters and Matters of Parental Responsibility, repealing Regulation (EC) No.1347/2000 (hereinafter "Regulation 2201", colloquially known as "Brussels II *Bis*").[11] Regulation 2201 came about as a result of the view that the scope of Regulation 1347, as it affected children, was too narrow. The more ambitious aim of Regulation 2201 was to create a single European instrument securing the free move-

---

[8] And see Domicile and Matrimonial Proceedings Act 1973, s.8(1) and (2).

[9] Law Reform (Miscellaneous Provisions) (Scotland) Act 1980, s.20. See previously *Acutt v Acutt*, 1935 S.C. 525.

[10] May 29, 2000, OJ 2000 L160/19. The relevant Scottish secondary legislation is The European Communities (Matrimonial Jurisdiction and Judgments) (Scotland) Regulations 2001 (SSI 2001/36); and Act of Sederunt (Ordinary Cause Rules) Amendment (European Matrimonial and Parental Responsibility Jurisdiction and Judgments) 2001 (SSI 2001/144).

[11] November 27, 2003, OJ 2003 L338/1. See also Council Regulation (EC) No.2116/2004 concerning Jurisdiction and the Recognition and Enforcement of Judgments in Matrimonial Matters and the Matters of Parental Responsibility, repealing Regulation (EC) No.1347/2000, as regards treaties with the Holy See (December 2, 2004, OJ 2004 L367/1). The relevant Scottish secondary legislation is The European Communities (Matrimonial and Parental Responsibility Jurisdiction and Judgments) (Scotland) Regulations 2005 (SI 2005/42) and Act of Sederunt (Ordinary Cause Rules) Amendment (European Matrimonial and Parental Responsibility Jurisdiction and Judgments) 2005 (SSI 2005/135).

ment, both of matrimonial judgments and parental responsibility judgments. Regulation 2201 came into force fully on March 1, 2005, repealing Regulation 1347.

The "Brussels rules" apply, with direct effect, among all Member States of the EU, with the exception of Denmark.[12] Necessary amendments have been made to the 1973 Act, the UK domestic statute dealing with allocation of jurisdiction in matrimonial matters.

Rules of jurisdiction after March 1, 2005: Council Regulation 2201/2003

12–06 The starting point is the 1973 Act, as amended first by The European Communities (Matrimonial Jurisdiction and Judgments) (Scotland) Regulations 2001 (SI 2001/36) (taking account of Regulation 1347), and more recently by The European Communities (Matrimonial and Parental Responsibility Jurisdiction and Judgments) (Scotland) Regulations 2005 (taking account of Regulation 2201).

The rules of Scottish domestic jurisdiction now are contained in section 7(2A) of the 1973 Act, to the effect that the Court of Session has jurisdiction to entertain an action for divorce or separation,[13] if and only if:

(1) the Scottish courts have jurisdiction under Regulation 2201; or

(2) the action is an excluded action and either of the parties to the marriage is domiciled in Scotland on the date when the action is begun.

Article 3, Regulation 2201

12–07 Turning first, therefore, to jurisdiction under Regulation 2201, the bases of jurisdiction are contained in Article 3, to the following effect: in matters relating to divorce, legal separation or marriage annulment, jurisdiction shall lie with the courts of the Member State:

(a) in whose territory:

---

[12] Protocol No.5 on the position of Denmark (OJ 1997 C340/101), in terms of which Denmark shall not take part in the adoption of proposed measures pursuant to Title IIIa of the Treaty establishing the European Community. See also 1973 Act, s.12(5)(b).

[13] There continue to be special rules of jurisdiction in relation to declarators of nullity of marriage, where one party was dead at the date of the action, and that party was domiciled at death in Scotland, or had been habitually resident there for one year before death (s.7(3A), 1973 Act). So too for actions of declarator of marriage (s.7(3), 1973 Act).

— the spouses are habitually resident, or
— the spouses were last habitually resident, insofar as one of them still resides there, or
— the respondent is habitually resident, or
— in the event of a joint application, either of the spouses is habitually resident, or
— the applicant is habitually resident if he or she resided there for at least a year immediately before the application was made, or
— the applicant is habitually resident if he or she resided there for at least six months immediately before the application was made, and is either a national of the Member State in question or, in the case of the UK and Ireland, has his or her "domicile" there[14];

(b) of the nationality of both spouses or, in the case of the UK and Ireland, of the "domicile" of both spouses.

"Excluded action"[15]

Secondly, the Scottish courts will have jurisdiction if the action is **12–08** an "excluded action" and either party is domiciled in Scotland on the date when the action is begun. An understanding of this qualification requires, therefore, an examination of the meaning of "excluded action", which is defined in SSI 2001/36,[16] as "an action in respect of which no court of a Contracting State has jurisdiction under the Council Regulation and the defender is not a person who is (i) a national of a Contracting State (other than the United Kingdom or Ireland); or (ii) domiciled in Ireland."[17] The main point to make here is that, in connection with actions of divorce, the pre-existing (that is, pre-March 1, 2001) Scottish jurisdictional ground of one year's habitual residence of either party in Scotland, has ceased to be available.

Conflicting jurisdictions

The common law position had been that if a Scots or English court **12–09** had jurisdiction in a consistorial action by one party and the other party was proceeding with another action in a foreign court, that fact would not prevent the first party from proceeding with the first action unless a very strong case was submitted.[18] The 1973 Act set

---

[14] In terms of Art.3.2, for the purposes of Regulation 2201, "domicile" shall have the same meaning as it has under the legal systems of the UK and Ireland.
[15] Regulation 2201, Art.7 provides for the continuing application of residual national rules of jurisdiction.
[16] In reg.2(5)(d). See also 1973 Act, s.12(5)(d).
[17] As to jurisdiction in nullity, see below.
[18] *Sealey v Callan* [1953] P. 135.

out for England,[19] and Scotland,[20] respectively, a dual system of mandatory and discretionary sists for the treatment of instances of conflicting jurisdictions in consistorial causes.

Mandatory sists

12–10 Where, before proof has begun in an action of divorce in the Court of Session, or sheriff court, a party shows that an action of divorce or nullity relating to the same marriage is proceeding in a related jurisdiction (that is within England and Wales, Northern Ireland, Jersey, Guernsey (including Alderney and Sark) and Isle of Man)[21] and, broadly speaking, that the parties resided together after the marriage and last resided together in that other jurisdiction, and that either party was habitually resident in that other jurisdiction throughout the year ending with the date on which they last resided together before that other action was begun, the Scottish court must sist the action (Sch.3 para.8).

Discretionary sists

12–11 Where, before proof has begun in any consistorial action in the Court of Session or sheriff court, it appears that there are other proceedings relating to the marriage in another jurisdiction (*i.e.* within or outside Great Britain) and that the balance of fairness (including convenience) between the parties is such that it is appropriate for those other proceedings to be disposed of before further steps are taken in the Scottish action, the court may if it thinks fit sist the action (Sch.3 para.9).[22]

There may be cultural considerations as a result of which the Scots forum may think that the balance of fairness and convenience lies in permitting an action here to proceed, for example, if the litigant has little hope of a satisfactory remedy in the competing jurisdiction.[23] However, many cases do not exhibit a cultural clash,

---

[19] 1973 Act, s.5 and Sch.1.

[20] *ibid.*, s.11 and Sch.3.

[21] *ibid.*, Sch.3 para.3.

[22] The principles and practice in commercial and consistorial causes now resemble each other. See Schuz, "The Further Implications of *Spiliada* in Light of Recent Case Law: Stays in Matrimonial Proceedings" (1989) 38 ICLQ 946. Also P.R. Beaumont, "Conflicts of Jurisdiction in Divorce Cases: *Forum Non Conveniens*" (1987) 36 ICLQ 116.

[23] *Shemshadfard v Shemshadfard* [1981] 1 All E.R. 726; *Thyssen-Bornemisza v Thyssen-Bornemisza* [1995] 1 All E.R. 58; *Hemain v Hemain* [1988] 2 F.L.R. 388 (wife sought from English court an injunction to restrain H from pursuing legal proceedings in a foreign country; although as in commercial actions, such a remedy would be granted only if the other proceedings were vexatious or oppressive, injunction was granted—"Hemain injunction"); *Bloch v Bloch* [2003] 1 F.L.R. 1 ("Hemain injunction" not granted); *Breuning v Breuning* [2002] 1 F.L.R. 888; and *Otobo v Otobo* [2003] 1 F.L.R. 192.

and in such cases the controversial issue is the extent to which personal or juridical advantage to one party ought to be taken into account.[24] On the other hand, the Matrimonial and Family Proceedings Act 1984 has changed this situation to a significant extent, in that a party may apply to a Scots or English court for financial provision despite the existence of an antecedent foreign divorce worthy of recognition in Scotland or England. Use of the 1984 Act is subject to strict jurisdictional requirements, and there have been few cases. Nevertheless, the provision should result in a smaller number of cases being defended, apparently on substance, when the true reason is financial.[25] It means also that some cases which pre-date the 1984 Act and which bear upon judicial advantage are no longer a safe guide.[26]

These rules are a manifestation in consistorial actions of a system of allocation of jurisdiction which depends on the use of judicial discretion. Such an approach traditionally has commended itself to UK courts in commercial actions also. It stands in contrast to the continental European preference for a system of ranking concurrent proceedings on the basis of priority of process (*lis pendens*). Since the Brussels regime has been extended, in operation and influence, from commercial law to family law,[27] it follows that the Brussels-preferred system of allocating jurisdiction among competing legal systems operates to solve this problem in appropriate cases.[28] The *lis pendens* system as provided for by Regulation 2201 for use in matrimonial matters (and matters of parental responsibility) is set out below. The Brussels system must apply in such cases where the interested legal systems are EU Member States,[29] but on occasion difficulties may arise in delimiting the ambit of operation of each contrasting system of rules, and further in stating with confidence the system which operates within the territories of the UK.

Schedule 3 contains provisions relating to sisting of actions in Scotland. In terms of Schedule 3 paragraph 7, there is a duty on the pursuer or on any other person who has entered appearance in a consistorial action in either the Court of Session or the sheriff

---

[24] *De Dampierre v De Dampierre* [1987] 2 All E.R. 1; the need for a judicial disposal with regard to heritable property within the jurisdiction may tend to dissuade that forum from sisting, *e.g. Mitchell v Mitchell*, 1993 S.L.T. 123; and *Butler v Butler (No.2)* [1997] 2 All E.R. 822, CA (the only matrimonial residence—which belonged to the wife—was in America; moreover, "all their life together had been centred in Florida", *per* Sir Stephen Brown P. at 825).

[25] Consider *Quazi v Quazi* [1980] A.C. 744 and contrast *Tahir v Tahir*, 1993 S.L.T. 194 (and see *Tahir v Tahir (No.2)*, 1995 S.L.T. 451).

[26] *e.g. K v K* [1986] Fam. Law 329 and *Gadd v Gadd* [1985] 1 All E.R. 58.

[27] See Ch.1, above.

[28] See para.7–36, above.

[29] 1973 Act, s.11(2).

court in which proof has not begun, to give notice of any proceedings relating to, or capable of affecting the validity of, that marriage in another jurisdiction, whether within or outside Great Britain.

Lis pendens *system under Brussels regime*

12–12 The rules on *lis pendens* currently are contained in Regulation 2201, Article 19: where proceedings relating to divorce, legal separation or marriage annulment between the same parties are brought before the courts of different Member States, the court second seised shall of its own motion stay its proceedings until such time as the jurisdiction of the court first seised is established.[30] The same system applies to concurrent proceedings relating to parental responsibility concerning the same child and involving the same cause of action.[31]

Delimitation of the rule contained in Article 19

12–13 There is no difficulty in appreciating the differences between the Brussels system and that provided by the 1973 Act, and their respective strengths and weaknesses. One of the most challenging tasks for conflict lawyers is to form a defensible view of which set of rules applies in hybrid or borderline cases, for example where one spouse initiates a divorce action in the court of a Member State, say, Scotland, founding on a ground under Article 3 of Regulation 2201; and in response the other spouse argues that the court of a non-EU country, say, Iowa, USA, is a more appropriate forum, and pleads for a stay or sist of the Scottish proceedings. Whilst the UK courts are experienced in using their discretion to adjudicate between contending courts on the grounds of suitability and justice, the question arises whether a Scots court would be entitled to accede to a plea for a sist in these circumstances, since it could be argued that by doing so it would be defeating the legitimate expectations of the pursuer and would be adopting a

---

[30] This is a re-working of the rule contained in Regulation 1347, Art.11. See also the provision in Regulation 2201, Art.16, of a common approach to identifying the date at which a court shall be deemed to be seised. A good early example of interpretation of the priority of process rule, against the background of the technicalities of French process, is *Chorley v Chorley* (*Divorce: Jurisdiction*) [2005] 1 W.L.R. 469, in which the question posed in both conflicting jurisdiction (England and France), was whether the first phase of French divorce proceedings, termed the "*raquete*", was to be taken as an initiation of "proceedings" or an entirely separate process. The Court of Appeal upheld the husband's argument that the commencement of the French "*raquete* process" rendered the French court first seised in law.

[31] See, however, the different rule adopted with regard to children (Art.15), permitting by way of exception transfer of the case to a Member State court "better placed to hear the case".

"non-Brussels" plea in litigation which the pursuer legitimately has founded as a Brussels case. This difficulty has been met with in the commercial sphere,[32] where it has been decided that it would be against the spirit of the Brussels regime for the court addressed to exercise its discretion in the manner requested. The ambit of the *lis pendens* rule therefore may be wider than at first thought.[33]

If, by virtue of the factual circumstances, no Member State court has jurisdiction under Article 3, and for this reason, or for a reason of practical convenience, the parties (say, a "European" married couple who are not of common nationality or domicile, and who have been habitually resident in a non-EU state, say Iowa, USA) resort to the court of Iowa which, by its own rules, may take jurisdiction in the case, recognition in an EU state of the resultant Iowa decree will be governed, not by Regulation 2201, but by the pre-existing (residual) divorce recognition rules of that EU state.

Intra-UK conflicts of jurisdiction

There is much debate in the commercial arena concerning the **12–14** continuing competence of the plea of *forum non conveniens* among the legal systems of the UK. The same problem arises in the family law context. The question is whether the system of mandatory sists within the UK has been affected by the system of *lis pendens* put in place by Regulations 1347 and 2201. Recourse must be made to relevant secondary legislation. There does not appear to have been a repeal of the mandatory stay system, but the systems under the 1973 Act, Schedule 3 paragraph 8 and Regulation 2201, Article 19 do not differ in essence, and so the point is academic.

B. CHOICE OF LAW

At common law, when only the courts of the husband's domicile **12–15** had jurisdiction, no problem of choice of law could arise because the *lex domicilii* and the *lex fori* were the same, and so the potentially applicable laws always coincided. Under the new statutory jurisdiction, however, those laws may be different. It may be contrary to principle, therefore, to apply the *lex fori* both to

---

[32] *Re Harrods (Buenos Aires) Ltd (No.2)* [1992] Ch 72; and *Owusu v Jackson* [2005] 1 Ll Rep. 452.

[33] No conceptual problem appears to have been noticed by the court in *Breuning v Breuning* [2002] 1 F.L.R. 888, in which, though jurisdiction was laid in England one month after the coming into force of Reg.1347, no inhibition was felt about the possible incompetence of acceding to a request for a discretionary stay in favour of South Africa. It has also to be said that discussion of jurisdiction focussed upon domicile in the classic sense, and upon habitual residence with reference to the 1973 Act, s.5, rather than upon Reg.1347, Art.2.

substance and procedure, but in practice, the courts in Scotland and England, once seised of jurisdiction, will apply their own domestic law to grounds of divorce.[34] The divorce rules reflect the policy of the forum at any given time; the parties (or at least one of them) has selected the forum; and it is easier and less expensive for the forum to use its own law. Moreover, a whole new range of problems would be opened up if one had to consider how "foreign" a case need be before the forum would yield its function here. The situation is quite different with regard to choice of law in nullity cases, where the ground of nullity is bound to refer back to some earlier stage of the matrimonial history, and that stage is likely to have a conflict rule of its own (eg that alleged defects of form must be referred to the *lex loci celebrationis* and defects of legal capacity to the ante-nuptial domicile of each).[35]

The Vienna Action Plan[36] called for measures to be taken within five years of the entry into force of the Treaty of Amsterdam, to examine the possibilities of drawing up a legal instrument on the law applicable to divorce. In March 2005, the EU Commission published a Green Paper on Applicable Law and Jurisdiction in Divorce Matters[37] ("Rome III"), seeking responses from interested parties, principally on the matter of choice of law in divorce actions. The subject currently is not governed by any Community rule. The Commission cites two contradictory reasons for initiating discussion on harmonisation of choice of law in divorce, namely, first, that under the *lis pendens* system one party may hasten to begin divorce proceedings in country A, in order to ensure the application to the substance of the question of a particular law, which it may be predicted the courts of country A will apply; and second, that because of the lack of legal certainty, an "international" married couple cannot predict which system of divorce law will apply in any given European divorce forum.

The strictness of the *lis pendens* system, as opposed to the discretionary method used in non-EU cases based upon the *forum non conveniens* principle, compounds any tactical implications which the current state of non-harmonised choice of law rules may generate.

Action to harmonise choice of law rules in divorce is said to be justified by the fact that Regulation 2201 offers seven possible forums for divorce, which could encourage forum-shopping, if each of the forums were free to retain its own approach to choice of law. The current proposals therefore could be said to be an answer to a

---

[34] See *Zanelli v Zanelli* (1948) 64 T.L.R. 556 and *Warrender* above, and discussion generally in Cheshire & North, pp.639 *et seq*.
[35] See below nullity paras 12–36 *et seq*.
[36] See Ch.1, above.
[37] March 14, 2005, COM (2005) 82 final.

problem of the Commission's own making by its incursion into family law.

The Green Paper seeks views on the desirability of introducing party autonomy into this area of the law; and asks consultees to consider the problems of "Community citizens" living in a non-EU Member State, and to assess whether the current diversity of choice of law rules in divorce in different Member States, together with the rule on *lis pendens*, may lead to an unseemly race to the court. The Commission hopes to gauge the degree of support for a variety of possible responses to this subject, *e.g.* retention of the *status quo* on the ground of insufficient seriousness or frequency of incident the problem; introduction of harmonised choice of law rules based on a set of uniform connecting factors such as common nationality, or spouses' last common habitual residence[38]; introduction of a limited degree of party choice of applicable law; and, remarkably, reconsideration of the jurisdiction rules in matrimonial matters, so as to restrict, or alternatively, to add to the grounds so recently set down in Regulation 2201. In particular, concern is expressed regarding the residual jurisdiction rule contained in Regulation 2201.[39] A radical variation on taking the jurisdiction route to attempt to solve this problem would be to allow bilateral party choice of court in divorce cases; the current rule represents usually the choice of one party. Attention might be paid to the virtues and vices of the *lis pendens* system itself, and consideration given to the possibility of allowing, in exceptional circumstances, transfer of jurisdiction in a divorce action to a court of another Member State.[40]

C. RECOGNITION OF FOREIGN DIVORCES

Introduction

The basic principle underlying the recognition of foreign divorces, **12–16** at common law and by statute until European intervention, is universality of status, based upon the connecting factor of domicile.[41] A foreign decree of divorce granted by the court of the husband's domicile earned recognition at common law as being regarded as the court pre-eminently appropriate, and equivalent to a decree *in rem*,[42] receiving extraterritorial recognition and being

---

[38] The question is asked whether these harmonised rules should apply also to legal separation and/or marriage annulment.

[39] See para.12–08, above, relating to Art.7.

[40] *cf.* Art.15 relating to parental responsibility.

[41] See Ch.6.

[42] *cf. Salvesen or von Lorang v Administrator of Austrian Property* [1927] A.C. 641, *per* Viscount Dunedin at 662–663 in the matter of decrees of nullity.

regarded everywhere as having terminated the marriage. Through operation of common law development, the grounds upon which a foreign divorce court would be regarded as competent in Scotland and England were enlarged greatly from that first basis of husband's domicile.[43]

Recognition in Scotland of a divorce granted by a court of an EU Member State (apart from Denmark) depends upon the interlocking scheme of jurisdiction and recognition contained in Regulation 2201. Recognition of Danish decrees, and non-EU decrees, continues to be regulated by the Family Law Act 1986.

It is a feature of the harmonisation instruments in the area of International Private Law that doubt arises about the application of the harmonised rules within multi-legal system states, and in particular as between the legal systems of the UK. Such doubt may arise as a result of lack of direction from secondary legislation. The problem always is to what extent the pre-existing rules remain operative. In the absence of any legislative initiative by the Scottish and/or Westminster Parliaments to expand on the guidance given in Article 66 of Regulation 2201, in relation to Member States having two or more legal systems, it is presumed that the Family Law Act 1986, section 44(2) (effectively providing a system of mutual recognition) still regulates the matter of recognition in one part of the UK of a consistorial decree granted in another part.

Declarators

12–17 Although a decree *in rem* requires no further approbation in any legal system where recognition or application is desired, nevertheless in order to test the validity of a foreign decree of divorce in a case of doubt, the proper procedure is not to raise an action of declarator with a crave specifically directed to the validity of the foreign decree, but rather a declarator as to the status of the petitioner (*e.g.* that the petitioner is free to marry). A decree in such a petition achieves the same effect, but is preferable because it enables the court to grant a declarator as to the petitioner's status without pronouncing directly upon the quality of the foreign decree.[44] The Registration of Births, Deaths and Marriages (Scotland) Acts apply to Scots births, deaths and marriages, but even if a marriage took place in Scotland, a foreign decree of divorce cannot be registered or made effective indirectly in such a manner.[45]

In terms of the Family Law (Scotland) Act 2006, section 37, jurisdiction to grant declarator of recognition of decrees of divorce,

---

[43] See para.12–18, below.
[44] *Arnott v Lord Advocate*, 1932 S.L.T. 46; *McKay v Walls*, 1951 S.L.T. (Notes) 6; *Sim v Sim*, 1968 S.L.T. (Notes) 15.
[45] *Smart v Registrar General*, 1954 S.C. 81 (contrast *Arnott*, above).

nullity or separation granted outwith a Member State of the EU, is given to the Court of Session and sheriff court.[46] Strictly, a foreign consistorial decree is equivalent to decree *in rem*, and requires no further approbation. However, for the avoidance of doubt, the 2006 Act has endowed the Scots courts with power to grant such declarators.

Regulation 2201

In terms of Article 21 of Regulation 2201, a judgment given in a Member State shall be recognised in the other Member States without any special procedure being required; in particular, no special procedure shall be required for updating the "civil-status records" of a Member State, on the final award of a consistorial judgment from another Member State. However, any interested party may apply for a decision that the judgment be or be not recognised.[47]

Recognition of foreign decrees of divorce at common law

At common law, a foreign decree of divorce which had been **12–18** granted by a court of competent jurisdiction and was not subject to challenge on any of certain grounds (no notice, fraud, duress, ground of divorce against public policy—a ground of challenge more theoretical than real) would be regarded as having the same effect in Scotland as a decree granted by the Court of Session. The number of courts regarded as competent increased gradually, from the court of the husband's domicile,[48] court recognised by that of the husband's domicile,[49] and through *Travers v Holley*,[50] to the decree of a court the jurisdictional basis of which was similar to that of the English or Scots court (even though the foreign court had not proceeded on that ground).[51] English and Scots courts also

---

[46] *cf.* for England, Family Law Act 1986, s.55. See *e.g. Abbasi v Abbasi* [2006] All E.R. (D.) 92 (wherein the Court of Appeal authorised the exercise of discretion by the judge of first instance to refer the question of the validity of a talaq divorce to a court in Pakistan).

[47] This must be read subject to an understanding that the rules governing recognition under Regulation 2201 admit few opportunities for successful challenge. In the light of this it is difficult to appreciate in what circumstances Art.21.4 might be useful.

[48] *Le Mesurier* [1895] A.C. 517; *Shaw v Gould* (1868) L.R. 3 (HL) 55.

[49] *Armitage v Att.-Gen.* [1906] P. 135; thus far and no further—*Mountbatten v Mountbatten* [1959] P. 43.

[50] [1953] P. 246.

[51] It is very important to realise that in divorce recognition the forum addressed is not concerned with the grounds upon which the foreign court assumed jurisdiction (*Robinson-Scott* [1958] P. 71), but rather with whether the foreign court is competent in terms of UK recognition rules. The inroad made upon this principle by *Travers v Holley*, above, is now historical.

recognised decrees of divorce granted in the Dominions or Colonies where the courts assumed jurisdiction under the Indian and Colonial Divorce Jurisdiction Acts. The common law development culminated in the famous case of *Indyka*[52] in which the House of Lords, by a variety of lines of reasoning including wife's nationality, wife's residence, and real and substantial connection of the marriage with the court which granted that decree, decided to recognise a Czechoslovakian decree of divorce, even though by the date of that decree and at the date of the English litigation the husband was domiciled in England. It could be said that this decision reinstated the so-called ground of matrimonial domicile which had been in abeyance since *Le Mesurier* in 1895. The fame and influence of the case was short-lived because deliberations on the subject of divorce recognition conducted at the Eleventh Session of the Hague Conference resulted in a degree of international agreement, implemented in the United Kingdom by the Recognition of Divorces and Legal Separations Act 1971. The 1971 Act retained the "liberality" of *Indyka*, but at the same time was productive of greater certainty than obtained at common law after *Indyka*.

The 1971 Act was repealed *in toto* by the Family Law Act 1986, wherein now are contained (sections 44 to 51) the relevant rules for recognition of overseas (non-EU and Danish) decrees of divorce, legal separation and annulment (and possibly also of intra-UK decrees). Certain changes to the recognition rules were made by the 1986 Act, but the later scheme of statutory rules does not differ fundamentally from the earlier one.

Recognition of divorces (annulments and legal separations) under the Family Law Act 1986

12–19 In terms of section 44(1) of the 1986 Act, no divorce or annulment obtained in any part of the British Islands shall be regarded as effective in any part of the United Kingdom unless granted by a court of civil jurisdiction. Under section 44(2), subject to section 51 of the Act, the validity of any divorce, annulment or judicial separation granted by a court of civil jurisdiction in any part of the British Islands shall be recognised throughout the United Kingdom.[53]

Overseas divorces, annulments and legal separations

Sections 44 to 51 apply only to overseas divorces obtained outside the EU, and in Denmark.[54]

---

[52] [1969] 1 A.C. 33. Scots cases following this trend shortly thereafter are *Galbraith*, 1971 S.C. 65 and *Bain*, 1971 S.C. 146.

[53] Note intra-UK mutual recognition (also found in 1971 Act), subject to s.51(1) and (2) (prior irreconcilable decision or "no marriage to terminate"). Contrast *Shaw v Gould* (1868) L.R. 3 (H.L.) 55.

[54] 1986 Act, s.45(2).

46. (1) The validity of an overseas divorce, annulment or legal separation obtained by means of proceedings shall be recognised if—

    (a) the divorce, annulment or legal separation is effective under the law of the country in which it was obtained[55]; and

    (b) at the relevant date either party to the marriage—

        (i) was habitually resident in the country in which the divorce, annulment or legal separation was obtained; or

        (ii) was domiciled in that country[56]; or

        (iii) was a national of that country.

(2) The validity of an overseas divorce, annulment or legal separation obtained otherwise than by means of proceedings shall be recognised if—

    (a) the divorce, annulment or legal separation is effective under the law of the country in which it was obtained;

    (b) at the relevant date—

        (i) each party to the marriage was domiciled in that country; or

        (ii) either party to the marriage was domiciled in that country and the other party was domiciled in a country under whose law the divorce, annulment or legal separation is recognised as valid; and

    (c) neither party to the marriage was habitually resident in the United Kingdom throughout the period of one year immediately preceding that date.

(3) In this section "the relevant date" means—

    (a) in the case of an overseas divorce, annulment or legal separation obtained by means of proceedings, the date of the commencement of the proceedings;

    (b) in the case of an overseas divorce, annulment or legal separation obtained otherwise than by means of proceedings, the date on which it was obtained.

---

[55] See *Emin v Yeldag* [2002] 1 F.L.R. 956.

[56] In terms of the 1986 Act, s. 46(5) "domicile" is to be understood either according to the law of the foreign country in family matters or the law of the forum of the relevant part of the UK.

The Family Law Act 1986, in its treatment of the recognition of non-EU consistorial decrees, differentiates between divorces and annulments obtained by means of proceedings (section 46(1)) and divorces and annulments[57] obtained otherwise than by means of proceedings (section 46(2)). A stricter test for recognition applies in the latter case because there is concern that before such divorces may be recognised in the UK, there must be a strong connection between both parties and the legal culture which provides such relatively informal methods of divorce. Hence, section 46(2) provides that the divorce must be effective under the law of the country in which it was obtained and at the relevant date (*i.e.* the date on which it was obtained[58]) each party must have been domiciled[59] in that country or either party domiciled in that country and the other party domiciled in a country the law of which would recognise the divorce as valid, *and* neither party[60] must have been habitually resident in the United Kingdom throughout the period of one year immediately preceding the date on which the divorce was obtained.

With regard to the meaning in this context of the connecting factor of domicile, section 46(5) provides that a party to a marriage shall be treated as domiciled in a country if he was domiciled in that country either according to the law of that country in family matters or according to the law of the part of the United Kingdom in which the question of recognition arises. It is unusual for the forum to yield to any other law in the interpretation of connecting factors generally, and of this factor in particular.[61]

Conversion of judicial separation

12–21 Section 47 regulates cross-proceedings and divorces following legal separations. A generous attitude towards the conversion of legal separations into divorces is manifested by section 47(2): where a legal separation, the validity of which is entitled to recognition by virtue of the provisions of section 46 of the Act or of subsection (1) above, is converted, in the country in which it was obtained, into a divorce which is effective under the law of that country, the validity of the divorce shall be recognised in Scotland whether or not it would itself be entitled to recognition by virtue of those provisions.[62]

---

[57] See para.12–39 relating to nullities.
[58] s.46(3)(b).
[59] s.46(5).
[60] The prior rule had withheld recognition if *both* parties had been habitually resident in the UK for one year before pronouncement of divorce (Domicile and Matrimonial Proceedings Act 1973, s.16).
[61] *cf. Re Annesley* [1926] Ch. 692.
[62] See analogous provision in Regulation 2201. See also para.12–31, below.

Proof of facts relevant to recognition

For the purpose of sections 46 and 47 of the 1986 Act, section 48 **12–22** provides that any finding of fact on the basis of which jurisdiction was assumed in the proceedings shall, if both parties to the marriage took part in the proceedings, be conclusive evidence of the fact found; and in any other case, shall be sufficient proof unless the contrary is shown.[63]

Refusal to recognise

Section 51, reproduced below, narrates the bases on which recogni- **12–23** tion may be refused:

51. (1) Subject to section 52 of this Act, recognition of the validity of—

   (a) a divorce, annulment or judicial separation granted by a court of civil jurisdiction in any part of the British Islands, or

   (b) an overseas divorce, annulment or legal separation,

   may be refused in any part of the United Kingdom if the divorce, annulment or separation was granted or obtained at a time when it was irreconcilable with a decision determining the question of the subsistence or validity of the marriage of the parties previously given (whether before or after the commencement of this Part) by a court of civil jurisdiction in that part of the United Kingdom or by a court elsewhere recognised or entitled to be recognised in that part of the United Kingdom.

   (2) Subject to section 52 of this Act, recognition of the validity of—

   (a) a divorce or judicial separation granted by a court of civil jurisdiction in any part of the British Islands, or

   (b) an overseas divorce or legal separation,

   may be refused in any part of the United Kingdom if the divorce or separation was granted or obtained at a time when, according to the law of that part of the United Kingdom (including its rules of private international law and the provisions of this Part), there was no subsisting marriage between the parties.

---

[63] "Finding of fact" includes a finding that either party to the marriage (a) was habitually resident in the country in which the divorce, annulment or legal separation was obtained; (b) under the law of that country was domiciled there; or (c) was a national of that country.

(3) Subject to section 52 of this Act, recognition by virtue of section 45 of this Act of the validity of an overseas divorce, annulment or legal separation may be refused if—

(a) in the case of divorce, annulment or legal separation obtained by means of proceedings, it was obtained—

(i) without such steps having been taken for giving notice of the proceedings to a party to the marriage as, having regard to the nature of the proceedings and all the circumstances, should reasonably have been taken; or

(ii) without a party to the marriage having been given (for any reason other than lack of notice) such opportunity to take part in the proceedings as, having regard to those matters, he should reasonably have been given; or

(b) in the case of a divorce, annulment or legal separation obtained otherwise than by means of proceedings—

(i) there is no official document certifying that the divorce, annulment or legal separation is effective under the law of the country in which it was obtained; or

(ii) where either party to the marriage was domiciled in another country at the relevant date, there is no official document certifying that the divorce, annulment or legal separation is recognised as valid under the law of that other country; or

(c) in either case, recognition of the divorce, annulment or legal separation would be manifestly contrary to public policy.[64]

---

[64] See, *e.g.* recently *Ahmed v Ahmed*, 2006 S.L.T. 135. Older cases, decided in relation to the 1971 Act, s.8 may still be helpful: *Hack v Hack* (1976) 6 Fam. Law 177; *Newmarch v Newmarch* [1978] 1 All E.R. 1; *Joyce v Joyce and O'Hare* [1979] 2 All E.R. 156; *Kendall v Kendall* [1977] Fam. 208. The ground of a foreign divorce is potentially or in theory a ground for non-recognition but in practice our courts have accepted foreign divorces on grounds unknown to them (*Perin*, 1950 S.L.T. 51; *Pemberton v Hughes* [1899] 1 Ch. 781). (Contrast non-recognition of Maltese annulments in *Chapelle* [1950] P. 134; *Gray v Formosa* [1963] P. 259; *Lepre* [1965] P. 52.) It is different if coercion is used and the will of one party is overborne by an external agency to obtain a divorce (*Re Meyer* [1971] P. 298). But possibly means and ground might merge in the case of a person divorced against his will (and against his spouse's will) for reasons such as alleged heresy or

Recognition of divorces (annulments and legal separations) under Regulation 2201/2003

A defining feature of any Brussels instrument, commercial or **12–24** consistorial, is the general prohibition of review of jurisdiction of the court of origin by the legal system in which recognition is sought. Article 24 of Regulation 2201 states that the jurisdiction of the court of the Member State of origin may not be reviewed, and further, that the test of public policy may not be applied to the jurisdiction rules set out in the Regulation. There is no opportunity for challenging the decision of the court of the Member State of origin in its application of Article 3 to the facts of the case.[65] Article 24 is consonant with the overarching principle contained in preamble (21), that the recognition and enforcement of judgments given in a Member State should be based on the principle of mutual trust, and that the grounds for non-recognition should be kept to a minimum. Moreover, recognition of a judgment may not be refused because the law of the Member State in which recognition is sought would not allow divorce, legal separation or marriage annulment on the same facts. Further, a judgment may never be reviewed as to its substance.[66]

The grounds of non-recognition are very limited, and are contained in Article 22. They are concerned solely with public policy, natural justice, due process, and *res judicata*. It is important to be familiar with the precise grounds of challenge available:

Article 22

A judgment relating to a divorce, legal separation or marriage annulment shall not be recognised:

(a) if such recognition is manifestly contrary to the public policy of the Member State in which recognition is sought;

(b) where it was given in default of appearance, if the respondent was not served with the document which instituted the proceedings or with an equivalent document in sufficient time and in such a way as to enable the respondent to arrange for his or her defence unless it is determined that the respondent has accepted the judgment unequivocally;

(c) if it is irreconcilable with a judgment given in proceedings between the same parties in the Member State in which recognition is sought; or

---

apostasy (abandonment of religious faith) in a religious country (Muslim *hisbah* divorces). *Cf.* refusal of recognition of a dissolution of marriage in *Viswalingham* (1980) 1 E.L.R. 15, CA. See Clive, pp.586–587.

[65] Therefore, for the first time in the history of this branch of conflict rules, examination of the facts of the case against the relevant jurisdictional rules is not permissible. Contrast the limited opportunity for challenge on this ground under Council Regulation 44/2001, Art.35(1).

[66] Art.26. Contrast *Gray v Formosa* [1963] P. 259.

(d) if it is irreconcilable with an earlier judgment given in another Member State or in a non-Member State between the same parties, provided that the earlier judgment fulfils the conditions necessary for its recognition in the Member State in which recognition is sought.

Recognition of same sex "divorce"

12–25 It is inevitable that the question of the validity of the termination of a same sex marriage will arise for decision by a court in the UK.[67]

Under the 1986 Act, the matter is likely to be addressed under section 51(3)(c) (public policy). It is possible, though unlikely, that the principle of *res judicata* might be relevant.[68] Assuming that the same sex marriage in question satisfied the UK conflict rules as to form and capacity, it has been argued that the "marriage" itself would be recognised in the UK. The next step, therefore, is recognition of the dissolution of that "marriage", by means of a divorce satisfying section 46 of the 1986 Act. If, on the other hand, the antecedent "marriage" is not worthy of recognition by UK conflict rules, there arises the question why the parties should be anxious to have the divorce recognised in the UK.

If the dissolution of the same sex "marriage" emanates from an EU court (with the exception of Denmark), then three questions arise: (a) does such a divorce fall within the scope of Regulation 2201? (b) if so, to what extent do the courts of Member States have a discretion to refuse to recognise such a divorce decree? and (c) among such cases, how is the delimitation made between application of recognition rules in Regulation 2201, and those in the Civil Partnership Act 2004, Part 5?[69] Since neither "divorce" nor "marriage" is defined in Regulation 2201, it will be argued that same sex divorces fall within the scope of that instrument. In turn, this means that a Scottish court, as the court addressed for recognition purposes being prohibited from reviewing the jurisdiction of the court of origin,[70] and similarly prohibited from refusing recognition on the ground that Scots law would not grant a matrimonial remedy on the same facts, can rely only on Article 22, above. If, on the other hand, the Scots court is the court petitioned under Article 3 of Regulation 2201, for a same sex divorce, it is clear that the Scots court cannot refuse to hear the case, but the question of the grant of the remedy, and the public policy implications thereof, will not arise unless the "marriage" itself

---

[67] *cf.* para.11–12, above.
[68] *cf.* generally *Vervaeke v Smith* [1983] A.C. 145.
[69] See para.12–48, below.
[70] Reg.2201/2003, Art.24.

satisfies Scots conflict rules as to essential and formal validity. If, finally, as a hypothesis, there is requested of the Scots court the grant of a "divorce" of a "marriage" of two, say, Dutch domiciliaries habitually resident in Scotland, there is a clear difficulty in that Scots domestic law makes no provision for such a decree. It may be different, in future, if as a result of the Rome III negotiations,[71] the courts of Member States are required to apply harmonised choice of law rules in divorce.

Re-marriage: Family Law Act 1986, section 50

When recognition of a foreign consistorial decree depended upon **12–26** the decree having emanated from the court of the parties' (necessarily common) domicile, and capacity to marry also (as now) was governed by the law of the domicile, there would usually be a coincidence of the two laws (unless a new domicile had been acquired in the interval between the granting of a divorce and the date of re-marriage), and no conflict would arise with regard to a person's legal capacity to (re-)marry.

However, since the recognition rule in Scots and English conflict of laws has widened to accept consistorial decrees from the domicile (in either sense),[72] habitual residence, or nationality, of either party, while the capacity to marry rule has remained the same (requiring of the party intending to marry capacity to marry by his/her ante-nuptial domicile), a problem may arise for the forum in prioritising its own rules in this area. Tension inevitably will arise on occasion.

At common law,[73] a persuasive case was made to the effect that a person whose personal law considered him to be already married, should be regarded as legally incapable of re-marriage in the United Kingdom no matter that the Scots or English court might view as valid a purported divorce pre-dating the desired re-marriage. In other words, the forum would defer to the personal law in the matter of recognition of antecedent decrees. *Contra*, in *Perrini*,[74] with little argument, Sir George Baker, President of the Family Division, upon finding the antecedent New Jersey nullity worthy of recognition by English conflict rules, concluded that a party thereto might re-marry in England.

In a provision now repealed (1971 Act, section 7) it was enacted that the recognition rule of the forum should take precedence over the capacity to marry rule, where the antecedent decree was that of divorce and where the re-marriage took place in the United

---

[71] See choice of law, para.12–15, above.
[72] Family Law Act 1986, s.46(5).
[73] *Padolecchia* [1968] P. 314. See *R v Brentwood Superintendent Registrar of Marriages, ex parte Arias* [1968] 2 Q.B. 956.
[74] [1979] Fam. 84.

Kingdom.[75] Now the case is governed by the Family Law Act 1986, section 50, which provides that:

50.—Where, in any part of the United Kingdom—

> (a) a divorce or annulment has been granted by a court of civil jurisdiction, or
> (b) the validity of a divorce or annulment is recognised by virtue of this Part,

the fact that the divorce or annulment would not be recognised elsewhere shall not preclude either party to the marriage from re-marrying in that part of the United Kingdom or cause the re-marriage of either party (wherever the re-marriage takes place) to be treated as invalid in that part.

The opposite situation (where the divorce is recognised by a party's personal law but not by the forum) is not catered for, but help may be had by reference to discussions of the Incidental Question,[76] and in particular to *Schwebel v Ungar*,[77] in which the Canadian forum, using a *lex causae* approach, deferred to the Israeli law of the antenuptial domicile of the woman, where Ontarian law and Israeli law differed as to the validity of an Israeli *ghet*, and thereby the Ontarian court held valid a re-marriage of the woman in Ontario.

There is no provision equivalent to section 50 in Regulation 2201, presumably because in a situation where it is intended that recognition of EU divorces among Member States will be almost automatic, such provision would be unnecessary. However, it is not impossible that a "section 50 situation" could arise in a European context; the answer in the instant case would depend upon the conflict rules of the forum in which the problem (of whatever kind) arose.[78]

Recognition of overseas extra-judicial divorces

12–27　Not all foreign divorces are judicial: it may be found rather that the divorce has been obtained by legislative process,[79] or by religious divorce, the most common[80] of which are the Muslim *talaq* (or

---

[75] UK restriction caused difficulties in *Lawrence v Lawrence* [1985] Fam. 106.

[76] See para.4–06, above.

[77] (1964) 48 D.L.R. (2d.) 644. Ritchie J does state, however, that the decision was exceptional, and was a particular response to the peculiar facts of the case.

[78] Art.22(d).

[79] *Manning* [1958] P. 112.

[80] *Lee v Lau* [1964] 2 All E.R. 248 gives an example of the Chinese *chop* (document signed by parties agreeing to dissolve their marriage was authenticated by the "chop" or seal). *Quazi* [1979] 3 All E.R. 897 contains reference to a Thai *khula*.

talak) and the Jewish *ghet*[81] (or *gett*). Initial non-recognition by the English courts of extra-judicial divorces[82] gave way quickly to a less strict attitude, which would recognise such divorces provided that they were competent by the law of the husband's domicile,[83] no matter that the marriage[84] and/or the divorce[85] had taken place in England.[86]

The test of recognition against the law of the husband's domicile was retained by sections 2 to 6 of the 1971 Act. As has been noted, the 1971 Act was repealed *in toto* by the Family Law Act 1986. Nevertheless, not only have some interpretative decisions[87] survived to guide later cases, but also the interpretation of the word "proceedings" handed down in two important cases decided under the 1971 Act (*Quazi*[88] and by way of contrast, *Chaudhary*[89]) arguably remain as the key interpretative guidance to distinguish between cases falling respectively now under the Family Law Act 1986, section 46(1) and under section 46(2). In *Chaudhary*, concerning a "bare" *talaq*, Oliver L.J. attempted to make such a distinction and produced a form of words which often is quoted: "[i]n the context . . . of a solemn change of status, it does seem to me that the word ["proceedings"] must import a degree of formality and at least the involvement of some agency, whether lay or religious, of or recognised by the state, having a function that is more than simply probative, although *Quazi v Quazi* clearly shows that it need have no power of veto."[90] In *Quazi*, the House of Lords held that compliance with the Pakistan Muslim Family Laws Ordinance 1961 involving notification to the wife and to a public authority and the compulsory elapse of a 90-day reconciliation period (but with no compulsion to attempt to achieve reconciliation), amounted to "proceedings", although essentially the divorce

---

[81] See, for example, Gordon, *Foreign Divorces: English Law and Practice* (1988); Hamilton, *Family, Law and Religion* (1995).

[82] *R. v Hammersmith Superintendent Registrar* [1917] 1 K.B. 634 in which the English forum refused to recognise the purported termination by *talaq* performed in London of a marriage between an Indian man and an English woman.

[83] See, e.g. *Maher* [1951] 2 All E.R. 37 (*talaq* not recognised) and *Russ* [1963] P.87 (original and later *talaqs* recognised in a matrimonial history which displays the need for a scheme of regulatory conflict rules). The decision in *Makouipour*, 1967 S.L.T. 101 suggests that the Scots rule was the same as the English one.

[84] *Har-Shefi (No. 2)* [1953] P. 220.

[85] *Sasson* [1924] 1 A.C. 1007 (British subjects but married in Alexandria).

[86] In *Qureshi* [1972] Fam. 173 both the marriage and the religious divorce took place in England. The divorce was recognised but it was felt that some legislative restriction was necessary.

[87] *Hack v Hack* (1976) 6 Fam. Law 177; *Newmarch v Newmarch* [1978] 1 All E.R. 1; *Joyce v Joyce & O'Hare* [1979] 2 All E.R. 156; *Kendall v Kendall* [1977] Fam 208.

[88] [1979] 3 All E.R. 897. *Cf. Ahmed v Ahmed*, 2006 S.L.T. 135.

[89] [1984] 3 All E.R. 1017.

[90] *per* Oliver L.J. at 1031 (distinguishing, at 1030, "proceedings" from "procedure" or "ritual") (and the latter terms, it is submitted, differ from each other).

was a unilateral act by the husband and was a remedy which no public authority could deny him.

Public policy

12–28 Public policy as a ground of non-recognition of an overseas divorce is particularly significant with regard to extra-judicial decrees. Section 51 of the 1986 Act permits non-recognition if the divorce is "manifestly contrary to public policy". While section 51(3)(a) concerns itself with challenges on grounds of lack of notice or lack of opportunity to take part in the case of "proceedings" divorces, such provisions were thought unsuitable in relation to non-judicial divorces; however, section 51(3)(b), which applies only to non-proceedings divorces, states that recognition may be refused if there is no official document certifying that the divorce is effective under the law of the country in which it was obtained or, where either party was domiciled in another country at the relevant date, there is no official document certifying that the divorce is recognised as valid under the law of that other country.[91]

This subject tends to resolve itself into a consideration of whether the religious divorce can be said to be a "proceedings" divorce or an "otherwise than by means of proceedings" divorce; whether, if the latter, section 46(2) (jurisdiction) and section 51(3)(b) (authentication) can be satisfied; whether section 51(3)(c) (public policy) can be said to have any application[92]; and finally whether the Matrimonial and Family Proceedings Act 1984 has any part to play in the situation.[93] Opinion in the religious communities whence such divorces spring may be thought not to be convinced of the rightness of the "proceedings" distinction, nor of the feasibility of obtaining official certificates to satisfy section 51(3)(b).

The impulse behind the *Quazi* litigation was financial[94] in that, if the Pakistan *talaq* was recognised, as the law then stood, the British court could not add financial provisions to it. Now, in terms of the Matrimonial and Family Proceedings Act 1984,[95] such provision may be made after any divorce or annulment in a case where the Scots or English court satisfies the strict terms of that Act. Consequently it may be that the validity of religious divorces will be less often the subject of debate.[96] It has even been the case that

---

[91] 1986 Act, s.51(3)(b).

[92] Bearing in mind that the public policy challenge is always potentially available: Norrie, "The Raven and the Writing Table: Recent English decisions on recognition of the Talaq" (1986) J.L.S.S. 158 and 208.

[93] *Tahir v Tahir*, 1993 S.L.T. 194.

[94] *Cf. Ahmed v Ahmed*, 2006 S.L.T. 135 (exceptional circumstances, in which the point at issue was the standing of a Scottish divorce obtained in 1994, in the face of earlier dissolution of the marriage by Pakistan law.

[95] See paras 13–23, below.

[96] *Tahir v Tahir*, above. *Cf. Ahmed v Ahmed*, above.

reduction of a later Scottish divorce has been sought on the basis of recognition of an earlier overseas religious divorce. However, it has been pointed out that the grant of reduction of a decree *in foro* by a Scots court is a matter within the judicial discretion of the court, and it may be that in all the circumstances, including especially financial, reduction is not warranted.[97]

One notable development in English conflict rules in this area of religious divorces is the enactment of the Divorce (Religious Marriages) Act 2002, by section 1 of which an insertion is made in the Matrimonial Causes Act 1973, to the following effect: if a decree of divorce has been granted but not made absolute, and the parties to the marriage (a) were married in accordance with (i) the usages of the Jews or (ii) any other prescribed religious usages; and (b) must co-operate if the marriage is to be dissolved, then on the application of either party, the court may order that a decree of divorce is not to be made absolute until a declaration made by both parties that they have taken such steps as are required to dissolve the marriage in accordance with those usages is produced to the court. Such an order may be made by the court only if it is satisfied that in all the circumstances of the case it is just and reasonable to do so. The order may be revoked at any time. The background to this legislation is the importance attached to religious divorce in certain religious laws, particularly those of Judaism. If the religious divorce is not obtained, the wife, in the view of her religion, would have the status of a "chained woman" (*agunah*), a status which forbids her re-marriage under Jewish law, and any issue of a subsequent union would be regarded under Jewish law as illegitimate unto the tenth generation.

Equivalent legislation for Scotland has been implemented by the Family Law (Scotland) Act 2006, section 15,[98] which amends the Divorce (Scotland) Act 1976, section 3, to permit postponement of the grant of a decree of divorce where religious impediment to re-marry exists. If, in any Scots divorce action in which irretrievable breakdown of a marriage has been established, one party ('the applicant') is prevented from entering into a religious marriage by virtue of a requirement of the religion of that marriage, and the other party to the divorce can act so as to remove, or enable or contribute to the removal of, the impediment which prevents that marriage, that Scots divorce court may, upon application by the applicant, and if satisfied that it is just and reasonable to do so, postpone the grant of decree until it is satisfied that the other party has so acted to remove the impediment, etc.

---

[97] *Ahmed v Ahmed*, above.

[98] See also the Divorce (Religious Bodies) (Scotland) Regulations 2006 (SI 2006/253).

Transnational divorces

12–29 In terms of section 44(1) of the 1986 Act, no divorce or annulment obtained in any part of the British Islands shall be regarded as effective in any part of the United Kingdom unless granted by a court of civil jurisdiction.[99] Should the divorce, being part of a religious and/or legal procedure, be seen to have taken place in two countries, in order to qualify for recognition in the UK, it is essential that no part of the "proceedings" have taken place in the United Kingdom.[1] Although the wording of section 46 of the 1986 Act might suggest that what matters henceforward is whether the divorce is valid where it is completed,[2] recent decisions show that dual location divorces do not commend themselves as complying with the Act.[3]

Brussels regime

12–30 In *Maples v Maples*,[4] it was made clear that no extra-judicial divorce can be tested for recognition in the UK except by reference to the terms of the 1986 Act.[5] In view of the EU family law harmonisation programme, it is necessary now to determine the extent of application, if any, of Regulation 1347, and its successor Regulation 2201, to recognition of extra-judicial divorces. This must be done by reference to the terms of the Regulations, and to their respective preambles.

Preamble (9) of Regulation 1347 states that the scope of the Regulation should cover "civil proceedings and non-judicial proceedings in matrimonial matters in certain States, and exclude purely religious procedures." Article 1.2 of Regulation 1347 states that "[o]ther proceedings officially recognised in a Member State shall be regarded as equivalent to judicial proceedings." The preamble to Regulation 2201 omits specific reference to religious procedures, and in recital (7) advises that the scope of this

---

[99] *Sulaiman v Juffali* [2002] 1 F.L.R. 479: irrespective of parties' domicile(s) and religion, an informal divorce obtained in the UK otherwise than by way of proceedings in a court of civil jurisdiction is not to be recognised. The policy applies indiscriminately to all informal divorces, irrespective of the nature of the parties' religious or other beliefs.

[1] *R. v Secretary of State for the Home Dept, ex p. Fatima; ex p. Bi* (transnational talaq) [1984] 2 All E.R. 458.

[2] Pilkington, "Transitional Divorces under the Family Law Act 1986" (1988) 37 ICLQ 131. See, however, *Berkovits v Grinberg* [1995] 2 All E.R. 681, *per* Wall, J. at 690 *et seq.*

[3] *Sulaiman v Juffali* and *Berkovits v Grinberg*, above. However in both cases part of the divorce took place in England, and so the question of recognition of transnational divorces no part of which takes place in the UK, remains open.

[4] [1987] 3 All E.R. 188.

[5] As opposed to the Foreign Judgments (Reciprocal Enforcement) Act 1933. See Ch.9 regarding commercial judgments.

Regulation covers "civil matters, whatever the nature of the court or tribunal". There has been no attempt to date to apply the Regulation to recognition of a religious divorce.[6] Article 1.1 of Regulation 2201 (scope) states that the Regulation shall apply "whatever the nature of the court or tribunal, in civil matters relating to divorce, legal separation or marriage annulment." The system of recognition depends upon jurisdiction having been assumed in terms of Article 3 of the Regulation, which states that jurisdiction shall lie with the courts of a Member State, broadly speaking, on the grounds of habitual residence of one or both parties.[7] For the *ghet* to fall under Regulation 2201, therefore, the rabbinical court would have to satisfy Article 1.1 (scope), which *ex facie* it would seem to do. In sum, the terms are somewhat ambivalent, and might be apt to include divorces involving the participation by a religious court or tribunal, such as the Jewish letter of divorcement (*ghet*) issued by the rabbinical court. A case could be presented that Article 1.1 can be interpreted so as to include religious divorces, but arguably this was not the intention of the EU draftsmen.[8] It should be borne in mind that a UK court has greater discretion under the 1986 Act than it has under Regulation 2201.

II. JUDICIAL SEPARATION

All statutory rules which govern, in divorce and annulment, **12–31** domestic jurisdiction and recognition of foreign decrees, and the common law approach to choice of law, apply also to judicial separation. Note should be made of section 47(2) of the 1986 Act, concerning conversion of legal separation into divorce.[9]

Judicial separation is a remedy on the decline domestically,[10] and a foreign judicial separation in relation to the validity of which there lingers a conflict of laws doubt is a poor remedy indeed. Those countries such as Spain, Italy and Ireland, which were

---

[6] But see *Sulaiman v Juffali* [2002] 1 F.L.R. 479 in which the question whether the English court had jurisdiction in the wife's petition for divorce (contested by the husband on the ground that the marriage already had been validly dissolved by bare *talaq* pronounced in England and registered in Saudi Arabia in the *Sharia* court three days later), was determined by the Family Division of the High Court according to Art.2 of Regulation 1347/2000. But the recognition issue was settled by application of the Family Law Act 1986, s.44(1). It was sufficient to preclude recognition that *talaq* had been pronounced in England (*cf. Berkovits*, above).

[7] See para.12–07, above.

[8] If membership of the EU continues to expand, and comes to include predominantly Muslim countries, the applicability of the Regulation to religious divorces will become an important issue.

[9] *cf.* Reg.2201/2003, Art.5.

[10] Clive, p.362.

opposed to divorce in principle in their domestic laws, now have yielded on the matter.

III. NULLITY OF MARRIAGE

A. THE JURISDICTION OF SCOTS COURTS

Introduction

12–32 The treatment of annulment of marriage in the conflict of laws has been attended by greater complexity, doubt, difficulty and interest than has the treatment of divorce. One reason has been the void/voidable distinction which is not observed in all systems or, if observed, may differ in content. Some systems may have other classifications peculiar to themselves.[11] Some systems may grant an annulment where others would grant divorce (*e.g.* the remedies in the area of physical incapacity).[12]

While, as has been noted, the grounds of divorce available in a system at any time will reflect its policy at that time, the grounds of annulment will be linked to an earlier matter such as alleged lack of capacity, physical or legal, or an absence of consent: each of these factors will attract the application of a conflict rule of the forum which is called upon to judge the validity of the marriage. Therefore, while reasons of cost and convenience may justify application by the forum of its own law in granting divorce, the subject of choice of law in nullity rightly demands a different approach.

Further, while an annulment of a void marriage merely declares the position, legal systems will vary in the effect which they accord (prospective only, or dating back to purported marriage) to a nullity decree pertaining to a voidable marriage. It would seem that this is a matter properly for the forum which granted the decree: the recognising court should accept the effect as an integral part of the decree.[13]

Statutory intervention in jurisdiction (Domicile and Matrimonial Proceedings Act 1973, as amended) and recognition (1986 Act and Regulation 2201), together with the abolition of the unity of

---

[11] *Merker* [1963] P. 283. (Held that the English forum should not concern itself with the German distinction between marriages null and void, on the one hand, and non-existent marriages, on the other).

[12] It is no longer necessary for the UK court to classify the *genus* of foreign consistorial decree before knowing which rules of recognition, common law or statutory, to apply, because the rules of recognition of divorces and nullities are now contained in the same statute: Family Law Act 1986, Pt II; Cheshire & North, p.663.

[13] Social Security Decision No. R(G) 1/85.

domicile between husband and wife, have removed many of the difficulties and sources of doubt in Scots and English conflict rules relating to nullity. In domestic terms, the family law (Scotland) Act 2006, section 4 has extended jurisdiction in actions of declarator of marriage or nullity of marriage to the Sheriff Court.

Jurisdiction at common law

A decree of nullity of a voidable marriage clearly effects a change **12–33** in the status of the parties, but a decree of nullity of a void marriage does not have any such effect because the parties never were married. For this reason, in the past, both Scots and English courts assumed jurisdiction on a wider basis[14] in actions of nullity involving void marriages than in voidable marriages.[15] The distinction between void and voidable, which might not have been present in the law of the granting country, created difficulties as to jurisdiction in that a decision had to be made upon the nature of the marriage as void or voidable (by which law?) before it could be said whether the court had jurisdiction.[16] This is a variation on the problem of circularity which not infrequently arises in conflict problems.[17]

Development of grounds of jurisdiction

Rules of jurisdiction up to March 1, 2001

The position was simplified by the Domicile and Matrimonial **12–34** Proceedings Act 1973 which provided in sections 5 (England), 7 (Scotland), and 13 (Northern Ireland) that the only competent grounds for a declarator of marriage, or a declarator of nullity of marriage, were as follows:

(1) Domicile of either party in Scotland on the date when the action was begun; or

---

[14] *e.g.* in Scots law the assumption of jurisdiction by the forum *qua locus celebrationis* was permitted only if the marriage was thought to be void (*Prawdziclazarska*, 1954 S.C. 98). In England that ground was initially used with regard to both void and voidable marriages. It was rejected in respect of voidable marriages by the House of Lords in *Ross Smith* [1963] A.C. 280 but continued to be used with regard to void marriages, as can be seen from *Padolecchia* [1968] P. 314.

[15] Scots authorities at common law include: *Miller v Deakin* (1912) 1 S.L.T. 253; *Lendrum v Chakravarti*, 1929 S.L.T. 96; *Macdougall v Chitnavis*, 1937 S.C. 390; *Prawdziclazarska*, 1954 S.C. 98; *Aldridge*, 1954 S.C. 58; *Woodward*, 1958 S.L.T. 213 (also reported as *AB v CD*, 1957 S.C. 415); *Orlando v Castelli*, 1961 S.L.T. 119; *Balshaw v Kelly*, 1967 S.C. 63; Walton, *A Handbook of Husband and Wife According to the Law of Scotland*, 3/410; T.B. Smith, *Short Commentary on the Law of Scotland* (1962) pp.307–308.

[16] *Prawdziclazarska*, above.

[17] E.B. Crawford, "The Uses of Putativity and Negativity in the Conflict of Laws", 2005 ICLQ (54) 829.

(2) Habitual residence of one year of either party prior to the date when the action was begun; or

(3) If one party has died, that he or she either—

    (a) was domiciled in Scotland at death, or

    (b) had been habitually resident in Scotland throughout the period of one year ending with the date of death.

This eliminated any distinction between void and voidable marriages as regards jurisdiction.

Rules of jurisdiction after March 1, 2001: Council Regulation 2201/2003

12–35 As with jurisdiction in divorce, the starting point is the 1973 Act, as amended.[18]

The rules of Scottish domestic jurisdiction in actions of *declarator of marriage* now are contained in section 7(3) of the 1973 Act, and remain the same as the pre-March 1, 2001 position.[19]

The rules of Scottish domestic jurisdiction in actions of *declarator of nullity of marriage*, however, now are contained in section 7(3A) of the 1973 Act, to the effect that the Court of Session has jurisdiction to entertain such an action, if and only if:

    (a) the Scottish courts have jurisdiction under Regulation 2201[20]; or

    (b) the action is an excluded action[21] and either of the parties to the marriage is domiciled in Scotland on the date when the action is begun.[22]

The action for declarator of nullity brought in *Singh v Singh*,[23] indicates that the Regulation applies notwithstanding that the defender was of Indian domicile (the pursuer being of Scots domicile). The court held that it had jurisdiction under section 7(3A)(a) (there being jurisdiction under Article 2.1.a of Council Regulation 1347/2000, then applicable, on the basis of the pursuer's habitual residence in Scotland). Alternatively, if the Council Regulation were restricted to cases where both parties could found jurisdiction in a Member State, the judge held that the action

---

[18] See para.12–06, above.

[19] Similarly, the rules of jurisdiction of the Scots court in a petition for declarator of death continue to be governed by the Presumption of Death (Scotland) Act 1977, s.1(3) and (4).

[20] See para.12–07, above.

[21] s.7(3B).

[22] There are special provisions for the situation where either party is dead at the date of raising the action.

[23] 2005 S.L.T. 749.

would have been an excluded one and the Court of Session would have had jurisdiction under section 7(3A)(b)(a) (domicile in Scotland on the date when the action is begun).[24]

B. Choice of Law

Which law is the court to apply in determining the validity of a **12–36** marriage in an action of nullity of marriage? Principle indicates that the court should look at the defect alleged and decide whether it relates to essentials or form. If it relates to form, reference should be made to the *lex loci celebrationis*, and if it relates to essentials, the reference should be to the law of the domicile.

But which domicile is to apply if the parties do not have a common domicile? It is submitted that the law of the domicile of each party applies as regards capacity to marry and matters up to the date of the ceremony but that as regards essentials and matters after the ceremony (*e.g.* impotence) the only law which could have been applied during the days of unity of domicile was that of the domicile of the alleged husband. Such a statement elicits immediately the response that there would be no unity of domicile if the marriage was void and of course today the domiciles of women, married or not, are ascertained independently of the domicile of any other person. It should be borne in mind when reading the older cases that an added difficulty was that the unity of domicile rule between husband and wife required that the domicile of the wife followed that of the husband *ex lege* if the marriage was valid or voidable,[25] but not if the marriage was void, although in that case it might be found on the facts that the woman had changed her domicile upon going to live with the man.

It is suggested that where the parties have different domiciles, reference should be made to the law of the domicile of the party alleged to have no capacity, but that if by that law the marriage is valid, reference should then be made to the law of the domicile of the other party.

Particular difficulty arises where the defect alleged is absence of consent or physical incapacity. In these areas, there is little judicial guidance, although much discussion.[26] Sometimes the forum has

---

[24] The judge accepted counsel's submissions on this interpretation of these new rules of jurisdiction, in respect of which it was said that there was no authority in either Scotland or England (see paras 10–11).

[25] And if so would not change upon pronouncement of declarator of nullity but only upon acquisition of a different domicile independently thereafter—*De Reneville* [1948] 1 All E.R. 56. Such difficulties are to be seen in Maltese Nullity Cases, *Chapelle*, *Lepre* and *Gray v Formosa*, above.

[26] *e.g.* Law Com. Working Paper No. 89, *Choice of Law Rules in Marriage* and Scot. Law Com. Memo No.64, *Choice of Law Rules in Marriage* (Choice of Law in Nullity Suits).

applied its own law without question,[27] often because the question of application of foreign law was not raised; in other cases, there is valuable discussion.[28] The decisions in *Ponticelli* and *Szechter* favour the domicile (in *Ponticelli*, a case of physical incapacity, that of the domicile of the aggrieved party; in *Szechter*, a marriage of compassionate convenience, the domicile, as it happened, of all parties at the time of the marriage[29]). In *H v H* the English forum, finding the possibly applicable laws, those of England and of Hungary, to be similar, stemming from the common parentage of the canon law, honestly and explicitly chose its own law as the law with which it was familiar.

In principle there seems no reason why, subject to public policy, a Scots court should not grant the remedy of annulment on a ground unknown to it, if it is a ground of the *lex causae* (the common domicile, the domicile of the complainer, or possibly the domicile of the defender).

Physical incapacity

12–37 The point is well made, in *Ross-Smith*, *per* Lord Reid[30] that the ground of wilful refusal may found an action of divorce for desertion in some systems, and in others may give rise to no remedy. Arguably, it is wrong for the forum to grant a remedy where none is available by a law of closer connection.

Impotence is more likely generally among legal systems to found an action for nullity. In Scots law it will render a marriage voidable. The two grounds of impotence and wilful refusal to consummate are different in nature and it might be thought appropriate to have different applicable laws in any system of conflict rules, yet North,[31] noting that the grounds are likely to be found in the alternative in many petitions, recommends that there be one conflict rule for all alleged defects of physical incapacity.

It could be argued that a remedy should be given if such is available under the personal law of either, notwithstanding that this may result in a larger number of annulments.

---

[27] *Buckland* [1968] P. 296; *Kassim* [1962] P. 224.

[28] *Ponticelli* [1958] P.204; *H v H* [1954] P. 258; *Szechter* [1971] P. 286.

[29] The case is less useful than at first appears because it presented no conflict of laws, English law and Polish law both agreeing that the marriage was void. The court relied upon a brief statement from the expert on Polish law who was in hospital at the date of the case, and there are hints in the judgment that the forum considered that its own policy in such a case was a relevant consideration.

[30] [1963] A.C. 280 at 306.

[31] See discussion, Cheshire & North, pp.649–651. But see Clive, pp.132–133, who argues that impotency and wilful refusal should have the same choice of law rule, but it should be the same choice of law rule as applies in divorce (namely, application of *lex fori*).

Mental element: error, lack of consent, unilateral mental reservation

In the Scots law of marriage, there must be "an agreeing mind". **12–38**
Scots law does not favour giving legal effect to unilateral mental
reservation, yet Lord Dunpark in *Akram*[32] was required by the facts
of the case to grant an annulment to Muslim parties who had
"married" in a civil ceremony in Glasgow, upon evidence given
that neither had considered the formalities to amount to marriage
from the viewpoint of their religion.

Parties may marry out of a sense of family duty if that is the
pattern of their cultural background. In each of the two cases of
Mahmud[33] and *Mahmood*,[34] the Court of Session granted annulments of Muslim arranged marriages, at the instance of pursuers
who argued respectively that he and she had entered into marriage
without the (Scottish) requisite of free will but out of a sense of
family loyalty or under threat of being cut off from the family.[35] It
does not appear that in either case was the issue of domicile raised;
nor did the Scots court make any reference to foreign law. It would
seem that the Scots domestic law of the forum was used but the
court was mindful of the cultural background: in both cases the
parties were of Pakistani culture living in Scotland. It was appreciated that their wills would be more easily overborne as a result of
the family piety which formed part of their background. Hence, the
forum appears to have interpreted its own law in the light of a
background acknowledged to be different. It did not apply the law
of the domicile (which might have upheld the marriage) but in any
event no query as to the possibility of domicile being other than
Scots was raised. Paradoxically, the care accorded to the background may have resulted in a decision at odds with that which
would have been reached in a legal system of Muslim culture. The
approach is hybrid therefore in these two cases and there is no
discussion of choice of law. Similarly in *Sohrab v Kahn*,[36] Lord
McEwan granted decree of nullity of a pretended marriage on the
ground of the woman's lack of consent, induced by duress, and for
reasons of defects of formal validity; there was much evidence on

---

[32] 1979 S.L.T. (Notes) 87. *Cf. Orlandi v Castelli*, 1961 S.C. 113.
[33] 1994 S.L.T. 559.
[34] 1993 S.L.T. 589.
[35] A more extreme variation is exemplified by parental wishes to take a daughter
out of a UK jurisdiction in order to arrange a marriage in Pakistan: *M v B* [2005]
EWHC 1681 (consent to remove refused where the (adult) daughter had learning
difficulties such that she was incapable of understanding the meaning of consent
to marry); or where the party who, it is surmised, may be induced to marry, is
under the age of sixteen years, in which event the case may present as an
abduction or wardship case: *Re KR (a child) (abduction: forcible removal by
parents)* [1999] 4 All E.R. 954.
[36] 2002 S.L.T. 1255.

the detail of the Muslim wedding ceremony, and marriage customs. Although his Lordship's decision on lack of consent was reached after careful consideration of factual evidence of Muslim practice and parties' actings and statements in relation thereto, there is no indication that Lord McEwan applied any law other than Scots to determine the quality of consent which he deemed requisite for a valid marriage.

A seemingly more significant decision (overtaken by events on appeal) is that of *Hakeem v Hussain*,[37] in which Lord Clarke held, at first instance, that a civil marriage was not void merely because the parties to it did not regard it as having any religious significance. A distinction was drawn between consent to marriage for the purposes of the civil law, and the parties' private views on the relationship of a Scottish civil marriage ceremony and a religious marriage prescribed by their own faith. This distinction, while useful (*e.g.* when contrasted with the outcome in *Akram v Akram*[38]) in effectively preventing the exploitation of Scots civil marriage, is a fine one, some would say almost too fine to make. Reliance was placed on a statement by Professor Clive that "[e]verything turns on the distinction between an intention to assume the legal relationship of husband and wife and an intention not to get married at all. If the parties intended to get married . . . then they will be married even if their marriage was for a limited purpose and they had no intention of living together or assuming the normal social roles of husband and wife. If they intended not to get married at all, but merely to go through an empty ceremony they will not be married."[39]

While Clive admits that parties may not draw this distinction clearly in their minds, he writes that it is the crucial distinction. This central distinction is difficult to grasp; the difference between marrying without the intention of assuming the normal roles, on the one hand, and, on the other, merely going through a ceremony with no intention to get married at all, is one which may not convince. Perhaps the inference which could be taken from Lord Clarke's decision (which, however, was overturned) was that marriages entered into in Scotland for an identifiable purpose,[40] albeit not "matrimonial" (whatever that may mean), should be upheld. This may still be the case, but it must now be noted that in a long and careful judgment on appeal,[41] Lord Penrose, while agreeing

---

[37] 2003 S.L.T. 515, and on appeal, unreported, October 13, 2005.

[38] 1979 S.L.T. (Notes) 87.

[39] *Husband and Wife*, para.07.047. A further variation is that the argument is advanced that one or both parties believed that the cerfemony was merely an engagement ceremony: *Alfonso-Brown v Millwood* [2006] All E.R. (D.) 420.

[40] As in, *e.g. Hakeem*, so that the defender's visa could be granted if the immigration authorities considered that he was married to the pursuer.

[41] The main opinion was delivered by Lord Penrose, Lords Marnoch and Macfadyen concurring (unreported, October 13, 2005).

with Lord Clarke that parties' motives on entering into marriage
are not a determinative factor, nevertheless held that "there may
be cases in which the religious convictions of the parties may affect
the consent exchanged in a regular marriage ceremony to the
extent of wholly undermining it."[42] Lord Penrose was in no doubt
that the parties wished it to be understood that the registry office
ceremony was a formal marriage; but the critical question in an
annulment is whether at the moment of seeming acceptance of/
acquiescence in the civil ceremony, they intended to become
husband and wife. Since, in the view of the appellate court, an
agreement that the parties would not become husband and wife in
any real sense until some further condition was satisfied in the
indefinite future was not a marriage, the appeal was allowed, and
decree of nullity granted.

This is an active area of consideration in Scots family law. In all
cases of this type in which annulment has been granted, the forum
has been conscious of the public policy aspect, in particular, the
abuse or exploitation of the Scots institution of marriage, as
entered into by means of a civil ceremony, with accompanying
formalities. Insofar as this most recent decision reverts to a
criterion of assessing the existence of matrimonial consent on a
subjective basis, it is in line with earlier Scots law marriage
precedents.[43] While it is an established rule of domestic Scots law
that *unilateral* mental reservation to marriage with a particular
person cannot found an action of nullity, the court in cases such as
those under discussion is required to deal with instances of *bilateral*
mental reservation on the ground that, at best, the Scottish civil
ceremony is merely a precursor to a marriage ceremony fully
recognised as such by the parties in terms of their religious views.[44]
This latest judicial stance is a retrenchment to what might be
regarded as an incontrovertible meaning of consent (*i.e.* subjective). On the other hand, it is impossible not to sympathise with the
distinction which Lord Clarke made at first instance: if the parties
register themselves as married persons, having utilised Scottish
marriage procedures, they have purported to consent to enter the
institution for which the formalities were designed, *viz*; marriage in
Scots law. Such marriage has public law and private law consequences. It is unreasonable that parties should hope to enjoy the
public law consequences of the married status in Scotland, but
should choose not to recognise the private law consequences. In
these cases, the parties appear to wish to have the benefit of the
incidents of marriage without acquiring the status of married
parties.

---

[42] Para.36. Lord Penrose made reference to *Brady v Murray*, 1933 S.L.T. 534.
[43] Such as *Akram*, 1979 S.L.T. (Notes) 87 (*per* Lord Dunpark at 88), and *Brady v
Murray*, 1933 S.L.T. 534.
[44] *i.e.* a form of betrothal or condition precedent to "full" religious marriage.

Notable for its raising of the conflict implications which might be expected to attend such a case is the decision of Temporary Judge R.F. Macdonald Q.C. in *Singh v Singh*,[45] to the effect that the law governing the issue of consent to marry is the law of the domicile of the party alleging lack of consent. The decision provides a discussion of choice of law upon the issue of duress relating to marriage. The judge declined to follow an *obiter dictum* of Lord Guthrie in *Di Rollo v Di Rollo*,[46] which had favoured the application of the *lex loci celebrationis* to the question of consent. The pursuer, a UK citizen, had been brought up in Edinburgh and expressed the intention to live in Scotland for the foreseeable future; there was no challenge to the inference of Scots domicile. She had accompanied her mother to India to visit relations, only to be coerced into marriage at the mother's instance during the holiday in India. The judge applied to the substance of the case[47] Scots law in the matter of the requirement and content of consent to marry, being the law of the pursuer's domicile. Hence this decision brings Scots law further along a path which, it is submitted, is the correct one *quoad* choice of law; but it does not afford an example of application by the Scots forum, after proof, of a *foreign* marriage law *qua lex causae*. In the instant case, the court was satisfied that the threat from the pursuer's mother was sufficient to cause the will of the pursuer to be overborne and vitiated her consent to marry.

The robust English view of consent to marriage, namely that parties of sound mind should be held to their bargain, is seen in the notable House of Lords decision of *Vervaeke v Smith*.[48]

A statutory response

The Family Law (Scotland) Act 2006 seeks to address the problems encountered in this area in the following manner[49]:

---

[45] 2005 S.L.T. 749.

[46] 1959 S.L.T. 278.

[47] Making reference to *Mahmood* and *Mahmud*, above.

[48] [1983] 1 A.C. 145.

[49] See also Asylum and Immigration (Treatment of Claimants etc) Act 2004, ss.21 and 22, the aim of which is to ensure that a District Registrar shall not enter particulars of an intended marriage in the marriage notice book, nor complete a Marriage Schedule, unless satisfied that a party to the intended marriage in Scotland who is subject to immigration control has an entry clearance granted expressly for the purpose of enabling him to marry in the UK, or has the written permission of the Secretary of State to marry in the UK. As of April 2006, the Home Office has partially suspended these rules as a response to a High Court decision *per* Silber J that the requirement to apply for a certificate of approval to marry is incompatible with Arts 12 and 14 of the ECHR because, with regard to Art.12, it affected the rights of substantially many more people than necessary to achieve the legislative purpose of preventing sham marriages, and with regard to

Section 38(2) directs the question whether a person has consented to enter into a marriage to the law of the domicile of that person immediately before the marriage. This provision will make clear the basic rule in the general case, but the inclusion in section 2 of the Act of a particular rule concerning void marriages (to be inserted as section 20A of the Marriage (Scotland) Act 1977) represents an attempt to address the problems which recently have troubled the Scots courts. Section 2 provides a rule which insists upon its own operation, i.e. is of an overriding nature, where the marriage, the validity of which is in question, was solemnised in Scotland.

Such a marriage shall be void if, at the time of the marriage ceremony, a party to the marriage who was capable of consenting to the marriage purported to give consent, but did so by reason only of duress or error (*i.e.* coerced marriage: section 20A(2)). Error is defined for the purposes of the legislation as (a) error as to the nature of the ceremony; or (b) a mistaken belief held by a person that the other party at the ceremony with whom the first party purported to enter into a marriage was the person whom the first party had agreed to marry (section 20A(5)).

Further, the marriage shall be void if at the time of the marriage ceremony, a party to the marriage was incapable of (a) understanding the nature of marriage; and (b) consenting to the marriage (*i.e.* lack of understanding: section 20A(3)). However, thirdly, if a party to a marriage purported to give consent to the marriage other than by reason only of duress or error, the marriage shall not be void by reason only of that party's having tacitly withheld consent to the marriage at the time when it was solemnised (*i.e.* sham marriages: section 20A(4)).

This clearly is a statutory response[50] to the courts' difficulty, outlined above, and establishes a criterion of consent, *objectively construed*,[51] to marriage.

Art.14, it amounted to direct discrimination on the grounds of religion and nationality which was not justified in the interests of immigration control: *R. (on the application of Baiai and others) v Secretary of State for the Home Department* [2006] EWHC 823 (Admin).

[50] See *Akram, per* Lord Dunpark at 89: "It must be for Parliament to decide whether this abuse should be made a statutory offence or whether legislation should preclude parties from challenging the legal effect of any formal ceremony of marriage on the ground that they knowingly but tacitly withheld their true consent to marriage." Statute exists or is in contemplation where this subject is met with in its criminal law or immigration law context: Asylum and Immigration (Treatment of Claimants etc) Act 2004, ss.19–25. See also 2005 Home Office and Foreign & Commonwealth Office Consultation on proposals to create a specific criminal offence relating to forced marriage: "Forced marriage: a wrong not a right"; see also public information campaign launched in March 2006 by the joint Home Office and Foreign & Commonwealth Office Forced Marriage Unit.

[51] *cf.* generally commercial contracts: *Muirhead &Turnbull v Dickson* (1905) 7 F. 686

Section 2 of the 2006 Act introduces a mandatory provision of the *lex loci celebrationis*, where the *lex loci* is Scottish.

C. Recognition of Foreign Decrees of Nullity

12–39 Until 1986, recognition of foreign decrees of nullity developed at common law, following a pattern similar to that found in relation to recognition of foreign divorces prior to 1971.[52] The only challenges were on the grounds of no jurisdiction, fraud, or that the ground on which the foreign nullity was granted was *contra bonos mores*.[53] Error by the foreign court as to its own law or any other law was not a ground of challenge.[54]

The Law Commissions concluded[55] that there was no convincing argument for retaining common law regulation of recognition of nullity decrees. As a result, the Family Law Act 1986 (sections 44 to 54) was applied to the recognition of foreign divorces and annulments.

Since the coming into force of Regulations 1347 and 2201, the 1986 Act applies only to the recognition of annulments obtained outside the EU, and in Denmark; the Brussels regime applies to recognition of all other EU annulments in the same manner as it applies to recognition of EU divorces.[56]

---

at 694 *per* L.P. Dunedin: "Commercial contracts cannot be arranged by what people think in their inmost minds. Commercial contracts are made according to what people say."

[52] *e.g. cf. Law v Gustin* [1976] 1 All E.R. 113 with *Indyka* [1969] 1 A.C. 33: law of close connection. See also *Perrini* [1979] 2 All E.R. 323. Instances of foreign extrajudicial annulments are rare and no case has arisen in recent years. However, *Di Rollo*, 1959 S.C. 75, concerning an extrajudicial annulment, is to the effect that the validity of a marriage good by the *lex loci celebrationis* will not be affected by the decision of a church tribunal. The court held that, for the *Armitage* principle then applicable (see para.12–18, above) to apply, there would have to have been a decision of a court (not a tribunal) recognised by the court of the husband's (Italian) domicile. One must consider now the effect of Family Law Act 1986, s.46(1) and (2) in relation to extra-judicial annulments but there have been few, if any, cases. It could be that decisions of the Roman Catholic Rota might come to be adjudicated upon under the 1986 Act. Presumably such a decision would be a "proceedings" annulment, to be judged according to s.46(1). Whether a religious annulment is capable now of being governed by Reg.2201 is debateable. See para.12–30, above. In the case of the Roman Catholic Rota, see also Council Regulation (EC) No.2116/2004 concerning Jurisdiction and the Recognition and Enforcement of Judgments in Matrimonial Matters and the Matters of Parental Responsibility, repealing Regulation (EC) No.1347/2000, as regards treaties with the Holy See (December 2, 2004, OJ 2004 L367/1).

[53] *Gray v Formosa*; *Lepre*; *Chappelle*, above. These cases provide rare instances of a successful challenge on policy grounds of the substance of the foreign ground of nullity.

[54] *Merker* [1963] P. 283.

[55] Law Com. No.137; Recognition of Foreign Nullity Decrees and Related Matters; Scot. Law Com. No.88 (1984).

[56] 1986 Act, s.45(2).

IV. Dissolution of Civil Partnership

A. Jurisdiction of Scots Courts under the Civil Partnership Act 2004

Part 3 of the Act applies to civil partnerships registered in **12–40** Scotland, and Part 5 applies to civil partnerships formed and dissolved abroad (dissolution and separation: sections 117 to 122; and nullity: sections 123 and 124).

Part 3—dissolution in Scotland of a civil partnership: jurisdiction

In terms of section 117, an action for the dissolution of a civil **12–41** partnership may be brought in the Court of Session or in the sheriff court. Though section 117 in its terms does not restrict the jurisdiction which it confers to actions concerning civil partnerships registered in Scotland, Part 5 of the Act (sections 225 to 227) lays down particular rules of jurisdiction of the Scottish courts in respect of civil partnerships formed abroad, and so by inference it would seem that Part 3 jurisdiction must be restricted to those civil partnerships registered in Scotland, or possibly in the UK.[57] The jurisdictional link, therefore, for the first time in the treatment of the subject, is based on the location of the occurrence of an event, rather than upon a personal connection between one or both parties and the forum.[58]

Under section 117, the Scottish court may grant decree if, but only if, it is established that the civil partnership has broken down irretrievably. Irretrievable breakdown is taken to be established by proof of certain factors such as unreasonable behaviour, desertion, or non-cohabitation, all on the model of the domestic divorce law of Scotland as contained in the Divorce (Scotland) Act 1976. A register of decrees of dissolution will be maintained at the General Register Office.

Part 5—civil partnerships formed or dissolved abroad

This Part makes provision for "overseas relationships", which are **12–42** defined as specified relationships,[59] or as relationships which meet the general conditions, AND which are registered in a country outside the UK by two people who under the relevant law (qv) are

---

[57] For "abroad" is not defined. Section 225(1)(c) confers residual jurisdiction on the Scottish courts.

[58] As will be seen, *locus registrationis* in Scotland will regulate capacity and form, but domicile safeguards are inserted where the *locus registrationis* is overseas. See para.12–43, below.

[59] Defined in s.213, and by reference to Sch.20, as augmented by The Civil Partnership Act 2004 (Overseas Relationships) Order 2005 (SI 2005/3135).

of the same sex at the time when they do so, and neither of whom is already a civil partner or lawfully married.[60] The Act describes in these provisions a set of factual/legal circumstances which is a sufficient approximation to the institution of civil partnership in UK law as to justify the attachment to those circumstances of (a) recognition in the UK; and (b) availability of domestic remedy. Thus:

Chapter 2—overseas relationships treated as civil partnerships

(i) General rule—section 215

12–43 In order to have an overseas relationship treated as a civil partnership, the parties must have had legal capacity under the *locus registrationis*,[61] and have met all the formal requirements of the *locus*.

(ii) Persons domiciled in a part of the UK—section 217

By section 217 persons domiciled in Scotland will not be treated as having formed a civil partnership if, at the time of registration, they were not eligible in terms of section 86[62] to register such a relationship in Scotland.[63] This section reinstates for parties domiciled in a part of the UK the traditional rule that the law of the domicile regulates legal capacity to enter into domestic relationships. In this way, the registration of an overseas relationship receives a different treatment from the registration of a civil partnership within the UK, in respect of the latter of which essential validity (including capacity) and formal validity are both governed by the *lex loci registrationis*. As a result of this section it is clear that while the *locus registrationis* is a sufficient test to deal with partnerships registered in the UK, it has been thought appropriate to use the traditional connecting factor of domicile where parties, one of whom is domiciled in a part of the UK, have purported to enter into a civil partnership abroad.

---

[60] Defined in s.214, thus: the general conditions are that under the relevant law (being the law of the place of registration, including its conflict rules—s.212(2)) (a) neither of the parties is already a party to such a relationship, or lawfully married; (b) the relationship is of indeterminate duration; and (c) the effect of entering into the relationship is that the parties are either treated as married, or treated as a couple either generally or for specified purposes.

[61] Being the law of the place of registration, including its rules of private international law (ss.212 and 215), although by s.216(1) the parties are not to be treated as having formed a civil partnership in such circumstances if at the time of registration they were not at that date of the same sex under UK law.

[62] See para.11–37, above.

[63] The same principle applies to English domiciliaries (s.217(2)) and Northern Irish domiciliaries (s.217(5)).

By inference, it must be that a Scots court in seeking to establish whether parties, neither of whom who was at the point of registration domiciled in a part of the UK, have validly created a civil partnership abroad, must apply the *lex loci registrationis*, including its rules of private international law.

(iii) Public policy—section 218

All of the above is subject to the usual public policy discretion of the forum, which will justify non-recognition of a capacity existing under the *lex loci registrationis*.

Part 5, Chapter 3—dissolution of civil partnerships formed abroad: jurisdiction of the Scottish courts

Section 225 provides that the Court of Session and, in qualifying **12–44** cases, the sheriff court has jurisdiction to entertain an action for the dissolution of a civil partnership formed abroad, or for separation of such partners,[64] if (and only if):

(a) the court has jurisdiction under regulations made under section 219 of the Act (that is, to correspond to Regulation 2201, Article 3)[65]; or

(b) if no court has jurisdiction under (a) above, and either civil partner is domiciled in Scotland on the date when the proceedings are begun; or

(c) the following conditions are met—

   (i) the two people concerned registered their partnership in Scotland,[66]

   (ii) no court has jurisdiction under (a) above; and

   (iii) it appears to the court to be in the interests of justice to assume jurisdiction in the case.[67]

---

[64] For declarators of nullity, jurisdiction is restricted to the Court of Session; see s.225(3).

[65] Detailed rules, laid under s.219 of the 2004 Act, are proposed in draft SSI, The Civil Partnership (Jurisdiction and Recognition of Judgments) (Scotland) Regulations 2005, regulation 4. These rules, which attempt to align the rules on jurisdiction in respect of dissolution and annulment of civil partnerships, and separation of partners, with the corresponding rules for marriage contained in Council Regulation 2201/2003, were intended to come into force on December 5, 2005, but have not yet been implemented. Equivalent rules applying in England and Wales, and Northern Ireland, implemented on December 5, 2005, are contained in The Civil Partnership (Jurisdiction and Recognition of Judgments) Regulations (SI 2005/3334).

[66] There is a precedent for this in that at common law in Scotland *locus celebrationis* was regarded as a good ground of jurisdiction in annulment of marriage if it was averred that the marriage was void: *Prawdziclazarska*, 1954 S.C. 98.

[67] *i.e.* the residual rules of national jurisdiction. *Cf.* Reg.2201/2003, Art.7.

Conflicting jurisdictions

12–45 Provision is made in section 226 for the resolution of cases of conflicting jurisdiction, corresponding to the system of mandatory and discretionary sists contained in Schedule 3 to the Domicile and Matrimonial Proceedings Act 1973.[68] However, it may be expected that any regulations introduced in terms of section 219 will adopt the system of *lis pendens*, which is characteristic of the Brussels regime. A potential categorisation difficulty is capable of arising in civil partnership cases as well as in divorce, separation and nullity cases regarding delimiting the sphere of operation of different regulatory regimes, that is to say, to identify which partnership dissolution cases are governed by section 219 regulations, and which are governed by the rules of court to be introduced under section 226.[69]

B. Choice of Law

12–46 There is no direct reference in the 2004 Act to choice of law. Currently in divorce actions in Scotland the choice of law made by the forum is always the *lex fori*. In the case of civil partnerships registered in Scotland, the civil partnership is void if, and only if, the parties were not eligible to register (see section 86), or, being eligible, either of them did not validly consent to its formation.[70]

The minor differences between the body of provisions governing civil partnerships registered in England and Wales, and Northern Ireland, from those which are to obtain with regard to civil partnerships registered in Scotland, have resulted in a covert choice of law direction in section 124, *viz*: where two people have registered as civil partners of each other in England and Wales, or Northern Ireland, and wish to have that relationship declared null in Scotland, it is enacted that their civil partnership is to be regarded as void (or voidable) if it would be void (or voidable) in England and Wales, or Northern Ireland, respectively.[71] This must mean that a Scottish dissolution forum must apply to a civil partnership registered in England and Wales, or Northern Ireland, those provisions in the Act which have been particularly crafted for those jurisdictions.

By the same token where (by implication of the Act) two people seek a dissolution of their partnership in a Scots court (*per* sections

---

[68] For England and Wales, see the Family Proceedings (Civil Partnership: Staying of Proceedings) Rules 2005 (SI 2005/2921). Equivalent rules for Scotland have not yet been made.

[69] See also para.12–48, below.

[70] s.123.

[71] For grounds of voidability, see ss.50–51. *Cf.* s.174 for Northern Ireland.

225 to 227), said partnership being "an apparent or alleged overseas relationship", section 124(7) directs that the civil partnership is void if the relationship is not an overseas relationship or, being an overseas relationship, the parties are not to be regarded under Chapter 2 of Part 5 (overseas relationships treated as civil partnerships) as having formed a civil partnership. Further, section 124(8), in regard to overseas relationships, provides that the civil partnership is voidable if it is voidable under the relevant law,[72] or, either of the parties being domiciled in England and Wales or Northern Ireland, if the circumstances fall within sections 50 or 174 (grounds on which a civil partnership is voidable, in England and Wales, and Northern Ireland, respectively).

C. Recognition of Foreign Decrees of Dissolution, Annulment and Separation of Civil Partnership

Decrees obtained in the UK

By section 233,[73] no dissolution or annulment of a civil partnership **12–47** obtained in one part of the UK is effective in any part of the UK unless obtained from a court of civil jurisdiction. Likewise[74] if such a judicial dissolution etc is obtained from a court in one part of the UK, it shall be recognised throughout the UK subject to the principles of *res judicata* and avoidance of irreconcilable judgments.

Decrees obtained overseas

A distinction is likely to be made between recognition of decrees **12–48** obtained from courts of EU Member States (except Denmark), and those from non-EU states. In the former case, section 234(2) permits rules of recognition of EU decrees to be introduced, mirroring those which obtain currently in relation to matrimonial decrees under Regulation 2201[75] The rules of recognition of non-

---

[72] s.124(10) defines relevant law as the law of the country or territory where the overseas relationship was registered, including its rules of private international law. This therefore amounts to reference to the use of that law, including its conflict rules.

[73] *cf.* Family Law Act 1986, s.44(1).

[74] *ibid.*, cf. s.44(2).

[75] Detailed rules, laid under section 219 of the 2004 Act, are proposed in draft SSI, the Civil Partnership (Jurisdiction and Recognition of Judgments) (Scotland) Regulations 2005, Part 2, regulations 5 to 11. These rules, which attempt to align the rules on judgment recognition in respect of dissolution and annulment of civil partnerships, and separation of partners, with the corresponding rules for marriage contained in Council Regulation 2201/2003, were intended to come into force on December 5, 2005, but have not yet been implemented. Equivalent rules applying in England and Wales, and Northern Ireland, implemented on December 5, 2005, are contained in the Civil Partnership (Jurisdiction and Recognition of Judgments) Regulations (SI 2005/3334).

EU decrees[76] follow closely the provisions for recognition (and refusal thereof) of overseas consistorial decrees which are contained in the Family Law Act 1986, sections 46 and 51. The mirroring continues in sections 237 and 238,[77] but one notable novelty is contained in section 237(2)(b)(ii), which addresses the interesting issue of the proper resolution of the following situation: what is to happen where (i) a party has purported to enter into a civil partnership in a jurisdiction in which he is not domiciled; and (ii) one or both parties to the purported partnership is/are domiciled in a country which does not recognise such relationships between two persons of the same sex; (iii) this relationship, presumably legally constituted according to the *lex loci registrationis*,[78] has broken down; (iv) the parties have obtained a dissolution order from a court in the *locus registrationis*, and now seek to have that order recognised in the UK? Section 237(2) permits the Lord Chancellor or the Scottish Ministers to make provision for such cases, but it is uncertain whether provision is necessary, and it is difficult to predict the nature of the modifications to be made. If the difficulty in the case described is one of capacity to enter into a new partnership, section 238 already provides a solution. If it is rather a matter of the wisdom of according recognition to such a dissolution, section 236(3)(c) permits withholding recognition on the grounds of public policy. However, if the effect of withholding recognition of a dissolution would be to recognise the continuing existence (according to Scots conflict rules) of a legal relationship which is forbidden by the domicile of one of the parties, such an outcome seems counter-productive.

Since there is to be a dual system, with provision for one set of rules for recognition of EU decrees, and another set for non-EU decrees, it will be important to delimit the scope of operation of each set of rules. Moreover, it will require to be clarified, as regards, eg, the recognition of EU decrees, when Regulation 2201 applies, and when section 234, of Part 5 of the 2004 Act applies. By which law is the relationship to be characterised as "marriage" or "partnership"? Upon that categorisation rests the decision as to which set of jurisdiction and recognition rules apply. Thus, for example, if a Scottish court is called upon to recognise a Dutch dissolution of a Dutch same sex relationship, the relationship in the eyes of Dutch law amounting to "marriage" (and therefore attracting in the Netherlands application of Regulation 2201), but conversely the same relationship in the eyes of Scots law amounting rather to "civil partnership" (attracting application of Part 5 of the 2004 Act)—is the Scots forum to prefer its own approach to

---

[76] s.235 (grounds for recognition); s.236 (refusal of recognition).

[77] *cf.* Family Law Act 1986, ss.46(5) and 50, respectively.

[78] Bearing in mind s.124(10).

characterisation and consequences? A further dilemma of delimitation might arise in relation to conflicting proceedings concerning the same relationship, in order to decide which set of conflicting jurisdiction rules should apply (i.e. those in Regulation 2201, or those in the 2004 Act).

To what extent does the restrictive attitude to public policy-founded refusal of recognition contained in Regulation 2201 apply in the context of the decision to recognise, or not, the foreign termination of a registered partnership?[79] The body of UK rules, extant and proposed, may be criticised as deficient in explicitness and structure, and less than comprehensive, even though embodied in complex, lengthy legislation.

Cessation of *de facto* cohabitation

De facto relationships, by definition, do not require formalities at **12–49** the point of commencement, or conclusion, but a court may be asked to make proprietary and/or financial provision to a "cohabitant", during or at the cessation of the *de facto* relationship, and therefore must ascertain by the relevant applicable law, whether the claimant qualifies as a cohabitant. For this purpose, the length of the period, and nature, of the alleged cohabitation will be relevant.[80] The Family Law (Scotland) Act 2006, section 28, empowers the court to make certain financial provision orders "where cohabitants cease to cohabit otherwise than by reason of the death of one (or both) of them". The test of cessation therefore is a factual one. Similarly, application to the court by the survivor for provision upon intestacy will be possible upon proof of the death intestate of a predeceasing cohabitant, domiciled in Scotland.[81]

Summary 12—Consistorial Causes

1. Jurisdiction **12–50**

Allocation of jurisdiction

Divorce, judicial separation and nullity: Domicile and Matrimonial Proceedings Act 1973, sections 7 and 8, as amended.

Civil partnership: Civil Partnership Act 2004, sections 117, 121, 123, and 225 to 227.

---

[79] 2004 Act, s.236(3)(c). *Cf.* para.12–25 above.
[80] For Scots law, see Family Law (Scotland) Act 2006, ss.25–30. See Ch.11, above.
[81] See further Chs 13 and 14, below.

Conflicting jurisdictions

Divorce, judicial separation and nullity:
—Outside the Brussels regime, and within the United Kingdom: the matter is governed by the Domicile and Matrimonial Proceedings Act 1973, Schedule 3 (mandatory and discretionary sists).
—Under Regulation 2201: a *lis pendens* system operates (Article 19).

Civil partnership: Civil Partnership Act 2004, sections 219 and 226.

2. Choice of law

Divorce and judicial separation: Scots law as the *lex fori* determines grounds as well as procedure, but see proposed changes in Rome III.

Nullity: grounds of nullity pertaining to form are governed by the *lex loci celebrationis*. Grounds of nullity pertaining to legal capacity are governed by the ante-nuptial domicile(s). Subject to the speciality that the Family Law (Scotland) Act 2006, section 2 imposes certain overriding rules of Scots law pertaining to consent in cases where the purported marriage was solemnised in Scotland. It is suggested that grounds pertaining to physical incapacity should be governed by the domicile of the aggrieved party or possibly of either party; in respect of grounds pertaining to consent possibly governed by the law of the domicile of the party averring absence of consent. The forum may use its own law for a variety of reasons including failure by either side to offer to prove foreign law.

Civil partnership: limited guidance is contained in the Civil Partnership Act 2004, section 124.

3. Recognition of overseas decrees

Divorce, judicial separation and nullity (including extrajudicial divorces etc)
—Outside the Brussels regime, and within the United Kingdom: the matter is governed by sections 44 to 51 of the Family Law Act 1986.
—Under Regulation 2201: Articles 21 to 27 apply.

Civil partnership

—Intra-UK decrees, and non-EU decrees: Civil Partnership Act 2004, sections 233 and 234(1), respectively.
—EU decrees: Civil Partnership Act 2004, section 234(2) applies.

CHAPTER 13

PROPRIETARY AND FINANCIAL CONSEQUENCES OF MARRIAGE AND OTHER ADULT RELATIONSHIPS

I. PROPRIETARY CONSEQUENCES

A. PROPERTY RIGHTS OF MARRIED PERSONS

The effect of marriage upon the property rights of parties thereto **13–01** differs from one legal system to another. Certain systems imply that, in the absence of an express marriage contract between the parties, marriage creates a "community of goods" between the spouses.

Under domestic Scots law, marriage *per se* has no effect upon the property rights of spouses. The Family Law (Scotland) Act 1985, section 24 states that marriage shall not of itself affect the respective rights of parties to the marriage in relation to their property.[1]

The different approaches taken by legal systems to the effect of marriage upon the property rights of spouses have the potential to produce conflict of laws problems. Attempts to resolve such problems, and to reconcile the differences in approach, were made by the Hague Conference on Private International Law, in 1978, resulting in a Convention on the Law Applicable to Matrimonial Property Regimes (which the United Kingdom did not sign).[2] The subject of matrimonial property is the focus of renewed international harmonisation efforts, now within the EU, *sub nom.* "Brussels III".[3] In advance of harmonised rules, Scots conflict rules of matrimonial property have been placed on a legislative footing in terms of the Family Law (Scotland) Act 2006, section 39.

---

[1] There is therefore in Scots law a system of separation of property, except for (i) piecemeal legislative provision, such as the Family Law (Scotland) Act 1985, s.25 (presumption of equal share in household goods); (ii) "equalisation" provisions which obtain at termination of marriage by divorce; and (iii) the modifying effect upon the death intestate of a predeceasing spouse of the survivor's claim for legal rights in his/her moveable estate, a very long established feature of Scots law.

[2] The Convention is of limited effect, entering into force (on September 1, 1992) in only three countries.

[3] *qv*, para.13–16, below.

When dealing with a question of matrimonial property rights having cross-border implications, one of the first issues to ascertain is whether a "matrimonial property regime" was established upon marriage, either by operation of law, or by contract. There are three possibilities:

(1) (default) statutory regime imposing community of goods;
(2) private marriage contract; or
(3) absence of statutory or contractual provision.

By virtue of the 2006 Act, section 39(6)(b), it is clear that the Scots conflict matrimonial property rules provided thereby are subject to the spouses' contrary agreement. It is therefore apparent that these new rules do not trump private marriage contract provisions. Since, as will be explained below, the traditional approach of Scots and English conflict rules has been to assimilate the effect of statutory codes to that of private marriage contracts, and since any other construction would be productive of great difficulty, it is assumed that the provisions contained in section 39 shall apply only where there is no private regime, statutory or contractual. Discussion of section 39, therefore, is postponed to the appropriate point in the text.

Marriage contracts: statutory community of goods

13–02 In certain countries there is a statutory code which, in the absence of a written marriage contract, establishes a community of goods between husband and wife. Such a code is likely to have the same legal effect as a private marriage contract. In order to avoid the operation of statutory community of goods, parties may exclude, or opt out of, the community of goods (if permitted so to do by the statutory regime).[4]

The leading case of *De Nicols v Curlier*[5] shows that failure by spouses to enter into an express marriage contract may mean that, by default, they become subject to the property regime laid down by the law in terms of which they may be presumed to have entered the marriage relationship.[6] The rights which spouses acquire under

---

[4] *Shand-Harvey v Bennet-Clark* (1910) 1 S.L.T. (Sh.Ct) 133; the choice in this case was unaffected by a subsequent change of domicile.

[5] *(No.1)* [1900] A.C. 21 (moveables); *(No.2)* [1900] 2 Ch. 410 (immoveables).

[6] There may be argument about the basis on which this law is to be identified. Moreover, any given regime of community rules will provide for the extent of its own application, *e.g. De Nicols*, above, *per* Lord Macnaghten at 33: "Community of goods in France is constituted by a marriage in France according to French law, not by married people coming to France and settling there. And the community must commence from the day of the marriage. It cannot commence from any other time." *Cf.* Clive, p.256. "Late entry" usually therefore will be precluded.

the statutory regime are thought to vest at the point of contracting; no matter where the parties subsequently may reside, their property rights are not affected by subsequent change(s) of domicile.[7] This doctrine is known as immutability of property rights. The most famous Scottish (House of Lords) case on the topic, *Lashley v Hog*,[8] appears *prima facie* to be inconsistent with the theory of immutability. In *Lashley*, Hog of Newliston, domiciled in Scotland, removed to England and became domiciled there. While in England he married an Englishwoman and the parties had a number of children, including Thomas Hog, and a daughter who became Mrs Lashley, the litigants. Upon his wife's death in 1760, Hog returned to Scotland where he died domiciled. Mrs Lashley then claimed not only *legitim* (due to a child of the marriage), but also a share in the *communio bonorum* of her parents' marriage to which at that date (and until (Dunlop's) Marriage Act 1855[9]) the representatives of a predeceasing wife could lay claim, standing in their mother's place.[10] The *communio bonorum* was vestigial evidence of community of property in Scots law;[11] the law of England had no equivalent.

The House of Lords, in upholding Mrs Lashley's claim, might be thought to have admitted the possibility that matrimonial property rights may change upon change of domicile, since the law of England, the domicile at marriage, contained no such property claim.[12] If, on the other hand, the case is regarded as a succession case, which is plausible, it was proper for Scots law, as the law of the deceased's domicile at death, to regulate Mrs Lashley's claim.[13]

If it is to be argued by one or both parties that the foreign community of property regime has extra-territorial effect, such as to purport to extend to foreign *immoveable* property, this, if not admitted,[14] must be proved, the onus lying on the married pair, or the survivor as the case is more likely to be.[15] The *lex situs* in its

---

[7] At the date when these grand illustrative cases were handed down, the conjugal unit had one conjoined domicile. Since this is no longer the case, difficulties may arise.

[8] (1804) 4 Paton 581.

[9] Intestate Moveable Succession (Scotland) Act 1855, s.6.

[10] Of the surviving three children, Mrs Lashley alone claimed under this head, her brother Alexander having received advances from their father during his lifetime. In the circumstances, it was not in the succession interests of her brother Thomas to argue in favour of the application of Scots law.

[11] It was a claim by Mrs Bell's daughter for her deceased mother's share in the "goods in communion" which occasioned the House of Lords decision on continuance of domicile of origin: *Bell v Kennedy* (1868) 6 M. (H.L.) 69.

[12] There was no matrimonial property regime in England, a fact which enabled the House of Lords a hundred years later in *De Nicols* to distinguish *Lashley*.

[13] See Ch.18. *Cf.* Walton, *A Handbook of Husband and Wife according to the Law of Scotland* (3rd ed.) pp.352–354.

[14] *De Nicols (No. 2)* [1900] 2 Ch. 410.

[15] *Callwood* [1960] A.C. 659: widow unable to prove that Danish community of property regime extended to Great Thatch Island in the British Virgin Islands.

discretion may accept that the devolution of land is to be regulated by some legal system other than its own,[16] *i.e.* the *lex situs* may acquiesce in a foreign community of property regime.

Although it seems clear that the survivor may claim under the terms of a matrimonial regime,[17] private or statutory, no matter that the predeceaser died domiciled in another legal system (that is to say, it can confidently be expected that the matter will be regarded as one of matrimonial property rather than succession), if, rather, the question is whether the survivor has the option to choose between the rights conferred by a matrimonial property regime, and rights conferred by means of succession to the deceased's estate, the point seems to be regarded as one of succession, to be determined, in principle and in detail, by the law of the deceased's last domicile.[18]

Marriage contracts: private marriage contracts

13–03 In the absence of a default system of community of goods, or even within such a system if the system itself permits, parties may enter into a private marriage contract, for example selecting a bespoke system of community of property, or of separation of property.

Proper/governing law

13–04 "Rights in property arising out of a matrimonial relationship" are excluded from the Rome Convention.[19] Hence, marriage contracts are governed by common law, though a marriage contract involving trusts will be regulated by the Recognition of Trusts Act 1987.[20] Consequently, the proper law of a private marriage contract is either the law by which the parties expressly, or by implication, agree that it is to be governed, or failing any such express or implied agreement, the law with which the contract has the most real and substantial connection.[21]

---

[16] *De Nicols (No. 2)*, above; *Chiwell v Carlyon* (1897) 14 S.C. 61 (South Africa) (land in Cornwall, being community property by the law of South Africa, devolved according to that law) (details to be found at Cheshire & North, p.1023).

[17] Contrast absence of English regime in *Lashley*.

[18] *Re Mengel's Will Trusts* [1962] Ch. 791; contrast *Re Allen's Estate* [1945] 2 All E.R. 264.

[19] Contracts (Applicable Law) Act 1990, Sch.1; Rome Convention, Art.1.2.6.

[20] Implementing 1986 Hague Convention on the Law Applicable to Trusts and on their Recognition; *qv* 18–53, below.

[21] Following the common law rules of Scotland/England for commercial contracts. For marriage contract examples, see *Chamberlain v Napier* (1880) 15 Ch. D. 614; *Re Fitzgerald* [1904] 1 Ch. 573; *Re Mackenzie* [1911] Ch. 578; *Re Hewitt* [1915] 1 Ch. 228; *Brown v Brown* (1913) 2 S.L.T. 314; *Eadie's Trs v Henderson* (1919) 1 S.L.T. 253; *Goold Stuart's Trs v McPhail*, 1947 S.L.T. 221; *Iveagh v IRC* [1954] Ch. 364; *Duke of Marlborough v Att.-Gen. (No.1)* [1945] Ch. 78 ("presumption" in favour of matrimonial, *i.e.* husband's, domicile applied); *Re Bankes* [1902] 2 Ch. 333 ("presumption" rebutted); *R v R* [1995] 1 F.C.R. 745.

Capacity to enter into a marriage contract

As regards immoveables, capacity to enter into a marriage contract **13–05** is governed by the *lex situs*.[22] As regards moveables there is no recent case, but arguing by analogy from the topic of commercial contracts, application of the putative proper law (that is, the law which would govern if the contract were valid) commends itself.

In earlier days, an argument was adduced that a distinction could be drawn between void and voidable marriage contracts; in the former case, capacity was referable to the law of the domicile of the granter at the date of the purported grant,[23] and in the latter, the question was whether by the law of the domicile of the granter at the date of the purported revocation, s/he had capacity to revoke.[24] It may still be thought best to express the matter in the form that revocability is an issue for the putative proper law of the contract, whereas capacity to revoke is an issue for the *lex domicilii* at the time of the purported revocation of the party/parties wishing to revoke. Later English consensus[25] construes all cases as supporting a reference to the putative proper law, but it is arguable that the law of the domicile should be applied, until such time at least as the House of Lords reviews the case of *Cooper*.[26]

The case of *Sawrey-Cookson*[27] is instructive in a number of aspects: a Scotswoman granted in Scotland a unilateral antenuptial marriage settlement in Scots form in anticipation of her marriage to an Englishman. A few years later, she wished to revoke it. As the proper law of the deed was Scots, Scots law determined its revocability *sua natura*, but her capacity to revoke was to be referred to her English domicile at the date of proposed revocation. She also had executed in England, after her marriage, a ratification of the settlement: *that* deed had an English proper law, and its effect and its revocability, as well as her legal capacity to revoke, were to be determined by the law of England.

Formal validity

It is sufficient that the deed complies in form either with the **13–06** proper law or with the law of the place where the marriage contract was executed.[28]

---

[22] *Black v Black's Trs*, 1950 S.L.T. (Notes) 32.
[23] *Re Cooke's Trusts* (1887) 3 T.L.R. 558; *Cooper v Cooper* (1888) 15 R. (H.L.) 21; *Black v Black's Trs*, 1950 S.L.T. (Notes) 32.
[24] *Viditz v O'Hagan* [1900] 2 Ch. 87; *Sawrey-Cookson's Trs* (1905) 8 F. 157.
[25] Morris, 16-011; Dicey and Morris, 28-037; Cheshire & North, pp.1025–1026. Also Morris, "Capacity to Make a Marriage Settlement Contract in English Private International Law" (1938) 54 LQR 78.
[26] (1888) 15 R. (HL) 21. See Clive, p.321, and Anton with Beaumont, p.579, where may be found a discussion at length.
[27] *Sawrey-Cookson v Sawrey-Cookson's Trs* (1905) 8 F. 157.
[28] *Guepratte v Young* (1851) 4 De G. & Sm. 217; *Van Grutten v Digby* (1862) 31 Beav. 561; *Re Bankes* [1902] 2 Ch. 333.

Essential validity

13-07 Essential validity is governed by the *lex situs* as regards immoveables.[29] As regards moveable property, it is governed by the proper law,[30] being the law with reference to which the contract was made, and which the parties intended to govern their rights and liabilities, or failing such ascertainable or deemed intention, by the law of most real and substantial connection, objectively construed.[31] Thus, for example, the proper law applies to all questions of substance such as:

(1) the validity of the provisions of the deed;
(2) the property rights of the parties; and
(3) whether the deed is revocable *sua natura*.

The meaning of the terms of the contract (including possibly identification of the property to be affected by the contract) is determined by the law governing interpretation of the contract (which might be expressed by the parties, or could be inferred from the language of the deed; failing which the putative proper law will apply).[32]

Effect of a change of domicile on a private marriage contract

13-08 A change of domicile does not affect the contractual rights of the parties,[33] though, as stated above, it may affect the capacity of the parties to revoke an existing agreement. This means that the rights of third parties, for example the husband's creditors, whose claims

---

[29] *Tezcan v Tezcan* (1992) 87 DLR 503 (BCCA).

[30] Scottish cases: *Countess of Findlater & Seafield v Seafield Grant*, February 8, 1814, F.C.; *Williamson v Taylor* (1845) 8 D. 156; *Scott v Sinclair* (1865) 3 M. 918; *Earl of Stair v Head* (1844) 6 D. 904; *Corbet v Waddell* (1879) 7 R. 200; *Brown's Trs* (1890) 17 R. 1174; *Brown* (1913) 2 S.L.T. 314; *Lister's J.F. v Syme*, 1914 S.C. 204; *Battye's Trs*, 1917 S.C. 385; *Montgomery v Zarifi*, 1918 S.C. (HL) 128; *Eadie's Trs v Henderson* (1919) 1 S.L.T. 253; *Goold-Stuart's Trs v McPhail*, 1947 S.L.T. 221; *Stevenson v Stevenson's Trs* (1905) 13 S.L.T. 457; *Black's Trs*, 1950 S.L.T. (Notes) 32; *Lashley v Hog* (1804) 4 Paton 581. English cases: *Van Grutten v Digby* (1862) 31 Beav. 561; *Chamberlain v Napier* (1800) 15 Ch. D. 614; *Re Hernando* (1884) 27 Ch. D. 284; *Re Fitzgerald* [1904] 1 Ch. 573; *Re Mackenzie* [1911] 1 Ch. 578; *Re Hewitt* [1915] 1 Ch. 228; *Re Duke of Marlborough v Att.-Gen. (No. 1)* [1945] Ch. 78. Irish case: *Re Lord Cloncurry's Estate* [1932] I.R. 687.

[31] See Ch.15, below. Consider *Re Bankes* [1902] 2 Ch. 333, and see also *Chamberlain v Napier* (1880) 15 Ch. D. 614 (Scots and English law governed different parts of the deed).

[32] *Corbet v Waddell* (1879) 7 R. 200; *Hope Vere v Hope Vere* (1907) 13 S.L.T. 774, aff'd by HL (1907) 15 S.L.T. 361; and *Drummond v Bell-Irving*, 1930 S.C. 704.

[33] *Shand-Harvey v Bennet Clark* (1910) 1 S.L.T. (Sh.Ct) 133. Contrast Belgian authority: *Duyrewaardt v Barber* (1992) 43 R.F.L. (3d.) 139 (B.C.C.A.), though see special circumstances, related and explained in Dicey and Morris, Fourth Cumulative Supplement to the 12th ed. (1997), p.171.

may be good by their own laws (*i.e.* by the law(s) governing the debt(s)), may be prejudiced by the pre-existing rights of the debtor's spouse under another law governing the debtor's marriage contract or matrimonial regime, in terms of which the spouse's rights have vested.[34]

Effect of divorce

There is a difficulty here in that it is clear that any forum, if **13–09** properly seised of jurisdiction in divorce, will apply its own law to the grounds of divorce and to the rules of property distribution upon divorce.[35] A Scots court probably will endeavour to give effect to parties' wishes as expressed by their contract, provided that the contract is valid, essentially and formally, and that the parties had capacity to enter into it.[36] Alternatively, the means and property of parties, to which the court will apply its own rules of distribution, might first have been determined (ie diminished) by the matrimonial property provisions of a foreign law.[37] It is possible that English courts are more dismissive than Scots courts of earlier arrangements made by private contract,[38] rendering the identity of the forum, and identification of the proper law as between Scots law and English law,[39] the more significant.[40] A legal system might have policy objections to agreements which envisage, or seek to regulate, ante-nuptially, property effects of the termination of the

---

[34] See, *e.g. Shand-Harvey v Bennet-Clark*, above.

[35] See, for Scots law, Family Law (Scotland) Act 1985, s.14(2)(h) (power to grant an incidental order, including an order setting aside or varying any term in an antenuptial or postnuptial marriage settlement) (but such an order may be made only if justified by the principles set out in s.9 of the Act); also ss.16 and 17 (judicial power to vary contractual terms agreed by parties to come into effect in the event of divorce or nullity).

[36] See Anton with Beaumont, pp.589–590; Clive, pp.255 and 321–322.

[37] Clive, p.256. But see *contra*, for English law, Clarkson & Hill, p.508. See also *S v S* [1997] 2 F.L.R. 100; *N v N* [1999] 2 F.L.R. 745; and *C v C* [2001] 1 F.L.R. 624. Note, however, that insofar as these authorities concern the staying of English divorce proceedings on a *forum conveniens* basis, they have been overtaken by the *lis pendens* system in Article 19 of Council Regulation 2201/2003. In view of recent controversial English divorce awards (*Miller v Miller*, and *McFarlane v McFarlane* [2006] UKHL 26); and *Martin-Dye v Martin-Dye* [2006] All E.R. (D) 369, generous to the weaker economic party, it is beyond doubt that the incidence of antenuptial ("prenuptial") settlements will increase, and the extent to which they may influence the terms of the divorce decree will become a pressing issue. The recent trend of English decisions is obviously significant in terms of choice of forum (*i.e.* in EU terms, forum first seised).

[38] *R v R* [1995] 1 F.C.R. 745; and see *F v F* [1995] 2 F.L.R. 45, and discussion and criticism thereof by Clarkson & Hill, p.508, who point out that such a summary dismissal hardly accords with parties' reasonable expectations.

[39] *R v R* [1995] 1 F.C.R. 745.

[40] See *e.g. Drummond v Bell-Irving*, 1930 S.C. 704; and *Montgomery v Zarifi*, 1918 S.C. (HL) 128.

marriage about to be entered into, but this seems unlikely in modern circumstances.[41]

No marriage contract

13–10 At common law, where parties did not make a private marriage contract, and did not impliedly consent to be governed by a statutory code, the rights of the husband and wife in *immoveables* was governed by the *lex situs*.[42] With regard to *moveables*, the test was more complex. It was essential to distinguish two different issues: *first*, what was the touchstone against which parties' rights were to be tested?;[43] *second*, could parties' rights change through the course of their marriage, following, for example, changes of domicile?[44]

Initially, there was a presumption to the effect that the rights of parties are/were to be determined by the law of the husband's domicile at the time of the marriage, but it seems clear that this presumption, or any more modern formulation of it, might be rebutted if there was express agreement that another law would govern, or if there was implied agreement to that effect, in that there was proof that the parties intended to set up home shortly in another legal system having a distinct matrimonial property regime (or having none), and they did in fact carry out their intention reasonably promptly. The guide was *Re Egerton*,[45] where not only did the parties after the marriage fail to effect their proposed removal to France, from the husband's domicile in England, until two years had elapsed, but it was held also that mere agreement to change to French domicile did not carry any inference that the parties had agreed to adopt French matrimonial property law. Nevertheless, Roxburgh, J left open the possibility of the use of intended matrimonial home as the base test in a suitable case.[46] In the normal case, though, the most likely applicable law would have been the matrimonial domicile (that is, in this context, the domicile of the married pair immediately after the marriage).

The question whether the rights of parties in property acquired during the marriage must be referred always and only to that law first "chosen" was something other than the *Egerton* issue. Civilian

---

[41] Yet see Clarkson, p.507.

[42] *Welch v Tennent* (1891) 18 R. (H.L.) 72.

[43] *i.e.* what was the first regulator of rights in moveables, at the point of marriage? Did rights "crystallise" at that point?

[44] *i.e.* was it possible that their rights in moveables acquired at different times during the marriage were governed by different laws?

[45] [1956] Ch. 593.

[46] Though the legal system to which the parties remove, at whatever speed and with whatever degree of decisiveness, may not admit "late entry". *Cf.* para.13–02, above.

systems typically prefer the "immutability" rule, by which the law governing matrimonial property rights at the outset, whatever that law may be, continue to regulate rights in acquisitions, wherever and whenever acquired, and no matter that the parties have changed domicile once or several times since marriage. The question was argued with full and learned citation of authority in the South African case of *Frankel v The Master*,[47] in which the decision (that the German law of the husband's domicile at the date of marriage would regulate the parties' rights in property *inter se* at all times thereafter even though within four months of marriage they had settled in Johannesburg, South Africa) was described as "a tribute which logic pays to certainty". Immutability is a principle which has merits and demerits: it has the merit of certainty, but the governing law thus identified may be that of the one legal system in the world to which the parties, erstwhile refugees, would not return.

The South African case of *Sperling v Sperling*[48] reveals that the South African conflict rules are disposed to apply the rules of that (initial and continuing) *lex causae* as they may prevail from time to time, *i.e.* if retrospective changes are made in the *lex causae*, the forum, subject to public policy, would accept them, demonstrating a very faithful allegiance to the chosen connecting factor and to the doctrine of "immutability".

In the United States mutability prevails, so that rights of parties in acquisitions during the course of marriage are referred to the domicile of the parties at the time of each acquisition.[49]

It is probable[50] that a middle path was taken in England and Scotland.[51] The only guide was the old case of *Lashley v Hog*,[52] which, on one reading, might be said to support the argument that property rights may change upon a change of domicile. It is just as likely, however, that *Lashley* properly is understood as a succession case.

The Scots position immediately before the 2006 Act, therefore, probably was that although (future) rights might change with a change of domicile, the domicile change must be effected by *both*

---

[47] (1950) 1 S.A.L.R. 220 (South Africa).
[48] 1975 (2) S.A. 707. Morris, p.435.
[49] See Davie, "Matrimonial Property in English and American Conflict of Laws" (1993) 42 ICLQ 855.
[50] Though see expressed doubts and exceptions: Cheshire & North, pp.1019–1021.
[51] Clive, p. 256, seems prepared to countenance, indeed approve, mutability, subject to protection of vested rights, in any case in which the significant features of *De Nicols* are absent. See *Kennedy v Bell* (1864) 2 M. 587, *per* the Lord Ordinary reported at 588.
[52] (1804) 4 Pat. 581; though see also *Clarke v Newmarsh* (1836) 14 S. 488; *Duchess of Buckingham v Winterbottom* (1851) 13 D. 1129; *Roe*, 1916 32 Sh.Ct Rep. 30; *Frankel v The Master* (1950) 1 S.A.L.R. 220 (South Africa); *Chiwell v Carlyon* (1897) 14 S.C. 61; *Re Bettinson* [1956] Ch. 67; *Re Egerton* [1956] Ch. 593.

parties, and vested rights in earlier acquired property would not be prejudiced.[53]

Family Law (Scotland) Act 2006, section 39

13–11 The following rules are laid down in section 39:

By section 39(1), the rights of spouses to each other's immoveable property arising by virtue of the marriage shall be determined by the *lex/leges situs*.[54] Moreover, by section 39(4), any question relating to the use of the contents of a matrimonial home, or to the use or occupation of a moveable matrimonial home, shall be determined by the law of the country in which the home is situated (for the time being, it is presumed, as the case may be).

By section 39(2), the rights of spouses to each other's moveable property arising by virtue of the marriage shall be determined by the law of the common domicile. The relevant time at which domicile is to be ascertained is not specified: it may be a reference to the domicile of the spouses at the date of acquisition of the property in question, or possibly to the immediate post-nuptial domicile. Section 39(5) provides that a change of domicile by one or both spouses shall not affect a right in moveable property which, immediately before the change, has vested in either spouse.[55] By section 39(3), where the parties are domiciled in different countries (when?), the spouses shall be taken to have the same rights in each other's moveable property arising by virtue of the marriage as they had immediately before the marriage (by which law?). This is an obscure provision, also subject to the provision on vested rights contained in section 39(5). It may mean that the parties are to be taken to have adopted for the future the matrimonial property rules existing in their respective antenuptial domiciles; but what if these systems are mutually inconsistent?

Section 39 shall not apply in relation to the law on aliment, financial provision on divorce, transfer of property on divorce or succession.

The need to legislate on these matters, after many years of quiescence, introducing provisions of variable clarity and quality, was not obvious, and in any event the wisdom of so doing in Scots law is doubtful in view of imminent EU developments.

---

[53] Dicey and Morris, Rule 150 (though noting a difference in Scots position, pp.1084–1085); Cheshire & North, pp.1019–1021. *Cf.* Clive, 14.127 *et seq.*

[54] *Ex facie* this appears simply to be a reiteration of the common law position. The advisability of encasing it in legislation is not beyond doubt since the phrase "arising by virtue of the marriage" not only begs the question, but raises the spectre of an incidental question on the point whether the marriage itself is valid. Admittedly, the same could be said of the rule at common law, but the absence of case law suggests that few problems have arisen.

[55] This is thought to be the common law rule of Scots and English law where there is no statutory or private regulation of matrimonial property.

B. Property Rights Arising from other Adult Relationships

Types of cohabitation—"*de facto*" and "*de iure*"

In the following discussion, *de facto* cohabitation is intended to **13–12** mean relationships not formalised by legal ceremony or registration process, but nevertheless attracting, to a greater or lesser extent as the case may be, financial/proprietary/succession consequences which arise by operation of law where the relationship in question satisfies the definition of cohabitation laid down by the legal system purporting to regulate that relationship. Of such a type is the cohabitation relationship to which are attached property, etc. consequences by the Family Law (Scotland) Act 2006, sections 25 to 30.

De iure cohabitation, on the other hand, denotes a relationship which is formally registered in accordance with the legal system which creates and regulates it. Of such a type is registered partner status.

De facto cohabitants, cohabiting in Scotland

In terms of Scots domestic law, sections 25 to 30 of the Family Law **13–13** (Scotland) Act 2006, endow "cohabitants"[56] with certain rights (*e.g.* in household goods, *per* section 26 and, *per* section 27, in money derived from a household allowance on property acquired out of such money). Section 28 states that where cohabitation ends otherwise than by death, a Scottish court may award a capital sum to the applicant, and grant an order in respect of any economic burden of caring for a child of the cohabitants. Application is permitted, *per* section 29, to the court by the survivor for provision on the death intestate of his/her cohabitant.[57]

It is implicit that application may be made for the rights provided for in the Act whenever Scots law is the *lex causae*. But the Act does not specify, from a conflict of laws perspective, when, or in what circumstances, the rights created therein should apply.

---

[56] "Cohabitant" means either member of a couple consisting of (a) a man and a woman who are (or were) living together as if they were husband and wife; or (b) two persons of the same sex who are (or were) living together as if they were civil partners: section 25(1). Further, *per* s.25(2), in determining whether a person is a cohabitant of another person, the court shall have regard to (a) the length of the period during which the parties have been living together (or lived together); (b) the nature of their relationship during that period; and (c) the nature and extent of any financial arrangements subsisting, or which subsisted during that period. It is unclear whether a Scottish forum will be prepared to take into account any period of cohabitation spent abroad (cf. and contrast *Walker v Roberts*, 1998 S.L.T 1133).

[57] See the Family Law (Scotland) Act 2006 (Commencement, Transitional Provisions and Savings) Order 2006 (SI 2006/212).

By inference, and arguing by analogy from the use of the matrimonial domicile in marriage cases, Scots law would be the *lex causae* in relation to rights arising during the cohabitation where the cohabitation is occurring in Scotland. This immediately raises temporal issues which, given the mobility of persons today, are not academic. At least it is clear that in respect of the rights of the survivor on the death intestate of the predeceaser, Scots law, if it is the *lex ultimi domicilii*, must be the *lex causae*.[58]

If a case were to arise with an actual or potential conflict of laws dimension (eg as regards the property consequences of cohabitation in Scotland of one or more foreign domiciliaries), guidance in solving such problems will require to be drawn from general conflict principles governing capacity to enter into legal relationships, recognition of status and its incidents, and public policy.

The 2006 Act contains no jurisdiction or choice of law rules with regard to *de facto* cohabitation. Thus, it remains uncertain in Scots law which law, for example, governs an individual's legal capacity to attain the status of cohabitant (for the purposes of section 25); and in what factual circumstances a Scottish court would be entitled to apply the provisions in the Act covering the personal, financial and proprietary consequences of cohabitation. The essential antecedent question, not addressed in the Act, is in what circumstances the Scottish courts have jurisdiction to rule on the financial/proprietary rights of cohabitants (including the question as to the extent of competence of the Scottish courts to regulate the distribution of cohabitants' foreign assets upon termination of their relationship).[59]

At this point one might summarise the position by stating that the 2006 Act introduces into Scots domestic law significant new rules relating to cohabitation *without* enacting when those rules shall apply. The provisions are incomplete. This is not to say that Scots conflict of laws cannot provide guidance and remedy, but it is regrettable to leave these important matters to speculation. Silence about jurisdiction is the most difficult to fill.[60]

De facto cohabitants, cohabiting outside Scotland

13–14 With regard to the proprietary consequences of a foreign *de facto* cohabitation, and in particular, the effect, if any, upon moveable and immoveable property situated in Scotland, it is likely that, in the first instance, the Scottish court would apply the "proper law of the cohabitation" (law of closest connection) to determine whether

---

[58] s.29(1)(b)(i).
[59] See Carruthers (2005), paras 2.51—2.62. Also *McKie v McKie* [1933] I.R. 464.
[60] Presumably jurisdiction could be established upon the presence of property within Scotland.

the statutory regime imposed by that law purported to have extraterritorial effect upon property belonging to the cohabitants and situated abroad. If the statutory regime (say, of community of property between cohabitants), or a private contractual arrangement between the cohabitants[61] did purport to affect *all* property belonging to the couple, the Scottish *lex situs* nevertheless would retain absolute control over any property situated within Scotland, and would have an undeniable right to recognise, or not, the purported extraterritorial proprietary effects of the statutory regime, and the purported effect of the parties' contractual arrangements. It is probable that the Scottish *lex situs* would recognise the purported proprietary effects of a *de facto* cohabitation, *inter partes*, but possibly not in the event of a competing claim to property in Scotland by a third party such as a creditor.[62]

The question whether a Scottish court would be entitled to apply the provisions of the Family Law (Scotland) Act 2006 to cohabitants would seem to rest upon the Scottish court having jurisdiction (the basis of which is not clear), and upon the individuals satisfying the section 25 meaning of cohabitants.

Foreign "*de iure*" cohabitants

Scots domestic law currently does not make provision for registered heterosexual partnerships. With regard to foreign *de iure* cohabitants, it is likely that the attitude of the Scots court would be similar to that outlined above in relation to *de facto* cohabitants cohabiting outside Scotland. In both instances, the likelihood of recognition is greater now that Scots law contains provision regulating certain proprietary and financial consequences of cohabitation, and same sex civil partnership.   **13–15**

It is likely that the Scots court would take a similar approach to that outlined above in relation to *de facto* cohabitants cohabiting outside Scotland. In both instances, the likelihood of recognition is greater now that Scots law contains provision (actual and proposed) regulating certain proprietary and financial consequences of cohabitation.

---

[61] *cf.* statutory recognition of private contractual arrangements in a matrimonial context: Family Law (Scotland) Act 1985, ss.14(2)(h), 16 and 17, and Family Law (Scotland) Act 2006, s.39(6)(b).

[62] At least where the third party, say, the creditor, is relying on *Scots* law. If, however, the proper law of the debt between the creditor and the debtor (*i.e.* the cohabitant) were, say, Dutch law, it would *not* be contrary to the reasonable expectations of the creditor to apply Dutch law rather than Scots law, and therefore, to prefer the claim to moveable property in Scotland of, say, the Dutch cohabitant (*cf. North Western Bank v Poynter, Son & Macdonald* (1894) 22 R. (H.L.) 1; *Scottish Provident Institution v Robinson* (1892) 29 S.L.R. 733).

Civil Partnership

13–16 In the case of civil partnerships registered in England, the property and financial consequences are detailed in Civil Partnership Act 2004, Part 2, Chapter 3. Part 3, Chapter 3, of the 2004 Act (civil partnership: Scotland) makes provision with regard to occupancy rights and tenancies. As regards the financial consequences of a civil partnership (registered in Scotland?), or of the death intestate of a civil partner (by inference, domiciled at death in Scotland), section 261(2) and Schedule 28 of the 2004 Act extend to civil partners, *mutatis mutandis*, the rules contained in the Succession (Scotland) Act 1964 concerning intestate and testate succession; rights in moveable property and money conferred by the Family Law (Scotland) 1985, and also the financial relief provisions of that Act upon dissolution of a relationship; and certain other miscellaneous legislative provisions concerning, *inter alia*, bankruptcy, damages, and housing. The new rights will arise whenever Scots law is the governing law, though there may well be doubt as to when this will be the case.[63]

Generally, with regard both to registered partnerships and regulation of *de facto* cohabitation, there is little if any express guidance on choice of law, which is a serious lack.

C. Proposed EU Green Paper: "Brussels III"

13–17 A European project is under way concerning *jurisdiction* and *judgments* in the area of matrimonial property. The proposal is at an early stage, with a Green Paper expected in 2006.[64] The preparatory research conducted in each Member State encompassed not only rules of matrimonial property, but also the property consequences for unmarried, cohabiting couples. The Hague Programme, however, refers only to *matrimonial* property issues. It is not clear whether the legislation soon to be proposed in this area will be restricted to the property of married persons (the rules, internal and conflict of laws, in several Member States concerning the property of unmarried, cohabiting parties being uncertain, underdeveloped, or on the brink of change), or whether the Programme has been drafted in deliberately opaque terms, to draw the focus away from the complex and controversial topic of the legal consequences of cohabitation. On current understanding, it is likely that complementary rules on *choice of law* will be produced, of equivalent scope (whatever that may be).

---

[63] *cf.* the position in relation to *de facto* cohabitants under the 2006 Act.
[64] The multi-annual programme adopted by the European Council at its meeting in the Netherlands on November 4 and 5, 2004, para.3.4.2. (Draft Multiannual Programme (Brussels, 27 October 2004) (JAI 408, 13993/04–LIMITE) (henceforth the "Hague Programme").

II.FINANCIAL CONSEQUENCES

A. Maintenance Obligations

Jurisdiction

The allocation of jurisdiction intra-EU is determined by Council **13–18** Regulation 44/2001. In terms of the Regulation, a person normally is sued in the country in which s/he is domiciled (Article 2), but one of the derogations to that rule concerns matters relating to maintenance. Article 5.2 states that: "A person domiciled in a Member State may, in another Member State, be sued . . . in matters relating to maintenance, in the *courts for the place where the maintenance creditor is domiciled or habitually resident* or, if the matter is ancillary to proceedings concerning the status of a person, in the court which, according to its own law, has jurisdiction to entertain those proceedings, unless that jurisdiction is based solely on the nationality of one of the parties." Thus, maintenance creditors can opt to sue either in the court for the Member State where the debtor is domiciled, or in the Member State where s/he (the creditor) is domiciled or habitually resident. The option is thought to confer an advantage on the maintenance creditor (the claimant payee), who is perceived as the weaker party.

What is a "matter relating to maintenance"? According to *Van den Boogard v Laumen*,[65] if a court judgment: "is designed to enable one spouse to provide for himself or herself or if the needs and resources of each of the spouses are taken into consideration in the determination of the amount, the decision will be concerned with maintenance. On the other hand, where the provision awarded is solely concerned with dividing property between spouses, the decision will be concerned with rights in property arising out of the matrimonial relationship and will not therefore be enforceable under the Brussels regime.[66]

Where Council Regulation 44/2001 does not apply, allocation of jurisdiction in matters relating to maintenance will be governed by rule 2(e) of Schedule 8 of CJJA 1982.[67]

Choice of law

Where a Scots court has jurisdiction in respect of a maintenance **13–19** claim, it will apply Scots law to the substance of the question.[68] This rule has been placed on a statutory basis by Family Law (Scotland)

---

[65] Case C-220/95 [1997] All ER 517. Also *De Cavel v De Cavel (No. 1)* Case 143/78 [1979] E.C.R. 1055 and *(No. 2)* Case 120/79 [1980] E.C.R. 731; and *Farrell v Long* Case C-295/95 [1997] All E.R. (E.C.) 449.

[66] Art.1.1; see Jenard and Schlosser Report, p.87. See now Council Regulation 44/2001, Art.1.2.a. *Cf.* Regulation 2201/2003, Art.1.3.e, and recital 8.

[67] See the Civil Jurisdiction and Judgments Order 2001 (SI 2001/3929).

[68] Family Law (Scotland) Act 1985, ss.1–7.

Act 2006, section 40, and is subject to the Maintenance Orders (Reciprocal Enforcement) Act 1972 (*qv*).

Enforcement of maintenance orders intra-UK

13–20 The Maintenance Orders Act 1950 governs the registration and enforcement of aliment or maintenance orders intra-UK.

Recovery of maintenance orders under Maintenance Orders (Reciprocal Enforcement) Act 1972, as amended[69]

13–21 For many years the enforcement of foreign maintenance orders for spouses and children gave rise to such practical difficulties that in many cases it was impossible to recover any sum whatsoever. As between Great Britain and the Commonwealth there have been statutory provisions since 1920 (Maintenance Orders (Facilities for Enforcement) Act 1920), but these were never entirely satisfactory,[70] and the 1920 Act did not apply to Scotland.

The Maintenance Orders (Reciprocal Enforcement) Act 1972,[71] was intended to facilitate the recovery of maintenance by or from persons in the UK, from or by persons in other countries.

Part I of the 1972 Act provides a system of registration and enforcement in the United Kingdom of maintenance orders made in reciprocating (mainly Commonwealth) countries.[72] The 1972 Act contains both "incoming" and "outgoing" registration provisions. Incoming orders are governed by sections 6 to 11 (section 6: registration in Scotland, *per* sheriff court, of maintenance order from reciprocating country; section 8: enforcement thereof; section 9: variation thereof[73]). Under these statutory rules, no provision is made to permit refusal to enforce such an order on the ground of public policy. This matter was raised in *Sethi*,[74] in which the husband sought reduction of the 1986 registration in Scotland of a maintenance order obtained against him by his wife in India. Lord Weir refused to accede to his request, holding that the terms of section 6 were mandatory, and observing that the pursuer ought to have challenged the original order (rather than its enforcement) as contrary to public policy.

Part II of the 1972 Act provides for reciprocal enforcement of claims for the recovery of maintenance in "Convention countries", being countries party to the 1956 New York (UN) Convention on

---

[69] By the Maintenance Orders (Reciprocal Enforcement) Act 1992.
[70] *Peagram* [1926] 2 K.B. 165; *Harris* [1949] 2 All E.R. 318.
[71] Providing for accession by the UK to the 1956 United Nations (New York) Convention on the Recovery Abroad of Maintenance.
[72] This replaces the Maintenance Orders (Facilities for Enforcement) Act 1920.
[73] *Killen v Killen*, 1981 S.L.T. (Sh.Ct) 77.
[74] 1995 S.L.T. 104.

the Recovery Abroad of Maintenance. Part II provides procedure for the transmission, not of maintenance *orders* (as in Part I), but of maintenance *claims*.

Part III of the 1972 Act deals with countries which are neither reciprocating countries, nor "Convention countries". Special bilateral arrangements may be made with countries, and if this is done, an Order in Council may be made under Part III, applying modified provisions of the 1972 Act to the country in question.[75]

Where the maintenance order emanates from a foreign legal system which does not fall to be regulated by the 1972 Act, the holder may seek "decree conform" from the Court of Session.[76]

Recovery of maintenance orders intra-EU

At present, a maintenance order may be enforced under the **13–22** Brussels regime, in the same way as ordinary commercial debts.[77] The main enforcement route within the EU is the general commercial enforcement procedure provided in Regulation 44/2001, but there is an alternative European Enforcement Order for Uncontested Claims,[78] which includes claims for maintenance payments.

Where EU Member States are party also to the 1956 New York Convention and/or the 1973 Hague Convention, questions of priority of instrument may arise. Such questions are answered at present by Council Regulation 44/2001, Article 67, to the effect that the maintenance creditor may choose which regime to follow.[79] In many cases, proceeding under Council Regulation 44 will be the preferred option.[80]

---

[75] *e.g.* Reciprocal Enforcement of Maintenance Orders (United States of America) Order 1995 (SI 1995/3345). Of particular significance are the arrangements made under this Part in relation to countries signatory to the 1973 Hague Convention on the Recognition and Enforcement of Decisions relating to Maintenance Obligations: see Reciprocal Enforcement of Maintenance Orders (Hague Convention Countries) Order 1993 (SI 1993/593).

[76] *qv* para.9–09.

[77] See paras 9–36 *et seq.*

[78] Regulation (EC) No 805/2004 of the European Parliament and of the Council of April 21, 2004 creating a European Enforcement Order for Uncontested Claims (OJ L143, 30/04/2004, pp.15–39). See paras 9–78 *et seq.*, above.

[79] See Anton with Beaumont at pp.562–563; Aird and Jameson note at para.20.46; and Clarkson & Hill, p.437. See below, however, changes under consideration in Proposal for Council Regulation on jurisdiciotn, applicable law, recognition and enforcement of decisions and co-operation in matters relating to maintenance obligations. COM (2005) 649 final, Proposal Art. 49.

[80] There are two valuable features of the Council Regulation 44/2001 enforcement route: it applies not just to court orders, but also to "authentic instruments", including registered Minutes of Agreement (Civil Jurisdiction and Judgments (Authentic Instruments and Court Settlements) Order 1993 (SI 1993/604); and now also Civil Jurisdiction and Judgments (Authentic Instruments and Court Settlements) Order 2001 (SI 2001/3928)); and under no circumstances can the foreign judgment be reviewed as to its substance (Reg.44, Art.36).

Proposal for a Council Regulation on jurisdiction, applicable law, recognition and enforcement of decisions, and co-operation in matters relating to maintenance obligations

13–23 A Green Paper was issued by the EU Commission in April 2004 on Maintenance Obligations, with a view to presenting a proposal for a Regulation on Maintenance Obligations.[81] The proposal was issued in December 2005.[82] According to the Commission, "[t]he recovery of maintenance claims in the Member States accounts for a vast mass of litigation as a result of the fragile state of family relationships". The Commission claims it is "a Community problem as a result of the free movement of Community citizens." There is doubt about the true volume of cases, but, nevertheless, there is an underlying economic imperative since Member States are concerned about the considerable sums which they may have to pay out to make up for the defaults of maintenance debtors.

The content of the proposed rules is underpinned by three aims, namely: simplification, certainty and effectiveness. What is envisaged is an instrument ambitious in scope, delivering "more than cosmetic changes to current mechanisms"[83]: the proposed Regulation deals with jurisdiction, applicable law, recognition and enforcement of decisions, and co-operation. The objective is that "[w]ithout damage to debtors' rights, a creditor should be able to obtain a decision enforceable throughout the territory of the European Union."[84]

With regard to jurisdiction, it is proposed to replace the rule contained in Article 5.2 of Council Regulation 44/2001 with those proposed in Articles 3 (general jurisdiction), 4 (prorogation of jurisdiction), and 5 (appearance of defendant). Article 6 concerns residual jurisdiction where no court of a Member State has jurisdiction pursuant to Articles 3 to 5. Articles 7 to 9 (*lis pendens*; related actions; seising of a court) mirror those contained in Council Regulation 44/2001.

The provisions on applicable law are contained in Chapter III, and are restricted to the determination of the law applicable to maintenance obligations, and should not determine the law applicable to the establishment of the family relationships on which the maintenance obligations are based (Article 12).[85] The principal

---

[81] COM (2004) 254 final.

[82] COM (2005) 649 final.

[83] Communication from the Commission to the Council calling on the Council to provide for measures relating to maintenance obligations taken under Art.65 of the Treaty establishing the European Community to be governed by the procedure laid down in Art.251 of that Treaty (COM (2005) 648 final), para.1.2.1 (hereinafter "Communication from the Commission to the Council").

[84] COM (2005) 649 final, Explanatory Memorandum, para.1.2.3.

[85] Proposal, recital 13.

choice of law rule (Article 13) is that maintenance obligations shall be governed by the law of the country of habitual residence of the creditor, though Article 13.2 makes provision for application of the law of the forum in certain circumstances. Article 13.1 and 13.2 are subject to 13.3, which permits application of a law of close connection, in particular that of the common nationality of creditor and debtor. Use of the connecting factor of nationality is not typical in the UK. Given the nature of the problem, it is not likely that the maintenance creditor and debtor will be habitually resident in the same country. While this is a variant of the rule of commonality which is becoming a favoured connecting factor in the drafting of choice of law rules, obviously the use of nationality is problematic with regard to multi-legal system States, such as the UK.

Notwithstanding the rules contained in Article 13, (restricted) party autonomy is permitted by Article 14.

The law designated by the Regulation shall be applied whether or not it is the law of a Member State; the universality principle (Article 18). Article 19 precludes the operation of *renvoi*. Article 20 contains the public policy exception, but derogates from this by stating that application of a provision of the law of a Member State designated by the Regulation shall not be refused on a public policy ground.[86]

By Article 25 a decision given in a Member State and enforceable there shall be recognised and enforceable in another Member State without the need for a declaration of enforceability, and without any possibility of opposing its recognition. There shall be no review of substance, except that at its own initiative, the Member State of enforcement may decide to limit the enforcement of the decision of the court of origin to partial enforcement, if complete enforcement would impact upon a part of the debtor's assets which is not attachable according to the law of the Member State of enforcement.

Article 33 lists the grounds upon which partial or total refusal or suspension of the enforcement of the decision of the court of origin may, at the request of the debtor, be granted (*e.g.* the debt has prescribed). By Article 34, at the request of the creditor, the court of origin may make an order for monthly direct payments addressed to the debtor's employer in another Member State, or to the bank in another Member State in which the debtor has an account. Furthermore, the creditor may ask the court of enforcement temporarily to freeze a bank account belonging to the debtor and situated in another Member State. These provisions, if implemented, would make more speedy and effective the enforcement of

---

[86] *cf.* Council Regulation 2201/2003, Art.25 (differences in applicable law). Note the erosion of Member State discretion.

maintenance obligations than the enforcement of any other pecuniary obligation, and therefore provide evidence of the Commission's determination to deliver its promise. Implementation and administration of the provisions of the proposed Regulation shall be assisted by "central authorities" in each Member State (Articles 40 to 47).

Procedure for implementing the proposed Regulation

A maintenance obligation "generally arises from a family relationship, but also [has] financial aspects, since the obligation generates a claim for a sum of money."[87] Strictly, therefore, this proposal has "aspects relating to family law", such as to bring it within the meaning of Article 67.5 of the Treaty establishing the European Community, which would mean that the (now standard) co-decision procedure is not applicable, and the proposed Regulation would require to be adopted by the Council, acting unanimously after consulting the European Parliament.

Given the hybrid status of maintenance obligations, there is a problem of characterisation. For example, maintenance is included within the scope of Council Regulation 44/2001 (even though family law matters are not included in that instrument), but is excluded from the scope of Council Regulation 2201/2003 (which concerns family law matters). The Commission has noted that where a matter is not concerned with the core aspects of family relationships, rigid application of Article 67.5 may be unsatisfactory.[88] In seeking an escape route from the strict application of Article 67.5, the Commission has called on the Council, in accordance with the second indent of Article 67.2, to decide, under the so-called *passerelle* manoeuvre, that the procedure established by Article 251 of the Treaty establishing the European Community (*i.e.* the co-decision procedure) is applicable in relation to maintenance obligations.

It should be noted that the UK and Ireland will require to opt-in to the Regulation if it is to apply in those States.

Hague Conference initiatives

Simultaneously, the Hague Conference has been engaged in preparatory work for a new, comprehensive Convention on Maintenance Obligations, building on the best features of the existing Hague Conventions[89] in the area of maintenance, and seeking to

---

[87] Communication from the Commission to the Council, Annex—Council Decision, recital 5.

[88] *ibid.*, para.2.

[89] *e.g.* 1973 Hague Convention on the Recognition and Enforcement of Decisions relating to Maintenance Obligations (falling under Pt III of the 1972 Act).

involve in this project the participation of non-Member States of the Conference, including in particular signatory states to the 1956 New York Convention. Discussions are expected to crystallise in 2007. According to the EU Commission, the exercises under way at the Hague and in Europe, respectively, are not contradictory, but complementary. Justification for specific Community solutions rests upon the different level of integration between EU Member States, compared with that between non-Member countries, and the scale of the objectives pursued by the EU. The European Community takes part in the Hague negotiations, and possibly in certain specific matters solutions adopted by the Hague Conference "could produce results which might prove transposable within the European Union".[90] However, ultimately, as among EU Member States, it is intended that the resultant EU Regulation on maintenance obligations would take precedence over any other international instrument.[91] The aim is simplicity and this requires "putting an end to the diversity of sources of the law in this field."[92] Consequently, not only shall the proposed Regulation, in relations among Member States, take precedence over relevant conventions and treaties to which Member States are parties (Article 49), but it shall replace, in matters relating to maintenance obligations, Council Regulation (EC) No 44/2001, and Council Regulation (EC) No 805/2004 (European Enforcement Orders). However, if the UK should decide not to opt in to the Proposal, these instruments will continue to apply in this matter.

B. Financial Provision upon Termination of Marriage and other Adult Relationships

Termination of marriage by foreign divorce

Provided that a foreign divorce is recognised in Scotland as valid, **13–24** and that the Scots court has jurisdiction,[93] any lack in the terms of the foreign decree in the matter of property distribution/financial provision now may be supplied.[94] It was not always so. There used to be a difficulty in that, if a foreign divorce was entitled to recognition in Scotland, the Scots courts could not award financial provision to one of the parties, since *ex hypothesi* the parties were no longer married to each other, and s/he had no title to ask, nor the Scottish/English court any jurisdiction to grant, an order which it thought desirable to append to the foreign decree. The problem

---

[90] COM (2005) 649 final, Explanatory Memorandum, para.1.1.2.
[91] COM (2005) 649 final, Proposal, Art.49.
[92] Explanatory Memorandum, para.1.2.1.
[93] Matrimonial and Family Proceedings Act 1984, s.28.
[94] *ibid.*, s.29.

was compounded by the proper reluctance of any foreign court otherwise competent to terminate the marriage (in the view of Scots/English law), to make an award in relation to immoveable property outside its territory. Hence, no provision would be made with regard to immoveable property in Scotland or England. As a result, as happened in *Torok*,[95] an unseemly race to the courthouse door might ensue. Law Commission discussion followed[96] and resulted in the enactment of provisions clothing the Scots and English courts with jurisdiction to make property provision in suitable cases. All were agreed that the rules must be strict, but separate legislative provision within the Matrimonial and Family Proceedings Act 1984 was made for Scotland and England, respectively, with the result that the same end was achieved by different rules.

The Scottish Law Commission "preferred legislation which identified certain cases as inappropriate in advance"; the Commission did not believe that actions for financial provision after foreign divorce would be frequent in Scotland and it did not favour the introduction of a special set of procedural rules for this limited situation.[97] The Scottish provisions are available after foreign divorce, or annulment,[98] and are contained in sections 28 and 29, stipulating a number of strict jurisdictional criteria, and additional conditions which must be satisfied before an award may be made. In Scotland, the remedy may be sought in the Court of Session or sheriff court.[99] A rare example in Scots law of the use of these provisions is *Tahir*.[1]

For England, the Law Commission preferred a solution which permitted the court, guided by a list of factors, to eliminate cases where an award would be inappropriate. In England, a party must first seek the leave of the court to apply for financial relief, which leave shall not be granted unless the court thinks there is substantial ground for the making of an application for such an order; further, the leave may be conditional.[2] Under the English rules, parties may apply for financial provision after foreign divorce, annulment or legal separation. Thus far, there have been a few English cases,[3] often to the effect that it is inappropriate to supply

---

[95] [1973] 1 W.L.R. 1066.
[96] *Financial Relief after Foreign Divorce*, Law Com. Working Paper No. 77.
[97] Miller, Annotations to Statute, Pt IV, General Note.
[98] s.29A, inserted by Family Law (Scotland) Act 1985.
[99] s.30.
[1] 1993 S.L.T. 194; and *Tahir (No. 2)* 1995 S.L.T. 451.
[2] 1984 Act, s.13.
[3] *e.g. Macaulay v Macaulay* [1991] 1 All E.R. 865; *Chebaro v Chebaro* [1987] Fam. 127; *Garcia v Garcia* [1991] 3 All E.R. 451; *M v M* [1995] 7 C.L. 64; *Jordan v Jordan, The Times*, July 29, 1999; *Emin v Yeldag* [2002] Fam Law 419; and *A v S* [2002] EWHC 1157.

the remedy,[4] or that the English court should not interfere where a foreign appropriate forum has made satisfactory provision.[5] The English provisions are contained in Part 3 of the Matrimonial and Family Proceedings Act 1984, and the Scottish provisions in Part 4.

Termination of civil partnership by foreign dissolution

In relation to financial provision available upon the foreign dissolu- **13–25** tion of a civil partnership, the Civil Partnership Act 2004 provides, in section 125 and Schedule 11, that where a civil partnership has been dissolved or annulled abroad, and the dissolution or annulment is entitled to be recognised as valid in Scotland, the Scots court may entertain an application by one of the former civil partners, or former ostensible civil partner, for an order for financial provision. The jurisdictional requirements and conditions clearly are modelled upon those contained in the Matrimonial and Family Proceedings Act 1984, sections 28 and 29. In such a case, the Scots court may make property orders in terms of the provisions of the Civil Partnership Act 2004. As with divorce,[6] the court will apply its own domestic law, *mutatis mutandis*, after taking jurisdiction in terms of section 125 of the Civil Partnership Act 2004[7] (financial provision after overseas proceedings). As regards civil partnerships dissolved or annulled in Scotland, there is provision in the 2004 Act in Schedule 28, Part 2 (and section 261), whereby the benefits conferred upon married persons by the Family law (Scotland) Act 1985 are extended, *mutatis mutandis*, to civil partners. Financial provision on termination of *de facto* cohabitation otherwise than by death is discussed above at paragraph 13–12.

---

[4] *Hewitson v Hewitson* [1995] 1 All E.R. 472: the Court of Appeal held that the purpose of the 1984 Act was to provide a remedy in exceptional cases, where persons divorced in foreign jurisdictions had been deprived of financial relief, which it would be proper for the English court to supply, *not* to provide financial relief claimed to arise from the status of cohabitation, even if the parties previously had been married. The sequel came before QBD in 1999, reported at [1999] Fam. Law 450, on the matter of alleged promise by the man to maintain the woman, including questions of the evidencing thereof, jurisdiction in which matter the English court yielded to the Californian court of the matrimonial domicile, which had also been the divorce forum, and which had made a clean-break order.

[5] *Holmes v Holmes* [1989] 3 All E.R. 786.

[6] Although there is a Green Paper on applicable law and jurisdiction in divorce matters, issued by EU Commission in 2005, the harmonisation plan does not extend, currently, to harmonisation of financial consequences of divorce.

[7] Sch.11, Pt 3 (Disposal of Applications).

370 International Private Law

Summary 13—Proprietary and financial consequences of marriage and other adult relationships

Property of married persons

1. Statutory community of goods

13–26 A foreign community of goods may have the same effect as a formal marriage contract, by creating indefeasible contractual rights in moveable and immoveable property, in the latter case subject to the acquiescence of the *lex situs*.

2. Private marriage contracts

The proper law is the law intended by the parties either expressly or by implication and, failing that, the law with which the deed has closest connection. It is usually presumed to be the law of the domicile of the granter. The 1980 Rome Convention has no application.

Capacity to grant a marriage contract is thought to be governed by the law of the domicile of the granter, or perhaps by the putative proper law.

Capacity to revoke a marriage contract is governed either by the putative proper law, or by the law of the domicile of the revoker at the date of purported revocation.

Formal validity—proper law or place of execution.

Essential validity—proper law (being the *lex situs* in relation to immoveables).

Divorce brings into operation the forum's own property provisions to apply on termination of marriage, but it is thought that a Scots forum would endeavour to respect the terms of the marriage contract.

3. No marriage contract

The Family Law (Scotland) Act 2006, section 39 has laid down a statutory rule concerning applicable law in relation to the rights of spouses to each other's immoveable and moveable property arising by virtue of the marriage.

Essentially, as at common law, questions in relation to immoveable property shall be determined by the *lex situs*.

Rights in each other's moveable property arising by virtue of the marriage shall be determined by the law of the common domicile (without specification as to tempus inspiciendum); and failing such common domicile, the spouses shall be taken to have the same rights to such property as they had immediately before the marriage.

A change of domicile by one or both spouses shall not affect a right in moveable property which immediately before the change has vested in either spouse.

Questions in relation to the contents of a matrimonial home shall be determined by the *lex situs* of the home.

Section 39 shall not apply to the law on aliment, financial provision on divorce, or transfer of property on divorce or succession; nor shall it apply to the extent that spouses agree otherwise.

Property rights arising from other adult relationships

Provision is made in the Family Law (Scotland) Act 2006 for **13–27** conferring upon cohabitants certain rights in property and upon death intestate of a predeceasing cohabitant, exigible where Scots law is the *lex causae*.

Maintenance obligations

Jurisdiction of the Scots courts rests upon Council Regulation **13–28** 44/2001, Articles 2 and 5.2, and otherwise upon CJJA 1982, Schedule 8, as amended.

Enforcement of orders intra-UK is governed by the Maintenance Orders Act 1950.

The Maintenance Orders (Reciprocal Enforcement) Act 1972, as amended, applies: Part I to reciprocating countries, Part II to 1956 New York Convention countries, and Part III to countries with which the UK has made bilateral arrangements.

Enforcement of orders intra-EU is governed mainly by Council Regulation 44/2001, subject to the exercise by parties of the option of proceeding under the 1972 Act, if applicable.

Financial provision upon termination of marriage and other adult relationships

Matrimonial and Family Proceedings Act 1984 permits a Scots court to make an award of financial provision following recognition of a foreign divorce or nullity.

Section 125 of the Civil Partnership Act 2004 endows the court with an equivalent power in relation to civil partnerships dissolved overseas.

CHAPTER 14

CONFLICT RULES AFFECTING CHILDREN

STATUS, PARENTAL RIGHTS AND RESPONSIBILITIES, ABDUCTION, GUARDIANSHIP AND ADOPTION

I. STATUS

LEGITIMACY

Legitimacy is the status acquired at birth by an individual born of **14–01** persons (a) whose marriage to each other is recognised as valid by Scots conflict rules[1]; or (b) in accordance with the conflict rule stated below.

The status of legitimacy may continue to be relevant in Scots conflict cases, even though in domestic law the Law Reform (Parent and Child) (Scotland) Act 1986 began a process of removing distinctions between children on the basis of having been born inside or outside marriage, by enunciating "the general principle of legal equality of children irrespective of their parents' marriage or lack of marriage to each other".[2] This process was completed by the Family Law (Scotland) Act 2006, which, by section 21, abolishes the status of illegitimacy. Section 21(2)(a) enacts a substitution in the 1986 Act, to the following effect:

> "No person whose status is governed by Scots law shall be illegitimate; and accordingly the fact that a person's parents are not or have not been married to each other shall be left out of account in—
>
> (a) determining the person's legal status; or

---

[1] The child of a voidable marriage which has been annulled has the status of legitimate child in Scots and English domestic law. See Law Reform (Miscellaneous Provisions) Act 1949, s.4; and Matrimonial Causes Act 1973, s.16 (providing for English law that decrees of nullity do not have retrospective effect).

[2] D. Nichols, *Annotations to Statute*, 1986 Act, s.1.

(b) establishing the legal relationship between the person and any other person."

This begs the question of when a person's status is governed by Scots law. There is a mutually dependent relationship between domicile and status in this area, domicile having been ascribed at birth according to status, but until the advent of the 2006 Act in Scotland, and still in England, the status of the individual was/is required to be/must be identified before domicile could/can be ascribed.[3] Since in terms of the 2006 Act, section 22, the domicile of a child at birth is ascribed according to the rules contained therein, and not according to status as having been born inside marriage or not, one must conclude that if, in terms of section 22, the child's domicile is Scots, his/her status cannot be one of illegitimacy. But if, by that section, his/her domicile is found to be other than Scots, his/her status must be determined by that other personal law,[4] whether or not it contains a distinction between legitimate and illegitimate.[5] Questions of legitimacy are most likely to arise now in relation to matters of testate succession, where the testator's intention must first be ascertained before identification of those entitled to succeed.[6] In the case of deeds executed after commencement of the 1986 Act, the Scots rule of construction will presume that the granter did not intend to make any distinction between children on the ground of status.[7]

Declarators of status

14–02 The Law Reform (Parent and Child) (Scotland) Act 1986 makes provision for declarators of status. By the 2006 Act, Schedule 2, the

---

[3] Domicile depended on legitimacy, but, as domicile determined status, legitimacy depended on domicile. There was, therefore, a problem of circularity of reasoning, which was apparent in theory but seemingly not often encountered in practice. See solutions suggested by Wolff (2nd ed.), p.109, and Anton (1st ed.) pp.345–346. Leslie, *Encyclopaedia*, p.239 pointed out that whether a posthumous child, or a child whose father is unknown, is legitimate, depended on the content of the mother's domicile on that matter.

[4] Reinforced by 2006 Act, s.41.

[5] Whether the status of illegitimacy by a foreign legal system of a party's personal law would be found to be against Scots public policy would depend upon the matter being capable of being raised in a Scots forum, and upon the context in which the matter arose. The existence of 2006 Act, s.41 suggests, however, that a foreign status of illegitimacy would not, *per se*, offend Scots public policy.

[6] See Ch.18.

[7] Law Reform (Parent and Child) (Scotland) Act 1986, s.1. The precursor of this provision, repealed by the 1986 Act, was the Law Reform (Miscellaneous Provisions) (Scotland) Act 1968 which reversed the common law presumption that the granter intended to favour only the legitimate. By the 1968 Act, the domestic rule of Scots law, in the case of deaths intestate after November 25, 1968, is that illegitimate children succeed to their parents' estate along with legitimate children. This rule therefore will apply to the succession to the intestate moveable estate of a deceased person dying domiciled in Scotland.

declarators which may be sought, in terms of section 7 of the 1986 Act, in the Court of Session or Sheriff Court, are those of "parentage or non-parentage". In domestic Scots law, therefore, the concept of illegitimacy, and associated terminology, has been removed. In Scots conflict law, the rule is as follows:

— a child born anywhere of a marriage valid in the view of Scots conflict law is legitimate;
— a child not born of a marriage valid by Scots conflict law is legitimate if he is legitimate by the law of the domicile of *each* parent at the date of his birth.[8] This rule is subject to the qualification that in the case of *intestate succession to immoveables* or *succession to a title of honour,* the child must be legitimate also by the *lex situs* or the law of the title, if such law so requires[9] (that is to say, the requirements of the *lex situs* or the law of the title, whatever they may be, must be satisfied[10]); and
— in the case of the child of a putative marriage,[11] his/her status will depend upon the law of the domicile of the innocent "spouse"; that is, he/she will be legitimate if that law recognises such marriages, and/or concedes that the issue thereof are legitimate.[12]

LEGITIMATION

Legitimation is the means by which the status of legitimacy is acquired by an illegitimate person subsequent to birth. The concept is no longer relevant in Scots domestic law, but may be **14–03**

---

[8] Dicey and Morris, Rule 99; though Anton with Beaumont, p.488 notes the absence of Scots authority. Separation of the issue of status from the issue of validity of marriage was a late development in English law and was not seen generally until *Re Bischoffsheim* [1948] Ch. 79. Children of polygamous marriages were considered legitimate in English law in advance of changes in the law permitting full recognition of the marriages whence they sprang: *Bamgbose v Daniel* [1955] A.C. 107. See *Khoo Hooi Leong* [1926] A.C. 529; *Hashmi* [1971] 3 All E.R. 1253; and *Motala v Att.-Gen.* [1990] 2 F.L.R. 261.

[9] Since the Law Reform (Parent and Child) (Scotland) Act 1986, there is no such requirement by domestic Scots law. As to succession to titles, see Legitimation (Scotland) Act 1968, s.8(4).

[10] *Birtwhistle v Vardill* (1840) 7 Cl. & F. 895; *Re Don's Estate* (1857) 4 Drewry 194; and *Shedden v Patrick* (1854) 1 Macq. 535 (although this may not be necessary as regards testate succession to land: *Re Grey's Trusts* [1892] 3 Ch. 88).

[11] According to Scots law, one contracted in the *bona fide,* but erroneous, belief on the part of one or both parties that they are free to marry; the error must be one of fact and not of law (Walker, *Principles of Scottish Private Law* (4th ed., 1988), p.285).

[12] *Smijth* (1918) 1 S.L.T. 156.

relevant where there is a foreign *lex causae*. There are two principal methods of legitimation and the Scots conflict rules are as follows:

Legitimation by subsequent marriage (*per subsequens matrimonium*)

14-04 It is thought that the conflict rule of Scots common law required capacity in the father so to legitimate the child by the law of the father's domicile only at the date of the marriage, and not necessarily at any earlier date.[13] What mattered therefore was whether the law of the father's domicile at marriage contained a doctrine of legitimation. This is confirmed by the somewhat circuitously worded section 5(2) of the Legitimation (Scotland) Act 1968.[14]

Legitimation was not part of English common law. English domestic law was inimical to legitimation, cleaving to the doctrine of indelibility of bastardy and being particularly hostile where succession to English land was concerned. It followed that the English conflict rule was strict. A child would be regarded as legitimated by the marriage of its parents only if the father had capacity so to legitimate by the law of his domicile *both* at the date of the child's birth *and* at the date of the subsequent marriage.[15] This rule was altered by the Legitimacy Act 1926, which introduced legitimation into English domestic law by section 1. In terms of section 8, the father need have such capacity by the law of his domicile only at the date of the marriage.[16] The English rules now are contained in the Legitimacy Act 1976, sections 2 and 3.

Legitimation by recognition (*per rescriptum principis*)

14-05 The English common law rule still applies so that a child will be regarded as having been legitimated in this manner only if its father had power so to legitimate him both at the date of the child's birth and at the date of the act of recognition.[17] The Scots

---

[13] See *Udny* (1869) M. HL 89; *Munro* (1837) 16 S. 18 confirmed by HL on appeal (1840) 1 Rob. 492; *McDouall v Adair* (1852) 14 D. 525; *Aikman* (1859) 21 D. 757; aff'd (1861) 23 D. (H.L.) 3; and *Blair v Kay's Trs*, 1940 S.L.T. 464.

[14] Legitimation does not have retrospective effect under Scots law: Legitimation (Scotland) Act 1968, ss.1, 4, 5(3). R.D. Leslie, *Stair Memorial Encyclopaedia*, p.239.

[15] *Re Goodman's Trusts* (1881) 17 Ch. D. 266.

[16] *cf. Re Askew* [1930] 2 Ch. 259: since English law at the date in question would not have considered the child to be legitimate, the benefit of legitimate status was conveyed to the child through operation of the doctrine of *renvoi*.

[17] *Re Luck's Settlement Trusts* [1940] Ch. 864. See also *Kelly v Marks*, 1974 S.L.T. 118.

conflict rule, less strict, probably is the same as that which obtains in cases of legitimation by subsequent marriage, requiring capacity to legitimate only at the date of act of recognition.[18]

II. PARENTAL RIGHTS AND RESPONSIBILITIES

The Borras Report[19] stated that family law, including the law in **14–06** relation to children, should form part of the phenomenon of European legal integration. For several years there has existed a number of international conventions dealing with child matters, including: the 1961 Hague Convention concerning the Powers of Authorities and the Law Applicable in respect of the Protection of Minors (to which the UK is not a party); the 1980 Hague Convention on the Civil Aspects of International Child Abduction[20]; the 1980 Council of Europe Convention on the Recognition and Enforcement of Decisions concerning Custody of Children[21]; and the 1996 Hague Convention on Jurisdiction, Applicable Law, Recognition, Enforcement and Co-operation in respect of Parental Responsibility and Measures for the Protection of Children.[22] Arguably, no European intervention in relation to parental rights and responsibilities would have been necessary had all the EU Member States ratified the 1996 Hague Convention, but in September 1995 the Council of Ministers of the EU concluded that it was necessary to make provision for parental responsibility matters, in the form of measures supplementary to those laid down in the 1996 Convention.[23] The only perceived benefit of introducing special EU rules in addition to the Hague rules was that it would fill the gap where any Member State decided not to ratify the 1996 Hague Convention, and also that it would confer jurisdiction on the European Court of Justice to interpret the provisions and thereby bring some uniformity of interpretation. The Borras Report concluded in 1998 that the negotiating and drafting work had been laborious, but fruitful (paragraph 10): the result was

---

[18] Anton with Beaumont, p.495.
[19] A. Borras, Explanatory Report on the Convention on Jurisdiction and the Recognition and Enforcement of Judgments in Matrimonial Matters and in Matters of Parental Responsibility (OJ 1998 C221/27) (henceforth "Borras Report").
[20] See paras 14–27 *et seq.*, below.
[21] See para.14–27, below.
[22] See para.14–24, below.
[23] Borras Report, para.9.

Council Regulation 1347/2000,[24] itself succeeded rapidly by Council Regulation 2201/2003.[25]

BACKGROUND

Council Regulation 1347/2000

14–07 Regulation 1347 set out rules for jurisdiction and recognition and enforcement of judgments in matrimonial matters and matters of parental responsibility for the children of both spouses rendered on the occasion of the matrimonial proceedings. The instrument did not cater for all children, or for all parental responsibility issues. Whilst it covered both biological and adopted children of the couple, it did not provide for the more general concept of "children of the family" (a term familiar in Scots law, but not in all other Member States). It was soon apparent that a further instrument was required, with a wider remit concerning children.

French Access Initiative[26]

On July 3, 2000, France presented an initiative for a Council Regulation on the mutual enforcement of judgments on rights of access to children. The initiative was to facilitate, through the abolition of (*exequatur*) procedural hurdles, the exercise of cross-border rights of access in the case of divorced or separated couples. However, the Justice and Home Affairs Council of the EU felt that work on the French initiative could proceed only in parallel with extension of the scope of Regulation 1347. Therefore the Commission presented on March 27, 2001 a working document on the mutual recognition of decisions on parental responsibility. Ultimately, Regulation 1347 was repealed by Regulation 2201.

COUNCIL REGULATION 2201/2003

14–08 Since March 1, 2005, jurisdiction, recognition and enforcement of judgments on parental rights and responsibilities have been governed by Regulation 2201. The prime importance of Regulation

---

[24] Council Regulation (EC) No. 1347/2000 on Jurisdiction and the Recognition and Enforcement of Judgments in Matrimonial Matters and in Matters of Parental Responsibility for Children of Both Spouses (henceforth "Regulation 1347").

[25] Council Regulation (EC) No. 2201/2003 concerning Jurisdiction and the Recognition and Enforcement of Judgments in Matrimonial Matters and in Matters of Parental Responsibility for Children of Both Spouses, repealing Regulation (EC) No. 1347/2000 (henceforth "Regulation 2201"). See Practice Guide for the Application of the New Brussels II Regulation (Commission Services in consultation with the European Judicial Network in Civil and Commercial Matters) (henceforth "Practice Guide").

[26] Initiative of the French Republic with a view to adopting a Council Regulation on the Mutual Enforcement of Judgments on Rights of Access to Children (OJ 2000 C234/7).

2201 *quoad* proceedings relating to children, lies in its severing of the link with matrimonial proceedings. Regulation 2201 covers judgments on parental responsibility over a child, irrespective of his parents' marital status, thereby ensuring equality of treatment for all children. The objective of Community action in Regulation 2201 is to protect the child's best interests, and to give expression to the child's fundamental right to maintain on a regular basis a personal relationship and direct contact with both parents, as laid down in Article 24 of the Charter of Fundamental Rights of the EU.[27]

Regulation 2201 lays down rules on jurisdiction (Chapter II), recognition and enforcement (Chapter III), and cooperation between central authorities (Chapter IV) in the field of parental responsibility, and contains specific rules on child abduction and access rights.[28] The Regulation applies to *all* civil matters concerning the "attribution, exercise, delegation, restriction or termination of parental responsibility."[29] In contrast to Regulation 1347, Regulation 2201 applies to all decisions on parental responsibility issued by a court of a Member State. However, the following matters are not included in the scope of the Regulation: criminal aspects of child protection; criminal offences committed by children; adoption, emancipation, the child's names; measures taken as a result of criminal offences committed by children; and maintenance obligations.[30] The Regulation does not apply to general public law issues concerning education, health, immigration or asylum.[31] Nor does it apply, within private law, to paternity issues, since establishing parenthood is thought to be quite different from the matter of attributing parental responsibility.[32]

Mostly parental responsibilities relate to a child's person, but they may relate also to a child's property.[33] It may be necessary to take certain protective measures concerning a child's property, for example to appoint a person or group to assist and represent the child in relation to that property. The Regulation applies to any such protective measure that may be necessary for the administration or sale of the property (*e.g.* if the child's parents are in dispute about the property). Measures relating to the child's property which are not protective in nature are not covered by the Regulation. Whether or not a measure is protective will be decided on a case-by-case basis.

---

[27] Reg.2201, Proposal Explanatory Memo, p.2.
[28] Arts 1.1.b; 1.2; and 2.7.
[29] Art 1.1.b.
[30] See recitals 10 and 11, and Art.1.3. The last is perhaps surprising since maintenance obligations and parental responsibilities often are dealt with in the same court action (but maintenance obligations are covered by Reg.44/2001 as a civil and commercial matter).
[31] Though see text at n.37, below.
[32] Recital 10.
[33] See para.14–50 below.

Parental responsibility

14–09 For the purposes of Regulation 2201, "parental responsibility" means "all rights and duties relating to the person or property of a child which are given to a natural or legal person by judgment, by operation of law or by an agreement having legal effect. The term shall include rights of custody and rights of access."[34] The list of matters in Article 1.2 concerning the attribution, exercise, delegation, restriction or termination of "parental responsibility" is illustrative, not exhaustive. The expression covers not only rights of custody[35] and access,[36] but also matters such as guardianship and the placement of a child in a foster family, or in institutional care (covering cases where a specific matter of parental responsibilities is a "public law" measure).[37] The holder of parental responsibilities may be a natural person, or a legal person. The term parental responsibilities is used in the 1996 Hague Convention (*qv*), and the Borras Report says that it has a "degree of unifying potential".[38]

Rules of jurisdiction in Regulation 2201

14–10 Chapter II, Section 2 lays down rules of jurisdiction concerning parental responsibility. The jurisdiction rules listed in Articles 8 to 15 establish a complete system of grounds of jurisdiction to determine the courts of which Member States are competent. The question which court is competent within a particular Member State (*e.g.* sheriff court or Court of Session) is answered by domestic procedural rules.[39] The grounds of jurisdiction in matters of parental responsibility are said to be shaped in light of the best interests of the child, "in particular the criterion of proximity".[40]

Article 8—general jurisdiction[41]

14–11 "The fundamental principle of the Regulation is that the most appropriate forum for matters of parental responsibility is the relevant court of the Member State of the habitual residence of the

---

[34] Art.2.7.

[35] Art.2.9: "Rights of custody" shall include rights and duties relating to the care of the person of a child, and in particular the right to determine the child's place of residence.

[36] Art.2.10: "Rights of access" shall include the right to take a child to a place other than his habitual residence for a limited period of time.

[37] Art.1.2.

[38] Para.24.

[39] Practice Guide, p.11.

[40] Recital 12: "This means that jurisdiction should lie in the first place with the Member State of the child's habitual residence, except for certain cases of a change in the child's residence or pursuant to an agreement between the holders of parental responsibility."

[41] Practice Guide, p.12.

child".[42] The concept of habitual residence is not defined, but will be determined by the judge in each case on the basis of factual elements, and in light of the objectives and purpose of the instrument. Once a competent court is seised, in principle it retains jurisdiction even if the child acquires habitual residence in another Member State during the course of the proceedings.[43] This important principle is effected by Article 9 *et seq.* The competence of jurisdiction is determined at the time the court is seised; a change of habitual residence while the action is proceeding does not generally entail a change of jurisdiction.

Article 9—continuing jurisdiction of child's former habitual residence[44]

The Practice Circle made clear that when a child moves from one **14–12** Member State to another, it is often necessary to review access or contact arrangements. Article 9 "encourages the holders of parental responsibility to agree upon the necessary adjustments of access rights before the move."[45] Any person who can no longer exercise access rights (because of the removal of the child to a new habitual residence) can apply for an appropriate adjustment of access rights by the court which granted them (*i.e.* the former habitual residence of the child) for a period of three months following the move. During this three-month period, the courts of the new Member State do not have jurisdiction in matters of access rights. Article 9 deals only with access rights; it does not apply to other matters of parental responsibility.

For Article 9 to apply, the following conditions must be satisfied:

(1) The courts of the Member State of origin must have issued a decision on access rights (otherwise the Member State of the child's new habitual residence would have jurisdiction under Article 8);
(2) The removal of the child to the new habitual residence must be lawful (otherwise, see Article 10);
(3) It is operative only during the three-month period immediately following the child's physical removal;
(4) The child must have acquired habitual residence in the new Member State during the three-month period (otherwise the Member State of origin would have Article 8 jurisdiction);

---

[42] Practice Guide, p.12.
[43] *ibid.*
[44] *ibid.*
[45] *ibid.*, p.13.

(5) The holder of the access rights must still be habitually resident in the Member State from which the child was removed (the Member State of origin); and

(6) The holder of the access rights must not have accepted the change of jurisdiction.[46]

Articles 10 and 11—jurisdiction in cases of child abduction; return of the child

14–13 These provide special rules requiring closer examination (*qv*).

Article 12—prorogation of jurisdiction

14–14 This provides very limited scope to seise a court of a Member State in which the child is not habitually resident. The basis of prorogation is that the matter of parental responsibility is connected with a related, pending consistorial proceeding, or that the child has a substantial connection with that Member State.[47] Article 12 covers two quite different situations: Article 12(1) and (2) provide for the related consistorial proceedings ground, whereas Article 12(3) provides for the substantial connection ground. The reference in Article 12(1)(b) to the "superior interests of the child" should be explained. This differs from the term "best interests of the child" in Article 12(3)(b). However, since the non-English versions of the Regulation employ identical wording in both paragraphs, no significance is thought to attach to the difference in wording in the English text.

Article 13—jurisdiction based on child's presence

14–15 If it should be impossible to determine the child's habitual residence, and if Article 12 does not apply, then Article 13 allows a Member State court to decide matters of parental responsibilities in relation to a child who is present in that Member State.[48] This would be capable of applying to refugee and asylum children.[49]

Article 14—residual jurisdiction

14–16 If no court has jurisdiction pursuant to Articles 8 to 13, then the Member State court may found its jurisdiction on the basis of its own national rules.[50]

---

[46] Practice Guide, p.13–14.

[47] *ibid.*, p.16. *cf. C v FC* [2004] 1 F.L.R. 317.

[48] Practice Guide, p.17.

[49] *cf.* ss.10 and 12 of the Family Law Act 1986, and at common law in Scotland *Oludimu*, 1967 S.L.T. 105.

[50] *i.e.* ss.9–18, Family Law Act 1986, at para.14–44 below. *Cf.* the operation of the Domicile and Matrimonial Proceedings Act 1973 in cases where consistorial jurisdiction cannot be exercised under Art.3 of Reg.2201/2003.

Article 15—transfer to a court better placed to hear the case

Exceptionally, a court which is seised of a case (the court of origin) **14–17** may transfer it, in whole or in part, to a court of another Member State if that Member State is "better placed" to hear the case. Once a case has been transferred to the second Member State, it cannot be further transferred to a third Member State (recital 13). This admission, though tentative, of the principle of judicial discretion, at the heart of a new Brussels regime instrument, is worthy of remark. The circumstances in which the discretion may be exercised, and how it shall be done, are set out in Article 15(2) to 15(6).[51]

Conflicting jurisdictions

Generally, the treatment of allocation of jurisdiction in a case of **14–18** concurrent proceedings is determined by the *lis pendens* principle.[52] Hence, where proceedings relating to parental responsibility concerning the same child and involving the same cause of action are brought before courts of different Member States, the court second seised shall of its own motion stay its proceedings until such time as the jurisdiction of the court first seised is established.

Recognition and enforcement of judgments

As in the case of consistorial decrees, mutual recognition is a main **14–19** objective of the Regulation, and the grounds of non-recognition of judgments relating to parental responsibility are relatively few. These are contained in Article 23: a judgment relating to parental responsibility shall not be recognised:

   (a) if such recognition is manifestly contrary to the public policy of the Member State in which recognition is sought taking into account the best interests of the child[53];

   (b) if it was given, except in case of urgency, without the child having been given an opportunity to be heard, in violation of fundamental principles of procedure of the Member State in which recognition is sought;

   (c) where it was given in default of appearance if the person in default was not served with the document which instituted the proceedings or with an equivalent document in sufficient time and in such a way as to enable that person to

---

[51] Practice Guide, pp.18–21.
[52] Art.19. See paras 12–12 and 12–13 above.
[53] This "public policy" clause is unusual in the qualification, "taking into account the best interests of the child"; by which law are the best interests of the child to be determined? Presumably this must lie within the discretion of the forum, probably applying its own law.

      arrange for his or her defence unless it is determined that such person has accepted the judgment unequivocally;

(d) on the request of any person claiming that the judgment infringes his or her parental responsibility, if it was given without such person having been given an opportunity to be heard;

(e) if it is irreconcilable with a later judgment relating to parental responsibility given in the Member State in which recognition is sought;

(f) if it is irreconcilable with a later judgment relating to parental responsibility given in another Member State or in the non-Member State of the habitual residence of the child provided that the later judgment fulfils the conditions necessary for its recognition in the Member State in which recognition is sought; or

(g) if the procedure laid down in Article 56 has not been complied with.

The jurisdiction of the court of the Member State of origin may not be reviewed, nor may the test of public policy be applied to the rules relating to jurisdiction.[54]

Enforceability

Article 28: Enforceable judgments

14–20 A judgment on the exercise of parental responsibility in respect of a child given in a Member State which is enforceable in that Member State and has been served, shall be enforced in another Member State when, on the application of any interested party, it has been declared enforceable there. However, in the United Kingdom, such a judgment shall be enforced in England and Wales, in Scotland or in Northern Ireland only when, on the application of any interested party, it has been registered for enforcement in that part of the UK.

Where application for a declaration of enforceability has been made, the court shall give its decision without delay. Submissions by the child, or by the person against whom enforcement is sought, will not be admitted at this stage. The judgment may not be reviewed as to its substance,[55] and the application may be refused only on the ground of one of the reasons specified in Articles 22 to 24. Article 33 sets out the rules for appealing against the decision.

---

[54] Art.24.
[55] Art.31.

Rights of access

The 1980 Hague Convention does not guarantee the enforcement **14-21** of access rights in the same way as it seeks to uphold custody rights, but Article 21 of that instrument binds Central Authorities to promote the peaceful enjoyment of access rights and the fulfilment of any conditions to which the exercise of those rights shall be subject. They shall take steps "to remove, as far as possible, all obstacles to the exercise of such rights".[56] The French Initiative on Rights of Access[57] having expedited agreement on parental responsibilities generally, it is not surprising to find a specific provision (Article 48) in Regulation 2201, concerned with making practical arrangements for the exercise of rights of access.

International co-operation

Implementation of Regulation 2201 is facilitated by the provisions **14-22** of Chapter IV (cooperation between Central Authorities in matters of parental responsibility).

Disconnection

Finally, it is necessary to consider the disconnection clause[58] which **14-23** specifies the relationship of Regulation 2201 with other cognate instruments, and ranks them *inter se*. By far the most important point to note is that while Regulation 1347 was subordinate to the 1980 Hague Convention, Regulation 2201 takes precedence over it.[59]

This means that where child abduction matters arise under international instruments, the rules of the 1980 Hague Convention

---

[56] Art.21. *Cf. Re J (A Minor)* [1989] 3 All E.R. 590; *C, Petr* [1997] G.W.D. 23–1132; and *Donofrio v Burrell*, 2000 S.L.T. 1051. See Norrie, "The Hague Convention, Rights of Contact, and s. 2(3) and (6) of the Children (Scotland) Act 1995", 1997 S.L.T. 173. *Cf.* Council of Europe Convention (*qv*), Art.11: *Joffre*, 1992 G.W.D. 27–1522; and *Re H* [1994] 1 All E.R. 812. For a UK example, see *Clarke v Clarke*, 1993 G.W.D. 16–1030. See Crawford, 1992 J.R. 192.

[57] At para.14–07, above.

[58] See Arts 59–63, in particular Art.60.

[59] By means of the European Communities (Matrimonial and Parental Responsibilities Jurisdiction and Judgements) (Scotland) Regulations (SSI 2005/42), appropriate amendments have been made to relevant legislation, including in this regard the Child Abduction and Custody Act 1985, the Family Law Act 1986, and the Children (Scotland) Act 1995. The purpose of the secondary legislation is to ensure that domestic legislation complies with Regulation 2201, to the effect that: the 1985 Act will operate so as to give precedence to relevant provisions of the Regulation over those of the 1980 Hague Convention; the 1995 Act will operate subject to the rules of jurisdiction contained in the Regulation; and under the 1986 Act, it is possible for a Scots court to sist an action when transferring jurisdiction to the court of another Member State under Art.15 of Regulation 2201.

are subject to the overriding direction of Regulation 2201 in a qualifying case.[60]

1996 HAGUE CONVENTION

14–24 A further development in this area of the conflict of laws is the 1996 Hague Convention on Jurisdiction, Applicable Law, Recognition, Enforcement and Co-operation in respect of Parental Responsibility and Measures for the Protection of Children. The 1996 Convention was signed on April 1, 2003 by the then 14 EU Member States. Only after ratification or accession by any individual Member State, however, will the 1996 Convention enter into force in that Member State. While the EU has given Member States authority to sign the Convention, it has not yet given permission to accede to or ratify it, and so the Convention is not yet in force in the UK.

It is hoped that the Convention will make a valuable contribution to the protection of children in parental responsibility and child protection cases that transcend the boundaries of Europe, and complement Community rules. Its quadruple nature as a conflict of laws instrument is notable.

One of the great merits of the Convention is its comprehensive scope in terms of subject matter, applying equally to the protection of a child's person and property. It applies to all children, from birth to 18 years, and deals with both public law and private law matters, where these are not expressly excluded from the Convention as having been covered already by other Hague Conventions. The Convention is limited to matters of child protection or child law matters, and does not cover matters of general application having some tangential child law implications which have their own private international law rules.

The provisions on jurisdiction and recognition and enforcement of judgments concerning parental responsibility are similar in design and content to those in Regulation 2201. The main ground of jurisdiction under the 1996 Convention is the Contracting State of the habitual residence of the child (Article 5), and there are various subsidiary bases of jurisdiction (Articles 7 to 14).

Unlike Regulation 2201, the 1996 Hague Convention lays down rules concerning applicable law (Articles 15 to 22), the general rule being that the *lex fori* shall apply.

Article 61 of Regulation 2201 ranks the Regulation above the relevant provisions of the 1996 Convention where the child is habitually resident in an EU Member State.

---

[60] *i.e.* abduction of a child from one EU Member State to another EU Member State, both of which are parties to the 1980 Hague Convention. See paras 14–34 *et seq.*, below.

III. INTERNATIONAL CHILD ABDUCTION

HISTORICAL BACKGROUND

At common law in Scotland questions of custody were regarded as **14–25** pertaining to status.[61] Accordingly, the court of the father's domicile was regarded as the court of pre-eminently suitable jurisdiction.[62] Custody orders made by the court of the father's domicile were accorded the greatest respect.[63] As time passed, this was tempered by an appreciation that the Scots court, in granting an order or withholding recognition of a foreign custody order, should regard as paramount the best interests of the child, and should be sensitive also to the need to return the child to the "natural" forum, if foreign, there to have the substantive custody issue determined.[64] This remains the approach of the Scots court in its treatment of incoming common law cases of alleged child abduction.[65]

In England the custody jurisdiction was regarded as a manifestation of the protection afforded by the State to its residents, or alternatively by the national law in exchange for the allegiance of its nationals. To this was added a measure of judicial discretion.[66] Moreover, the English courts were doubtful about the suitability of domicile as a connecting factor in these cases given that the determination of domicile is not a speedy exercise.[67] In the matter of recognition, as the law developed, the English courts too displayed great concern for the best interests of the child in

---

[61] The terminology has changed. For English law, see the Children Act 1989. For Scotland, the Children (Scotland) Act 1995 replaces "custody" and "access" with "residence" and "contact": the new language speaks of "parental responsibilities" and "parental rights". In the context of intra-U.K. custody matters, strictly one should speak of a "Part 1 Order" (that is, under Family Law Act 1986, Pt 1).

[62] Hence the Scots court would consider itself of pre-eminent jurisdiction if the father was of Scots domicile: *Ponder*, 1932 S.C. 233; *McLean*, 1947 S.C. 79; *Re B's Settlement* [1940] Ch. 54; *Brown*, 1948 S.L.T. 189; *Babington*, 1955 S.C. 115; *Kitson*, 1945 S.C. 434; *McShane*, 1962 S.L.T. 221; and *Shanks*, 1965 S.L.T. 330. Crawford, "International Child Abduction" (1990) 35 J.L.S.S. 277.

[63] *Westergaard*, 1914 S.C. 977; *Radoyevitch*, 1930 S.C. 619.

[64] *McKee* [1951] A.C. 352; *Battaglia*, 1967 S.L.T. 49; *Sargeant*, 1973 S.L.T. (Notes) 27; *Kelly v Marks*, 1974 S.L.T. 118; *Lyndon v Lyndon*, 1978 S.L.T. (Notes) 7; *Campbell v Campbell*, 1977 S.L.T. 125; and *Thomson, Petr*, 1980 S.L.T. (Notes) 29.

[65] See para.14–47, below.

[66] *Kermot* [1965] Ch. 217; *Re P* [1965] Ch. 568; *Re H (No.1)* [1966] 1 All E.R. 886; *Re E* [1967] Ch. 287; *Re T* [1968] Ch. 704; *Re A* [1970] Ch. 665; and *Fabbri (No.1)* [1962] 1 All E.R. 35. There was also a jurisdiction if the child was resident in Scotland and the protection of the court was needed in the interests of the child: *Oludimu*, 1967 S.L.T. 105.

[67] See, *e.g. Re P (GE) (An Infant)* [1964] 3 All E.R. 977, *per* Lord Denning at 980–981.

preference to adherence to a rigid rule of recognition.[68] Between the courts of the neighbouring UK legal systems, it was said that neither system was avid of jurisdiction,[69] but there is no doubt that in this area of the conflict of laws there was a degree of friction.[70]

CURRENT RULES

14–26 International child abduction disputes now fall into three categories:

> (1) cases regulated by international instrument;
> (2) intra-UK cases; and
> (3) cases governed by common law rules.

The rules to be applied will depend largely on the identity of the country(ies) to/in and from which the child has been (wrongfully) removed/retained.[71] In the context of the international instruments, not only must the circumstances fall within those covered by the particular instrument, but the date of the circumstances must post-date the coming into effect of the instrument in the relevant country(ies).[72]

CASES REGULATED BY INTERNATIONAL INSTRUMENT

Cases falling under the 1980 Hague Convention and/or the Council of Europe Convention

14–27 There has been a great change in the civil law governing cross-border child abduction cases as a result of the 1980 Hague Convention on the Civil Aspects of International Child Abduction,[73] and the 1980 Council of Europe Convention on Recognition and Enforcement of Decisions concerning Custody of Children and on the Restoration of Custody of Children.[74] The United Kingdom

---

[68] *McKee* [1951] A.C. 352; *J v C* [1970] A.C. 668.

[69] *Re B's Settlement* [1940] Ch. 54; *Re X's Settlement* [1945] Ch. 44.

[70] Contrast, later, *e.g. Davidson v Davidson*, 1997 G.W.D. 2–39.

[71] See E.B. Crawford, *Butterworths Scottish Family Law Service* (1996), Ch.5, "International child abduction and questions of custody".

[72] *Kilgour*, 1987 S.L.T. 568.

[73] Convention on the Civil Aspects of International Child Abduction, signed at The Hague on October 25, 1980.

[74] Convention on Recognition and Enforcement of Decisions concerning Custody of Children and on the Restoration of Custody of Children, signed by the UK and several other States (including all the other EC countries except Denmark) at Luxembourg on May 20, 1980 (sometimes called the European or Luxembourg Convention).

became party to both Conventions by virtue of the Child Abduction and Custody Act 1985. Part 1, Schedule 1 to the Act implements the Hague Convention, and Part 2, Schedule 2 implements the Council of Europe Convention.

A number of countries are party to both Conventions. If a case is capable of falling under both Conventions, a litigant may choose which instrument to invoke.[75] Both Conventions apply to persons under 16, but the Hague seeks to uphold custody *rights*[76] (whether or not there has been a "custody order"), where there has been wrongful removal[77] of a child habitually resident in a Contracting State from the legal system of his habitual residence,[78] or wrongful retention[79] of him outside the legal system, whereas the Council of Europe Convention is concerned with registration and enforcement of custody *decisions*. Under the Council of Europe Convention, a decision will be denied recognition only on one or more of certain stated grounds, relating to jurisdiction, natural justice, or welfare of the child.[80] The assumption is that a custody decision given in one Contracting State should be recognised and enforced in all others. Nevertheless, the grounds under the Hague Convention for refusing to return the child are narrower than are those available under Council of Europe Convention to refuse recognition and enforcement of the foreign decision. However, in general, if there is an option, a litigant should proceed under the Hague Convention, in respect of which there is a substantial body of case law in Scotland, England, and elsewhere in Europe.[81] A selection of interpretative cases is footnoted.[82] Both instruments, of which the

---

[75] See Child Abduction and Custody Act 1985, s.16(4)(c). Consider conflict of jurisdiction *between* the operation of the Conventions: *Re S (a minor) (custody: habitual residence)* [1997] 4 All E.R. 251 (Hague and Europe); *Re R* [1997] 1 F.L.R. 663 (Hague (Child's Views)) and Europe (A 10(1)(b)). A case illustrating conflict *within* the operation of *one* Convention is *Re O (Child Abduction: Re Abduction)* [1997] 2 F.L.R. 712.

[76] Although the terms "custody" and "access" have been replaced, in Scots law, by "residence" and "contact", the 1980 Hague Convention utilises the "old" terminology.

[77] See Hague Convention, Art.3, below.

[78] See discussion of habitual residence generally at Ch.6, above. Also *Dickson*, 1990 S.C.L.R. 692; *Cameron v Cameron (No.1)*, 1996 S.L.T. 306; *Cameron v Cameron (No. 2)*, 1997 S.L.T. 206; *Watson v Jamieson*, 1998 S.L.T. 180; *D v D*, 2001 S.L.T. 1104; *Al-Habtoor v Fotheringham* [2001] EWCA Civ. 186; *W & B v H (Surrogacy)* [2002] 1 F.L.R. 1008; *W, Petr* 2003 G.W.D. 28-772; *M, Petr* 2005 S.L.T. 2; and *Mark v Mark* [2005] 3 All ER 912.

[79] See Hague Convention, Art.3, below.

[80] See Arts 9 and 10 (Sch.2), below.

[81] I.L.S. Balfour and E.B. Crawford, "The Hague Convention on International Child Abduction: Recent Scottish Cases" (1996) SLPQ 411. Reference may be made to *ww.incadat.com* (the international child abduction database).

[82] These footnotes contain many important authorities, but the body of case law grows daily.

Hague Convention is by far the more prominent, now are subject to the overriding authority of Regulation 2201 in a qualifying EU case.[83]

Substance of the 1980 Hague Convention

14–28 By section 4 of the Child Abduction and Custody Act 1985, the courts having jurisdiction to entertain applications under the 1980 Hague Convention shall be in Scotland, the Court of Session, and in England and Wales, or in Northern Ireland, the High Court.

The following provisions of the Convention are of prime importance:

Article 3

14–29 The removal[84] or the retention[85] of a child is to be considered wrongful where:

    (a) it is in breach of rights of custody[86] attributed to a person,[87] an institution or any other body, either jointly or alone, under the law of the State in which the child was habitually resident[88] immediately before the removal or retention[89]; and

    (b) at the time of removal or retention those rights were actually exercised,[90] either jointly or alone, or would have been so exercised but for the removal or retention.

---

[83] Art.60. See paras 14–34 *et seq.*, below.

[84] *Taylor v Ford*, 1993 S.L.T. 654; *McCarthy v McCarthy*, 1994 S.L.T. 743; *Perrin v Perrin*, 1995 S.L.T. 81; *Seroka v Bellah*, 1995 S.L.T 204; *Hunter v Murrow*, 2005 EWCA Civ. 976.

[85] *Findlay v Findlay*, 1994 S.L.T. 709; *Findlay (No.2)*, 1995 S.L.T. 492; *M, Petr*, 2000 G.W.D. 32–1242; and *Re H* [1991] 3 All E.R. 230.

[86] *Bordera*, 1995 S.L.T. 1176; *McKiver*, 1995 S.L.T. 790; *Pirrie v Sawacki*, 1997 S.L.T. 1160; *Re H (Rights of Custody)* [2000] 2 All E.R. (HL) 1; *Re G (Rights of Custody)* [2002] 2 F.L.R. 703; and *Re P (Abduction: Acquiescence)* [2004] 2 F.L.R. 1057 and *Re D. (a child) (abduction: custody rights) (CA)* [2006] All E.R. (D) 355.

[87] This could include, *e.g.* grandparents. See *Re O (A minor) (Child Abduction: Custody Rights), The Times*, June 24, 1997, *per* Cazalet J. In Scotland grand-parents may seek a parental responsibilities and rights order under Children (Scotland) Act 1995, s.11; see also *Re M (Minors) (Residence Order: Jurisdiction)* [1995] 1 F.L.R. 495, CA.

[88] See Ch.6, above. Also *Robertson v Robertson*, 1988 S.L.T. 468, on the question of the state of knowledge required in the "consenting" parent before consent to children's becoming habitually resident in a country, or acquiescence therein, can be established.

[89] *Cameron v Cameron*, 1996 S.L.T. 306; *Moran v Moran*, 1997 S.L.T. 541; *Watson v Jamieson*, 1998 S.L.T. 180.

[90] *Urness v Minto*, 1994 S.L.T. 988. See also *A.J. v F.J.*, unreported, April 29, 2005, Second Division.

The rights of custody mentioned in subparagraph (a) above may arise by operation of law or by reason of a judicial or administrative decision, or by reason of an agreement having legal effect under the law of that State.[91]

Article 12

Where a child has been wrongfully removed or retained in terms of **14–30**
Article 3 and, at the date of the commencement of the proceedings before the judicial or administrative authority of the Contracting State where the child is, a period of less than one year has elapsed from the date of the wrongful removal or retention, the authority concerned shall order the return[92] of the child forthwith.[93]

The judicial or administrative authority, even where the proceedings have been commenced after the expiration of the period of one year referred to in the preceding paragraph, shall also order the return of the child, unless it is demonstrated that the child is now settled in its new environment.[94]

Where the judicial or administrative authority in the requested state has reason to believe that the child has been taken to another state, it may stay the proceedings or dismiss the application for the return of the child.

Article 13

Notwithstanding the provisions of the preceding Article, the judi- **14–31**
cial or administrative authority of the requested State is not bound to order the return of the child if the person, institution or other body which opposed its return establishes that:

(a) the person, institution or other body having the care of the person of the child was not actually exercising the custody rights at the time of removal or retention, or had con-

---

[91] *Findlay*, 1994 S.L.T. 709; *Findlay (No.2)*, 1995 S.L.T. 492; *Perrin*, 1995 S.L.T. 81; *Seroka v Bellah*, 1995 S.L.T. 204; *Bordera*, 1995 S.L.T. 1176; *McKiver*, 1995 S.L.T. 790; *Urness v Minto*, 1994 S.L.T. 988; *Zenel v Haddow*, 1993 S.L.T. 972; *Taylor v Ford*, 1993 S.L.T. 654; *McCarthy*, 1995 S.L.T. 1176; *Dickson*, 1990 S.C.L.R. 693; *Cameron*, 1996 S.L.T. 306; *Moran*, 1997 S.L.T. 541; *Pirrie v Sawacki*, 1997 S.L.T. 1160; *Re S (A minor) (Custody: Habitual Residence)* [1997] 4 All E.R. 251, HL; and *Fourman v Fourman*, 1998 G.W.D. 32–1638.

[92] That is to say, return to the jurisdiction of habitual residence, not to the custody of the other parent; *Findlay*, 1994 S.L.T. 709 and 1995 S.L.T. 492.

[93] See *Re S (Minors: Abduction; Wrongful Retention)* [1994] 1 All E.R. 237, *per* Wall J. at 249.

[94] *Perrin*, 1995 S.L.T. 81; *Soucie*, 1995 S.L.T. 414; *O'Connor*, 1995 G.W.D. 3–113; and *Cannon v Cannon* [2004] EWCA Civ. 1330 (concealment of child), and *Re C (a child) (abduction: settlement)* [2006] EWHC 1229 (Fam).

sented[95] to or subsequently acquiesced[96] in the removal or retention; or

(b) there is a grave risk[97] that his or her return would expose the child to physical or psychological harm or otherwise place the child in an intolerable situation.[98]

The judicial or administrative authority may also refuse to order the return of the child if it finds that the child objects to being returned and has attained an age and degree of maturity at which it is appropriate to take account of its views.[99]

In considering the circumstances referred to in this Article, the judicial and administrative authorities shall take into account the information relating to the social background of the child provided

---

[95] See *Robertson v Robertson*, 1998 S.L.T. 408; *Re C (Abduction: Consent)* [1996] 1 F.L.R. 414; *C v C*, 2003 S.L.T. 793; *H v H*, 2006 G.W.D. 18–361.

[96] *Zenel v Haddow*; *Soucie*; *Robertson*, all above; *Re A (minors)* [1992] 1 All E.R. 929. *Contra* important H.L. decision of *Re H* [1997] 2 All E.R. 225: acquiescence depends on *actual state of mind and subjective intention* although this approach will be subordinated to any impression the bereft parent had given by clear and unequivocal actings. However, acquiescence cannot be inferred from oral or written remarks made by someone who had just suffered the wrongful removal of children. See also *Re B (Abduction) (Art.13 Defence)* [1997] 2 F.L.R. 573; *Re M (Abduction: Acquiescence)* [1996] 1 F.L.R. 315; *J v K*, 2002 S.C. 450; *T v T*, 2003 S.L.T. 1316; *M v M*, 2003 S.L.T. 330; and *Re P (Abduction: Acquiescence)* (2004) 2 F.L.R. 1057.

[97] This is an immensely important phrase. The court will be slow to find grave risk proved. The onus lies on the party averring risk (the abducting parent) (*Whitley*, 1992 G.W.D. 15–843 and 22–1248), and the *tempus inspiciendum* is the time at which the case comes to the Scots court: it is not open to the court to ponder the effect of improvements which could be made in conditions in the legal system of habitual residence: *Macmillan*, 1989 S.L.T. 350 (*contra* Regulation 2201, Art.11.4, *qv*). See generally *Murphy*, 1994 G.W.D. 32–1893; *Slamen*, 1991 G.W.D. 34–2041; *Matznick*, 1998 S.L.T. 636; *Starr v Starr*, 1999 S.L.T. 335; *I, Petr*, 1999 G.W.D. 21–972; *Q, Petr*, 2001 S.L.T. 243; *Re W (Abduction: Domestic Violence)* [2004] 2 F.L.R. 499; *D v D*, 2001 S.L.T. 243; *I, Petr*, 2004 S.L.T. 972; and *S v B* [2005] All E.R. (D) 37. The first English decision upholding the grave risk argument was as late as 1995: *Re F (Minor: Abduction: Rights of Custody Abroad)* [1995] 3 All E.R. 641, *per* Butler Sloss L.J. at 648. See also now *Re M (Psychological Harm)* [1997] 2 F.L.R. 690; *Re O (A Minor)* [1996] 6 C.L. 73; and *Re S (Abduction: Custody Rights)* [2002] F.LR. 815. The terms of Art.13 mean that the child may have to be returned though conditions are not ideal (*Viola*, 1988 S.L.T. 7): the principle of paramountcy of the child's best interests does not apply. But see *Re C (a child) (abduction: settlement)* [2006] EWHC 1229 (Fam.).

[98] *Re R (Abduction: Immigration Concern)* [2005] 1 F.L.R. 33.

[99] *Urness v Minto*; *O'Connor*, both above; *Marshall*, 1996 S.L.T. 429; *Cameron (No.2)*, 1997 S.L.T. 206; *Matznick*, above; *Singh v Singh*, 1998 S.L.T. 1084; *W v W*, 2003 S.L.T. 1253; and *Re H* [2005] All E.R. (D) 17. The court must be sure it understands the child's views, and that the child understands its options: his true wish may be to stay with one parent, wherever that parent may choose to be. Also *Re S (A minor) (Child Abduction: Delay)* [1998] 1 F.C.R. 17; *W v W*, 2003 S.L.T. 1253; and *Re J (Children: abduction: child's objections to return)* [2004] EWCA Civ. 428.

by the central authority or other competent authority of the child's habitual residence.

Role and function of Central Authorities

Article 7 provides for the involvement of Central Authorities. **14–32** Their function, in summary, is to facilitate the smooth working of the Convention by helping a parent locate a child, and obtain legal advice. The Central Authority for Scotland is the Civil Justice Department (Private International Law branch) of the Scottish Executive, and for England and Wales is the Child Abduction Unit of the Office of Official Solicitor and Public Trustee.

Central Authorities exist in every Contracting State, but the speed with which applications for assistance are dealt with varies from country to country.[1] Central Authorities shall bear their own costs, and shall not require payment from applicants towards the costs and expenses of proceedings.[2] However, a Contracting State may limit its assumption of costs to those covered by its system of legal aid and advice.[3]

Substance of the Council of Europe Convention

Before the coming into effect of Regulation 1347, and its suc- **14–33** cessor, Regulation 2201, the Council of Europe Convention, which had received substantial support from European states, played a useful, but subsidiary role in securing the recognition and enforcement of "custody decisions" among signatory states. In principle, a "custody decision" of a signatory state ought to be enforced in another signatory state. This Convention, rare among modern instruments, admits a challenge on the grounds of jurisdiction, essentially where the child's connection with the State addressed is stronger than with the State of origin, through the connecting factor of habitual residence.[4] Likewise, in the case of decisions made in absence of the defendant, recognition may be refused if the competence of the decision-making authority was not founded on the habitual residence of the defendant, or the last common habitual residence of the parents (at least one parent being still habitually resident there), or on the child's habitual residence. Otherwise, recognition depends upon the decision not being subject to challenge on the grounds of natural justice; *res judicata*

---

[1] The UK has a good record in the speedy treatment of and discouragement of abductions. Concern is felt that even at this date in Europe, some countries show undue favour to their *own* parent and/or are slow to process cases in an area where, above all, speed is desirable.

[2] Though they may require payment of expenses incurred or to be incurred in implementing the return of the child: Art.26.

[3] See *Matznick v Matznick*, 1998 S.L.T. 636.

[4] Art.10(c).

in the State addressed; manifest incompatibility with the fundamental principles of the law relating to the family and children in
the State addressed; or a change in circumstances having an effect
upon the welfare of the child.[5]

Since in terms of Regulation 2201, Article 60, the Council of
Europe Convention is subordinated to Regulation 2201, the
already minor contribution made by the Council of Europe Convention must be reduced further, since Regulation 2201, in its
application to parental responsibility matters, principally is concerned with recognition and enforcement of parental responsibility
orders emanating from EU Member States. That being so, the
Council of Europe Convention's ambit of operation must be
limited, *first*, geographically, to those signatory states which are not
currently EU Member States. *Thereafter*, it would be defined by
subject matter (custody decisions), where for some reason it was
thought necessary, or advantageous, to use the Council of Europe
rather than the 1980 Hague Convention.

Cases falling under Regulation 2201/2003

14–34 The 1980 Hague Convention has been ratified by all EU Member
States and applies in relations between Member States. However,
the 1980 Convention now is supplemented by certain provisions of
Regulation 2201, which operate in cases of child abduction
between Member States, and which take precedence. To that
extent therefore (in relations between Member States, in matters
covered by Regulation 2201), the rules of the Regulation prevail
over the rules of the 1980 Hague and Council of Europe Conventions. Regulation 2201 aims to deter wrongful removal or retention
of children between Member States, and if abduction should occur,
it aims to ensure the prompt return of a child to his Member State
of origin.[6] However, the existence of the Regulation provides
another example of the "layering" of potentially relevant conflict
rules, which is characteristic of many areas of international private
law at this period of its development, and which may be productive
of advantage (though certainly of complexity).

Recital 17 states that in cases of wrongful removal or retention
of a child, the child must be returned without delay; to this end, it
is expressly stated that the 1980 Hague Convention continues to
apply, as complemented by the provisions of Regulation 2201, and
by Article 11 in particular.[7]

---

[5] Examples of cases decided under the 1980 Council of Europe Convention are: *F
v F (minors)* [1989] Fam. 1; *Re R* [1990] 1 F.L.R. 387; *Re S (Abduction; European
Convention)* [1996] 1 F.L.R. 660; *Re O* [1997] 2 F.L.R. 712; *Dehn v Dehn*, 1998
G.W.D. 2–59; G.W.D. 35–705 *Campins-Coll, Petr*, 1989 S.L.T. 33 and *S v S*, 2004
G.W.D. 35–705.

[6] Practice Guide, p.28.

[7] See *Vigrent v Michel and another* [2006] EWCA Civ. 630, the first case governed
by the Regulation to reach the Court of Appeal.

Recital 17 summarises the position. The courts of the Member State to/in which the child has been wrongfully removed/retained[8] should be able to oppose the child's return in specific, duly justified cases (in the normal way under the 1980 Hague Convention). Where such a court decides not to return a child by reason of Article 12 or 13 of the 1980 Hague Convention, it must inform the court of the Member State in which the child was habitually resident prior to the wrongful removal or retention (recital 18). However, the decision not to return the child is little more than a provisional protective decision because such a decision may be superseded by a subsequent decision of the court of the Member State in which the child was habitually resident prior to the wrongful removal or retention. If that subsequent decision (by the court of the former habitual residence) requires that the child be returned to his habitual residence, return must take place without special procedure for decree recognition/enforcement thereof in the court of the state to/in which the child was wrongfully removed/retained.

Where a child is "abducted" from one Member State (Member State of origin) (henceforth "MSO") to another Member State (the requested Member State) (henceforth "RMS"), the Regulation ensures that the courts of the MSO retain jurisdiction to decide on the question of custody, notwithstanding the abduction. Once a request for the return of the child is lodged with a court in the RMS, the RMS will apply the 1980 Hague Convention as complemented by the Regulation in order to make a decision, which, as explained, is in the nature of a provisional decision.

Article 10—Jurisdiction in Cases of Child Abduction

The 1980 Hague Convention does not contain direct or indirect **14–35** rules of jurisdiction. Article 10 of Regulation 2201 lays down intra-EU rules for child abduction cases, to determine which EU Member State has jurisdiction to decide "custody issues". As a deterrent to intra-EU child abduction, Article 10 ensures that the courts of the MSO (state in which the child was habitually resident before the abduction) remain competent after the abduction, to decide on matters of custody.

The RMS (the state to which the child has been abducted) may exercise jurisdiction over the child only in narrowly defined circumstances, namely, if:

(1) the child has acquired habitual residence in the RMS, AND all those with custody rights have acquiesced in the abduction; OR

---

[8] Defined in Art.2.11.

(2) the child has acquired habitual residence in the RMS and has resided there for at least one year after those persons with custody rights learned, or should have learned,[9] of the child's whereabouts; AND the child has settled in the new environment; AND one of the following conditions is met:

    (i) the bereft parent has not lodged a request for return of the child within a year of being able to locate the child;

    (ii) the bereft parent has lodged a request for return of the child, but has withdrawn that request;

    (iii) Article 11.7 (qv) has been satisfied;

    (iv) the MSO has issued a decision which allows the child to remain in the RMS.[10]

Under Article 10.a, the child would require to be returned to the court of his habitual residence, meaning that the outcome is in line with the Hague regime. The terminology is more specifically tied to jurisdiction; one may even see the beginnings of an attempt to define in an international instrument the time at which one habitual residence might be said to be supplanted by another, which is one of the most controversial matters in abduction cases, not only in law, but in fact.

Article 10.b is intended to keep a jurisdictional balance. It is extremely difficult to tear jurisdiction away from the courts of the child's original habitual residence, a feature which is a great help to the bereft parent. Jurisdictional competence will shift to the RMS *only* if the bereft parent acquiesces, or is indifferent, or does not discharge the duty of enquiry.[11] Article 10.b enumerates rules of specificity, the sum of which appears to hint at a desire to hone the ground of jurisdiction founded on "habitual residence" of the child. While the opening words of the Article uphold the claim of the court of the jurisdiction whence the child has been wrongfully removed/retained, the remaining parts of the Article afford justifications for departing from that position. Article 10 recognises the conceptual difficulties which the concept of habitual residence contains, namely, that as time goes on, it may be perverse to refuse to recognise a situation which in factual terms is incontestable.

From the abductor's point of view, one assumes that if acquiescence is not proved under Article 10, the matter still could be argued under Article 13 of the 1980 Hague Convention, since

---

[9] Practice Guide, p.30.

[10] Note the imposition upon a parent by this term of the Regulation of a duty of enquiry.

[11] Although under the Hague regime, in England and Scotland, unexplained inactivity by the bereft parent is likely to give rise to judicial comment, and sometimes may contribute to a defence of acquiescence. See *contra J v K*, 2002 S.C. 450.

Regulation 2201,[12] although demoting the Hague Convention, does not extinguish it.

Article 11—Return of the Child

In any case brought in an EU Member State under the 1980 Hague **14–36** Convention, in respect of the wrongful removal or retention of a child to or in another Member State, the provisions of Article 11.2 to 11.8 apply.

Article 11.2—Child's opportunity to be heard

Regulation 2201 "reinforces"[13] the child's right to be heard. Recital **14–37** 19 lays down the principle that giving audience to the child plays an important role in the application of the Regulation. When a court is applying Articles 12 and 13 of the 1980 Hague Convention, it may refuse to order the child's return if it finds that the child objects to being returned, and has attained an age and maturity at which it is appropriate to take account of its views. Article 11.2 of the Regulation goes further than Article 13 of the Hague Convention, by "ensuring" that the child is given the opportunity to be heard, "unless this appears inappropriate having regard to his or her age or degree of maturity". Hence, there can be discerned a slight shift in emphasis.

Article 11.3—6-week deadline

Article 11.3 is somewhat tautological: the court "shall act expedi- **14–38** tiously . . . using the most expeditious procedures available in national law." The RMS must issue a decision (and, implicitly, enforce that decision) no later than six weeks after the lodging of the application for return of the child.

Article 11.4—Future arrangements

This is an interesting provision, showing how strictly Article 13.b of **14–39** the Hague Convention is to be construed in intra-EU cases. Regulation 2201 reinforces the principle that the RMS shall order the immediate return of the child by restricting the Article 13.b exceptions to a minimum.[14] The Regulation requires the return of the child to the MSO even in cases where a return would expose the child to physical or psychological harm, so long as the authorities of the MSO have made "adequate arrangements" to secure the child's protection following his return. The RMS cannot refuse to return a child on Article 13.b grounds if it is shown that

---

[12] Art.60.
[13] Practice Guide, p.33.
[14] Practice Guide, p.32.

"adequate arrangements have been made to secure the protection of the child after his or her return". The child should always be returned to the MSO if he can be adequately protected there.[15]

How will it be established that adequate arrangements have been made? Is this an evidentiary issue? Adequate arrangements under Article 11.4 mean more than procedures existing in theory in the MSO to safeguard the child; it must be established that the authorities in the MSO have taken definite measures to protect the child in question. Central Authorities will play a vital role in assessing whether or not adequate protective measures are in place.

Article 11.5—Bereft parent's opportunity to be heard

14–40 As well as the child having an opportunity to be heard, so too a court cannot refuse to return a child unless the bereft *parent* (the party requesting return of the child) has been given the opportunity to be heard. Arguably the application for return of the child is itself an opportunity to be heard, but Article 11.5 seems to envisage something more.

Article 11.6 and 11.7—RMS's refusal to return the child

14–41 In most cases, the RMS is likely to order return of the child to the MSO (ie it will not find an Article 13 ground to be established). But, in exceptional cases, where the RMS decides that the child shall not be returned to the MSO, special procedures must be followed, as laid down in Article 11.6 and 11.7.

Within one month of the (provisional protective) decision not to return the child, the RMS must transmit a copy of its decision to the court of the MSO (either directly or via the Central Authorities). The MSO must notify the parties, and invite them to make submissions within three months, as to whether or not they wish the MSO to examine the question of custody. If no submissions are made, the MSO shall close the case. However, if one or both parties make(s) submissions, the MSO must examine the case, in which event all parties (including, if appropriate, the child) must be given an opportunity to be heard.[16] The judge in the MSO is expected to take account of the reasons of the judge in the RMS for not returning the child. This process may result in a peremptory order for return to the MSO, as explained.

Article 11.8—Subsequent decision of MSO

14–42 Article 11.8 is the crucial provision of Article 11. Following the provisional decision issued by the RMS, if the court of the MSO, upon application by the bereft parent (as described above), makes

---

[15] *cf.* argument and outcome in *Q, Petr*, 2001 S.L.T 243, and contrast *tempus inspiciendum* approach in *Macmillan*, n.97 above.

[16] Art.42.

a decision which entails the child's return to that State, this decision *must* be directly recognised and enforced in the RMS, without need for further procedure.[17] It is not possible for the RMS to oppose the recognition and enforcement of such a judgment, which is to be directly recognised and enforceable in the other Member States. Article 11.8 allows, in effect, for the non-return order of the RMS to be subverted.

INTRA-UK CASES

Amendments made to the Family Law Act 1986 pursuant to Regulation 2201

The Family Law Act 1986, when brought into force, made pro- **14–43** vision for the allocation of jurisdiction within the UK in all matters relating to children, including rules for deferring to a court more appropriate, and for mutual recognition and enforcement, after registration, of Scots parental responsibility orders in England and *vice versa*. In light of the coming into force of Regulation 2201, and amending secondary legislation,[18] Part I of the Family Law Act 1986 now must be taken to apply only where jurisdiction cannot be founded under the Regulation.[19]

By SSI 2005/42, the provisions of Chapter III of the 1986 Act (Jurisdiction of courts in Scotland) are subject to the provisions of Regulation 2201, Chapter II (Jurisdiction), Section 2 (parental responsibilities) and Section 3 (common provisions). This means that the pre-eminent provisions with regard to jurisdiction in matters of parental responsibilities, in a qualifying (ie intra-EU) case, are to be found in Articles 8 to 15 of Regulation 2201. Those provisions set out in Chapter III of the 1986 Act (principally, sections 9 to 14, below) are relegated to the status of residual national rules (an important change which can be discerned only after careful examination of SSI 2005/42). This view is adduced on the basis that Regulation 2201 is to be taken to effect allocation of jurisdiction between the territorial units of a Member State, as well as between Member States.[20] In this instance, to assume the operation of Regulation 2201 in intra-UK cases is the less complex interpretative option.

SSI 2005/42 makes no mention, however, of sections 27 to 29 of the 1986 Act, covering registration and enforcement of parental

---

[17] Arts 40 and 42.
[18] The European Communities (Matrimonial and Parental Responsibility Jurisdiction and Judgments) (Scotland) Regulations 2005 (SSI 2005/42).
[19] See Art.14, Reg.2201/2003.
[20] See generally N. Lowe, "The Family Law Act 1986–A Critique" [2002] Fam Law 39.

responsibility orders intra-UK, and so it is to be assumed that these provisions continue to operate intra-UK, in qualifying cases (*qv*), irrespective of the recognition and enforcement provisions in Regulation 2201 (Chapter III).

For the reduced number of cases to which the 1986 Act now applies, the most important provisions, paraphrased in places for brevity or clarity, are as follows:

Chapter III—Jurisdiction of court in Scotland

Section 9: Habitual residence of the child

14–44 An application for a parental responsibilities order otherwise than in matrimonial proceedings[21] may be entertained by (a) the Court of Session if, on the date of the application, the child[22] concerned is habitually resident in Scotland; or (b) the sheriff, if, on that date, the child concerned is habitually resident in the sheriffdom.

Section 10: Presence of the child

An application for a parental responsibilities order may be entertained by (a) the Court of Session if, on that date, the child is (i) present in Scotland and (ii) not habitually resident in any part of the U.K.; or (b) the sheriff if, on that date, the child is (i) present in Scotland; (ii) not habitually resident in any part of the U.K.; and (iii) either the pursuer or the defender in the application is habitually resident in the sheriffdom.

Section 11: Relevant matrimonial proceedings

The jurisdiction of a court to entertain an application under sections 9, 10, or 15(2) is excluded if, on the date of the application, matrimonial proceedings in respect of the marriage of the parents of the child are continuing in a court in any part of the UK (unless that other court has made an order under the 1986 Act enabling the custody proceedings to be taken in Scotland).

Section 12: Emergency jurisdiction

Notwithstanding that any other court, within or outside Scotland, has jurisdiction to entertain an application for a parental responsibilities order, the Court of Session or the sheriff shall have jurisdiction if—(a) the child concerned is present in Scotland or in the sheriffdom on the date of the application; and (b) the Court of

---

[21] See *Dorward v Dorward*, 1994 S.C.L.R. 928. Section 13 provides for jurisdiction ancillary to matrimonial proceedings.

[22] A person who has not attained the age of 16: s.18(1).

Session or sheriff considers that, for the protection of the child, it is necessary to make such an order immediately.

Section 14: Power to refuse application or sist proceedings

There is power in the court to refuse application or to sist proceedings[23] or to exercise its powers under Article 15 of Regulation 2201 where the matter has been determined already in other proceedings[24]; or where concurrent proceedings regarding the same matters are continuing, and where it would be more appropriate for those matters to be determined in proceedings outside Scotland or in another court in Scotland, and such proceedings are likely to be taken there; or where it is proper to exercise its powers under Article 15, Regulation 2201.[25]

Section s.17: Orders for delivery of child

This empowers the Court of Session or sheriff court generally to make an order for delivery of a child from one parent to the other when the order is not sought to implement a parental responsibility order, if, but only if, the Court of Session or sheriff would have had jurisdiction to make a parental responsibilities order.

Chapter V—Recognition and Enforcement

Section 25(1): A parental responsibilities order made by a court in **14–45** any part of the UK in force in respect of a child who has not attained 16 years, shall be recognised (except for its enforcement provisions) in any other part of the UK as if made by the appropriate court in that part . . . (3) A court in a part of the UK in which a parental responsibility order is recognised shall not enforce the order unless it has been registered in that part of the UK as if made by the appropriate court to that part.

Section 26: An order relating to parental responsibilities or parental rights in relation to a child which is made outside the UK shall be recognised in Scotland if the order was made in the country where the child was habitually resident.[26]

---

[23] *Messenger v Messenger*, 1992 S.L.T. (Sh. Ct) 29 (sist refused); contrast *Hill v Hill*, 1991 S.L.T. 189. See *B v B*, 1998 S.L.T. 1245.

[24] *Al-Najjar, Petr*, 1993 G.W.D. 27–1661.

[25] Inserted by SSI 2005/42, reg.4.

[26] Note statutory change to common law rule. The statutory rule now is subject to Arts 21–27, 41.1 and 42.1 of Reg.2201.

Section 27(1) and (2): Any person on whom rights are conferred by a parental responsibility order may apply to the court which made it for the order to be registered in another part of the UK.[27]

Section 29(1): Where a parental responsibility order has been registered under s.27, the registering court shall have the same powers to enforce the order as if it had itself made the order and had jurisdiction to make it; and proceedings for enforcement may be taken accordingly.

Section 32: "The appropriate court" in relation to England and Wales or Northern Ireland means the High Court, and in relation to Scotland, means the Court of Session.

Chapter VI—Miscellaneous and supplemental

14–46 Various miscellaneous powers are granted to safeguard the child and ensure the effective operation of the Act:

Section 33: Power to order disclosure of a child's whereabouts (from any person whom the court has reason to believe may have relevant information).

Section 34: Power to order recovery of a child, including authority to enter and search any premises where the person acting in pursuance of the order has reason to believe the child may be found, and to use such force as may be necessary to give effect to the purpose of the order.[28]

Section 35: Powers to restrict removal of a child from the jurisdiction of the court.[29]

Section 37: Where there is in force an order prohibiting or otherwise restricting the removal of a child from the UK or from

---

[27] It became clear in *Woodcock v Woodcock*, 1990 S.L.T. 848 that, in the view of the Scots court, s.29 did not deprive the court of its discretion and duty to ensure that natural justice was observed. See D. Edwards, "A Domestic Muddle: Custody Orders in the United Kingdom" (1992) 41 I.C.L.Q. 444. See also *Rellis v Hart*, 1993 S.L.T. 738; *Messenger v Messenger*, 1992 S.L.T. (Sh.Ct) 29; and *Re B (Minors) (Residence Order)* [1992] 3 All E.R. 867.

[28] s.34 was enacted without prejudice to any existing power of the court. The Scots court has common law powers: *Edgar v Fisher's Trs* (1893) 21 R. 59; *Guthrie*, 1954 S.L.T. (Sh.Ct) 58; *Fowler v Fowler (No.2)*, 1981 S.L.T. (Notes) 78; and *Abusaif*, 1984 S.L.T. 90.

[29] On occasion a custodial parent may seek the court's permission to relocate with the child outside the Scottish jurisdiction (see Children (Scotland) Act 1995, s.2(3)). For England, see *Payne v Payne*, 2001 CLY 596, and 2005 Fam Law 781 (permanent removal); and *Re A (a child) (Temporary Removal from Jurisdiction)* [2004] EWCA Civ. 1587. Unusually, parents may agree, by means of submitting to a judicial decree in these terms, that a child shall not be taken to a country which is not party to the 1980 Hague Convention, and agree sanctions to operate in the event of breach thereof. Such an agreement has been upheld by the Court of Appeal in *Whyte v Whyte* [2005] EWCA Civ. 858.

any specified part of it, the court by which the order was made may require any person to surrender any UK passport which has been issued to, or contains particulars of, the child.

Section 41: Habitual residence after removal without consent, etc.

(1) Where a child who:

    (a) has not attained the age of 16, and

    (b) is habitually resident in a part of the UK, becomes habitually resident outside that part of the UK in consequence of circumstances of the kind specified in section 41(2) below, he shall be treated for the purposes of this Part II of the Act as continuing to be habitually resident in the UK for the period of one year beginning on the date on which those circumstances arise.[30]

(2) The circumstances referred to in (1) above exist where the child is removed from or retained outside, or himself leaves or remains outside, the part of the UK in which he was habitually resident before his change of residence:

    (a) without the agreement of the person or all the persons having, under the law of that part of the UK, the right to determine where he is to reside, or

    (b) in contravention of an order made by a court in any part of the UK.

(3) A child shall cease to be treated by virtue of section 41(1) as habitually resident in a part of the UK if, during the period there mentioned:

    (a) he attains the age of 16, or

    (b) he becomes habitually resident outside that part of the UK with the agreement of the person(s) mentioned in section 41(2)(a) above and not in contravention of an order made by a court in any part of the UK.

CASES GOVERNED BY COMMON LAW RULES

The facts of the case, including geography[31] and timing of events,[32] **14–47** may render it one for common law regulation.

---

[30] This protection is inserted to offset the advantage of the passage of time which otherwise generally operates in favour of a parent who removes a child.

[31] Abductions from and to certain parts of the world are always likely to be common law cases. Otherwise, in judging whether any international instrument is applicable, the initial act complained of must take place after the coming into force of the relevant instrument between the countries in question (*Kilgour v Kilgour*, 1987 S.L.T. 568; *Re H* [1991] 3 All E.R. 230, HL).

[32] It is obviously possible for a case to qualify as an abduction where the "child" is approaching the age of 16. These cases may overlap with issues of forced marriage: *cf. Re KR (a child) (abduction: forcible removal by parents)* [1999] 4 All E.R. 954.

Incoming common law cases[33] are dealt with in Scotland on a fair-minded basis of return of the child to a court of closer connection, if it is obvious that such a court exists.[34] On the other hand, if not convinced of the existence of a more appropriate forum, or if unsure about the conditions which await the child on return, the Scots court will retain the child and decide the custody issue.[35] Many years have elapsed from the era when the decree of the court of the father's domicile was entitled to unquestioned acceptance.[36]

As regards outgoing common law cases, Scots law, obviously, is unlikely to be able to influence the handling of such cases, and advice to parents is of a practical nature, seeking to stop the "abductor" from removing the child beyond the jurisdiction of the Scots courts.[37] Removal of a child to a non-Convention country of a very different culture from the UK will render unlikely a foreign court order directing return of the child to Scotland.

Application of Hague Convention principles to non-Convention cases

14–48 An interesting question is whether Scots and English courts should treat "non-Convention" incoming cases with a Convention-type approach. A Scots common law case of significance is *Calleja v Calleja*,[38] where the court opined that "physical or moral injury" (the terminology of the older common law cases) might not be the best expression in modern times, preferring the "psychological harm" wording used in the Hague Convention, Article 13 (while not applying it directly[39]).

There were some early indications that an English court in its discretion might wish to take as much of the Hague Convention as it felt appropriate in a particular case.[40] However, there was

---

[33] Involving non-Convention countries or involving Convention countries, but in circumstances where the Convention(s) does/do not apply.

[34] *Lyndon*, 1978 S.L.T. (Notes) 7; *Campbell*, 1977 S.C. 103; *Thomson, Petr*, 1980 S.L.T. (Notes) 29.

[35] *Sinclair*, 1988 S.L.T. 87 (in the days before Germany became a Convention country); and see *Basinski*, 1993 G.W.D. 8–533.

[36] *McKee v McKee* [1951] A.C. 352 at 365. See also Family Law Act 1986, s.26.

[37] Family Law Act 1986, ss.17 and 33–37; and *Robertson*, 1911 S.C. 1319. In Scotland the police can become involved only if a crime has been committed—in effect, only if Child Abduction Act 1984, s. 6 applies. The first source of advice if the destination is a non-Convention country is the Foreign and Commonwealth Office, and then "Reunite", a UK charity specialising in International Child Abduction.

[38] 1997 S.L.T. 579. See also *Perendes v Sim*, 1998 S.L.T. 1382.

[39] 1997 S.L.T. 579 at 603.

[40] *Re F (Minor; Abduction; Jurisdiction)* [1990] 3 All E.R. 97: see Crawford, 1992 JR. 177 at 191; *D v D* [1994] 1 F.L.R. 137, CA; *Re A (Minors; Abduction)* [1996] 1 All E.R. 24; *Re S* [1994] 1 F.L.R. 297; and *Re Z (Abduction: Non-Convention Country)* [1999] 1 F.L.R. 1270.

cautious retrenchment by the Court of Appeal in *Re A* (*Abduction; non-convention country*)[41] (where the non-Convention country was the United Arab Emirates). The need for comity, and the relativist cultural approach, retreated in favour of the welfare principle. Similarly, in *Re P*[42] the Court of Appeal held that it was not bound to apply the spirit of the Convention to a non-Convention case.

Most recently in *In re J*[43] the House of Lords applied a "best interests of the child" ("non-Convention") approach in a case involving what would have been termed under the Hague Convention "wrongful retention" by the mother of the child in England, the family having lived in Saudi Arabia and the parents, having divorced, having remarried in accordance with Shariah law.[44]

Whether under a Convention or not, the weight given to the views of the child must increase as the child grows older. There is a danger also since in some legal systems girls may be of marriageable age earlier than 16 years. Parents may be in agreement that they wish to remove the child from the UK to, for example, India, in order to have the child married there. In an instance of this type,[45] Singer J. in the Family Division of the High Court held that the courts in England, while not insensitive to the traditions and concepts of family authority held by minority communities, must nevertheless uphold the integrity of the individual child or young person, whose views must prevail in the "highly personal context of an arranged or forced marriage. Accordingly, the courts would not permit what was, at best, the exploitation of an individual, and might, in the worst case, amount to outright trafficking for financial consideration."

UK-Pakistan Consensus on Child Abduction

A protocol was reached in 2003, reflecting agreement between senior members of the UK judiciary and the Pakistan judiciary, in the matter of protection of children from the harmful effects of

---

[41] *The Times*, July 3, 1997. But contrast the approach taken earlier in *Re S* [1994] 1 F.L.R. 297, CA (where children were ordered to be returned to Pakistan, the English court being aware that the mother would lose custody in certain predetermined circumstances; and in making such order the court thereby deferred to the Muslim interpretation of children's welfare on the view that it was not substantially different from a welfare test: (1994) 2 New L.J., issue 17). Contrast generally *Osborne v Matthan (No.3)*, 1988 S.L.T. 1264. See also *Re A* [1996] 1 All E.R. 24; *Re JA (A minor) (Abduction: non-convention country)* [1998] 2 F.C.R. 159; and *Re J (A child)(Return to foreign jurisdiction)* [2005] 3 All E.R. 291 (HL).

[42] *(A Minor: Abduction) The Times*, July 19, 1996.

[43] *In re J (A Child) (Custody Rights: Jurisdiction)* [2006] 1 A.C. 80.

[44] See speech by Baroness Hale of Richmond, at paras 21 *et seq*.

[45] *Re KR (a child) (abduction: forcible removal by parents)* [1999] 4 All E.R. 954.

wrongful removal or retention, and having the aim of promoting judicial co-operation between the legal systems concerned.[46]

THE CRIMINAL LAW ASPECT OF INTERNATIONAL CHILD ABDUCTION

14–49 The Child Abduction Act 1984 amends the criminal law of England[47] and Scotland[48] relating to the abduction of children (*i.e.* the taking or sending of a child under the age of 16 out of the United Kingdom without the appropriate consent, where there is in force a parental responsibility order, or a UK order prohibiting the removal of the child from the UK).

These provisions were conceived as English measures, but it was feared that their effectiveness would be weakened if a parent or other person could take a child abroad from a Scottish airport or port without fear of criminal sanction. Hence, section 6, of application to Scotland only, was inserted at a late stage into the 1984 Act.[49] Scots law on this subject comprises, in addition to section 6 (which defines the offence, the penalties being specified in section 8), the common law crimes of *plagium* (child stealing) and abduction.[50] The matter has been considered by the Scottish Law Commission,[51] which recommended abolition of *plagium*, reform of abduction, and the creation of a statutory offence of taking or detaining a child under 16 from the control of any person having lawful control of that child, but there has been no implementing legislation.

IV. GUARDIANSHIP AND ADMINISTRATION OF A CHILD'S PROPERTY

GUARDIANSHIP

14–50 At common law in Scotland, there were three classes of guardians, *viz*: (1) tutors; (2) curators; and (3) curators *bonis* and/or *ad litem*. The Age of Legal Capacity (Scotland) Act 1991 removed the common law classification of children into pupils and minors, and replaced tutors and curators with "guardians" (defined as parent-

---

[46] See [2003] Fam. Law 199. See also comments at [2004] Fam. Law 359 and 609, and [2006] 1 F.L. 5, where it is reported that the Protocol, at least "in spirit", has been used in 52 cases.
[47] Pt 1 of the Act.
[48] Pt 2 of the Act.
[49] See Wilkinson and Norrie, pp.263–264.
[50] Both criminal and civil aspects may arise from one set of circumstances: *Deans v Deans*, 1988 S.C.L.R. 192 (Sh.Ct).
[51] Scot. Law Com. Memo No. 67; Scot. Law Com. No. 102 (1987).

substitutes). Curators *ad litem* and curators *bonis* still may be appointed by the court.[52] Many important changes in substance and terminology were made by the Children (Scotland) Act 1995; appointment and removal of guardians came to be regulated by sections 7 (Appointment), section 8 (Revocation and termination of appointment), and section 11(2)(h) (Judicial appointment or removal of guardians). Under the 1995 Act, an application can be made to the Court of Session or sheriff court for an order in relation to parental responsibilities and rights, by any person who claims an interest (section 11(3)(a)(i)). Such an interest may be genetic or emotional or professional and might include, therefore, a step-parent, grandparent, medical/social services professional, or even the child himself or herself.

Under Regulation 2201, the definition of parental responsibility, and of the holder thereof, is apt to cover a person who in Scots law would be regarded as a guardian,[53] and so the opinion can be ventured that the pre-existing jurisdictional rules of Scots law contained in the Family Law Act 1986, sections 9 to 12, henceforward take the function, in relation to guardianship, as for other aspects of parental responsibility, of residual national rules.[54]

Jurisdiction to administer a child's property[55]

At common law, jurisdiction in the Scots courts to appoint a **14–51** guardian by whatever name, was founded on the child's domicile or residence in Scotland, or on the ownership by the child of property in Scotland.[56] Section 16 of the Family Law Act 1986[57] conferred jurisdiction on the Scots court to entertain an application for guardianship, if the child in question was habitually resident in Scotland. With regard to orders concerning the administration of a child's property, the Children (Scotland) Act 1995, sections 9, 10, and 14 now apply, the last of which has conflict of laws implications. Section 14 provides that:

(1) The Court of Session shall have jurisdiction to entertain an application for an order relating to the administration of a child's property if the child is habitually resident in, or the property is situated in, Scotland.

(2) A sheriff shall have jurisdiction to entertain such an application if the child is habitually resident in, or the property is situated in, the sheriffdom.

---

[52] Age of Legal Capacity (Scotland) Act 1991, s.1(3)(f).
[53] Art.1.2.b and e.
[54] Art.14, Reg.2201/2003.
[55] See Reg.2201/2003, recital 9, and Art.1.2.e.
[56] *Hay* (1861) 23 D. 1291; as to *curators bonis* in insanity, see *Reid* (1887) 24 S.L.R. 281.
[57] Amended by Age of Legal Capacity (Scotland) Act 1991, Sch.2, para.46. As to s.16(3), "any other ground of jurisdiction", see Anton with Beaumont, p.565.

(3) Subject to subsection (4) below, any question arising under this Part of this Act:

    (a) concerning:

        (i) parental responsibilities or parental rights; or

        (ii) the responsibilities or rights of a guardian,

        in relation to a child shall, in so far as it is not also a question such as is mentioned in paragraph (b) below, be determined by the law of the place of the child's habitual residence at the time when the question arises[58];

    (b) concerning the immediate protection of a child shall be determined by the law of the place where the child is when the question arises[59]; and

    (c) as to whether a person is a validly appointed or constituted guardian of a child[60] shall be determined by the law of the place of the child's habitual residence on the date when the appointment was made (the date of death of the testator being taken to be the date of appointment where an appointment was made by will), or the event constituting the guardianship occurred.

Section 14(4) subjects the choice of law rule (in favour of the application of the law of the child's habitual residence), to the discretion of the Scots forum which, in making an order in relation to guardianship, is required, in terms of the 1995 Act, to regard the welfare of the child as the paramount consideration.

Sections 9, 11, 13 and 14 of the 1995 Act are rendered subject to the jurisdiction rules contained in Regulation 2201.[61]

Recital 9 of Regulation 2201 distinguishes between (i) measures for the protection of a child concerning the designation and functions of a person or body having charge of a child's property, representing or assisting him, and measures concerning the administration, conservation and disposal of his property; and (ii) measures relating to the child's property which do not concern his protection. Whilst the former are governed by Regulation 2201, the latter are governed by Regulation 44/2001 (failing which as to scope, by section 14 of the 1995 Act).

V. ADOPTION

14–52 *Adoption* is the form of procedure by which a person (the adoptee), becomes a member of the family of another person (the adopter). It has been said that adoption is a culture-specific legal entity. In

---

[58] Note choice of law rule regarding parental responsibilities.

[59] Note choice of law rule regarding child protection.

[60] This amounts to a rule of recognition.

[61] SSI 2005/42, reg.5. (For Arts 8–15, see paras 14–11 *et seq.*, above.)

this, it is perhaps unlike anything else so far studied under the heading of personal status, for while it is true that there are different types of marriage (monogamous, polygamous, etc.), and there are different methods of divorce (judicial, extrajudicial, etc.), the status of being married, or of being divorced, arguably has an agreed core of incidents. However, when considering recognition of foreign adoption orders, one of the difficulties which arises is that some legal systems favour "full" adoption, in which an individual who has the status of adopted person thereby extinguishes all links of parental influence, rights of aliment, support, property and succession, with his biological family, whereas other systems favour "simple" adoption, in which the break from the biological family is less absolute. Further, there is a difference between adoption by strangers, and adoption by blood relatives. In the latter case, contact with the biological family obviously will continue. Valid adoptions frequently bring in train benefits of citizenship, meaning that the topic often is closely linked with immigration issues.[62]

Within the domestic laws of Scotland and England, the state has a much stronger role in adoption than was the case in earlier days, and the subject of adoption now straddles public and private law. The topic is likely to have an enhanced public profile in the conflict of laws, in view of the increased opportunity to "rescue" children from overseas, which may give rise to controversial cases often lacking in statutory or Convention regulation.

The principal domestic legislation, for Scotland, is the Adoption (Scotland) Act 1978,[63] and the Children (Scotland) Act 1995, Part 3; and, for England, the Adoption and Children Act 2002.[64] For both legal systems, the Adoption (Intercountry Aspects) Act 1999 applies, bringing into force the 1993 Hague Convention on Protection of Children and Co-operation in Respect of Intercountry Adoption.[65] Since the Convention with which the 1978 Act was

---

[62] *Re H* [1983] 4 F.L.R. 85; and contrast *Re B (Adoption Order: nationality)* [1999] 1 F.L.R. 907.

[63] Most of the provisions came into effect on September 1, 1984, and the remainder on February 1, 1985. Though see Adoption and Children (Scotland) Bill, introduced March 27, 2006, which would repeal the 1978 Act, except Part IV.

[64] Certain provisions (having a "UK" remit) are relevant in Scotland, for example, s.83(7), which regulates the bringing into the UK of a child who is habitually resident outside the British Islands, for the purpose of adoption by a person who is habitually resident in the British Islands ("British resident"), and the bringing into the UK of such a child adopted by a British resident under an external (non-Hague Convention) adoption.

[65] See the Adoption of Children from Overseas (Scotland) Regulations 2001 (SSI 2001/236); the Intercountry Adoption (Hague Convention) (Scotland) Regulations 2003 (SSI 2003/19); and the Foreign Adoptions (Scotland) Regulations 2003 (SSI 2003/67).

concerned[66] has been superseded by the 1993 Hague Convention, certain provisions of that Act have been repealed, but many remain in force, including certain provisions of conflict of laws interest, for example concerning the jurisdiction of the Scots courts to make adoption orders,[67] and concerning overseas (sometimes known as "regulated") adoptions.[68]

Currently, there is proceeding through the Scottish Parliament the Adoption and Children (Scotland) Bill (introduced March 2006), which proposes certain changes in domestic law, and which contains in Chapter 6 provision concerning adoptions with a foreign element, including restrictions on bringing children into the UK for adoption; and restrictions on removal of children for adoption outwith Great Britain.

RECOGNITION OF ADOPTION ORDERS

Intra-UK

14–53   There is reciprocal recognition of adoption orders intra-UK.[69]

Foreign adoptions

14–54 It is necessary to categorise foreign adoptions as:

> (1) Hague Convention adoptions, regulated for the UK by the Adoption (Intercountry Aspects) Act 1999;
> (2) overseas adoptions, *i.e.* granted in countries designated by the Secretary of State; and
> (3) adoption orders at common law.

Convention Orders

14–55 This area now is governed by the 1993 Hague Convention. The aim of the Convention is to improve certainty, orderliness and fairness in intercountry adoption, and to attempt to stop the trafficking of children.[70] To this end, as with the 1980 Hague Convention on

---

[66] The 1965 Hague Convention on Jurisdiction, Applicable Law and Recognition of Decrees relating to Adoptions, which was ratified only by Austria, Switzerland and the UK.

[67] 1978 Act, ss.14(2) and 56(3). As to expansion of grounds of jurisdiction under the 2002 Act (ss.41 and 48), see Clarkson & Hill, pp.445–446. Where it has jurisdiction, the Scottish/English forum will apply its own law to the substance of the case.

[68] *e.g.* Annulment by Court of Session of such an adoption (s.47). See also s.49, and generally Pt VI.

[69] See s.38(1)(c), Adoption (Scotland) Act 1978, and Adoption and Children Act 2002, s.105.

[70] *i.e.* it has a criminal law remit also; see s.14, 1999 Act.

international child abduction the Central Authorities of Contracting States play an important facilitating and safeguarding role.[71]

Framework

The 1993 Convention shall apply where a child habitually resident **14–56** in one Contracting State ("the State of origin") has been, is being, or is to be moved to another Contracting State ("the receiving State"), either after his adoption in the State of origin by spouses or a person habitually resident in the receiving State, or for the purposes of such an adoption in the receiving State, or in the State of origin.[72] By Article 2(2), the Convention covers only adoptions which create a permanent parent-child relationship. Certain agreements, for example of Central Authorities in the State of origin and the receiving State, must be obtained; the Convention ceases to apply if these agreements have not been given before the child attains the age of 18 years.[73]

Requirements for intercountry adoptions

In terms of Article 4, an adoption within the scope of the **14–57** Convention shall take place only if the competent authorities of the State of origin have established that the child is adoptable, and have determined, after giving due consideration to placement of the child within the State of origin that an intercountry adoption is in the child's best interests. Presumably the criteria of "adoptability" (in all its aspects) and what is in the child's best interests must be tested according to the domestic law of the State of origin.

Further, the competent authorities of the State of origin must ensure that the persons, institution, and authorities whose consent is necessary for adoption have been counselled and informed of the effects of their consent, in particular on the matter whether the adoption will result in the termination of the legal relationship between the child and his family of origin; that such persons etc have given their consent freely in the required form, not induced by payment, and their consent has not since been withdrawn; and that the consent of the mother, where required,[74] has been given only after the birth of the child. Further, the authorities must ensure that the child has been counselled and informed of the effects of the adoption; that consideration has been given to the child's wishes and opinions; and that his consent, where required,[75] has been given freely in the required legal form, uninduced by

---

[71] Ch.3, Arts 6–13.
[72] Art.2(1).
[73] Art.3.
[74] This requirement surely must be a requirement of the State of origin.
[75] As above.

payment. These latter requirements are to be given effect having regard to the age and degree of maturity of the child.

In terms of Article 5, a Convention adoption shall take place only if the competent authorities of the receiving State have determined that the prospective adoptive parents are eligible and suited to adopt; have been counselled, as may be necessary; and have determined that the child is or will be authorised to enter and reside permanently in that State. Presumably "eligibility", in all its aspects, must be tested according to the domestic law of the receiving State.

Jurisdiction—applications to adopt

14–58 By Article 14, persons habitually resident in a Contracting State who wish to adopt a child habitually resident in another Contracting State[76] shall apply to the Central Authority in the state of their habitual residence.

If that Central Authority is satisfied that the applicants are eligible, and suited to adopt, it shall prepare a background report, to be transmitted to the Central Authority of the State of origin. If *that* Central Authority is satisfied that the child is adoptable, *it* shall prepare a background report (*e.g.* on the child's medical history and cultural background), ensuring that consents have been obtained in accordance with Article 4; and shall determine whether the envisaged placement is in the best interests of the child. This report shall be transmitted to the Central Authority of the receiving State, with proof that the necessary consents have been obtained (taking care not to reveal the identity of the natural parents, if in the State of origin these identities may not be disclosed).

In terms of Article 17, any decision in the State of origin that a child should be entrusted to prospective adoptive parents, may be made only if the Central Authority of that State has ensured that the prospective adoptive parents agree; that the Central Authority of the receiving State has approved such a decision, where such approval is necessary by the law of that State or by the Central Authority [*sic*] of the State of origin; that the Central Authorities of both States have agreed that the adoption will proceed; and that, in accordance with Article 5, the prospective adoptive parents are eligible and suited to adopt, and that the child is or will be authorised to enter and reside permanently in the receiving State. The Central Authorities of both States shall take all necessary steps to obtain permission for the child to leave the State of origin, and to enter and reside permanently in the receiving State.

---

[76] This is the (only) qualifying scenario. See, therefore, para.14–60 below regarding cases falling outside this set of circumstances.

Where the adoption is to take place after the transfer of the child to the receiving State, and it appears to the Central Authority of that State that the continued placement of the child with the prospective adoptive parents is not in the child's best interests, such Central Authority shall take the necessary measures to protect the child (which may include arranging temporary care, or a new placement, or, as a last resort, arranging the return of the child to the State of origin, if his interests so require). Having regard to the age and degree of maturity of the child, he shall be consulted, and where appropriate, his consent to these measures obtained.[77]

Recognition and effects of adoption

An adoption certified by the competent authority of the State of the adoption (being the State of origin, or the receiving State, as the case may be), as having been made in accordance with the Convention, shall be recognised as having operation of law in the other Contracting States.[78] The recognition of an adoption may be refused in a Contracting State only if the adoption is manifestly contrary to its public policy, taking into account the best interests of the child.[79]

What does recognition of an adoption connote? In terms of Article 26(1), the recognition of an adoption includes recognition of (a) the legal parent-child relationship between the child and his/her adoptive parents; (b) parental responsibility of the adoptive parents for the child; and (c) the termination of a pre-existing legal relationship between the child and his/her biological parents, *if* the adoption has this effect in the Contracting State where it was made. By Article 26(2), where an adoption has the effect of terminating a pre-existing legal parent-child relationship, the child shall enjoy in the receiving State, and in any other Contracting State where the adoption is recognised, rights equivalent to those resulting from adoptions having this effect in each such state.[80] Conversely, by Article 27(1), where an adoption granted in the State of origin is *less than full*, it may, in the receiving State which recognises the adoption under the Convention, be converted into a *full adoption* (a) if the law of the receiving State so permits; and (b) if the consents referred to in Article 4 have been, or are, given for the purpose of such adoption. If so, recognition of the conversion

---

[77] Art.21.

[78] Art.23.

[79] Art.24.

[80] Hence, if an adoption is carried out under a law which operates "full adoptions", then that full status shall be enjoyed in the receiving State and essentially in all other Contracting States. However, Art.26(3) provides that the child shall have the benefit of any *more favourable* provision which is in force in a recognising Contracting State.

will be guaranteed by Article 23 in the same way as recognition of any other qualifying adoption.

General provisions

14–59 Chapter VI contains general provisions, of an administrative or a policy[8] nature. By Article 28, the Convention does not affect any law of the State of origin which requires that the adoption of a child habitually resident within that State take place in that State, or which prohibits the child's placement in, or transfer to, the receiving State prior to adoption.

The 1993 Convention is an important contribution in an area of law which is difficult to regulate. Its provisions appear to contain many safeguards for the child, and for those whose consent to intercountry adoption is necessary. Its value will be judged according to the degree of international support which it commands.[82] The dual responsibility of the State of origin and the receiving State is a notable characteristic. The Convention contains *ex facie* fewer conflict rules than might be expected; indeed they must be searched out, and/or inferred. For example, there is no chapter specifically devoted to jurisdiction. It would appear that the only criterion to enable parties to utilise the adoption process provided is that the parties be habitually resident in a Contracting State, and that the child be habitually resident in another Contracting State. But perhaps this approach to jurisdiction provision is appropriate in the circumstances which the Convention seeks to address. The main challenge for the draftsmen was the crafting of recognition provisions which are apt to cover recognition of a status which varies from country to country, some adoption laws effecting full adoption, and others only simple adoption. The most notable

---

[81] *e.g.* Art.32: no-one shall derive improper financial or other gain from an activity related to an inter-country adoption.

[82] As of June 1, 2006 there are 69 Contracting States to the 1993 Convention. An interesting aspect of the 1993 Convention is that recognition of adoptions from certain specified countries can be suspended because of concerns about child trafficking. Clearly this can have severe consequences in the case of adoptions which are in course when the ban is imposed. In *R (on the application of Thomson) v Minister of State for Children* [2006] 1 F.L.R. 175 claimant British citizens unsuccessfully applied for judicial review of a decision by the Secretary of State to impose a temporary suspension on intercountry adoptions from Cambodia, and forbidding them to proceed. This problem is addressed for England, Wales and Northern Ireland in the Children and Adoption Bill 2005, clauses 9–12 which make provision concerning the suspension of intercountry adoptions where, in the view of the Secretary of State, it would be contrary to public policy to permit the bringing of children into the UK by British residents, whether the case falls within the 1993 Hague Convention, or not. It is possible for a Contracting State itself to lay a ban on adoptions if it is concerned that too many outward adoptions are taking place from that State (HL Research Paper 06/07, February 7, 2006).

absence is of any express mention of choice of law amid much facilitative and precautionary provision. There are many problems of a factual and evidential nature in this branch of the conflict of laws, eg location of the biological parents of a child, and obtaining sufficient evidence of their consent to removal of the child, and in any given case such problems are likely to be as, or more, acute than the legal problems.

Overseas adoptions

An "overseas adoption", being an adoption of such a description as **14–60** the Secretary of State may by order specify, and being a description of adoptions of children from designated countries,[83] has equivalent effect in Scotland to a Scottish adoption. Regulation is by the Adoption (Scotland) Act 1978. Upon application, however, the Court of Session may order that such adoptions shall cease to be valid in Great Britain on the ground that the adoption is contrary to public policy, or that the authority which purported to authorise the adoption was not competent to entertain the case.[84]

Many countries designated for this purpose also are party to the 1993 Hague Convention, but an adoption from such a signatory State still may be treated as an overseas adoption if, for some factual reason, the adoption does not satisfy the particular requirements of the 1993 Convention.[85]

Adoption orders at common law

Where a foreign adoption does not qualify as a Convention **14–61** adoption under the 1999 Act, or as an overseas adoption under the 1978 Act, a question of recognition will arise at common law. In such a case, where the matter falls to be decided without statutory guidance, there is support for application of old principles of recognition on the basis of domicile, or "recognition by"[86] the law of domicile[87] (of the adoptive parents, or one of them[88]).

---

[83] 1978 Act, s.65 designated countries include all western European countries, most members of the Commonwealth and UK dependent territories, South Africa, USA; on or after April 5, 1993, China is a designated country (SI 1993/690). See also Adoption and Children Act 2002, s.87 and cl.73 of Adoption and Children (Scotland) Bill 2006.

[84] 1978 Act, s.47(2)(a).

[85] Clarkson & Hill, p.449.

[86] On analogy of *Armitage v Att.-Gen.* [1906] P. 135 (divorce) and *Abate* [1961] P. 29 (nullity), though this principle has ceased to apply in "proceedings" divorce and nullity recognition: Family Law Act 1986, s.46(1).

[87] *Re Wilson (dec'd)* [1954] Ch. 733; *Re Wilby (dec'd)* [1956] P. 174; *Re Marshall (dec'd)* [1957] Ch. 507: and *Re Valentine's Settlement* [1965] Ch. 831. See Morris, p.249; Dicey and Morris, pp.891 (Rule 106) *et seq.*; Sir Peter Cheshire & North, pp.767 *et seq.* Sir Peter North queries whether it is right to concentrate exclusively

Recognition of an adoption order at common law does not necessarily require giving effect to all the incidents of that adoption.[89] Moreover, a foreign adoption may be denied recognition if recognition would be contrary to public policy.

Summary 14—Conflict rules affecting children

14–62 1. Legitimacy

A child is legitimate if born in a marriage valid by Scots conflict rules, or otherwise if it is legitimate by the law of the domicile of each parent.

2. Legitimation

A child is regarded as having been legitimated by the marriage of its parents or by an act of recognition if its father had power so to legitimate it by the law of his domicile at the date of the marriage or recognition.

3. Parental Responsibilities

Allocation of jurisdiction and conflicting jurisdictions

Regulation 2201, Articles 8 to 15; failing which Family Law Act 1986, sections 8 to 18. See also 1996 Hague Convention, Articles 5 to 14.

Choice of law

See 1996 Hague Convention, Articles 15 to 22.

Recognition and enforcement of parental responsibility orders

Regulation 2201, Articles 21 and 23; failing which Family Law Act 1986, sections 27 to 29.
  See also 1996 Hague Convention, Articles 23 to 28.

4. Guardianship and Administration of Property

Regulation 2201/2003, supplemented by the Children (Scotland) Act 1995, section 14.

---

on the domicile of the adopters, ignoring the domicile of the child or of the natural parents, but accepts that if domicile of adopters is the main jurisdictional criterion, the "recognition by" extension should be accepted. See Wilkinson and Norrie discussion, pp.581 *et seq.*
[88] Clarkson & Hill, p.450.
[89] See Ch.10, above.

5. International Child Abduction

The primary legislation in the UK is the Child Abduction and Custody Act 1985, bringing into effect the 1980 Hague Convention and the 1980 Council of Europe Convention. Of these, the more important instrument is the Hague Convention, but in a qualifying (intra-EU) case this is complemented by Regulation 2201, Articles 10 and 11.

In incoming common law cases, the Scottish court will act in what it perceives in its discretion to be the best interests of the child, and has shown willingness to return the child to a forum which it deems to be the natural forum in the circumstances.

6. Inter-country Adoption

The relevant legislation for Scotland is the Adoption (Scotland) Act 1978, and the Adoption (Intercountry Aspects) Act 1999. For English law, the 1999 Act is supplemented by the Adoption and Children Act 2002 (certain provisions of which have UK-wide implications).

The principal categories of foreign adoption are "Convention" adoptions (under the 1993 Hague Convention, and governed by the 1999 Act); "overseas" adoptions (governed by the Adoption (Scotland) Act 1978); and common law adoptions.

CHAPTER 15

THE LAW OF CONTRACTUAL OBLIGATIONS

I. GENERAL MATTERS AND GOVERNING LAW

CLASSIFICATION

The question whether a conflict case is to be treated as pertaining **15–01** to contract, or to some other legal category, is determined by the *lex fori*.[1] It is not essential for allocation of the problem to the class of contract for conflict purposes that all the domestic requirements of the *lex fori* for constitution of a contract be present. It is sufficient that there are present, in the view of the forum, the elements of a contractual obligation.[2]

CHOICE OF LAW

Choice of law rules in contract are contained mainly in the EC **15–02** Convention ("the Rome Convention") on the Law Applicable to Contractual Obligations, opened for signature on June 19, 1980 (henceforth "Rome I"), the rules of which "apply to contractual obligations in any situation involving a choice of law between the laws of different countries". [3] Rome I was brought into force in the United Kingdom, with effect from April 1, 1991, by means of the

---

[1] *De Nicols v Curlier* [1900] A.C. 21; *Earl of Stair v Head* (1846) 6 D. 904; and *Krupp Uhde GmbH v Weir Westgarth Ltd*, unreported, May 31, 2002 (Lord Eassie).

[2] *Re Bonacina* [1912] 2 Ch. 394 (though one might say of that case that there was sufficient of a contract to satisfy the (Italian) law which would govern if there were a contract ("putative proper law"). *Cf.* Private International Law (Miscellaneous Provisions) Act 1995, s.9(2).

[3] The phrase "contractual obligations" may receive an autonomous meaning from decisions of the European Court of Justice in the manner of interpretation of the special jurisdiction provisions in contract contained in Brussels Convention, Art.5(1) (as amended by Council Regulation 44/2001). See *Société Jakob Handte et Cie GmbH v Société Traitements Mecano-Chimiques des Surfaces* [1992] E.C.R. 1–3967; and *Atlas Shipping Agency (UK) v Suisse Atlantique Societe D'Armament SA* [1995] C.L.Y.B. 707 (implied promise held to fall within the scope of Lugano Convention, Art.5.1). Also Rome I, Art.18.

Contracts (Applicable Law) Act 1990, in respect of contracts entered into after that date.[4]

The courts of Contracting States must apply the rules in Rome I to any qualifying case, regardless of whether the applicable law(s) thereunder is/are that of a Contracting State.[5] Hence Rome I has the characteristic of "universality". Rome I applies also in the case of conflicts of laws between the different jurisdictions of the UK.[6]

Although the provisions of Rome I do not differ greatly from the pre-existing common law rules of Scotland and England, it would be dangerous to regard its terms as a codification of common law rules.[7] Where Rome I does not apply (Article 1: scope), or where Rome I is silent on an issue, the common law continues to apply, as it does to all contracts entered into before 1 April 1991.[8] As a result, Scots and English conflict rules in contract are found largely in statute,[9] but partly also in the common law; the common law should be regarded as the backdrop.[10]

The common law rules of contract are a well-furnished part of English and Scots conflict law, and are considered to be a notable (primarily English[11]) contribution to the subject. Consequently, Rome I did not receive an unqualified welcome in the UK, being regarded by some as unnecessary or undesirable.[12] Rome I permitted certain reservations (*i.e.* exclusion of particular provisions) by individual Contracting States, an opportunity which the UK utilised.[13]

Contracts (Applicable Law) Act 1990[14]

15–03 Rome I establishes uniform choice of law rules for contractual obligations among Contracting States, such rules to be applied by

---

[4] Art.17 (no retrospective effect).

[5] Art.2.

[6] 1990 Act, s.2(3) (Art.19.2 of Rome I would have permitted multi-legal system States to exclude the operation of the Convention between/among the constituent legal systems).

[7] Cheshire & North, pp.536–537.

[8] *Zebrarise Ltd v De Nieffe* [2005] 1 Ll's Rep. 154.

[9] Contracts (Applicable Law) Act 1990, implementing Rome I, and the Contracts (Applicable Law) Act 1990 (Commencement No.2) Order 2004 (SI 2004/3448), implementing the Brussels Protocol *qv* n.16 below.

[10] Consider, *e.g.* terms of Rome I, Arts 10 (discharge) and 11 (capacity).

[11] Anton with Beaumont, p.260; Leslie, *Encyclopaedia*, p.247.

[12] L. Collins, "Contractual and non-Contractual Obligations—EEC Preliminary Draft Convention" (1976) 25 ICLQ 35; F.A. Mann, "The Proper Law of the Contract—an Obituary" (1991) 107 L.Q.R. 353; but see Jaffey (1984) 33 ICLQ 531, and P.M. North, "The EEC Convention on the Law Applicable to Contractual Obligations (1980): Its History and Main Features", reprinted in *Essays in Private International Law* (ed. North, 1993).

[13] The UK availed itself of its right not to apply Art.7.1 (mandatory rules of another law of close connection) and Art.10.1.e (consequences of nullity of contract).

[14] See also Kaye, *The New Private International Law of Contract of the European Community* (1993); and Plender & Wilderspin, *The European Contracts Conven-*

the courts of Contracting States in any contract case having foreign (not necessarily European) elements.

With regard to interpretation, the Giuliano and Lagarde Report on the Rome Convention[15] (henceforth "Giuliano & Lagarde") may be considered in ascertaining the meaning and effect of any provision.[16] Any such question shall be determined in accordance with the principles laid down by the European Court of Justice, and any relevant decision of that court; judicial notice shall be taken of relevant decisions and opinions of the ECJ. Since 1990 a body of Scottish and English decisions interpretative of Rome I has accumulated. Since March 1, 2005, appellate courts in the United Kingdom have been permitted to refer cases raising issues concerning the interpretation of Rome I to the ECJ for decision,[17] and it may be expected, in light of the Brussels Protocol, that a body of ECJ decisions will develop (possibly demonstrating methods of purposive interpretation different from those to which the UK is accustomed).

Ratification of Rome I does not prejudice the application of other international conventions to which a Contracting State is, or becomes, a party (*e.g.* Conventions on Carriage).

Scope of Rome I

In terms of Article 1, Rome I shall not apply to[18]:　　　　　　**15–04**

(a) questions involving the status or legal capacity of natural persons, without prejudice to Article 11 (*qv*);

(b) contractual obligations relating to:

— wills and succession;

— rights in property arising out of a matrimonial relationship;

— rights and duties arising out of a family relationship, parentage, marriage or affinity, including maintenance obligations in respect of children who are not legitimate[19];

---

tion: *The Rome Convention on the Choice of Law for Contracts* (2nd ed., 2001).

[15] OJ 1980 C282, 31.10. 1980.

[16] 1990 Act, s.3(1), (2) and (3)(a).

[17] The Contracts (Applicable Law) Act 1990 (Commencement No.2) Order 2004 (SI 2004/3448). The Brussels Protocol 1998, permitting such references, could not come into force earlier as it had not been ratified by all the EU Member States. Sufficient ratification now has occurred (by UK, and all other EU Member States except the most recent accessions).

[18] Art.1.2, 1.3 and 1.4.

[19] Maintenance obligations generally are excluded from the scope of Rome I (contrast Council Regulation 44/2001, Art.5.2). But see Giuliano & Lagarde, p.11.

(c) obligations arising under bills of exchange, cheques and promissory notes and other negotiable instruments to the extent that the obligations under such other negotiable instruments arise out of their negotiable character[20];

(d) arbitration agreements and agreements on the choice of court[21];

(e) questions governed by the law of companies[22] and other bodies corporate or unincorporate such as the creation, by registration or otherwise, legal capacity, internal organisation or winding-up of companies and other bodies corporate or unincorporate and the personal liability of officers and members as such for the obligations of the company or body;

(f) the question whether an agent is able to bind a principal, or an organ to bind a company or body corporate or unincorporate, to a third party[23];

(g) the constitution of trusts and the relationship between settlors, trustees and beneficiaries[24];

(h) evidence and procedure, without prejudice to Article 14.

The rules of Rome I do not apply to contracts of insurance which cover risks situated in the territories of EU Member States.[25] This exclusion, however, does not apply to contracts of re-insurance.

IDENTIFICATION OF THE GOVERNING LAW OF A CONTRACT

15–05 Although a contract may contain elements connecting it with a number of different legal systems, if it is closely analysed, it will be found that its main elements can be localised, and that it has, or is deemed to have, a closer connection with one particular law than with any other law. This law, the governing law, was known at common law as the "proper law of the contract". Its successor

---

[20] *i.e.* not simply because payment under a contract was made by cheque. Characterisation as a negotiable instrument is governed by the *lex fori*. See Giuliano & Lagarde, p.11.

[21] The UK delegation did not favour this exclusion.

[22] *i.e.* concerning internal operation of the entity; contracts made with such bodies and not otherwise excluded are subject to Rome I.

[23] But contracts made between agent and principal *are* governed by Rome I. See paras 15–40 *et seq.* below; and Giuliano & Lagarde, p.13.

[24] See Recognition of Trusts Act 1987.

[25] In order to determine whether a risk is situated in these territories the court shall apply its internal law. There is sectoral (*i.e.* specific) provision for the subject of insurance.

under the 1990 Act is termed "the applicable law". It is the legal centre of gravity of the contract, and in it there is to be found the origin and determinant of the rights and obligations of the contracting parties.

Nature of the governing law

The proper/applicable law must be determined according to the **15–06** facts as they exist at the date of making the contract, and not taking into account actings after the conclusion of the contract.[26] It is generally thought that a contract must have a governing law from the outset: the governing law is held to attach at the time the contract is concluded, even though it may not be visible and may require subsequently to be identified. Therefore it has been said that the proper law cannot float:[27] a contract cannot be "anarchic" since, should a problem arise immediately upon conclusion thereof, there must be a law to determine the existence and extent of a remedy.[28]

(a) More than one proper/applicable law

There are unusual cases in which different parts of a contract may **15–07** have closer connections with different systems of law. There is no reason why the provisions of a contract should not be severable,[29] and the result, exceptionally, is that different proper/applicable laws may govern different parts of a contract. This remains the position in terms of Rome I, Article 3.1.

(b) Change of governing law

By agreement, the parties may change the proper/applicable law **15–08** after conclusion of the contract. This is confirmed by Rome I, Article 3.2, subject to the proviso that such variation shall not

---

[26] *Compagnie Tunisienne de Navigation v Compagnie d'Armement Maritime* [1970] 3 All E.R. 71; *James Miller & Partners Ltd v Whitworth Street Estates (Manchester) Ltd* [1970] 1 All E.R. 796 (though since the parties by their subsequent conduct had acquiesced in Scottish arbitration proceedings, Scots law governed the curial procedure).

[27] See *The Armar* [1981] 1 All E.R. 498; *E.I. du Pont de Nemours v Agnew (No.2)* [1987] 2 Ll Rep. 585 (C.A.); and *Libyan Foreign Bank v Bankers' Trust Co.* [1987] 2 F.T.L.R. 509.

[28] *The Armar* [1981] 1 All E.R. 498. Though see Plender & Wilderspin, para.5-06, arguing that it is the purpose of Art.3 to allow maximum scope to party autonomy, and must be taken to permit that which it does not forbid; hence, in their view, a floating choice of law clause *is* permissible under Rome I.

[29] Cheshire, *International Contracts*, (1948), p.42; Schmitthoff, 3/106; Wolff, p.422; *Greer v Poole* (1880) 5 Q.B.D. 272; *Adelaide Electric Supply Co. v Prudential Ass. Co.* [1934] A.C. 122 at 151; *Re Int. Trustee* [1937] A.C. 500; *Mount Albert Borough Council* [1938] A.C. 224; *Forsikringsaktieselskapet Vesta v Butcher* [1986] 2 All E.R. 488, at 504–505, aff'd [1988] 1 Ll Rep. 19, at 29–33, 34–35, CA; and [1989] 2 W.L.R. 290, HL; and *Libyan Arab Foreign Bank v Bankers' Trust Co.* [1987] 2 FTLR 509.

prejudice the contract's formal validity, or adversely affect the rights of third parties.

(c) Change in substance of governing law

15–09 The proper/applicable law of a contract is not static and does not remain fixed or frozen according to the provisions of that law at the date of formation of the contract. The applicable law, as it stands from time to time, governs. Changes in substantive law may bring private law advantages and disadvantages, respectively, to the parties.[30]

COMMON LAW CHOICE OF LAW RULES IN CONTRACT

15–10 As explained above, well-established common law principles and approaches remain of use in cases which fall outside the scope of Rome I, and also may be called in aid for amplification of Rome I, or where the 1990 Act is silent.

Ascertaining the proper law[31]

Party autonomy: choice of proper law

15–11 At common law, parties' expressed intention determined the proper law of a contract.[32] The guideline was taken to be that set down by Lord Wright in *Vita Food Products Inc. v Unus Shipping Co.*,[33] namely that (a) the law selected has been chosen in good faith; (b) the choice is legal; and (c) the choice is not contrary to public policy.[34] Opinion varied as to whether there required to be some factual connection between the choice of law and the facts of the contract.[35] The absence of reported cases where the validity of

---

[30] *Re Chesterman's Trusts* [1923] 2 Ch. 466; and *Kahler v Midland Bank Ltd* [1950] A.C. 24.

[31] When referring to the proper law, the past tense of the verb is preferred, although there are cases, limited in number, which continue to be regulated by the common law rules.

[32] *e.g. Earl of Stair v Head* (1844) 6 D. 904; *The Nina* (1867) L.R. 2 P.C. 38; *British Controlled Oilfields v Stagg* [1921] W.N. 319; *Jones v Oceanic Steam Navigation Co.* [1924] 2 K.B. 730; *Anselme Dewavrin v Wilson* (1931) Ll Rep. 289; *Feist v Société Intercommunale* [1934] A.C. 161; *Vita Food Products v Unus Shipping Co.* [1939] A.C. 277; *Ocean Steamship Co. v Queensland State Wheat Board* [1941] 1 K.B. 402; *Stirling's Trs v Legal & General*, 1957 S.L.T. 73; *English v Donnelly*, 1958 S.C. 494; *Golden Acres v Queensland Estates* (1969) St. R. Qd. 738 (Australia); and *Queensland Estates v Collas* [1971] St. R. Qd. 75.

[33] [1939] A.C. 277, 290.

[34] The requirements were readily understood, but equally readily, or wilfully, were queried: at what point does (legitimate?) self-interest extinguish or grievously impair good faith? "Legal" by which law?

[35] Cheshire was of the view that an unconnected choice would be ineffective: see Cheshire & North (11th ed.), pp.471–472.

an express choice of law was disputed suggests that, in practice, the parties' agreement would rule: parties, for their own reasons, might wish to choose a "neutral" law. A self-interested choice, lacking in good faith, and/or contrary to public policy (of the forum) would be struck down by the court.[36]

Parties' choice was limited to the choice of a law having sufficiently well developed rules on contract to serve the purpose of the choice.[37] Parties might not choose as governing law, for example the "rules of comity of nations", which would be inappropriate, or insufficient, to provide an answer to the problems which may arise.[38] Particular provisions of a foreign law might be expressly incorporated as terms of a contract: this is not the same as making the whole of that foreign law the proper law.[39]

Determination of proper law in absence of express choice of law

At common law there were subjective and objective approaches to **15–12** the determination of the proper law. The subjective approach sought to find the intention of the parties, albeit never expressed: "[t]he proper law is the law which the parties either expressly or impliedly have chosen to govern their contractual relations."[40] The search, therefore, was for supposed intention, the hypothesis being that the parties had entertained an intention. The objective approach preferred to treat as the proper law the law with which the contract had the most real and substantial connection objectively, considering the facts of the case as a whole. The court, therefore, supplied the (reasonable) intention. An example of the latter approach is provided by *The Assunzione*[41] in which it was said that Italian law was the law which just and reasonable persons ought to have chosen had they thought about the matter.[42] A significant common law case, in the decade preceding the 1990 Act, is the House of Lords decision in *Amin Rasheed Shipping Corp. v Kuwait Ins. Co. The Al Wahab.*[43]

---

[36] But the principal authority is Australian: *Golden Acres v Queensland Estates* (1969) St. R. Qd. 738 (Australia); and *Queensland Estates v Collas* [1971] St. R. Qd. 75.

[37] See paras 15–13 and 15–49, below.

[38] P. Stone, p.235.

[39] Dicey and Morris, para.32-086. See *Amin Rasheed* [1984] A.C. 50, *per* Lord Wilberforce at 69–70; and *Vesta v Butcher* [1988] 1 Ll Rep. 19, aff'd on other grounds [1989] A.C. 852.

[40] *Re United Railways of Havana and Regla Warehouses Ltd* [1958] 1 Ch. 724, *per* Wynn-Parry J. at 756; see also *R v Int Trustee* [1937] A.C. 500; *cf. Zebrarise Ltd v De Nieffe* [2005] 1 Ll's Rep. 154.

[41] [1954] P. 150.

[42] *Boissevain v Weil* [1949] 1 K.B. 482, aff'd [1950] A.C. 327, *per* Lord Denning: the proper law of a contract "depends not so much on the place where it is made, nor even on the intention of the parties, or on the place where it is to be performed, but on the place with which it has the most substantial connexion" (at 490).

[43] [1983] 2 All E.R. 884.

Where no expressed choice was made, the court would derive help from certain indications or pointers such as:

Locus contractus

The *locus contractus* is the place where, technically, a contract is deemed to have been concluded, and is determined by the *lex fori*. A contract may be entered into face to face,[44] but the circumstances, especially in conflict cases, are likely to be more complex. In the case of a contract entered into by exchange of documents posted in different places, the locus is the place where the acceptance is posted,[45] but where a contract is entered into by instantaneous means of communication, the locus is the place where the acceptance is received.[46] The latter principle was approved, in 1982, by the House of Lords in *Brinkibon Ltd v Stahag Stahl und Stahlwarenhandelgesellschaft GmbH*,[47] subject to a warning that in view of technological advances, the rule may have to give way on occasion to considerations of where the risk should lie.[48]

At common law, ascertainment of the *locus contractus* was a first step to finding the proper law of the contract. However, where challenged by another contending law, the *locus contractus* rarely would prevail as governing law.[49] Where, on the other hand, the *locus contractus* and the place of performance of the contract coincided, it would be rare for a different law to be the proper law.

Submission to a particular jurisdiction

A contractual term by which the parties agreed to submit to the jurisdiction of a particular court was considered to indicate, in general, that the law of that court was the proper law. The converse, however, was not true: choice of a particular law did not render the parties subject to the jurisdiction of the courts of that legal system if they were not otherwise subject thereto.[50]

Arbitration clauses

Until 1968, an arbitration clause was held to be a very important factor in ascertaining the proper law: if differences were to be

---

[44] *Rutherford & Son v Miln & Co.*, 1941 S.C. 125.

[45] *Benaim v Debono* [1924] A.C. 514.

[46] *Entores Ltd v Miles Far East Corp.* [1955] 2 Q.B. 327; *Mauroux v Pereira* [1972] 1 W.L.R. 962; *Brinkibon Ltd v Stahag Stahl und Stahlwarenhandelgesellschaft GmbH* [1982] 1 All E.R. 293. See para.15–43, below.

[47] [1982] 1 All E.R. 293.

[48] See, *per* Lord Wilberforce in *Brinkibon* above, at 296: "[n]o universal rule can cover all such cases; they must be resolved by reference to the intention of the parties, by sound business practice and in some cases by a judgment where the risks should lie."

[49] See Lord Mansfield's second presumption, n.56, below.

[50] *N.V. Kwik Hoo Tong Handel Maatschappij v James Findlay & Co. Ltd* [1927] A.C. 604; *Dunbee Ltd v Gilmour & Co.* [1968] 2 Ll Rep. 394.

settled by arbitration in a particular place, or by an arbiter to be appointed in such a place, it was presumed that the parties intended that their rights should be governed by the law of that place.[51] Morris, in 1968,[52] stated that "there is an almost irrebuttable presumption that the law of that country is the proper law of the contract as a whole". Decisions of the House of Lords of 1970[53] show, however, that although an arbitration clause was still a very strong factor, it was not conclusive and might give way to other indications. Moreover, they show that the law of the arbitration was not necessarily the same as that of the proper law: its procedure might be governed by a law different from that of the proper law (which it was required to apply to the substance of the dispute), and in that event, procedure, including review of the arbiter's award, would be governed by the (curial) law of the arbitration.[54]

Language

On occasion, the court derived help from the terms or language in which the contract was framed to determine the proper law.[55]

Presumptions

Presumptions traceable to Lord Mansfield in the 1760s sometimes were used, for example in favour of the *lex loci contractus*, if the

---

[51] *Hamlyn & Co. v Talisker Distillery* (1894) 21 R. (H.L.) 21; *Girvin Roper & Co. v Monteith* (1895) 23 R. 129; *Spurrier v La Cloche* [1902] A.C. 446; *Austrian Lloyd Steamship Co. v Gresham Life Ass. Soc.* [1903] 1 K.B. 249; *Robertson v Brandes Schonwald & Co.* (1906) 8 F. 815; *Johannesburg Municipal Council v D. Stewart & Co.*, 1909 S.C. (H.L.) 53; *Kirchner & Co. v Gruban* [1909] 1 Ch. 413; *Pena Copper Mines v Rio Tinto Co. Ltd* (1911) 103 L.T. 846; *Norske Atlas Insurance Co. Ltd v London General Insurance Co. Ltd* (1972) 43 T.L.R. 541; *Perry v Equitable Life Assoc. Soc.* (1929) 45 T.L.R. 468; *Kennedy v London Express* [1931] I.R. 532; *National Bank of Greece and Athens v Metliss* [1958] A.C. 509; *Tzortzis v Monark Line* [1968] 1 W.L.R. 406.

[52] Morris Cases, p.280.

[53] *Compagnie Tunisienne de Navigation v Compagnie d'Armement Maritime* [1970] 3 All E.R. 71; and *James Miller & Partners Ltd v Whitworth Street Estates (Manchester) Ltd* [1970] 1 All E.R. 796.

[54] See also *Astro Vencedor v Babanaft* [1971] 2 Q.B. 588; *Tracomin SA v Sudan Oil Seeds Co. Ltd (No. 2)* [1983] 2 All E.R. 129; *Astro Venturoso Compania Naviera v Hellenic Shipyards S.A. (The Mariannina)* [1983] 1 Ll Rep. 12; *Furness Withy (Australia) v Metal Distributors (U.K.) (The Amazonia)* [1990] 1 Ll Rep. 236.

[55] *The Industrie* [1894] P. 58 (reference to "Act of God" or "the Queen's Enemies" helped Lord Esher M.R. to reach the conclusion that the charterparty in English form for the carriage of goods on a German ship had an English proper law. He placed reliance not on any one fact but on all of them together, but nevertheless he found it noteworthy that the terms used were applicable to English and not to German law. The case is an exception to carriage by sea cases decided at about that date, where the preference in case of doubt was for the law of the flag (though the law of the flag may be meaningless in the circumstances; *Compagnie Tunisienne*, above).

See also *Re Pilkington's Trusts* [1937] Ch. 574 (whole phraseology of deed indicated a Scots deed).

contract was to be performed where made; otherwise the *lex loci solutionis*[56]; the law of the flag in a contract of affreightment, if no closer connection with another law was demonstrated; the more effective law,[57] that is, the law which favours validity of the contract, or validity of a particular clause; the *lex situs* in cases concerning immoveables[58]; or the place where a professional person practises.[59]

By the mid to late twentieth century,[60] use of these presumptions had fallen from favour.

ROME I—CHOICE OF LAW RULES IN CONTRACT

Identification of the applicable law

Choice of applicable law by the parties

15–13 Rome I permits freedom of choice of applicable law by the parties,[61] but engrafts on to the chosen system "mandatory rules"[62] of other systems. Thus, in the first instance:

Article 3: Freedom of choice

1. A contract shall be governed by the law chosen by the parties. The choice must be express or demonstrated with reasonable

---

[56] *Chatenay v Brazilian Submarine Telegraph Co.* [1891] 1 Q.B. 79; *Re Missouri SS Co.* (1889) 42 Ch. D. 321; *Hansen v Dixon* (1906) 23 T.L.R. 56; *Mackintosh v May* (1895) 22 R. 345; *Kremezi v Ridgway* [1949] 1 All E.R. 662; *Benaim v Debono* [1924] A.C. 514; *Mauroux v Soc. Com Abel Pereira* [1972] 1 W.L.R. 962.

[57] This presumption seems to have been rarely used. The germ of the idea may be seen in *Hamlyn v Talisker Distillery* (1894) 21 R. (H.L.) 21. It is potentially unfair and liable to encourage *ex post facto* reasoning. See May L.J. in *Monterosso Shipping Co. L.A. v International Transport Workers' Federation* [1982] 3 All E.R. 841 at 848, upon comments made in *Coast Lines Ltd v Hudig & Veder Chartering NV* [1972] 2 Q.B. 34. See also *P & O v Shand* (1865) 3 Moore P.C. (N.S.) 272 and *Re Missouri SS Co.* (1889) 42 Ch. D. 321.

[58] *Mount Albert Borough Council v Australasian etc. Life Ass. Soc.* [1938] A.C. 224. Exceptionally, another law was held to apply usually in situations where the cases were concerned with personal rights arising from contracts involving land, rather than real rights in land. *Cood* (1863) 33 Beav. 314; *BSA Co. v De Beers* [1910] 2 Ch. 502; *Liquidator of the Salt Mines Syndicate Ltd* (1895) 2 S.L.T. 489. An unusual Scottish example is *Hamilton v Wakefield*, 1993 S.L.T. (Sh.Ct) 30. See also in jurisdiction *Webb v Webb* [1994] Q.B. 696.

[59] *R. v Doutre* (1884) 9 A.C. 745; *Re Maugham* (1885) 2 T.L.R. 115.

[60] See *Coast lines v Hudig & Veder Chartering* [1972] 2 Q.B. 34, *per* Lord Denning, 44.

[61] And subsequent variation thereof within the terms of Art.3: *ISS Machinery Services Ltd v Aeolian Shipping SA ("The Aeolian")* [2001] 2 Ll Rep. 641.

[62] See para.15–17, below. *Cf.* provisions in English/Scots law in pre-1990 Act days, often termed "overriding legislation of the forum", such as Unfair Contract Terms Act 1977, s.27 and Timeshare Act 1992.

certainty[63] by the terms of the contract or the circumstances of the case. By their choice the parties can select the law applicable to the whole, or a part only, of the contract.

2. The parties may at any time agree to subject the contract to a law other than that which previously governed it, whether as a result of an earlier choice under this Article or of other provisions of this Convention. Any variation by the parties of the law to be applied made after the conclusion of the contract shall not prejudice its formal validity under Article 9 or adversely affect the rights of third parties.

3. The fact that the parties have chosen a foreign law, whether or not accompanied by the choice of a foreign tribunal, shall not, *where all the other elements relevant to the situation at the time of the choice are connected with one country only, prejudice the application of rules of the law of that country which cannot be derogated from by contract*, hereinafter called "mandatory rules".[64]

4. The existence and validity of the consent of the parties as to the choice of the applicable law shall be determined in accordance with the provisions of Articles 8, 9 and 11.

Parties may choose,[65] by means of Article 3, only the law of a country (ie a body of State law), capable of ascertainment, and capable of answering any problem which may arise concerning the contract; as at common law, adequacy of a system to answer a question arising out of a contract is an essential prerequisite. Rome I does not contemplate, or permit, choice of a non-State system of law, such as the *lex mercatoria*, or a body of religious law.[66]

---

[63] This provision includes not only cases of express choice (encompassing an express choice of law contained in General Conditions of Sale in an auction catalogue, deemed to have been accepted by all bidders: *Morin v Bonham & Brooks Ltd* [2004] 1 Ll Rep. 702), but also cases where the choice can be inferred through, for example, earlier course of dealing or standard conditions of the trade; see Giuliano & Lagarde, p.17. The court may not infer a choice of law, however, which the parties might have made, if they had no clear intention of making a choice. Contrast approach at common law.

[64] Emphasis added.

[65] The issue whether a party later may be heard to say that his consent to a contract including a choice of law and jurisdiction clause, was not real or genuine, or existent at the time of purported conclusion of the contract, was raised in *Horn and Linie GmbH & Co. v Panamericana Formas E Impresos SA, Ace Seguros SA* [2006] EWHC 373 (Comm.), before Morison J., who held that in the circumstances the defendants must be held to the choice which they had expressly made: "I can think of no good reason why it would be reasonable to judge the consent of the Defendants otherwise than by the law of their choice" (para.19). As to law governing validity of choice itself and scope of clause, see *Finance One Public Co. Ltd v Lehmann Bros Special Financing Inc.*, 414 F. 3d 325 (2nd cir. 2005).

[66] See *Shamil Bank of Bahrain EC v Beximco Pharmaceuticals Ltd* [2004] 1 W.L.R. 1784, *per* Potter L.J., at para.48; references to Sharia law merely reflected the

Moreover, it would not be acceptable for parties to choose, under authorisation of Rome I, the common law of England or Scotland pertaining to contract as it stood prior to the coming into force of Rome I, *i.e.* parties cannot use Rome I to contract out of Rome I.

The parties' choice is subject to the provisions of Article 3.3 (an anti-avoidance provision), as well as to the "mandatory rules" of the forum (Article 7.2),[67] and the public policy of the forum (Article 16).

Determination of applicable law in the absence of choice of law

Article 4: Applicable law in the absence of choice

15–14 1. To the extent that the law applicable to the contract has not been chosen in accordance with Article 3, the contract shall be governed by the law of the country[68] with which it is most closely connected. Nevertheless, a severable part of the contract which has a closer connection with another country may by way of exception be governed by the law of that other country.

2. Subject to the provisions of paragraph 5 of this Article, it shall be presumed that the contract is most closely connected with the country where the party who is to effect the performance which is characteristic of the contract has, at the time of conclusion of the contract, his habitual residence, or, in the case of a body corporate or unincorporate, its central administration.[69] However, if the

---

Islamic religious principles according to which the Bank did business; the form of words used did not incorporate Sharia law as the governing law of the contract. The attempt was inept, procedurally as well as substantively. Also *Halpern v Halpern* [2006] All E.R. (D.) 389 wherein, however, Clarke J., at para.51, noted that parties' desire to have a dispute regulated by a body of non-State law (in the instant case Jewish law) could be fulfilled by their submission to arbitration, provided that the agreement to arbitrate should itself be enforceable under a national system of law.

[67] The UK exercised its right not to accept Art.7.1, the terms of which are as follows: "When applying under this Convention the law of a country, effect may be given to the mandatory rules of the law of another country with which the situation has a close connection, if and in so far as, under the law of the latter country, those rules must be applied whatever the law applicable to the contract. In considering whether to give effect to these mandatory rules, regard shall be had to their nature and purpose and to the consequences of their application or non-application." This provision was regarded by a number of delegations with misgiving, as novel and uncertain (Giuliano & Lagarde, p.27).

[68] At common law, the "law" (*i.e.* system of law) most closely connected. *cf. Rossano v Manufacturers' Life Insurance Co.* [1963] 2 Q.B. 352 (the Egyptian "country" of closest connection fell back to a position of no importance against the Ontarian law of closest connection). See Cheshire & North, pp.567–568.

[69] *Sierra Leone Telecommunications Co. Ltd v Barclays Bank plc* [1998] 2 All E.R. 820 (performance of the obligation of repaying a sum deposited in a bank account was made through the branch where the account was kept, and therefore the applicable law was the law of the country where the account was kept).

contract is entered into in the course of that party's trade or profession, that country shall be the country in which the principal place of business is situated or, where under the terms of the contract the performance is to be effected through a place of business other than the principal place of business,[70] the country in which that other place of business is situated.

3. Notwithstanding the provisions of paragraph 2 of this Article, to the extent that the subject matter of the contract is a right in immovable property or a right to use immovable property it shall be presumed that the contract is most closely connected with the country where the immovable property is situated.

4. A contract for the carriage of goods shall not be subject to the presumption in paragraph 2. In such a contract if the country in which, at the time the contract is concluded, the carrier has his principal place of business is also the country in which the place of loading or the place of discharge or the principal place of business of the consignor is situated, it shall be presumed that the contract is most closely connected with that country. In applying this paragraph single voyage charter-parties and other contracts the main purpose of which is the carriage of goods shall be treated as contracts for the carriage of goods.

5. Paragraph 2 shall not apply if the characteristic performance cannot be determined, and[71] the presumptions in paragraphs 2, 3 and 4 shall be disregarded if it appears from the circumstances as a whole that the contract is more closely connected with another country.

Article 4.2

The provisions of Article 4.2, which are derived from Swiss conflict **15–15** rules, have excited much comment, some of it adverse. While it is true that at common law the *lex loci solutionis* usually was preferred to the *lex loci contractus* (where they differed), and that while in identifying the place of performance, "performance" by means of manufacture or creative work was rated more meaningful than "performance" by way of payment made by the other party,[72] Rome I introduced a significant change in its choice of the connecting factor of *habitual residence* of the characteristic performer. It may be felt that such a choice of connecting factor is idiosyncratic.[73]

---

[70] See *Ennstone Ltd v Stanger Ltd* [2002] 1 W.L.R. 3059.

[71] Meaning "in addition" *or* "alternatively"; Art.4.5 comprises two gates which, independently of each other, may open the way to an unfettered consideration in the old style of all potentially relevant factors and indications.

[72] Giuliano & Lagarde, p.20.

[73] See discussion by Blaikie, "Choice of Law in Contract, 'Characteristic Performance' and the EEC Contracts Convention", 1983 S.L.T. 241. Also *Ophthalmic Innovations International (UK) Ltd v Ophthalmic Innovations International Inc* [2005] I L Pr 10.

The concept of *"characteristic performance"* itself was new to the UK in 1990. Giuliano & Lagarde explain it thus: "[i]n addition it is possible to relate the concept of characteristic performance to an even more general idea, namely the idea that his performance refers to the function which the legal relationship involved fulfils in the economic and social life of any country. The concept of characteristic performance essentially links the contract to the social and economic environment of which it will form a part." Make of that what you may. It seems that under Rome I manufacture is more characteristic than payment; provision of a service more characteristic than payment for the service; performance by a banker of his side of a contract with a customer as more characteristic than the customer's obligation.[74] The tendency is to favour the party effecting the "positive" performance rather than the reciprocal pecuniary obligation.

The relative strengths of Article 4.2 and 4.5[75]

15–16 It is permitted to disregard Article 4.2 if characteristic performance cannot be determined;[76] or if it appears from the circumstances as a whole that the contract is more closely connected with another country.[77] It is this latter clause of Article 4.5 which permits UK courts to draw upon the pre-existing body of common law case law concerning determination of the proper law of a contract.

The relationship between Articles 4.2 and 4.5 (*i.e.* their relative strengths) has been a matter of controversy. According to Article 4.5, the presumptions in Articles 4.2, 4.3 and 4.4 shall be disregarded if it appears from the circumstances as a whole that the contract is more closely connected with another country. The EU Commission favours the approach taken in the decision of the Dutch Hoge Raad in *Société Nouvelle des Papeteries de l'Aa SA v BV Machinenfabriek BOA*,[78] which applied the Dutch law of the place of business of the sellers as the applicable law in circumstances where all other contacts were with French law. The

---

[74] *Bank of Baroda v Vysya Bank Ltd* [1994] 2 Ll Rep. 87. See also *Ark Therapeutics Plc v Time North Capital Ltd* [2006] 1 All E.R. (Comm) 138 (a "unilateral contract").

[75] See J. Hill, "Choice of Law in Contract under the Rome Convention", 2004 (53) ICLQ 325; and S. Atrill, "Choice of Law in Contract: the Missing Pieces of the Article 4 Jigsaw", 2004 (53) ICLQ 549.

[76] As in *Print Concept GmbH v GEW (EC) Ltd* [2001] EWCA Civ. 352, in which Longmore L.J. held that the supply of products, rather than their onward sale, was the performance characteristic of the contract. (This having been decided, there was no need to employ Art.4.5.)

[77] *cf. Kenburn Waste Management Ltd v Bergmann, The Times*, July 9, 2001 (and on appeal [2002] EWCA Civ. 98), concerning a negative obligation, the nature of which made it justifiable in the view of the English forum to displace Art.4.2.

[78] September 25, 1992.

contract for the sale of a paper press by a Dutch seller to a French buyer had been negotiated and completed in France; the press had been delivered to the buyer in France, there to be assembled by him; the order had been placed in France with the French agent of the Dutch seller; and payment was to be made in French francs. The buyer having failed to pay, the sellers elected to sue him in the Netherlands, using the special jurisdiction in contract then extant.[79] Jurisdiction was challenged by the French parties, arguing that the place of performance (being the obligation to pay) was in France. In terms of Brussels I, Article 5.1, it was necessary for the forum of a Contracting State first to identify the applicable law, and by that law to determine whether the legal system of the forum was the place of performance of the obligation in question. On this rationale, the Dutch court, applying Article 4.2, found Dutch law to be the applicable law. The decision represents a strong preference for the certainty which application of Article 4.2 delivers, over the possible benefits of appropriateness inherent in displacement of Article 4.2 by means of Article 4.5 and the discretion which the latter provision confers. It will be noted, however, that in the instant case, the decision permitted the forum to apply its own Dutch law.

The wording of Article 4.5, and choice of the verb "disregard",[80] suggest that a variety of interpretative approaches might justifiably be taken.[81]

An early English case interpretative of Article 4.2 is *Bank of Baroda v Vysya Bank*,[82] concerning a letter of credit. The contract between the issuing and the confirming Banks was English law, *per* Article 4.2. Although the applicable law of the principal contract (for which the inter-Bank contract was facilitative) would have been governed by Indian law *per* Article 4.2, Mance J. (as he then was) held that, for clarity and simplicity, it was desirable that all aspects of this contractual nexus be governed by the same applicable law (English law). Article 4.5 was the means by which to secure this result.

The line of English authority evinces a preference for use of Article 4.5 in order to confer a wider discretion upon the forum in its identification of the applicable law, a discretion which, in a

---

[79] Brussels I, Art.5.1.

[80] See generally *Definitely Maybe (Touring) Ltd v Marek Lieberberg Konzertagentur GmbH* [2001] 4 All E.R. 283, *per* Morison J., at 287/8; *Credit Lyonnais v New Hampshire Insurance Co.* [1997] 2 Ll Rep. 1, *per* Hobhouse L.J., at 5; *Samcrete Egypt Engineers and Contractors SAE v Land Rover Exports Ltd* [2001] EWCA Civ. 2019; and *Iran Continental Shelf Oil Co. v IRI International Cooperation* [2002] EWCA Civ. 1024.

[81] See Clarkson at 223.

[82] [1994] 2 Ll Rep. 87. See also *P.T. Pan-Indonesian Bank TBK v Marconi Communications International Ltd* [2005] 2 All E.R. (Comm) 325.

number of instances, is seen to result in the choice of English law as the applicable law.[83] In contrast, the effect of the Dutch *Papeteries* decision is that Article 4.2 should be displaced only if the factor of the habitual residence of the characteristic performer has "no real value" as a connecting factor.

The leading Scots case is *Caledonia Subsea Ltd v Micoperi Srl*,[84] which at first instance and on appeal shows a clear preference for adhering to the Article 4.2 presumption.[85] The circumstances revealed a factual and legal nexus with Egyptian law, but the business of the characteristic performer was situated in Scotland. Lord President Cullen's opinion gives firm dominance to the Article 4.2 presumption: "I consider that the presumption under para 2 should not be "disregarded" unless the outcome of the comparative exercise referred to in para 5 . . . demonstrates a clear preponderance of factors in favour of another country."[86] The outcome of holding to Article 4.2 was application of the forum's own law. In order for the forum to "walk home", it is not necessary always to have resort to Article 4.5.

More rarely is difficulty encountered in ascertaining the "characteristic performance", or in identifying the party who is to effect that.[87] In *Ennstone*,[88] in which issues of contract and delict arose, in circumstances where expert advice was proffered in England, and acted upon in Scotland, the English forum held that with regard to the contractual claim, the applicable law should be determined by reference only to Article 4.2 (resulting in a finding of English applicable law). The court was not minded to take account of the final clauses of Article 4.2, which permit application of the law of a legal system other than that of the situation of the principal place of business, if performance is to be effected through a different place of business.

---

[83] e.g. *Bank of Baroda v Vysya Bank* [1994] 2 Ll. Rep. 87; *Definitely Maybe (Touring) Ltd. v Marek Lieberberg Konzertagentur GmbH* [2001] 4 All E.R. 283, *per* Morison J. at 287/8; see also *per* Hobhouse L.J. in *Credit Lyonnais v New Hampshire Insurance Co.* [1997] 2 Ll. Rep. 1, *obiter* at 5; *Samcrete Egypt Engineers and Contractors SAE v Land Rover Exports Limited* [2002] C.L.C. 533; and *P.T. Pan-Indonesian Bank TBK v Marconi Communications International Ltd* [2005] 2 All E.R. (Comm) 325. But see comments of Lawrence Collins in *Opthalmic Innovations Ltd v Opthalmic Innovatins International Inc.* [2005] I.L.Pr. 10.

[84] 2002 S.L.T. 1022. Also *William Grant v Marie Brizard Espana SA*, 1998 S.C. 536. Contrast *Ferguson Shipbuilders Ltd v Voith Hydro*, 2000 S.L.T 229, *obiter per* Lord Penrose.

[85] cf. *Krupp Uhde GmbH v Weir Westgarth Ltd*, unreported, May 31, 2002 (Lord Eassie).

[86] 1029G.

[87] See *Iran Continental Shelf Oil Co. v IRI International Cooperation* [2002] EWCA Civ. 1024; *Hogg Insurance Brokers Ltd v Guardian Insurance Co.* [1997] I Ll Rep. 412; and *Apple Corps Ltd v Apple Computer Inc.* [2004] EWHC 768.

[88] *Ennstone Ltd v Stanger Ltd* [2002] 1 W.L.R. 3059. Contrast *Iran Continental Shelf Oil Co. v I.R.I. International Co-operation*, above.

Restrictions on choice of law: mandatory rules

The approach which Rome I has adopted to the subject of party **15–17**
autonomy has been to allow choice of law, but to circumscribe that
choice by means of the compulsory application of rules of certain
other laws. There are two types of mandatory provision, internal
and overriding. While the French text of Rome I makes clear in its
use of the terms *"dispositions impératives"* (Article 3.3) and *"lois de
police"* (Article 7) that there is a difference between types of
mandatory provision, this difference is not apparent in the English
language text.

The meaning of the phrase "mandatory rules" in relation to
Article 3.3 is "rules which cannot be derogated from by contract"
(ie domestically).[89] See *Caterpillar Financial Services Corp. v SNC
Passion* [2004] 2 Ll.'s Rep. 99. The meaning in Article 7 is rules
which "must be applied whatever the law applicable to the
contract" (ie conflictually). The latter usage used to be termed in
UK law "overriding legislation of the forum", which legislation
applied no matter what the content of the foreign proper law, and
therefore was a type of directory provision, which superimposed
itself upon, or countermanded, normal conflict rules.

A court of a Member State must take its own view on the
question whether a rule of its domestic law is an (overriding)
mandatory provision for the purpose of Article 7.2. Article 3.3
secures application of the mandatory rules of the law of a country
to which "all other elements [apart from the parties' choice of law]
relevant to the situation at the time of the choice are connected".
Article 7.2 provides for application of the rules of the law of the
forum in a situation where they are mandatory irrespective of the
law otherwise applicable to the contract. Article 7.1, which permits
"effect to be given"[90] to the (overriding) mandatory rules of the law
of another country with which the situation has a close connection,
does not apply in the UK, reservation having been entered in
respect of this provision.

II. INCIDENTS OF A CONTRACT

The proper/applicable law, though it governs all essential matters, **15–18**
does not necessarily govern, or solely govern, all the incidents of a
contract. In cases regulated by the 1990 Act, the applicable law will
govern most issues, but another law may govern a particular

---

[89] See *Caterpillar Financial Services Corporation v SNC Passion* [2004] 2 Ll Rep. 99.
[90] "In considering whether to give effect to these mandatory rules, regard shall be
had to their nature and purpose, and to the consequences of their application or
non-application."

incident as an alternative to the applicable law, in addition to it, or, in substitution for it.[91]

ESTABLISHING THE FACT OF AGREEMENT

15–19 At common law, the question whether a contract has been formed is governed by the law which would be the governing law of the contract if it were held that a contract had been validly concluded (the putative proper law[92]), exemplified in *Albeko Schuhmaschinen & Co v Kamborian Shoe Machine Co. Ltd.* [93]

This rule covers the question whether there has been any consent to contract, and the question whether there has been sufficient agreement to constitute a binding bargain of sorts. Hence, questions of substance as to what constitutes acceptance, as well as "technical" questions, such as the effect of posting an unqualified acceptance (whether or not that acceptance is received by the offeror), are referred to the putative applicable law.

Article 8 of Rome I affirms the common law position (though without reference to the term *lex loci contractus*), and supplements it as follows:

Article 8: Material validity

1. The existence[94] and validity of a contract, or of any term of a contract, shall be determined by the law which would govern it under this Convention if the contract or term were valid.

2. Nevertheless a party may rely upon the law of the country in which he has his habitual residence to establish that he did not consent if it appears from the circumstances that it would not be reasonable to determine the effect of his conduct in accordance with the law specified in the preceding paragraph.

The reason for the inclusion of the discretionary power in Article 8.2 was fear of the consequences of operation of a rule of some legal systems that silence imports acceptance.[95]

---

[91] *e.g.* material validity (Art.8); formal validity (Art.9); contractual capacity (Art.11).
[92] See generally *Mackender v Feldia* [1967] 2 Q.B. 590 and *Euro-Diam Ltd v Bathurst* [1987] 2 All E.R. 113, aff'd [1990] 1 Q.B. 1.
[93] (1961) 1111 L.J. 519. See also *The Parouth* [1982] 2 Ll Rep. 351, CA.
[94] Covering, therefore, cases such as *Albeko* where the issue is the legal effect of non-arrival of an acceptance.
[95] See Giuliano & Lagarde, p.28. An appeal could be made to public policy (under Art.16) even in relation to Art.8.1.

CAPACITY TO CONTRACT

Early Scots and English cases indicated that contractual capacity **15–20** was governed by the *lex loci contractus*,[96] but preference later was shown for the putative proper law.[97] Cheshire, when he delivered the David Murray Lecture[98] at the University of Glasgow in 1948 suggested, *first*, that a contract is not void for incapacity if the parties are fully capable by the putative proper law (that is, the law objectively ascertained, for parties cannot confer on themselves capacity by simple choice of a law unconnected) and, *second*, that a party who is incapable by the putative proper law should not succeed in pleading incapacity if he is of full capacity by the law of his domicile.

This topic in practice is not simple, and there are conflicting policy considerations.[99] Article 11 of Rome I lays down a provision which is remarkably specific in its terms.[1]

Article 11: Incapacity

In a contract concluded between persons who are in the same country, a natural person who would have capacity under the law of that country may invoke his incapacity resulting from another law only if the other party to the contract was aware of this incapacity at the time of the conclusion of the contract or was not aware thereof as a result of negligence.

Where the case does not fall within the complex prerequisites of Article 11, the common law applies.

FORMAL VALIDITY

At common law a contract is formally valid if it complies with the **15–21** provisions of either the proper law or the *lex loci contractus*.[2] Essentially, the position is the same under Rome I, but the provisions are more detailed:

---

[96] *Male v Roberts* (1800) 3 Esp. 163; *McFeetridge v Stewarts & Lloyds Ltd*, 1913 S.C. 773.

[97] *Bondholders Securities Corp. v Manville* (1933) 4 D.L.R. 699; *Charron v Montreal Trust* (1958) 15 D.L.R. (2d) 240; *Bodley Head Ltd v Flegon* [1972] 1 W.L.R. 680.

[98] Printed as Cheshire, *International Contracts* (1948).

[99] See Morris, *Conflict of Laws* (1993), pp.269–271 and J. Blaikie, "Capacity to Contract: *McFeetridge v Stewarts & Lloyds* Revisited", 1984 S.L.T. (News) 161. For Scottish domestic position, see Age of Legal Capacity (Scotland) Act 1991; D. Nichols, "Can They or Can't They? Children and the Age of Legal Capacity (Scotland) Act 1991", 1991 S.L.T. 395, 399–400. These provisions will apply where the contract has a (putative) Scottish applicable law, subject to the provisions of Art.11.

[1] See commentary *per* Cheshire & North, pp.594–595.

[2] *Guepratte v Young* [1851] 4 De G. & Sm. 217; *Van Grutten v Digby* (1862) 31 Beav. 561; *Purvis's Trs. v Purvis's Exrs* (1861) 23 D. 812 (see, *per* L.J.-C. Inglis at 831) (testamentary writings); *Valery v Scott* (1876) 3 R. 965. See Leslie, pp.257–258.

Article 9: Formal validity

1. A contract concluded between persons who are in the same country is formally valid if it satisfies the formal requirements of the law which governs it under this Convention or of the law of the country where it is concluded.

2. A contract concluded between persons who are in different countries is formally valid if it satisfies the formal requirements of the law which governs it under this Convention or of the law of one of those countries.

3. Where a contract is concluded by an agent, the country in which the agent acts is the relevant country for the purposes of paragraphs 1 and 2.

4. An act intended to have legal effect relating to an existing or contemplated contract is formally valid if it satisfies the formal requirements of the law which under this Convention governs or would govern the contract or of the law of the country where the act was done.

5. The provisions of the preceding paragraphs shall not apply to a contract to which Article 5 applies, concluded in the circumstances described in paragraph 2 of Article 5. The formal validity of such a contract is governed by the law of the country in which the consumer has his habitual residence.

6. Notwithstanding paragraphs 1 to 4 of this Article, a contract the subject matter of which is a right in immovable property or a right to use immovable property shall be subject to the mandatory requirements of form of the law of the country where the property is situated if by that law those requirements are imposed irrespective of the country where the contract is concluded and irrespective of the law governing the contract.

ESSENTIAL VALIDITY

15–22 The essential validity of a contract (*i.e.* its provisions) is governed by its proper/applicable law (or putative proper/applicable law).[3] Essential validity includes all questions pertaining to substance, and

---

[3] A selection of common law cases is noted: *Jacobs Marcus & Co. v Credit Lyonnais* (1884) 12 Q.B.D. 589; *The Leon XIII* (1883) 8 P.D. 121; *Hansen v Dixon* (1906) 23 T.L.R. 56; *Kremezi v Ridgway* [1949] 1 All E.R. 662; *Equitable Trust Co. of New York v Henderson* (1930) 47 T.L.R. 90; *Société des Hotels Reunis v Hawker* (1913) 29 T.L.R. 578; *Re Bonacina* [1912] 2 Ch. 394; *Re Helbert Wagg* [1956] Ch. 323; *McCormick v Rittmeyer* (1869) 7 M. 854; *Gow v Caledonian Scrap Company* (1893) 8 Sh.Ct Rep. 65; *Keiner* [1952] 1 All E.R. 643; *Hamlyn v Talisker Distillery* (1894) 21 R. (HL) 21; *St Pierre v South American Stores* [1937] 3 All E.R. 349; *Amin Rasheed Shipping Corp. v Kuwait Ins. Co., The Al Wahab* [1983] 2 All E.R. 884; *Monterosso Shipping Co. Ltd v International Transport Workers' Federation* [1982] 3 All E.R. 841; *Gill and Duffus Landauer Ltd v London Export Corp. GmbH* [1982] 2 Ll Rep. 627; *Astro Venturoso Compania Naviera v Hellenic Shipyards SA (The Mariannina)* [1983] 1 Ll Rep. 12; *Armour v Thyssen Edelstahlwerke AG*, 1986 S.L.T. 94; 1990 S.L.T. 891; *Zahnrad Fabrik Passau GmbH v Terex Ltd*, 1986 S.L.T. 84.

to the rights and obligations of the parties generally: the need for consideration; excuses for non-performance; interest;[4] acquiescence; rejection of goods as disconform to contract[5]; retention of payment[6]; liability for damages; *jus quaesitum tertio*; the effect of a moratorium; the effect of war; the effects of exemption and indemnity clauses, etc. The proper/applicable law therefore determines all questions as to the rights of parties and defences, subject to the qualification that contractual rights may not be enforceable if illegal[7] or contrary to public policy of the forum, and subject to the rules concerning "mandatory provisions" introduced by Rome I. Article 10 provides as follows:

Article 10: Scope of the applicable law

1. The law applicable to a contract by virtue of Articles 3 to 6 and 12 of this Convention shall govern in particular:[8]

    (a) interpretation;

    (b) performance;

    (c) within the limits of the powers conferred on the court by its procedural law, the consequences of breach, including the assessment of damages[9] in so far as it is governed by rules of law;

    (d) the various ways of extinguishing obligations, and prescription and limitation of actions;

    (e) [the consequences of nullity of contract.][10]

2. In relation to the manner of performance and the steps to be taken in the event of defective performance regard shall be had to the law of the country in which performance takes place.

Effect of statutory provisions

At common law, the general rule is that statutory provisions, **15–23** whether Scottish, British or foreign, affect a contract only if they are part of the proper law[11]; or if they regulate the enforcement of

---

[4] *Parken v Royal Exchange Assurance Co.* (1846) 8 D. 365.

[5] *Benaim & Co. v Debono* [1924] A.C. 514; *Sellar & Sons v Gladstone & Co.* (1868) 5 S.L.R. 417; *Gow v Caledonian Scrap Co.* (1892) 8 Sh.Ct Rep. 65.

[6] *cf. Bank of East Asia Ltd v Scottish Enterprise*, 1997 S.L.T. 1213.

[7] See discussion below.

[8] The list is not comprehensive.

[9] *cf.* at common law *D'Almeida Araujo Lda v Becker & Co. Ltd* [1953] 2 Q.B. 329.

[10] By UK reservation Art.10.1.e does not apply in UK conflict rules because the consequences of nullity are regarded as pertaining to rules of restitution. See Ch.16, below.

[11] *Kleinwort Sons & Co. v Ungarische Baumwolle* [1939] 2 K.B. 678; *Vita Food Products v Unus Shipping Co.* [1939] A.C. 277; *Arab Bank v Barclays Bank* [1954] A.C. 495; *English v Donnelly*, 1959 S.L.T. 2; *Metliss v National Bank of Greece & Athens* [1958] A.C. 509; *Adams v National Bank of Greece & Athens* [1961] A.C. 255; *Rossano v Manufacturers Life Ins. Co.* [1963] 2 Q.B. 352.

rights under a contract in a particular place where the contract is to be performed, that is, if they are of a procedural nature or regulate social policy there. Hence, excuses or defences attributable to statutes which are not part of the proper law are not operative or effective in a British forum,[12] unless the existence of such defences in the *lex fori* is sufficient to prompt an argument upon public policy (Article 16), or mandatory provision of the forum (Article 7.2).

By virtue of Article 10 of Rome I, statutes forming part of the applicable law apply (subject to the mandatory rules of other laws, statutory or not). As to "manner of performance" and "steps to be taken in the event of defective performance", the law, statutory or not, of the country in which performance takes place may regulate.[13]

CONSTRUCTION OR INTERPRETATION

15-24 At common law the construction or interpretation of a contract is determined by the law selected or declared by the parties to govern that aspect of the contract. In the absence of a clause providing for interpretation, the law indicated by the contract will apply; in the majority of cases, this will be the proper law, but that law does not necessarily apply and probably will not apply if the contract is written in a language different from that of the proper law.[14]

Article 10.1.a of Rome I refers the matter of interpretation to the applicable law of the contract.

DISCHARGE

15-25 The problem here is the extent to which obligations under a contract may be affected, or even completely discharged, by subsequent events, including the insolvency of a contracting party,

---

[12] *Kleinwort Sons & Co. v Ungarische Baumwolle* [1939] 2 K.B. 678, *Rossano*, both above; contrast *Metliss and Adams*, above; see also *Kahler v Midland Bank Ltd* [1950] A.C. 24.

[13] Giuliano & Lagarde suggest (p.33) that the court may consider whether such law has any relevance to the manner of performance, and has discretion whether to apply it in whole or in part "so as to do justice between the parties". It is generally thought that the provision is intended to refer to minor matters such as the definition of "normal business hours", where it would seem appropriate to take into account local business practice. The law of the place of performance seems unlikely to be granted any fuller role under this Article.

[14] *Bonython v Com. of Australia* [1951] A.C. 201; [1952] A.C. 493; *The Assunzione* [1954] P. 150; *Re Helbert Wagg* [1956] Ch. 323; *Corocraft Ltd v Pan American Airways Inc.* [1969] 1 Q.B. 616; *The Alexandria* [1972] 1 Ll Rep. 399; *Woodhouse A.C. Israel Cocoa Ltd v Nigerian Produce Marketing Co. Ltd* [1972] A.C. 741; *Alan v El Nasr Export* [1972] 2 Q.B. 189.

particularly if such events take place in, or are governed by, a law other than the proper/applicable law.

A general discharge of obligations, or some other act purporting to discharge obligations, is effective if it is effective under the proper/applicable law of the contract. Thus, the proper law determines the effect of war, supervening impossibility, moratorium, confiscatory and other legislation.[15] Similarly the effect of novation, delegation,[16] and acceptilation must be determined by the proper/applicable law of the principal obligation (rather than that of the derivative agreement[17]).

The same principle applies with regard to the universal discharge of all obligations following upon a statutory bankruptcy (conducted under the same law as the proper law of the principal obligation). Likewise, a discharge under a trust deed will also be a complete discharge, if granted under the same law as the proper law of the principal obligation. If, however, the proper law differs from the law of the bankruptcy or the trust deed, a discharge would have no extra-territorial effect[18] except that under the British bankruptcy statutes a discharge in a Scots (or Northern Irish) sequestration will be effective as a discharge in England in respect of a claim arising from any contractual obligation, regardless of its proper law.[19]

A discharge in a Scots sequestration would bar all right of action in a Scots court on an obligation by the bankrupt granted before the sequestration, whether it is governed by Scots law or some other law, but a discharge under a foreign bankruptcy or under a Scots trust deed would not have this effect unless it were granted under the same law as the proper law of the debt.[20]

Where the discharge arises in the context of collective insolvency proceedings in relation to a debtor whose main interests are centred in an EU Member State, account must be taken of Council

---

[15] *Watson v Renton* (1792) M. 4582; *Ellis v McHenry* (1871) L.R. 6 C.P. 228; *Jacobs v Credit Lyonnais* (1884) 12 Q.B.D. 589; *Gibbs v Société Industrielle* (1890) 25 Q.B.D. 399; *Re Anglo-Austrian Bank* [1920] 1 Ch. 69; *Swiss Bank Corp. v Boehmische Industrial Bank* [1923] 1 K.B. 673; *Employers Liability Assurance Corp v Sedgwick Collins & Co* [1927] A.C. 95; *Perry v Equitable Life Ass.* (1929) 45 T.L.R. 468; *Mount Albert B.C.* [1938] A.C. 224; *Re United Railways of Havana & Regla Warehouses Ltd* [1961] A.C. 1007; *Adams v National Bank of Greece & Athens* [1961] A.C. 255.

[16] *Re United Railways of Havana & Regla Warehouses Ltd* [1961] A.C. 1007.

[17] See R.D. Leslie, *Stair Memorial Encyclopaedia*, p.277.

[18] See *Gibbs & Son v Société Industrielle et Commerciale des Metaux* (1890) 25 Q.B.D. 399.

[19] For England, see Insolvency Act 1986, s.281(1): "an English bankruptcy releases the debtor from all debts provable in bankruptcy; and these debts are not . . . limited to those which are governed by English law". For Scotland, see Bankruptcy (Scotland) Act 1985, ss.54 and 55(1).

[20] Dicey & Morris, Rule 166.

Regulation (EC) No 1346/2000 on Insolvency Proceedings.[21] Article 4.2. of the Regulation states that the law of the State of the opening of proceedings (the *lex concursus*[22]) (regarding main or secondary proceedings, respectively[23]) shall determine the effects of insolvency proceedings upon current contracts to which the debtor is party (paragraph e), and on creditors' rights after closure of such proceedings (paragraph k). As regards contracts relating to immoveable property, however, the effect of insolvency proceedings on a contract conferring the right to acquire or use such property, is governed solely by the law of the Member State within the territory of which the property is situated (Article 8[24]).

The relationship between Council Regulation 1346/2000 and Rome I is not clear, Article 10.1.d of the latter instrument referring to the applicable law of the contract, "the various ways of extinguishing obligations and prescription and limitation of actions."

EFFECT OF ILLEGALITY UPON THE SUBSTANCE OF A CONTRACT

15–26 The common law position is that a contract will not be enforceable in Scotland or England if:

    (a) it is illegal according to the proper law of the contract[25];

    (b) it offends against the public policy of the *lex fori*[26] in that:

        (i) it offends against conceptions of British justice or morality;

        (ii) it involves enforcement of foreign penal or revenue laws; or

---

[21] May 29, 2000. The Regulation applies only to collective insolvency proceedings where the centre of the debtor's main interests is located in the EU; recitals 13 and14.

[22] Recital 23.

[23] Council Regulation (EC) No 1346/2000, Art.3. See Ch.17, below.

[24] *cf.* recital 25.

[25] *Heriz v Riera* (1840) 11 Sum. 318; *Hope* (1857) 8 De G.M. & G. 731; *Rousillon* (1880) 14 Ch. D. 351; *Re Missouri SS Co.* (1889) 42 Ch. D. 321; *Kaufman v Gerson* [1904] 1 K.B. 591; *Société des Hotels Reunis v Hawker* (1914) 30 T.L.R. 423; *Ralli Bros. v Compania Naviera* [1920] 2 K.B. 287; *Trinidad Shipping Co.* [1920] A.C. 888; *Foster v Driscoll* [1929] 1 K.B. 470; *De Beeche v South American Stores* [1935] A.C. 148; *R. v International Trustee* [1937] A.C. 500; *O'Toole v Whiterock Quarry Co.*, 1937 S.L.T. 521; *Kahler v Midland Bank* [1950] A.C. 24; contrast *Kleinwort v Ungarische Baumwolle* [1939] 2 K.B. 678; *Addison v Brown* [1954] 1 W.L.R. 779; *Arab Bank v Barclays Bank* [1954] A.C. 495; *Prodexport State Co. v Man* [1973] Q.B. 389.

[26] It may be that the forum in refusing to enforce a contract on this ground will seek affirmation from another law of close connection; *cf. Lemenda Trading Co. Ltd v African Middle East Petroleum Co. Ltd* [1988] Q.B. 448, and see Clarkson & Hill, p.560.

(iii) it might prejudice the interests of Great Britain with a friendly foreign State[27]; or

(iv) its terms are in breach of international exchange control regulations.[28]

The suggestion that illegality by the law of the place of performance renders a contract, or any provision thereof, unenforceable in an English forum arises from the decision in *Ralli Bros v Compania Naviera Sota y Aznar*.[29] The case concerned the carriage of jute on a Spanish ship from Calcutta to Barcelona, at a rate of freight which, *en route*, became illegal by the Spanish law of the nationality of the ship[30] (taken to be the law of the place of performance). The proper law of the contract of carriage was English. Since the English forum refused to enforce the contractual rate of freight, the inference may be drawn that, if the proper law of a contract is English, illegality by the *lex loci solutionis* is likely to render the contract unenforceable in England. There is debate about whether this rule is one of English domestic or English conflict law, but it seems reasonable, and in accordance with principle, further to infer from the decision that the *effect* of illegality by the *lex loci solutionis* is a matter which an English court would refer to the applicable law.[31]

Other examples of non-enforcement in England of a contract illegal by the law of the place where actings under the contract were carried out[32] may be explained on policy grounds (to avoid affront to a friendly country). Any authority to the effect that a contract will not be enforced if it is illegal according to the *lex loci contractus* is outdated and untenable.[33]

Rome I does not make express provision regarding the matter of illegality, but a rule can be inferred by reference to Article 8, namely, a contract which in its terms breaches its own applicable law will not be enforced. It could be argued that contravention of any other law has no import, but there must be considered as potentially relevant, mandatory rules under Article 3.3 or 7.2, and account must be taken of the public policy of the forum (Article 16), contravention of any of which may lead to unenforceability of the contract in the UK.[34] Had not the UK made a reservation with

---

[27] *Regazzone v K.C. Sethia* [1958] A.C. 301.

[28] *i.e.* it contravenes the International Monetary Funds Agreement—the Bretton Woods Order in Council 1946. See para.15–33, below.

[29] [1920] 2 K.B. 287.

[30] An example of supervening (as opposed to initial) illegality of contractual terms (by the law of the place of performance).

[31] *cf.* Reynolds, "Illegitimacy by *Lex Loci Solutionis*" (1992) 108 L.Q.R. 553.

[32] *Regazzone v K.C. Sethia* [1958] A.C. 301. *Cf. Foster v Driscoll* [1929] 1 K.B. 470.

[33] See *Re Missouri S.S. Co.* (1889) 42 Ch. D. 321, *per* Fry L.J. at 342.

[34] *Soleimany v Soleimany* [1999] QB 785. See Clarkson, pp.247–250; and Cheshire & North, pp.600–603.

regard to Article 7.1, UK courts would have had access to that provision, to assist in cases where, initially or subsequently, there was illegality by some law of close connection (other than the applicable law).[35]

MISCELLANEOUS

Evidence and procedure

15–27 Rules of evidence and procedure fall within the province of the forum, for reasons of long held tradition and convenience. Rome I upholds this by excluding such matters from its scope (Article 1.2.h), but the exclusion is subject to Article 14, as follows:

Article 14: Burden of proof, etc.

1. The law governing the contract under this Convention applies to the extent that it contains, in the law of contract, rules which raise presumptions of law or determine the burden of proof.

2. A contract or an act intended to have legal effect may be proved by any mode of proof recognised by the law of the forum or by any of the laws referred to in Article 9 under which that contract or act is formally valid, provided that such mode of proof can be administered by the forum.

Exclusion of *renvoi* (Article 15)

15–28 The application of the law of any country specified by Rome I means the application of the rules of law in force in that country other than its rules of private international law.

"Ordre public" (Article 16)

15–29 The application of a rule of the law of any country specified by Rome I may be refused only if such application is manifestly incompatible with the public policy ("*ordre public*") of the forum.

III. SPECIAL CONTRACTS

15–30 All the special contracts referred to below, as regards essential validity, are governed by their applicable law.

A. IMMOVEABLES

15–31 At common law, the *lex situs* is the proper law of a contract concerning rights *in rem* in immoveable property.[36] Rome I, Article 4.3 supplies a presumption to similar effect: to the extent that the

---

[35] *cf.* notable Dutch decision, *Cie européenne des pétrôles SA v Sensor Nederlands BV* Hague 1982 (1983) 23 Int Legal Mat 66 (see Dicey & Morris, para.12-42).

[36] *Hamilton v Wakefield*, 1993 S.L.T. (Sh.Ct.) 30.

subject matter of a contract is a right in immoveable property, or a right to use immoveable property, it shall be presumed that the contract is most closely connected with the country where the immoveable property is situated. The presumption contained in Article 4.3, like that in Article 4.2, may be disregarded in terms of Article 4.5, if it appears from the circumstances as a whole that the contract is more closely connected with another country.

B. Contracts for the Carriage of Goods

Common Law

Contracts of affreightment, or other maritime contracts, are governed by the proper law in the usual common law way. However, if there was no express choice of law and no clear inference as to governing law, the cases show that a strong contender was the law of the flag,[37] the law of the flag being either: **15–32**

(a) the law of the country whose flag the ship wears; or
(b) if the nationality of the ship includes more than one system of law, the law of the country or place of the port of registration.[38]

It was stated in *The Assunzione*[39] that the presumption would be used only as a matter of last resort if the various factors were so evenly balanced that there was no other conclusive indication of proper law, but even that role or function is potentially useful and is worthy of note.[40] The rule applies both to contracts made before the voyage, such as charterparties, and also to contracts made during the voyage, such as repairs instructed by the master at a foreign port.[41] In the case of the former, there is a greater likelihood that the proper law will be expressly stated or necessarily implied from the documents, whereas in the latter, there is a

---

[37] *Lloyd v Guibert* [1865] L.R. 1 Q.B. 115; *The Karnak* [1869] L.R. 2 P.C. 505; *The San Roman* (1872) L.R. 3 A. & E. 583; *Chartered Mercantile Bank of India v Netherlands India SN Co.* (1883) 10 Q.B.D. 521; *The August* [1891] P.328; *The Industrie* [1894] P.58; *The Stettin* (1889) 14 P.D. 142; *The Adriatic* [1931] P. 241; *The Torni* [1932] P. 78; *The St Joseph* [1933] P. 119; *The Njegos* [1936] P.90; *Kadel Chajkin Ltd v Mitchell Cotts & Co.* [1947] 2 All E.R. 786; *The Metamorphosis* [1953] 1 W.L.R. 543; *The Assunzione* [1954] P. 150; *Compagnie Tunisienne de Navigation v Compagnie d'Armement Maritime* [1970] 3 All E.R. 71; *Coast Lines v Hudig & Veder Chartering NB* [1972] 2 Q.B. 34.

[38] Dicey and Morris, pp.1411–1413, where it is suggested also that certain situations may justify the court in lifting the veil of incorporation.

[39] [1954] P. 150.

[40] See also *Coast Lines* above, *per* Lord Denning at 44.

[41] *The Gaetano & Maria* (1882) 7 P.D. 137.

greater chance that the presumption will apply. The presumption is still effective, but it has less importance than in the past.

Rome I

15-33 Article 4.4 provides a specific presumption in respect of contracts for the carriage of goods (not persons[42]), as follows:

A contract for the carriage of goods shall not be subject to the presumption in Article 4.2. In such a contract, if the country in which, at the time the contract is concluded, the carrier has his principal place of business is also the country in which the place of loading or the place of discharge or the principal place of business of the consignor is situated, it shall be presumed that the contract is most closely connected with that country. In applying this paragraph single voyage charter-parties and other contracts the main purpose of which is the carriage of goods shall be treated as contracts for the carriage of goods.[43]

The presumption contained in Article 4.4, like that in Article 4.2, may be disregarded in terms of Article 4.5, if it appears from the circumstances as a whole that the contract is more closely connected with another country.

The terms of Rome I are subordinate to the terms of other Conventions to which a Contracting State is, or may become a party (Article 21). Hence, for example carriage of goods by sea continues to be regulated by the Hague-Visby Rules in terms of the Carriage of Goods by Sea Act 1971.[44]

C. CONSUMER CONTRACTS

Common law

15-34 At common law, there was no such species as "consumer" for the purpose of the conflict of laws.[45] However, prior to the 1990 Act, British domestic legislation sought to recognise and compensate

---

[42] Contracts of carriage of persons, if not governed by other Convention, are subject to Art.4.2; they are generally excluded from the consumer contract provision (Art 5.4.a) except that (Art 5.5) the latter applies to "a contract which, for an inclusive price, provides for a combination of travel and accommodation".

[43] But charters by demise, where the contract is for the hire of the ship rather than for the carriage of goods, are not covered by the special presumption in Art.4.4, but rather by Art.4.2, the characteristic performance being delivery of the ship by the ship owner: Kaye, p.200.

[44] A list of countries in which the Hague-Visby rules are in force is set out in the Carriage of Goods by Sea Act 1971 (Parties to Convention) Order 1985, as amended by SI 2000/1103.

[45] Though see *English v Donnelly*, 1958 S.C. 494 (Scots hire-purchase legislation held to apply irrespective of the proper law of the contract). *Cf.* generally *Stirling's Trs v The Legal and General Assurance Society Ltd*, 1957 S.L.T. 73.

cases of uneven bargaining power, principally in the cases of consumers and employees. An early example of conflict of laws awareness in a domestic statute is the Unfair Contract Terms Act 1977,[46] which contains in section 27(1) a self-denying provision, and in section 27(2) an overriding provision.

Rome I

Article 5 of Rome I is specific and, in the absence of choice of law **15–35** by the parties, fixes as the applicable law the law of the country of the consumer's habitual residence. Moreover the consumer cannot, by choice of law, be deprived of the mandatory rules of that law, provided that the case falls within the circumstances described in Article 5.2.

Article 5: certain consumer contracts

1. This Article applies to a contract the object of which is the **15–36** supply of goods or services to a person ("the consumer") for a purpose which can be regarded as being outside his trade or profession, or a contract for the provision of credit for that object.

2. Notwithstanding the provisions of Article 3, a choice of law made by the parties shall not have the result of depriving the consumer of the protection afforded to him by the mandatory rules of the law of the country in which he has his habitual residence:

— if in that country the conclusion of the contract was preceded by a specific invitation addressed to him or by advertising, and he had taken in that country all the steps necessary on his part for the conclusion of the contract[47]; or
— if the other party or his agent received the consumer's order in that country[48]; or
— if the contract is for the sale of goods and the consumer travelled from that country to another country and there gave his order, provided that the consumer's journey was arranged by the seller for the purpose of inducing the consumer to buy.[49]

3. Notwithstanding the provisions of Article 4, a contract to which this Article applies shall, in the absence of choice in accordance with Article 3, be governed by the law of the country in

---

[46] As amended by Contracts (Applicable Law) Act 1990, s.5, Sch.4, para.4.See also Employment Protection (Consolidation) Act 1978; Wages Act 1986.
[47] Doorstep selling and mail order. See generally, Smith, paras 4–46—4–48.
[48] For example consumer approaches foreign seller, *e.g.* at a trade fair.
[49] "Cross-border excursion selling".

which the consumer has his habitual residence if it is entered into in the circumstances described in paragraph 2 of this Article.

4. This Article shall not apply to:

(a) a contract of carriage;
(b) a contract for the supply of services where the services are to be supplied to the consumer exclusively in a country other than that in which he has his habitual residence.

5. Notwithstanding the provisions of paragraph 4, this Article shall apply to a contract which, for an inclusive price, provides for a combination of travel and accommodation.

If the mandatory rules of the consumer's habitual residence are less favourable than those of the applicable law, it has been suggested[50] that the supplier would be prevented from setting up the less favourable rules of the habitual residence.

It is not clear what is the relationship in the area of consumer protection between Articles 5 (mandatory rules of the law of the country in which the consumer is habitually resident) and 7. Is Article 7 available to protect the consumer in a case where, in the circumstances, s/he fails to qualify for Article 5 protection? It may be expected that the Commission in a future instrument would aim to deliver this result.

D. Employment Contracts

D. Common law

15–37 The proper law of the contract was usually, but not necessarily, the law of the country where the contract was concluded (often the place of residence or business of the employer), but in some cases it was held that the contract had more connection with the law of the place where it was to be performed and, accordingly, that that law was the proper law. The older common law cases do not present a clear picture.[51] A noteworthy decision is *Sayers v International Drilling Co.*,[52] in which it was held that where a company

---

[50] Smith, para.4–51; see also Stone, p.268 and Kaye, p.213.
[51] *Arnott v Redfern* (1825) 2 Car. & P. 88; *South African Breweries Ltd v King* [1899] 2 Ch. 173: [1900] 1 Ch. 273; *Re Anglo-Austrian Bank* [1920] 1 Ch. 69; *Serra v Famous Lasky Film Service* [1922] W.N. 44.
[52] [1971] 1 W.L.R. 1176.

employs employees of varying nationalities to work in various places in the world, the proper law is the place where the employer, the common denominator, is situated.

Rome I

Article 6: individual employment contracts   **15–38**

1. Notwithstanding the provisions of Article 3, in a contract of employment a choice of law made by the parties shall not have the result of depriving the employee of the protection afforded to him by the mandatory rules of the law which would be applicable under paragraph 2 in the absence of choice.
2. Notwithstanding the provisions of Article 4, a contract of employment shall, in the absence of choice in accordance with Article 3, be governed:

(a) by the law of the country in which the employee habitually carries out his work in performance of the contract, even if he is temporarily employed in another country; or
(b) if the employee does not habitually carry out his work in any one country, by the law of the country in which the place of business through which he was engaged is situated; unless it appears from the circumstances as a whole that the contract is more closely connected with another country, in which case the contract shall be governed by the law of that country.

As with consumer contracts, the weaker party (the employee) should have the best outcome from his point of view. If the rules of the "chosen" law confer greater benefit on him in the instant case than do the rules of the place of habitual employment, the court should not "insist on the letter of the Convention".[53]

The provision is specific and leans towards application of the law of the place where the employee habitually carries out his work, not only in securing to him the benefit of the mandatory provisions of that law, but also in identifying that law as the applicable law in the absence of choice.[54]

---

[53] Smith, para.4-65; see also Kaye, p.228.
[54] *Shekar v Satyam Computer Services Ltd* [2005] I.C.R. 737. Consider CJG Morse, "Consumer Contracts, Employment Contracts and the Rome Convention" (1993) 41 ICLQ 1.

E. INTERNATIONAL SALE OF GOODS[55]

15–39 There have been various attempts by the Hague Conference on Private International Law to regulate contracts for the sale of goods, including: 1955 Convention on the Law Applicable to International Sales of Goods; 1958 Convention on the Law governing Transfer of Title in International Sales of Goods; and 1958 Convention on the Jurisdiction of the Selected Forum in the case of International Sales of Goods.[56] Other international efforts in this area include the 1980 United Nations Convention on Contracts for the International Sale of Goods (also known as the Vienna Convention[57]). These Conventions aim to harmonise the substantive domestic laws of Contracting States in one particular area of law, and in so doing to provide an alternative to the traditional conflict of laws method of resolving disputes. None, however, has been adopted by the UK.

By the Uniform Law on International Sales Act 1967,[58] the UK implemented two Conventions, namely, the Uniform Law on the International Sale of Goods, and the Uniform Law on the Formation of Contracts for the International Sale of Goods.[59] Since Article 21 of Rome I saves the application of international Conventions to which a Contracting State is, or becomes, a party, this means that, in theory, the two Uniform Law Conventions take precedence over the solution dictated by the general provisions of Rome I. But in practice, parties very rarely agree to adopt, for application to their contract, the body of substantive rules contained in the Uniform Laws (assuming such a choice is competent[60]). Additionally, certain factual conditions must be fulfilled before the corpus of Uniform Law rules shall operate,[61] and these uniform rules are, in any event, subordinate to the mandatory provisions of the law which otherwise would have been applicable. Hence, the option is not wholly attractive. Not only is the UK party only to a minority of these Conventions, but those Conventions which it has implemented are not in their substantive rules comprehensive (eg while passing of risk is treated, passing of property is not).

---

[55] See J.J. Fawcett, J. Harris, and M. Bridge, *International Sale of Goods in the Conflict of Laws* (2005, OUP).

[56] The 1955 Convention entered into force in nine States, but not in the UK. The two 1958 Conventions did not enter into force.

[57] Not, however, adopted by the UK.

[58] amended by the Sale and Supply of Goods Act 1994, Sch.2, para.3

[59] Both concluded at The Hague on July 1, 1964.

[60] See Green Paper: choice of body of "non-State" law.

[61] See 1967 Act, Sch.1, Art.1.

F. AGENCY

Common law

As between principal and agent living in the same country, the **15–40** rights of the parties were governed by the proper law of their contract which was usually, but not necessarily, the *lex loci contractus*, being the law of the place where the relationship was constituted (that place usually being where the principal carried on business). Where the principal and agent lived in different countries there was no such presumption.[62] The reasoning in *Chatenay v Brazilian Submarine Telegraph Co.*[63] suggests that the likelier choice of proper law in such cases would be that of the place where the contract was being carried out.

As between principal and third party, the question whether a third party might sue a Scots principal, having contracted with an agent (for a then unnamed principal), was held by the Scots court in *Girvan Roper & Co v Monteith*[64] to be a dispute arising under the contract, and referred to the English proper law of that contract, an outcome which does not seem unreasonable.[65]

Rome I

Article 1.2.f excludes from the scope of Rome I the central **15–41** question whether an agent is able to bind a principal, or an organ to bind a company or body corporate or unincorporated, to a third party.[66] Other contractual aspects of agency, including disputes between principal and agent, will be subject to Rome I,[67] and identification of the applicable law for such matters are regulated by Article 3 or 4, as the case may be.[68]

---

[62] *Pattison v Mills* (1828) 1 Dow & Cl. 342; *Albion Insurance Co. v Mills* (1828) 3 W. & S. 218; *Millar v Mitchell Cadell & Co.* (1860) 22 D. 833; *Bennett v Inveresk Paper Co.* (1891) 18 R. 975; *Maspons y Hermano v Mildred* (1882) 9 Q.B.D. 530; *Delaurier v Wyllie* (1889) 17 R. 167; *Sinfra Ltd* [1939] 2 All E.R. 675; *Mauroux v Soc. Com Abel Pereira* [1972] 1 W.L.R. 962; *Maclaine Watson & Co. Ltd v International Tin Council* [1988] Ch. 1; *J H. Rayner (Mincing Lane) Ltd v Dept of Trade and Industry* [1989] Ch. 72, 187, CA.

[63] [1891] 1 Q.B. 79.

[64] (1895) 23 R. 129.

[65] See Cheshire & North, p.549; and Anton with Beaumont, p.308.

[66] Giuliano & Lagarde, p.13.

[67] "The exclusion affects only the relationships between the principal and third parties, more particularly the question whether the principal is bound vis-à-vis third parties by the acts of the agent in specific cases . . . principal-agent, and agent-third party relationships in no way differ from other obligations and are therefore included within the scope of the Convention" (Giuliano & Lagarde, p.13).

[68] Consider, generally, *Presentaciones Musicales SA v Secunda* [1994] Ch. 271.

Commercial Agents

15–42　The activities of commercial agents in Great Britain[69] are regulated by the Commercial Agents Directive 1986,[70] brought into effect in Great Britain by the Commercial Agents (Council Directive) Regulation 1993.[71]

The 1986 Directive was introduced due to differences in the national laws of EU Member States concerning commercial representation, and the resultant inhibition upon conclusion and operation of commercial representation contracts where principal and commercial agents were established in different Member States. Since conflict of laws rules in the matter of commercial representation do not remove inconsistencies in national law, some degree of harmonisation of substantive law was required. The Directive gives priority to the legal relationship between commercial agent and principal.

The 1993 Regulation, as amended, has the general effect of protecting the agent, whereas domestic Scots law might be said to have shown particular awareness of the potential liabilities of the principal, and therefore, to be more protective of the latter party.[72] A commercial agent is defined in regulation 2(1) as "a self-employed intermediary who has continuing authority to negotiate the sale or purchase of goods on behalf of another person (the 'principal'), or to negotiate and conclude the sale or purchase of goods on behalf of and in the name of that principal."[73] By schedule to the Regulations, it is made clear that the type of agent to which this applies is one who devotes "substantially the whole of his time to representative activities". It is a complex matter to decide as regards any individual whether the Regulation applies.[74]

It has been seen that the relationship between principal and agent is subject to Rome I. In a British forum, it is likely that the Regulation (application whereof is determined by the location of the activities of the agent, and not by personal law factors pertaining to the principal or agent) will have the status of mandatory provisions for the purposes of Rome I. In terms of Regulation 1, courts are directed to apply the law which the parties

---

[69] Separate provision exists for Northern Ireland, and Ireland. As to the latter, see E.C. Commercial Agents Regulations 1994 (SI 33/1994), as to which see *Kenny v Ireland ROC Ltd* [2005] 1 E.H.C. 241.

[70] EC Council Directive 86/653 ([1986] OJ L382/17) on the Co-ordination of the Laws of the Member States relating to Self-employed Commercial Agents.

[71] SI 1993/3053, amended by SI 1993/3173 and SI 1998/2868.

[72] See generally F.P. Davidson and L. Macgregor, *Commercial Law in Scotland* (2003), paras 2.2 *et seq.*

[73] Though see express exclusions from this category in reg.2. As to definition of commercial agent, see *Parks v Esso Petroleum Co. Ltd* [2000] EU LR 25; contrast *Kenny*, above.

[74] See *McAdam v Boxpak Ltd*, 2006 S.L.T. 217.

have agreed (*i.e.* under Rome I, Article 3) will govern their agency contract, to the extent that the choice is the law of a Member State. But it may be assumed, given the nature of the Directive, that there will be equivalent derivative/secondary legislation in each Member State, respectively, and that such legislation will share the characteristic of being mandatory in nature. Therefore, in any case where the activities of the agent are being performed in an EU state, it seems likely, regardless of the applicable law under Rome I (be it the law of an EU Member State, or otherwise), that the contract will be subject to the mandatory rules of the (EU) forum (Rome I, Article 7.2), and possibly of the law of another EU Member State under Articles 3.3 or 7.1. This important point (that parties whose activities take place in a Member State cannot evade the protective provisions concerning commercial representations by choosing as the applicable law under Rome I the law of a non-EU State) was confirmed by the ECJ in *Ingmar GB Ltd v Eaton Leonard Technologies Inc*.[75]

In cases where the agent's activities are to be performed outside the EU, presumably the effectiveness of a choice of law clause in the principal-agent contract (even where those parties have Scottish connection), for application of the law of a non-EU Member State, will depend upon the rules of the *lex fori*. If ensuing litigation should take place in Scotland in respect of such a scenario, it would seem difficult as a matter of interpretation for the Scots court to hold that the Regulations (which govern the activities of commercial agents *in Great Britain*) are mandatory under Article 7.2. This suggests that a rule, or provision, may be mandatory for one purpose, but not for another.[76]

IV. ELECTRONIC COMMERCE

The internet and cyberspace pose problems[77] in many areas of civil **15–43** law, including delict (particularly damage to reputation[78]), property (instantaneous property transfer and intellectual property rights[79]), but in particular with regard to electronic transacting, especially formation of contract and all the consequences flowing therefrom. Technological developments also have repercussions in matters of evidence, procedure and remedies.[80] Cyberspace is, as Gale notes,[81]

---

[75] [2001] All ER (D) 448. See *SME Reissue (2002), Agency and Mandate*, L.J. Macgregor, para.48.
[76] *cf.* explanation of mandatory provisions, para.15–17 above.
[77] See generally Edwards and Waelde, *Law & the Internet: a framework for electronic commerce* (2nd ed., 2000).
[78] *Western Provident v Norwich Union* [1997] New L.J. Digest 1277 (defamation by e-mail: agreement to pay £450,000 damages and costs).
[79] *Shetland Times Ltd v Wills*, 1997 S.L.T. 669.
[80] L. Edwards and C. Waelde, Ch.14, Stuart Gale, "The Impact of Information Technology Upon Civil Practice and Procedure".
[81] p.9.

not a lawless place (if it *is* a place), but a place characterised by its "anarchic climate and shifting players."[82]

Electronic advances have removed the firm basis of understanding and acting on the assumption that the world is divided into legal systems based on territorial areas, and have thrown into confusion certain established methods of approaching and solving conflict problems. This does not mean that "traditional" rules may not be adapted to service the electronic age. As McBryde has written, "[e]lectronic commerce is not new. Telegrams and telexes have been methods of entering into contracts for many years."[83] The conflict of laws was able to accommodate such "remote" methods of contracting by identifying what it deemed to be the *lex loci contractus* and the proper law.[84] UK government policy, recognising the growth of electronic commerce, is to encourage and facilitate such transactions and to attempt to safeguard UK interests. One of the main concerns is to secure the principle of "medium neutrality", *i.e.* to ensure that there is no difference in legal effectiveness between traditional and electronic methods of transacting.

There follows an outline of the legislative responses of more recent years to the developments which have occurred.

ELECTRONIC SIGNATURE: ELECTRONIC COMMUNICATIONS ACT 2000

15–44 The Electronic Communications Act 2000 is part of the legislative framework to facilitate and encourage confidence in electronic transactions. It sought to implement certain provisions of the EU Electronic Signatures Directive (adopted on December 13, 1999),[85] which was intended to facilitate the use of electronic signatures and to provide for their legal recognition throughout the EU. The 2000 Act is in three Parts. Part I makes arrangements for registering providers of cryptography support services, providing eg electronic signature services and confidentiality services,[86] and Part II provides for the legal recognition of electronic signatures, regulating the process under which such signatures may be "generated, communicated or verified".[87]

---

[82] p.7.
[83] McBryde, *The Law of Contract in Scotland* (2nd ed., 2001), para.5-83.
[84] *Entores v Miles Far East Corp.*; *Brinkibon v Stahag Stahl*, above.
[85] (1999/93/EC) OJ L13/12, January 19, 2000.
[86] The use of cryptography can secure confidentiality, and provide a means for delivering a signature electronically. By s.7 of the 2000 Act, electronic signatures can be admitted as evidence in court.
[87] Pt III has been repealed; see Communications Act 2003.

Electronic Commerce Directive

The EU Electronic Commerce Directive, adopted on May 4, **15–45** 2000,[88] encourages the development of electronic commerce in the internal market. There is "no overlap in the detailed provisions" of the Electronic Commerce Directive and the 2000 Act.[89] Two main areas addressed in the Directive are ensuring legal validity of electronic contracts and limiting the liability of intermediary service providers.

Recital 58 makes clear that while the Electronic Commerce Directive does not apply to services supplied by providers established in non-EU States, nevertheless, in view of the global dimension of electronic commerce, it is appropriate to ensure that European rules are consistent with international rules. Globalisation necessitates consultation between the EU and major non-EU trading entities such as the WTO, the OECD and UNCITRAL. However, development of the EU internal market requires co-ordination at EU level of regulatory measures so as not adversely to affect the competitiveness of European industry.

Article 1.4 of the Directive declares that it does *not* establish additional rules on private international law, nor does it deal with the jurisdiction of courts.[90] However, Article 9 (treatment of contracts) begins with the requirement that Member States shall ensure that their legal systems allow contracts to be concluded by electronic means, and that their legal requirements do not create obstacles for the use of electronic contracts, nor deprive them of legal effectiveness by reason of their having been made by electronic means. Article 9.2 permits Member States to make certain exceptions[91] to this *desideratum* in respect of all or certain contracts falling into one of the following categories:

(a) contracts that create or transfer rights in real estate, except for rental rights;

(b) contracts requiring by law the involvement of courts, public authorities or professions exercising public authority;

(c) contracts of suretyship granted and on (*sic*) collateral securities furnished by persons acting for purposes outside their trade, business or profession;

---

[88] Directive 2000/31/EC of the European Parliament and of the Council of June 8, 2000 on certain legal aspects of information society services, in particular electronic commerce, in the Internal Market (OJ L178, July 17, 2000, 1–16) (henceforth "EU Electronic Commerce Directive").

[89] Explanatory Note to the 2000 Act, p.6.

[90] *cf.* Electronic Commerce Directive, recital 23 and recital 55.

[91] Member States who make such exceptions are required to submit to the Commission every five years a report explaining why they consider it necessary to maintain excluded category/ies of contract.

(d) contracts governed by family law or by the law of succession.

THE ELECTRONIC COMMERCE (EC DIRECTIVE) REGULATIONS 2002

15–46 Certain provisions of the Electronic Commerce Directive have been implemented in the UK by the Electronic Commerce (EC Directive) Regulations 2002.[92] The 2002 Regulations seek to promote the internal market in Europe, by securing the free movement of "information society services", meaning, essentially, all commercial online services.[93] The 2002 Regulations apply to those who advertise or sell goods or services online to businesses or consumers. Generally the Regulations require online service providers to comply with certain information requirements, which can be divided into three categories: (i) information requirements, which require providers to give full information about themselves to "end users";[94] (ii) commercial communications requirements; and (iii) electronic contracting requirements, which require the online services provider to provide end users with a description of the different technical steps to be taken to conclude a contract online.

For present purposes, the principal feature of interest is the limited guidance as to choice of law applicable to online services. The 2002 Regulations direct that UK-established services providers must comply with UK laws, even if they are providing those services in another EU Member State, and they prevent the UK from restricting the provision in the UK of online services from another EU Member State. The regulatory structure is authorised by regulation 4 of the 2002 Regulations, but it does not apply to those fields set out in the Schedule to the Electronic Commerce Directive (the Schedule permitting, in such excluded fields, the contracting parties freedom to choose the applicable law and not affecting the law applicable to a consumer contract, so that the consumer may not be deprived of the mandatory rules otherwise applicable to his situation by the law of the Member State in which he has his residence).[95] Otherwise parties are free to choose the law applicable to individual contracts. The 2002 Regulations do not deal with the matter of jurisdiction.[96]

---

[92] SI 2002/2013.

[93] Electronic Commerce Directive, recital 18.

[94] These information requirements are in addition to existing requirements, such as contained in the Consumer Protection (Distance Selling) Regulations 2000 (SI 2000/2334).

[95] Electronic Commerce Directive, recital 55.

[96] Jurisdiction must be determined according to normal commercial rules, *i.e.* Council Regulation 44/2001.

CONSUMER PROTECTION (DISTANCE SELLING) REGULATIONS 2000[97]

The 2000 Regulations regulate "distance contracts", which are **15–47** defined generally as any contracts concerning goods or services concluded between a supplier and a consumer under an organised distance sales or service provision scheme run by the supplier, who, for the purpose of the contract, makes exclusive use of one or more means of distance communication, up to and including the moment at which the contract is concluded.[98] The Regulations are without conflict of laws content, except to the extent that regulation 25(1) prohibits contracting out of the consumer protection provisions of the Regulation, and regulation 25(5) stipulates that the Regulations shall apply if the contract has a close connection with the territory of a Member State, notwithstanding any contract term which applies or purports to apply the law of a non-Member State.[99] The effect of these provisions is to secure for the consumer in his electronic dealings the same protections as have been constructed in relation to traditional forms of consumer contract.

APPLICATION OF ROME I TO ELECTRONIC COMMERCE TRANSACTIONS

None of these complex modern instruments addresses sys- **15–48** tematically the conflict of laws implications of electronic contracting, and so the conclusion must be that, for the time being, electronic contracts (their constitution and effects) are susceptible to treatment by Rome I. The absence of bespoke conflict rules regarding electronic contracts is noticeable, particularly when one considers the exponential growth of electronic contracts, and the fact that a far higher number of contracts have international implications than has been the case with traditional contracts, especially consumer contracts. The challenge is to interpret Rome I in a manner compatible with modern electronic conditions. Murray[1] has argued that the analysis which is required in the electronic context of "www" is "when, what, where?" (when is the contract made; what is made; and where is it concluded?).

The questions to be answered are the same as arise with regard to "traditional" contracts. With regard to electronic contracting, (conflict) disputes are likely to concern: (i) pre-contractual issues,[2]

---

[97] SI 2000/2334, implementing Directive 97/7/EC of the European Parliament and of the Council of May 20, 1997 on the protection of consumers in relation to distance contracts (OJ L144, June 4, 1997, p.19) ("Distance Selling Directive").

[98] Reg.3(1).

[99] *cf.* Distance Selling Directive, reg.12(2).

[1] "Entering into Contracts Electronically: the Real WWW" in L. Edwards & C. Waelde, *Law and the Internet—a framework for electronic commerce* (2nd ed., 2000).

[2] Note, however, that Art.1.2(i) of the Rome I Regulation (*qv* para.15–49, below) provides that the Regulation shall not apply to obligations arising out of a pre-contractual relationship. The matter now is dealt with expressly in Rome II, Art.9C, Council Approved Version. See Ch.16, below.

including advertising, and the process of negotiation, culminating in an argument by one/both parties that *consensus* has been reached; (ii) evidencing that *consensus* has been reached between identified parties; (iii) ascertaining the identity of the governing law and assessing the substantive validity of the contract, including any choice of court and/or choice of law clauses; (iv) performance-related issues, including the main obligation and counter-obligation (supply and payment); and (v) post-contractual issues of dispute resolution, including application of relevant rules of jurisdiction (because however great the extent and rapidity of technological change, carrying with it the impression that territorial frontiers no longer are significant, it is the case that, ultimately, a remedy must be pursued in the court of some territorial law unit).

The first matter to be ascertained is whether the contracting parties have made a choice of law, express or demonstrated with reasonable certainty.[3] If such a choice is evident, the body of law applicable to the contract will be augmented, in the usual way, by the mandatory rules of another system of law, in terms of Rome 1, Articles 3.3. and 7.2. It may be that in the act of ordering online one party accepts the other's express choice of law. Whether the parties have reached *consensus* is governed, in the usual way, by the putativity principle in Rome I, Article 8.

As to formal validity, Rome I, Article 9.1 provides that for contracts "concluded between persons who are in the same country" it is sufficient that the contract comply with the formal requirements of the applicable law, or of the law where it is concluded. This provision demonstrates the extent to which territorial situation remains important in traditional contracts, but at the same time reveals its inappropriateness with regard to electronic contracting.[4] The qualifications contained in Article 9.1 are unlikely to be satisfied in electronic contracts, and therefore one is led to the rule of alternative reference in Article 9.2, to the effect that if persons "are in different countries", it is sufficient to comply with the formal validity rules of the applicable law, or the law of one of those countries. In view of possible difficulties of definition of presence in a country, it would surely be preferable to apply the applicable law of the putative contract.

With regard to contractual capacity, it has been seen that Article 11 supplies a specific rule, applicable in cases of "face-to-face" contracting, which obviously is not helpful in the case of remote transactions. The answer, for electronic commerce, would be to apply the putative applicable law to the question of capacity.

In terms of Article 4 of Rome I, the online supplier of goods or services is likely to be the characteristic performer of the contract;

---

[3] Rome I, Art.3.1.
[4] See Electronic Commerce Directive, recital 55.

the problem then is to identify his habitual residence or principal place of business. Article 4.5 gives scope to the court to identify the applicable law on a wider basis and, by utilising the common law approach, it reasonably could justify consideration of "remote" factors beyond the contemplation of the courts of the common law era, for example place of internet service providers.

If, as in many cases of online transacting, the purchaser/user is a "consumer", he will have the benefit of Rome I, Article 5, especially Article 5.3, which secures application of the law of the consumer's habitual residence in the absence of choice of law, provided that any of the three indents in Article 5.2 are present, namely:

— if in that country the conclusion of the contract was preceded by a specific invitation addressed to him or by advertising, and he had taken in that country all the steps necessary on his part for the conclusion of the contract; or
— if the other party or his agent received the consumer's order in that country; or
— if the contract is for the sale of goods and the consumer travelled from that country to another country and there gave his order, provided that the consumer's journey was arranged by the seller for the purpose of inducing the consumer to buy.

There may be particular difficulties in interpreting Article 5 in the context of e-commerce, for example the words, "specific invitation addressed to him or by advertising". Much will depend upon judicial interpretation of the adjective "specific". Unless the "web-vertisement", by some verbal or language indication, purports to restrict its ambit, the nature of the electronic world suggests that the online provider contemplates transacting with any consumer, regardless of his territorial situation. The changes in the rules of jurisdiction brought about by Regulation 44/2001 have resulted in those rules moving ahead of the choice of law rules in this matter.[5]

---

[5] Regulation 44/2001, Art.15 states that: "1. In matters relating to a contract concluded by a person, the consumer, for a purpose which can be regarded as being outside his trade or profession, jurisdiction shall be determined by this Section, without prejudice to Art.4 and point 5 of Art.5, if: (a) it is a contract for the sale of goods on instalment credit terms; or (b) it is a contract for a loan repayable by instalments, or for any other form of credit, made to finance the sale of goods; or (c) in all other cases, the contract has been concluded with a person who pursues commercial or professional activities in the Member State of the consumer's domicile or, *by any means, directs such activities* to that Member State or to several States including that Member State, and the contract falls within the scope of such activities." (Emphasis added.)

V. PROPOSED CHANGES TO ROME I

15–49 On 14 January 2003 the EU Commission published a Green Paper entitled, "Conversion of the Rome Convention of 1980 on the Law Applicable to Contractual Obligations into a Community Instrument and its Modernisation."[6] The Commission sought views on whether Rome I should be converted into a Regulation, and upon whether, in any event, the substantive provisions ought to be amended in light of experience.

The Commission pointed out that at Community level, Rome I is the only international private law instrument still in the form of an international treaty, and suggested that in this important commercial area, the rules of jurisdiction on the one hand, and of choice of law, on the other, should not be governed by different types of instrument. Proceeding by Regulation (rather than, say, by Directive) is said to be appropriate where an entire subject area (the private international law of contractual obligations) is to be harmonised (not simply a particular aspect of that area), and being directly applicable, means that harmonisation measures would enter into force in all Member States contemporaneously. The separate argument that a Regulation would achieve the desirable aim of clothing the ECJ with jurisdiction to hear appeals on matters concerning the interpretation of Rome I (with the aim of having legal concepts common to Brussels and Rome interpreted in like manner), is less persuasive now that the Brussels Protocol is in force. The Commission argued that conversion of the instrument would promote consistency, transparency, certainty, and speed. On the other hand, it might be anticipated that there would be a diminution in the autonomy of individual Member States, and less opportunity for States to enter reservations.[7]

There are thought to be advantages in amending the terms of Rome I in areas which the case law of Member States suggests is capable of giving rise to problems.

In December 2005 the Commission presented a Proposal for a Regulation of the European Parliament and the Council on the law applicable to contractual obligations (Rome I).[8] The following commentary is offered:

Article 1—*Scope*: Despite earlier discussion about the wisdom of continuing to exclude arbitration agreements and agreements on

---

(Art.15 provides additional grounds of jurisdiction where a contract has been concluded by a consumer (as defined), and broadly speaking, brings about a situation in which a consumer may be sued by the other party to the contract only in the courts of the Member State in which the consumer is domiciled, though a consumer may raise proceedings in the other's party's domicile, or in his own. This benefit can be secured only if any of the conditions in Art.15.1 is satisfied.)

[6] COM (2002) 654.

[7] Green Paper, para.3.2.11.

[8] COM (2005) 650 final (hereinafter "the Proposal").

choice of court from the scope of the instrument, this exclusion remains in the Proposal. The question whether an agent is able to bind a principal, an issue excluded from the scope of the 1980 Rome Convention, receives in the Proposal separate treatment *per* Article 7. It is noteworthy that, *per* Article 1.2(i), obligations arising out of a pre-contractual relationship are excluded from the scope. The explanation is that such matters (*e.g.* standards of conduct at the pre-contractual stage and good faith in negotiating[9]) generally are regarded in civilian legal systems as pertaining to tort or restitution; therefore, by default, such matters would be referred to the Rome II Regulation (*qv*), if and when it comes to fruition.

Article 3—*Freedom of choice*: In this important provision certain changes are proposed, some of which represent an expansion of choice, and others curtailment. By Article 3.2, parties may choose as the applicable law a body of law other than a national law (*e.g.* UNIDROIT Principles of International Commercial Contracts), or the rules of a Convention, such as the 1980 Vienna Convention. More significant is the proposed presumption in Article 3.1 that if the parties have agreed to confer jurisdiction on a court or tribunal of a Member State to hear and determine disputes that have arisen or may arise out of the contract, they shall be presumed also to have chosen the law of that Member State. Therefore under this Proposal, there is a rebuttable presumption that choice of court denotes choice of law. At common law, and under the 1980 Convention (Article 4.5), the position was that, in the discretion of the forum, choice of court *might* denote choice of law. There is no indication of the factors which, if proved, might serve to rebut the presumption. Choice of court, therefore, may supply choice of law; but it remains the case that choice of law cannot, in itself, supply choice of court.[10] Insofar as this proposed presumption adds to the principles which govern identification of the applicable law, if implemented, it could be said to sit uneasily with the rewritten principles set out under the proposed Article 4 for identification of applicable law in the absence of choice. Moreover, by whom and on what basis would the presumption be rebutted?

Article 4—*Applicable law in the absence of choice*: It is proposed to re-cast Article 4 quite significantly. This is not surprising, given the variation in the approach taken by the courts of Member States to the interpretation of Article 4.2 of the 1980 Rome Convention, and its relationship with Article 4.5. There is a desire to reduce uncertainty and to reduce opportunity for Member State discretion. Consequently, Article 4 is "type-specific", *e.g.* Article 4.1.a, a contract of sale shall be governed by the law of the country in

---

[9] An area termed *culpa in contrahendo* from the German common law.
[10] Though see *Shekar v Satyam Computer Services Ltd* [2005] I.C.R. 737 (employment tribunal, *per* Mr P T Wallington, at para.52).

which the seller has his habitual residence. Such a formulation has the effect of removing, for the general rule, the connecting factor present in the 1980 Convention of "habitual residence of the party who is to effect the performance which is characteristic of the contract." New rules are proposed in relation to contracts relating to intellectual or industrial property rights; franchise contracts; and distribution contracts. There is of course a "sweeper" provision (Article 4.2), which states that contracts not specified in Article 4.1 shall be governed by the law of the country in which the party who is required to perform the service characterising the contract has his habitual residence at the time of conclusion of the contract. Where that service cannot be identified, the contract shall be governed by the law of the country with which it is most closely connected.[11]

Bearing in mind the symbiosis between jurisdiction and choice of law, it should not go unnoticed that the effect of the proposed new rule governing choice of law in the case of contracts of sale is inconsistent with the effect of the re-drawn Council Regulation 44/2001, Article 5.1, which identifies place of delivery of the goods/provision of services as the location of the special jurisdiction. Thus, in the case where there is no choice of law, and no choice of court, litigation will proceed in the "buyer's forum", applying the "seller's law."

Article 5—*Consumer contracts*: These provisions too have undergone significant change in the Proposal. Most notably, freedom of choice of law no longer is permitted. Provided that the contract falls to be regulated by Article 5 (which is determined by Article 5.2 and 5.3), it shall be governed by the law of the Member State in which the consumer has his habitual residence. It is notable that the definition of consumer contract, referring to a person who "by any means directs such activities" to the Member State of the habitual residence of the consumer, now mirrors the wording adopted, after much debate between the consumer and business lobbies, in Council Regulation 44/2001, Article 15.

Article 7—*Contracts concluded by an agent*: Under the 1980 Rome Convention, the contractual relations between principal and agent fall to be governed by Articles 3 or 4, as appropriate; so too is determined the applicable law of the contract between the agent and the third party. Article 7 proposes a rule to govern the contract between principal and agent (Article 7.1); the relationship between the principal and third parties, whether the agent has acted within or outside his powers (Article 7.2 and 7.3); and the relationship between the agent and the third party, whether the agent has acted within or outside his powers (Article 7.4). Care will require to be

---

[11] Note the attenuation of the discretion currently enjoyed by the forum in terms of Art.4.5, which the Commission is anxious to curtail.

taken to avoid creating inconsistencies with the rules proposed in Rome II concerning *negotiorum gestio*.

Article 8—*Mandatory rules*: The background here is the difficulty occasioned by use of the term "mandatory rule" in the English text, to mean both "domestic" mandatory rules (*"dispositions imperatives"*), on the one hand, and, on the other, "overriding" mandatory rules, which the forum insists on applying in a conflict situation, whatever the (foreign) law otherwise applicable to the issue, and the content thereof (*"lois de police"*). The proposed Article 8 offers a definition of mandatory rules which appears to match the meaning of *lois de police*. The proposed Article 3.4 has the same wording as Article 3.3 of the 1980 Rome Convention, and in its reference to "mandatory rules" means domestic mandatory rules. Hence there is no improvement as far as the English language version is concerned. Article 8.2 (mandatory rules of the forum) replicates Article 7.2 of the Rome Convention. Article 8.3 replicates Article 7.1 of the Convention, in respect of which under the Convention state reservation is permitted (and utilised by the UK); no reservation is possible where the instrument takes the form of a Regulation.

A further point to note is that in terms of proposed Article 3.5 where the parties choose the law of a non-Member State, that choice shall be without prejudice to the application of such "mandatory rules of Community law as are applicable to the case." This provision is new, and not explained.

Article 10—*Formal validity*: The effect of the Proposal is to increase the number of laws by which formal validity may be tested.

Article 11—*Scope of applicable law*: That which was optional under Rome I, that is to say, "the consequences of nullity of the contract", would require to be regulated by the applicable law under Article 3 or 4.

Article 13—*Voluntary assignment and contractual subrogation*: In commenting on the proposed Article 13, it is desirable to identify the flaws in Article 12 of the 1980 Convention. Where a creditor who has a claim against a debtor assigns his right to pursue that claim to a third party assignee, the Rome Convention supplies guidance as to the governing law of the contract between the original parties (debtor and creditor), and between creditor and assignee. Article 12.2 of the Convention, concerning the rights between assignee and debtor, refers to the "law governing the right to which the assignment relates"; this is replaced in the proposed Article 13.2 by the "law governing the original contract". The effect of this is that while the new rule would apply to contractual assignments of contractual rights, it would no longer apply to contractual assignments of non-contractual rights.

The Convention does not deal with the problem of rights of competing assignees. This omission is addressed, though not expressly, by the proposed Article 13.3, which refers to "the law of the country in which the assignor . . . has his habitual residence at the material time." Under the current Scots rule, such competitions would be resolved, as a general rule, by application of the law governing the right assigned (exceptionally by application of the law under which all competing claimants base their claims). Article 13.3, therefore, the rationale of which is not clear, is a departure from the existing Scottish rule. Moreover, what is the material time?

UK position—It is not yet clear whether the UK will opt in to the proposed Regulation. Criticism has been expressed by UK commentators.[12] Therefore, it seems likely that some change will require to be made to the Proposal before it is acceptable to legal opinion in the UK. If the UK, ultimately, should decide not to opt in, the "layering" feature which is characteristic of modern conflict of laws quickly would become apparent, since courts in the UK would continue to apply the Rome I Convention in qualifying cases. Qualifying cases heard in another EU forum (with the exception of any other dissident State(s)), whether or not involving British parties or performance in Britain, would be determined in accordance with the Regulation. Thirdly, a complex contractual matrix falling for decision in a UK court might involve anterior obligations determined according to the Regulation. Further, the extent to which ECJ jurisprudence built up on interpretation of the Regulation on points common to both instruments, or upon differences between them, would influence British courts is likely to be problematic.

VI. MONEY OBLIGATIONS

15–50 This area concerns the answers which the conflict of laws provides to the problem of currency value fluctuation. It is important to distinguish between the substance of an obligation, on the one hand, and the currency which, by agreement of the parties, is to be used to make payment in respect thereof, on the other.[13]

MONEY OF ACCOUNT

15–51 The money of account of a contract is the *amount of money* due by the debtor, and in which his obligation must first be calculated. In accordance with general principles, the debtor's obligation to pay is

---

[12] *e.g.* Financial Markets Law Committee, Issue 121 (April 2006).
[13] *Adelaide Electric Supply Co. v Prudential Ass. Co.* [1934] A.C. 122; *Auckland Corp. v Alliance Ass.* [1937] A.C. 587; *Mount Albert BC v Australasian Temperance and General Mutual Life Ass.* [1938] A.C. 224; *Bonython v Commonwealth of Australia* [1951] A.C. 201; *National Mutual Life Ass. of Australasia v A.G. for New Zealand* [1956] A.C. 369.

governed by the proper law of the contract which decides the money of account by which the substance of the obligation is to be calculated. Money of account is the currency in which the obligation is measured. It tells the debtor how much he has to pay.[14]

MONEY OF PAYMENT

The money of payment of a contract is the *kind of money* which the debtor must proffer in order to discharge his obligation. In other words, it is the currency in which the money of account is to be paid. This is a matter of performance and therefore is governed by the *lex loci solutionis*. Money of payment is the currency in which the obligation is to be discharged. It tells the debtor by which means he is to pay.   **15–52**

In modern practice the money of account and money of payment usually are the same, agreed between the parties at the outset. A party to a contract may cover the risk of changes in the exchange rate between his own currency and the currency of payment by arranging a forward exchange contract with a third party (usually a bank) to hedge the exchange risk. In earlier decades, this aim was achieved by use of "gold clauses", linking the obligation to the value of gold, but in more recent years a substantial body of law and practice has developed in the structuring of *derivatives* of the basic concept of covering forward exchange risk. Parties may make a forward purchase of currency to safeguard their exposure, or if the period of time is considerable, seek, through a bank, a swop contract, if an equal and opposite risk can be found.

EXCHANGE CONTROL REGULATIONS[15]

Subject to the International Monetary Fund Agreement (the Bretton Woods Agreement) among members of the IMF (to respect the currency regulations of each), exchange control legislation may affect and even invalidate contractual obligations which contravene them, if: **15–53**

(1) the legislation forms part of the governing law of the contract[16]; or

---

[14] *Woodhouse Ltd v Nigerian Produce Ltd* [1971] 2 Q.B. 23 at 54, aff'd [1972] A.C. 741, *per* Lord Denning.

[15] Exchange control regulations, though removed in the UK in 1979, may yet be important in international transactions.

[16] Provided that the exchange control legislation of the applicable law is not oppressive thereby offending the public policy of the forum. See *Re Helbert Wagg & Co. Ltd* [1956] Ch. 323, where the legislation was a genuine measure to protect the German economy.

(2) the legislation forms part of the law of the place of performance, and the governing law is English[17]; or

(3) the legislation is part of English law and is applicable to the contract in question.[18]

Revalorisation laws (laws revaluing a particular currency) apply only to contracts and debts whose governing law is the law of the country concerned.[19]

DECREES IN FOREIGN CURRENCY

15–54 The judiciary in both England and Scotland in the past thirty years have changed their attitude towards the competence of granting a decree expressed in foreign currency.

The earlier position, uncompromising and long-held,[20] was that a decree must be expressed in sterling. The modern position is that the decree may be expressed in the currency which best expresses a party's loss. If conversion must be made, it should be done at the latest date procedurally possible.[21]

VII. WHERE CONTRACT MEETS OTHER AREAS OF LAW

PROPERTY

15–55 The terms of a contract, valid by the governing law of the contract, nevertheless may contravene, in detail or in policy, the law of some other interested legal system, most frequently in practice that of the *situs* of moveable property[22] which is the subject of the contract. Thus, while property may have passed according to the

---

[17] *cf. Ralli Bros* principle referred to above at para.15–26 and see Dicey and Morris, Rule 212. There is no Scots authority.

[18] *i.e.* mandatory provision of the forum; see Rome I, Art.7.2. *Cf.* at common law, *Boissevain v Weil* [1950] A.C. 327.

[19] *Anderson v Equitable Life Ass. Co.* (1926) 41 T.L.R. 123; *Re Schnapper* [1936] 1 All E.R. 322; *Kornatzki v Oppenheimer* [1937] 4 All E.R. 133.

[20] *Hyslops v Gordon* [1824] 2 Shaw App. 451; *Re United Railways of Havana and Regla Warehouses* [1961] A.C. 1007.

[21] *Commerzbank Aktiengesellschaft v Large*, 1977 S.L.T. 219; *The Despina/ The Folias* [1979] 1 W.L.R. 783; *North Scottish Helicopters Ltd v United Technological Corp. Inc. (No. 2)*, 1988 S.L.T. 778. See also Private International Law (Miscellaneous Provisions) Act 1995, Pt I—interest on judgment debts and arbitral awards may be expressed in a currency other than sterling (England and Wales only). See further, para.8–21, above.

[22] *i.e.* the law of the situation of the property at the point of contracting, or more likely, the law of the subsequent situation of the property at litigation. See *e.g. Hammer and Sohne v HWT Realisations Ltd*, 1985 S.L.T. (Sh. Ct) 21.

contractual applicable law, it may not have passed according to the governing law in property, namely, the *lex situs* of the goods at the time when ownership is purported to have passed, or subsequently. The forum in such cases may require, in adjudicating between or among parties claiming under different heads of law, to rank its own conflict rules. This matter is discussed further at Chapter 17 below.

DELICT

This encounter is examined at paragraph 16–24, below. It occurs in **15–56** cases where parties engaged in litigation arising out of an allegedly delictual situation are linked by a pre-existing contractual relationship, commonly that of employer and employee, or carrier and passenger. The defender may adduce a defence in contract to a claim laid in delict, and the task then for the court is to prioritise the forum's own conflict rules in these areas, and to assess their interaction.

RESTITUTION/UNJUST ENRICHMENT

This third area of the law of obligations[23] (variously termed **15–57** restitution, unjust/unjustified enrichment, quasi-contract, and encompassing also the topic of *negotiorum gestio*) is one which has given rise in recent years to much academic writing in the UK. It is sufficient to note that in cases arising under the head of unjust enrichment, in which, as between the parties in dispute, there existed an element or semblance of a contract, there is judicial and academic support for applying to the restitutionary problem the putative proper/applicable law of that contract.[24] These cases are termed "relational" restitution cases.

SUMMARY 15—THE LAW OF CONTRACTUAL OBLIGATIONS

1. General

15–58

Classification of a matter as contractual or otherwise is currently determined by the *lex fori*.

Whether or not there is deemed to be agreement such as to constitute a contract is determined by the putative proper/applicable law (subject to Rome I, Article 8.21).

---

[23] See Ch.16.
[24] *Caterpillar Financial Services Corporation v SNC Passion* [2004] 2 Ll's Rep. 99.

Choice of law is governed by Rome I, where it applies, embodied in the Contracts (Applicable Law) Act 1990, amplified by the common law where Rome I is silent. Cases which, by type or time, are outside the scope of Rome I, are governed by common law rules.

2. Incidents of contract

Capacity is governed by the proper/applicable law, but a person's domicile may be relevant (see also Rome I, Article 11).

Material validity is governed by the putative proper/applicable law (Rome I, Article 8).

Formal validity is governed either by the proper/applicable law, or the *lex loci contractus* (Rome I, Article 9).

Essential validity is governed by the proper/applicable law (Rome I, Article 10).

Interpretation is governed by the proper/applicable law (Rome I, Article 10.1.a).

Discharge, and consequences of breach are governed by the applicable law (Rome I, Article 10.1.d and c).

Illegality by the applicable law will result in unenforceability of the contract or the offending term thereof in a UK forum, depending on the content of the applicable law on the matter. Where there is illegality by some other law, a UK court may derive assistance, in a suitable case, from Articles 7.2 or 16.

3. Particular contracts

Special rules pertain to the following particular contracts:

  (a) immoveables;
  (b) contracts for the carriage of goods;
  (c) consumer contracts;
  (d) employment contracts;
  (e) international sale of goods;
  (f) agency.

4. Electronic commerce

The following legislation must be borne in mind:

  (a) Directive 2000/31/EC of the European Parliament and of the Council of 8 June 2000 on certain legal aspects of information society services, in particular electronic commerce, in the Internal Market (EU Electronic Commerce Directive);
  (b) Electronic Communications Act 2000;
  (c) Consumer Protection (Distance Selling) Regulations 2000 (SI 2000/2334); and

(d) Electronic Commerce (EC Directive) Regulations 2002 (SI 2002/2013).

5. Hybrid cases

Cases may arise which require the forum to consider the interaction of its conflict rules of contract, with those in cognate areas such as delict and property.

6. Proposal for a Regulation of the European Parliament and the Council on the Law Applicable to Contractual Obligations (December 2005).

CHAPTER 16

THE LAW OF NON-CONTRACTUAL OBLIGATIONS

I. DELICT

INTRODUCTION

Although the commission of a delict imposes an obligation on the **16–01** delinquent to make reparation to the victim, there has been no question to date[1] of giving effect to any intention, expressed by or ascribed to the parties to an action, as to choice of law to govern liability, its constitution and consequences. There is no evidence in Scots or English law of any choice having been made by parties,[2] except the indirect or limited choice by the pursuer of the forum in which to sue, and in any event, in most cases, delictual events are not contemplated or anticipated.[3] The applicable law therefore is determined independently of the parties' intentions.[4]

CHOICE OF LAW THEORIES

There are various theories as to the law(s) which should be applied **16–02** in cases involving delicts with foreign elements, and in particular, delicts committed in foreign countries.[5]

(1) The *lex fori* theory

According to this theory, the court should apply only its own **16–03** (substantive as well as procedural) law. The objections, however, are that:

---

[1] Though see P.M. North, "Torts in the Dismal Swamp: Choice of Law Revisited" in *Essays in Private International Law* (North ed., 1993), p.69.

[2] Though see *Morin v Bonham & Brooks Ltd* [2004] 1 Ll Rep. 702, a case raising issues in contract and tort: the Court took note of the law governing the contract in identifying the applicable law in tort.

[3] It is thought that the existence in English and Scots law before 1995 of the rule of double actionability (*qv*) acted as a disincentive to bringing litigation in the UK.

[4] See, however, Proposal for an EU Council Regulation on the law applicable to non-contractual obligations (henceforth "Rome II") COM (2003) 427 final (2003/0168) COD, Art.10. See para.16–29, below.

[5] See, *e.g.* CGJ Morse, *Torts in Private International Law* (1978).

(a) it could result in a decree for damages being granted in respect of an act which was not delictual in the place where it was committed; and

(b) it would encourage forum shopping.

(2) The *lex loci delicti* theory

16–04 According to this theory, the court should apply the law of the place where the delictual act was committed. The objections, however, are that:

(a) it might result in the court having to grant a decree for damages for an act which was not delictual by its own law;

(b) the *locus delicti* may be entirely fortuitous and/or difficult to determine[6]; and (therefore)

(c) it may lead to a grossly unjust result.

(3) The double actionability theory

16–05 Until the coming into effect of the Private International Law (Miscellaneous Provisions) Act 1995,[7] Scots and English courts applied a choice of law rule which was a combination of theories (1) and (2), entitled the "rule of double actionability" (for detail see below). The House of Lords decision in *Boys v Chaplin*[8] has multiple *rationes*, but by general agreement, raises to prominence the speeches of Lords Hodson and Wilberforce, to the effect that the double rule, requiring actionability as a tort by the *lex fori*, and civil liability by the *lex loci delicti*, remained, but that flexibility should be inserted by introducing the notion that a particular issue and its applicable law might be segregated from the law generally applicable to the claim. The English courts, in the years immediately preceding the 1995 Act, became rather bolder in the exercise of this discretionary exception.[9] But this willingness to make the rule more flexible was not evident in Scottish judicial practice.[10]

(4) The proper law theory

16–06 According to this theory the rights of the parties should be governed by the proper law of the delict, that is, the law with which, objectively, it has the closest connection. Parties' rights and liabilities should be judged according to the social environment in which the delict was committed.

---

[6] See para.16–18, below.

[7] All references in this chapter to the "1995 Act" are to this statute.

[8] [1971] A.C. 356, affirming [1968] 2 Q.B. 1.

[9] *Johnson v Coventry Churchill International Ltd* [1992] 3 All E.R. 14; *Red Sea Insurance Co. Ltd v Bouygues SA* [1994] 3 All E.R. 749, P.C.

[10] See *e.g. James Burrough Distillers plc v Speymalt Whisky Distributors Ltd*, 1989 S.L.T. 561.

The progenitor of the theory was Morris, writing in 1949 to 1952,[11] just after the Scots decision of *McElroy v McAllister*[12]; a case which demonstrated that operation of the double actionability rule could work adversely so as to supply an outcome which, it can reasonably be assumed, would not have been the desire of either (Scottish) *lex fori* or (English) *lex loci delicti* system necessarily involved by virtue of application of the double rule.

(5) The obligation theory

This theory originated in the judgment of Holmes J. in *Slater v Mexican National Railroad Co.*,[13] and was to the effect that though the conduct in question may not be struck at by the domestic law of the forum, delictual actings give rise to an *obligatio* which follows the person and may be enforced wherever the alleged wrongdoer may be found. The *lex loci delicti*, the source of the obligation, determines the existence and extent of the obligation. **16–07**

(6) The American Experience

Until the 1960s, the preferred approach in the USA was strict adherence to sole application of the *lex loci delicti*. When this was plainly unsuitable, recourse sometimes was had to the device of manipulative characterisation to secure a different result. However, from the early 1960s there emerged a new and broader, unorthodox, approach, similar to the proper law theory.[14] **16–08**

It is scarcely appropriate to dispose in a few sentences of such creativity, but for present purposes it suffices to be aware of this major development, and to note that there is an identifiable homeward trend in decisions where the court has applied "non-orthodox" methodologies (that is, rule-selecting rather than jurisdiction-selecting). The Law Commissions in their thorough review of Scots and English rules, and in their suggestions for possible reform thereof, thought that the American "revolution", though interesting, and giving due warning against over-rigidity of choice of law connecting factor, was more suited to the inter-state, than the international, situation, and they decided against recommending adopting such approaches in the UK.[15]

---

[11] Morris, "The Proper Law of a Tort" (1949) 12 M.L.R. 248, expanded in (1951) 64 Harv. L.Rev. 881. Lord Denning MR, sitting in the Court of Appeal in *Chaplin v Boys*, supported the proper law approach.

[12] 1949 S.C. 110.

[13] 194 U.S. 120 (1904).

[14] Famously in *Babcock v Jackson* 12 N.Y. 2d 473, 191 N.E. 2d 279 (1963). Also *Macey v Rozbicki* 18 N.Y.2d 289, 221 N.E. 2d 380 (1966); *Griffith v United Airlines Inc.* 203 A. 2d 796 (1964); *Tooker v Lopez* 12 N.Y. 2d 569, 249 N.E. 2d 394 (1969); *Reich v Purcell* 67 Cal. 2d 551, 423 P. 2d 727 (1967); *Kell v Henderson* 26 A.D. 2d 595, 270 N.Y.S. 2d 552 (1966); *Bernhard v Harrah's Club* 128 Cal. Rptr. 215, 546 P.2d 709 (1976). See Ch.3 regarding policy evaluation methods.

[15] Scot. Law Com. Consultative Memo. No. 62 and Law Com. Working Paper No. 87, *Private International Law: Choice of Law in Tort and Delict* (1984) 4.35–4.54.

A. CHOICE OF LAW IN DELICT: COMMON LAW RULES

16–09 The choice of law rules applied by Scots courts at common law varied according to the place where the delict was committed:

Delicts committed within Scotland

16–10 As regards delicts committed within Scotland having foreign elements (eg through connection of parties), Scots law applied, irrespective of whether there was a right of action in delict under the personal law of the alleged wrongdoer and/or victim.[16] The English courts applied an equivalent rule.[17] One might say of such cases simply that the *lex fori* applied, or alternatively that, since there was a coincidence of the *lex fori* and *lex loci delicti*, this was another example of operation of the double actionability rule (*qv*).

Where the opposing parties shared the same personal law, it might have been thought that the occurrence of allegedly delictual conduct in a different country (which also happened to be the *lex fori*) should result at least in the possibility of displacement of the *lex fori* by a law of closer connection to the parties, for it could be said that the parties were walking in a bubble of their own law, or, more elegantly, that they were "politically and psychologically insulated from their geographical environment."[18] Nevertheless, in *Szalatnay-Stacho v Fink* the English court applied to the substantive issue English law, stating that the principle of comity of nations did not compel or entitle the court to apply foreign (in this case Czech) law to acts done in England, even though both parties to the litigation were Czech. An exception to a general choice of law rule in delict, based on factors common to the parties (a rule of commonality), has been a feature of other legal systems, and has been suggested for adoption by EU Member States in Rome II.[19]

Delicts committed furth of Scotland (other than on the high seas)

Scots law[20]

The Scots courts referred, in the first place, to the *lex loci delicti* as the origin of the pursuer's right, if any. If, by that law, the conduct

---

[16] *Convery v The Lanarkshire Tramways Co.* (1905) 8 F. 117.

[17] *Szalatnay-Stacho v Fink* [1947] 1 K.B. 1; *cf. Fayed v Al-Tajir* [1987] 3 W.L.R. 102.

[18] Morris, p.289.

[19] See para.16–29, below.

[20] The following is a selection of leading Scottish cases: *Goodman v LNWR* (1877) 14 S.L.R. 449; *Rosses v Bhagvat Sinhjee* (1891) 19 R. 31; *Evans & Sons v Stein & Co.* (1904) 7 F. 65; *Thomson v Kindell*, 1910 S.L.T. 442; *Soutar v Peters* (1912) 1 S.L.T. 111; *Naftalin v LMS*, 1933 S.C. 259; *McElroy v McAllister*, 1949 S.C. 110; *MacKinnon v Iberia Shipping Co.*, 1955 S.C. 20; *Rodden v Whatlings Ltd*, 1961 S.C. 132; *Mitchell v McCulloch*, 1976 S.L.T. 2; *James Burrough Distillers plc v Speymalt Whisky Distributors Ltd*, 1989 S.L.T. 561; and *Wm Grant and Sons Ltd v Glen Catrine Bonded Warehouse Ltd*, 1995 S.L.T. 936. *Cf.* in Australia, *Breavington v*

was actionable, the court referred to Scots law as the *lex fori* to ensure that it was actionable also by that law.[21] The rule of Scots common law was that an act committed outside Scotland would be actionable as a delict in the Scots courts if:

(a) it was actionable[22] as a delict by the *lex loci delicti* at the date of the action; and

(b) it was actionable as a delict by the *lex fori* at the date of the action; and

(c) both systems of law conferred a right of action on the same person in the same capacity for substantially the same remedy.

This *rule of double actionability* regulated the heads under which damages might be claimed, and governed questions of remoteness.[23]

English law[24]

In the past, the English courts adopted a slightly different (more **16–12** forum-dominant) approach from that of the Scots courts, but in the end, they arrived at a similar result. In the first place, they looked for actionability according to the *lex fori*.[25] If that condition was satisfied, they referred to the *lex loci delicti*. The conflict rule which

---

Godleman (1988) 80 A.L.R. 362; and contrast in Canada, *Tolofson v Jensen* (1994) 120 DLR (4th) 289.

[21] See J.M. Thomson, "Delictual Liability in Scottish International Private Law" [1976] 25 ICLQ 873; Law Com. Working Paper No. 87, *Private International Law: Choice of Law in Tort and Delict*, Scot. Law Com., Consultative Memo. No.62 (1984).

[22] *i.e.* in general, and in the particular circumstances.

[23] Thus in *Mitchell v McCulloch*, 1976 S.L.T. 2, a claim under certain heads of damage could not be pursued in Scotland in so far as those heads were not allowed by the *lex fori* although recognised by the *lex loci delicti*.

[24] The following is a selection of leading English cases: *Dobree v Napier* (1839) 2 N.C. 781; *The Halley* (1868) L.R. 2P.C. 193; *Phillips v Eyre* (1870) L.R. 6 Q.B. 1; *The Mary Moxham* (1876) 1 P.D. 107; *Machado v Fontes* [1897] 2 Q.B. 231; *Carr v Fracis Times & Co.* [1902] A.C. 176; *Canadian Pacific Ry v Parent* [1917] A.C. 195; *Walpole v Canadian Northern Ry* [1923] A.C. 113; *McMillan v Canadian Northern Ry* [1923] A.C. 120; *Isaacs & Sons Ltd v Cook* [1925] 2 K.B. 391; *The Waziristan* [1953] 1 W.L.R. 1446; *Boys v Chaplin* [1969] 2 All E.R. 1085, [1971] A.C. 356; *John Walker & Sons Ltd v Henry Ost & Co. Ltd* [1970] 1 W.L.R. 917; *Church of Scientology of California v Commissioner of Police for the Metropolis (No.1)* (1976) 120 Sol. J. 690; *MacShannon v Rockware Glass Ltd* [1978] 1 All E.R. 625; *Def Lepp Music v Stuart-Brown* [1986] R.P.C. 273; *Black v Yates* [1991] 4 All E.R. 722; *Tyburn Productions Ltd v Conan Doyle* [1991] Ch. 75; *Johnson v Coventry Churchill International Ltd* [1992] 3 All E.R. 14; *Red Sea Insurance Co. Ltd v Bouygues SA* [1994] 3 All E.R. 749, PC.

[25] A requirement traceable to *The Halley* (1868) L.R. 2 P.C. 193 and much regretted by many as the tale unfolded.

was applied for many years was based on the opinion of Willes J. (later Lord Penzance) in *Phillips v Eyre*[26] in which, after saying that, in order to found a suit in England, a tort must be actionable by the *lex fori*, he said that it must also be "not justifiable" according to the *lex loci delicti*. As a result, the choice of law rule of English law prior to *Boys v Chaplin*,[27] was that an allegedly tortious act committed in a foreign country would be actionable as such in England only if it was both:

(a) *actionable* as a tort according to English law; and
(b) *not justifiable* according to the law of the country where it was committed.

This can be seen to be an unusual choice of law rule, concerned rather with the laying down of jurisdictional requirements in a broad sense, and placing the main emphasis on the *lex fori*, both as a gatekeeper *and* to judge the substance if the case was allowed to proceed through the gate, in a manner not generally found in other conflict rules.

A difficulty was introduced by *Machado v Fontes*[28] in which the words *not justifiable* were held to include an act which was wrongful in general (ie criminal) terms, but which did not confer a civil right of action by the *lex loci delicti*. It is thought that this case, which had no influence in Scotland[29] and was rejected in the leading and notorious case of *McElroy v McAllister*,[30] was overruled in *Boys v Chaplin*[31] and that, thereafter, in the basic rule a difference merely in approach was apparent between the Scottish and English rules, but little difference in result.[32]

Operation of the double rule, however, is subject to the important *caveat* that, from the date of *Boys*, the English courts, unlike the Scots, displayed willingness (albeit sporadically and rather more in the latter years just before the enactment of the 1995 Act) to use discretion in applying a *flexible exception* to the double rule, namely a particular issue might be held to be governed by the law of the country which, as regards that issue, had the most significant relationship with the occurrence and the parties. While Scotland adhered to the double rule strictly, it was accepted in England[33]

---

[26] (1870) L.R. 6 Q.B. 1.

[27] [1971] A.C. 356.

[28] [1897] 2 Q.B. 231.

[29] See, however, earlier approach in *McLarty v Steele* (1881) 8 R. 435.

[30] 1949 S.C. 110; see R.D. Leslie, *Stair Memorial Encyclopaedia*, p.293.

[31] Though see Leslie, *ibid*.

[32] The approach of the Scottish courts was more careful to respect the rules of the *lex loci delicti*; Scots law required *delictual* liability; English law required *civil* liability (see J. Blaikie, 1995 S.L.T. (News) 23).

[33] *Johnson v Coventry Churchill International Ltd* [1992] 3 All E.R. 14.

that the effect of the flexible exception was not only that the *lex loci delicti* might be displaced in favour of the *lex fori*, but also that the reverse process might take place (ie the *lex fori* could be displaced in favour of the *lex loci delicti*), and that this could be done in relation not solely to an issue, but to the whole claim.[34]

Defences

In actions based on the double actionability rule, possible defences **16–13** might be grouped as follows: no liability under the *lex fori*[35]; no liability under the *lex loci delicti*,[36] or express exclusion of a civil law claim by that law in favour, for example, of a compensation scheme[37]; operation of a time-bar under the *lex fori* or *lex loci delicti*[38]; absence in the *locus delicti* of the head of damages claimed[39]; or indemnification of the alleged wrongdoer either by the *lex fori* or the *lex loci delicti*.[40]

Defences on the merits of the type *volenti non fit injuria* or contributory negligence were available to the defender if competent under either *lex fori* or *lex loci delicti*,[41] so long as not a matter of purely local procedure in the *lex loci delicti*.[42] Procedural defences of the *lex fori* (but not of the *lex loci delicti*) also were available.

In sum these common law rules operated to the advantage of the defender.

Maritime delicts

This category of delict is excluded from the scope of the 1995 Act **16–14** (meaning that the common law still applies), if it was not governed at common law by the double rule (by inference of section 14(2)). If it was governed at common law by the double rule, then it will be

---

[34] *Red Sea Insurance Co. Ltd v Bouygues SA* [1994] 3 W.L.R. 926.
[35] *The Halley* (1868) L.R. 2 P.C. 193; see in Scotland *McElroy v McAllister*, 1949 S.C. 110 and *Mitchell v McCulloch*, 1976 S.L.T. 2.
[36] *Goodman v LNWR* (1877) 14 S.L.R. 449; *Rosses v Bhagvat Sinhjee* (1891) 19 R. 31; *Naftalin v LMS*, 1933 S.C. 259; *McElroy v McAllister*, 1949 S.C. 110; *MacKinnon v Iberia Shipping Co.*, 1955 S.C. 20; *The Mary Moxham* (1876) 1 P.D. 107; *Isaacs & Sons Ltd v Cook* [1925] 2 K.B. 391; *The Waziristan* [1953] 1 W.L.R. 1446.
[37] *Phillips v Eyre* (1870) L.R. 6 Q.B. 1; *Machado v Fontes* [1897] 2 Q.B. 231; *Walpole v Canadian Northern Ry* [1923] A.C. 113; *McMillan v Canadian Northern Ry* [1923] A.C. 120.
[38] *Goodman v LNWR* (1877) 14 S.L.R. 449; *McElroy v McAllister*, 1949 S.C. 110.
[39] *Naftalin v LMS*, *McElroy v McAllister* and *MacKinnon v Iberia Shipping Co.*, 1955 S.C. 20.
[40] *Phillips v Eyre*, above; *Carr v Fracis Times & Co.* [1902] A.C. 176.
[41] *cf. Anderson v Eric Anderson Radio & TV Pty Ltd* (1965) 114 C.L.R. 20 (Australia).
[42] *Scott v Seymour* (1862) LJ 61: requirement of the Neapolitan *locus* that criminal proceedings should precede civil ones could be ignored in the English forum.

governed now by the Private International Law (Miscellaneous Provisions) Act 1995.

(a) *Incidents internal to a ship on the high seas*: the incident is regarded as having occurred within the country whose flag the ship flies. If the action is raised in Scotland, the Private International Law (Miscellaneous Provisions) Act 1995 (*qv*) is thought to apply to such cases, and the *locus* will be the place at which the ship is registered.[43]

(b) *Incidents external to a ship on the high seas*: the Private International Law (Miscellaneous Provisions) Act 1995 does not apply here, because in such cases the courts always have applied a general maritime law, so-called.[44] It may be doubted, however, whether such a body of law truly exists. It is perhaps rather more likely in these cases that the forum applies its own law, whether or not by its own name.[45] A UK forum may require to apply provisions in the Merchant Shipping Act 1995 to a question, for example of the liability of the shipowner(s), within the ambit of operation laid down by that Act.

(c) *Incidents in foreign territorial waters*: In the past the double rule applied,[46] and therefore it would seem that the statutory rules brought in by the Private International Law (Miscellaneous Provisions) Act 1995 now apply.[47] According to Dicey & Morris, the applicable law for the purposes of section 11 will be the law of the country in whose territorial waters the incident occurs.[48] Where, however,

---

[43] Dicey & Morris, 35-066/067.

[44] *Boettcher v Carron C.* (1861) 23 D. 322; *Aberdeen Artic Co. v Sutter* (1862) 4 Macq. 355; (1862) 24 D. (HL) 4; *The Amalia* (1863) 1 Moore P.C. (N.S.) 471; *The Submarine Telegraph Co. v Dickson* (1864) 15 C.B. (N.S.) 759; *The Leon* (1881) 6 P.D. 148; *Chartered Mercantile Bank of India v Netherlands India Steam Navigation Co.* [1883] 10 Q.B.D. 521; *Currie v McKnight* (1897) 24 R. (HL) 1; *Kendrick v Burnett* (1897) 25 R. 82; *S.S. Reresby v SS Cobetas*, 1923 S.L.T. 719; *The Tubantia* [1924] P. 78; *Sheaf Steamship Co. Ltd v Compania Transmediterraneanae*, 1930 S.C. 660; *Chung Chi Cheung v R.* [1929] A.C. 16; *HMS King Alfred* [1914] P. 84. *Cf.* Dicey & Morris, 35-070.

[45] *The Esso Malaysia* [1974] 2 All E.R. 705 (applying *Davidsson v Hill* [1900–1903] All E.R. 997); see *Lally v Comex (Diving) Ltd*, May 5, 1976, OH, unreported, cited in Leslie, p.299.

[46] *MacKinnon v Iberia Shipping Co. Ltd*, 1955 S.C. 20. This was an accident internal to a ship lying in the territorial waters of San Domingo. San Domingo, as the littoral state, was the *locus delicti*. The Scots forum applied the double rule in circumstances where arguably a proper law of delict approach would have been more suitable. Dicey & Morris, 35-073, note that the Scots forum took the *locus delicti* to be the littoral state, rather than the law of the flag.

[47] Rodger, *Annotations to the Private International Law (Miscellaneous Provisions) Act 1995*; Dicey and Morris, 35-072.

[48] 35-072. Except that in a UK forum, the provisions of the Merchant Shipping Act 1995 will apply *qua* mandatory rules of the forum by virtue of the Private International Law (Miscellaneous Provisions) Act 1995, s.14(4).

there is no significant link with the littoral state (which one might think would not infrequently be the case), it is suggested[49] that use may be made of the rule of displacement in section 12 of Private International Law (Miscellaneous Provisions) Act 1995, normally in favour of the law of the flag.

B. CHOICE OF LAW IN DELICT: STATUTORY RULES

PRIVATE INTERNATIONAL LAW (MISCELLANEOUS PROVISIONS) ACT 1995

This significant Act[50] sprang from the work and consultation **16–15** undertaken by the Law Commissions in the 1980s,[51] in turn prompted by long-running academic discussion and speculation. Latterly, the question was asked whether legislative reform was necessary, in view of the remarkable flexibility and creativity displayed by English judges. The Act was precipitated by an unexpected opportunity arising in the parliamentary timetable, and was not universally welcomed[52] since it might have been possible to bring the law forward through judicial creativity alone (though North was of the view that the point had been reached when the legislature must intervene).[53]

The 1995 Act applies only to acts or omissions which occur after the commencement date of May 1, 1996.[54] All issues excluded from

---

[49] 35-073.

[50] CGJ Morse, "Torts in Private International Law: A New Statutory Framework" (1996) ICLQ 888; J. Blaikie, "Foreign Torts and Choice of Law Flexibility", 1995 S.L.T. 23; J. Blaikie, "Choice of Law in delict and tort: reform at last!" (1997) 1 (3) Edin.L.Rev., 361; B.J. Rodger, "Whisky Galore—*Por Favori*", 1996 S.L.T. (News) 105; B.J. Rodger, "The Halley Holed—and Now Sunk", 1996 SLPQ 397; P.J. Rogerson, "Choice of Law in Tort: A Missed Opportunity?" [1995] ICLQ 650. There exist international Conventions in the area of civil liability, to which the UK is not party, *e.g.* Hague Convention on the Law Applicable to Traffic Accidents (1971), and Hague Convention on the Law Applicable to Products Liability (1973).

[51] Law Com., Working Paper No. 87 and Scot. Law Com. Consultative Memo. No. 62 (1984) *Private International Law: Choice of Law in Tort and Delict* (Joint Working Paper), Law Com. No. 193 and Scot Law Com. Memo. No. 129 (1990), *Private International Law: Choice of Law in Tort and Delict*. There were important changes on the way to enactment, but there was no alteration in the general aim or purpose.

[52] P. Carter, "Choice of Law in Tort and Delict" (1991) 101 L.Q.R. 405; P. Carter, "The Private International Law (Miscellaneous Provisions) Act 1995" (1996) 112 L.Q.R. 190.

[53] "Torts in the Dismal Swamp: Choice of Law Revisited" in *Essays in Private International Law* (North ed., 1993), p.88.

[54] The date of the act or omission, not the date of harm, determines whether the old or new rules apply. See Morse, *op. cit.*, n.53 at p.888 and *Re T and N Ltd* [2005] EWHC 2990 (Ch).

operation of the Act by date,[55] or by section 13 (issues arising in any defamation claim),[56] or by section 14,[57] will be governed by the pre-existing common law rule, respectively narrow (Scots) or broad (English). The double rule is abolished by section 10 (subject to section 13), to be replaced as governing law by the *lex loci delicti* (not so called) (section 11). The *lex loci delicti* itself is subject to a rule of displacement (section 12). With the exception of defamation claims, the 1995 Act marked a significant new era of choice of law rules in tort and delict in the UK.

Section 9: characterisation, etc.

16–16 Removal of the first limb of the double rule means that incidents occurring abroad and imposing liability there (but not in Scotland) may give rise to successful damages claims in a Scottish court; so too even where the "wrongful" act which resulted in personal injury or damage to property elsewhere was done in Scotland, eg, ecological/environmental delicts (assuming a suit can be taken and is taken in Scotland). But there is an important proviso: in order for the 1995 Act to apply, the issue must be viewed by the forum as an issue relating to tort or delict. Any issue which fails to be characterised by the forum as an issue relating to tort or delict *ex hypothesi* will be governed neither by the common law nor the statutory choice of law rules in tort or delict, because it will not have qualified as a delictual issue.[58]

Since it cannot be that the forum will allow an action to proceed only if the foreign rule is identical to the rule of the forum, classification is to be made "for the purposes of private international law".[59] This assumes an enlightened approach on the part

---

[55] A few notable cases requiring to be treated at common law by reason of date include: *Kuwait Airways Corporation v Iraqi Airways Company* [2002] 3 All E.R. 209 (in respect of which see Carruthers & Crawford 2003 (52) ICLQ 761); *Ennstone Building Products Ltd v Stanger Ltd* [2002] EWCA Civ. 916; *Base Metal Trading Limited v Shamurin* [2003] EWHC 2419, and on appeal [2004] EWCA Civ. 1316; and *Re T and N Ltd* [2005] EWHC 2990 (Ch).

[56] At para.16–21, below.

[57] At para.16–22, below.

[58] In *Douglas v Hello! Ltd (No. 2)* [2005] EWCA Civ 595, 4 All E.R. 128 (concerning a claim for breach of confidence) the Court of Appeal confirmed that the parties were correct to have no regard to s.9(1) of the 1995 Act. The claim for breach of confidence was to be categorised, not as a tort, but as a restitutionary claim for unjust enrichment. The Court of Appeal held (para.96) that, "[w]e have concluded . . . albeit not without hesitation, that the effect of shoe-horning this type of [invasion of privacy] claim into the cause of action of breach of confidence means that it does not fall to be treated as a tort under English law, see *Kitechnology BV v Unicor GmbH* [1995] IL Pr 568." By contrast, it appears that the matter of pre-contractual liability (known as *culpa in contrahendo*, having been expressly excluded from the scope of the proposed Rome I Regulation, must fall, by inference, within the scope of the proposed Rome II Regulation.

[59] s.9(2): "The characterisation for the purposes of private international law issues arising in a claim as issues relating to tort or delict is a matter for the courts of the forum". But contrast s.9(4). *Cf.* Ch.15, above; *Bonacina* [1912] 2 Ch. 394.

of the forum but, nevertheless, use may be made of section 9 as protection against, or escape from, the consequences of removal of *lex fori* application under the double rule.

Section 11: the general rule

The *lex loci delicti* in this legislative version of the choice of law rule is not so named; section 11(1) sets out the basic rule in English rather than Latin, as follows: **16–17**

11. (1) The general rule is that the applicable law is the law of the country in which the events constituting the tort or delict in question occur.[60]

(2) Where elements of those events occur in different countries, the applicable law under the general rule is to be taken as being:

(a) for a cause of action in respect of personal injury caused to an individual or death resulting from personal injury, the law of the country where the individual was when he sustained the injury[61];

(b) for a cause of action in respect of damage to property, the law of the country where the property was when it was damaged[62]; and

(c) in any other case, the law of the country in which the most significant element or elements of those events occurred.[63]

The most significant consequence of the 1995 Act is that it is no longer necessary for the pursuer to show that the actions complained of are actionable as a delict or tort by the *lex fori*. The long reign of *The Halley*[64] is almost over.

Double locality delicts: ascertaining the locus delicti[65]

In some cases at common law a problem arose as to whether allegedly delictual conduct spread over intervals of time and place was to be regarded as having been committed at (i) the place **16–18**

---

[60] *e.g. Equitas Ltd v Wave City Shipping Co. Ltd* [2005] 2 All E.R. (Comm.) 301.

[61] *e.g. Hulse v Chambers* [2002] 1 All ER (Comm) 812.

[62] *e.g. West Tankers Inc v RAS Riunione Adriatica DI SICURTA (The Front Comor)* 2005 EWHC 454.

[63] *e.g. Protea Leasing Ltd v Royal Air Cambodge Ltd* [2002] EWHC 2731 (improper management and conduct of business); and *Morin v Bonham & Brooks Ltd* [2004] 1 Ll Rep 702.

[64] (1868) LR 2 PC 193.

[65] See J.M. Carruthers and E.B. Crawford, "Variations on a Theme of Rome II: Reflections on Proposed Choice of Law Rules for Non-Contractual Obligations", 2005 Edin. L.R. 65 (Pt I), and 238 (Pt II); see Pt II, p.242.

where it began, or was instigated; (ii) the place where it ended and its effects were felt; or (iii) either/both places.[66] In many potentially helpful English cases[67] the point at issue was one of jurisdiction,[68] and when that point had been settled, no further discussion of *locus* was made for the purposes of choice of law.

Not infrequently at common law such problems of ascertaining the *locus delicti* were resolved by means of the forum paying close attention to the nature of the delict or tort in question,[69] and/or to the manner in which the complaint was framed. More generally, the court might resort to a consideration of where the *substance* of the alleged tort took place.[70] Much may depend therefore on (i) localisation of the actings which *constitute* the tort or delict; or (ii) the precise description in the pleadings of the wrongdoing alleged (*e.g.* the putting on the market of a product/medication without due warning, rather than the negligent manufacture thereof).[71]

---

[66] *Dow Jones & Company Inc. v Gutnick* [2002] High Court of Australia 56 *per* Kirby, J. at para.140: to adopt the law of the place of the wrong as the applicable law in international tort claims "is not the end of the inquiry, it is merely the beginning. It leads immediately to the additional question of identifying the place of the wrong . . . much controversy can exist in relation to the proper identification of where the place of the wrong is." But contrast *Jameel v Dow Jones & Co. Inc.* [2005] EWCA Civ. 75.

[67] *R. v Peters* (1886) 16 Q.B.D. 636; *George Monro Ltd v American Cyanamid & Chemical Corporation* [1944] 1 K.B. 432; *Bata* [1948] W.N. 366; *Jenner v Sun Oil Co.* (1952) 2 D.L.R. 526 (defamatory broadcast in USA heard in Canada); *Cordova Land Co. Ltd v Victor Bros. Inc.* [1966] 1 W.L.R. 793; *R. v Hart, Millar & Robert Millar (Contractors) Ltd* [1969] 3 All E.R. 247; *Distillers Co. (Bio Chemicals) Ltd v Thompson* [1971] A.C. 458. See consideration by P. Carter, in *Transnational Tort Litigation: Jurisdictional Principles* (McLachlan and Nygh eds, 1996), Ch.7, "Defamation".

[68] See *Diamond v Bank of London & Montreal* [1979] Q.B. 333, in which it was accepted that an alleged misrepresentation received by instantaneous means within the jurisdiction of the English forum had been made within that jurisdiction. *Cf. Ark Therapeutics Plc v True North Capital Ltd* [2006] 1 All E.R. (Comm) 138, para.58. See also, with regard to Council Regulation 44/2001, Art.5.3, *Henderson v Jaouen* [2002] 2 All E.R. 705, where the victim suffered in England a deterioration in his condition originally brought about by an accident in France. See, for Canada, *Bangoura v Washington Post*, 2005 (25) T.L.W.D. 2522–006 (CA C Ont.) [2005] O.J. No. 5428).

[69] In *Soutar v Peters* (1912) 1 S.L.T. 111, the delict alleged being that of seduction, the Sheriff felt justified in noting that the defender's arts and wiles had been practised before the couple crossed the border into England (where no such tort existed, and where the act took place), so as to secure a result of coincidence of Scots *lex fori* and Scots *lex loci delicti*, whereby the conduct complained of was capable of giving rise to delictual remedy.

[70] *Metall and Rostoff A.G. v Donaldson Lufkin & Jenrette*; *Morin v Bonham & Brooks Ltd* [2004] 1 Ll Rep. 702. See discussion at Carruthers and Crawford, Pt II, pp.240 *et seq*. *Cf. Protea Leasing Ltd v Royal Air Cambodge Ltd* [2002] EWHC 2731.

[71] *cf. Castree v Squibb* [1980] 1 W.L.R. 1248; *Distillers Co. (Biochemicals) Ltd v Thompson* [1971] A.C. 458.

One of the last cases to be decided at common law, *Ennstone Building Products Ltd v Stanger Ltd*,[72] in which, as to the tortious issue, it was necessary to identify the *locus delicti*, in circumstances where advice was given in England and acted upon in Scotland. Keane L.J. accepted the argument that where the tort consists in essence in the giving of negligence advice, the tort is committed where the advice is received (*i.e.* in this case, England).

A great deal of the difficulty engendered in common law cases has been removed by the introduction in the 1995 Act of detailed rules, in section 11(2), which define where the country in which the events constituting the tort or delict occur is to be taken to be.[73] However, section 11(2)(c) caters for residual cases, and therefore admits judicial discretion. Cases of difficulty still may arise. A recent illustration[74] is provided by *Morin v Bonham & Brooks Ltd*,[75] in which the purchaser of a classic car at auction in Monaco (his interest in the auction having been raised by an entry in a catalogue delivered to the purchaser in London), subsequently sued in tort on the basis of alleged misrepresentation in the matter of a false odometer reading. The Court of Appeal, upholding the view of Hirst Q.C., considered that although elements constituting the alleged tort occurred both in England and in Monaco, the most significant elements occurred in Monaco, and accordingly, by virtue of section 11(2)(c) of the 1995 Act, the law applicable to the torts allegedly committed by Bonham & Brooks (Monaco) Ltd was Monegasque law.

Section 12: the rule of displacement

In the pre-legislative consultation period much attention was paid **16–19** to the height of the threshold at which the forum should be permitted to depart from the law generally applicable under section 11 in favour of another law. At one stage, a high threshold was favoured (in the verbal formulation that the general rule could be departed from only if there was an "insignificant connection" between the law indicated by the general rule and the relevant factors of the case).[76] The position settled upon is that the general rule may be departed from only if it is "substantially more appropriate" for some other law to govern, as follows:

---

[72] [2002] EWCA Civ. 916. *Cf. Diamond v Bank of London & Montreal* [1979] Q.B. 333.

[73] *e.g. Anton Durbeck GmbH v Den Norske Bank ASA* [2002] EWHC 1173 (QBD Commercial Court, June 13, 2002, and [2006] 1 Ll's Rep. 93); and *Morin v Bonham & Brooks Ltd* [2004] 1 Ll Rep. 702.

[74] See also *Anton Durbeck GmbH v Den Norske Bank ASA*, above.

[75] [2004] 1 Ll Rep. 702. See Carruthers and Crawford, Pt 1, pp.84 *et seq.*

[76] Law Com./Scot. Law Com. Consultative Memo. No. 62 "Private International Law: Choice of Law in Tort and Delict" (1984), paras 3.9 *et seq.*

12. (1) If it appears, in all the circumstances, from a comparison of—

    (a) the significance of the factors which connect a tort or delict with the country whose law would be the applicable law under the general rule; and

    (b) the significance of any factors connecting the tort or delict with another country,

That it is substantially more appropriate for the applicable law for determining the issues arising in the case, or any of those issues, to be the law of the other country, the general rule is displaced and the applicable law for determining those issues or that issue (as the case may be) is the law of that other country.

    (2) The factors that may be taken into account as connecting a tort or delict with a country for the purposes of this section include, in particular, factors relating to the parties, to any of the events which constitute the tort or delict in question or to any of the circumstances or consequences of those events.

The decision to displace is a matter for the discretion of the forum; upon the frequency and boldness of the forum's exercise of its discretion depends the strength of the general rule. The words "substantially more appropriate" sound a warning against overuse. The decision to displace will be based on the preponderance and distribution of factors. The list of factors is not exhaustive. Morse argues that, if the surrounding circumstances can include "factors relating to the parties" (section 12(2)) it may be possible to segregate pairs of parties, so that a different applicable law may apply between different pairs of litigants even where all claims arise out of the same incident.

There may be displacement in respect of a particular issue as well as in respect of the whole claim. Displacement may be in favour of the forum or of a third (or conceivably more) law(s). A *lex loci delicti* rule with no exit route would have resulted in the court chafing under restriction and seeking to avoid by means of manipulative characterisation, or use of public policy, the choice of law indicated by the rule.[77] As the legislation has been framed, loss of forum control by abolition of the double rule is mitigated by the opportunity available to the forum to "block" application of the *lex loci delicti* through use of this displacement provision (as well as by the public policy provision in section 14, or by forestalling it through use of the characterisation provision in section 9).

---

[77] Morse, *op. cit.*, p.897.

Cases interpretative of sections 11 and 12 of the 1995 Act

A number of English cases have been handed down since the entry **16–20** into force of the 1995 Act. Particularly useful guidance can be had from *Roerig v Valiant Trawlers Ltd*,[78] in which a Dutch claimant, Ms Roerig, brought proceedings on behalf of herself and her children, as dependants of the deceased Dutchman, Mr Van de Plas. Mr Van de Plas had been killed whilst working on an English-registered trawler owned by the English-registered defendant company. The central issue was whether, in assessing damages for loss of dependency, collateral benefits resulting from the loss should be deducted from the award of damages. Under Dutch law, all benefits received by a claimant, including social security provision and personal accident insurance payments, were deducted from awards of compensation payable to the victims of accidents and/or their dependants. In contrast, under English law, collateral benefits were to be disregarded by the forum. At first instance, Reddihough, J. concluded that the applicable law in tort was English law, the applicable law under section 11, the fatal accident having occurred on board an English-registered vessel. The defendant appealed, arguing that the facts justified displacement of the general rule. The decision of Waller, L.J. serves as a useful guide to the steps which a court should take in deciding whether or not to displace the general rule. His Lordship stated that "[t]he first exercise is to identify the issue in relation to which it might be suggested that the general rule should not be applicable."[79] Thereafter, "the next task is to identify the factors which connect the tort with England and those that connect the tort with Holland."[80] The factors which connected the case with England were three-fold: (1) the events occurred aboard a boat registered in England; (2) the skipper of the boat was English; and (3) the defendant company was English. The factors which connected the case with Holland were manifold: (1) the deceased was a Dutchman; (2) his death would lead to damage being suffered in Holland by his Dutch dependants; (3) the incident occurred when the deceased was under the supervision of a Dutch fishing master; (4) the deceased was on board the trawler in his capacity as an employee of a Dutch company; (5) insofar as the boat set off from a Dutch port and was expected also to land its catch at a Dutch port, the vessel was on a Dutch fishing expedition; and (6) the defendant was a subsidiary of a Dutch company. An important task for the forum is to assess the *significance* of the contacts: "What then is the significance of the

---

[78] [2002] 1 Ll Rep. 681. *cf. Ark Therapeutics Plc v True North Capital Ltd* [2006] 1 All E.R. (Comm) 138.

[79] Para.12 (ii).

[80] Para.12(iii).

Dutch factors when compared to the significance of the English factors which might make it substantially more appropriate for Dutch law to determine the loss of dependency issue?"[81] This requires the court to make a value judgment.

The Court of Appeal considered that the circumstances lay below the threshold for displacement, declaring that, "The general rule [in section 11] is not to be dislodged easily." "Substantially" is to be strictly construed. It could *not* be said in *Roerig* that it was "*substantially* more appropriate" for the issue of loss of dependency to be governed by Dutch law simply because the claimant or the deceased was Dutch. Accordingly, the defendant's appeal was dismissed: the applicable law was held to be English law.

Courts must be careful not to displace the general rule too readily, particularly where they are displacing in favour of the *lex fori*.[82] However, many would agree with the decision of Garland J. in *Edmunds v Simmonds*[83] to displace the Spanish law applicable under section 11 in favour of the English law of the forum. The circumstances were that Ms. Edmunds was a passenger in a car which she and Mrs Simmonds had rented whilst on holiday in Spain. During one journey, when the defendant was at the wheel, the car was involved in a collision with a Spanish lorry. Ms Edmunds suffered very severe head injuries, and sued the defendant in England to recover damages. Liability was clear. The debate concerned the size of the award of damages. According to the general rule in section 11, Spanish law was the applicable law. In terms of section 12, however, the question arose whether it was "substantially more appropriate" to apply English law. Garland J. recounted the factors which, respectively, connected the tort with Spain and with England. The factors connecting the tort with Spain were four-fold: (1) the collision occurred in Spain; (2) both vehicles involved in the collision were Spanish; (3) the driver of the second vehicle was Spanish; and (4) both insurers were Spanish. The factors which connected the tort with England were fewer in number: (1) the complainant and the defendant were both English; and (2) the complainant's damages, particularly the major heads of cost of care and loss of future earnings (being "consequences of the event" constituting the tort), arose in England. Garland J. determined that the applicable law was English law. With regard to

---

[81] Para.12 (iv).

[82] *cf.* Rome I, Art.4.2/4.5, discussed above at para.15–16. *Cf. Dovuoch Ltd & Ors v The Mauritius Union Assurance Co. Ltd* [2006] EWCA Civ. 389.

[83] [2001] 1 W.L.R. 1003. *Cf. Harding v Wealands* [2005] 1 All E.R. 415, and [2006] UKHL 32. In not dissimilar circumstances in *Hulse v Chambers* [2002] 1 All E.R. (Comm) 812, the parties in their suit in England did not seek displacement of the Greek *lex loci delicti*, but sought to argue that English law should govern quantification of damages *qua lex fori*. No attempt was made to argue that English law was, by virtue of s.12, the *lex causae*.

the weight to be given to the Spanish nationality of the car insurers, Garland J drew support from the unreported case of *Hamill v Hamill*,[84] that insurers of hire cars in tourist areas must contemplate that the majority of hirers will be foreign.

In *Glencore International A.G. and Others v Metro Trading International Inc.*,[85] concerning a tortious action in relation to property, Moore-Bick L.J. refused to displace (in favour of English law) the general rule applying the Fujairahan *lex situs* of property at the time when it was damaged. Similarly, in *Anton Durbeck GmbH v Den Norske Bank ASA*,[86] concerning alleged wrongful arrestment of a vessel in Panama (the decision to arrest having been made in London), the court held that the most significant element of the tort was the physical arrest, and it refused to be persuaded by arguments that it would be substantially more appropriate to apply English law.

Another example of a dual locality scenario under the 1995 Act is *Morin v Bonham & Brooks Ltd*, discussed above, but raising also questions in relation to section 12.[87] The Court of Appeal having found the applicable law under section 11(2)(c) to be Monegasque law,[88] applied that law to the tort claim. However, had the decision been to opposite effect (ie that the *locus* was England), it would have been open to the defendant to seek to argue by virtue of section 12 that the factor of English *locus* should be displaced by the Monegasque law of closest connection.[89]

Section 13: defamation claims

Particular disquiet[90] was felt by the British Press that, as a result of loss of forum control which is a concomitant of the 1995 Act, its freedom might be compromised if, following publication of material in a UK newspaper, it were possible for a suit for defamation for a delict "unknown", or as yet unknown, to the forum, to be brought in the UK[91] by a party aggrieved by the dissemination

16–21

---

[84] July 24, 2000.

[85] [2001] 1 Ll Rep. 284.

[86] 2002 W.L. 1039584 (QBD Commercial Court, June 13, 2002) *per* Nigel Tearpe Q.C., for the purposes of the decision or jurisdiction, confirmed *per* Clarke J. at [2006] 1 Ll's Rep. 93.

[87] [2004] 1 Ll Rep. 702. See Carruthers and Crawford, Pt 1, pp.84 *et seq.*

[88] See double locality delicts, above.

[89] The interesting point is raised that "[i]n general terms it would seem odd, if an express choice of law [in favour of Monegasque law, governing the contract between the parties] were not at least relevant to the governing law of a tort." Further, "[i]t may be open to argument that [the non-exclusive jurisdiction clause in favour of the Monegasque courts] itself constitutes a 'factor connecting the tort' to Monaco" (*per* Mance L.J., para.23). These points were left open by the Court of Appeal, being *obiter*.

[90] misplaced: Morse, *op. cit.*, n.53, at p.892. See also Clarkson, p.270.

[91] As to the jurisdictional rules in this area, see Ch.7, above.

incidentally of the material elsewhere. This lobby was successful at a late stage, with the following result:

13. (1) Nothing in this Part applies to affect the determination of issues arising in any defamation claim.

(2) For the purposes of this section "defamation claim" means—

(a) any claim under the law of any part of the United Kingdom for libel or slander or for slander of title, slander of goods or other malicious falsehood and any claim under the law of Scotland for verbal injury; and

(b) any claim under the law of any other country corresponding to or otherwise in the nature of a claim mentioned in paragraph (a) above.

The result is that liability for allegedly delictual actings under the head of defamation claims continues to be judged by the double actionability rule.[92] Few (if any) cases have been litigated upon the point whether section 13, in principle, applies to a given claim, but the limits of the category of "defamation claims" are not free from doubt. The circumstances which allegedly give rise to a claim for verbal injury also may raise related issues, for example, of privacy and confidentiality. Not only would such issues be excluded from the scope of section 13, but they might be excluded altogether from treatment as delictual issues.[93]

In applying the common law rule to defamation claims, there may be particular difficulties in ascertaining the *locus delicti*,[94] though clear favour has been shown to the place of harm. Thus, in *Evans & Sons v Stein & Co.*,[95] a useful common law authority, the allegedly defamatory letters complained of, while in transit from Scotland to their destination in England were "as safe as if they

---

[92] *cf.* early example of *McLarty v Steele* (1881) 8 R. 435. See Norrie, *Defamation and Related Actions in Scots Law* (1995), pp.188–191.

[93] *cf. Douglas v Hello! Ltd (No. 6)* [2005] EWCA Civ. 595, 4 All E.R. 128; and *Campbell v Mirror Group Newspapers Ltd* [2004] 2 A.C. 457, and [2005] UKHL 61.

[94] Especially as regards defamation and the internet: see Law Com., "Aspects of Defamation Procedure" (2002), and Scoping Study No. 2 "Defamation and the Internet: A Preliminary Investigation" (December 2002), Pt IV (Jurisdiction and Applicable Law).

[95] (1904) 7 F.65. And see earlier *Longworth v Hope* (1865) 3 M. 1049. See also *Parnell v Walter* (1889) 16 R. 917 and *Thomson v Kindell* (1910) 2 S.L.T. 442; *cf. Diamond v Bank of London & Montreal Ltd* [1979] 1 All E.R. 561 (fraudulent misrepresentation by telex was held to have been committed where received); and support for place of acting by CA in *Armagas Ltd v Mundogas SA* [1986] A.C. 717, point not considered in HL.

were still locked up in the defender's desk". The *locus delicti* was the place of receipt (but the content of the letters was not actionable there, because of the lack of "publication").

One main concern in relation to defamation is the response which the law will make to the challenge which technology lays down. Communication of defamatory or offensive material may be made instantaneously by a system which knows no territorial bounds, and into which all may enter.[96]

Section 14: Savings

Section 14 delimits the sweep of the new rules, as follows: **16–22**

(1) Nothing in this Part applies to acts or omissions giving rise to a claim which occur before the commencement of this Part.

(2) Nothing in this Part affects any rules of law (including rules of private international law) except those abolished by section 10 above.

(3) Without prejudice to the generality of subsection (2) above, nothing in this Part—

    (a) authorises the application of the law of a country outside the forum as the applicable law for determining issues arising in any claim in so far as to do so—

        (i) would conflict with principles of public policy; or

        (ii) would give effect to such a penal, revenue or other public law as would not otherwise be enforceable under the law of the forum; or

    (b) affects any rules of evidence, pleading or practice or authorises questions of procedure[97] in any proceedings to be determined otherwise than in accordance with the law of the forum.

(4) This Part has effect without prejudice to the operation of any rule of law which either has effect notwithstanding the rules of private international law applicable in the particular circumstances or modifies the rules of private international law that would otherwise be so applicable.[98]

---

[96] Consider C. Waelde and L. Edwards, "Defamation and the Internet: a Case Study of Anomalies and Difficulties in the Information Age" (1996) 10 (2) *Intl Review of Law Computers and Technology*, and Norrie, Ch.13.

[97] See Ch.8, above. Also J.M. Carruthers, "Substance and Procedure in the Conflict of Laws: A Continuing Debate in relation to Damages", 2004 (53) ICLQ 691; and J.M. Carruthers, "Damages in the Conflict of Laws—The Substance and Procedure Spectrum", 2005 JPrIL 323. See also *Harding v Wealands*, above.

[98] This is a formulation or description of "mandatory rules" as met in Contract. It is not clear whether the rules referred to are those of the forum, or of a third law, but probably the former. See Morse, *op. cit.*, n.53, at p.901.

INTRA-UK CASES

16–23 The relationship of section 9(6)[99] of the 1995 Act with section 14(2)[1] has raised queries.

One interpretation of section 9(6) is that even if the harm occurs entirely in one part of the United Kingdom and is litigated there, the forum can displace its own law by use of section 12,[2] in circumstances which appear to justify this, for example, where all parties involved share a common foreign connection.

The opposite interpretation[3] arises from the thought that section 10 abolishes only the double actionability rule (and, by inference, the flexible exception), leaving in place any rules which operated outside the double rule. The dilemma is whether to categorise an intra-Scottish delict (having foreign connections) as one to which the double rule applied.[4] If the rule hitherto applied to govern such delicts taking place entirely within Scotland *is* regarded as being a manifestation of the double rule (which it *can* be, by reason of coincidence of the two laws), it *would* be affected by section 10. It appears probable, given the ambitious aims of the statute, that this bolder interpretation is correct.

Moreover, the new rules apply, in qualifying cases, where the competing laws before a "UK" forum are those of different UK legal systems, in the same way as they do where the competing laws are those of a UK legal system and a foreign system, or two or more foreign systems. Whether the intra-UK position will be regulated by the proposed harmonised choice of law rules (*qv*) in Rome II remains to be seen.[5]

MISCELLANEOUS MATTERS

Where delict meets contract

16–24 Although delictual actings usually are not premeditated, it may happen that there is a pre-existing relationship between the alleged wrongdoer and the victim. They may stand to each other, for example, in the relationship of employer/employee, or carrier/passenger, and, as a result, the defender in an action founded in

---

[99] "This Part applies in relation to events occurring in the forum as it applies in relation to events occurring in any other country".

[1] "Nothing in this Part affects any rules of law (including rules of private international law) except those abolished by section 10".

[2] See North, p.86, criticising an earlier version of the reforms which had proposed a special rule for intra-UK torts.

[3] *cf.* Clarkson & Hill, p.259. But see Morse, *op. cit.*, p.890.

[4] See para.16–10, above.

[5] See para.16–29, below.

delict may wish to try to use a term of the contract agreed between the parties to oust or mitigate his potential delictual liability.[6]

The problem will arise, for example, when a Scots employee has entered into an employment contract under which he has agreed to waive certain provisions of Scots law regarding the law of damages for personal injuries, and has agreed instead to accept the provisions of some other (presumably less favourable) law, or an exclusion or limitation of liability on the part of the employer. If such a person is injured through an act of negligence for which his employer *prima facie* is responsible, is his right of action to be regarded as a right based on delict governed by the conflict rules stated, or as a contractual right governed (ie limited) by the provisions of the contract? In *Sayers*,[7] the judges took different views, but it is suggested that if the approach of Lord Denning MR in that case, and of Lord Kissen in *Brodin*,[8] is followed, the Scots courts will treat the matter, first, as one involving delict and apply the conflict rules of delict prior to those of contract.[9]

Hence, applying the choice of law rule in delict (common law, or under the 1995 Act, as the case may be), the court would decide whether contractual exclusion or limitation of delictual liability on the part of the alleged wrongdoer would be permitted by the delictual *lex/leges causae*. Only if such a defence is allowed according to the delictual *lex/leges causae* would the court proceed to consider whether the contract and/or contractual term in question is valid by its own applicable law, as determined by Rome I, and relevant in the circumstances.[10]

Title and interest to sue

This is normally a matter of procedure to be determined by the *lex* **16–25** *fori*, but examples of more manipulative classification in the United States have demonstrated that this largely procedural subject,

---

[6] *cf. Matthews v Kuwait Bechtel Corpn* [1959] 2 All E.R. 345. See *Coupland v Arabian Gulf Petroleum Co.* [1983] 3 All E.R. 226.

[7] *Sayers v International Drilling Co.* [1971] 1 W.L.R. 1176. See also *Comex Houlder Diving Ltd v Colne Fishing Co. Ltd*, 1987 S.L.T. 443 (right of contribution under Law Reform (Miscellaneous Provisions) (Scotland) Act 1940, s.3(2)).

[8] *Brodin v A/R Seljan*, 1973 S.L.T. 198. In this case no doubt an element of policy was present. Lord Kissen was not inclined to the view that the thrust of the provisions of the UK Law Reform (Personal Injuries) Act 1948 could be displaced by the Norwegian contract of employment of a sailor injured in Scotland by a fellow employee, who sued his employer in Scotland.

[9] *Coupland v Arabian Gulf Petroleum Co.* [1983] 3 All E.R. 226; *Henderson v Merrett Syndicates Ltd (No.1)* [1994] 3 All E.R. 506 (domestic law). See Morse, *Torts in Private International Law*, pp.187 *et seq.*; North, "Contract as a Tort Defence in the Conflict of Laws", reprinted in *Essays, op. cit.*, n.1, above, p.89: "The availability of the contractual defence is a matter of tort law but the validity of the contract in which it is to be found is a matter of contract law" (p.108).

[10] Consider, *Essays* in *Private International Law* (North ed., 1993), pp.103–104.

which is of the first importance in every sense, may merge into a matter of substance. For example, claims within the family may be regarded as pertaining to the law of domestic relations and may be referred to the domicile. While title to sue in a technical sense is procedural, interest to sue is a substantive matter; sometimes this distinction is not clearly drawn, and the expression "title to sue" may encompass both aspects.[11]

Survival of Action

16–26 Under Scots law, before the Damages (Scotland) Act 1976,[12] an executor might continue an action raised by the deceased, but he could not raise an action for damages if the deceased had not commenced such an action during his lifetime. In terms of the 1976 Act, section 2, as amended, there is transmitted to the executor of a deceased person the like rights to damages (including a right to damages by way of *solatium*) in respect of personal injuries sustained by the deceased as were vested in him immediately before his death. To enforce such a right, the executor shall be entitled to bring an action; or if an action for that purpose had been brought by the deceased but had not been concluded before his death, to be sisted as pursuer in that action (section 2A). However, under section 2(2), there shall not be transmitted to the executor a right to damages by way of compensation for patrimonial loss attributable to any period after the deceased's death. In determining the amount of damages by way of *solatium* payable to an executor by virtue of section 2, the court shall have regard only to the period ending immediately before the deceased's death (section 2(3)).[13] Under section 3, there shall not be transmitted to the executor of a deceased person any right which has accrued to the deceased before his death, being a right to (a) damages by way of *solatium* in respect of the death of any other person, under the law in force before the commencement of the Act; or (b) a loss of society award.[14] Under the double rule there was a problem if such survival of actions was allowed by the *lex loci delicti*, but was not allowed by the *lex fori* as in *McElroy*, or *vice versa*. No such difficulty will arise *per se* where the conflict rule

---

[11] *FMC Corporation v Russell*, 1999 S.L.T. 99. See E.B. Crawford, "The Adjective and the Noun: Title and Right to Sue in International Private Law", 2000 J.R. 347. See para.8–05, above.

[12] As amended by the Damages (Scotland) Act 1993.

[13] Similarly by s.2(4), claims for damages pertaining to defamation allegedly sustained by the deceased shall be transmitted to the executor only if an action for damages had been brought by the deceased before his death and not concluded by then.

[14] See generally Damages (Scotland) Act 1976 (*e.g.* provisions for avoidance of multiplicity of actions).

provides for one governing law, so long as it is accepted that the matter is one which properly belongs to the law of reparation and not to that of succession or procedure.

Exclusion of *renvoi*

Section 9(5) of the 1995 Act provides that the applicable law to be **16–27** used for determining the issues arising in a claim shall exclude any choice of law rules forming part of the law of the country or countries concerned. This echoes the common law approach.[15]

DAMAGES

Subject to one's preferred *ratio* of *Boys*, there are two main **16–28** elements in the assessment of damages:[16]

  (a) determination of liability, which is a matter of *substance* to be determined in accordance with the delictual *lex causae*. The applicable law will determine all matters such as remoteness of damage and the heads under which damages may be claimed; and

  (b) quantification of the amount of damages, which is a matter of *procedure* to be determined by the *lex fori* alone.[17]

The result of section 14(2) and (3)(b) of the 1995 Act seemingly is that there is no change in this area, but the matter of distinguishing between issues of substance and of procedure has revealed itself to be more complex than at first appears.[18] Moreover the rationale for the distinction may be subject to criticism.[19]

ROME II[20]

In search of European agreement on a choice of law rule in tort and delict[21]

The proposed Regulation of the European Parliament and Council **16–29** on the Law Applicable to Non-Contractual Obligations ("Rome II")[22] encompasses non-contractual obligations[23] arising out of a

---

[15] *cf. McElroy v McAllister*, 1949 S.C. 110, *per* Lord Russell at 126. *Cf.* para.5–07, above.

[16] *Kohnke v Karger* [1951] 2 All E.R. 179; *D'Almeida Araujo v Becker & Co. Ltd* [1953] 2 Q.B. 329 (contract); *Boys v Chaplin* [1971] A.C. 356; *Mitchell v McCulloch*, 1976 S.L.T. 2.

[17] But see *Harding v Wealands* [2005] 1 All E.R. 415.

[18] *e.g. Roerig*, above.

[19] *Harding v Wealands* [2005] 1 All E.R. 415. Also J.M. Carruthers, "Substance and Procedure in the Conflict of Laws: A Continuing Debate in relation to Damages", 2004 (53) ICLQ 691; and J.M. Carruthers "Damages in the Conflict of Laws—The Substance and Procedure Spectrum", 2005 JPrIL 325. See *Re T and N Ltd* [2005] EWHC 2990 (Ch.) at paras 45 *et seq*.

[20] Latest proposal at time of writing is Proposal for a Regulation of the European Parliament and the Council on the law applicable to non-contractual obligations

tort or delict, or from restitutionary claims under the heads of unjust enrichment and agency without authority, *negotiorum gestio* and now, though not originally, *culpa in contratendo*.[24]

As with Rome I, there are certain exclusions from the scope of the proposed instrument.[25] The choice of law rules proposed, if adopted, will have universal application, that is, they must be applied in qualifying cases in any EU forum regardless of whether the contending laws are those of EU Member States or not.[26]

It appears to be clear, although it was not always so, that the UK, having decided to opt in to the Rome II negotiations, is likely to be bound by the outcome.[27] It seems unlikely that the UK will opt to disapply Rome II in intra-UK cases.[28]

A general description of the shape of the proposed instrument would emphasise that: Article 3—*General rule* (for obligations arising out of a tort or delict): The proposal contains a rule of general application (Article 3), applicable where no choice of law has been made under Chapter IV, designating as applicable the law of the country in which the damage occurs[29] (termed, in recital 7, the *lex loci delicti commissi*, but more accurately being the *lex loci damni*), irrespective of the country in which the event giving rise to the damage occurred (*i.e.* the place of acting), and irrespective of the country or countries in which the indirect consequences of that event occur. Article 3.1 is subject to a commonality clause, to the effect that the obligation shall be governed instead by the law of the common habitual residence of the alleged wrongdoer and the

---

(May 19, 2006) (9142/06) (JUSTCIV 118 CODEC 455) (hereinafter "Council Approved Version").

[21] See J.M. Carruthers and E.B. Crawford, "Variations on a Theme of Rome II: Reflections on Proposed Choice of Law Rules for Non-Contractual Obligations", 2005 Edin. L.R. 65 (Pt I), and 238 (Pt II).

[22] See earlier Amended Proposal of February 21, 2006 (COM (2006) 83 (final). See earlier still Draft Report Revised Version on the proposal for a European Parliament and Council regulation on the law applicable to non-contractual obligations ("Rome II") (COM (2003) 427-C5-0338/2003-2003/0168 (COD)) (April 5, 2004), Rapporteur Diana Wallis MEP (hereinafter "the Wallis Report"); and House of Lords European Union Committee HL Paper No. 66 (April 7, 2004) (henceforth "the Scott Report").

[23] See Council Approved Version, recital 5: for the purposes of the Regulation non-contractual obligation should be understood as an autonomous concept.

[24] A resumé of what is proposed for this secondary category is contained in paras 16–30 *et seq*, below.

[25] Art.1.2.

[26] Art.2.

[27] Carruthers and Crawford, Pt I, p.68; and Counsel Approved Version, recital 22.

[28] See authorisation in Art.21.2.

[29] According to Council Approved Version, recital 7, "A connection with the country where the direct damage occurred (*lex loci damni*) strikes a fair balance between the interests of the person causing the damage and the person sustaining the damage, and also reflects the modern approach to civil liability and the development of systems of strict liability."

victim at the time when the damage occurs (Article 3.2), if such commonality is present. Overriding *both* of these rules, Article 3.3 provides the forum with discretion to apply the law of manifestly more close connection.

A difference between the civilian and UK approaches is the evident preference of the former for fixed, certain rules, contrasted with the UK preference for flexibility. As explained, English courts have shown confidence in utilising discretion in choice of law in tort, in order to find what they consider to be the most appropriate law.[30] It is trite to say that in crafting a rule for choice of law in delict the balance has to be struck, where desired, at some point on the line between certainty and flexibility.[31] As the negotiations *sub nom* Rome II have advanced, the English background of the European Parliamentary *rapporteur* has become evident.

Application of the general rule is modified in appropriate cases by a series of tort-specific rules contained in Articles 4 to 8a (covering product liability; unfair competition and acts restricting free competition; environmental damage; and infringements of intellectual property rights; and industrial action).[32] The tort-specific rules are more familiar to civilian lawyers than to UK lawyers; such an approach has never featured in Scots and English choice of law rules in delict/tort, apart from the defamation exception contained in section 13 of the 1995 Act.

A specific-category approach has its drawbacks in that there will always be potential for argument where the categorisation is debateable in a particular case, or where the factual and legal circumstances straddle more than one category, or where the categories themselves seem inadequate for the complexity of the situation. Moreover, the presence of an abundance of categories will be likely to weaken the so-called general rule. However, recital 9 of Council Approved Version states that specific rules should be laid down for special torts/delicts, where the general rule does not allow a reasonable balance to be struck between the interests at stake.

Chapter IV—*Freedom of choice*: Whether, and to what extent, party autonomy should be permitted in the area of non-contractual

---

[30] Carruthers and Crawford, Part II, pp.254–259. Council Approved Version, Art.26B requires the Commission, not later than four years after the Regulation enters into force, to submit a report on its application. In particular, the report shall consider non-contractual obligations arising out of traffic accidents and out of violations of privacy and rights relating to personality, including defamation.

[31] However, it must be appreciated that even choice *ex post facto* is not necessarily *informed* choice; permission to choose the applicable law *after* the event is no guarantee that advantage will not be taken of the weaker party. See further Carruthers and Crawford, Part I, pp.82 *et seq.*

[32] Recital 16, while respecting the intentions of parties, protects "weaker parties" by imposing certain conditions on the choice (*i.e.* restricting choice to choice *ex post*). "Weaker parties" must be taken to mean, at least, consumers and employees, who otherwise would have been the parties most likely to be asked to make an ex ante choice.

obligations has been the subject of much discussion. In this latest formulation, there is sanctioned freedom of choice ex post (*i.e.* after the event giving rise to the damage occurred).[33] The link in thought and policy between Rome II and the Rome Convention is evidenced by the similarity of drafting found in Chapter IV of Rome II and Article 3 of the Convention (*viz* the choice must be expressed or demonstrated with reasonable certainty by the circumstances of the case; and it may not affect the rights of third parties).

Furthermore, where "all the parties are pursuing a commercial activity", Article 3A.1 permits choice *ex ante* (*i.e.* by agreement freely negotiated *before* the event giving rise to the damage occurred).[34]

Where parties have chosen the applicable law in terms of Chapter IV, the choice will be subject to the mandatory rules of the law of another country wherein all the other elements relevant to the situation at the time when the event giving rise to the damage occurs are located.[35]

A further, novel, restriction upon party choice is contained in Chapter IV, Article 3A.3, namely, that where all the elements relevant to the situation at the time when the event giving rise to the damage occurs, are located in one or more EU Member States, the parties' choice of applicable law other than that of the Member State(s) in question, shall not debar the application of provisions of Community law, where appropriate as implemented in the Member State of the forum, which cannot be derogated from by contract.

The applicable law (whether found by application of Article 3, or the tort-specific rules, or party choice) is subject to the overriding mandatory provisions of the *lex fori* (Article 12).

Once identified, the scope of the applicable law is set down in Article 11, covering, *e.g.* the basis and extent of liability, including vicarious liability; exemption from, limitation or division of liability; and the existence, nature and assessment of damages or the remedy claimed.

As is normal in these instruments, there is an exclusion of *renvoi* clause (Article 20) and a public policy saving (Article 22). *Per* Article 23, the proposed Regulation shall not prejudice the application of acts of the institutions of the European Communities which, in relation to particular matters, lay down choice-of-law rules relating to non-contractual obligations.

---

[33] *cf.* 1980 Rome Convention, Art.3.3, and proposed Rome I Regulation, Art.3.4.

[34] Scott Report, Evidence: E.B. Crawford and J.M. Carruthers, p.104.

[35] Paradoxically, the connecting factor offered in Rome II for "non-relational" cases is the very one in respect of the quality of which, in the UK, we have had misgivings regarding its lack of potential, its inappropriate nature, or inadequate character. It is notorious that the place of enrichment as a criterion has been productive of much trouble, but see *Douglas v Hello! Ltd (No. 6)* [2005] EWCA Civ. 595; 4 All E.R. 128.

II. UNJUST ENRICHMENT

Since the latter part of the twentieth century this area of law in its **16–30** domestic aspect has been the subject of much academic exploration and discussion in England and Scotland, of an intensity which is surprising to those whose education in the matter consisted of a brief review of "quasi-contract"[36] Initially the writing was concerned with the topic in its domestic law aspect, but increasingly there has been interest in its conflict dimensions.[37] Conflictually, the relative paucity of decisions[38] on jurisdiction[39] and choice of law[40] affords opportunity for speculation as to applicable law[41] and reason for caution. To date, the area has been a common law hybrid, governed neither by Rome I, nor by the Private International Law (Miscellaneous Provisions) Act 1995.

Existing Choice of Law Rules

Rule 200 of Dicey and Morris proposes that: **16–31**

---

[36] See P. Birks, *Introduction to the Law of Restitution* (1989); P. Jaffey, *The Nature and Scope of Restitution* (2000); A. Jones, *Restitution and European Community Law* (2000); A.S. Burrows, *The Law of Restitution* (2002); Goff and Jones, *The Law of Restitution* (2002); and R. Evans-Jones, *Unjustified Enrichment* (2003), Vol. 1. There are historical and essential differences between English and Scots domestic law, including the presence in Scots, but not English law—with the associated potential for interesting conflict consequences—of a well developed rule of *negotiorum gestio*. How will an English forum react to a claim under a head unknown to it? Though see D. Sheehan, "*Negotorium Gestio*: A Civilian Concept in the Common Law?" (2006) (55) ICLQ 253.

[37] See discussion by J. Blaikie, "Unjust Enrichment in the Conflict of Laws", 1984 J.R. 112; see also R.D. Leslie, "Unjustified Enrichment in the Conflict Laws" (1998) 2 Edinburgh Law Review, 233.

[38] But see *Batthyany v Walford* (1887) 36 Ch.D. 269; *Cantiere San Rocco v Clyde Shipbuilding and Engineering Co. Ltd* [1924] A.C. 226; *Fibrosa Spolka v Fairbairn Lawson* [1943] A.C. 32; *Re Jogia (A Bankrupt)* [1988] 1 W.L.R. 484; *Arab Monetary Fund v Hashim (No.9)* [1993] 1 Ll Rep. 543; *El Ajou v Dollar Land Holdings plc* [1993] 3 All E.R. 717 and [1994] 2 All E.R. 685; *Macmillan Inc. v Bishopsgate Investment Trust plc (No. 3)* [1996] 1 W.L.R. 387; *Baring Bros & Co. Ltd v Cunninghame D.C.*, 1996 G.W.D. 25–1405; *Strathaird Farms v G.A. Chattaway & Co.*, 1993 S.L.T. (Sh.Ct) 36; *Kleinwort Benson Ltd v Glasgow D.C.* [1995] All E.R. (E.C.) 514; and [1997] 4 All E.R. 641.

[39] *Kleinwort Benson v City of Glasgow Council* [1997] 4 All E.R. 641 to the effect that a claim based on unjust enrichment is to be classified as neither contractual nor delictual; see also *Strathaird Farms v G.A. Chattaway & Co.*, 1993 S.L.T. (Sh.Ct.) 36.

[40] *Baring Bros & Co Ltd v Cunninghame D.C.*, above; *Macmillan Inc. v Bishopsgate Investment Trust plc (No. 3)* [1996] 1 W.L.R. 387 (CA); *Arab Monetary Fund v Hashim* [1996] 1 Ll Rep. 589 (CA); and *cf. Douglas v Hello! Ltd (No. 6)* [2005] EWCA Civ. 595, 4 All E.R. 128 (the issue of breach of confidence was being treated as restitutionary).

[41] Even to the extent of arguments in favour of *renvoi*: *Barros Mattos Junior v MacDonalds Ltd* [2005] I.L.Pr. 47, *per* Collins J. at para.121.

(1) The obligation to restore the benefit of an enrichment obtained at another person's expense is governed by the proper law of the obligation.

(2) The proper law of the obligation is (*semble*) determined as follows:

    (a) If the obligation arises in connection with a contract, its proper law is the law applicable to the contract;

    (b) If it arises in connection with a transaction concerning an immovable (land), its proper law is the law of the country where the immovable is situated (*lex situs*);

    (c) If it arises in any other circumstances, its proper law is the law of the country where the enrichment occurs.[42]

Whilst there is general support among commentators for paragraphs (2) (a) and (b) of Rule 200 there is also general doubt[43] about the wisdom of paragraph (2)(c); this particular minor rule, or default position, has provided something of an opportunity for commentators to tilt at giants.[44]

Paragraph (2)(c) is to the effect that where there is a contract, an element of contract or semblance of a contract between the parties, their alleged non-contractual rights and obligations will be governed by the law governing the anterior or underlying contractual relationship. This approach may be said to reflect the prevailing view within and outside the UK, and those who subscribe to it term such cases "relational restitution cases".[45] Notably, however, the authors of Cheshire and North seem unconvinced both generally, and on the particular ground[46] that insofar as parties can choose the applicable

---

[42] In *Douglas v Hello! Ltd (No. 6)* [2005] EWCA Civ. 595; 4 All ER 128 the Court of Appeal characterised the claimant's claim relating to invasion of privacy *not* as a tort, but rather as a restitutionary claim for unjust enrichment. Giving general approval to the Dicey & Morris preferred connecting factor of "place where the enrichment occurred", the Court, by inference, proceeded to hold in effect that England was the place of enrichment, based upon publication in England of the offending material (paras 96–102).

[43] J. Blaikie, *Unjust Enrichment and the Conflict of Laws* (1984) J.R. 112; Bird, J. in Rose (ed)., *Restitution and the Conflict of Laws* (1995); R.D. Leslie, *Unjustified Enrichment and the Conflict of Laws* (1998) 2 Edin. L.R. 233; Cheshire and North, Ch.20; G. Panagopoulos, *Restitution in Private International Law* (2000); and A. Briggs, *The Conflict of Laws* (2002), Ch.7.

[44] But see decision of Lawrence Collins J. in *Barros Mattos Junior* above, in which approval was not given to any mechanical application of the law of the place of enrichment. Generally this area provides an opportunity for creation of "a principled and reasoned approach to the question of the proper choice of law rule for restitutionary issues." (Panagopoulos, *Restitution in Private International Law* (2000), p.111).

[45] Briggs, p.196. See discussion by J. Bird, "Choice of Law", in *Restitution and the Conflict of Laws* (F. Rose ed., 1995). Though the proportion of "non-contractual" relationship cases is likely to be small, other antecedent events may concern, *inter alia*, tort, property or trusts.

[46] See Cheshire & North, pp.679, 686, 691–692.

law of their contract, it would follow that they can choose, indirectly (possibly inadvertently) and perhaps with inappropriate effect, the law to govern related restitutionary obligations.

Through the lens of *contract*, the subject of applicable law governing the consequences of nullity of a contract (which must frequently provoke questions of unjust enrichment) is excluded from the scope of Rome I by virtue of United Kingdom reservation.[47] However, looked at through the lens of *restitution*, the embryonic conflict rule in relational cases points to the putative applicable law of the underlying contract or semblance of contract, to which Rome I is likely to apply. Hence there is tension and circularity.

Few conflict lawyers[48] have the appetite for challenging a *lex situs* rule where it appears to be the obvious and ineluctable one (Rule 200(2)(b)).

Thus it is in the residual case (2)(c) (termed "non-relational restitution"[49]), that disagreement among scholars emerges. Enrichment may "occur" in several places, and those places may be artificial or casual. From this arises the school of thought which favours flexibility, *i.e.* application of the law of closest and most real connection. It is clear that this is an unregulated area, one of the precious few, where commentators have enjoyed giving rein to untrammelled creativity and serious thought as of new to the formulation of appropriate choice of law rule(s) for this area.[50] Though "it is not now disputed that there is a choice of law rule, or rules, for restitutionary claims",[51] authorities are ambivalent. There is "domestic instability [which] is reflected in the emerging rules of private international law"[52] and there are large and largely undiscussed issues of how equity should be treated in conflict rules and theory. In short in the UK we are somewhat nonplussed and the state in which we gather to consider the EU proposed solution is one of disarray.

---

[47] *i.e.* reservation with regard to Art.10.1(e). See objections recorded in Giuliano & Lagarde Report, OJ C282 31.10.80, p.33.

[48] Though one is J.M. Carruthers, *The Transfer of Property in the Conflict of Laws* (2005).

[49] Briggs, p.198.

[50] See in particular Cheshire & North, Ch.20, where is to be found a magisterial and comprehensive review of the possibilities, concluding, with regard to unjust enrichment, that the obligation to make restoration is governed by the proper law of the obligation, giving great discretion to the judge. There are few, if any, lines of thought which the authors do not pursue, but the very exercise of considered and reflective review emphasises the embryonic nature of the conflict "rule" in England.

[51] Briggs, p.191.

[52] Briggs, p.192. See also Explanatory Memorandum accompanying the Commission Proposal for Rome II, p.21, which states, "[s]ince these obligations are clearly distinguished by their own features from torts and delicts, it has been decided that there should be a special section for them."

It seems, therefore, that two opposing points of view reasonably can be held upon the desirability of seeking to harmonise on a European basis choice of law rules in this area: one view is that such an exercise is premature, and another cautiously welcomes the introduction of some measure of certainty and order in an area where views are not entrenched. The problem, however, lies in the *detail* of the rules proposed, which at least in their first formulation were strongly criticised. Moreover, one of the greatest difficulties is drafting a workable choice of law rule which is apt to cover all possible restitutionary scenarios.

ROME II

In search of European agreement on a choice of law rule in non-contractual obligations arising otherwise than out of tort and delict (unjust enrichment and *negotiorum gestio*)

The original proposal

16–32 In Article 9 of the EU Commission's first version of Rome II (henceforth "the Commission Proposal") (now revised—see below), the mode of treating "restitution" in choice of law was to encompass in one article all topics with which the Commission aimed to deal, under this head, namely unjust enrichment and agency without authority. The consequence of this drafting decision was to produce a cumbrous and lengthy, yet not comprehensive, multi-paragraph rule.

Article 9 of the Commission Proposal established a cascade of rules, flowing down five steps.[53] Pre-eminence was given to the law governing the underlying relationship, if any, between the parties (Article 9.1). Nevertheless, where the parties had a common habitual residence at the time when the event giving rise to the damage occurred, the applicable law should be the law of that country (Article 9.2). Article 9.3 then provided a specific rule for unjust enrichment, and Article 9.4 a specific rule for actings without authority. However, both of these were subject to the overriding rules of underlying relationship and common habitual residence (Article 9.1 and 9.2). In turn, *all* of these rules were subject to Article 9.5, which contained in familiar words the displacement rule that, where it was clear from all the circumstances that the non-contractual obligation was manifestly more closely connected with another country, the law of that other country should apply.[54] Hence,

---

[53] See generally J.M. Carruthers and E.B. Crawford, *Conflict of Laws Update*, 2004 S.L.T. (News) 19.

[54] None of these rules was to apply to intellectual property rights (Art.9.6 of the Commission Proposal), but the exclusion did not appear in the Revised Proposal, Art.9A or 9B.

the drafting formulation employed should be described not as a cascade, but rather as a stream running uphill.

The Commission produced a later, revised version of the proposal, creating a division between Article 9A (unjust enrichment) and Article 9B (*negotiorum gestio*). The change took into account criticisms of the original versions of Article 9.

At the time of writing, Article 9 has been re-cast and currently survives.[55] It seems to be much more satisfactory to treat the two topics of unjust enrichment and *negotiorum gestio* separately, albeit in a similar structure to each other[56]; and further, in both instances, there should be separate treatment of relational and non-relational cases.

Council Approved Version, Chapter III, Article 9A (unjust enrichment)

The general thrust of Article 9A is to apply to relational cases the **16–33** law governing the relationship previously existing between the parties, be it contractual, delictual or other; and to non-relational cases, the law of the common habitual residence at the time when the event giving rise to unjust enrichment occurs, failing which the law of the country in which the event takes place[57]; and in both relational and non-relational cases to permit reversion to judicial discretion where it is clear from all the circumstances of the case that the non-contractual obligation arising out of unjust enrichment is manifestly more closely connected with another country.

It is notable that there is to be no express application of the *lex situs* in cases where the unjust enrichment is connected with a transaction concerning immoveable property. Presumably in the operation of this proposed Article, the applicable law in such cases would be likely to be the *lex situs*, at least by operation of Article 9A.1.

---

[55] Contained in Council Approved Version (which, subject to certain additional provisions, replicates Art.9 of the Amended Proposal of February 21, 2006 (COM) (2006) (83 final)).

[56] Although it cannot be said that the Scots courts prior to 1995 showed the same inclination, and since 1995 have had very little opportunity so to do. The wealth of writing devoted to the subject of choice of law in tort and delict is disproportionate to the number of cases of this type arising before the courts. One, unreported, Scottish case is *Banks v CGU Insurance plc*, November 5, 2004, *per* Lady Smith, but the case principally concerns the plea of *forum non conveniens*.

[57] Paradoxically, the connecting factor offered is the very one in respect of which the quality of which, in the UK, we have had misgivings. It is notorious that the place of enrichment, which previously has been a favoured criterion, has been productive of much trouble; but see *Douglas v Hello! Ltd (No. 6)* [2005] EWCA Civ. 595; 4 All E.R. 128.

Council Approved Version, Chapter III, Article 9B (negotiorum gestio)

16–34 The formulation of choice of law rules by which to deal with cases of *negotiorum gestio* presents a challenge. Within the UK such cases are rare, and so seldom do they have a conflict dimension that one might say the subject was arcane. Moreover, controversy will arise only if the *content* of the potentially applicable laws varies (although variation, admittedly, is likely). Interesting points where there might be a variation between domestic laws include:

(a) the circumstances which justify an individual person becoming an agent or *gestor*;

(b) the *gestor*'s right to payment, or only to reimbursement, and the effect thereon of the *gestor*'s efforts having proved fruitless or detrimental;

(c) the right of action by an individual reasonably employed by the *gestor* to sue the beneficiary (*ie* principal) direct;

(d) the standard of care to be exercised by the *gestor*, and liability of the *gestor* to the principal if that standard is not exhibited; and

(e) whether the *gestor*, having intervened, must attempt to bring matters to a conclusion, and the legal consequences of quitting the task prematurely.

In relational cases of *negotiorum gestio*[58] under Article 9B.1, the law governing the relationship (where there is one), be it contractual, delictual or other, shall apply. In non-relational cases, by Article 9B.2, the law of the common habitual residence at the time when the event giving rise to the loss or damage occurs, shall apply, failing which,[59] by Article 9B.3, the applicable law shall be the law of the country in which the action (*i.e.* that performed without due authority in connection with the affairs of another person) took place. There is discretion in Article 9B.4 permitting recourse in both relational and non-relational cases to the law of the country of manifestly more close connection.

Council Approved Version, Chapter III, Article 9C (culpa in contrahendo)

16–35 The phrase *culpa in contrahendo*, originating in German customary law, signifies those rules of national legal systems concerning the standard of conduct required by parties in pre-contractual negotia-

---

[58] One must speculate that examples of this would be, *e.g.* actings by a parent/guardian on behalf of a child concerning his property; or where an agent acts, on an ongoing basis, by virtue perhaps of a power of attorney.

[59] *i.e.* where the applicable law cannot be determined under either Art.9B.1 or 9B.2.

tions. Whether a contract comes into existence or not, it can be seen that issues such as adequate disclosure, misrepresentation, and duty to display good faith and decent dealing, have a hybrid character within the law of obligations.[60] In many European systems, such questions as regarded as delictual or restitutionary. In recital 15a of the Council Approved Version, it is explained that, for the purposes of the proposed Regulation, *culpa in contrahendo* is an autonomous concept, and should not necessarily be interpreted within the meaning of national law. Further, the recital explains that the provision in this subject (Article 9C) "covers only non-contractual obligations presenting a direct link with the negotiations prior to the conclusion of a contract". Hence, the relevant (delict) provisions of proposed Rome II (*i.e.* Article 3, *etc.*) should apply if during the negotiations of a contract a person suffers personal injury. This must surely be taken to mean that if one of the parties in course of negotiation suffers (physical) injury through lack of care by the defendant, Article 3 would apply. However, for the type of situation which can be characterised as pertaining to *culpa in contrahendo*, as illustrated above, a special rule is provided in Article 9C, which, confusingly (by referring to the putative applicable law of the (putative) contract), diverts attention from the non-contractual character of the obligation. The special choice of law rule formulated for such cases leads to the same result as would have eventuated had such cases of *culpa in contrahendo* been characterised as cases of relational unjust enrichment. Moreover, under the solution currently proposed, though the topic falls under Rome II (non-contractual obligations), the (restitutionary) choice of law rule, in its content as it applies to *culpa in contrahendo*, is indistinguishable from the "putative applicable law" solution to problems of material validity of contract contained in Rome I, Article 8.

SUMMARY 16—THE LAW OF NON-CONTRACTUAL OBLIGATIONS

1. Choice of law in delict

The main rules are contained in the Private International Law **16–36** (Miscellaneous Provisions) Act 1995, Part III, which (in section 10) abolishes the former rule of double actionability. The statutory rules apply only where the act or omission giving rise to the claim occurred after the commencement date (May 1, 1996). They do not apply (section 13) to the determination of issues arising in a

---

[60] At the current state of development in Scots law such circumstances often are treated purely as contractual, the issue being whether *consensus in idem* has been reached in the circumstances: *e.g. W.S. Karoulias S.A. v The Drambuie Liqueur Company Ltd* [2005] CSOH 112.

defamation claim of whatever date, which continue to be governed by the common law.

The rule of double actionability is replaced by a rule of application of the law of the country in which the events constituting the tort or delict in question occur, as defined (section 11), subject to a rule of displacement (section 12) if another law is substantially more appropriate to determine the issues arising in the case, or any of those issues.

2. Issues presenting elements both of contract and delict

Such a problem will be approached, first, from the delictual aspect, by ascertaining whether by the conflict rule in delict, liability of the defender can be ousted or mitigated by a contractual term. If so, it is necessary to ascertain according to the contractual applicable law whether the contractual term is valid and effective.

3. Damages

Substantive aspects such as heads of liability are governed by the delictual *lex causae*.

Procedural aspects (including at present quantification) are governed by the *lex fori* alone.

4. Choice of law rules in unjust enrichment

These rules are somewhat under-developed in Scots and English law, but there is a measure of agreement that restitutionary claims closely allied to a contract (relational cases) should be governed by the applicable law, or putative applicable law, governing that contract. In other (non-relational) cases, support has been given to application of the law of closest connection, however identified, or of the *lex situs* in cases concerning immoveable property.

5. Harmonisation

Negotiations with the aim of creating harmonised choice of law rules in non-contractual obligations, to be applied in EU forums, are at an advanced stage (Rome II). Political agreement was reached at the European Council meeting at end April, 2006, on the articles of the Draft Regulation. In 2006, the draft instrument will be forwarded to the European Parliament for a second reading.

If/when implemented, the Regulation shall apply to events (and presumably omissions) giving rise to damage occurring after its entry into force (Article 27).

CHAPTER 17

THE LAW OF PROPERTY

Different rules govern the transfer of property according to whether **17–01** the transfer in question is universal (or general) in nature, that is, affecting an individual's entire estate, such as upon the event of marriage, insolvency or death, or particular (or special) in nature, that is, affecting one or more specific assets, by means of gift, sale, mortgage etc. This chapter will examine, first, the rules governing particular transfers of property, and second, the rules which apply to general transfers in the event of insolvency.

I. PARTICULAR TRANSFERS OF PROPERTY

A. TERMINOLOGY AND CLASSIFICATION

This is one of the very few areas of Scots and English international **17–02** private law which rests mainly on the common law, being largely untouched by statute and convention. This is both refreshing and alarming. The contributions of writers are influential.[1]

Note should be taken of the following differences in terminology:

(a) domestic Scots law—heritage and moveables;
(b) domestic English law—real and personal property;
(c) conflict of laws—immoveables and moveables.[2]

The forum uses the terms and classification immoveable and moveable to endeavour to accommodate within a "more universal and natural distinction"[3] differences in property categorisations adopted by different legal systems.

---

[1] See J.M. Carruthers, *The Transfer of Property in the Conflict of Laws* (2005); P.A. Lalive, *The Transfer of Chattels in the Conflict of Laws* (1951); and G. Zaphiriou, *The Transfer of Chattels in Private International Law* (1951).

[2] *Macdonald*, 1932 S.C. (HL) 79, *per* Lord Tomlin at 84; *cf. Re Hoyles, Row and Jagg* [1911] 1 Ch. 179, *per* Farwell L.J. at 185. But see *Re Cutcliffe* [1940] Ch. 565 and Dicey and Morris, 22-004 *et seq.*

[3] Dicey & Morris, 22-004: a distinction made in the conflict of laws upon the factual difference between moveable and immoveable property and not on technical nicety or historical basis (e.g. Scots law of "fixtures" where, in domestic law, a right over what is physically moveable is regarded as being a right over an immoveable).

Property is always classified for the purposes of a conflict case as moveable or immoveable in accordance with the rules of the *lex situs* (*qv*) as they apply for the purpose of the conflict of laws.[4]

Examples can be cited of cases where the classification of property arrived at as a result of the application of the conflict rule of a legal system differs from that accorded by its domestic law, for example English leaseholds[5]; foreign land[6] and mortgages over land;[7] stocks and shares;[8] Scots bonds and dispositions in security[9]; and land held upon trust for sale.[10]

A problem of classification may arise between categories of legal problem, for example as between property and contract, and property and restitution.[11] A claim for restitution of property is a claim to which, if there are conflict elements, it may be appropriate for the conflict rules of property to be applied in preference to the rules of contract. The characterisation proposed in the pleadings of parties may not be that which is adopted ultimately by the court as evidenced by the manner in which it chooses to resolve the dispute.[12]

The initial characterisation of a cause of action by the forum (*e.g.* as being one of intestate succession to moveable property) will indicate to that court the identity of its choice of law rule, and the applicable law to apply (*i.e.* last domicile of the deceased). But to follow through the application of the *lex causae*, recharacterisation of

---

[4] See Leslie, *Encyclopaedia*, pp.315 and 316. *Ross v Ross's Trs*, July 4, 1809, F.C.; *Hall's Trs v Hall* (1854) 16 D. 1057; *Macdonald*, above.

[5] *Freke v Carbery* (1873) L.R. 16 Eq. 461; *Re Gentili* (1875) I.R. 9 Eq. 541; *Duncan v Lawson* (1889) 41 Ch.D. 394; *Pepin v Bruyere* [1902] 1 Ch. 24; *De Fogassieras v Duport* (1881) 11 L.R. Ir. 123.

[6] *Re Berchtold* [1923] 1 Ch. 192; *Macdonald*, 1932 S.C. (HL) 79.

[7] *Marquess of Breadalbane's Trs* (1843) 15 S.J. 389; *Downie v Downie's Trs* (1866) 4 M. 1067; and *Monteith v Monteith's Trs* (1882) 9 R. 982.

[8] *Moss's Trs v Moss* (1916) 2 S.L.T. 31; but see Anton (1st ed.), pp.387–388; *Re Hoyles, Row & Jagg* [1911] 1 Ch. 179; *Macmillan Inc. v Bishopsgate Investment Trust plc (No. 3)* [1996] 1 All E.R. 585, CA.

[9] The chameleon nature of these security rights has caused difficulties (*e.g. Train v Train's Exr* (1899) 2 F. 146; *cf. Moss's Trs v Moss* (1916) 2 S.L.T. 31. See Anton, pp.387–388 and explanation by R.D. Leslie, *Stair Memorial Encyclopaedia*, above, p.318.). Such bonds were immoveable by the conflict rule of Scots law, although moveable in the succession of the creditor in the domestic law of Scotland in terms of the Titles to Land Consolidation (Scotland) Act 1868, s.117, as amended. The standard security, which replaced them in terms of the Conveyancing and Feudal Reform (Scotland) Act 1970 is a heritable security which forms a heritable debt in the estate of the debtor, and is not subject to legal rights in the estate of the creditor.

[10] The interest of a beneficiary in such land in Scotland or England is immoveable until the power of sale is exercised. *Murray v Champernowne* [1901] 2 I.R. 232; *Re Lyne* [1919] 1 Ch. 80; *Re Berchtold* [1923] 1 Ch. 192; *Re Cartwright* [1929] Ch. 90; *Re Cutcliffe's Will Trusts* [1940] Ch. 565; *Re Middleton* [1947] Ch. 583; *Re Stoughton* [1941] I.R. 166.

[11] Leslie, *Encyclopaedia*, p.312.

[12] See *Macmillan Inc. v Bishopsgate Investment Trust plc (No. 3)* [1996] 1 All E.R. 585.

the property by use of the domestic law of the *lex causae* occasionally may be necessary.[13] Thus, characterisation of the nature of property, whether or not straightforward at the outset, conceivably may require to be revisited at a later stage.

Meaning of *lex situs*

The *lex situs* in relation to immoveable property (being the law of **17–03** the place where the property is situated), besides being capable of clear identification, is generally thought to have an unassailable claim to be applied, as of right and common sense. It has the advantage of requiring, in most cases, no further definition or qualification, except to say that to be true to the supremacy of the *lex situs*, the forum may have to be prepared to include in its definition the conflict rules of the *lex situs* and thereby to be open to the concept of *renvoi*.[14]

In disputes concerning moveable property, there is an important temporal element to the ascertainment of the *lex situs*. Although it is the nature of the *situs* of a moveable to change, at any given time the situation of a corporeal moveable normally is fixed. The *lex situs* (or *lex loci rei sitae*) of a corporeal moveable, for the purposes of conflict of laws assessment of title thereto, is the law of the place where the property is situated at the time of the transaction in question,[15] *i.e.* when ownership or other proprietary right is alleged to have passed.

In the case of goods in transit, the *situs* of which is casual, fortuitous or transient,[16] a more flexible approach requires to be taken. Property will be classified as being in transit if it has left the country of despatch without having arrived at its intended destination.

A more difficult concept is the *situs* of incorporeal moveables. Since by nature an intangible right has no physical location, the practice has been to impute to such property an artificial legal *situs*, according to the choice of law rule of the forum.[17] Rules have emerged in terms of which certain classes of intangible rights have been accorded fictional *situs*, for example a money debt is deemed to be situated at the place where the debtor resides and, it is presumed, where the debt may be enforced[18]; registered shares generally are

---

[13] As explained by Leslie, *Encyclopaedia*, p.318.

[14] *Re Duke of Wellington (dec'd)* [1947] Ch. 506, aff'd [1948] Ch. 118; see para.5–13, above.

[15] See, *per* Staughton L.J. in *Macmillan Inc. v Bishopsgate Investment Trust plc (No. 3)* [1996] 1 W.L.R. 387 at 400.

[16] *Standard Chartered Bank Ltd v IRC* [1978] 1 W.L.R. 1160.

[17] *Smelting Company of Australia Ltd v IRC* [1897] 1 Q.B. 175.

[18] *English, Scottish & Australian Bank Ltd v IRC* [1932] A.C. 238; *Banque des Marchands de Moscou (No.3)* [1954] 1 W.L.R. 1108; and *Jabbour v Custodian of Israeli Prop.* [1954] 1 W.L.R. 139.

deemed to be situated in the country in which they can be effectively dealt with as between the shareholder and the company[19]; and rights of action in contract, delict or unjustified enrichment are deemed to be situate in the country in which they can be effectively pursued.

Whilst it would be possible to argue, as with immoveables, so with moveables, that the reference to the law of the *situs* includes a reference to its rules of international private law, a possibility that was kept alive by Slade J. in *Winkworth v Christie, Manson & Woods Ltd*,[20] the decision of Staughton L.J. in *Macmillan Inc v Bishopsgate Investment Trust plc (No. 3)*[21] states that the argument in favour of *renvoi* has been abandoned.

It is important to be clear about the meaning of the *lex situs* in different contexts, in view of the importance which traditional conflict rules place upon this connecting factor in the resolution of title disputes.

Alienability of property

17–04 The *lex situs* decides whether or not property is alienable, and determines also the nature of any document or other thing connected with property, such as title deeds or keys.[22] In *Duc de Frias v Pichon*[23] the saleability of sacred vessels stolen from a monastery in Spain was referred to the law of France, their situation at the time of the sale in question: by French law they could be sold, but not by Spanish law.

The assignability of incorporeal moveable property is a more complex matter, discussed at para.17–22, below.

B. Immoveable Property

Capacity and powers

17–05 Capacity and power generally to transact in relation to land are governed by the *lex situs*.[24]

---

[19] *Brassard v Smith* [1925] A.C. 371; *R v Williams* [1942] A.C. 541. If there should be more than one share register the *situs* will be the country in which the transaction, according to the ordinary course of business, would be registered. See *Macmillan Inc v Bishopsgate Investment Trust plc (No. 3)* [1996] 1 W.L.R. 387. Difficulties arise where the place of the issuer's incorporation differs from the place where the share register is maintained, and from the place where the shareholding can be dealt with effectively as between the investor and the issuer.

[20] [1980] 1 Ch. 496, 514.

[21] [1996] 1 W.L.R. 387, 405.

[22] *Duc de Frias v Pichon* (1886) 13 *Journal du Droit International* 593; *Lushington v Sewell* (1827) 1 Sim 435; *Stewart v Garnett* (1830) 3 Sim 398; *Dominion Bridge Co. v British American Nickel Co. Ltd* (1925) 2 D.L.R. 138.

[23] (1886) 13 *Journal du Droit International* 593.

[24] *Bank of Africa Ltd v Cohen* [1909] 2 Ch. 129 (but this case has been criticised: see Carruthers, above, 4.04); *Ogilvy v Ogilvy's Trs*, 1927 S.L.T. 83; *Black v Black's Trs*, 1950 S.L.T. (Notes) 32; *Bondholders Securities Corp. v Manville* (1933) 4 D.L.R. 699; *Charron v Montreal Trust Co.* (1958) 15 D.L.R. (2d.) 240. See now (rarely in this connection) Rome I, Art.11.

Contracts

A distinction should be drawn between an agreement to transfer an **17–06** interest in land or other immoveable property, or otherwise transact in relation to such property (concerning only personal rights), and the actual transfer/conveyance of a right *in rem* in immoveable property (concerning real rights).[25]

As regards the essential validity of contracts in relation to immoveable property, the rights of the parties are governed by the governing law of the contract which will usually,[26] but not necessarily,[27] be the *lex situs*. This has been reinforced by the Contracts (Applicable Law) Act 1990, Article 4.3 for the (many) cases which the Act regulates.

The formal validity of contracts the subject matter of which is a right in immoveable property or a right to use immoveable property is subject to the mandatory requirements of form of the *lex situs* (Article 9.6).

Real rights of property

The existence and nature of real rights in land are governed by the **17–07** *lex situs*.[28] Any question pertaining to the creation, including alienability, acquisition (including by means of prescription[29]), use, disposal, gift,[30] or transfer of an interest in immoveable property, its effect on the proprietary rights of any person claiming, by any law, to be interested therein, presently is governed by the *lex situs*.

All deeds of title must comply with the *lex situs* both as regards form[31] (including formalities of execution) and essentials.[32]

---

[25] *cf. e.g. Hamilton v Wakefield*, 1993 S.L.T. (Sh. Ct) 30 in which the question which was raised was whether the initial contract to transfer heritage in Scotland, valid by English law, was acceptable to Scots law, though the offer and acceptance were not in writing nor probative, the acceptance having taken the form of the fall of the auctioneer's hammer. Sheriff Jessop held that the Scottish proper law of the contract recognised the obligation as enforceable: later conveyance of the land must be in accordance with Scots solemnities.

[26] *Cood* (1863) 33 Beav. 314; *Re Smith* [1916] 2 Ch. 206; see also *Mackintosh v May* (1895) 22 R. 345.

[27] *British South Africa Co. v De Beers Consolidated Mines Ltd* [1912] A.C. 52.

[28] Dicey and Morris, Rule 115.

[29] *Beckford v Wade* (1805) 17 Ves. Jun. 87 (positive prescription); *Re Peat* (1869) L.R. 7 Eq. 302; *Pitt v Lord Dacre* (1876) 3 Ch. D. 295 (negative).

[30] *Cochrane v Moore* (1890) 25 Q.B.D. 57; *Re Korvine's Trusts* [1921] 1 Ch. 343. Whether or not a gift will be recognised as effective must be a matter for the *lex situs* at the time of alleged donation, which will decide all questions of proprietary rights. Personal rights as between donor and donee may be governed by the proper law of the gift, which need not necessarily be the *lex situs*.

[31] *Adams v Clutterbuck* (1883) 10 Q.B.D. 403. This is reinforced by Rome I, Art.9.6.

[32] *Norton v Florence Land and Public Works Co.* (1887) 7 Ch. D. 332.

Real rights in security

17–08 The grant of a security interest over immoveable property must comply with the *lex situs* both as regards form and essentials. [33]

If, however, a security over land in Scotland is taken by a foreign creditor by way of equitable mortgage, or some other form of security not known to Scots domestic law, while it cannot prevail against a valid security in Scots form, nevertheless it may confer a preference on the holder over unsecured creditors in a Scots bankruptcy or liquidation. If there are no securities valid by the *lex situs*, or if after such securities have been satisfied, there are no prior claims valid by that law, there will then be a competition between purely personal rights,[34] which will be determined by the law common to the litigants, if there is one, or failing that, by the *lex situs*.

C. MOVEABLE PROPERTY

Preliminary

17–09 For the purpose of the resolution of conflict disputes, and comprehension of the reasoning adopted, it is important to note certain distinctions concerning:

  (a) *nature of the property*: different rules apply to the treatment of corporeal moveables (choses in possession/chattels, *e.g.* motor vehicle, book etc) from that of incorporeal moveables (choses in action, *e.g.* a money debt, or the interest under a life insurance policy);

  (b) *nature of the purported transfer*: different rules govern voluntary assignations (*e.g.* by means of gift, sale, exchange or otherwise) from those which govern involuntary assignations (by virtue of diligence or bankruptcy); and

  (c) *basis of the dispute*: contractual or proprietary? Contractual rights involve the rights of the parties to a transfer of moveables *only as between themselves*, and are purely personal. Proprietary rights may, and usually do, involve questions with third parties relating to rights in the object which is the subject of the transfer and are real rather than

---

[33] For a rare illustration of the prevailing of another law over the *lex situs*: *Carse v Coppen*, 1951 S.C. 233 (but see now the Companies (Floating Charges and Receivers) (Scotland) Act 1972). Also *Ballachulish Slate Quarries v Menzies* (1908) 16 S.L.T. 48.

[34] *Re Courtney, ex p. Pollard* (1840) Mont. & Ch. 239; *Coote v Jecks* (1872) L.R. 13 Eq. 597; *Ex p. Holthausen* (1874) L.R. 9 Ch. App. 722; *Re The Anchor Line (Henderson Bros) Ltd* [1937] Ch. 483.

personal, *i.e.* rights enforceable *against all the world* (*contra mundum*). Certain types of transfer have an existence which is independent of contract (*e.g.* donations), whereas other transfers are rooted in contract (*e.g.* conditional sale agreements). Whilst personal rights are governed by the law governing the contract, proprietary questions are referred to the applicable law in property.[35] This chapter is concerned mainly with the existence and ranking of proprietary (real) rights, rather than with contractual (personal) rights.

CORPOREAL MOVEABLES

The laws which might be applied in order to determine conflict **17–10** questions relating to the validity of the creation, acquisition, use and/ or transfer of rights in corporeal moveables are:

(a) *lex domicilii* (of transferor and/or transferee)[36];
(b) *lex loci actus* (the law of the place where the transaction/ transfer took place)[37];
(c) *lex actus* (proper law of the transfer, being the law of deemed closest connection therewith); and
(d) *lex situs*.

In the past, the maxim *mobilia sequuntur personam* (questions of moveable property are governed by the personal law) operated in questions relating to corporeal moveables. It is now recognised that the maxim is principally a rule of succession on death[38] (namely, that succession, testate or intestate, to moveable estate is regulated by the law of the deceased's last domicile).

The development of the law to date shows the increasing influence of the *lex situs*; the *lex situs* generally has final control over title to corporeal moveables and determines all questions involving proprietary rights.[39] Counsel's attempt in 1980 in *Winkworth v Christie, Manson & Woods Ltd*[40] failed to persuade the court of the possible existence of a proper law of property based on law of closest connection, and it seems such a suggestion is yet premature.[41]

---

[35] See *Glencore International AG v Metro Trading International Inc. (No. 2)*[2001] 1 All E.R. (Comm) 103.
[36] See suggestions in *Sill v Worswick* (1791) 1 H.B. 1 665, at 690, and *Re Ewin* (1830) 1 Cr. & J. 151 at 156.
[37] As suggested by Kay L.J. in *Alcock v Smith* [1892] 1 Ch. 238 at 267.
[38] *Provincial Treasurer for Alberta v Kerr* [1933] A.C. 710 at 721 (and *cf. Bank voor Handel en Scheepvaart N.V. v Slatford* [1953] 1 Q.B. 248, *per* Devlin J. at 257).
[39] *Re Anziani* [1930] 1 Ch. 407; *Bank voor Handel en Scheepvaart NV v Slatford* [1953] 1 Q.B. 248; *Jabbour v Custodian of Israeli Absentee Property* [1954] 1 W.L.R. 139.
[40] [1980] 1 All E.R. 1121.
[41] Though see Carruthers' suggested "*lex proprietatis*" in *The Transfer of Property in the Conflict of Laws*, Chs 5, 8 and 9. *Cf. Glencore International AG v Metro Trading International Inc (No. 2)*[2001] 1 All E.R. (Comm) 103.

Account may require to be taken of special rules pertaining to particular types of property, for example aircraft[42] and ships (in respect of which, voluntary transfers and contractual rights generally are governed by the law of the flag, being normally the applicable law, though in cases involving third parties such as creditors, the *lex situs* will apply[43]).

The validity of a transfer

17–11 In this area of conflict of laws, the most difficult, though most common, problem will be that concerning the ranking of competing claims to the same property. It is necessary therefore to consider first the validity of each particular, potentially contending claim, and the transfer upon which it is based. Each transfer of specific moveable assets must be considered as regards:

> (a) alienability of property (see above);
> (b) legal and proprietary capacity of transferor and transferee[44];
> (c) formal validity of transfer (if the transfer is by means of contract, see Chapter 12, paragraph 15–21 above; if otherwise than by means of contract (*e.g.* by gift) the governing law would be, by analogy, the *lex loci actus* or the *lex actus* (proper law of the transfer, being the law of deemed closest connection therewith).

Rules for determining proprietary rights

17–12 As a general rule, proprietary rights are governed by the *lex situs*. In a question between an "original" owner and a subsequent transferee, the latter will be preferred if he has acquired a title valid by the *lex situs* at the time of the transfer in question, or if he has acquired from an intermediate owner who has obtained such a title, that is, one which extinguishes the rights and title of the original owner.[45]

---

[42] UNIDROIT Convention on International Interests in Mobile Equipment and Aircraft Equipment Protocol (2001).

[43] *Schultz v Robinson & Niven* (1861) 24 D. 120; *Simpson v Fogo* (1863) 1 H. & M. 195; *Liverpool Marine Credit Co. v Hunter* (1867) L.R. 4 Eq. 62; *Hooper v Gumm* (1867) L.R. 2 Ch. 282; *Castrique v Imrie* (1870) L.R. 4 HL 414.

[44] The proprietary capacity of the transferor (ie entitlement to deal with the property) is governed by the *lex situs*; the legal capacity of the transferor (*i.e.* age, insanity etc), one might suggest, could be governed by the putative applicable law (being the *lex situs*) or by the transferor's personal law. As to the capacity of the transferee, some assistance can be derived from *Republica of Guatemala v Nunez* [1927] 1 K.B. 669, C.A. Compare generally, legal capacity of a beneficiary to succeed, para.18–10, below.

[45] *Todd v Armour* (1882) 9 R. 901; *Inglis v Usherwood* (1801) 1 East 515; *Cammell v Sewell* (1860) 5 H. & N. 728; *Castrique v Imrie* (1870) L.R. 4 HL 414; *Re Korvine's Trusts* [1921] 1 Ch. 343; *Re Craven's Estate (No.1)* [1937] Ch. 423; *Princess Paley Olga v Weisz* [1929] 1 K.B. 718; *Winkworth v Christie, Manson & Woods Ltd* [1980] 1 All E.R. 1121.

Thus, if a valid transfer has taken place in the country in which an object was situated at that time, any proprietary rights which it confers on the transferee will be recognised in Scotland, whether the transfer took place by way of public or private sale, order of court,[46] Act of Parliament or its equivalent, donation, pledge or otherwise.

Fraud/sale by non-owner

A transferee will *not* obtain good title to the property in question if **17–13** he has been guilty of fraud or if he has acquired from a non-owner (*e.g.* a thief), *unless* that transfer or a subsequent transfer under a new *lex situs* was valid according to the *lex situs*. In the case of stolen property or transfers by non-owners, the general principle is that a transferee takes the property subject to all restrictions on the right of the transferor, *unless* the *lex situs* at the time of the purported transfer, or a subsequent *lex situs*, has had an overriding effect which extinguishes any prior rights.[47]

The case of transfer "tainted" by fraud is singled out only for emphasis, not because the choice of law rule applied differs from any other purported transfer case.

Exceptions to the situs *rule*

Certain exceptions to the *situs* rule were conceded by the defendant **17–14** in the leading case of *Winkworth*; namely:

> "The first 'if goods are in transit and their *situs* is casual or not known, a transfer which is valid and effective by its proper law will (semble) be valid and effective in England'[48] . . . The second exception . . . arises where a purchaser claiming title has not acted *bona fide*.[49] The third exception is the case where the

---

[46] *Castrique v Imrie* (1870) L.R. 4 HL 414.

[47] *Freeman v The East India Co.* (1822) 5 B. & Ald. 617; *Mehta v Sutton* (1913) 108 L.T. 514; *Goetschius v Brightman* (1927) 245 N.Y. 186; *Universal Credit Co. v Marks* (1932) 163 A. 810; *Century Credit Corp. v Richard* (1962) 34 D.L.R. (2d.) 291 (also reported Morris Cases, p.357, and see discussed at Cheshire & North, pp.946–947); *Winkworth v Christie, Manson & Woods Ltd*, above.

[48] The proper law of the transfer, being the law having closest connection to the transfer, seems an appropriate contender. In ascertaining that law, account will be taken of the country of despatch, and the country of intended destination. See Carruthers, above, paras 3.32–3.35. *Cf.* by analogy, para.15–32, above.

[49] However surely an explanatory gloss is needful: any requirement of good faith on the part of the transferee in order that title shall pass should depend entirely on the content of the *lex situs* (see Carruthers, above at 8.38 *et seq*). A more general point is that there is a division among legal systems between those favouring the instant transaction (*en fait des meubles, la possession vaut titre*), and those which find it impossible to disregard a *vitium reale* in the subject matter purported to be transferred (*i.e.* that stolen property has an ineradicable taint: *nemo dat quod non habet*). Clearly the well-informed art thief should seek to dispose of his spoils in the former.

English court declines to recognise the particular law of the relevant *situs* because it considers it contrary to English public policy. The fourth exception arises where a statute in force in the country which is the forum in which the case is heard obliges the court to apply the law of its own country . . . Fifthly . . . special rules might apply to determine the relevant law governing the effect of general assignments of movables on bankruptcy or succession."[50]

Competing claims to the same property

17–15 There may arise a question of competing claims to property, each claimant purporting to derive title from the same (*i.e.* original) "owner". If all such claims, each valid by its own governing law as to substance and form, be governed by the *same* law, a Scots or English forum will apply that law to determine which claim succeeds.[51] However, in competitions between voluntary and involuntary transfers, or between transfers having *different* governing laws, competing proprietary claims are governed by the *lex situs*.

Where contract meets property[52]

17–16 Where there is a collision between a legal system's rules, conflict and/or domestic, of contract and property, the property rules have prevailed, at least if the dispute is one of proprietary right.

The terms of a contract, valid by the governing law of the contract, may contravene the law of some other interested legal system. In a purely contractual sphere, this is regulated by the "mandatory rules" provisions of Rome I, and by its preservation of the forum's public policy. However choice of law rules of property typically may

---

[50] *Winkworth v Christie, Manson & Woods Ltd*, above, at 501. See also *Glencore International AG v Metro Trading International Inc (No. 2)* [2001] 1 All ER (Comm) 103.

[51] *North Western Bank Ltd v Poynter Son & Macdonald* (1894) 22 R. (H.L.) 1: [1895] A.C. 56. In the time-honoured (but later, by the speaker, amended) words of Lord Watson, at 75: "[w]hen a moveable fund, situated in Scotland admittedly belongs to one or other of two domiciled Englishmen, the question to which of them it belongs is *prima facie* one of English law." The gloss is that the reference to "two must be taken to mean "two men claiming under the same English law". *City Bank v Barrow* (1880) 5 A.C. 64; *Robertson & Baxter v Inglis* (1898) 25 R. (HL) 70; *Connal & Co. v Loder* (1868) 6 M. 1095; *Dinwoodie's Exr v Carruthers' Exr* (1895) 23 R. 234.

[52] See para.15–55. Background writing: see K. Reid and G. Gretton, "Retention of Title in Romalpa Clauses", 1983 S.L.T. (News) 77; "Retention of Title: Lord Watson's Legacy", 1983 S.L.T. (News) 105; Stewart, "Romalpa Clauses: Choosing the Law", 1985 S.L.T. (News) 149; P. Sellar, "Romalpa and Receivables—Choosing the Law", 1985 S.L.T. (News) 313; H. Patrick "Romalpa: the International Dimension", 1986 S.L.T. (News) 265 and 277; Clark, "All-Sums Retention of Title", 1991 S.L.T. 155; CGJ Morse, "Retention of Title in English Private International Law" [1993] J.B.L. 168; and G. McCormack, *Reservation of Title* (2nd ed., 1996).

impinge, and there have been cases in Scotland[53] concerning the effect of advanced or elaborate forms of retention/reservation of title ("Romalpa") clauses,[54] which, while acceptable, say, by the governing law of the contract of which they form part, are found to contravene the principles of the Scottish *lex situs*, where was situated, at the time of conclusion of the contract or thereafter, the subject matter of the contract.

Much interest in this area was shown in Scotland in the 1980s and 1990s. Although it seemed that Scotland was being true to its own law, both domestic (that generally there can be no security without possession), and conflict (that the validity of security rights are judged by the *lex situs*), there was a problem of its being out of step in international commercial terms. A solution, by means of change in forms of security, was considered, originally by the Halliday Committee for Scotland in 1986,[55] and the Diamond Committee[56] for England (though the growth of Romalpa clauses did not occasion an equivalent flurry of conflict cases on the point in that jurisdiction). Another solution might have been to redefine the *lex situs* in these cases to be, say, the place of despatch in terms of the contract,[57] or thirdly, to place the problem in a wider context of distribution in bankruptcy (for such was often the situation which brought the case to court). However, in *Armour v Thyssen Edelstahlwerke A.G.*[58] the House of Lords ruled that, in the courts below, the nature of the retention of title clause in the contract in question had been misconstrued; that it could not be offensive to Scots law as a security right without possession, because on a true construction only possession and not property was transferred before payment. There the matter rests at present (though the Department of Trade and Industry produced in 1994 a consultation paper entitled "Security over Moveable Property in Scotland"[59]).

---

[53] *Hammer and Sohne v HWT Realisations Ltd*, 1985 S.L.T. (Sh.Ct) 21; *Zahnrad Fabrik Passau GmbH v Terex Ltd*, 1986 S.L.T. 84; *Armour v Thyssen Edelstahlwerke AG*, 1986 S.L.T. 452, and in HL, 1990 S.L.T. 891; *Emerald Stainless Steel Ltd v Southside Distribution Ltd*, 1983 S.L.T. 162; *Deutz Engines Ltd v Terex Ltd*, 1984 S.L.T. 273; *Pfeiffer Weinkellerei-Weinenkauf Guibti v Arbuthnot Factors Ltd* [1988] 1 W.L.R. 150.

[54] So-called because of the name of the case in which such a clause was first noted: *Aluminium Industrie Vaasen B. v Romalpa Aluminium Ltd* [1976] 1 W.L.R. 676 (conflict issues not discussed).

[55] Scot. Law Com. Report by Working Party on *Security Over Moveable Property*, chaired by Professor J.M. Halliday, March 1986.

[56] *A Review of Security Interests in Property* by Professor A. Diamond (1989)

[57] Stewart, 1985 S.L.T. (News) 149.

[58] 1990 S.L.T. 891.

[59] Department of Trade and Industry, *Security Over Moveable Property in Scotland: A Consultation Paper* (1994). See commentary by Murray, "Security over Moveable Property", 1995 S.L.T. (News) 31. However, one of the items in the seventh Programme of the Scotish Law Commission for the period 2005–2009 is "Assignation of and Security over Intangible Assets".

INCORPOREAL MOVEABLES

17-17 This is an area where further complexities are present,[60] concerning the transfer of such rights as: debts, bank accounts, insurance policies, decrees, claims for damages, interests in trust estates, shares, and causes of action.[61] Problems of a more modern nature include the treatment of securities held with an intermediary.

Situs

17-18 As explained above, such rights have their *situs* at the place where the right is enforceable.[62]

Choice of Law

17-19 The possible laws which might govern assignations of incorporeal rights, and questions arising therefrom, are as follows:

(a) *lex domicilii* of the creditor or the debtor;
(b) *lex loci actus* (the law of the place where the transaction takes place: the law of the paper transfer);
(c) *lex actus* (the proper law of the transfer or assignation, being the law of deemed closest connection therewith);
(d) *lex situs* of the incorporeal right (normally the residence of the debtor); or
(e) proper law of the right.

One difficulty in the early cases[63] is that the reason for application of a particular *lex causae* by the *lex fori* is not clear (eg where the *lex*

---

[60] See *Carse v Coppen*, 1951 S.L.T. 145, *per* Lord President Cooper at 148; Morris, "The Transfer of Chattels in the Conflict of Laws" (1945) 22 B.Y.B.I.L. 232.

[61] *Clare & Co. v Dresdner Bank* [1915] 2 K.B. 576; *Joachimson v Swiss Bank Corporation* [1921] 3 K.B. 110; *Swiss Bank Corporation v Boechmische Industrial Bank* [1923] 1 K.B. 673; *New York Life Insurance Co. v Public Tr.* [1924] 2 Ch. 101; *Richardson v Richardson* [1927] P. 228; *Sutherland v Administrator of German Property* (1934) 50 T.L.R. 107; *Arab Bank Ltd v Barclays Bank* [1954] A.C. 495; *Re Helbert Wagg* [1956] Ch. 323; *Re Banque des Marchands de Moscou* [1954] 1 W.L.R. 1108 at 1115; *Reuter v Mulhens* [1954] Ch. 50; *Westminster Bank Trustee Co. (Channel Islands) Ltd v National Bank of Greece* [1971] 2 W.L.R. 105; *Colombiana de Seguros v Pacific Steam Navigation Co.* [1965] 1 Q.B. 101; *Trendtex Trading Corporation v Credit Suisse* [1982] A.C. 679; *Macmillan Inc. v Bishopsgate Investment Trust plc (No. 3)* [1996] 1 All E.R. 585; and *Raiffeisen Zentralbank Osterreich AG v Five Star General Trading LLC and Others* [2000] 2 Ll Rep. 684; [2001] 1 Ll Rep. 597.

[62] See para.17-03, above; *e.g. Jabbour v Custodian of Israeli Prop.* [1954] 1 W.L.R. 139; *Kwok Chi Leung Karl v Commissioner of Estate Duty* [1988] 1 W.L.R. 1035, PC; *Power Curber International Ltd v National Bank of Kuwait SAK* [1981] 3 All E.R. 607.

[63] See more recently *Trendtex Trading Corp. v Credit Suisse* [1982] A.C. 679 *Macmillan Inc. v Bishopsgate Investment Trust plc (No. 3)* [1996] 1 W.L.R. 387; and *Raiffeisen Zentralbank Osterreich AG v Five Star General Trading LLC and Others* [2000] 2 Ll Rep. 684; [2001] 1 Ll Rep. 597.

domicilii, the *lex loci actus* and the *lex situs* coincide). Thus, in the early leading case of *Republica de Guatemala v Nunez*,[64] concerning both the formal validity of an assignation and the legal capacity of the assignee to take (the flaw alleged being infancy), both issues were referred to the law of Guatemala which, on a revisionist view, has been said to be the (putative) proper law of the assignation.[65]

Effect of Contracts (Applicable Law) Act 1990

Although the principal concern of this Chapter is the proprietary, **17–20** rather than contractual, aspects of transfers, in relation to the assignation of incorporeal moveables of a contractual nature (*e.g.* a contractual debt[66]), it is difficult to sever the proprietary aspect from the contractual aspect, since the property right is a right arising under contract. Contractual assignations[67] of incorporeal moveable rights (whether of contractual or non-contractual nature) are governed by Article 12 of the Contracts (Applicable Law) Act 1990.[67a]

Article 12 Voluntary assignment

1. The mutual obligations of assignor and assignee under a **17–21** voluntary assignment of a right against another person ("the debtor") shall be governed by the law which under this Convention applies to the contract between the assignor and assignee.

2. The law governing the right to which the assignment relates shall determine its assignability, the relationship between the assignee and the debtor, the conditions under which the assignment can be invoked against the debtor and any question whether the debtor's obligations have been discharged.

The validity of a contractual assignation falling outside the scope of Rome I is governed by the common law rules of assignation. Likewise, non-contractual assignations, even of a contractual right such as a money debt are not governed by Rome I, but fall to be governed by the common law rules of assignation. It is important, therefore, to distinguish between contractual and non-contractual assignations of incorporeal moveable rights.[68]

Assignability

As regards contractual assignations, Article 12.2 of Rome I applies **17–22** to the effect that assignability is governed by the applicable law of the right to which the assignation relates.

---

[64] [1927] 1 K.B. 669.

[65] An earlier and similar authority is *Lee v Abdy* (1886) 17 Q.B.D. 309 where it was clear that the putative proper law was the law of Cape Colony, South Africa.

[66] Rights which are capable of being assigned can be contractual, or non-contractual, *e.g.* the benefit arising under a right of copyright, or a right to sue (*Trendtex Trading Corp v Credit Suisse*, above.

[67] An assignation of property can be contractual, but might also be effected in a non-contractual manner, *e.g.* by gift or bequest.

[67a] *Waldwiese Shiftung and Another v Lewis* [2004] EWHC 2589.

[68] See Carruthers, above, Ch.6, paras 6.12 *et seq.*

As regards non-contractual assignations (*e.g.* by means of gift), assignability is governed by the proper law of the right[69] (*i.e.* to the same result as Article 12.2). The common law rule is clearly seen in the case of *Pender*,[70] in which the assignability of an insurance policy, taken out with reference to the English Married Women's Property Act 1882, was categorised by the Scots court as an assignation of a Scottish right, as to which assignability and the separate issue of capacity to assign were referred to Scots law *qua*, respectively, the law of closest connection and the domicile of the transferor. By Scots law the married woman granter was under a personal incapacity to assign the benefits of such a policy. Hence, her purported assignation to a Bank was ineffective.

These facts illustrate that within the one broad heading of assignability, the issue of capacity to assign (regulated by the personal law of the purported transferor) may take precedence. "In other words, the rule as to assignability is subordinate to the rule governing capacity to assign; personal (in)capacity to assign must be regarded as an essential component of assignability."[71] In *Pender*, the two *leges causae* (law of closest connection and the domicile of the transferor) coincided in Scotland, but clearly this might not always be the case, even if now a less strict approach is taken to the question of the law governing capacity to assign.

Capacity to grant or to accept an assignation

17–23 In the past, the *lex loci actus* or the law of the domicile was applied, but it is submitted that capacity to make or to accept an assignation of incorporeal moveable property should be governed by the proper law of the transfer or by the proper law of the right,[72] perhaps according to whichever confers capacity earlier. In the case of contractual assignations, the putative governing law of the contract now is thought to apply, and account also must be taken of Rome I, Article 11,[73] in a qualifying case.

Formal validity

17–24 At common law, there were three possibly applicable laws, to the effect that an assignation, contractual or non-contractual, would be formally valid if it complied with any one of the *lex loci actus*, the

---

[69] *Grant's Trs v Ritchie's Exr* (1886) 13 R. 646; *Pender v Commercial Bank of Scotland Ltd*, 1940 S.L.T. 306; *Campbell Connelly & Co. Ltd v Noble* [1963] 1 W.L.R. 252; *Libertas-Kommerz GmbH v Johnson*, 1977 S.C. 191. (As to Scots domestic law on assignability of floating charges, see Lucas, "The Assignation of Floating Charges", 1996 S.L.T. (News) 203.)

[70] 1940 S.L.T. 306.

[71] Carruthers, above, para.6.08.

[72] *Lee v Abdy*; *Republica de Guatemala v Nunez*, both above.

[73] See Ch.15.

proper law of the assignation, or the proper law of the right assigned.[74]

In cases of contractual assignations regulated by the Contracts (Applicable Law) Act 1990, Article 9 governs formal validity.[75]

Triangular relationship

Typically, cases involving incorporeal moveable rights concern a **17–25** triangular scenario, where a creditor in an original claim against a debtor assigns his right to pursue that claim to a third party assignee. The contract between the original parties (debtor and creditor) has a governing law, ascertained by reference to Article 3 or 4 (so long as the contract falls within the scope of Rome I; if not, the relationship is governed by the proper law of the right, being the law where the right may be enforced). The assignation (from creditor to assignee) has its own law (Article 12.1). The third side of the triangle is the relationship between assignee and debtor. Currently, Article 12.2 refers both the assignability of the right assigned, and the relationship between the assignee and the debtor, to the law governing the right.

It is important in any conflict case to ascertain *which* parties the dispute concerns.

Relationship between the assignor and the assignee

In the case of contractual assignations, the relationship between the **17–26** assignor and assignee falls, as a contractual matter, within Rome I, Article 12.1, in terms of which "[t]he mutual obligations of assignor and assignee under a voluntary assignment of a right against another person ('the debtor') shall be governed by the law which under this Convention applies to the contract between the assignor and assignee."

This means that the applicable law of the assignation governs, determined in accordance with the rules and presumptions contained in Rome I (Articles 3 and 4).

In the case of non-contractual assignations, matters of essential validity are governed at common law by the proper law of the assignation,[76] but an assignation will be essentially valid also if it complies with the proper law of the right transferred.[77]

Relationship between the assignee and the debtor

As between assignee and debtor (*i.e.* under the right transferred): **17–27**

---

[74] *Republica de Guatamala v Nunez*, above; *Stirling's Trs v The Legal & General Assurance Society*, 1957 S.L.T. 73.

[75] See earlier, *Scottish Provident Institution v Cohen* (1888) 16 R. 112; and *Bankhaus H. Aufhauser v Scotboard Ltd*, 1973 S.L.T. (Notes) 87.

[76] *Scottish Provident Institution v Cohen* (1888) 16 R. 112; *Libertas-Kommerz GmbH v Johnson*, 1977 S.C. 191.

[77] *Re Anziani* [1930] 1 Ch. 407.

"[I]t is easy to understand why the intrinsic validity of the assignment should be governed by the proper law of the assignation; but, when issues of validity (other perhaps than mere formal validity) arise between the assignee and the other party to the original contract, the argument in support of the application of the proper law of the assignation, in preference to the proper law both of the original contract and of the debt claimed, is in my opinion, inconsistent with both logic and equity."[78]

Assuming that the right in question is assignable (this being the first matter of essential validity), Rome I, Article 12.2 states, in relation to contractual assignations, that the law governing the right to which the assignment relates (*i.e.* the proper law of the right) governs the relationship between the assignee and the debtor, the conditions under which the assignment can be invoked against the debtor and any question whether the debtor's obligations have been discharged.

Relationship between competing assignees

17–28 Questions involving competing proprietary rights must be considered as regards:

    (a) the debtor's liability under the right in question;
    (b) the validity of each assignation, as to form and essentials; and
    (c) the ranking of competing claims *inter se.*

There is a gap in the current provision, to which the Rome I Green Paper[79] turns its attention, namely, the competing rights of third parties (eg two or more competing assignees, by virtue of voluntary and/or involuntary assignation(s)). Questions arise of ranking of competing claims to the original right. Currently, these points must be dealt with by each Member State according to its own conflict rules. In Scotland, the *lex situs* regulates the proprietary rights of the parties and governs in particular (a) the debtor's liability to pay; and (b) competitions between assignations valid by their own proper laws; and between voluntary and involuntary assignations and diligences. There are, however, certain qualifications to this rule: in a competition between two or more assignations having the same proper law and derived from the same debtor, or between a

---

[78] *per* Lord Hunter in *Bankhaus H. Aufhauser v Scotboard Ltd*, 1973 S.L.T. (Notes) 87 at 89.
[79] "Conversion of the Rome Convention of 1980 on the Law Applicable to Contractual Obligations into a Community Instrument and its Modernisation" COM (2002) 654.

voluntary and an involuntary assignation both governed by the same proper law, the parties' rights are governed and regulated by that law.[80] This rule applies only to the determination of the rights of creditors *inter se* when they hold assignations with the *same proper law*.[81] However, the rights of creditors *inter se* holding under assignations with *different proper laws* are governed by the *lex situs*.[82] Any question of priority between the holders of voluntary and involuntary transfers,[83] such as arising as a result of diligence, also are governed by the *lex situs*. The EU Commission asks whether a future instrument should specify the law applicable in such a case, and sets forward for consideration possible Community solutions.

In practice, questions are solved as follows:

(1) The debtor's liability will be determined by the *lex situs* of the right which is the subject of the subsequent assignation(s).

(2) Assuming the right in question is enforceable against the debtor, the following process is applied:

(a) the validity of each assignation, contractual or non-contractual, is determined by its governing law[84];

(b) if there is more than one valid assignation, and each competing assignation has the same proper law, that law will regulate the rights of assignees *inter se*;

(c) if there is more than one valid assignation, and the competing assignations have different proper laws, or if there is a competition between voluntary and involuntary transfers, such as diligence, priority will be regulated by the *lex situs*.

BILLS OF EXCHANGE AND NEGOTIABLE INSTRUMENTS[85]

Bills of Exchange

Conflict rules in relation to bills of exchange were laid down early, **17–29** by statute, in terms of the Bills of Exchange Act 1882.[86] There are excluded (Article 1.2.c) from Rome I: "Obligations arising under

---

[80] cf. *North Western Bank v Poynter Son & Macdonald* (1894) 22 R. (HL) 1, *per* Lord Watson at 12.

[81] *Scottish Provident Institution v Robinson* (1892) 29 S.L.R. 733; *Dinwoodie's Exr v Carruthers' Exr* (1895) 23 R. 234; *Forbes v Official Receiver in Bankruptcy*, 1924 S.L.T. 522; *Republica de Guatemala v Nunez*, above.

[82] *Le Feuvre v Sullivan* (1855) 10 Moore P.C.389; *Kelly v Selwyn* [1905] 2 Ch. 117.

[83] *Strachan v McDougle* (1835) 13 S. 954; *Donaldson v Ord* (1855) 17 D. 1053; *Re Maudslay* [1900] 1 Ch. 602; *Re Queensland Mercantile and Agency Co.* [1892] 1 Ch. 219; *Jabbour v Custodian of Israeli Property* [1954] 1 W.L.R. 139.

[84] See *e.g. Scottish Provident Institution v Cohen* (1888) 16 R. 112.

[85] For modern specialised treatment, see Proctor, *International Payment Obligations— A Legal Perspective*, Ch.27, Negotiable Instruments and Ch.28 (letters of credit).

[86] The meaning of bills of exchange is defined in ss.3 and 4.

bills of exchange, cheques and promissory notes and other negotiable instruments to the extent that the obligations under such other negotiable instruments arise out of their negotiable character." It seems that the qualifying phrase "to the extent that . . . negotiable character" applies only to "other negotiable instruments": bills of exchange, cheques and promissory notes are excluded from Rome I without reservation.[87] A commercial letter of credit is not a negotiable instrument and is not subject to exclusion as above.[88]

Conflict rules concerning bills of exchange are contained in the 1882 Act, section 72[89] the general effect of which as regards foreign bills is to make the validity of each of the interdependent contracts depend upon its *own law* and not on the law of the bill. This "several laws" approach attracts widespread international agreement, which as Dicey and Morris say[90] cannot be said of many areas of conflict rules. Equally clearly, the nature and purpose of bills are likely to lead to conflict situations. Section 72 applies well-established conflict rules to bills as follows:

(1) the formal validity of a bill and of each indorsement is governed by the law of the place where it is made[91] but it will be sufficient for enforcement of payment in this country that the law of the UK is complied with. Lack of a stamp in accordance with the law of the place of issue does not make a bill invalid here;

---

[87] Giuliano and Lagarde, p.11.

[88] Conflict cases on letters of credit include the following: *Offshore International SA v Banco Central SA* [1976] 3 All E.R. 749 (E.B. Crawford, "Oil on Troubled Waters: proper law of letter of credit" (1977) 22 J.L.S.434); *Power Curber International Ltd v National Bank of Kuwait SAK* [1981] 3 All E.R. 607; *United City Merchants (Investments) Ltd v Royal Bank of Canada* [1983] 1 A.C. 168, HL; *Bank of Baroda v Vysya Bank* [1994] 2 Ll Rep. 87 (with reference to Art.4.2 of Rome Convention, characteristic performance was held to be that of the confirming bank). See also *P.T. Pan Indonesia Bank Ltd v Marconi Communications* [2005] 2 All E.R. (Comm) 325.

[89] Cases after the Act: *Re Marseilles Extension Railway and Land Co.* (1885) 30 Ch. D.598; *Re Commercial Bank of South Australia* (1887) 36 Ch.D. 522; *Bank of Montreal v Exhibit Trading Co. Ltd* (1906) 22 T.L.R. 722; *Guaranty Trust Co. of New York v Hannay* [1918] 1 K.B. 43, 2 K.B. 623; *Alcock v Smith* [1892] 1 Ch. 238; *Embiricos v Anglo Austrian Bank* [1904] 2 K.B. 870; [1905] 1 K.B. 677; *Koechlin et Cie v Kestenbaum Bros* [1927] 1 K.B. 889; *Moulis v Owen* [1907] 1 K.B. 746; *Re Francke and Rasch* [1918] 1 Ch. 470; *Koch v Dicks* [1933] 1 K.B. 307; *Bank Polski v Mulder* [1941] 2 K.B. 266; [1942] 1 K.B. 497; *Cornelius v Banque Franco-Serbe* [1941] 2 All E.R. 728; [1942] 1 K.B. 29; *Syndic in Bankruptcy of Khoury v Khayat* [1943] A.C. 507.

[90] Para.33–327.

[91] A contract is made (s.21) when the instrument is delivered in order to give effect to the contract: delivery means transfer of possession, actual or constructive (Dicey and Morris, 33-335). The Act has put the *lex loci contractus* in a dominant position in matters of form and interpretation and Dicey and Morris recommend that "gaps" in the Act be filled by ascribing to this law regulation of capacity and everything pertaining to the formation of the contract.

(2) essential validity is governed by the law of the place where the bill and indorsements are made. The word used in the Act is "interpretation" of the drawing, indorsement, acceptance or acceptance *supra* protest of a bill[92] but it may be thought[93] that this term relates not merely to construction but to all questions of essential validity[94];

(3) procedure as to protest on dishonour, etc., is governed by the law of the place where the *act is done*[95];

(4) the due date is determined by the law of the place where the bill is payable.[96]

The 1882 Act does not provide conflict rules to govern all conflict questions which might arise in relation to a bill, and leaves aside, in particular, capacity and the proprietary as opposed to the contractual aspects.[97] In their residual contractual aspect, they will be governed by common law contractual rules, and not by Rome I.

Negotiable Instruments

The conflict rules on this subject are based on the conflict rules **17–30** relating both to the law of contract and the law of property. A negotiable instrument is an order involving a contract to pay money to a person to be named or to his order to be signified by endorsation of the document. No intimation to debtor is required, and the debtor is not affected by defects in the title of a prior holder. A document recognised as being a negotiable instrument has certain privileges which do not apply to documents not recognised as such, in that a holder acquiring a document not having this characteristic does not necessarily acquire a good title even if he acquires it in good faith and for value.

The general view is that the question whether or not a particular document is to be regarded as a negotiable instrument is to be determined by the law of the place where its negotiation takes place, which will almost invariably be the *lex fori*.[98] It is suggested that for a

---

[92] Provided that where an inland bill is indorsed in a foreign country the indorsement as regards the payer shall be interpreted according to the law of the United Kingdom (s.72(2)).

[93] Though see Anton with Beaumont, p.390; and the views of Proctor to the effect that contractual questions which cannot be brought within the terms of the Act must be referred to the common law conflict rules of contract.

[94] *Alcock v Smith* [1892] 1 Ch. 238; *Embiricos v Anglo Austrian Bank* [1904] 2 K.B. 870; *Koechlin et Cie v Kestenbaum Bros* [1927] 1 K.B. 889.

[95] s.72(3).

[96] s.72(5).

[97] Dicey and Morris 33-329; Proctor, p.464.

[98] Dicey and Morris, para.33-318 consider that negotiability will be determined by the place of negotiation which will be the place of situation of instrument at time of delivery; *cf.* Anton (1st ed.), p.419 and (2nd ed.), pp.387–388. Giuliano and Lagarde at p.11 favour the application of the conflict rules of the forum—*obiter*, because characterisation as negotiable is not an issue governed by the Rome Convention.

document to be regarded as a negotiable instrument, the true test is that it must be recognised as such by the *lex fori* but possibly it should also have that quality according to the law under which it was created.[99]

Shares and other securities[1]

17–31 Questions of choice of law may arise in relation to (a) the effect of transfers as regards the issuing company; (b) the effect of transfers as between the parties themselves (*i.e.* issuer and investor); and (c) the situation of shares for the purposes of inheritance tax, stamp duties, income tax and other similar matters.

Choice of law rules in relation to shares and other securities traditionally were based upon the assumption of a direct relationship between the issuer and the investor, evidenced, in the case of registered securities, by registration of the investor's name in the books of the issuer, and in the case of bearer securities, by physical possession by the investor of a certificate. The following rules apply to directly-held securities.[2]

Normally the *situs* of shares of a company is the place where the company is registered and the share register is kept.[3]

In order to divest the transferor and give the transferee a good title which will be effective as a real right against third parties, it is essential to comply with the *lex situs*.

The rights of the parties merely as between themselves (that is contractual rights) are regulated by the law of the place where the transfer takes place which is usually the proper law of the transfer and may be quite different from the *lex situs* of the shares.

Technological developments, and market demands, however, have led to the development of a more efficient holding pattern namely, one which permits holding via an intermediary, and which allows for the transfer of interests by means of electronic book-entry to securities accounts. The traditional, materialized system in many instances has been replaced by a dematerialized (electronic), intermediated holding system.

---

[99] *Goodwin v Robarts* [1876] 1 A.C. 476; *Picker v London and County Banking Co.* (1887) 18 Q.B.D. 515; *London Joint Stock Bank v Simmons* [1892] A.C. 201.

[1] See Carruthers, above, Ch.7.

[2] *Williams v Colonial Bank* (1888) 38 Ch.D. 388 (right to hold share certificates distinguished from substantive rights in shares); *Colonial Bank v Cady and Williams* [1890] 15 A.C. 267; *Brassard v Smith* [1925] A.C. 371; *Baelz v Public Tr.* [1926] Ch. 863; *London and South American Inv. Trust v British Tobacco Co.* [1927] 1 Ch. 107; *Erie Beach Co. Ltd v A.G. for Ontario* [1930] A.C. 161; *R. v Williams* [1942] A.C. 541; *Re Middleton* [1947] Ch. 583; *Fry* [1946] Ch. 312; *Macmillan Inc. v Bishopsgate Investment Trust plc (No. 3)* [1996] 1 W.L.R. 387. See also *International Credit and Investment Co. (Overseas) Ltd v Adham* [1994] 1 B.C.L.C. 66. But consider Stevens, "The Law Applicable to Priority in Shares" (1996) 112 L.Q.R. 198.

[3] Recently confirmed in *Macmillan Inc. v Bishopsgate Investment Trust plc (No. 3)* [1996] 1 W.L.R. 387.

The choice of law rule traditionally applied to govern the proprietary aspects of a transfer of shares or other securities (namely, the law of the *situs* of those shares or other right) is not easily applied to the transfer of "intermediated securities". To meet the demands of the global financial market for certainty and predictability of securities transactions, there was agreed in 2002 a Hague Convention on the Law Applicable to Certain Rights in respect of Securities Held with an Intermediary. The purpose of the Convention is to harmonise rules of choice of law concerning rights in respect of intermediated securities. The Convention applies in all cases where securities are held with an intermediary (ie where securities are credited to a securities account), but it has no application to directly held securities, which continue to be governed by pre-existing, national choice of law rules. The primary rule of choice of law is contained in Article 4 of the Convention, and gives effect to an express agreement on governing law between an account holder and its immediate intermediary, subject however to the requirement that the law chosen will apply only if the relevant intermediary has, at the time of the agreement, a qualifying office in the state the law of which has been chosen. If the applicable law is not determined under Article 4, Article 5 contains a series of "fall-back" rules. Article 6 deliberately severs any link with traditional *situs* thinking, insofar as it is expressly stated that in determining the applicable law under the Convention no account should be taken, *inter alia*, of the place where the issuer is incorporated, the place where securities certificates are located, or the place where a securities register is located or maintained.

Intellectual property rights

Though this heading encompasses a number of different types of **17–32** right, including copyright, patents, and trademarks, each appears to be treated in broadly the same way, in that the *situs* is taken to be the country in which they may be effectively transferred, *i.e.* the legal system of their creation.[4] Intellectual property rights have a definite connection with a particular place,[5] and if created in Britain are effective only in Britain unless they receive effect in foreign countries under the conflict rules there applicable. Provision is made in Scotland for the recognition of rights acquired under foreign patents.[6]

---

[4] See J.J. Fawcett & P. Torremans, *Intellectual Property and Private International Law*, p.490.
[5] *Campbell Connolly & Co. Ltd v Noble* [1963] 1 W.L.R. 252.
[6] And see *Pearce v Ove Arup Partnership Ltd* [1997] 3 All E.R. 31; English court bound to accept jurisdiction in respect of alleged breach of a foreign statutory intellectual property right, the Brussels Convention having overridden the *Moçam-*

The goodwill of a business is deemed to be situated in the legal system of the situation of the asset to which the goodwill is attached.[7]

Governmental seizure of property

17–33 The territoriality principle applies, but this in turn may have private law repercussions outside the territory. The topic is treated at paras 3–04/05, above.

II. UNIVERSAL TRANSFERS OF PROPERTY: INSOLVENCY[8]

THEORIES

17–34 In the development of this subject, favour has been shown to one or other of two main theories or approaches, which will be outlined before attention is turned to recent international legislative development.

Unity of bankruptcy

17–35 According to this theory, a bankruptcy should be one and indivisible and, when a person is sequestrated or grants a trust deed for his creditors, the process should attach and convey to the trustee in bankruptcy all property, wherever situated, belonging to the bankrupt with the result that only one bankruptcy should be permissible. A separate bankruptcy in each country should not be permissible.

At common law, the Scots courts favoured the unity theory[9] and therefore would not grant a sequestration if the bankrupt already had been sequestrated in another country, unless perhaps for some reason the foreign bankruptcy was no longer effective or was of strictly limited effect.

Separate bankruptcies

17–36 This theory is the opposite of the unity theory. By it the bankrupt's assets should be distributed separately in each jurisdiction for the benefit of creditors in that jurisdiction; hence it should be permiss-

---

bique rule, and the defendant being "domiciled" in the UK. Contrast *Tyburn Productions Ltd v Conan Doyle* [1990] 3 W.L.R. 167. See also *Coin Controls Ltd v Suzo International (UK) Ltd* [1997] 3 All E.R. 45. But see criticism of both cases by Collier, *All E.R. Annual Review 1997*, pp.78–80.

[7] *IRC v Muller & Co Margarines Ltd* [1901] AC 217, *per* Lord Macnaghten at 224. Contrast dissenting judgment of LC Halsbury at 240. *Cf. R.J. Reuter Co Ltd v Mulhens*, 1954 Ch. 50, 95–96.

[8] For a full treatment of this subject see I.F. Fletcher, *Insolvency in Private International Law* (2nd ed, 2005, OUP).

[9] See *Goetze v Aders & Co.* (1874) 2 R. 100; *Bank of Scotland v Youde* (1908) 15 S.L.T. 847. See also *Hume's Trs v Hume's Trs*, 1926 S.L.T. 214 (recognition in Scotland of South African order of sequestration of moveable funds wherever situated).

ible to have separate bankruptcies.[10] This is the "territoriality" approach, favoured at common law in England.[11] The English courts declined to allow the existence of concurrent proceedings, or the factor of priority of date to be decisive in the question whether there should be a stay of English bankruptcy proceedings.[12]

Universality of bankruptcy

Under this principle, a bankruptcy should receive extra-territorial **17–37** effect, and therefore, unless it clearly confers a very territorially limited title on the trustee, it should be regarded as passing to the trustee all estate, moveable and immoveable, in the country where it was granted and all moveable estate abroad. Immoveable estate abroad is not included at common law. At common law, both the Scots and English[13] systems accepted this theory, which is the logical result of the unity theory. "Unity" and "universality" therefore mean, as it has been well put, "one set of proceedings (unity) effective in every jurisdiction (universality)".[14]

EU DEVELOPMENTS: INSOLVENCY REGULATION[15]

Council Regulation 44/2001

Bankruptcy and similar proceedings in relation to insolvent com- **17–38** panies do not fall within the scope of Council Regulation (EC) 44/2001.[16] However, a company winding up can occur when a company is solvent, as well as when insolvent, and in the former case, Regulation 44/2001 will apply, directing the matter by way of the exclusive jurisdiction provision of Article 22.2 to the one court which is defined for constitutional purposes as the "seat" of the company.[17] Company winding-up is excluded from the intra-U.K. allocation effected by the Civil Jurisdiction and Judgments Acts 1982

---

[10] *Re Artola Hermanos* (1890) 24 Q.B.D. 640; see recently *Re Thulin* [1995] 1 W.L.R. 165 (bankruptcy proceedings in England and Sweden).

[11] *Re Artola Hermanos* above; *Felixstowe Dock & Railway Co. v US Lines Inc.* [1988] 2 All E.R. 77; *Re Thulin,* above. Smart, *"Forum Non Conveniens in* Bankruptcy Proceedings" [1989] J.B.L. 126.

[12] Cheshire & North (12th ed.), p.907.

[13] *i.e.* in England the status and claims of a foreign trustee would be accepted provided that there were no English proceedings.

[14] D.McKenzie-Skene, "The EC Convention on Insolvency Proceedings" (1995) 4 *European Review of Private Law,* 182.

[15] See Fletcher, above, pp.339 *et seq.*

[16] Art.1.2.b. This reiterates the position under the 1968 Brussels Convention. See *Gourdain v Nadler* [1979] E.C.R. 733 [4]. Consider *Thoars' J.F. v Ramlort Ltd,* 1998 G.W.D. 20–1040; and successful reclaiming motion, 1998 G.W.D. 29–1504; see note by E.B. Crawford, 1999 J.R. 203.

[17] CJJA, s.43, and Council Regulation 44/2001, Art.60.

and 1991, Schedule 4,[18] and must be governed by the rules contained in the Insolvency Act 1986.

Council Regulation 1346/2000

17–39 The Council of Europe produced in 1990 a Convention on Certain International Aspects of Bankruptcy (the Istanbul Convention), which was not signed by the UK, perhaps in anticipation of EU intervention in this area. The Convention was overtaken by Council Regulation (EC) on Insolvency Proceedings 1346/2000, which came into force on May 31, 2002.[19] The Regulation affects a number of areas pertaining to insolvency proceedings including jurisdiction and applicable law. Being directly applicable in all EU Member States except Denmark, it affects the substance of Scots law with effect from that date.[20]

The aim of the Insolvency Regulation is to put in place a framework for the administration of cross-border insolvencies within the EU, applicable to the insolvency of natural and legal persons. In the manner of many EU instruments of recent years in the conflict of laws, the scheme of the Regulation is to provide at the outset rules on jurisdiction, justifying rules of recognition and enforcement. However, the Regulation contains also provisions as to applicable law and co-operation where there is more than one set of bankruptcy proceedings.

The new international approach is a compromise between the unity and territoriality approaches, to the effect that insolvency proceedings may be opened in more than one Member State, but only one set of proceedings may have extra-territorial effect. Any other proceedings will have only intra-territorial effect.

The Regulation applies to "collective insolvency proceedings involving the appointment of a liquidator".[21] For the purposes of the UK, this comprises winding up by or subject to the supervision of the court; creditors' voluntary winding up with confirmation by the court; administration; voluntary arrangements under insolvency legislation; and bankruptcy or sequestration.[22] Notably, the Regulation does not apply to receivership since that essentially is an action at the instance of one creditor, and is not a collective procedure.

---

[18] See now Civil Jurisdiction and Judgments Order 2001 (SI 2001/3929).
[19] See D. McKenzie-Skene, "The EC Convention on Insolvency Proceedings" (1996) 4 *European Review of Private Law* 181 at pp.182–183, wherein will be found details of the predecessor Convention.
[20] See W.W. McBryde, "Insolvency Jurisdiction", 2004 S.L.T. (News) 185.
[21] Art.1.
[22] Annex A.

Jurisdiction rules under Council Regulation 1346/2000

Main proceedings (Article 3)

The Regulation applies to any debtor having the centre of his main **17–40** interests in a Contracting State.[23] It is obvious that the connecting factor of "centre of a debtor's main interests" is the crux of the matter; the centre of main interests must first be identified, and found to be within the EU (except Denmark) before the Regulation applies.[24]

Article 3.1 provides that the courts of the Member State within the territory of which the centre of a debtor's main interests (henceforth "COMI") is situated shall have jurisdiction to open insolvency proceedings (the "main proceedings"). In the case of a company, or legal person, the place of the registered office shall be presumed to the centre of its main interests, in the absence of proof to the contrary.[25] This means that the Regulation may apply to a company incorporated outside the EU as long as the COMI is situated within the EU.[26]

There is no presumption in relation to individuals, but recital 13 contributes the thought that the COMI should correspond to the place where the debtor conducts the administration of his interests on a regular basis, being therefore ascertainable by third parties (ie potential creditors) (recital 13).[27]

Although a debtor reasonably may be held to have interests in one, or more than one, Member State(s), the Regulation does not apply unless one of these business bases can be said to be the "centre" of his interests. The criterion assumes that a debtor has only one centre of main business interests,[28] but this is not always so.

---

[23] See *Skjevesland v Geveran Trading (No. 4)* [2003] B.P.I.R. 924; *Re BRAC Rent-A-Car International* [2003] EWHC 128; 1 W.L.R. 1421; *Re Daisytek-ISA Ltd* [2004] BPIR 30; and *Re Salvage Association* [2003] EWHC 1028. Also *Eurofood IFSC Ltd*, below; centre of main interests has all autonomous meaning, and must therefore be interpreted in a uniform way.

[24] Preamble, recital 14.

[25] See *Eurofood IFSC Ltd*, ECJ, May 2, 2006: where a debtor company is a subsidiary company whose registered office and that of its parent company are situated in the different Member States, the presumption that the COMI of the subsidiary Is situated in the Member State in which *its* registered office is situated can be rebutted only if factors, both objective and ascertainable by third parties enable it to be established that the actuality is different from that which location at that registered office is deemed to reflect.

[26] Recital 14. There is no conclusive definition of this important term but, with regard to companies, Art.3.1 provides a rebuttable presumption that it is the place of the registered office.

[27] *e.g. X v Fortis Bank (Nederland)* NV ((HR (NL)) Hoge Raad (NL) (January 9, 2004) [2004] I L Pr 37.

[28] G. Maher and B. Rodger, "Jurisdiction in Insolvency Proceedings", 2003 (48) JLSS 26, at p.30.

Determination of the COMI will necessitate that a detailed factual inquiry be conducted.[29] Some help can be had from *Re Daisytek-ISA Ltd*,[30] which concerned a petition for administration orders to be made in an English court in respect of the English holding company of a pan-European group of companies, many of the members of which had registered offices in France and Germany. The English court had to perform a balancing exercise, assessing the size and importance of interests administered in England and elsewhere, respectively. The court held that there was sufficient evidence to rebut the presumption that the place of the registered office was the COMI, with the result that the English forum was competent. A large majority of potential creditors by value knew that many important functions of the group companies were carried out in England.

There is no temporal element in the COMI criterion, whereas in business life one would expect to find that the centre of main interests of an individual or company might change over time. This was recognized in *Shierson v Vlieland-Boddy*,[31] where the English court took account of the fact that the debtor's centre of main interests had moved from England to Spain. The precise question whether the relevant date for identifying the centre is that of the request to open proceedings, has been referred to the ECJ by the Bundesgerichtshof in *Re Opening of Insolvency Proceedings*.[32] It seems likely that interpretation of COMI will vary from Member State to Member State, and more references to the ECJ can be anticipated.[33]

Averments as to jurisdiction must acknowledge the primacy of the Regulation, and in a qualifying case, at the outset must aver in an insolvency petition that the COMI is in the forum petitioned.

Allocation of jurisdiction within the UK

17–41 It is said that territorial jurisdiction within a Member State must be established by the national law of the Member State concerned (recital 15) (*i.e.* if the centre of the debtor's main interests is in the

---

[29] *e.g. Re Ci4Net.com.Inc, Re DBP Holdings*, Chancery Division (Companies Court) (8 June 2004) [2004] EWHC 1941.

[30] [2004] BPIR 30.

[31] Ch. D. (November 26, 2004) [2004] EWHC 2752; [2005] B.C.C. 416. Followed in *Cross Construction Sussex Ltd v Tseliki* [2006] All E.R. (D.) 334.

[32] (IX ZB 418/02) BGH (Germany) (November 27, 2003); [2005] I L Pr 4.

[33] See *Staubitz-Schreiber* (January 17, 2006) Case C-104: decision by ECJ that Art.3.1 must be interpreted as meaning that the court of the Member State within the territory of which the centre of the debtor's main interests is situated at the time when the request is lodged to open insolvency proceedings retains jurisdiction to open those proceedings if the debtor moves the centre of his main interest to the territory of another Member State after the request has been lodged, but before the proceedings are opened.

UK, "UK national law" must determine the further allocation).
However, the effect of this is unclear in the UK or any other multi-
legal system context for there is no equivalent in this context to the
Civil Jurisdiction and Judgments Act 1982, Schedule 4 to serve to
allocate jurisdiction among the courts of the constituent units of the
UK. It has been suggested[34] that, assuming it can be established that
the COMI is in the UK, the allocation thereafter will be done
according to the pre-existing (ie non-Regulation) domestic insolvency rules (see below).

Secondary proceedings

To protect the diversity of interests, the Regulation allows "second-   **17–42**
ary proceedings" to be opened in parallel with the main proceedings.
Jurisdiction in respect of secondary proceedings is conferred upon
the legal system of a Member State in which the debtor has an
"establishment".[35] More than one set of secondary proceedings may
take place concurrently. Secondary insolvency proceedings, as well as
protecting local interests, serve a useful purpose in cases of complex
estates which are difficult to administer as a unit, or where there is
wide variation in the laws of the jurisdictions in which the debtor has
assets. The liquidator in the main proceedings may request the
opening of secondary proceedings if it seems to him that efficient
administration of the estate so requires.[36]

Effect of main and secondary proceedings

The main proceedings have extraterritorial effect, encompassing all   **17–43**
of the debtor's assets. Article 3.1, therefore, can be seen to enshrine
the principle of universality.

The effect of secondary proceedings is limited to assets situated
within the State in which they are opened (*i.e.* intra-territorial effect
only).

Given the different consequences attaching to main and secondary
proceedings, respectively, it is important for a court to make clear
the capacity in which it is acting.

Relationship between main and secondary proceedings

There must be co-operation between the liquidator in the main   **17–44**
proceedings and the liquidator(s) in the secondary proceedings
(Article 31). A creditor may lodge his claim both in the main

---

[34] G. Maher and B. Rodger, "Jurisdiction in Insolvency Proceedings" 2003 (48) JLSS
26, at 30.
[35] Art.2(h): an "establishment" shall mean any place of operations where the debtor
carries out a non-transitory economic activity with human means and goods (*i.e.* the
mere presence of assets in a Member State will not confer jurisdiction). There must
be an element of permanence to the establishment, but a branch office is not
necessary to constitute an "establishment".
[36] Preamble, recital 19.

proceedings and in any secondary proceedings (Article 32). The main liquidator can request that the secondary proceedings be stayed (Article 33). The stay will be refused only if it is manifestly of no interest to the creditors in the main proceedings. In the event of a stay, the main liquidator must guarantee the interests of creditors in the secondary proceedings. Any surplus assets in the State of secondary proceedings following payment of claims in that State must be remitted to the main liquidator (Article 35).

Choice of law rules under Council Regulation 1346/2000 (Articles 4 and 28)

17–45 The Regulation harmonises conflict rules, not substantive rules. Article 4 directs that the applicable law shall be the law of the State in which the proceedings (main[37] or secondary,[38] respectively) are opened (the *lex concursus*). In other words, the opening, conduct and closure of the proceedings [39] will be conducted according to the law of the forum. This is the same as the pre-existing rule of Scots law.

Under Article 4.2 the *lex concursus* determines many essential matters, including the ascertainment of assets and liabilities; the lodging and verification of claims; the ranking of claims; distribution of proceedings; the debtor's and liquidator's powers; the conditions for, and effects of, closure of insolvency proceedings (in particular by composition); and creditors' rights after closure.

Articles 5–15

17–46 Importantly, however, account must be taken of Articles 5 to 15 which provide, by way of exception, that certain other laws shall take precedence over the *lex concursus*. For example, the effect of insolvency proceedings on a contract conferring the right to acquire or make use of immoveable property shall be governed solely by the law of the State in which that property is situated[40]; and their effect upon employment contracts shall be governed solely by the law of the State applicable to the contract of employment.[41]

It is obvious that the admission of a claim, if contractual, depends upon the validity of the claim according to its own (contractual) governing law, but in an EU context, each EU forum must apply to this question the relevant provisions, if applicable, of Rome I.

More complex is Article 7 (the opening of insolvency proceedings against the purchaser of an asset shall not affect the seller's rights

---

[37] Art.4.
[38] Art.28.
[39] Recital 23.
[40] Art.8, and recital 25.
[41] Art.10, and recital 28.

based on a reservation of title where at the time of opening proceedings the asset is situated within the territory of a Member State other than the State of opening proceedings). Similarly, in Article 5 (third parties' rights *in rem*), the opening of insolvency proceedings shall not affect the rights *in rem* of creditors or third parties in respect of assets (of all types) belonging to the debtor which are situated at that date within the territory of another Member State.

Therefore, although the *lex concursus* is said to govern the opening, conduct and closure of the insolvency proceedings, Articles 5 to 15 represent substantial, albeit defensible, derogations from the basic *lex concursus* rule.

Recognition rules under Council Regulation 1346/2000 (Articles 16–26)

The principle in Article 16 is that any judgment opening insolvency **17–47** proceedings handed down by a court of a Member State having jurisdiction under Article 3 shall be recognised in all the other Member States without those other Member States being able to review the jurisdiction of the court of the Opening State.[42] Recognition of proceedings, however, shall not preclude the opening in another Member State of secondary proceedings. There is therefore a system of recognition of judgments opening insolvency proceedings. Article 25 lays down the principle of mutual recognition of judgments concerning the course and closure of insolvency proceedings. Grounds for non-recognition are minimal. In terms of Article 26, a State may refuse to recognise the opening of insolvency proceedings, or a judgment from such proceedings, only if it is manifestly contrary to its own public policy.[43]

There is one notable exception to the "revenue law exception",[44] namely, as a result of the promotion of equal treatment of creditors, recognition of the entitlement of tax authorities (and social security authorities) domiciled, habitually resident or having a registered office in a Member State other than the State of the opening of proceedings, to lodge claims in writing in any proceedings (Article 39).

In terms of Article 40, when insolvency proceedings are opened in a Member State, there is a duty upon the court of that State having jurisdiction, or the liquidator appointed by it, immediately to inform known creditors having their habitual residence, domicile, or registered office in the other Member States. This seems hardly capable of being satisfied. Not only in a complex case are assets and

---

[42] *Eurofood IFSC Ltd*, above.
[43] *ibid.*, above, paras 62–64.
[44] Ch.3, above.

creditors, known and unknown, likely to be found in more than one EU Member State so that provisions such as Article 40 seem unrealistic of attainment even within Europe, but also it is likely that assets and/or creditors will exist outside Europe, so that there will be an uneasy co-existence between the EU regulated area and the pre-existing national rules.

It is plain from the exceptions to be found in the Regulation that the drafting of a harmonised EU approach to the regulation of cross-(EU)-border insolvencies, has proved more difficult than har-monisation drafting in other areas.

IMPACT OF EU INSOLVENCY REGULATION ON PRE-EXISTING NATIONAL LAW

17–48 The Regulation applies only to collective insolvency proceedings opened after May 31, 2002. Proceedings opened prior to that date are unaffected, and are governed by the residual provisions of Scots domestic law.

As has been explained, the key to understanding the operation of the Regulation is as follows: if it can be said that the centre of a debtor's main interests lies within a Contracting State, collective insolvency proceedings in respect of the debtor must be governed by the Regulation (even where in a multi-legal system State such as the UK, allocation within that State, eg as between Scotland and England, is governed by pre-existing national rules). If, however (and only if), the centre of the debtor's main interests cannot be said to be in any Contracting State, "non-Regulation proceedings" still may be taken in Scotland if a ground of jurisdiction is available under the residual provisions of Scots domestic law.[45] The consequences of such proceedings (choice of law and recognition) will be determined by the pre-existing national rules. In such cases, the jurisdiction of the Scots court would be founded upon the provisions of the Bankruptcy (Scotland) Act 1985, and the Insolvency Act 1986, as amended.[46]

If the centre of the debtor's main interests is situated in another Contracting State, main proceedings cannot be opened in Scotland, even though jurisdiction appears to exist in terms of the 1985 or 1986 Acts. The jurisdiction of the Contracting State where the debtor's main interests are centred obliterates the jurisdiction other-wise available to the Scots court under residual national legislation (but without prejudice to the jurisdiction of the Scots court in

---

[45] Companies Act 1985, Bankruptcy (Scotland) Act 1985, Insolvency Act 1986, and Enterprise Act 2002. See McBryde, above.
[46] See Insolvency (Scotland) Regulations 2003 (SI 2003/2109); and Insolvency (Scotland) Amendment Rules 2003 (SI 2003/2111).

relation to secondary proceedings—which would, of course, be governed by the Regulation).

INTRA-UK SITUATION

Within the UK, early authority was to the effect that a bankruptcy **17–49** should proceed in a single jurisdiction.[47] By the Insolvency Act 1986, section 426, provision was made for reciprocal recognition of insolvency proceedings in the constituent parts of the UK.[48] This did not necessitate enforcement of such orders in respect of property situated in that other part,[49] but section 426(4) enjoins mutual assistance between UK courts.[50] Otherwise, the general principles emphasising the supremacy of the *lex situs* apply. *Galbraith v Grimshaw*[51] is authority for the view that the "no dating back" rule applies in Scottish/English as in foreign bankruptcy situations,[52] being peculiar to each system's bankruptcy rules.

There is mutual recognition of receivers within the United Kingdom in terms of the Insolvency Act 1986, s.72.

Since May 31, 2002, however, whenever the centre of the debtor's main interests is located within the UK, proceedings must fall within the scope of the Regulation, with attendant consequences.[53] Further,

---

[47] *Cooper v Baillie* (1878) 5 R. 564: see, *per* Lord Gifford at 570: "[u]nless there is good cause to the contrary, a strictly English bankruptcy should go on in England and a Scotch bankruptcy in Scotland": the place of sequestration may be a matter of indifference, but sometimes as here, the results may be very different. Parties should not be able to take advantage of the specialties of the UK situation and may be interdicted from doing so: *Lindsay v Paterson* (1840) 2 D. 1373; *Royal Bank of Scotland v Assignees of Scott Stein & Co.*, January 20, 1813, F.C.

[48] A bankruptcy order made in one part of the UK must be recognised in another: Insolvency Act 1986, s.426(1) and (2). Fletcher and Crabb, annotating the statute, sum up "thus a complete intra-United Kingdom system of reciprocal enforcement is established in respect of bankruptcy, winding up, receivership and the administrative order and voluntary arrangement procedures". They also note the beginnings of international co-operation in s.426(5). But see *Thoars' J.F.*, above. The IPL dimension is not altogether clear.

[49] s.426(2); but see also s.426(3).

[50] The scheme for mutual assistance extends to Channel Islands, Isle of Man, and any foreign country designated by the Secretary of State: Co-operation of Insolvency Courts (Designation of Relevant Countries and Territories) Order 1986 (McBryde, pp.226 *et seq.*). Such help, of course, was always available at common law: *e.g. Re Kooperman* [1928] W.N. 101; *Obers v Paton's Trs* (1897) 24 R. 719. See, generally, Cheshire & North (12th ed.), pp.915–916. These days, the innocuous verb "assist" will require to be interpreted according to the complexities of modern business.

[51] [1910] A.C. 508.

[52] In *Galbraith*, an HL decision, the effect was to frustrate the "relation back" or "dating back" domestic rules of both England and Scotland. See criticism in Anton with Beaumont, p.734.

[53] On a strict interpretation, therefore, in such a situation, the proceedings must be regarded as "Regulation proceedings" (*pace* Maher and Rodger, at p.30).

since April 4, 2006, account must be taken of the Cross-Border Insolvency Regulations 2006 (regulation 7).[54]

GENERAL PRINCIPLES GOVERNING "NON-REGULATION" INSOLVENCY PROCEEDINGS IN SCOTLAND

The statutory background[55]

17–50 The internal law of Scotland pertaining to bankruptcy differs in substance and terminology from that of England.[56] The old law was contained in the Bankruptcy (Scotland) Act 1913, which was repealed *in toto* by the Bankruptcy (Scotland) Act 1985 which came into effect mainly on April 1, 1986 and completely on December 29, 1986.[57] The rules now are contained in the Bankruptcy (Scotland) Act 1985 (see, having particular conflict significance: section 9—jurisdiction[58]; section 10—concurrent proceedings; section 16—petitions for recall of sequestration; and section 17—recall of sequestration). The Insolvency Act 1986 is concerned with corporate insolvency law for Scotland (Part 4),[59] and England, but in relation to individual insolvency law, for England only.

Appointment of trustee

17–51 The interim and the permanent trustee, being an insolvency practitioner, must reside within Scotland (or within the sheriffdom[60]) and may be removed if either of these conditions is found not to be satisfied.[61]

Property vested in the trustee

17–52 Section 31 of the 1985 Act confers upon the trustee in bankruptcy "the whole estate of the debtor" as at the date of sequestration, and wherever situated,[62] for the benefit of the creditors. There is no

---

[54] SI 2006/1030; see below.
[55] See I. Fletcher, "The Genesis of Modern Insolvency Law—An Odyssey of Law Reform" [1989] J.B.L. 365.
[56] See *Scots Commercial Law* (Forte ed., 1997), Ch.7, pp.209 *et seq.*
[57] W McBryde, *Bankruptcy* (2nd ed.), p.11. See generally, on the subject of bankruptcy, McBryde, *op. cit.*; F.P. Davidson and L. Macgregor, *Commercial Law in Scotland* (2003), Ch.8.
[58] Broadly speaking, in the case of individual and entities, based upon proof of an established place of business in Scotland. Alternatively, in the case of individuals, based upon habitual residence in Scotland; and in the case of entities, formation under Scots law and proof that at any time it carried on business in Scotland.
[59] See St J. Clair and Lord Drummond Young, *The Law of Corporate Insolvency in Scotland* (3rd ed., 2004); Greene and Fletcher, *The Law and Practice of Receivership in Scotland* (2004) Collins, *Essays in International Litigation and the Conflict of Laws*, Chap. XII, "Floating Charges, Receivers and Managers and the Conflict of Laws".
[60] ss.2(2)(a), (b) and 24(d), 1985 Act.
[61] ss.3(b), 29(6) and 29(9)(a), 1985 Act.
[62] s.31(8).

territorial limitation, but in respect of property situated abroad it is for the foreign *lex situs* to determine the effect which it gives to Scottish sequestration.[63] Whether property situated abroad falls to the trustee "must depend in the last resort on the *lex situs . . .* For no Act of Parliament can of its own force and effect transfer property situated, *e.g.* in France from the bankrupt to the trustee".[64]

Applicable law

As noted above, any rights acquired by the trustee in bankruptcy are **17–53** subject to the overriding provisions of the *lex situs*.[65] Otherwise, the forum applies its own domestic law, and matters of administration also are governed by the *lex fori*.[66]

A creditor who recovers assets abroad may rank in Scotland if he makes available what he has recovered.[67] There is no difference in principle in ranking simply because the claim is foreign,[68] though ranking in general is the function of the *lex fori*.[69] If, however, he does not claim, it would seem that, if he obtained the assets before the date of the bankruptcy, they cannot be recovered but, if he obtained them after that date and he is subject to the jurisdiction in bankruptcy in Scotland, the trustee may recover the assets.[70] A claim in a Scots sequestration will subject a creditor to the jurisdiction of the Scots court by reconvention.[71]

Discharge

Discharge is governed by the *lex fori*. Discharge has the same effect **17–54** territorially as the original bankruptcy. A discharge under a "UK" bankruptcy will excuse the subject of the order from suit in the

---

[63] Or *vice versa*: *Murphy's Trs v Aitken*, 1983 S.L.T. 78, *sub nom. Morley's Trs v Aitken*, 1982 S.C. 73: English trustee in bankruptcy took Scottish heritage subject to any inhibitions registered against the bankrupt prior in date to trustee's appointment.

[64] Dicey and Morris, 31-024.

[65] *Re Reilly* [1942] I.R. 416.

[66] *cf. Bank of Credit and Commerce International SA (No. 10)* [1996] 4 All E.R. 796.

[67] This is not expressly laid down in the 1985 Act (ss.48 and 49), but seems clear at common law: *cf. Clydesdale Bank v Anderson* (1890) 27 S.L.R. 493, *per* Lord Shand at 504.

[68] *Re Kloebe* (1884) 28 Ch.D. 175 (succession).

[69] Which may disadvantage foreign creditors, *e.g.* if their claims have prescribed by the law of the forum, but not by their own proper applicable law: see *Re Lorillard* [1922] 2 Ch. 638 (succession), which has been the subject of criticism. See for Scots law as to unfair preferences Bankruptcy (Scotland) Act 1985, s.36.

[70] *Stewart v Auld* (1851) 13 D. 1337; *Wilsons (Glasgow and Trinidad) Ltd v Dresdner Bank* (1913) 2 S.L.T. 437; *Murphy's Trs.*, 1933 S.L.T. 632; *Re Courtney, ex p. Pollard* (1840) Mont. & Ch. 239; *Re Oriental Island S.S. Co.* (1874) L.R. 9 Ch. App. 557; *Ex p. Robertson* (1875) L.R. 20 Eq. 733; *Thurburn v Steward* (1871) L.R. 3 P.C. 478; *Ex p. Melbourn* (1870) L.R. 6 Ch. App. 64; *Banco de Portugal v Waddell* [1880] 5 A.C. 161; *Re Anchor Line (Henderson Bros) Ltd* [1937] Ch. 483; *Rousou* [1955] 1 W.L.R. 545. Cheshire & North, pp.908–911.

[71] *Barr v Smith* (1879) 7 R. 247; *Wilsons (Glasgow and Trinidad) Ltd*, above; Anton with Beaumont, p.734, and *cf.* generally the salutary tale of incautious greed: *Guiard v De Clermont* [1914] 3 K.B. 145 (Morris (3rd ed.), p.113).

United Kingdom in respect of a foreign debt or obligation,[72] though its effect in a foreign court will be a matter for decision in accordance with the foreign bankruptcy/contract conflict rule.

Cross-Border Insolvency Regulations 2006[72a]

In 1997 UNCITRAL adopted a Model Law on Cross-Border Insolvency, offering a legislative framework for adoption by States. By virtue of the 2006 Regulations, this Model Law was adopted for Great Britain. To an extent this overlaps with the rules in Council Regulation 1346/2000, albeit that the latter govern only the coordination of insolvency proceedings within the EU. The Model Law is capable of providing a complementary regime of regulation and co-operation outside the EU: "[t]his will place Great Britain, by virtue of the operation of section 426 of the Insolvency Act 1986 in the unique position of having a suite of statutory procedures available in cross-border insolvency cases, as well as the flexibility of common law."[72b] Henceforth, by rule 3 of the 2006 Regulations, "British insolvency law" shall apply, with such modification as the context requires, for the purpose of giving effect to the provisions of the 2006 Regulations. In the case of conflict, the provisions of the 2006 Regulations shall prevail. Less clear is the interaction between the Model Law and Council Regulation 1346/2000.[72c]

In terms of the Model Law, the person administering a foreign insolvency may initiate an insolvency proceeding in Great Britain in relation to a debtor who is the subject of the foreign proceedings, and participate in those British proceedings regarding that debtor. The Model Law establishes criteria for deciding whether foreign insolvency proceedings are to be recognised elsewhere, and if so, whether as "main" or "non-main" proceedings (depending on whether the foreign proceedings are taking place in the country where the main operations of the debtor are located); and sets out

---

[72] See McBryde, p.415; and Dicey and Morris, Rules 170 and 171. Also Ch.15, and *Gibbs & Sons v La Société Industrielle et Commercialle des Metaux* (1890) 25 Q.B.D. 399.

[72a] SI 2006/1030 (entry into force April 4, 2006). See also Act of Sederunt (Rules of the Court of Session Amendment No. 2) (UNCITRAL Model Law on Cross-Border Insolvency) 2006 (SSI 2006/199), Act of Sederunt (Sheriff Court Bankruptcy Rules 1996) Amendment (UNCITRAL Model Law on Cross-Border Insolvency) 2006 (SSI 2006/197) and Act of Sederunt (Sheriff Court Company Insolvency Rules 1996) Amendment (UNCITRAL Model Law on Cross-Border Insolvency) 2006 (SSI 2006/200).

[72b] Explanatory Memorandum to 2006 Regulations, para 7.4. See *McGrath & Ors v McMahon & Ors, Re HIH Casualty and General Insurance Ltd & Ors* [2006] EWCA Civ. 732.

[72c] With regard to this difficult issue, there has been procrastination: the ranking provisions have not been included within the Model Law "for the time being", but are promised "as soon as it is practicable and possible" (Explanatory Memorandum to 2006 Regulations, para.7.20).

the effects of recognition, and the relief available to a foreign representative.

A British court may grant discretionary relief for the benefit of any recognised foreign proceedings, although it must be satisfied that the interests of local creditors are adequately protected. Recognition of foreign proceedings does not prevent local creditors from initiating or continuing insolvency proceedings in Britain concerning the same debtor.

Rules also are provided to permit foreign creditors to commence and participate in insolvency proceedings in Britain. The Model Law seeks coordination between courts in different States in relation to concurrent insolvency proceedings concerning the same debtor, and authorises courts in one State to seek assistance from courts and representatives in another.[72d]

RECOGNITION IN SCOTLAND OF NON-EU (OR DANISH) INSOLVENCY PROCEEDINGS

In the case of insolvency proceedings not governed by Council **17–55** Regulation 1346/2000, pre-existing national rules apply. In general, such foreign insolvencies are recognised in Scotland, subject to the overriding control of the Scottish forum *qua lex situs*.[73] Such a foreign insolvency receives effect in Scotland provided that the court is regarded as having had jurisdiction, but only from the date of the bankruptcy. There is no retrospective or dating back effect in Scotland. The Scots rules as to illegal preferences apply only to Scots bankruptcies in Scotland and a foreign trustee does not have the right to cut down preferences, because the effect of a foreign bankruptcy in Scotland is prospective only.[74] Similarly, a Scots sequestration takes effect abroad but only from its date onwards so that it does not operate to cut down preferences already obtained there,[75] *i.e.* ranking or entitlement to rank is governed by the law under which the sequestration/bankruptcy order is granted.

Jurisdiction

The foreign court will be regarded as competent if it has assumed **17–56** jurisdiction on grounds similar to those assumed in Scotland provided that the bankrupt was a party to the proceedings.[76]

[72d] Explanatory Memorandum to 2006 Regulations, paras 7.7—7.17.

[73] *Murphy's Trs v Aitken*, 1983 S.L.T. 78.

[74] *Goetze v Aders* (1874) 2 R. 150.

[75] *Galbraith v Grimshaw* [1910] A.C. 508.

[76] *Wilkie v Cathcart* (1870) 9 M. 168; *Gibson v Munro* (1894) 21 R. 840; *Obers v Paton's Trs* (1897) 24 R. 719; *Re Davidson* (1873) L.R. 15 Eq. 383; *Re Lawson* [1896] 1 Ch. 175; *Re Anderson* [1911] 1 K.B. 896; *Re Craig*, 86 LJ Ch. 62; *Bergerem v Marsh* (1921) 125 L.T. 630.

Scots heritage

17–57 Scots heritage does not pass to the trustee under a foreign bankruptcy. Nevertheless, the court may assist the trustee in such a bankruptcy to deal with heritage in Scotland,[77] and if so the Scots heritage will pass subject to any charges attaching to the property under the Scots *lex situs*.[78]

Moveables in Scotland

17–58 The Scots courts will recognise and enforce the right of a foreign trustee to all the bankrupt's moveable property without further process,[79] with the result that all such property is attached and falls to the trustee in preference to the claims of creditors who may have attached the assets after the date of the bankruptcy.[80] The rights of Scots creditors who have taken action such as diligence in Scotland prior to the date of the foreign bankruptcy are not adversely affected because the foreign bankruptcy, assuming it is recognised, is regarded as taking effect only from its date onwards. The *lex situs* controls the situation and the Scots statutory provisions about dating back apply only to Scots bankruptcies. (See now the 1985 Act, sections 34 to 37.)

Competing claims

Competing claims are decided by the *lex fori* of the bankruptcy.[81]

Discharge

17–59 A discharge has the same effect territorially as the original award of bankruptcy. A discharge in bankruptcy will have the effect of discharging a contractual obligation[82] only if it was granted under the same law as the proper law of the obligation.[83]

---

[77] *Rattray v White* (1842) 4 D. 880; *Araya v Coghill*, 1921 S.C. 462. The English courts apply the same principle: *Re Kooperman* [1928] W.N. 101.

[78] *Murphy's Trs v Aitken*, 1983 S.L.T. 78.

[79] *Araya v Coghill*, 1921 S.C. 462.

[80] *Goetze v Aders* (1874) 2 R. 150; *Phosphate Sewage Co. v Molleson* (1876) 3 R. (HL) 77, 5 R. 1125, 6 R. (HL) 113; *Obers v Paton's Trs* (1897) 24 R. 719; *Salaman v Tod*, 1911 S.C. 1214; *Hume's Trs*, 1926 S.L.T. 214.

[81] *Re Courteney, ex p. Pollard* (1840) Mont. & Ch. 239; *Re Anchor Line (Henderson Bros) Ltd* [1937] Ch. 483; *Scottish Union & National Insurance Co. v James* (1886) 13 R. 928.

[82] *Gardiner v Houghton* (1862) 2 B. & S. 743; *Ellis v McHenry* (1871) L.R. 6 C.P. 228.

[83] *Bartley v Hodges* (1861) 1 B. & S. 375; *Gibbs & Son v Société Industrielle* (1890) 25 Q.B.D. 399.

SUMMARY 17—THE LAW OF PROPERTY

I. Particular transfers of property

1. Classification and alienability

The nature of property as moveable or immoveable, and whether it **17–60** is alienable, is determined by the *lex situs*.

2. Importance of the *lex situs*

According to current rules, the *lex causae* to determine questions of title is the *lex situs*, being the law of the situation of the property at the time of the transfer allegedly giving rise to the claim.

3. Immoveable property

(a) Proprietary rights in respect of immoveable property are governed by the *lex situs*;

(b) Contracts concerning immoveables are governed by their applicable law, usually the *lex situs* (see also Contracts (Applicable Law) Act 1990, Rome I Articles 4.3 and 9.6);

(c) Security rights in respect of immoveable property must comply with the *lex situs*.

4. Moveable Property

(a) Corporeal moveables:

Care must be taken to distinguish rights *in rem* from rights *in personam*.

Title validly conferred by the *lex situs* at the time of the purported transfer prevails, subject to any overriding effect according to a subsequent *lex situs*. The *lex situs* generally governs competing claims.

(b) Incorporeal moveables:

(a) *Situs* is the place where the right may be enforced.

(b) Assignability is governed by the proper law of the right.

(c) Capacity is governed by the proper law of the right or *lex loci actus* or *lex actus*.

(d) Formal validity is governed by the *lex loci actus* or the proper law of the assignation or the right.

(e) Essential validity the proper law of the assignation or of right.

(f) As regards contractual assignations, see Rome I, Article 12.

II. Universal transfers of property: insolvency

1. Theories

Unity; separation; universality of bankruptcy.

2. EU Council Regulation 1346/2000

It establishes a system to regulate cross-border EU insolvencies where the centre of a debtor's main interests is situated within an EU Member State (except Denmark).

It sets up a system of main proceedings (having extra-territorial effect) and secondary proceedings (limited to assets situated in the State where the secondary proceedings are opened).

Pre-existing national rules of Scots law concerning jurisdiction, applicable law, and recognition and enforcement must be read subject to the Regulation.

3. "Non-Regulation" proceedings

The residual national rules are contained in the Bankruptcy (Scotland) Act 1985 (personal insolvency), and the Insolvency Act 1986 (corporate insolvency), and the Enterprise Act 2002.

(a) Jurisdiction depends generally on habitual residence at the relevant time or place of business in Scotland.

(b) The whole estate of the debtor (subject in the case of foreign immoveables to the foreign *lex situs*) shall vest as at the date of sequestration in the permanent trustee for the benefit of the creditors.

(c) Administration is governed by the *lex fori*.

(d) Discharge is governed by the *lex fori*.

4. Recognition of "non-Regulation" foreign insolvency proceedings.

In general, such foreign insolvencies are recognised in Scotland subject to the overriding control of Scots law *qua lex situs*, but recognition will be prospective only.

CHAPTER 18

THE LAW OF SUCCESSION

I. MATTERS PERTAINING TO BOTH TESTATE AND INTESTATE SUCCESSION

CONFIRMATION AND PROBATE

The general principle is that a person is not entitled to take any **18–01** administrative act in the estate of any deceased person who has left assets in Scotland until he has obtained confirmation in Scotland. Confirmation constitutes title to all moveable and immoveable estate in Scotland of a deceased Scottish domiciliary. There must be property in Scotland before confirmation may be granted. The same principles apply in England where probate is granted in testate cases and letters of administration in intestate cases.[1]

The granting of confirmation (or probate, or letters of administration) confers authority on the executor to intromit with assets only in Scotland, England or the country where such title was granted, but not with assets in any other country i.e. before the executor can have authority to intromit with such assets he must complete title according to the *lex loci rei sitae/lex situs*. Within the UK there used to be a system of resealing of the grant of authority in one jurisdiction in the other constituent parts, if there were assets to be dealt with there, but by the Administration of Estates Act 1971, section 3(1) resealing was dispensed with, provided the deceased died domiciled in the legal system which issued the authority. Thus, confirmation or probate or letters of administration granted in any UK jurisdiction operates directly in the others, though obtaining confirmation to Scottish estate and separate probate/letters to English estate is still competent.[2]

If the deceased died domiciled in a Commonwealth country, and if probate or letters of administration have already been granted in such a country, it is not necessary to apply for confirmation to estate in Scotland. Instead the probate or letters may be resealed in

---

[1] See E. Scobbie, *Currie on Confirmation* (8th ed., 1995), para.14-33.
[2] *ibid.*, para.14-41; see generally para.14-35.

Edinburgh.[3] (Reciprocal arrangements have been made for the resealing of Scottish confirmations in Commonwealth countries.) Before resealing can take place, an inventory of the deceased's estate in Scotland must be lodged.[4] Resealing does not have any retrospective effect, with the result that a resealed confirmation or probate is effective in the country where it was resealed only from the date of resealing onwards, not from the date of the original confirmation or probate.

If the deceased died domiciled outside the Commonwealth and if probate, letters of administration or similar authority has already been granted abroad, the Scots courts will follow the law of the domicile as regards the appointment of the executor,[5] and confirmation will be granted in Scotland to such a person already appointed under the law of the domicile, or to the person entitled to appointment as such under that law. Unless the estate is small, a petition for the appointment of the administrator as executor dative will be required.

If the deceased died domiciled outside the Commonwealth, but probate or letters of administration have not been granted in the courts of the domicile, and there is property to be administered in Scotland, it is necessary to prove that the will is valid according to the law of the domicile, or that the person seeking appointment as executor dative is the person entitled to the office of administrator by that law.[6]

---

[3] Resealing of probates in Scotland is competent under the Colonial Probate Act 1892 and the Colonial Probate (Protected States and Mandated Territories) Act 1927. If resealing is competent under these Acts, it does not matter that the executor could not have been appointed as such executor in the country where resealing takes place. But see Currie para.15-02, explaining that obtaining Scottish confirmation may be preferable, *e.g.* to obtain title to individual items of estate.

[4] Currie, para.14-13.

[5] Some systems, however, know no interposition of executor between deceased and heir, in which case Scots law must be guided by the rules of the *lex situs* or the personal law, though its accommodation of the foreign law must inevitably be approximate because, first, the personal law will be taken to be the law of the domicile of the deceased, though the choice of the foreign law is likely to be in favour of the application of the law of the nationality to all property, moveable and immoveable. Secondly, the foreign system would have that property pass directly to the heir. Whatever the rule of the personal law, property in Scotland or England cannot pass without confirmation, probate or letters having been obtained by the party entitled. See, generally, Cheshire & North, p.975. On the other hand, Scots law will accept as executor the person identified by the personal law whether or not such a person would be entitled to act under Scots domestic law: Currie, para.2.36.

[6] For example, on procedure and more complex cases, see Currie, paras 2.37 *et seq.* For styles see *Currie on Confirmation of Executors, Supplement to the Eighth Edition* (1996).

The following is a summary of the position.[7]

Country of deceased's domicile—procedure

(a) Scotland—Confirmation is title to assets in Scotland, **18–02** England, and Northern Ireland.

(b) England—Probate or letters of administration are immediately effective in Scotland as regards title to property (Administration of Estates Act 1971).

(c) Northern Ireland—As for (b) above, but a separate inventory must be lodged of the deceased's estate in Scotland.

(d) Channel Islands and the Isle of Man[8]—There is no procedure for resealing, and therefore confirmation in Scotland is required.

(e) Commonwealth—Resealing under Acts of 1892 and 1927 above. A separate inventory must be lodged of the deceased's estate in Scotland, but separate Scottish confirmation is unnecessary.

(f) Other foreign countries[9]:

    (i) If probate or letters have already been granted: an inventory must be lodged in Scotland, in which executor refers to probate or letters as his title, and confirmation will be granted.

    (ii) If no probate or letters have been granted, an opinion may be required as to the validity of the will (if any) or

---

[7] See Currie, Ch.15. Older cases: *Hutchison v Aberdeen Bank* (1837) 15 S. 1100; *Marchioness of Hastings v Executors of Marquess of Hastings* (1852) 14 D. 489; *Whiffin v Lees* (1872) 10 M. 797; *Ewing v Orr-Ewing* [1883] 9 A.C. 34; *Rodger v Adam's Trs* (1885) 1 Sh. Ct Rep. 202; *New York Breweries Co. v Att.-Gen.* [1899] A.C. 62; *Re the Duchess of Orleans* (1859) 1 Sw. & Tr. 253; *Re Tucker* (1864) 3 Sw. & Tr. 585; *Re Coode* (1867) L.R. 1 P. & D. 449; *Re Earl* (1867) L.R. 1 P. & D. 450; *Re Hill* [1870] L.R. 2 P. & D. 89; *Re Briesemann* [1894] P. 260; *Re Von Linden* [1896] P. 148; *Re Achillopoulos* [1928] 1 Ch. 433; *Re Leguia* [1934] P. 80; *Re Humphries* [1934] P. 78; *Re Schulhof and Wolf* [1948] P. 66; *Re O'Grady* (1941) 75 I.L.T.R. 119; *Re Welsh* [1931] I.R. 161; *Re Dyas* [1937] I.R. 479; *Re Rea* [1902] I.R. 451. More recent cases include: *Irwin v Caruth* [1916] P. 23; *Re Rankine* [1918] P. 134; *Burns v Campbell* [1952] 1 K.B. 15; *Re Wayland* [1951] 2 All E.R. 1041; *Re Kaufman* [1952] 2 All E.R. 261; *Finnegan v Cementation Co.* [1953] 1 Q.B. 688; *Re Yahunda* [1956] P. 388; *Bowler v Mowlem* [1954] 1 W.L.R. 1445; *IRC v Stype Investments (Jersey) Ltd* [1982] Ch. 456.

[8] See, generally, *Administration of Foreign Estates* (Pugh ed., 1988).

[9] *Administration of Foreign Estates, op. cit.*, is a compilation of essays on matters of death, succession and administration in France, Italy, Spain, Portugal, Jersey, Guernsey, Isle of Man and the State of Florida, selection of countries on the doleful rationale that it is not unlikely that British residents/nationals/domiciliaries may die in any of these countries while on holiday or on longer term stay, and where in addition, they may have second homes. See also Hayton, *European Succession Law* (chapters on the succession of various countries, contributed by experts in each system). For Republic of Ireland, see W. Binchy, *Irish Conflict of Laws* (1988), Ch.24.

persons entitled to appointment as executor: an inventory must be lodged in Scotland, and confirmation will be granted.

The court may take evidence upon the question of the domicile of the deceased (Colonial Probate Act 1892, section 22). A foreign declarator of death is not conclusive in Scotland so that in a contested case proof of death may be necessary.[10]

The 1973 Hague Convention concerning the International Administration of the Estates of Deceased Persons has been signed, but not ratified by the UK.[11]

ADMINISTRATION AND DISTRIBUTION OF ESTATE

18–03 *Administration* of a deceased's estate is governed by the *lex fori*, which is, in effect, the *lex situs* of the assets, not the *lex domicilii* of the deceased.[12] Thus, in the case of debts which have prescribed by the law of domicile, but not by the *lex fori* or *vice versa*, it is the *lex fori* which determines whether they may be admitted and which determines priorities.[13] The incidence of debts as between moveables and immoveables probably is determined by the *lex situs* of the immoveables.

Administration comprises all steps of procedure in completion of title and all the duties of the executor up to the stage of bringing the estate to the point of division. It includes obtaining confirmation (or probate or letters of administration), payment of capital transfer/inheritance tax, collection of assets, and payment of debts. In English law there is a presumption that, if a bequest is declared to be "free of duty" or is expressed in similar terms, such an expression covers only duties imposed by UK law unless the testator has indicated a contrary intention.[14] There is no such presumption in Scots law where the courts approach the matter

---

[10] *Simpson's Trs v Fox*, 1951 S.L.T. 412.
[11] See EU Commission Green Paper on Wills and Succession (2005) COM 2005 65 final. See para.18–05, below. As well as initiating a debate on choice of law in succession, the Green Paper consults on seemingly administrative matters, such as whether automatic recognition should be given in all EU Member States of the designation and functions of executor: should such a person be furnished with a certificate to describe his powers? Should the heir have a certificate as evidence of his status? Such matters surely beg important, substantive questions.
[12] *cf. Weinstock v Savnat (NSW)* [2006] 3 C.L. 79.
[13] *Re Lorillard* [1922] 2 Ch. 638. This case is not without its critics: if the debts were still exigible by their own laws, perhaps the forum was overreaching itself by refusing to admit the claims; *Re Kloebe* (1884) 28 Ch. D. 175; *Re Manifold* [1962] Ch. 1.
[14] *Re Goetze* [1953] Ch. 96; *Re Nesbitt* [1953] 1 W.L.R. 595; *Re Scott* [1915] 1 Ch 592.

purely as one of interpretation of the testator's intention.[15] If the will is silent generally about the matter of duties, taxes are paid out of the residue of the estate; and failing residue, out of the legacies, which will have to be abated.[16]

Distribution involves the division of the estate among the beneficiaries, and is governed by the *lex successionis*. When the deceased dies domiciled abroad, the assets in Scotland normally are remitted to the country of the domicile for distribution, or *vice versa*, but this is not essential. Distribution at the *situs* in accordance with the *lex successionis* is sufficient. The procedure in the *forum rei sitae* is termed the *ancillary administration*; that in the *lex successionis* is termed the *principal administration*.

Classification between matters of administration and of distribution is governed by the *lex fori*.[17]

A decree of the court of the deceased's domicile determining a question of succession to moveables is a decree *in rem* entitled to international recognition and conclusive against other claimants.[18]

THE SCISSION PRINCIPLE

This phrase refers to the split nature of the "UK" (as opposed to European) conflict rule in succession, which differentiates between the law governing succession to moveables (ultimate domicile) from that governing succession to immoveables (*lex situs*). **18–04**

Whether this distinction should continue to be made is a question under consideration.[19] Professor Meston's view[20] is that "all property ought to devolve according to the deceased's last domicile and that the role of the *lex situs* should disappear," noting the unimplemented recommendation to this effect in the Scottish Law Commission Report No. 124.

---

[15] *Maclean's Trs v McNair*, 1969 S.L.T. 146; *Scottish National Orchestra Society Ltd v Thomson's Exrs*, 1969 S.L.T. 325.

[16] See generally Barr, Biggar, Dalgleish and Stevens, *Drafting Wills in Scotland* (2005).

[17] *Ewing v Orr-Ewing* [1885] 10 A.C. 453; *Grant v Gordon Falconer & Fairweather*, 1932 48 Sh. Ct Rep. 155; *Scottish National Orchestra Society Ltd v Thomson's Exrs*, 1969 S.L.T. 325; *Re Kloebe* (1884) 28 Ch. D. 175; *Re Lorillard* [1922] 2 Ch. 638; *Re Achillopoulos* [1928] Ch. 433; *Re Wilks* [1935] Ch. 645; *Re Goenaga* [1949] P. 367; *Re Manifold* [1962] Ch. 1; *Re Weiss* [1962] P. 136.

[18] *Ewing v Orr-Ewing* [1883] 9 A.C. 34, [1885] 10 A.C. 453; *Enohin v Wylie* (1862) 10 H.L.C. 1; *Doglioni v Crispin* (1866) L.R.1 (HL) 301; *Re Trufort* (1887) 36 Ch. D. 600.

[19] See, earlier, Morris, "Intestate Succession to Land in the Conflict of Laws" (1969) 85 L.Q.R. 839; *Some Miscellaneous Topics in the Law of Succession*, Scot. Law Com. Memo. No. 71 (1986) considers private international law aspects in Pt 6. Later consideration in Scot. Law Com. Report No. 124. See most recently EU Commission Green Paper on Succession & Wills COM (2005) 65 final, below.

[20] M.C. Meston, *The Succession (Scotland) Act 1964* (5th ed., 2002), p.113.

The Succession (Scotland) Act 1964 removed many differences which previously had existed domestically between succession to heritage and succession to moveables. However, remnants of the distinction remain in domestic law, and permeate Scots conflict rules of succession. It can lead to difficult cases and the possibility of error, particularly where property is chameleon in character, changing its nature according to the context in which it is encountered; the result may be seen as unfair: a widow may benefit twice.[21] The 1989 Hague Convention on the Law Applicable to the Estates of Deceased Persons, to which the United Kingdom has not acceded, proceeds on the principle of unity (*i.e.* of one law governing succession to all types of property).

EU GREEN PAPER ON SUCCESSION AND WILLS[22]

18–05 As will be seen, the conflict rules of Scots and English law in the area of succession are well-settled and understood, and rest largely on the common law. The statutory rules concerning formal validity of wills are flexible and generous and accord with international norms. There is administrative cooperation between Scotland and England. The choice of law rules provide certainty and predictability (subject to the uncertainty which ascertainment of domicile by its nature may entail).

Succession conflict rules were excluded from early EU harmonisation processes. Whilst harmonisation of choice of law rules concerning formal validity of wills has been accomplished,[23] efforts to harmonise the rules concerning essential validity have proved less successful: the 1989 Hague Convention received little support and was not acceptable to the UK.[24]

As regards the EU, the 1998 Vienna Action Plan placed among its priorities the adoption of a European instrument concerning conflict rules of succession.[25] The Hague Programme called upon the EU

---

[21] *Train* (1899) 2 F. 146: see criticisms in Anton (1st ed.), pp.387–388; *Re Collens* (*dec'd.*) [1986] All E.R. 611, in which, however, scission was adhered to, following *Re Rea* [1902] 1 I.R. 451, and *Re Ralston* [1906] V.L.R. 689.

[22] (2005) COM 2005 65 final. See also Commission Staff Working Paper, Annex to the Green Paper on Succession and Wills (SEC (2005) 270), and Opinion of the European Economic and Social Committee on the Green Paper on Succession and Wills (2006/C 28/01).

[23] 1961 Hague Convention on the Conflicts of Laws Relating to the Form of Testamentary Dispositions, leading to 1963 Wills Act.

[24] See Lord Chancellor's Department: Hague Convention on Succession: Consultation Paper (1990). Difficulties which arise in attempting to harmonise laws of succession are considered by Robertson, "International Succession Law. A Co-ordinated Approach" (1989) 34 J.L.S. 377.

[25] See generally Chapter 1. Also E.B. Crawford and J.M. Carruthers, "Conflict of Loyalties in the Conflict of Laws: The Cause, the Means and the Cost of Harmonisation", 2005 J.R. 251.

Commission to present a Green Paper covering jurisdiction, applicable law, and recognition, together with administrative measures relating to wills. A consultation process took place in summer 2005 to elicit opinion in the Member States, not only upon the scope of the instrument (choice of law and/or administration), but also on the detail of proposed rules. It is envisaged that a Community instrument will emerge.[26] This initiative is said to be justified by the growing mobility of EU citizens in an area without internal frontiers, and the increasing frequency of personal unions between nationals of different Member States, together with the fact of acquisition of property situated in the territories of different States, which property ultimately will form part of the deceased's estate.

It can be assumed that the instrument will determine its own scope; identify legal systems interested in the administration of an estate; make provision as to applicable law[27] (which may include party choice of law) to govern matters of substance; and remove administrative and practical barriers to the winding up of estates.

Debate is not invited on the merits of the principle of universality. It is assumed that the harmonised rules will be of universal application (*i.e.* will apply in any EU forum, whatever the identity—EU or not—of the applicable law(s)).

It is not clear what the attitude of the Scottish Executive and UK delegation generally will be as to the principle of harmonisation (and particularly to the question whether the UK should "opt-in" to the initiative),[28] to say nothing of the detail of the provisions. After consideration of expert opinion, the Justice 1 Committee of the Scottish Parliament concluded that the proposals as "fundamentally flawed and unnecessary", and strongly urged the U.K. Government not to opt in to any draft instrument which should emerge following the conclusion of the consultation processes.[29]

LEGAL RIGHTS

Such rights (of family members of the deceased to claim against **18–06** the will, or in intestacy, a reserved portion of the deceased's estate, *i.e.* rights of indefeasible family provision) are both rights of

---

[26] A European Parliament report is scheduled for adoption in the Legal Affairs Committee in June 2006 and for adoption in the Plenary Session in September 2006, whereas the Parliament, it is expected, will call upon the Comission, during 2007, to submit a legislative proposal to Parliament in order to deal with succession and wills.

[27] It can be predicted that the scission principle utilised in Scots and English conflict rules will not find favour, preference currently resting on habitual residence of deceased at death. See Draft Report PE 367.975v02–00 (French language only).

[28] See Ch.1, above.

[29] Press Release October 6, 2005, Scottish Parliament.

succession and restrictions on testamentary powers. The subject of legal rights, being a matter of substance, is regulated by the law of the deceased's domicile at the date of his death as regards moveables,[30] and by the *lex situs* at the date of death, as regards immoveables.[31]

Scotland

18–07 Legal rights consisting in Scots domestic law of rights of surviving spouse (*ius relicti/relictae*) and children (*legitim*) arise now only out of moveables, and in conflict terms only if the deceased died domiciled in Scotland. Legal rights in Scots law, exigible now only out of moveable estate and available therefore only where the deceased died domiciled in Scotland, can be claimed in intestate or testate succession, though in the former case (intestacy), they do not arise until prior rights have been satisfied, and in the latter case (testacy), they cannot be taken in addition to any bequest under the will.[32] Since the law of Scotland knows no legal rights in heritage, the Scots *lex situs* is immune from any such claim, domestic or foreign.[33]

Collation

18–08 Collation is an equitable doctrine which requires a potential beneficiary, who has received advances from the deceased during his lifetime, to throw these advances notionally into the pot for division if he wishes to participate in that division. Since September 10, 1964, collation in Scots law has been restricted to collation *inter liberos*.[34] In England the equivalent principle was "hotch pot", but the rule was removed from English law by the Law Reform (Succession) Act 1995, section 1(2).

In conflict law, this subject should be regarded, it is submitted, as a matter of substantive succession law, applicable therefore in relation to moveable property if the *lex ultimi domicilii* contains such a rule pertaining to moveable property. With regard to immoveables, the rules of the *lex situs* on the matter will govern.[35]

---

[30] *Bell v Kennedy* (1868) 6 M. (H.L.) 69; *Trevelyan v Trevelyan* (1873) 11 M. 516; *Train v Train's Exrs* (1899) 2 F. 146; *Macdonald v Macdonald*, 1932 S.C. (H.L.) 79; *Re Groos* [1915] 1 Ch. 572.

[31] *Bell v Kennedy* (1868) 6 M. (H.L.) 69: consider *Lashley v Hog* (1804) 4 Pat. 581; *Re Ogilvie* [1918] 1 Ch. 492; *Re Collens (dec'd)* [1986] 1 All E.R. 611.

[32] The claimant is "put to his election". This may not be the case in all legal systems. The matter is one of substance, to be determined by the *lex successionis*. See "approbate and reprobate", below.

[33] Meston, p.135.

[34] See Gloag and Henderson, para.43.06.

[35] *Hay-Balfour v Scotts* (1793) 3 Pat. 300; *Robertson*, February 16, 1816, F.C.; *Robertson v McVean*, February 18, 1817, F.C.; *Dundas v Dundas* (1830) 2 Dow & Cl. 349 H.L.; *Hewitt's Trs v Lawson* (1891) 18 R. 793; *Brodie v Barry* [1813] 3 Ves. & B. 127; *Orrell v Orrell* (1871) 6 Ch. App. 302; *Brown's Trs v Gregson* 1920 S.C. (H.L.) 87.

England

In English domestic law a person who is dissatisfied by the terms of **18–09** a will, and/or the rules of intestacy and who falls within the list of persons named in the relevant legislation, may apply, within six months of the grant of representation, to the court for the making of a discretionary order for payment or property transfer out of the estate, in terms of the Inheritance (Provision for Family and Dependants) Act 1975: the list of parties entitled to claim has been extended by the Law Reform (Succession) Act 1995, section 2(3) to include a cohabitant if the cohabitation has subsisted for at least two years prior to death.[36] These rules, being substantive rules of English domestic succession law, apply where English law is the *lex successionis* (i.e. where the deceased died domiciled in England and Wales).[37]

CAPACITY OF BENEFICIARIES

The law of the deceased's last domicile, as regards moveables, and **18–10** the *lex situs*, as regards immoveables, determine legal capacity to succeed, as well as the substantive matter of class and order of persons who succeed. English cases, however, suggest that the legal capacity of a particular beneficiary to succeed to moveables is governed by the law of the deceased's last domicile *or* the law of his own domicile according to which of those laws he acquired full capacity at the earlier age.[38] There seems no reason why a similar rule should not apply in Scotland.

Capacity to grant a discharge to trustees or executors is governed by the law of the domicile of the beneficiary (moveables) or the *lex situs* (immoveables).[39]

II. INTESTATE SUCCESSION

IMMOVEABLE ESTATE

All questions of succession are governed by the *lex situs*.[40] The **18–11** provisions of the Succession (Scotland) Act 1964 as to the deceased's house (section 8) apply to all cases where a deceased

---

[36] And to civil partners, in terms of s.71 and Sch.4 of the Civil Partnership Act 2004.

[37] *e.g. Gully v Dix* [2004] 1 WLR 1399; *Robinson v Bird* [2003] EWHC 30 (Ch); *Morgan v Cilento*, 2004 EWHC 188; and *Agulian & Another v Cyganit* [2006] EWCA Civ. 129.

[38] *Doglioni v Crispin* (1866) L.R. 1 (HL) 301; *Re Hellman's Will* (1866) L.R. 2 Eq. 363; *Re Goodman's Trusts* (1881) 17 Ch. D. 266; *Re Hall* [1914] P. 1; *Re Schnapper* [1928] Ch. 420; *Re Hagerbaum* [1933] I.R. 198; in Scots law see *Seddon* (1891) 20 R. 675; *Atherstane's Trs* (1896) 24 R. 39; *Webb v Clelland's Trs* (1904) 41 S.L.R. 229; and *Ogilvy v Ogilvy's Trs*, 1927 S.L.T. 83.

[39] *Ogilvy v Ogilvy's Trs*, 1927 S.L.T. 83.

[40] *Nisbett v Nisbett's Trs* (1835) 13 S. 517; *Train* (1899) 2 F. 146; *Fenton v Livingstone* (1859) 3 Macq. 497; *Re Gentili* (1875) L.R. 9 Eq. 541.

person, irrespective of his domicile, died intestate, the owner of a (qualifying) house in Scotland.[41]

MOVEABLE ESTATE

18–12 The rule is that succession is governed by the law[42] of the deceased's domicile at the date of his death,[43] irrespective of the law of the country of birth, death, or domicile of origin or where the moveables are situated. The applicable law is that law (of the domicile) at the date of death, and not after the date of death.[44]

PRIOR RIGHTS

18–13 "Prior rights" is a reference to those rights, introduced in the 1964 Act, which are capable of arising in Scots domestic law in cases of intestacy, and comprise the right of a surviving spouse to:

(a) An interest in a qualifying dwelling-house[45] under section 8 (or to a cash equivalent under section 8(2), which from a conflict viewpoint will be regarded as immoveable also). Where the value of the house exceeds a certain sum (updated from time to time[46]) the survivor is entitled to receive the permitted sum in lieu of the house. This substitute, too, Professor Meston,[47] after consideration, would ascribe to the immoveable category *qua surrogatum*

---

[41] *cf.* Meston, p.133; Leslie, "Prior Rights in Succession: The International Dimension", 1988 S.L.T. (News) 105; *Some Miscellaneous Topics in the Law of Succession*, Scot. Law Com. Memo. No. 71 (1986); and Miller, "Family Provision on Death—The International Dimension" (1990) 39 ICLQ 261.

[42] Which will be a civil law, not a body of religious law, unless the content of the law of the domicile is co-terminous with religious law: *Al-Bassam v Al-Bassam* [2004] EWCA Civ. 857. *cf. Halpern v Halpern* BLD 280306089.

[43] *Brown* (1744) Mor. 4604; *Bruce v Bruce* (1790) 3 Paton 163; *Lashley v Hog* (1804) 4 Paton 182: *Nisbett* (1835) 13 S. 517; *Newlands v Chalmers' Trs* (1832) 11 S. 65; *Maxwell v McClure* (1857) 20 D. 307, affd 3 Macq. 852; *Re Rea* [1902] 11.R. 451; *Lynch v Provisional Government of Paraguay* (1871) LR2P&D 268.

[44] In *Lynch v Provisional Government of Paraguay*, above where a government sought to confiscate assets of the deceased in England and purported to alter the succession after the date of death, such provision was ineffective in England. However, it must be said that such governmental order would not be given effect in a British court for the reason also that it would fall foul of the rule that confiscations *extra territorium* have no effect. Moreover, the qualifying phrase "at death" may have been intended merely to fix the date at which the *domicile* was to be identified.

[45] Defined in s.8(4).

[46] See Prior Rights of Surviving Spouse (Scotland) Order 2005 (SSI 2005/252).

[47] Meston, p.134.

for immoveable, and therefore to regulation by the *lex situs,* i.e. *lex situs* not *lex domicilii* determines entitlement. No right *qua* Scottish prior right nor any *surrogatum* arises if the (otherwise qualifying) dwelling-house is situated outside Scotland.

(b) A right to the furniture and plenishings. This right is classified as a right to moveables, and hence is exigible only if the deceased died domiciled in Scotland. Further, in Dr Leslie's submission, the furniture and plenishings must be those contained in the qualifying dwelling-house which is the subject of section 8, and which must be situated in Scotland.[48]

(c) A right to a cash sum, which, though apparently moveable, is to be borne rateably out of both the heritable and moveable parts of the estate. Hence, if the deceased died domiciled in Scotland, the sum is apportioned between his moveables *wherever situated*, and his heritage *in Scotland*. However, if domiciled outside Scotland, then the whole sum is to be taken from any heritage in Scotland.

CADUCIARY RIGHTS

Difficulties may arise with regard to the succession to assets in **18–14** Scotland in the estate of a person who died, intestate and without relatives, domiciled in a foreign country. The assets may be claimed both by the British Crown, on the basis of claimant to *bona vacantia*, and by the government of the country where the deceased died domiciled, which may claim as a universal successor or heir. In such a case, reference is made to the law of intestate succession in the country of the deceased's domicile, and the right claimed by the foreign government is analysed and classified by the *lex fori*; if it is a true right of succession it will be recognised and its claim preferred, but if it is merely a right to *bona vacantia*, under a *jus regale*, the *lex loci rei sitae* will apply as the matter is one of property law and the right of the foreign (non-*situs*) government

---

[48] Leslie, referring therein to contrary view in Scot. Law Com. Memo. No. 71, para. 6.2: the difference resides in whether one directs attention to the factual qualifications contained in s.8(4) or to the clear territorial restriction imposed by the conflict rule. So, if the deceased spouse died domiciled in Scotland, is the survivor entitled to the furniture and plenishings contained in an otherwise qualifying dwelling-house which is excluded by its foreign situation from forming the subject of a prior right to the house? Answer and authority seems to be absent. Perhaps the balance of the sense of the statute suggests that the house must be in Scotland and the furniture in question must be within it, and for a successful claim to be made by the survivor, the deceased spouse must have died domiciled in Scotland.

will not be recognised,[49] and the estate will fall to the British Crown, *i.e.* exchequer.

The case of *Maldonado*[50] is renowned for the unaccustomed generosity of the forum (the Court of Appeal) in yielding to the foreign law of the domicile the power to classify the nature of its own claim, and accepting that classification, as expressed in the following words: "[t]here might be a case where a so-called right of succession claimed by a foreign State could be shown to be in truth no more than a claim to *bona vacantia* . . . but this has not been shown to be such a case. On the contrary, it has been found (and the Crown has accepted the finding) that the State of Spain is, in the eye of Spanish law, the true heir."[51]

If the foreign rule is simply to the effect of conveying the ownerless property to its fisc, the UK forum *qua situs* would prefer that the property fall into the UK exchequer, and can give effect to that preference. In 1986, the Scottish Law Commission proposed that the claim of the British Crown in such cases should be regarded as a claim in succession, as should the claim of a foreign State of the domicile of the deceased.[52] After consultation, it was decided *not* to recommend any such change, partly because there was no compelling need for it and partly because it would be undesirable to have the State succeed to such property on a different basis in Scotland from that on which it acquired it in England.[53]

III. TESTATE SUCCESSION

INTRODUCTION

18–15 The conflict rules are two dimensional (or three dimensional if one includes the *renvoi* aspect) in the sense that they depend both on *time(s)* (date of execution of the will and date of death) and *place* (situation of immoveable and moveable estate belonging to deceased at death). A will is an inchoate or ambulatory document in that, in the domestic sense, one cannot know a testator's final intention until the date of his death (unless he should lose mental capacity beforehand to such an extent that a later will is invalid or evidence of testamentary intention being lacking) and, in the

---

[49] *Re Barnett* [1902] 1 Ch. 867; *Re Musurus* [1936] 2 All E.R. 1666; *Goold Stuart's Trs v McPhail* 1947 S.L.T. 221; *Re Maldonado* [1954] P. 223.

[50] [1954] P. 223.

[51] Jenkins L.J. at 248–250.

[52] Scot. Law Com. Memo. No. 71 (*Some Miscellaneous Topics in the Law of Succession*) (1986), para.6.13.

[53] See Scot. Law Com. Report No. 124 on Succession (1990), para.10.10.

conflict sense, one cannot know whether the provisions of the will are essentially valid until the date of his death because only then can the legal system of his last domicile, the judge of the provisions, be identified.

CAPACITY OF THE TESTATOR

Legal capacity and proprietary capacity

The conflict rule of Scots law upon legal capacity (*i.e.* age, sanity **18–16** etc) is thought to be[54] that the law of the testator's domicile *at the date of the will*, as regards moveables, and the *lex situs*, as regards immoveables, governs. In domestic law, in the matter of mental capacity, a testator need not be of sufficient mental capacity to test at the date of death: his will made earlier, in time of lucidity, is sufficient.

Proprietary capacity (*i.e.* entitlement to bequeath property), on the other hand, regulating a testator's freedom of testation, is obviously the correlative of the rule on legal rights, and is governed by the testator's domicile *at death* in relation to moveables, and the *lex situs* in relation to immoveables.

The point is well demonstrated by *Re Groos*[55] in which a lady of Dutch domicile made a will before her marriage to another Dutch domiciliary. The terms of the will indicated that her intention was to make her future husband her heir or universal legatee so far as this could be done, in preference to any children who might be born. The will made mention of the children's *legitima portio* under Dutch law, but that potential entitlement never became an actual entitlement in the events which followed. Some years after their marriage, the couple came to England and acquired a domicile there. The testatrix died, survived by her husband and five children. The children could not dispute the terms of their mother's will because her proprietary capacity was judged finally in accordance with her English domicile at death, and by that law had been expanded, since English law at that date permitted freedom of testation. It was established that by Dutch law marriage itself did not revoke a will.[56]

---

[54] The case of *Re Fuld* [1968] P. 675 suggests that legal testamentary capacity is governed by the law of the domicile at the date of execution of the will. Scot. Law Com. Memo. No. 71 at para.6.14 also takes the view that this is or should be the rule. No doubt the matter will be clarified when a suitable legislative opportunity arises. The minimum age of testing in Scots domestic law is 12 years: Age of Legal Capacity (Scotland) Act 1991, s.2(2).

[55] *Re Groos, Groos v Groos* [1915] 1 Ch. 572. (See earlier *In the Estate of Groos* [1904] P. 269.) In the factual circumstances which in the end obtained, the estate by Dutch domestic law should have been distributed in the proportion three quarters to the children as their legitimate portion, and one quarter to the husband.

[56] As to conflict rules pertaining to revocation of a will by marriage, see below.

FORMAL VALIDITY OF WILLS

Common law

18–17 At common law in England, as regards immoveables, a will had to be formally valid according to the *lex situs*, but as regards moveables English law insisted upon compliance with the law of the testator's domicile at the date of his death[57] although as time went on that law was interpreted to include a law recognised by the law of the domicile at the date of death (thereby providing the genesis of *renvoi* thinking in England). In *Bremer v Freeman*[58] a will made in Paris in English form by an Englishwoman then domiciled in England was held to be invalid because it was not also valid by the law of France which was the law of her domicile at the date of her death. The decision showed that a change of domicile could have the effect of invalidating a will as to form. As a result the Wills Act 1861 was passed.

The difficulty referred to in the preceding paragraph did not arise in Scotland,[59] because the conflict rule of Scots common law was that a will was regarded as being formally valid if it had been executed in accordance with any of the following laws, that is as regards:

(a) Immoveables

　　(i) the lex situs

(b) Moveables

　　(i) the law of the place of execution[60];
　　(ii) the law of the testator's domicile at the date of execution of the will;
　　(iii) the law of the testator's domicile at the date of his death.[61]

---

[57] *Bremer v Freeman* (1857) 10 Moore P.C. 306; *Re Groos* [1904] P. 269; *Re Grassi* [1905] 1 Ch. 584; *De Fogassieras v Duport* [1881] 11 I.R.Ir. 123; *Murray v Champernowne* [1901] 2 I.R. 232; *Re Moses* [1908] 2 Ch. 235; *Re Schroeder* [1949] I.R. 89.

[58] (1857) 10 Moo. P.C. 306.

[59] See generally: *Purvis' Trs v Purvis' Exrs* (1861) 23 D. 812; *Connel's Trs v Connel* (1872) 10 M. 627; *Bradford v Young* (1884) 11 R. 1135; *Macdonald v Cuthbertson* (1890) 18 R. 101; *Chisholm v Chisholm*, 1949 S.C. 434; *Irving v Snow*, 1956 S.C. 257.

[60] *Re Purvis's Trs* (1861) 23 D. 812 (will made by Scots domiciliary in the Dutch East Indies).

[61] *cf.* at later date *Chisholm*, 1949 S.C. 434: opinion, *per* Lord Ordinary Guthrie that a will made by a testator then domiciled in England which had been typed and signed, but not witnessed should receive effect in Scotland if it complied with Scots law which was the law of his domicile at the date of his death.

Wills Act 1861 (Lord Kingsdown's Act)

This Act was the result of *Bremer v Freeman* (1857) and was not **18–18** essential as regards Scots law, but it applied to both Scotland and England and provided that:

    (a) a will should not be held to be revoked nor should its construction be altered by reason of a change of domicile of the testator;

    (b) various options against which the formal validity of a will could be tested were provided in addition to the common law rules stated above.

Nevertheless, there remained certain defects in the law.

Wills Act 1963

The law was altered by the Wills Act 1963, which repealed the 1861 **18–19** Act, and came into operation on January 1, 1964 as regards the will of a person who died after that date. The 1963 Act represents the modern law on the subject and is the result of deliberations at the Hague culminating in the 1961 Hague Convention on the Conflict of Laws relating to the Form of Testamentary Dispositions. The Act contains the following rules as to formal validity:

(a) General rule (section 1(1))

A will is to be regarded as validly executed in form if it complies **18–20** with any of the following laws:

    (i) *lex loci actus*—the law of the place of execution[62];

    (ii) *domicile*—the law of the testator's domicile at the date of execution or at his death;

    (iii) *residence*—the law of the testator's habitual residence at the date of execution or at his death;

    (iv) *nationality*—the law of the testator's nationality at the date of execution or at his death (if he was a national of more than one country, then possibly compliance with either (any) of those laws will suffice[63]).

In each case the law in question is the internal law of the country.[64]
    Clearly the list of applicable laws is long and the choice wide, but it is still possible for a testator to err. In *Re Kanani*[65] an English

---

[62] Even if the testator was on a temporary visit there. Cheshire & North, p.988, citing *Re Wynn* [1983] 3 All E.R. 310.

[63] Cheshire & North, p.988; F.A. Mann, "The Formal Validity of Wills in Case of Dual Nationality" (1986) 35 ICLQ 423

[64] s.6(1); though see Morris, p.453.

[65] (1978) 122 S.J. 611.

national and domiciliary, on holiday in Switzerland, made a will written in his own handwriting on the writing paper of his hotel. His death occurred shortly afterwards. The will was invalid as to form because it did not comply with English requirements and, although Swiss law recognised holograph wills, such wills had to be entirely holograph and the printed heading of the hotel on the writing paper was fatal to the will's validity.

(b) Additional rules (section 2)

18–21 A will is also to be regarded as validly executed in form in the following circumstances:

> (i) **Ship or aircraft** (section 2(1)(a)) The internal law of the place of registration of the ship or aircraft or law with which the ship or aircraft is most closely connected, on which ship or aircraft the testator was when he made the will.[66]
>
> (ii) **Immoveables**—the *lex situs* (section 2(1)(b))

(c) Other relevant provisions (sections 2 to 6)

18–22
> (i) **Revocation** (section 2(1)(c)). If a will purports to revoke a will valid in form under the Act, it shall itself be regarded as valid in form and thus revoking the earlier will, if it conforms to any law by reference to which the revoked will would be valid.[67]
>
> (ii) **Powers** (section 2(1)(d), and (2)). If a will exercises a power of appointment, it shall be regarded as valid in form if it conforms with the law governing the essential validity of the power. Further, (section 2(2)), a will which exercises a power of appointment shall not be treated as improperly executed by reason only that its execution was not in accordance with any formal requirements contained in the instrument creating the power.[68]
>
> (iii) **Foreign law** (section 3). Where a law in force outside the United Kingdom falls to be applied in relation to a will, any requirement of that law, whereby special formalities are to be observed by testators of a particular description, or

---

[66] If the aircraft was on the ground, or the ship in territorial waters, it will be sufficient that the testator complied with the law of the place of execution (Cheshire & North, p.988). In the alternative, the testator may comply with the law of closest connection.

[67] Hence, a will dealing with immoveables and valid by the *lex situs* will be revoked by a later will valid by the *lex situs* (not therefore the *Alberti* situation [1955] 1 W.L.R. 1240).

[68] This is a notably generous rule, demonstrating *dépeçage*.

witnesses are to possess certain qualifications, shall be treated as a formal requirement only.

(iv) **Construction** (section 4). The construction of a will shall not be altered by reason of any change of domicile of the testator after the date of execution of the will.

(v) **Interpretation** (section 6). This section defines *inter alia* "internal law" as the law which would apply in a case where no question of the law in force in any other territory or state arose.[69] Section 6(2) provides a solution where doubt arises in a multi-legal system state about which law to apply as the "internal law".

"International wills"

The Administration of Justice Act 1982, section 27 (not yet in force) provides that the Annex to the Convention on International Wills, concluded at Washington on October 26, 1973, shall have the force of law in the UK. **18–23**

> "The Annex is set out in Schedule 2 to the Act. It provides in article 1 that a will shall be valid as regards form, irrespective of the place where it was made, of the location of the assets and of the nationality, domicile or residence of the testator, if it complies with articles 2 to 5. The will must be in writing and signed or acknowledged by the testator in the presence of two witnesses and of an 'authorised person' (a solicitor or notary public: section 28) who must then attest the will in the presence of the testator. The authorised person must attach to the will a certificate in the form prescribed by article 10 authenticating the will and its due execution. The will may (but need not) be deposited for safe custody in the Principal Registry of the Family Division. That Registry will keep a list of the states which have ratified the Washington Convention and will keep district probate registries informed."[70]

A UNIDROIT Convention on the Establishment of a Scheme of Registration of Wills was drawn up at Basle in 1972,[71] with the aim of reaching agreement on a form of will which would have *international validity*. Provisions (Administration of Justice Act 1982, sections 23 to 25, not yet in force) are in place to allow the UK to comply with its requirements and thereby to ratify. This therefore is something of a dead letter.

---

[69] *i.e.* there is to be no scope for *renvoi* in matters covered by the Act (in the subject area which gave rise to *renvoi*). But the matter is to be revisited in the Green Paper.

[70] Morris and North, *Cases and Materials on Private International Law*, p.581.

[71] Dicey and Morris, 27–037/8.

However, the impetus towards some type of *international register* of wills (misguided though this is[72]) has been resurrected in the Green Paper.

DUTY OF A SOLICITOR TO ACT TIMEOUSLY UPON INSTRUCTIONS TO MAKE A WILL

18–24 Such duty will be categorised, and its existence tested, as a matter of potential *delictual* liability. The conflict aspect of the subject must be governed therefore by the applicable law determined in accordance with Private International Law (Miscellaneous Provisions) Act 1995, sections 11 and 12.[73]

ESSENTIAL VALIDITY OF WILLS

18–25 The essential validity of a will, that is, the validity of its provisions as to devolution of property, is governed by the proper law of the will, which, in general terms, in the case of immoveables is the *lex situs*,[74] and in the case of moveables is the law of the testator's domicile, both at the date of his death.

Essential validity is concerned with all matters pertaining to the validity and enforceability of the provisions of a will. Thus it deals with the extent to which the provisions of a will are valid, or may be affected adversely by any of the following matters:

   (a) the extent to which the provisions are affected by statutory provisions as to accumulation of capital and income, and perpetuities[75];
   (b) claims for legal rights[76];
   (c) conditions as to marriage or religion attached to bequests[77];
   (d) bequests contrary to public policy;
   (e) bequests for religious or charitable purposes[78];

---

[72] This idea has only superficial attractions, and is subject to many flaws. Upon whom would the duty lie to register a will? What would be the effect of failure to register? Would a registered will trump a subsequent unregistered will? Such a register inevitably would be partial and unsatisfactory.

[73] See for England, H.L. decision in *White v Jones* [1993] 3 All E.R. 481 and in Scotland, *Holmes v Bank of Scotland*, 2002 S.L.T. 544.

[74] *Philipson-Stow v IRC* [1961] A.C. 727; see earlier *Nelson v Bridport* (1846) 8 Beav. 547 and *Re Miller* [1914] 1 Ch. 511.

[75] *Fordyce v Bridges* (1848) 2 Ph. 497.

[76] *Re Groos* [1915] 1 Ch. 572.

[77] *Ommanney v Bingham* (1936) 3 Paton 448.

[78] *Boe v Anderson* (1862) 24 D. 732; *Ferguson v Marjoribanks* (1853) 15 D. 637; *Hewit's Trs v Lawson* (1891) 18 R. 793; *Re Elliot* (1891) 39 W.R. 297; *Re De Noailles* (1916) 114 L.T. 1089; *Re Egan* (1918) LJ 633; *Re Dawson* [1915] 1 Ch. 626.

(f) the extent to which provisions may be affected by considerations of capital transfer tax/inheritance tax[79];

(g) proof of survival[80];

(h) the operation of the *conditio si testator sine liberis decesserit*[81];

(i) election, or approbate and reprobate[82];

(j) lapse of testamentary gifts to spouse upon the occurrence of subsequent divorce or annulment[83]; and

(k) rules of forfeiture ("the unworthy heir").[84]

The distinction between formal validity and essential validity is clear in theory, but in exceptional cases, it may not be easy to distinguish between them. In the case of *Re Priest*,[85] the English forum classified its own rule that bequests would be rendered void if the will in which they were made was witnessed by the spouse of a beneficiary, as a rule of substance, governed, therefore, by the testator's last domicile.[86]

CONSTRUCTION OR INTERPRETATION

Just as the distinction between formal validity and essential validity **18–26** is clear in theory, but occasionally the one aspect may tend to merge with the other, in the same way, the distinction between essential validity and construction in practice may tend to con-

---

[79] *Philipson-Stow v IRC* [1961] A.C. 727; *Levick's Will Trusts* [1963] 1 W.L.R. 311. British capital transfer tax/inheritance tax is payable on transfers of property (unless it falls below the exemption limits): (a) made by a deceased who died domiciled in the UK no matter where the property was situated, and (b) situated in the UK no matter where the deceased died domiciled. See statutory extension of meaning of domicile (extending to residence in the UK in 17 out of the previous 20 years of assessment): Inheritance Tax Act 1984, s.267. Transfers of value between spouses are exempt (Inheritance Tax Act 1984, s.18(1)), but if only the transferor spouse is domiciled in the UK the transfer is only partially exempt. See D.R. Macdonald, *Succession* (3rd ed., 2001), para.12.26.

[80] *Re Cohn* [1945] Ch. 5.

[81] But see Anton (1st ed.), p.536 and Anton with Beaumont, pp.694–695; but see again R.D. Leslie, *Stair Memorial Encyclopaedia*, p.348.

[82] *Re Ogilvie* [1918] 1 Ch. 492. See *Hewit's Trs v Lawson* (1891) 18 R. 793.

[83] Such a provision was enacted for English domestic law in the Law Reform (Succession) Act 1995, and applicable therefore by this reasoning where the gift was of moveable property and the deceased died domiciled in England, or where the gift was of immoveable property situated in England.

[84] See *Re DWS (deceased)* [2001] 1 All E.R. 97: further, and criticism thereof Law Com. No. 295 (2005).

[85] [1944] Ch. 58.

[86] See also *Irving v Snow*, 1956 S.C. 257, in which a will, though null and void under Scots law because of the prohibition on notarial execution by a party interested in the will, was held to have been validly executed since it satisfied the English legal requirements of the *lex loci actus*.

verge. The importance of the distinction lies in the fact that essential validity is governed by the law prevailing at the date of death, whereas construction is governed by the law intended by the testator, which may or may not be the same.

Construction answers the question—what do the provisions *mean*?

Essential validity answers the question—*to what extent* are the provisions of a will *valid and enforceable*?

The general principle is that a will must be construed in accordance with the law by reference to which it was written, that is, the legal system contemplated by the testator, which may or may not be the same as the proper law of the will. The testator's intention, deemed or actual, is the paramount consideration[87] and will take precedence over the law of his domicile[88] or the *lex situs* of his property.[89] English authorities are *Philipson-Stow v IRC*[90] and *Levick*.[91] In *Philipson-Stow*, Lord Denning said "whilst I would agree that the *construction* of the will depends on the intention of the testator, I would say that in no other respect does his intention determine the law applicable to it".[92]

The following are working rules:

(1) If there is an express declaration as to the law to be applied, that law normally will regulate the construction of the will.

(2) In the absence of such a declaration, the law to be applied may be clearly inferred from the language of the will.[93] The use of technical terms of a particular law usually indicates that the will should be construed by that law.[94]

In the special case of a will dealing with a bequest of immoveables expressed in the technical terms of the law of a country other than the *lex situs*, the meaning of the will is first ascertained according to the law indicated by the will

---

[87] *Re Nesbitt* [1953] 1 W.L.R. 595 (domestic case); *Re Scott* [1915] 1 Ch. 592 (conflict case).

[88] *Re Allen* [1945] 2 All E.R. 264.

[89] *Mitchell & Baxter v Davies* (1875) 3 R. 208; *Smith* (1891) 18 R. 1036; *McBride's Trs*, 1952 S.L.T. (Notes) 59; *Re Price* [1900] 1 Ch. 442 (subject always to the ultimate practical pre-eminence of the *lex situs*).

[90] [1961] A.C. 727.

[91] [1963] 1 W.L.R. 311.

[92] [1961] A.C. 727, HL at 760–761. As to the future availability, if any, of party autonomy in succession, see Green Paper.

[93] *Re Goetze* [1953] Ch. 96; *Re Cunnington* [1924] 1 Ch. 68; *Re Price* [1900] 1 Ch. 442, *per* Stirling J. at 453; *Re Allen's Estate* [1945] 2 All E.R. 264.

[94] *Re McMorran* [1958] Ch. 624; *Re Manners* [1923] 1 Ch. 220; but see *Bradford v Young* (1885) 29 Ch. D. 617 in which the use of some technical terms of Scots law was held by the CA, disapproving court below, to be insufficient indication of the testator's intention to have the will construed by that law.

and the court then endeavours to translate it and give effect to it in terms which will make sense and be effective according to the *lex situs*.[95]

(3) If a will is expressed in popular language which gives no guide as to its construction, it will be construed according to the *lex fori*.[96]

(4) Otherwise, there is a presumption that the law of the testator's domicile at the date of the will shall apply as regards moveables and probably also as regards immoveables because presumably he had that law in mind.[97] In exceptional cases, however, if the language of the will does not clearly indicate any particular law, the law of the domicile at the date of death has been applied.[98]

(5) The Wills Act 1963, section 4, which repeats in substance the corresponding provisions of the 1861 Act, provides that the construction of a will is not to be affected by a change of domicile.

The width and variety of these "rules" (or guides) suggest that it is more important to be aware of the distinction between essentials and construction, to note that the *lex successionis* may not necessarily be the law which governs construction, and to be cognisant of those matters which have been assigned to the category of "interpretation", than to place great reliance on any one of the "presumptions".

Conflict problems involving the following matters are solved by the application of the rules as to construction:

(a) whether a will in general terms exercises a power of appointment;

(b) application of *conditio si institutus sine liberis decesserit*.

In *Mitchell & Baxter v Davies*[99] the question was of the type to which the Scottish *conditio si institutus sine liberis decesserit* applies, and having been assigned by the Scots forum to the category of "interpretation", was referred to the Scots law of the will, rather than to the English law of the deceased's last domicile.

(c) accretion or intestacy as a result of the absence of a survivorship clause or a destination-over.

---

[95] *Studd v Cook* (1883) 10 R. (HL) 53; *Cripps' Trs v Cripps*, 1926 S.C. 188; *Re Miller* [1914] 1 Ch. 511.

[96] *Griffith's J.F. v Griffith's Exrs* (1905) 7 F. 470.

[97] *Philipson-Stow v IRC* [1961] A.C. 727, *per* Lord Denning at 761–762 (so long as the construction does not conflict with the rules of the *lex situs*).

[98] *Re Cunnington* [1924] 1 Ch. 68: French domicile *qua* domicile at death applied. But the testator's domicile at testing was unclear. However, the will in question was made only four years before his death when it might be assumed his domicile was likely to be French.

[99] (1875) 3 R. 208.

The question whether accretion to the survivors of a list of eight residuary legatees (as was the French rule), or whether the shares of the two predeceasers, neither of whom had left issue, should fall into intestacy (the English rule), was classified by the English forum, in the case of *Re Cunnington*,[1] as a matter of interpretation. The case illustrates also the relative weakness of the "working rules" to identify the law which should regulate interpretation since the French law of the domicile at death was taken to be the law governing construction, there being no indication to the contrary.

Construction of destinations

18–27 To determine the validity of a claim of a beneficiary in testate succession, it will be necessary to ascertain, according to the law governing interpretation of the will, the testator's intention with regard to that beneficiary or class of beneficiaries, but there may arise thereafter the separate issue of ascertaining the status of the claimant (ie whether he qualifies as a member of that class, eg of the legitimate/legitimated).

If the destination is to the "heirs", "children", "issue", "next-of-kin", etc., of a *named beneficiary*, the question whether a particular person falls within that class is determined by the law regulating his status. The law to which the latter question should be referred may be the subject of controversy. If the succession to the estate of X, domiciled in country A, opens only to the legitimate children of Y, domiciled in country B, and a question arises as to whether or not a person is a legitimate child of Y, by which law is such a question determined? Scots and English conflict rules diverge in this matter. Scots law favours the application of B law[2] to determine the status of the children of Y,[3] whereas English law prefers application of A law[4] (in each case subject to the respect necessarily paid to the *lex situs* or law of a title).

If the destination is to the "heirs", "children", "issue", "next-of-kin", etc. of the *testator*, the beneficiaries are identified by the *lex domicilii* of the testator, usually the same law as that which governs the interpretation of the will.

---

[1] [1924] 1 Ch. 68.
[2] See Family Law (Scotland) Act 2006, s.41.
[3] *Mitchell's Trs v Rule*, 1908 S.L.T. 189; *Smith's Trs v Macpherson's Trs*, 1926 S.C. 983; *Goold Stuart's Trs v McPhail*, 1947 S.L.T. 221; *Spencer's Trs v Ruggles*, 1981 S.C. 289; *Wright's Trs v Callander*, 1993 S.L.T. 556; *Salvesen's Trs*, 1993 S.L.T. 1327. See Crawford, 1994 S.L.T. (News) 225 and Leslie, 1995 S.L.T. (News) 264. In *Spencer's Trs*, above, the question at issue was whether adopted children could succeed but since it was established that the testator did not intend to benefit adopted children, the second stage of debating by which law the validity of a foreign adoption should be judged was not reached.
[4] *Campbell v Campbell* (1866) L.R. 1 Eq. 383; *Re Fergusson's Will* [1902] 1 Ch. 483.

REVOCATION OF WILLS

It is necessary to consider the effect upon a will of a later will, of **18–28** the marriage of the testator, of a change of domicile, etc. The following cases must be noted.

(a) New will

The revocation of the old will depends on the validity and scope of **18–29** the new will.[5]

This simple and obvious statement contains within it a number of difficulties, for example as to the scope of the new will, and its validity as to form and essence. It is possible that the new will may be formally defective with regard to the testator's immoveable property, with the result that a prior will (if extant), valid by the *lex situs*, may continue to regulate the immoveable succession, while the new will regulates the succession to moveables.[6] The matter alternatively might be one of inference and interpretation, as when, without express revocation, the testator makes provision in a later will in relation to property included in an earlier one.

Further, a will may be regarded as having been revoked in one country, but not in another.[7] If the testator has assets in different countries, the *lex situs* in each case will prevail and will decide which will is to be regarded as the last will as regards assets within its jurisdiction. It follows that different wills may relate to assets in different countries. This can be seen in *Re Manifold*.[8]

---

[5] *Cameron v Mackie* (1833) 7 W. & S. 16; *Cottrell* (1872) L.R. 2 P. & D. 397.

[6] *Re Alberti* [1955] 1 W.L.R. 1240.

[7] *Richmond's Trs v Winton* (1864) 3 M. 95.

[8] [1962] Ch. 1. A testatrix domiciled in Cyprus made two wills, the first valid by the laws of England and Cyprus, and the second valid only by the law of England. Probate was granted on the first will in Cyprus, but it was held that, as regards assets in England, the Wills Act 1861 must have an overriding effect and that probate must be granted on both wills. Thereafter, the administrators in England of the English estate were directed to distribute the assets in England according to the terms of the later will, on the basis that it had, in the English view, superseded the earlier will, and as if the assets in England were the whole estate, the legacies to abate rateably so far as necessary. In the case of *Re Alberti* [1955] 1 W.L.R. 1240 a testator made a will in England dealing, *inter alia*, with real estate in England. Later he made a holograph will in Switzerland which was invalid by English law although valid by the *lex loci* and which purported to revoke all previous wills. It was held that the English will was still effective as regards the English real estate because only a will valid by the *lex situs* could revoke the earlier will. A different outcome now would transpire, but simply because of the expansion of laws governing formal validity of wills, rather than by operation of Wills Act 1963, s.2(1)(c).

(b) A revocation clause

18–30 The effect of such a clause is considered in light of all the circumstances.[9]

Again this seems a very broad guide, but it can happen on occasion that the circumstances reveal quite clearly what was the testator's intention. Thus, in *Re Wayland*[10] where the testator had separate wills to deal with his English and his Belgian estate, it was apparent that when he made a new English will, its revocation clause was intended to apply only to previous English wills. Before and after making that new English will, he corresponded with his Belgian lawyer about the safekeeping of his Belgian will.

(c) Acts involving revocation

18–31 The effectiveness of a purported act of revocation depends upon the law of the testator's domicile at the date of the revocation.

An excellent example is provided by *Velasco v Coney*[11]: the English testatrix, who had taken Italian domicile on marriage, instructed her English solicitor to destroy her will, previously made by her in accordance with both English and Italian law. This he did, but not in her presence as required by English law. The English court decided that such an act of revocation was sufficient to satisfy its conflict rules if the act amounted to revocation by the domicile of the testatrix at the date of the act of purported revocation—a practical decision, and the policy of the court being to "lean towards giving effect to the intention of the testatrix." By Italian law, her letter or mandate containing her instructions to revoke would have been sufficient even without the physical destruction which in fact happened.

(d) Change of domicile

18–32 This has no effect, as to form or construction of the will.[12]

However, change of domicile is of fundamental importance in the final outcome, for the essential validity of the will falls to be judged by a testator's last domicile.[13]

---

[9] *Re Barker* [1995] 2 V.R. 439: the question whether extrinsic evidence may be adduced to prove the intention of the testator with regard to the revocation of an earlier will in so far as the latter dealt with property in another country is a matter of evidence to be determined by the *lex fori* and a matter of construction to be determined by the law of testator's domicile.

[10] [1951] 2 All E.R. 1041.

[11] [1934] P. 143.

[12] Wills Act 1963, s.4.

[13] *Re Groos, Groos v Groos* [1915] 1 Ch. 572.

(e) Subsequent marriage

The effect of the marriage of the testator upon a previous will is **18–33** determined by the law of the domicile of the testator immediately after the marriage.[14]

Any rule of revocation by subsequent marriage is regarded in Scots and English conflict rules as a matter of matrimonial law rather than the law of succession.[15] Since the domestic laws of Scotland and England differ on this matter, though their conflict rules agree, this means, in an English/Scottish context, that if a testator domiciled in England makes a will before his marriage, and is of English domicile immediately after marriage, the will is revoked and cannot revive on subsequent acquisition of Scots domicile. *Contra*, the English courts will uphold any will made by a Scots domiciliary before marriage even though he may die domiciled in England, provided that his immediate post-nuptial domicile was Scottish.[16]

By English domestic law, an ante-nuptial will is revoked by marriage of the testator, unless the will was made in contemplation of that marriage. Marriage *per se* does not revoke by Scots law an earlier made will, but if children are born, no provision having been made in the will for such an eventuality, it will be open to them to seek to have applied the presumption *conditio si testator sine liberis decesserit*. The *conditio si testator* or equivalent in a conflict context is regarded as a matter of substance, available, therefore, in the Scots view only if such a rule forms part of the domestic succession law of the *lex successionis* (ie being Scots law, or any law containing an equivalent provision).

CONVERSION

Conversion (rules to be applied to determine the nature of property where immoveables have been converted into money or *vice versa*) is determined, it would seem, by the law of the testator's domicile at the date of his death and not by the *lex situs*.[17]

---

[14] Its effect upon any provisions in respect of immoveables must surely be determined by *lex situs* (*Re Caithness* (1890) 7 T.L.R. 354).

[15] *Westerman v Schwab* (1905) 8 F. 132; *Re Martin* [1900] P. 211; *cf. Re Groos* [1915] 1 Ch. 572.

[16] *Re Reid* (1866) L.R. 1 P. & D. 74.

[17] *Hall's Trs v Hall* (1854) 16 D. 1057. See para.18–13, above, in relation to prior rights and *surrogatum*.

APPROBATE AND REPROBATE OR ELECTION

18–34 The question whether or not a beneficiary must elect between a bequest under a will and an interest outside the will is determined by the law of the testator's domicile at the date of his death,[18] subject to the view of the *lex situs* as regards foreign land.[19]

POWERS OF APPOINTMENT AND POWERS OF APPORTIONMENT[20]

18–35 A testator may give to his executors a power to deal with the estate or part of it, as the latter may decide. This may serve the purpose of a trust without going so far as to create a trust.

General and special powers

Terms: Donor, donee, appointee

18–36 *Conflict problems*: Are the capacity of the donee and the validity of the exercise of a power in form and essentials to be governed by the law of the will conferring the power or by the law of the domicile of the donee or by the law of the will by which the power is exercised? Must the law of the power also be the law of its exercise?[21] Lord Justice-Clerk Thomson in *Durie's Trs v Osborne*[22] expressed the matter as follows: the question is whether we should regard the donee as a free agent exercising the choice given to him by a testament in accordance with his own law, or as "a cog in the machinery of the donor's deed. In sheer logic there is much to be said for both views", but if intention be the vital matter, "it seems better to look to a man's own law than to one arbitrarily imposed on him". In the absence of specific indications to the contrary, there is no reason why it should be assumed that the donor intended to dictate that only his law should apply. The Lord Justice-Clerk in that case was hesitant about the use in Scotland of the more ample English authority in this area.

---

[18] *cf. Re Allen's Estate* [1945] 2 All E.R. 264 (interest outside the will consisted of rights under South African community of property. Husband/testator died domiciled in South Africa, and wife was put to her election between provisions to which she was entitled under community and under will, respectively).

[19] *Murray v Smith* (1828) 6 S. 690; *Alexander v Bennet's Trs* (1829) 7 S. 817; *Hewit's Trs v Lawson* (1891) 18 R. 793; *Brown's Trs v Gregson*, 1920 S.C. (H.L.) 87; *Trotter v Trotter* (1829) 3 Wils. & Sh. 407; *Dundas v Dundas* (1830) 2 Dow & Cl. 349; *Douglas Menzies v Umphelby* [1908] A.C. 224; *Re Ogilvie* [1918] 1 Ch. 492; *Allen's Estate* [1945] 2 All E.R. 264; *Re Mengel* [1962] Ch. 791.

[20] See generally Barr, Biggar, Dalgleish and Stevens, *Drafting Wills in Scotland* (2005) .

[21] See Lord Justice-Clerk Moncrieff in *Kennion v Buchan's Trs* (1880) 7 R. 570 at 573, quoting in turn Lord Brougham in *Tatnall v Hankey*, 2 Moore P.C. 342.

[22] 1961 S.L.T. 53 at 61.

General powers or *powers of appointment* (unrestricted choice to be exercised by donee) as distinguished from *Special powers* or *powers of apportionment* (donee's choice restricted to particular class of persons).

The general principles to be elicited from English and Scottish authorities are as follows.[23]

General powers

The fund is regarded as being the property of the donee, so that **18–37** the same rules apply to a deed by the donee exercising the power, as to the donee's own will.[24]

Special powers

This is more usual, since a wide discretion in the form of a general **18–38** power might be void as a delegation to another of the power to test.

The fund is regarded as being still the property of the donor or his trustees and the donee as his or their agent so that the validity of a deed exercising the power is governed by the same rules as apply to the original will of the donor. The *lex situs* will apply as regards immoveables to all aspects except form and construction.

The undernoted rules state the position only as regards moveables:

Capacity

The exercise of the power will be valid if the donee has capacity by **18–39** the law of his domicile, but it may be sufficient that he has capacity by the law of the trust. This will certainly be the case as regards a special power.[25]

Formal validity

It is sufficient both as regards general and special powers that any **18–40** deed exercising the power comply with the law of the trust or any law by which the donee's own will would be formally valid.[26] The provisions of the Wills Act 1963 as to the various permissible forms apply to wills exercising powers and section 2(2) provides that a

---

[23] And see further Anton with Beaumont, pp.696–698.
[24] See *Durie's Trs v Osborne*, 1961 S.L.T. 53, following *Anderson v Collins* (1913) 1 S.L.T. 219.
[25] *Gould v Lewal* [1918] 2 Ch. 391; *Re Langley's Settlement Trusts* [1962] Ch. 541.
[26] *Kennion v Buchan's Trs* (1880) 7 R. 570; *Anderson v Collins* (1913) 1 S.L.T. 219— ruling law that of donee; *Durie's Trs v Osborne*, 1961 S.L.T. 53; *Re Price* [1900] 1 Ch. 442; *Barretto v Young* [1900] 2 Ch. 339; *Re Wilkinson's Settlement* [1917] 1 Ch. 620; or perhaps the *lex situs*: Anton with Beaumont, p.696.

will exercising a power is not to be treated as having been improperly executed merely because it does not comply with formal requirements of the deed conferring the power.

Essential validity

General powers

18–41 The essential validity of a will exercising a general power is determined by the law of the will itself, that is, the law of the testator's domicile at the date of his death, as regards moveables.[27] The law of the will conferring the power is irrelevant in this case. The *lex situs* applies as regards immoveables.

Special powers

18–42 The essential validity of a will exercising such a power is determined by the law (that is the proper law) governing the deed which confers the powers.

Construction

The following presumptions apply.

General powers

18–43 A will exercising such power is construed according to the law which governs the construction of the will itself[28] (not the deed conferring the power), that is, it is presumed that the law of the testator's/donee's domicile applies. That law determines whether a will in general terms without mentioning a power in fact operates as an exercise of the power.[29]

Special powers

18–44 According to the older English cases the rule is that the construction of a deed exercising a special power must be governed by the law conferring the power.

Revocation

18–45 A deed revoking the exercise of a power will be effective (*i.e.* as regards essentials) if it complies with either the law of the deed conferring the power or the law of the donee's domicile at the date of revocation.[30]

---

[27] *Pouey v Hordern* [1900] Ch. 492; *Re Pryce* [1911] 2 Ch. 286; *Re Waite's Settlement Trust* [1958] Ch. 100; *Re Khan* [1965] 3 W.L.R. 1291.

[28] *Durie's Trs v Osborne*, 1961 S.L.T. 53; *Re Price* [1900] 1 Ch. 442; *Re Khan* [1965] 3 W.L.R. 1291; *Gould v Lewal* [1918] 2 Ch. 391; *Re McMorran* [1958] Ch. 624; *Re Waite's Settlement Trust* [1958] Ch. 100; *Re Fenston's Settlement* [1971] 1 W.L.R. 1640.

[29] Though see further Anton with Beaumont, p.697.

[30] *Velasco v Coney* [1934] P. 143.

TRUST ESTATES

Common law

Prior to the Recognition of Trusts Act 1987, the following were the **18–46** common law principles.

(a) Domicile

Most matters were governed by what was known for convenience **18–47** as the "domicile" of the trust, that is, the proper law of the trust deed or the law of the country with which it had the closest connection. Thus, it was the court of the domicile of the trust which had jurisdiction to determine an application to vary the trust purposes under the Trusts (Scotland) Act 1961.[31] Broadly speaking, the law of the domicile of a trust would be the law of the country in which the testator's will was lodged and a grant of confirmation or probate was first obtained, *i.e.* from the court of his last domicile.

(b) Capacity to create a trust

The *lex situs* applied as regards heritage[32]; otherwise the law of the **18–48** granter's domicile would apply.

(c) Formal validity

It was sufficient that the deed comply with either the proper law of **18–49** the trust or the law of the place of execution.[33]

(d) Essential validity

Trustees' powers and variation of trust purposes were governed by **18–50** the law of the domicile of the trust. So too were matters of construction.

(e) Change of domicile

In exceptional cases the domicile of a trust might be changed.[34] **18–51**

---

[31] As to what constitutes a Scottish trust see Duncan and Dykes, *Principles of Civil Jurisdiction* (1911), p. 213 quoted with approval by Lord President Clyde in *Clarke's Trs*, 1966 S.L.T. 249 at 251. As to domicile of a trust under the 1968 Convention and the 1982 Act, see Anton and Beaumont, p.116. As to definition of trust for the purposes of Recognition of Trusts Act 1987, see Sch. to the Act, Art.2.

[32] *Black*, 1950 S.L.T. (Notes) 32.

[33] *Thomson v Thomson* (1917) Sh. Ct Rep. 84; *Re Pilkington's Will Trusts* [1937] 1 Ch. 574.

[34] Cheshire (8th ed.), pp.577–578; Anton (1st ed.), p.481; *Duke of Marlborough v Att.-Gen.* [1945] Ch. 78; *Baroness Lloyd*, 1963 S.L.T. (Notes) 40; *Seale's Marriage Settlement* [1961] Ch. 574; *Weston's Settlements* [1969] 1 Ch. 223; *Re Windeatt's Will Trusts, Petr* [1969] 1 W.L.R. 692.

(f) Sales of Scots Heritage by English Trustees

18–52 The powers of sale conferred upon Scots and English trustees by the Scots and English Trusts Acts applied only to Scots and English trustees and land in Scotland and England respectively. If an English will did not confer express power[35] of sale, power to sell land in Scotland might be obtained at the discretion of the court by procedure as follows[36] in two stages.

> (1) in England the trustees applied to the Court of Chancery for power to apply to the Court of Session, which would normally be granted if it was considered expedient and in the interests of the trust estate to do so;[37]
>
> (2) in Scotland the trustees then applied to the Court of Session craving power of sale under the *nobile officium*.

Retrospective sanction was not usually granted.[38] Whether this procedure, after the advent of the Recognition of Trusts Act 1987,[39] is still required is, on the best authority, unclear.[40]

Recognition of Trusts Act 1987[41]

18–53 The Act applies to trusts regardless of their date of creation, subject to individual state reservation and to the *caveat* that the Act shall not affect the law governing acts or omissions of trustees before the coming into force of the Act on August 1, 1987.

---

[35] If power express, no further authorisation from a Scots court was required: *Phipps v Phipps's Trs* (1914) 1 S.L.T. 239 (though there the trustee's power to sell Scottish heritage was not express but deduced by inference from the testator's use of the words "all other my real estate whatsoever, wheresoever").

[36] See, *e.g.* the following: *Allan's Trs* (1896) 24 R. 238 and 718; *Pender's Trs* (1903) 5 F. 504 and 1907 S.C. 207; *Harris's Trs*, 1919 S.C. 432; *Laurie's Trs, Petrs* 1946 S.L.T. (Notes) 31; *Campbell-Wyndham-Long's Trs Petrs*, 1952 S.L.T. 43; *Prudential Ass. Co.*, 1952 S.L.T. 121; Anton (1st ed.), pp.483–484.

[37] *Forrest* (1910) 54 S.J 737; *Georges* (1921) 65 S.J 311.

[38] *Dow's Trs, Petrs*, 1947 S.L.T. 293; *Prudential Ass. Co.*, 1952 S.L.T. 121.

[39] The Act applies within the constituent parts of the UK as well as outside the UK, though it is not comprehensive in the matter of choice of law in relation to trusts (Art.14; Art.15). While the applicable law of the trust (determined by Arts 6 and 7) shall govern its validity, construction, effects, administration, and in particular *inter alia* the power of trustees to administer or to dispose of trust assets, to create security interests therein or to acquire new assets (Art.8(d)), Anton with Beaumont, pp.630 *et seq.* note the limiting "thread" of its provisions, namely that "the validity of such an instrument or contract would require to be assessed under its *lex causae* or proper law" (p.635).

[40] Anton and Beaumont at p.643, quoting informal view of Halliday; Halliday, *Conveyancing Law and Practice* (2nd ed., 1997, by Talman), para.2-83.

[41] See Dicey and Morris, Ch.29; J. Harris, "The Hague Trust Convention" (Hart Publishing, 2002); and D. Hayton, "The Hague Convention on the Law Applicable to Trusts and on their Recognition" (1987) 36 ICLQ 260.

This Act has given effect in UK law to the 1986 Hague Convention on the Law Applicable to Trusts and on their Recognition, the purpose of which is to "ensure the international recognition of trusts and to obtain the adoption by States (even those which do not themselves have the trust concept)" [42] of a uniform choice of law rule relating to the validity, and many other aspects, of trusts.

In terms of section 1(1), the provisions of the Convention as set out in the Schedule to the Act shall have the force of law in the U.K. Section 1(2): those provisions shall, so far as applicable, have effect not only in relation to the trusts described in Articles 2 and 3 of the Convention, but also in relation to any other trusts of property arising under the law of any part of the United Kingdom or by virtue of a judicial decision whether in the United Kingdom or elsewhere.

The definition of "trust" in Article 2 of the Schedule to the Act is designed not only to cover the notion of trust in the Anglo-American legal systems and the different notions in other systems such as Scotland, but also "trust-like concepts", yet to develop.

The statutory rules are not concerned with preliminary issues relating to the testamentary instrument which purports to convey assets to a trust (Article 4).

A trust shall be governed by the law chosen by the settlor, expressly or impliedly (Article 6), or, failing such choice, by the law of closest connection (Article 7). That law (Article 8) shall govern the validity, construction, effects and administration of the trust, and in particular shall govern matters itemised in a list ((a) to (j)) in Article 8, including appointment and removal of trustees, their rights among themselves, rights to administer and dispose of trust assets, to create security interests in the trust assets[43] or to acquire new assets, powers of investment, and liability of trustees to beneficiaries. It will be remembered[44] that Article 8 does not always supply the answer.

If the law identified as a result of the application of Article 7 has no knowledge of the trust concept, the Convention "self-destructs",[45] and shall not apply (Article 5); if such a result should happen after express or implied choice, then Article 7 must apply to identify the appropriate law.

Article 11 enjoins recognition of trusts falling within the scope of the Convention and the Act, and regulates the effect of such

---

[42] R.D. Leslie, "Trusts in Private International Law: Recognition of Trusts Act 1987" (1988) 33 J.L.S.S. 27 (see also A.E. Anton, "The Recognition of Trusts Act 1987", 1987 S.L.T. (News) 377–385).

[43] Would there be *Romalpa* problems? See saving clause in favour of the *lex situs* in Art.15(d).

[44] See above discussion of powers of English/Scottish trustees to purchase Scottish/English land at para.18–52, above.

[45] Raymond Smith, 5/90.

recognition.[46] In this way, the provisions are consistent with the title of the Act, albeit that the Act, despite its name, is concerned primarily with choice of law.

These rules apply in suitable cases in the UK court whether or not the trust arises under the law of a contracting state, and also within the UK, but only to "trusts created voluntarily and evidenced in writing" (Article 3).[47]

SUMMARY 18—THE LAW OF SUCCESSION

Testate and Intestate Succession

1. Confirmation

18–54 The Scots courts follow the law of the domicile of the deceased as regards title to administer moveables. If probate or letters of administration have been granted under that law, confirmation is granted to the same persons as executors for the purposes of estate in Scotland. If there has been no grant of administration, the person entitled to appointment under the law of the domicile is confirmed to deal with property in Scotland. In the absence of statutory provision, a foreign executor must seek confirmation in Scotland in order to deal with Scottish estate. Confirmation or probate granted in any of the UK jurisdictions operates directly in the other jurisdictions, and resealing will suffice in the case of Commonwealth countries.

2. Administration and distribution

Administration, being a matter of procedure, is governed by the *lex situs* of the asset (termed the *lex fori*).

Distribution, being a matter of substance, is governed by the law of the succession (explained below).

The *lex fori* determines classification between administration and distribution.

3. The scission principle

This principle, by which a different choice of law rule (the *lex situs*) applies to succession to immoveables, from that (deceased's last

---

[46] But note Art.11(d), preserving the conflict rules of property of any relevant *lex situs* to determine third party rights in relation to trust assets which have passed, as a result of a trustee's breach of trust, into his hands, provided those hands were innocent and that innocence is of importance to the *lex situs*.

[47] See commentary upon this restriction, Anton with Beaumont, pp.635 *et seq.*, and Raymond Smith, 5/88.

domicile) which applies to succession to moveables, operates in Scots and English choice of law rules, but a unitary rule obtains in most other legal systems.

4. Existence and extent of legal rights

These are determined by the law of the domicile of the deceased at death as regards moveables, and the *lex situs* as regards immoveables.

Intestate Succession

1. The laws governing intestate succession are: **18–55**

   (a) immoveables: the *lex situs* at the date of death;
   (b) moveables: the law of the deceased's domicile at the date of death.

2. prior rights in moveable property available by Scots domestic law arise if the deceased died domiciled in Scotland; the prior right to the house if the qualifying house is situated in Scotland.

3. Caduciary rights—the question whether a foreign government may succeed when there are no relatives, depends on whether or not, in the view of the forum, under the law of the deceased's domicile it has the right to succeed as *last heir* as opposed to acquiring right to *bona vacantia*.

Testate Succession

Note the two-dimensional nature of the conflict rules (relevance of time and space).

1. Capacity

Legal testamentary capacity appears to be governed by the law of **18–56** the domicile of the testator at the date of the will as regards moveable property, and the *lex situs* at that date as regards immoveables.

Proprietary testamentary capacity is governed by the law of the last domicile of the deceased as regards moveable property, and the *lex situs* as regards immoveables.

2. Formal Validity

Under the Wills Act 1963 a will is to be regarded as validly executed in form if it complies with any one of the following laws:

   (a) place of execution;
   (b) domicile of testator at date of will or death;

(c) habitual residence of testator at date of will or death;
(d) nationality of testator at date of will or death;
(e) place of registration of ship/aircraft;
(f) *lex situs* (immoveables).

3. Essential Validity

The essential validity or legality of the substance of the provisions of the will is governed by the following laws as at the date of the death of the testator:

(a) immoveables—the *lex situs*;
(b) moveables—the law of the testator's domicile.

4. Construction

The testator's intention takes precedence and there are a number of working rules to identify the law to be applied as his deemed intention in the matter of construction, if his intention is not express.

5. Revocation of Wills

(a) new will—the extent of revocation of a previous will depends on the validity and scope of a new will;
(b) the effect of a revocation clause is determined according to the circumstances;
(c) the effect of a purported act of revocation depends on the law of the testator's domicile (regarding moveables; or the *lex situs* relating to immoveables) at that date;
(d) the effect of a subsequent marriage is determined by the law of the domicile of the testator immediately after the marriage;
(e) a change of domicile has no effect on a will (subject to the rule that essential validity relating to moveables is governed by the law of the testator's last domicile).

6. Trusts

See Recognition of Trusts Act 1987.

Law Reform

The 1989 Hague Convention on the Law Applicable to the Estates of Deceased Persons was not ratified by the UK.

EU Green Paper on Succession and Wills (2005)—negotiation is ongoing.

AFTERWORD

Thus concludes our report for 2006. It is a truism that this must be an interim summary, despite its compendious character. We draw an analogy with the judgment in a domicile case: depending on the nature of the point in issue, the *tempus inspiciendum* may be at the end of the life of the *propositus*, or at some point in the course of it, without benefit of sight of the whole. So it is with any description of international private law rules at present. The extent and success of the harmonisation outcome is not yet available to view.

"European" conflict rules continue to advance through the current phase of active change towards harmony, or such harmony as the non-physical world can achieve. National disparities are scarcely to be tolerated; all unevenness smoothed out. The observer marvels at the fixity of purpose and range of the EU harmonisation project, notes the sometime political purpose, and the oft-time political method, ponders the ambition, and strives to record the "current" position in the knowledge that the formulation of proposed rules in any given area is in flux until enacted; and even then, supervised by an overarching, supranational court, and provided with a catalogue of supranational (autonomous) meanings, is subject to variation in implementation through problems of interpretation suggested by the obligatorily inventive minds of lawyers in combat.

We are mindful of the signal successes of the European harmonisation project, beginning with and stemming from the 1968 Brussels Convention on jurisdiction and judgment enforcement, and extending to matters of choice of law and improvements in procedure. At the same time, UK specialist conflict opinion, we venture to say, is in a state of surprise, apprehension, potential affront, and frustration, yet cognisant of the extra complexity which we should bring about by choosing to stand aside from EU instruments under production, or by electing to apply special, intra-UK rules in certain areas.

To the creation, modification or reassessment of certain rules, new or proposed, UK legal expertise has contributed; in others, we see the germ of time past. And what might have been the course of development of our conflict rules had they been permitted to remain parochial?

This book is vouched, as it must be, by extensive and rigorous citation of legal authority, primary and secondary, but the sentiment which in this postscript, and throughout, we have sought to express can be rendered poetically:

> *Time present and time past*
> *Are both perhaps present in time future,*
> *And time future contained in time past.*
> *If all time is eternally present*
> *All time is unredeemable.*
> *What might have been is an abstraction*
> *Remaining a perpetual possibility*
> *Only in a world of speculation.*
> *What might have been and what has been*
> *Point to one end, which is always present.*
> *Footfalls echo in the memory*
> *Down the passage which we did not take*
> *Towards the door we never opened*
> *Into the rose-garden.*[1]

---

[1] T.S. Eliot (1888-1965): *Four Quartets*, "Burnt Norton" (1936).

INDEX

Abduction of children
  categorisation, 14–26
  common law rules, 14–47
  criminality, 14–49
  EU
    Council Regulation 2201/2003,
      14–34—14–42
    Hague Convention 1996,
      14–27—14–33
    historical background, 14–25
    intra-UK cases, 14–43—14–46
    non-Convention cases, 14–48
Access to children, 14–21
Actionability, 8–03
Ad factum praestandum, 9–12
Administration of estates
  capacity of beneficiaries, 18–10
  choice of law, 18–03
  confirmation and probate
    general principles, 18–01
    procedure, 18–02
  intestacy
    caduciary rights, 18–14
    immoveable property, 18–11
    moveable property, 18–12
    prior rights, 18–13
  nature of legal rights, 18–06—18–9
  overview, 18–54
  powers of appointment
    construction and interpretation,
      18–43—18–44
    essential validity, 18–41—18–42
    formal validity, 18–40
    general and special powers,
      18–36—18–38
    legal capacity, 18–39
    revocation, 18–45
  proposals for reform, 18–05
  scission principle, 18–04
  trusts
    common law, 18–46—18–52
    statutory provisions, 18–53
  wills
    construction and interpretation,
      18–26—18–28
    conversion of property, 18–33
    elections, 18–35
    essential validity, 18–25
    formal validity, 18–17—18–24
    legal capacity, 18–16
    revocation, 18–29—18–33
    scope for conflict rules, 18–15

Administration of estates—*cont.*
  wills—*cont.*
    statutory provisions, 18–18—18–24
Adoption
  domicile of origin, 6–06
  overview, 14–52
  recognition of foreign decrees
    common law, 14–61
    Hague Convention 1996,
      14–55—14–59
    intra-UK cases, 14–53
    overseas adoptions, 14–60
Agency, 15–40—15–42
Alienability of property, 17–04
American policy evaluation theories,
  3–01
Annulment of marriage
  choice of law, 12–36
  grounds
    lack of "agreeing mind", 12–38
    physical incapacity, 12–37
  jurisdiction
    common law, 12–33
    overview, 12–32
    statutory developments,
      12–34—12–35
  recognition of foreign decrees
    overview, 12–31
    Regulation 2201/2003, 12–24
    statutory provisions, 12–19—12–23
  relevance of time, 4–05
Anti-suit injunctions, 7–47—7–48
Anton Piller **orders**, 7–58
Appointments
  construction and interpretation,
    18–43—18–44
  essential validity, 18–41—18–42
  formal validity, 18–40
  general and special powers,
    18–36—18–38
  legal capacity, 18–39
  revocation, 18–45
  statutory provisions, 18–22
Arbitration awards
  choice of law, 15–12
  procedure for enforcement, 9–77
  significance, 9–76
Armed services
  domicile, 6–31
  evidence, 8–12
  immunity from suit, 7–03
Arrestment, 7–58
Asset preservation, 7–57

Asylum seekers, 6–30

Bankruptcy
anti-suit injunctions, 7–47
discharge of contractual obligations,
    15–25
EU
    choice of law, 17–45—17–46
    impact, 17–48
    jurisdiction, 17–38—17–44
    recognition rules, 17–46
intra-UK cases, 17–49
jurisdiction, 7–09
non-EU proceedings in Scotland
    discharge, 17–59
    heritage in Scotland, 17–57
    jurisdiction, 17–56
    moveable property, 17–58
    statutory background,
        17–50—17–55
priority of creditors, 8–22
separate theory, 17–36
unity theory, 17–35
universality principle, 17–37
Bequests
capacity of testator, 18–16
determination of domicile, 6–20
Bigamy, 11–07
Bills of exchange, 17–29
Bona vacantia, 18–13
British Nationality, 6–38

Caduciary rights, 18–13
Capacity. *see* **Legal capacity**
Carriage of goods, 15–32—15–33
Characterisation, 4–02—4–04, *see also*
    Classification
delicts, 16–16
marriage, 11–9—11–10
Children
adoption
    domicile of origin, 6–06
    overview, 14–52
    recognition of foreign decrees,
        14–53—14–61
domicile
    of origin, 6–06
    statutory rules, 6–26—6–27
guardianship
    appointments, 14–50
    jurisdiction, 14–51
illegitimacy
    domicile of origin, 6–06
    legitimation, 14–03—14–05
international abduction
    categorisation, 14–26

Children—*cont.*
international abduction—*cont.*
    common law rules, 14–47
    criminality, 14–49
    Hague Convention 1980,
        14–27—14–33
    historical background, 14–25
    intra-UK cases, 14–43—14–46
    non-Convention cases, 14–48
    Regulation 2201/2003,
        14–34—14–42
legitimacy
    domicile of origin, 6–06
    legitimation, 14–03—14–05
    polygamous marriages, 11–04
    status, 14–01—14–02
overview, 14–62
parental rights and responsibilities
    EU law, 14–07—14–24
    overview, 14–06
status
    legitimacy, 14–01—14–02
    legitimation, 14–03—14–05
Choice of court clauses
Hague Convention 2005, 7–31—7–34
prorogation rules, 7–29—7–30
Choice of law
administration of estates, 18–03
alienability of property, 17–04
annulment and separation, 12–31,
    12–36
civil partnerships, 13–16
classification of property, 17–02
cohabitation, 13–16
consistorial actions, 12–15
contractual obligations
    common law, 15–10—15–12
    EU law, 15–02—15–09,
        15–13—15–17
    incidental questions, 15–18
corporeal moveables, 17–10
delicts
    EU proposed harmonisation,
        16–29
    intra-UK cases, 16–23
    maritime delicts, 16–14
    statutory rules, 16–15—16–22
    theories, 16–02—16–08
dissolution of civil partnerships,
    12–46
immoveable property
    legal capacity, 17–05
    real rights, 17–07
    security interests, 17–08
incidental questions, 4–06
incorporeal moveables, 17–19
indicated by *lex fori*, 4–01

Choice of law—*cont.*
insolvency
EU, 17–45—17–46
Scots law, 17–53
intellectual property rights, 17–32
intestacy
caduciary rights, 18–13
immoveable property, 18–11
moveable property, 18–12
prior rights, 18–13
maintenance obligations, 13–19
moveable property
corporeal moveables, 17–15
incorporeal moveables,
17–18—17–23
negotiable instruments, 17–30
powers of appointment
construction and interpretation,
18–43—18–44
essential validity, 18–41—18–42
formal validity, 18–40
general and special powers,
18–36—18–38
legal capacity, 18–39
revocation, 18–45
private marriage contracts, 13–04
shares, 17–31
special contracts
agency, 15–40—15–42
carriage of goods, 15–32—15–33
consumer contracts, 15–34—15–36
electronic commerce,
15–43—15–49
employment contracts,
15–37—15–38
immoveable property, 15–31
money obligations, 15–50—15–54
sale of goods, 15–39
time, relevance of, 4–05
trust estates
common law, 18–46—18–52
statutory provisions, 18–53
unjust enrichment, 16–31
EU proposals for reform,
16–32—16–35
wills
construction and interpretation,
18–26—18–28
conversion of property, 18–33
essential validity, 18–25
formal validity, 18–17—18–24
legal capacity, 18–16
revocation, 18–29
Civil partnerships
defined, 11–35

Civil partnerships—*cont.*
dissolution
choice of law, 12–46
financial provision, 13–25
jurisdiction, 12–41—12–45
recognition of foreign decrees,
12–47—12–48
legal capacity, 11–37
overview, 11–42
property rights, 13–16
recognition of same sex "divorces",
12–25
significance, 11–13
statutory requirements, 11–36
Classification
contractual obligations, 15–01
examples, 4–04
"false conflicts", 4–03
significance, 4–02
Cohabitation
cessation, 12–49
commencement and termination,
11–40
family provision, 18–09
meaning, 11–39
overview, 11–42
property rights
de facto and *de iure* distinguished,
13–12
de facto in Scotland, 13–13
de facto outside Scotland, 13–14
de iure foreign cohabitants, 13–15
significance, 11–13
statutory provisions, 11–38
uncertainty of law, 11–41
Collation, 18–08
Commercial agents, 15–42
Common law conflict rules
choice of law for delicts
delicts committed furth of
Scotland, 16–11—16–13
delicts committed in Scotland,
16–10
contractual obligations
choice of law, 15–10—15–12
proof of existence, 15–19
enforcement of foreign decrees,
9–08—9–13
foreign adoption, 14–61
international child abduction, 14–47
jurisdiction
annulments, 12–33
consistorial actions, 12–02
contractual obligations, 7–04

Common law conflict rules—*cont.*
  property rights in marriage
    no marriage contract,
      13–10—13–11
    private marriage contracts, 13–04
  recognition of foreign divorces,
    12–18
  special contracts
    agency, 15–40
    carriage of goods, 15–32
    consumer contracts, 15–34
    employment contracts, 15–37
    transfers of property, 17–02
    trust estates, 18–46—18–52
    validity of marriage, 11–27—11–29
Community of goods, 13–02
Compromises, 8–24
Confirmation
  general principles, 18–01
  procedure, 18–02
Confiscatory laws, 3–04—3–05
Conflict of laws. *see* **International
  private law**
Connecting factors
  delicts, 16–19
  domicile
    British Nationality, 6–38
    disadvantages attaching to relevant
      factors, 6–36—6–37
    habitual residence, 6–40
    residence, 6–39
  relevance of time, 4–05
  significance, 4–01
Consistorial actions
  see also **Annulment of marriage;
    Dissolution of civil
    partnerships; Divorce;
    Separation**
  anti-suit injunctions, 7–47
  choice of law, 12–15
  jurisdiction
    common law, 12–02
    conflicting jurisdictions,
      12–09—12–14
    current grounds, 12–04—12–08
    statutory extension, 12–03
  polygamous marriages, 11–03
  private marriage contracts, 13–09
Consumer contracts, 7–20—7–22,
  15–34—15–36
Contractual obligations
  choice of law
    common law, 15–10—15–12
    EU law, 15–02—15–09,
      15–13—15–17

Contractual obligations—*cont.*
  classification, 15–01
  construction and interpretation,
    15–24
  corporeal moveables, 17–16
  discharge, 15–25
  domicile, 6–03
  essential validity, 15–22
  evidence, 15–27
  exclusion of *renvoi*, 5–07, 15–28
  formal validity, 15–21
  illegality, 15–26
  immoveable property, 17–06
  incidental questions, 15–18
  incorporeal moveables, 17–20
  jurisdiction under Reg. 44/2001, 7–13
  legal capacity, 15–20
  overview, 15–58
  private marriage contracts
    changes of domicile, 13–08
    choice of law, 13–04
    effect of divorce, 13–09
    essential validity, 13–07
    formal validity, 13–06
    legal capacity, 13–05
  procedure, 15–27
  proof of existence, 15–19
  public policy, 15–29
  relationship with other areas of law
    delicts, 15–56, 16–24
    property rights, 15–55
    restitution, 15–57
  Scots jurisdiction, 7–04
  special contracts
    agency, 15–40—15–42
    carriage of goods, 15–32—15–33
    consumer contracts, 15–34—15–36
    electronic commerce,
      15–43—15–49
    employment contracts,
      15–37—15–38
    immoveable property, 15–31
    money obligations, 15–50—15–54
    sale of goods, 15–39
  statutory provisions, 15–23
Corporeal moveables
  choice of law, 17–10
  conflicts with contract law, 17–16
  lex situs and lex loci rei sitae, 17–10,
    17–15
  proprietary rights, 17–12—17–14
  validity of transfer, 17–11
Country, meaning of, 1–05
Curators, 14–50
Currencies, 8–21, 15–54

Damages
calculation, 8–20
currency, 8–21
delict, 16–28
Debtors, 6–29
Declarators
of fact, 9–02
legitimacy, 14–02
recognition of foreign divorces,
12–17
Decrees. *see* **Enforcement of foreign
decrees**
Defamation
choice of law, 16–21
jurisdiction under Reg. 44/2001, 7–15
Delicts
choice of law
common law rules, 16–09—16–14
EU proposed harmonisation,
16–29
intra-UK cases, 16–23
maritime delicts, 16–14
statutory rules, 16–15—16–22
theories, 16–02—16–08
damages, 16–28
exclusion of *renvoi*, 5–07, 16–27
jurisdiction under Reg. 44/2001,
7–14
overview, 16–36
relationship with contract, 15–56,
16–24
Scots jurisdiction, 7–04
Solicitor's duty, 18–24
survival of action, 16–26
title to sue, 16–25
Diligence, 8–23
Diplomats
domicile, 6–30
immunity from suit, 7–03
Disadvantaged parties, 7–18
Discretionary (consistorial) sists,
12–09, 12–11
Dissolution of civil partnerships
choice of law, 12–46
financial provision, 13–25
jurisdiction, 12–41—12–45
recognition of foreign decrees,
12–47—12–48
Distance selling, 15–47
Divorce
financial provision, 13–24
recognition of foreign decrees
capacity to re–marry, 12–26
common law, 12–18
declarators, 12–17

Divorce—*cont.*
recognition of foreign decrees—*cont.*
extra–judicial divorces,
12–26—12–30
Regulation 2201/2003, 12–24
same sex relationships, 12–25
statutory provisions, 12–19—12–23
relevance of time, 4–05
Domicile
armed services, 6–31
asylum seekers, 6–30
capacity to marry
dual domicile theory, 11–16
matrimonial domicile theory,
11–17
of choice
burden of proof, 6–08
intention, 6–10
loss, 6–22
requirements, 6–07
residence, 6–09
standard of proof, 6–11
classification, 6–05
connecting factors
British Nationality, 6–38
disadvantages attaching to relevant
factors, 6–36—6–37
habitual residence, 6–40
residence, 6–39
debtors, 6–29
diplomats, 6–30
factors determining change
bequests, 6–20
burial and cremation directions,
6–21
declaration of intention, 6–16
deposit of moveables, 6–17
lairs, 6–21
nationality, 6–13
newspapers, 6–18
old age, 6–19
political and social commitments,
6–15
residence, 6–14
general meaning, 6–02
invalids, 6–32
jurisdiction under 44/2001, 7–11
legal capacity
married women, 6–25
incapaces, 6–24
minors, 6–26—6–27
legal implications, 6–01
old age, 6–33
of origin, 6–06
prisoners, 6–28
private marriage contracts, 13–08

Domicile—*cont.*
reform, 6–34
relevance of time, 4–05
revocation of wills
change of domicile, 18–32
purported acts, 18–31
Scots jurisdiction, 7–04
statutory definition, 6–03
technical rules, 6–04
trust estates, 18–47, 18–51
validity of wills, 18–20
Double actionability
choice of law theory, 16–05
defamation, 16–21
possible defences, 16–13
Double locality delicts, 16–18
Double *renvoi* theory, 5–06

Elections, 18–35
Electronic commerce
application of Rome I, 15–48
distance selling, 15–47
online services, 15–46
proposed changes, 15–49
signatures, 15–44
significance, 15–43
validity and liability, 15–45
Employment contracts, 7–23—7–26
Enemy aliens, 7–03
Enforcement of foreign decrees
see also **Recognition**
arbitration awards
procedure, 9–77
significance, 9–76
calculation of damages, 8–20
classes of decree
declarators of fact, 9–02
interdicts, 9–03
judgments affecting status, 9–05
judgments *in personam*, 9–06
judgments *in rem*, 9–04
currencies, 8–21
diligence, 8–23
EU principles
Council Regulation Reg 44/2001,
9–44—9–59
general principles, 9–37—9–38
Lugano Convention 1988,
9–60—9–75
order for payment procedure, 9–93
recognition rules, 9–39—9–43
small claims procedure,
9–87—9–92
statutory provisions, 9–36
uncontested claims, 9–78—9–86
international child abduction, 14–45

Enforcement of foreign decrees—*cont.*
judgments *in personam*, 9–06
legal basis
common law rules, 9–08—9–13
general principles, 9–07
maintenance obligations
intra-UK cases, 13–20
reciprocal enforcement
agreements, 13–21
overview, 9–94
parental rights and responsibilities,
14–20
priority of creditors, 8–22
protection of trading interests,
9–34—9–35
reciprocal agreements, 9–21—9–33
registration
Commonwealth judgments,
9–15—9–20
English and Irish judgments, 9–14
English law principles
domicile
founding principles, 6–01
of origin, 6–06
statutory definition, 6–03
technical rules, 6–04
domicile of choice, 6–09
enforcement of foreign decrees
declarators of fact, 9–02
legal basis, 9–07
enlightened view of classification,
4–02
financial provision on divorce, 13–24
harmonisation, 1–06—1–08
illegal contracts, 15–26
jurisdiction
pre–trial measures, 7–58
residual rules, 7–55
parental consent to marriage, 11–33
succession, 18–09
Essential validity
bills of exchange, 17–29
capacity to marry
dual domicile theory, 11–16
exceptions to general rule,
11–19—11–22
matrimonial domicile theory,
11–17
requirements of *lex loci*, 11–18
contractual obligations, 15–22
electronic commerce, 15–45
form distinguished, 11–14
immoveable property, 17–06
matters arising during marriage,
11–23

Essential validity—*cont.*
powers of appointment,
18–41—18–42
private marriage contracts, 13–07
special contracts, 15–30
trust estates, 18–50
wills, 18–25
EU conflict rules
consistorial actions
conflicting jurisdictions,
12–12—12–14
recognition of EU decrees, 12–24
contractual obligations,
15–13—15–17
delicts, 16–29
dissolution of civil partnerships,
12–47—12–48
enforcement of foreign decrees
Regulation 44/2001, 9–44—9–59
general principles, 9–37—9–38
Lugano Convention 1988,
9–60—9–75
order for payment procedure, 9–93
recognition rules, 9–39—9–43
small claims procedure,
9–87—9–92
statutory provisions, 9–36
uncontested claims, 9–78—9–86
harmonisation, 1–06—1–09
insolvency
choice of law, 17–45—17–46
jurisdiction, 17–38—17–44
recognition rules, 17–47
international child abduction,
14–27—14–43
jurisdiction
Brussels Convention 1968,
7–05—7–06
choice of court clauses,
7–28—7–34
Regulation 44/2001, 7–08—7–49
identifying areas of operation,
7–50—7–52
Lugano Convention 1988, 7–07
maintenance obligations
enforcement, 13–22—13–23
jurisdiction, 13–18
parental rights and responsibilities
background, 14–07
Council Regulation 2201/2003,
14–08—14–23
Hague Convention 1996, 14–24
property rights in marriage, 13–01,
13–17
recognition of foreign decrees
annulment and separation, 12–39
extra–judicial divorces, 12–30

EU conflict rules—*cont.*
recognition of foreign decrees—*cont.*
harmonisation, 12–16
procedure, 12–17
Regulation 2201/2003, 12–24
same sex relationships, 12–25
service of documents, 8–10
taking of evidence abroad,
8–13—8–15
unjust enrichment
choice of law, 16–30
proposals for reform,
16–32—16–35
Evidence
contractual obligations, 15–27
determination by *lex fori*, 8–12
pre-trial preservation, 7–56
presumptions of law and fact, 8–19
proof of foreign law, 8–17—8–18
taking abroad
within EU, 8–13—8–15
outside EU, 8–16
Exchange control
illegal contracts, 15–26
money obligations, 15–53
Exclusion of foreign law. *see* **Rules of exclusion**
Exclusive jurisdiction
choice of court clauses, 7–30
Council Regulation 44/2001, 7–27
Exequatur, 9–79, 9–83
Expropriation, 3–04—3–05

"False conflicts", 4–03
Foreign court theory of *renvoi*, 5–06
Foreign decrees. *see* **Enforcement of foreign decrees**
Form of action
determined by *lex fori*, 4–01
procedure, 8–04
Formal validity
bills of exchange, 17–29
contractual obligations, 15–21
electronic commerce, 15–45
incorporeal moveables, 17–24
marriage
exceptions to general rule,
11–26—11–29
general presumption, 11–30
general rule, 11–24
religious celebration, 11–25
powers of appointment, 18–40
private marriage contracts, 13–06
trust estates, 18–49
wills
common law, 18–17
statutory, 18–19

Forum non conveniens
identifying areas of operation,
7–50—7–52
significance, 7–45
when available, 7–46
Forum shopping, 7–44
Fraud
corporeal moveables, 17–13
enforcement of foreign decrees, 9–12
Freezing orders, 7–58

General powers of appointment,
18–36—18–38
Ghet **divorces**, 12–26—12–30
Governing law. *see* **Choice of law**
Guardianship
appointments, 14–50
jurisdiction, 14–51

Habitual residence
connecting factor, 6–40
defined, 6–02
harmonisation, 6–01
international child abduction, 14–46
parental rights and responsibilities,
14–15
Harmonisation
consistorial actions, 12–15
EU, 1–06—1–09
foreign divorces, 12–16
property rights in marriage, 13–01
History
early civilisations, 2–01
French statute theory, 2–02
Scotland, 2–03—2–04

Illegal contracts, 15–26
Illegitimate children
domicile of origin, 6–06
legitimation, 14–03—14–05
Immoveable property
administration of estates, 18–04
classification of transfers, 17–02
contractual obligations, 15–31, 17–06
intestacy, 18–11
legal capacity, 17–05
real rights, 17–07
security interests, 17–08
wills, 18–17
Immunity from suit, 7–03
Immutability of property rights
no marriage contract, 13–10
private marriage contracts, 13–02
Incidental question, 4–06

Incorporeal moveables
assignability, 17–22
choice of law, 17–19
contractual obligations, 17–20
formal validity, 17–24
legal capacity, 17–23
lex situs and lex loci rei sitae, 17–18
triangular scenario, 17–25—17–28
voluntary assignments, 17–21
Inhibition, 7–58
Injunctions, 7–58
Insolvency
anti-suit injunctions, 7–47
discharge of contractual obligations,
15–25
EU law
choice of law, 17–45—17–46
impact, 17–48
jurisdiction, 17–38—17–44
recognition rules, 17–47
intra-UK cases, 17–49
jurisdiction, 7–09
non–EU proceedings in Scotland
discharge, 17–59
heritage in Scotland, 17–57
jurisdiction, 17–56
moveable property, 17–58
statutory background,
17–50—17–55
overview, 17–60
priority of creditors, 8–22
theories
separate theory, 17–36
unity of bankruptcy, 17–35
universality of bankruptcy, 17–37
Insurance jurisdiction, 7–19
Intellectual property rights, 17–32
Intention
domicile of choice
determining factor, 6–16
general requirement, 6–07
meaning, 6–10
mental incapacity, 6–24
Interdicts, 9–03
Internal law theory of *renvoi*, 5–04
International child abduction
categorisation, 14–26
common law rules, 14–47
criminality, 14–49
Hague Convention 1980,
14–27—14–33
historical background, 14–25
intra-UK cases, 14–43—14–46
non-Convention cases, 14–48
Regulation 2201/2003, 14–34—14–42

International private law
  harmonisation, 1–06—1–09
  history, 2–01—2–04
  scope, 1–01—1–02
  terminology, 1–03—1–04
International wills, 18–23
Intestacy
  caduciary rights, 18–13
  immoveable property, 18–11
  moveable property, 18–12
  polygamous marriages, 11–05—11–06
  prior rights, 18–13
Invalids, 6–32

Judgments
  affecting status, 9–05
  in personam, 9–06
  in rem, 9–04
Judicial separation
  overview, 12–31
  Regulation 2201/2003, 12–24
  statutory provisions, 12–19—12–23
Jurisdiction
  abduction of children
    Council Regulation 2201/2003,
      14–35
    intra-UK cases, 14–44
  adoption, 14–58
  annulment of marriage
    common law, 12–33
    overview, 12–32
    statutory developments,
      12–34—12–35
  anti-suit injunctions, 7–47—7–48
  arbitration awards, 9–76
  Brussels Convention 1968,
    7–05—7–06
  choice of court clauses
    Hague Convention 2005,
      7–31—7–34
    prorogation rules, 7–29—7–30
  consistorial actions, 12–04—12–08
    common law, 12–02
    conflicting jurisdictions,
      12–09—12–14
    statutory extension, 12–03
  Council Regulation 44/2001
    consumer contracts, 7–20—7–22
    contractual obligations, 7–13
    defamation, 7–15
    defendant's domicile, 7–11
    delicts, 7–14
    disadvantaged parties, 7–18
    employment contracts, 7–23—7–26
    exclusive jurisdiction, 7–27

Jurisdiction—*cont.*
  Council Regulation 44/2001—*cont.*
    general rule, 7–10
    identifying areas of operation,
      7–50—7–52
    insurance, 7–19
    lis pendens, 7–36—7–44
    ranking of rules, 7–49
    related actions, 7–17
    scope, 7–09
    significance, 7–08
    special matters, 7–16
    submission to jurisdiction, 7–35
  determined by *lex fori*, 4–01
  dissolution of civil partnerships,
    12–41—12–45
  English law, 7–55
  forum non conveniens
    significance, 7–45
    when available, 7–46
  general principles, 7–02
  guardianship, 14–51
  insolvency, 17–38—17–44, 17–56
  Lugano Convention 1988, 7–07
  maintenance obligations, 13–18
  overview, 7–59
  parental rights and responsibilities,
    14–10—14–18
  pre-trial measures
    preservation of assets, 7–57
    preservation of evidence, 7–56
    remedies, 7–58
  restrictions on parties, 7–03
  Scots law
    common law rules, 7–04
    Modified Convention, Sch.4, 7–53
    Sch.8, 7–54
  significance, 7–01
Jus civile, 2–01
Jus gentium, 2–01
Justice Theory, 3–01

Lairs, 6–21
"Law of a country", 1–05
Legal capacity
  see also **Status**
  assignment of incorporeal moveables,
    17–23
  beneficiaries, 18–10
  civil partnerships, 11–37
  contractual obligations, 15–20
  domicile, 6–04
    married women, 6–25
    incapaces, 6–24
    minors, 6–26—6–27
  immoveable property, 17–05

Legal capacity—*cont.*
marriage
dual domicile theory, 11–16
exceptions to general rule,
11–19—11–22
matrimonial domicile theory,
11–17
polygamous relationships, 11–11
requirements of *lex loci*, 11–18
powers of appointment
private marriage contracts, 13–05
remarriage after foreign divorce,
12–26
status distinguished, 10–07
testators
trust estates, 18–48
Legitimacy
domicile of origin, 6–06
legitimation, 14–03—14–05
polygamous marriages, 11–04
status, 14–01—14–02
Lex actus
corporeal moveables, 17–10
defined, 1–04
incorporeal moveables, 17–19
Lex causae
actionability, 8–03
assignability of incorporeal
moveables, 17–22
classification
examples, 4–04
"false conflicts", 4–03
classification of property, 17–02
defined, 1–04
determination of substantive law,
4–01
heads of damage, 8–20
incidental questions, 4–06
justification for disapplication, 8–01
limited territorial effect of statutes,
3–07
presumptions of law and fact, 8–19
public policy, 3–06
relationship between delict and
contract, 16–24
relevance of time, 4–05
Scots law, 3–08
traditional approach, 1–02
Lex concursus, 17–46
Lex domicilii
administration of estates, 18–03
beneficiaries, 18–27
collation, 18–08
consistorial actions, 12–15
corporeal moveables, 17–10
defined, 1–04
incorporeal moveables, 17–19

Lex fori
administration of estates
caduciary rights, 18–13
calculation of damages, 8–20
choice of law for delicts, 16–03
consistorial actions, 12–15
contractual obligations, 15–01
defined, 1–04
determination of evidence, 8–12
domicile, 6–04
double actionability, 16–13
"false conflicts", 4–03
incidental question, 4–06
procedure
actionability, 8–03
form of action, 8–04
prescription, 8–06—8–08
public policy, 3–06
significance, 4–01
wills
construction and interpretation,
18–26
Lex loci actus
corporeal moveables, 17–10
defined, 1–04
incorporeal moveables, 17–19, 17–23
validity of wills, 18–20
Lex loci celebrationis
annulments, 12–36, 12–38
classification
difficulties, 4–02
examples, 4–04
consistorial actions, 12–15
defined, 1–04
marriage
essential validity, 11–14
formal validity, 11–24
requirement of capacity, 11–18
relevance of time, 4–05
religious celebration of marriage,
11–25
renvoi, 5–07
Lex loci contractus
agency, 15–40
choice of law, 15–12
classification, 4–04
defined, 1–04
relevance of time, 4–05
Lex loci delicti
choice of law, 16–04
defined, 1–04
double actionability, 16–13
"false conflicts", 4–03
public policy, 3–06
relevance of time, 4–05
statutory rules, 16–15—16–22
Lex loci rei sitae, 18–13

Lex loci solutionis
  choice of law, 15–12
  defined, 1–04
Lex patriae
  defined, 1–04
  double *renvoi* theory, 5–06
  partial *renvoi* theory, 5–05
Lex situs and lex loci rei sitae
  administration of estates
    capacity of beneficiaries, 18–10
    choice of law, 18–03
    collation, 18–08
    intestacy, 18–11
    nature of legal rights, 18–07
    scission principle, 18–04
  alienability of property, 17–04
  classification, 4–04
  classification of property, 17–02
  contractual obligations, 15–55
  corporeal moveables, 17–10, 17–15
  defined, 1–04
  determination of connecting factor,
    4–01
  double *renvoi* theory, 5–06
  immoveable property, 15–31
    contractual obligations, 17–06
    legal capacity, 17–05
    real rights, 17–07
    security interests, 17–08
  incorporeal moveables, 17–18, 17–19
  intellectual property rights, 17–32
  meaning, 17–03
  powers of appointment
    essential validity, 18–41
    special powers, 18–38
  relevance of time, 4–05
  renvoi, 5–07
  shares, 17–31
  unjust enrichment, 16–31, 16–34
  wills
    construction and interpretation,
      18–26
    revocation, 18–29
Lex successionis
  classification
    examples, 4–04
    "false conflicts", 4–03
  construction and interpretation of
    wills, 18–26
  defined, 1–04
  family provision, 18–09
Limitations, 8–09
Lis pendens
  conflicts under Reg. 44/2001,
    7–36—7–41

Lis pendens—*cont.*
  consistorial actions, 12–12
  identifying areas of operation,
    7–50—7–52
  interpretation of Reg. 44/2001,
    7–42—7–43
  negative declarations, 7–44
  parental rights and responsibilities,
    14–18
Local Law Theory, 3–01
Locus celebrationis, 4–01
Locus contractus, 15–12

Maintenance
  choice of law, 13.19
  enforcement intra–UK, 13.20
  intra-EU cases, 13.22—13.23
  jurisdiction, 13.18
  overview, 13.26
  reciprocal enforcement agreements,
    13.21
Mancini's Theory, 3–01
**Mandatory (consistorial) (common
  law) sists**, 12–09—12–10
Mareva injunctions, 7–58. *See also*
  Freezing orders
Maritime delicts, 16–14
Marriage
  see also **Annulment of marriage;
    Consistorial actions; Divorce**
  capacity to marry
    dual domicile theory, 11–16
    exceptions to general rule,
      11–19—11–22
    matrimonial domicile theory,
      11–17
    requirements of *lex loci*, 11–18
  consent
    mental state of parties, 11–30
    parents, 11–32—11–34
  defined, 11–01
  domicile, 6–04, 6–25
  essential validity other than capacity,
    11–23
  essentials and form distinguished,
    11–14
  formal validity
    exceptions to general rule,
      11–26—11–29
    general presumption, 11–30
    general rule, 11–24
    religious celebration, 11–25
  maintenance obligations
    choice of law, 13–19
    enforcement intra–UK, 13–20
    intra-EU cases, 13–22—13–23

Marriage—*cont.*
  maintenance obligations—*cont.*
    jurisdiction, 13–18
    overview, 13–26
    reciprocal enforcement
      agreements, 13–21
  overview, 11–42
  parental rights and responsibilities
    EU law, 14–07—14–24
    overview, 14–06
  polygamous relationships
    bigamy, 11–07
    capacity to marry, 11–11
    characterisation, 11–09—11–10
    consistorial actions, 11–03
    legitimacy, 11–04
    recognition, 11–02
    social security benefits, 11–08
    status, 11–05
    succession, 11–04
  property rights
    EU initiative, 13–17
    no marriage contract,
      13–10—13–11
    overview, 13–01, 13–26
    private marriage contracts,
      13–03—13–09
    statutory community of goods,
      13–02
  revocation of wills, 18–33
  same sex relationships, 11–12
Mental incapacity, 6–24
Methodology
  applications of classification, 4–04
  classification, 4–02—4–03
  incidental question, 4–06
  objectives, 4–07
  overview, 4–01
  relevance of time, 4–05
Minors. *see* **Children**
Money obligations
  currencies, 15–54
  exchange control, 15–53
  money of account, 15–51
  money of payment, 15–52
Moveable property
  administration of estates, 18–04
  classification of transfers, 17–02
  corporeal moveables
    choice of law, 17–10
    conflicts with contract law, 17–16
    proprietary rights, 17–12—17–14
    validity of transfer, 17–11
  incorporeal moveables
    assignability, 17–22
    choice of law, 17–19

Moveable property—*cont.*
  incorporeal moveables—*cont.*
    contractual assignments, 17–20
    formal validity, 17–24
    legal capacity, 17–23
    lex situs and lex loci rei sitae, 17–18
    triangular scenario, 17–25—17–28
    voluntary assignments, 17–21
  insolvency, 17–58
  notable distinctions, 17–09
  relationship with contract, 15–55
  Scots jurisdiction, 7–04
  wills
    formal validity, 18–17

Nationalisation, 3–04—3–05
Nationality
  defined, 6–02
  determination of domicile
    British Nationality, 6–38
    general principles, 6–13
  validity of wills, 18–20
Natural justice
  enforcement of foreign decrees, 9–12
  illegal contracts, 15–26
Natural persons, 10–02
Negative prescription, 8–08
Negotiable instruments, 17–30
Nullity of marriage. *see* **Annulment of marriage**

Obligation theory, 16–07
Order for payment procedure, 9–93
Ordre public. *see* **Public policy**
Overseas adoptions, 14–60

Partial renvoi theory of *renvoi*, 5–05
Parties, 8–05
Penal laws
  capacity to marry, 11–21
  illegal contracts, 15–26
  rules of exclusion, 3–03
Polygamous marriages
  bigamy, 11–07
  capacity to marry, 11–11
  characterisation, 11–09—11–10
  consistorial actions, 11–03
  legitimacy, 11–04
  recognition, 11–02
  social security benefits, 11–08
  status, 11–05—11–06
  succession, 11–04
Positive prescription, 8–07

Powers of appointment
construction and interpretation, 18–43—18–44
essential validity, 18–41—18–42
formal validity, 18–40
general and special powers, 18–36—18–38
legal capacity, 18–39
revocation, 18–45
statutory provisions, 18–22
Preliminary questions
contractual obligations, 15–18
methodology, 4–06
Prescription, 8–06—8–08
Presumptions
contractual obligations, 15–12
domicile, 6–04
exclusive jurisdiction, 7–30
law and fact, 8–19
validity of marriage, 11–30
Prisoners, 6–28
Probate
general principles, 18–01
procedure, 18–02
Procedure
actionability, 8–03
confirmation and probate, 18–02
contractual obligations, 15–27
enforcement of foreign decrees
minimum standards for EEO, 9–84
orders for payment, 9–93
small claims, 9–87—9–92
exclusion of foreign rules, 4–01
form of action, 8–04
limitations, 8–09
meaning, 8–02
prescription, 8–06—8–08
recognition of foreign divorces, 12–17
service of documents
within EU, 8–10
outside EU, 8–11
set–off and compromise, 8–24
substantive rights distinguished, 8–01
title to sue, 8–05
Proof
contractual obligations, 15–19
domicile, 6–04
domicile of choice
relevant factors, 6–08
standard of proof, 6–11
foreign law, 4–01, 8–17—8–18
Proof of foreign law, 4–01, 8–17—8–18
Proper law theory, 16–06
Property rights
bills of exchange
statutory provisions, 17–29

Property rights—*cont.*
civil partnerships, 13–16
cohabitation
de facto and *de iure* distinguished, 13–12
de facto in Scotland, 13–13
de facto outside Scotland, 13–14
de iure foreign cohabitants, 13–15
immoveable property
contractual obligations, 17–06
legal capacity, 17–05
real rights, 17–07
security interests, 17–08
intellectual property, 17–31
marriage
EU initiative, 13–17
no marriage contract, 13–10—13–11
overview, 13–01, 13–26
private marriage contracts, 13–03—13–09
statutory community of goods, 13–02
moveable property
corporeal moveables, 17–10—17–16
determination of domicile, 6–17
incorporeal moveables, 17–17—17–28
Scots jurisdiction, 7–04
negotiable instruments, 17–30
overview, 17–60
relationship with contract, 15–55
shares, 17–31
testamentary capacity, 18–16
transfers of property
alienability, 17–04
meaning of *lex situs*, 17–03
terminology, 17–02
Prorogation of jurisdiction
choice of court clauses, 7–29—7–30
parental rights and responsibilities, 14–14
Protection of trading interests, 9–34—9–35
Public policy
capacity to marry, 11–21
contractual obligations, 15–29
enforcement of foreign decrees, 9–12
recognition of extra–judicial divorces, 12–28
recognition of status, 10–05
rules of exclusion, 3–06

Recognition of foreign decrees
see also **Enforcement of foreign decrees**
adoption
common law, 14–61
Hague Convention 1996, 14–55—14–59
intra-UK cases, 14–53
overseas adoptions, 14–60
annulment and separation
overview, 12–31
Regulation 2201/2003, 12–24, 12–39
statutory provisions, 12–19—12–23
arbitration awards, 9–77
dissolution of civil partnerships, 12–47—12–48
enforcement of foreign decrees, 9–10
EU principles, 9–39—9–43
foreign divorces
capacity to re–marry, 12–26
common law, 12–18
declarators, 12–17
extra–judicial divorces, 12–26—12–30
Regulation 2201/2003, 12–24
same sex relationships, 12–25
statutory provisions, 12–19—12–23
universality of status, 12–16
insolvency
EU law, 17–46
Scots law, 17–55
international child abduction, 14–45
legitimation, 14–05
parental rights and responsibilities, 14–19
status, 10–05
Registration
civil partnerships, 11–37
foreign decrees
Commonwealth judgments, 9–15—9–20
English and Irish judgments, 9–14
Religious celebration of marriage, 11–25
Remedies. *see* **Procedure**
Renvoi
case studies, 5–09—5–13
contractual obligations, 15–28
delicts, 16–27
history, 5–02
meaning and significance, 5–01
scope, 5–07—5–08
theories
foreign court theory, 5–06
internal law theory, 5–04
partial *renvoi* theory, 5–05

Res judicata, 9–13
Residence
defined, 6–02
domicile of choice
connecting factor, 6–39
determining factor, 6–14
general requirement, 6–07
meaning, 6–09
habitual residence
adoption, 14–58
connecting factor, 6–40
defined, 6–02
harmonisation, 6–01
international child abduction, 14–46
parental rights and responsibilities, 14–15
relevance of time, 4–05
Restitution. *see* **Unjust enrichment**
Revenue laws
domicile, 6–03
exclusion of jurisdiction under Reg. 44/2001, 7–09
illegal contracts, 15–26
rules of exclusion, 3–02
Revocation
powers of appointment, 18–45
wills
change of domicile, 18–32
express clauses, 18–30
marriage, 18–33
new wills, 18–29
purported acts, 18–31
statutory provisions, 18–22
Royal marriages, 11–20
Rules of exclusion
see also **Theories**
confiscatory laws, 3–04
penal laws, 3–03
public policy, 3–06
revenue laws, 3–02
statute law, 3–07

Sale of goods
contractual obligations, 15–39
electronic commerce, 15–47
Same sex relationships
see also **Civil partnerships**
marriage, 11–12
recognition of same sex "divorces", 12–25
Savigny's Theory, 3–01
Scission principle, 18–04
Search warrants, 7–58
Security for costs, 7–03

Service of documents
within EU, 8–10
outside EU, 8–11
Set-off, 8–24
Shares, 17–31
Sist of mandatory
foreign pursuers, 7–03
Small claims procedure, 9–87—9–92
Social security benefits, 11–08
Special powers of appointment,
18–36—18–38
State parties
immunity from suit, 7–03
status, 10–03
Status
see also Legal capacity
children
legitimacy, 14–01—14–02
legitimation, 14–03—14–05
defined, 10–01
effects arising must be distinguished,
10–06
enforcement of foreign decrees, 9–05
exclusion of jurisdiction under Reg.
44/2001, 7–09
legal capacity distinguished, 10–07
natural persons, 10–02
non–natural parties, 10–03
overview, 10–08
polygamous marriages, 11–05—11–06
public policy, 10–05
universality theory, 10–04, 12–16
Statute law
ambit of statutes, 3–07
exclusion of foreign rights, 3–06
Submission to jurisdiction
Reg. 44/2001, 7–35
**Substance (distinguished from
procedure)**, 8–01
Succession
administration and distribution,
18–03
capacity of beneficiaries, 18–10
confirmation and probate
general principles, 18–01
procedure, 18–02
intestacy
caduciary rights, 18–13
immoveable property, 18–11
moveable property, 18–12
prior rights, 18–13
nature of legal rights, 18–06—18–09
overview, 18–54
polygamous marriages, 11–04
powers of appointment

Succession—*cont.*
powers of appointment—*cont.*
construction and interpretation,
18–43—18–44
essential validity, 18–41—18–42
formal validity, 18–40
general and special powers,
18–36—18–38
legal capacity, 18–39
revocation, 18–45
proposals for reform, 18–05
renvoi
case studies, 5–09—5–13
scope, 5–07—5–08
scission principle, 18–04
trust estates
common law, 18–46—18–52
statutory provisions, 18–53
wills
construction and interpretation,
18–26—18–28
conversion of property, 18–33
elections, 18–35
essential validity, 18–25
formal validity, 18–17—18–24
legal capacity, 18–16
revocation, 18–29—18–33
statutory provisions, 18–18—18–24

Talaq divorces, 12–26—12–30
Tempus inspiciendum, 4–05
Territorial Theory, 3–01
Theories
see also Rules of exclusion
bankruptcy
unity, 17–35
capacity to marry
dual domicile theory, 11–16
matrimonial domicile theory,
11–17
choice of law for delicts
double actionability, 16–05
lex fori, 16–03
lex loci delicti, 16–04
obligation theory, 16–07
proper law theory, 16–06
US experience, 16–08
explanations of territorial effect,
3–01
French statute theory, 2–02
insolvency
separate bankruptcies, 17–36
universality of bankruptcy, 17–37
renvoi
foreign court theory, 5–06
internal law theory, 5–04

Theories—*cont.*
  renvoi—*cont.*
    partial *renvoi* theory, 5–05
    universality of status, 10–04, 12–16
Time factors
  choice of law, 4–05
  limitation of actions, 8–09
Title to sue
  delicts, 16–25
  procedure, 8–05
Torts. *see* **Delicts**
Transfers of property
  alienability, 17–04
  corporeal moveables, 17–11
  incorporeal moveables
    assignability, 17–22
    contractual assignments, 17–20
    voluntary assignments, 17–21
  meaning of *lex situs*, 17–03
  terminology, 17–02
Transnational divorces, 12–29
Trust estates
  common law, 18–46—18–52
  jurisdiction, 7–04
  statutory provisions, 18–53

Uncontested claims, 9–78—9–86
Universality of status, 10–04, 12–16
Unjust enrichment
  choice of law, 16–31
  EU
    proposals for reform,
      16–32—16–35
    Rome I, 16–30
  relationship with other areas of law,
    15–57

Validity. *see* **Essential validity; Formal
  validity**
Vested or Acquired Right Theory, 3–01

Wills
  changes of domicile, 18–18
  construction and interpretation,
    18–26—18–28
  conversion of property, 18–33
  elections, 18–35
  essential validity, 18–25
  formal validity, 18–17
  legal capacity, 18–16
  revocation, 18–29—18–33